ADAPTED PHYSICAL ACTIVITY, RECREATION AND SPORT

Crossdisciplinary and Lifespan

ADAPTED PHYSICAL ACTIVITY, RECREATION AND SPORT
Crossdisciplinary and Lifespan

FOURTH EDITION

Claudine Sherrill
Texas Woman's University

Madison, Wisconsin • Dubuque, Iowa • Indianapolis, Indiana
Melbourne, Australia • Oxford, England

Book Team

Editor *Chris Rogers*
Developmental Editor *Scott Spoolman*
Production Editor *Suzanne M. Guinn*
Designer *Eric Engelby*
Art Editor/Processor *Rachel Imsland*
Photo Editor *Robin Storm*
Permissions Editor *Mavis M. Oeth*
Visuals/Design Developmental Consultant *Marilyn A. Phelps*
Visuals/Design Freelance Specialist *Mary L. Christianson*
Publishing Services Specialist *Sherry Padden*
Marketing Manager *Pamela S. Cooper*
Advertising Manager *Jodi Rymer*

WCB Brown & Benchmark

A Division of Wm. C. Brown Communications, Inc.

Vice President and General Manager *Thomas E. Doran*
Editor in Chief *Edgar J. Laube*
Executive Editor *Ed Bartell*
Executive Editor *Stan Stoga*
National Sales Manager *Eric Ziegler*
Director of CourseResource *Kathy Law Laube*
Director of CourseSystems *Chris Rogers*
Director of Marketing *Sue Simon*
Director of Production *Vickie Putman Caughron*
Imaging Group Manager *Chuck Carpenter*
Manager of Visuals and Design *Faye M. Schilling*
Design Manager *Jac Tilton*
Art Manager *Janice Roerig*
Permissions/Records Manager *Connie Allendorf*
Consulting Editor *A. Lockhart*

Wm. C. Brown Communications, Inc.

President and Chief Executive Officer *G. Franklin Lewis*
Corporate Vice President, President of WCB Manufacturing *Roger Meyer*
Vice President and Chief Financial Officer *Robert Chesterman*

The credits section for this book begins on page 700 and is considered an extension of the copyright page.

Cover Image: Courtesy of the Junior Orange Bowl and the Sports Ability Games. Illustration by Mena

Copyedited by Mary Monner

Dedicated to my parents, Ivalene and Robert
Sherrill, of Logansport, Indiana

BRIEF
CONTENTS

Contents

A P P E N D I X E S

Foreword: Reflections on the New Title

The title change for this fourth edition reflects changes of the last two decades, particularly the emergence and influence of an international movement. The term *adapted physical education* in the old title is interpreted by most sectors as referring to school-based instruction and the ages from birth to 21 specified by federal legislation. Today's professional works with people of all ages in many settings. Physical educators, kinesiologists, recreators, occupational and physical therapists, music and dance therapists, and others adapt physical activity for all age groups.

Adapted physical activity was first proposed as the appropriate term for our body of knowledge in 1973, when the International Federation of Adapted Physical Activity (IFAPA) was founded in Montreal, Canada. The board of directors that created this new term included President Clermont Simard of Quebec, Vice President Robert L. Eason of the University of New Orleans, Julian Stein and John A. Nesbitt of the United States, Gudrun Doll-Tepper of Germany, Jean-Claude DePotter of Belgium, Eileen McLeish of England, David Jones of Australia, and Jean Claude Pageot and Fernand Caron of Canada. IFAPA meets every 2 years in various countries throughout the world and has many regional affiliates.

In 1984, the first professional journal to disseminate and extend our body of knowledge was created by Human Kinetics of Champaign, IL. This journal is called the *Adapted Physical Activity Quarterly (APAQ)*.

In 1986, the Adapted Physical Activity Council (APAC) of the American Alliance for Health, Physical Education, Recreation, and Dance (AAHPERD) was created by the merger of two structures, one of which dated back to 1905 and the early influence of Swedish medical gymnastics. Today, we support our profession when we join and attend meetings of APAC, which is housed within the Association for Research, Administration, Professional Councils and Societies (ARAPCS) of AAHPERD.

Clearly, adapted physical activity is the name of the present and the future. It is broad and inclusive and emphasizes the theory and practice of adaptation. It recognizes that adaptations are needed for all persons with psychomotor problems, not just those labeled as disabled. Professionals in a number of fields and disciplines can make these adaptations. Adapted physical activity is especially linked to recreation and sport (not necessarily adapted recreation or adapted sport).

Recreation is retained in the title of this text for many reasons. The word *recreation* emphasizes a state of mind and reminds us that the purpose of adapting physical activity is to develop attitudes, appreciations, and habits that will contribute to an active, healthy lifestyle and rich, satisfying leisure. My first 15 years of university teaching experience were focused dually on therapeutic recreation and physical education. The partnership of these two professions is crucial to lifespan programming.

Sport has been added to the title in recognition of the right of all persons to engage in competitive sport. Whereas sport can be educational, recreational, or competitive, the term increasingly refers to competition. I have participated in all of the quadrennial international Paralympics summer events since 1984 (New York, Korea, and Spain) and in all of the Special Olympics summer events since 1979 (New York, Louisiana, Indiana, Minnesota). Cerebral palsy and les autres sports, in particular, have captured my imagination because they address the broadest spectrum of individual differences. Athletes and coaches in the disabled sport movement have contributed significantly to adaptation theory and practice. Sport is woven throughout the book and has especially strong coverage in the chapters on disability in Part 3.

Crossdisciplinary is a more accurate descriptor of the book's approach than multidisciplinary. Our body of knowledge does come from many fields, but the goal is to integrate content across disciplines into a broad-based theory that can guide professionals in the many fields that adapt physical activity. The term *multidisciplinary,* however, appears in federal law. This was the rationale for use of *multidisciplinary* in the title of earlier editions.

The word *lifespan* in the title reflects the revived interest in many fields of serving persons of all ages. This text includes a new chapter on infants, toddlers, and early childhood, and much content in other chapters is directed toward this area. Content has been expanded throughout to encompass problems of adults, but the chapters on fitness and other health impaired conditions have been especially strengthened.

PREFACE

This fourth edition has been revised extensively to meet the diverse needs of undergraduate and graduate students, as well as beginning and experienced professionals. The intent was to develop a comprehensive, multipurpose resource that can serve as a textbook for several of the courses offered by colleges and universities and as a reference book throughout the professional's career.

This book can be used for basic adapted physical activity, recreation, and sport courses or for specialized courses on (a) assessment, (b) programming, (c) administration, (d) individual differences and disabilities, and (e) infants, toddlers, and early childhood. It is also perhaps the strongest resource available on the sport and disabled athlete movement and sport classification. The broad coverage affords professors the freedom to select content that meets individual needs and interests.

Adapted physical activity attitudes, knowledge, and skills must be *infused* into all courses. After university students are introduced to the content of this text in a basic course, their competencies should be further enhanced by a teacher training *infusion model* in which individual differences are addressed in every course. A goal is for this textbook to be used as a resource in every class. To achieve this, adapted physical activity proponents must share this text with regular education colleagues and emphasize infusion of content into daily lesson plans.

Public Law 101–476, the Individuals with Disabilities Education Act of 1990, brought major changes, all of which are incorporated into this text. Chief among these is the mandate that we use person-first terminology, thereby according persons with disabilities dignity and respect.

In the 1990s, regular and adapted physical educators will increasingly work as partners in the delivery of services to meet individual needs. More and more persons with disabilities will be in regular settings, and mainstream professionals will need considerable knowledge and skills for coping with wide ranges of behaviors and abilities. The content of this text is based on the belief that both regular and adapted physical activity personnel need competencies in seven areas:

P Planning

A Assessment

P Prescription/Placement

T Teaching/Counseling/Coaching

E Evaluation

C Coordination of Resources

A Advocacy

I call the knowledge comprising these areas the PAP-TE-CA model. It would be helpful if this acronym spelled something meaningful, but we shall have to settle for its spirited rhythm. It is a mnemonic device that effectively assures memory of the services that guide competency development.

Organization of Fourth Edition

This fourth edition begins with a list of competencies related to job functions. This list can guide self-evaluation and the development of a personal learning plan. Organization of the fourth edition into three parts is similar to that of the third edition. Titles of these sections have been changed, however.

Part 1: Foundations

Part 1 includes nine chapters, four of which are new. All have been rewritten. "Foundations" presents information everyone should know prior to involvement with individual differences. For graduate students and experienced teachers, there is much new material also. A theoretical framework for our profession is proposed, and problems, issues, and trends are highlighted.

Chapter 1 establishes the rationale for adapted physical activity; defines it; specifies core areas of knowledge and basic job functions; identifies underlying theories, principles, and models; and states 10 characteristics that distinguish adapted from regular physical activity service delivery. It also includes a brief history and proposes a philosophy.

Chapter 2 emphasizes celebration of individual differences and promotion of positive attitudes. Eight case studies are presented to focus learning on human beings, not disabilities. Prejudice, stigmatization, and stereotyping are discussed, and four attitude theories are presented to guide classroom and community practices: (a) contact, (b) persuasive communication, (c) social cognitive, and (d) reasoned action.

Chapter 3 identifies settings for either practica experiences or employment. Special attention is given sport organizations for persons with disabilities since these are featured as major resources throughout the book. The remainder of the chapter covers all the basics needed for success in a first practicum. For advanced students, adaptation and creativity theory are proposed, with special emphasis on ecological task analysis.

Chapter 4 focuses on advocacy and the worldwide human rights movement. Legislation that guides adapted physical activity service delivery is discussed, and the individualized education program (IEP) and the individualized family service plan (IFSP) are introduced.

Chapter 5 centers on writing goals and objectives, observation techniques to guide global assessment, and information relevant to age-appropriate programming in the cognitive, affective, and psychomotor domains.

Chapter 6 posits that self-concept and motivation are greater concerns in adapted than regular physical activity. The purpose of this chapter is to guide the development of a philosophy that supports humanistic service delivery practices. Assessment of self-concept and pedagogy for enhancing self-concept are thoroughly covered. Several psychosocial theories are explained.

Chapter 7 presents purposes and types of assessment, methods of data collection, assessment procedures, and illustrative instruments. Three theories are explained: (a) normal curve, (b) personal best, and (c) sport classification.

Chapter 8 contrasts least restrictive environment and regular education initiative placement approaches, discusses service delivery for regular education as well as special education students, and describes school district and individual planning. Transitional and inclusive models are described. All of the PAP-TE-CA services except assessment are discussed with respect to job functions.

Chapter 9 reviews the biomechanical, exercise science, and motor learning foundations of adaptation and covers behavior management. Development of teacher creativity is emphasized.

Part 2: Generic Service Delivery

Part 2 is designed for professors who wish to focus on goals, objectives, and pedagogy instead of disabilities. It provides in-depth pedagogy for achieving nine goals of adapted physical activity. The section includes eight chapters. One is new, and four have been totally rewritten.

Chapter 10 describes assessment and programming for nonambulatory locomotion, abnormal retention of reflexes, and delayed emergence of protective and equilibrium reactions. It presents the Milani-Comparetti assessment system and sensorimotor integration pedagogy. The chapter concludes with basic neurology and selected theories related to reflexes, reactions, and stereotypic patterns.

Chapter 11 covers assessment and teaching of basic locomotor and object control skills, including writing goals and objectives and developing task cards and lesson plans. Both qualitative and quantitative assessment is included.

Chapter 12 covers assessment and teaching of perceptual-motor abilities. A model is followed that includes attention, sensation, cognition, memory, and perceptual-motor abilities. Ecological task analysis is emphasized.

Chapter 13 includes everything needed to assess and program for lifespan wellness and fitness. Emphasis is on *persons with low fitness* and adaptations needed. American College of Sports Medicine (ACSM) guidelines are highlighted.

Chapter 14 covers postures, appearance, and muscle imbalance. Content is especially important for persons working with physical disabilities and low fitness.

Chapter 15 presents content related to the goal of relaxation, reduction of hyperactivity, and control of stress.

Chapter 16 describes adapted dance and dance therapy. This content is particularly relevant to persons with low self-concept, poor mental health, and/or problems of social acceptance.

Chapter 17 focuses on water activities for beginners and/or slow learners. Emphasis is on perceptual-motor learning in the water. Two instructional models (Sherrill and Halliwick) are presented.

Part 3: Individual Differences, with Emphasis on Sport

Part 3 is designed for persons who want in-depth knowledge of disabilities and basic information on incidence, prevalence, etiology, illustrative behaviors, and programming concerns and strategies. Sport classification is presented as the assessment approach. There are 10 chapters, and all but Chapter 18 follow more-or-less the same outline. Chapter 18 covers content relative to extending PL 101–476 assessment and programming to infants, toddlers, and early childhood. Topics of Chapters 18 through 27 are

Chapter 18 Infants, Toddlers, and Young Children: The New Emphasis

Chapter 19 Other Health Impaired Conditions

Chapter 20 Learning Disabilities, Attention Deficits, and Hyperactivity

Chapter 21 Mental Retardation and Special Olympics

Chapter 22 Serious Emotional Disturbance and Autism

Chapter 23 Wheelchair Sports and Orthopedic Impairments

Chapter 24 Les Autres Conditions and Amputations

Chapter 25 Cerebral Palsy, Stroke, and Traumatic Brain Injury

Chapter 26 Deaf and Hard-of-Hearing Conditions

Chapter 27 Blindness and Visual Impairments

New Chapters in Fourth Edition

New chapters, offering content not in the third edition, are

Chapter 2 Celebrating Individual Differences and Promoting Positive Attitudes

Emphasis on Sports for Individuals with Disabilities

Whereas some authors develop separate chapters and books on sports for athletes with disabilities, this text treats sports as an integral part of adapted physical activity. Over 150 pages of text on sport have been included in this fourth edition, as well as outstanding photographs of athletes with disabilities in competition.

Pedagogical Devices

This text offers numerous pedagogical devices designed to help students blend theory with practice. Among these are

- *Chapter objectives to guide study*
  Objectives at the beginning of each chapter may form the basis for written assignments or may be used as essay questions on an examination. Or an objective may be assigned to a student who prepares an oral report for class, makes a tape recording or videotape, or develops a slide presentation.

- *Learning activities embedded in each chapter*
  These activities are designed to ensure that practicum experiences supplement classroom theory. Use of these activities works especially well in contract teaching.

- *Subject index that can be used as a dictionary for looking up spelling of words*
  The subject index can also be used as a testing device. A card for every word in the index is made and color-coded (if desired) by chapter. Students randomly draw cards from the stack for a particular chapter and talk or write for 60 sec on the subject drawn. The subject index can also be used in studying for the final exam; students should be able to spell and discuss every word in the index.

- *Name index for becoming familiar with authorities in adapted physical activity and related disciplines*
  The name index can be used the same way as the subject index. Emphasis on learning names (i.e., primary sources) is probably more appropriate for graduate than undergraduate students.

- *Numerous photographs and line drawings*
  Approximately 230 photographs and 200 line drawings enrich the text. Test questions can be drawn from figure captions since these descriptions provide double emphasis of facts.

- *American Psychological Association (APA) format*
  Adherence to APA writing style provides a model for students who wish to acquire research and publication skills.

- *Appendixes on prevalence and incidence statistics and medications*
  The statistics in Appendix A are helpful in preparing term papers and in documenting the need for adapted physical activity service delivery. Appendix B on medications is valuable in understanding individual needs and in working in a crossdisciplinary setting.

- *Appendix on assessment information*
  Appendix C presents information useful in making placement decisions, programming, and writing IEPs. It summarizes text tables that can be used for class assignments.

- *Appendixes on sources of information*
  Appendixes D, E, and F provide readers with over 100 addresses to write for additional information.

- *Appendix on history of adapted physical activity, recreation, and sport*
  Beginning in 1817 with the establishment of the first residential schools in the United States, the chronology of over 100 events presented in Appendix G includes the initiation of services, enactment of legislation, and formation of organizations.

- *References to reinforce understanding of primary sources*
  The reference list at the end of each chapter comprises recommended reading for persons who wish more in-depth coverage. Students should be encouraged to learn names of journals and to stay abreast of new issues as they are published.

ACKNOWLEDGEMENTS

To the many individuals and agencies who shared in this adventure, a heartfelt thank you. I am especially grateful to *Julian Stein,* who served as major reviewer and advisor for the first edition and who has been my mentor for many years; to *Bill Hillman* and the other members of the National Consortium on Physical Education and Recreation for Individuals With Disabilities (NCPERIWD) who have expressed faith in my ideas and leadership; to *Janet Wessel* of I Can and the ABC curriculum whose work forms the basis of the PAP-TE-CA service delivery model in this textbook; and to *G. Lawrence Rarick,* whose rare combination of research abilities and humanistic beliefs serves as a model for us all.

To Creators of Our Knowledge Base

I am indebted to the many persons who are creating the adapted physical activity knowledge base and to the editors of the journals that disseminate this knowledge. Work that appears in the *Adapted Physical Activity Quarterly* and *Palaestra: The Forum of Sport, Physical Education, and Recreation for the Disabled* significantly affects my thought, creativity, and commitment. My thanks to the editors of these journals for their service and scholarship: *Geoffrey Broadhead,* Kent State University; *Greg Reid,* McGill University; and *David Beaver,* Western Illinois University. Writers who particularly have stimulated my thinking are Terry Rizzo, Walter E. Davis, Allen Burton, Dale and Beverly Ulrich, Gail Dummer, Ted Wall, E. Jane Watkinson, Martin E. Block, and Patricia Krebs.

To My Students

Most important, I thank my students at the Texas Woman's University, who keep me involved in research and practicum experiences, and the parents who trust us with their children. Each edition brings new students as well as memories of past ones who have shared and grown with me and significantly affected the contents of this book. I wish I could mention all their names, but a few will have to do: Karen DePauw, Luke Kelly, Jim Rimmer, Sarah Rich, Boni Boswell, Wanda Rainbolt, Ellen Lubin Curtis-Pierce, Jo Ellen Cowden, Garth Tymeson, Tom Montelione, Jim Mastro, April Tripp, Ellen Kowalski, Carol Pope, Ron Davis, and Leslie Low.

To My Support Network

For her photography and assistance with the many aspects of production, I thank *Rae Allen.* I am indebted also to *Annetta Simpson,* my typist, and to many artists: *Mary Jane Cardenas* and *C. David Mathis,* first edition; *Molly Pollasch,* second edition; *Dr. Diann Laing,* third edition; and *Lin Hampton* and *Lisa West,* fourth edition. I am grateful also to the outstanding staff of Brown & Benchmark, whose editing, production, and marketing excellence make them the leaders in creating a knowledge base for adapted physical activity.

To My Resource Persons

Special recognition is extended to *Wynelle Delaney,* DTR, who coauthored Chapter 16, "Adapted Dance and Dance Therapy;" *Jeff Jones, Carol Mushett, Dr. Ken Richter, Kim Grass, Ruth Burd,* and *Duncan Wyeth,* who shared their expertise on cerebral palsy sports; *Patricia Krebs,* who assisted with the chapter on mental retardation; *Charles Buell, Rosie Copeland,* and *James Mastro,* who taught me about blindness and visual impairments; *David A. Stewart* and *Gina Olivia,* who reviewed the chapter on deaf and hard-of-hearing conditions and offered valuable suggestions; *Abu Yilla* and *Don Drewry,* wheelchair athletes who shared their knowledge; *Inge Morisbak* of Norway, who helped with winter sports; *Terry Rizzo* and *April Tripp,* who assisted with content on attitudes and social acceptance; and *David Reams,* who helped obtain the artwork for the textbook cover.

To My Role Models

Acknowledgments can be complete only if they extend backward in time to those persons who sparked the initial enthusiasm in teaching and writing: *Dr. Harry A. Scott* of Teachers College, Columbia University, who spoke of competency-based teaching in the early 1950s; *Dr. Josephine Rathbone,* also of Teachers College, who instilled in me a deep concern for the right of all persons to efficient and beautiful bodies; and *Dean Anne Schley Duggan,* Texas Woman's University, who taught me to hear the different drummer and to keep step to the music—however measured or far away.

—Claudine Sherrill

COMPETENCIES

A *competency* is adequate and suitable philosophy, attitude, knowledge, or skill to perform a specific job function or task. Study of this textbook will result in the competencies necessary to (a) perform the job functions indigenous to direct service delivery, (b) conduct research to further the knowledge base of adapted physical activity, and (c) serve as a leader and professional educator in in-service and college and university settings.

Competencies Related to Advocacy (Action Aimed at Promoting, Maintaining, or Defending a Cause)

1.1 Philosophy that supports

    1.11 The right of all persons to (a) high-quality physical education instruction and (b) lifespan sport, fitness, and recreation

    1.12 Assessed individual differences (not characteristics of people with disabilities) as the basis for adapted physical activity

1.2 Attitude of accepting and appreciating individual differences

1.3 Knowledge of

    1.31 Individual differences associated with normal curve theory and with various disabilities: myth and reality

    1.32 State physical education requirements and indicators of high-quality instruction

    1.33 Laws that eliminate barriers and protect rights

    1.34 Lifespan sport, fitness, and recreation opportunities in a variety of settings

    1.35 Theories, models, and strategies relevant to acceptance and appreciation of individual differences

1.4 Skill in

    1.41 Increasing comfort and communication among people with limited exposure to individual differences

    1.42 Applying attitude and behavior management theories to promote acceptance and appreciation of individual differences

    1.43 Using advocacy strategies in the 5 L model (Look at me, Leverage, Literature, Legislation, Litigation)

    1.44 Working with the press and media

Competencies Related to Coordination of Resources

2.1 Philosophy that supports

    2.11 Resource utilization as a means of learning and personal growth as well as improving service delivery to others

    2.12 Multidisciplinary and crossdisciplinary cooperation

    2.13 Partnerships between persons with and without disabilities in promoting lifespan sport, fitness, and recreation

2.2 Attitude of self-confidence in human relationships

2.3 Knowledge of

    2.31 Many types of resources (e.g., organizations, athletes with disabilities, special educators, related services personnel, parents)

    2.32 Many types of settings for learning about and using resources

    2.33 Models and theories that impact on resource coordination

2.4 Skill in

    2.41 Locating, contacting, and establishing rapport with resources

    2.42 Bringing resources together (e.g., planning meetings or introducing people to each other)

    2.43 Serving as a chair or participant in meetings and projects

    2.44 Working with administrators and parents

Competencies Related to Planning

3.1 Philosophy that supports critical thinking about

    3.11 Nature of adapted physical activity (APA); its philosophy, goals, and characteristics; core areas of knowledge; job roles and functions; service delivery; eligibility requirements for APA services

    3.12 Nature of human beings, the values of physical activity, and the rights of individuals and families

    3.13 Desirable student, parent, teacher, and administrator behaviors

    3.14 APA theories, models, principles, and practices

    3.15 Law, the role of government, morality, and personal ethics

3.2 Attitude of responsibility for critical thinking as the basis for

   3.21 Planning APA learning experiences for self and others

   3.22 Decision making in all aspects of direct service delivery

   3.23 Evaluating effectiveness

3.3 Knowledge of planning for (a) individual students; (b) classrooms, schools, and school districts; (c) communities; and (d) organizations and agencies

3.4 Skill in

   3.41 Decision making regarding variables to be assessed, procedures to be followed, and resources to be used

   3.42 Prioritizing and establishing goals

   3.43 Writing behavioral objectives to achieve goals

   3.44 Matching activities to objectives

   3.45 Calculating instructional time for objectives and activities

   3.46 Writing instructional units and lesson plans

   3.47 Addressing transitional education concerns and monitoring systems that maximize active lifestyles

   3.48 Creating behavior management plans

Competencies Related to Assessment

4.1 Philosophy that supports assessment as the key to individualizing and adapting

4.2 Attitude of commitment to assessing both individuals and environments

4.3 Knowledge of

   4.31 Instruments and protocols for assessing performance in nine goal areas

   4.32 Scientific and psychosocial foundations that relate to assessment (e.g., biomechanics, exercise physiology, motor learning, human development, sport sociology)

4.4 Skill in

   4.41 Using various types of assessment

   4.42 Interpreting assessment data

   4.43 Decision making based on data collection and interpretation

   4.44 Making referrals for further assessment

Competencies Related to Prescription

5.1 Philosophy that supports

   5.11 Individualized education programs (IEPs) as vehicles for curricular prescription for people with and without disabilities

   5.12 Exercise prescriptions as guides for fitness training

   5.13 Lesson plans as means of achieving prescribed objectives

5.2 Attitude of accountability

5.3 Knowledge of

   5.31 Parts of an IEP and of procedures in the IEP process

   5.32 Parts of an exercise prescription

   5.33 Parts of a lesson plan and of environmental variables to be manipulated

   5.34 Exercise indications and contraindications for specific conditions

   5.35 Models that guide school district decision making

   5.36 Support services and placement options

5.4 Skill in

   5.41 Making placement decisions

   5.42 Writing IEPs, exercise prescriptions, and lesson plans

Competencies Related to Teaching, Counseling, and Coaching

6.1 Philosophy that supports

   6.11 Adaptation, creativity, and individualization as theories that guide instruction

   6.12 Counseling as an integral part of teaching and sport psychology as an integral part of coaching

   6.13 Self-concept and self-actualization as central constructs

   6.14 Humanistic teaching practices

   6.15 Inclusion, normalization, and least restrictive environment (LRE) strategies

6.2 Attitude of celebrating individual differences and lifespan ability to learn and change

6.3 Knowledge of

   6.31 Adaptation, creativity, and individualization theories, models, processes, principles, and pedagogy

   6.32 Scientific and psychosocial foundations of adaptation (e.g., biomechanics, exercise physiology, motor learning and control, human development, psychology, sociology, behavior management)

   6.33 Assessment, curriculum, instruction, and evaluation practices that contribute to good teaching

   6.34 Counseling theory, weaving together sport, psychology, rehabilitation counseling, and movement therapy

   6.35 Pedagogy related to sensorimotor integration, reflexes, reactions, perceptual-motor learning, and play and game behaviors

   6.36 Pedagogy related to motor performance, dance, aquatics, sports, and games

   6.37 Pedagogy related to fitness, healthy lifestyle, postures, appearance, muscle imbalance, and relaxation

6.38 Pedagogy related to self-concept, social acceptance, inclusion, sport socialization, lifespan active leisure, and motor creativity

6.39 Individual differences in growth, development, and function that impact on teaching, counseling, and coaching

6.4 Skill in

6.41 Adapting instruction for individual differences (age, performance) and for achievement of specific goals

6.42 Using ecological and traditional task and activity analysis

6.43 Motivating students and athletes to personal bests and managing individual and group behaviors

6.44 Socializing persons into active, healthy lifestyles and sport

6.45 Applying knowledge in all aspects of teaching, counseling, and coaching

Competencies Related to Program Evaluation

7.1 Philosophy that supports continuous evaluation as an integral part of service delivery

7.2 Attitude of

7.21 Striving for personal best while accepting that the best can always be improved

7.22 Seeking ways to improve and being open to ideas for change

7.3 Knowledge of

7.31 Instruments and protocols for program evaluation

7.32 Evaluation theories, models, principles, and strategies

7.4 Skill in

7.41 Using evaluation instruments and protocol and, when necessary, developing new ones

7.42 Applying evaluation theories, models, principles, and strategies

Competencies Related to Research

8.1 Philosophy that supports research as the method of choice for improving service delivery and for creating the knowledge base of a profession and discipline

8.2 Attitude of responsibility for

8.21 Reading research to stay abreast of new knowledge

8.22 Conducting research to contribute to the knowledge base

8.3 Knowledge of

8.31 Journals and books that publish research

8.32 Meetings where research is presented

8.33 Research methods and strategies, including statistics

8.34 Computer- and hand-search techniques for locating research

8.35 Topics on which research in needed

8.4 Skill in

8.41 Locating, reading, understanding, and applying research

8.42 Reviewing research related to selected topics

8.43 Conducting and reporting research

Competencies Related to Conducting In-service or College/University Professional Education Courses

9.1 Philosophy that supports adapted physical activity training for professionals and parents

9.2 Attitude of helpfulness in assisting adults to achieve personal goals in relation to adapted physical activity competencies

9.3 Knowledge of

9.31 Content in adapted physical activity textbooks and journals

9.32 Roles, service delivery areas, specific job functions, and competencies

9.33 Best practices and models of direct service delivery

9.34 Pedagogy for adult education

9.4 Skill in

9.41 Motivating adults to accept personal responsibility for learning

9.42 Helping adults acquire favorable attitudes about individual differences

9.43 Individualizing content and learning experiences for adults

PART

I

Foundations

Chapter

1

Quality Physical Education and Active Lifestyle

FIGURE 1.1

What an individual *can* be, he *must* be. He must be true to his own nature. This need we may call self-actualization.—Abraham Maslow (1970, p. 46).

After you have studied this chapter, you should be able to:

1. Discuss contributions of a good physical education program to the cognitive, affective, and psychomotor domains.

2. Identify poor teaching practices and problems that must be eliminated for physical education to meet the needs of all students.

3. Contrast definitions and purposes of regular and adapted physical education. Discuss the knowledge base and teacher training for each.

4. Contrast theories, principles, models, philosophy, and practices and discuss their relationship to each other. Discuss examples of each in the adapted physical activity knowledge base.

5. Differentiate between the terms *adapted* and *adaptive*.

6. Identify and discuss seven adapted physical activity services.

7. Assess your present level of knowledge and develop a personal learning plan that is competency based.

8. Develop a philosophy of adapted physical activity that includes (a) purpose and goals, (b) beliefs about who should be eligible for services, and (c) other basic beliefs. Discuss similarities and differences between your beliefs and those presented in the text.

9. Identify and discuss 10 characteristics of adapted physical activity. Evaluate the mnemonic device and propose some alternatives.

10. Trace the history of adapted physical activity through five stages.

In physical activity, everyone fails at one time or another—by coming in last on the relay team, by missing the basket or the field goal that would have tied the game, by choking and struggling in the swimming pool. Failure often results in labels: clumsy, awkward, uncoordinated, disabled. How long does a label, once internalized, endure? What effect does a label have on growth and development? In particular, how does failure affect body image and self-concept? The improved self-concept that results from a carefully planned progression of successful movement activities may be the greatest contribution that physical education can offer the education process (Craft & Hogan, 1985; Gruber, 1986).

Self-concept refers to all the opinions, feelings, and beliefs that a person holds about self (see Figure 1.1). The self contains many dimensions (e.g., scholastic, behavioral, physical appearance, athletic, social, global), and persons may feel good about some dimensions and bad about others. *Body image* is a similar construct that refers to opinions, feelings, and beliefs about different parts of the body.

Good Teaching Is Adapting

Good teaching implies *adapting* the curriculum to individual needs so as to minimize failure and preserve ego strength. In a sense, *all good physical education is adapted physical education.* Regular physical education includes students with a wide range of individual differences. Some students are *average* or *gifted,* while others are classified as needing *special education* because of a particular disability, such as mental retardation or orthopedic impairment.

Many students with disabilities are excellent athletes and can participate successfully in regular physical education. An individual in leg braces may be able, without adaptations, to engage successfully in swimming, gymnastics, or archery. A pupil with a congenital amputation of the arm may be a star soccer player; some have excelled in baseball, basketball, and football! On the other hand, many students have problems that require individual attention if physical education is to be a pleasant and self-actualizing experience. Perceptual-motor deficits, low fitness, awkwardness, obesity, asthma, and poor eyesight are only a few of the problems that students exhibit daily.

The integration of students with disabilities into as many school activities as possible is a current trend. Physical education, art, and music are often the curriculum areas in which such integration occurs first. The success of integration depends in large part upon the quality of the regular physical education program and the extent to which it meets individual differences. A sound understanding of regular physical education contributes to the innovation of effective, comprehensive curricular models for individuals who are clumsy or disabled.

What Is Physical Education?

Physical education is an *academic subject* similar to reading, arithmetic, and social studies. It is *instructional* and should offer a planned sequence of *new* material each day. Participation should be *required,* as it is in other subjects, and missed sessions should be rescheduled. The teacher is responsible for lesson plans that include clear statements of objectives, learning activities, motivational techniques, and evaluation procedures. Physical education is not play, nor is it recess or athletics.

Textbooks and school curriculum guides offer definitions of physical education that differ according to the writer's philosophy. Definitions also appear in law and in policies and guidelines of educational agencies. The following definition of physical education was developed in conjunction with federal law that assured students with disabilities the right to free, appropriate physical education instruction:

(i) The term means the development of:
  (A) Physical and motor fitness;
  (B) Fundamental motor skills and patterns; and
  (C) Skills in aquatics, dance, and individual and group games and sports (including intramural and lifetime sports).

FIGURE   1.2

Behaviors in all three educational domains contribute to physical education knowledge, skills, attitudes, and habits.

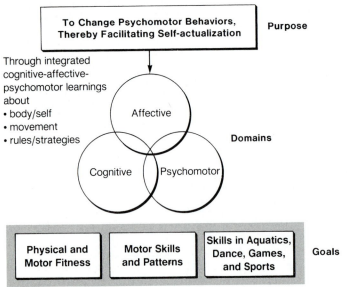

(ii) The term includes special physical education, adapted physical education, movement education, and motor development. (20 U.S.C. 1401 [16]) (*Federal Register,* August 23, 1977, p. 42480)

Physical education instruction contributes to development in all three of the commonly recognized domains of behavior: *cognitive* (intellectual skills), *affective* (feelings, opinions, attitudes, beliefs, values, interests, desires), and *psychomotor* (motor and fitness performance). Schema for these domains are widely known and explained in detail in the three well-known taxonomies of educational objectives (Bloom 1956; Harrow, 1972; Krathwohl, 1964). Figure 1.2 presents the purpose, domains, and goals for which the physical educator is responsible.

While physical education instruction traditionally has focused on the psychomotor domain, psychomotor behaviors occur within an integrated framework of cognitive-affective-psychomotor interrelationships. *Psychomotor* thus refers to all *the integrated cognitive-affective-psychomotor behaviors related to the human body and its movement.*

Purpose of Physical Education

The primary purpose of physical education instruction is to change psychomotor behaviors, thereby facilitating self-actualization, particularly as it relates to understanding and appreciation of the body (and the self) in motion and at rest. Physical education is not limited to vigorous activities but includes instruction in relaxation, opportunities for creative expression, practice in sports that will enhance leisure throughout the lifespan, and participation in large-muscle games that teach cooperation and social skills.

Self-actualization, as used in this text, is defined as making actual, or realizing, all of one's psychomotor potentialities (Maslow, 1968, 1970). This lifelong process begins

with dependence and other-directedness in infancy and progresses to independence and inner-directedness. Self-actualization philosophy emphasizes internal rather than external motivation and stresses personal responsibility for an active, healthy lifestyle and meaningful leisure. The self-actualizing person feels good about self and has confidence in movement abilities (i.e., has a positive self-concept); has positive attitudes toward exercise and physical activity; has the knowledge, skills, and fitness to participate in desired activities; has friends with whom to share exercise and physical activity; and has the creativity and perceptual-motor function to solve psychomotor problems and reach goals. What kind of physical education program contributes to these outcomes?

A Model Physical Education Program

In a model physical education program, students are taught in classes not larger than 25 to 30 pupils (the same size deemed appropriate for other school-based learning activities). Individual needs and interests are identified, and instruction is adapted accordingly. The teacher views teaching, guidance, and counseling as inseparable processes, and each student is helped to develop interest and skill in activities in which he or she can experience success. Dance and such individual sports as bowling, tennis, and golf are introduced early in the elementary grades.

Warm-up exercises and equipment are individualized. Each student, for instance, aspires to a different number of bent-knee sit-ups, depending upon his or her abdominal strength. Individuals with low strength execute their sit-ups with hands on their thighs, while the more athletically inclined undertake the traditional sit-up, with hands clasped behind the neck. In learning racket games, awkward students use shorter rackets, while the better coordinated begin with rackets of standard length.

The official rules of such games as volleyball and softball are adapted, and learning—not recreation or competition—is the main goal. For example, in classes based upon the principle of success, all pupils are not required to stand behind the baseline when they serve a volleyball. Each stands at a point on the court where he or she is most likely to get the ball over. Well-coordinated students accept the official rule of hitting the ball one time, while the less athletic may volley it multiple times. In softball, an inning may be played by time rather than by three outs. The pressures inherent in striking out are thereby deemphasized so that equal turns at bat and optimal skill development are possible.

The well-skilled athlete can learn and practice official rules in after-school athletic programs or in league play. The instructional period in a model physical education program is a time when games are modified in accordance with individual differences. All students are accepted for what they are—awkward, uncoordinated, obese, skinny, or gifted. Students must have no doubt about what is more important to the teacher—the game or the individual. When teaching is based upon the concept of individual differences, students seldom fail.

Poor Teaching Practices

Many physical activity settings, however, are antithetical to learning. Such practices as choosing up sides, playing elimination games, and expecting all students to engage in the same activities contribute to failure. Consider the following incidents that occur frequently:

"What shall we play today?" asks the teacher. "Kickball" is the unanimous choice of the third-grade class. Wishing to be democratic and to encourage the development of leadership as well as the ability to follow, Mr. A poses the expected question: "Who wants to be leader?" Nearly everyone's arm rises, and some children chime, "I do," "I do," "I do."

"Billy, you be the leader for Team 1. Jerry, you can be the leader for Team 2. Now let's choose up sides quickly." One by one, the children are chosen—first Billy's and Jerry's best friends, then their friend's best friends. The skilled children are always among the first to be chosen, and there is much laughter and enthusiasm. Clearly, the needs of the majority of the class are being met.

Now, only Jimmy and Darol are left. Skinny or obese, it doesn't really matter—they are different from the others, a little less coordinated, a little slower maturing. Does anyone remember that they were the last boys to be chosen yesterday and the day before that? Mr. A was an outstanding athlete in college and a varsity player on several teams. Never in his life has he been chosen last. How could he possibly understand how it feels?

Jimmy and Darol stand there, waiting, hoping, trying to smile and act as though they don't care, wanting to cry, just wishing it were over. Everyone staring—or do they even notice? "Oh, well," shrugs Jimmy, "this way I won't have to come up to bat."

Circle dodgeball—the children's favorite. Dodge, twist, jump! At all costs, avoid the ball. Try harder than last time. Won't help. The other kids always try to hit me first. They know I'm easy to put out. And so I join the circle—eliminated again.

Jump rope—got to run in without the rope touching me. Got to concentrate. Got it. 1–2–3–4, I can jump until I miss. Leah and Amy and all my friends make it to 100. 6–7–8. Ooops, miss. And so I go to the end of the file again to wait my turn. 97–98–99–100 . . . and on and on—I'm glad my friends are so good—they've tried to help me—but PE is just a time when I wait a lot for a turn that never lasts very long.

D-O-N-K-E-Y. Another elimination game. Part of the tradition of sports. Each time the kid in front of me makes a basket and I don't, I get a letter on me. I'm not very good. Usually, I get eliminated first. If no one's watching, I can sneak around the fence and have a smoke.

Ann has made an A on every written test in physical education she's ever taken. When she hits a ball in tennis class and it fails, as usual, to go where she intended, she knows before the teacher ever tells her that her elbow was bent, that the racket face was closed, or that she swung too soon. In fact, Ann knows a lot about tennis—on the verbal level. It's just that her body won't do what her mind says—it never has.

This year, Peter's parents sent a note from their physician to have their son excused from physical education. They are sensitive persons, concerned about their action, worried about the values he'll never derive from guided motor activities. But every day for 6 years, Peter's physical education has started the same way—two laps around the football field. Peter is 5 ft tall, 160 lb of rounded, squatty body, undeniably obese. He can't run,

and each day he dies a little when subjected to the ridicule of his classmates. In the beginning, his learning disability was his obesity. Now, more and more, it's his attitude.

Mike tries—he really does. Every muscle in his body reveals effort—he's tense, anxious, eager to please. In the agility race, he hits his head on the beam he is trying to duck under, trips over the rope he must jump, twists his neck as he tries the required forward roll, and then gamely runs toward the finishing line. The other teams finished seconds ago. The cheering is over. It's quiet. The team members tolerate him, hoping they won't have him next time. What is his learning disability—space perception, poor coordination, just plain awkwardness?

And what does the physical educator say? "Good! All the teams ready? Let's do that relay again! Mike, you exchange places with John." John was on the winning team, and it is only fair to Mike's team to give them a chance to win. Does the teacher hear the barely audible slurs—the "Ugh, do we have to have him?" as Mike reluctantly joins the new group?

The teams are evened up now! Ready—set—go! Kids love relays. They are an integral part of physical education, and everyone must participate, abide by the rules, run the same distance.

These anecdotes provide insight into relationships between positive and negative movement experiences and self-concept. Most of the adults who shared these experiences believed that their physical education had not been adapted to individual needs. They were unaware that many methods exist for ameliorating awkwardness (see Figure 1.3).

The Challenge to Change

Poor teaching and administrative practices are responsible for many psychomotor problems. Parents, and society at large, however, also shape the attitudes and practices that underlie healthy, active lifestyles and leisure. The 1990s are recognized as a time when America must give renewed attention to education. *AMERICA 2000: An Education Strategy* states that there will be "major change in our 110,000 public and private schools, change in every American community, change in every American home, change in our attitude about learning" (U.S. Department of Education, 1991, p. 5).

This change must encompass physical education instruction and home-school-community partnerships that support wellness and fitness. It must also strengthen active involvement in sport, dance, and aquatics throughout the lifespan. Inclusion of physical activity in leisure as persons grow older depends largely on perceived success in childhood and subsequent attitudes toward body, self, and movement.

Adapted physical education is one approach to increasing the quality and quantity of positive movement experiences. This is an area of study that prepares professionals to help resolve psychomotor problems that limit success. Some of these problems are associated with disability, but others are linked with environment and lifestyle.

What Is Adapted Physical Activity?

Adapted physical activity is a crossdisciplinary body of knowledge directed toward identification and solution of psychomotor problems throughout the lifespan. These problems may be within the individual or the environment. Thus, the adapted physical activity body of knowledge, when applied,

FIGURE   1.3

Awkward children often achieve more success in foot-eye coordination tasks than in hand-eye coordinations.

encompasses *attitudes* supportive of individual differences and adaptation and a *service delivery system* designed to ameliorate problems.

In this text, the terms *adapted physical activity* and *adapted physical education* are used interchangeably. However, *education* generally refers to school-based programs and to ages birth to 21 years, whereas *activity* refers to all kinds of programs for all age groups. Regardless of which term is used, a definition should include believing, doing, and knowing components.

Believing Component

The believing component of adapted physical activity is an attitude, a way of teaching in both integrated and special class environments, that is reflected in the beliefs and practices of teachers who adjust learning experiences to meet individual needs and assure optimal success. An *attitude* is an enduring set of beliefs charged with emotion that predisposes a person to certain kinds of behaviors. Attitudes typically involve feelings about people, especially people who are different, and how they should be treated and/or educated. The adapted physical activity attitude embraces individual differences and enjoys the challenge of helping persons achieve self-actualization through exercise and sport. Like birthdays and other good things, individual differences are celebrated!

Doing Component

The doing component of adapted physical activity is more than classroom instruction. It is a *comprehensive service delivery system* designed to ameliorate problems within the psychomotor domain. A service delivery system is a classroom, school, agency, or community model used to individualize the provision of services to people with different needs. The term evolved out of federal legislation in the 1970s and is widely used in special education and the helping professions, particularly those that support multidisciplinary programming. A service delivery system is a way of offering a continuum of services, regardless of educational placement, rather than associating one set of services with regular physical education and another set of services with adapted physical education.

The services delivered depend on the philosophy of the school system, residential facility, or agency that employs the teacher. Typically, however, these services are

P Planning

A Assessment

P Prescription/Placement

T Teaching/Counseling/Coaching

E Evaluation

C Coordination of resources

A Advocacy

An acronym to help remember these services is PAP-TE-CA. These services, with the exception of the last two, are the same as those comprising the widely used Achievement-Based Curriculum (ABC) model, on which I CAN is based (Wessel, 1977; Wessel & Kelly, 1986). The ABC and I CAN models were developed to guide personnel preparation and service delivery that would result in quality physical education for all students.

The PAP-TE-CA model emphasizes that advocacy and the coordination of resources are two umbrella services that must be added to the ABC or I CAN models to assure differently abled persons equal opportunity for self-actualization through physical activity (see Figure 1.4). The adapted physical activity PAP-TE-CA model also stresses the importance of counseling skills in teaching and coaching persons with psychomotor problems. Coaching has been added to extend the model's applicability to sport and recreation programs.

The comprehensive service delivery system is directed toward two types of students: (a) those classified as special education (i.e., disabled) under state and federal law and (b) those not so classified (i.e., regular or average). According to federal law, students classified as special education must be assessed annually by a multidisciplinary team and have an individualized education program. This procedure, explained further in Chapter 4, determines whether students receive adapted physical education services in a regular class, a special class, or a combined placement setting. Many students, however, do not meet special education eligibility requirements and yet have fitness, coordination, and/or medical problems that require adapted physical activity services. Adapted physical education, therefore, should not be conceptualized as a placement or setting; rather, it is a composite of beliefs (i.e., attitudes) and practices (i.e., comprehensive service delivery system) designed to assure high-quality physical education for all students. These services are delivered in many settings.

FIGURE 1.4

Services included in the adapted physical activity delivery system.

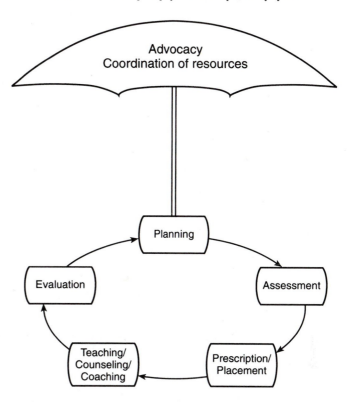

Knowing Component and Core Areas of Knowledge

The knowing component of adapted physical activity is the *crossdisciplinary body of knowledge* that focuses upon identification and remediation of problems within the psychomotor domain in individuals who perform below age-level expectations and/or need help in overcoming aspirational, attitudinal, or environmental barriers. Central to gaining this knowledge is emphasis on problem-solving skills (Hogan, 1990).

The core areas of knowledge in adapted physical activity that enable educators to deliver services and to understand individual differences are

1. Individual differences in human growth, development, and function, including the neurological bases of motor function.
2. Attitude, interpersonal relations, and communication theory.
3. Law, human rights, and advocacy theory.
4. Scientific foundations of adaptation, including biomechanics, exercise physiology, and motor control theory.
5. Psychosocial foundations of adaptation, including self-actualization, self-concept, motivation, social competence, and behavior management theory. This area also includes theories and approaches to normalization, integration, inclusion, and least restrictive environment.

6. Service delivery theory, including the traditional bodies of knowledge taught in assessment, curriculum, instruction, and evaluation courses.

7. Counseling theory, weaving together sport psychology, rehabilitation counseling, and movement therapy.

8. Adaptation, creativity, and individualization theory, based on a thorough understanding of movement, fitness, sports, games, dance, and aquatics. Adaptation requires a knowledge of rules, skills, strategies, and exercise and the ability to use task, activity, and games analysis. Illustrative of evolving theory in this area is work on ecological task analysis (Davis & Burton, 1991) and perceptual-motor learning (Burton, 1990; Burton & Davis, 1992). This area also encompasses the sport and disabled athlete movement, including assessment approaches for sport classifications and the design and adaptation of equipment.

9. Philosophy, history, and problem solving in relation to every core area, with emphasis on the great thinkers and researchers as models for helping to clarify and shape personal philosophy and understand current issues and emerging trends.

This textbook is designed to develop beginning-level knowledge and skills in each of these areas. Much research is needed to develop theories, principles, and models in each area. A trend of the 1990s is a new emphasis on *theorizing,* the process of identifying related facts, concepts, and statements and synthesizing them into conceptual frameworks or theories that help individuals to become better teachers and service providers (Reid, 1989).

The rapidly expanding knowledge base of adapted physical activity includes theories, principles, models, philosophy, and practices. A review of these terms may help you to set goals for learning about adapted physical activity.

Theories, Principles, and Models

Theories, principles, and models are studied in each of the core areas. Some of these have been borrowed from other professions and disciplines, but others are evolving specifically in relation to adapted physical activity service delivery.

Theories are clusters of interrelated facts, statements, or concepts that are systematically organized around a central theme. The purpose of a theory is to describe, explain, or predict some phenomenon like development or learning (Bigge, 1982; Salkind, 1985). The knowledge explosion has made it increasingly impossible to remember the millions of isolated bits of information that have been generated. The synthesis of related facts and ideas into theories helps make greater sense of the world and enhances problem solving.

Illustrative theories of particular interest in adapted physical education are Muska Mosston's teaching style theory (Mosston & Ashworth, 1986), G. S. Don Morris's games design theory (Morris & Stiehl, 1989), and various motor learning theories (Hoover & Wade, 1985; Reid, 1989). These and many other theories are explained later in this text.

Good teachers seek to understand the theory underlying their classroom practices. In many cases, the theory

that guides physical education curriculum and instruction has not been tested with individuals who are clumsy and/or disabled. Much research and critical thinking are needed to resolve this problem.

Principles are fundamental truths or basic laws that guide education or explain mechanical processes and natural phenomena. Illustrative of these are the overload principle studied in exercise physiology, Newton's three laws of motion (inertia, acceleration, and reaction) in biomechanics, and Fitt's law in motor learning. Most principles that guide instruction and classroom management can be traced back to Edward Thorndike's three laws of learning (effect, exercise, and readiness), B. F. Skinner's principles of operant conditioning, and Robert Gagne's principles of learning conditions and hierarchy (Bell-Gredler, 1986).

Adapted physical educators must know all the principles that guide regular education, plus those that guide service delivery to students with psychomotor problems. For example, principles of motor development (see Chapter 18) and of movement coordination and control (Burton, 1990) must be used in adapting instruction to meet special needs. Likewise, human rights principles guide placement and curriculum design. The best known of these is the *normalization principle* of Wolfensberger (1972), which states that the living, learning, and working conditions of people with disabilities should be as close as possible to the norms of able-bodied society.

Models are unifying structures or examples. Figure 1.2, for example, is a model that brings together ideas about the purpose, domains, and goals of physical education. Figure 1.4 is a model that shows the relationships among the seven types of services provided through adapted physical education. Writers often create models to unify and emphasize especially important bits of information. The term *model* also refers to exemplary programs, designs, and patterns. Several curriculum models are explained later in this text. Among these are the I CAN curriculum model of Janet Wessel and Luke Kelly, the PREP curriculum model of Jane Watkinson and Ted Wall, and the GAMES DESIGN model of G. S. Don Morris and Jim Stiehl.

Sometimes, the words *model* and *theory* are used interchangeably. The knowledge base in adapted physical activity is said to come from both a medical model and an educational model (i.e., both medical and educational theory).

Medical Model

Historically, physical education evolved from a medical model, in that physicians were the first to develop and teach school and university exercise programs. Physicians also wrote the first physical education textbooks. An understanding of individual differences and of how exercise and sport affect these differences can be obtained by reading sources used by physicians, therapists, and other medical personnel.

From the medical model, we learn the definitions of conditions, their etiologies (i.e., causes), and symptoms/signs. The medical model is often called a categorical approach, in that its emphasis is on categories of human beings clustered together because of common pathology.

Educational Model

In sharp contrast to the medical model, the educational model focuses on individual differences and the competencies a teacher or coach needs to individualize instruction and training. The educational model evolved with the development of the social sciences (psychology, sociology, education) in the early 1900s but did not gain widespread acceptance until the Education of the Handicapped Act in the 1970s. This federal legislation mandated that decisions regarding students with disabilities would be based on comprehensive assessment of individual needs by a multidisciplinary team rather than on a medical diagnosis.

Reliance on the educational model leads physical educators to look beyond categorical classifications like mental retardation, learning disabilities, and orthopedic impairments. Although certain behaviors are associated with each of the major disabling conditions (see Part 3 of this text), individual differences make labels almost useless in the instructional setting. Describing a student in terms of specific learning strengths and weaknesses is much more relevant than saying that he or she is mentally retarded, physically disabled, blind, or asthmatic. From the educational model, we learn competencies needed to provide individuals with needed services. The educational model is sometimes called the *generic* or noncategorical model.

Philosophy and Practices

Figure 1.5 shows how a knowledge of theories, principles, and models affects philosophy of teaching and service delivery. *Philosophy* is a system of values and beliefs that guides behaviors. Derived from the Greek word *philosophia,* its literal meaning is love of truth. Philosophy evolves as we critically analyze theories, principles, and models and integrate what is personally meaningful with our experience and knowledge.

Values typically pertain to truth, goodness, justice, and beauty, whereas *beliefs* are convictions at a more concrete level. Consider, for example, your basic beliefs about people who are disabled or clumsy. What should be the nature of their physical education? Who should teach them? Where? How? What kind of recreation and sport opportunities should be made available? How? Why? One purpose of this book is to help you clarify your values and develop a strong philosophy about physical education and individual differences.

Practices are techniques, methods, strategies, or pedagogies used in service delivery, instruction, or therapy. While good teaching practices are important to all students, they are especially critical when individuals are clumsy and/or disabled or have low self-esteem. Think of the most difficult child you ever tried to teach. What practices worked? Why? What practices did not work? Why?

Practices may be designated as primarily educational or therapeutic. Education is derived from the Latin word *educatus* (*e* [out] + *duc* [lead] + *atus* [to]) and thus means to lead or guide an individual into active learning. Much of education is motivation, helping persons to believe in themselves and their capacity for change in relation to new skills, knowledge, attitudes, practices, and habits. Therapy comes from the Greek word *therapeia,* meaning treatment. Its primary aim is not teaching but the application of treatment modalities (i.e., ice, heat, exercise, medication) to make a person who is sick or disabled well and/or as functional as possible. Therapy is typically something done to or for persons, whereas education involves helping persons to do for themselves.

Should school-based adapted physical education be education or therapy? What practices belong equally to education and therapy? What practices are unique to each discipline? Figure 1.5 shows that education and therapy overlap. Unique blends must be created to assure that all individuals, particularly those with severe disability, develop the competencies needed for productive employment and leisure.

Individual Differences: The Unifying Theme

Adapted physical activity does not categorize human beings as disabled or nondisabled, as do eligibility procedures for special education placement. Instead, it analyzes individual differences associated with problems in the psychomotor domain. Additionally, adapted physical activity provides services for people with disabilities who are or aspire to be gifted athletes and who compete in specially designed sports, such as wheelchair basketball and tennis, that meet their needs.

Adapted physical activity theory pertains primarily to individual differences. These may be *developmental,* as is the case with most clumsy children, or *acquired,* as occurs with spinal cord and head injuries, amputations, and some sensory impairments. All adapted physical activity specialists thus are *developmentalists* with strong backgrounds in human growth and development and the neurological bases for normal and abnormal motor functioning. The knowledge base of adapted physical activity, however, extends beyond developmental theory.

How Does *Adapted* Differ from *Adaptive?*

Some persons confuse the adjectives *adapted* and *adaptive.* These words should not be used interchangeably. *Adapt* means to make suitable—to adjust, accommodate, or modify in accordance with needs. These needs may be developmental or environmental. Educators *adapt* curriculum content, instructional pedagogy, assessment and evaluation methodology, and physical environment, but they also help students to adapt. Thus, instruction is continuously being *adapted;* it is an active, ongoing process. In contrast, *adaptive* is used to describe behaviors.

Jean Piaget (1896–1980), perhaps the best known of all child psychologists, based his developmental theory upon the concept that *adaptation* is the fundamental characteristic of human life (Phillips, 1969; Piaget, 1962). According to Piaget, there are two types of adaptive behaviors: assimilation and accommodation. Assimilation occurs when an organism incorporates sensory input (like food) into the system, and both the food and the person are changed in the process (i.e., the change is interactive). Piaget defines *play* as almost entirely assimilative. Accommodation occurs when sensory input does not change, but perceptual-motor abilities do (i.e., they mature), and the self becomes more like the environment. Piaget states that imitation is nearly pure accommodation. Behavior is most adaptive when assimilation and accommodation are in balance, but this balance is always

FIGURE 1.5

A structure of knowledge model for the adapted physical activity
specialization and/or courses that focus on direct service delivery.

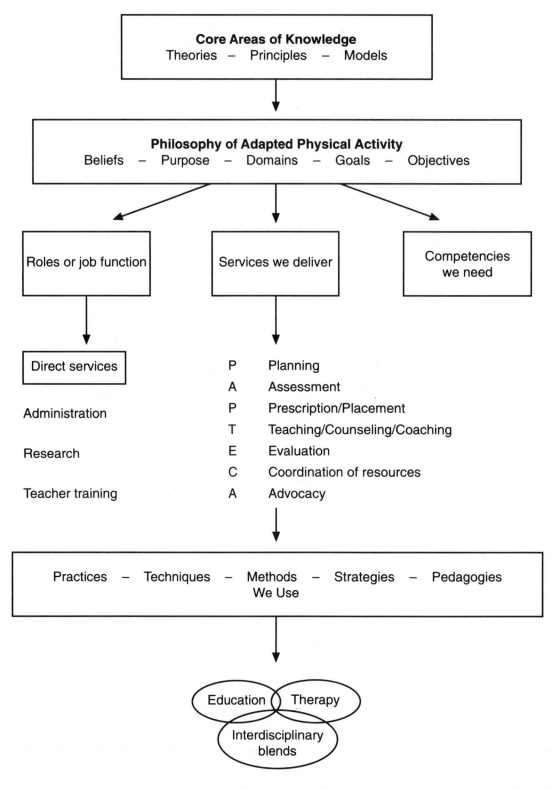

temporary because growth and development consist of continuous adapting (i.e., shifting back and forth between assimilation and accommodation).

In summary, education is *adapted,* but behaviors are
adaptive. Deficits in adaptive behavior are problems of de-

velopment, maturation, learning, and social adjustment that
result in individuals' failure to meet standards of personal
independence and social experience expected of their age
group and culture. Adapted physical education thus aims to
remediate deficits in adaptive behavior.

Table 1.1
A continuum of placement options for physical education instruction.

Students may be assigned to levels part or full time for a varying number of days or weeks. For example, a student might be assigned to Level IV 1 day a week, Level III 2 days a week, and Level II 2 days a week during a basketball unit. The assignment might change during a dance and rhythm unit.

Level I: Regular Physical Education
This system accommodates all students (both regular and special education) who meet certain eligibility criteria (e.g., perform at the 30th percentile or better; are able to benefit from group instruction when student-teacher ratio is 30:1). Criteria are typically established by local or state education agency. Curriculum and instruction decisions center around majority needs. Adaptations are made, as needed, for all students. Special education and adapted physical education support services are made available.

Level II: Partially Integrated Physical Education
A system comprised of many creative methods of combining special needs students with regular students. Curriculum and instruction decisions center around special needs students. This system is often implemented by an adapted physical education (resource room) specialist.

Level III: Separate Physical Education
A system in which students with similar instructional needs and/or disabling conditions are clustered together and taught separate and apart from others.

Level IV: One to One
A tutorial system in which one teacher works with one student.

Adapted Physical Activity Services

The adapted physical activity service delivery system is concerned with the same services as the regular curriculum except that advocacy and coordination of resources are added umbrella responsibilities. Counseling is a more important component in teaching persons with psychomotor problems than in regular physical education.

The individualized education program (IEP), the written legal document that guides the services of special education students, cannot be equated with any one service. The IEP results from a process prescribed by law that encompasses several of these services. See Chapter 4 for further information.

A description of seven services that comprise adapted physical activity follows. Use PAP-TE-CA as the key to remembering these.

Planning

Planning entails identifying appropriate physical education goals in accordance with school and community philosophy as well as individual needs. After available instructional time is calculated, the teacher estimates the number of objectives each student can probably achieve within the school year and then selects the specific objectives. Finally, the specific adapted physical education services needed to achieve objectives are planned. Planning also includes decision making about facilities and equipment and determinations of whether class sizes permit high-quality instruction. Planning denotes concern for budget, the number of personnel who can be employed, and how their time can best be used. Planning can be for an entire school system, a school, a single class, or an individual.

Assessment

Assessment is the combined process of testing, measuring, and evaluating persons and ecosystems (environments). It is an integral part of the teaching-learning process and occurs continuously. Assessment is needed to determine the best physical education placement for students: mainstream, separate, or combined. Once students are assigned to classes, assessment is needed to determine the *present level of psychomotor performance;* this serves, then, as the basis for planning. Also, evaluation procedures must be established for periodic determination of the effectiveness of the physical education program.

Prescription/Placement

Prescribing is the written recommendation of exercise and/or instructional activities based on the assessed needs of students. Prescription entails writing out the content to be taught (i.e., services to be delivered) and stating how much, when, and where, just as a physician states the medication to be taken, time of day, and amount per dose. Prescribing also includes specifying the educational environment likely to promote optimal development and learning (see Table 1.1). The more placement options a school can provide, the better that individual needs are served.

Placement can refer to either the scheduling and class assignment process or to grouping students into squads, teams, or partners within an already-established class. Because learning partners and classmates are so important to self-esteem and feelings of competence, adapted physical education emphasizes the joint process of prescribing/placing.

Teaching/Counseling/Coaching

Teaching/counseling/coaching is the process whereby psychomotor behaviors are changed to promote optimal performance. In adapted physical activity, teaching is often called *intervention.* Intervention means interfering with (or coming between, modifying) some undesirable physical, emotional, and/or social behavior to bring about a specific positive change. Each teacher contact that is directed toward changing behavior is considered an intervention.

Adapted physical education is often considered *developmental teaching* because the learning activities or interventions are adapted to the student's developmental motor, fitness, or play level. This is generally achieved through *ecological task analysis,* which is defined as problem solving to identify task and environmental variables so that they can be altered to assure success as challenges are made progressively more difficult.

In adapted physical activity, teaching and counseling are considered inseparable. To resolve problems pertaining to fitness, sport, and leisure, teachers must be good listeners and possess skills that help students to believe in themselves and their ability to overcome problems. Teachers must know how to create support networks to provide continuous feedback as students strive to change. Moreover, teachers must be skilled in values clarification, able to offer information about alternative choices, and knowledgeable about ways to help students help themselves. *Counseling* thus is a helping process in which teachers use individual and small-group talk, interaction, and movement to facilitate self-actualization in relation to fitness, sport, and leisure. Peer counselors may be trained to use these modalities also. Physical educators should take at least one counseling course and have some counseling skills. It is important to recognize when a student's problems extend beyond personal counseling abilities and time and to know procedures for referral to a certified school or community counselor.

Coaching can be volunteer or salaried. If persons with disabilities are to be given equal access to sports (developmental, recreational, competitive) during their leisure time, professionals must be willing to coach and be skilled in training adult, sibling, and peer volunteers. Professionals must also know how to promote attitude change that will lead to integration of persons with disabilities into school and community programs.

Sport involvement is often a family activity, and there should be a continuum of opportunities, ranging from affiliation with a sport organization for persons with disabilities to full integration in a regular program. Professionals assist with decision making, ascertaining that persons understand the differences between developmental, recreational, and competitive sports. The goal of coaching varies from socializing persons with disabilities into active lifestyles through developmental sports to helping them win and/or achieve personal bests in high-level, fierce competition.

Evaluation

Evaluation is the continuous process of determining student gain and program effectiveness. Although evaluation should be ongoing, it typically is emphasized the last few days of an instructional unit or school term. Evaluation is conducted in relation to set goals, and results are used to determine whether or not goals have been achieved. This process, in turn, leads to modification of the instructional system before the cycle is begun anew (see Figure 1.4).

Coordination of Resources

For physical education to improve quality of life, it must be carried over into daily living activities and leisure. The adapted physical educator therefore identifies community, home, and agency resources that can be utilized by persons with disabilities during after-school and weekend hours and then facilitates and coordinates the use of such resources.

Advocacy

Advocacy entails defending, maintaining, or promoting the rights of all human beings to high-quality physical activity and the use of school and community resources. It includes teaching able-bodied persons about the laws that govern human rights and working for stronger legislation. Most important, advocacy involves changing society's attitudes and aspirations about persons who are different or disabled.

Adapted Physical Education Competencies

Each of the adapted physical activity services just discussed can be broken down into specific tasks. Since 1972, the American Alliance for Health, Physical Education, Recreation, and Dance (AAHPERD) has supported a competency approach for preparing individuals to teach adapted physical education. A *competency* can be defined as adequate, suitable, or sufficient skill, behavior, or knowledge to perform specific services or functions. The word is derived from the Latin *competere,* meaning to meet or to agree; this emphasizes that job functions and professional abilities must agree.

AAHPERD has published two sets of competencies, one in 1972 and one in 1981, to guide the preparation of adapted physical education teachers. These are found in various sources (AAHPERD, 1973; Hurley, 1981; Sherrill, 1988), but a new set will probably appear in the 1990s. Competencies related to job functions and services described in this text are presented at the beginning of this book. You may wish to assess your skills in relation to these competencies.

Roles or Job Functions

Services that professionals perform depend on the role or job function for which they are employed. In the public schools, roles are usually designated as (a) direct service delivery, (b) related services delivery, and (c) administrative. *Direct service delivery* refers to contact with a student or client in which attention is directed toward development or function (i.e., causing a permanent change in knowledge, skills, attitudes, and the like). In contrast, *related services delivery* refers primarily to various kinds of therapy that are required for a student to benefit from instruction. *Administrative* roles vary by school district but often emphasize assessment, curriculum development, supervision of less experienced teachers, consulting, and program evaluation.

Table 1.2
Goals of adapted physical activity classified according to domains.

Affective Domain Goals

Positive Self-Concept. To strengthen self-concept and body image through activity involvement; to increase understanding and appreciation of the body and its capacity for movement; to accept limitations that cannot be changed and to learn to adapt environment so as to make the most of strengths (i.e., to work toward self-actualization).

Social Competency. To reduce social isolation; to learn how to develop and maintain friendships; to demonstrate good sportsmanship and self-discipline in winning and losing; to develop other skills necessary for success in the mainstream, including appropriate social behaviors (i.e., how to interact with others—sharing, taking turns, following, and leading).

Fun/Tension Release. To improve attitude toward exercise, physical activity, and sports, dance, and aquatics so that involvement represents fun, recreation, and happiness; to improve mental health through activity involvement; to learn to release tensions in a healthy, socially acceptable manner; to reduce hyperactivity and learn to relax.

Psychomotor Domain Goals

Motor Skills and Patterns. To learn fundamental motor skills and patterns; to master the motor skills indigenous to games, sports, dance, and aquatics participation; to improve fine and gross motor coordination for self-care, school, work, and play activities.

Physical Fitness. To develop the cardiovascular system; to promote ideal weight; to increase muscular strength, endurance, and flexibility; to improve posture.

Leisure-Time Skills. To learn to transfer physical education learnings into habits of lifetime sports, dance, and aquatics; to become acquainted with community resources for recreation; to expand repertoire of and/or to refine skills in individual and group games and in sports, dance, and aquatic activities.

Cognitive Domain Goals

Play and Game Behaviors. To learn to play spontaneously; to progress through developmental play stages from solitary and parallel play behaviors up through appropriate cooperative and competitive game behaviors; to promote contact and interaction behaviors with toys, play apparatus, and persons; to learn basic game formations and mental operations needed for play; to master rules and strategies of simple games.

Perceptual-Motor Function and Sensory Integration. To enhance visual, auditory, tactile, vestibular, and kinesthetic functioning; to reinforce academic learnings through games and perceptual-motor activities; to improve cognitive, language, and motor function through increased sensory integration.

Creative Expression. To increase creativity in movement and thought; when posed a movement problem, to generate *many* responses, *different* responses, *original* responses; to learn to imagine; to embellish and add on; to risk experimentation; to devise appropriate game strategy; to create new games, dances, and movement sequences.

As a practicum experience for this chapter, arrange to visit some public or private schools and observe professionals who are employed in different roles. Talk to both regular and adapted physical educators to extend your understanding of the roles, services, and competencies associated with direct service delivery.

Philosophy of Adapted Physical Activity

Philosophy evolves from moral reasoning. Some persons believe as they do because they embrace the laws of society, whereas others are guided by personal conscience and integrity. Much of contemporary adapted physical activity has its roots in the federal legislation of the 1970s, but commitment to the idea of quality physical activity for all persons extends beyond law into your personal value system.

A professional philosophy typically includes statements of belief about the purpose and goals of education, the nature of the student, the behaviors of the teacher, the service delivery system, and adapted physical activity pedagogy. These beliefs may reflect what currently exists but more typically indicate what should be.

Purpose and Goals

In adapted physical activity, the terms *purpose, goal,* and *objectives* are used in very specific ways. A *purpose* is the overall aim or intention. The purpose of adapted physical activity is the same as that of regular activity: to change psychomotor behaviors, thereby facilitating self-actualization.

Goals are broad, global statements that are long range in nature, whereas *objectives* are short term and often written in behavioral format. These definitions come from federal legislation that guides the development of individualized education programs (IEPs). Long range refers to annual, semiannual, or quarterly statements that guide instruction. Table 1.2 presents nine goal areas. Usually, time permits work on only three or four goals. Therefore, teachers must use assessment data to select the goals most appropriate for each individual.

Each goal then is broken down into specific, short-term objectives that require 3 to 5 hours for achievement. Often, lesson plans allocate only 5 or 10 minutes per session to an objective, so work continues over several weeks. For example, consider the goal of developing a good self-concept in the athletic domain. An objective might be: *Given opportunity to engage in a leisure activity like skiing for 30 minutes and to evaluate success after the activity, student will say at least one good thing about self* (see Figure 1.6). If the goal were to develop fitness, then the objective might be: *Given instructions to do as many sit-ups as possible in 30 seconds, student will complete 25.*

FIGURE 1.6

Students with severe mental retardation can be taught skiing when skills
are task analyzed and variables are manipulated.

Purpose and goals are integral parts of a philosophy. They determine the kind of assessment administered and thus establish the framework of opportunity. Objectives are not part of a philosophy; they are tools or vehicles for accomplishing goals.

Each of the nine goal areas in Table 1.2 contributes to self-actualization in one of three domains (affective, psychomotor, or cognitive). Consider different persons with disabilities. What three or four goals might be best for each one? Can you think of ways to assess performance in each goal area? If not, then you cannot use the goal because programming is based on assessment. Your competencies thus shape the philosophy that guides your service delivery.

Nature of the Student

Whom should adapted physical education serve? The answer is an important part of your philosophy. In this text, the target population is both regular and special education students who have psychomotor problems that affect success. Assignment to adapted physical education should not be based on presence of a disability but rather on psychomotor performance.

Normal curve or individual differences theory posits that, for every 100 students administered a test, 68% will make average or normal scores (i.e., letter grades ranging from $C-$ to $C+$) (see Figure 1.7). The other 32% will be evenly divided between the A/B and D/F letter-grade categories and can be described as either above average or gifted, or below average or delayed/clumsy. Any student whose physical education performance repeatedly falls below average on tests or whose performance looks clumsy to an expert observer should receive adapted physical education assistance. Clumsiness, or physical awkwardness, is the inability to perform culturally normative motor activities with ac-

ceptable proficiency (Wall, 1982). Clumsiness denotes performance below the 50th percentile (see Figure 1.7). The average score or mean is the same as the 50th percentile.

Students who perform poorly in the psychomotor domain typically have low self-esteem about their bodies and movement capacities. These feelings of inadequacy may carry over into social relationships because success in sports and games is valued highly in our society, particularly by children and adolescents. Students with low self-esteem often feel helpless about changing themselves and/or the environment. They see themselves as clumsy, fat, or unfit/unattractive forever and powerless to change. This, in turn, may lead to disliking and avoiding physical activity. A large part of adapted physical education is therefore changing the way persons feel about themselves.

In some school systems, part of physical education instructional time is spent in game play and competition. When this is the case, students who cannot safely or successfully participate in games like basketball, football, and soccer may be scheduled for alternative instructional units. In this regard, all students should have access to instruction in sports that will carry over into their use of leisure time. This often means instruction, practice, and competition in sports specific to a disability, such as wheelchair basketball, tennis, track, and distance racing for persons with lower-limb impairments; beep baseball and goalball for persons with visual impairments; and boccia and team handball for individuals with cerebral palsy.

Some students are so severely disabled that they cannot benefit from group instruction in a regular physical education setting. These individuals are typically multi-disabled, with various combinations of mental retardation (IQs below 35), physical disabilities (inability to sit or

FIGURE 1.7

A normal curve is a mathematical model that shows where 100 or more students will score if given a standardized test. Along the baseline are standard deviation marks ($\pm\sigma$) that divide the curve into 3%, 13%, and 68% areas. Underneath the baseline of the curve is a percentile equivalents scale showing that the 50th percentile is synonymous with the concepts of 0, mean, and average score.

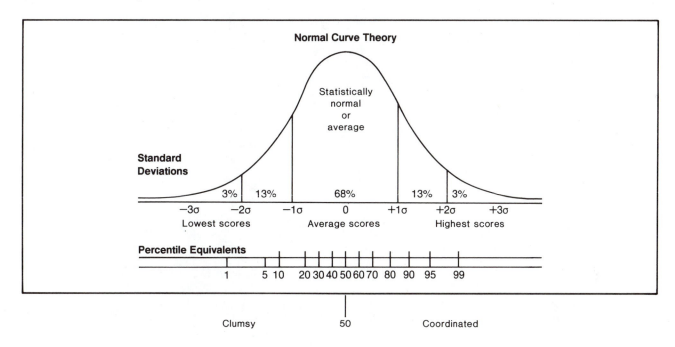

walk unassisted), language deficits (inability to understand and/or respond appropriately to speech), total or almost total blindness and/or deafness, and medical problems like seizures and heart defects. Adapted physical activity philosophy posits that these students, like their less disabled peers, have the right to high-quality physical education instruction. They are typically taught on a one-to-one basis or with three or four classmates.

Basic Beliefs

In summary, students receiving adapted physical education (like regular physical education) have widespread individual differences. Regardless of the nature of the student, adapted physical activity philosophy affirms that

1. All students can benefit from physical education in one or more of nine goal areas.
2. All students can learn.
3. All students should be assured the right to high-quality physical education instruction that will enhance their self-esteem and contribute to good mental health.
4. All students should receive instruction in sports, dance, and aquatics that will carry over into their use of leisure time and contribute to an active, healthy lifestyle.
5. All students should be provided adequate physical activity to assure health and fitness for daily living and to benefit from instruction.

Characteristics of Adapted Physical Education

Similarities and differences between adapted physical education and regular physical education vary according to school system, school, and teacher. In general, however, 10 major characteristics are apparent, with the first letter of each characteristic combining to spell FAMILY SEAZ. This mnemonic device will enhance memory of the characteristics.

F—Federally Mandated Legislative Base

The Individuals with Disabilities Education Act (IDEA), which is reauthorized approximately every 3 years, provides the basis for adapted physical activity service delivery for special education students. The IDEA rules and regulations include physical education as a part of special education, which is defined as:

. . . specially designed instruction, at no cost to parents or guardians, to meet the unique needs of a child with a disability, including—

(A) instruction conducted in the classroom, in the home, in hospitals and institutions, and in other settings; and
(B) instruction in physical education. (Individuals with Disabilities Education Act, 20 U.S.C., Chapter 33, Section 1401)

Thus, special education students are assured adapted physical activity services if assessment indicates this need and the recommendation is written into the individualized education program (IEP). In contrast, regular education students are

FIGURE 1.8

Teachers in early childhood units must have a strong background in motor development since young children with disabilities often perform motorically as infants and toddlers. This 3-year-old with Down syndrome must improve *hand grasp and release* and *visual pursuit and tracking* before ball-handling skills are introduced.

not provided this legal protection. No IEP is required to guide their education. Adapted physical educators must therefore advocate and work toward adapted physical education services for any student who needs them, regardless of eligibility under federal law.

A—Assessment

Adapted physical activity begins with assessment of needs and identification of problems. Without this process, there can be no scientifically based individualizing and adapting. Whereas assessment is important in regular physical education, it is critical in adapted physical education. Note that all three definitions of adapted physical activity (believing, doing, knowing) are dependent on assessment of individual needs and/or problems.

M—Multidisciplinary/Crossdisciplinary

Federal law uses the term *multidisciplinary* to emphasize that many disciplines must work together in assessment and programming. This book includes *crossdisciplinary* in its title to emphasize that the adapted physical activity knowledge base integrates content across disciplines.

I—Inclusive of Infancy and Postsecondary Ages

Many adapted physical activity specialists work in early childhood and infant stimulation units (Figure 1.8). Others provide services for persons ages 18 to 21 in vocational education and alternative work/study settings. Still others are employed in community-based and residential programs that offer physical activity, fitness, and leisure services for persons over 21. Adapted physical education thus encompasses a lifespan approach.

L—Low or Different Psychomotor Performance

Adapted physical activity is mainly concerned with psychomotor performance that is below average (i.e., below the 50th percentile) or different from the norm. Low performance is not synonymous with having a disability. Many students with disabilities have the potential of becoming excellent athletes, assuming that they have access to appropriate sports (e.g., wheelchair events, beep baseball). If a person's innate functional capacity requires adapting a sport to permit safe and successful participation, the adapted physical educator is usually the one who teaches the skills, rules, and strategies of the "different" sport.

Y—Yes, Sport Training and Competition

Sports are an integral part of every culture. They contribute to an active lifestyle, good mental health, and rich, satisfying use of leisure time. Thus, sport associations have evolved to meet the needs of specific disabilities. Among these are the U.S. Cerebral Palsy Athletic Association (USCPAA), the U.S. Association for Blind Athletes (USABA), the National Wheelchair Athletic Association (NWAA), and Special Olympics International (SOI). Table 3.1 provides names of comparable international sport associations (see Chapter 3). An important goal of adapted physical education is to help students develop leisure-time skills that contribute to lifelong involvement in sports. To achieve this, the teacher helps students to match their abilities to the appropriate organization and socializes them into sport as early as possible.

S—Services Emphasis

The emphasis in adapted physical education, like in special education, is on providing a continuum of services, rather than simply adapting instruction. One student may need many services, while another may require only a few. In some instances, a student needs only *direct services* (i.e., those that pertain directly to instruction, like special education and physical education), whereas for others, *related services* are important. Related services are provisions like transportation and physical and occupational therapy that are required to assist a student to benefit from direct services. Related services cannot be a substitute for direct instruction. Related services are always supplementary. Physical education services (remember the acronym PAP-TE-CA) are direct services.

E—Ecological Orientation

Much of the success of students in the mainstream depends upon the teacher's skill in removing architectural, attitudinal, and aspirational barriers (i.e., facilitating the favorable interrelationships that contribute to social acceptance and good self-concept and, subsequently, to effective learning). Adapted physical education is, therefore, concerned with *ecology* (the science of relationships between organisms and their environment).

An *ecosystem* is the total environment or lifespace environment of an individual (see Figure 1.9). This includes the attitudes and practices of everyone the student contacts: members of the family, neighborhood, school, and community. The adapted physical educator recognizes that changing the behavior of a student is not enough; the entire ecosystem must be changed.

A—Accountability

The concept of accountability, when applied to the teaching process, means that a particular program, method, strategy, or intervention can be demonstrated to cause a significant positive change in one or more behaviors. While all teachers are more or less accountable to administrators and parents, the adapted physical educator is expected to maintain written records on each student that document specific progress toward preestablished objectives. More about the accountability movement in education is found in the works of Lessinger (1970), Sherrill (1988), and Turnbull (1975, 1990).

Z—Zero Reject and Zero Fail

Zero Reject emphasizes the right of all students, regardless of severity of disability, to high-quality physical education instruction. No student is rejected from free, public school programming, and no student is excused from class participation. Zero Fail captures the idea of success-oriented physical education, with adaptations so that every student can achieve.

FAMILY SEAZ: A Mnemonic Device

To facilitate remembering the 10 characteristics of adapted physical education just discussed, try visualizing a large family at the seashore. For *F*, visualize a father in an Uncle Sam uniform to remember *federally mandated legislative base*. For *A*, think of aunts sticking their toes in the water and *assessing* the temperature. For *M*, conceptualize a mother in many colors, talking about her multiple roles in today's society: *multidisciplinary*. For *I*, visualize *inclusive* of all ages: a baby in the water, a teenager, a grandfather. And so on! This learning technique is called a *mnemonic device*. The more ridiculous you make the visualization, the easier you will remember the characteristics. Ask your teacher to discuss the many kinds of mnemonic devices and think of creative ways to remember the content of this chapter.

History of Adapted Physical Activity

Many issues concerning the future growth and direction of adapted physical activity can be clarified by a brief review of the profession's history. Contemporary adapted physical activity has its roots in both a medical and an educational model, and the sport movement has had an impact on both models.

The origin of the medical model, or the use of exercise in physical rehabilitation, is usually attributed to Per Henrik Ling (1776–1839) of Sweden. Ling, a fencing master with a disabled arm, studied the effect of exercise on his own rehabilitation and subsequently developed the system of exercise known as medical gymnastics. This system emphasized specific movements for each part of the body performed to the command of an instructor (e.g., "Ready—1, 2, 3, 4")

FIGURE   1.9

Ecosystem of a child, showing the influence of persons in the family, community, neighborhood, and school.

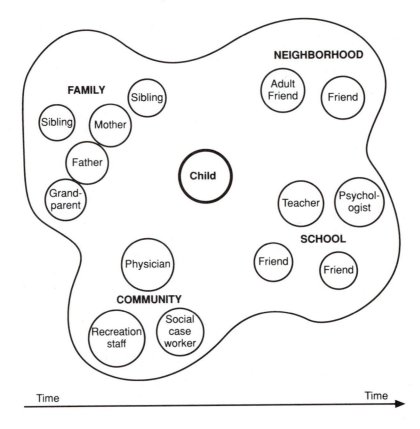

in militaristic fashion. Its purpose extended beyond rehabilitation to embrace health, control, and bodily perfection. Medical gymnastics was recommended for all students, not just those ill or disabled.

The origin of the educational model, or the use of sensorimotor or perceptual-motor activity to remediate mental and sensory defects, is usually attributed to Jean-Marc Itard (1775–1839), a French physician known as an authority on deafness. Itard is recognized for his attempt to educate Victor, a 12-year-old boy found naked, wild, and nonverbal in 1800. Although Victor, called the Wild Boy of Aveyron, remained functionally retarded, Itard and his followers believed that Itard's innovative sensorimotor training program was effective in ameliorating the condition. This training model was subsequently used in residential facilities but received little attention in public schools until special education evolved as a profession.

The formation of a professional organization is typically the event that marks the beginning of a profession. The American Medical Association was formed in 1847, and the National Education Association in 1870. The Association for the Advancement of Physical Education began in 1885. By 1905, the therapeutics interest group/section/council was established within the physical education organization. Thus, adapted physical activity has a long, rich history. It existed before professional organizations were formed for recreation

(1906), occupational therapy (1917), physical therapy (1921), and special education (1922).

Adapted physical activity has survived many name changes and philosophical differences. In the United States, this service delivery system seems to have evolved through five stages.

Stage 1, Medical Gymnastics: Before 1900

Prior to the 1900s, all physical education was medically oriented and preventive, developmental, or corrective in nature. The physical education curriculum was comprised primarily of that which we know today as gymnastics, calisthenics, body mechanics, and marching or military-like exercise drills. University physical educators were generally *physicians* who applied known principles of medicine to the various systems of exercise. The purpose of physical training (or physical culture, as the profession was called then) was to prevent illness and/or to promote the health and vigor of the mind and body.

Stage 2, Transition to Sports: 1900–1930

The gradual transition from medically oriented physical training to sports-centered physical education occurred in the early 1900s. Factors influencing this change were (a) the introduction of sports into American culture and, subsequently, the physical education curriculum; (b) the application of psychological and sociological theory to education, resulting in the conceptualization of the *whole child;* (c) the trend away from medical training as appropriate teacher preparation for physical educators; and (d) the advent of compulsory physical education in the public schools.

State legislation making physical education mandatory in the public schools increased the number of students to be taught and brought new problems. What, for instance, would be done if a student were ill or disabled, or lacked the physical stamina to participate in the regular curriculum? The solution was to divide physical education into two branches: (a) *regular* and (b) *corrective* or *remedial.*

Stage 3, Corrective Physical Education: 1930–1950

Between the 1930s and the 1950s, both regular and corrective physical education served mostly what are known today as normal students. Assignment to physical education was based on a thorough medical examination by a physician, who determined whether a student should participate in the regular or corrective program. Corrective classes were comprised primarily of limited, restricted, or modified activities related to health, posture, or fitness problems. In many schools, students were excused from physical education. In others, the physical educator typically taught several sections of regular physical education and one section of corrective physical education each day. Leaders in corrective physical education continued to have strong backgrounds in medicine. Persons preparing to be physical education teachers generally completed one university course in corrective physical education.

Veterans returning from World War II were instrumental in initiating a name change. They pointed out that amputations and spinal cord injuries could not be corrected. They also emphasized the potential of sports in rehabilitation and started various wheelchair sports.

Stage 4, Adapted Physical Education: 1950–1970

During the 1950s and 1960s, the population served in public school corrective/adapted physical education broadened to include persons with all disabilities. Instrumental in this change was the trend away from residential school placement. This resulted in increased enrollment of students with disabilities, particularly mental retardation, in the public schools. The values that such children and youth could derive from participation in sports, dance, and aquatics adapted to their special needs were increasingly recognized. The following definition evolved in the early 1950s:

Adapted physical education is a diversified program of developmental activities, games, sports, and rhythms suited to the interests, capacities, and limitations of students with disabilities who may not safely or successfully engage in unrestricted participation in the vigorous activities of the general physical education program. (Committee on Adapted Physical Education, 1952, p. 15)

This definition was viable throughout the next two decades since adapted physical education teaching practices paralleled the special education procedure of segregating students with disabilities in separate classes and/or special schools.

FIGURE 1.10

The National Advisory Committee on Physical Education and Recreation for Handicapped Children was created by Congress to guide personnel preparation in the 1970s. *Top, left to right:* Fred Humphrey, William Wolfe, John Nesbitt, George Valos. *Bottom, left to right:* Robert Holland, Janet Wessel, and Rafer Johnson.

During this era, many names were proposed (special, developmental, and remedial) and used as textbook titles.

Through the efforts of President John F. Kennedy, his sister Eunice Kennedy Shriver, and his brother Senator Edward Kennedy, physical educators became increasingly aware of mental retardation. Special Olympics was created in 1968. The human rights movement of the 1960s led to federal legislation that addressed inequities in public school education and prohibited segregation.

Stage 5, Adapted Physical Activity: 1970–Present

Since 1970, countries throughout the world have passed legislation to guarantee rights to persons with disabilities. The United Nations designated 1981 as International Year of the Disabled. This stage marked the shift from educating persons with disabilities in separate or special settings to an emphasis on least restrictive educational environments and integration. The concepts of service delivery systems and multidisciplinary programming emerged in conjunction with federal legislation. Labeling students (e.g., special, disabled) fell into disrepute, and the normalcy of individual differences and the responsibility of teachers to adapt for differences were increasingly emphasized.

Although in 1967 legislation was enacted to fund the training of physical education and recreation specialists to serve students with disabilities, money to implement the law did not become available until 1970. Colleges and universities thus began developing an academic specialization or major in adapted physical education during the 1970s (see Figure 1.10). Typically, this specialization was offered only at the graduate level, although some undergraduate programs encouraged double majors in special education and physical education.

Some authorities began to see adapted physical activity as a merger between special education and physical education, whereas others saw it as an evolving crossdisciplinary body of knowledge. In 1973, the International Federation of Adapted Physical Activity (IFAPA) was founded in Canada. Professionals from around the world lent strength to the crossdisciplinary conceptual framework by sharing research and practices.

If history fascinates you and/or you need more background to clarify your philosophical beliefs, see Appendix G. A detailed history of adapted physical activity can be found in *Leadership Training in Adapted Physical Education* (Sherrill, 1988).

Issues and Trends

This chapter has provided an overview of adapted physical activity as an evolving specialization and service delivery system. Embedded in the presentation of definitions, nature, scope, philosophy, and history are both issues and trends. A list of issues stated as questions with alternative answers follows. Think about various options, read other references, and make up your own mind about each issue. The decisions you and your generation make will set the trends for the future.

1. **What is adapted physical activity?**

   - A service delivery system that includes assessment, placement, prescriptive and developmental teaching, and fitness and leisure counseling
   - A program of medically prescribed therapeutic exercise, education, and adapted physical activities
   - A diversified program of developmental activities, games, sports, and rhythms suited to the interests, capabilities, and limitations of students with disabilities who may not safely or successfully engage in unrestricted participation in the vigorous activities of the general physical education program

2. **Whom should adapted physical education serve?**

   - Students with disabilities defined in federal legislation
   - Students who meet special education eligibility requirements under state policy and federal legislation
   - Students who consistently perform below the 50th percentile in tests and observations of physical and motor fitness, motor skills and patterns, and aquatics, dance, and sports

3. **Where do adapted physical activity specialists deliver services?**

   - A separate setting
   - An integrated setting
   - A continuum of placements: separate, combined, and mainstreamed

4. **What are the goals and objectives of adapted physical education?**

   - Same as regular physical education
   - Goals same, but objectives prioritized differently
   - Both goals and objectives different

5. **What is the best name for the public school service delivery system?**

   - Adapted physical education
   - Developmental physical education
   - Special physical education

6. **Which of the following does adapted physical activity favor?**

   - Accepting and appreciating individual differences
   - Reducing individual differences
   - Ignoring individual differences

References

American Alliance for Health, Physical Education, Recreation, and Dance. (1973). *Professional preparation in adapted physical education, therapeutic recreation, and corrective therapy.* Washington, DC: Author.

Bell-Gredler, M. (1986). *Learning and instruction: Theory into practice.* New York: Macmillan.

Bigge, M. L. (1982). *Learning theories for teachers* (4th ed.). New York: Harper & Row.

Bloom, B. (Ed.). (1956). *Taxonomy of education objectives. Handbook I: Cognitive domain.* New York: David McKay.

Burton, A. W. (1990). Applying principles of coordination in adapted physical education. *Adapted Physical Activity Quarterly, 7* (2), 126–142.

Burton, A. W., & Davis, W. E. (1992). Issues related to balance in adapted physical education: Assessment and intervention strategies. *Adapted Physical Activity Quarterly, 9* (1), 14–46.

Committee on Adapted Physical Education. (1952). Guiding principles for adapted physical education. *Journal of Health, Physical Education, and Recreation, 23,* 15.

Craft, D. H., & Hogan, P. I. (1985). Development of self-concept and self-efficacy: Considerations for mainstreaming. *Adapted Physical Activity Quarterly, 2* (4), 320–327.

Davis, W. E., & Burton, A. W. (1991). Ecological task analysis: Translating movement behavior theory into practice. *Adapted Physical Activity Quarterly, 8,* 154–177.

Federal Register, August 23, 1977, PL 94–142, the Education for All Handicapped Children Act.

Gruber, J. J. (1986). Physical activity and self-esteem development in children: A meta-analysis. In G. A. Stull & H. E. Eckert (Eds.), *American Academy of Physical Education Papers No. 19.* (pp. 30–48). Champaign, IL: Human Kinetics.

Harrow, A. (1972). *A taxonomy of the psychomotor domain.* New York: David McKay.

Hogan, P. I. (1990). Problem-based learning and personnel preparation in adapted physical education. *Adapted Physical Activity Quarterly, 7* (3), 205–218.

Hoover, J. H., & Wade, M. G. (1985). Motor learning theory and mentally retarded individuals: A historical review. *Adapted Physical Activity Quarterly, 2* (3), 228–252.

Hurley, D. (1981). Guidelines for adapted physical education. *Journal of Physical Education, Recreation, and Dance, 52,* 43–45.

Individuals with Disabilities Education Act of 1990, 20 U.S.C., Chapter 33.

Krathwohl, D. (Ed.). (1964). *Taxonomy of education objectives. Handbook II: Affective domain.* New York: David McKay.

Lessinger, L. (1970). *Every kid a winner: Accountability in education.* New York: Simon & Schuster.

Maslow, A. (1968). *Toward a psychology of being* (2nd ed.). Princeton, NJ: Van Nostrand.

Maslow, A. (1970). *Motivation and personality* (2nd ed.). New York: Harper & Row.

Morris, G. S. D., & Stiehl, J. (1989). *Changing kids' games.* Champaign, IL: Human Kinetics.

Mosston, M., & Ashworth, S. (1986). *Teaching physical education* (3rd ed.). Columbus, OH: Merrill.

Phillips, J. (1969). *The origins of intellect: Piaget's theory.* San Francisco: W.H. Freeman.

Piaget, J. (1962). *Play, dreams, and imitation in childhood.* New York: W.W. Norton.

Reid, G. (1989). Ideas about motor behavior research with special populations. *Adapted Physical Activity Quarterly, 6* (1), 1–10.

Salkind, N. J. (1985). *Theories of human development.* New York: John Wiley & Sons.

Sherrill, C. (Ed.). (1988). *Leadership training in adapted physical education.* Champaign, IL: Human Kinetics.

Turnbull, H. R. (1975). Accountability: An overview of the impact of litigation on professionals. *Exceptional Children, 41,* 427–433.

Turnbull, H. R. (1990). *Free appropriate public education: Law and education of children with disabilities.* Denver: Love Publishing.

U.S. Department of Education. (1991). *AMERICA 2000: An education strategy.* Washington, DC: Author.

Wall, A. (1982). Physically awkward children: A motor development perspective. In J. Das, R. Mulcahy, & A. Wall (Eds.), *Theory and research in learning disabilities* (pp. 253–268). New York: Plenum.

Wessel, J. (Ed.). (1977.) *Planning individualized education programs in special education.* Northbrook, IL: Hubbard.

Wessel, J., & Kelly, L. (1986). *Achievement-based curriculum in physical education.* Philadelphia: Lea & Febiger.

Wolfensberger, W. (1972). *The principle of normalization in human service.* Toronto: National Institute of Mental Retardation.

CHAPTER

2

Celebrating Individual Differences and Promoting Positive Attitudes

FIGURE 2.1

A life situation for consideration: (*A*) Bob (on crutches) and Joe (in the wheelchair) are 10-year-olds with normal intelligence. Both are average or better students in their fourth-grade classroom but have had little opportunity to learn sports, dance, and aquatics. (*B*) Jim is 5 years old and obviously small for his age; he learns slowly but tries hard to please. (*C*) Dick has a brace on one leg and lots of problems with asthma. Your principal asks you to integrate these children into your regular physical education classes, which typically have 25 to 30 students. How do you feel about this?

B

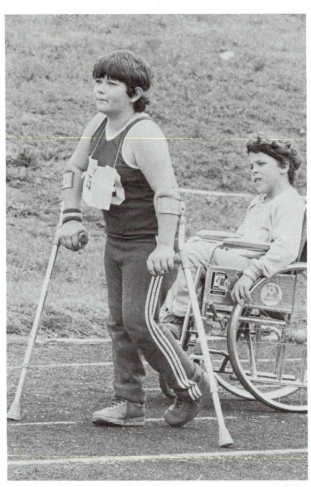

A

C

After you have studied this chapter, you should be able to:

1. Discuss the wide range of individual differences associated with eight disabilities and the importance of developing a *person-first* philosophy.

2. Cite guidelines for interacting with and speaking and writing about persons with disabilities. Find and discuss examples that support and violate these guidelines.

3. Initiate contact with persons who have disabilities and establish equal-status relationships. Describe your attempts and the goals you have set.

4. Discuss issues pertaining to semantics, labeling, and categorizing. Consider the past, present, and future.

5. Define attitude, discuss its components, and explain the role of specificity in attitude change.

6. Discuss problems in being different and associated attitudes and behaviors. Identify and discuss theories related to these problems.

7. Discuss attitude assessment and describe some available instruments.

8. Explain four theories that can be applied to guide attitude change and discuss strategies associated with each.

9. Given a student who is low in social acceptance, discuss the techniques you would use to ameliorate this problem. Cite theories and research to support your approach.

Sport holds a mirror to our life
all that we can know
> *of joy*
> *or sadness*
finds its counterpart in sport
we learn not only how we move
> *but how we feel*
> *and think*
> *and struggle*
> *how we are tormented*
> *triumph*
> *and then find peace*
as we absorb the
> *mood*
> *drama*
> *and emotion*
which are the essences of our sport
> *so we discover*
> *all the inward stresses*
> *that move our being*
(Price, 1970, p. 13)

Beliefs such as those reflected in the preceding poem make strong advocates for physical education, recreation, and sport. Adapted physical activity educators are also advocates for persons who are differently abled (see Figure 2.1). Much of the focus is on changing attitudes and practices so that all individuals have opportunities for growing and developing through sport, dance, aquatics, movement education, and exercise.

This chapter presents information useful in developing advocacy skills and working in integrated settings. The chapter begins with accounts of eight individuals who have overcome various problems. The role of physical activity and sport in expressing individuality and uniqueness is explored, as is the personal meaning of disability. Guidelines are suggested for interacting with differently abled persons and helping self and others acquire positive attitudes. The chapter content comes from two knowledge clusters believed to be important in adapted physical activity: (a) individual differences theory and (b) attitude, interpersonal relations, and communication theory.

Case Studies and Anecdotes

Case studies and anecdotes are presented in this section to introduce several conditions and personalize human beings who have these conditions. Included are accounts of asthma and health problems, clumsiness, learning disabilities, mild and severe mental retardation, cerebral palsy, traumatic spinal-cord injury, and deafness. The case-study approach emphasizes the importance of thinking about individuals, not conditions, when studying adapted physical activity.

Carl Rogers (1902–1987), the father of modern-day counseling and humanistic teaching, stated that friendship (i.e., a caring, trusting relationship) is an important ingredient in teaching:

In my judgment, the warm, subjective, human encounter of two persons is more effective in facilitating change than the most precise art or technique growing out of learning theory or operant conditioning. (cited in Buscaglia, 1975, p. 287)

This chapter challenges physical educators to view themselves as friends, advocates, and facilitators of change. We focus now on what some differently abled people feel and think.

Asthma and Health Problems

• *I was a sickly child, missing approximately 1 week of every 6 weeks of school because of various combinations of asthma, colds, and respiratory illness. My earliest memories center on looking out the window at the other kids, engaged in fast, wonderful, vigorous games, and wanting desperately to be with them and like them. I was skinny and unfit. Exercise almost always made me wheeze, and I hated my lungs and what I perceived to be an inefficient body that wouldn't let me do and be what I wanted. I read a lot and made good grades, but I didn't feel good about myself.*

By high school, I seemed magically to have outgrown my asthma. Physical education became my favorite class, and the after-school sports program was my life. I felt suddenly alive, really alive. My mind and body were finally working together, and I believed I could do everything. I never achieved the skill level of my friends who had rich, active childhoods, but I made up for this with enthusiasm and extra effort. I felt like my PE teacher liked me for myself, not because I made good grades or was one of her best athletes. She spent a lot of time talking with us kids. We all had a lot of problems, but we would never have gone to the school counselor.

When it was time to enter college, I agonized over whether to major in physical education or medicine. Physical education won. I loved the active life (sports, aquatics, primitive camping), and somehow I felt that PE had made me a happy, whole, integrated person. PE had also helped me to make friends and feel that people cared about me. I worshiped my PE teachers and wanted to be just like them: to help others as they had helped me.

When I got to college, I found out I wasn't as good (skill wise) as other PE majors. I made As on knowledge tests and Cs on skill tests. Amount of effort didn't seem to matter, especially in hand-eye coordination activities. Field hockey provided some success, primarily because I trained so hard I could run longer and faster than my peers. But I wanted to be with my friends and play on the varsity basketball, volleyball, and softball teams!

I discovered that self-esteem is multidimensional. I felt good about myself as a studious, fit individual, but I mourned the highly skilled athlete that day by day I failed to become. It often seemed that I loved physical education more than any of my athlete friends did. They took for granted what I wanted so much. •

These words, from the author of this textbook, illustrate that sports and games can be meaningful to persons who are not well skilled and/or who have health and fitness problems. As indicated in Chapter 1 (Table 1.2), physical education can accomplish many goals. Chief among these is the opportunity to share the fun and excitement of the sport setting and to be with peers perceived as popular, healthy, and happy. Persons who miss school frequently and/or lack the stamina to engage in vigorous activities often feel left out. Physical education, if properly conducted, provides an environment in which meaningful contacts are made with significant others. These contacts should lead to shared afterschool and weekend experiences in sports. The process of making and keeping friends, and thereby feeling included rather than excluded, is called *social competency* in this text. This goal requires that teachers play an active role in helping students to care about each other and to structure their leisure to include physical activity with friends.

Asthma, diabetes, obesity, cancer, cardiovascular disorders, seizures, and similar problems are called *other health-impaired (OHI)* conditions and are covered in Part 3 of this book. Federal legislation defines OHI conditions as "Limited strength, vitality, or alertness due to chronic or acute health problems which adversely affect a child's educational performance" (*Federal Register,* August 23, 1977, p. 42478). *Acute* means rapid onset, severe symptoms, and a short course; *chronic* means of long duration. Asthma, for example, is a chronic condition that is typically *managed* by medication and healthful living practices (i.e., balanced diets and regular eating, sleeping, and exercise practices). Occasionally, however, an acute episode (i.e., an asthma attack) may occur. How individuals cope with acute and chronic OHI conditions varies widely.

Conditions like asthma, diabetes, obesity, and cardiovascular disorders require individualization in regard to exercise. Both perceived and real limitations must be addressed, and students often need extra help in achieving physical education goals and in developing attitudes and habits conducive for lifelong health and fitness. Typically, however, school district budgets are too limited to classify students with these problems as needing special education and thereby justify extra money for special programming. The knowledge and creativity of the regular physical educator determine the extent that special needs are met. In such cases, regular physical educators are said to be delivering adapted physical education services.

Clumsiness

• *In about the third grade, I could neither catch nor throw a ball with the proficiency that would enhance my self-concept. By the time I finished third grade, I had come to detest that ball because it was the source of all those feelings of inadequacy, which, at the time, mattered most. One day, after an eternity of missed catches, inaccurate throws, strikeouts, and being chosen last (or being told by the team captain to play in the outfield because the ball seldom got that far), I managed to get that damned ball when nobody was looking. Intent upon punishing that ball for all it had done to me, I took it to the farthest corner of the playground and literally buried it. For a while, I felt good because I knew my spheroid enemy, in its final resting place, couldn't hurt me any more. Unfortunately, our class soon got a new ball.* (Eichstaedt & Kalakian, 1987, p. 89) •

These memories come from Leonard (Lennie) Kalakian, professor of physical education at Mankato State University in Minnesota, who has coauthored an excellent adapted physical education textbook: *Developmental/Adapted Physical Education: Making Ability Count.* In a telephone interview, Dr. Kalakian said:

Yes, I was a clumsy child. It took a long time to find a sport I was really good at, but eventually I became an All-American Gymnast. Obviously, sport and movement were very important to me. When it came time to enter the university, I majored in physical education.

Clumsiness, or physical awkwardness, was defined in Chapter 1 as inability to perform culturally normative motor activities with acceptable proficiency. The prevalence of clumsiness for regular education students who have no sensory, motor, emotional, or learning problems is estimated at 10 to 15%. Prevalence of clumsiness for special education students is much higher.

Clumsiness is related to perceptual-motor function, sensory integration, and information processing. A clumsy student may demonstrate an acceptable level of proficiency in a *closed skill* (one done in a predictable environment that requires no quick body adjustments) but perform miserably in an *open skill* (one done in an unpredictable, changing environment that requires rapid adjustments). Thus, clumsiness is typically evidenced in activities of balance, bilateral coordination, agility, and ball handling, particularly in game settings.

Clumsiness is caused by both human and environmental constraints (limitations). Among these are insufficient opportunities for instruction and practice; delayed or abnormal development of the nervous, muscular, or skeletal systems; genetically imposed body size and motor coordination limitations; and problems related to space, equipment, surfaces, noise, visibility, weather, allergens, improper clothing, and rules or instructions.

The effect of clumsiness on an individual's mental health depends largely on the personal meaning of sport and movement. How significant others in the ecosystem view sport and value physical prowess affects how clumsy persons feel about themselves. If, for example, the father or mother is an athlete, expectations are probably high that a child will do well in sports. If one's best friend is on a team, achieving similar status may be terribly important. Attitudes toward self, based largely on perceived competence and beliefs about what significant others hold important, predispose individuals toward active or passive lifestyles. This, in turn, may help to decrease or increase clumsiness.

Clumsiness is particularly debilitating because it is a global manifestation that is easily identified but poorly understood. Everyone can pick out "the clumsy kid" in an activity; typically, such persons endure a lot of teasing. No one wants them on their team. The teacher may repeatedly single them out for special help. The ecosystem of clumsy children is different from that of classmates; thus, clumsiness is a psychosocial problem as well as a physical one. Some children, like young Lennie, express their individualities and uniqueness through action. They keep trying new activities until they find one compatible with their body build and motor coordination. Others withdraw and seek success and self-esteem in other areas.

For clumsy students, the development of positive self-concept is an especially important goal. Through individual and small-group movement activities and counseling, students learn to accept limitations that cannot be changed and to adapt the environment so as to make the most of their strengths. Achievement of this goal requires small class sizes so teachers can work individually with students.

Clumsiness is a disability in most physical education classes, yet is not defined as a disability in special education legislation. Adapted physical activity educators need to consider what is a disability in a movement setting and should not be governed by eligibility criteria derived by special educators for classroom academic work.

Learning Disabilities

Learning disabilities (LD) is the special education condition most prevalent in the United States. Almost 45% of the students receiving services have a specific learning disability. By definition, these students have normal or better intelligence quotients (i.e., they are not mentally retarded). Students with LD are identified on the basis of significant discrepancies between intellectual abilities and academic achievement. Specific problems are diagnosed in the ability to listen, think, speak, read, write, spell, or do mathematical calculations. Typically, students with LD demonstrate an uneven learning profile: They are good in some subjects and bad in others.

Don, a high school counselor, was diagnosed as having a learning disability in the fourth grade. Subsequently, he received individual assistance with math and other problems in a resource room for 3 years. He recalls:

• *I was the fourth boy in a family where education was really important. My father was a university professor, and my mother was a librarian. I don't remember being different until the second or third grade. I loved to read, and it was easy for me, but there were crazy little discrepancies in my learning pattern. Like I didn't memorize the alphabet until I was 7 years old. I just couldn't remember the sequence. My parents thought I would never learn to tie my shoes. I'd watch and I'd listen, but I just couldn't make my fingers do what I wanted.*

But math was what made my life really miserable. In the fourth grade, we started having story problems. You know, things like: "Your car is going 50 miles an hour. It takes 5 hours to drive from Dallas to Austin. How many miles will you drive?" The longer and more complex those sequences got, the more I was lost. In the fourth grade, I brought home a D in arithmetic. Everything else was Bs and Cs, but my parents had a fit. They said my IQ was 125 and I wasn't trying. The school gave me a bunch of tests and assigned me to a resource room 1 hour a day. Although I hated to admit it, I was having trouble remembering and dealing with sequences in my other classes also. Like in gym, this teacher would tell us we were going to work in stations. Then he'd talk on and on about what to do at each station. By the time he finished, I'd have forgotten where to start. I just followed whoever was next to me and copied them.

Everybody kept telling me to try harder, to concentrate, to have a better attitude. I was so humiliated and so hurt, mainly because my parents didn't believe in me. I made up my mind that I would conquer math if it killed me. I quit going out to play after school. All I can remember in junior high and high school is studying. I managed to get dismissed from the special education roll and maintain a C average in math, but only with extraordinary effort.

I used to have terrible migraine headaches and feel so tense all the time. I was so scared I wouldn't have the grades to get into college. Life just wasn't much fun. No, I wasn't very good at PE, but I wasn't bad either, considering I never practiced. I never had a weight problem, so PE just wasn't very important to me. No one in my family cared much about sports. Looking back, I know I missed a lot. •

Analysis of this passage shows that physical education has not been very meaningful in Don's life. As an adult, he has no physical activity leisure skills and interests. He eventually learned relaxation and stress reduction techniques in course work to become a counselor but remains unaware that this learning could have been part of regular PE instruction made available to students with special tension control needs.

The many individual differences among students with LD allow for few generalizations. Although many have average or better intelligence, some have borderline IQs (70 to 90 range) that further intensify learning problems and stress. Some are hyperactive, have attention deficit disorders, and display perceptual-motor problems. Others do not. Many are deficient in balance, fine motor coordination, and agility stunts involving total body coordination. Listening and thinking deficits affect all areas of life, especially social relations. Students with LD often need extra help in developing appropriate play and game behaviors and in acquiring the social competency for acceptance.

Mild Mental Retardation

• *Eric Tosado is an 18-year-old middle-distance runner from Puerto Rico. Handsome, tall, and slender, Eric easily passes for normal, as do many persons with mild mental retardation. He reads at about the sixth-grade level, attends high school, works part-time, and has many friends. Eric competes in both able-bodied (AB) track and Special Olympics. He has over 50 trophies from various AB road races and is a gold medalist in the 1,500-m and 3,000-m events of the International Summer Special Olympics Games. Although Eric is a special education student, he has never thought of himself as handicapped in sports. For many years, he avoided Special Olympics because he didn't want to be associated with "the retarded movement." Eric says, "But I love to run so much that I thought, why lose an opportunity to compete? I'm good in able-bodied competition, and I often win local-type races. Teachers kept telling me I could be the best in the world if I entered Special Olympics. It was a way to test myself in international competition, to have opportunities I couldn't find elsewhere. And now I am so glad I made the choice. There's no reason a person can't compete in both AB road races and Special Olympics." Eric's gold medalist times were 4:14.3 in the 1,500 m and 9:38 in the 3,000 m. About the role of sports in his life, Eric says:*

It's hard to grow up mentally retarded. A lot of people tease you when you have trouble in studies. Once, when I was little and was upset, a teacher said, 'Let's go out and run.' He told me I was good at running, and this made all the difference in my life. It's really important to feel good at something. It helps you accept the bad stuff you can't change. Running makes me feel good physically, but competing and winning is what makes me feel good mentally.

Eric clearly expresses his individuality and uniqueness in both AB sport and Special Olympics. Strongly motivated to train hard and perform well, he is an excellent role model for persons who aspire to become runners. Like many persons with mild disability, Eric is intensely aware of the *stigma* (i.e., undesired differentness) of mental retardation (MR) and thus reluctant to be associated with activities for the MR population. In sociological terms, he is coping with *role ambiguity:* whether to pass for normal or to take advantage of opportunities offered to persons with MR. Good

FIGURE 2.2

Persons with Down syndrome have distinct features.

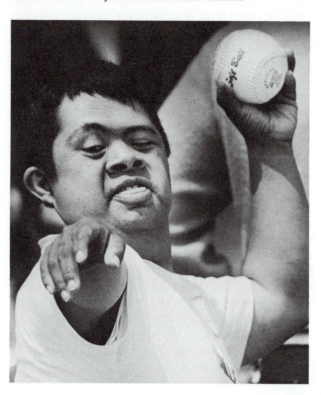

counseling can help Eric to realize that he can be himself and do what he wishes; it is not necessary to choose between roles.

Mental retardation is a condition of impaired intellectual and adaptive behavior function that is documented by a score of 70 or less on a standardized intelligence test and an assessment of personal and vocational independence. Approximately 3% of the world's population is mentally retarded, and most of these individuals pass as normal once they have left school. Approximately 90% of all MR conditions are classified as mild. By adulthood, persons with mild MR typically function academically somewhere between the third and sixth grades. Cognitively, their greatest deficits are in the areas of abstract thinking, concept formation, problem solving, and evaluative activity.

Severe Mental Retardation

• *In the same school with Eric, the same age, and also classified as mentally retarded, is a boy we shall call Juan, who has Down syndrome. Approximately 10% of all persons with mental retardation are born with this chromosomal abnormality, which has distinct physical characteristics (see Figure 2.2). Juan has close-set, almond-shaped, slanting eyes, a flattening of the bridge of the nose, and an abnormally small oral cavity. He is not as tall as other boys of his age and has short limbs with small, stubby fingers and toes. He appears loose jointed because ligaments are lax and muscle tone tends to be poor. Juan has an intelligence quotient of about 45, functions at the first-grade level, and will probably always need to live and work in a sheltered environment. Like Eric, Juan is a special education student and eligible for Special Olympics.* •

In physical appearance, intellectual functioning, and motor ability, however, Eric and Juan are totally different. Whereas Eric can pass for normal, except when called on to read or to do abstract thinking, Juan has been treated as special since birth. There are real problems in assigning both boys the same diagnostic label: mentally retarded. This is why federal law now requires that an individualized education program (IEP) be developed separately for each student. Each person, regardless of label, has distinctly different needs. No two persons with Down syndrome are the same, even though the syndrome causes similar physical appearance. Likewise, no two persons with MR are the same.

Whereas appropriate physical education goals for Eric may be physical fitness, leisure-time skills, positive self-concept, and social competency, Juan probably needs help primarily in play and game behaviors, perceptual-motor function, and sensory integration. Special attention will probably be important for him to master the mental operations needed to understand game formations, rules, and strategies and to appreciate the differences between cooperation and competition. He will also need continued guidance on what to watch for during demonstrations, how to listen to instructions, and how to integrate information from all the senses into meaningful wholes.

Through Special Olympics, many persons have developed good attitudes toward mental retardation. Special Olympics, however, is only one of many sport organizations designed to serve persons who are differently abled. Only persons with mental retardation are eligible to participate in Special Olympics. Therefore, physical educators need to know how to match disabilities with organizations. More about these organizations appears in Part 3 of this text.

Cerebral Palsy

Cerebral palsy (CP) is a group of neuromuscular conditions caused by damage to the motor areas of the brain. There are many types of CP and many degrees of severity, ranging from mild incoordination to muscle tone so abnormal that a person cannot use a manual wheelchair and must therefore ambulate in a motorized chair. More information on CP is presented in Chapter 25.

CP is the most common orthopedic disability seen in the public schools. Because of the many individual differences within CP, a classification system is necessary for describing persons and assessing their abilities. The U.S. Cerebral Palsy Athletic Association uses eight such classifications.

• *Nancy Anderson, a world-class athlete in her middle 30s, is a Class 2 CP, which means that she uses a wheelchair for daily living activities. She can take a step or two, with assistance, to transfer from wheelchair to bed or toilet but is unable to ambulate on crutches. Nancy's motor problems are expressed largely as athetosis (involuntary, purposeless, repeated movements of head and limbs), but she also has spasticity (abnormal muscle tightness and exaggerated reflexes). She thus lacks motor control for participation in sports unless rules and equipment are adapted. This combination of motor problems also makes fine motor coordi-*

nation like writing difficult, but Nancy uses a word processor and types approximately 24 words a minute. She feeds herself but needs a helper to cut up food. Through speech therapy, Nancy has learned to talk, but experience is needed to understand her speech. Nancy has a bachelor's degree from Michigan State University, lives independently in her own apartment, and writes professionally. Her passion, however, is sports.

Nancy was introduced to swimming at age 3 by her parents. In the beginning, she simply did exercises in the water to increase range of motion and strength, but eventually, Nancy learned to swim. After introduction to CP sports competition, Nancy began to train seriously, and today she is a top U.S. swimmer in her classification (see Figure 2.3). Illustrative of her times are 1:00.1 in the 25-m free stroke and 1:02.4 in the 25-m back stroke. CP sports rules mandate different distances for swimming and track for each classification. These are the distances appropriate for a Class 2 CP.

Nancy also competes in field events (shot put, club throw, discus) and boccia, a team sport that involves throwing balls at a target ball. She wheels a 60-m dash in 34.01 sec and completes the 100-m dash in 1:00.54. She sees sports as a means of expressing her competitiveness and takes advantage of every opportunity to excel.

Nancy expresses her philosophy in the following song, which is featured in a commercial videotape of athletes with disabilities:

LOOK AT ME
*In the beginning, no one thought I could.
In the beginning, I wondered if I should.
But in the beginning, I just knew I would—
If I really tried my best,
Put myself through every test
Never settled for any less—
My Personal Best.*

CHORUS:

*Look at me—I'm going stronger, faster, farther
than they thought I could.
Look at me—I'm going stronger, faster, farther
than some wished I would.
Look at me—I'm going stronger, faster, farther
than I dreamed I could
Wait and see—I'll better my best yet.*
(Reprinted with permission from Nancy Anderson and Terry N. Terry, THE MESSAGE MAKERS, Lansing, Michigan.)

Traumatic Spinal-Cord Injury

• *Rick Hansen, a Canadian, is one of the best-known spinal cord injured athletes in the world. Not only is he an international-level competitor, but Rick is acknowledged as a creative and courageous advocate for wheelchair sports. The first to wheel around the world (24,901 miles through 34 countries), he has generated millions of dollars for wheelchair sports, raised awareness levels, and stimulated research and action to enhance the lives of individuals with disabilities (see Figure 2.4). The Rick Hansen Centre at the University of Alberta, Edmonton, Canada, a major wheelchair sports training and research facility, is but one of his many contributions.*

FIGURE 2.3

Nancy Anderson, a world-class swimmer with cerebral palsy, receives last-minute tips from Coach Marybeth Jones, puts on a nose clip, and mentally prepares to win.

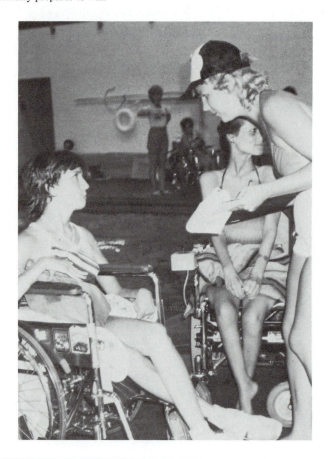

FIGURE 2.4

Rick Hansen wheeling on the Great Wall of China during his Man in Motion tour.

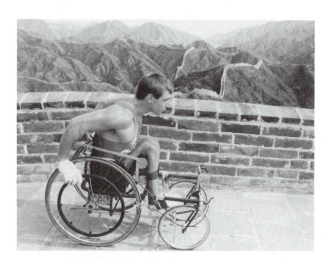

Rick was a teenager with three obsessions: fishing, hunting, and sports. His life changed drastically at age 15, when a ride in the back of a pickup truck ended in an injury to the spinal cord at thoracic segments 10 and 12. The result was flaccid paralysis of the hip, leg, and foot muscles, loss *of sensation from about the waist down, and changes in bladder, bowel, and sexual function. This condition is variously called a spinal-cord lesion, a lower motor neuron disorder, and paraplegia. Flaccidity refers to loss of muscle tone, loss of or reduction in tendon reflexes, atrophy (wasting away) of muscles, and degeneration of muscle tissue.*

After the accident, Rick spent approximately 7 months in hospitals and rehabilitation centers to learn how to handle all of the changes in his body. This included mastering wheelchair techniques, learning to use leg braces and crutches, and going to the bathroom in a different way. It also included much loneliness, self-evaluation, and periodic depression. Because Rick was younger than the average person who sustains spinal-cord injury, there were few persons his age to socialize with in the rehab centers.

Making the transition from rehab center to home also was hard, however. His was the only wheelchair in the small rural town, and he opted to ambulate on crutches and braces for many months. Returning to the gymnasium was the hardest of all. Rick stated:

. . . going back into the gym was devastating. I avoided it as long as I could. Then one day I screwed up my courage and peeked through the door. There they were: Bob Redford and the volleyball team. Same coach, same guys, only now I was on crutches and out of it. It was going to be awful. (Hansen & Taylor, 1987, p. 40)

• *This first experience ended with Rick rushing out of the gym, jumping into his car, and driving out into the country for a long cry. Looking back, Rick says he underestimated his friends. After initial shyness, his friends were fine. Rick, however, had to learn to cope with new experiences, allow persons to help him with things he couldn't handle, and become creative in devising alternative ways to achieve goals and meet needs. The following passage illustrates his growing acceptance of self and his understanding of the importance of adapting:*

There's nothing wrong with being carried down a bank by your friends so you can go swimming. What's wrong with taking your clothes off and going in shorts and letting people see that you've got skinny legs? It's no big deal. I had to realize that there weren't too many things I used to do that I couldn't do again, but that some of it wouldn't be the same. All I really had to do was adapt. . . .
(Hansen & Taylor, 1987, p. 43)

As might be expected, Rick became involved in wheelchair basketball, then track, and later marathoning. He won the Boston marathon, completing the course in 1 hr, 48 min, and 22 sec, as well as other marathons and races throughout the world. He discarded the crutches and braces (a slow, inefficient method of ambulation for most persons with spinal cord injuries) and made life in a wheelchair adventurous and self-actualizing. He completed a degree in physical education at the University of British Columbia, married a physiotherapist named Amanda Reid, and developed into the mature, creative individual who today serves as a model for thousands of others who are learning to problem solve and move in alternative ways.

Sport is the way both Rick Hansen and Nancy Anderson express their individuality and uniqueness. These elite athletes both use a wheelchair and have many of the same personality characteristics: a love of competition, willingness to train hard, good self-esteem, tremendous perseverance, and strong commitment to become the best they can be. Their conditions and movement capacities, however, are very different. Nancy has an upper motor neuron disorder that manifests itself in spasticity and athetosis. Rick has a lower motor neuron disorder that manifests itself in flaccidity and loss of sensation. Nancy's total body is involved; Rick has perfect control of his upper extremities. Nancy is dependent upon others for transportation; Rick can drive anywhere in a car adapted with hand controls and brakes.

Is Nancy more like you or Rick? Is Rick more like you or Nancy? On what bases would you make such comparisons: gender, method of ambulation, speech fluency, creative writing ability, amount of travel, interest in basketball versus swimming? Teachers learn not to categorize human beings as disabled and nondisabled but rather to celebrate and appreciate their many similarities and differences as human beings.

Deafness

Persons who are deaf or hearing impaired also demonstrate individual differences in motor performance and fitness. Dis-

FIGURE 2.5

Dr. David Stewart signing instructions to a student. Stewart's research on children who are deaf has focused on appropriate test administration.

ability for a deaf person is primarily environmental and depends on the two-way interactions possible in a given setting. Because most hearing people cannot use sign language, the world is divided for a deaf person. There is the deaf community, where people share a common language, similar values, and positive attitudes toward deafness; here, one is free of disability. Then there is the hearing world, which is uncertain and unpredictable; sometimes, one is disabled and sometimes not.

There is much controversy in educational circles concerning the best school placement for students who are deaf or hearing impaired: separate classes where sign is used, mainstream classes, or some combination. The question is similar to that addressed in bilingual education: Can children be taught better in their native language, or should they be exposed only to English? The issue is complicated for students who are deaf because their primary language at home probably depends on whether or not their parents are deaf. The sensitive physical educator must be aware of this citizenship in two worlds and the inherent problems.

Dr. David Stewart, a professor in the College of Education at Michigan State University and author of *Deaf Sport: The Impact of Sports Within the Deaf Community,* was born deaf (see Figure 2.5). The cause of his deafness is unknown, although genetics is suspected. An operation for otitis media at age 4 improved his ability to hear for a while, but his hearing has progressively deteriorated since that time, and he is now profoundly deaf. Dr. Stewart has written about himself and the importance of sports:

• *I am bilingual in American Sign Language and English and proficient in the use of various forms of English signing. I am culturally Deaf and socialize within the Deaf community. I have a hearing wife and three hearing daughters and spend much time socializing with hearing members of society. I rely heavily on sign interpreting at meetings. In noisy environments with individuals who do not sign, I generally resort to writing or to slow, exaggerated spoken conversations. I have a 95-decibel hearing loss in both ears; yet, I can use the phone with amplification if I am talking about a familiar topic with people I know. My preference is to use a Telecommunication Device for the Deaf (TDD). I empathize with other deaf individuals dealing with the challenges of a hearing and speaking society. I sympathize with hearing individuals who spend much time trying to understand the various ramifications of deafness. If someone were to ask what my biggest asset in communication is, I would respond that it is my ability to respond to a wide range of communication demands. I do not impose my communication standards on others, and I accord full respect to those with whom I communicate.*

My confidence in deafness as a facilitator of a treasured lifestyle is a result of many years of interacting in both the Deaf and hearing communities. In particular, my involvement in sports has been critical. When I was 14 years old, I had a keen interest in becoming a basketball player because a lot of my friends were interested in that sport. I followed them to my first basketball practice in high school. I didn't have a clue what the coach was saying or what was expected of me. The techniques for doing lay-ups and for following through on a shot went right past me. Because I was a fast learner, I remember saying to myself that, if only the coach would take me aside and explain a few things, then I would fit right into the team picture. I didn't realize at that time that I should have confronted the coach with my own strategies for becoming a good basketball player. Instead, I found other interests and let a chance to obtain a lifelong skill disappear.

Confronting a coach and putting forth my own objectives for learning and playing a game was a skill I learned many years later, when I became involved with other deaf athletes in various deaf sport activities. Within deaf sport, communication is not a special consideration, and objectives for participating in sport are clearly focused.

Many deaf persons gravitate toward deaf sport activities because communication is restricted in hearing sports. In addition, the bond forged through a commonality of experiences in deafness increases the likelihood of obtaining social gratification in deaf sport. Hence, the deaf are a linguistic and cultural minority. •

Many students who are deaf participate in integrated physical education. They have a right to full understanding of class instructions, officiating calls, and comments from team members. A certain degree of maturity is required, however, to confront the individual in authority with the idea that he or she is not getting the lesson across. Sometimes, pretending to understand or somehow fading into the background is easier. The physical educator must create an environment of open, honest, and effective communication. The presence of an interpreter is just as important in physical education as in classroom subjects. To learn, one must understand.

Knowing that opportunities for full participation and socialization in after-school hearing sports may be limited for students who are deaf or hearing disabled, physical educators should be knowledgeable about deaf sports and able to refer students. The choice of whether to participate during leisure time in deaf or hearing sports or both belongs to the student, and the decision should be treated with respect and dignity. Sports are more than motor skills and fitness; they are a vehicle for making and keeping friends. This requires equal access to communication in all class and after-school activities.

Today, an increasing number of hearing persons are enrolling in sign language courses. Dr. Stewart points out that he is proficient in American Sign Language and various forms of English signing. How much do you know about the different kinds of sign language? See Chapter 26 for further information.

Ideas to Consider

The preceding case studies were presented to stimulate critical thought about individual differences. Among the ideas you may wish to consider are (a) how the personal meaning of physical activity varies from person to person; (b) how the nine goals of adapted physical activity presented in Chapter 1 are illustrated in these accounts; (c) how the persons served by adapted physical education may differ from those served by special education; (d) how misleading it is to lump all persons with disabilities into a category called "handicapped," "disabled," or "impaired"; (e) how a health impairment like asthma, diabetes, and obesity can be just as disabling as mental retardation and cerebral palsy; (f) how a person with a disability may feel more similar to you and me than to other persons with a disability; (g) how labeling a condition as disabling and providing federal and state monies for special services relates to politics—who decides what condition gets the money and how; (h) how much you can learn by becoming personally acquainted with persons of your own age who have disabilities; and (i) how the persons described in this chapter are similar or different from other individuals with disabilities that you have known.

In this section, you have been introduced to several kinds of individual differences: asthma and other health impairments, clumsiness, learning disabilities, mental retardation, cerebral palsy, traumatic spinal cord injury, and deafness. If you wish to know more about these or other specific conditions, check the index at the end of the book for the page numbers in Part 3 of the text where the conditions are described in detail. The index can also serve as a spelling aid and guide for assessing your vocabulary in relation to adapted physical activity.

Guidelines for Interacting

The best way to learn about individual differences—and, thus, to prepare to teach adapted physical activity—is to become personally acquainted and closely associated with several persons with disabilities. As meaningful relationships develop, you become increasingly able to interact with others as *whole persons,* rather than as people with problems or disabilities. Through such interactions, you clarify your beliefs concerning individual differences and refine your philosophy with regard to service delivery. The following guidelines may be helpful in the early stages of getting acquainted:

1. *Remember that each person who is disabled is different, and no matter what label is attached for the convenience of others, is still a totally "unique" person.*

FIGURE   2.6

Joannie Hill, Denton State School teacher, demonstrates comfort in giving and receiving love. Persons with severe mental retardation often rely on touch and physical closeness to communicate feelings.

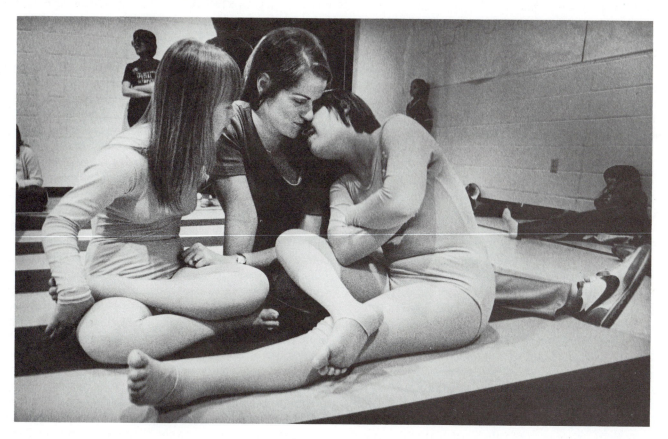

2. *Remember that persons with disabilities are persons first and disabled individuals secondly. These persons have the same right to self-actualization as any others—at their own rate, in their own way, and by means of their own tools.*

3. *Remember that persons with disabilities have the same needs that you have, to love and be loved, to learn, to share, to grow, and to experience, in the same world you live in. They have no separate world. There is only one world (see Figure 2.6).*

4. *Remember that persons with disabilities have the same right as you to fall, to fail, to suffer, to decry, to cry, to curse, to despair. To protect them from these experiences is to keep them from life.*

5. *Remember that only those with disabilities can show or tell you what is possible for them. We who love them must be attentive, attuned observers.*

6. *Remember that persons with disabilities must do for themselves. We can supply the alternatives, the possibilities, the necessary tools—but only they can put these things into action. We can only stand fast, be present to reinforce, encourage, hope, and help, when we can.*

7. *Remember that persons with disabilities, no matter how disabled, have a limitless potential for becoming—not what we desire them to become, but what is within them to become.*

8. *Remember that all persons with disabilities have a right to honesty about themselves, about you, and about their condition. To be dishonest with them is the most terrible disservice one can perform. Honesty forms the only solid base upon which all growth can take place. And this above all—remember that persons with disabilities need the best you possible. In order for them to be themselves, growing, free, learning, changing, developing, experiencing persons—you must be all of these things. You can only teach what you are. If you are growing, free to learn, change, develop, and experience, you will allow them to be.* (Buscaglia, 1975, pp. 19–20)

Only by interacting on an authentic and equal-status basis can professionals acquire the attitudes and knowledge to help children and youth accept and appreciate individual differences. To be authentic is to be real and genuine, comfortable in a relationship, and able to share and trust. *Equal-status relationships* are those involving friendship with individuals of approximately the same age. Both individuals contribute in equal amounts to the relationship, learn from each other, and find contact satisfying and self-actualizing.

Find some persons with disabilities on your campus or in your community, explore areas of mutual interest, and discover some things that each of you can do better than the other. Have long talks, do activities together, and perhaps you will become friends.

If we believe in the right of persons with disabilities to participate fully in society, then we must be their friends. Approximately 10% of the world's people have disabilities. Do 10% of your personal friends have disabilities? As models for children and youth, what is our responsibility?

Semantics and Definitions

In interactions with differently abled persons, one of the first dilemmas is what to call their disabilities. Numerous terms have evolved to describe individual differences. Professionals use words carefully because they know words have the power to hurt people or make them angry, particularly when reference is being made to an undesired differentness.

Semantics (the study of the meaning of words) is important in deciding which terms are best under various circumstances. Language not only is a means of communication, but it shapes the way persons perceive and experience the world. The meaning of words not only varies by country and culture but from person to person within the same family or social group.

The connotation of words also changes with time. For example, persons with mental retardation were once called "*feebleminded*" and classified by school personnel as *idiots* (severe), *imbeciles* (moderate), and *morons* (mild). Official terminology then shifted to *trainable* (severe or moderate) and *educable* (mild). In the 1980s, the categories of *profound, severe, moderate,* and *mild* were used to describe severity of mental retardation, but now the trend is toward differentiating only between mild and severe conditions. Who knows what tomorrow will bring? Persons with physical disabilities were designated by federal legislation as *crippled* for many years, while persons with learning disabilities were called *brain-injured.* Changes in terminology are typically launched by either professional organizations or legislation.

World Health Organization Definitions

As world events bring professionals from many countries together, international definitions are supplanting those of legislation and tradition. Today, a growing number of persons are accepting the definitions of the World Health Organization (1980):

Impairment—any disturbance of, or interference with, the normal structure and function of the body

Disability—the loss or reduction of functional ability and/or activity

Handicap—a condition produced by societal and environmental barriers

Analysis of Meanings

Of the preceding terms, *impairment* is the broadest and most neutral. Nevertheless, several synonyms have been proposed (limitation, challenge, inconvenience, disadvantage) as persons seek to describe themselves and others in a positive way. Advocates of individual differences theory support the phrase *differently abled* as a means of emphasizing differences (the full spectrum of abilities) rather than limitations.

Disability evokes mixed feelings because the Latin prefix *dis* means apart, asunder, aside, or away and connotes negation, lack, or invalidation. Words that begin with *dis*— *disaffirm, disbelief, discontent, dishearten, disown*—all convey a negative feeling. Some persons remember that, in Latin mythology, Dis is the god of the underworld, the equivalent of Pluto in Greek mythology. Still others confuse *dis* with *dys,* which means diseased, difficult, faulty, or bad (e.g., *dysentery, dysmenorrhea, dyslexia, dysplasia*). In spite of these problems, disability seems to be the word of choice among athletes with impairments. References to *disabled sport* and the *disabled sport movement* are common.

Handicap, the most controversial of these words, is defined in dictionaries as a race or contest in which, to equalize chances of winning, a disadvantage is imposed on superior contestants or an advantage is given to inferior ones. Handicap is derived from the Anglo-Saxon phrase *hand-n-cap,* which according to dictionaries, originally referred to drawing lots from a cap before horse races. Today, several sports (e.g., golf, bowling) use handicaps to help equalize competition. Some persons, however, insist that the word *handicap* evolves from the cap in the hand of a beggar. Such widely differing views show the importance of integrating semantics into the adapted physical activity knowledge base.

The varied use of *handicap* is also illustrative of how professions define words differently. The World Health Organization, by defining this term as "a condition produced by societal and environmental barriers," supports the social psychology viewpoint. Beatrice Wright, a leading scholar in the psychosocial aspects of disability, emphasizes that it is not the condition that handicaps an individual but the personal meaning attached to the condition. Personal meaning comes largely from the way persons are treated by society, especially significant others. Every differently abled person can describe architectural, attitudinal, and aspirational barriers that must be overcome daily. According to Wright (1983):

If people with a disability are unable to participate in some activities that are highly valued, their space of free movement is restricted. Part of the restriction may be due to the physical limitation itself. A person who is deaf may not enjoy nuances of music. A person with limb or heart impairments may avoid walking more than modest distances. However, part of the restriction has its source in socially derogatory attitudes— attitudes that say, in effect, "You are less good, less worthy because of the disability. It is something to be ashamed of, to be hidden, and made up for." Devaluation is expressed sometimes subtly, sometimes bluntly, and sometimes viciously. (p. 17)

In sharp contrast to the sociology view, the federal law used *handicapped* to describe special education students until 1990. During that year, an amendment called Public Law 101–476, the Individuals with Disabilities Education Act, was passed that legally changed the terminology to *disabled.* The federal law (see Chapter 4) officially defines several categories of disabilities (e.g., mental retardation, learning disabilities, orthopedic impairments, and deafness).

Gradually, the terms *special education* and *disabled* have come to mean the same thing. This is very confusing inasmuch as assessment procedures often identify a student as needing special education in some areas and not others. A child disabled in reading and spelling may not be disabled in math and physical education, or vice versa. *Disability* thus is a relative term that changes with federal legislation and school policy. When the economy is good and ample money is available for education, a definition may be broad so that all persons with special needs can be declared eligible to receive help. When money is tight, eligibility criteria are narrowed so that only students with the most severe conditions are diagnosed as disabled.

A healthy way to think of handicaps and disabilities is that we all have some. Depending upon our needs, interests, goals, and aspirations, any mental or physical limitation can be perceived as a handicap. If one aspires to be outstanding in any area of endeavor, possessing only average abilities is a handicap. Short stature, if it prevents one from making the varsity basketball team, is a disability. Asthma and other respiratory problems are disabilities if one desires to socialize but cannot breathe when friends smoke. Finger dexterity becomes a disability if the time required to type school assignments is so great that it eliminates recreation.

The terms *exceptional* and *special* are also used to denote persons who are different. Dictionary definitions indicate that *exceptional* means uncommon, rare, or forming an exception, and *special* means (a) distinguished by some unusual quality, uncommon, noteworthy, or (b) particularly favored or loved, as a special friend. *Exceptional* encompasses giftedness as well as undesired differentness and derives its popularity from the name of the professional organization to which most special educators belong: the Council for Exceptional Children. *Special* not only connotes special education eligibility but also evokes an image of Special Olympics (sports training and competition for persons with mental retardation) in many persons' minds. The common term *special populations* can refer to any group with special needs (e.g., the aged, the disadvantaged or poor, the disabled, juvenile delinquents).

Labeling

In general, slogans like "Label jars, not people" and "Labeling is disabling" summarize good practices in relation to individual differences. The implications of labeling are so vast that some sources include entire chapters on labeling theory. A major problem in calling persons disabled is that it lumps them together in a single category that emphasizes an undesired difference. This takes away from their individuality and humanity. None of us likes to be remembered by or categorized on the basis of one strength or weakness. We want to be thought of as whole people, constantly changing, with many individual differences. For an excellent review of research on labeling, see Davis & Rizzo (1991).

Labels contribute to negative self-concept. The following poem expresses the feelings of a 6-year-old boy who is just becoming aware of his differentness:

LABELS

There are labels in my shirts;
    They tell me front and back,
My "P.F. Flyers" make me run faster on the track.
    "Billie the Kid" made my pants
And "Bonnie Doon" my socks.
    Momma says "Mattel" made my brightly colored
      blocks.
There are labels on most all things,
    And that is plain to see.
But Momma, why's there a label on me?

          Jean Caywood
          Physical Education Instructor
          Plano, Texas

Categorizing

Social and professional situations call for the use of names. Labels and categories are appropriate only in regard to funding. There must be terms to designate persons who meet eligibility criteria for special services and to maintain records for financial reimbursement. Likewise, terms are necessary to guide the writing of textbooks that describe individual differences. Teachers are expected to be able to identify and describe such conditions as mental retardation, learning disabilities, and cerebral palsy. For these reasons, there must be categories, and categories must have names.

The use of categories, however, is fraught with difficulties because every person within a category is different. Textbook knowledge is intended to create awareness, to help us become better observers, and to know what to look for. The only way to know about real people is to observe and assess each one individually.

Guidelines for Speaking and Writing

Traditionally, textbooks have presented physical, mental, social, and emotional characteristics for each disability. This practice is changing. By definition, a *characteristic* is a highly stable quality, a constituent or trait, that is difficult or impossible to change. The purpose of education is change. Therefore, we should focus on assessing and describing specific, observable behaviors rather than characteristics. *Behaviors* are actions that change constantly in relation to internal and external variables. We should not assume that certain categories of people will evidence the same behaviors. We should assess carefully and list only what we see.

The language we choose depends largely on whether we are traditionalists or futurists (see Figure 2.7). Our choices, however, are powerful because they affect the way people think and feel. The following are some criteria to guide writing and speaking about differently abled persons:

1. Do not refer to a disability unless it is crucial to the story.
2. Avoid portraying persons with disabilities who succeed as superhuman. This implies that persons who are disabled have no talents or unusual gifts.

FIGURE 2.7

Duncan Wyeth, center, is an internationally known advocate for persons with and without disabilities working together on appropriate language and other issues.

3. Do not sensationalize a disability by saying "afflicted with," "victim of," and so on. Instead, say, "person who has multiple sclerosis," "person who had polio."

4. Avoid labeling persons into groups, as in "the disabled," "the deaf," "a retardate," "an arthritic." Instead, say, "people who are deaf," "person with arthritis," "persons with disabilities."

5. Where possible, emphasize an individual, not a disability. Say, "people or persons with disabilities" or "person who is blind," rather than "disabled persons" or "blind person."

6. Avoid using emotional descriptors, such as "unfortunate," "pitiful," and so on. Emphasize abilities, such as "uses a wheelchair/braces," (rather than "confined to a wheelchair"), "walks with crutches/braces" (rather than "is crippled"), "is partially sighted" (rather than "is partially blind").

7. Avoid implying disease when discussing disabilities. A disability such as Parkinson's disease may be caused by a sickness but is not a disease itself; nor is the person necessarily chronically ill. Persons with disabilities should not be referred to as "patients" or "cases" unless they are under medical care (Research and Training Center on Independent Living, 1990).

Individual Differences and Social Psychology

Knowing as much as possible about the social aspects of being perceived as different is important. Much depends on whether the perceived difference is desirable (giftedness) or undesirable (impairment) and on how great the difference is.

Persons with disabilities have one thing in common: They are different on some observable physical, mental, or emotional parameter. Social psychology theory posits that, if someone is different from the norm, even on a dimension that is generally evaluated positively, he or she will have problems with social acceptance (Katz, 1981). This "mere difference hypothesis" also applies to discrepancies between expected and perceived attributes of objects, like taste, color, temperature, and sound. Judgments about something's acceptability depend on the size of the differences. Small discrepancies may be considered pleasant surprises (i.e., "a nice change"), but large differences typically result in negative feelings. Small wonder then that persons with disabilities sometimes want to be like everyone else! But is it good to want to be like everyone else? Is it possible?

An often-used approach to differentness is emphasizing the many ways that persons are similar and promoting the development of further similarity. This pedagogy tends to support the idea that being different is bad, whereas being like everyone else is good. The philosophy of this text celebrates individual differences and the importance of understanding and accepting ourselves as we are: a unique and wonderful combination of strengths and weaknesses. The following poem captures the feelings of many persons who are different:

ON BEING DIFFERENT

Watching without sight,
Running without legs,
Conversing without voice,
Loving without prejudice,
Ofttimes it is belief that makes it happen . . .
      What's the difference in being different?
Acts which are naive, those deemed grand,
Small, tall, some with, some without,
Some who can, some who can't . . .
      What's the difference in being different?
Thinking, feeling, acting, sharing,
moving, gaming, loving, romping,
You and I, not the same but
yet the same because we are by fate just people . . .
      What's the difference in being different?
Oh for the chance to share my dreams,
to hold hands, to join in happiness,
to play your games, to taste the differences in life,
and not be scorned and turned away . . .
      What's the difference in being different?
                              —Dave Compton
                        (July 1975). *Leisurability, 2,* 27.

Social psychology addresses the structure of groups, how they are formed and changed, how they influence individuals, and vice versa. Of particular interest is what it feels like to be a member of a minority group, how one is treated (both real and imagined treatment), and why. Social psychologists posit that the status of individuals with a disability is the same as that of a devalued minority group (Wright, 1983).

Research has also shown that attitudes toward persons with disabilities are related to attitudes toward minority groups like Blacks, Hispanics, the economically disadvantaged, and the aged. These findings can be explained partly in *ethnocentricity* (i.e., an attitude that one's race, culture, or nation is superior to all others) and partly in such folk adages as "one should stick to his or her own kind" and "birds of a feather flock together." Persons with undesirable attitudes toward disabilities may not so much be influenced by the impairment as its quality of differentness. Many persons feel fear or anxiety when exposed to someone or something different, unfamiliar, or new.

Attitude Theory

Attitude formation and change are often considered the most important focus of adapted physical activity. *Attitude theory* is defined as the body of knowledge pertaining to how people think, feel, and act in regard to psychological objects. *Attitude* is derived from the Latin word *aptitude* (meaning "fitness," "faculty"), which, in turn, comes from the word *aptus* (meaning "fit," "apt," "suited"). This derivation suggests that attitudes and behaviors are reciprocally related. Attitudes indicate one's fitness or predisposition to either approach or avoid something. Approaching or avoiding behaviors, in turn, evoke new attitudes about self and environment. The attitude-behavior relationship can be conceptualized as a continuous circle with change occurring in both directions.

Attitude theories tend to be complex because they involve many components (Ajzen & Fishbein, 1980; Horne, 1985; Jones, 1984; Triandis, 1971; Yuker, 1988; Zimbardo, Ebbesen, & Maslach, 1977). The *cognitive component* is the opinions or beliefs a person holds about some object. Opinions represent the first level of belief formation; they are the early judgments held before we are certain of our beliefs. The *affective component* of an attitude is emotion or feelings about an object or one's likes and dislikes. The *behavioral component* of an attitude is behavioral intentions (i.e., one's inclination to approach, avoid, or continue deliberation).

Attitudes may be directed toward many kinds of psychological objects: self, other persons, a racial or ethnic group, religion, a disability, an undesired difference, exercise, physical activity, an idea, a behavior, or a situation. The more global a psychological object is, the more difficult it is to measure attitude toward it and plan change. When we feel uncomfortable about something or dislike it, we should analyze and pinpoint the specific variables causing unfavorable affect. Logically, for example, disliking a whole person is rather silly, although we sometimes say, "I hate myself" or "I dislike so-and-so." We should determine the specific behaviors causing our attitudes and then take steps to change these behaviors. An often-used motto in education is "Accept people, change behaviors!"

Problems in Being Different

Unfortunately, many persons are not logical in the ways they think, feel, and act toward persons who are different. Among the problems confronting persons with disabilities are prejudice, discrimination, stigmatization, and stereotyping (Sherrill, 1986; Wright, 1983). These problems affect every aspect of adapted physical activity service delivery. Some problems are caused by attitudes; others by behaviors. Often, in real life, it is difficult to separate attitudes from behaviors.

Prejudice and Discrimination

Prejudice refers to an unfavorable opinion or feeling formed beforehand and without knowledge, thought, or reason. The word is derived from Latin (*pre + judicium*), meaning, literally, "judgment before." Prejudice is an attitude that predisposes persons to avoid situations that may entail contact with disabilities. All kinds of reasons may be offered ("I'm too busy;" "I don't have the skills"), but the underlying problem may be fear and/or unwillingness to take risks. Prejudice is also associated with an authoritarian personality syndrome. Prejudiced persons tend to be conceptually rigid, preoccupied with power and morality, and rejecting of individuals and groups who represent different abilities, races, religions, socioeconomic classes, and value systems.

The first authority to write extensively about prejudice was Gordon Allport (1897–1967), an American psychologist with special interest in individuality, motivation, and the process of becoming. Among his many works is a book entitled *The Nature of Prejudice,* published in 1954. This was the year that the U.S. Supreme Court ruled in favor of integrated public schooling for students of different racial origins. Allport was one of the first to propose that prejudice could be reduced and attitudes changed by meaningful contact among persons who are different.

Persons with disabilities are sometimes prejudiced against others with dissimilar disabilities. Thus, some athletes with physical disabilities express considerable prejudice toward Special Olympians. They feel that persons with mental retardation cannot be athletes in the same sense as individuals with other disabilities; moreover, they strongly oppose their games being held at the same time and place as Special Olympics. Their reasons are complex. Many, however, are reacting to deep hurts caused by persons mistakenly thinking they are mentally retarded just because they have other disabilities.

The generalization of mental retardation prejudice to other disabilities by the general public is called the *spread phenomenon.* The spread phenomenon can be curtailed by teaching parents and children about individual differences within disabilities. For example, Special Olympics is only for persons with mental retardation. Separate sport organizations exist for other disabilities. Most persons, however, also want acceptance in integrated recreation and sport. They want to be known by name and judged on a personal basis. Generalization causes hurt and anger (see Figure 2.8).

The term *spread* also refers to "the power of single characteristics to evoke inferences about a person" (Wright, 1983, p. 32). In assessment theory, this is called the halo or pitchfork effect. Make an *A* on the first test a teacher administers, and he or she is likely to invest you with a halo symbolic of all kinds of positive attributes and abilities. Make a *D,* and your pitchfork (i.e., that one weakness) may influence how you are viewed and treated all year long.

Persons not knowledgeable about individual differences theory often generalize from one disability a vast array

FIGURE 2.8

Persons with disabilities want to be known by name. These international-level athletes represent five disability groups. They have little in common except love for sports and exceptionally high skill.

of expectations about personality and behavior. Chief among these is the belief that disability implies incompetence in all or several areas of life. Spread typically leads to *discrimination,* making a distinction in favor of or against persons based on the group, class, or category they belong to rather than on individual merit. *Prejudice thus refers to beliefs and feelings, whereas discrimination connotes acts.*

Stigmatization

Stigmatization refers to discriminatory or unjust treatment directed toward persons perceived as different. First conceptualized by Goffman (1963), stigma theory defines stigma as an undesired differentness, an attribute perceived as discrediting, a failing, a shortcoming, or a handicap. Underlying stigma theory are fear of individuals who are different from oneself, the equating of differentness with inferiority and/or danger, and the belief that persons with stigmata (plural of *stigma*) are not quite human and, thus, need not be accorded the same acceptance, respect, and regard given others.

The word *stigma* is Greek and means, literally, "tatoo mark." It can be traced back to such practices as branding slaves and criminals and forcing persons believed to be inferior or bad to wear distinguishing clothes or symbols (e.g., Nazis requiring Jews to wear a star; swimming teachers requiring students who are seizure-prone to wear red caps). Today, the concept of stigma has been broadened to include any physical, mental, or social attribute or assistive device that results in unfair or bad treatment (e.g., color of skin, eyeglasses, crutches, obesity, speech impairment, mental retardation).

Stereotyping

Stereotyping refers to conceptualizing and/or treating persons the same without regard for their individuality. Stereotypes are assigned primarily to persons and groups about whom little is known: Stereotypes may be good or bad—the problem is that they depersonalize. Generally, stereotypes are learned from authority figures (parents, journalists, textbook

writers) and tend to be more rigid than beliefs developed on our own. The broader the categories used in stereotyping, the less likely the stereotypes are to be accurate.

Assessment of Attitudes and Planning for Change

Attitude change begins with assessment of attitude components and related behaviors. Attitude instruments are typically called surveys, adjective checklists, opinionnaires, inventories, rating scales, and sociometric measures. Attitude measures are never called *tests,* a term properly used only when there are right and wrong answers and the domain examined is cognitive. Responses to attitude inventories are not considered right or wrong, good or bad, but only a reflection of feelings or beliefs at a given time. This fact is important to convey to subjects before conducting an attitude assessment; otherwise, persons may tend to give socially desirable ("right") answers rather than the truth, a phenomenon called *response bias.*

One way to avoid response bias in research is to tell subjects not to write their names on inventories. This assures that their responses are anonymous and that they cannot be judged or held accountable for expressed attitudes. In an instructional setting, where the goal is to improve attitudes, anonymity is not possible because teachers must know the baseline attitudes of each student and be able to chart change. In these situations, attitude must be assessed in a warm, positive climate in which students feel safe to be themselves. This is facilitated by teachers who are able to convey that they accept and care about each individual, regardless of attitudes and behaviors.

Table 2.1 describes instruments that measure attitudes toward persons with disabilities. In adapted physical education, Dr. Terry Rizzo is the recognized pioneer in this area (see Figure 2.9) (Rizzo, 1984; Rizzo & Vispoel, 1991; Rizzo & Wright, 1987).

Some attitude instruments are associated with a particular theory, but the study of attitude in physical education has tended to be haphazard and atheoretical. This trend is changing; for an excellent review of attitude theories that guide adapted physical educators, see Tripp and Sherrill (1991).

Physical educators need to be concerned about attitudes toward (a) self (self-concept) and the body (body concept), (b) movement and exercise, and (c) others (social competency and acceptance concepts). Four approaches to attitude change—(a) contact theory, (b) persuasive communication theory, (c) social cognitive theory, and (d) reasoned action theory—are described in the sections that follow. These theories can be applied to attitude change in relation to any psychological object. The emphasis in this chapter, however, is on attitudes toward persons with disabilities.

Contact Theory

Contact theory posits that contact between individuals with differences produces positive attitudes when interactions are frequent, pleasant, and meaningful. Gordon Allport (1954) is acknowledged as the pioneer who created the structural

Table 2.1
Types of attitude inventories.

Social Distance Measures

1. *Cowell Personal Distance Scale*—Uses a 7-point scale to indicate acceptance (e.g., into my family, as a next-door neighbor, into my school).

2. *Siperstein Friendship Activity Scale*—Uses a 4-point Likert scale to measure behavioral intentions in regard to 15 activities.

3. *Aufsesser Ranking of Disabilities Protocol*—Requests *ranking* of 10 disabilities from high to low to express friendship and self-affliction preferences and provides *checking* criteria that explain rankings.

4. *Bagley and Greene PATHS (Peer Attitudes Toward the Handicapped Scale)*—Uses a 5-point social distance scale (in my home, in another group, in no group, outside of class, at home) to rate descriptions of 30 students.

Cowell, C. (1958). Validating an index of social adjustment for high school use. *Research Quarterly, 29,* 7–18. (Appears in Barrow, McGee, and Tritschler, 1989, p. 261.)

Siperstein, G., Bak, J., & O'Keefe, P. (1988). Relationship between children's attitudes toward and their social acceptance of mentally retarded peers. *American Journal of Mental Retardation, 93* (1), 24–27.

Aufsesser, P.M. (1982). Comparison of the attitudes of physical education, recreation, and special education majors toward the disabled. *American Corrective Therapy Journal, 36,* 35–41.

Bagley, M., & Greene, J. (1981). *Peer attitude toward the handicapped scale.* Austin, TX: PRO-ED.

Teacher Attitude Measures

1. *Rizzo Physical Educators' Attitude Toward Teaching the Handicapped (PEATH-II) Inventory*—Uses a 5-point Likert scale (strongly disagree, disagree, undecided, agree, strongly agree) to respond to 12 statements with embedded blanks, such as "Teaching students labeled as ____ in my regular PE classes with nonhandicapped students will disrupt the harmony of the class."

2. *Jansma & Shultz Mainstreaming Attitude Inventory for Physical Educators*—Uses a +3 to −3 point scale (strongly disagree, disagree, slightly disagree, slightly agree, agree, strongly agree) to respond to 20 items about a 10-year-old boy.

Rizzo, T. L. (1984). Attitudes of physical educators toward teaching handicapped pupils. *Adapted Physical Activity Quarterly, 1,* 263–274.

Also note the Rizzo sources in the "References" at the end of this chapter or contact him at California State University at San Bernardino, 5500 University Parkway, San Bernadino, CA 92407–2397.

Jansma, P., & Shultz, B. (1982). Validation and use of a mainstreaming attitude inventory with physical educators. *American Corrective Therapy Journal, 36,* 150–157.

Agree/Disagree Opinion Scale

1. *Attitudes Toward Disabled Persons Scale (ATDP)*—Uses a +3 to −3 point scale (I agree very much to I disagree very much) to respond to 30 items. This scale has generated more publications than any other.

Yuker, H., Block, J., & Younng, J. (1966). *The measurement of attitudes toward disabled persons.* Albertson, NY: Human Resources Center.

Adjective and Phrase Checklists

1. *Siperstein Adjective Checklist for Describing Classmates*—Asks students to circle as many adjectives as they wish to describe a peer. List includes 16 positive and 18 negative adjectives.

2. *Children's Attitudes Toward Handicapped Scale (CAHS)*—Asks students to respond to 20 descriptors of a peer by circling one of three phrases for each (e.g., are lots of fun, are fun, are not any fun).

Same source as Siperstein Friendship Activity Scale. These can be ordered from Dr. Gary Siperstein, Center for the Study of Social Acceptance, University of Massachusetts, Boston, MA 02125.

Rapier, J., Adelson, R., Carey, R., & Croke, K. (1972). Changes in children's attitudes toward the physically handicapped. *Exceptional Children, 39,* 219–223.

Bipolar Adjective Opposites Scale

1. *Spreen's Semantic Differential Protocol for Attitude Measurement*—Asks university students to respond to six disabilities by rating 22 bipolar adjective opposites (e.g., strong-weak, fast-slow). A 7-point scale is used for each rating.

Rees, L. M., Spreen, O., & Harnadek, M. (1991). Do attitudes towards persons with handicaps really shift over time? Comparison between 1975 and 1988. *Mental Retardation, 29* (2), 81–86.

FIGURE 2.9

Dr. Terry Rizzo talks to children about attitudes and emphasizes the importance of contact between people representing all kinds of individual differences.

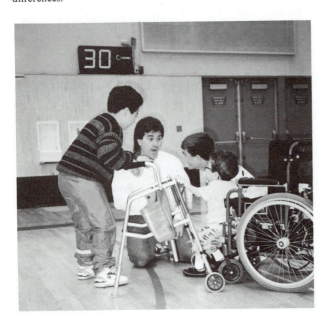

framework for this theory, which serves as the basis of integration practices in schools and communities. Early theorists focused only on getting persons together in the same physical setting. Today, contact at the observational and casual interaction levels is known to be not enough to create positive attitudes (Amir, 1969; Archie & Sherrill, 1989; Ibrahim, 1968; Jones, 1984).

Research indicates that integration does not promote positive attitudes unless specific interaction experiences are planned and the environment is carefully structured (Horne, 1985; Jones, 1984). Favorable conditions that tend to promote the development of positive attitudes are (a) equal-status relationships, (b) a social and instructional climate that requires frequent contacts, (c) cooperative rather than competitive or individual activities, (d) contacts that are pleasant and rewarding, (e) modeling of positive attitudes by teacher and significant others, and (f) scientifically planned and applied persuasion.

Figure 2.10 presents a model based on contact theory for use in research and instruction to guide attitude and behavior change. The model begins with teacher preparation through assessment, planning, and training strategies that help teachers feel competent. Two factors are especially important in teacher preparation: (a) the promise of support services, if needed, and (b) an equal-status relationship with an adult who has some kind of disability. *Equal status* infers a mutually satisfying association in which both individuals contribute in equal amounts, building on each other's strengths. Teachers, in turn, prepare students to interact with each other.

Structuring integrated physical activities for students demands much creativity. Contacts must be frequent, interactive, pleasant, and focused on common, meaningful goals that promote respect. In the beginning, these contacts

may be brief, but programming should gradually increase the duration of interaction. Partner activities typically are first, followed by small-group cooperative games. The equal-status criterion dictates that partners should be systematically assigned so that they have as much in common as possible; often, these commonalities must be pointed out, explored, and confirmed. The closer the match between abilities, the easier this is, but physical educators often have no control over the range of individual differences in a class.

Partnerships in which one person gives and the other receives assistance do not have the same impact as partnerships in which giving and taking are reciprocal. In addition, opportunities for following and for leading should be equal. Regardless of the degree of equal status possible, teachers must use praise and rewards creatively. *Interactive* means that time must be planned for listening or making sense of signs and gestures.

Most research shows that social acceptance is facilitated by cooperative rather than competitive or individual activities (Johnson & Johnson, 1986). When integration is practiced in a competitive game structure, social acceptance increases only in those teams that win and are rewarded (Lott & Lott, 1960). In other words, players who feel good about a game outcome tend to generalize this feeling to everyone and everything associated with the game.

Ultimately, structured contacts in the instructional setting should result in attitude and behavior changes (see Figure 2.10). Social acceptance implies that contacts become voluntary, spontaneous, equal status, and generalized. For example, social acceptance would be indicated by the person with a disability being included in after-school activities with increasing frequency and duration.

Persuasive Communication Theory

The use of persuasion to change attitudes is a common approach. Persuasion can be through direct methods (lectures, one-to-one talks, small-group discussions, films, presentations by persons who are disabled) or indirect methods (personal contact, role playing, or simulating activities of persons who are different). Thus, a body of knowledge has emerged called persuasive communication theory. Carl Hovland, Director of the Yale University Communication Research Program, is acknowledged as the father of this theory, also called the Yale approach, which was first posited in the early 1950s.

Proponents of persuasive communication theory define attitudes as multidimensional. Attitude change is posited to progress through four stages: (a) opinion change, (b) perception change, (c) affect or emotional change, and (d) action change. Information is carefully designed to (a) catch attention, (b) increase comprehension, and (c) promote acceptance.

Assessment of Opinions

Application of persuasive communication theory begins with assessment of opinions about a particular attitude object (Yuker, 1988). Instruments that could be used are the Attitudes Toward Disabled Persons (ATDP) scale of Yuker, Block, and Younng (1966) and the Adjective Checklist for Describing Classmates of Siperstein (1980).

FIGURE   2.10

Model for attitude change based on contact theory.

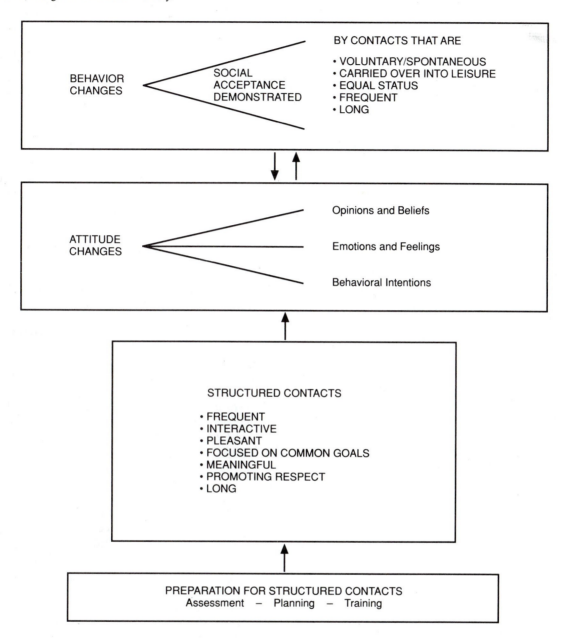

The ATDP scale measures beliefs about whether persons with disabilities are the same as nondisabled individuals or whether they are different and need special treatment. A high score indicates belief that a disability is only one of the thousands of attributes characterizing each human being and thus is of little importance. Figure 2.11 shows examples of ATDP items.

Each opinion measured by ADTP taps into the recognition that a disability does not change the essence of humanness (i.e., that individuals with disabilities have the same constellations of individual differences as other people). Responses enable the teacher to determine whether students judge persons with disabilities on the basis of one attribute (the disability) or as individuals with the same spread of differences as others.

The adjective checklist is based on the assumption that adjective choice reveals opinions and feelings. Many such checklists are available for attitude measurement, but the Siperstein (1980) checklist in Figure 2.12 was developed specifically for use with schoolchildren and has provided data for several published studies. Either the name of a particular child or a category (e.g., mental retardation) can be placed in the blank to elicit responses. After using this checklist, students should be helped to understand the fallacy of generalizations. For example, a term like *slow* is relative. Does it mean slow in running, slow in learning, or slow in giving affection? Also, because a person is slow on one dimension does not mean that he or she should automatically be judged slow on other dimensions.

FIGURE   2.11

Sample ATDP items.

---

1. Disabled people are the same as anyone else.

Strongly agree	Agree	Slightly agree	Neutral	Slightly disagree	Disagree	Strongly disagree
+3	+2	+1	0	−1	−2	−3

(The most favorable response on this item is "strongly disagree." In scoring, the −3 value is changed to a +3.)

---

2. Disabled people are as happy as nondisabled ones.

Strongly agree	Agree	Slightly agree	Neutral	Slightly disagree	Disagree	Strongly disagree
+3	+2	+1	0	−1	−2	−3

(The most favorable opinion is indicated by "strongly agree.")

FIGURE   2.12

Siperstein adjective checklist for describing classmates.

If you had to describe _____ to your classmates, what kinds of words would you use? Below is a list of words to help you. CIRCLE the words you would use. You can use as many or as few words as you want. Here is the list:

healthy	neat	careful
slow	lonely	glad
sloppy	pretty	stupid
clever	cruel	careless
alert	proud	dishonest
alright	weak	smart
crazy	bright	unhappy
greedy	bored	mean
cheerful	helpful	ugly
honest	dumb	happy
ashamed	friendly	kind
	sad	

Variables in Attitude Change

Figure 2.13 depicts the variables, processes, and effects pertaining to persuasive communication theory. Once opinions are assessed, *independent variables* can be manipulated to facilitate change in attitudes. Hovland's theory, simplified, posits that three sets of independent variables determine attention, comprehension, and acceptance of information and cause attitude change. These sets of variables are source factors (*who* presents the information), message or content factors (*what* is presented), and audience factors (*who* receives the information). The independent variables listed in column 1 of Figure 2.13 are illustrative of those shown by research to relate to opinion change.

Many source factors influence opinion change. Chief among these is the extent that listeners perceive the speaker to be knowledgeable (e.g., have actual experience and thus expertise), trustworthy (e.g., have no hidden motives and thus tell it as it is), and likable. If the speaker is perceived to hold high status and/or to be valued by one's significant others, then the content is likely to receive more attention than if status is perceived as average or low. Persons with disabilities who are successful athletes or professionals are among the most powerful sources.

Demographic variables like race, religion, gender, age, and occupation are more important to some persons than others. Matching characteristics of a speaker with those of the audience is often strategic. Adolescents, for example, may be more influenced by peers than adults. One secret to attitude change is knowing the source variables most signifi-

FIGURE 2.13

Model depicting persuasion theory.

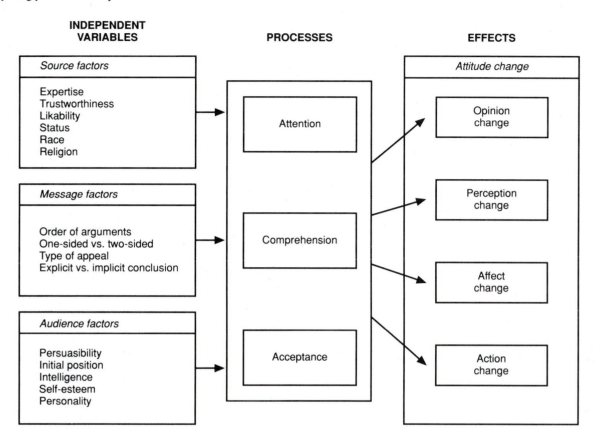

cant to a particular group. A particularly exciting research study published in *Mental Retardation* by a second grader tells how she used *kid power* (her own persuasiveness) to change the attitudes of her class (Turnbull & Bronicki, 1986).

Message factors that influence comprehension are listed in Figure 2.13. Illustrative questions that should be asked about message factors are

1. **In planning the order of arguments, should the strongest come first or last?**
   Answer: First, in most cases.

2. **Should the argument be one-sided or two-sided?**
   Answer: Generally, two-sided (i.e., both pros and cons) is best, especially when (a) students are opposed to the desired position and/or (b) students will be exposed later to counterarguments.

3. **What type of appeal (emotional vs. factual) is more effective?**
   Answer: Depends on the audience and the topic under discussion.

4. **Which type of conclusion (explicit or implicit) is better?**
   Answer: Explicit; explain clearly the attitudes and behaviors desired and the recommendations for achieving them. Use implicit conclusions (e.g., make up your own mind) only with a very intelligent, mature audience.

Figure 2.13 also indicates that several audience variables are related to opinion change: (a) persuasibility, (b) initial position, (c) intelligence, (d) self-esteem, and (e) personality. How these relate, however, depends on the nature of the psychological object, the intensity of the initial position, the function the attitude plays in one's life, and the perceived consequences of change.

Space does not permit further elaboration on persuasive communication theory. However, attempting to modify attitudes by means of persuasion techniques is both an art and a science based on an extensive body of research literature that continues to grow and change. Like all evolving knowledge, Hovland's work has been criticized, challenged, and expanded. Many attitude-change theories have their roots in persuasive communication theory but dispute some small part of it. For example, *channel* (the listening, receiving environment or *how* the message is delivered) is now accepted as an additional independent variable to be manipulated. In summary, persuasive communication theory focuses on the cognitive domain and addresses opinion change. The assumption is that opinion changes lead to desired modifications of perception, affect, and action.

Social Cognitive Theory

Social cognitive theories focus on the importance of situational or environmental factors, especially those of a social nature. They posit that attitudes are formed primarily from total life experiences rather than from the passive cognition emphasized in persuasive communication theory.

Whereas persuasive communication theory was derived mainly by one person (Carl Hovland at Yale), social cognitive theories have come from many persons. Some of these theories focus mostly on attitudes, whereas others center on social behaviors. Each contributes to a better understanding of social competency and acceptance, one of the major goals of adapted physical education. See the article by Tripp and Sherrill (1991) for a review of the work of social cognitive theorists. Kurt Lewin, whose work is associated with the Massachusetts Institute of Technology and the University of Michigan, is acknowledged as the major pioneer in the early evolution of social cognitive attitude theories.

Field or Ecological Theory

Lewin's field theory of personality evolved from the Gestalt psychology of the 1930s, which posited that behavior is determined, not by stimulus-response methodology or passive cognition, but by the total environmental field or life space. This field consists of an organized system of psychosocial stresses or forces, analogous to a gravitational or electromagnetic field, which must be kept in balance.

According to Lewin (1951), behavior can be understood only by analyzing the total field, or life space, today called the ecosystem. Life space consists of the total psychological world (i.e., everything that is seen, heard, sensed, or inferred). *Field theory,* then, emphasizes analysis of the individual, the environment, and the interactions between the two and working for change by altering person-by-situation interactions. Lewin's field theory has been particularly influential in the evolution of rehabilitation counseling and in the creation of theories pertaining to interpersonal relations, group dynamics, and social learning.

Socially Based Needs

Central to all social cognitive theories is the belief that attitude change is motivated by socially based needs: (a) the need to compare oneself to similar others to evaluate achievement or worth, (b) the need for approval and acceptance by significant others, and (c) the need to reduce discrepancies between one's own beliefs and group norms. Attitudes are strongly influenced by the norms and goals of groups to which people belong or aspire to belong. This is especially true in adolescence, when the need for group affiliation is very strong. Within most groups, various pressures cause members to behave, think, feel, and dress alike.

Complex reward and punishment systems exist within group structures. People often are unaware of these. They simply know that they feel good when in compliance with group expectations and bad otherwise. Areas particularly dominated by group mores are friendships and treatment of minorities. Some groups are open, whereas others are closed. When a person becomes friends with someone who is different and unacceptable to his or her group, a state of *cognitive dissonance* exists (i.e., there is a discrepancy between one's personal attitudes and the normative position of the group).

To reduce cognitive dissonance, an individual chooses from three alternatives: (a) change one's position in the direction of the norm, (b) try to influence the group norm, or (c) reject the group as irrelevant. Values clarification in individual and small groups often helps students to cope with group dynamics processes. For instance, how might you guide group discussion in a physical education class that contains some students who are social isolates?

The higher an individual's position in the social structure, the more likely that he or she can cause attitude change. This is because persons tend to imitate leaders and significant others. In this respect, the social cognitive theories incorporate the basic tenet of persuasive communication theory: that persons pay attention, comprehend, and accept the ideas and demands of significant others. Cliques, gangs, and other subgroups set the norms for behavior in the school and community. Attitude-change strategies must focus on the leaders of such subgroups, because changing the attitudes of leaders results in similar changes in group members. For example, if a leader agrees to be a partner or tutor for a student with a disability, others will probably volunteer also.

Perceptions and Interpersonal Relations

Attitude change is strongly influenced by perceptions of advantages and disadvantages. These are often social in nature. For example, consider some of the questions that people ask themselves: If I change my attitude, will the teacher respect and like me more, or less? Will my friends respect and like me more, or less? How will attitude change affect my family members? Persons consider consequences and usually make decisions in the direction of the attitude held by whomever is their most significant and/or powerful other.

Some persons are better than others at accurately perceiving the attitudes and behaviors of the people in their life space. *Interpersonal relations theory* focuses on observing other individuals and learning to understand why they think, feel, and act as they do (Selman, 1980). Structured contacts with partners and small groups help individuals become better observers of body language and more sensitive to tone of voice and meaning of words. Popular techniques are (a) repeating in your own words what you think someone said before giving a response and (b) mirroring or shadowing the movements of a partner in follow-the-leader type games. Chapter 16 on dance therapy offers other ideas for sensitivity training. The goal is to reinforce the understanding that how we *perceive* others to feel and act toward us influences our attitudes and behaviors toward them, and vice versa.

Interpersonal relations theory also teaches analysis of situational factors through vicarious experience. Simulating disabilities (e.g., spending a day in a wheelchair or on crutches, wearing a blindfold or earplugs to create seeing and hearing impairments) sensitizes persons to how varying situational demands affect attitudes and behaviors. A good strategy is to have people try their simulated disabilities in different settings with varied goals (e.g., participate in a team sport, an individual sport, a recreational partner activity, a cooperative game, a competition). This helps them to analyze the effects of different situations on interpersonal relations.

FIGURE 2.14

Puppets and dolls with disabilities can be used to facilitate understanding of wheelchairs and architectural barriers in the integrated setting.

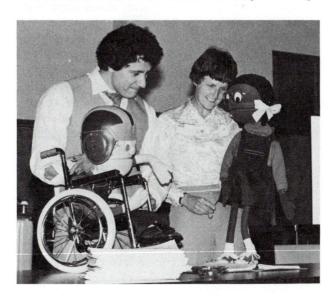

Role playing is another vicarious experience that helps persons understand and empathize with unfamiliar and/or undesirable conditions. In such activities, persons are assigned the roles they least understand and most fear or dislike. Role playing can be spontaneous sociodrama, or it can be structured as a group assignment to write and present a play, dialogue, or monologue.

Puppet shows accomplish the same purpose. Puppets, dolls, or stuffed animals can be designed so that they are different in appearance or abilities. These promote analysis as well as the sharing of ideas and feelings. Kids on the Block is a set of commercial puppets with published scripts that has been widely used to promote attitude change about persons with disabilities (see Figure 2.14) (Aiello, 1988; Gilfoyle & Gliner, 1985).

Locus of Control

Locus of control (LOC) is important in the social cognitive theories. LOC is the extent that persons view themselves as having power over their destiny, as opposed to fate, chance, and powerful or significant others. Persons who attribute events to fate, chance, or other persons are governed by an external LOC. In contrast, persons who believe that their personal ability and effort make things happen are guided by an internal LOC.

Persons with external LOC are more motivated by socially based needs than those with internal LOC. Children, for example, are characterized by external LOC and depend more on parents and significant others for direction than do adults. Teachers can promote the development of internal LOC by giving students choices (e.g., "Would you like to play alone or with Bob?" "Shall we work on running today or jumping?" "What size ball do you want me to throw you?") As children practice and gain confidence in decision making, they become increasingly self-reliant. People with internal LOC are not easily influenced by sources that teach prejudice and discrimination.

Behaviorism

Social cognitive attitude theorists do not agree about whether change strategies should be directed toward attitudes or behaviors. Most theorists believe that attitude change leads to behavior modification, but Daryl Bem's (1972) self-perception theory posits that attitudes develop as a result of behaviors, not vice versa. According to Bem, self-perceptions are based on memories of thoughts, feelings, and actions. Parents use this approach when they insist that children try unfamiliar food or experiences. The assumption of "Try it, you'll like it" leads to some persons feeling good about the exposure (contact) and developing good attitudes. Others do not. The difference seems to be in how carefully the experience is structured to create feelings of mastery, success, and pleasure. Fun, praise, and reward should be built into the contact experience.

Albert Bandura, a psychology professor at Stanford University in California, is today's leader in social cognitive theorizing. Bandura (1977, 1986) emphasizes changing behaviors through (a) modeling and learning by observing others, (b) structured direct experiences, and (c) analytical, self-reflective, and self-regulatory thought that uses imagery and mental rehearsal to focus on things as they should be, not as they are. While social and observational learning is a behavioral perspective, Bandura's recent publications establish him as a leader in interactionism. His social cognitive theory posits that human functioning is best explained in terms of "a model of triadic reciprocality in which behavior, cognitive and other personal factors, and environmental events all operate as interacting determinants of each other" (Bandura, 1986, p. 18).

Interactionism

Bandura's focus as a social-learning theorist is primarily in the cognitive rather than the affective domain. He does, however, discuss attitude, noting that the assumption that attitudes determine behavior is only partially true. Bandura emphasizes that experiences accompanying changes in behavior also alter attitudes:

Both attitudinal and behavioral changes are best accomplished by creating conditions that foster the desired behavior. After people behave in new ways, their attitudes accommodate to their actions. . . . If the new practices are advantageous, adopters either alter their attitudes to coincide with their new behavior or they construe their behavior in a manner consistent with their traditional beliefs. (Bandura, 1986, p. 160)

Bandura's primary contribution to attitude theory is thus the interactionist perspective that helps us dismiss unproductive arguments about which occurs first (attitudes or behaviors) and encourages new theorizing about bidirectionality and reciprocality.

In summary, the social cognitive theories, although embodying distinct differences, are becoming increasingly interactive. These theories are particularly helpful to educators because they suggest practical applications for facilitating social competency and acceptance. Because social interactions increase the complexity of human behaviors, developing models that show relationships between and among

FIGURE 2.15

Theory of reasoned action approach to attitude assessment and behavior change. Note that beliefs, attitudes, intentions, and behaviors are separate components. (Icek Ajzen/Martin Fishbein, *Understanding Attitudes and Predicting Social Behavior,* © 1980, pp. 8, 84. Adapted by permission of Prentice Hall, Englewood Cliffs, New Jersey.)

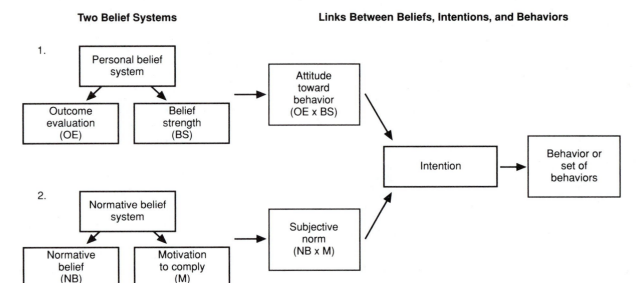

all of the operating attitude and behavior components is difficult. Teachers must become increasingly bold in constructing their own models, hypothesizing how components interrelate, and theorizing about change through social cognitive interactions.

Theory of Reasoned Action

The theory of reasoned action, proposed in the 1970s by Martin Fishbein, University of Illinois, and Icek Ajzen, University of Massachusetts, emphasizes the link between (a) two belief systems, (b) intentions, and (c) actual behaviors. This approach is vastly different from others and merits careful study. The term *reasoned action* implies that most behaviors are performed for a reason: People think about the consequences of their actions and deliberately decide to achieve some outcomes and avoid others.

Attitude in this theory is conceptualized as unidimensional and defined as overall feeling or general evaluation of a behavior (e.g., the behavior of adapting instruction). In this theory, unlike others, attitude toward the person is not considered important. Instead, the focus is on attitude toward one's behaviors in relation to this person.

The theory of reasoned action posits that two belief systems interact to cause a behavioral intention, which, in turn, will result in a behavior or set of behaviors. The two belief systems are (a) personal beliefs and (b) normative beliefs. These are examined in relation to some behavior (e.g., adapting physical education instruction, losing weight, changing jobs).

Personal beliefs pertain to probable outcomes/consequences of a behavior and are broken down into two components. Component 1 is an evaluation of whether the outcome is likely to be good or bad. Component 2 is a prediction about whether the outcome will really occur (certain or uncertain). The numerical scores for Component 1 (outcome evaluation) and Component 2 (belief strength) are multiplied to obtain a score for attitude toward behavior.

Normative beliefs pertain to perceptions about what significant others think you should do and your motivation to comply with their beliefs. The numerical scores for these two components are multiplied to obtain a score called the subjective norm.

Figure 2.15 depicts the parts of the theory of reasoned action. The two belief systems, just described, are personal beliefs and normative beliefs. The links between beliefs and intention are designated as the *attitude toward behavior* and the *subjective norm* and are expressed as numerical scores that can be used to predict intention level (e.g., 20%, 40%, 60%). From this predicted level, the probability of behavior is inferred.

Let's apply the theory of reasoned action to a typical physical education setting in which we want to predict probable behaviors of a physical education teacher who has been assigned a 14-year-old boy with cerebral palsy. The boy has normal intelligence, good speech, and Class 4 functional motor ability (i.e., no involvement of upper extremities, but needs wheelchair for ambulation; see Chapter 25 on cerebral palsy). There are 27 other 14-year-olds in the class, all of whom are able-bodied (AB) and represent the usual wide range of sport skills. The teacher has no assistant. The boy, Joe, arrives on the first day of the spring term, accompanied by an individualized education program (IEP), written by a multidisciplinary team in accordance with federal law and school district policy. This IEP briefly states Joe's annual physical education goals, including short-term instructional objectives. The teacher notes that these are compatible with

Table 2.2
A teacher's personal beliefs about adapting instruction for a disabled student in a mainstream class.

My Adapting Instruction for Joe Will Result in These Outcomes/Consequences:	Outcome Evaluation (OE)			Belief Strength (BS) That Outcome Will Occur			Attitude (A)
	Good		Bad	Certain		Uncertain	OE × BS = A
1. Joe will achieve goals.	③	2	1	3	②	1	6
2. Other students will achieve their goals (i.e., Joe's presence will not interfere with learning of nondisabled students).	③	2	1	③	2	1	9
3. Adaptations needed will increase pressures on me so I'm more tired at night, maybe grouchy.	3	2	①	3	②	1	2
4. I'll have to give up some of my recreation to find the extra time needed for planning and individualizing.	3	2	①	3	②	1	2
5. The principal will be pleased and give me a merit raise.	③	2	1	3	2	①	3
Total Attitude Toward Behavior Score							22

Note. Highest possible total attitude score is 45.

Table 2.3
A teacher's normative beliefs about adapting instruction for a disabled student in a mainstream class.

My Significant Others Believe I Should Adapt Instruction for Joe:	Normative Belief (NB)			My Motivation to Comply (M)			Subjective Norm (N)
	Yes		No	Strong		Weak	NB × M = N
1. My spouse or housemate	3	2	①	3	②	1	2
2. My mother	3	②	1	3	②	1	4
3. My principal	③	2	1	3	②	1	6
4. My best friend	3	2	①	3	②	1	2
5. Other teachers in my school	3	②	1	3	②	1	4
Subjective Norm Score							18

Note. Highest possible score, when there are five significant others, is 45.

those of the regular education students. For Joe to achieve these goals, however, the teacher will have to adapt instruction. The question is, will he or she do this? How can classroom behavior be predicted?

According to the theory of reasoned action, two inventories should be administered to the teacher: (a) one to determine personal beliefs about adapting instruction and (b) one to determine normative beliefs about adapting instruction. Each inventory would include 5 to 7 items, each of which would be rated on two 3-point scales. From these scores, an attitude toward behavior and a subjective norm would be derived, which, in turn, could be used to predict strength of intention to adapt instruction and probable actual behavior.

Table 2.2 presents an example of how personal beliefs about adapting instruction might be measured. Each of the five items represents an outcome or consequence of adapting instruction. Note that there are separate items in relation to the consequences for (a) Joe, (b) regular education students, and (c) the teacher. Note also that both positive and negative consequences are included. In the first response column of the inventory (Outcome Evaluation), the teacher circles the numbers to express his or her overall feeling about each outcome. In the second response column (Belief Strength), numbers are circled to indicate degree of certainty that the outcome will occur. The third column (Attitude) would not appear on the actual inventory. It is included here simply to illustrate how the attitude score is derived.

Table 2.3 presents an example of how normative beliefs about adapting instruction might be measured. Each of the five items represents a significant other. In the first response column (Normative Belief), numbers are circled to indicate the degree of probability that significant others will support the behavior. In the second response column (Motivation to Comply), the teacher circles numbers to indicate degree of motivation. The third column (Subjective Norm) would not appear on the actual inventory but is included to show how this score is derived.

The attitude score of 22 out of 45 (48.9%) from the first inventory and the subjective norm score of 18 out of 45 (40%) from the second inventory are then examined in terms of the relative importance of these two variables. This provides insight into the relationship between attitude, subjective norm, and intention. In this example, the teacher's commitment to adapting instruction, as expressed by intention, ranges somewhere between 40 and 49%. With such a low intention level, the teacher probably will not do much adapting in relation to the boy's special needs. This kind of information is valuable in that it helps (a) teacher trainers assess where more work on belief and attitude change are needed, (b) principals assess which teachers are likely to do the best job and which teachers need more inservice training, and (c) prospective teachers to assess themselves and set personal change goals.

The theory of reasoned action, in its entirety, has not yet been tested in relation to physical education teacher behaviors. Parts of the theory have been examined by Terry Rizzo (1984), who developed an instrument called Physical Educators' Attitude Toward Teaching the Handicapped (PEATH). The theory of reasoned action has, however, been subjected to study in relation to exercise adherence (Dishman, 1988), predicting and understanding weight loss (Ajzen & Fishbein, 1980), and several other behaviors. The theory has been included in this chapter to emphasize the complexity of attitude formation, change, and measurement and to encourage readers to undertake research in relation to beliefs, attitudes, intentions, and behaviors. Beliefs and attitudes are important because they affect intentions and behaviors. Models such as that presented in Figure 2.15 are needed to guide both teaching and research.

Summary of Attitude Theories

Four groups of attitude theories have been described: (a) contact theory, (b) persuasive communication, (c) social cognitive theories, and (d) reasoned action. Use of these theories will help you plan all aspects of service delivery, and they will be particularly helpful in advocacy activities. It is important for you to feel comfortable with theories and theorizing. Feel free to criticize these theories, test them, play with them, and propose changes. Consider each brick in our wall of knowledge about individual differences, attitudes, and behaviors. Each generation of teachers and researchers leaves its mark on this wall. Are you ready to begin? Try it; you'll like it!

References

Aiello, B. (1988). The Kids on the Block and attitude change. In H. E. Yuker (Ed.), *Attitudes toward persons with disabilities* (pp. 223–229). New York: Springer.

Ajzen, I., & Fishbein, M. (1980). *Understanding attitudes and predicting social behavior.* Englewood Cliffs, NJ: Prentice-Hall.

Allport, G. W. (1954). *The nature of prejudice.* Cambridge, MA: Addison-Wesley.

Amir, Y. (1969). Contact hypothesis in ethnic relations. *Psychological Bulletin, 71,* 319–342.

Archie, V., & Sherrill, C. (1989). Attitudes toward handicapped peers of mainstreamed and nonmainstreamed children in physical education. *Perceptual and Motor Skills, 69,* 319–322.

Bandura, A. (1977). *Social learning theory.* Englewood Cliffs, NJ: Prentice-Hall.

Bandura, A. (1986). *Social foundations of thought and action: A social cognitive theory.* Englewood Cliffs, NJ: Prentice-Hall.

Barrow, H., McGee, R., & Tritschler, K. (1989). *Practical measurement in physical education and sport* (4th ed.). Philadelphia: Lea & Febiger.

Bem, D. J. (1972). Self-perception theory. In L. Berkowitz (Ed.), *Advances in experimental social psychology* (Vol. 6, pp. 2–62). New York: Academic Press.

Buscaglia, L. (1975). *The disabled and their parents: A counseling challenge.* Thorofare, NJ: Charles B. Slack.

Davis, W. E., & Rizzo, T. L. (1991). Issues in the classification of motor disorders. *Adapted Physical Activity Quarterly, 8* (4), 280–304.

Dishman, R. (Ed.). (1988). *Exercise adherence: Its impact on public health.* Champaign, IL: Human Kinetics.

Federal Register, August 23, 1977, PL 94–142, the Education for All Handicapped Children Act.

Eichstaedt, C., & Kalakian, L. (1987). *Developmental/adapted physical education* (2nd ed.). New York: Macmillan.

Gilfoyle, E., & Gliner, J. (1985). Attitudes toward handicapped children: Impact of an educational program. *Physical and Occupational Therapy in Pediatrics, 5* (4), 27–41.

Goffman, E. (1963). *Stigma: Notes on the management of a spoiled identity.* Englewood Cliffs, NJ: Prentice-Hall.

Hansen, R., & Taylor, J. (1987). *Rick Hansen: Man in motion.* Vancouver: Douglas & McIntyre.

Horne, M. (1985). *Attitudes toward handicapped students: Professional, peer, and parent reactions.* Hillsdale, NJ: Lawrence Erlbaum.

Ibrahim, H. (1968). Prejudice among college athletes. *Research Quarterly, 39,* 556–559.

Johnson, D. W., & Johnson, R. T. (1986). Mainstreaming and cooperative learning strategies. *Exceptional Children, 52,* 553–561.

Jones, R. L. (Ed.). (1984). *Attitudes and attitude change in special education: Theory and practices.* Reston, VA: Council for Exceptional Children.

Katz, I. (1981). *Stigma: A social psychological analysis.* Hillsdale, NJ: Lawrence Erlbaum.

Lewin, K. (1951). *Field theory in the social sciences.* New York: Harper.

Lott, B. E., & Lott, A. J. (1960). The formation of positive attitude toward group members. *Journal of Abnormal and Social Psychology, 61,* 297–300.

Price, L. (1970). *The wonder of motion.* Reston, VA: American Alliance for Health, Physical Education, Recreation, and Dance.

Research and Training Center on Independent Living. (1990). *Guidelines for reporting and writing about people with disabilities* (3rd ed.). Lawrence, KS, University of Kansas.

Rizzo, T. L. (1984). Attitudes of physical educators toward teaching handicapped pupils. *Adapted Physical Activity Quarterly, 1,* 267–274.

Rizzo, T. L., & Wright, R. G. (1987). Secondary school physical educators' attitudes toward teaching students with handicaps. *American Corrective Therapy Journal, 41,* 52–55.

Rizzo, T. L., & Vispoel, W. P. (1991). Physical educators' attributes and attitudes toward teaching students with handicaps. *Adapted Physical Activity Quarterly, 8* (1), 4–11.

Selman, R. L. (1980). *The growth of interpersonal understanding.* New York: Academic Press.

Sherrill, C. (1986). Social and psychological dimensions of sports for disabled athletes. In C. Sherrill (Ed.), *Sports and disabled athletes* (pp. 21–33). Champaign, IL: Human Kinetics.

Siperstein, G. (1980). *Instruments for measuring children's attitudes toward the handicapped.* Unpublished manuscript, University of Massachusetts, Boston.

Stewart, D. A. (1991). *Deaf sport: The impact of sports within the deaf community.* Washington, D.C.: Gallaudet University Press.

Triandis, H. (1971). *Attitude and attitude change.* New York: John Wiley & Sons.

Tripp, A., & Sherrill, C. (1991). Attitude theories of relevance to adapted physical education. *Adapted Physical Activity Quarterly, 8* (1), 12–27.

Turnbull, A., & Bronicki, G. J. (1986). Changing second graders' attitudes toward people with mental retardation: Using kid power. *Mental Retardation, 24* (1), 44–45.

Yuker, H. (Ed.). (1988). *Attitudes toward persons with disabilities.* New York: Springer.

Yuker, H., Block, J., & Younng, J. (1966). *The measurement of attitudes toward disabled persons.* Albertson, NY: Human Resources Center.

World Health Organization. (1980). *International classification of impairments, disabilities, and handicaps: A manual of classification relating to the consequences of disease.* Geneva, Switzerland: Author.

Wright, B. (1983). *Physical disability—A psychosocial approach* (2nd ed.). Philadelphia: Harper & Row.

Zimbardo, P., Ebbesen, E., & Maslach, C. (1977). *Influencing attitudes and changing behavior* (2nd ed.). Reading, MA: Addison-Wesley.

Chapter

3

Getting Started: Settings, Resources, Adaptation, and Creativity

FIGURE 3.1

Two models that guide teaching/coaching practices. The medical model guided service delivery in the 1970s and 1980s. The social minority model is recommended for the 1990s.

Medical Model	Social Minority Model
• Disability is equated with being defective, inferior, or less than.	• Disability is equated with being different; different is *not* less than, it is simply being different.
• A wide spectrum of biological/psychological anomalies and deficits exists.	• There is only one shared experience: social stigma.
• Terminology tends to be very negative.	• Terminology tends to be positive or neutral with person-first emphasized.
• Discussion is about defects, problems, or characteristics.	• Discussion is about individual assessment data, personal strengths and weaknesses.
• Goal is to give advice/prescription to patient.	• Goal is to empower individual to assume active role in self-actualization.
• Graphics are passive. 	• Graphics are active. 

After you have studied this chapter, you should be able to:

1. Make decisions about the settings where you want to obtain practicum experiences and/or part- or full-time employment.

2. Identify and discuss kinds of educational placements. Explain the difference between least restrictive environment, integration, and mainstreaming. Make plans for observing students in each kind of placement.

3. Explain the structure of the international and national sport movements for athletes with disabilities. Discuss how persons associated with these movements can serve as resources.

4. Identify resources for learning about adapted physical activity. Develop a semester plan or contract for getting acquainted with resources from many disciplines.

5. Explain adaptation theory. Discuss how adaptation theory guides service delivery.

6. Define *variable* and discuss categories of variables that are manipulated in accordance with adaptation theory.

7. Explain creativity theory and discuss relationships among creative behaviors, adaptation, and service delivery.

8. Identify and discuss five indicators of effective teaching. Develop a plan to use these as criteria for self-evaluation.

9. Identify human variables that are considered enduring and stable versus those that are more easily changed.

Individual differences, adaptation, and creativity are the three areas of knowledge that serve as the foundation for adapted physical activity service delivery. This chapter presents resources and concepts in relation to these areas to assist in planning observations and practicum experiences that will supplement and enrich your study of the text. Approximately 50% of the homework for an adapted physical activity course should be experiential (see Figure 3.1).

Settings for Practica and Employment

Where can you learn about individual differences? There are many places, both in school and out, including (a) the regular school setting; (b) the separate school setting; (c) recreation, sport, and camp settings; (d) hospitals and rehabilitation centers; (e) infant and early childhood settings; and (f) sport organization programs. Planning field trips, practicum experiences, or in-service training in one or more of these settings is important for experienced professionals as well as beginners. It is always exciting to observe others, share ideas, and engage in mutual problem solving.

The Regular School Setting

How a community provides schooling for students with special needs depends on its philosophy. Before the 1970s, most communities funded two types of schools: (a) special education and (b) regular education. Students with disabilities were thus segregated from peers and placed in homogeneous groupings. In the past two decades, many changes have occurred. Some communities still fund separate schools, but most have expanded regular schools to include a continuum of placements: (a) self-contained classes, (b) resource teacher arrangements, and (c) full or partial integration into regular classes.

Least Restrictive Environment Principle

The goal is to place each student in his or her least restrictive environment (LRE) for each school subject. An environment is considered least restrictive when it (a) matches individual abilities with appropriate services and (b) preserves as much freedom as possible. The LRE principle is interpreted in different ways. Students are typically placed in regular classes unless assessment procedures justify the restrictions of a more sheltered environment.

Seldom are placements all in the same setting. Today's special education student may be in a self-contained classroom part of the day and in regular classrooms the other part. Various resource teacher models are implemented to bridge the gap between placements. The resource teacher is typically a certified special educator who serves students with disabilities in the regular classroom (the in-class model) or in a resource room (the pull-out model, in which students go to a special room for part of their instruction).

For you to gain perspective concerning the overall educational process and how special and regular education interface, your field trips and practica should involve observations of the same student in several different school subjects. The special education director of a school system or individual principals can make arrangements for this kind of experience.

Integrated Placements

Most special education students in a regular school setting receive physical education in an integrated class (see Figure 3.2). Often, the physical educator has no knowledge that these students are receiving special education services in other classes. Students with disabilities are often placed in regular

FIGURE 3.2

Key concepts for differentiating between integrated, mainstreamed, and least restrictive environment placements.

Least Restrictive Environment

    In regular, resource, separate, or other environment

    Must be based on assessment

    Must include support services

Mainstreamed

    In some type of regular education

    Must be based on assessment

    Must include support services

Integrated

    In regular education

    May or may not be based on assessment

    May or may not include support services

physical education for several reasons. First, the level of severity of most conditions is mild or moderate, and administrators believe that regular physical educators can cope with a wide range of individual differences. Second, use of the regular physical educator to teach students with disabilities is less expensive than employing specialists. Third, federal law states that students with disabilities must be afforded the opportunity to participate in the regular physical education program available to nondisabled peers unless a multidisciplinary educational team indicates that specially designed, separate instruction is needed.

An integrated placement is not necessarily in compliance with the LRE principle (Broadhead, 1985; Heikinaro-Johansson & Telama, 1990; Lavay & DePaepe, 1987; Loovis, 1986). Integration simply means that students are together in the same school or class. This may or may not be sound programming. Questions to ask when observing students with disabilities in an integrated setting are (a) Are they being treated like everyone else? (b) Are they actively involved in movement, with the same opportunity to learn as their classmates? (c) Are they safe? (d) Can they achieve goals with minimal or no assistance? and (e) Can they assume some personal responsibility for their successes and failures? If the answers to these questions are yes, the students are probably appropriately placed. If not, the LRE may be one of the many designs for separate or combined placement. Implementation of the LRE principle in physical education, however, requires considerable creativity and the support of parents and administrators. Legislation designed to promote LRE placement is discussed in Chapter 4.

Although sometimes used as synonyms, *integrated* and *mainstreamed* theoretically are not the same. Whereas integrating means combining, mainstreaming denotes a process by which students are placed in settings that represent different degrees of integration and that provide support services needed for success. Originally, *mainstreaming* was a term created by special educators to describe the *right way* to integrate (i.e., the careful matching of abilities with environmental demands and the provision of support services to facilitate success). This concept was the basis for the evolution of the LRE principle in the 1970s.

Professionals use mainstreaming to refer to the LRE process, but laypersons often consider mainstreaming and integration to be synonyms. This leads to many misunderstandings (Dybwad, 1980; Lavay, Foret, Dempsey, & Loovis, 1987). How each school system defines terms thus must be clarified. Regular physical education in the 1990s is increasingly integrated, but the support services often are not present to make it mainstreamed.

In every regular physical education class of 30 students, 3 are likely to be classified by the school system as special education, a figure based on the 10 to 11% of all students in the public schools who meet special education eligibility requirements. Additionally, many nonspecial education students can benefit from adapted physical education instruction. In a regular physical education class with 30 pupils, the following conditions probably are present:

3 to 5 special education conditions (i.e., physical, mental, sensory impairments)

3 to 5 clumsiness conditions (based on Cratty's [1989] 10 to 15% estimate)

3 to 5 asthma, diabetes, and other health impairments not usually of concern to special educators but requiring special attention in the regular physical education setting

<u>**3 to 5**</u> weight conditions that need special programming

12 to 20 total students who need adapted physical education services (40 to 66% of total class)

Thus, regular physical education classes are a good place to observe individual differences. Often, special education students fit into activities better than clumsy, health-impaired, and weight-impaired students. The point is that special education assessment and placement procedures often are not meaningful in the physical education context. Educators have to adapt to the needs of all students, not just those with a special education label.

Separate and Combined Placements

There are many designs for separate and combined adapted physical education placement. Some pertain to nonspecial education students, others to students in wheelchairs or with special sport instruction needs, and still others to students with severe disabilities.

Nonspecial education students who are clumsy, have weight problems, or are coping with various health impairments should have opportunities for separate, part-time instruction—for example, 1 day a week in separate physical education and 4 days a week in regular physical education. This plan permits students with like conditions or problems to meet and work together. It recognizes the need for support networks, strong adult models, and individual and small-group counseling to actualize psychomotor potential.

Students eligible for wheelchair sports need occasional separate units of instruction to learn the skills, rules, and strategies of wheelchair activities. Otherwise, they are being denied the right to learn lifetime sports, a violation of the normalization principle, since able-bodied peers typically are provided opportunities to practice team and individual sports in the class setting. This same philosophy applies to students with visual impairments who are eligible for sports like beep baseball and goal ball that are not included in the regular curriculum.

Students with severe disabilities require one-to-one and small-group instruction that is not possible in most integrated classrooms. These individuals are usually taught by itinerant adapted physical activity specialists who serve two or more schools.

The Separate School Setting

Separate schools may be public or private, day or residential. These facilities typically serve one special population or address the needs of individuals with multiple disabilities. Best known, perhaps, are residential schools for students who are blind, deaf, or mentally retarded. Philosophies vary widely about the maintenance of such facilities, but almost every state or province has one or more separate schools. Visits and/or volunteer work at such schools are excellent learning experiences.

The nature of residential facilities for persons with mental retardation has changed drastically over the past two decades. Whereas most individuals were once institutionalized in large, centralized facilities, today only those with severe retardation (IQs of 35 and under) and multiple disabilities are served in this manner. Only 5% of all persons with mental retardation have IQs of 35 and below, and most of these individuals reside with parents or in small-group homes. Thus, state schools today house very few people.

With regard to special schools for persons with sensory impairments, the logic is different. These schools typically serve the full spectrum of ability levels, field excellent sport teams, and generate loyal alumnae groups (Butterfield, 1991; Stewart, 1991). Nevertheless, placement in such schools is controversial, with strong proponents on each side of the argument. Reasons for selecting a state school over a local placement are diverse, but the inadequacies of small school districts are commonly cited as an explanation.

Some schools and universities are known worldwide for their special services. Among these are *Gallaudet University* in Washington, DC, the only liberal arts institution in the world for persons who are deaf, and *Perkins School for the Blind* in Boston, Massachusetts. Most professionals recognize these names and aspire to visit these and similar sites.

Recreation, Sport, and Camp Settings

Municipal parks and recreation settings offer both segregated and integrated activities. Communities that employ therapeutic recreation specialists provide excellent prac-

FIGURE 3.3

Winter sports training at Beitostølen, internationally known center near Oslo, Norway.

ticum experience. In some communities, parent-professional organizations like the ARC (formerly named the Association for Retarded Citizens) and the Learning Disability Association of America (LDA) have developed recreation and camp programs. These and similar organizations are usually listed in the phone book and offer opportunities for getting to know parents as well as children and youth with disabilities. Local addresses can also be obtained from national organizations.

Several private facilities offer year-round programs of recreation, sport training and competition, outdoor education, and wilderness camping (see Figure 3.3). Perhaps the best known of these is *Beitostølen,* located in central Norway, approximately 150 mi north of Oslo. Its founder, Erling Stordahl, who himself is blind, created a model for serving all disabilities that has been followed in many parts of the world. The *Courage Center* in Golden Valley, Minnesota, and the *Breckenridge Outdoor Education Center for the Handicapped* in Colorado are illustrative of similar centers in the United States that provide sport and recreation training and experience. Summer internships for university students are often available at these and other centers.

In Canada, the *Rick Hansen Centre* at the University of Alberta in Edmonton is internationally known as a model site for research and for the training of athletes with disabilities and their coaches. Founded by physical educator Robert Steadward, who is currently president of the International Paralympic Committee (IPC), the Rick Hansen Centre benefited greatly from the advocacy activities of Rick Hansen, the athlete described in Chapter 2.

Hospitals and Rehabilitation Centers

Whereas hospitals typically provide short-term treatment and/or surgery, rehabilitation centers may house patients for months. *Rehabilitation,* derived from the Latin word *habilitus,* meaning "ability," is a comprehensive, interdisciplinary process directed toward restoring ability, health, and independence. Among the persons who spend considerable time in rehabilitation centers are those recovering from spinal cord

FIGURE 3.4

Sir Ludwig Guttman, the father of wheelchair sports.

injuries, traumatic brain injuries, strokes, burns, amputations, heart attacks, drug abuse, and mental illness. Interdisciplinary teams in rehabilitation centers typically include physicians, nurses, psychiatrists, psychologists, counselors, social workers, therapists (occupational, physical, music, art, dance, recreation), nutritionists, prosthetists, and the like (Jochheim, 1990). A recent development is the employment of sports coordinators, often individuals in wheelchairs, as part of the rehabilitation team.

An increasing number of rehabilitation centers offer sport programs (Hutzler, 1990). Some sponsor teams and regularly hold meets and tournaments. Practica in this kind of setting offer a wide array of experiences. The best-known facility of this nature—the *Stoke Mandeville Sports Centre* in Aylesbury, England—is where neurosurgeon Sir Ludwig Guttmann introduced the concept of wheelchair sports as part of the rehabilitation of World War II veterans (see Figure 3.4). Today, the Stoke Mandeville Sports Centre is the world headquarters for wheelchair sports for athletes with spinal paralysis.

Rehabilitation programs for substance abuse and mental illness rely heavily on dance and aquatics therapy, as well as sports. Movement and psychomotor therapy is often used in the treatment of persons with emotional and behavioral disorders. For more information on the use of these modalities, refer to Chapter 16, "Adapted Dance and Dance Therapy," and Chapter 17, "Adapted Aquatics," in Part 2 of this text and use the Index to look up specific topics.

Infant and Early Childhood Settings

Many facilities offer infant and early childhood training programs. These may be public or private, in a separate building or attached to a school that serves other age groups, and separate or integrated. Many day-care centers serve a wide spectrum of individual differences.

Universities with medical schools and/or health allied training centers often provide exemplary programs for this age group. Likewise, children's hospitals, parent professional organizations, and voluntary health associations offer follow-up and outpatient programs.

Sport Organization Programs

Sport can be recreational, educational, or competitive. In the 1990s, attention is increasingly focused on the right of persons with disabilities to competitive sport opportunities. As in able-bodied sport, age 8 or 9 is generally the recommended time for beginning competition. Sport camps, training programs, and meets offer excellent practica experience.

Today, school-based adapted physical education programs are expected to develop sports skills, knowledges, and strategies so that students with disabilities have the same opportunities as able-bodied youth for recreation and competition. To achieve this goal, you must have a knowledge of sport organizations and contacts with athletes who are disabled. Plan volunteer work with sport organizations and clubs that serve individuals with disabilities. If clubs of this type do not exist in your community, then the university can be a powerful force in initiating programs.

The nature of sport organizations for athletes with disabilities varies throughout the world (Brasile, 1990; Paciorek & Jones, 1989; Sherrill, 1986; Vermeer, 1987). International sport organizations, however, can provide some structure and guidance to national and local sport groups. The organization of the disabled sport movement is similar to that of the able-bodied. International games, held every 4 years, are run by a central committee analogous to the International Olympic Committee (IOC) that governs the Olympic Games for able-bodied athletes. This central committee determines which sports are most appropriate for each disability, how competitive events should be organized, and which rules must be followed.

Table 3.1 presents the names of international organizations that govern two or more Olympic sports, their equivalents in the United States, and the population served by each. Addresses of these organizations appear in Appendix D. University libraries should be encouraged to purchase the rule books of these organizations. From an advocacy standpoint, paying membership dues to as many sport organizations as possible ensures knowledge of changing rules and policies and offers the opportunity for active involvement in shaping the future of sports for athletes with disabilities.

Sports for Deaf Persons

Table 3.1 shows that the deaf population was the first to organize an international sport movement. Since the 1920s, deaf athletes have regularly held competitions. Because of the importance of sign language, deaf athletes hold their events

Table 3.1
International sport organizations and U.S. equivalents with dates of founding.

International	United States	Population Served
Comite International des Sports des Sourds (CISS), 1924	*American Athletic Association for the Deaf (AAAD), 1945*	Sports for deaf athletes (i.e., hearing loss of 55 decibels or greater in the better ear)
International Stoke Mandeville Wheelchair Sports Federation (ISMWSF), 1957	*National Wheelchair Athletic Association (NWAA), 1956*	Wheelchair sports for spinally impaired
International Sports Organization for Disabled (ISOD), 1963	*No equivalent. The United States has three separate organizations:*	Wheelchair and ambulatory sports for amputees (nine classes) and les autres (six classes)
	National Handicapped Sports (NHS), 1967	
	U.S. Les Autres Sports Association (USLASA), 1986	
	Dwarf Athletic Association of America (DAAA), 1986	
Cerebral Palsy International Sports and Recreation Association (CP-ISRA), 1978	*U.S. Cerebral Palsy Athletic Association (USCPAA), 1978*	Wheelchair and ambulatory sports for eight different cerebral palsy classes
International Blind Sports Association (IBSA), 1981	*U.S. Association for Blind Athletes (USABA), 1976*	Sports for three classes of visual impairment
Special Olympics International (SOI), 1968	*Special Olympics International (SOI), 1968*	Sports for athletes with mental retardation
International Sports Federation for Persons with Mental Handicaps (INAS-FMH), 1988	*No U.S. equivalent*	Sports for athletes with mental handicaps

Note. National Handicapped Sports (NHS) is a powerful U.S. sport organization that governs winter sports and other events for several disability groups.

separately from those of other disabled groups. International games are conducted quadrennially in the year after the regular Olympics. Videotapes of these games can be obtained from Gallaudet University, 7th & Florida NE, Washington, DC 20002.

Sports for Persons with Physical Disabilities

Table 3.1 shows that four international organizations govern Olympic sports for athletes with physical disabilities: International Stoke Mandeville Wheelchair Sports Federation (ISMWSF), International Sports Organization for Disabled (ISOD), Cerebral Palsy International Sports and Recreation Association (CP-ISRA), and International Blind Sports Association (IBSA). Visual impairments are included within the umbrella term *physical disability*. These organizations cooperate to conduct the Paralympics every 4 years. Both summer and winter Paralympics are held in the same year as the regular Olympics and, whenever possible, in the same country. Summer Paralympics was held in Spain in 1992. The next one will be in Atlanta, Georgia, in 1996. *Paralympics* originally was a term used only by the spinal cord injured population and represented the compounding of two words, *paraplegia* and *Olympics*. Since 1988, the term has been redefined to include athletes with a variety of disabilities. *Para* (a Latin prefix meaning "attached to") now signifies that the Paralympics are attached to, or held together

with, the Olympic Games. Videotapes of the Paralympics and of national and local sport events can be obtained from individual organizations.

The term *les autres* (French, meaning "the others") has evolved to describe locomotor disabilities not served by ISMWSF, CP-ISRA, and IBSA. Les autres includes such diverse conditions as dwarfism, muscular dystrophy, polio, and many kinds of muscular-skeletal-nervous disorders. In most countries, the same organization governs les autres athletes. In the United States, however, separate organizations have evolved to meet the needs of amputees, dwarfs, and people with les autres conditions (see Table 3.1).

In the United States, winter sports and fitness activities are promoted by National Handicapped Sports (NHS), an organization founded in 1967 and called the National Handicapped Sports and Recreation Association (NHSRA) until 1989. This organization works closely with the President's Council on Physical Fitness and Sports, the Aerobics and Fitness Association of America, and the U.S. Ski Association. NHS offers fitness instructor and ski instructor certification training and makes available videotapes and publications.

As shown in Table 3.1, six different national U.S. organizations sponsor two or more sports for athletes with physical disabilities: National Wheelchair Athletic Association (NWAA), National Handicapped Sports (NHS), U.S.

Les Autres Sports Association (USLASA), Dwarf Athletic Association of America (DAAA), U.S. Cerebral Palsy Athletic Association (USCPAA), and U.S. Association for Blind Athletes (USABA). Each organization has its separate rule books and eligibility requirements. Staying abreast of these is a formidable task.

At the local level, there is a trend toward forming sport clubs that permit athletes with different disabilities to train together and share the same coaches, facilities, and equipment. During competitions, however, only athletes with the same disability and identical classifications compete against each other. While athletes who are blind, cerebral palsied, and paralyzed might compete, for example, in the same heat, they are not competing against each other. Each is competing against either his or her best time or that of others with the same disability and classification.

Sports for Persons with Mental Handicaps

Table 3.1 shows that two organizations govern sports for persons with mental handicaps. Special Olympics International (SOI), founded in 1968 by Eunice Kennedy Shriver (the sister of President John F. Kennedy), has branches in over 90 countries and holds international summer and winter competitions every 4 years in the year prior to the regular Olympics (see Figure 3.5). Thus far, all international meets have been held in the United States. The International Sports Federation for Persons with Mental Handicaps (INAS-FMH) is a relatively new organization of European origin.

Eligibility requirements for Special Olympics participation, published in 1989, indicate that persons must be at least 8 years old and (a) classified as mentally retarded or (b) identified as handicapped because they experience cognitive delays and have significant learning or vocational problems. If of school age, they must be receiving specially designed instruction for at least 50% of their instructional day. Thus, Special Olympics does not serve individuals with physical impairments unless their primary disability is mental.

Special Olympics programs are operative in almost every community. State offices offer opportunities for training to become certified as coaches in various Special Olympics sports, and volunteers are welcomed in all program areas. Certification training is a good activity to coordinate with adapted physical education course work.

Disability-Specific Organizations

The disability-specific organizations empirically test which sport activities are most appropriate for each disability, make decisions about adaptations, write official rule books, and develop instructional materials and programs for teachers, coaches, and recreators. These organizations also serve as the policymakers through representation on the Committee on Sports for the Disabled (COSD), a structure of the U.S. Olympic Committee (USOC), which has its headquarters in Colorado Springs, Colorado.

In addition to multisport structures, organizations like the National Beep Baseball Association promote involvement of a single disability group. Beep baseball is a sport

FIGURE   3.5

International Special Olympics competition attracts athletes from over 90 countries. (Photo courtesy of Helen Brush Photography, Santa Monica, CA.)

for persons who are blind and is described in Chapter 27, "Blindness and Visual Impairments," in Part 3.

Disability-General or Combined Organizations

Organizations formed around a single sport usually adhere to a disability-general or combined philosophy. Wheelchair basketball and tennis, for instance, require only that players have permanent lower limb impairments that prevent success in able-bodied sport. These broad eligibility criteria make it relatively easy to develop local teams.

Illustrative of organizations with disability-general philosophy are the National Wheelchair Basketball Association and the National Foundation of Wheelchair Tennis. Addresses of these and many other organizations appear in Appendix D.

Programs offered by disability-general groups offer excellent practicum experiences because they provide contact with many kinds of individual differences. For instance, at a wheelchair basketball game, you will see athletes with amputations, spinal cord injuries, cerebral palsy, and les autres conditions.

Integrated Sports Programs

Many persons with disabilities are able to train and compete with able-bodied athletes. Every sport setting therefore holds potential as a practicum site. In accordance with the LRE principle, many schools are integrating their competitive sport programs. Adapted physical activity specialists then serve as liaisons between coaches and potential athletes. Athletes with disabilities need to practice with school and community teams to gain experience for disability-specific and disability-general competition.

Human Resources for Learning

So now you know where to go to observe individual differences and to become involved in field experiences. A good class project is to develop a directory with names, addresses, phone numbers, and maps to local facilities in each of the six practicum categories.

FIGURE 3.6

Athletes with disabilities are excellent resources and should be used in university and public school team teaching.

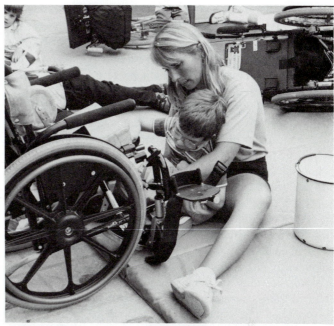

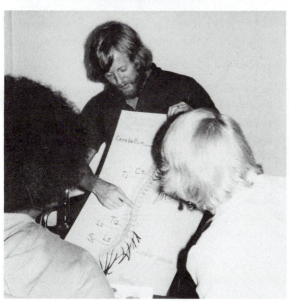

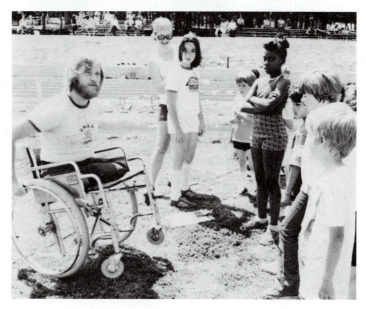

The next step in learning about individual differences is to identify human resources who can offer guidance in observation and field experiences. A university teacher is one such resource, but many additional resources are needed to make adapted physical activity rich and exciting. Among the best resources are (a) athletes with disabilities, (b) adapted physical education specialists, (c) regular physical educators, (d) special educators, (e) related services personnel, and (f) parents and family members.

Athletes with Disabilities

The number of athletes with disabilities is growing. These individuals can help you make contact with sport organiza-tions and can supply schedules of events to assist in planning your personal calendar. They can give lectures on wheelchair technology, assistive devices, and adapted equipment (see Figure 3.6). Because the rules and strategies of adapted sport are continuously changing, athletes with disabilities are more likely to have up-to-date information than published sources. They also offer a pool from which to draw personal and professional friends. No resource is more powerful in terms of knowledge and attitude development.

Coaches and athletic trainers in the disabled sport movement also make excellent resources. In addition to their coaching knowledge, many of these individuals are also family members of athletes with disabilities and can share perspectives gained from years of trial and error.

Adapted Physical Education Specialists

Many school districts employ adapted physical education specialists, who usually have a bachelor's degree in regular physical education and a master's degree in adapted physical education. These specialists work primarily in four roles: (a) direct service delivery, (b) consulting and resource room functions, (c) in-service training, and (d) administration.

Direct service delivery was defined in Chapter 1 as PAP-TE-CA (planning, assessment, prescription/placement, teaching/counseling/coaching, evaluation, coordination of resources, and advocacy). Services are often directed toward students with severe disabilities who cannot be integrated full-time into regular physical education. Because there are often only a few such students in a school, adapted physical education specialists typically are assigned two or three schools and are called itinerant teachers.

Consulting and resource room assignments are special types of service delivery analogous to those used in special education with mild and moderate problems. Adapted physical education *resource teachers* serve a single school and team-teach with regular physical educators. Like special educators, they may use in-class or pull-out models (Jenkins & Heinen, 1989). *Consulting teachers* usually travel from school to school, doing some direct service delivery but mostly meeting with regular physical educators and helping them learn how to adapt instruction.

In-service training and administration are roles that specialists perform in addition to direct service delivery (Tymeson, 1988). In-service training refers to planning and conducting workshops and learning experiences for school district personnel. Administration involves many tasks, most of which center on planning, supervising, and evaluating for an entire community.

Adapted physical educators hold membership in the Adapted Physical Activity Council (APAC) of the American Alliance for Health, Physical Education, Recreation, and Dance (AAHPERD). This council is located within the Association for Research, Administration, Professional Councils and Societies (ARAPCS). Inasmuch as AAHPERD is comprised of seven independent professional associations, be sure to indicate ARAPCS when paying membership dues. At state and national AAHPERD conferences, special sessions are offered on adapted physical education as well as on therapeutic recreation and dance for special populations. From 1966 to 1981, AAHPERD provided an Office on Programs for the Handicapped, directed by Dr. Julian Stein. This office enabled AAHPERD members with concerns about special populations to receive direct services, and many professionals continue to advocate for its reinstatement (Rizzo & Davis, 1991; Sherrill, 1988).

Adapted physical educators who are especially interested in advocacy and grant writing belong to the National Consortium for Physical Education and Recreation for Individuals With Disabilities (NCPERIWD), which was founded in 1972 by Lou Bowers, a physical education professor at the University of South Florida, and Bill Hillman, a therapeutic recreation specialist employed by the Bureau of Education for the Handicapped (the U.S. government agency now called the Office of Special Education Programs). This organization promotes, stimulates, encourages, and conducts professional preparation and research in physical education and recreation for individuals with disabilities.

The International Federation for Adapted Physical Activity, (IFAPA), founded in 1973 in the Canadian province of Quebec, provides opportunities for worldwide sharing. This federation, which has branches in various regions of the world, holds a conference every 2 years. Published proceedings make excellent supplementary textbooks (Berridge & Ward, 1987; Doll-Tepper, Dahms, Doll, & Selzam, 1990; Eason, Smith, & Caron, 1983).

Adapted physical educators subscribe to specialized journals like *Adapted Physical Activity Quarterly* (*APAQ*), *Palaestra: The Forum of Sport and Physical Education for the Disabled,* and the *Journal of Clinical Kinesiology,* formerly the *American Corrective Therapy Journal.* The year 1984 marked the beginning of both *APAQ* and *Palaestra,* strong recognition that adapted physical activity was becoming increasingly scholarly and versatile (see Figure 3.7). Addresses for these journals appear in Appendix F.

Many adapted physical educators are also active in the Council for Exceptional Children (CEC), read its journals, and rely on its excellent Department of Governmental Relations for leadership in legislation and advocacy. Both the CEC and AAHPERD national headquarters are located in Reston, Virginia (near Washington, DC).

Regular Physical Educators

Regular physical educators teach both regular and special education students in the integrated setting, adapting pedagogy, equipment, and environment as needed. They also may be assigned classes of adapted physical education for students with severe psychomotor problems. Involvement in Special Olympics, cerebral palsy sports, wheelchair sports, and other special events is common.

If the school system does not have an adapted physical education specialist, regular physical educators perform all of the tasks normally expected of a specialist. To fulfill these responsibilities, they may ask their principals to bring in a consultant for a few days or to fund participation in workshops, conferences, or courses in adapted physical education. When a school district has 30 to 40 students with severe psychomotor problems, regular physical educators often band together and ask their administration to employ a full-time adapted physical education specialist.

Regular physical educators receive the *Journal of Physical Education, Recreation, and Dance* and the *Research Quarterly for Exercise and Sport* when they join AAHPERD. They also read *The Physical Educator, Perceptual and Motor Skills,* and other specialized journals.

Special Educators

Special educators are helpful resources. Like adapted physical educators, they deliver direct services (PAP-TE-CA) and can offer insight into the overall curricular framework. Special educators typically hold membership in the Council for

FIGURE 3.7

Dr. Claudine Sherrill (*right*) and Dr. Wanda Rainbolt survey resources for learning.

Exceptional Children (CEC), which publishes the excellent resource journals *Exceptional Children* and *Teaching Exceptional Children*.

CEC is subdivided into 14 divisions, each with its own officers, conference programs, and journals. Illustrative of these separate structures are Division for Early Childhood, Division for Learning Disabilities, Council for Educational Diagnostic Services, and Teacher Education Division. Like AAHPERD, CEC has state organizations and student memberships. At the university level, there are often student CEC clubs. A good crossdisciplinary activity is for physical education majors to attend CEC campus meetings and offer to conduct a program on adapted physical education.

Special educators also belong to organizations that focus on one condition. One of the oldest and most influential of these is the American Association on Mental Retardation (AAMR), founded in 1876. AAMR publishes two research-oriented journals: *Mental Retardation* and the *American Journal of Mental Retardation.* AAMR also establishes the official terminology and definitions used in mental retardation.

Another excellent resource is the *Journal of Special Education*. The special education profession offers many rich resources, and many physical education majors elect courses in this area. In some states, adapted physical educators are required to earn special education certification.

Related Services Personnel

Related services personnel broadly refers to all school employees (except special educators and physical educators) who assist with education, including therapy, of students with disabilities. Federal legislation explains **related services** as

. . . transportation and such developmental, corrective, and other supportive services . . . as may be required to assist a child with a disability to benefit from special education. . . . (Individuals with Disabilities Education Act of 1990, Sec. 1401)

Among the related services most relevant to helping students benefit from adapted physical education are therapeutic recreation, occupational therapy, physical therapy, corrective therapy, and the arts. These professions historically have been associated with the medical model, but many changes are occurring. Inviting related services personnel to lecture and observing these professionals in the field are ways of remaining current.

Therapeutic Recreation Specialists

Therapeutic recreation (TR) is a specialization within the broad discipline of recreation. Most therapeutic recreators (TRs) belong to their parent organization, the National Recreation and Park Association (NRPA), and consider themselves recreation and leisure specialists. NRPA began as the Playground Association of America in 1906 and thus has a rich history of resources. The official journal of NRPA is *Parks and Recreation.*

Early terms for TR were hospital recreation, medical recreation, and recreation therapy. Since 1967, the date of the founding of the National Therapeutic Recreation Society (NTRS), the official name of the profession has been therapeutic recreation. There is no one definition that professionals universally embrace. O'Morrow and Reynolds (1989) explain:

Therapeutic recreation is multifaceted and multidimensional. We cannot help but feel that maybe there is no one definition or purpose of therapeutic recreation because of the many variables operating: persons, needs, settings. (p. 114)

TRs belong to two organizations: (a) NTRS, which is an official structure within the NRPA, and (b) the American Therapeutic Recreation Association (ATRA), which was founded in 1984. NTRS publishes *Therapeutic Recreation Journal;* thus far, ATRA has published only newsletters. The two organizations offer slightly different definitions of TR. NTRS uses the following definition.

Therapeutic recreation—is service delivery that facilitates the development, maintenance, and expression of an appropriate leisure lifestyle for individuals with physical, mental, emotional, or social limitations . . . Three specific areas of professional services are employed to provide this comprehensive leisure ability approach toward enabling appropriate leisure lifestyles: therapy, leisure education, and recreation participation. (National Therapeutic Recreation Society, 1982, p. 1)

This NTRS definition is broad, encompassing service delivery in accordance with both medical and educational models, and is particularly favored by community recreation proponents. Such specialists are typically employed by facilities financed by taxes (residential and day-care centers run by government agencies, schools, and parks and recreation departments) and are not directly concerned with generating revenues to pay bills or their salaries.

In contrast, many TRs are employed by private hospitals and rehabilitation centers or work in private practice. These individuals prefer a definition acceptable to health insurance companies that pay fees for treatment and therapy. Key concepts in a definition that meets these needs are intervention, health, and well-being. ATRA thus adopted the following definition.

Therapeutic recreation—is the application, by qualified professionals, of appropriate intervention strategies, using recreation services to promote independent functioning and to enhance optimal health and well-being of individuals with illnesses and/or disabling conditions. Therapeutic recreation places a special emphasis on the development of an appropriate leisure lifestyle as an integral part of that independent functioning. (American Therapeutic Recreation Association, 1984, p. 2)

Central to both definitions is the promotion of positive leisure lifestyles. Leisure encompasses thoughts, feelings, attitudes, and behaviors. Traditionally, leisure was defined as discretionary or nonwork time. Contemporary theorists point out that leisure can be a state of mind that influences perception during both work and nonwork time. TRs focus, therefore, on helping persons to (a) assess life satisfaction; (b) set goals for learning and participating in activities that are healthy, pleasurable, satisfying, and self-actualizing; and (c) achieve these goals. Several professions share TR's interest in leisure: occupational therapy, education, and physical education.

TRs are competent in widely diversified program areas, such as music, dance, art, drama, horticulture, camping, and sports. They are also skilled in leisure education and counseling and assist persons in making the transition from institutions or schools to community recreation. TRs utilize all possible community resources (both human and physical) to make leisure rich, varied, satisfying, and self-actualizing.

The greatest difference between adapted physical educators and TRs lies in the scope of the program each is qualified to conduct. Adapted physical educators are responsible only for physical activities and the state of mind related to such activities. TRs are responsible for 10 or more widely diversified program areas. Both professions emphasize carryover values and use of community resources. Leisure-time education and counseling are performed by both types of specialist.

Occupational Therapists

The related service that is broadest in scope and most likely to overlap physical education services, particularly in infancy and early childhood programs, is *occupational therapy*

(OT). In its early years, OT focused mainly on activities of daily living (ADL), particularly on the rehabilitation of arm and hand skills relevant to self-care, work, and leisure. Often, arts and crafts activities were the medium through which goals were achieved. OT, however, has changed tremendously. The official definition of OT is

Occupational therapy—is the therapeutic use of self-care, work, and play activities to increase independent function, enhance development, and prevent disability. (Hopkins & Smith, 1988, p. 4)

Whereas, in the past, OT was prescribed and directed by a physician, the American Occupation Therapy Association (AOTA) no longer requires this practice. Occupational therapists (OTs) now can determine treatment on the basis of their own assessments.

Traditionally, OTs worked in hospitals and rehabilitation centers. Today, over one third of the OTs in the United States work in school settings. Much of their focus is on infants, toddlers, and young children who need assistance in learning self-care activities to benefit from special education instruction (see Figure 3.8). OT has embraced a broad and holistic philosophy that enables its practitioners to do almost anything. Concurrently, the profession has developed high-quality training programs and certification standards.

Two levels of OTs work in schools and other settings: (a) registered occupational therapists (OTRs) and (b) certified occupational therapy assistants (COTAs). In addition to meeting other requirements, both must pass stiff national examinations (mostly multiple choice) to be eligible for employment. States that require licensure currently accept the professional organization's quality-control system. The major textbook used in OT training is *Willard and Spackman's Occupational Therapy* (Hopkins & Smith, 1988). The journal published by the professional organization is the *American Journal of Occupational Therapy.*

Of particular interest are the many contributions that OTs are making in the area of *sensorimotor integration.* Best known is the work of Jean Ayres (1972), which has popularized the use of the vestibular and tactile sense modalities. In accordance with Ayres's procedures, many OTs are now using equipment previously thought to belong in gymnasiums: scooterboards, cage balls (called therapy balls), and balancing apparatus.

Physical Therapists

Traditionally, *physical therapy (PT)* has been defined as treatment that uses heat, cold, light, water, electricity, massage, ultrasound, exercise, and functional training. Physical therapists (PTs) devote much of their time to gait training and wheelchair use. Many work in sports medicine and orthopedic rehabilitation. They use therapeutic exercise to relieve pain, prevent deformity and further disability, develop or improve muscle strength or motor skills, and restore or maintain maximal functional capacities. *Functional training* refers to teaching the patient to use crutches, prostheses, and braces.

Most PTs work within a medical model. This means that they carry out an exercise prescription written by a phy-

FIGURE 3.8

A revolving plate designed by an occupational therapist allows students who have no arm and hand control to eat independently.

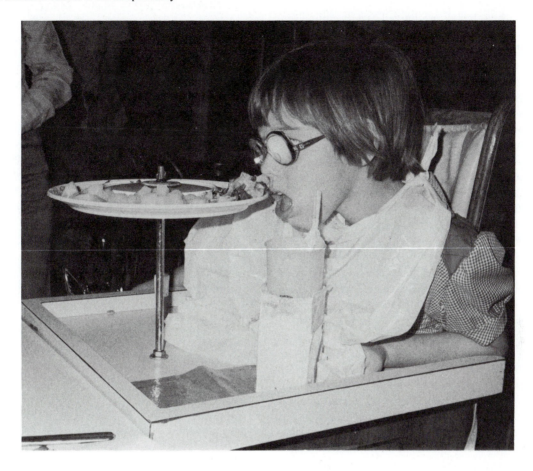

sician. They also work with very sophisticated equipment, like that used in functional electrical stimulation (FES) which enables individuals with paralyzed legs to walk or use limbs, actions previously deemed impossible. State and national certification requirements are changing, however. Some states permit PTs to work without a physician prescription.

Among the best-known PT authorities is Berta Bobath, who, with her physician-husband Karel, has developed many of the treatment procedures used with infants and children who have cerebral palsy. This treatment is based on the *inhibition* of abnormal reflex activity and the *facilitation* of higher level righting and equilibrium reflexes.

PTs belong to the American Physical Therapy Association (APTA), which publishes the journal *Physical Therapy*. Like OTs, they must pass a national certification examination administered by their national organization; there is also a system for certifying PT aides.

Corrective Therapists

Corrective therapy is an alternative certification area for persons who are especially interested in therapeutic exercise. Its definition is

Corrective therapy—is the applied science of medically prescribed therapeutic exercise, education, and adapted physical activities to improve the quality of life and health of adults and children by developing physical fitness, increasing functional mobility and independence, and improving psychosocial behavior. The corrective therapist evaluates, develops, implements, and modifies adapted exercise programs for disease, injury, congenital defects, and other functional disabilities. (Purvis, 1985, p. 5)

Persons especially interested in corrective therapy affiliate with an organization called the American Kinesiotherapy Association, Inc. (new name in 1988), which publishes *Clinical Kinesiology*. Previously known as the *American Corrective Therapy Journal* (1967–1987) and the *Journal of the Association for Physical and Mental Rehabilitation* (1946–1966), this resource was the first periodical to evolve for adapted physical activity. Over the years, several adapted physical educators have served as its editor and board members (e.g., B. Robert Carlson and Peter Aufsesser of San Diego State University; Julian Stein, retired, George Mason University).

Arts Educators and Therapists

The arts are extremely helpful in assisting persons with disabilities to benefit from special education instruction and to live rich, full lives (Groves, 1979; Roswal, Sherrill, & Roswal, 1988; Sherrill, 1979). The National Dance Association (NDA) of AAHPERD is an extremely supportive resource on dance for special populations. Periodically, articles on this topic appear in the *Journal of Physical Education, Recreation, and Dance* (see November/December 1989 issue), and conference programs are offered.

Dance, although now recognized as a discipline separate from physical education, has traditionally been part of the training of the well-rounded physical educator. Chapter 16 focuses on the use of dance.

Many educators believe that the arts (appropriately adapted) are particularly valuable in teaching self-help skills, language, and socialization. An arts-oriented approach to adapted physical activity blends music, dance, drama, and the visual/graphic arts with the teaching of movement. The resulting emphasis on movement exploration to a variety of sounds and tempos (music); colors, shapes, and textures (art); and thematic ideas (drama) stimulates creative behaviors and builds self-confidence.

Also acting as proponents of the arts are several professions, each of which has its own organization: *music therapy* (1950), *dance therapy* (1966), and *art therapy* (1969). By utilizing the expertise of arts educators and therapists, adapted physical educators can enrich learnings about the body and its capacity for creative movement and artistic expression (see Figure 3.9).

Crossdisciplinary Teamwork

The helping professions, including adapted physical activity, have changed tremendously in recent years. As the knowledge explosion continues and the economy of the nation ebbs and flows, professionals must become increasingly adept at coping with transience. Persons who work in the psychomotor domain, regardless of disciplinary affiliation, have much to gain through unification and cooperation. New models of person-centered service delivery systems are replacing traditional unidisciplinary systems.

Crossdisciplinary interactions should begin in the undergraduate years. Consider the commonalities among the helping professions: (a) each has its earliest roots in medicine; (b) each is extending its scope in response to new legislation; and (c) each is dedicated to the self-actualization of persons with disabilities.

Professional boundaries among disciplines are becoming more and more ambiguous (Blumenkopf, Levangie, & Nelson, 1985). The following are some common ambiguities and misconceptions:

1. Therapists often see themselves as responsible for *individualized* exercise and physical educators for *group* exercise. This is not a valid perception since adapted physical educators, like special educators, work on a one-to-one basis when needed.

2. Cane- and crutch-walking procedures and wheelchair transfers were once believed to belong to the therapies, but now many public school physical educators teach them.

3. Recreation specialists often believe that theirs is the major discipline concerned with play, but OTs also consider play a major goal.

4. Sensory integration therapy is conducted by many professionals. Its originator, Jean Ayres, stated that it "may be carried out by educators, psychologists, or health-related professionals" (1972, p. ix).

5. Adapted physical educators sometimes naively assume that physical and occupational therapy curricula do not include content on legislation and writing individualized education programs (IEPs). Therapists change their curricula in accordance with new legislation, just as educators do.

These commonalities emphasize the importance of every professional developing as many skills as possible. During economic crises, when job markets narrow, the major criteria for employing adapted physical educators will be breadth and depth of competence, excellence in work performance, high energy level, and good personality (i.e., the demonstrated ability to get along well with others).

Parents and Family Members

In the ecological approach to service delivery, adapted physical educators not only serve students with disabilities but also work with parents, siblings, and significant others (peers, teachers, and friends). The only way to teach the whole child is to understand the total social environment in which he or she lives. Such desired social outcomes of physical education as self-worth, acceptance by others, and rich, full leisure depend more upon family and neighborhood interactions than on school training. Thus, the teaching-learning process must be a partnership between school and family.

Adapted physical education courses can be enriched by inviting parents, siblings, and persons with disabilities to speak and/or participate in discussions about their needs, interests, and concerns. Case studies, biographies, and autobiographies about persons with disabilities also enable physical educators to better understand the persons they teach.

Adaptation Theory

Adapted physical activity takes its name from the process of adapting. It seems fitting, therefore, to call this body of knowledge *adaptation theory*. Ernst Kiphard of Germany was the first to suggest that a theory of motor adaptation should be evolved to describe the work of adapted physical educators. Kiphard (1983) stressed individual and environmental interactions as a means of maintaining homeostasis (a state of dynamic equilibrium). Persons not only adapt to the environment but they alter and change the environment each time they respond (i.e., adaptation is a reciprocal process).

Adaptation is the process by which individuals and the environment reciprocally change one another. The process is continuous, dynamic, and bidirectional. The purpose of education is to change the behaviors of a student, but the teaching-learning process results in changes in both students and teachers. A student can cause a teacher to feel excited, enthusiastic, proud, happy, and successful or bored, anxious, frustrated, disappointed, and depressed. Sometimes, it is not what we do and say that affects another person but their perception of these things, the individual meaning they attach

FIGURE   3.9

The arts are an excellent medium for learning about the body and its capacity for movement.

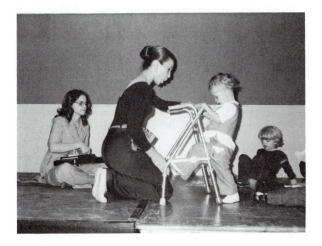

FIGURE   3.10

Categories of variables that interact in the teaching-learning process.

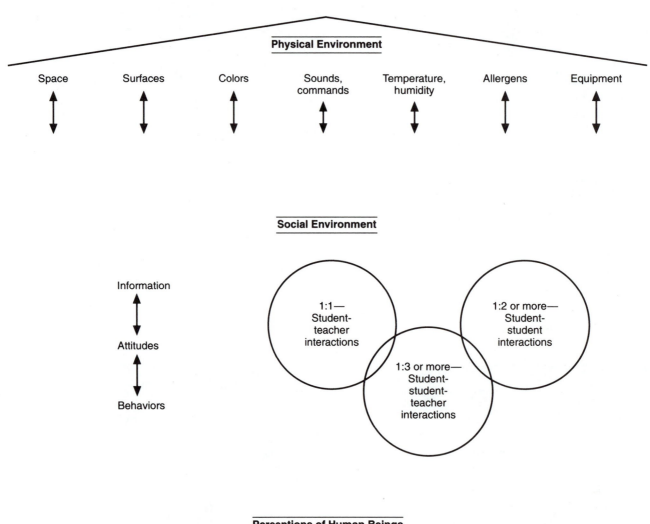

Time on Task and Number of Trials

Physical Environment

| Space | Surfaces | Colors | Sounds, commands | Temperature, humidity | Allergens | Equipment |

Social Environment

Information

Attitudes

Behaviors

1:1— Student-teacher interactions

1:2 or more— Student-student interactions

1:3 or more— Student-student-teacher interactions

Perceptions of Human Beings

What We See	What We Hear	What We Smell	What We Feel
Facial expression	Voice	Perfumes	Close/distant
Gestures	Footsteps	Soap/water	Light/heavy touch
Postures	Gestures	Bad breath	Firm/weak grasp
Clothing/style	Clothing	Perspiration	Short/long contact
Height/weight	Background		Friendly/unfriendly
Body proportions	Distracting		
Eye contact, how much	Facilitating		
Locomotion, how much			

to each phenomenon. What we expect others to do affects their behavior as well as our own perceptions. Motivation (the internal state that directs us toward some goal) is affected by literally thousands of variables, all in constant interaction with one another.

Interacting Variables

The science and art of adapting physical activity are inextricably linked with decision making about variables. A *variable* is a dimension of a human being, relationship, task, or environment that can be defined, observed, assessed, and acted upon. In adapted physical activity, thousands of variables are operative. Figure 3.10, for example, shows several categories of variables that interact in the teaching-learning process. Time or trials is featured as a major instructional variable because research shows that *time on task* determines amount of learning. Teachers make many decisions about use of time that students either honor or sabotage.

The seven variables with bidirectional arrows beneath them emphasize that adaptation of these variables is continuous, dynamic, and bidirectional. For example, space factors determine the kinds of movements and games that can be taught. Human beings interact with space, however, to change it in many ways. Adapted physical activity specialists take time to analyze these factors and determine conditions under which students learn best. They recognize that information, actions, and attitudes/feelings influence each other.

The interlocking circles show how interpersonal relations affect teaching and learning. Each represents a different kind of relationship. Beneath the circles are lists of human variables that teachers and students perceive in different ways. Most of these can be altered to enhance learning, but some, like height and body proportions, are relatively stable. Teachers give careful attention to these variables, altering self and environment in accordance with students' assessed needs.

Consider, for example, how what you wear may affect approach/avoidance behaviors. What do students see, hear, smell, and feel while you are teaching? How does this vary from student to student?

The following variables can be altered to promote success:

1. **Physical environment variables.** These include

    a. Space—open, closed; blank or structured by lines, ropes, or barriers; large or small; moving like a swing or escalator, or stationary.

    b. Lighting—bright, dull; direct, indirect; positioning to avoid looking into the sun.

    c. Sound—loud, average, soft; clear, muffled; use of music and various kinds of accompaniment to guide or structure movement.

    d. Support, wall, and ceiling surfaces—their stability and colors; their influence on sound, lighting, and movement. The support surface, for example, can be moving or stationary when the goal is to enhance balance. Or the walls and ceilings can be made to move.

    e. Mirrors—how big, where.

    f. Number and nature of distractors—objects in the room that do not relate directly to instruction.

    g. Allergens, pollens, molds, dust.

    h. Temperature and humidity.

2. **Object or equipment variables.** Balls, for example, can be described in terms of the following categories:

    a. Size—small, medium, large, or 8-inch, 10-inch, 13-inch.

    b. Weight—light, medium, heavy, or 5 oz, 1 lb, or 6 lb.

    c. Color—blue ball against white background, yellow or orange ball against a black background.

    d. Surface—*smooth* like a balloon or leather ball; *rough* with tiny indentations like a basketball; *cushy* with many soft, rubber, hairlike projections; consistent or changing.

    e. Texture—soft, firm, or hard; consistent or inconsistent.

    f. Sound—silent, beeping loud or soft, jingling with bells, or rattling with noisemakers.

    g. Shape—round, oblong, or irregular.

    h. Movement—stationary or moving.

3. **Action or performance variables.** Objects that move must be acted upon to operationalize the following factors:

    a. Speed—fast, medium, slow; constant or changing.

    b. Pathway—horizontal, vertical, arc.

    c. Direction—constant, changing; to midline, preferred side, or nonpreferred side; forward, backward; to a target or unspecified.

    d. Height—way above head, eye level, chest or waist level, ground level.

    e. Accuracy—no error, some error, lots of error.

    f. Force—hard, medium, soft.

4. **Psychosocial variables.** This refers to attitudes/feelings about self and others. It encompasses nature and number of persons sharing the space, how they are perceived by the teacher and the learner, and how they affect learning. Is only one person recognized as the teacher, or are several individuals helping and sometimes giving conflicting directions? Are peers viewed as supportive, indifferent, neutral, or hostile? What are expectations, reactions, and actions?

5. **Instructional or informational variables.** These include teaching style, type of feedback, method of presenting new material, level of assistance during practice, structured use of time, and physical distance between learner and teacher. Of particular importance is model type. The model may be the teacher or a student who is similar or dissimilar to the learner. Models may be silent or verbal.

6. **Learner variables.** These include interest, previous experience, level of sport socialization, personal meaning of a new skill or activity, modality preferences, learning style, self-concept, strengths and weaknesses, and demographics like age, gender, race, and socioeconomic class. Strengths and weaknesses can be categorized by domains (cognitive, affective, psychomotor) or by specific fitness and movement abilities.

Adaptation theory posits that professionals who are knowledgeable about variables are able to match abilities with content and teaching style to create optimal learning opportunities. *Adapt* means to make suitable, to adjust, or to modify

FIGURE   3.11

The adaptation process. Note that a task is analyzed into variables.
Variables are analyzed into factors. Factors are analyzed into levels that
are designated when writing goals.

The Adaptation Process

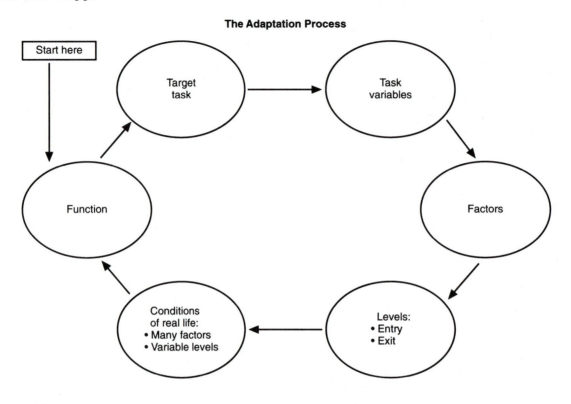

Illustrative Ecological Task Analysis

Variables	Factors	Levels
1. Ball	Size	Large, medium, small
	Momentum	None, slow, fast
	Height	Waist, higher, lower
2. Model or demonstration	Type	Live, videotaped
	Age	Same age, older, younger
	Pattern	Forehand, backhand
3. Verbal instructions	Duration	Short, medium, long
	Timing	Concurrent, before
4. Reinforcers	Type	Verbal, smile, touch
	Timing	Immediate, delayed
	Frequency	Every trial, every three trials

in accordance with individual needs. *Adaptation is individualization.* For some persons, *adapt* may mean to make a task easier, but for others, the challenge is to make it harder or more interesting. For most, *adapt* simply means to find another way: to experiment, discover, create!

Ecological Task Analysis

The adaptation process starts with *function* (e.g., ability to perform activities of daily living, work, or play). Depending upon its complexity, function can be specified as *tasks* (locomotor, nonlocomotor, and object manipulation), *problem-solving processes* (skills, strategies, rules, interpersonal relations), or *lead-up activities* (games, drills, relays, races, or routines). Figure 3.11 shows the process of (a) specifying a function; (b) selecting a target task; (c) analyzing the task into variables, factors, and levels; and (d) determining the conditions requisite to success.

The adaptation process can be applied to planning, assessment, or instruction. These are often interwoven and occur simultaneously rather than sequentially. Whenever possible, the student is involved in each step. The process of analyzing variables into factors and levels and making decisions about entry, practice, and exit levels is called *ecological task analysis* (*ETA*). In explaining the theory underlying task analysis, Davis and Burton (1991) emphasized that ETA focuses on relationships between the learner and the ecosystem, not on parts. Thus, the adaptation process creates new relationships as variables, factors, and levels are altered to enhance success.

Figure 3.11 shows that, ultimately, many factors and levels comprise the conditions requisite to performing self-care, play, or work functions. *Condition* is defined as the combination of relationships that students must handle to be successful in real life. For example, to play simple ball games, they must cope with changing speeds and directions of the other players as well as the ball. If outdoors, they must also cope with variable ground, lighting, and sound relationships.

Instructional objectives, to be effective, must specify conditions. If the *function* is to play a tennis lead-up game and the *task* is to strike a ball, then the objective might be *"Given certain conditions, the student will strike a tennis ball over the net so that it lands inside the boundary lines."* The conditions might be (a) a regulation racquet, (b) an outdoor court with good surface, (c) 15 trials not facing the sun and 15 trials facing it, (d) wind factor not more than 10 mph, and (e) balls directed at slow and medium speeds so that they land in front of the student into three areas designated as midline, left, and right. Conditions in a terminal objective should be as close as possible to the normal game setting.

Assessment and ecological task analysis are interwoven in the adaptation process of moving the student from entry to exit level. For most beginners in racquet sports, for example, the easiest ball-size level is large. The easiest momentum level may be none, so practice consists of running three steps forward and striking a suspended motionless ball. Waist high is the easiest height level for most persons. Teachers involve students in helping to select the easiest levels and then summarize findings into a prescription that describes the entry-level condition and specifies number of practice trials. For some variables, there is general agreement about a complexity continuum from easy to difficult (Morris, 1980). However, what is easy for one person may not be easy for another. Therefore, assessment encompasses cooperative teacher-student problem solving to determine the order in which tasks are taught.

Variable Practice Conditions

Consistent success under a prescribed condition signals that it is time to reassess, determine the next level of complexity, and move on. The end result of this process should be competency in *functions* related to sport and game success. Research shows that having students practice at many levels under variable conditions is wise (Eidson & Stadulis, 1991; Weber & Thorpe, 1989). If success is not obtained within a few trials, the conditions should be changed to find another set of relationships more conducive to learning. As success is achieved under more and more conditions, retention must be considered with old practice conditions interspersed with new ones.

Adaptation and Service Delivery

Adapting is important in all aspects of service delivery. Each of the seven services comprising the PAP-TE-CA model in Chapter 1 (planning, assessment, prescription/placement, teaching/counseling/coaching, evaluation, coordination of resources, and advocacy) are made more viable by appropriate adaptation. Although these services are described in considerable detail later in the text, an overview of adapting in relation to each is presented here to assist in planning practicum experiences.

Planning

Most university students have little control over the people they are assigned for practicum work. Planning thus requires getting ready for anything. Visiting ahead of time, getting acquainted with staff and facilities, and acquiring general information about the neighborhood and such variables as ethnic group, socioeconomic status, and leisure-time practices are helpful.

Whenever possible, obtain photograph and videotape clearance for your practicum student. Access to files is also essential. Discussing these needs with supervisory personnel and sharing ideas about responsibilities and benefits creates the structure for an optimal practicum experience.

Planning, after the initial meeting, involves getting acquainted, establishing rapport, and cooperatively agreeing on goals. For example, assume that you are assigned an 8-year-old named Bob who is receiving physical education in an integrated setting. A unit on catching and throwing is underway, and Bob's catching proficiency is far below that of his classmates.

Planning involves gathering information about relevant variables so that time and space can be used wisely. Instructional planning is often enhanced by asking Who? What? Where? When? and How? Let's consider each of these in relation to Bob:

Who? The *who* is obviously Bob, but this question also involves thinking through yours and Bob's relationship to the other students in the class. Should lessons be confined to interactions only between Bob and you (i.e., a pull-out type of instructional arrangement), or should part of each class period be spent with other students? If the answer is other students, then which ones, how many, and in what roles?

What? The *what* is primarily the motor skill of catching because a multidisciplinary diagnostic team has already indicated that this is a major goal for the year. Specifics about catching, however, will be determined cooperatively by you and Bob as part of instructional assessment.

Where? The *where* is the location you select or are assigned for your one-to-one interactions with Bob. Negotiate for a private space with as few distractors as possible. Make a list of other important variables. What kind of equipment is needed? Do you want the same location for each lesson, or is it desirable to schedule different learning stations?

When? The *when* is the number of minutes allocated to physical education instruction each day. For example, if your time allotment is 30 min, how much of this

FIGURE   3.12

Physical educators need suitcases on wheels to transport their homemade equipment.

time each day should be devoted to catching? Your decisions will depend largely on assessment data. The *when* variable can also involve your motivating Bob to spend after-school and weekend time on catching.

How? The *how* (pedagogy) should be related to assessment data and determined cooperatively by you and Bob. Find out what kinds of balls, gloves, backboards, and related equipment are available and the procedures to be used in reserving them. Often, you must create or purchase your own equipment. The practicum experience is a good time to begin your personal suitcase (preferably one with wheels) with homemade balls and other novel objects that enhance goal attainment (see Figure 3.12). *How* also involves planning to ascertain that Bob has balls at home for practice and that parents and significant others are motivated to help him.

In summary, planning is extremely complex because it relates to every aspect of service delivery. There is daily, weekly, and semester planning. Some of this is done by the teacher alone, but much of it is cooperative.

Assessment

Assessment involves examination of both the environment and the individual to determine what needs to be changed and what can remain the same. Environment is total lifespace (physical, social, and psychological) and can be broken down

into hundreds of variables, each of which may affect behavior. Consider, for instance, how light and noise factors influence test results of persons with different disabilities.

In Bob's case, the goal is to learn to catch. Goals must be operationalized by breaking them down into behavioral objectives. Prior to establishing objectives, however, explore personal meaning. Does Bob care about learning to catch? Do his friends know how to catch? Does he have opportunities to play catching games? What kind of instruction has he already had? Where? By whom? Has he had previous experiences that cause fear, anxiety, or doubt? Through question-and-answer interactions, teacher and student together cooperatively agree on the goal, verbalize it, and perhaps write it or sign a contract indicating intent to teach and learn.

Assessment is individualized to focus on strengths as well as weaknesses. What kinds of objects can the student catch? What movement variables must be addressed? The best way to find out is usually to ask the student and/or engage in cooperative problem solving. Together, teacher and student identify present level of performance, determine learning style, and work out details concerning pedagogy. This process should be activity oriented, fun, and free from anxiety. Encourage the student to discuss what task requirements he or she wants and/or needs. If Bob says, "Hey, I think I can catch that big yellow ball," then you may say, "Good, where do you want me to stand when I throw it?" Then a few tosses may be exchanged before other variables are brainstormed.

The level of task difficulty appropriate for Bob is established by experimenting with balls with varying object dimensions (size, weight, shape, color, texture, sound) and movement dimensions (speed, force, direction, pathway, height at moment of contact). Environmental and instructional variables also are considered. Environmental variables include (a) postures (sitting, standing, running), (b) use of glove/nature of glove, (c) lighting, (d) noise control and/or choice of verbal cues, (e) assistive devices to help with balance, and (f) floor or ground surface. Instructional variables that relate to task difficulty include amount of assistance needed, nature of assistance, length and wording of verbal instructions, and use of demonstrations. Thus, assessment focuses not only on what the student can do but also on environmental and instructional variables to be manipulated.

Prescription/Placement

Prescription/placement in the instructional setting refers to prescribing the objectives to be met and the activities needed for learning to occur. Specific behavioral objectives are cooperatively set by teacher and student, and amount of practice time and effort are agreed on. A behavioral objective is a specific statement that includes (a) condition, (b) observable behavior, and (c) criterion level. For example,

Condition: Given a ball of a certain size, weight, color, texture, and sound, thrown in a certain way from a set distance,

Observable behavior: Bob will perform a two-hand mature catch

Criterion level: in 7 out of 10 trials.

To achieve this objective, Bob may sign a contract in which he agrees to do 50 catches, with various balls under a variety of conditions, every class period for 6 weeks. Or he may agree to go to the catching station and practice a certain number of minutes three times a week. An important part of individualization is the student's understanding of both objective and process.

Teaching/Counseling/Coaching

Adaptation in teaching/counseling/coaching is synonymous with individualization. This is easy in a one-to-one practicum setting, but individualization does not necessarily mean teaching one-to-one. Learning to individualize in group settings is important since teachers are often responsible for 20 or more students.

For example, while working with Bob on catching, you could consider pedagogies that might be used in assisting 30 students to meet personalized objectives with regard to catching. One approach is creative utilization of gymnasium space so that many different stations, each offering a progressively more difficult level of challenge, are operative. Another is to encourage students to assume partial responsibility for their learning by using contracts, task cards, and videotape technology. Partner and small-group feedback permits students to help one another.

Movement education is an approach that permits many students to work simultaneously on the same skill but at their own level of difficulty. In movement education, the teacher asks questions that guide students in discovering the ways their bodies can move and how they can use movement elements (time, space, force, and flow) in new and different ways. For example, a movement education session on catching could involve every person having one or more balls and the teacher asking questions about the following:

Time (fast, slow concepts; rhythms). Can you throw your ball into the air somewhere in front of you and then very swiftly run and catch it? Can you do this same thing but change the toss so you can move very slowly and still catch it? Can you do this same thing except toss the ball against a wall and catch the rebound?

Space (concepts of level—high, low). How high can you throw your ball into the air and make a successful catch? Try some different-sized balls. What difference does this make? Find a partner and see how low you can toss the ball to him or her and still have a successful catch. How far away do you need to stand from each other? Can you toss a ball so it arrives at exactly waist height for your partner?

Force (concepts of hard, soft; heavy, light). What makes it hurt when you catch a hard ball? How can you change a toss so that it does not hurt? Can you toss and catch a ball with different body parts? How about just your wrist and fingers? Now how about a toss and catch that uses shoulders, elbows, wrists, and fingers? Which way results in a soft throw? a hard throw?

FIGURE 3.13

Barbara Wood of Homer, New York, challenges her first-graders to find how many ways they can toss objects in the air and catch them with a cup.

Flow (concepts of graceful vs. jerky; free vs. floor-bound). Can you follow through in the direction of your toss—let your whole body flow with the movement? Can you relax when you catch and pull the ball in toward you? Try jumping up as you catch a fly ball. Now try catching the same kind of ball but play like your feet are glued to the floor. What is the difference in the feeling?

In movement education, there is no right or wrong answer, so the teacher does not make corrections or give demonstrations. The secret is to generate questions that motivate each student to discover all he or she can about catching. Often, novel tasks, such as catching objects thrown into the air with a large cup are helpful (see Figure 3.13). Such a task promotes hand-eye coordination as well as creativity in thinking up items that can be tossed and caught. Movement exploration involves few discipline problems because there is no set formation and only two rules: (a) stay on task, and (b) respect other persons' space and objects.

Another approach to individualizing learning is to create games in which several students can participate fully while functioning with different levels of skill. An illustrative game for practicing catching skills is *Dodge or Catch*. This is a variation of dodgeball and can be played as either an individual or team game. The formation is free, with students allowed to move wherever they want except when a ball is in their hands, during which time one foot is "frozen" to the floor. The goal of the game, like in dodgeball, is to throw the ball and hit someone below the chest. In *Dodge or Catch,* however, the student can either dodge or reach out and catch the throw. There can be several balls of different sizes and shapes in motion, and point systems can be created. Numerous variations are possible.

Counseling goes hand in hand with teaching, a recognition that students with movement or fitness problems need someone to talk to. Counseling in adapted physical education uses the knowledge base of sport psychology. Students are helped with relaxing, focusing, imaging, and the like.

Coaching, properly planned and conducted, follows the same principles as teaching and counseling. Adaptation is the key to success as each athlete is helped to achieve a personal best. Coaches are sensitive to individual differences in participation incentives and other psychosocial parameters, as well as improvement in skill and fitness (Brasile & Hedrick, 1991; Jones, 1988; Stewart, 1991).

Evaluation

Evaluation is individualized by permitting students to help decide what criteria must be met for each letter grade. Various schemes can be agreed upon, with different percentages for effort, improvement, and achievement. Here, as in sport competition, the emphasis should be on achieving one's personal best (PB) rather than comparison with classmates and/or norms. Given a student like Bob, for example, what percentage of his grade should be based on effort, improvement, and achievement? What other criteria should be used in grading? Evaluation should also be directed toward teachers. What criteria should be established for you as the teacher?

Coordination of Resources and Advocacy

Coordination of resources and advocacy also are individualized in accordance with each student's needs. In regard to catching, for instance, the child may be referred to a vision specialist or optometrist. Parents may be encouraged to set up home training programs and to build innovative equipment. The teacher advocates both for the student and for high-quality physical education and recreation experiences.

Considerations in Adapting

The preceding section does not mention Bob's disability because such information often is not relevant to the adaptation process. Adapting should be based on assessment, with no preconceived ideas about what persons can or cannot do. A philosophy of adapting for individual differences and the evolution of successful service delivery practices should be based on principles or guidelines that apply across several areas. The following are ideas to consider.

Affordances and Constraints

Adaptation requires thinking about the strengths and weaknesses of persons in environmental or functional terms. To do this, you must strive to increase your awareness of variables that serve as constraints and affordances to performance and learning. *Constraints* are interactions between persons and environments that serve as limitations; constraints must be accepted or overcome. *Affordances* are interactions that facilitate goal achievement; affordances must be maximized. Each student must be afforded the combination of variables that best facilitates goal attainment. This is achieved through ecological task analysis.

Affordances and constraints are relatively new educational terms that help capture the idea of simultaneously working with human and environmental variables rather than stressing one or the other. Begin using these terms, and practice thinking about affordances and constraints.

Adapting in Different Domains

When a student is placed in a group setting, the adaptation process may need to be directed toward goals in the affective and cognitive domains instead of, or in addition to, the psychomotor domain. For example, to participate in games, a student must have cognitive skills, such as understanding game formations and such play concepts as chase, flee, safe, you're out. Adapting instruction to teach the mental operations for mastering rules and strategies is much harder than focusing exclusively on skills or fitness. Success in a gymnasium is often perceived as feeling good about oneself. This attribute is related to game performance and to social interactions with peers as well as to perceived efficacy in motor skills. Sometimes, the structure of a class needs to be temporarily changed or adapted to permit work toward goals of social competency and acceptance.

Cooperative, Reciprocal Process

Adapting, regardless of the setting and goals, is a cooperative, reciprocal process shared by teacher and student(s). When students have a role in assessing and planning, they are more likely to support and advance instructional activities. While collaborative decision making is more time consuming than authoritarian patterns, the potential outcomes are richer and lead more directly to self-actualizing individuals who care about each other and know how to work together.

Normalization

Adapting should also be related to the goal of *normalization*. This term, widely used in special education and rehabilitation, means to make available to differently abled individuals conditions as close as possible to that of the group norm (average). It does not mean to make a person normal or like everyone else. The changes involved in activity adaptation should be minimal so that games resemble those played by the able-bodied (AB) as much as possible. Wheelchair basketball, tennis, and handball are examples of adapted sports with minimal changes.

Normalization requires that adapting be a process applied to all students in the class, not just those with disabilities. Part of creating a warm, positive classroom climate is teaching students that adapting is fun, good, and beneficial to all. Thus, the teacher may involve students in the adapting process by challenging, "How can we change this game (or drill) so that everyone has fun?" or "Is there a way to adapt our gymnasium environment (e.g., lighting, temperature, smell, placement of objects) so that it is more pleasant and/or makes learning easier?" or "This is the way I usually give this test. Are there some ways we can adapt the testing procedures so everyone has a better chance at success?"

Use of Social Criteria

Adapting, in relation to normalization, also supports the use of social criteria when making decisions about appropriate conditions, apparatus, dress, games, sports, and toys. Care should be taken that students will not be teased or ridiculed because of adaptations. For example, a group of teenagers with severe retardation might enjoy *Ring Around the Rosy* because it is appropriate to their mental ages (2 to 7 years). If such persons, however, go home or to their sheltered work environments and say, "I had a good time at the club meeting last night when we played *Ring Around the Rosy*," this will likely cause smiles. Appropriate adaptation would be selection of a simple square or social dance activity.

Sport Classification Systems

Adaptation involves using functional classification systems to structure activity so that everyone has an equal opportunity to participate in sports and learn about cooperation and competition. Fairness in team sports depends on the balance of abilities among teams. There are many ways to achieve this balance. One way is to assign points to different ability levels and then require that the combination of players in the game at any given time must not surpass a set sum (e.g., 12 points). Wheelchair basketball is a game governed by this type of classification system. Rules require that every player be classified as a 1, 2, or 3, depending upon his or her functional abilities. Players on the floor cannot total more than 12 points. This system allows teams to use their members as they wish, with various combinations of classifications on the floor.

Another approach is to require that one player with low functional ability be in the game at all times. Regardless of approach, the key is to eliminate the practice of having persons sit on the bench or serve as scorekeepers and managers. Classes (as opposed to after-school sport structures) must afford all students an equal opportunity to participate. This demands adaptations. Students must be helped to understand that the purpose of team sports in the instructional setting is different from that in the recreational or competitive setting.

Principles of Adapting

In summary, several principles guide the process of adapting:

1. Adapting should be based on assessment of affordances and constraints and include examination of the person, the environment, and interactions between the two.
2. Adapting is achieved through *individualization*. This is manipulation of variables and the changing of task requirements and environmental conditions so that each person can succeed.
3. Adapting requires prioritizing goals and attending to needs in the cognitive and affective domains that affect success in physical activity.
4. Adapting, regardless of environmental setting and goals, is a cooperative, reciprocal process shared by teacher and student(s).
5. Adapting should advance the goal of normalization. This means that adapting is used to make available opportunities as close as possible to the group norm (average). For example, adapting should entail minimal change in the structure, rules, equipment, and strategies of sports for persons with disabilities so that the opportunities afforded are as similar as possible to those of regular sport.
6. Adapting should be based on social criteria so that individuals are treated with dignity and respect. Adapting should never result in ridicule or teasing.
7. Adapting should use functional sport classification systems to equalize abilities when activities involve competition.

Creativity Theory

Adaptation, individual differences, and creativity are the essential ingredients of adapted physical education. What is the meaning of creativity and the specific behaviors we must strive to develop in order to be creative? The following are two definitions:

Creativity—is "the ability to transcend traditional ideas, rules, patterns, relationships, or the like, and to create meaningful new ideas, forms, methods, interpretations, etc.; originality, progressiveness, or imagination." (Random House Dictionary, 1987, p. 473)

Creativity—is "a process of being sensitive to problems, deficiencies, gaps in knowledge, missing elements, disharmonies, and so on; identifying the difficulty; searching for solutions, making guesses, or formulating hypotheses about the deficiencies; testing and retesting them; and finally communicating the results." (Torrance, 1974, p. 8)

The definition of Paul Torrance, retired professor from the University of Georgia, was selected to supplement the dictionary explanation because Dr. Torrance is the acknowledged pioneer in the development and assessment of creativity in teachers and schoolchildren (Torrance, 1962, 1974, 1981). Torrance's definition encompasses both the affective and cognitive domains and is behavioral in its approach. Note that the dictionary defined creativity as an "ability," whereas Torrance defined it as a "process."

Creativity can be analyzed into specific, observable, measurable behaviors in each domain (cognitive, affective, and psychomotor). Table 3.2 presents cognitive and affective behaviors that are important in adapted physical education. The table's four cognitive creative behaviors have a well-established knowledge base (Guilford, 1952; Torrance, 1962; Williams, 1972). Less attention has been given to affective domain components (Williams, 1972). The five affective behaviors in Table 3.2 reflect the author's beliefs about the attitudinal-behavioral composites essential in working with individual differences.

As we shall see in the next sections, adapting, as an approach to service delivery, is largely dependent upon the behaviors of fluency, flexibility, originality, and elaboration (cognitive domain) and acceptance, imagination, curiosity, caring, and courage (affective domain). The body of knowledge being developed on creative behaviors is called *creativity theory*. Much research is needed in this area.

Table 3.2
Behaviors in the creative process.

Behavior	Meaning
Cognitive	
1. Fluent thinking: To think of the *most*	Generation of a quantity, flow of thought, number of relevant responses
2. Flexible thinking: To take *different* approaches	Variety of kinds of ideas, ability to shift categories, detours in direction of thought
3. Original thinking: To think in *novel* or unique ways	Unusual responses, clever ideas, production away from the obvious
4. Elaborate thinking: To *add on* to	Embellishing upon an idea, embroidering upon a simple idea or response to make it more elegant, stretching or expanding upon things or ideas
Affective	
1. Acceptance: To reach out and embrace	To feel a sense of identity and empathy with others, accept self and others in spite of weaknesses, generally feel good about life and human beings, perceive differences among people as inevitable and normal
2. Imagination: To have power to envision	To see each human being as unique, different from all others; visualize what this person can become, dream about things that have never happened; feel intuitively that this person can grow, develop, and succeed; have a mind that reaches beyond barriers and boundaries
3. Curiosity: To have a problem-solving mind	To be inquisitive and wonder, toy with ideas, open to alternatives; seek new and different ways; ponder the mystery of things
4. Caring: To be driven to action	To become involved; find the inner resources to endure and persist until solutions are found; have faith in ability to bring order out of chaos, find missing pieces, derive solutions
5. Courage: To be willing to take risks	To devise and try new strategies; expose oneself to failure and criticism; support and defend persons, ideas, or things that are different or unpopular

Cognitive Creative Behaviors

Cognitive creative behaviors are *f*luency, *f*lexibility, *o*riginality, and *e*laboration (FFOE). These four behaviors act as a "foe" to boredom and burnout and are important for professionals to develop.

The illustrations of fluency, flexibility, originality, and elaboration that you are about to read may seem far-out, by adult standards, but they work with children—not just those with problems, but all children. Most students need many more repetitions to learn skills than their interest and concentration can sustain. Part of adapting is trying enough different ways, with abundant enthusiasm, to maintain student interest.

Fluency

Fluency is the generation of a large number of relevant, workable ideas and was illustrated in the earlier discussion on adaptation and teaching Bob to catch. A large number of variables was generated in specified categories: (a) student, (b) object or equipment, (c) movement, (d) physical environment, (e) psychosocial, and (f) task, activity, and event dimensions. Consider each of these categories and others relevant to service delivery. Can you add to the list of variables? The larger the number of relevant variables, the more fluent the teacher. Fluency is also seen in the number of different games, drills, and movement education challenges that you can devise for practicing a particular skill, and in the many different ways you can word a question, give instructions, and explain a problem. The more synonyms known, the more fluent you are. Persons who know sign language are more fluent than those who rely entirely on verbal communication. The essence of fluency is *find another way*.

Flexibility

Flexibility is making change with ease, especially about different categories and kinds of ideas. It is adaptability to changing situations and stimuli, freedom from inertia or blockage of thought, and spontaneous shifting of mind-set. Flexibility in teaching Bob was illustrated by the ability to shift categories during assessment and brainstorming processes. In getting acquainted with Bob, the teacher can switch from the category of interests (does Bob want to learn to catch?) to relevance (do Bob's friends play catch?) to sport socialization (what kind of lessons has Bob already had in catching?). The teacher also shifts easily among the following categories of variables in discovering the kinds of balls Bob could catch: (a) size, (b) weight, (c) color, (d) direction, (e) path, (f) postures, and (g) lighting.

Flexible persons do not usually list all possibilities in one category and then move in orderly fashion to another category; instead, they move back and forth among categories with ease. This helps them to plan and teach in a holistic manner (i.e., see the whole, synthesize parts from many categories, combine them to make a new whole).

Originality

Originality pertains to unusual, new, and clever ideas, such as different kinds of balls and gloves during the individualized skill assessment or goal/objective-setting phase. The teacher wants to motivate the student and/or maintain his or her interest. The balls and gloves might have velcro strips on them to make catching easier, or they might have bells embedded in them and painted faces to enhance interest and motivation. Balls might smell and taste good, like an orange or marshmallow, and be offered as a reward for effort and/or success.

Unique starting and stopping signals, lighting conditions, and background music also can enhance interest. Putting game elements together in new and different ways to create adapted sports and new recreational play activities is also originality. Consider, for instance, how an egg-tossing game might be devised to reinforce and motivate catching skills. Originality might playfully be thought of as the crazy things a teacher does to keep from going crazy when skill mastery requires lots of repetition.

Elaboration

Elaboration refers to the richness of interesting details or extras supplied. Think about the last lecture you attended. Did the speaker just state facts, or did he or she supplement points with anecdotes, illustrations, examples, poems, or problem-solving exercises? During catching practice, for example, elaboration might be evidenced by the use of imagery and metaphors: "Run to meet the ball . . . play like it's a bolt of lightning . . . if you don't stop it, the forest will catch on fire;" "Reach out for the ball . . . think of it as a puppy or child falling out of a window . . . don't wait for it to come to you . . . go after it, gently, gently, now draw it in toward your chest."

The idea of catching might be embellished by coordinating skill practice with a story, music, drama, costumes, or puppets (see Figure 3.14). After each successful catch, various reinforcers might make the experience more elegant. Catching practice with a wind machine or electric fan on at one station and flickering lights at another station are embellishments, particularly when interwoven with a story.

Affective Creative Behaviors

The five affective domain creative behaviors are acceptance, imagination, curiosity, caring, and courage (see Table 3.2). These behaviors stem from feelings and emotions, rather than ideas and thoughts, and highlight sensitivity to human needs and situational problems. Sensitivity varies among individuals, but good self-concept and confidence in your abilities are related to creative behaviors. Teachers have to believe in themselves and expect success.

Acceptance

Acceptance is favorable reception. Teacher acceptance can be defined as behaviors showing that a student is perceived and treated as capable, worthy, agreeable, and welcome. Acceptance is often measured in terms of approach and avoid-

FIGURE 3.14

A child who is fearful or doesn't want to play needs a teacher with creative behaviors. Here, the puppet says, "Please let me play with you . . . I want to roll you a pretty ball."

ance behaviors. Certainly, you must approach, and be relatively close to, a student to assess his or her abilities and plan how to adapt instruction. You can be close to a student in many ways: (a) physically (hug, touch), (b) visually (smile, eye contact), (c) auditorially (warm, pleasant voice), and (d) mentally (an affinity for each other's ideas, thoughts, beliefs; a similar learning or problem-solving style, and so on). List the things that teachers say and do that help you to feel capable, worthy, agreeable, and welcome and prioritize them in terms of importance. How does your ranking of items compare with those of classmates? The specific behaviors of acceptance probably have different meanings for different individuals.

The state of acceptance between two persons provides the environmental readiness for other creative behaviors. Some teachers, however, find it easy to accept persons (and things) that are different in appearance, sound, smell, and touch, whereas others find it hard. Which are you? This pertains partly to flexibility, the ability to shift back and forth between categories of similarity and dissimilarity in people, foods, cars, beds, and the like. Some persons prefer sameness, whereas others like to liven up their existence with new and different things, people, and experiences. Which are you?

Acceptance is also closely related to empathy, an innate quality that varies from person to person and is not well understood. *Empathy* is identification with or vicarious experiencing of the feelings, thoughts, and attitudes of another. Empathy is often explained as the ability to walk in another's shoes, to see and feel the world as another does. Thus, it encompasses both sensitivity and responsivity. "Awareness Days" to enhance understanding of individual differences often include challenges to able-bodied (AB) persons to spend a day in a wheelchair or to play a game while blindfolded or wearing earplugs. Such simulated activities promote empathy and, thus, acceptance.

Imagination

Imagination is the power to envision things and people as different from what they are. Within the adapted physical activity context, imagination is the ability to visualize all that a person can become. Although imagination can dwell on the negative, the emphasis in teaching is on positive thinking. Are you an optimist or a pessimist?

Consider the effect of teacher expectations. If a teacher imagines that a student can do something, does this make it easier? What behaviors convey that the teacher imagines the student to be a leader, an athlete, or a scholar in the future? For instruction to be adapted, the process must be imagined. You must intuitively feel good about the capacity of students to change and have a clear view of the direction to lead.

Curiosity

Curious behaviors are inquisitive and searching. Some persons seem to be fascinated by the unknown; they spend a lot of time analyzing how and why things work. Others can solve problems, if challenged to do so, but typically are not curious enough to ask questions. Which are you? Some persons are interested in how the human mind works and spend a lot of time thinking about behaviors. Others are more fascinated by machines or laboratory apparatus. Which is more like you? Within the adapted physical activity context, curiosity is spontaneous involvement in problem-solving behaviors in order to answer self-generated questions.

Caring

Caring has many definitions, each of which connotes the ability to feel deeply and intensely. For our purposes, *caring* is operationally defined as having feelings and beliefs so strong that you get involved in positive action directed toward making things better for an individual or group. As used in this model of creative behaviors, caring is a complex emotion. It is intertwined with faith in your ability to create, in the probability that people and things will change in the desired direction, and in the meaning of life. Caring also is linked with the inner resources to endure and persist until solutions are found (i.e., caring enough usually evokes the stamina to keep going).

Courage

Courage is the quality that enables you to try something new, to delve into the unknown, and to expose self to failure or criticisms. Because the essence of creativity is finding new, different, and original ways to assure success for people with

problems, the probability is high that at least several of the attempts will fail or receive criticism. Courage enables you to work alone, if need be, in the generation of new ideas and solutions.

Courage is needed also in adapted physical activity specialists who act as advocates for persons with disabilities and who fight for removal of attitudinal, aspirational, and architectural barriers (see Figure 3.15). Proposals to change the environment, even when changes clearly benefit the lives of persons with disabilities, are often met with criticism because of the expense and inconvenience involved. To create and adapt, you must be able to withstand pressures from those who prefer traditional ways. Likewise, to become a close friend of someone different in appearance and abilities requires the courage to withstand peer pressures and the advice of significant others. To create is to dare to take risks.

Indicators of Effective Teaching

Five indicators of effective teaching have been identified by research (Jewett & Bain, 1985; Siedentop, 1983):

1. Development of a warm, positive climate
2. Appropriate matching of content to student abilities (i.e., adapting and ensuring success-oriented learning)

3. High percentage of time devoted to lesson objectives
4. High rates of on-task behaviors
5. Use of strategies that contribute to on-task behaviors but do not violate presence of a warm, positive climate

The creative behaviors described in the preceding section are basic to effective teaching. Assess yourself on which creative behaviors you would most likely exhibit in relation to each indicator.

Human Variables and Change

Effective teaching is largely dependent upon an understanding of human variables and change processes. The term *variable* refers to anything that can be changed. Variables differ, however, in the ease with which they can be changed.

Words used to describe human variables that are considered enduring or stable are *trait, ability, belief, attitude, emotion,* and *habits.* Variables that can be changed more easily are called *state* or *mood, skill, knowledge, opinion, feeling,* and *practices.* These terms can be conceptualized as pairs of bipolar opposites (i.e., they are on opposite poles of a continuum varying in stability).

Careful definition of these terms enhances effective goal setting. A *trait* is a distinguishing characteristic, feature, or quality, whereas a *state* or *mood* is a temporary condition that varies with circumstances. *Ability* is a stable characteristic, genetically defined and unmodifiable by practice or experience, whereas *skill* is a movement or competence dependent upon practice and experience (Schmidt, 1988). *Knowledge* is facts, scope of information, or cognition and, like skill, is dependent upon practice and experience. *Belief* is certainty or a conviction held with complete confidence, whereas *opinion* is a judgment held as true but without absolute conviction. *Attitude* is a position or bearing indicating action, feeling, or mood. *Emotion* and *feeling* refer to affective states or dispositions, with emotion denoting the more intense state. *Habit* is an acquired behavior pattern regularly followed until it becomes a way of life, whereas a *practice* is a way of doing something (e.g., your teaching practices).

Adapted physical activity can be directed toward changing any variable. In writing goals and objectives and determining the amount of time needed to cause change, however, it is helpful to know whether a variable is defined as fluctuating or stable.

Teachers, like many other persons who work to create change, find the following prayer useful:

God, grant me the *serenity* to accept the things I cannot change, the *courage* to change the things I can, and the *wisdom* to know the difference.

—Reinhold Niebuhr

References

American Therapeutic Recreation Association. (1984). *Newsletter, 1,* 2.

Ayres, A. J. (1972). *Sensory integration and learning disorders.* Los Angeles: Western Psychological Services.

Berridge, M., & Ward, G. (Eds.). (1987). *International perspectives on adapted physical activity.* Champaign, IL: Human Kinetics.

Blumenkopf, M., Levangie, P., & Nelson, D. (1985). Perceived role responsibilities of physical therapists and adapted physical educators in the public school setting. *Physical Therapy, 65* (7), 1046–1051.

Brasile, F. M. (1990). Wheelchair sports: A new perspective on integration. *Adapted Physical Activity Quarterly, 7* (1), 3–11.

Brasile, F. M., & Hedrick, B. N. (1991). A comparison of participation incentives between adult and youth wheelchair basketball players. *Palaestra, 7* (4), 40–46.

Broadhead, G. (1985). Placement of mildly handicapped children in mainstream physical education. *Adapted Physical Activity Quarterly, 2,* 307–313.

Butterfield, S. A. (1991). Physical education and sport for the deaf: Rethinking the least restrictive environment. *Adapted Physical Activity Quarterly, 8* (2), 95–102.

Cratty, B. J. (1989). *Adapted physical education in the mainstream* (2nd ed.). Denver: Love.

Davis, W. E., & Burton, A. W. (1991). Ecological task analysis: Translating movement behavior theory into practice. *Adapted Physical Activity Quarterly, 8* (2), 154–177.

Doll-Tepper, G., Dahms, C., Doll, B., & Selzam, H. von (Eds.). (1990). *Adapted physical activity.* Berlin: Springer-Verlag.

Dybwad, G. (1980). Avoiding misconceptions of mainstreaming, the least restrictive environment, and normalization. *Exceptional Children, 47* (2), 85–88.

Eason, R., Smith, T., & Caron, F. (Eds.). (1983). *Adapted physical activity: From theory to application.* Champaign, IL: Human Kinetics.

Eidson, T. A., & Stadulis, R. E. (1991). Effects of variability of practice on the transfer and performance of open and closed motor skills. *Adapted Physical Activity Quarterly, 8,* 342–356.

Groves, L. (Ed.). (1979). *Physical education for special needs.* London: Cambridge University Press.

Guilford J. (1952). *A factor analytic study of creative thinking.* Report from the psychological laboratory, No. 8, University of Southern California.

Heikinaro-Johansson, P., & Telama, R. (1990). Downstream or upstream with mainstreaming? Handicapped students at Finnish schools. In G. Doll-Tepper, C. Dahms, B. Doll, & H. von Selzam (Eds.), *Adapted physical activity* (pp. 159–165). Berlin: Springer-Verlag.

Hopkins, H., & Smith, H. (1988). *Willard and Spackman's occupational therapy* (7th ed.). Philadelphia: J.B. Lippincott.

Hutzler, Y. (1990). The concept of empowerment in rehabilitative sports. In G. Doll-Tepper, C. Dahms, B. Doll, & H. von Selzam (Eds.), *Adapted physical activity* (pp. 43–51). Berlin: Springer-Verlag.

Jenkins, J., & Heinen, A. (1989). Students' preferences for service delivery: Pull-out, in-class, or integrated models. *Exceptional Children, 55,* 516–523.

Jewett, A., & Bain, L. (1985). *The curriculum process in physical education.* Dubuque, IA: Wm. C. Brown.

Jochheim, K. A. (1990). Adapted physical activity—An interdisciplinary approach, premises, methods, and procedures. In G. Doll-Tepper, C. Dahms, B. Doll, & H. von Selzam (Eds.), *Adapted physical activity* (pp. 15–22). Berlin: Springer-Verlag.

Jones, J. A. (Ed.). (1988). Training guide to cerebral palsy sports (3rd ed.). Champaign, IL: Human Kinetics.

Kiphard, E. (1983). Adapted physical education in Germany. In R. Eason, T. Smith, & F. Caron (Eds.), *Adapted physical activity: From theory to application.* Champaign, IL: Human Kinetics.

Lavay, B., & DePaepe, J. (1987). The harbinger helper: Why mainstreaming doesn't always work. *Journal of Physical Education, Recreation, and Dance, 58* (7), 98–103.

Lavay, B., Foret, C., Dempsey, S., & Loovis, M. (1987). Issues: Is mainstreaming in physical education, recreation, and dance working? *Journal of Physical Education, Recreation, and Dance, 8* (58), 14–15.

Loovis, E. M. (1986). Placement of handicapped students: The perpetual dilemma. *Adapted Physical Activity Quarterly, 3,* 193–198.

Morris, G. S. D. (1980). *Elementary physical education: Toward inclusion.* Salt Lake City, UT: Brighton.

O'Morrow, G., & Reynolds, R. (1989). *Therapeutic recreation: A helping profession* (3rd ed.). Englewood Cliffs, NJ: Prentice-Hall.

National Therapeutic Recreation Society. (1982). *Philosophical position statement.* Alexandria, VA: Author.

Paciorek, M. J., & Jones, J. A. (1989). *Sports and recreation for the disabled: A resource manual.* Indianapolis: Benchmark Press.

Purvis, J. (1985). A new description of corrective therapy. *American Corrective Therapy Journal, 39* (1), 4–5.

Rizzo, T. L., & Davis, W. E. (1991). From the back of the physical education bus: The functional exclusion of adapted physical education. *Journal of Physical Education, Recreation, and Dance, 62* (6), 53–55.

Roswal, P., Sherrill, C., & Roswal, G. (1988). A comparison of data-based and creative dance pedagogies in teaching mentally retarded youth. *Adapted Physical Activity Quarterly, 5,* 212–222.

Schmidt, R. (1988). *Motor control and learning.* Champaign, IL: Human Kinetics.

Sherrill, C. (Ed.). (1979). *Creative arts for the severely handicapped.* Springfield, IL: Charles C. Thomas.

Sherrill, C. (Ed.). (1986). *Sport and disabled athletes.* Champaign, IL: Human Kinetics.

Sherrill, C. (Ed.). (1988). *Leadership training in adapted physical education.* Champaign, IL: Human Kinetics.

Siedentop, D. (1983). *Developing teaching skills in physical education.* Palo Alto: Mayfield.

Stewart, D. A. (1991). *Deaf sport: The impact of sports within the deaf community.* Washington, DC: Gallaudet University Press.

Torrance, E. P. (1962). *Guiding creative talent.* Englewood Cliffs, NJ: Prentice-Hall.

Torrance, E. P. (1974). *Torrance tests of creative thinking.* Bensenville, IL: Scholastic Test Service.

Torrance, E. P. (1981). *Thinking creatively in action and movement.* Bensenville, IL: Scholastic Test Service.

Tymeson, G. (1988). In-service teacher education: A review of general practices and suggested guidelines for adapted physical education teacher trainers. In C. Sherrill (Ed.), *Leadership training in adapted physical education* (pp. 401–410). Champaign, IL: Human Kinetics.

Vermeer, A. (Ed.). (1987). *Sports for the disabled: Proceedings of International Congress on Recreation, Sports, and Leisure.* Haarlem, Netherlands: Uiteverj de Vrieseborch.

Weber, R. C., & Thorpe, J. (1989). Comparison of task variation and constant task methods for severely disabled in physical education. *Adapted Physical Activity Quarterly, 6,* 338–353.

Williams, F. (1972). *Total creativity program.* Englewood Cliffs, NJ: Educational Technology Publications.

CHAPTER

4

Advocacy, the Law, and the IEP

FIGURE 4.1

Advocacy requires knowledge of laws that mandate rights. (DD = Developmental Disabilities; PE-R = Physical Education and Recreation; MR = Mental Retardation; MR–MH = Mental Retardation–Mental Health.)

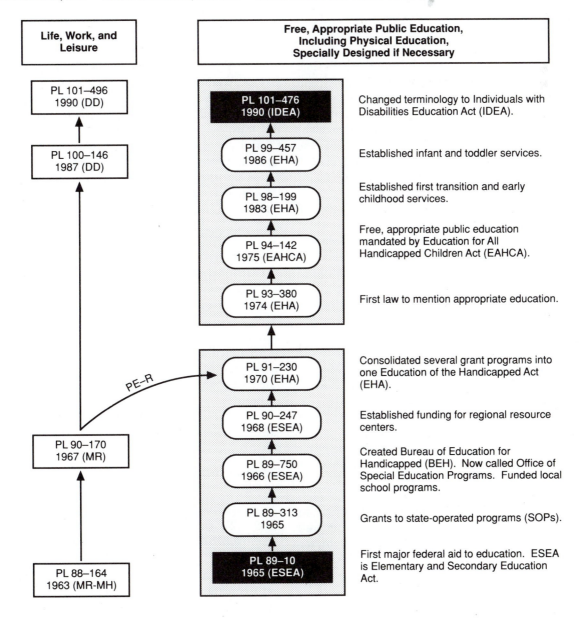

Life, Work, and Leisure

Free, Appropriate Public Education, Including Physical Education, Specially Designed if Necessary

PL 101–496
1990 (DD)

PL 100–146
1987 (DD)

PL 90–170
1967 (MR)

PL 88–164
1963 (MR-MH)

PL 101–476
1990 (IDEA) — Changed terminology to Individuals with Disabilities Education Act (IDEA).

PL 99–457
1986 (EHA) — Established infant and toddler services.

PL 98–199
1983 (EHA) — Established first transition and early childhood services.

PL 94–142
1975 (EAHCA) — Free, appropriate public education mandated by Education for All Handicapped Children Act (EAHCA).

PL 93–380
1974 (EHA) — First law to mention appropriate education.

PE–R

PL 91–230
1970 (EHA) — Consolidated several grant programs into one Education of the Handicapped Act (EHA).

PL 90–247
1968 (ESEA) — Established funding for regional resource centers.

PL 89–750
1966 (ESEA) — Created Bureau of Education for Handicapped (BEH). Now called Office of Special Education Programs. Funded local school programs.

PL 89–313
1965 — Grants to state-operated programs (SOPs).

PL 89–10
1965 (ESEA) — First major federal aid to education. ESEA is Elementary and Secondary Education Act.

After you have studied this chapter, you should be able to:

1. Define advocacy, identify causes, and discuss five advocacy behaviors. Summarize your experiences in advocacy and make a personal plan for growth in this area.

2. Find out about the physical education requirement in your state and contrast it with recommendations by organizations and authorities. Suggest improvements.

3. Discuss how various minority groups have striven for equal opportunity and consider the role of adapted physical education in this struggle.

4. Discuss landmark laws of the 1970s and describe how each influenced change.

5. Summarize basic concepts underlying legislative advocacy and describe resources. Know where to find resources, both written and human.

6. Explain current RA, ADA, DDA, and IDEA legislation. Give examples of how each of these is changing lives.

7. Discuss the legislative basis of practices in adapted physical education.

8. Differentiate between the IEP and the IEP process. Identify and explain the parts of each. Create an original story or play to illustrate them.

9. Discuss different kinds of placement and the legislative basis of each.

10. Discuss the state plan in relation to IDEA and funding of adapted physical education. State strategies for improving local education agency (LEA) delivery of services.

Much of the adapted physical activity professional's time and energy is spent in advocacy for individual dignity and equality. *Advocacy* is action aimed at promoting, maintaining, or defending a cause. Adapted physical activity specialists typically are advocates for two causes: (a) the right to high-quality physical education instruction and (b) the elimination of attitudinal, aspirational, and architectural barriers that limit opportunity, especially in regard to sport, dance, aquatics, fitness, and leisure.

Figure 4.1 summarizes some of the laws discussed in this chapter. Effective advocates know laws and use them to assure equal opportunity. History shows that children and youth with disabilities do not receive good physical education unless someone fights for them. Likewise, adults with disabilities need advocates for their right to independence, productivity, and integration into community life, work, and leisure.

The knowledge base underlying advocacy is fraught with numbers and abbreviations. Because numbers of laws change approximately every 3 years, it is better to focus on abbreviations: MR-MH (Mental Retardation-Mental Health), DDA (Developmental Disabilities Act), and ESEA, EHA, EAHCA, and IDEA (each explained in Figure 4.1). Not shown but also important are RA (Rehabilitation Act) and ADA (Americans with Disabilities Act).

Law forms the basis for good service delivery. Everything done in adapted physical education has its roots in law. Planning, assessment, and placement are particularly affected by law, and these are emphasized in this chapter. Implementation depends on money, and this chapter aims to increase awareness of how taxes, grants, and fund-raising are linked to desirable school practices. When money is tight, for example, school districts reduce services. Advocacy skills are needed to assure compliance with law in relation to physical education and to help with fund-raising.

Education is primarily the responsibility of local and state governments and rests on their ability to generate money. Laws and policies thus vary widely. Only a small percentage of school funding comes from the federal government, and this must be justified as necessary for the general welfare (health and education) of a particular group, such as the economically disadvantaged or the disabled. Both special education and adapted physical education are funded mainly by local money, and services are influenced by attitudes and aspirations.

The Physical Education Requirement

Adapted physical educators are advocates for both regular and adapted physical education. Advocacy begins with learning about the state physical education requirement and examining its implementation in local schools. Principals who value physical education in the regular program and who champion services needed by students with disabilities should be identified and used as models. Persons not aware of the importance of adapted physical education need to be provided with guidelines from professional organizations and authorities.

The American Alliance for Health, Physical Education, Recreation, and Dance (AAHPERD) recommends the following minimum instructional requirements:

Elementary schoolchildren should have a daily *physical education program of 30 minutes a day, five times a week—or a total of 150 minutes a week. The size of the class should be consistent with that of other classes in the school.*

Secondary school students should have daily *physical education programs which are equal in length and class size to other classes. (AAHPERD, 1980, v-3)*

The Canadian Association for Health, Physical Education, and Recreation (CAHPER) and the International Council for Health, Physical Education, and Recreation (ICHPER) also endorse the policies of daily physical education instruction and 150 to 300 minutes per week of physical education activities. Increasingly, physical educators are learning to be advocates for these recommendations and for better methods of enforcing state laws at the local level.

State laws should be equally applicable to everyone, regardless of disability. Many persons, however, are still being denied equal opportunity. A federal law called the Individuals with Disabilities Education Act (IDEA) mandates that physical education services, specially designed if necessary, be made available to students with disabilities. This law was called the Education of the Handicapped Act (EHA) until 1990; its best-known amendment was PL 94–142 or EHA-Part B.

IDEA also mandates that students participate in regular physical education unless a legal procedure called the individualized education program (IEP) process judges them too disabled to benefit from such placement. This means that most students with disabilities are placed in regular physical education classes. The quality of regular physical education is thus a concern of adapted physical activity advocates.

Regular programs must be monitored to ascertain that students with fitness and coordination problems are not sitting on benches or serving as assistants. Many students not eligible for special education services can benefit from this advocacy also.

Advocacy Behaviors—The Five Ls

Advocacy can be broken down into several tasks or behaviors known as the five Ls: (a) look at me, (b) leverage, (c) literature, (d) legislation, and (e) litigation.

Look at Me—Individual Action

First and foremost, advocacy involves setting a good example, modeling a positive attitude toward both physical activity and persons with disabilities. Each time adapted physical activity professionals are seen in a friendship relationship with persons who are disabled, this is advocacy. Each time professionals support a candidate running for public office and become actively involved in promoting education and human rights as campaign issues, they are demonstrating advocacy.

Leverage—Group Action

Leverage refers to group action as a means of gaining advantage in the fight for human rights. Whereas one individual can make a small difference, a professional organization can create pressures that make elected officials vote in desired ways. Adapted physical activity professionals therefore belong to organizations like AAHPERD and the Council for Exceptional Children (CEC) and expect part of their membership dues to be applied toward advocacy activities. They are also active in organizations run jointly by parents and professionals, such as the Parent Teachers Association (PTA), ARC, formerly the Association for Retarded Citizens, and the Learning Disability Association of America (LDA). Only by joining together with persons who have similar concerns can sufficient leverage be created to make a difference.

Leverage also can be wielded by supporting or boycotting businesses and industries. For example, buying products from stores that employ persons with disabilities is an advocacy activity. Knowing the companies that financially support sport organizations for athletes with disabilities guides advocates in their choice of what brands to buy.

Literature

Literature refers to assertiveness in writing advocacy articles for newspapers and journals, in conducting research, and in using the written word to promote, maintain, or defend a cause. Letters to the editor of a newspaper and to elected officials are particularly powerful forms of advocacy. Chain letters can be initiated to further a cause. Research concerning the efficacy of physical education and recreation programs and/or attitudes toward persons who are different can lead to the publication of findings that advance specific advocacy goals.

Legislation

Legislation is the preparation and enactment of laws at the local, state, and national levels. Advocates must know the laws at each level of government that affect education and human rights and must monitor school and agency administrators to be sure that these laws are enforced. Advocacy also involves acquainting others (especially parents) with laws and encouraging them to become involved in the legislative process.

Legislation is closely related to finance because laws cannot be implemented without money. Sometimes, laws contain passages about the amount of money needed to make them viable. IDEA, for example, specifies the amount of money that should be made available to implement each of its sections. Raising the money, however, is achieved through enactment of laws that pertain to taxation and other sources of revenue (e.g., state lotteries, parking meters, highway toll fees, and special service charges). Most state and local government money comes from taxes; therefore, most advocates for high-quality education are also advocates for tax laws.

Advocates must be involved in the politics of taxing and spending. Although raising taxes is unpopular, the money to run schools and social services is largely dependent upon such government revenue. Legislation thus not only encompasses the making of laws about education and human rights but also the enactment of laws that generate money. Advocates need to be assertive in deciding how federal (as well as state and local) money is spent, must monitor appropriations carefully, and must ascertain that education (especially physical education) gets its fair share.

Litigation

Litigation is the use of the judicial process (i.e., due process hearings, lawsuits, court action) to force compliance with laws and/or the government's Constitution. Advocates encourage parents and persons with disabilities to use due process procedures when rights are violated. These procedures, which are described in IDEA and other laws, include a hierarchy of activities that begin with an impartial due process hearing and end with court action in response to a lawsuit filed by an attorney.

Usually, problems are resolved in the early stages of formal negotiation, and lawsuits are not necessary. Sometimes, however, governmental agencies, schools, and business and industry do not obey laws unless forced to do so. Two classic lawsuits show the impact of litigation under such circumstances. The principle of school integration is derived from the 1954 case of *Brown v. Board of Education of Topeka, Kansas*. In this litigation, the U.S. Supreme Court ruled that the doctrine "separate but equal" in the field of public education was unconstitutional and deprived the segregated group (Blacks) of rights guaranteed by the 14th Amendment.

The principle of *zero reject,* or free appropriate public education for all children, has its roots in the 1972 class action suit of *Pennsylvania Association for Retarded Citizens (PARC) v. Commonwealth of Pennsylvania*. The court ruling that no child can be excluded from public school programs led directly to enactment of PL 94–142 in 1975. This case continues to serve as the basis for challenging the constitutionality of excluding children with severe disabilities from public school programs.

For further discussion of litigation, consult the writings of Weintraub, Abeson, Ballard, and LaVor (1976) and Turnbull (1990), or contact your professional organization. Many state education agencies can provide lists of special advocacy groups that keep abreast of litigation. Another source is the National Information Center for Children and Youth with Disabilities, P.O. Box 1492, Washington, DC 20013.

Advocacy, A Way of Life

Advocacy is a way of life. It governs the way we teach, influences the friends we select, and affects the products we buy. To be a good advocate, we must believe in ourselves, in the democratic process, and in the power of individuals to create change. We must *care* enough to learn about legislation and litigation and to use these processes to improve quality of life.

The five Ls also are important in the human rights movement. Concern for life, liberty, and the pursuit of happiness extends beyond people with disabilities to other minority groups who share similar problems of inequality. To be an effective advocate, it is helpful to have a sense of history and to understand how events relate to one another. There is a definite trend toward minority groups working together at the grass roots level.

The Human Rights Movement

History shows that equality of opportunity does not come easily. The Civil War (1860s) was fought to achieve the right of all males, regardless of race or color, to vote. Approximately 50 years later, in 1920, women won the right to vote. Persons of color, women, individuals with disabilities, and other minorities are all related in the sense that their rights are often violated. One way or another, they are denied cit-

izenship privileges, including equal opportunities for education and physical activity. Why does this happen? What can you, as a professional, do?

Advocacy for equal and/or appropriate physical education is but one link in the chain of events whereby minority groups have fought discrimination. From 1950 to 1980, several groups sequentially achieved access to equal education. Figure 4.2 shows the relationship between the U.S. Constitution and early laws.

Blacks

The human rights movement intensified after World War II, with the battle against school segregation culminating in the already mentioned 1954 federal Supreme Court case *Brown v. Board of Education of Topeka, Kansas*. This litigation resulted in the ruling that the doctrine of "separate but equal" schooling for Black students was unconstitutional in that it violated the 14th Amendment. According to the 14th Amendment:

No state shall make or enforce any law which shall abridge the privileges or immunities of citizens of the United States, nor shall any State deprive any person of life, liberty, or property, without due process of law; nor deny to any person within its jurisdiction the equal protection of the laws.

In spite of the Supreme Court's ruling that segregated education was unconstitutional, most local school districts did not change their policies and practices. Thus, the 1960s brought the demonstrations, boycotts, and violence now known as the civil rights movement. President John F. Kennedy urged the enactment of federal legislation to end the widespread discontent, and shortly after his assassination, the Civil Rights Act of 1964 (PL 88–352) was passed by the 88th Congress.

Women

In the 1960s, the groundwork was also laid for legislation to prevent sex discrimination in education. These efforts resulted in Title IX of the Educational Amendments Act of 1972 (PL 92–318). Thus, the doctrine of separate but equal found unconstitutional for Blacks in 1964 was also declared illegal for women. The 14th Amendment was cited as the basis for making school physical education programs coeducational and for upgrading girls' and women's athletic programs.

Persons With Disabilities

The 1960s were also a time of beginning awareness of mental retardation (MR). President John F. Kennedy was particularly interested in MR because his oldest sister (Rose) had this condition. In 1961, he created the first President's Panel on Mental Retardation. Most persons with MR were served by residential facilities in the 1960s, and this panel worked to upgrade conditions and increase awareness of alternative living arrangements. Acting on the panel's recommendations, President Kennedy encouraged enactment in 1963 of the first major MR legislation, the Mental Retardation Facilities and Community Mental Health Centers Construction Act.

FIGURE 4.2

The human rights movement is rooted in the Constitution and based on two concepts: (*A*) federal aid is a necessary intervention, and (*B*) separate but equal is not constitutional. (MR–MH = Mental Retardation–Mental Health; ESEA = Elementary and Secondary Education Act.)

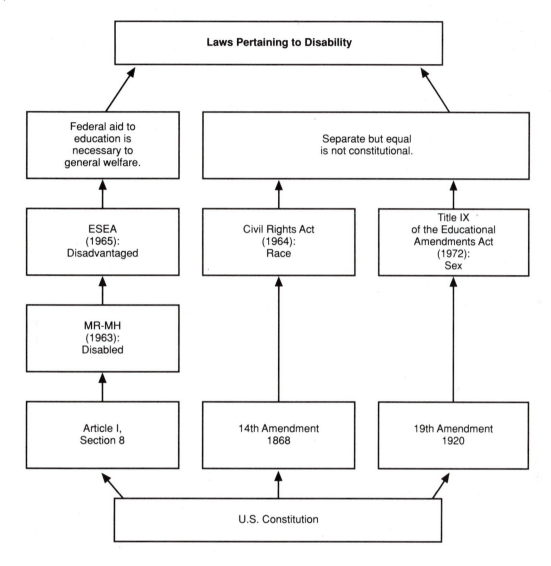

Amendments to this law in 1967 initiated the advocacy movement for physical education and recreation (PE-R) for persons with disabilities. Specifically, the Mental Retardation Amendments of 1967 (PL 90–170) provided funds for university training programs to teach physical educators and recreators how to work with individuals with MR. In 1970, funding of PE-R training was switched to EHA (see Figure 4.1), and authorization of grants for graduate programs and research in PE-R continues today under IDEA. The legislation introduced by Kennedy was periodically reauthorized and is now known as the Developmental Disabilities Act (DDA). Figure 4.1 shows that two tracks were established early, one to improve living conditions and one to improve education.

Through the example set by the Kennedy family, professionals began to take an active interest in MR. Many physical educators became involved in Special Olympics, the sport movement for persons with MR, founded in 1968 by Eunice Kennedy Shriver, a sister of President Kennedy. Senator Edward Kennedy of Massachusetts has led the battle in Congress for legislation to protect the rights of persons with disabilities and to improve education (see Figure 4.3).

The Disadvantaged or Poor

The 1960s also brought concern about disparities in education provided by rich and poor school districts. Local and state governments either could not or would not do anything about the welfare of many disadvantaged students. Therefore, the federal government began to intervene, using legislation as a means of enhancing the education and health of disadvantaged and/or minority group children. The Democratic party spearheaded this movement, citing Article 1, Section 8, of the U.S. Constitution as its basis for action. This article, still

FIGURE 4.3

Eunice Kennedy Shriver and Edward Kennedy in the 1960s were among the first advocates for physical education and recreation for people with disabilities.

used as the constitutional basis for federal intervention in education, is often called the General Welfare Clause. Abbreviated, Section 8 states:

The Congress shall have the power To . . . provide for the common Defense and general Welfare of the United States . . . To make all laws which shall be necessary and proper for carrying into Execution the foregoing Powers. . . .

The first federal law to provide substantial aid to education was the Elementary and Secondary Education Act (ESEA) of 1965. This legislation provided funds for *compensatory education* for disadvantaged students. It also made available money for innovative and/or exemplary local school district physical education programs like Project ACTIVE and Project PEOPEL (Sherrill & Hillman, 1988), which were designed for students with disabilities.

Landmark Laws of the 1970s

In the 1970s, a new era for adapted physical activity and sport for athletes with disabilities evolved because of the advocacy movement and resulting legislation and litigation. Three landmark laws were enacted that all adapted physical activity professionals should know well. The constitutional basis for important parts of each of these laws was the 14th Amendment.

PL 93–112: The Rehabilitation Amendments

PL 93–112, enacted in 1973 but not implemented until its rules were printed in the *Federal Register* in 1977, includes many mandates but is best known for Section 504, often called the "Nondiscrimination Clause" (*Federal Register,* May 4, 1977). Section 504 states:

No otherwise qualified handicapped individual . . . shall, solely by reason of his handicap, be excluded from participation in, be denied the benefits of, or be subjected to discrimination under any program or activity receiving Federal financial assistance.

This means that schools conducting interscholastic athletics and extraclass activities must provide qualified students with disabilities an equal opportunity with nondisabled peers for participation. Such opportunities must be given in the least restrictive environment, which is generally the regular program. Persons with artificial limbs or one eye or kidney cannot be barred from sport competition. Likewise, athletic events in public places receiving federal funds (almost all do) must be accessible to all spectators, including those in wheelchairs. All facilities do not have to be accessible as long as programs are accessible. Students with disabilities must have access to at least one playing field, gymnasium, and swimming pool if able-bodied (AB) students are provided opportunities for sports, dance, and aquatics programs.

Accessibility refers to communication (the ability to understand) as well as architecture; hence, interpreters for persons who are deaf must be available as well as braille or tape-recorded signs/directions for persons who are blind. This type of accessibility should be kept in mind when planning workshops, tournaments, and meets.

The Office of Civil Rights (OCR) is responsible for administering the Rehabilitation Act (RA), which undergoes a number change each time it is amended. OCR does not, however, take action until a specific complaint for noncompliance is registered. Most schools, agencies, and universities prefer to handle Section 504 problems rather than have to cope with legal action. Therefore, institutions that receive federal funds designate one of their staff as a 504 compliance officer. This person is contacted regarding problems related to physical, learning, living, and work environments.

Institutions also establish 504 committees or councils, which serve as advisory and advocacy bodies. Such committees often conduct awareness programs and assess barriers. Membership on the 504 committee is a good volunteer activity for students who want to learn advocacy skills.

PL 94–142: The Education for All Handicapped Children Act

PL 94–142, the Education for All Handicapped Children Act (EAHCA), later called Part B or Chapter II of the Education of the Handicapped Act (EHA), was enacted in 1975. It was not implemented, however, until its rules were printed in the *Federal Register* in 1977 (*Federal Register,* August 23, 1977). This law provided the first legal basis for adapted physical education. It required that physical education services, specially designed if necessary, be made available to students declared eligible by the IEP process and that these be free, appropriate, and in the least restrictive environment. PL 94–142 separated *direct services* (i.e., required special education) from *related services* (not required unless proven

FIGURE 4.4

Athletes with cerebral palsy are part of the national advisory committee of the U.S. Cerebral Palsy Athletic Association, which meets at the U.S. Olympic Training Center. Pictured from left to right are Dick Hosty, Ken Wells, Wendy Shugal, and Sal Ficara. (Photo courtesy of U.S. Cerebral Palsy Athletic Association)

needed as a *prerequisite* to benefiting from special education). By including physical education as a part of the special education definition, PL 94–142 specified physical education as a direct and, therefore, required service.

In terms of its contributions to special education as a whole, PL 94–142 mandated five rights that changed the nature of public schooling for children and youth with disabilities:

1. Right to a *free* education
2. Right to an *appropriate* education
3. Right to *nondiscriminatory* testing, evaluation, and placement procedures
4. Right to be educated in the *least restrictive environment*
5. Right to *procedural due process* of the law

PL 94–142 also authorized the federal government to award the 50 states an annual sum of money based on the number of students with disabilities they served. These grants (variously called formula-based, entitlement, or statutory) were permanently authorized and therefore not subject to debate every 3 to 5 years, as are discretionary grants, the more common type of federal funding. Because the amount of money for each state was based on the number of students with disabilities, PL 94–142 carefully defined disabilities and established an IEP protocol for documenting nondiscriminatory testing, evaluation, and placement procedures.

PL 94–142 protected against overlabeling and overcounting by mandating that no more than 12% of the total school-age population of a state can be counted as disabled in the funding formula.

PL 94–142 was a momentous achievement. By the early 1980s, official government documents called it EHA-B, since it was an amendment to EHA. Since 1990, it has been called IDEA-Part B or Subchapter II. It is reauthorized about every 3 years and assigned a new number.

PL 95–606: The Amateur Sports Act

When the U.S. Olympic Committee (USOC) was reorganized in the 1970s and plans made for better promotion and coordination of amateur athletics, sports for athletes with disabilities were included in the master plan. Specifically, PL 95–606, the Amateur Sports Act of 1978, charged the USOC

to encourage and provide assistance to amateur athletic programs and competition for handicapped individuals, including, where feasible, the expansion of opportunities for meaningful participation by handicapped individuals in programs of athletic competition for able-bodied individuals. (Article II, 13, p. 2)

Today, athletes with disabilities use the U.S. Olympic Training Center at Colorado Springs (see Figure 4.4), and their sport organizations are assisted by USOC. New role models are emerging from within the ranks of persons with disabilities. Contemporary adapted physical education exposes students to these role models and uses them as resources.

Within the USOC, the Committee on Sports for the Disabled (COSD) is responsible for policy development in relation to disabled sports. Organizations that sponsor two or more sports of Olympic caliber for citizens with disabilities are governed by this committee. Names and addresses of these organizations appear in Appendix D.

The COSD meets semiannually. Its goals are to (a) enlist increasing support from and involvement by the national governing bodies of able-bodied sports, (b) promote more aggressively the concept of sports for persons with disabilities, (c) exert more influence internationally on sports and disability, (d) foster more and better research on sports for individuals with disabilities, (e) enhance the status of athletes within the USOC, and (f) obtain a fair share of USOC funds.

Basic Concepts and Resources of Advocacy

Effective advocacy requires an understanding of (a) how laws are numbered, (b) the difference between authorization and appropriation, (c) the procedures by which a bill becomes a law, (d) the protocol followed in determining rules and regulations for implementation of a law, (e) how copies of laws can be obtained, (f) enforcement of laws, (g) ways to find your congresspersons, and (h)the importance of the *Annual Report to Congress.* An understanding of basic concepts pertaining to federal laws will generalize to state-level legislative action since all states but one (Nebraska) are organized like the federal government with a Senate and House of Representatives.

The Numbering of Laws and Bills

How does a law like PL 94–142 derive its number? The first number indicates the Congress that enacted it. The second number states the law's rank or order. For example, PL 94–142 was the 142nd bill passed by the 94th Congress.

A Congress keeps the same number for a 2-year period. The number changes at the beginning of each odd-numbered year. The first Congress was 1789–1790, reminding us that George Washington was inaugurated in 1789. We celebrated the U.S. Constitution's 200th birthday in 1987; this was the Bicentennial, and the 100th Congress (1987–1988) was in progress. Can you use this information to determine the number that bills passed this year will have?

Congress changes its number every 2 years because the entire membership of the House of Representatives ($N = 435$) is elected every 2 years. Members of the Senate hold 6-year terms, and one third of the Senate's 100 members are elected every 2 years.

Before enactment, bills have separate Senate and House of Representatives numbers. This is because the two structures of Congress consider and pass bills independently. For example, the influential Americans With Disabilities Act, enacted in 1990, was Senate (S) 933 and House of Representatives (HR) 2273. After both Houses passed the bill and it was signed by the president, the Americans With Disabilities Act became PL 101–336. Knowing HR and S numbers is important in advocacy activities pertaining to getting a law passed. When you write a letter to a congressperson, for example, urging him or her to vote for a law, it is essential to cite the law's number. Advocacy organizations can generally supply these numbers.

Authorization and Appropriation

Almost all laws involve the granting of money to carry out particular programs or initiatives. Two terms are used to designate decision making about money: authorization and appropriation. *Authorization* is the authoring of a mandate that empowers Congress to grant money, up to a specified ceiling level, to carry out the intent of a law. *Appropriation* is decision making about the actual amount to be given each year to particular programs or initiatives. Authorization is like promising an ice-cream cone contingent upon whether or not there is money to pay for it. In contrast, appropriation is like handing someone a dollar and saying, "Buy your ice-cream cone." Authorizations always involve greater sums of money than appropriations.

Authorization comes from specific laws like IDEA and may be formula-based (permanent) or discretionary (usually established for 3-year periods). In contrast, appropriation is determined year by year in conjunction with the preparation of the overall government budget. Only the president can initiate the annual appropriations bill, but both Houses must agree on expenditures. Once decisions are made, the money appropriated for a particular program is given to the federal agency responsible for overseeing that program. If advocates want federal money to be spent on programs for persons with disabilities, they must be assertive in conveying this wish to their congresspersons.

Enactment of Laws

Except for the annual appropriations bill, which is the president's responsibility, members of Congress are responsible for writing bills and introducing them to the Senate and House of Representatives. Much of this work is done by legislative aides, and input from individuals and professional organizations is welcomed. Committees and subcommittees from both branches of Congress study proposed bills, conduct hearings, gather testimony, and make numerous revisions. Over 95% of the 10,000 to 15,000 new bills introduced every 2 years die at the subcommittee level because of lack of support. The other 5% advance to the floor, are voted upon, and (if approved by both the House and the Senate) are signed by the president and become laws. Advocates can monitor how their legislator votes and who speaks for and against bills by reading the *Congressional Record,* a daily periodical found in most university libraries.

Many bills are reauthorizations of earlier legislation. IDEA legislation is typically reauthorized (i.e., updated or amended) every 3 to 5 years. Various advocacy groups monitor the rewording of laws and typically keep educators informed through organizations like AAHPERD and CEC.

Occasionally, adapted physical activity professionals are requested to participate in letter-writing campaigns or telephone action.

The separate parts of a law are designated as either permanent or discretionary. The parts of IDEA that are permanent continue without reauthorization. These are Subchapter II (PL 94–142, Assistance for Education of All Handicapped Individuals) and Subchapter VIII (Infants and Toddlers With Disabilities). These parts (also known as B and H) are permanent because their funding and authorization are formula-based rather than a set sum agreed upon at the discretion of Congress. For example, IDEA-Part B states that special education funding for each state shall be a maximum of 40% of the national average per pupil expenditure in public elementary and secondary schools.

The discretionary parts of IDEA can be revised, deleted, or expanded every 3 to 5 years at the discretion of Congress. Discretionary status also means that the amount of money to be authorized for implementation of programs can be raised, lowered, or left the same. For example, grants to universities to fund personnel training in special education, physical education, and related services are discretionary. The amount authorized is usually around $2 million. Far less than this is actually appropriated.

Rules and Regulations

After a bill is signed into law by the president, a period of several months is required for the federal agency responsible for implementation to write the official rules and regulations. Until these are published, a law cannot be enforced. Laws are usually relatively brief. The complete text of PL 94–142 was only 17 pages long (see Weintraub, Abeson, Ballard, & LaVor, 1976). The rules and regulations for implementation, published in the *Federal Register* almost 2 years after enactment, required 45 pages.

The *Federal Register* is the official government publication for disseminating (a) the rules and regulations that govern implementation of laws, (b) notices pertaining to grant applications, (c) presidential proclamations and executive orders, and (d) information about other government business. Published daily (except weekends), the *Federal Register* is an 8 1/2-by-11-inch newspaper-like periodical that is available in most university libraries. Copies of a particular *Federal Register* can be obtained from your congressperson. Many university teachers own a copy of the August 23, 1977, *Federal Register,* which serves as the primary source for PL 94–142 theory and practice.

Hearings must be held throughout the nation so that all interested persons can offer suggestions and recommendations for implementing a new law. Written and oral testimony presented at hearings is used in formulating proposed rules. After these proposed rules are published in the *Federal Register,* more hearings are held and experts are brought to Washington, DC, to help with decision making. The final official rules and regulations are then published in the *Federal Register.* An important advocacy role is presence at public hearings and the submission of both oral and written testimony. Encouraging parents to participate in hearings is essential also.

FIGURE 4.5

Formats used in writing and recording law. Can you describe each source? Do you know where each source can be found?

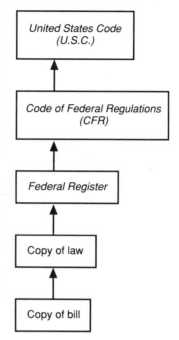

Obtaining Copies of Laws and Bills

Advocates obtain copies of laws and bills so that they know firsthand what is going on. They share these with parents and others who may be less assertive in obtaining copies. A powerful strategy is carrying a copy of the law or its rules and regulations (the *Federal Register*) to meetings where policy and/or compliance are to be discussed. Monitoring bills when they are in draft stage and assisting professional organizations in providing input are also important.

Copies of IDEA legislation, soon after enactment, can be purchased from CRR Publishing Company, P.O. Box 1905, Alexandria, VA 22313–1905, or from the National Association of State Directors of Special Education, (703) 519–3800. Copies can also be obtained through your legislator. Copies of established laws appear in legal reference books like the *Code of Federal Regulations (CFR)* and the *United States Code (U.S.C.).* These multivolume sets of books can be found in most university libraries.

The *CFR* and *U.S.C.* codify (i.e., systematize and classify) everything on a particular topic into the same bound volume. The *CFR,* which is published annually, codifies the laws from the previous 12 months. EHA and IDEA information is codified in Volume 34 of the *CFR.* The *U.S.C.,* which is published every 6 years, codifies legislation over a longer time period. EHA and IDEA information is codified in Volume 20 of the *U.S.C.*

Knowledge of the *CFR* and *U.S.C.* helps in understanding the referencing system used in finding laws and citing particular passages. For example, the definition of physical education in EHA is referenced as 34 *CFR,* 300.14 or 20 *U.S.C.* 1401 [16]. Figure 4.5 summarizes the formats in which law is written.

Single copies of all House bills and committee reports can be obtained by calling the U.S. House of Representatives Document Room at (202) 225–3456. Additional copies may be obtained by writing the House Document Room, U.S. House of Representatives, Washington, DC 20515. Include a self-addressed mailing label. Copies of Senate bills and reports may be obtained by writing the U.S. Senate Document Room at Hart Office Building, B-04, Washington, DC 20510, and including a self-addressed mailing label.

Up-to-date information on pending federal legislation can be obtained by calling the U.S. Legislative Status Office at (202) 225–1772. You must know the bill's number and title.

Enforcement of Laws

Once a law is enacted, many years are required for 100% compliance. Often, if no one points out that rights are being violated, no attempt is made to enforce the law. The parts of IDEA that pertain to physical education are not being enforced in many school districts. One reason is that parents have not forced compliance. Perhaps they do not understand the law, or they may not appreciate the importance of physical education in the health, fitness, and happiness of their children.

Teachers, if they want to keep their jobs, often cannot challenge school administrators directly. There are many ethical dilemmas (Churton, 1987; Loovis, 1986; Minner, Prater, & Beane, 1984). A viable approach to improved law enforcement is to work through parents, acquainting them with publications that describe the success of other parents (Kennedy, French, & Henderson, 1989) and getting them involved in sport and recreation activities that heighten their awareness of the values of physical education.

IDEA legislation gives parents tremendous power. Procedures are outlined whereby parents can present complaints with respect to any matter relating to the educational placement or to the provision of a free, appropriate public education (20 *U.S.C.* 1415). If problems are not resolved, parents can request that a formal due process hearing be conducted by the local education agency (LEA). If the outcome at this level is not satisfactory, parents may then request the state education agency (SEA) to conduct a due process hearing. If parents dislike SEA decisions, they then have the right to initiate litigation (i.e., file a civil action suit in the courts).

Advocates help parents to understand and use their power. They provide support for resolving differences without formal due process hearings and civil court action if possible. The following is a list of hierarchical steps that parents should follow when they are unhappy with service delivery (Kennedy et al., 1989):

1. Talk to your child's teacher to see if adjustments or changes can be made.
2. Talk to other school personnel who are aware of your child's needs (e.g., counselor, nurse, psychologist, educational diagnostician, principal, special education director) to discuss alternatives and solutions.
3. Discuss concerns with professionals outside the school who know your child (e.g., psychologist, neurologist, family physician). These individuals may have ideas to solve the problem or may document support for your position.
4. Request that a child study team meeting (IEP meeting) be convened to discuss alternatives.
5. Write a letter to the school principal or special education director, requesting a meeting.
6. Write a similar letter to the superintendent of schools. Include with this letter a copy of all previous correspondence with school personnel and document your efforts to solve the problem.
7. Notify the school board of the problem.
8. Contact state and local chapters of parent and advocacy organizations for advice and assistance.
9. Contact the SEA for information and advice.

If these steps do not produce satisfactory enforcement of the law in parents' minds, then the due process hearing and litigation options should be taken. This may be the only way that some students will receive appropriate physical education and thus have their rights to health, fitness, and leisure skills upheld.

Finding Your Congress Persons

Citizens in every state elect two senators and several representatives who shape the legislation of this country. These persons maintain offices in Washington, DC, and in various cities throughout their state. Everyone is welcome to visit these offices, and advocates use this approach to get acquainted with legislative aides and advance the IDEA cause. While a face-to-face meeting with congresspersons is preferable, their legislative aides usually represent the first level of access.

If you know the names of your congresspersons, you can reach them in Washington, DC, by telephoning the Capitol Operator at (202) 224–3121. Or you can contact them by writing to the following addresses: U.S. Senate, Washington, DC 20510 or U.S. House of Representatives, Washington, DC 20515.

To obtain names of congresspersons, as well as information about other government officials, books like the *United States Government Manual* and the *Official Directory of the Congress* can be ordered from the Superintendent of Documents, U.S. Government Printing Office, Washington, DC 20402. The telephone number for ordering documents by mail is (202) 783–3238. Libraries and local offices of political parties have these and other directories.

Annual Report to Congress

The U.S. Department of Education is required each year to publish the *Annual Report to Congress,* which describes (a) progress made in implementation of IDEA legislation, (b) national and state statistics pertaining to service delivery, and (c) needs (met and unmet). This report, published since 1979, typically is about 300 pages long and is the best primary source available for staying abreast of IDEA.

FIGURE 4.6

Follow the yellow brick road to somewhere over the rainbow: A model summarizing laws, outcomes, and advocacy behaviors. (MR–MH = Mental Retardation–Mental Health; ESEA = Elementary and Secondary Education Act; EHA = Education of the Handicapped Act; EAHCA = Education for All Handicapped Children Act; IEP = Individualized Education Program; IFSP = Individualized Family Service Plan.)

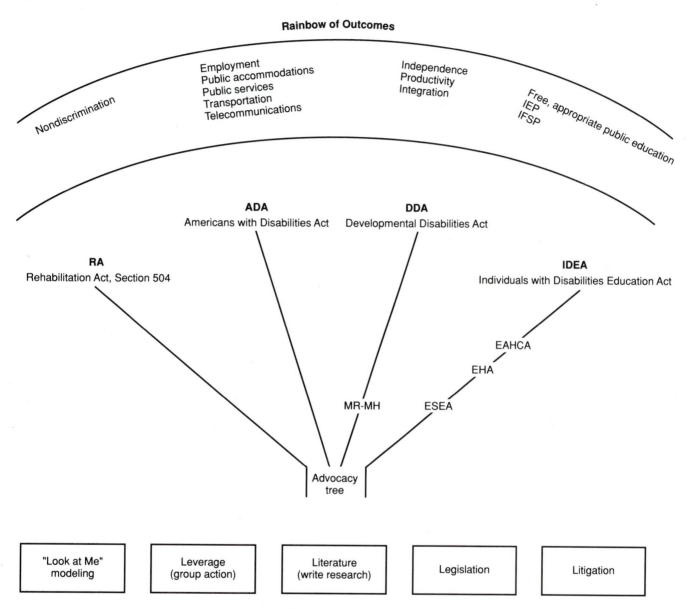

The Yellow Brick Road of Advocacy Stepping Stones

The *Annual Report to Congress* can be obtained at no cost by writing or telephoning the Division of Innovation and Development, Office of Special Education Programs, Switzer Building, Washington, DC 20202, telephone (202) 205–9864. Copies of these reports are also available at many university libraries through the computer-based information network of the Education Resources Information Center (ERIC).

The *Annual Report to Congress* summarizes what each state is doing with respect to IDEA implementation and thus enables advocates to compare their state with other states. It also provides statistics on the number of children and youth served by age, condition, and educational setting for each state. *This resource is a must for advocates.*

Current RA, ADA, and DDA Legislation

Figure 4.6 summarizes four tracks of legislation that are important in the 1990s. Each has a different number every 3 to 5 years.

The Rehabilitation Act

The Rehabilitation Act (RA), described earlier, continues to address discrimination against persons with disabilities. It is helpful, however, only when the offending agency or facility receives federal funds. In such cases, proven discrimination may result in withdrawal of federal funds.

Americans With Disabilities Act

The Americans With Disabilities Act (ADA) (PL 101–336) was passed in 1990. The purpose of this law is to end discrimination against persons with disabilities and to bring them into the economic and social mainstream of American life. The law addresses five areas in which discrimination was rampant in the 1980s: (a) employment in the private sector, (b) public accommodations, (c) public services, (d) transportation, and (e) telecommunications.

Some examples follow. All facilities, whether or not they receive federal funding, must provide equal access and equal services to persons with disabilities. This includes playgrounds, swimming pools, health spas, bowling alleys, golf courses, gymnasiums, and the like. Separate but equal will not be tolerated. Under ADA, persons with disabilities can no longer be denied insurance or be subject to different conditions based on disability alone. The nation's telephone services are being remodeled so that persons with hearing and /or speech impairments have services functionally equivalent to individuals without impairments.

The ADA is heralded as a landmark law that will do for persons with disabilities what the Civil Rights Act did for persons of color. The rules and regulations for the ADA will be written in the early 1990s, and everyone will have the opportunity to provide input via oral and written testimony at public hearings. For additional information, contact the U.S. Department of Justice, Civil Rights Division, Coordination and Review Section, P.O. Box 66118, Washington, DC 20035–6118.

Developmental Disabilities Assistance and Bill of Rights Act

The Developmental Disabilities Assistance and Bill of Rights Act (DDA) of 1990 (PL 101–496) emphasized three goals (independence, productivity, and integration into the community) and mandated that state-level Developmental Disabilities Councils direct their efforts toward achievement of these goals. DDA activities are regulated and funded by the U.S. Department of Health and Human Services. Goals are achieved through (a) individual and family support, including federal funds for child welfare and older Americans; (b) education; (c) employment; (d) income, including the Supplemental Security Income and the Social Security Disability Insurance programs; (e) housing; and (f) health, including Medicaid programs.

Unlike IDEA, which defines disabilities categorically (e.g., mental retardation, severe emotional disturbance), the DDA uses the following definition:

Developmental disability *is a severe, chronic disability which:*

(1) is attributable to a mental or physical impairment or combination of mental and physical impairments;

(2) is manifested before the person attains age twenty-two;

(3) is likely to continue indefinitely;

(4) results in substantial functional limitations in three or more of the following areas of major life activity: (a) self-care, (b) receptive and expressive language, (c) learning, (d) mobility, (e) self-direction, (f) capacity for independent living, and (g) economic self-sufficiency; and

(5) reflects the person's need for a combination and sequence of special, interdisciplinary, or generic care, treatment, or other services which are of lifelong or extended duration and are individually planned and coordinated. (Section 102(5) of PL 100–146)

Community programs that can show success in helping persons with developmental disabilities achieve independence, productivity, and integration may apply for grants. Physical activity and recreation programs, if properly conducted, can promote these goals.

IDEA Legislation

The Individuals With Disabilities Education Act (IDEA) is the legislation that guides policies and practices in educating students with disabilities. This legislation, first passed in 1970, has been updated and/or amended every 3 to 5 years. The most recent reauthorization is PL 101–476, enacted in 1990. Figure 4.7 presents its eight parts.

Age Range Covered by IDEA

The age range covered by IDEA is from birth to 21 years of age. IDEA-Part B (PL 94–142) provides for ages 3 to 21 years, and IDEA-Part H provides for infants and toddlers, defined as individuals from birth to age 2.

IDEA-Part C emphasizes the importance of secondary and postsecondary education and transitional services for youth with disabilities. The law defines *youth with disabilities* as persons who are 12 years of age or older or who are enrolled in the seventh or higher grade in school. *Transitional services* refers to assistance in making the transition from traditional-school-based education to vocational training, competitive employment, independent living, and use of community resources to meet health, fitness, and leisure needs. Special funding is available under IDEA-Part C to encourage schools to develop transitional services, but the federal special education money for ages 3 to 21 comes from IDEA-Part B.

Definitions

To be an effective advocate and good teacher, you must know sections of IDEA that relate to physical education. Direct quotations from the law are used in the sections that follow. Physical educators should cite these direct quotations in term papers and research projects as well as in public meetings where policy is discussed.

FIGURE 4.7

Parts of IDEA (Individuals with Disabilities Education Act) of 1990.

Subchapter or Part		Title
I	A	General Provisions, including definitions
II	B	Assistance for Education of All Handicapped Individuals
III	C	Centers and Services to Meet Special Needs (like regional resource centers, early childhood, programs for children with severe disabilities, and secondary and transitional services)
IV	D	Training Personnel
V	E	Research
VI	F	Instructional Media
VII	G	Technology, Educational Media, and Materials
VIII	H	Infants and Toddlers with Disabilities

The rules and regulations for IDEA include the same definitions (with only a few exceptions) found in PL 91–230 (1970) and PL 94–142 (1975). Selected definitions follow. After each direct quotation, a brief discussion highlights key ideas.

Special Education Definition

PL 101–476, Sec. 1401 (16), states:

(16) The term special education *means specially designed instruction, at no cost to parents or guardians, to meet the unique needs of a child with a disability, including—*

(A) instruction conducted in the classroom, in the home, in hospitals and institutions, and in other settings; and

(B) instruction in physical education.

Physical education is the only school subject mentioned in this definition. Essentially, this definition makes specially designed physical education a component of special education. This is why adapted physical educators hired to teach separate classes, usually of children with severe disabilities, are often salaried by IDEA-Part B monies and considered members of the special education staff. In some states, persons taking such positions are required to have separate teacher certification in special education and physical education. A better requirement is a graduate degree or state certification specifically in adapted physical education.

Definitions of Disabilities

PL 101–476, Sec. 1401a (1), states:

(1) The term children with disabilities *means children—*

(A) with mental retardation, hearing impairments including deafness, speech or language impairments, visual impairments including blindness, serious emotional disturbance, orthopedic impairments, autism, traumatic brain injury, other health impairments, or specific learning disabilities; and

(B) who, by reason thereof, need special education and related services.

Table 4.1 presents definitions of disabilities from the *Federal Register* (August 23, 1977, p. 42478). Current legislation combines deaf and hard of hearing conditions. The definitions and abbreviations in Table 4.1 are about the same for every state because they are used in head counts for funding purposes.

IEP Definition

The individualized education program (IEP) is one of the most important concepts of IDEA legislation. Key words in the 1990 definition are in bold print.

(20) The term individualized education program *means* **a written statement** *for each child with a disability developed in any meeting by a* **representative** *of the local educational agency or an intermediate educational unit who shall be qualified to provide, or supervise the provision of, specially designed instruction to meet the unique needs of children with disabilities, the* **teacher,** *the* **parents or guardian** *of such child, and whenever appropriate, such* **child,** *which statement shall include (A) a statement of the present levels of educational* **performance** *of such child, (B) a statement of* **annual goals,** *including short-term instructional objectives, (C) a statement of the specific educational* **services** *to be provided to such child, and the extent to which such child will be able to participate in regular education programs, (D) a statement of the needed* **transition** *services for students beginning no later than age 16 and annually thereafter (and, when determined appropriate for the individual, beginning at age 14 or younger), including, when appropriate, a statement of the interagency responsibilities or linkages (or both) before the student leaves the school setting, (E) the projected* **date** *for initiation and anticipated duration of such services, and (F) appropriate objective criteria and* **evaluation** *procedures and schedules for determining, on at least an annual basis, whether instructional objectives are being achieved. (PL 101–475, Sec. 1401 (20)*

This definition includes *what* the IEP is (a written statement developed in a meeting), *who* must be present at the meeting (four types of persons), and the required contents of the IEP. There are five sections for students under

Table 4.1
Definitions of disabilities that appear in federal law.

Mentally retarded (MR) means significantly subaverage general intellectual functioning existing concurrently with deficits in adaptive behavior and manifested during the developmental period, which adversely affects a child's educational performance.

Orthopedically impaired (OI) means a severe orthopedic impairment which adversely affects a child's educational performance. The term includes impairments caused by congenital anomaly (e.g., clubfoot, absence of some member, etc.), impairments caused by disease (e.g., poliomyelitis, bone tuberculosis, etc.) and impairments from other causes (e.g., cerebral palsy, amputations, and fractures or burns which cause contractures).

Specific learning disability (LD) means a disorder in one or more of the basic psychological processes involved in understanding or in using language, spoken or written, which may manifest itself in an imperfect ability to listen, think, speak, read, write, spell, or do mathematical calculations. The term includes such conditions as perceptual handicaps, brain injury, minimal brain disfunction, dyslexia, and developmental aphasia. The term does not include children who have learning problems which are primarily the result of visual, hearing, or motor handicaps, of mental retardation, or of environmental, cultural, or economic disadvantage.

Seriously emotionally disturbed (ED) means a condition exhibiting one or more of the following characteristics over a long period of time and to a marked degree which adversely affects educational performance:

(A) An inability to learn which cannot be explained by intellectual, sensory, or health factors;

(B) An inability to build or maintain satisfactory interpersonal relationships with peers and teachers;

(C) Inappropriate types of behavior or feelings under normal circumstances;

(D) A general pervasive mood of unhappiness or depression; or

(E) A tendency to develop physical symptoms or fears associated with personal or school problems.

The term includes children who are *schizophrenic*. The term does not include children who are socially maladjusted, unless it is determined that they are seriously emotionally disturbed.

Visually handicapped (VH) means a visual impairment which, even with correction, adversely affects a child's educational performance. The term includes both partially seeing and blind children.

Deaf (D) means a hearing impairment which is so severe that the child is impaired in processing linguistic information through hearing, with or without amplification, which adversely affects educational performance.

Hard of hearing (HH) means a hearing impairment, whether permanent or fluctuating, which adversely affects a child's educational performance but which is not included under the definition of "deaf" in this section.

Deaf-blind (DB) means concomitant hearing and visual impairments, the combination of which causes such severe communication and other developmental and educational problems that they cannot be accommodated in special education programs solely for deaf or blind children.

Other health impaired (OHI) means limited strength, vitality or alertness, due to chronic or acute health problems, such as a heart condition, tuberculosis, rheumatic fever, nephritis, asthma, sickle cell anemia, hemophilia, epilepsy, lead poisoning, leukemia, or diabetes, which adversely affect a child's educational performance.

Speech impaired (SI) means a communication disorder, such as stuttering, impaired articulation, a language impairment, or a voice impairment, which adversely affects a child's educational performance.

Multihandicapped means concomitant impairments (such as mentally retarded blind, mentally retarded orthopedically impaired, etc.), the combination of which causes such severe educational problems that they cannot be accommodated in special education programs solely for one of the impairments. The term does not include deaf-blind children.

Note. In 1981, autistic children were officially classified as other health impaired rather than seriously emotionally disturbed. In 1990, autism and traumatic head injury were recognized as separate categories.
Note. Definitions from *Federal Register*, August 23, 1977, PL 94–142, the Education for All Handicapped Children Act.

---

age 16 and six for those over 16. The sections can be remembered by the acronym PAST-DE, conceptualized as follows:

P—Performance, present level

A—Annual goals, including short-term objectives

S—Services to be provided

T—Transition services

D—Dates and duration

E—Evaluation to determine whether objectives are achieved

To remember PAST-DE, think about how the age of ignorance about educating students with disabilities is past history or dead (DE).

The IEP is an official special education document. Its main purpose is to document the placement decision. This decision has two parts. First, evidence must be presented to show that the student meets entry-level criteria to be classified as having a disability in the subject matter under consideration. Second, evidence must be presented to support the specific services designated (regular class, resource room, separate class, etc.) as the least restrictive placement. By law, the IEP must encompass physical education. This inclusion is generally a mention of the type of physical education placement (regular, adapted, or some combination) and a description of psychomotor performance. Most IEP forms do not have space for a complete delineation of physical education goals, objectives, and services.

The physical education section must be brief because all subject matter areas are included in the IEP. Each school district uses a different form, but most special education IEPs are about three to four pages long. Research shows that school districts vary widely on time spent writing IEPs, with a range of from 13 to 150 short-term objectives written for each student. The median number was 22 and 27 in two large-scale studies.

In many school districts, the three-to-four-page special education IEP represents a summary of IEPs written by specialists in different areas. The adapted physical educator, for instance, may be expected to write a physical education IEP. Figure 4.8 shows a sample physical education IEP written for a 5-year-old student with mild cerebral palsy. Note that this one-page form includes the components of an IEP as required by IDEA.

Free Appropriate Public Education Definition

Free appropriate public education is defined in IDEA Part A as follows:

(18) The term free appropriate public education *means special education and related services that (A) have been provided at public expense, under public supervision and direction, and without charge, (B) meet the standards of the State educational agency, (C) include an appropriate preschool, elementary, or secondary school education in the state involved, and (D) are provided in conformity with the individualized education program required under section 1414(a)(5) of this title. (PL 101–475, Sec 1401 (18)*

The term *appropriate* has caused considerable debate, resulting in several lawsuits. In one of these (*Board of Education of Hendrick Hudson Central Schools District v. Rowley,* 458 US, 176, 1982), the U.S. Supreme Court declared that *appropriate education was personalized instruction with sufficient support services to permit the student to benefit educationally from instruction.* Now called the Rowley standard, this decision clarifies that a school is not required to maximize a student's potential for learning. Rather, the IDEA sets forth a "basic floor opportunity" for students with disabilities. *Appropriate* depends on standards established by state education agencies. One characteristic of appropriate instruction is congruency with what is written on the IEP.

Physical Education Mentions in IDEA

Physical Education Definition

Page 42480 of the August 23, 1977, *Federal Register* states:

(2) Physical education *is defined as follows:*
  (i) The term means the development of:
    (A) physical and motor fitness;
    (B) fundamental motor skills and patterns; and
    (C) skills in aquatics, dance, and individual and group games and sports (including intramural and lifetime sports).

  (ii) The term includes special physical education, adapted physical education, movement education, and motor development.

This definition differentiates physical education from such related services as occupational and physical therapy. The term *skills,* as used in IDEA, encompasses mental and social (as well as physical) skills needed to learn rules and strategies. Nowhere in IDEA is there a definition specifically for adapted physical education.

Physical Education Requirement

Page 42489 of the August 23, 1977, *Federal Register* states:

121a.307 Physical Education
(a) General. *Physical education services, specially designed if necessary, must be made available to every handicapped child receiving a free appropriate public education.*

This passage, together with the mention of physical education in the special education definition, comprises the legal basis for adapted physical education service delivery for students with disabilities. Whether a specially designed program is needed is determined by IDEA-Part B eligibility procedures, which are described later in the chapter.

Integration in Regular Physical Education

Page 42489 of the August 23, 1977, *Federal Register* states:

(b) Regular physical education. *Each handicapped child must be afforded the opportunity to participate in the regular physical education program available to nonhandicapped children unless:*
  (1) the child is enrolled full-time in a separate facility; or
  (2) the child needs specially designed physical education, as prescribed in the child's individualized education program.

The intent is to place each student in his or her least restrictive environment based on individual assessment data and multidisciplinary deliberation. To justify segregation, the IEP process must document that the present level of performance, goals, and objectives are such that needs cannot be met in the regular physical education setting.

Special Physical Education

Page 42489 of the August 23, 1977, *Federal Register* states:

(c) Special physical education. *If specially designed physical education is prescribed in a child's individualized education program, the public agency responsible for the education of that child shall provide the service directly, or make arrangements for it to be provided through other public or private programs.*

Specially designed physical education, as defined, does not have to be full-time placement in a separate class. It can refer to specific conditions imposed upon regular class placement, like limited class size, the presence of an assistant for one-to-one instruction, and the availability of wheelchairs and other special or adapted equipment. Just as special education is taught by a certified special education teacher, specially designed physical education should be planned and, when possible, implemented by an adapted physical activity specialist.

FIGURE 4.8

A sample Physical Education IEP (Individualized education program) form.

```
┌─────────────────────────────────────────────────────────────────────┐
│        ADAPTED AND DEVELOPMENTAL PHYSICAL EDUCATION - IEP             │
│              Alief Independent School District                        │
│                                                                       │
│  Parent Signature of Approval _____  Date _____         │
│                                                                       │
│  Name ___Amy S.___   Date _1-15-93_  School _Washington Elem._        │
│                                                                       │
│  D.O.B._7-3-87_ Age _5_ Grade _Early Childhood_ Classification _OI_   │
│                                                                       │
│  APA Specialist _C. Pope_  Projected Starting Date of Services 9-1992 │
│                                                                       │
│  Instructional P.E. Arrangement 1/1 APA Specialist 3 times weekly-15 min. │
│                                 1/15 Regular PE  2 times weekly - 30 min. │
│  Physical Abilities/Disabilities Mild Cerebral Palsy - L. side, hemiplegic │
│      spastic, ambulatory_____  Related Services  OT, PT               │
└─────────────────────────────────────────────────────────────────────┘
```

PRESENT LEVEL OF PSYCHOMOTOR PERFORMANCE	ANNUAL GOALS
Amy walks independently and climbs stairs with assistance. Uses a wide base of support and carries arms in high guard position. Has developed some protective extension of arms and equilibrium reactions. Amy rolls a 10" ball for distance of 8-10'; hits a suspended swinging ball; throws (RH) with a flinging motion; creeps up an inclined mat and log rolls down; walks a 6" beam with assistance, and balances momentarily on one foot. She is just entering the associative play stage and appears to have had little experience interacting with other children; plays no group games.	1. Develop fundamental movement patterns to age appropriate level. 2. Improve social interaction skills to cooperative play stage. 3. Learn 10+ low organized games. 4. Improve postures in all positions.

SHORT TERM OBJECTIVES	(METHODS/ACTIVITIES)

1. Interact with 3+ classmates each regular PE class
2. Perform a broad jump (2-ft. takeoff and land) for a distance of 8"
3. Maintain balance on one foot for 3-5 seconds
4. Jump down from a height of 10-12"
5. Kick a 10" stationary ball while standing
6. Throw a bean bag 5' using overarm pattern
7. Walk a 5' balance beam (6" wide) on floor unassisted
8. Stand up from supine position in less than 10 seconds
9. Track and catch a 10" ball rolled from 10'
	Command teaching style
	Physical prompts as needed
	Insist on eye contact
	Reinforce-random schedule
	See the following pages of *Adapted PE Guide:*
	  Movement Skill-pp.1-9
	  Bean Bag Games - p.22
	
	Note: This section generally refers to school curriculum guide or a favorite book that describes method in detail.

Table 4.2
IEP process as required by IDEA, adapted to show roles of regular and adapted physical education instructors.

Phase 1 *Child Find*	District-wide screening process for all children in all school subjects. (1) Usually done by regular physical education instructor or classroom teacher.	(2) Usually conducted at beginning of school year but can occur anytime. (3) Often informal, resulting from observation and/or conference with parent.	(4) Parent can initiate process instead of teacher.
Phase 2 *Initial Data Collection and Pre-IEP Meeting*	Begins with referral for further testing to determine if adapted physical education/special education services are needed. (1) Request special education director to determine pupil's eligibility for special services.	(2) Contact parents for consent to test and/or collect eligibility data. (3) Data collection usually done by regular physical education instructor.	(4) Pre-IEP meeting to determine need for more extensive testing. (5) Written report of findings.

Phase 3 *Admission to Special Education, Including Adapted Physical Education*	**Comprehensive Individual Assessment**
	Initiated by written report signed by referral committee—see Phase 2.
	(1) Special education director assigns persons to do assessment.
	(2) Notification of rights to parents.
	(3) Obtain parent consent for comprehensive assessment by multidisciplinary team.
	(4) Comprehensive individual assessment with psychomotor part done by adapted physical education specialist.
		IEP Meeting
		(1) Procedural safeguards must be observed in planning meeting.
		Consider:
		  (a) who must be present,
		  (b) time and place, and
		  (c) native language.
		(2) Presentation and analysis of assessment data by different team members.
		(3) Agreement on present level of functioning.
			(4) Decision making concerning:
			  (a) goals and objectives,
			  (b) services,
			    (i) educational placement,
			    (ii) interventions,
			    (iii) et cetera,
			  (c) dates/timeline,
			  (d) evaluation plan.
			(5) Write IEP.
			(6) Sign IEP.

Phase 4 *Program Implementation With Annual Program Review*			
Phase 5 *Dismissal From Special Education Into Full-Time Regular Education*			

Role in Transitional Services

The following is suggested under projects in IDEA-Part C, Sec. 1425 (b):

(10) specially designed or adapted physical education and therapeutic recreation programs to facilitate the full participation of youths with disabilities in community programs.

The IEP Process

The IEP process (sometimes called the child study or ARD [Admission, Review, Dismissal] process) is a series of public school procedures that culminates in the written IEP. These procedures are directed toward finding unserved children with disabilities, *admitting* them to the school district's special education program, providing them with special services, *reviewing* their progress at least annually, and subsequently *dismissing* them from special education. The precise roles of regular and adapted physical educators are not discussed in IDEA and thus vary by school district. In most instances, however, the physical educator is expected to contribute expertise in the identification and solution of problems in the psychomotor domain.

Five Phases of the IEP Process

Table 4.2 depicts five phases of the IEP process: (a) child find (identification of students who may be eligible for special education services, including adapted physical education); (b) initial data collection and pre-IEP meeting; (c) formal admission to special education, including *comprehensive individual assessment* and the official *IEP meeting;* (d) program implementation with annual program review, for the purpose of evaluating the effectiveness of the learning activities in achieving goals and objectives; and (e) dismissal from the special education program into regular education. This last phase may seem idealistic, but it demonstrates IDEA philosophy that students should, if possible, be integrated into regular education.

Regulations Relating to Dates

IDEA requires that an IEP must be in effect *before* students with disabilities can receive special education. This is because the IEP process is the means by which eligibility for services is determined and educational placement is assigned.

Parental consent is required before comprehensive individual assessment for special education (including adapted physical education) placement can begin. Once this consent is obtained, most states require that the IEP process be completed in 30 to 60 days.

IDEA also requires that the written IEP be officially reviewed once each year. Many states require more frequent reviews. The purpose of these reviews is to analyze the student's educational progress and to make revisions in the IEP.

IEP Meeting and the Adapted Physical Education Specialist

In general, participants in IEP meetings represent four types of roles: (a) parental, (b) administrative, (c) instructional, and (d) diagnostic. Most adapted physical activity authorities believe that a physical educator should be present at the IEP meeting to provide input concerning performance and needs in the psychomotor domain. If, however, a physical educator cannot be released from teaching responsibilities to attend, he or she should submit written recommendations to the special education director and, when possible, confer with the parents before the meeting and ask them to serve as advocates for physical education.

The primary purpose of the IEP meeting is to determine for each school subject whether the student should be assigned a regular, special, or combined educational placement. If the school district employs an adapted physical education specialist, this person is typically responsible for assessment and making a recommendation about physical education placement. If no specialist is available, the regular physical educator is expected to perform these tasks or, in some instances, the student is just automatically placed in regular physical education without consideration of needs.

IEP Principles and Practices

The IEP and the IEP process are praiseworthy concepts that have shaped and changed practices in the field. Most of the principles that guide school district practices in relation to assessment, evaluation, and placement have their roots in the IEP process and thus come from IDEA-Part B. Among the most important of these principles are the following:

1. A student shall be considered nondisabled (i.e., normal) until sufficient evidence is presented that he or she meets criteria to be labeled disabled. This principle is similar to that followed in a court of law:

All persons are considered innocent until proven guilty. Educational classification is a legal procedure with due process requirements.

2. The regular education placement (i.e., integration) shall be considered the most appropriate placement for each student until evidence is presented, through the IEP process, that special services are required and that these services cannot be provided in the regular classroom.

3. A student may be declared disabled in one curricular area but not another. The placement decision for each subject matter area must therefore be made separately and independently from all others.

4. Placement decisions shall be based on comprehensive assessment data generated by instruments that are valid for the purpose for which they are being used.

5. The evaluation procedures used in making placement decisions must meet the six criteria stated in IDEA. (These six criteria are discussed later in the chapter.)

6. Placement decisions must be based on multidisciplinary data and made by teams of experts rather than one person.

7. School districts should make available a continuum of placements and services so that students in separate education settings can be moved into progressively more integrated environments.

8. Placement decisions must be reviewed at least once each year to determine whether the student is ready yet for a more integrated environment and to update goals and objectives.

9. Every student shall be placed in his or her least restrictive environment.

10. Due process procedures to protect the rights of every student shall be clearly delineated.

These principles are discussed briefly in the sections that follow. More extensive coverage is provided in Chapters 7 and 8, on assessment and service delivery.

Services for Infants and Toddlers

The EHA of 1986 (PL 99–457) was the first federal legislation to mandate early intervention services for infants and toddlers with disabilities, defined as individuals from birth to age 2 years. Rules and regulations for this law were published in the *Federal Register* June 22, 1989. Instead of an IEP, early intervention services for infants and toddlers with disabilities are guided by an *individualized family service plan (IFSP)*. This plan is described in Chapter 18, "Infants, Toddlers, and Young Children: The New Emphasis."

The IFSP, like the IEP, must be based on multidisciplinary assessment and developed by a multidisciplinary team, including the parent or guardian. IDEA-Part H does not specifically mention adapted physical education, but these services may be provided under special education since IDEA-Part A includes physical education as a part of special education.

Especially significant in the regulations are the role of the family in the decision-making process and the strong preference shown for services in integrated settings. On the issue of integration, the *Federal Register* (June 29, 1989) states:

(b) Location of Services. *To the extent appropriate, early intervention programs must be provided in the types of settings in which infants and toddlers without disabilities will participate . . . it is important that efforts be made to provide early intervention services in settings and facilities that do not remove the children from natural environments (e.g. the home, day-care centers, or other community settings). Thus, it is recommended that services be community-based, and not isolate an eligible child or the child's family from settings or activities in which children without disabilities would participate. (Sec. 303.12)*

Due Process and Education

Due process (the right of an individual to fair treatment) is guaranteed under the 5th and 14th Amendments to the U.S. Constitution. The 5th Amendment, which applies only to federal government, states, "No person . . . shall be deprived of life, liberty, or property without due process of law." The 14th Amendment extends this concept to state government operations, stating, "nor shall any State deprive any person of life, liberty, or property without due process of law."

In general, law distinguishes between two types of due process: substantive and procedural. *Substantive* due process requires that a state have a valid goal, like protection from disease, before it can deprive an individual of the right to life, liberty, or property, as in requiring vaccinations before children can attend school (Appenzeller, 1983). *Procedural* due process guarantees a person the right and a meaningful opportunity to be heard and to protest before action can be taken in regard to his or her life, liberty, or property (Turnbull, 1976). Assignment to special education is considered action in regard to basic constitutional rights.

IDEA-Part B makes many references to procedural due process. Proper procedures in regard to assessment/evaluation, the parents' role in the IEP process, and the right to an impartial due process hearing are described in detail. Of particular importance to physical educators is the requirement that schools must give parents written notice that their child has been referred for assessment and that parents must give written consent before such assessment can be undertaken. The written notice to parents should include reasons for the referral, information about who will administer tests, names and descriptions of tests or data collection protocols, and a statement of parents' rights. In most school systems, this paperwork is under the jurisdiction of the director of special education. School administrators have the responsibility of ensuring that teachers understand due process.

A Continuum of Services and Least Restrictive Environment

The concept of a continuum of education services was introduced by Evelyn Deno (1970) and subsequently woven into the legislative rules and regulations. Figure 4.9A shows Deno's original cascade system of special education services, while Figure 4.9B shows an adaptation to physical education. An inverted triangle shape was used to depict the idea of a series of downward waterfalls (the meaning of *cascade*), beginning large at the top (Level I) and becoming progressively smaller (Level VI). Deno's cascade system of special education services thus emphasized that most special education students would be placed in regular classes but that many alternatives would be made available by each school district.

Today, Levels I, II, and III of these models are receiving the most attention, regardless of how severely disabled the student is. At each of these levels, resource teachers (or adapted physical education specialists) are being used in new and creative ways. Increasingly, dual- and team-teaching, with regular and adapted physical educators paired, is viewed as a model for providing supplementary instructional services and/or helping students to make the transition from full- or part-time segregated placement to full- or part-time integrated placement. Adapted physical educators are also used as consultant teachers who instruct regular educators on how to assess, teach, and evaluate students with disabilities.

Mainstreaming

The concept of a continuum of educational services was created to help explain the philosophy and practices of *mainstreaming,* the process by which students are placed in settings representing different degrees of integration, depending upon their assessed needs. Philosophically, mainstreaming (when properly defined) can only work when a wide variety of settings and support services are available. The idea is to match each student's abilities with clusters of services that permit him or her to learn best. Levels within the cascade system thus may represent places within a building, types of programs, or clusters of services.

The term *mainstreaming* (a process) should be differentiated from *mainstream* (a place), but both mean the presence of supportive services to enable students to benefit from instruction in a designated environment. Because mainstreaming, as a concept, was not well understood, the experts who wrote PL 94–142 did not use the term *mainstreaming* in either the law or its rules and regulations.

Least Restrictive Environment

Instead of *mainstreaming,* the term *least restrictive environment* (*LRE*) is used in legislative rules and regulations. The U.S. Department of Education (1989) stated in this regard:

The least restrictive environment provision of the Education of the Handicapped Act, as amended, created a presumption in favor of educating children with handicaps in regular education environments. . . . The statute and its implementing regulations require that, first, educational services appropriate for each child be defined annually in an Individualized Education Program (IEP), and, second, an educational placement be selected from a continuum of alternatives so that the individually appropriate education can be delivered in the setting that is least removed from the regular education environment, while simultaneously offering the greatest interaction with children who are not handicapped. (p. 21)

FIGURE   4.9

(*A*) Deno's cascade system of special education services. (*B*) Sherrill's cascade system of adapted physical education services. Levels I, II, and III utilize adapted physical educators as resource room or consultant teachers.

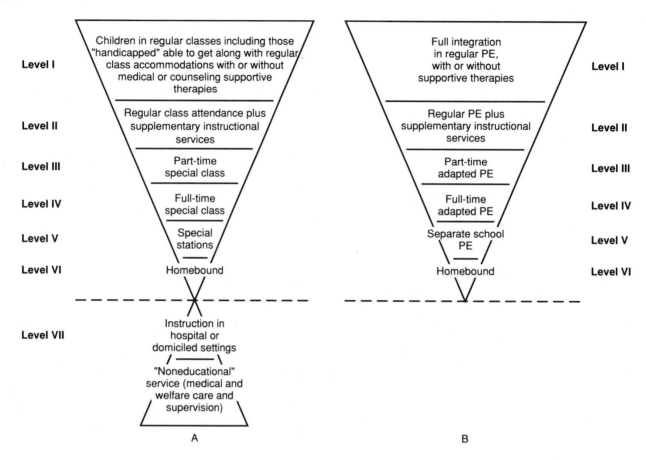

A

B

LRE, as currently defined, thus requires two decisions for every curricular subject: (a) what services (i.e., content, activities) are appropriate and (b) where and how can they be delivered (i.e., taught) so that interaction with children who are not disabled is greatest.

The LRE for each student must be determined individually, depending upon the setting in which the most learning is likely to occur—mentally, physically, and socially. Separate one-to-one instruction in a resource room may be the LRE for a student with severe disability, whereas partial integration in a regular class with a peer tutor may be the LRE for another.

The LRE also varies in terms of curriculum content and teaching style. For a student in a wheelchair, the regular classroom during a soccer or football unit might be the most restrictive environment, whereas the same classroom during an archery or swimming unit might be least restrictive. For students with severe emotional disturbance who need externally imposed limits, a movement education setting might be more restrictive (i.e., permitting less learning) than a command-style follow-the-leader class.

The Regular Education Initiative

The *regular education initiative* is the term used to describe the goal of keeping as many students in regular education as possible. The following passage serves as the basis for this initiative:

The state has established . . . (B) procedures to assure that, to the maximum extent appropriate, handicapped children, including children in public or private institutions or other care facilities, are educated with children who are not handicapped, and that special classes, separate schooling, or other removal of handicapped children from the regular educational environment occurs only when the nature or severity of the handicap is such that education in regular classes with the use of supplementary aids and services cannot be achieved satisfactorily. (20 U.S.C., 143)

To comply with IDEA, school districts split the placement of students among several settings and name the placement according to the location where most instruction is received.

The U.S. Department of Education (1989) has established the following definitions:

Regular class placement—The student receives special education and related services for 20% of the school day or less.

Resource room placement—The student spends from 21% to 60% of the school day with special education and related services personnel.

Special class placement—The student spends 61% or more of the school day in special education.

Using these definitions, the U.S. Department of Education (1989) estimated that about 27% of all special education students are served in regular classes and about 43% are served in resource rooms. Thus, about 70% receive a substantial amount of their education in the integrated or regular setting.

Special monetary incentives are available to encourage administrators to comply with the regular education initiative. Thus, when students need full- or part-time separate physical education instruction, strong supportive evidence is required to obtain such a placement.

Instead of using the now outdated all-or-none placement philosophy, physical educators must learn to negotiate for split placements so that students can spend some time with adapted physical education specialists (e.g., 1 or 2 days a week) and still be classified as having regular or resource room placements. Table 4.3 shows innovative thinking about placement and support services (Block & Krebs, 1992).

Evaluation Procedures in IDEA

IDEA has also contributed to the improvement of evaluation (sometimes called assessment) procedures, particularly as they pertain to placement. Physical educators, because of their potential role in placement decision making, should know the legal bases for evaluation. The August 23, 1977, *Federal Register*, pages 42496–42497, states:

121a532 **Evaluation procedures.**
State and local education agencies shall ensure, at a minimum, that:
(a) Tests and other evaluation materials
    (1) are provided and administered in the child's native language or other mode of communication, unless it is clearly not feasible to do so;
    (2) have been validated for the specific purpose for which they are used; and
    (3) are administered by trained personnel in conformance with the instructions provided by their producer;
(b) Tests and other evaluation materials include those tailored to assess specific areas of educational need and not merely those which are designed to provide a single general intelligence quotient;
(c) Tests are selected and administered so as best to ensure that when a test is administered to a child with impaired sensory, manual, or speaking skills, the test results accurately reflect the child's aptitude or achievement level or whatever other factors the test purports to measure,

Table 4.3
A continuum of support to ensure success in regular education placement. (RPE = Regular physical education; APE = Adapted physical education.)

Level 1: *No Support Needed*
1.1 Student can make necessary modifications on his or her own.
1.2 RPE teacher feels comfortable working with student.
Level 2: *APE Consultation*
2.1 No extra assistance needed.
2.2 Peer tutor watches out for student.
2.3 Peer tutor assists student.
2.4 Paraprofessional assists student.
Level 3: *APE Direct Service in RPE 1 to 2 Times/Week*
3.1 Peer tutor watches out for student.
3.2 Peer tutor assists student.
3.3 Paraprofessional assists student.
Level 4: *Part-Time APE and Part-Time RPE.*
4.1 Flexible schedule with reverse mainstreaming.
4.2 Fixed schedule with reverse mainstreaming.
Level 5: *Reverse Mainstreaming in Special School*
5.1 Students from special school go to regular school for RPE.
5.2 Nondisabled students go to special school for RPE.
5.3 Students with and without disabilities meet in community for recreation training.

Note. From Block & Krebs, 1992.

rather than reflecting the child's impaired sensory, manual, or speaking skills (except where those skills are the factors which the test purports to measure);
(d) No single procedure is used as the sole criterion for determining an appropriate educational program for a child;
(e) The evaluation is made by a multidisciplinary team or group of persons, including at least one teacher or other specialist with knowledge in the area of suspected disability; and
(f) The child is assessed in all areas related to the suspected disability, including, where appropriate, health, vision, hearing, social and emotional status, general intelligence, academic performance, communicative status, and motor abilities. (20 U.S.C. 1412[5]0)

The U.S. Department of Education reports that parents lodge more official complaints about placement than any other area. Many of these complaints are related to the evaluation procedures used in decision making. Of particular concern to physical educators is the general lack of physical education tests validated for the specific purpose of placement.

Funding of Adapted Physical Education

Whether a school district initiates and maintains a high-quality adapted physical education program is often dependent upon funding. Therefore, physical educators must understand methods of public school funding and problems involved in the equalization of educational opportunity for all children.

The cost of educating students with disabilities is about 2.3 times more than that of educating the nondisabled. In recognition of this fact, IDEA-Part B provides that federal grants be awarded to state education agencies (SEAs). These federal monies must be spent only for the *excess cost* of special education (including adapted physical education) over the average per-pupil expenditure in regular education. These are called flow-through monies because the SEA keeps about 25% of them and distributes the other 75% to local education agencies (LEAs).

Adapted physical educators employed to serve only students with disabilities are often salaried by IDEA-Part B flow-through monies. There are, however, many other ways of funding adapted physical educators. A philosophically sound approach is for regular education to contribute toward the salary of adapted physical educators the monies that would be spent on regular physical education if the student had not been placed in a separate setting. Then, special education monies are applied only toward the excess cost.

Regardless of where the monies come from, if adapted physical education is written into the student's IEP, the school administration must find a way of providing the needed services. The law is clear that related service (physical and occupational therapy) cannot substitute for physical education instruction. *The regular physical educator is responsible for teaching students with disabilities if no adapted physical education specialist is available.* This explains why so many regular physical educators are undertaking graduate work in adapted physical education; they might not wish to become specialists, but they do graduate work because they need additional knowledge to fulfill the expectations of their school systems.

The State Plan and Adapted Physical Education

IDEA requires every SEA to develop a *state plan* that describes specifically how IDEA will be implemented in that state. This state plan is then submitted to the U.S. Department of Education every 3 years; this official document enables the state government to receive federal funds to supplement the cost of quality education for students with disabilities.

Ideally, the state plan should include all of the mentions of physical education that appear in IDEA regulations. If, however, SEA personnel are not knowledgeable and/or supportive of physical education, they may neglect writing out procedures for implementing physical education mandates. If the state plan does not include these procedures, then IDEA cannot be enforced in regard to physical education. It is, therefore, imperative that university classes teach physical educators about the state plan and that a copy of it be available for study. A copy can be obtained from a local special education administrator or by writing the state education agency.

Before a state plan is filed with the federal government, it must be made available to all interested persons, and public hearings must be held to allow individuals and special interest groups to offer input. Input may involve agreement or disagreement with changes or the pointing out of inconsistencies between the state plan and IDEA. The dates of these public hearings, by law, are announced in newspapers of the large cities in which they are held. The SEA decides which cities these shall be, but everyone is free to attend and speak. In addition to attending public hearings, physical educators and parents should submit written testimony to the SEA concerning the state plan. Deadlines for receiving these letters are also published.

The process for becoming involved in the state plan is outlined in Figure 4.10. It is appropriate for university classes to attend public hearings and write individual letters. Ideally, physical educators take parents of children with disabilities to these hearings to speak in favor of physical education mandates and the values their children have derived from physical education instruction. Only by caring and acting at the state level can IDEA be translated into action.

Need for State Laws

IDEA forms the legal basis for adapted physical education only for students declared disabled by IEP eligibility procedures. Many, many other students have psychomotor problems serious enough to merit adapted physical education intervention. Federal law cannot be passed to improve the general education system for nondisabled students since education is not a power given to the U.S. government by the Constitution.

The only way to ensure high-quality physical education, including adapted physical education when needed, for all students is through state legislation. Many states have or are working on legislation that parallels IDEA. Physical educators should work actively with state legislators to ensure that the physical education passages in IDEA are included and expanded to encompass nondisabled students in state law.

Advocacy for Needed Legislation

This chapter has emphasized the importance of federal and state laws in shaping adapted physical education. These laws are not static because implementation depends on funding, which may change annually. New laws are needed year by year to actually appropriate the money for use.

The following is a list of strategies that physical educators can use in advocating for needed legislation:

1. Get to know your state and federal legislators. Let them know you vote for them specifically because they support legislation favorable to education and/or equal opportunity for persons with disabilities.

2. Visit your legislator in his or her office in the Capitol. Get to know the legislator's staff by name and personality; usually, they are the ones responsible for compiling materials, reading and answering letters sent to the legislator, and keeping him or her informed.

3. Make frequent contacts with legislators. The best communication is face-to-face, but telephone calls, telegrams, and letters are crucial when bills are ready for a vote.

FIGURE 4.10

The legislative process for influencing the rules and regulations of the state plan. This series of steps occurs once every 3 years. The resulting 3-year plan governs all aspects of state education agency (SEA) and local education agency (LEA) compliance with the Individuals with Disabilities Education Act.

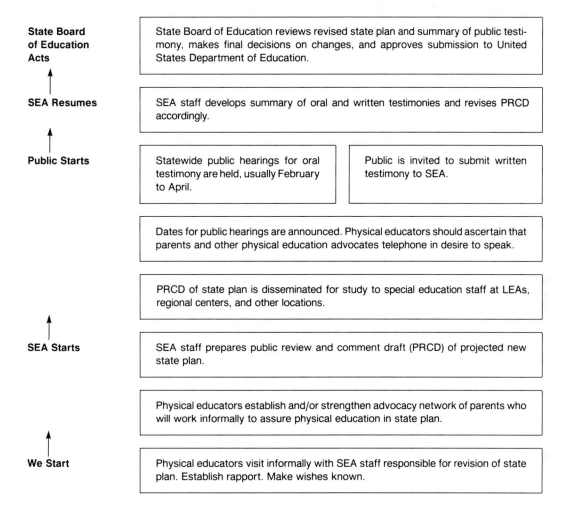

State Board of Education Acts — State Board of Education reviews revised state plan and summary of public testimony, makes final decisions on changes, and approves submission to United States Department of Education.

SEA Resumes — SEA staff develops summary of oral and written testimonies and revises PRCD accordingly.

Public Starts — Statewide public hearings for oral testimony are held, usually February to April.

Public is invited to submit written testimony to SEA.

Dates for public hearings are announced. Physical educators should ascertain that parents and other physical education advocates telephone in desire to speak.

PRCD of state plan is disseminated for study to special education staff at LEAs, regional centers, and other locations.

SEA Starts — SEA staff prepares public review and comment draft (PRCD) of projected new state plan.

Physical educators establish and/or strengthen advocacy network of parents who will work informally to assure physical education in state plan.

We Start — Physical educators visit informally with SEA staff responsible for revision of state plan. Establish rapport. Make wishes known.

4. Do not mail form letters; make contents brief and personal. Be sure to mention the law by name and number and state specifically which passage you wish to retain or change.

5. Develop parent advocacy corps for physical education. Take different kinds of stationery to Special Olympics and other sport practices and ask parents who are waiting to jot letters to their legislators. Offer to speak at meetings of parent groups, inform them about IDEA, and ask them to visit, telephone, and write legislators specifically on behalf of physical education.

6. Become a member of parent and other advocacy groups for persons with disabilities and encourage them to invite legislators to speak at their meetings. Volunteering to be program chairperson will guarantee that the invitations are extended. Legislators, as well as candidates running for office, are particularly willing to speak during election years.

7. Become personal friends with people who are disabled and encourage them to advocate for physical education.

8. When you write to a legislator, be sure to ask for an answer in which he or she states intent to support or not to support your request. When you speak to a legislator, do the same.

9. Invite legislators, with the approval of your administration, to visit your adapted physical education program and/or to be a dignitary in the opening or closing ceremonies of Special Olympics, Cerebral Palsy Sports, or other events.

10. Keep abreast of funding issues, especially which parties and which persons support federal and state funding favorable to education. Find out how your legislator votes on critical issues by reading newspapers or the *Congressional Record* or by telephoning his or her office. Let your legislator know when you approve, as well as when you disapprove.

11. Get to know the state directors of physical education and special education and their staff, all of whom are part of the SEA, and encourage them to communicate with legislators.

12. Be sure local and state meetings of physical educators include legislative updates concerning action that may affect adapted physical education. Exhibit bulletin boards showing progress made in implementation of laws. Encourage officers of local and state physical education organizations, as well as members, to maintain close contact with their legislators.

References

American Alliance for Health, Physical Education, Recreation, and Dance. (1980). *Shaping the body politic: Legislative training for the physical educator.* Reston, VA: Author.

Appenzeller, H. (1983). *The right to participate: The law and individuals with handicapping conditions in physical education and sports.* Charlottesville, VA: The Michie Co.

Block, M. E., & Krebs, P. L. (1992). An alternative to least restrictive environments: A continuum of support to regular physical education. *Adapted Physical Activity Quarterly, 9* (2), 97–113.

Churton, M. (1987). Impact of the Education of the Handicapped Act on adapted physical education: A 10–year overview. *Adapted Physical Activity Quarterly, 4*(1), 1–8.

Deno, E. (1970). Special education as developmental capital. *Exceptional Children, 37* (3), 229–237.

Federal Register, May 4, 1977, PL 93–112, the Rehabilitation Act of 1973, Section 504.

Federal Register, August 23, 1977, PL 94–142, the Education for All Handicapped Children Act.

Federal Register, June 22, 1989, PL 99–457, the Education of the Handicapped Act.

Kennedy, S. O., French, R., & Henderson, H. L. (1989). The due-able process could happen to you! Physical educators, handicapped students, and the law. *Journal of Physical Education, Recreation, and Dance, 60* (8), 86–93.

Loovis, E. M. (1986). Placement of handicapped students: The perpetual dilemma. *Adapted Physical Activity Quarterly, 3* (3), 193–198.

Minner, S., Prater, G., & Beane, A. (1984). Provision of adapted physical education: A dilemma for special educators. *Adapted Physical Activity Quarterly, 1* (4), 282–286.

Sherrill, C., & Hillman, W. (1988). Legislation, funding, and adapted physical education teacher training. In C. Sherrill (Ed.), *Leadership training in adapted physical education* (pp. 85–103). Champaign, IL: Human Kinetics.

Turnbull, H. R. (1976). Accountability: An overview of the impact of litigation on professionals. In F. J. Weintraub, A. Abeson, J. Ballard, & M. LaVor (Eds.), *Public policy and the education of exceptional children* (pp. 362–368). Reston, VA: Council for Exceptional Children.

Turnbull, H. R. (1990). *Free appropriate public education: Law and the education of children with disabilities.* Denver, CO: Love Publishing.

U.S. Department of Education. (1989). *To assure the free appropriate public education of all handicapped children: Annual report to Congress on the implementation of the Education of the Handicapped Act.* Washington, DC: Author.

Weintraub, F. J., Abeson, A., Ballard, J., & LaVor, M. (1976). *Public policy and the education of exceptional children.* Reston, VA: Council for Exceptional Children.

CHAPTER
5

Goal Setting and Age-Appropriate Programming

FIGURE 5.1

The Individuals with Disabilities Education Act of 1990 mandates services from birth to age 21. The Americans with Disabilities Act of 1990 emphasizes lifespan programming.

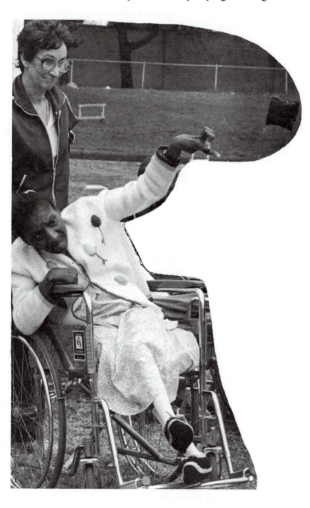

After you have studied this chapter, you should be able to:

1. Differentiate between goals and objectives and show competence in writing each. State criteria for evaluating an objective.

2. Discuss three domains and nine goal areas that are relevant to assessment and programming. Describe ways to prioritize goals.

3. Compare functional and developmental approaches to programming and discuss the merits of an interactionist approach.

4. Discuss lifespan perspectives and the implications of various life stages for programming.

5. Discuss observational assessment in natural settings as a guide to programming. Describe a model that helps structure observations.

6. Identify four channels of development and state behaviors to look for in each. Explain why and how cognition is important in teaching motor skills, games, and sports.

7. Identify Piaget's four stages of cognitive development, the ages associated with each, and the implications for programming adapted physical activity.

8. Identify stages and levels in rules understanding and conformity. Discuss how disability and moral development interact to affect game and sport behaviors.

9. Explain levels of social play used in adapted physical activity assessment and programming. Explain the relationship between competition and social comparison and use it to justify the age at which children should start team sport competition.

10. Discuss levels of motor development and how they relate to cognitive, moral, and social development. Document practice in using the assessment and programming model and the summary observation form.

Goals determine the outcome of teaching. They direct assessment, the writing of IEPs, and the planning of service delivery. Therefore, this chapter begins with a discussion of goals. After consideration of goals, teachers must decide whether a functional, developmental, or interactional frame of reference guides their decision making, so this chapter also explains these perspectives. Chapter focus then shifts to age-appropriate programming as the basis for implementing the normalization principle (see Figure 5.1).

Utilizing Goals in Adapted Physical Activity

Goals are guides to action that include intention, purpose, and meaning (Davis, 1989). Usually, goals are expressed as broad, global statements in relation to a specific action like observation, teaching, or performance. For example, when you observe a group of students, your goals determine what you look for and what you see. When you teach, your goals determine what you say and do. When you perform a motor skill or pattern, the goal determines product or outcome. When you write a term paper or an individualized education program (IEP), goals determine the content.

Goals guide programs as well as individuals. Consider, for instance, the following statement:

Goals derive from beliefs. Goals are broad statements of intent that describe the kinds of outcomes that a program strives to achieve. . . . The physical educator must carefully consider four important issues when attempting to develop goals for a physical education program: (1) an emphasis on outcomes; (2) commitments to both equity and quality; (3) doing a few things well; and (4) socializing students into the role of participant. (Siedentop, Mand, & Taggart, 1986, p. 132)

Typically, curriculum committees are established at the district or school level to develop and/or revise goals that are common to everyone involved in the educational process. Some states have set forth goals or common elements that all curricula must target. Teachers work within this general goal framework when they assess and establish goals for classes and individuals. Clearly, goals are the essence of planning.

Planning is the first step in service delivery; thus, goals are the first concern of professionals. There are two types of planning: (a) program, referring to decision making about community-school-home relationships, and (b) instructional, referring to decisions made about one class or individual. This chapter focuses on instructional planning.

Model to Guide Instructional Planning

Figure 5.2 presents a model to guide instructional planning. At the top of the model are reminders that educators must plan (a) *who* to teach, (b) *what* behaviors and environmental variables are targeted for change, and (c) *how* to facilitate changes. The center portion of the model highlights three behavioral domains and specifies goal areas for each. The intent is to show that physical education can address many goals.

This model guides decision making about assessment. It helps professionals to determine what to look for during observational assessment and what instruments to administer to describe present level of performance in the IEP.

Since the content of physical education is movement, the nine goal areas in Figure 5.2 all pertain to movement. Affective domain goals emphasize the beliefs, attitudes,

FIGURE 5.2

Instructional model for adapted physical activity.

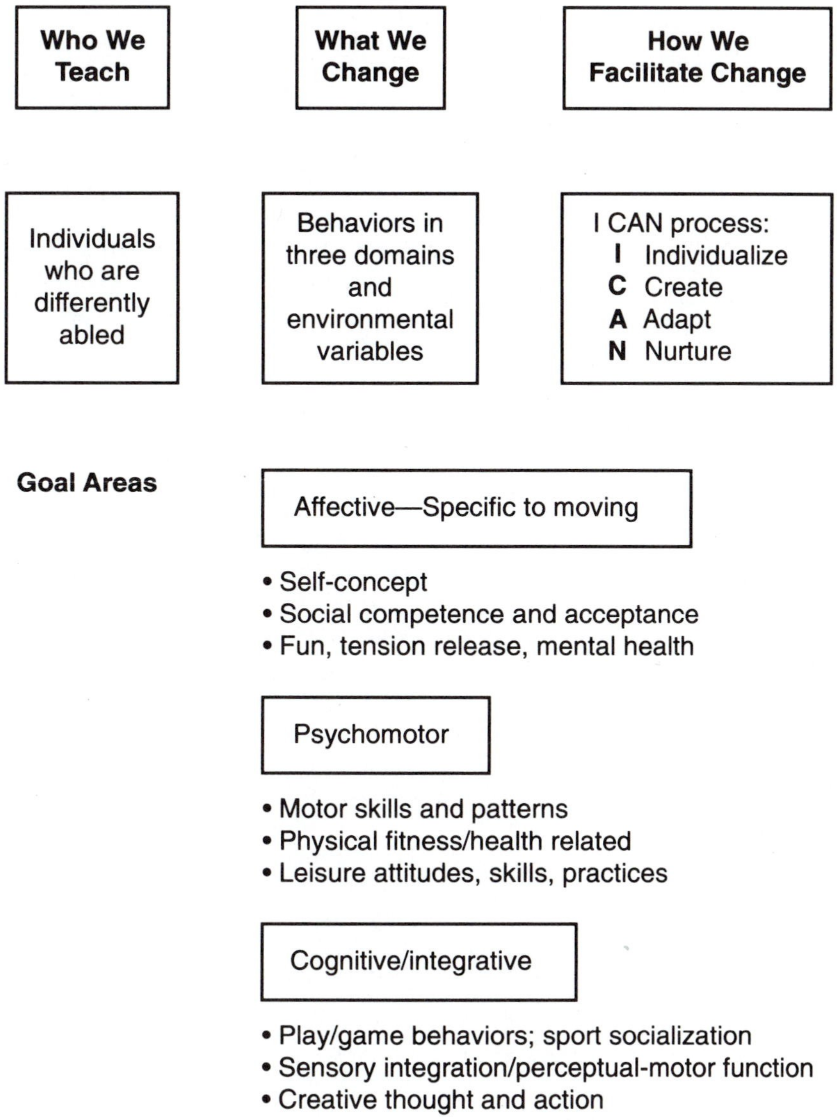

Who We Teach	What We Change	How We Facilitate Change
Individuals who are differently abled	Behaviors in three domains and environmental variables	I CAN process: **I** Individualize **C** Create **A** Adapt **N** Nurture

Goal Areas

Affective—Specific to moving

- Self-concept
- Social competence and acceptance
- Fun, tension release, mental health

Psychomotor

- Motor skills and patterns
- Physical fitness/health related
- Leisure attitudes, skills, practices

Cognitive/integrative

- Play/game behaviors; sport socialization
- Sensory integration/perceptual-motor function
- Creative thought and action

and intentions associated with a healthy, active lifestyle. Psychomotor domain goals emphasize basic skills and fitness and the generalization of these abilities to leisure functioning. Cognitive domain goals are consistent with cognitive psychology constructs that indicate that cognition integrates the various kinds of learning into usable *functions* (to play a game), *abilities* (to balance well enough to perform activities of daily living (ADL) or sports), or *processes* (creating or problem solving).

Your beliefs about the teaching-learning process determine which two or three of these goals are the most important. The student's level of function, age, environmental constraints, and affordances also have an impact on decision making.

Some persons believe that low self-concept about the body and its capacity for movement limit ability to learn motor skills and develop fitness. These persons typically prioritize self-concept as the most important goal because they view it as an antecedent of effective learning. This prioritization means that they will alter environmental variables so as to control what people say and do to the learner. Particular attention also will be given to eliminating physical barriers to success and planning order of difficulty in which learning tasks are presented.

Other persons believe that inappropriate behaviors, such as aggression, hyperactivity, or lack of responsiveness, as in depression or cognitive delays, are the major problems that prevent effective learning of motor skills. These persons would probably prioritize social competence and acceptance as the most important goal.

In summary, what you believe influences what you decide to assess. You need to remain open to individual differences and to keep assessment broad enough to identify all the areas that impact on healthy, active lifestyle.

The short time allocated to physical education instruction allows systematic work on only three or four goals. In addition to considerations already discussed, other questions requiring attention are

1. Should all goals be in areas of weakness, or should goals be divided among strengths and weaknesses? Should you emphasize doing a few things well or attaining minimal competence in a number of things?

2. What is the minimal level of motor skill proficiency that should be attained before skills are linked together into games and related to leisure function? How much time should be spent on practice of skills in a nongame context?

3. How can you teach for active, healthy lifestyle? Proportionately, how much attention should be given to beliefs, attitudes, intentions, skills, and fitness? How much should families and communities be involved? How are persons socialized into sport and/or active lifestyle?

4. Should goals be directed toward motor *skills,* such as running, jumping, and throwing, or toward perceptual-motor *abilities,* such as balance, coordination, and motor planning, that underlie skills?

Three Aspects of a Goal

Goals include three aspects: intention, purpose, and meaning (Davis, 1989). *Intention* refers to aim with respect to some life function. *Purpose* refers to making a behavior (belief, attitude, or skill) functional (i.e., achieving enough proficiency or competence that it enhances function). *Meaning* refers to the link between the behavior and the function as perceived by the learner; this is the significance of the task or the motivation that drives action.

Intentions vary, depending on focus (lifespan or lesson) and timeline (lifespan or present). For example, intention may be to demonstrate (a) healthy, active lifestyle, (b) functional competence in a game or sport, or (c) functional competence in an activity of daily living (ADL), such as running to catch a bus, leaping to cross a mud puddle, or balancing to avoid a fall. Often, professionals think only of purpose when writing goals and forget that be-

haviors must enable functions in order to be relevant. To check that students grasp the meaning of a task, you need to frequently ask, "Why are we practicing this?"

Prioritizing Goals

Figure 5.3 depicts three students. Child A in Figure 5.3A is age 6, is partially sighted, has minor learning problems, expresses lots of fear about new experiences, and is an only child of parents who tend to be overprotective. Child B in Figure 5.3B is age 10, has three brothers and athletic parents, has been adopted as mascot of the local wheelchair basketball team, talks about basketball all the time, but refuses to try other sports and to recreate with able-bodied peers. Child C in Figure 5.3C is age 9, has severe mental retardation, does not play spontaneously, has a mild congenital heart defect, and lives with a mother and older sister who are not athletic.

Which of the nine goal areas in Figure 5.2 would you plan to assess for each? Hypothesize some assessment data for each and, based on these data, select four goals for each child.

This process is fun and probably relatively easy. In real life, however, decisions about goals are made in IEP meetings, where parents, other teachers, and sometimes the child cooperatively determine goals. Sometimes, there is agreement, but often, goals differ. When this is the case, a goals prioritization instrument can guide discussion and resolve conflict. The Goals of Adapted Physical Education Scale (GAPES) in Table 5.1 is such an instrument, with confirmed validity and reliability (Sherrill & Montelione, 1990).

Administer GAPES to yourself and some friends. Think either of students in general or a specific student, such as Child A, B, or C in Figure 5.3. Read the definitions of each goal carefully before you check which of each pair of goals you prefer. The technique used in this instrument is *paired-comparison.* Every goal has been paired against each of the other eight goals in round-robin tournament fashion. The result is 36 pairs. In each pair, you check the goal you consider most important.

When done, count and make sure you have 36 checks. Then use the definition section of Table 5.1 as your tabulation sheet. Place a tally mark in front of the goal definition for each time you have checked it as a preferred goal in the list of 36 pairs. The highest number of tallies a goal can receive is 8; the lowest number is 0.

When tallying is completed, identify the three or four goals most important to you. There is not enough time in adapted physical education to work equally on all goals. This process enables you to prioritize use of instructional time.

FIGURE   5.3

Three students with distinctly different needs. Which goals would you set for each?

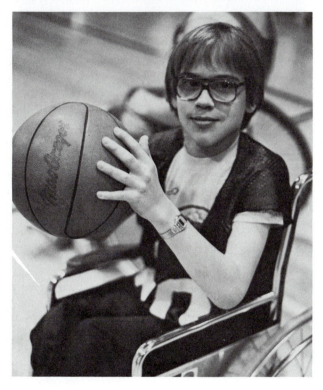

Table 5.1
Long-range goals of adapted physical education scale (GAPES), a paired-comparison ranking.

Let us assume that the *purpose* of adapted physical education is to change psychomotor behaviors (i.e., to remediate or ameliorate specific problems that interfere with success and/or optimal functioning in the regular physical education setting as well as in the home and community). What, then, are our long-range goals that guide program planning? What are our priorities?

The following goals of adapted/developmental physical education are representative of those accepted by educators, parents, and students. On the next page, you are asked to rank these goals, using the definitions that follow. Please read these definitions carefully before beginning the ranking. *Note that all of these goals are to be achieved through movement.*

A. *Positive Self-Concept.* To develop a positive self-concept and body image through activity involvement; to increase understanding and appreciation of the body and its capacity for movement; to accept limitations that cannot be changed; to learn to adapt environment so as to make the most of strengths (i.e., to work toward self-actualization).

B. *Fun/Tension Release.* To have fun, recreation, happiness; to release tensions in a healthy, socially acceptable manner; to reduce hyperactivity and learn to relax; to improve mental health and attitude toward exercise and/ or physical education.

C. *Creative Expression.* To increase creativity in movement and thought; when posed a movement problem, to generate *many* responses, *different* responses, *original* responses; to learn to imagine, to embellish and add on; to risk experimentation; to devise appropriate game strategy; to create new games, dances, and movement sequences.

D. *Motor Skills and Patterns.* To learn fundamental motor skills and patterns; to master the motor skills indigenous to games, sports, dance, and aquatics participation; to improve fine and gross motor coordination for self-care, school, work, and play activities.

E. *Play and Game Skills.* To learn to play (i.e., to progress through developmental play stages from solitary and parallel play behaviors up through appropriate cooperative and competitive game behaviors; to promote contact and interaction behaviors with toys, play apparatus, and persons; to learn basic game formations and mental operations needed for play; to master rules and strategies of simple games.

F. *Physical Fitness.* To develop the cardiovascular system; to promote ideal weight; to increase muscular strength, endurance, and flexibility; to improve postures.

G. *Social Competency.* To learn appropriate social behaviors (i.e., how to interact with others—sharing, taking turns, following, and leading); to reduce social isolation; to learn how to develop and maintain friendships; to demonstrate good sportsmanship and self-discipline in winning and losing; to develop other skills necessary for acceptance by peers in the mainstream.

H. *Leisure-Time Skills.* To learn to transfer physical education learnings into habits of lifetime sports, dance, and aquatics; to become acquainted with community resources for recreation; to expand repertoire of individual and group games and sports, dance, and aquatic activities and/or to refine skills.

I. *Perceptual-Motor Function and Sensory Integration.* To enhance visual, auditory, tactile, vestibular, and kinesthetic functioning; to reinforce academic learnings through games and perceptual-motor activities; to improve cognitive, language, and motor function through increased sensory integration.

GAPES: A Paired-Comparison Ranking

Choose between two adapted physical education goals. Of each pair presented, check the goal you see as more important for adapted physical education to achieve. This choice is meant to reflect your opinion of adapted physical education in general and not that of any specific institution. Do not omit any!

Pair		Choices	
1	—Leisure-time skills	or	—Motor skills and patterns
2	—Play and game skills	or	—Creative expression
3	—Leisure-time skills	or	—Creative expression
4	—Positive self-concept	or	—Leisure-time skills
5	—Social competency	or	—Motor skills and patterns
6	—Social competency	or	—Positive self-concept
7	—Fun/tension release	or	—Social competency
8	—Perceptual-motor function and sensory integration	or	—Creative expression
9	—Physical fitness	or	—Fun/tension release
10	—Physical fitness	or	—Play and game skills
11	—Play and game skills	or	—Leisure-time skills
12	—Motor skills and patterns	or	—Play and game skills
13	—Social competency	or	—Play and game skills
14	—Fun/tension release	or	—Creative expression
15	—Play and game skills	or	—Perceptual-motor function and sensory integration
16	—Positive self-concept	or	—Fun/tension release
17	—Play and game skills	or	—Fun/tension release
18	—Physical fitness	or	—Leisure-time skills
19	—Positive self-concept	or	—Physical fitness
20	—Leisure-time skills	or	—Perceptual-motor function and sensory integration
21	—Social competency	or	—Physical fitness
22	—Social competency	or	—Creative expression
23	—Motor skills and patterns	or	—Positive self-concept
24	—Social competency	or	—Leisure-time skills
25	—Motor skills and patterns	or	—Physical fitness
26	—Motor skills and patterns	or	—Fun/tension release
27	—Perceptual-motor function and sensory integration	or	—Physical fitness
28	—Creative expression	or	—Physical fitness
29	—Perceptual-motor function and sensory integration	or	—Motor skills and patterns
30	—Fun/tension release	or	—Leisure-time skills
31	—Creative expression	or	—Positive self-concept
32	—Motor skills and patterns	or	—Creative expression
33	—Play and game skills	or	—Positive self-concept
34	—Social competency	or	—Perceptual-motor function and sensory integration
35	—Perceptual-motor function and sensory integration	or	—Positive self-concept
36	—Fun/tension release	or	—Perceptual-motor function and sensory integration

Table 5.2
Illustrative objectives for selected goals as they might appear in a curriculum guide or an IEP.

Goal	Objectives
A. *To Demonstrate Positive Self-Concept in Relation to Fitness, Motor, and Leisure Performance*	1. To improve score on selected domains of a standardized self-concept test by a set amount 2. To demonstrate understanding and appreciation of self by stating accurately one's personal best time, distance, or score on selected tasks like mile run, 50-yd dash, overarm throw 3. To demonstrate belief in ability to improve through hard work by stating high (but realistic) levels of aspiration on selected tasks 4. To demonstrate pride by describing daily practice and/or workout sessions 5. To demonstrate commitment to change by showing chart kept over several weeks and/or diary that describes time spent in exercise, games, sports, and dance and/or a diet plan

B. *To Demonstrate Functional Competence in Selected Play and Game Behaviors*	1. To progress from the parallel play to the interactive play stage by showing five characteristics of interactive play
	2. To participate successfully in five selected games by
	  a. Remaining on task for the entire game without verbal prompting from teacher or peers
	  b. Following all rules without prompts
	  c. Not being tagged, made "it," or sent to prison more often than other players
	3. To demonstrate ability to get into the following formations with nine other students within a count of 10 sec: single circle, file, line, double circle
	4. To demonstrate appropriate use of the following play objects and apparatus by playing for 3 min in response to "Show me how you play with this:" ball, racket, tricycle, stall bars, balance beam, minitrampoline

C. *To Demonstrate Functional Competence in Selected Motor Skills and Patterns*	1. To perform three of four components of a mature run, throw, and jump 2. To increase overarm throw distance by 10 ft 3. To decrease 50-m dash speed by .50 sec 4. To demonstrate the first five steps or focal points in a task analysis or learning progression

D. *To Demonstrate Functional Social Competence in Physical Education Setting*	1. To demonstrate at least three kinds of positive interacting behaviors during every 20-min class
	  a. Initiating conversation
	  b. Answering questions
	  c. Asking questions
	  d. Offering assistance
	  e. Asking for assistance
	  f. Congratulating or praising another
	2. To cope with losing games or failing to achieve desired motor or fitness goal by not crying, pouting, whining, or similar behavior for 3 consecutive days
	3. To lead group in warm-up or follow-the-leader game, speaking loudly enough to be heard
	4. To decrease number of behavior problems exhibited during a 20-min class

Note. "To demonstrate functional competence" means to perform within an average range for one's age and gender.

FIGURE   5.4

Checklist for evaluating objectives that you write for class practice.

CHECKLIST FOR EVALUATING OBJECTIVES				
	Objectives			
Criteria	1	2	3	4
1. Describes learner behavior, not teacher behavior				
2. Describes product, not process (i.e., the terminal behavior, not the learning activity)				
3. Includes a verb that specifies a definite, observable behavior				
4. Contains a single learning outcome, not several				
5. Contains three parts: condition, observable behavior, and criterion level				
6. Matches assessment data to specified behavior				
7. Focuses on functions that are usable and relevant in everyday life				
8. Selects product that is achievable through 4 to 5 hours of instruction and practice				

Writing Objectives

Table 5.2 offers examples of goals and objectives. Whereas goals are long range (annual, semiannual, or quarterly), objectives are short term, usually defined as requiring 4 to 5 hr for achievement. *Objectives,* which result from breaking goals down into measurable, observable tasks, are statements that contain three parts: (a) conditions; (b) one specific, observable behavior; and (c) a criterion level for success.

Conditions are missing from the objectives in Table 5.2, so examples of how the environmental conditions for testing might be described follow:

For Objective A1: Given the Harter Self-Perception Scale in accordance with instructions in the manual,

For Objective A4: Given a notebook to use as an activity journal, daily reminders to write in the journal, and a deadline for submitting it,

For Objective B1: Given 5 min in a 10-ft-by-10-ft room with five pieces of play apparatus (tricycle, wagon, long rope, life-size rag doll, cloth tunnel) in designated places and three children (A, B, and C) present,

For Objective C2: Given a regulation softball, a wall target (60 by 40 inches in size) set at a designated distance and height, the command, "Throw as hard as you can," and three trials,

The one specific observable behavior in an objective is denoted by an action verb (e.g., *demonstrate, show, participate, run, score, perform*). This verb states what the student should be able to do at the end of the instructional unit. The criterion level for success is a statement of something specific, such as distance thrown, score made, or number of components passed. In Table 5.2, find the criterion level in each objective and underline it. Is criterion level missing from any objective?

Now that you can identify the parts of an objective, select some of the goals you wrote for the children in Figure 5.3 and break them into objectives. Use the format in Table 5.2 so that the relationship of objectives to goals is clear. State whether the objectives are for Child A, B, or C. Figure 5.4 presents a checklist of criteria to determine whether or not your objectives are correctly written.

Writing goals and objectives correctly is important in the development of an IEP. Remember the six parts of an IEP:

P—Performance, present level

A—Annual goals, including short-term objectives

S—Services to be provided

T—Transition services

D—Dates and duration

E—Evaluation to determine whether objectives are achieved

Writing goals and objectives begins with assessment of present level of performance. Also important in writing IEPs and individualizing service delivery are frames of reference.

Frames of Reference

A *frame of reference* is an approach to education or treatment that is based on your philosophy and theoretical knowledge base (Hopkins, 1988; Mosey, 1986). Synonyms for frame of reference are *approach, perspective,* and *value orientation.* This section highlights three frames of reference: (a) functional, (b) developmental, and (c) interactional. Each represents a different body of knowledge. While a delivery system could be based on one perspective, good professionals utilize information from each frame of reference to individualize and adapt instruction.

Professionals must have a good understanding of both function and development. *Function,* derived from the Latin *functio* (meaning "activity," "performance"), refers to the acts, tasks, or activities that a person can perform. *Development,* derived from the French *desveloper* (meaning "to unwrap"), refers to changes that occur throughout the lifespan (i.e., the unwrapping or evolving of the human being).

Functional Frame of Reference

The functional frame of reference focuses on the functions needed for success in a specific job or activity. Assessment determines whether or not the person can perform these functions. Then education and treatment are directed toward mastery of task or activity components that comprise the function.

The pedagogy used is typically *behavior management* (i.e., a precisely planned, systematic application of cues and consequences to guide the student through a series of tasks or activities that are ordered from easy to hard). Behavior management begins with analysis of an age-appropriate function. This may be either an ecological task analysis like that discussed in Chapter 3 or a traditional analysis that breaks a task into smaller, teachable steps (see Table 5.3). Next, the teacher determines the cues and consequences to be used. A *cue* is a command or instruction telling the student what to do. A *consequence* is immediate feedback designed to either increase or decrease a behavior.

For example, in teaching a target throw, using the functional approach and behavior management, the teacher models (demonstrates) the task and gives a simple cue like, "Jim, pick up the ball." If the student imitates correctly, the consequence is an immediate reward (i.e., verbal praise, "Good boy!" or a reinforcer known to be especially effective with that student). If the student does not make the desired response within 5 sec, a correction procedure is initiated (e.g., "No, watch me pick up the ball. I pick up the ball with my fingers. Jim, pick up the ball"). Learning is primarily by repetition. These same cues and corrective strategies are used until the student is successful in a set number of trials. Then, the instruction proceeds to the next task in the easy-to-hard sequence (e.g., "Watch how I face the target. See my forward leg. Jim, face the target with your leg forward.")

In the functional approach, little or no attention is given to the student's chronological age or to whether he or she has progressed through the normal developmental levels or stages associated with the function to be taught. The functional approach, in its pure form, is generally used in adolescent or adult programs that serve individuals with severe disabilities. Underlying the functional frame of reference is the philosophy that tasks, activities, and pedagogy should be age-appropriate.

Table 5.3
Traditional task analysis of target throw for person with severe mental retardation.

Short, Easy Chain	Longer, Harder Chain	Hardest Chain
	10. Praise self; say "Good, I threw the ball."	10. Same
	9. Look where ball goes.	9. Same
	8. Follow through.	8. Same
	7. Release ball.	7. Same
	6. Swing throwing arm forward.	6. Add trunk rotation.
	5. Swing throwing arm backward.	5. Add trunk rotation.
4. Look where ball goes.	4. Assume shoulder-to-target stance.	4. Same
3. Release ball.	3. Look at target.	3. Same
2. Pick up ball.	2. Pick up ball.	2. Same
1. Look at ball.	1. Look at ball.	1. Same

Note. Steps are taught separately and linked together by forward or backward chaining.

Developmental Frame of Reference

The developmental frame of reference focuses on the abilities and skills that society expects individuals to have at certain chronological ages. This approach has its roots in the traditional body of knowledge taught in such courses as developmental psychology, human development, and motor development (Illingworth, 1983; Payne & Isaacs, 1991; Salkind, 1985). In this approach, standardized assessment instruments with norms are used to determine whether or not a person is performing at or near the level of others the same age. Then, education and treatment are directed toward learning age-related skills, knowledge, and strategies. Any pedagogy, including behavior management, may be used. The same developmental sequence is followed, however, for all students, with the entry level into the sequence individualized. A *developmental sequence* is a list of tasks or activities in which items are ordered according to the mean chronological age that each is achieved by normal infants and children (see Table 5.4).

Central to developmental theory is the assumption that learning proceeds in a spiral, upward direction, with performance at each level dependent on knowledge and skill acquired at earlier levels. For example, persons are taught a long jump only after they have mastered jumping down from a 1-ft height and demonstrated that they can perform stand-to-squat and squat-to-stand position changes without losing balance. This is because these tasks are developmentally easier than the long jump. Likewise, persons are taught tosses at floor targets before wall targets because downward tosses,

Table 5.4
Developmental sequence for teaching/testing throwing.

Task	Criterion to Pass	Average Age (in Months)
1. First voluntary grasp	Grasps objects, holds 5 sec	4–5
2. First voluntary release	Releases object on command	10–11
3. Throw (hurl) playground ball	Travels 5 ft forward	24–29
4. Throw (hurl) tennis ball	Travels 7 ft forward	24–29
5. Throw tennis ball	Shows trunk rotation, follow-through; ball travels 10 ft	42–47
6. Use underarm toss to hit wall target from 5 ft	Hits target two of three trials with tennis ball	42–47

Note. Distance objectives (i.e., "Throw hard!") are worked on before accuracy objectives.

aided by gravity, require less strength and thus are developmentally easier than horizontal tosses.

The developmental frame of reference is particularly applicable to infants, toddlers, and young children. A knowledge of the developmental milestones normally achieved at each age enables professionals to plan and deliver appropriate assessment, teaching, and evaluation services.

Interactional Frame of Reference

During the school years (i.e., from birth until age 21, according to federal law), development and function are inseparable. This is because regular education is organized by grades, with each grade level representing a mixture of chronological age and function. Although some special education students are placed in nongraded, self-contained classrooms that serve several age groups, development remains an important consideration. The goal is to move as many special education children into integrated settings as possible. To do this, the teacher must be ever mindful of whether students are functioning at levels comparable to regular education students of more or less the same age. Adherence to the principle of normalization also requires that teachers know what is normal or average for chronological age groups. Students must be afforded the same opportunities to learn, develop, and function as others within the same life stage.

Thus, development and function are two sides of the same coin. Development is a vertical or longitudinal perspective. The developmental frame of reference focuses on how far up the age-related continuum of motor skills a person can progress. In contrast, function is a horizontal perspective. The functional frame of reference focuses on environmental demands and the functions required to perform at adequate levels. Good teachers move back and forth between

these two frames of reference, utilizing both in their daily service delivery. *The combination of these two approaches is an interactional or individual differences perspective.*

Age and Disability

The age at which a disability occurs affects programming. Age at onset of problem or condition is therefore always included in educational and medical records. The broadest classifications in this regard are *congenital* (born with) and *acquired* or *adventitious* (occurring after birth). Life stages, however, are a more precise approach to describing development and planning service delivery.

Life Stages

Seven life stages provide the structure for studying the changes that occur in human beings. Some of these are depicted in Figure 5.5.

1. **Embryo** (from the second to the end of the eighth week after conception). This is the stage during which all body parts and internal organs are formed.

2. **Fetus** (from the beginning of the ninth week after conception to birth). This is the stage during which body structures begin to function. Of primary importance is the evolution of nervous system function and the process of *myelination*. Myelin is the fatlike protein and lipid substance that forms the covering of axons (nerve fibers) and enables them to transmit impulses. The formation of myelin (myelination) begins in the spinal cord during midfetal life (about the 16th week after conception) and continues until nerve fibers are covered in all parts of the central nervous system at about 30 years of life. Perception, cognition, and action (all of life's functions) are dependent upon myelination.

3. **Early childhood** (0 to 5 years). This stage is broken down into infants and toddlers (0 to 2 years) and preschoolers (3 to 5 years). From a movement perspective, the most important developmental function is the suppression or integration of primitive reflexes and the emergence of reactions and voluntary movement patterns. *Reflexes* are specific, involuntary, muscle-tone responses to stimuli. Infants are born with about 30 primitive reflexes that are suppressed or integrated according to an inborn biological timetable that is more or less the same for all children. *Reactions* are involuntary postural patterns that enable righting, equilibrium, and protective movements (see Figure 5.5). *Voluntary movements* are the locomotor and nonlocomotor actions that individuals initiate and control of their own volition.

From an overall perspective, cognitive and language development are often considered most important. In the early years, however, movement, cognition, and language training must be integrated for optimal effects.

4. **Middle childhood** (ages 6 to 8 years). This stage typically refers to children in the primary grades (i.e., Grades 1 to 3).

FIGURE 5.5

(*A*) Normal infant at 7 weeks of age exhibits no protective extension of the arms. Many adults with severe cerebral palsy have this same problem. When they fall, the arms do not automatically respond with the parachute reaction. (*B*) Same infant at 16 weeks of age is beginning to show parachute reactions. (*C*) Same infant at 24 weeks of age, showing equilibrium or tilting reactions. These reactions are gradually refined over the next 5 years. Note the compensatory movement and the increased muscle tone on the lowered side.

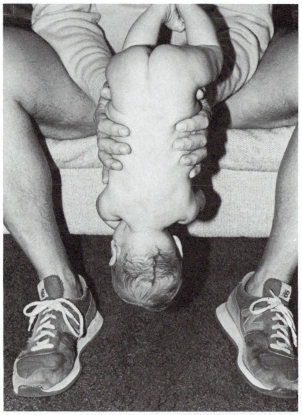

A

B

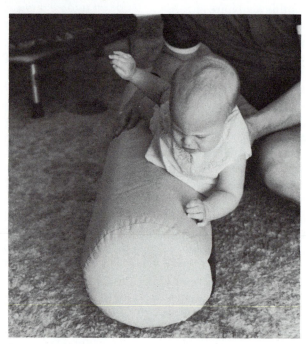

C

5. **Late childhood** (ages 9 to 12 years). This stage typically refers to children in the intermediate grades (i.e., Grades 4 to 6) but may encompass children in middle schools (Grades 6 to 9). Biologically, a person is considered a child until puberty, but sociologically, the terminology changes at about age 12 or 13 to teenager or adolescent.

6. **Adolescence** (age span depends on whether biological or sociological perspective is taken). Biologically, this is the period in life during which persons become functionally capable of reproduction. In temperate climates, this averages at age 12 to 15 in girls and age 13 to 16 in boys. In hot and cold climates, puberty occurs later. Sociologically, adolescence is usually defined as the secondary school years (i.e., Grades 9 to 12, or 10 to 12).

The exact period of adolescence, however, is relative, depending on the time required to make the transition from childhood dependence to adult independence. Wright (1983) states that disability, in many cases, tends to prolong the adolescent period. This extended adolescence is acknowledged by federal legislation that makes available free, appropriate public schooling for persons with disabilities until age 21.

7. **Adulthood.** Biologically, this stage is usually divided into three time periods: early (ages 18 to 35 years), middle (35 to 60 years), and late (60 and up). Like adolescence, adulthood is relative from a psychosocial standpoint. Wright (1983) emphasizes:

When circumstances prolong the period of economic dependence, postpone independent living, or disallow sufficient emotional separation from the parent, the position of the individual as an adult (no matter what his or her age) is apt to be tenuous and, like that of the adolescent, marginal between adulthood and childhood. (p. 252)

Programming for Adults

Although adapted physical activity has typically focused on school-aged persons, the trend is to broaden and consider needs of all ages. Particular attention is given to the *transition* from school to community-based activities and the development of lifetime leisure interests and habits.

Most adults with disabilities live (a) independently, (b) with a spouse or significant other, or (c) in a small-group home with six or more others (generally called clients by the professionals who serve them). Most persons with severe disabilities are eligible for financial assistance and other services, but physical activity and recreation are often forgotten. Persons with disabilities, who are taught to be self-advocates, must learn to advocate for and specifically request help with physical activity and recreation. To achieve this, positive attitudes and habits of daily vigorous activity must be deeply ingrained in children and youth.

Adults with disabilities tend to be underemployed and underpaid. This means they have more free time than peers for physical activity and recreation but less money to spend. This must be kept in mind when programming. Adults should be involved in cooperative assessment of activity needs and interests and subsequent programming. Adapted phys-

ical activity professionals need to acquaint adults with options and resources and to provide encouragement to try new things. Also important is working with the attitudes of people in the community so that they are accepting and helpful.

Transportation is often a concern. Persons who cannot drive may need help with alternative transportation. Fitness and recreational vans can come to homes or neighborhood centers or to community facilities. Adapted physical activity professionals should carry good liability insurance if they do the driving.

Most chapters in this text take a lifespan approach. Space limitations, however, do not permit lengthy discussion. The best way to learn to work with adults is to commit several hours a week to recreating with someone your age or older and/or to affiliate with a group home and offer services. Concerns of adults with disabilities are the same as those of everyone else: sexuality, work satisfaction, decent salary, nice home, friends, and good health. An active lifestyle contributes to each of these.

Age discrimination is as ugly as disability discrimination. In general, sports cannot be categorized as more appropriate for one chronological age group than another. Social interests, fitness, motor skills, and self-esteem are common factors underlying adult activity choices. The principle of normalization should be remembered, with persons given equal opportunities to learn, recreate, and compete.

Observation in Natural Environments

The best way to learn about development and function is to observe persons in natural environments. Identify some physical activity settings in which you can observe and assess individuals of different ages. Your presence will always have some effect on behaviors: Some persons like to be watched and perform at their best in front of an audience; others hate it. Sometimes, it is best to enter into the activity; in such cases, you are called a *participant-observer*.

The best natural environments for observation of adolescents and adults are sport events and activities at recreation and fitness centers. To plan observations, obtain schedules of wheelchair basketball and tennis games, Special Olympics training sessions, and the like.

For children and youth, a room or outdoor area full of apparatus and play equipment makes an excellent initial assessment environment (see Figure 5.6). There should be ladders and ropes to climb, ramps or slides for moving up and down, bars to hang and swing from, balance beams and interesting surfaces to navigate, tunnels, and a variety of movement challenges like swinging bridges, structures that rock, and walls made of tires or heavy cargo nets. The apparatus should provide access for wheelchairs and be appropriate for all kinds of individual differences.

This kind of setting allows observation of whether or not persons know how to play, like to play, or have the language and motor skills to play. Most persons, given this environment, will demonstrate the full repertoire of their locomotor movement patterns. They will run, jump, leap, hop, climb, swing, roll, slide, and the like. Moreover, you can observe the personal meaning of each movement pattern, determine which movements are favorites and why, and develop

FIGURE 5.6

Play apparatus should be used to teach and/or reinforce language concepts. Here, Dr. Ellen Lubin Curtis-Pierce, authority in early childhood adapted physical activity uses the London trestle tree apparatus to teach concepts of *up* and *down*, while simultaneously working on arm and shoulder strength.

a list of movement strengths and weaknesses. To assess object play (including the use of balls, striking implements, targets, and hoops), place additional equipment around the room.

To assess social interactions, introduce two to five persons to a play or sport environment at the same time. Observe who initiates interactions, listen to what they say to each other, and note the kind of partner and small-group activities that evolve.

When possible, videotape observations. Videotapes provide study aids for beginning teachers and are especially helpful in university classes to focus attention on real persons and environments instead of imagined ones. Videotapes also provide permanent records of locomotor and object control abilities. As such, they can be used to justify placement decisions and guide programming.

Model to Guide Observation and Programming

Figure 5.7 depicts a model to guide the study of school-aged persons. This model can serve as the background for completing class assignments designed to promote understanding of differently abled students (e.g., development of case studies) or can provide the beginning structure for whole-part-whole assessment and programming. The model emphasizes that assessment and programming must attend to cognitive, moral, social, and motor channels. To use this model, make a copy for every person you plan to observe. Then, when observation is complete, draw a circle around the descriptor in each channel that best represents present level of performance. Be able to cite anecdotes that support your decision making.

Figure 5.7 shows that development is a continuous process. Each age (see left-hand column) is associated with specific milestones, tasks, or functions that are societal expectations. Children normally progress upward through definite stages or levels from birth to adulthood.

Developmental theory posits that the sequence of milestones/tasks is uniform but that the rate of development varies. For example, adults with severe mental retardation may function at a cognitive level of 2 to 3 years of age. Their progress is very slow and may even appear frozen.

To interpret what this means for programming, find ages 2 to 3 on the assessment and programming model in Figure 5.7 and read horizontally across. The figure shows that persons with a mental age or cognitive level of 2 to 3 years

FIGURE 5.7

Sherrill's assessment and programming model: cognitive-moral-social-motor developmental channels.

Average Age	Piaget's Stages of Cognitive Development	Kohlberg's Levels of Moral Development	Levels of Social Play Development	Levels of Motor Development
Adult		Universal ethical principles		Increasingly advanced sport skills
16				
15				
14				
13				
12	Formal mental operations		Individualized leisure preferences	
11				
10		Conventional rule conformity—flexible adherence, common sense	Team sports	
9				
8	Concrete mental operations		Individual/dual sports, relays, and lead-up games	Beginning sport skills
7				
6			Low organized games and movement education	Skill combinations
5		Rules are regarded as sacred and absolute—rigid adherence	Cooperative play	Skip
4			Associative play	Hop
3	Preoperational mental operations	No comprehension of rules		Jump
2			Parallel play	Run
1		Responds to "no"		Walk
8 months			Peek-a-boo games	Creep / Crawl / Roll / Righting reactions
6 months			Solitary play	Voluntary movement
4 months				
Birth	Sensorimotor mental operations	No comprehension of language	Unoccupied	Reflexes

are primarily in the sensorimotor stage of reasoning, unlikely to understand rules beyond "yes" and "no," seldom able to initiate and sustain meaningful play interactions, and likely to have a repertoire of locomotor motor skills that includes only roll, crawl, creep, walk, and run. There are, of course, many individual differences within this range of abilities and some exceptions.

Some persons progress faster up some channels than others because of a combination of genetic and environmental factors. Few children in our society actualize their potential, partly because they do not have the internal motivation and partly because teachers and parents do not know how to help. Children with disabilities are more likely to have uneven development across channels than peers. Therefore, assess each channel separately and identify strengths to build on.

Cognitive Development and Function

Cognitive development, the first channel in Figure 5.7, depicts the evolution of the mental operations that collectively are called intelligence, knowledge, thought, or cognition. Five processes contribute to cognition: (a) comprehension, (b) application, (c) analysis, (d) synthesis, and (e) evaluation (Bloom, 1956). (To remember, use the first letter of each word to form the acronym CAASE; think, we need to make a case for cognition or intelligence as the basis for learning physical activity.)

Approaches to developing and using intelligence (i.e., CAASE) are either convergent, divergent, or mixed. *Convergence* refers to memorizing the one best or right answer or to precise imitation of a demonstration. *Divergence* refers to generation of many possible answers and finding new, original ways. Creative expression, one of the goals of physical education, is the ability to use both convergence and divergence in mental operations. Thus, creativity is a part of cognition and can be assessed in relation to CAASE.

Although, neurologically, cognition and perception are separate, they tend to be lumped together because cognition cannot occur without perception and vice versa. Cognitive function is generally accepted as the major determinant of learning in each channel. This is because learning moral, social, and motor tasks is dependent upon perception and other mental operations. To learn a new motor skill, a child must be able to see and imitate, hear and follow directions, or engage in spontaneous exploratory motor activities that provide meaning about the body and space/time relationships. Assessment of cognition therefore begins with placing the student into one of the four stages of mental operations proposed by Jean Piaget, the Swiss psychologist considered by many the father of developmental psychology.

The assessment and programming model in Figure 5.7 shows the four stages of cognitive development: sensorimotor, birth to age 2; preoperational, ages 2 to 7; concrete mental operations, ages 7 to 11 or 12; and formal or abstract operations, ages 11 or 12 and above. The horizontal line between ages 7 and 8 in the model is the barrier that must be crossed before persons are mentally, socially, and emotionally ready to function as team members in competitive sport activities. This is also approximately when they change from

being egocentric (I-centered) to empathetic (able to understand the view or role of another) and when they begin to make social comparisons ("Am I as good as others, better, or worse?"). At this age, they also acquire skills for analyzing reasons why. Most persons with moderate mental retardation (IQs from 35–40 to 50–55) never cross this barrier. Persons with mild mental retardation, in contrast, are usually able to participate successfully in team competition but at older ages than peers. A brief description of each stage follows.

Sensorimotor (Ages 0 to 2)

The sensorimotor stage is a time of rapid change. Sensory integration (organizing and deriving meaning from sensory stimuli) begins at birth, long before voluntary movement is possible. The tactile sensory system clues the infant to wet versus dry diapers, comfortable versus uncomfortable surfaces, and hot versus cold conditions. It also receives and interprets pain stimuli. The kinesthetic (body position) and vestibular (equilibrium) sensory systems work together to give meaning to all kinds of movement (reflex, voluntary, and externally imposed). Likewise, visual, auditory, olfactory (smell), and gustatory (taste) sensory systems operate so that the child acquires an elementary understanding of self/not self and begins to attach meaning to persons and objects in the environment. Along with meaning comes an understanding of cause and effect (i.e., crying brings attention, waving bye-bye brings praise, reaching for certain objects causes the "no" word).

Sensorimotor input from voluntary movement does not begin until about 4 months of age. Motorically, infants are controlled by reflexes (involuntary motor responses to environmental stimuli) and stereotypical movement patterns. This means that they can use body parts for voluntary movement only after reflexes governing these parts are suppressed or integrated. This integration process follows an inborn timetable that is about the same for all infants except those with reflex disorders (e.g., cerebral palsy). The horizontal line at about the 4-month period in the assessment and programming model in Figure 5.7 thus indicates the major barrier to be crossed for infants to perform voluntary movements. Once this barrier is crossed, only about 4 months are required for independent sitting, rolling, crawling, and creeping patterns to emerge. Each additional pattern brings new sensory information for the brain to process and assign meaning.

The first 2 years of life are thus primarily a time of sensory integration, the development of beginning locomotor and object control patterns, and the emergence of comprehension. The ability to imitate is acquired during these years, and children learn appropriate responses to yes/no and short commands like "Come here," "Sit down," and "Throw me the ball."

Preoperational (Ages 2 to 7)

The preoperational years are lumped together because development focuses on the acquisition of language. By age 2, most children have acquired a speaking vocabulary of about 300 words and are beginning to use speech as a means of communication. The major developmental task during these years is *representation,* learning to link meaning to objects and subsequently to symbols (like pictures, written words, and gestures/signs) that represent words.

Mental operations of comprehension, application, analysis, synthesis, and evaluation (CAASE) are all dependent upon the ability to derive meaning from sounds, sights, and other sensory stimuli by relating them to similar units in the short- and long-term memory. Thought at this stage is preoperational largely because of memory limitations. From ages 2 to 7, most children progress slowly, from ability to think about or remember only one thing at a time to a sequence of three or four things. For example, the mental operation of matching or grouping things according to a given characteristic (e.g., color, shape, size) depends on ability to mentally handle two things at once and draw a relationship (alike or different) between them. Thereafter, the ability to handle three things at once (and more) develops rapidly.

Ages 2 to 7 is the time when children begin to learn through verbal input (auditory perception). Nevertheless, spontaneous movement exploration, seeing and imitating, and trial and error remain the three best approaches to motor learning. Most children are not ready to learn games that involve more than one or two rules or concepts until about age 7. They simply cannot yet grasp relationships between their own and others' actions, space and time, and rules and penalties.

The ability to think and act creatively (i.e., fluency, flexibility, originality, elaboration) first occurs in the preoperational stage. Standardized tests for measuring creativity are available for ages 3 years and up (Jay, 1991; Sherrill, 1986; Torrance, 1981). A minimum IQ (50 to 60) appears necessary for creative thought to occur; otherwise, the relationship between intelligence and creativity is low. Creativity seems to be strongly related to children's perception—how keenly they observe the world, what kind of meaning they derive from it, and how free they feel to express this meaning.

The preoperational period is called perceptual-motor in that judgments are based on perception rather than reasoning. Classification of objects, for example, is generally based on surface appearance rather than underlying function. Children can match objects on the basis of overall appearance (e.g., "Find two things on this page that are exactly alike"), color, and shape long before they can find two things in a cluster (e.g., truck, airplane, apple) that have the same function. Perceptions are egocentric or I-centered. Everything is perceived in relation to the self, rather than objectively by logical reasoning. For example, in games, children of this age all want to be "it." Often, they do not realize that being "it" may be a penalty for failure to avoid being caught.

Out of perceptual-motor learning come the initial mental operations necessary for understanding the directions to low organized games, movement education, and most sports. Among these mental operations are classification, seriation, number concepts, conservation, and reversibility.

Ability in *classification* is needed before children can successfully engage in team competition (i.e., differentiate between teammates and opponents). It is also essential to game strategies that involve position play. Students must be

FIGURE 5.8

Challenging young children to pull different-colored valentines from the wall and put them in a basket teaches classification, while offering practice in reach-grasp-release.

able to differentiate between offensive and defensive moves and to match their use to the situation. The easiest games involving classification are hide-and-seek, guessing, and retrieval games (see Figure 5.8). In the latter, objects of different colors or shapes are scattered all over the wall or floor and the students are challenged, "Who can run and pick up the most reds?"

Seriation, usually called *sequencing* in physical education, is the ability to remember sequences, as in *I'm Going to Grandmother's House. I'm Going to Grandmother's House* (GH) is a game in which each child repeats in correct order what other children have said and then adds something new. For example, Child 1 says, "I'm going to GH and I'm taking my toothbrush." Child 2 says, "I'm going to GH and I'm taking my toothbrush and my dog." Child 3 says, "I'm going to GH and I'm taking my toothbrush, my dog, and my pajamas." Until children acquire this ability, they cannot remember game rules, such as what happens in softball after three strikes, after three outs, or when a fly ball is caught.

Until students master *number concepts,* scoring has little meaning. Likewise, such movement education challenges as "Can you balance on three body parts?" are not understood. In addition, children do not comprehend the idea of trials and trying to improve over a set number of opportunities.

Ability in *conservation* relates to generalization (i.e., understanding that a ball is a ball and can be thrown and caught, regardless of its color, size, and shape). Much of perceptual-motor training pertains to object constancy (i.e., an object is the same whether upside down, rotated, or hidden in a background in which it is out of context). Movement education challenges like "How many ways can you move?" or "How many shapes can you make with your body?" help to develop conservation. The ability to understand pretend roles, like being "It" or being the fox or chickens in *What Time Is It, Mr. Fox?,* also rests on conservation concepts (i.e., people can assume roles, but they have not really changed). For example, in *What Time Is It, Mr. Fox,* all the children (chickens) run from one baseline to another when Mr. Fox answers, "Midnight." Those children whom Mr. Fox tags must change roles from pretend chickens who are fleeing to little foxes who help Mr. Fox tag others.

Reversibility is the basic ability needed to play all the early childhood games that involve a quick change of direction of one player (i.e., when tagged) or the entire group (in running away from "It" after a cue word) or a quick change of speed (*Red Light, Green Light*). Until students develop this mental operation, they cannot change roles within a game (i.e., switch from someone who is fleeing from "It," after being tagged, to someone who is "It" and now performs a chasing role).

Many physical educators take these mental operations for granted. They evolve with no special training in children without disabilities. Their absence, however, brings chaos when trying to teach the simplest of childhood games. The development of these mental operations is delayed, often by several years, in children with mental retardation and related conditions. Many children with severe disabilities display mental operations that appear to be frozen at the preoperational level.

Concrete Mental Operations (Ages 7 to 11)

Persons in the concrete operational stage can demonstrate problem solving based on logic as long as the task is concrete rather than abstract. They can remember and reproduce four to seven items in a sequence (the same as most adults) and draw relationships between many things. Because learning is centered around concrete objects and experiences, educators must emphasize the salient points to look for in a demonstration and to listen for in a lecture (i.e., help is needed with cue selection). Concrete operations allow generalization to and from identical things and experiences, but not similar ones.

Simultaneous seeing and hearing (i.e., reliance upon the visual and auditory systems and the use of observational learning) becomes the motor learning modality of preference. Children no longer have to learn everything by personal trial and error. At ages 7 to 11, they can consider alternatives and analyze the probable consequences of actions. They begin to analyze the reasons things happen as they do (attributions) and to develop personal belief systems

in this regard (e.g., is winning a game or making an *A* on a test the result of effort, ability, luck, or powerful others?).

Formal Mental Operations (Ages 11 and up)

According to Piaget, children's mental operations begin to acquire adult characteristics at about age 11 or 12. Intelligence becomes increasingly logical and abstract, allowing adolescents to think in terms of ideas rather than things and people. They become capable of problem solving in the scientific sense and can hypothesize and examine alternatives.

Formal in formal mental operations refers to the acquisition of form or structure in thought and, hence, the ability to consistently use one or more systems. Persons can follow a set form in writing letters, term papers, and research manuscripts and in composing art, music, dance, and other products. Likewise, they can apply the scientific method of testing hypotheses to problem solving and use abstract algebraic formulas in explaining and predicting phenomena. Persons in this stage can mentally manipulate symbols and conditions that have not been experienced and have no concrete meaning. Many persons of average intelligence do not function comfortably in this stage. Most can use form or system in some but not all cognition.

Implications of Cognitive Development for Moral, Social, and Motor Function

Assessment of a person's cognitive stage allows inferences to be drawn about moral, social, and motor functioning. Then, adaptations can be made to assure success in various physical activity placements. Level of cognition is an indicator of how much individual help will be needed to follow visual demonstrations and derive meaning from verbal explanations. Level of cognition also gives an idea of the problem-solving or creative abilities (see Figure 5.9).

From elementary through secondary school levels, physical education curriculums devote an increasing amount of time to games and sports. Level of cognition, in combination with moral development, offers insight into capacity to learn the rules and strategies of game play.

Moral Development and Function

Moral development refers to changes in knowledge and compliance pertaining to rules and standards of conduct. To participate in even the simplest game, persons must understand and abide by rules. Likewise, class discipline requires making students aware of rules, the penalties for breaking rules, and the rewards for following them. Little attention has been given to the developmental aspects of morality (Bredemeier & Shields, 1987). Experts agree, however, that individuals progress from levels of naiveté and egocentricism to unselfish concerns for human rights and universal ethical principles. This progress is age- and experience-related (Kohlberg, 1984; Piaget, 1932). Morality is situation-specific. Individuals may function at one level in sport settings and at another level in everyday life settings.

Table 5.5 shows broad levels of moral development that can be used in assessment. These are a simplification of the work of Lawrence Kohlberg of Harvard University, the foremost theorist on moral development. Kohlberg believes

FIGURE 5.9

Level of cognition is an indicator of how much help will be needed in problem-solving activities. Here, Barbara Wood of Homer, New York, school system teaches balancing, throwing, and spelling.

that an individual's cognitive thought processes parallel his or her moral reasoning. According to Kohlberg, many persons never achieve full formal operational cognition; these persons are likewise unable to live by and be guided by abstract ethical principles. Persons who do reach the universal ethical principles stage seldom do so before age 20; most are in middle or old age.

Simple Game Rules

Moral development and function can be assessed by observing game and class behavior in relation to rules and by describing problem situations and asking, "What would you do?" and "Why?" Until persons understand language (words, gestures, signs), there can be no morality. By age 1, however, most children have been programmed to understand "no," primarily for their own safety. Watching young children play with dolls offers insight into their exposure to punishment and rewards, for most children will treat the dolls as they have been treated.

By age 4, most children can understand games having one or two rules and can follow simple classroom rules. Their motivation for following such rules is essentially egocentric: to avoid punishment and/or to secure the favor of someone powerful. Some children test limits far more than others; this is probably more a manifestation of energy and activity levels than cognition and morality. Social learning is

Table 5.5
Developmental stages in rules conformity.

Stages	Level
Premoral	1. **Punishment and obedience.** Right and wrong are determined solely by physical consequences. Children obey rules to avoid punishment.
	2. **Egocentrism.** Right is determined by what satisfies one's personal needs. Some understanding of reciprocity may be present: "You scratch my back and I'll scratch yours." Children conform to receive rewards.
Conventional Rule Conformity	3. **Pleasing others.** Behavior is determined by reinforcement or lack of it from significant others. Children conform to obtain approval.
	4. **Rigid adherence to rules that gradually becomes more flexible.** In early stages of rules comprehension (ages 4 to 7 years), rules are regarded as sacred and absolute; they cannot be broken by anyone for any reason. *From about age 7 on, rules become increasingly relative and flexible.* Persons conform to avoid censure by authority.
	5. **Participation in rule-making.** Right and wrong are determined by society and reflect strengths and weaknesses of lawmakers. Persons expect the right to help shape rules that affect their daily living and take this responsibility seriously. They usually abide, however, by existing laws while waiting for change to occur. Persons conform to maintain respect of social community.
Ethical Principles	6. **Personal ethics and integrity.** Right and wrong are based on personal conscience rather than the laws of society or rules of a game. Persons conform to maintain self-respect and integrity.

tremendously important in the shaping of early morality, and most persons model fairly closely what they see and hear.

Conventional Morality

Kohlberg suggests that conventional flexible rule conformity does not begin until about age 9. Until then, children are inconsistent in their understanding of rules and their moral reasoning about the purpose of rules. They are ambiguous in that they often break rules but, at the same time, seem to believe that game rules are sacred and absolute. This helps to explain the many arguments and confusions that occur in play, especially when children remember the rules in different ways and/or when an adult attempts to alter a familiar game structure.

FIGURE 5.10

An infant should be exposed to many peek-a-boo type games to learn about object permanence. Here, a 7-month-old infant learns to pull off the bear hat to find her mother's face. Since peek-a-boo is developmentally the first game children learn, it should be taught to 3- and 4-year-old students with severe disabilities and others who never learned it.

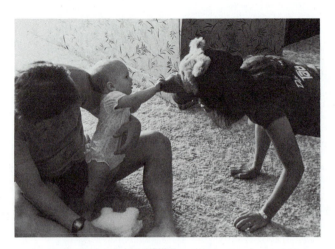

Inasmuch as the underlying philosophy of adapted physical activity is to change or adapt games to meet individual needs, anticipating the reactions of the players is important. They may balk at game adaptations or perceive them as "special favors" or even as "put-downs." Some children would rather fail than feel singled out as needing a particular adaptation. Therefore, games must be adapted for *all* persons rather than only for the one or two with disabilities. To increase social competence, it is sometimes necessary to decrease the conceptual rigidity of children, thereby assisting their progress toward conventional morality.

Conventional morality develops in conjunction with (a) cognitive reasoning about relationships and (b) increasing ability to empathize and see the world from the perspective of others. Most persons follow the conventions of good conduct because they have learned to care about other people and property. They feel a need to be good in their own eyes and those of others. At the first level of conventional morality, people tend to believe that everyone else is good also and shares common values. The occasional "bad" person is dismissed as an exception who will someday receive his or her just reward. At the second level of conventional morality, there is recognition of individual differences in other persons' morality and appreciation of the need to work out compromises and adhere to rules that seem to be best for the majority. At the third level of conventional morality, rules tend to be relative and situational. Persons must therefore learn to reason what is the right behavior in many different kinds of situations.

Good Sportsmanship

Morality is the basis for becoming good sports persons (i.e., exhibiting good sportsmanship). Consider the following statement:

To be educated in sport means something more than being a skilled competitor. It means valuing the rules, the traditions, and the rituals of a sport. It means playing fairly. It means

appreciating good competition and the efforts of teammates and opponents. These values *and* attitudes *have behavioral dimensions that teachers can observe and teach to students. Students do not automatically know what it means to be a good sports person. They have to be taught. . . . (Siedentop, Mand, & Taggart, 1986, p. 200)*

Many persons with mental impairments have the motor skills and fitness to participate in games and sports but lack the necessary understanding of rules and appropriate social interactions. This fact should be considered in placement decisions and in planning instructional intervention. Appropriate goal areas are social competence and play and game behaviors. Moral development is an important part of adapted physical activity.

Social Development and Function

The social play developmental channel in the assessment and programming model in Figure 5.7 shows that children progress from an unoccupied status at birth to solitary play at about 6 months and peek-a-boo games with adults shortly thereafter (see Figure 5.10). Peek-a-boo is the first game that most children learn; children with severe disabilities may be considerably delayed in playful responses to adult movement, but eventually, most do react with smiles or laughs. Solitary play typically begins when infants gain enough voluntary control over their hands to grasp, pound, or shake objects. This leads to social interactions with adults, who instigate further object manipulation. Infants with cerebral palsy or other conditions that delay or impede object manipulation progress up the social play channel very, very slowly.

Levels of Social Play

Since the 1930s, various stages and levels of social play development have been posited. Piaget (1952, 1962) suggested that young children move progressively through stages designated as practice play (primarily sensorimotor), symbolic play (experimentation with language and movement, including real or imagined playmates and situations), and rules

Table 5.6
Developmental stages in social play.

Stages	Level
Preplay	1. **Autistic or unoccupied.** Plays with own body or with objects, but without apparent purpose. Lies, sits, or wanders about aimlessly. Exhibits stereotyped or repetitive behaviors.
Practice Play	2. **Onlooker.** Watches others at play, seems interested, follows activity with eyes.
	3. **Solitary play.** Plays alone with definite goal/purpose. Ignores others in close proximity. Reactions to toys/stimuli can be classified as approach or avoidance.
Symbolic Play	4. **Parallel play.** Plays independently, but shows awareness and occasional interest in others. Brings toys and/or establishes play space near others.
	5. **Associative play (interactive).** Initiates contacts with others. Interacts on playground apparatus and in "playing house" or other make-believe games. Talks with others. Interactions can be classified as positive or negative and as dyads, triads, and the like.
Rules Play	6. **Cooperative play.** Shares toys and apparatus. Participates in simple organized games; understands game formation and base or safety line; knows game goal and can switch roles (chase/flee, tag/dodge, roll/catch). Optimal group size seems to be three to six.
	7. **Increasingly complex games play.** Engages in progressively more complex, organized games to lead-up games to regulation team sports. Concurrently engages in progression of movement activities demanding self-competition (self-testing), partner competition, and group competition. Individual preferences emerge for team vs. individual vs. no competition.

Note. Adapted from Parten (1932) and Piaget (1952, 1962). See checklist for assessing social play in Chapter 18.

play (see Table 5.6). Children with severe mental retardation may, however, be frozen in a preplay stage because they lack the cognition for voluntary action. Parten (1932) and many other researchers (Levy, 1978) have examined Piaget's ideas and posited play levels for use in assessment and programming. Most research has focused on the symbolic and rules play stages.

Symbolic play, which normally begins at age 2 (the same time as preoperational cognition), is broken down into parallel play and associative play. *Parallel play* is awareness and interest in others, but individuals have insufficient ma-

FIGURE 5.11

Group games, like cageball, demand social readiness and self-confidence.

turity to initiate and sustain interactions with others of same functional level. The child establishes a play space close to other children, may watch the others and occasionally interact, but essentially plays independently. Depending on language development, social training, and observational learning ability, this level describes normal children between ages 2 and 4. *Associative play* is the name given the next developmental level, when children have developed the language and social skills to make and sustain associations with others. Associative play often centers on make-believe and show-and-tell activities. Lots of talk or sign language is involved as children explore the things they can do together. Associative play typically extends from ages 3 to 5 or until children begin to devise and apply rules.

Rules play begins at about age 5 and is broken down into cooperative play and games play. *Cooperative play* (ages 5 to 7) refers primarily to an understanding of and willingness to follow basic rules of sharing, taking turns, being nice to each other, and starting and stopping on cues. Cooperative play activities have a set structure that everyone follows, a clearly defined purpose, and one or two specific rules or game concepts. Examples of cooperative play are *Follow the Leader; Simon Says; Musical Chairs; Hide and Seek; Red Light, Green Light;* and *Keep the Cageball Up* (see Figure 5.11). In these games, everyone is essentially doing the same thing, usually in response to a leader. There is no changing

5   Goal Setting and Age-Appropriate Programming   **119**

FIGURE 5.12

Questions about interest and involvement in sports from instrument
developed by Susan Greendorfer and John Lewko.

1. How much do you play sports after school and on weekends?

5	4	3	2	1
Very much	A lot	Some	Not much	Not at all

2. How important is it to you that you participate in sports?

1	2	3	4	5
Not important	Not too	In between	Somewhat	Very important

3. How much do you like playing sports?

5	4	3	2	1
Very much	A lot	Some	Not much	Not at all

4. In general, how good are you at sports?

1	2	3	4	5
Not good at all	Not good	In between	Good	Very good

5. How easy is it for you to learn new sports skills?

5	4	3	2	1
Very easy	Somewhat easy	Average	Not very easy	Not easy at all

of roles like, for example, fleeing one minute and then (after being tagged) having to switch to a chasing role. *Games play,* the next level, denotes the social maturity to engage in increasingly complex games governed by many rules and concepts and requiring a changing of roles. These are called *low organized games.*

The emergence of concrete mental operations at around age 7 to 8 creates the possibility of understanding all of the interpersonal relationships required in cooperative and competitive sports, relays, and games. Assessment at this level entails observation of how many persons a student can cooperate and/or compete with at one time. Developmental theory posits that students move from partner relationships to triads (threesomes) to team play involving increasingly larger groups. Discipline problems occur when students are expected to function at levels they are not yet ready for.

Most individuals are not ready psychologically for organized team sport competition until about age 8 (i.e., concrete mental operations fully functional). This is because competition involves social comparison (judging whether one is as good as others, better, or worse), making judgments about why (attributions analysis—effort, ability, luck), and establishing personal value systems about cooperation and competition, right and wrong, and the like (Coakley, 1986; Passer, 1986). Clearly, assessment of social development after age 8 becomes complex.

Social development at all ages depends largely on the environment, the nature and number of persons present and willing to interact, and opportunities for social or observational learning. The class structure of physical education is essentially social. Chapter 2, which emphasizes attitudes, dwells on the importance of social acceptance to game and sport success and positive self-concept. Acquisition of basic play and game behaviors in preschool and primary grades is a prerequisite for developing the social skills necessary for effective participation in partner, small-group, and team activities.

Social competence, one of the goals of adapted physical education, refers to the ability to initiate contacts and make and keep friends who have the same leisure preferences as oneself. Without skills in this area, motor abilities and game/sport knowledge are relatively meaningless.

Sport Socialization

Another social development goal is sport socialization, the process of becoming interested in sport as an active leisure pastime and learning how to perform sport roles. Nondisabled children often become socialized into the same sports as their parents and siblings. Development as an athlete evolves for them as naturally as passing from one social play level to another. Many individuals with disabilities, however, are dependent upon friends, teachers, and agency personnel for socialization into sport (Lugo & Sherrill, 1992; Sherrill, Pope, & Arnhold, 1986; Sherrill & Rainbolt, 1986).

How do you know when students have been socialized into sport? Sport socialization has been operationally defined as the sum of answers to five questions (see Figure 5.12). Ask these questions of children whom you are observing. Take time for discussion after each question and ask, "Why?"

A Sport Interest Inventory has guided most of the research in this area and is fun to administer (Greendorfer

& Lewko, 1978). The inventory contains about 40 questions; the number is flexible because some teachers want to ask about various opportunities and barriers to participation. Some of the key questions that are asked in relation to father, mother, siblings, teachers, or friends are:

1. How important is it to your _____ that you be good in sports?
2. How important is it to your _____ that you play sports?
3. How much does your _____ play sports?
4. How much does your _____ play sports with you?
5. How much has your _____ helped you learn how to play sports?

Sport socialization depends on several variables: (a) opportunity set—availability of instruction, facilities, equipment, transportation, and persons to play with; (b) personal variables—values, motivation, ability, health, fitness, and free time; and (c) significant others—influence of family, friends, teachers, and others. Leisure-time skills is one of the main goals of adapted physical education. Sport socialization is one way to achieve this goal. Much research is needed in this area.

Social Comparison and Competition

From a psychological standpoint, competition is social comparison, a means of judging whether you are as good as everyone else and developing opinions about your competence in various domains. This, in turn, influences self-concept, mental health, and whether or not an activity is fun. Table 5.7 presents developmental levels to guide the teaching of cooperation and competition. Concepts of cooperation and personal best should be developed before those of competition.

Sport has different meanings to persons, depending upon whether it is individual, dual, or team and primarily recreational or competitive. These meanings change with age because there is a developmental hierarchy in the way persons judge their competence.

Before age 5, most children do not understand competition because they are not yet developmentally able to make social comparisons. All sport is therefore recreational. Persons at this level of development (both the very young and the developmentally delayed) engage in sport to please parents and to feel good. Typically, they perform to the best of their ability but have no set goals other than to have fun. They do not understand winning and losing but instead base judgments of self-competence on (a) simple task mastery (either I did it or I did not, or the coach let me play or the coach did not) and (b) the feedback of significant others, mainly parents. Much of the early Special Olympics philosophy (e.g., the huggers at the finish line in track and swimming) was based on the assumption that most persons with mental retardation function at this level. Today, Special Olympics philosophy and practices have changed to emphasize assessing athletes individually and determining whether or not they understand concepts of winning.

Table 5.7
Developmental levels in cooperation-competition continuum.

Levels	Explanation
Egocentric	1. **Individual and group play.** Thinks only of self. Lacks maturity to empathize and cooperate.
Cooperation	2. **Cooperative organized play.** Cooperates with others to achieve a mutual goal, like winning a relay or tagging the most persons.
Personal Best	3. **Goal-directed self-competition.** States level of aspiration and tries to attain this specific goal. Teacher or coach may establish goal also. The concept of *personal best* is emphasized.
Individual or Dual Competition	4. **Individual competition.** Competes with one opponent in individual sports like track, swimming, bowling, golf, and tennis. Competes against others also in trying to make the best score in fitness, track, and self-testing activities.
	5. **Dual or doubles competition.** Competes in dual sports like doubles in tennis, badminton, and table tennis. Cooperates with partner in doubles tennis, with team in bowling, and in other situations demanding a limited number of interactions.
Team Competition and Cooperation	6. **Team competition.** Cooperates with team members while concurrently competing with opponents. The smaller the team, the easier the learning progressions in cooperation and competition.

From ages 5 to 7, children achieve the cognitive capacity to make social comparisons. This skill gradually improves. Children naturally strive to become the best they can be. They begin to link the way others feel about them to personal judgments about whether they are the best or worst in the group. This is the age when they begin social discrimination by calling others names (baby, sissy, stupid) and become concerned about favoritism ("Teacher likes him [or her] better than me."). Cooperation, not competition, should be emphasized at this age, with the teacher praising children for helping others, sharing the ball, and taking turns.

The concept of personal best should be introduced around age 7 or 8, with children encouraged to state *level of aspiration* before undertaking tasks in which success depends on numbers. For example, the teacher may ask each child to write his or her anticipated score (level of aspiration) on a daily contract or in a secret place before responding to such challenges as (a) "How many sit-ups can you do in 30 sec?" (b) "How fast can you run the 50-yd dash?" and (c) "How far can you throw the softball?" By comparing aspirations with actual scores, children are helped to focus

FIGURE   5.13

Ideally, team competition should be introduced at about the third-grade level, when children are socially and cognitively mature enough to handle complex interactions with teammates and opponents.

newly evolving comparison skills on a personal best rather than on the goal of being better than others.

Throughout the concrete mental operations stage, children tend to judge themselves in terms of what they see and hear because they cannot yet use logic to reason why they feel good or bad about an experience. The primary motivation in sport from ages 7 to about 11 is to be as good as or better than everyone else. The challenge of playing one's best while simultaneously comparing performance to others is fun for most children (see Figure 5.13). The four reasons, from most to least important, that children ages 7 to 14 give for enjoyment of sport are (a) comparing skills against others, (b) personal accomplishment, (c) improving skills, and (d) excitement of the game (Wankel & Kreisel, 1985). Less important reasons, from high to low, are (a) doing the skills of the game, (b) being on a team, (c) being with friends, (d) winning, (e) getting rewards, and (f) pleasing others. Fun and leisure-time decisions to remain involved in sport are thus linked with feeling good about self.

In adapted physical activity, however, one of the main concerns is children who fail. Almost no research is available to describe the psychosocial development of children whose social comparisons always tell them that they are performing below average. One approach to this problem is to stress competition against self instead of others.

Attributions Analysis

At about age 11 or 12, children begin to use attributions analysis to logically explain why they feel good or bad about

a performance and how they will plan for the future. The four attributions generally used and the questions children ask are as follows:

1. **Effort.** "Did I try hard enough?" "Did I try as hard as everyone else?" "Did I do my best?"

2. **Ability.** "Am I clumsy, dumb, average, gifted?" "How do I compare with my peers?" "Who should I compare myself to—others with my same condition (e.g., cerebral palsy, blindness) or people in general?"

3. **Fate, luck, powerful others.** "Does chance or fate favor me?" "Am I lucky or unlucky?" "How does this compare to how chance favors others?" "Did I have any control over my performance, or was it manipulated by some powerful other (God, the devil, a coach, or parent)?"

4. **Task difficulty.** "Was the task too hard or time consuming?" "Was it harder for me than for others?" "Was it appropriate for me?"

Thus, logical thought is closely interwoven with social comparison. Help children separate who they are from what they can do. They must understand that they are loved for many reasons, not just because they are as good or better than others in particular tasks.

Personal-Best Analysis

Adolescence is when approaches to sport become diversified. Some persons continue to use social comparison as the main method of self-evaluation. Others internalize and use a personal-best philosophy. Understanding of personal best matures rapidly from about 8 on, the age when most children can differentiate between ability and effort. Several years are needed for accurate assessment of self against objective criteria. Time is also needed to learn how to select appropriate criteria.

Four developmental levels thus can be used to assess psychosocial development in relation to sport: (a) egocentric (not developmentally ready to make social comparisons), (b) social comparisons predominant, (c) attributions analysis predominant, and (d) personal-best analysis predominant. Development depends on both maturation and learning. Progression from level to level requires careful teaching similar to that used in facilitating motor skills and fitness.

Motor Development and Function

The last channel of development on the assessment and programming model in Figure 5.7 depicts the progression from reflex dominance to increasingly advanced sport skills. Levels include (a) reflex dominance, (b) righting reactions emergence, (c) basic motor skill mastery, and (d) sport skill competence. Progress up this channel is usually assessed as normal, delayed, or abnormal. *Abnormal* describes severe conditions in which some of the major reflexes are not integrated and motor skill remains partially reflex-dominated. *Delayed* motor development is slowness in achieving motor milestones. For example, the motor development of children with mental retardation tends to lag 3 to 6 years behind that designated as normal or average.

Many standardized assessment instruments are available for examining reflexes, reactions, and motor skills. These are covered in later chapters (see "Tests" in the Index). At the initial assessment level, however, observation of locomotor and nonlocomotor skills in a play or sport environment is the best approach. At this level, simply note what persons can and cannot do and indicate whether or not development is at the expected age level.

Responsivity Problems

Another area important to observe is responsivity to stimuli. Four descriptors are used: (a) hyper (over, above, too much), (b) average, (c) hypo (under, too little), and (d) fluctuating, inconsistent, or labile. Persons who are hyperactive or hypoactive need special environmental adaptations, and teachers should ask questions about (a) energy levels and similar states of parents and siblings; (b) side effects of drugs, prescribed and nonprescribed; (c) presence of headache or illness; and (d) other variables (personal and environmental) that might affect responsivity. Appendix B provides information about medications that might be mentioned.

Inattention, impulsivity, and hyperactivity are considered separate responsivity disorders. They often occur together but may appear independently of each other. Because these often contribute to learning disabilities, they are described in detail in Chapter 20. Age affects each of these, and programming must be sensitive to the amount of time a person can concentrate and remain on task.

Synthesizing Observational Data

Obviously, much can be learned about persons by observing them in natural settings. This chapter has reviewed behaviors associated with various age groups and emphasized matching goals to assessment data and ascertaining that learning activities are age appropriate. The observation form on page 124 will help synthesize data from observations as a prerequisite to (a) formal assessment (see Chapter 7) and (b) describing present level of psychomotor performance in an IEP.

References

Bloom, B. (Ed.). (1956). *Taxonomy of educational objectives, Handbook I: Cognitive domain.* New York: David McKay.

Bredemeier, B., & Shields, D. (1987). Moral growth through physical activity: A structural/developmental approach. In D. Gould & M. R. Weiss (Eds.), *Advances in pediatric sport sciences, Volume 2* (pp. 143–165). Champaign, IL: Human Kinetics.

Coakley, J. (1986). When should children begin competing? A sociological perspective. In M. R. Weiss & D. Gould (Eds.), *Sport for children and youths* (pp. 59–63). Champaign, IL: Human Kinetics.

Davis, W. E. (1989). Utilizing goals in adapted physical education. *Adapted Physical Activity Quarterly, 6,* 205–216.

Greendorfer, S. L., & Lewko, J. H. (1978). Role of family members in sport socialization of children. *Research Quarterly, 49,* 146–153.

Hopkins, H. (1988). Current basis for theory and philosophy of occupational therapy. In H. Hopkins & H. Smith (Eds.), *Willard and Spackman's occupational therapy* (7th ed.) (pp. 38–42). Philadelphia: J. B. Lippincott.

Illingworth, R. S. (1983). *The development of the infant and young child* (8th ed.). Baltimore: Williams & Wilkins.

Jay, D. (1991). Effect of a dance program on the creativity of preschool handicapped children. *Adapted Physical Activity Quarterly, 8* (4), 305–316.

Kohlberg, L. (1984). *The psychology of moral development: The nature and validity of moral stages.* San Francisco: Harper & Row.

Levy, J. (1978). *Play behavior.* New York: John Wiley & Sons.

Lugo, A.A., & Sherrill, C. (in press). Sport socialization of secondary youth with cerebral palsy. *Adapted Physical Activity Quarterly.*

Mosey, A. C. (1986). *Psychosocial components of occupational therapy.* New York: Raven Press.

Parten, M. (1932). Social participation among preschool children. *Journal of Abnormal and Social Psychology, 27,* 243–269.

Passer, M. W. (1986). When should children begin competing? A psychological perspective. In M. R. Weiss & D. Gould (Eds.), *Sport for children and youths* (pp. 55–58). Champaign, IL: Human Kinetics.

Payne, V. B., & Isaacs, L. D. (1991). *Human motor development: A lifespan approach* (2nd ed.). Mountain View, CA: Mayfield Publishing.

Piaget, J. (1932). *The moral judgment of the child.* New York: Harcourt, Brace & World.

Piaget, J. (1952). *The origins of intelligence in children.* New York: International Universities Press.

Piaget, J. (1962). *Play, dreams, and imitation in childhood.* New York: W. W. Norton.

Salkind, N.J. (1985). *Theories of human development* (2nd ed.). New York: John Wiley & Sons.

Sherrill, C. (1986). Fostering creativity in handicapped children. *Adapted Physical Activity Quarterly, 3* (3), 236–249.

Sherrill, C., & Montelione, T. (1990). Prioritizing adapted physical education goals: A pilot study. *Adapted Physical Activity Quarterly, 7,* 355–369.

Sherrill, C., & Rainbolt, W. (1986). Sociological perspectives of cerebral palsy sports. *Palaestra, 2* (4), 20–26, 50.

Sherrill, C., Pope, C., & Arnhold, R. (1986). Sport socialization of blind athletes: A preliminary study. *Journal of Visual Impairment and Blindness, 80* (5), 740–744.

Siedentop, D., Mand, C., & Taggart, A. (1986). *Physical education teaching and curriculum strategies for grades 5–12.* Palo Alto, CA: Mayfield.

Torrance, E. P. (1981). *Thinking creatively in action and movement: Examiner's manual.* Bensenville, IL: Scholastic Testing Service.

Wankel, L. M., & Kreisel, P. (1985). Factors underlying enjoyment of youth sports: Sport and age group comparisons. *Journal of Sport Psychology, 7* (1), 51–64.

Wright, B. (1983). *Physical disability—A psychosocial approach* (2nd ed.). New York: Harper & Row.

SUMMARY OBSERVATION FORM BY _____

1. Name of Person Observed _____

2. Gender _____   3. Chronological age _____

4. Dates of observation, setting, number of children present, available equipment, and other conditions.

   _____

   _____

   _____

5. Circle motor skills and patterns student used.

Log roll	**Walk**	**Ascend stairs**	**Strike**	**Serve**
Crawl	**Run**	**Descend stairs**	**Bat**	**Catch**
Creep	**Jump down**	**Hang from bar**	**Bounce**	**Kick**
Scoot	**Jump over**	**Climb**	**Dribble**	**Trap**
Rise-to-stand	**Leap**	**Dodge**	**Pivot**	**Dribble, feet**
Stand-to-lie	**Hop**	**Throw**	**Volley**	**Tag**

   Others _____

6. In general, compared to peers of same age, how would you rank motor skills and patterns?
   Superior   **Average**   **Below average**   **Bottom 10 %**

7. Which was preferred hand in throwing/striking?   **R   L   Neither**

8. Which was preferred foot in kicking?   **R   L   Neither**

9. Which motor skills and patterns were used most?

   _____

10. What is major method of ambulation?
    Independent   **Assistive device**   **Crutches**   **Wheelchair**

11. In general, compared to peers of same age, how would you rank activity level?
    Hyperactive   **High**   **Average**   **Low**   **Hypoactive**

12. What health problems, interactions, or other variables seemed to be contributing to high or low energy level?

    _____

13. Which stage best describes mental operations?
    Sensorimotor   **Preoperational**   **Concrete**   **Formal**

14. What level best describes rules understanding and compliance?
    No comprehension   **Pleasing others**   **Rigid adherence**   **Flexible adherence**

15. What best describes language and communication ability?
    Highly verbal   **High average**   **Average**   **Low average**   **Very quiet**

16. What best describes social play level?
    Solitary   **Parallel**   **Associative**   **Cooperative**

17. What best describes readiness level on cooperation-competition continuum?
    Egocentric   **Cooperation**   **Personal best**   **Individual or dual competition**   **Team competition**

18. Circle the one phrase that seems to best describe initiative, understanding of instructions, and mental flexibility.

Initiative	**Understanding of instructions**	**Mental flexibility**
A self-starter	Grasps instructions	Leads in generating new ideas
Has considerable initiative	Understands after asking questions	Shows excitement about new ideas
Average	Average	Prefers the old and familiar
Responds to prodding	Confused, but tries	Resents change
Relies entirely on others	Confused and helpless	Perseverates

19. Who did the student interact with the most? One person or several?

    _____

    _____

20. In programming for this student, what three physical education goal areas seem to be his or her major strengths? Why?

    _____

    _____

    _____

21. What three physical education goal areas seem to be his or her major weaknesses? Why?

    _____

    _____

    _____

CHAPTER

6

Humanism, Self-Concept, and Motivation: Philosophy and Pedagogy

FIGURE   6.1

Warm, subjective, human encounters with persons with disabilities in a variety of settings are essential to teacher training. There must be quiet times to talk together, to listen, and to feel. (*A*) Dance instruction in a leotard is a part of normalization. (*B*) Risk recreation activities are as important for persons with disabilities as they are for the able-bodied. (*C*) Teachers cheer an athlete who is mentally retarded and has cerebral palsy on to victory.

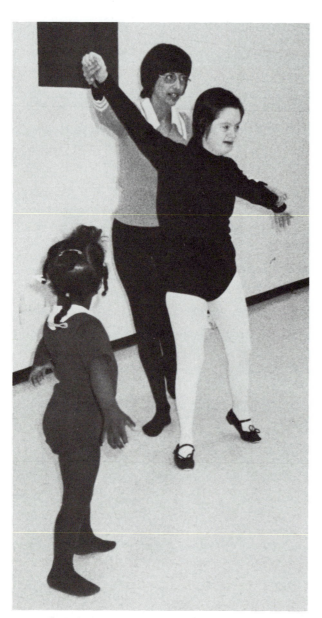

A

B

C

After you have studied this chapter, you should be able to:

1. Discuss humanistic philosophy, trace its evolution from the 1950s to the present, and identify the theories that form its basis.

2. Discuss the special pedagogical needs of students with low motor ability, fears, and phobias. Identify theories that provide guides to action. Relate your discussion to persons you have known.

3. Describe good teaching practices for persons of various ages with poor self-concept and/or low motivation. Link practices with theories.

4. Explain how normalization theory guides beliefs and practices in relation to integration and mainstreaming. What other theories relate to integration?

5. Consider the PAP-TE-CA service delivery model. Which theories guide practices in relation to each of its seven parts? Give examples.

6. Explain the three parts of self-concept and its many domains or dimensions. Discuss the issue of whether self-concept is unidimensional, multidimensional, or hierarchical. What do you think? Why?

7. Describe development of self-concept and changes that occur with age. Identify and discuss assessment instruments appropriate for different ages.

8. Discuss pedagogical implications of self-concept for all children and strategies especially appropriate for those with low self-concept.

9. Identify and explain motivation theories. Relate each to good teaching practices and give concrete examples of their use.

10. Link names like Maslow, Rogers, Bandura, and Harter with theories and the practices they guide. When theories can be explained by a model, be able to draw and discuss the models.

We deeply believe in and are committed to a philosophy of modern humanism; a way of looking at individuals . . . which supremely values the dignity and worth of all human beings.
—Rosalind Cassidy and Stratton F. Caldwell

Adapted physical education extends the humanistic qualities of prizing, caring, trusting, and respecting to all children and youth, with emphasis on those who are clumsy and/or have disabilities (see Figure 6.1). Adapted physical activity professionals must be master teachers who systematically apply pedagogy that empowers students to become the best they can be. This is possible only when philosophy evolves from carefully considered theories.

Regular and adapted physical activity have the same purpose and goals. Goals are, however, prioritized differently. In regular education, many assumptions are made. First, students are assumed to have sufficient self-concept, social competency, and mental health to benefit from instruction that employs traditional methodology and provides direct corrective feedback. A second assumption is that students have the play and game behaviors needed to get into a game formation, to follow basic rules, and to derive expected outcomes (fun, enjoyment, satisfaction). A third assumption is that sensory input and perceptual processes are intact and that students can handle a vast amount of stimuli at one time. Finally, it is assumed that students can generalize skills and fitness developed in school to lifespan behaviors supportive of good health and leisure.

In adapted physical activity, no assumptions are made. Goals are individualized and based on assessment data. Differently abled students have many more needs than regular students. These may be developmental or acquired because of gradual demoralization experiences in physical education (Robinson, 1990). Perceived failure in activities that seem easy to others may result in low self-esteem and learned helplessness that must be remediated before traditional instruction can be effective.

Regular and adapted physical activity differ primarily in philosophy and pedagogy (i.e., the way we teach and how). These are the concerns of this chapter. The philosophy that guides adapted physical education is deeply rooted in the understanding and appreciation of individual differences, of the importance of adaptation and individualization, and of the creativity needed to effectively help each individual become fully functional and human. This philosophy, called humanism or humanistic education, influences all aspects of service delivery.

Humanistic Philosophy

Humanistic philosophy, as used in this text, has its roots in humanistic psychology, the body of knowledge that pertains to helping persons become fully human (i.e., to realize and develop their human potential). This movement began in the 1950s with the self-actualization theory of Abraham Maslow and the fully functioning self theory of Carl Rogers. These persons and their followers were rebels against the Freudian methods that prevailed in psychiatry as well as the sickness and disease theories that dominated medicine.

The 1950s were full of change. This was the era when public schools began serving students with disabilities and special education was evolving into a profession. School personnel were developing an educational model to guide service delivery that would soon replace the medical model in which physicians made placement and other decisions. War veterans were convincing the public that they might be disabled but that they were not sick. Observation in the public schools revealed that here, too, students might have disabilities but

FIGURE   6.2

Humanistic service delivery begins with philosophy and practices that are based on three sets of theories.

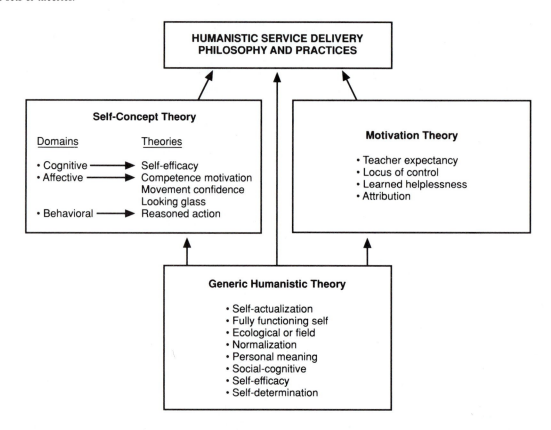

were not sick. Blacks, active in civil rights pursuits, gained access to integrated education in 1954. Everywhere, attitudes were changing about the nature of human beings.

Maslow, Rogers, and followers posited that human nature is essentially good and that development (unless delayed, interrupted, or distorted) moves naturally toward a healthy, self-actualizing personality. They were among the first to focus on psychological and physical health rather than on pathology, sickness, and disability, as was then the practice. From their works were derived such guidelines as "It's ability that counts, not disability" (motto of National Handicapped Sports) and "Sports by ability, not disability" (motto of the U.S. Cerebral Palsy Athletic Association).

Humanistic philosophy is a global instructional approach that emphasizes self-concept, relationships with others, intrinsic motivation, and personal responsibility. Its central tenet is *holism*, the careful planning of each learning experience to meet the needs of the whole person. In physical education, this means that movement and fitness activities are taught and conducted in ways that promote and preserve self-esteem. Self-concept is not conceptualized as a concomitant or incidental goal but as a primary concern.

Humanistic philosophy is the hallmark of adapted physical education because of the nature of the students served. Students with low motor skills and fitness typically have little faith in their ability to overcome these problems. They tend to be self-conscious, poorly motivated, and strongly influenced by past failures and disappointments. Many perceive physical activity as having few benefits; for them, it is

not easy, fun, relaxing, or satisfying. They are unlikely to develop active lifestyles unless the instructional approach helps them to feel good about themselves and their capacity for change.

Humanism and Religion

Humanism, as used in educational philosophy, has no connection with religious beliefs. It does not mean believing in human beings instead of God (Reilly & Lewis, 1983). Instead, as explained on previous pages, humanism is a specific approach to service delivery that has its roots in the humanistic psychology movement of the 1950s. Most adapted physical educators with this orientation believe deeply in God.

Theoretical Basis of Humanism

Although many theories provide the knowledge base for humanistic service delivery, the self-actualization theory of Abraham Maslow (1908–1970) and the fully functioning self theory of Carl Rogers (1902–1987) are the pioneer works that gave humanistic psychology its initial impetus. These and related theories are called *organismic* in that they focus on the whole organism as a unified system (i.e., they are holistic). Also important to contemporary humanism are theories that stress interactions between the environment and people: (a) field or ecological, (b) normalization, (c) personal meaning, (d) social cognitive, (e) self-efficacy, and (f) self-determination. Figure 6.2 shows the theories discussed in this chapter.

FIGURE   6.3

Self-actualization theory evolved out of Maslow's hierarchy of human needs.

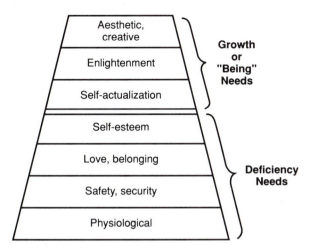

Self-Actualization Theory

Self-actualization theory evolved out of Maslow's hierarchy of human needs, first formulated as motivation theory in Maslow's text *Motivation and Personality* (1954). This hierarchy of needs looked like a pyramid, with physiological needs like hunger and thirst at the bottom and aesthetic and creative needs at the top (see Figure 6.3). The needs are arranged in a hierarchy to illustrate Maslow's contention that motivation is concentrated primarily on one level at a time. According to Maslow, individuals cannot move to a higher level until at least a minimal degree of satisfaction is derived at the lower level.

Maslow hypothesized two sets of needs: (a) deficiency needs and (b) growth or "being" needs. Distinctly different processes are required to meet these needs. *Deficiency needs* require external help. Parents, teachers, and significant others should provide as much gratification of these needs as possible, according to Maslow. "*Being*" *needs* are intrinsically motivated once a person achieves self-esteem. These "being" needs drive the great thinkers to enlighten the world (see the enlightenment level of the hierarchy) and likewise impel artists and creators to use their talents. Maslow posited, however, that only a small percentage of the adult population ever achieves self-actualization, which explains why the really great thinkers, artists, and creators in the history of the world number so few.

Maslow's hierarchy has implications for physical education pedagogy. One is that deficiency needs should be addressed in a particular order. Teachers should ascertain that (a) nutritional and fluid needs are being met, (b) prescribed medications have been taken, and (c) temperature, lighting, and other environmental conditions are conducive to physiological well-being.

Concern about safety needs includes psychological security as well as physical safety. Freedom from fear, anxiety, and confusion is a prerequisite for attending to and learning subject matter. Students must not be afraid of teachers or of failure. The safety mandate of Maslow's hierarchy thus guides educators to select assessment and learning tasks that build trust, faith, and confidence. Students must be helped to perceive the teacher as a partner in learning and classmates as a support group.

The love and belonging step has been interpreted as emphasizing the social basis of learning. Students need to be loved, appreciated, and accepted for who they are rather than what they can or cannot do. If love is unconditional, then persons can become intrinsically motivated to do their best because they are not worried about pleasing the teacher and being liked. Maslow's writing emphasizes the fragility of the inner being. Self-actualization theory suggests that the whole person (the self) must feel safe, loved, and accepted before the ego can survive objective, corrective feedback directed at specific behaviors. Only when love and belonging needs are met is the student able to benefit from formal motor skill and fitness instruction that enhances competence, mastery, achievement, and other outcomes related to esteem.

According to Maslow (1970, p. 45), "satisfaction of the self-esteem need leads to feelings of self-confidence, worth, strength, capability, and adequacy, of being useful and necessary in the world." Once this need is met, individuals are internally motivated to become all that they can be. Concurrently, they feel responsible for making the world a better place to live. Good teaching, according to Maslow's theory, is not changing the person but rather manipulating the environment so that needs are met.

Maslow's second contribution to humanistic psychology is not as well known as his hierarchy of human needs but is tremendously important. This is his qualitative research on the nature of psychological health and how it can be achieved. After an intensive study of self-actualizing people, Maslow proposed criteria that distinguish between self-actualizers and nonself-actualizers. His findings offer a composite model to help us each become the best we can be. Some of these markers are:

1. Positive self-acceptance
2. Positive acceptance of others in general
3. Capacity for intimate relationships
4. Sense of identity with all humanity
5. Spontaneity of thought, feeling, and action
6. Thought processes that are independent, creative, ethical, and democratic
7. Realistic orientation to life

Self-actualizing is thus largely concerned with relationships. It is not an egotistical process but an ecological one. The self can be actualized only to the extent that we feel at home in the world, identify with all humanity, and care for the ecosystem. In humanistic physical education, the teacher uses movement experiences to develop desired behaviors.

Regular education is based on the belief that nondisabled students can develop these behaviors and become self-actualizing without concrete, specific help from teachers. This may be the case when development is normal and no illness or disability intensifies deficiency needs. Adapted physical activity, however, is concerned with people who have psychomotor problems. A different teaching philosophy and pedagogy are needed when the process of becoming entails conquering problems (clumsiness, perceptual-motor deficits, health impairments) rather than the self evolving naturally. Maslow's theory thus has been extended and refined by many leaders in the search for ways to help teachers, students, and athletes become self-actualizing (Sherrill, Silliman, Gench, & Hinson, 1990).

Fully Functioning Self Theory

Carl Rogers, recognized worldwide as the father of humanistic counseling, systematically applied self-actualization theory to teaching, counseling, and rehabilitation. Of his many contributions, the one most relevant to adapted physical activity is the idea of the fully functioning self. Rogers posited that self-concept is the central concept in psychology and provides the best perspective for understanding an individual's behavior.

Rogers hypothesized that all of us has an ideal self and a real or actual self. The more congruent these two selves are, the more fully functioning and self-actualizing we are. According to this theory, teachers must spend time talking to students and helping them clarify the self they really want to be. Personal goal setting is an important part of this theory. Teachers must know how to ask the right questions to motivate students to assess themselves, set goals, and follow through.

Rogers posited that people come to know themselves through experiences, including verbal feedback from others. To maintain or enhance congruence between ideal self and real self, people tend to seek out experiences that confirm the self they want to be and avoid experiences that cause discrepancy. The clumsy child who wants to become a good athlete may avoid practice and block out corrective feedback because these experiences are painful. They heighten realization of how separate the ideal and the real selves are. Creating a make-believe world and daydreaming about the self are easier. Knowledge of this phenomenon helps teachers to understand why the behaviors of so many students seem counterproductive to the logical approach to acquiring motor competence.

When persons cannot cope with discrepancies between experiential feedback (kinesthetic, visual, verbal) and the ideal self, they develop *defense mechanisms* of distortion and denial. *Distortion* alters the meaning of the experience (i.e., the individual begins to perceive self and world as he or she wants to see it rather than how it really is). *Denial* removes or blocks from consciousness things that are hurtful. Illustrative of distortion and denial are findings that self-concept scores of youth with physical disabilities on a physical appearance scale are higher than the norm for able-bodied youth (Sherrill, Hinson, Gench, Kennedy, & Low, 1990).

When disability causes the body to look different and/or limits motor prowess, distortion and denial may be mechanisms for trying to keep the self integrated and psychologically healthy. According to Rogers, these mechanisms lead to conceptual rigidity and maladjustment. They are like putting bandaids on a wound rather than treating it. Sooner or later, the wound festers. Rogers therefore developed a system of counseling techniques to help persons modify

the way they conceptualize themselves. This system, described in his most famous book (Rogers, 1951), was first called *client-centered therapy* and later referred to as *person-centered therapy* (Hall & Lindzey, 1978; Shilling, 1984). The approach is also called Rogerian counseling or teaching.

Rogers applied his theory directly to teaching in his book *Freedom to Learn* (1969). In it, he described teachers as facilitators and stressed that the warmth, empathy, and genuineness of teachers make students free to learn (see Figure 6.4). He emphasized that students learn to use freedom and to become internally motivated only when they are given freedom. From Rogers comes many of the indicators of good teaching that are taught in education courses (Reilly & Lewis, 1983) and also the belief that teaching and counseling should be inseparable.

Implications of the fully functioning self theory (also called person-centered theory) for adapted physical activity are many. Threads of this theory run throughout the text. First and foremost, however, is the principle that self-concept should be the central concern in planning and implementing service delivery. Second is the principle that physical educators should have the counseling skills to help students resolve problems in the psychomotor domain. Sport psychology courses are increasingly becoming the source of training in this area. Techniques for enhancing the performance of athletes need to be generalized to persons with disabilities (Asken & Goodling, 1986; Hanrahan, Grove, & Lockwood, 1990; Ogilvie, 1985), and perhaps even more important, to clumsy children.

Ecological or Field Theory

Ecological theory pertains to interactions between an individual and everything in his or her ecosystem. An interactionist approach blends strategies for changing both the individual and the environment. Kurt Lewin's field theory is acknowledged as the forerunner of ecological theory. Lewin's work (1951) was the first to blend the tenets of individual and social psychology and thus is considered by many to be the theoretical basis of contemporary rehabilitation psychology (Cook, 1987; Golden, 1984). It also has played a meaningful role in adapted physical activity.

Lewin's work was consistent with Gestalt theory in that he believed the total pattern, or *field,* of events determines behavior. Lewin coined the term *lifespace* to refer to all of the external and internal forces acting on an individual. Lifespace consists of the total psychological world (i.e., everything seen, heard, sensed, or inferred). Field theory then emphasizes analysis of the individual, the environment, and interactions between the two. Change is promoted by altering person-by-situation interactions.

Lewin has had many followers, two of the most influential being Roger Barker who wrote *Ecological Psychology* (1968), and Urie Bronfenbrenner, who wrote *The Ecology of Human Development* (1979). Many leaders in perceptual-motor remediation have been influenced by James J. Gibson's ecological theory of affordances (1977) and visual perception (1979).

The implication of ecological theory for adapted physical activity is the assessment of psychomotor problems

FIGURE 6.4

No variable is more important than the personality of the teacher in working with students who have poor self-concepts and low motivation.

from both environmental (situational) and personal perspectives. Good pedagogy involves action directed toward changing each. Ecological theory also creates the framework for families and professionals working together and for collaborative models in which many disciplines cooperate. Perhaps, however, the greatest impact of ecological theory is its implications for integration and normalization.

Normalization Theory

Normalization refers to making available to persons with disabilities living, learning, and working conditions as close as possible to the norms of able-bodied society. Normalization theory does not mean making such individuals normal, as it has sometimes been incorrectly conceptualized, but rather affording them access to the same environment and opportunities as their able-bodied peers.

Success in sports competition, especially in events like the Boston Marathon, in which elite athletes with dis-

abilities compete side by side with those who are nondisabled, is believed to be normalizing in the sense that it changes perceptions. It alters the way we see persons with disabilities as well as the way they see themselves. Fred McBee, coauthor of *The Continental Quest* (McBee & Ballinger, 1984) and a wheelchair user, described how the 1978 Boston Marathon changed his life. He conveys his feelings as George Murray (Figure 6.5) finished first in this race—before any of the able-bodied runners:

For his friend, Fred McBee, that day would change his life. . . . He'd seen the gimps come from wheezing through the 40-yd dash in shaking, quaking, rattletrap wheelchairs, to winning the greatest 26.2-m race in the world. From a bunch of convalescing cripples out for a little recreation, they'd become muscled, highly fit gimps out for blood. (McBee & Ballinger, 1984, p. 2)

McBee earlier explained that only persons in wheelchairs can use such words as *gimps* and *cripples;* they are

FIGURE 6.5

George Murray, of Florida, is one of the best-known wheelchair marathoners in the world. (Photo courtesy of Top End Wheelchair Sports, Inc.)

part of the "in-language" of the wheelchair athlete community but are never appropriate for an outsider.

Normalization theory was introduced to the United States from Sweden by Bengt Nirge in the late 1960s and is recognized as a major factor in the deinstitutionalization of persons with mental retardation and their subsequent social integration into the community (Nirge, 1969, 1980). Wolf Wolfensberger, who began the citizen advocacy movement within ARC (formerly called the Association for Retarded Citizens), has devoted a lifetime to expanding and operationalizing normalization theory (Wolfensberger, 1972, 1991). Among his contributions is an instrument called PASSING that permits the objective evaluation of services provided by school, recreation, or community programs (Wolfensberger & Thomas, 1983).

Although initially applied only to mental retardation issues, normalization theory is now widely used in relation to all disabilities in which persons are perceived as looking or behaving differently. Wolfensberger (1972) stated that three principles underlie normalization theory:

1. Behavioral and appearance deviancy can be reduced by minimizing the degree to which persons with disabilities are treated differently from able-bodied persons.
2. Conversely, deviancy is enhanced by treating persons as if they were deviant.

3. To the degree that they are grouped together and segregated from the mainstream of society, individuals will be perceived as different from others and will tend to behave differently.

Wolfensberger's work focuses on the social devaluation of people who are different and the negative roles that society assigns them. He stresses that we must use culturally valued means to enable people to live culturally valued lives. There are seven core themes of normalization:

1. Normalization is concerned with identification of unconscious (usually negative) dynamics that contribute to the devaluation and oppression of certain groups and promotes conscious strategies for remediating devalued social status.
2. Normalization focuses on the creation of valued social roles and the elimination of negative role expectancies.
3. It is not enough to use approaches that are normal or neutral; we must select means and tools that enhance the image of persons who are devalued.
4. The developmental model, properly implemented, can lead to tremendous client growth because of its positive presumptions about human potential, its high demands and expectancies, and its requirement of effective pedagogies.
5. Normalization recognizes that imitation is one of the most powerful learning mechanisms known and provides models that will help people function in appropriate and valued ways.
6. Social imagery strongly influences role expectancies; therefore, the social image of devalued people must be enhanced.
7. A number of supports are needed for *personal,* valued, social integration of a devalued person to be successful. Integration must be personal and social rather than physical. (paraphrased from Wolfensberger & Thomas, 1983, pp. 24–27)

Clearly, many humanistic practices have their roots in normalization. This theory particularly supports integration; the use of person-first terminology; careful, systematic selection of models; and concentrated work on attitude change.

Personal Meaning Theory

Personal meaning theory, attributed to Beatrice Wright, stresses that it is the personal meaning of a disability that is important rather than the disability itself. This personal meaning is derived from a host of psychosocial factors "that underlie the way disability as a value loss is perceived and reacted to by other people, as well as the self" (Wright, 1983, p. 6). Author of *Physical Disability—A Psychological Approach* (1960) and a second edition with a modified title, *Physical Disability—A Psychosocial Approach* (1983), Wright acknowledges that Kurt Lewin and Carl Rogers most influenced her thinking. Wright is considered the leading theorist in contemporary rehabilitation psychology. The implications of personal meaning theory in disability are dis-

Table 6.1
Movement Purposes Inventory.

In physical education, I use movement to

1. Release tension.
2. Feel healthier.
3. Discover what I can and cannot do.
4. Encourage my teammates to do their best.
5. Have a special feeling of excitement.
6. Take part in activities with my friends because I enjoy playing with them.
7. Become better at things like throwing, catching, and hitting.
8. Work with others in games and sports.
9. Explore the space around me.
10. Learn about my country by doing such things as clogging, folk, and square dancing.
11. Have fun.
12. Help me to keep my weight right.
13. Compete with myself or with my team.
14. Improve my speed and skill in games.
15. Test my skill and courage.
16. Develop and maintain a healthy heart and lungs.
17. Express my thoughts and feelings.
18. Feel like a complete person.
19. Develop strong muscles.
20. Feel good.
21. Know more about watching sports and games.
22. Improve my balance and flexibility.

Note. The possible responses vary, with yes/no appropriate for elementary schoolchildren and 3- to 5-point numerical scales appropriate for older students.

cussed in Chapter 2. The teacher must be especially aware of the social environment in learning.

Personal meaning theory, as used in regular physical education, also has implications for adapted physical education. Ann Jewett and Linda Bain in *The Curriculum Process in Physical Education* (1985) describe a personal meaning curriculum model as one of seven basic curricular structures. This model stresses that the purposes and processes of physical education vary for each individual and change in relation to situational needs.

The application of personal meaning theory to adapted physical education leads to formal and informal assessment of personal meaning in relation to the activities to be taught. Students should be actively involved in planning their instructional program, encouraged to set goals, and taught how to monitor their progress.

The personal meaning of movement and sport can be assessed in several ways. One is to ask students why they move. Ennis (1985) developed an instrument for this purpose that includes 22 reasons (see Table 6.1). Reasons probably change with class content (e.g., soccer, folk dance, movement education) and structure (e.g., competition, cooperation, individual). Ennis reported that Items 11 and 14 received the highest ratings by middle school students.

Research shows that fun is the reason most children give for participation in youth sports (Wankel & Sefton, 1989). To facilitate the development of an active lifestyle, teachers need to explore with students the personal meaning of fun. For some individuals, this seems to have a social basis, whereas for others, it seems to be challenge or mastery oriented.

Another approach to assessing personal meaning is the use of instruments that measure the importance of sports and physical appearance (Fox & Corbin, 1989; Harter, 1985, 1988). For example, students may be given pairs of items like those that follow and asked to circle the one of each pair that better describes how important something is to them:

Some teenagers don't think that being athletic is that important	BUT	Other teenagers think that being athletic is important.
Some teenagers think that how they look is important	BUT	Other teenagers don't care that much about how they look.
		Harter (1988)

Only by caring about personal meaning can you personalize instruction. Know and accept that physical activity and competence are not the central constructs in everyone's lives. For some persons, finding a job, acquiring a close friend or lover, or gaining access to a social group may be foremost. Take the time to listen and to show the link between physical activity and other goals.

Personal meaning is extremely important in self-concept theory (discussed later in the chapter) because it provides insight into the ideal or desired self. Asking students to state their level of aspiration or to rate importance of a particular domain or activity enables you to examine the discrepancy between actual and ideal self.

Social Cognitive Theory

Social cognitive theory, proposed by Albert Bandura, supports the humanistic perspective. Bandura (1986) emphasizes that human functioning can best be explained in terms of "a model of triadic reciprocality in which behavior, cognitive and other personal factors, and environmental events all operate as interacting determinants of each other" (p. 18). He states that *social cognitive* is a replacement label for his earlier theory of social learning. Bandura is recognized as one of the five leading theorists who have most influenced contemporary education practices (Bell-Gredler, 1986). His self-efficacy theory provides the theoretical framework for many adapted physical activity practices.

Self-Efficacy Theory

Bandura (1977) proposed self-efficacy theory as a conceptual framework for changing fearful and avoidant behaviors. As such, it has considerable relevance for low-skilled individuals (Craft & Hogan, 1985). According to Bandura (1986), *perceived self-efficacy* is "a judgment of one's capacity to accomplish a certain level of performance" (p. 391). It is concerned, not with skills, but with what we think we can do with these skills. Self-efficacy is also defined as a situation-specific form of self-confidence.

FIGURE   6.6

Model showing antecedent events used in Bandura's self-efficacy model to change efficacy expectations.

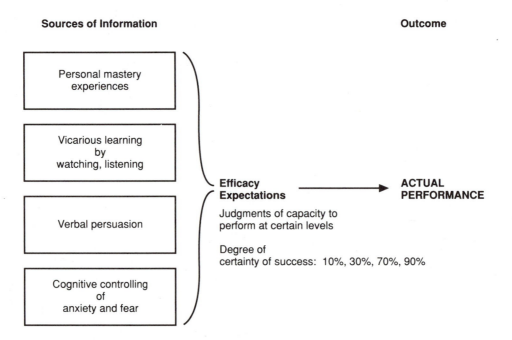

Self-efficacy is typically measured with a yes/no response scale in relation to specific questions (e.g., "Can you jump over a 3-ft height?" "Can you run a 12-min mile?" "Can you score 7 out of 10 on a volleyball serve test?"). Another approach is to ask students their degree of certainty that they can do something: 0%, 20%, 40%, 60%, 80%, 100%. An *efficacy expectation* is a good predictor of actual performance. If a student expresses a negative efficacy expectation, the humanistic teacher does not force him or her to try the task. Instead, the reasons for the belief are explored, and four antecedent events are used to change the belief (see Figure 6.6). Partner- or team-teaching practices are helpful when implementing self-efficacy theory because they allow giving students with negative expectancies a choice. The students can either go to the resource teacher station for help or stay and watch the successful performances of others. A time limit, however, is placed on the watching option (also called symbolic modeling or vicarious learning by Bandura).

Figure 6.6 shows the four sources of information posited by Bandura as determinants of an efficacy expectation. Of these, Bandura believed that personal mastery experiences were the most important. He stressed that success raises expectations of further success and discussed structuring the environment to ensure efficacy. Students should be taught to visualize themselves and others coping successfully with the phobia or fear. Performance accomplishments thus can be direct or indirect. As a pioneer in social learning theory, Bandura believed strongly in partner follow-the-leader type activities called *participant modeling*. He also supported cognitive training to control anxiety and to cope with stress.

Self-efficacy theory seems similar to the self-concept theories described later in the chapter, but Bandura (1986) pointed out several differences. Mainly, self-efficacy is more cognitively oriented. It is a *judgment* that one can do something, regardless of whether the consequences are pleasant. A skilled combat soldier may judge himself to be efficacious but derive neither pleasure nor self-esteem from his work. In contrast, according to Bandura, most self-concept theories emphasize feelings. This is not entirely true in that new approaches treat self-concept as an attitude with cognitive, affective, and behavioral dimensions.

Self-Determination Theory

Maslow's self-actualization theory in the 1950s stressed the importance of independent and creative thought processes. Since then, many theories pertaining to self-determination and intrinsic motivation have been developed. Vallerand and Reid (1990) provided an excellent review of these, with applications to special populations. Highlighted in their review is the self-determination and intrinsic motivation theory of Deci and Ryan (1985), also called cognitive evaluation theory. This theory posits that several types of forces initiate, direct, and sustain behaviors. The more intrinsic and self-determining the force, the more positive the consequences.

Motivation refers to all of the forces (internal and external) that focus behaviors, start and stop them, and determine their frequency and duration. Deci and Ryan (1985) distinguish between three types of motivation: (a) intrinsic, (b) extrinsic, and (c) amotivation. *Intrinsic motivation* refers to forces that are 100% self-determined; these come directly from voluntary activity and are experienced as fun, pleasurable, and satisfying. *Extrinsic motivation* may be self- or other-determined, depending on who sets the goals and establishes rewards and sanctions; these forces are focused on either obtaining rewards or avoiding sanctions. *Amotivation* refers to absence of forces because no cognitive link is established between behavior and outcomes. This may occur because mental function is frozen at or below the level of

FIGURE 6.7

Model depicting parts of the self-concept based on the theory of reasoned action. We have belief systems for several separate domains (e.g., physical appearance, athletic competence, social competence).

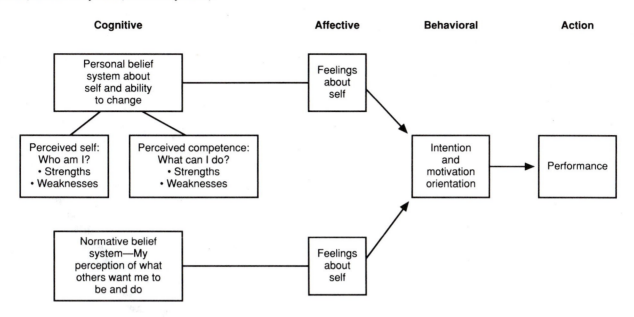

a 7- or 8-month-old infant or because life experiences are so confusing and overpowering that persons no longer try to make sense of cause-effect relationships.

Obviously, many variables influence motivation to engage in physical activities. Humanistic teachers strive to make activities intrinsically rewarding through adaptations that assure success, fun, and satisfaction. They provide abundant choices in order to promote feelings of self-determination, and much of their verbal feedback requires problem solving (e.g., "That was great! Why is your performance so good today? How many times have you practiced that? Have you shown your mother that you can do this? What part of that skill is the easiest for you? What part is the hardest?").

Humanistic teachers deemphasize tangible rewards like tokens, ribbons, and trophies because research shows that such reinforcement eventually leads to dependence on others for motivation. Feedback is used to praise effort as well as success (e.g., "I can tell you worked really hard on that." "I can see you are concentrating." "You remembered all the instructions."). Feedback also frequently mentions fun (e.g., "What was the most fun about that?" "Isn't this fun?").

Self-Concept Theory

Self-concept refers to all of the beliefs, feelings, and intentions that a person holds in regard to self. Figure 6.7 shows the cognitive, affective, and behavioral dimensions of self-concept. Many theories have been posited to explain self-concept, describe its development, and enhance its function. This is because self-concept is believed to be the mediator of both affect (life satisfaction and happiness) and motivation. As such, it has a direct bearing on learning and other behaviors.

The difference between the "I Am" and "I Can Do" selves is important in self-concept theory. Persons may feel good or bad about themselves because of gender ("I am a female"), race ("I am an Afro-American"), home ("I live in the poor part of town"), family ("My parents are uneducated [or criminals or whatever]"), appearance ("I am fat"), disability or illness ("I have asthma"), and a host of other variables. Likewise, persons may feel good or bad about themselves because of what they can or cannot do (see Figure 6.7).

Educators are particularly interested in perceived competence theory, but individuals need to be loved and accepted, not only for what they can do, but simply because they exist. This quality is called unconditional love or acceptance. In achievement-oriented families and cultures, some persons grow up feeling that they are loved only for what they can do, and hence their lives are meaningful only in relation to their doing selves. Psychologists tell us that equal emphasis should be placed on the being self.

How persons feel about their being and doing selves depends partly on what they perceive others think of these selves. Two systems thus influence the selves that determine happiness and motivation. Both of these belief systems are affected by environmental-genetic interactions. Perceptions of what significant others think and want may or may not be accurate. According to Carl Rogers, parts of these belief systems may be distorted or denied.

Self-concept in school and movement settings is typically defined operationally in terms of beliefs, feelings, and intentions that can be measured by standardized instruments. Many different domains or dimensions of self can be measured (e.g., physical appearance, athletic competence, scholastic competence). Basic information about self-concept that is essential to planning and conducting humanistic adapted physical education follows. Topics covered are terminology, development of self-concept, principles of self-concept formation, issues regarding self-concept, profiling, pedagogical implications for teachers, and descriptions of major instruments.

Self-Concept Terminology

Some persons use *self-concept, self-worth, self-esteem, self-regard,* and *self-perception* (perceived competence) as synonyms, whereas others make sharp distinctions. In general, self-concept or ego identity is considered the broadest construct and includes both cognitive ("I am a female." "I am an athlete." "I weigh 110 pounds.") and evaluative (good or bad) dimensions (i.e., opinions, beliefs, and feelings). Other terms tend to denote only the evaluative component of self-concept. The term used typically reflects the standardized instrument selected as best and the theory underlying the assessment approach.

Development of Self-Concept

The infant, held close to the person feeding him or her, first begins to perceive the difference between self and not-self at about 3 months of age. At about 8 months of age, this perception matures into recognition of the "I" as a being who can cause things to happen (i.e., smile and the other person smiles back; cry and you get action). In infancy and early childhood, self-concept is difficult to separate from body image, since early feelings about the body and its capacity for movement form the basis of self-concept.

Authorities disagree on the age when self-concept can be measured. Some believe than an accurate estimate of feelings about concrete aspects of the self can be obtained at about age 4 or 5 years. Pictorial inventories in which the child chooses between two drawings ("Which one is more like you?") are typically used until about age 8 (i.e., the emergence of third-grade thinking and evaluation capacity). Thereafter, standardized written inventories are typically used unless disability makes pictorial measures preferable.

Initially, self-concept is formed at home and includes only factors relating to home and family. By the second grade, however, the school and other interactions outside the home have begun to exert a major influence on self-concept formation. By this age, also, children with visible disabilities have come to realize that their appearance is different from that of their peers; this naturally affects self-concept. Thus, with increasing age and experience, the ego identity of individuals expands to include more and more domains or dimensions.

The concept of the self also becomes more stable and resistant to change as persons grow older. With young children, day-to-day (and sometimes moment-to-moment) variability is a problem in self-concept measurement. It is easy to change the young child's mind about self or almost anything. Every experience causes fluctuations because the self is not yet integrated by a formal system of thought. Understanding of these facts guides teachers to assess self-concept several times rather than once. Then an average is recorded as the estimate of real self.

The issue of stability must also be considered in evaluating self-concept change. Before age 8 (or the equivalent mental functioning), significant change scores may be obtained as a result of special programs of short duration. To ascertain that such self-concept changes are permanent, it is necessary to assess again about 1 month later. After age 8, self-concept becomes increasingly difficult to change. Long-term, intensive programs in which family and school work together are most effective in causing change.

Age and sex differences in self-concept seem to depend on the assessment instrument. Many assessment manuals report that self-concept is highest in the first grade and then begins to decline, at least until the third or fourth grade, when it stabilizes. The high early childhood self-concept probably relates to immaturity of evaluation processes; the child has not yet begun to compare self to others. Most research shows no gender differences or very small ones that are not interpreted as meaningful.

Progress from one life stage to another affects self-concept because persons must meet new societal expectations and adjust to changes in body (e.g., puberty, old age) and abilities. Transition into adolescence, with its challenge to succeed in romantic and job realms, may cause fluctuations in self-concept. Likewise, changing one's comparison group, as in the shift from high school to college or from one job to another, affects self-concept.

The longitudinal development of self-concept in persons with disabilities and/or health problems has received little study. Much depends on coping skills, social support, and the intensity and duration of stress. The comparison group that a person uses in evaluating self also makes a big difference. A clumsy child in a class of good athletes may have lower physical self-esteem than a clumsy child in a class with peers of similar ability. On the other hand, placement outside the mainstream may cause feelings of inferiority.

Principles of Self-Concept Formation

Five principles serve as guides to enhancing self-concept. Which of the following principles would you rely on the most as you teach differently abled students?

1. **Principle of Reflected Appraisals.** This principle emphasizes that children grow up seeing themselves as they *think* others see them. This has been called the looking-glass or mirror phenomenon. Every facial expression, gesture, and word of another is interpreted as having meaning for oneself. The more perceived significance of the other, the more influential the reflected appraisal. Because many persons do not interpret the feelings and actions of others accurately, you must work to assure real rather than distorted or denied perceptions.

   Reflected appraisal is feedback, and you must be aware of individual differences in sensitivity. Clarification is important: "I like you but I do not like this particular behavior." "You are a good person, but this behavior is not acceptable." Equally important is the O'Leary and Schneider (see reference list) principle "Catch 'em being good." The more frequently you can see students doing something well or behaving in a thoughtful, caring, responsible way, the more often the reflected appraisal (both conscious and subconscious) will be positive.

2. **Principle of Self-Attribution.** This principle, derived from behavioral theory, states that past behavior (i.e., feelings of efficacy or competency) affects the formation of self-concept. We make attributions about ourselves on the basis of our observations of a particular behavior. After eating a large meal, for instance, we think, "I was hungrier than I thought." After achieving a success, we infer, "Hey, I'm pretty good." Self-concept is thus based on analysis of overt behaviors and the circumstances under which they occurred. Implications for teaching are reminding students of past successes, encouraging analysis of reasons for success, and structuring situations so that the same conditions are present as when the remembered success occurred.

3. **Principle of Mastery Challenge or Perceived Competence.** This principle, derived from humanistic psychology, is future oriented, whereas the self-attribution principle is past oriented. *Mastery challenge* is the principle of making students feel safe, loved, and appropriately challenged so that they see themselves as competent before trying the task. If Maslow's hierarchy of needs is met by creating a warm, success-oriented environment, then persons are intrinsically motivated to reduce the discrepancy between what they can do and what they wish they could do. This is called the innate mastery challenge. Positive self-concept develops when persons set goals (consciously or unconsciously), expect to be successful, and then validate their expectancies.

   Shaping the environment so that Maslow's deficiency needs are met and persons perceive that they will be successful is a shared responsibility of everyone in the ecosystem; this is a holistic approach with everyone agreeing to provide social support. It also respects the freedom of a student to say, "I'm not ready yet. I want to do it but I can't by myself." This opens the way for teacher-student and peer partnerships based on the idea: "Trust me. I'll lead you through it. Together we can be successful. Then, when you are ready, you can try it alone."

4. **Principle of Social Comparison.** This principle, based on the social comparison theory of Leon Festinger (1954), states that self-concept is formed through the lifelong process of comparing oneself to others (see Figure 6.8). Between the ages of 5 and 7, children begin to make peer comparisons ("I'm better, [the same, or worse] than others"). This information source becomes increasingly important, peaking at about ages 10 to 11. Thereafter, persons tend to develop either a predominantly task or ego orientation. *Task-oriented* persons judge themselves in terms of effort ("I did the best I could"), whereas *ego-oriented* persons judge their self-worth by means of social comparison.

   Humanistic teaching tries to deemphasize social comparison and help persons feel good about their own ability and effort. Students are taught to monitor their

FIGURE   6.8

Social comparison theory states that self-concept is formed through the lifetime process of comparing self to others.

learning progress by charting scores and behaviors. Questions emphasized are, "Did you achieve your goal?" and "Did you make a personal best?" Nevertheless, everyone uses social comparison from time to time. When this is the case, ask questions to encourage students to think about whether they have selected a similar or appropriate other to use for comparison. Social comparison should involve more than outcomes; it should also include attributions (reasons) like effort, ability, and chance.

5. **Principle of Personal Meaning.** This principle emphasizes that self-concept is a structure with many dimensions that have unequal salience (prominence). There is a hierarchy of salience, and pedagogy must address what is central to personal goals and/or needs. These may be stable or vary by situation and/or task. A particularly important aspect of personal meaning is whether events and behaviors are internally or externally controlled. For most persons, internal control is linked with greater personal meaning.

Self-Concept Issues

Should physical educators be concerned with general self-concept or only the specific dimensions that relate to the physical self? Is there a difference between general and global self-concept? Which scales relate to physical education goals? Answers to these and other questions are important to planning physical education assessment and curriculum models. Beliefs about the nature of self-concept affect the selection of instruments.

The first issue is whether self-concept is unidimensional, multidimensional, or hierarchical. This question pertains mainly to scoring because all instruments measure several dimensions of the self (see Table 6.2).

In unidimensional self-concept theory, the self is the sum of all of its parts. Items measure both being and doing selves, and every item contributes equally to the total score, which is considered an estimate of the general, total self. In Table 6.2, the Piers-Harris Children's Self-Concept Scale (CSCS) and the Martinek-Zaichkowsky Self-Concept Scale

Table 6.2
The subscales comprising several self-concept inventories.

Piers-Harris (CSCS): The Way I Feel About Myself	Martinek-Zaichkowsky Self-Concept Scale (MZSC)	Harter Self-Perception Profile: What Am I Like	Marsh Self-Description Questionnaire (SDQ)
1. Behavior 2. Intellectual and school status	1. Behavioral, personal, and social characteristics	1. Behavioral conduct 2. Scholastic	*Academic* Math Reading General-school
3. Physical appearance and attributes 4. Anxiety	2. Ability in games, recreation, and sports 3. Personality traits and emotional tendency	3. Physical appearance 4. Athletic competence	*Nonacademic* Physical abilities Physical appearance Peer relations Parent relations
5. Popularity 6. Happiness and satisfaction	4. Home and family relationships and circumstances 5. Satisfaction and happiness	5. Social acceptance 6. Close friendship 7. Romantic appeal 8. Job competence 9. Global self-worth	*Global* Total academic Total nonacademic Total self General-self

Note. The Harter profile is the only inventory of this group that *never* uses a total score; it thus reflects belief that global self-worth (the last item) is not the sum of the parts. Harter and Marsh use the term *global* in different ways.

(MZSC) are illustrative of the unidimensional stance. Separate subscale scores can be calculated to guide goal setting, but the total score is always examined.

In multidimensional self-concept theory, the self is *not* the sum of all of its parts but rather a multifaceted structure that becomes increasingly complex. By about age 4, children have the ability to evaluate concrete aspects of the self: physical competence, cognitive competence, peer acceptance, and parental acceptance. They typically cannot separate the concrete from the abstract until about age 8, when a separate, global self-concept begins to emerge. This global self pertains to abstract feelings of overall happiness and life satisfaction, is related to competence feelings in specific domains, but is separate. Theorists taking this stance thus differentiate between global and general (total) self-concept. In Table 6.2, the Harter scale is illustrative of multidimensional philosophy.

In hierarchical self-concept theory, the idea of multidimensionality is extended by breaking the total self into major parts (e.g., academic and nonacademic) and then further analyzing each part into subcomponents. In Table 6.2, the Marsh Self-Description Questionnaire (SDQ) is illustrative of hierarchical philosophy. It blends unidimensional total score usage with multidimensional domain-specific measurement concepts.

The second self-concept issue is determining the major domains (dimensions, clusters, factors) of self-concept and the items that should be used to measure them. Table 6.2, which lists the subscales included in four of the best-known inventories, shows that there is general agreement about most (but not all) of the components. Physical educators must study both scales and items to decide which instruments are most appropriate for their needs. Most libraries have copies of the major self-concept manuals. Otherwise, they can be ordered from publishing companies.

Profiling

The construction of individual profiles enables the teacher to sit down with a student, discuss strengths and weaknesses, and set physical education goals. Scores of average, same-age students help in the interpretation of profiles. Inventory manuals typically give this information. Average scores (means) on self-concept tend to run high. On a 4-point scale, the means tend to fluctuate around 2.9. On an 80-item instrument, the average usually ranges between 45 and 55. On a 25-item instrument, the average falls between 19 and 21.

Figure 6.9 shows how self-concept scores are profiled. The solid line shows the average scores presented in the inventory manual for 14-year-olds (Harter, 1988). The broken line shows scores of a selected student whose self-concept in most areas is lower than that of peers. Consider what the dialogue between the teacher and student might be. How can physical education help strengthen areas of weakness?

Pedagogical Implications

Thus far, research with all of the instruments shows that the physical appearance scale is more closely related to global or general self-concept than any other scale. The physical appearance scale is also highly related to peer relations (popularity, social acceptance, close friendship). This has powerful implications for humanistic teaching. To help students feel good about their general or global selves, educators must help them understand, appreciate, like, and accept their bodies and various physical attributes. Feelings about the face, eyes, and hair are more powerful predictors of self-concept than other body parts. Complimenting students on these parts and noticing changes is, therefore, particularly important.

Self-concept assessment early in the school year provides a way of getting acquainted with the whole student. Generally, students' estimates of their physical appearance,

FIGURE   6.9

Harter's self-perception profile for adolescents. Individual student profile (broken line) compared with average scores (solid line) of 14-year-olds.

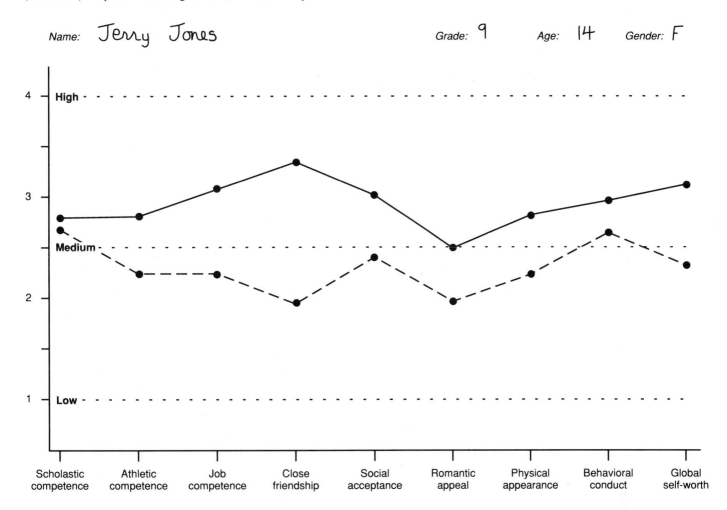

Name: Jerry Jones   Grade: 9   Age: 14   Gender: F

athletic competence, and social acceptance are good predictors of physical education interest and performance, so these measures are helpful in screening to find students who need special help.

Students' perceptions and feelings, as measured by self-concept scales, should be compared with their actual abilities in the physical education setting. Some students are really good at things, but do not seem to feel or know this. Other students think they are better than they really are. Regardless of the direction of the discrepancy, these students are denying or distorting reality and need special help in making the perceived and actual selves congruent.

Self-concept information should also be used in personalized goal setting. Periodically, ask students to write essays or make audio or videotapes about who they are and what they can do at present, what they want for the future, and how physical education can help them become the self they want to be. This serves as the basis for setting goals, breaking goals into objectives, deciding on activities, and agreeing on evaluation methodology.

Another approach is to ask students to identify problems that physical education can help resolve and then check to see if the problems match self-concept data. Among

problems that students often list are (a) "My asthma (or other condition) makes me miss a lot of school and I feel left out," (b) "I don't have the energy to do what everyone wants me to do," (c) "I feel depressed or blah a lot of the time," (d) "I have a lot of friends but no really close friend—I want someone to like me better than anyone else," and (e) "I feel scared (high-strung, nervous) so much of the time." Many students need help in making the connection between physical activity and mental health, tension release, friendships, and energy.

Asking students to keep physical activity journals or diaries is a good technique. Such self-reports should include duration and intensity of activity, whether it was done alone or with people, what goals the activity was directed toward (e.g., fun, relaxation, losing weight), and whether the goals were achieved.

Central to self-concept work in physical education is establishment of trust and an open, sharing relationship between students and teacher. Self-concept instruments, like the attitude measures discussed in Chapter 2, should never be called *tests* because this word traditionally infers right and wrong answers. Self-concept measures are called scales, inventories, or questionnaires. Students must understand that there are no right and wrong answers, only individual differences, and that these differences are what make us unique, wonderful, and interesting humans. Students also need to know that their responses will be held in confidence. If you feel that a student needs the services of a professional counselor, then the goal is to convince the student to go to a counselor and share. Never do the sharing for the student.

Descriptions of Major Self-Concept Instruments

Familiarity with several self-concept instruments allows wise choices to be made in planning the physical education assessment model. Descriptions of several instruments that have good validity and reliability follow. The *Mental Measurements Yearbook,* edited by Oscar Buros (old editions) and Conoley & Kramer (1989), provides more information about these instruments, including expert evaluation of pros and cons, and is found in the reference section of every library.

Piers-Harris Children's Self-Concept Scale

The Piers-Harris Children's Self-Concept Scale (CSCS), developed by Ellen Piers and Dale Harris in 1964, is a widely used measure of self-concept in Grades 3 to 12. It includes 80 items written at a third-grade reading level and yields separate scores for six areas (see Table 6.2). The revised manual emphasizes, however: "The single most reliable measure for the *Piers-Harris,* and the one with the best research support, is the total score" (Piers, 1984, p. 37).

Illustrative items are "I have a pleasant face" and "I am among the last to be chosen for games." Respondents circle either *yes* or *no* for each item. The test manual for this inventory (Piers, 1984) is available from Western Psychological Services, 12031 Wilshire Blvd., Los Angeles, CA 90025. An advantage of the CSCS is availability of computerized scoring and interpretation, which generates profiles of strengths and weaknesses in six areas.

Cratty Self-Concept Scale

Bryant Cratty, a physical educator at UCLA, developed the Cratty Self-Concept Scale specifically to measure dimensions of self-concept that discriminate between clumsy and well-skilled children in kindergarten through Grade 6. Most of the 20 questions comprising this scale are rewordings of Piers-Harris items. Because this scale is especially recommended for use in movement settings, it appears in its entirety in Figure 6.10.

Scoring of the inventory is directed by common sense, with 1 point given for each *yes* answer that reflects a good self-concept. Cratty defined *high self-concept* as a score of 16 or over and *low self-concept* as 14 and under. Average scores ranged between 14.1 and 15.7 for kindergarten to Grade 6, with no significant differences between grades or genders. This instrument is highly recommended for screening purposes.

Martinek-Zaichkowsky Self-Concept Scale

The Martinek-Zaichkowsky Self-Concept Scale (MZSC) was developed in 1977 by two physical educators, Thomas Martinek and Leonard Zaichkowsky, and has been used ex-

FIGURE 6.10

Cratty Self-Concept Scale.

1. Are you good at making things with your hands?	Yes/No
2. Can you draw well?	Yes/No
3. Are you strong?	Yes/No
4. Do you like the way you look?	Yes/No
5. Do your friends make fun of you?	Yes/No
6. Are you handsome/pretty?	Yes/No
7. Do you have trouble making friends?	Yes/No
8. Do you like school?	Yes/No
9. Do you wish you were different?	Yes/No
10. Are you sad most of the time?	Yes/No
11. Are you the last to be chosen in games?	Yes/No
12. Do girls like you?	Yes/No
13. Are you a good leader in games and sports?	Yes/No
14. Are you clumsy?	Yes/No
15. In games, do you watch instead of play?	Yes/No
16. Do boys like you?	Yes/No
17. Are you happy most of the time?	Yes/No
18. Do you have nice hair?	Yes/No
19. Do you play with younger children a lot?	Yes/No
20. Is reading easy to you?	Yes/No

From B. Cratty, N. Ikedo, M. Martin, C. Jennett, & M. Morris (1970). *Movement activities, motorability, and the education of children.* Springfield, IL: Charles C. Thomas.

tensively in physical education research (Gruber, 1985). This pictorial scale consists of 25 pairs of drawings (see sample item in Figure 6.11). Males and females are equally represented in the drawings. Six of the 25 items depict physical activities.

The MZSC is recommended for children in Grades 1 to 8 as a nonverbal, culture-free measure (Martinek & Zaichkowsky, 1977). Its pictorial format makes the MZSC especially valuable in assessing self-concepts of children who cannot read. Although the MZSC is designed as a nonverbal measure, explaining the items in individual and small-group administrations may be helpful. In regard to the sample item in Figure 6.11, for instance, you could say: "We see two children trying to do a push-up exercise. The child in the top picture has trouble doing the push-up. The child in the bottom picture is doing the push-up with ease. Which child is most like you?" Furthermore, when the inventory is administered

FIGURE   6.11

Sample item from Martinek-Zaichkowsky Self-Concept Scale.

individually, ask the child "Why?" or "How do you know that?" This is an excellent way to get acquainted with children and to cooperatively set goals for the year.

The MZSC is available from Psychologists and Educators, Inc., P.O. Box 513, Chesterfield, MO 63006. So far, most research has reported only total scores, but separate scores for five areas can be calculated (see Table 6.2).

Harter Self-Perception Instruments

Susan Harter and colleagues at the University of Denver have developed instruments for several different age groups (see Table 6.3). Additionally, there is an inventory specifically for students with learning disabilities in Grades 3 to 8 (Renick & Harter, 1988), which is appropriate also for normally achieving students. The items for athletic competence on this and the Self-Perception Profile for Children (Harter, 1985) are the same except for simplification of wording on one and deletion of one.

Harter's instruments are all characterized by a structured alternative-response format (see Figure 6.12). Only one box is checked. Students first indicate which of the two descriptions they are most like. Then, within this category, they check "Really True for Me" or "Sort of True for Me." This format reduces the chance that persons will give what they think are desirable responses rather than the truth.

Harter's instruments are different from most others in another way. From age 8 and up, one scale is designed to measure global self-worth. The global self-worth score is derived only from the five items in Figure 6.12, and this score is considered separate from the domain-specific self-perception scores. Items on Harter's inventories are never added together to make a total self-concept score.

The number of perceived competence scales increases for each age group. The pictorial scale for young children yields four scores: cognitive competence, physical competence, peer acceptance, and maternal acceptance. The childhood scale yields a global self-worth score and five domain scores: scholastic competence, social acceptance, athletic competence, physical appearance, and behavioral conduct. As shown in Table 6.2, the adolescent scale measures the same things as the childhood scale, plus close friendship, romantic appeal, and job competence. The college and adult scales measure all of these areas plus more.

Several of the Harter scales are appropriate for helping physical educators to operationally define and measure the goal of positive self-concept as it relates to movement, physical appearance, and social competency. For example, Harter uses the five items in Figure 6.13 to measure perceived competence in sports and games. The numerical value of each box is included in these examples to help you understand how items are scored. On the forms administered to students, however, the boxes are blank. Ideally, with clumsy and differently abled students, self-perception data should be collected through an interview technique that encourages students to talk about why they perceive their sport and game abilities as they do, how important these abilities are to them, and whether or not they want to set personal goals to improve.

For young children and/or those who have difficulty reading, the pictorial format can be used to determine feelings about physical competence and to set goals. Harter uses six pairs of pictures for this purpose.

Harter's self-perception instruments, as well as other inventories related to her theory of competence motivation, can be obtained from Dr. Susan Harter, Psychology Department, University of Denver, 2040 S. York St., Denver, CO 80208. These instruments increasingly are being used in physical education research (Gibbons & Bushakra, 1989; Hopper, 1988; Sherrill et al., 1990; Ulrich, 1987; Weiss, Bredemeier, & Shewchuk, 1985).

Ulrich Pictorial Perceived Physical Competence Scale

Beverly and Dale Ulrich, physical educators at Indiana University, have extended Harter's pictorial scales to include 21 pairs of pictures in the Ulrich Pictorial Perceived Physical Competence Scale (see Figure 6.14). Like Harter, they have developed separate test booklets for boys and girls (Ulrich & Ulrich, 1990). This extended scale holds tremendous promise for learning more, not only about young children, but also about students who are mentally retarded and learning disabled (Ulrich & Collier, 1990).

Table 6.3
Harter self-perception instruments.

Age Group	Self-Perception Instrument
4–7	Pictorial Scale for Perceived Competence and Social Acceptance for Young Children (Harter & Pike, 1984)—There are two versions of this instrument: (a) preschool/kindergarten and (b) first-/second-graders. For each, there are separate booklets for boys and girls.
8–13	Self-Perception Profile for Children (Harter, 1985)—This is a revision of the Perceived Competence Scale for Children, published in 1979.
Adolescents	Self-Perception Profile for Adolescents (Harter, 1988)
College Students	Self-Perception Profile for College Students (Neemann & Harter, 1986)
Adults	Self-Perception Profile for Adults (Messer & Harter, 1986)

FIGURE   6.12

Items that measure global self-worth.

Really True for Me	Sort of True for Me	Items		Sort of True for Me	Really True for Me
1	2	9. Some teenagers are often disappointed with themselves	BUT other teenagers are pretty pleased with themselves.	3	4
1	2	18. Some teenagers don't like the way they are leading their life	BUT other teenagers do like the way they are leading their life.	3	4
4	3	27. Some teenagers are happy with themselves most of the time	BUT other teenagers are often not happy with themselves.	2	1
4	3	36. Some teenagers like the kind of person they are	BUT other teenagers often wish they were someone else.	2	1
4	3	45. Some teenagers are very happy being the way they are	BUT other teenagers wish they were different.	2	1

Note. Numbers show scoring system and should not be used on inventory given to students.

FIGURE   6.13

Items that measure athletic competence.

Really True for Me	Sort of True for Me		Items			Sort of True for Me	Really True for Me
4	3	3.	Some teenagers do very well at all kinds of sports	BUT	other teenagers don't feel that they are very good when it comes to sports.	2	1
4	3	12.	Some teenagers think they could do well at just about any new athletic activity	BUT	other teenagers are afraid they might not do well at a new athletic activity.	2	1
4	3	21.	Some teenagers feel that they are better than others their age at sports	BUT	other teenagers don't feel they can play as well.	2	1
1	2	30.	Some teenagers don't do well at new outdoor games	BUT	other teenagers are good at games right away.	3	4
1	2	39.	Some teenagers do not feel that they are very athletic	BUT	other teenagers feel that they are very athletic.	3	4

Note. Numbers show scoring system and should not be used on inventory given to students.

FIGURE   6.14

Items included on the Ulrich Pictorial Perceived Physical Competence Scale.

Grade K	Grades 1 and 2

Harter's Original Six Items

Grade K	Grades 1 and 2
1. Swinging	1. Swinging
2. Climbing on jungle gym	2. Climbing on jungle gym
3. Skipping	3. Skipping
4. Running	4. Running
5. Tying shoes	5. Bouncing a ball
6. Hopping	6. Jumping rope

Ulrichs' Additional Fundamental Motor Skill Items

7. Jumping	7. Jumping
8. Kicking	8. Kicking
9. Throwing	9. Throwing
10. Catching	10. Catching
11. Am strong	11. Am strong
12. Bouncing a ball	12. Batting a ball

Ulrichs' Additional Sport-Specific Skill Items (Same for Grades K, 1, and 2)

Baseball:	13. Batting a baseball
	14. Throwing a baseball
	15. Catching a baseball
Basketball:	16. Dribbling a basketball
	17. Shooting a basketball
	18. Passing a basketball
Soccer:	19. Dribbling a soccer ball
	20. Kicking a soccer ball
	21. Soccer throw-in

FIGURE 6.15

Sample item from Ulrich Pictorial Perceived Physical Competence Scale.

Unlike the Martinek-Zaichkowsky pictorial instrument, which is described in the test manual as a nonverbal measure, the Harter-Ulrich approach requires that the pairs of pictures be explained to the student. Illustrative directions for Figure 6.15 are "This boy isn't very good at running." (Tester points to picture on the right.) "This boy is pretty good at running." (Tester points to picture on the left.) "Please point to the picture which is most like you." After the child points, the tester continues: "Are you a lot like this boy." (Tester points to a big circle.) "Or are you a little like this boy?" (Tester points to a little circle.) "Which one?" The tester must be sure that the item is understood and should find out what kinds of experience prompt the response. Students should be asked: "Have you ever done this skill? When? A lot or a little? Who taught you? Do you like doing this skill? Is it fun?"

The Ulrich pictorial scale can be obtained from Dr. Beverly Ulrich or Dr. Dale Ulrich, Kinesiology Department, Indiana University, Bloomington, IN 47405.

Self-Description Questionnaire I, II, III

Herbert Marsh of Australia has published self-concept inventories for three age groups: Self-Description Questionnaire-I (SDQ-I), for ages 8 to 12; SDQ-II, for ages 13 to 17; and SDQ-III, for age 16 to adult. Each SDQ assesses self-concept in three areas (academic, nonacademic, global) that are further broken down in hierarchical fashion. Marsh and Shavelson (1985) are accredited with developing the hierarchical model of multidimensional self-concept measurement. The SDQ is used in many countries and has provided data for much published research (Marsh, 1989).

Of particular interest to physical educators are the SDQ physical abilities and physical appearance subscales. The SDQ uses a 5-point rating response format: (a) false; (b) mostly false; (c) sometimes false, sometimes true; (d) mostly true; and (e) true. Illustrative items are "I like to run and play hard" and "I am good at sports."

The SDQ manuals and inventories are available from The Psychological Corporation, P.O. Box 839954, San Antonio, TX 78283–3954 (toll-free number 1–800–228–0752).

Physical Self-Perception Profile

Kenneth Fox and Chuck Corbin (1989) have developed a 30-item instrument specifically for physical educators to help guide high school and college students in understanding their physical selves and setting goals for improvement. The Physical Self-Perception Profile (PSPP) consists of five 6-item subscales: (a) global physical self-worth, (b) sports competence, (c) attractive body, (d) physical strength and muscular development, and (e) physical condition, fitness, and exercise ability. This instrument is based on hierarchical self-esteem theory (see Figure 6.16).

PSPP uses Harter's four-choice, structured, alternative-response scale. Illustrative of the items are those comprising the attractive body subscale in Figure 6.17. Scores on this scale correlate higher with global physical self-worth than do scores on other scales. This indicates that educators should consider physical attractiveness a major goal and help students to understand the relationship between fitness activities and attractiveness. The availability of separate PSPP scales to measure changing perceptions that result from instruction enables humanistic teachers to assess progress.

Fox and Corbin (1989) recommended that the PSPP be administered along with the (a) Rosenberg (1965) Global Self-Esteem Scale, (b) self-reports of physical activity, and (c) an instrument to measure the perceived importance of each physical subdomain. These instruments can be obtained from the Office for Health Promotion, Northern Illinois University, DeKalb, IL 60115.

Low Self-Concept and Physical Education

Self-concepts of students with disabilities are often lower than those of able-bodied peers. Inherent in low self-concept are expectations of failure, fear of letting teammates down during a crucial play, dread of being teased or singled out from others for correction and/or help with skills, and a growing reluctance to participate. It becomes increasingly easier to sit and watch others play and/or compete than to risk failure. Thus, many students may profess a desire to sit out or keep score when, deep inside, they long to participate and to be part of the group.

Before such students can be taught basic movement patterns, games, and sports in the traditional skill-oriented manner, they must be helped to change negative feelings about the self and taught methods of coping with the stresses related to fear of failure and lack of acceptance by others. Until they believe in themselves and trust in teachers and peers, students with low self-concepts are unlikely to put forth their best efforts in learning skills, rules, and strategies. Low self-concept tends to increase with age, often peaking in adolescence. Many factors are related to low self-concept, and you should learn as much about your students' home and school backgrounds as possible in an effort to identify and ameliorate causes.

Pedagogy in Relation to Low Self-Concept

Teaching practices that enhance self-concept generally also contribute to improvement of attitude toward movement and/or physical education. Ideally, the practices that follow

FIGURE 6.16

Hierarchical physical self-esteem model that guided the development of
the Physical Self-Perception Profile.

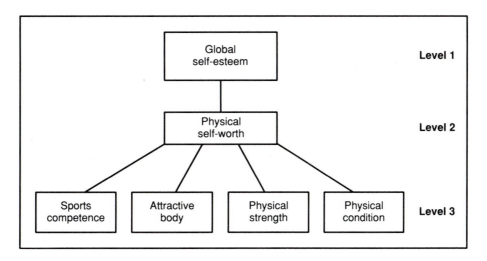

FIGURE 6.17

Items that measure attractive body.

Really True for Me	Sort of True for Me		Items			Sort of True for Me	Really True for Me
4	3	3.	Some people feel that, compared to most, they have an attractive body	BUT	others feel that, compared to most, their body is not quite so attractive.	2	1
1	2	8.	Some people feel that they have difficulty maintaining an attractive body	BUT	others feel that they are easily able to keep their body looking attractive.	3	4
1	2	13.	Some people feel embarrassed by their bodies when it comes to wearing few clothes	BUT	others do not feel embarrassed by their bodies when it comes to wearing few clothes.	3	4
4	3	18.	Some people feel that they are often admired because their physique or figure is considered attractive	BUT	others rarely feel that they receive admiration for the way their body looks.	2	1
1	2	23.	Some people feel that, compared to most, their bodies do not look in the best of shape	BUT	others feel that, compared to most, their bodies always look in excellent physical shape.	3	4
4	3	28.	Some people are extremely confident about the appearance of their body	BUT	others are a little self-conscious about the appearance of their body.	2	1

Note. Numbers show scoring system and should not be used on inventory given to students.

would be used with all students. Large class sizes and various other factors, however, often make the practices impractical for regular physical education, which is why they are described here as critical to effective teaching in adapted physical education.

1. **Conceptualize individual and small-group counseling as an integral part of physical education instruction.** Remember, the characteristics of a healthy counseling relationship are active listening, empathy, acceptance, willingness to become involved in another person's problems, and commitment to helping a person change in the way he or she chooses, which may or may not be the way you would choose. Listening to a student, asking questions to draw him or her out, and taking the initiative in following up when the student seems to withdraw are ways of showing that you genuinely care.

2. **Teach students to care about each other and to show that they care.** This is sometimes called *social reciprocity* and begins with the facilitation of one-to-one relationships, followed by increasingly complex social structures. *Reciprocity* is an interaction in which persons positively reinforce each other at an equitable rate, thereby increasing the probability of continuing interactions. Reinforcement can be facial and gestural expressions, verbal praise, or cheering for one another. Students typically model the teacher's behavior toward people who are different or disabled. Therefore, you must model encouragement, positive expectation, faith that the student really is exerting his or her best effort, and day-by-day acceptance of motor and social outcomes.

3. **Emphasize cooperation and social interaction rather than individual performance.** Plan lots of partner work. When necessary, assign partners who will bring out the best in one another rather than allowing chance to determine class twosomes. Match students with the same care used by computerized dating services. Remember, the creation of a friendship is often more valuable than any other factor in enhancing self-concept. Show awareness of emerging friendships and praise students for behaviors that help and support each other.

4. **Stress the importance of genuineness and honesty in praise.** Accept, but do not praise, motor attempts that are obviously unsuccessful. Instead, provide such input as: "Hey, this isn't like you. Tomorrow will be better." or "What's wrong? Let's try another way of throwing the ball!" or "I can tell you are upset by your performance today. You seem to be trying very hard and still not reaching your goal. How can I help?" Apply the same kind of sports psychology strategies to students with disabilities as you do to the able-bodied. In the real world of sport and competition, it is not effort that counts, but success. Therefore, structure lessons so as to build in success.

5. **Build in success through the use of task and activity analysis.** Also important is identifying the student's unique learning style. Does he or she learn best through visual or auditory input, or a combination of the two? Or must he or she learn kinesthetically through trial and error, trying alternative ways until one works? Motor planning and subsequent performance is enhanced in most students if the students talk aloud as they perform, giving themselves step-by-step directions. Remember, in many clumsy students, the mind grasps what is to be done motorically, but the body simply does not do what the mind wills. Therefore, do not repeatedly tell students what they are doing wrong. Ask questions and let them tell you. When possible, videotape or film and provide opportunities for students to watch and analyze their motor performance. Expect students to set their own goals but provide counseling in terms of realistic aspirations.

6. **Increase perceived competence in relation to motor skill and fitness.** There is no substitute for success. Perceived competence enhances intrinsic motivation to persevere. Competence, however, is typically perceived in terms of a reference group. Help students to compare their efforts, successes, and failures against others of similar abilities and disabilities, rather than the population as a whole. This is often more difficult than it sounds because many students with disabilities have not yet learned to accept their limitations and still model average performers. Yearning to be normal and, thus, to perform motorically as normal people leads to anger and depression, which ultimately must be worked through.

7. **Convey that you like and respect students as human beings, for themselves as whole persons, not just for their motor skills and fitness.** The bottom line is that many clumsy students will remain clumsy in spite of best efforts of self, teacher, and peers. This is the rationale for separate instructional settings and sport organizations like the U.S. Cerebral Palsy Athletic Association and Special Olympics. Students need realistic reference groups for forming opinions about themselves and for setting leisure-time use goals. Clumsiness and low skill do not have to be reasons for disliking and avoiding physical education. Too often, physical educators have equated skill with fun. The emphasis, instead, should be on using sport classifications to equalize abilities and on counseling to find and accept a realistic reference group. Movement is intrinsically fun and satisfying when one does not feel different from everyone else and embarrassed by that difference.

8. **Stress movement education and motor creativity rather than sports competition in the early stages of learning.** Many clumsy students can excel in fluency, flexibility, originality, and elaboration, largely because *try another way* is an intrinsic part of their lifestyles. Such students can find much satisfaction in choreographing original aerobic exercise, dance, gymnastics, and synchronized swimming routines. Likewise, clumsy students may be adept at creating new games and/or changing rules, strategies, and skills in existing ones. The teacher who truly values individual differences conveys this to students who, in

turn, learn to value themselves as the "different drummers in the physical education world." In this regard, the words of Henry David Thoreau remain timely:

If a man does not keep pace with his companions, perhaps it is because he hears a different drummer. Let him step to the music which he hears, however measured or far away.

9. **Enhance self-concept by leisure counseling directed toward achieving desired leisure lifestyle.** Help students to see the relationship between physical education instruction and present, as well as future, use of leisure time. Activities to be learned and practiced during class time ideally should be selected by the student rather than the teacher. Because many adults with disabilities are unable to find full-time employment, it is especially important that they learn early that leisure can be meaningful. Wholesome attitudes toward leisure contribute to good self-concept in persons who have an abundance of leisure time.

10. **Help students to feel that they are in control of many aspects of their lives.** They can change many of the things they do not like, providing they are willing to put forth enough effort. Other things they must accept and learn to manage. Teach coping strategies, assertiveness, and initiative.

11. **Apply theories that link the cognitive, affective, and behavioral dimensions of self-concept to motivation.** The self-efficacy theory of Bandura, for example, provides cognitive pedagogical approaches. The competence motivation theory that follows focuses on the affective domain.

Competence Motivation Theory

Competence motivation is the urge to engage in achievement-oriented activity as a means of feeling good and satisfying self-actualization needs. Competence motivation theory posits that persons engage in activity because certain behaviors (orientations) make them feel good. The more competent persons feel, the more they will sustain interest and persist in the activity. This, in turn, leads to high physical achievement.

Of the several competence motivation theories, the one best known in physical education is by Susan Harter (Weiss, 1987; Weiss, Ebbeck, McAuley, & Wiese, 1990). This is perhaps because she has not only proposed causally related variables but has also developed and validated instruments for testing the efficacy of the theory. Several physical educators have applied Harter's theory to physical education and sport. The competence motivation process can be explained mainly by four variables: (a) perceived competence, (b) perceived control, (c) motivation orientations, and (d) actual physical performance. The hypothesized relationships are depicted in Figure 6.18.

Perceived competence (high or low physical self-esteem, an evaluative judgment of adequacy) is interrelated with perceived control (internal, external, or unknown). These factors both influence motivation orientations and actual

physical achievement. Harter recommends measurement of five motivation orientations (see Figure 6.18). Preliminary research shows that the score on the challenge scale is most predictive of actual physical achievement, but this may vary with task and ability levels.

Teachers who aspire to increase the skill level of students must therefore be concerned with far more than corrective feedback. Individuals act in ways that are consistent with their (a) perceived competence, (b) perceived control, and (c) motivation orientations. Therefore, plan strategies that make students feel that they are competent and that they have at least partial control over task variables and outcomes. Ecological task analysis, when student and teacher jointly analyze variables and set goals, is a way of enhancing perceived internal control. With regard to the five motivation orientations, find ways to reinforce orientations that keep students intrinsically motivated and actively involved. Competence motivation theory essentially is a rationale for giving self-esteem equal attention with motor skill instruction.

Griffin-Keogh Movement Confidence Model

Closely related to competence motivation theory is the movement confidence model of Norma Griffin and Jack Keogh (1982). Of particular interest in adapted physical education is this model's applicability to assessing children's self-confidence about performing on playground apparatus (Crawford & Griffin, 1986) and engaging in various stunt-type activities like rope climbing, skateboarding, and stilt walking (Griffin & Crawford, 1989). In the gymnasium and swimming pool settings, fears and phobias often arise.

In coping with lack of self-confidence, this model indicates that three kinds of perception must be considered: (a) competence or adequacy, (b) enjoyment of moving sensations, and (c) harm or risk. There are two categories of the latter: (a) perceptions related to risk of personal injury and (b) perceptions related to the mental health factor of having to cope with unpleasant moving sensations. In helping students understand and work through fears of height, falling, dizziness, and other perceived risks, be aware of the separateness of these factors. The following formula summarizes the movement confidence model:

$$MC = (C - H1) + (E - H2)$$

where MC represents movement confidence, $C - H1$ represents perceived competence minus harm/personal injury factor, and $E - H2$ represents enjoyment minus harm/unpleasant moving sensation factor.

Figure 6.19 is illustrative of items used to measure movement confidence. Assessment instruments of this nature can be obtained from Dr. Michael Crawford, Department of Parks, Recreation, and Tourism, University of Missouri, Columbia, MO 65211 or Dr. Norma S. Griffin, School of HPER, University of Nebraska, Lincoln, NE 68588.

An especially important dimension of the movement confidence model is enjoyment. When students have phobias or express dislike of physical activity, give the goal area of fun/tension release/mental health high priority. Fun does not

FIGURE   6.18

Competence motivation theory.

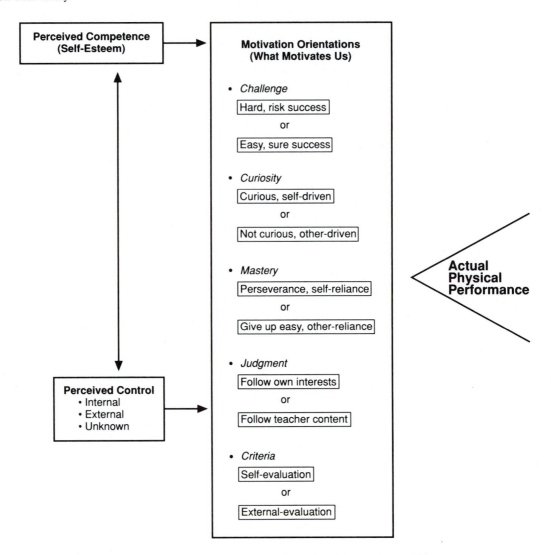

happen spontaneously for some students; it must be carefully taught. Researchers are focusing increasingly on the assessment of fun and on the analysis of enjoyment into discrete factors that can be enhanced (Wankel & Sefton, 1989).

Motivation Theories

Motivation refers to either the forces that cause behaviors or the internal state that focuses behaviors toward goal achievement. The first motivation theories were psychoanalytic (Freud, 1923) and behavioral (Hull, 1943); both assumed that behavior was motivated by biological drives to reduce inner tensions caused by a need for food, fluid, or sex. Maslow (1954) was among the first to challenge this assumption and assert that persons could be motivated by cognitive variables like needs for love, belonging, self-esteem, and self-actualization.

Today, cognitive approaches to motivation dominate. Among the theories of interest in adapted physical activity are (a) teacher expectancy, (b) locus of control, (c) learned helplessness, and (d) attribution.

Teacher Expectancy Theory

Expectancy theory embodies two basic assumptions: (a) persons will perform as they think others expect them to perform and (b) persons will expect of themselves what others expect of them. This theory, also called Pygmalion theory, takes its name from George Bernard Shaw's play *Pygmalion,* which was made into a famous Broadway play and later became the movie *My Fair Lady.* In *Pygmalion,* an English professor boasts that he can change an ignorant, unkempt young woman from the London slums into a beautiful, polished lady with perfect manners and flawless speech. Professor Higgins succeeds in achieving this with Eliza Doolittle, changing her from a person who makes a living by selling flowers on the street to a much-sought-after woman of high society. He does not, however, change the way he perceives and treats her, as indicated in Eliza's comments to one of her suitors:

. . . You see, really and truly, apart from the things anyone can pick up (the dressing and the proper way of speaking, and so on), the difference between a lady and a flower girl is not how

FIGURE 6.19

Sample item from instrument used in conjunction with Griffin-Keogh movement confidence model.

What I Am Like

Name _____ Age _____ Sex _____

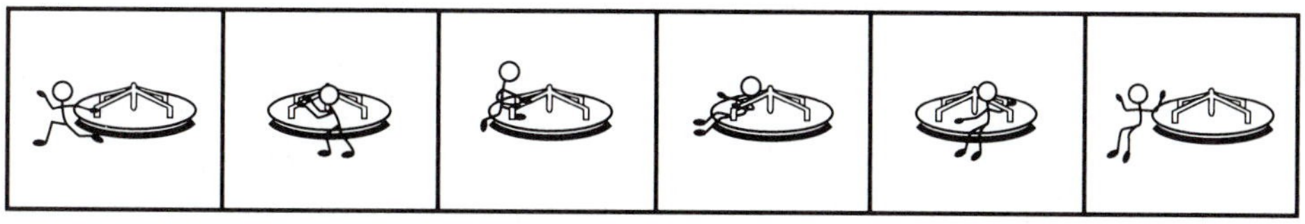

How sure are you that you could do this?

☐ I am very sure ☐ I am pretty sure ☐ I'm not very sure ☐ I know that I couldn't

How many times have you done this?

☐ I have done this a lot ☐ I have done this a few times ☐ I tried it once ☐ I've never done it

Now, for each sentence below, mark the box which best describes what you are like:

Really true for me	Sort of true for me				Sort of true for me	Really true for me
1. ☐	☐	Some kids are good at jumping onto moving things	BUT	other kids don't always do it so well.	☐	☐
2. ☐	☐	Some kids might slip and fall off the merry-go-round while it's moving	BUT	other kids can ride this and be safe.	☐	☐

she behaves, but how she's treated. I shall always be a flower girl to Professor Higgins, because he always treats me as a flower girl, and always will; but I know I can be a lady to you, because you always treat me as a lady, and always will.
—George Bernard Shaw, Pygmalion

This passage clearly illustrates the importance of positive thinking, believing, and acting. Just as coaches convey to their athletes the expectation that they will win, so must physical educators demonstrate belief in persons with disabilities. How perception of oneself influences motivation and success is called the *self-fulfilling prophecy;* persons unconsciously fulfill expectancies held by themselves and others.

Rosenthal and followers (Rosenthal & Jacobsen, 1968) have conducted so much research on Pygmalion theory that it is also called *Rosenthal theory.* The *Rosenthal effect* (i.e., the outcome of expectancy theory) is said to be operative in classes in which teachers communicate positive expectations to students. In physical education, Thomas Martinek, professor at the University of North Carolina at Greensboro, has spearheaded most of the research (Mar-

tinek, Crowe, & Rejeski, 1982). Among the most relevant of his studies is research on the effects of teacher expectation on self-concept.

Martinek and Johnson (1979) emphasize that physical educators typically expect more from and appear to care more about their good performers than others:

Within a physical education setting, high achievers have all the advantages—more attention, more praise, more acceptance, more intellectual stimulation, and better self-concept. It follows, then, that the physical education teacher should become sensitized to those behavior mechanisms that mediate expectation which perpetuates success and failure in children. (p. 69)

Physical attractiveness, as well as mental, physical, and social performance, has been shown to affect teacher and, later, employer expectations. Persons whose physical disability makes their appearance visibly different from that of peers often are exposed to low expectations and special treatment that sets them still further apart.

Locus of Control or Perceived Control

Locus of control (LOC), also called perceived control, is the perception of the connection or lack of connection between one's actions and their consequences. Julian Rotter (1966) posited that persons vary in LOC along an internal to external continuum. Some persons are in the middle, but others tend to be either internally or externally controlled. Internal LOC is belief and/or perception that events in one's life are dependent upon ability and effort. External LOC is the feeling that events in life are not based on one's actions but are a result of chance, fate, luck, or controls imposed by others, like task difficulty. Confused LOC is lack of understanding or inability to decide what causes events.

Several instruments have been developed to measure LOC: (a) Rotter's (1966) Internal-External (IE) Locus of Control Scale, which is appropriate for adolescents or older persons; (b) Children's Nowicki-Strickland (1973) Internal-External (CNSIE) Scale; (c) Preschool and Primary Nowicki-Strickland Internal-External (PPNSIE) Scale; (d) Adult Nowicki-Strickland Internal-External (ANSIE) Scale; and (e) Connell's (1980) Multidimensional Measure of Children's Perceptions of Control Scale. These enable assessment of persons' positions on the IE continuum and allow teachers to help external individuals to increase belief in their own ability and effort.

Child development theory emphasizes that LOC shifts from external to internal as students mature. The degree of this shift depends, however, on child rearing and classroom teaching practices and on such variables as health and disabilities that may prevent independent thought and action. Some persons remain more externally than internally controlled throughout life. This includes many normal persons as well as those with severe mental retardation or emotional disturbance.

Persons with disabilities want to control their own lives, just as do able-bodied persons. Humanistic teachers are careful not to do for such persons without first asking for permission or direction. When feeding persons with a disability, for instance, ask them to indicate what they want from the plate and in what order. Before assisting mobility-impaired persons, ask first if they want help and how help can best be given. The movie *Whose Life Is It Anyhow?* is an excellent resource for learning about LOC.

Because of the tendency of parents and society to overprotect persons with disabilities and deny them control of their own lives, physical educators need to stress independence, personal control, and responsibility. Remember expectancy theory. Expect persons to assume control over the situational factors in their lives, and gradually, they will assume that control.

Learned Helplessness

Learned helplessness is a composite of beliefs and behaviors that characterize many persons with external LOC (Dweck, 1980; Reid, 1987; Robinson, 1990; Seligman, 1975). It is a particular problem in a person with a severe disability or chronic illness when nothing the person does seems to ameliorate the condition. Likewise, learned helplessness has been associated with demoralization because of repeated failure in motor activities despite best efforts. When, over a period of time, persons come to believe that there is no relationship between effort and outcome, the result is reduced motivation, low self-esteem, and generalized depression. Physical educators must recognize the learned helplessness syndrome and work to prevent it.

Attribution Theory and Training

Attributions are causal inferences or perceptions of why things happen. Attribution theory focuses on the relationships between event outcomes (success vs. failure; winning vs. losing), beliefs about causes, and subsequent emotions and behaviors. Attribution theory, as begun by Bernard Weiner (1972), is an umbrella motivation theory subscribed to by most cognitive psychologists. It posits that the need to understand self, others, and the world in general is a major phenomenon in personal fulfillment and self-actualization.

Weiner identified four major causes that persons use to explain success and failure outcomes: (a) ability, (b) effort, (c) task difficulty, and (d) luck. He then categorized these according to three properties: (a) stability, (b) locus of causality, and (c) controllability. *Stability* is likelihood of endurance (i.e., failure attributed to a stable cause, such as lack of ability, is expected to continue). *Locus of causality* (internal or external) refers to whether the origin of the perceived cause is in the individual or the environment. *Controllability* is an attribute only of effort; everything else is uncontrollable and therefore likely to generate anger. Failure to try one's hardest, in contrast, typically results in guilt.

Attribution theory is so complex that defining each term by giving examples is helpful. Figure 6.20 presents the items used by Gail Dummer and associates (1987) to study the attributions of athletes with cerebral palsy. This model shows only the stability and locus of causality aspects of attribution. Immediately after their events, athletes used a 9-point response scale to rate each of the attributions in Figure 6.20. Additionally, they rated one attribution of affect ("I enjoy competition"), which was not in Weiner's model. These statements are appropriate for use in a school setting to find out how students explain their success and failure in specific physical education activities.

Little is known about the attributions of differently abled individuals in sport. Some evidence indicates that persons with severe disability and/or low skills use different attributions than able-bodied peers and thus need different motivational approaches. Persons with severe disabilities tend to explain their successes and failures more by luck and task difficulty than ability and effort. This is an indication of external locus of causality or control. They also seem uncertain about whether the reason is stable (task difficulty) or unstable (luck). Task difficulty is closely related to feelings about the person who required the task or determined its difficulty

FIGURE   6.20

Illustrative attributes organized according to Weiner's model.

Stability Factor

	Stable	Unstable
Internal	**Ability** I perform well because of my ability. I have special skills for this task.	**Effort** I tried hard. I was physically ready. I was mentally ready. I perform well in these situations. I used the right strategy.
External	**Task Difficulty** I spent a lot of time working on my skills.	**Luck** I was lucky. I was able to meet the challenge.

Locus of Causality Factor

(e.g., "The teacher doesn't like me. Otherwise, he [or she] wouldn't make the task so hard." or "The teacher doesn't give me the help I need.").

Low-skilled children often attribute poor performance to lack of innate ability (e.g., "I'm just not good enough"). This may be because of feelings of inferiority or the inability to differentiate between ability and effort. Children progress through several developmental levels in acquisition of attributional skills. Until age 5 or 6, children believe that effort and ability are the same; they evaluate themselves in terms of simple task mastery (e.g., "I did it" or "I didn't do it"). Between ages 7 and 9, children begin to understand effort. This leads to the misconception that effort is the sole determinant of outcome (e.g., if persons put forth the same effort, they will achieve equal outcomes). Around age 9, children can finally handle abstract thought and thus begin to accurately distinguish between effort and ability. At about age 12, this understanding matures, and children can analyze relationships between event outcomes and multiple causative factors.

Among students with cognitive disabilities, the ability to understand and use attributions to improve their performance may be delayed or frozen. Special educators recommend the use of attributional training or retraining to ameliorate this problem (Borkowski, Weyhing, & Turner, 1986). Procedures include (a) discussion of beliefs regarding the causes of failure and success; (b) instruction on the meaning of ability, effort, chance, and task difficulty; and (c) use of self-talk as a metacognitive and control strategy when doing tasks. Self-talk might resemble this:

Why did I goof or make a mistake last time? Maybe it was chance, but probably not. Maybe it was because the task was too hard. Probably not, because the teacher thinks I can do it. Maybe I just don't have the ability. This is silly. I have control over my ability. I can improve my ability. I can do this by effort. OK, now I am going to do this task again and try harder.

Attributional training requires that students talk through tasks with passages like this one. It also provides stories, poems, and mottos about effort and self-control and encourages visualization of the self expending effort and succeeding.

Judgments that teachers and significant others make about attributions are as important as self-judgments because they influence the way students are subsequently treated. If a teacher believes, for example, that a student has low ability, the level of difficulty is reduced. If the student does not appear to be trying hard enough, various motivational strategies are enacted. All classroom interactions obviously are dependent upon attributional analysis, and perceptions may be accurate or inaccurate. Emotional responses to attributions may be logical and valid or the opposite.

References

Asken, M., & Goodling, M. (1986). Sport psychology I: An introduction and overview. *Sports 'N Spokes, 12* (1), 12–16.

Bandura, A. (1977). Self-efficacy: Toward a unifying theory of behavioral change. *Psychological Review, 84* (7), 191–215.

Bandura, A. (1986). *Social foundations of thought and action: A social cognitive theory.* Englewood Cliffs, NJ: Prentice-Hall.

Barker, R. (1968). *Ecological psychology.* Stanford, CA: Stanford University Press.

Bell-Gredler, M. (1986). *Learning and instruction: Theory into practice.* New York: Macmillan.

Borkowski, J., Weyhing, R., & Turner, L. (1986). Attributional retraining and teaching of strategies. *Exceptional Children, 53* (2), 130–137.

Bronfenbrenner, U. (1979). *The ecology of human development.* Cambridge, MA: Harvard University.

Buros, O. (1978). *The eighth mental measurements yearbook.* Lincoln, NE: University of Nebraska Press.

Connell, J. P. (1980). *A multidimensional measure of children's perceptions of control.* Unpublished master's thesis, University of Denver.

Conoley, J. C., & Kramer, J. J. (Eds.). (1989). *The tenth mental measurements yearbook.* Lincoln, NE: University of Nebraska.

Cook, D. (1987). Psychological impact of disability. In R. Parker (Ed.), *Rehabilitation counseling: Basics & beyond,* (pp. 97–120). Austin, TX: Pro. Ed.

Craft, D., & Hogan, P. (1985). Development of self-concept and self-efficacy: Considerations for mainstreaming. *Adapted Physical Activity Quarterly, 2* (4), 320–327.

Crawford, M., & Griffin, N. S. (1986). Testing the validity of the Griffin/Keogh model for movement confidence by analyzing self-report playground involvement decisions of elementary schoolchildren. *Research Quarterly for Exercise and Sport, 57,* 67–78.

Deci, E. L., & Ryan, R. M. (1985). *Intrinsic motivation and self-determination in human behavior.* New York: Plenum.

Dummer, G., Ewing, M., Habeck, R., & Overton, S. (1987). Attributions of athletes with cerebral palsy. *Adapted Physical Activity Quarterly, 4* (4), 278–292.

Dweck, C. S. (1980). Learned helplessness in sport. In C. H. Nadeau, W. R. Halliwell, K. M. Newell, & G. C. Roberts (Eds.), *Psychology of motor behavior and sport—1979* (pp. 1–11). Champaign, IL: Human Kinetics.

Ennis, C. D. (1985). Purpose concepts in an existing physical education curriculum. *Research Quarterly for Exercise and Sport, 56* (4), 323–333.

Festinger, L. (1954). A theory of social comparison processes. *Human Relations, 7,* 117–140.

Fox, K. R., & Corbin, C. B. (1989). The physical self-perception profile: Development and preliminary validation. *Journal of Sport and Exercise Psychology, 11,* 408–430.

Freud, S. (1923). *The ego and the id.* London: Hogarth Press.

Gibbons, S., & Bushakra, F. (1989). Effects of Special Olympics participation on the perceived competence and social acceptance of mentally retarded children. *Adapted Physical Activity Quarterly, 6* (1), 40–51.

Gibson, J. J. (1977). The theory of affordances. In R. Shaw & J. Bransford (Eds.), *Perceiving, acting, and knowing: Toward an ecological psychology* (pp. 67–82). Hillsdale, NJ: Erlbaum.

Gibson, J. J. (1979). *The ecological approach to visual perception.* Boston: Houghton Mifflin.

Golden, C. (Ed.). (1984). *Current topics in rehabilitation psychology.* New York: Grune & Stratton.

Griffin, N. S., & Crawford, M. (1989). Measurement of movement confidence with a stunt movement confidence inventory. *Journal of Sport and Exercise Psychology, 11,* 26–40.

Griffin, N. S., & Keogh, J. F. (1982). A model for movement competence. In J. Kelso & J. E. Clark (Eds.), *The development of movement control and coordination* (pp. 213–236). New York: Wiley.

Gruber, J. J. (1985). Physical activity and self-esteem development in children: A meta-analysis. In G. A. Stull & H. E. Eckert (Eds.), *American Academy of Physical Education Papers No. 19* (pp. 30–48). Champaign, IL: Human Kinetics.

Hall, C., & Lindzey, G. (1978). *Theories of personality* (3rd ed.). New York: John Wiley.

Hanrahan, S., Grove, J. R., & Lockwood, R. (1990). Psychological skills training for the blind athlete: A pilot program. *Adapted Physical Activity Quarterly, 7* (2), 143–155.

Harter, S. (1985). *Manual for the Self-Perception Profile for Children.* Denver, CO: Author.

Harter, S. (1988). *Manual for the Self-Perception Profile for Adolescents.* Denver, CO: Author.

Harter, S., & Pike, R. (1984). The pictorial scale of perceived competence and social acceptance for young children. *Child Development, 55,* 1969–1982.

Hopper, C. (1988). Self-concept and motor performance of hearing-impaired boys and girls. *Adapted Physical Activity Quarterly, 5* (4), 293–304.

Hull, C. L. (1943). *Principles of behavior.* New York: Appleton-Century-Crofts.

Jewett, A., & Bain, L. (1985). *The curriculum process in physical education.* Dubuque, IA: Wm. C. Brown.

Lewin, K. (1951). *Field theory in the social sciences.* New York: Harper & Row.

Marsh, H. W. (1989). *Self-description questionnaire—I, II, III test manuals.* San Antonio, TX: The Psychological Corporation.

Marsh, H. W., & Shavelson, R. (1985). Self-concept: Its multifaceted, hierarchical structure. *Educational Psychologist, 20,* 107–125.

Martinek, T. J., & Johnson, S. (1979). Teacher expectations: Effects on dyadic interactions and self-concept in elementary age children. *Research Quarterly, 50,* 60–70.

Martinek, T. J., Crowe, P., & Rejeski, W. (1982). *Pygmalion in the gymnasium.* West Point, NY: Leisure Press.

Martinek, T. J., & Zaichkowsky, L.D. (1977). *Manual for the Martinek-Zaichkowsky Self-Concept Scale for Children.* Chesterfield, MO: Psychologists and Educators, Inc.

Maslow, A. (1954). *Motivation and personality.* New York: Harper & Row. (2nd ed. in 1970.)

McBee, F., & Ballinger, J. (1984). *The continental quest.* Tampa, FL: Overland Press.

Messer, B., & Harter, S. (1986). *Manual for the Self-Perception Profile for Adults.* Denver, CO: Authors.

Neemann, J., & Harter, S. (1986). *Manual for the Self-Perception Profile for College Students.* Denver, CO: Authors.

Nirje, B. (1969). The normalization principle and its human management implications. In R. Kugel & W. Wolfensberger (Eds.), *Changing patterns in residential services for the mental retarded* (pp. 179–195). Washington, DC: President's Committee on Mental Retardation.

Nirje, B. (1980). The normalization principle. In R. J. Flynn & K. E. Nitsch (Eds.), *Normalization, social integration, and community services* (pp. 31–49). Baltimore: University Park Press.

Nowicki, S., & Strickland, B. (1973). A locus of control scale for children. *Journal of Consulting and Clinical Psychology, 40,* 148–154.

Ogilvie, B. (1985). Sports psychologists and the disabled athlete. *Palaestra, 1* (4), 36–40.

O'Leary, K. D., & Schneider, M. R. (no date). *Catch'em being good.* (Videocassette and 16-mm film available from Research Press, Box 3177, Dept. S, Champaign, IL 61826.)

Piers, E.V. (1984). *Piers-Harris Children's Self-Concept Scale, revised manual.* Los Angeles: Western Psychological Services.

Reid, G. (1987). Motor behavior and psychosocial correlates in young handicapped performers. In D. Gould & M. R. Weiss (Eds.), *Advances in pediatric sport sciences, Volume 2* (pp. 235–258). Champaign, IL: Human Kinetics.

Reilly, R., & Lewis, E. (1983). *Educational psychology.* New York: Macmillan.

Renick, M. J., & Harter, S. (1988). *Manual for the Self-Perception Profile for Learning Disabled Students.* Denver, CO: Authors.

Robinson, D. W. (1990). An attributional analysis of student demoralization in physical education settings. *Quest, 42* (1), 27–39.

Rogers, C. R. (1951). *Client-centered therapy.* Boston: Houghton Mifflin.

Rogers, C. R. (1969). *Freedom to learn.* Columbus, OH: Charles E. Merrill.

Rosenberg, M. (1965). *Society and the adolescent self-image.* Princeton, NJ: Princeton University Press.

Rosenthal, R., & Jacobsen, L. (1968). *Pygmalion in the classroom.* New York: Holt, Rinehart, & Winston.

Rotter, J. B. (1966). Generalized expectancies for internal versus external control of reinforcement. *Psychological Monographs: General and Applied, 80* (1), 1–28.

Seligman, M. (1975). *Helplessness: On depression, development, and death.* San Francisco: W.H. Freeman.

Sherrill, C., Hinson, M., Gench, B., Kennedy, S., & Low, L. (1990). Self-concepts of disabled youth athletes. *Perceptual and Motor Skills, 70,* 1093–1098.

Sherrill, C., Silliman, L., Gench, B., & Hinson, M. (1990). Self-actualization of elite wheelchair athletes. *Paraplegia, 28,* 252–260.

Shilling, L. E. (1984). *Perspectives on counseling theories.* Englewood Cliffs, NJ: Prentice-Hall.

Ulrich, B. D. (1987). Perceptions of physical competence, motor competence, and participation in organized sport: Their interrelationships in young children. *Research Quarterly for Exercise and Sport, 58* (1), 57–67.

Ulrich, B. D., & Ulrich, D. A. (1990). *An expanded pictorial scale of perceived physical competence for young children.* Unpublished manuscript, Indiana University, Bloomington.

Ulrich, D. A., & Collier, D. H. (1990). Perceived physical competence in children with mental retardation: Modification of a pictorial scale. *Adapted Physical Activity Quarterly, 7* (4) , 338–354.

Vallerand, R. J., & Reid, G. (1990). Motivation and special populations: Theory, research, and implications regarding motor behaviour. In G. Reid (Ed.), *Problems in movement control* (pp. 159–197). Amsterdam: North Holland.

Wankel, L., & Sefton, J. (1989). A season-long investigation of fun in youth sports. *Journal of Sport and Exercise Psychology, 11,* 355–366.

Weiner, B. (1972). *Theories of motivation from mechanism to cognition.* Chicago: Markham.

Weiss, M. R. (1987). Self-esteem and achievement in children's sport and physical activity. In D. Gould & M. R. Weiss (Eds.), *Advances in pediatric sport sciences, Volume 2* (pp. 87–119). Champaign, IL: Human Kinetics.

Weiss, M. R., Bredemeier, B., & Shewchuk, R. (1985). An intrinsic/extrinsic motivation scale for the youth sport setting: A confirmatory factor analysis. *Journal of Sport Psychology, 7,* 75–91.

Weiss, M. R., Ebbeck, V., McAuley, E., & Wiese, D. (1990). Self-esteem and causal attributions for children's physical and social competence in sport. *Journal of Sport and Exercise Psychology, 12,* 21–36.

Wolfensberger, W. (1972). *Normalization.* Toronto: National Institute on Mental Retardation.

Wolfensberger, W. (1991). Reflections on a lifetime in human services and mental retardation. *Mental Retardation, 29* (1), 1–15.

Wolfensberger, W., & Thomas, S. (1983). *PASSING: Program analysis of service systems' implementation of normalization goals.* Ontario, Canada: National Institute on Mental Retardation.

Wright, B. (1960). *Physical disability: A psychological approach.* New York: Harper & Row.

Wright, B. (1983). *Physical disability: A psychosocial approach* (2nd ed.). New York: Harper & Row.

CHAPTER

7

Assessment: The Key to Individualizing and Adapting

FIGURE 7.1

Assessment of dynamic balance is a good way to start the year.

After you have studied this chapter, you should be able to:

1. Identify and discuss four purposes of assessment.

2. Contrast the following types of assessment: (a) formal/informal, (b) product/process, (c) norm/criterion, (d) standardized/content-referenced, (e) tests/instruments, and (f) self/other.

3. List and discuss seven planning procedures for assessment. Explain three criteria that good instruments meet.

4. Identify at least one test specifically designed for screening, one test for placement, and one test for student progress in the psychomotor domain. Discuss and be able to administer each.

5. Discuss instruments associated with various goal areas.

6. Identify and discuss three assessment theories. Discuss which is most meaningful to you and why.

7. Explain mean, median, mode, and standard deviation. Discuss application in relation to placement and the structuring of balanced class teams.

8. Explain the conversion of raw data to z scores. When are conversions necessary?

9. Identify and discuss three types of norms. Give examples of use in placement, grading, and awards.

10. Explain special considerations in assessment of persons with severe disabilities.

Some physical educators walk into the gymnasium in September, greet the students, and immediately begin teaching. They assume that all students have more or less the same needs and possess age-appropriate skills, fitness, and knowledge. Other physical educators begin each school year with 1 or 2 weeks of assessment activities (see Figure 7.1). They screen to determine which students are above and below the group average and arrange time for more comprehensive assessment of these individuals. These teachers explain the goals of physical education and the purposes of assessment. They encourage students to identify their own strengths and weaknesses and to set goals. The central theme of this beginning-of-the-year assessment unit is getting to know and care about oneself and others. This is the essence of individualized physical education.

Assessment refers to data collection, interpretation, and decision making. Federal law, however, uses the term *evaluation* to encompass these functions. *Assessment* and *evaluation* can thus be considered synonyms, although experts specify that assessment is the broader term (King-Thomas & Hacker, 1987; Salvia & Ysseldyke, 1991).

Four Purposes of Assessment

Assessment should be directed toward a specific purpose. Four purposes that entail different decision-making processes are (a) screening, (b) diagnosis and placement, (c) instruction and student progress, and (d) sport and activity classification.

Screening

Screening is the process used by regular educators to determine who needs referrals for further testing. It is typically done at the beginning of each school year. Screening in physical education is usually a group process but may be individual if a second teacher is available to cover the class. *Screening tests should never be called diagnostic.* In assessment theory, these terms have different meanings.

Screening is typically a pass-fail or yes-no protocol that requires only a few minutes per student. Consider, for instance, how long it would require to screen 100 students if each one took 15 min. To minimize time needed, stations are often set up, with students rotating to a new area as soon as they complete designated tasks. The choice of tasks is dictated by the goals and objectives of the regular physical education curriculum. Usually, however, stations are used to screen (a) balance; (b) ball skills, both hand-eye and foot-eye; (c) bilateral coordination and rhythm (mainly jumping, hopping, and imitation of movement skills); (d) visual motor control (pencil-paper and scissors tasks); and (e) skills on tricycle or bicycle and playground apparatus. Many school systems also screen vision, height, weight, postures, and cardiovascular fitness.

Screening can also be conducted during a group follow-the-leader activity or game. Of central importance to physical activity personnel is whether children can perform the gross motor skills expected of their age level and have the language and personal-social skills to benefit from instruction in the mainstream setting.

The Denver II, a revision and restandardization of the Denver Developmental Screening Test (DDST) by Frankenburg and Dodds (1967), is an excellent screening instrument that encourages observation of the whole child (see Figure 7.2). Physical educators are typically most concerned with pass/fail performance in relation to the 32 items comprising the Gross Motor Scale. The Denver II test form offers insight into how far a child lags behind 25%, 50%, 75%, and 90% of his or her peers. All 32 items can be screened in about 3 min of group follow-the-leader play. School systems set criteria for helping teachers decide whether or not a child should be referred for diagnostic testing. More information about Denver II appears on page 162.

FIGURE 7.2

Denver II (the revision of the Denver Developmental Screening Test).

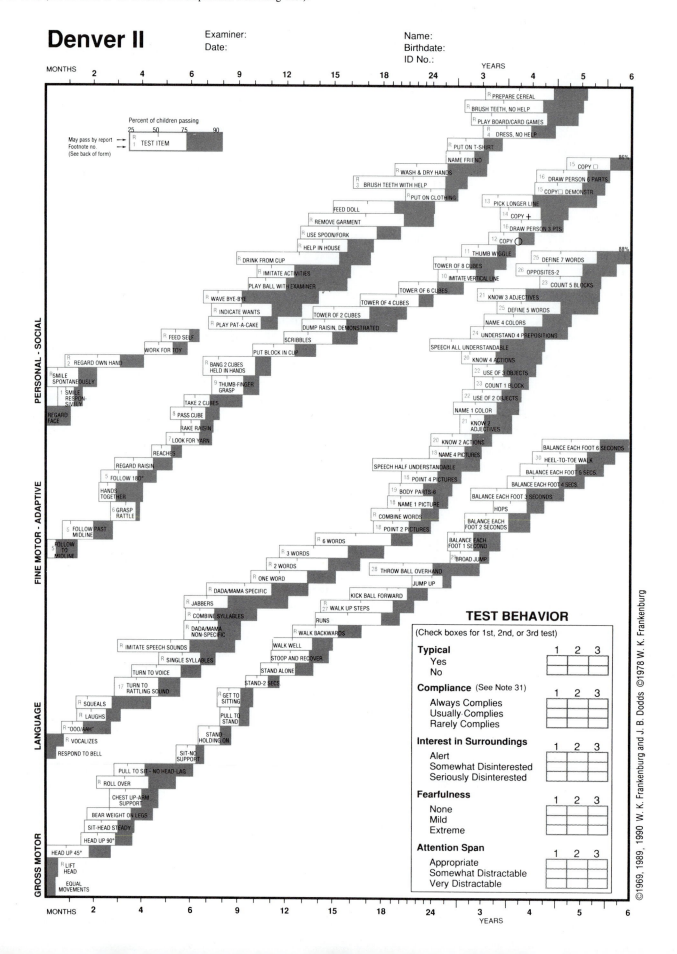

Diagnosis and Placement

Diagnosis is comprehensive, individual assessment by a specialist or group of specialists to determine placement and special services needs. Two assessment models guide diagnosis: (a) the individualized education program (IEP) model that is structured by law and uses diagnosis to obtain information for writing an IEP and (b) the regular education initiative (REI) or inclusion model that uses a variety of data-gathering approaches to identify students who need assistance or supplemental programming. The latter is often used to establish home and community programs for students with health, weight, or perceptual-motor problems. Diagnostic testing typically requires one or more hours for each person. Tests frequently used are the Bruininks-Oseretsky Test of Motor Proficiency (Long Form) (Bruininks, 1978) and the Test of Gross Motor Development (Ulrich, 1985).

When educators decide to place a student in a separate rather than a regular class, the assessment data must clearly show performance below the norms of chronological age-mates and/or inability to learn in a regular setting. This chapter explains norms and the simple statistics necessary for making placement decisions.

Instruction and Student Progress

Assessment of instruction and student progress occurs after placement, is done by the teacher, and can be individual or group. It identifies specific strengths and weaknesses to guide lesson planning and day-to-day instruction.

Some teachers administer only two or three tests a semester, but the best practice is continuous assessment, using line or bar graphs, to show day-to-day or week-to-week progress toward terminal objectives. Students should share in record keeping.

Data-based teaching is a specific type of assessment that is frequently used in adapted physical education. In this approach, teaching is directed by a task or ecological analysis. The teacher uses developmental sequences that list skills to be taught and records pass or fail for each trial. This process totally integrates teaching and assessment.

Sport and Activity Classification

Sport and activity classification is used to assign ability (or disability) classifications based on medical condition and/or functional capacity. First applied by sport organizations, classification is now widely used in adapted physical activity as a quick, efficient method of communicating general ability level and prescribing ecologically valid activities. One of the main purposes of classification is to assure equal opportunity in competition through balanced teams.

Authorities in all major areas except mental retardation, deafness, and learning disabilities have agreed on criteria and tests for assigning sport classifications. Furthermore, they have determined distances and times appropriate for each classification and ways of combining classifications to create balanced teams for sports like basketball, soccer, and handball. The resulting body of knowledge, known as *sport classification theory,* is important for adapted physical educators to master. Sport classification theory is discussed later in this chapter and in Part 3 of this text.

Six Types of Assessment

Types of assessment are so diverse that they are best described by several sets of bipolar terms: (a) formal versus informal, (b) product versus process, (c) norm versus criterion tests, (d) standardized versus content-referenced tests, (e) tests versus instruments, and (f) self versus other. The best assessment systems use combinations of all of these.

Formal versus Informal

Formal assessment is one in which students are aware that data are being collected. Typically, they are told the purpose and encouraged to do their best. Many individuals, however, experience anxiety in such situations and fail to give a true picture of what they can do. Formal assessment thus should be supplemented with informal data gathering within a game or play context as explained in Chapter 5.

When assessment is conducted as part of the IEP process, the protocol must be formal and adhere to legislative requirements. Written parental permission must be obtained. Among the legal specifications are (a) the tests must be validated for the specific purpose for which they are used, (b) the test administrator must be able to document training and skill in the protocol used, and (c) the tests must be administered in the student's native language or in sign if this is the preferred modality. No one procedure can be used as the sole criterion for placement, and decision making must reflect the consensus of a multidisciplinary team, the parents, and when possible, the student. Chapter 4 provides direct quotes from the law in relation to these requirements.

Formal assessment for placement purposes requires that test directions be followed precisely. This means that students may fail some items. The teacher must develop skill in helping students to handle such failures and to remain optimally motivated. When testing is for purposes other than placement, the humanistic teacher adapts the items and the environment so as to assure success.

Product versus Process

Assessment should involve both product and process. *Product* is the end result of performance—traditionally, a numerical measure (like distance or speed), the number performed (as in sit-up or push-up tests), or a numerical rating. In contrast, *process* refers to quality, form, or experience and generally relates to whether a movement pattern is mature or immature. Several checklists and pictorial instruments are included in Chapter 11 to encourage process evaluation. Other examples of process measures are journals, diaries, anecdotes, pictures, and film. Synonyms for product and process measures are, respectively, *quantitative* and *qualitative.*

Table 7.1
Illustrative percentile ranks: 50-yd dash norms.

	Boys Percentile Scores Based on Age Test Scores in Seconds and Tenths									Girls Percentile Scores Based on Age Test Scores in Seconds and Tenths							
	Age									Age							
Percentile	9–10	11	12	13	14	15	16	17+	Percentile	9–10	11	12	13	14	15	16	17+
100th	7.0	6.3	6.3	5.8	5.9	5.5	5.5	5.4	100th	7.0	6.9	6.0	6.0	6.0	6.0	5.6	6.4
95th	7.3	7.1	6.8	6.5	6.2	6.0	6.0	5.9	95th	7.4	7.3	7.0	6.9	6.8	6.9	7.0	6.8
90th	7.5	7.2	7.0	6.7	6.4	6.2	6.2	6.0	90th	7.5	7.5	7.2	7.0	7.0	7.0	7.1	7.0
85th	7.7	7.4	7.1	6.9	6.5	6.3	6.3	6.1	85th	7.8	7.5	7.4	7.2	7.1	7.1	7.3	7.1
80th	7.8	7.5	7.3	7.0	6.6	6.4	6.4	6.3	80th	8.0	7.8	7.5	7.3	7.2	7.2	7.4	7.3
75th	7.8	7.6	7.4	7.0	6.8	6.5	6.5	6.3	75th	8.0	7.9	7.6	7.4	7.3	7.4	7.5	7.4
70th	7.9	7.7	7.5	7.1	6.9	6.6	6.5	6.4	70th	8.1	7.9	7.7	7.5	7.4	7.5	7.5	7.5
65th	8.0	7.9	7.5	7.2	7.0	6.6	6.6	6.5	65th	8.3	8.0	7.9	7.6	7.5	7.5	7.6	7.5
60th	8.0	7.9	7.6	7.3	7.0	6.8	6.6	6.5	60th	8.4	8.1	8.0	7.7	7.6	7.6	7.7	7.6
55th	8.1	8.0	7.7	7.4	7.1	6.8	6.7	6.6	55th	8.5	8.2	8.0	7.9	7.6	7.7	7.8	7.7
50th	8.2	8.0	7.8	7.5	7.2	6.9	6.7	6.6	50th	8.6	8.3	8.1	8.0	7.8	7.8	7.9	7.9
45th	8.4	8.2	7.9	7.5	7.3	6.9	6.8	6.7	45th	8.8	8.4	8.2	8.0	7.9	7.9	8.0	8.0
40th	8.6	8.3	8.0	7.6	7.4	7.0	6.8	6.8	40th	8.9	8.5	8.3	8.1	8.0	8.0	8.0	8.0
35th	8.7	8.4	8.1	7.7	7.5	7.1	6.9	6.9	35th	9.0	8.6	8.4	8.2	8.0	8.0	8.1	8.1
30th	8.8	8.5	8.2	7.9	7.6	7.2	7.0	7.0	30th	9.0	8.8	8.5	8.3	8.2	8.1	8.2	8.2
25th	8.9	8.6	8.3	8.0	7.7	7.3	7.0	7.0	25th	9.1	9.0	8.7	8.5	8.3	8.2	8.3	8.4
20th	9.0	8.7	8.5	8.1	7.9	7.4	7.1	7.1	20th	9.4	9.1	8.9	8.7	8.5	8.4	8.5	8.5
15th	9.2	9.0	8.6	8.3	8.0	7.5	7.2	7.3	15th	9.6	9.3	9.1	8.9	8.8	8.6	8.5	8.8
10th	9.5	9.1	9.0	8.7	8.2	7.6	7.4	7.5	10th	9.9	9.6	9.4	9.2	9.0	8.8	8.8	9.0
5th	9.9	9.5	9.5	9.0	8.8	8.0	7.7	7.9	5th	10.3	10.0	10.0	10.0	9.6	9.2	9.3	9.5
0	11.0	11.5	11.3	15.0	11.1	11.0	9.9	12.0	0	13.5	12.9	14.9	14.2	11.0	15.6	15.6	15.0

Note. From *AAHPER Youth Fitness Test Manual,* 1976, by the American Alliance for Health, Physical Education, and Recreation.

Norm versus Criterion Tests

Both norm and criterion standards should be used in assessment. Norm-referenced instruments permit comparison of the individual's performance with a statistical standard. Criterion-referenced instruments enable comparison with a mastery standard.

Norm-Referenced Tests

Norm, an abbreviated form of the word *normal,* is a statistic that describes group performance and enables comparisons. *Norm-referenced* means that an instrument has been administered to several hundred persons and that statistics are available on the performance of chronological age groups and perhaps genders.

There are many kinds of norms: (a) percentile ranks, (b) standard scores, and (c) age equivalents. Best known of these are percentile ranks published by the American Alliance for Health, Physical Education, Recreation, and Dance (AAHPERD) (see Table 7.1). Percentile ranks extend from 0 to 100. The 50th percentile is the point above and below which 50% of the population scores. Any student who consistently scores below this point should receive special help. But when is performance low enough to warrant placement in a separate setting? Some states set the standard at the 30th percentile; others suggest the 15th percentile. Performance at the 15th percentile means that 85% of an individual's chronological peers score above him or her. Tables of percentile ranks can be found in most test manuals and in assessment textbooks.

Norm-referenced tests can be classified according to the population on which they are based: (a) regular education students or (b) students with disabilities. For placement decisions, regular education norms should be used, even though the student may be mentally retarded, blind, or physically disabled. When a student is placed in a regular class, the assumption is that he or she is not disabled in that particular school subject, regardless of medical condition. This means that performance must be equivalent to that of regular class members.

Several norm-referenced tests have been developed specifically for disabled populations, including the Project UNIQUE Physical Fitness Test (Winnick & Short, 1985) and fitness batteries for persons with various levels of mental retardation (AAHPERD, 1976a, b; Roswal, 1985) and blindness (Buell, 1973). These instruments permit comparison with others of similar disabilities. Such information is useful when instruction is conducted in separate settings and/or awards specifically for persons with disabilities are available.

Ideally, local school districts develop their own tables of percentile ranks for regular and separate education placements. Any test that yields numerical data can become a norm-referenced instrument if administered to enough persons. A rule of thumb when developing norms is that there must be at least 50 males and 50 females for every age or grade group represented. Once norms are developed and related statistics are computed, a test is considered standardized.

Criterion-Referenced Tests

Criterion-referenced tests are designed to measure mastery learning and/or assess achievement of developmental milestones, mature movement patterns, and minimal fitness levels. Usually, the format is a checklist, task analysis, or set of behavioral objectives. Data yielded are pass/fail rather than numbers.

Illustrative of a criterion-referenced approach is the AAHPERD (1988) health-related fitness test called Physical Best (see Table 7.2). In it, one mastery standard is set in each fitness domain for every age group. To pass, for example, 5–year-old girls must do a 1-mi walk/run in 14 min, whereas 18–year-old females must complete the distance in 10.5 min. These standards are, of course, subject to change. In some criterion-referenced tests, there is controversy about how high to set the standard. In others, as in the performance criteria that characterize a mature movement pattern, the standard is well accepted. For example, there is general agreement that four performance criteria must be met for a run to be judged mature. Thus, Ulrich (1985) developed the criterion-referenced test for the run shown in Table 7.3. Other criteria could be added to these, like "Eyes focused straight ahead (not on feet)," but research shows that most observers can only assess three or four things at one time. The key in this kind of criterion-referenced test is to identify the most important criteria. Ulrich's (1985) Test of Gross Motor Development (TGMD) includes excellent criteria for seven locomotor skills and five object control skills (see Chapter 11).

Criterion-referenced instruments related to motor skills typically emphasize process rather than product. They enable teachers to analyze the components of a skill and write objectives that focus on ameliorating weakness or immaturity of arm, leg, trunk, or head action. Activities can then be directed toward a particular criterion (e.g., "Demonstrate improved running form by bending elbows" or "Pass Criterion #2 on the run").

Criteria can also be set in relation to time and distance. Systems like I CAN (Wessel, 1976), Data-Based Gymnasium (Dunn, Morehouse, & Fredericks, 1986), and the Brigance Diagnostic Inventory (1978) all use lists of progressively more difficult tasks like that shown in Table 7.4. Such lists are particularly helpful in teaching students with severe disabilities. Instructional objectives can be worded: "Pass four of six items on the ball-rolling task analysis." If the test includes information on the age at which a student should be able to perform each task or item, the instrument is considered standardized.

Table 7.2
Illustrative criterion-referenced standards: AAHPERD Physical Best criteria.

	Test Item					
Age	1-mi Walk/ Run (minutes)	Sum of Skinfolds (mm)	Body Mass Index	Sit and Reach (cm)	Sit-up	Pull-up
			Girls			
5	14:00	16–36	14–20	25	20	1
6	13:00	16–36	14–20	25	20	1
7	12:00	16–36	14–20	25	24	1
8	11:30	16–36	14–20	25	26	1
9	11:00	16–36	14–20	25	28	1
10	11:00	16–36	14–21	25	30	1
11	11:00	16–36	14–21	25	33	1
12	11:00	16–36	15–22	25	33	1
13	10:30	16–36	15–23	25	33	1
14	10:30	16–36	17–24	25	35	1
15	10:30	16–36	17–24	25	35	1
16	10:30	16–36	17–24	25	35	1
17	10:30	16–36	17–24	25	35	1
18	10:30	16–36	17–24	25	35	1
			Boys			
5	13:00	12–25	13–20	25	20	1
6	12:00	12–25	13–20	25	20	1
7	11:00	12–25	13–20	25	24	1
8	10:00	12–25	14–20	25	26	1
9	10:00	12–25	14–20	25	30	1
10	9:30	12–25	14–20	25	34	1
11	9:00	12–25	15–21	25	36	2
12	9:00	12–25	15–22	25	38	2
13	8:00	12–25	16–23	25	40	3
14	7:45	12–25	16–24	25	40	4
15	7:30	12–25	17–24	25	42	5
16	7:30	12–25	18–24	25	44	5
17	7:30	12–25	18–25	25	44	5
18	7:30	12–25	18–26	25	44	5

Note. From AAHPERD *Physical Best,* 1988 by the American Alliance for Health, Physical Education, Recreation and Dance, pp. 28–29.

Table 7.3
Criterion-referenced test for a run from TGMD.

Performance Criteria	Trials	
	1	2
1. Brief period where both feet are off the ground	1	1
2. Arms in opposition to legs, elbows bent	0	1
3. Foot placement near or on a line (not flat-footed)	1	1
4. Nonsupport leg bent approximately 90° (close to buttocks)	0	0

Note. Under "Trials," 1 denotes pass, 0 denotes fail.

Table 7.4
Task-analysis test for rolling a ball.

	Task	Standard or Criterion
1.	Sit and roll or push a ball	Ball travels 1 ft
2.	Sit or stand and roll or push a ball	Ball travels 2 ft
3.	Same	Ball travels 5 ft
4.	Same except direct the ball toward a specific target 10 ft away	Ball travels 8 ft in direction of target
5.	Same	Ball travels 10 ft and touches target
6.	Same	Same except ball touches designated area on target

Standardized versus Content-Referenced Tests

Standardized tests are commercially published instruments with manuals that describe the performance of a standardization sample of several hundred persons. Statistics present information on both averages and individual differences. A norm-referenced test is always standardized. Criterion-referenced tests can be either standardized or teacher-made to assess the specific content or skills being taught.

Teacher-made tests are often called content-referenced because they are designed to measure what is being taught. Such tests permit the teacher to assess where a student falls in relation to the continuum of possible scores or behaviors. A content-referenced test becomes criterion-referenced when the teacher designates the scores required to pass or to earn particular letter grades.

Tests versus Instruments

Test, correctly defined, refers only to instruments for which there are right and wrong answers or mature and immature responses. A test is something that can be passed or failed. Many kinds of data are collected that do not fit this description (e.g., data about self-concept, attitudes, social behaviors, friendship choices, movement creativity). *Instrument* is a broader term than test and refers to inventories, rating scales, interview schedules, questionnaires, and other forms of data collection that do not yield right and wrong answers.

Self versus Other

Teacher-directed assessment is the traditional approach to data collection. In humanistic teaching, however, assessment responsibility is gradually shifted to the student. The simplest and best method of screening is often simply asking the student, "Can you do thus and so? What are your greatest strengths and weaknesses? What are you interested in learning? How can I (the teacher) best help you?"

Requiring students to grade or in some way evaluate their performance provides insight into their frame of reference, motivation, and attributions. Whenever possible, assessment should be a shared responsibility.

Planning Procedures

Each time assessment is planned, you should adhere to the following procedures:

1. Establish the specific purpose of the assessment.
2. Decide on the specific variables to be assessed.
3. Establish criteria for the selection of instruments or data collection protocols.
4. Review all available instruments and protocols that purport to assess the variables you selected.
5. Select the instruments or protocols to be used and state the rationale for selection (i.e., discuss how each meets every criterion).
6. Select the setting for the assessment.
7. Determine environmental factors to be considered and/or adapted.

Relating Assessment to Goals

Assessment should relate to the goals of the school system and/or teacher. If self-concept is an important goal, then dimensions of this variable should be assessed. If social competency or play and game behaviors are expected outcomes of instruction, then these variables should be broken into assessable components. If motor skills and patterns is the goal, then locomotor and object control skills should be examined.

Criteria for Selection of Instruments

The universally accepted criteria are validity, reliability, and objectivity. Other criteria may be added, depending upon special needs. All criteria are important, but federal law mentions only validity and states that instruments must be validated for the specific purpose for which they are used.

Validity comes from the Latin word for *strong.* It means founded on truth or fact and capable of being justified, supported, or defended. In regard to a test, validity refers to the extent that a test measures what it is supposed to measure. Think of the last exam you took. Did it measure what the teacher taught? If so, it was valid. Sometimes, there is a discrepancy between what teacher and students think has been taught.

Broadly generalizing, there are three kinds of validity. *Content validity* is demonstrated by showing the page number or place where test items and/or answers can be found in (a) source materials and (b) lesson plans, videotapes, and audiotapes that document what has been taught. Often, panels of experts are used to affirm content validity. *Criterion validity* is the extent that an instrument derives the same score/rank as another instrument or protocol believed to assess the same thing. *Construct validity* is the extent that statistics support three constructs: (a) the instrument discriminates between two groups known to be high and low in the attributes being measured; (b) the test items, when subjected to factor analysis, fall into logical clusters; and (c) the instrument is sensitive enough to show changes caused by instruction.

Reliability is also a statistical concept. There are two types: (a) stability and (b) internal consistency. Test-retest measures indicate stability of performance over several trials, also called *repeated measures reliability.* Alpha coefficients and other special formulae indicate internal consistency for a single administration. High internal consistency is evidenced when all items assessing a particular topic or skill elicit the same or consistent responses. The highest possible reliability coefficient is 1.00; thus, an .80 or .90 is considered high.

Objectivity, sometimes called interrater reliability, refers to several scorers or raters each perceiving a performance in the same way and giving the student the same rating or grade. This is especially important in observational assessment.

Reviewing Available Instruments

Every physical education professional should maintain a file of instruments with information about purpose, age range, validity, reliability, and objectivity. Some textbooks include copies of instruments. Most, however, do not because of copyright laws. In such cases, you must write to commercial companies and pay a small charge for sample copies.

The classic reference book for use in reviewing and evaluating instruments is the *Mental Measurements Yearbook,* edited by Buros (1938 to 1978 editions), Mitchell (1985), and Conoley and Kramer (1989). In spite of its title, the book includes reviews of many physical and motor measures and indicates where they can be ordered. It also includes a list of research studies related to each instrument.

Selecting Instruments

Many instruments measure the same things. Therefore, you must be able to show that your selected tools have higher validity and/or reliability than other possible choices. Moreover, to satisfy federal legislation, written documentation must show that the instrument is valid.

Do not make up diagnostic instruments by pulling items from several different sources. Doing so changes validity and reliability. Teachers who wish to create a new instrument may do so by enrolling in graduate studies and making this their thesis or dissertation. Properly done, this task requires thousands of hours.

Determining the Setting

Once the purpose of assessment is clarified and instruments selected, you must decide which setting will elicit the best performance:

1. Should data be gathered in an individual or group setting?
2. If group, how large? Does everyone take the instrument at the same time, or do some students watch or assist while others perform?
3. Should the setting be formal or informal? Should the students know they are being assessed?

Setting depends largely on the purpose of the assessment. Because testing in relation to placement is a legal process, it must be done in a formal context. Settings for other purposes should be individualized because students respond to assessment with different degrees of anxiety, frustration, and coping.

An informal setting, whenever possible, seems best. The Yellow Brick Road, a screening instrument to assess perceptual-motor strengths and weaknesses, illustrates a setting that maximizes abilities and minimizes anxiety (Kallstrom, 1975). The setting is based on the movie *Wizard of Oz.* Four stations are established for doing tricks that Oz characters request. In full costume, the cowardly lion gives instructions at one station, the scarecrow at another, the tin man at another, and munchkins at another. A yellow brick road made of contact paper stepping stones provides the structure for getting from one station to another. Periodically, music is played from the movie. Each child carries a ticket for admission to the stations on the way to finding the wizard. Reinforcement is provided by punching the ticket when each task is performed. When the ticket shows four punches, the reward is admission to a play area that is supervised by the wizard, who is also in costume.

This gamelike setting can be varied in as many ways as themes exist. What a wonderful way to be tested! For older students, a carnival or field day often achieves the same purpose.

Determining Environmental Factors

Students cannot be assessed within a vacuum. How they perform is influenced by hundreds of factors: weather, room temperature, allergens, gender and mood of the test administrator, and presence or absence of spectators (see Figure 7.3). Test administrators are likewise influenced by environmental factors, particularly when the assessment is primarily observational. In such cases, test administrators must place themselves where they can see best, where sun is not in their eyes, and where the angle of observation is most favorable.

In regular physical education, the tradition has been to keep all environmental factors constant (i.e., all students use the same equipment and follow uniform procedures). For some students, this practice inevitably results in failure.

Assessment, like learning, should be success oriented. Equipment should be altered in accordance with individual needs. In a test of striking, throwing, or catching ability, for instance, the characteristics of the striking implement and/or object are varied along a continuum from easy to difficult. Motor performance over several days or weeks is recorded on a profile sheet that describes assessment conditions. Figures 7.4 and 7.5 are examples of profile sheets. The date recorded in each box in these profile sheets indicates when there was success in 7 of 10 trials, the criterion established in the instructional objectives and written on the physical education IEP. Can you think of other ways to make assessment success oriented?

FIGURE   7.3

Test-condition variables that can be altered to attain success-oriented assessment.

Striking implement	Trajectory of object being struck	Size of object being struck	Object direction in fight	Weight of object being struck	Color of object being struck	Anticipation location	Speed object is traveling
Hand ↓ Paddle ↓ Bat	Horizontal ↓ Vertical ↓ Arc	Large ↓ Small	Right ↓ Left ↓ Center	Light ↓ Heavy	Blue ↓ Yellow ↓ White	How far must the performer move before striking the object	Slow ↓ Fast

FIGURE   7.4

Striking profile sheet for individual student.

Easy ————→ Difficult

		Color		
	Size	C_1	C_2	C_3
Easy ↓ Difficult	S_1	3/15		
	S_2		3/21	
	S_3		3/22	
	S_4		3/29	4/22

Key for object size

S_1 = Largest ball (18" diameter)
S_2 = Large ball (14" diameter)
S_3 = Small ball (12" diameter)
S_4 = Smallest ball (8" diameter)

Key for object color

C_1 = Blue
C_2 = Yellow
C_3 = White

FIGURE   7.5

Catching profile sheet for individual student.

Easy ————→ Difficult

		Angle of trajectory		
	Texture	A_1	A_2	A_3
Easy ↓ Difficult	T_1	3/15		
	T_2		3/21	
	T_3		3/22	
	T_4			4/22

Key for texture

T_1 = Balloon
T_2 = Nerf ball
T_3 = Rubber ball
T_4 = Softball

Key for angle of trajectory

A_1 = Horizontal plane
A_2 = Vertical plane
A_3 = Ball travels in arc

Recommended Instruments for Beginners

Practice in administering instruments that are designed for different purposes is helpful. Figures 7.6 to 7.10 present descriptions of tests that you should know. Additionally, Chapters 11 and 13, respectively, describe tests of motor skills and fitness.

Denver II

Since 1990, the Denver II has been the preferred test for screening children ages 1 month to 6 years on skills in four areas (personal-social, fine motor adaptive, language, and gross motor). The Denver II is a revision of the Denver Developmental Screening Test (DDST) which was first pub-

lished in 1967 and subsequently used in over 50 countries. Figure 7.2 on page 156 depicts a test form, and Figure 7.6 provides an overall test description.

Items are scored on the basis of formal and informal observation. When possible, parents are interviewed to ascertain the items that children perform at home. Persons administering Denver II need access to the *Denver II Screening Manual* and can benefit from the *Denver II Training Videotape,* but evaluating performance of the gross motor items is relatively straight forward. Assessment begins with obtaining the child's birth date and calculating the age in years, months, and days. Next a vertical age line is drawn on the test form. To determine if a child is developmentally at risk in the gross motor area, every item intersected by the age line should be tested. Additionally at least three items nearest

FIGURE 7.6

Denver II.

Purpose
To screen developmental delays in children from age 1 month to 6 years in four areas: gross motor, fine motor-adaptive, language, and personal-social.

Description
Norm referenced, with charts showing the age at which 25, 50, 75, and 90% of children can perform specific tasks.

The Denver II (Frankenburg, Dodds, & Archer, 1990) is a revision and restandardization of the DDST (Frankenburg & Dodds, 1967). Changes include an update in norms, removal or modification of troublesome DDST items, an 86% increase in language items, and the addition of a subjective behavior rating scale (Frankenburg, Dodds, Archer, Shapiro, & Bresnick, 1992). Whereas the DDST included 105 items, the Denver II includes 125 items.

The Denver II test form lists 32 gross motor items, 6 of which pertain to the number of seconds (1, 2, 3, 4, 5, 6) that a child can maintain a single leg balance.

The order of items on the Denver II test form reflects the developmental progression of the standardization sample (see Figure 7.2).

Scoring
Items are scored as pass, fail, refusal, or no opportunity to observe.

Validity
Final selection of 125 items was based on eight stringent criteria. Age placement of the individual items was guided by standardization data from more than 2000 children. Regression analysis determined the age at which 25, 50, 75, and 90% of children in various subgroups could perform each item.

Reliability
Four types of reliability were assessed: (a) inter-rater, (b) 5–10 min test-retest, different testers, (c) 7–10 days test-retest, same tester, and (d) 7–10 days test-retest, different testers. Mean percentage of agreement for most items was 100%, 90–99%, or 80–89%.

Primary Sources
Frankenburg, W. K., & Dodds, J. (1967). The Denver developmental screening test. *The Journal of Pediatrics, 71*, 181–191.
Frankenburg, W. K., Dodds, J., & Archer, P. (1990). *Denver II Technical Manual.* Denver, CO: Denver Developmental Materials, Inc.
Frankenburg, W. K., Dodds, J., Archer, P., Shapiro, H., & Bresnick, B. (1992). The Denver II: A major revision and restandardization of the Denver Developmental Screening Test. *Pediatrics, 89* (1), 91–97.

Address for Ordering
Denver Developmental Materials, Inc., P.O. Box 6919, Denver, CO 80206–0919.

to and totally to the left of the age line should be examined. Scoring is pass, fail, refusal, or no opportunity to observe (P, F, R, or NO).

Decision making about diagnostic test referral is based on counting the number of delays and cautions. A *delay* is defined as failing an item that 90% of age mates pass. A *caution* is defined as failing an item that between 75% and 90% of age mates pass. Test performance is generally considered *questionable* if a child has one delay and/or two or more cautions and *abnormal* if the child has two or more delays. Physical educators are expected to make recommendations about the need for referrals to administrators who, in turn, apply local or state criteria in making judgments.

Bruininks-Oseretsky Test of Motor Proficiency

The Bruininks-Oseretsky Test of Motor Proficiency (BOTMP) is widely used as a diagnostic instrument for making placement decisions (see Figure 7.7). This instrument purports to measure the specific abilities that underlie success in motor skills. *Motor proficiency* is not a synonym for motor performance; rather, it refers to the specific abilities on which performance is built. *The best definition of motor proficiency is the specific abilities measured by tests of running speed and agility, balance, bilateral coordination, strength, upper-limb coordination, response speed, visual-motor control, and upper-limb speed and dexterity.* This method of defining a constellation of abilities is called an operational definition and is frequently used in research.

A copy of the test manual is needed to administer the BOTMP. The item descriptions in the test manual give an operational definition of each factor—for example, bilateral coordination is what is measured by (a) jumps, (b) rhythmic tapping, and (c) index finger touching of body parts (i.e., a kinesthetic measure).

You need special training to score and convert BOTMP raw data to point scores and subsequently to standard scores. Figure 7.8 shows scoring for the long form. Norms are available for composite scores, but not for the individual factors. For the short form, norms are given in the test manual only for the total battery score. Broadhead and Bruininks (1982) have published means and standard deviations for short-form items.

FIGURE 7.7

Bruininks-Oseretsky Test of Motor Proficiency (BOTMP)—Placement.

Purpose
To assess motor performance of children from 4.6 to 14.6 years of age. Validated specifically for use in placement of students.

Description
Two forms are available: short and long.

Short Form
Norm referenced, with 14 items assessing eight factors: (a) running speed and agility, (b) balance, (c) bilateral coordination, (d) strength, (e) upper-limb coordination, (f) response speed, (g) visual-motor control, and (h) upper-limb speed and dexterity.

FIGURE 7.7 (continued)

Long Form of BOTMP
Same as short form, except with 46 items.

Scoring
Total test scores, subtest scores, and gross motor and fine motor composite scores can be derived. See Figure 7.8.

Validity
BOTMP is a revision of the well-known Lincoln-Oseretsky Test of Motor Proficiency. Content and construct validity is confirmed by similarity between factor analysis studies of BOTMP and works of Cratty (1967), Fleishman (1964), Guilford (1958), Harrow (1972), and Rarick, Dobbins, and Broadhead (1976).

Reliability
For short form: Test-retest *rs* ranging from .81 to .89 for 126 children. For long form: Test-retest *rs* ranging from .80 to .94. For the separate subtests, *rs* ranging from .15 to .89.

Primary Sources
Beitel, P. A., & Mead, B. (1980). Bruininks-Oseretsky test of motor proficiency: A viable measure for 3–5 year old children. *Perceptual and Motor Skills, 51,* 919–923.

Broadhead, G., & Bruininks, R. (1982). Childhood motor performance traits on the short form Bruininks-Oseretsky Test. *The Physical Educator, 39,* 149–155.

Bruininks, R. H. (1978). *Bruininks-Oseretsky test of motor proficiency manual.* Circle Pines, MN: American Guidance Service.

Bruininks, V., & Bruininks, R. (1977). Motor proficiency of learning disabled and nondisabled students. *Perceptual and Motor Skills, 44,* 1131–1137.

Address for Ordering
American Guidance Service, Circle Pines, MN 55014.

Bruininks-Oseretsky Test Items
(*Denotes items on short form)

Factor: Running Speed and Agility
Subtests: 1 on both long and short forms

*30-yard shuttle run

Factor: Balance
Subtests: 8 on long form, 2 on short form
 1. Standing on preferred leg on floor for 10 seconds
*2. Standing on preferred leg on balance beam for 10 seconds
 3. Standing on preferred leg on balance beam—eyes closed—for 10 seconds
 4. Walking forward on line on floor, 6 steps
 5. Walking forward on balance beam, 6 steps
 6. Walking forward heel-to-toe on line on floor, 6 steps
*7. Walking forward heel-to-toe on balance beam, 6 steps
 8. Stepping over response speed stick on balance beam

Factor: Bilateral Coordination
Subtests: 8 on long form, 2 on short form
*1. Tapping feet alternately while making circles with fingers, 90 seconds
 2. Tapping—Foot and finger on same side synchronized, 90 seconds

 3. Tapping—foot and finger on opposite side synchronized, 90 seconds maximum
 4. Jumping in place—leg and arm on same side synchronized, 90 seconds
 5. Jumping in place—leg and arm on opposite sides synchronized, 90 seconds
*6. Jumping up and clapping hands
 7. Jumping up and touching heels with hands
 8. Drawing lines and crosses simultaneously, 15 seconds

Factor: Strength
Subtests: 3 on long form, 1 on short form
*1. Standing long jump
 2. Sit-ups, 20 seconds
 3. Knee push-ups, 20 seconds—for all girls and boys under age 8
 4. Full push-ups—for boys age 8 and over

Factor: Upper-Limb Coordination
Subtests: 9 on long form, 2 on short form
 1. Bouncing a tennis ball 5 times and catching it with both hands
 2. Bouncing a tennis ball 5 times and catching it with preferred hand
*3. Catching a tennis ball 5 times with both hands tossed from 10 feet
 4. Catching a tennis ball 5 times with preferred hand tossed from 10 feet
*5. Throwing a tennis ball overhand at an eye-height target 5 feet away (1 practice and 5 trials)
 6. Touching a swinging ball with preferred hand, 5 trials
 7. Touching nose with index fingers—eyes closed, 90 seconds
 8. Touching thumb to index fingers—eyes closed, 90 seconds
 9. Pivoting thumb and index finger, 90 seconds

Factor: Response Speed
Subtest: 1 on both long and short forms

Stopping a falling stick with preferred thumb. The teacher holds the response speed stick against the wall and then drops it.

Factor: Visual-Motor Control
Subtests: 8 on long form, 3 on short form
 1. Cutting out a circle with preferred hand
 2. Drawing a line through a crooked path with preferred hand
*3. Drawing a line through a straight path with preferred hand
 4. Drawing a line through a curved path with preferred hand
*5. Copying a circle with preferred hand
 6. Copying a triangle with preferred hand
 7. Copying a horizontal diamond with preferred hand
*8. Copying overlapping pencils with preferred hand

Factor: Upper-Limb Speed and Dexterity
Subtests: 8 on long form, 2 on short form
 1. Placing pennies in a box with preferred hand, 15 seconds
 2. Placing pennies in two boxes with both hands
*3. Sorting shape cards with preferred hand
 4. Stringing beads with preferred hand
 5. Displacing pegs with preferred hand
 6. Drawing vertical lines with preferred hand
*7. Making dots in circles with preferred hand
 8. Making dots with preferred hand

FIGURE   7.8

Bruininks-Oseretsky Test of Motor Proficiency test score summary.
(*A*) Example of how BOTMP raw scores are converted to point scores.
(*B*) Example of conversion of students' point scores to norms.

SUBTEST 1: Running Speed and Agility Guide for Converting Raw Scores.

1. Running Speed and Agility SF*

TRIAL 1: 8.7 seconds   TRIAL 2: 7.5 seconds

Raw Score	Above 11.0	10.9-11.0	10.5-10.8	9.9-10.4	9.5-9.8	8.9-9.4	8.5-8.8	7.9-8.4	7.5-7.8	6.9-7.4	6.7-6.8	6.3-6.6	6.1-6.2	5.7-6.0	5.5-5.6	Below 5.5
Point Score	0	1	2	3	4	5	6	7	8	9	10	11	12	13	14	15

RECORD POINT SCORES FOR COMPLETE BATTERY ▼

RECORD POINT SCORES FOR SHORT FORM ▼

8

POINT SCORE SUBTEST 1 (Max: 16)

A

SAMPLE OF TEST SCORE SUMMARY FOR CHILD AGE 5 YEARS, 9 MONTHS

SUBTEST	POINT SCORE Maximum	POINT SCORE Subject's	STANDARD SCORE Test (Table 23)	STANDARD SCORE Composite (Table 24)	PERCENTILE RANK (Table 25)	STANINE (Table 25)	OTHER Age (Equiv.)
GROSS MOTOR SUBTESTS:							
1. Running Speed and Agility	15	8	21				7-8
2. Balance	32	16	13				5-2
3. Bilateral Coordination	20	9	23				7-11
4. Strength	42	5	11				4-11
GROSS MOTOR COMPOSITE			* 68 SUM	56	72	6	6-5
5. Upper-Limb Coordination	21	13	* 21				6-11
FINE MOTOR SUBTESTS:							
6. Response Speed	17	5	16				6-2
7. Visual-Motor Control	24	18	23				8-5
8. Upper-Limb Speed and Dexterity	72	27	20				6-8
FINE MOTOR COMPOSITE			* 59 SUM	64	92	8	6-8
BATTERY COMPOSITE			* 148 SUM	63	90	8	6-9

*To obtain Battery Composite: Add Gross Motor Composite, Subtest 5 Standard Score, and Fine Motor Composite. Check result by adding Standard Scores on Subtests 1–8.

Short Form

	POINT SCORE Maximum	POINT SCORE Subject's	STANDARD SCORE (Table 27)	PERCENTILE RANK (Table 27)	STANINE (Table 27)
SHORT FORM	98				

B

Table 7.5
Factors that widely used motor proficiency tests purport to measure.

Hughes Gross Motor Assessment (1979)	Bruininks-Oseretsky Test of Motor Proficiency (1978)	Cratty Six-Category Gross Motor Test (1969)	Project ACTIVE (Vodola, 1976) Basic Motor Ability Test
1. Static balance, eyes open	1. Running speed and agility	1. Body perception	1. Gross body coordination
2. Elementary ball handling	2. Balance	2. Gross agility	2. Balance/postural orientation
3. Static balance, eyes closed	3. Bilateral coordination	3. Balance	3. Eye-hand coordination
4. Leg strength and balance	4. Strength	4. Locomotor agility	4. Eye-hand accuracy
5. Object control	5. Upper-limb coordination	5. Throwing	5. Eye-foot accuracy
6. Aiming	6. Response speed	6. Tracking	
7. Dynamic balance	7. Visual-motor control		
	8. Upper-limb speed and dexterity		

Note. The Project ACTIVE test closely resembles the Basic Motor Fitness Test for Emotionally Disturbed and Mentally Handicapped Children by D. Hilsendager, H. Jack, & L. Mann in relation to the Buttonwoods Farm ED Project of Temple University.

The major decision with regard to the BOTMP is whether to use the long or short form. The long requires about 1 hr to administer, whereas the short takes about 20 min. In general, the short form is recommended as a screening instrument. The long form is used for diagnosis and placement because it is a better discriminator of students who need help (Verderber & Payne, 1987).

Research suggests that there is no such thing as general motor ability. Motor proficiency is multidimensional, and IEP goals should indicate specific factors (i.e., speed and agility, balance, bilateral coordination) rather than global motor proficiency. The focus of BOTMP factors suggests a perceptual-motor/sensory integration approach. Table 7.5 presents tests similar to the BOTMP that purport to measure basic abilities.

Tests of Motor Skills and Fitness

Several authorities prefer the goal areas of motor skills and fitness as the basis for placement and programming. The Test of Gross Motor Development (TGMD) of Dale Ulrich (Figure 7.9) and the Ohio State University Scale of Intra Gross Motor Assessment (OSU-SIGMA) of Michael Loovis and Walt Ersing (Figure 7.10) are examples of tests that focus on process rather than product. These tests are particularly helpful in instructional planning and measuring student progress. Additionally, the TGMD has been standardized and normed so that it can be used in placement. The TGMD is highlighted in Chapter 11.

To supplement process-oriented measures, tests that yield numerical scores should be administered. The overarm softball throw, standing long jump, 50-yd dash, and shuttle run offer a good four-item battery of product motor skill that, when coupled with a process measure like TGMD, make an excellent assessment for both placement and instruction. Norms are available on all of these items. Fitness tests that everyone should be able to administer are the four items comprising the AAHPERD Physical Best Test. These are highlighted in Chapter 13.

Other Instruments to Match Goal Areas

You should know how to administer instruments in all of the goal areas you consider important. Chapters 2, 5, and 6 therefore included descriptions of instruments related to the affective domain. The following are areas not covered elsewhere in the text.

Assessing Social Competency

The broad goal area of social competency is defined as follows: *to reduce social isolation; to learn how to develop and maintain friendships; to demonstrate good sportsmanship and self-discipline in winning and losing; to develop other skills necessary for success in the mainstream, including appropriate social behaviors (i.e., how to interact with others—sharing, taking turns, following, and leading).*

Tests and measurements textbooks (e.g., Barrow, McGee, & Tritschler, 1989; Kirkendall, Gruber, & Johnson, 1987) offer a few instruments directed toward these objectives. Don Hellison (1985), in his social development model designed for problem students, also offers assessment ideas, but overall, much work is needed in physical education to show potential contributions in this area.

Some standardized instruments, however, measure this goal area in a general way. Illustrative of these are the Walker-McConnell Scale of Social Competence and School Adjustment, the Behavior Evaluation Scale-2, and the Scale of Social Development. These instruments are available from Pro•Ed, 8700 Shoal Creek Blvd., Austin, TX 78758–6897.

Assessing Motor Creativity

Motor creativity is a broad goal area of particular value in assessing students, age 3 years and older, whose perceptual- and/or information-processing problems interfere with performance on traditional tests and affect motivation. Sherrill (1986a) has used motor creativity assessment primarily with students who are learning disabled or health impaired. *Motor creativity* is defined as *creative expression, a combination of*

FIGURE 7.9

Test of Gross Motor Development (TGMD).

Purpose

To identify children ages 3 to 10 years who are significantly behind their peers in the execution of 12 gross motor skill patterns.

Description

Two subtests are designed to assess different aspects of gross motor development: locomotion and object control. The results of the test provide both criterion- and norm-referenced interpretations. National representative norms are provided for both subtests and a gross motor development composite for children ages 3 to 10 years. The examiner is required to judge the presence or absence of 3 or 4 motor behaviors in each of 12 gross motor skills: run, gallop, hop, leap, horizontal jump, skip, slide, two-hand strike, stationary bounce, catch, kick, and overhand throw. Each skill is illustrated in the test manual.

Validity

Content validity was established by having three content experts judge whether the specific gross motor skills selected represented skills that are frequently taught to young children. Construct validity was established by testing the hypothesis that gross motor development would improve significantly across age levels. It was also supported by testing the hypothesis that children with MR would score significantly lower than peers of similar age. The test was also validated for instructional sensitivity. The results indicate that the test is sensitive to formal instruction in gross motor development.

Reliability

Test-retest reliability coefficients for the 12 gross motor skills ranged from .84 to .99. Interscorer reliability estimates for the skills ranged from .79 to .98 for 10 raters. Reliability of mastery decisions was reported also for samples using the total test score.

Primary Sources

Ulrich, D. A. (1984). The reliability of classification decisions made with the objectives-based motor skill assessment instrument. *Adapted Physical Activity Quarterly, 1*, 52–60.

Ulrich, D. A. (1985). *The Test of Gross Motor Development.* Austin, TX: PRO•ED.

Ulrich, D. A., & Ulrich, B. D. (1984). The objectives-based motor skill assessment instrument: Validation of instructional sensitivity. *Perceptual and Motor Skills, 59,* 175–179.

Ulrich, D. A., & Wise, S. L. (1984). The reliability of scores obtained with the objectives-based motor skill assessment instrument. *Adapted Physical Activity Quarterly, 1,* 230–239.

Address for Ordering

PRO•ED Publishing Co., 5341 Industrial Oaks Blvd., Austin, TX 78735.

thought and movement: when posed a movement problem, the ability to generate many responses, different responses, original responses; to learn to imagine; to embellish and add on; to risk experimentation; to devise appropriate game strategy; to create new games, dances, and movement sequences.

Several measures of motor creativity exist (Sherrill, 1986a). The most appropriate of these is the Test of Thinking Creatively in Action and Movement (TCAM) by E. Paul

FIGURE 7.10

Ohio State University Scale of Intra Gross Motor Assessment (OSU-SIGMA).

Purpose

To assess the qualitative aspects of 11 basic motor skills of children ages 2.5 to 14 years.

Description

Criterion referenced, with four levels of development specified for each motor skill. Specific criteria are stated for each level, with Level 1 designated as least mature. Teacher observes student in natural or test setting and rates performance of each skill as Level 1, 2, 3, or 4. The skills assessed are walking, stair climbing, running, throwing, catching, long jumping, hopping, skipping, striking, kicking, and ladder climbing.

Validity

Content validity by 11 experts who rated test, using 5-point Likert-type scale, on understandability and usefulness and by documentary analysis of the literature.

Reliability

None reported on student performance. Objectivity of scorers, however, was reported under this general heading with 13 judges viewing and rating the videotaped performance two times (1 week apart) of 12 children, ages 2.5 to 14 years. Resulting data, analyzed by Scott's Pi, produced test-retest scorer reliabilities ranging from .50 to 1.00 and intrajudge agreement ranging from .67 to 1.00.

Curriculum Available

Performance-based curriculum related to SIGMA (Loovis & Ersing, 1979). Contact Dr. M. Loovis at Cleveland State University, Cleveland, OH 44115.

Primary Sources

Ersing, W., Loovis, M., & Ryan, T. (1982). On the nature of motor development in special populations. *Exceptional Education Quarterly, 3* (1), 64–72.

Loovis, M. (1975). *Model for individualizing physical education experiences for the preschool moderately retarded child.* Unpublished doctoral dissertation, Ohio State University.

Loovis, M., & Ersing, W. (1979). *Assessing and programming gross motor development for children* (2nd ed.). Bloomington, IN: Tichenor Publishing.

Address for Ordering

Tichenor Publishing, P.O. Box 669, Bloomington, IN 47402-0669.

Torrance, a renowned authority on all kinds of creativity. TCAM has norms for children ages 3 to 8, but the items can be used with older age groups. This test requires about 20 min and no equipment but a wastebasket and lots of paper cups (Holguin & Sherrill, 1989).

TCAM includes four items. Item 1 focuses on how many different ways a student can move across a room. Torrance does not specify distance, but Wyrick (1968), in a similar test item, used 6 ft. A short distance avoids fatigue and puts the emphasis on new ways. This item and two others (3 and 4) are scored for both fluency (the frequency of responses) and originality (a 0 to 3 rating scale keyed to responses in the test manual that reflect whether the movement is common or infrequent). For example, hopping, skipping, and jumping receive 0 points because almost all students think of these. Frog, kangaroo, and various animal walks receive 1 point. Tumbling and spinning receive 2 points. Walking on knees backwards and running in circles receive 3 points.

Items 3 and 4 both pertain to possible uses of paper cups. Item 3 asks how many ways the student can put a paper cup in a wastebasket. Item 4 asks how many different things the student can do with a paper cup (i.e., imagine it is something else and show its use). Both fluency and originality scores are recorded. The following examples illustrate how 0, 1, 2, or 3 points are awarded:

0 points for hat, pencil, or jumping cup (response made by 10% or more of normative group)

1 point for spider, worm, and pop game (response made by 5 to 9% of normative group)

2 points for telescope, shoe cover, and nose cover (response made by 2 to 4% of normative group)

3 points for baseball bat, cow's milk, and dog's bowl (response made by 2% or less of normative group)

The imagination item (Item 2) requires children to pretend that they are six different things: a tree in the wind, a rabbit, a fish, a snake, a person driving a car, and a person trying to push an elephant. The child's response to each "Can you move like?" is scored on a 5–point scale as follows:

1 point—Child does not move.

2 points—Action is inadequate.

3 points—Action is adequate but without interpretation.

4 points—Action shows imagination.

5 points—Action tells a story beyond the assigned role.

Obviously, TCAM, especially Item 1, can elicit a lot of information about movement abilities. Torrance allows students to either tell or show responses. Sherrill has adapted TCAM to permit only showing. TCAM can be ordered from the Scholastic Testing Service, 480 Meyer Rd., Bensenville, IL 60106.

Other motor creativity protocols entail videotaping students on a multipurpose playground apparatus (rope, slide, ladder, balance beam, etc.) or in a room with various props (hoops, balls, ropes, scarves, broomsticks). The instructions are *"Show me all the different things you can do."* The prompt, *"Show me something new,"* is given every 60 sec. Videotapes of 3- to 5-min length provide a permanent record of children's movement vocabulary. Fluency and originality scores are derived by counting and rating responses using a Torrance protocol or by using a criterion-based motor creativity rating scale.

Interpretation of Data

Once data are collected, time must be spent on interpretation and on writing the results. Some school systems employ adapted physical educators and other specialists full-time to collect and interpret data. There is widespread agreement that adapted physical educators should have statistics and computer competencies.

Three bodies of knowledge provide basic facts needed for interpretation: (a) normal curve theory, (b) personal-best theory, and (c) sport classification theory. All three of these theories relate to everyday teaching. Normal curve theory allows comparison of students with one another to determine if they are performing at age-appropriate levels. Personal-best theory focuses attention on decision making in regard to individual goals. Sport classification theory introduces a communication system to guide program planning for persons who are clumsy or physically disabled.

Normal Curve Theory

The *normal curve* is a theoretical model derived by mathematicians that shows statistically how persons will place when tested. The model is based on the laws of chance and shows that scores, when graphed, depict a bell-shaped distribution (see Figure 7.11). This phenomenon occurs because, when large groups are tested, most persons (roughly 68%) score in the middle of the distribution. On Figure 7.11, the markers -1 SD to $+1$ SD indicate the middle 68% of the distribution, -2 SD to $+2$ SD indicate the middle 95% of the distribution, and -3 SD to $+3$ SD indicate the middle 99.7%. It can be seen that 68% of the population have IQs between 85 and 115 and can do between 19 and 39 sit-ups. These persons are considered statistically normal or average.

The laws of chance dictate that an equal number of persons score in the areas above and below the center point designated as 0 on the baseline of the normal curve model. Adapted physical educators are mainly concerned with people who score on the left-hand side of the curve.

Originally, normal curve theory was applied mainly to interpretation of intelligence tests because school placement was made solely on the basis of mental functioning. Persons scoring in the middle 68% of the distribution were placed in regular education. Those scoring in the upper 16% were assigned to advanced or faster-paced classes, whereas those scoring in the lower 16% were assigned to special education. Today, placement is typically based on achievement tests, but the concept is the same. The laws of chance and the resulting normal distribution of data can be applied to many human attributes. Thus, everyone involved in assessment and placement must understand normal curve theory.

Some states, for instance, have set placement criteria for assignment to adapted physical education. Illustrative of such criteria are

1. Score 1 standard deviation below the mean
2. Score 1.5 standard deviations below the mean
3. Score below the 30th percentile

What does all of this mean? Do you agree with these standards? In states where no universal placement criteria have been agreed on, school districts often set their own cutoff points. If asked to do this, how would you respond? Moreover, should placement decisions be based only on normal

FIGURE   7.11

This normal curve is the theoretical model that guides test interpretation and educational placement. The percentages inside the curve have been rounded off to facilitate memory. In reality, the 3% is 2.27%, the 13% is 13.59%, and the 34% is 34.13%. In reality, the shapes of the curves for the IQ and sit-up data also would be different. (SD = Standard deviation.)

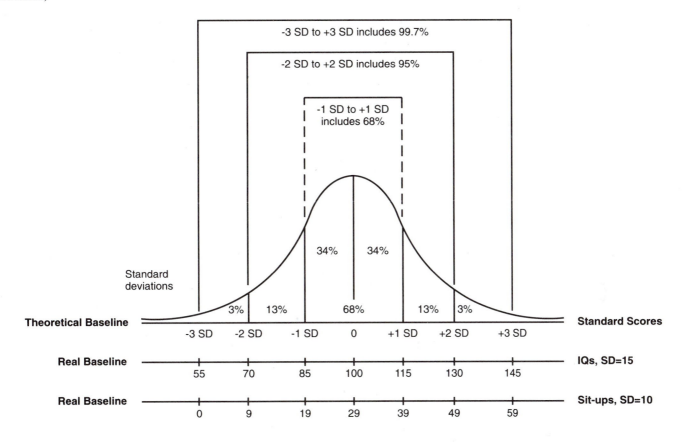

curve theory, or are there other considerations? The following sections should help you to develop the knowledge base needed to make and/or understand placement decisions.

The information also will enable you to interpret test results and use them to develop instructional objectives and to plan lessons. For every test administered, teachers are especially interested in two things: (a) average performance and (b) individual differences. Normal curve theory relates to both of these.

The normal curve is a model to aid with interpretation of real scores. To achieve this, the baseline (horizontal line) of the normal curve depicts only *standard scores* (-3, -2, -1, 0, $+1$, $+2$, $+3$), also called z scores. A standard score is a number that is used in *conversion, transformation,* and *interpretation.* During test interpretation, real scores are substituted for standard scores. For example, when sit-up data are being interpreted, the 0 and 1 might be replaced with 29 (an average sit-up score) and 10 (a measure of individual differences called a standard deviation). On a z-score scale, the mean is always 0, and the standard deviation is always 1.

Mean, Median, and Mode

Normal curve models always have a vertical line in the middle that is labeled 0. This 0 represents the mean, median, and mode. The *mean* is the average score on a test. The *median* is the midpoint of the scores, the point above and below which 50% of the group score. The *mode* is the one score made most frequently. When real data are graphed, the mean, median, and mode may not fall at precisely the same spot. With real data, especially when a test has only a few items, there may be more than one mode.

Thus, the theoretical model may or may not be a good fit for real data. The goodness of fit depends on whether the real data were collected from over 100 persons and are representative of the full range of individual differences in the population. Tests that are marketed for use in making placement decisions are administered to large groups so that the resulting data will fit the normal curve model.

The mean, median, and mode are called *measures of central tendency* because they describe the center, or middle, of the score distribution. Once teachers know the class

FIGURE 7.12

Transformation of z scores to real data for placement and teaching. The math calculations involve subtracting and adding the standard deviation (SD) to the mean (M), starting in the center of the curve and working outward. Also shown in this figure is the relationship between percentiles and standard deviations. (TGMD = Test of Gross Motor Development; BOTMP = Bruininks-Oseretsky Test of Motor Proficiency.)

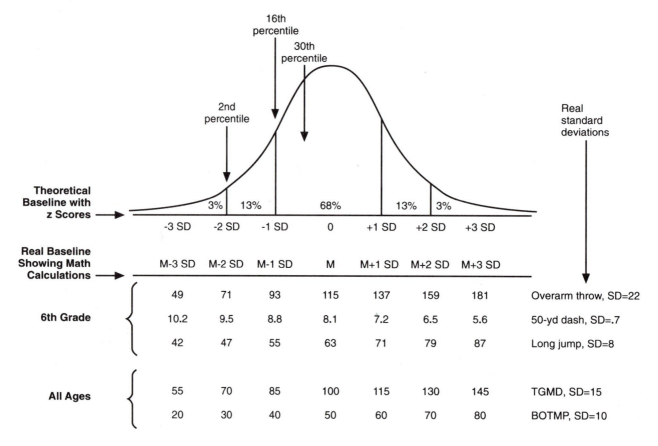

average, they are interested in whether their students mostly scored close to the mean or were spread out along the baseline. Note how the baselines of the normal curves in Figure 7.11 are divided by markers into equal spaces. Some baselines have 10 equal spaces, while others have 8, 6, 4, or 2. The number of spaces depends on the individual differences (i.e., spread of scores) and the number of persons tested. The normal curve model uses six equal spaces, but real data may result in any number.

Standard Deviations

Standard deviation (SD) is the term for a marker on the baseline that indicates the degree that scores deviate from the mean. A standard deviation is a *measure of variability* or individual differences. Standard deviations are written as -1, -2, and -3 to show how far scores deviate to the left and as $+1$, $+2$, and $+3$ to show how far scores deviate to the right. When real data are involved, the standard units (1, 2, 3) are transformed to actual values.

Figure 7.12 shows some real standard deviations and how they are used in calculations. To determine how far a real score deviates from its mean, the standard deviation is multiplied by 1, 2, or 3 and subtracted from or added to the

mean. Overarm throw data in Figure 7.12 illustrate this. The average throw for a Grade 6 boy is 115 ft. The standard deviation is 22. Thus, the calculations are $115 - 22 = 93$ and $115 + 22 = 137$. If the data are normally distributed, then the interpretation is that about 68% of Grade 6 boys throw between 93 and 137 ft. Any Grade 6 boy unable to throw 93 feet is performing below 1 standard deviation. To find out who is throwing below 1.5 standard deviations, subtract 33 (22 + 11) from the mean and get 82 ft. To find out who is throwing below 2 standard deviations, subtract 44 (2 × 22) from the mean and get 71 ft.

Applications

This information is useful in many ways. One application is the structuring of teams and practice groups. To equalize chances of winning, class teams should be balanced in terms of ability. If throwing is an important skill in the game being played, then an equal number of students scoring -1 or -1.5 standard deviations below the mean should be on every team. This is true also of persons scoring $+1$ or $+1.5$ standard deviations above the mean. In the old days, students scoring below 1 standard deviation would have been grouped together and taught separately. Today, the trend is to integrate them in carefully balanced teams or practice groups.

Another application pertains to decision making about special help and/or placement. Standard deviations are sometimes used as cutoff points for deciding when a student needs adapted physical education placement. Figure 7.12 shows what the -1 and -2 standard deviations cutoff points for Grade 6 boys on the overarm throw, 50-yd dash, and long jump would be. Most school systems, however, use standardized test batteries like the BOTMP and the TGMD for making placement decisions.

To aid in placement, the raw scores yielded by these batteries have been converted to *normalized standard scores* or quotients that have the same mean and standard deviation for each age group. To obtain a normalized standard score or quotient, simply use tables in the test manual. No math is involved.

For example, on the BOTMP, there are tables for converting (a) raw scores to point scores, (b) point scores to standard scores, and (c) battery composite standard scores to normalized standard scores. These normalized standard scores range from 20 and below to 80 and above. The mean is 50 and the standard deviation is 10 (Bruininks, 1978, p. 135). Figure 7.12 shows that the 1 standard deviation cutoff mark is 40 (M $-$ 1 SD).

Use of a cutoff has more meaning if standard deviations are equated with percentile ranks. The 1 standard deviation mark is the 16th percentile. This means that 16% of the test manual standardization sample scored below 40 and 84% scored above. If a cutoff of 1 standard deviation is used for placement, only a few students will receive the benefits of separate placement (i.e., about 16 out of every 100). This is perhaps an acceptable criterion if the regular physical educator who serves the other 84 students is assisted by an adapted physical education consultant and/or specially trained aides and peer tutors.

The TGMD conversions are less complicated than those of BOTMP. First, look up the standard scores for the locomotor and object control subtests and add them together for a summed standard score. Then, turn to the test manual page that converts summed standard scores to quotients. These motor quotients range from 46 to 154, similar to the system used in IQ test scoring. The mean is 100, and the standard deviation is 15 (Ulrich, 1985, p. 26). Figure 7.12 shows that the 1 standard deviation cutoff mark is 85, derived by subtracting 15 from 100.

These examples show that adapted physical education specialists who attend IEP meetings and assist with placement decisions need special training, not only in administering tests, but also in using test manuals to interpret data. Separate courses in assessment should be provided to teach about BOTMP, TMGD, and similar standardized tests. Criterion- and content-referenced tests are fine for teaching, but norm-referenced standardized tests should be used for placement decisions.

Standard Scores

The preceding section introduced the idea of standard scores. These are conversions or transformations of raw scores into equivalent units that permit adding different items or sub-scales. Whenever composite battery scores are needed, raw scores must be converted to standard scores because adding data yielded in different units, like seconds, feet, and counts of sit-ups or push-ups, is impossible.

There are many kinds of standard scores: z scores, stanines, and T scores, to name a few. Of these, z scores are most common because they are a part of normal curve theory. The -3, -2, -1, 0, $+1$, $+2$, $+3$ baseline of the normal curve shows standard scores, also called the standard scale of measurement. This scale always has a mean of 0 and a standard deviation of 1.

To convert raw scores to standard scores so that they can be added, the following formula is used:

$$z \text{ score} = \frac{\text{Student's score} - \text{Mean score}}{\text{Standard deviation}}$$

In Figure 7.12, for example, if an 11-year-old boy long-jumped a distance of 48 inches and the mean and standard deviation were 63 and 8, respectively, the calculation would be:

$$z = \frac{48 - 63}{8} \text{ or } \frac{-15}{8} = -1.88$$

In Figure 7.12, for a softball throw of 40, the age group mean and standard deviation are 115 and 22, respectively. Thus,

$$z = \frac{40 - 115}{22} \text{ or } \frac{-75}{22} = -3.41$$

For a 50-yd dash time of 9.8, the age group mean and standard deviation are 8.1 and .7, respectively. Thus,

$$z = \frac{9.8 - 8.1}{.7} \text{ or } \frac{+1.7}{.7} = 2.43, \text{ reversed to } -2.43$$

Note that in calculations that involve speed, a low score is considered better than a high score. Thus, the sign of the z score is always reversed.

Once the conversions are completed, the z scores can be added:

Long jump		-1.88
Overarm throw		-3.41
50-yd dash		$\underline{-2.43}$
	Sum	-7.72
	Average	-2.57 or 2.6

On the normal curve baseline, this z score will fall:

```
 -2.6
————+————————————————————————————————————
 -3     -2     -1      0     +1     +2     +3
```

This student's composite score falls about 2.6 standard deviations below the mean, which indicates that the individual definitely qualifies for adapted physical education placement in a separate class with a specialist.

FIGURE 7.13

Relationships between kinds of norms, the normal curve, and the stanine
bar graph with examples from the Bruininks-Oseretsky Test of Motor
Proficiency (BOTMP) and Ulrich's Test of Gross Motor Development
(TGMD).

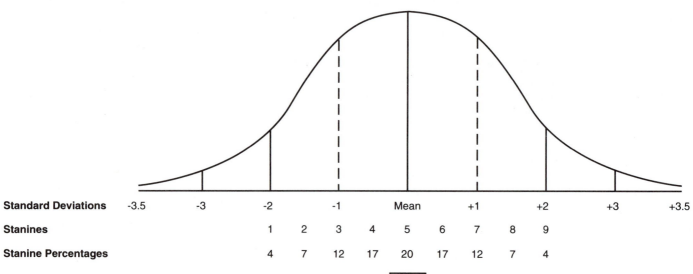

Standard Deviations	-3.5	-3	-2	-1	Mean	+1	+2	+3	+3.5
Stanines			1	2	3	4	5	6	7	8	9	
Stanine Percentages			4	7	12	17	20	17	12	7	4	

Stanine Model

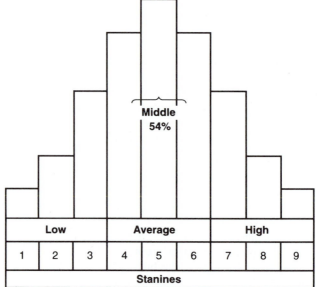

	Low			Average			High		
1	2	3	4	5	6	7	8	9

Stanines

Real World Applications

Below 32	32–37	38–42	43–47	48–52	53–57	58–62	63–67	Above 67

BOTMP Stanine Scores

Below 4	4–10	11–22	23–39	40–59	60–76	77–88	89–95	Above 95

BOTMP Percentile Ranks

1–4	5–6	7	8–9	10	11–12	13	14–15	Above 15

TGMD Stanine Scores

Table 7.6
Age equivalents for sample items on the Denver Developmental Screening Test (DDST).

DDST Item	25%	50%	75%	90%
		Ages		
Broad jump, 8.5 inches	2.0	2.8	3.0	3.2
5-sec balance, 1 foot	2.6	3.2	3.9	4.3
10-sec balance, 1 foot	3.0	4.5	5.0	5.9
Hops on one foot two times	3.0	3.4	4.0	4.9
Catches bounced ball two of three times	3.5	3.9	4.9	5.5
Heel-toe walk, four or more steps	3.3	3.6	4.2	5.0
Backward heel-toe walk, four or more steps	3.9	4.7	5.6	6.3

After z scores, the second most frequently used type of standard score in adapted physical education assessment is the stanine. *Stanine* is a contraction of the words *standard nine* and refers to a system of standard scores with a range of 1 to 9, a mean of 5, and a standard deviation of 1.96, which is typically rounded to 2. Figure 7.13 shows that the nine stanines equal the plus and minus 2 standard deviations of the mean area in a normal curve. Stanines of 4, 5, and 6 are interpreted as average. Stanines below 4 are low, and stanines above 6 are high. Stanines permit generalizations about which students fall within the middle 20%, 54%, 78%, and 92% of the mean (see stanine percentages line in Figure 7.13). They are more precise than z scores in describing placement but less precise than percentile ranks. Both BOTMP and TGMD provide the option of reporting data in stanines.

T scores are standard scores that range between 20 and 80 with a mean of 50 and a standard deviation of 10. To transform a z score to a T score, this formula is used:

$$T = 10(z) + 50$$

Norms

As mentioned earlier in the chapter, the three types of norms are (a) standard scores (e.g., z scores and stanines), (b) percentile ranks, and (c) age equivalents. Suppose, for example, that on the first subtest of BOTMP—running speed and agility—a child aged 5 years, 9 months made the following scores:

Raw score	Percentile	Stanine	Age equivalent
7.5 sec	72%	6	7.8

The raw score has little meaning until it is converted to one of the norms. A percentile of 72 means that the child scored higher than 72% of his or her agemates. The stanine of 6 means that the child scored in the high average range. The age equivalent of 7.8 indicates that the raw score was the midpoint score for all children 7 years, 8 months old. School records often state only one norm for each raw score. Regardless of whether the percentile, stanine, or age equivalent is reported, teachers are expected to be competent at interpretation.

Age equivalents are often given for subscales and test items but seldom for whole batteries. Criterion-referenced tests often use age equivalents. For example, the Denver Developmental Screening Test (DDST) states the age when 25%, 50%, 75%, and 90% of the population pass each item. To illustrate, the age equivalents for the last 7 of the 31 DDST items are presented in Table 7.6.

Often, the 75% column is used as the criterion for placement. For example, a 3-year-old who cannot perform a broad jump is functioning below 75% of agemates (i.e., he or she is scoring at the 25th percentile).

The TGMD gives the ages at which 60% and 80% of the standardization sample achieved the performance criteria for each of its seven locomotor and five object control skills. For example, 80% of the 3-year-olds met the first criterion for a run (a brief period where both feet are off the ground). Not until age 5, however, did 80% of children run with arms in opposition to legs, elbow bent. The BOTMP also provides a table for converting subscale scores into age equivalents.

In summary, most major placement instruments provide several kinds of norms: standard scores like stanines and z scores, percentiles, and age equivalents. Percentiles are the most common.

Placement and Awards

National award systems established by such structures as AAHPERD, the President's Council on Physical Fitness and Sports, and the Joseph P. Kennedy, Jr. Foundation are all based on normal curve theory. They recognize students who have worked hard to become outstanding when compared to others of the same age and ability (or disability).

In a sense, grades are like awards, and some teachers grade on the normal curve. This practice is typically followed in universities rather than in public schools. Even then, however, it is much misunderstood. To grade on a normal curve, teachers must either have access to norms in published test manuals or must develop their own norms, a feat that requires a minimum of 50 males and 50 females at each age level and considerable statistical knowledge.

Grading on a normal curve assures that half of the students will always fall below average. There are instances, as in teacher training, when this may be appropriate. We would like, perhaps, to identify the top 50% to teach our youth. With children, however, there seems to be no reason for grading on the normal curve. It is better to set mastery criteria and to consider effort as well as achievement.

FIGURE 7.14

Formation used to test running speed when personal-best theory is applied.

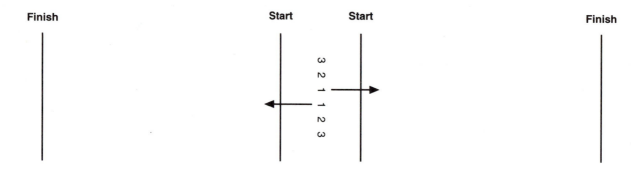

FIGURE 7.15

Example of interval goal-setting (IGS) model computation for the 50-yd dash and 60-sec sit-ups. (PB = Personal best.)

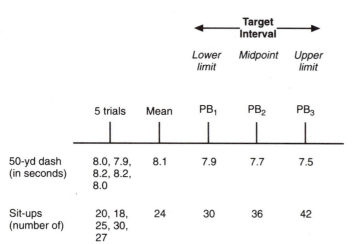

	5 trials	Mean	PB₁	PB₂	PB₃
50-yd dash (in seconds)	8.0, 7.9, 8.2, 8.2, 8.0	8.1	7.9	7.7	7.5
Sit-ups (number of)	20, 18, 25, 30, 27	24	30	36	42

Personal-Best Theory

Theory is needed for an understanding of how students perform in relation to their personal best. Sport competition has long capitalized on the concept of personal bests, and teachers need to follow this lead. Sherrill first used the idea of personal bests (PBs) with elementary schoolchildren in running the 50-yd dash. After the first trial, she pinned onto each child a card stating his or her time. Then instead of lining up students in the usual way and having them all run the same direction, she randomly assigned numbers and placed the students between two parallel starting lines, as in Figure 7.14. On the call of "Ones, on your mark, set, go," the ones ran in opposite directions, and each received their new times after crossing the finish line. Approximately 5 sec later, the call "Twos, on your mark, set, go" was given, and so on. This system requires two timers on each side and proceeds as efficiently as running heats. The obvious advantage is that it teaches students to compete against themselves and not others.

Another way to structure runs is to use staggered starts. Blindfolds also may be used as a way of emphasizing thinking only about one's own run. How many other ways can you create to teach and reinforce the personal-best concept?

The personal-best concept is hard to teach because children (at least the highly skilled ones) like to test their skills against others. At least half of class time, however, should be directed toward exploring personal bests.

Personal-best theory involves goal setting as well as testing. Students are taught to keep performance journals, with goals stated for each day or week. Research shows that persons who set specific goals are more motivated than those who set general goals or no goals. Moreover, telling one's goal to the teacher, a partner, or the class enhances performance even more.

Interval Goal-Setting Model

The interval goal-setting (IGS) model of O'Block and Evans (1984) helps to promote personal best. This model incorporates scores of the student's last five trials in setting a realistic interval for improvement. Figure 7.15 shows that the *target interval* is the range between one's previous personal best and a new upper boundary. Goals are illustrated for the 50-yd dash and sit-ups.

Calculations in this example are based on times of 8.0, 7.9, 8.2, 8.2, and 8.0 on the 50-yd dash and scores of 20, 18, 25, 30, and 27 on 60-sec bent-knee sit-ups. Building the IGS model begins with calculating the average (8.1 for the run and 24 for the sit-ups) and identifying the personal best (PB) of the five trials. This was 7.9 for the run and 30 for the sit-ups. PB1 is the lower limit of the new goal interval.

The midpoint or intermediate goal is determined by two steps. The first is finding the difference between the PB1 and the mean (M). This is called the difference score (D). The second step is either subtracting or adding D to PB1. For example,

Steps	50-yd dash	Sit-ups
PB1 − M = D	7.9 − 8.1 = .2	30 − 24 = 6
PB1 ± D = PB2	7.9 − .2 = 7.7	30 + 6 = 36

The upper boundary or long-term goal (PB3) is derived by subtracting or adding the difference score (D) to the new midpoint:

Steps	50-yd dash	Sit-ups
PB2 ± D = PB3	7.7 − .2 = 7.5	36 + 6 = 42

The subtract or add instruction obviously depends on the nature of the data. With a personalized IGS model in their physical education journal or on their clipboard, students can review their goals each class period.

Depending on how a student feels on a particular day, any of four goals might be vocalized:

1. I am going to better my average.
2. I am going to better my PB1.
3. I am going to better my PB2.
4. I am going to better my PB3.

This approach tells students that a range of performance is normal and acceptable. Everyone has good days and bad days. On good days PB1 or PB2 are goals until after PB2 is reached; then PB2 and PB3 become goals. On bad days (mood slumps, pollen or weather conditions for students with asthma, tensions and problems for students who are learning disabled or emotionally disturbed), the goal might simply be not to fall below average.

Criterion- and Content-Referenced Tests

Personal-best theory relates closely to criterion- and content-referenced testing. AAHPERD recognized the importance of this approach when it revised its health-related fitness test and named it the AAHPERD Physical Best Test. As shown in Table 7.2 on page 159, this test sets one minimum standard for each age group. Teachers are encouraged to individualize goal setting so that students with low fitness work toward this standard, while those with high fitness have the choice of setting more stringent standards or pursuing goals in other activity areas. The AAHPERD standards are the same for persons with and without disabilities.

Whereas the Physical Best Test relates to achieving a criterion level of fitness or beyond, personal-best theory challenges teachers to help students explore their personal best in hundreds of game, sports, dance, and aquatics activities. This includes not only motor skills but also knowledges, strategies, social behaviors, and use of leisure time. In areas that do not lend themselves to numerical measurement, creating lists of tasks or activities that can serve as criteria for pursuing a personal best is essential.

In gymnastics, considerable progress has been made in ordering activities according to degree of difficulty (see Figure 7.16). Lists like these indicate progression toward a personal best. The idea of difficulty ratings can be applied to the development of all kinds of instruments. Figure 7.17 presents the balance beam and floor exercise sports skills assessment instruments published by Special Olympics International. These checklists show how a task-analysis type

FIGURE 7.16

Difficulty ratings used by the U.S. Gymnastics Federation. Physical educators need to apply this idea to developing assessment checklists.

Balance Beam Locomotor Skills

Difficulty	Skills
____ .5	a. Slide forward or sideward
____ 1.0	b. Walk forward
____ 2.0	c. Plié walk (dip step) forward
____ 3.0	d. Step-hop forward (skip step)
____ 4.0	e. Walk backward
____ 5.0	f. Run forward
____ 6.0	g. Cross-step sideward

Floor Exercise Tumbling Skills

Difficulty	Skills
____ .5	a. Forward roll to stand
____ .5	b. Backward roll to knees
____ 1.0	c. Back roll to stand
____ 2.0	d. Pike forward or backward roll
____ 2.0	e. Straddle roll (forward or backward)
____ 3.0	f. Dive forward roll (pike)
____ 4.0	g. Handstand forward roll
____ 4.0	h. Back roll to headstand

of instrument (i.e., criterion- or content-referenced) can guide a student toward achievement of personal bests in various activities.

Sport Classification Theory

Assessment of persons with physical disabilities and/or visual impairments is especially difficult. The different levels of ability require a common vocabulary to designate function. Sport organizations for athletes with disabilities have developed such a vocabulary. Everyone in the disabled sport world, for instance, has a general idea about what a Class B1 person (blind) and a Class 3 person (cerebral palsy) can do and which sport activities are most appropriate.

The first thing that youth with disabilities learn when they become involved in sport is their classification. This is assigned after assessment by a certified classifier. Each sport organization has different requirements to become a classifier, but generally, both written and practical tests must be passed. The assessment used to assign a sport classification varies by organization but usually requires 15 to 30 min. For persons with visual impairments, the time is shorter because their sport classification is based on a standard test of visual acuity.

Issues

Assignment of sport classifications and use of these classifications in structuring teams is one of the most important principles in adapted physical activity. Sport classification theory has repeatedly been ranked as the sport topic on which

FIGURE 7.17

An illustrative activity analysis type of checklist based on idea of difficulty ratings.

Skills Assessment—Balance Beam

Test item 1, Level I: Balance beam skills
_____ Attempts to walk on the floor beam.
_____ Mounts the floor beam independently.
_____ Walks forward (toe-to-heel) on floor beam without assistance.
_____ Walks backward on floor beam.
_____ Performs slide steps on floor beam.
_____ Performs change of direction (¼ or ½ turns) on floor beam.
_____ Performs a "V"-seat balance on floor beam.
_____ Performs a straight-leg scale on floor beam.
_____ Changes level by squatting down and standing up.
_____ Dismounts the floor beam properly.
_____ Performs the Level I compulsory routine.

Test item 2, Level II: Balance beam skills
_____ Attempts to perform Level I compulsory routine on training beam (30–60 cm off the ground).
_____ Performs a knee scale mount onto training beam.
_____ Performs a Level I compulsory routine on training beam.
_____ Performs a lunge pose on training beam.
_____ Performs two other balance poses on training beam.
_____ Performs a straight jump on training beam.
_____ Performs dip steps on training beam.
_____ Performs a tuck-jump dismount off of training beam.
_____ Performs the Level II compulsory routine on training beam.

Skills Assessment—Floor Exercise

Test item 1, Level I: Floor exercise skills
_____ Attempts to perform a logroll.
_____ Performs a logroll without assistance.
_____ Performs a forward roll with assistance.
_____ Performs a forward roll to a standing position, without assistance.
_____ Performs a front scale balance skill.
_____ Performs a "V"-seat balance skill.
_____ Performs a lunge pose.
_____ Performs slide steps.
_____ Performs a straight jump.
_____ Performs the Level I compulsory routine.

Test item 2, Level II: Floor exercise skills
_____ Attempts to perform a forward-roll variation.
_____ Performs a forward-roll variation without assistance.
_____ Performs a backward roll without assistance.
_____ Performs a backward-roll variation.
_____ Performs a tripod stand.
_____ Performs a headstand.
_____ Performs a free "V"-seat balance skill.
_____ Performs a handstand.
_____ Performs a cartwheel.
_____ Performs a hurdle.
_____ Performs a stride leap.
_____ Performs a jump 180° turn.
_____ Performs combinations of Level I and II skills.
_____ Performs the Level II compulsory routine.

research is most needed (Richter, Ferrara, Adams-Mushett, & McCann, 1992; Sherrill, 1986b). Current issues that must be resolved are the following:

1. Should sport classifications be medical or functional?
2. Should sport classifications be specific to each disability (i.e., cerebral palsy, spinal cord injured), or should there be one system broad enough to include all disabilities?
3. Should there be a classification system for each different sport or a general system encompassing several sports?

Principles Underlying Classification

Two basic principles underlie classification theory. *First, in individual sports (like track and swimming), only athletes of the same classification compete against each other.* Although research is limited, existing evidence shows that sport classification is more important than age or gender when assigning persons to heats or events. If a school system does not have two students with the same classification, then a point system like the handicaps used in golf or bowling should be devised to equalize their competition. *Second, in team*

sports, the teams are scientifically structured, with each team having the same number of athletes from each class.

Point System in Team Sports

When students with disabilities are in integrated physical education, fairness in team sports depends on equal ability on each team. A point system similar to that used by the National Wheelchair Basketball Association ensures equality. A numerical value of 1, 2, or 3 points is assigned to each classification. Players on the floor cannot total more than 12 points. This allows each team to use its members as it wishes, with various combinations of classifications on the floor.

Medical Classification System

The medical classification system has been used worldwide for athletes with spinal cord injuries since the 1940s, when competitive sports were begun in England. Medical classification is anatomically based and assigned according to the level of spinal cord lesion (see Figure 7.18). The higher the lesion, the more severely impaired the function. The spinal cord is numbered into segments corresponding to the pairs of nerves that issue from it. If a segment is completely severed, the remaining function is known because the nerves from

FIGURE   7.18

Medical classification system adopted by the National Wheelchair Basketball Association (NWBA).

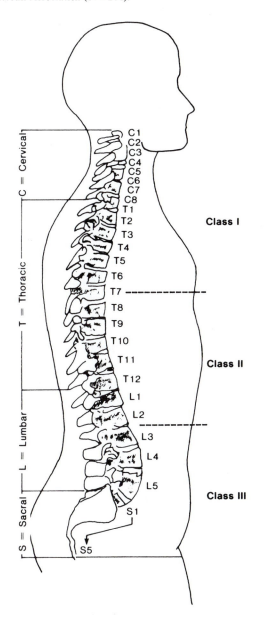

Class I

Class I. Complete motor loss at T7 or above or comparable disability that severely limits trunk mobility and balance and arm strength and range of motion.

Class II

Class II. Complete motor loss from T8 to L2 or comparable disability (including double leg hip amputee) that limits forward, backward, and sideward trunk mobility and balance.

Class III

Class III. Complete motor loss from L3 downward or comparable disability that limits sideward trunk mobility and balance and/or ambulatory speed, balance, and power compared to nondisabled peers. This classification includes persons who ambulate with limp or impaired gait.

this segment cannot innervate the movement of body parts or carry sensation. If the lesion is incomplete, however, muscle strength tests and observation must be used to determine the classification.

Functional Classification System

Functional classifications are assigned on the basis of what individuals can and cannot do in a sport setting. Function does not mean performance. *Function* is capability as judged by certified classifiers, who use standardized, written profiles (see Figure 7.19). When supplementary information is needed, muscle tests similar to those used in the medical classification system are administered.

There appears to be a trend, worldwide, toward using functional classifications (Curtis, 1991). Chapter 23 describes, in detail, new applications to wheelchair sports. In-

novative teachers and coaches are beginning to adapt functional classification systems to their school and community assessment needs. The system used by U.S. Cerebral Palsy Athletic Association (USCPAA) is presented in Figure 7.19 because more students have cerebral palsy than any other physical or sensory disability.

Since 1981, the USCPAA system has had eight classifications, Classes 1 to 4 for wheelchair users and Classes 5 to 8 for ambulatory athletes. Of the latter, only Class 5 athletes may use assistive devices like canes and crutches. Braces are not considered assistive devices. Figure 7.19 presents the functional profile for each classification. Adding a Class 9 for normal students with no coordination or balance problems and a Class 10 for gifted athletes allows this system to be used in a regular setting that serves all ability levels.

FIGURE   7.19

Sport classification profiles for persons with cerebral palsy.

Class	Description
1	Uses motorized wheelchair. Severe involvement in all four limbs, limited trunk control, and unable to grasp softball.
2	Propels chair with feet and/or very slowly with arms. Severe to moderate involvement in all four limbs. Uneven profile necessitating subclassifications as 2 Upper (2U) or 2 Lower (2L), with adjective denoting limbs having greater ability. Severe control problems in accuracy tasks.
3	Propels chair with short, choppy arm pushes but generates fairly good speed. Moderate involvement in three or four limbs and trunk. Can take a few steps with assistive devices, but is not functionally ambulatory.
4	Propels chair with forceful, continuous arm pushes, demonstrating excellent functional ability for wheelchair sports. Involvement primarily in lower limbs. Good strength in trunk and upper extremities. Minimal control problems.
5	Typically uses assistive devices (crutches, canes, walkers). Moderate to severe spasticity of either (a) arm and leg on same side (hemiplegia) or (b) both lower limbs (paraplegia).
6	Ambulates without assistive devices, but has balance and coordination difficulties. Moderate to severe involvement of three or four limbs.
7	Ambulates well, but with slight limp. Moderate to mild spasticity in arm and leg on same side (i.e., hemiplegic).
8	Runs and jumps freely without noticeable limp. Demonstrates good balance and symmetric form but has obvious (although minimal) coordination problems. Has normal range of motion.

Assessing Students With Severe Disabilities

A *severe disability* is defined as an IQ under 35 (i.e., a mental age between 0 and 3 years), serious emotional disturbance or autism, and/or multiple disabilities like deaf-blindness and cerebral palsy/mental retardation combinations. These persons are often nonverbal, nonambulatory, and dominated by primitive reflexes. Sometimes, they are ambulatory but cannot or will not stay in one place and attend to instructions. Obviously, assessment is a challenge. Standardized instruments often are not appropriate.

When assessing such individuals, first establish rapport. Even though they may appear oblivious of you, take the time to get acquainted. Talk to them like you would anyone else; try to initiate some kind of play, like peek-a-boo or copycat. If they make a movement, mirror them and see if they notice. *Mirroring* or reflecting another's movement shows acceptance and is especially recommended for persons who are autistic or emotionally disturbed.

Obtain background information from other persons and the files. Often, such students are on behavior manage-ment programs and respond to certain signs/words and reinforcers. Remember, no student is too severely disabled to receive physical education services. Assess play and game behaviors as well as motor skill, fitness, perceptual-motor function, and sensory integration.

Questions to guide assessment include:

1. Does the person attend to what you say or demonstrate? If not, does he or she respond to loud noises, light flashes, or other unusual stimuli (i.e., give evidence of seeing or hearing)? Keep trying until you find something.

2. What words/signs/gestures are understood? Often, these are on the individual's language board.

3. Does the person have some kind of expressive language (signs, words, pointing, eye blinks, facial expression)?

4. Can the person imitate? What kind of instructions will he or she follow?

5. What reinforcers (food, tokens, verbal praise, hug, touch) obtain the best responses?

6. What is the primary means of ambulation: (a) feet, (b) regular wheelchair, (c) motorized wheelchair? If regular wheelchair, is it propelled by hands or by feet?

7. How can muscle tone be described (normal, fluctuating, hypotonic, hypertonic)?

8. What primitive reflexes dominate or affect movement? Do head movements elicit associated movements? How can these reflexes be minimized or controlled?

9. If in a wheelchair, what is the disability? In most instances, it will be cerebral palsy, spina bifida, or muscular dystrophy.

10. If cerebral palsy, assign sport classification to obtain general idea of movement function. This primarily involves noting the type of ambulation, the hand-grasp function, and the range of motion (i.e., ability to independently move body parts). See Figure 7.20 and Chapter 25 on cerebral palsy.

11. Are there any contractures and/or abnormal postures or pain that need immediate attention?

12. Does the wheelchair and/or braces and assistive devices fit correctly? Is the person correctly positioned for physical education activities? Are body parts properly strapped?

These questions show that assessment competencies for students with severe disabilities are different from those of others. In general, criterion-referenced instruments (particularly the task-analysis types) work better than norm-referenced. Usually, the emphasis is on range of motion and postures, rather than strength and skills.

Instruments especially appropriate for certain kinds of severe conditions are described in Chapter 25 on cerebral palsy, Chapter 22 on emotional disturbance and autism, and Chapter 21 on mental retardation. For students who appear to be functioning motorically at the 0- to 5-year level, developmental inventories are useful.

FIGURE   7.20

Classification determines the type of projectile used with persons with cerebral palsy. (*A*) Class 2 lower athlete with no functional arm movements performing distance kick with 13-inch playground ball. (*B*) Class 2 upper athlete almost making bulls-eye with 5-oz soft shot. (*C*) Class 3 athlete performing club throw for distance.

A

B

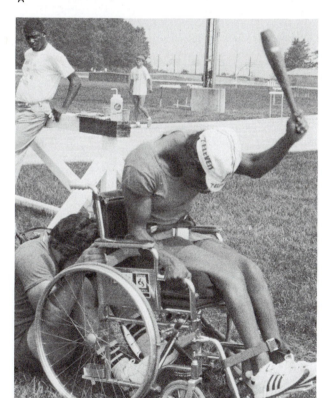

C

References

American Alliance for Health, Physical Education, and Recreation. (1976a). *Motor fitness testing manual for the moderately mentally retarded.* Washington, DC: Author.

American Alliance for Health, Physical Education, and Recreation. (1976b). *Special fitness test manual for the mildly mentally retarded* (2nd ed.). Washington, DC: Author. (First edition, 1968.)

American Alliance for Health, Physical Education, Recreation, and Dance. (1988). *Physical best: A physical fitness education & assessment program.* Reston, VA: Author.

Barrow, H., McGee, R., & Tritschler, K. (1989). *Practical measurement in physical education and sport* (4th ed.). Philadelphia: Lea & Febiger.

Brigance, A. (1978). *The Brigance diagnostic inventory of early development.* Woburn, MA: Curriculum Associates.

Broadhead, G., & Bruininks, R. (1982). Childhood motor performance traits on the short form Bruininks-Oseretsky Test. *The Physical Educator, 39,* 149–155.

Bruininks, R. H. (1978). *Bruininks-Oseretsky test of motor proficiency: Examiner's manual.* Circle Pines, MN: American Guidance Service.

Buell, C. (1973). AAHPER youth fitness test adaptation for the blind. In *Physical education and recreation for the visually handicapped.* Washington, DC: American Alliance for Health, Physical Education, and Recreation.

Buros, O. (1978). *The eighth mental measurements yearbook.* Lincoln, NE: University of Nebraska Press.

Conoley, J. C., & Kramer, J. J. (Eds.). (1989). *The tenth mental measurements yearbook.* Lincoln, NE: University of Nebraska Press.

Cratty, B. J. (1967). *Movement behavior and motor learning.* Philadelphia: Lea & Febiger.

Cratty, B. J. (1969). *Motor activity and the education of retardates.* Philadelphia: Lea & Febiger.

Curtis, K. A. (1991). Sport-specific functional classification for wheelchair athletes. *Sports 'N Spokes, 17* (2), 45–48.

Dunn, J., Morehouse, J., & Fredericks, H. (1986). *Physical education for the severely handicapped: A systematic approach to a data-based gymnasium* (2nd ed.). Austin, TX: Pro•Ed.

Fleishman, E. A. (1964). *The structure and measurement of physical fitness.* Englewood Cliffs, NJ: Prentice-Hall.

Frankenburg, W. K., & Dodds, J. B. (1967). The Denver Developmental Screening Test. *Journal of Pediatrics, 71,* 181–191.

Frankenburg, W. K., Dodds, J., & Archer, P. (1990). *Denver II technical manual.* Denver, CO: Denver Developmental Materials, Inc.

Frankenburg, W. K., Dodds, J., Archer, P., Shapiro, H., & Bresnick, B. (1992). The Denver II: A major revision and restandardization of the Denver Developmental Screening Test. *Pediatrics, 89,* (1), 91–97.

Guilford, J. P. (1958). A system of psychomotor abilities. *American Journal of Psychology, 71,* 164–174.

Harrow, A. J. (1972). *Taxonomy of the psychomotor domain: A guide for developing behavioral objectives.* New York: David McKay.

Hellison, D. (1985). *Goals and strategies for teaching physical education.* Champaign, IL: Human Kinetics.

Holguin, O., & Sherrill, C. (1989). Use of a motor creativity test with young learning disabled boys. *Perceptual and Motor Skills, 69,* 1315–1318.

Hughes, J. (1979). *Hughes basic gross motor assessment manual.* Yonkers, NY: G.E. Miller.

Kallstrom, C. (1975). *Yellow brick road manual.* Garland, TX: R & K. (Address for ordering is R & K, Inc., P.O. Box 461262, Garland, TX 75046.)

King-Thomas, L., & Hacker, B. (Eds.). (1987). *A therapist's guide to pediatric assessment.* Boston: Little, Brown and Company.

Kirkendall, D., Gruber, J., & Johnson, R. (1987). *Measurement and evaluation for physical educators* (2nd ed.). Champaign, IL: Human Kinetics.

Mitchell, J. (Ed.). (1985). *The ninth mental measurements yearbook.* Lincoln, NE: University of Nebraska Press.

Morris, G. S. D. (1980). *How to change the games children play* (2nd ed.). Minneapolis: Burgess.

O'Block, F., & Evans, F. H. (1984). Goal setting as a motivational technique. In J.M. Silva & R.S. Weinberg (Eds.), *Psychological foundations of sport* (pp. 188–196). Champaign, IL: Human Kinetics.

Rarick, G. L., Dobbins, D. A., & Broadhead, G. D. (1976). *The motor domain and its correlates in educationally handicapped children.* Englewood Cliffs, NJ: Prentice-Hall.

Richter, K., Ferrara, M., Adams-Mushett, C., & McCann, B. C. (1992). Integrated swimming classification: A faulted system. *Adapted Physical Activity Quarterly, 9,* 5–13.

Roswal, G. M., Dunleavy, A., & Roswal, P. (1985). Normative health-related fitness data for Special Olympians. In C. Sherrill (Ed.), *Sport and disabled athletes* (pp. 231–238). Champaign, IL: Human Kinetics. (For several privately printed books concerning tests and norms, contact Dr. Glenn Roswal, Department of HPERD, Jacksonville State University, Jacksonville, AL 36265.)

Salvia, J., & Ysseldyke, J. (1991). *Assessment* (5th ed.). Princeton, NJ: Houghton Mifflin.

Sherrill, C. (1986a). Fostering creativity in handicapped children. *Adapted Physical Activity Quarterly, 3,* 236–249.

Sherrill, C. (Ed.). (1986b). *Sport and disabled athletes.* Champaign, IL: Human Kinetics.

Ulrich, D. A. (1985). *Test of gross motor development.* Austin, TX: Pro•Ed.

Verderber, J., & Payne, V. G. (1987). A comparison of the long and short forms of the Bruininks-Oseretsky Test of Motor Proficiency. *Adapted Physical Activity Quarterly, 4* (1), 51–59.

Vodola, T. (1976). *Project ACTIVE maxi-model: Nine training manuals.* Oakhurst, NJ: Project ACTIVE.

Wessel, J. (1976). *I CAN—Primary skills.* Northbrook, IL: H. Hubbard. (Now available from Pro•Ed, Austin, TX.)

Winnick, J., & Short, F. (1985). *Physical fitness testing of the disabled: Project UNIQUE.* Champaign, IL: Human Kinetics.

Wyrick, W. (1968). The development of a test of motor creativity. *Research Quarterly, 39,* 756–765.

CHAPTER

8

Service Delivery: Placements and Job Functions

FIGURE 8.1

Good teaching involves all parts of the PAP-TE-CA model.

After you have studied this chapter, you should be able to:

1. Explain the PAP-TE-CA service delivery model and discuss how planning is affected by school district philosophy.

2. Contrast least restrictive environment (LRE) and regular education initiative (REI) philosophy.

3. Discuss support services and the importance of making available a continuum of placements. Identify various models and create some of your own.

4. Identify and discuss seven variables that should be considered in placement decisions (see Figure 8.1). Add some variables of your own.

5. Explain four steps in planning: (a) calculating instructional time, (b) planning use of time, (c) developing instructional units, and (d) making decisions about space, equipment, and resources.

6. Discuss how number of minutes of instructional time is used to determine number of objectives. Given assessment data, be able to develop a semester plan for service delivery and illustrative lesson plans.

7. Identify and explain some transitional mainstream models. Cite examples and research. Do the same for inclusive regular physical education models.

8. Explain how the services part of an IEP should be written. Identify at least five things that should be prescribed.

9. Discuss prescription in relation to lesson planning. What are three parts of a lesson plan? Given objectives for a student, develop a lesson plan.

10. Identify characteristics of a healthy counseling relationship and discuss them in relation to teaching.

11. Discuss program evaluation and document practice with the Checklist for Evaluating School District Adapted Physical Education.

T he service delivery model that guides adapted physical education appears in Figure 8.2. The services comprising this model (PAP-TE-CA) have been described throughout the text, and assessment was covered in detail in Chapter 7. The purpose of this chapter is to describe various kinds of placement and to build competencies in relation to job functions.

Planning at the School District Level

Planning can be a school system, school, or classroom function. However, since many adapted physical education specialists are employed to plan service delivery for an entire school district, we begin with planning at this level.

Figure 8.2 shows that the planning of adapted physical education depends on whether the school system follows the least restrictive environment (LRE) or the regular education initiative (REI) approach. Clearly, planning, assessment, and placement are dependent upon whether a continuum of physical education placements are made available or whether all students are placed in regular education. Many school districts apply REI philosophy in making physical education placements and LRE philosophy in making placements for other academic subjects. Let's briefly review these two approaches.

Least Restrictive Environment Approach

LRE philosophy is essentially the use of the individualized education program (IEP) or child study process to place students in their least restrictive environment for each content area. An environment is considered least restrictive when it (a) matches individual abilities with appropriate services and (b) preserves as much freedom as possible. For this philosophy to work, there must be a continuum of available placements for each subject matter area, and the LRE assignment

must be based on comprehensive assessment and collaborative parent-professional decision making. The LRE philosophy was created by special educators in the 1970s and operationalized by federal law, which described the IEP and procedures for making LRE placements.

A weakness in LRE conceptualization is that many school systems never created a continuum of placements for physical education. They placed all students either in separate adapted physical education or in integrated regular physical education. This, of course, was an improvement over the earlier practice of ignoring students with disabilities and providing them with no physical education. But a two-category system does not provide enough options for matching individual abilities with appropriate services.

Another weakness is that eligibility criteria for justifying LRE placement and/or services have typically been designed to identify cognitive or behavioral problems that interfere with academic achievement. Motor and health problems, unless associated with cognitive or behavioral deficits, have often been ignored. Many students, both special and regular education, who cannot succeed in a traditional physical education curriculum are assigned to regular education environments with the mistaken belief that such environments are least restrictive (i.e., abilities match the content to be taught). Historically, good physical educators have tried to accommodate such students and adapted instruction accordingly. Often, however, large class sizes, inadequate training, and lack of support services have defeated good intentions.

In summary, the LRE philosophy and IEP process are great ideas. Both are supported by law, but a double standard seems to exist in the interpretation of these constructs in relation to planning academic versus physical education

FIGURE 8.2

Planning, assessment, and prescription depend on whether the school
system follows the regular education initiative (REI) or least restrictive
environment (LRE) approach.

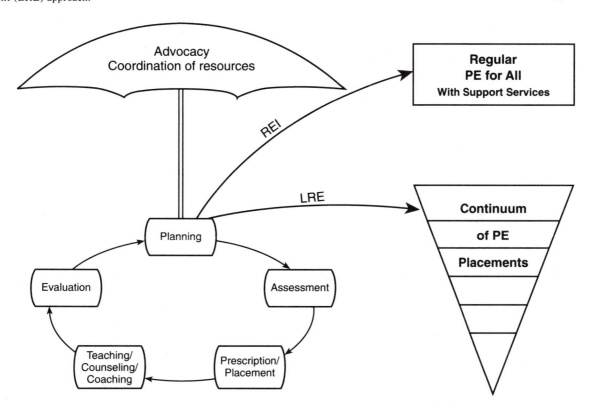

services. Physical educators need to understand LRE and IEP
concepts and to advocate that special educators extend their
beliefs to assessment, placement, and instruction in the psychomotor domain. Concurrently, physical educators must take
the initiative in making regular physical education the best
it can be for all of the students assigned this placement.

Regular Education Initiative Approach

The regular education initiative (REI) philosophy is the belief
that all or most students should be placed in the regular
classroom setting. Some proponents assert that any other
placement is discriminatory. Others take the stance that removal from the regular classroom is justifiable only if instruction with the use of supplementary aids and services is
documented as not successful. REI is a special education and
parent movement that began to have an impact in the 1980s
(Davis, 1989; Gartner & Lipsky, 1987; Jenkins, Pious, &
Jewell, 1990; Lilly, 1988; Stainback & Stainback, 1984).

The REI philosophy is currently the subject of much
debate among special educators. In contrast, the practice of
assigning almost everyone to regular physical education and
assuming that teachers will take the initiative in adapting
instruction is widespread.

Regardless of whether the LRE or REI approach is
operative in a particular community, regular physical educators should advocate and negotiate for at least one full-
time adapted physical educator in their school district. This
is because *support services* are an integral part of both the
LRE and REI approaches. Ideally, this specialist should be

funded from both the special education and regular education budgets and should assist all students with special psychomotor needs, not just those declared eligible by the IEP
process.

Support Services

The term *support services* (see Figure 8.2) refers to supplementary aids and services (the definition used in IDEA legislation, 20 *U.S.C.*, 143). This is usually the presence of extra
personnel in the regular classroom (e.g., adapted physical
education specialist, special educator, specially trained adult
aides, peer or crossage tutors). Extra personnel may also be
available in a nearby adapted physical activity resource room,
learning center, or counseling office. In the REI mode, students are not assigned to these separate areas but float in and
out as needed.

Support services may include things as well as
people. The availability of video cameras and monitors for
students to observe and analyze their movement patterns is
an aid to instruction. Likewise, the availability of machines
that pitch balls provides clumsy students with the thousands
of practice trials needed. To individualize instruction, there
must be much adapted equipment and sufficient space to set
up different stations for varying the time and space attributes that determine degree of difficulty of motor skills.
Likewise, computer and electronic technology can be used in
many creative ways to reinforce students' effort and ease
teacher load.

FIGURE 8.3

A continuum of placements for schools that implement least restrictive environment philosophy. The most imagination is needed at the "Part-time in Adapted PE" level, where students are making the transition into regular physical education.

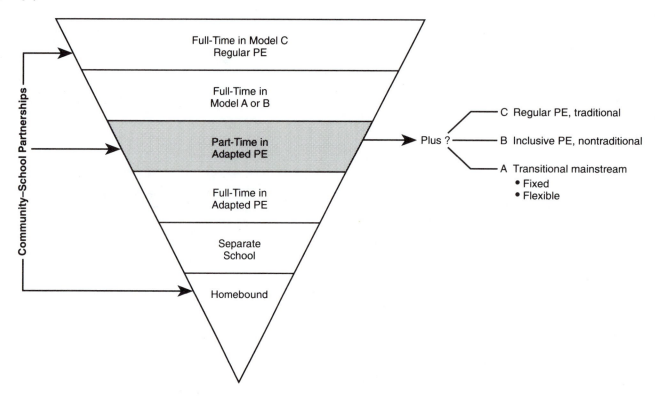

A Continuum of Placements

Support services are often not automatically provided. Regular physical educators must learn to ask, to negotiate, and to create. Success breeds success. The better a teacher is, the more likely he or she can convince the principal of the need for support services. Remember, support services cost extra money. Your requests will be weighed against others and sometimes be deferred. A positive and persistent attitude, coupled with a strong knowledge base of negotiation techniques, will eventually yield results. Warm, positive relationships with parents are also helpful. Parents often can find the time and energy to raise money, negotiate with the principal, and pose innovative alternatives.

The basic question to be posed to administrators is "Where is our school district adapted physical educator? Can you arrange for him or her to visit and help me?" Once this specialist is identified, he or she can act as a mediator in obtaining support services. If no specialists are employed by the school district, then regular educators can be advocates for the creation of such a position. Another basic question is "What in-service training can you provide for me in order to learn more about adapting instruction?"

A Continuum of Placements

For schools and school systems to plan services, decision makers must be aware of placement options. Figure 8.3 shows the different placements that might be used. Within the LRE philosophy, each step of this continuum is least restrictive for some students. Home- or hospital-bound instruction might

be the only option immediately after surgery and in long-term illnesses in which much time is spent in bed. Often, the physical education of persons in such situations is neglected, but play or recreational activities and a system for maintaining or building fitness should be provided. Terminally ill and medically fragile children, whether at home or in a hospital, need to sustain relationships with peers and physical education teachers, and creative school systems can make this possible.

Full-time adapted physical education in a separate or regular education school also depends on the philosophy and creativeness of the school system. Such programs usually follow a curriculum model like PREP (Watkinson & Wall, 1982), I CAN (Wessel, 1976), ABC (Wessel & Kelly, 1986), or ACTIVE (Vodola, 1976). These two steps of the continuum are well understood and need no further explanation.

Progressing up the continuum in Figure 8.3, the fourth step—part-time adapted physical education—represents the transition from separate to integrated placement. This critical step is analogous to the resource room concept in special education. Placement at this level demands two decisions: (a) How shall time be distributed between adapted and regular physical education? and (b) What shall be the nature of the regular physical education?

Figure 8.3 suggests that the answer to the second question should be Model A, B, or C. LRE philosophy requires having options, an area in many school systems in which imagination is nonexistent. However, it takes only one person to understand and advocate for a system like that in Figure 8.3.

Model A, a transitional mainstream program, is usually implemented by an adapted physical activity specialist. This is a system specially designed to integrate students with disabilities for the first time. Regular education students volunteer to help, receive special training, and are carefully selected for exemplary attitudes and peer teaching abilities. Among the variations of Model A that have been successful are (a) partners or peer tutors, (b) Unified Sports, and (c) reverse mainstream strategies. In these variations, the ratio of students with and without disabilities is equal.

Models B and C are conducted by regular physical educators. In these, the ratio of students with and without disabilities is about 1:10, the same as in society in general. If the ratio is smaller or there are special needs, then support services (usually teacher or peer aides) are supplied accordingly. Model B is a regular physical education class in which inclusion of all students is the main goal. Teaching style, content, and orientation are purposely designed to meet individual needs and assure success. This intent is much harder to implement than it sounds and requires training and experience. Model C is a class in which mastery of regulation sports or a designated fitness criterion is the main goal. Table 8.1 summarizes characteristics of regular and inclusive physical education models. Ideally, all schools have both models available because they teach different things. Often, however, this is not the case.

Mainstream Variables to Be Considered Prior to Placement

Planning service delivery begins with evaluation of regular physical education. Before making recommendations about placement, you need to know about class size, teaching style, skill performance level of students, and many other variables. Only by systematically examining such variables can you plan intelligently for differently abled students. Evaluation may result in placement in existing programs and/or the creation of new curriculum models.

Regular Class Size

When physical education classes contain over 30 students, it is difficult and perhaps impossible for one person to individualize and adapt. This is not only because of pupil-teacher ratio limitations but because space in the average gymnasium does not permit more than about five learning stations. *The optimal size for small-group interaction and skill practice is two to six students at a station.* There must be ample space between stations, particularly when balls are involved, to assure safety. Individualization implies personalization, and there should be the possibility within every class session of calling every student by name at least once, praising him or her for something, and engaging in personal talk. Class sizes larger than 30 build in defeat, contribute to teacher burnout, and intensify discipline problems.

Table 8.1
Two models used in regular physical education.

Regular (Traditional)	Inclusive (Nontraditional)
1. Regulation rules	Flexible rules
2. Do as I say	Find your own way
3. Focus on average	Focus on individual
4. Minimal competency expectancy for all	Individual personal-best expectancy

Class size should be negotiated. For students with attention deficit disorders, hyperactivity, and behavior problems, the maximum class size may be 10 or 12. For students with severe disabilities, the class size specification may also entail provision of a permanently assigned partner or aide. Class size should be matched with assessment data on social competence and learning style. Class size can be manipulated by decreasing the number of students or by increasing the number of teachers.

Teaching Style

Muska Mosston in 1966 introduced the idea of a spectrum of teaching styles in which students are given increasing freedom and responsibility for their own learning. Over the years, 11 teaching styles have evolved (Mosston, 1992; Mosston & Ashworth, 1986, 1990). In this chapter, several of these styles are loosely combined into two models: regular (Model C) and inclusive (Model B).

Method of judging student success is the major factor that distinguishes between Models C and B in Figure 8.3. In the regular style (also called command, practice, reciprocal, or self-check), all students must achieve a uniform standard or minimal competency level. The correct or efficient movement pattern is modeled and explained, and students are expected to approximate this pattern through on-task practice of specific, assigned activities. Feedback is largely corrective to enable students to meet age-appropriate minimum standards. Ultimately, each student passes or fails each task or step.

In the regular style, all students usually practice the same activity or participate in the same game. Sports and games are played by regulation rules to enhance generalization to leisure activities. Minimum health-related fitness standards are identical for everyone. Most traditional classes teach motor skills, fitness activities, and leisure competencies this way. The placement question then is, "Does the differently abled student, given his or her present level of performance, have a chance at achieving the required minimum competency set for each class objective?" If so, what kind of support services will this student need when placed in the regular class?

The inclusive teaching style is characterized by use of multiple performance standards or the criterion of everyone doing his or her best. Sports and games are not played by regulation rules; hence, the emphasis is not on mastering traditional sports. Instead, the major goal is getting to know and care about oneself and others through movement. Emphasis is on finding many ways of doing one skill, activity, or game, rather than one correct or efficient way. Feedback is facilitative rather than corrective, with students encouraged to explore their personal best and/or a collaborative best with a partner or small group.

In the inclusive style, students are given a choice about degree of difficulty. This means that every activity is task-analyzed from easy to difficult. Within the class, students are all performing at different levels. Traditional games are adapted so that there is no elimination and every student is maximally active.

With the inclusive style, differently abled students can be accommodated in regular physical education. Many regular physical educators, however, have never been taught how to adapt and include all students. Others find it difficult or impossible to apply this style because class size is too large or space is inadequate for parallel group activities of different difficulty levels. Finally, this style is inappropriate when the class goal is to learn regulation sports.

In conclusion, persons who make placement decisions should check on the teaching styles used in regular physical education. Ideally, every school has some classes representative of each style. Then the placement can be regular physical education with an inclusive teaching style. If no such classes exist, then regular physical education is probably not an appropriate assignment.

Skill Level of Regular Education Students

Whether or not students can succeed in a regular class taught in a traditional style depends on how close their performance is to the class mean (numerical average) on the skills, knowledges, strategies, and behaviors being taught. Persons who make placement decisions should have access to regular class statistics. These may be for a class, school, school district, or some larger conglomerate like several school districts from different parts of the country.

If running speed, for example, is important to success in the activities to be taught (e.g., low organized games), then a student's speed should be compared to that of the regular class student. Table 8.2 shows that, in the school system represented, the average 6-year-old boy runs the 50-yd dash in 9.9 secs. The standard deviation (SD) is included in the table to allow determination of whether a score meets the criterion of being no more than 1 standard deviation from the mean. This is a good criterion for deciding whether or not a student needs special help.

Means and norms are essential guides when making placement decisions involving regular classes governed by regulation teaching styles. A knowledge of the average student's skills, rules, strategies, and behaviors in the regular class lends insight into the probability of success for students with disabilities.

The ability to use rules and strategies in a game setting and/or to exhibit appropriate behaviors is difficult to assess by standardized tests that yield norms. In this area,

videotapes are recommended. Experts can then view videotapes of the differently abled student in several game settings and determine whether or not he or she can fit into and benefit from instruction in these settings.

Competition, Cooperation, or Individualistic Orientation

Orientation refers to whether the content in a particular class emphasizes competition, cooperation, or individual achievement. Two brothers, David and Roger Johnson (1975; Johnson, Johnson, Holubec, & Roy, 1984), both professors at the University of Minnesota, have spearheaded a comprehensive research movement that shows that classroom orientation significantly affects the differently abled person's social acceptance, performance level, and rate of learning. Their findings indicate that a cooperative goal structure is more appropriate for differently abled persons than the other two orientations.

Table 8.3 shows the desired characteristics of the cooperative learning structure. The recommended small-group size is two to six, depending on the students' social skills and the amount of time available to work on a particular task. The shorter the time, the smaller the group should be. Positive interdependence, the most important characteristic of the cooperative learning structure, is often promoted by joint reward systems, such as partner or group grades or points. The goal is to create a system whereby everyone helps everyone else, and success (task completion, winning, praise) is dependent upon everyone's contributions.

Many physical class activities can be taught and practiced using a cooperative group structure. For example, throwing, catching, and volleying practice can be structured around the challenge of which group can keep the ball in the air the longest while giving everyone an equal number of trials. Traditional team games can be changed so that a certain number of people must touch the ball (e.g., three or five passes) before it goes over the net or is used to make a basket or goal. Team bowling or shooting scores can be highlighted instead of individual ones.

Our society, however, expects most students to learn the rules, strategies, and skills of regulation team and individual sports before graduation. These activities are essentially competitive, even though cooperation with teammates is stressed. If the class goal is to teach mastery of regulation sports, then placement of a differently abled student in the class is inappropriate unless the ability to participate fully and to succeed can be documented in the assessment process.

Content to Be Taught

Like any other subject matter, the nature of physical education content varies by grade. Elementary school physical education is easier to adapt than secondary because the emphasis is on teaching basic skills, rules, and strategies and on developing minimum fitness. This content can be taught using traditional or nontraditional styles within competitive, cooperative, or individualistic orientations. In middle and secondary school, increasingly more time is spent teaching regulation sports that will generalize into lifelong leisure and

Table 8.2
50-yd dash times (in seconds) for grades 1 to 6. (SD refers to standard deviation.)

	Boys						Girls					
Grade	1	2	3	4	5	6	1	2	3	4	5	6
Age	6	7	8	9	10	11	6	7	8	9	10	11
Mean	9.9	9.3	8.8	8.5	8.2	8.1	10.3	9.5	9.2	8.7	8.6	8.3
SD	1.0	.9	.7	.7	.7	.7	1.0	.9	.9	.7	.6	.7
Percentiles												
95	8.4	8.1	7.8	7.5	7.4	7.1	8.9	8.2	8.0	7.6	7.7	7.2
75	9.2	8.7	8.3	8.1	7.8	7.7	9.5	8.9	8.7	8.3	8.2	7.8
50	9.9	9.2	8.8	8.6	8.2	8.0	10.2	9.3	9.2	8.7	8.6	8.3
30	10.4	9.6	9.0	8.9	8.6	8.4	10.9	9.7	9.5	9.0	9.0	8.7
25	10.6	9.9	9.1	9.0	8.6	8.5	11.0	9.9	9.6	9.1	9.1	8.8
15	11.0	10.2	9.4	9.3	8.9	8.8	11.3	10.4	9.9	9.5	9.4	9.1
5	11.6	11.0	9.9	9.6	9.5	9.3	12.0	11.1	10.8	10.1	9.8	9.5

Note. From Margie Hanson, *Motor Performance Testing of Elementary School Age Children*, p. 265, unpublished doctoral dissertation, University of Washington, Seattle.

Table 8.3
A comparison of cooperative and traditional learning groups.

Cooperative Learning Groups	Traditional Learning Groups
Positive interdependence	No interdependence
Individual accountability	No individual accountability
Heterogeneous	Homogeneous
Shared leadership	One appointed leader
Shared responsibility for each other	Responsibility only for self
Task and maintenance emphasized	Only task emphasized
Social skills directly taught	Social skills assumed
Teacher observes and intervenes	Teacher ignores group functioning
Groups process their effectiveness	No group processing

Note. From *Circles of Learning: Cooperation in the Classroom* (p. 10) by D. W. Johnson, R. T. Johnson, E. J. Holubec, & P. Roy, 1984, Alexandria, VA: Association for Supervision and Curriculum Development.

fitness practices. Curriculum at this level assumes that basic skills, rules, and strategies have been mastered, so accommodation of students without these abilities requires team-teaching and the running of parallel programs.

At the secondary school level, most good physical education programs use a multiactivity curriculum approach that covers several units over the school year. Ideally, some units teach regulation team sports, but others focus on fitness, movement education, dance, gymnastics, swimming, individual sports, and recreational games. The student with a disability may have potential for success in some of these but not others. Therefore, the IEP team should not assign secondary school students to generic regular physical education but rather to specific instructional units that are appropriate.

When full participation is not possible in regulation sport units, arrangements should be made for students to receive parallel instruction in sports specific to their disability (e.g., wheelchair basketball or handball) or to learn an individual sport not usually taught in regular physical education. An excellent approach is for school systems to employ athletes with disabilities to provide such instruction. The student not only benefits from new content but is introduced to role models and community resources. A growing number of athletes with disabilities are earning physical education degrees and qualify superbly for employment. If available athletes have not had teacher training, then special arrangements for in-service and supervision may be needed.

Disability-specific instruction often involves transportation to locations where special sports equipment and facilities are available. Budgeting for this is as important as transportation for the school's football team, but resources often are obtained only through advocacy and negotiation. Some school systems collaborate with community recreation programs, which make available transportation, facilities, and staff. This is an excellent way to facilitate transition from school to community resources, and many experimental mainstream programs can be devised.

The normalization principle must guide the planning of content. Differently abled students must be afforded the same opportunities as peers to learn lifetime leisure skills and to develop fitness and positive attitudes toward physical activity. This requires careful planning. Does the regular physical education program afford these opportunities?

Teacher Attitudes and Training

The attitudes and training of the regular physical education teacher ultimately determine success for the differently abled student. The availability of support services influences how teachers feel and their assessment of personal competency. Generally, we feel good about things we think we do well. Preservice and in-service training in adapted physical education enhances competence and contributes to good attitudes. A personality that is warm, friendly, and open to new people, ideas, and strategies creates a regular education climate that promotes humanistic learning for students with disabilities.

Adapted physical activity specialists are often assigned responsibility for in-service training of regular educators. This is why Chapter 2 emphasized learning as much as possible about attitudes.

Overall Program Quality

In summary, the overall quality of the regular physical education program affects planning, assessment, and placement. One role of the adapted physical education specialist is to serve as a liaison between regular physical education and special education and ascertain that students with disabilities are properly assessed and placed. At IEP meetings, information should be available, not only about the student, but about the regular education environment: (a) class sizes; (b) teaching styles; (c) skill level of regular education students; (d) competition, cooperation, or individualistic orientation; (e) content; (f) teacher attitudes and training; and (g) overall program quality.

Service Delivery for Regular Education Students

Many regular education students also need adapted physical activity services, but they are not eligible for help under the IEP-based special education model. Many school districts, however, want to serve students who are overweight, unfit, or clumsy, even though the law does not protect them. When a continuum of placements is available, there is no rule that only students with disabilities can have adapted physical activity. Upon the recommendation of the physical educator, principals or school counselors can initiate an assessment-placement process for regular education students similar to that used for students with disabilities.

Many regular education students need help as much or more than special education students. Families also need help. The 1990s offer opportunities for new, creative models for applying the content of this chapter to all persons, not just those with disabilities recognized by law.

Planning Instruction for the Year

Procedures involved in planning instruction include (a) calculating instructional time, (b) planning use of time, (c) developing instructional units, and (d) making decisions about space, equipment, and resources.

Calculating Instructional Time

Before determining number of objectives, calculate available instructional time for a specific class and/or student. Table 8.4, based on Wessel's (1977) I CAN system and the ABC curriculum (Wessel & Kelly, 1986), shows how the school calendar is used to do this for the academic year. Table 8.4 shows that the average student assigned to physical education 5 days a week (30 min a day) has 4,800 min (80 hr) of instructional time. This is 2,400 min (40 hr) a semester, a phenomenally short amount of time for the changing of behaviors.

Planning Use of Time

The next step is to decide how many objectives can be achieved in 2,400 min. Remember that students who are disabled or clumsy typically learn more slowly than their normal peers and that young students learn more slowly than older ones. Approximately 270 min (4.5 hr) are required for a preschool child with developmental delay to master one objective (Wessel & Kelly, 1986). Low-skilled students in elementary school and secondary school require about 210 min (3.5 hr) and 180 min (3 hr), respectively, per objective. To calculate number of objectives per semester, divide time needed to master one objective into total instructional time. For example, for elementary school:

$$\frac{2,400 \text{ min per semester}}{210 \text{ min per objective}} = 11.43 \text{ objectives per semester}$$

The next decision involves how many objectives should be selected from each goal area. Most IEPs include three or four goals, each broken down into three or four objectives. Time estimates often relate only to teaching motor and fitness skills; much research is needed on amount of time required to teach rules, strategies, and games. Research is also needed on amount of time required to increase cooperative behaviors and peer interactions and to decrease the many negative behaviors that constitute discipline problems.

Developing Instructional Units

The last step in group planning of time usage is to arrange objectives into instructional units and to specify the beginning and ending date of instruction for each unit. The IEP form, remember, requires a projected date for beginning service delivery. Legislation requires that progress on achievement of objectives must be reviewed for students with disabilities every 12 months. Many states require more frequent reviews. This should be considered in determining number of instructional units and duration of each unit. For convenience, assume that the periodic IEP review falls at the same time as the end of a semester (i.e., after about 2,400 min of instructional time).

Table 8.5 presents a sample semester plan for a student who requires approximately 270 min to achieve an objective (i.e., a preschool child who is slow or a student of any age who is severely mentally handicapped). In 16 weeks, stu-

Table 8.4
Calculating available instructional time for the year.

1. *Total number* of instructional weeks available: <u> 36 </u> weeks
   180-day school year = 36 instructional weeks
   230-day school year = 46 instructional weeks
   (Christmas, spring, summer vacations already excluded.)
2. Subtract 2 weeks of the total time available to allow for *cancelled physical education classes* resulting from conference time, psychological testing, swimming schedule, snow days, field trips, voting days (gym in use), holiday assemblies, beginning and end of school, and others.   <u> 2 </u> weeks
3. Subtract 2 weeks of the total time available to allow for flex time (unplanned adjustments that need to be made to allow for additional instructional needs).   <u> 2 </u> weeks
4. Total weeks available (#1 minus #2 and #3) =   <u> 32 </u> weeks (16 each semester)
5. Total days available:
   a. Multiply #4 by the number of physical education classes per week.   × <u> 5 </u> days gym/week
       = <u> 160 </u> days gym/year
   b. Multiply total number of days by the length (minutes) of your physical education class (instructional time—not dressing or set-up time).   × <u> 30 </u> min gym/day
       = <u>4,800</u> min gym/year

Table 8.5
Sample semester plan to guide service delivery.

Instructional Unit		Time in Minutes	Time Spent Each Week, in Minutes	Number of Weeks
1. Running games				
a. Motor skill—running		1,050	105	
b. Self-concept		450	45	
c. Social interactions		Embedded	Embedded	
d. Play and game concepts		Embedded	Embedded	
	Total	1,500	150	10
2. Aquatics				
a. Water entry and locomotion		270	67.5	
b. Breathing		270	67.5	
c. Self-concept and body image		60	15	
	Total	600	150	4
3. Creative movement/dance				
a. Portraying animals		100	50	
b. Moving to accompaniment		100	50	
c. Abdominal strength		100	50	
	Total	300	150	2

Note. a, b, c, and *d* refer to specific objectives. If 540 min are allocated, two objectives can be achieved. If 270 min are allocated, one objective can be achieved. If fewer than 270 min are allocated, there is not time for completion of one objective.

dents on this plan are expected to complete four full objectives and make progress toward six others. Develop some lists of objectives for hypothetical students and then show your competence in prioritizing and organizing these objectives into semester plans. *Remember that planning should always be done in units of minutes.*

    The amount of time required for a student to achieve an objective varies widely. The estimates of 270, 210, and 180 min for preschool, elementary, and secondary students are based on averages. Difficult objectives naturally require more time than easy ones. The art of writing objectives is enhanced by keeping in mind the number of minutes. Flexible time is needed for review and reinforcement of skills, knowledge, rules, and strategies learned in previous units. The planning of instruction is directed primarily toward new learning.

Other Decision Making

Planning also entails decision making about space, equipment, and resources. Size of class is tremendously important, since every student should have maximum on-task time. This means that, in a ball-handling unit, every student should have a ball and not be standing in line, waiting for a turn. It also means that every student has a chance to learn sports by practicing as a member of a regulation-size team, not by being one of 15 players scattered over the softball field. If too many students are assigned to a class in proportion to available space and equipment, selection of objectives and time planning are obviously affected.

In summary, planning reflects the philosophy of teacher, school, and community. Some of the processes involved in group planning are the same processes used for the IEP as required by legislation.

Prescribing/Placing

Prescribing, a term borrowed from the medical model, is the process of officially or formally recommending services. This includes *what* (the content or activities to accomplish objectives), *when, where, how much* (number of minutes or trials), and *by whom* (an adapted or regular physical educator). Each aspect of a prescription must relate to assessed needs.

Of particular importance to students with disabilities is the prescription of the instructional setting or model. This is often simply called placement. Prescription denotes more detail and structure. Figure 8.3 presented Models A, B, and C as placement options that every school or school district should make available. Examples of each of these kinds of models follow.

Transitional Mainstream Models

Students who are receiving most of their academic education in separate or resource room settings need exposure to a progression of integrated experiences to ensure success. The first level in a continuum of integration experiences is a transitional mainstream setting in which special attention is given to the ratio of students with and without disability, overall class size, and attitudinal preparation of everyone involved. Creative school personnel can devise all kinds of models. Descriptions of models to spark further creativity follow. Many others can be found in the literature (Aufsesser, 1991; Block & Krebs, 1992; Karper & Martinek, 1985; Karper, Martinek, & Wilkerson, 1985; Watkinson, 1987; Watkinson & Titus, 1986).

Reverse Mainstreaming

Reverse mainstreaming refers to the integration of nondisabled students into the facilities of students with disabilities (i.e., a separate school or class). Rarick and Beuter (1985) described the success of reverse mainstreaming in improving motor skills of students with mental retardation, ages 11 to 13 and 13 to 16, when nondisabled students (Grades 3 and 6) were brought to their facility. The ratio of disabled to nondisabled was approximately 1 to 3, and the teacher-pupil ratio

was 1 to 8. The program was conducted by two experienced adapted physical educators and one aide, using a station approach.

Titus and Watkinson (1987) also reported use of reverse mainstreaming. Their research focused on children, ages 5 to 10, with moderate mental retardation and minimal language ability integrated with nondisabled 5-year-olds from a local day-care center. The playroom had a variety of large and small apparatus as well as 10 vehicles (tricycles, wagons, and scooters). Lessons featured small-group instruction (teacher-pupil ratio of 1 to 4) for 15 min, followed by 7 1/2 min of free play. Findings indicated that exposure to the integrated program did not increase activity participation and social interaction.

Peer and Crossage Tutors

One of the best-known models of peer teaching is the PEOPEL (Physical Education Opportunity Program for Exceptional Learners) Project, which originated in Arizona and was disseminated through the National Diffusion Network and the Office of Special Education (Long, Irmer, Burkett, Glasenapp, & Odenkirk, 1980). In the PEOPEL model, nondisabled high school students complete a one-semester physical education careers class that trains them to work with peers who have disabilities. They are then assigned to PEOPEL classes, where they serve as peer tutors to provide individualized instruction based upon task-analyzed objectives. Generally, PEOPEL classes are comprised of 12 students with disabilities and 12 peer tutors under the supervision of an adult instructor. Statistical research (pretest-posttest design) shows that PEOPEL significantly improves the physical fitness of students with disabilities, as well as their attitudes toward physical education. It also facilitates mainstreaming and encourages peer tutors with special promise to choose physical education as their university major.

Project PEOPEL is no longer receiving federal funds, but the idea lives on. Many teachers throughout the country were trained to become PEOPEL facilitators and still conduct programs. Others simply use the idea of PEOPEL to innovate various kinds of "partners" curricula. One of the best resources for information on PEOPEL is Dr. Lee Burkett, Physical Education Dept., Arizona State University, Tempe, AZ 85287.

Many books and articles have been written on peer tutor models (Folio & Norman, 1981; Jenkins & Jenkins, 1981; Strain, 1981), but little research has been published in physical education. One excellent study (DePaepe, 1985) reported that peer teaching was the best of three models for youth with mental retardation. Webster (1987) showed that the presence of peer tutors had a positive effect on academic learning time of three persons with mental retardation.

PARTNERS clubs, used by Special Olympics International, are a variation of the peer tutor idea. They bring nondisabled students together with persons who are mentally retarded to practice skills and game strategies and encourage after-school and weekend activities using community resources (Krebs, 1990). This idea can be extended to all kinds of partnership relationships.

FIGURE 8.4

Research shows that children can often teach other children more effectively than adults can. In mainstream physical education, well-skilled children are often given special training to qualify as *peer teachers*.

Crossage tutor programs are effective in many communities (see Figure 8.4). Older students, designated as members of the "Honor PE Corps," are released from their classes one or two periods a day to work in elementary schools as physical education teacher aides. Such students generally are required to meet certain criteria and to complete after-school or weekend training programs. The honors corps often functions as a club (sometimes a subdivision of Future Teachers of America) and meets periodically for in-service training.

A related model is reciprocal teaching (the use of a partner), as explained by Mosston and Ashworth (1986), who note that even third-grade children are capable of observing and correcting one another's movement errors. Research shows that children *learn* through teaching. Students with disabilities need the opportunity to teach. Success in reciprocal teaching depends largely on preclass organization—the development of task cards or tangible instructions for pairs to follow with regard to learning objectives, principles of good performance, and the like.

Reciprocal and peer teaching generally involve *modeling* (learning through observing and imitating others). Modeling occurs incidentally in mainstream physical education, even without reciprocal teaching. A growing body of special education research substantiates that modeling modifies inappropriate behaviors and facilitates interactions among students with and without disabilities. Children are reinforced by being imitated, and they subsequently value the imitator more highly. The reverse may also be true. Modeling appears to be most effective when there is age and sex similarity.

Unified Sports

Unified Sports is a transitional mainstream model introduced by Special Olympics International (SOI) in the 1980s. Although developed by SOI (1989) specifically to promote integration of persons with and without mental retardation, the idea can be applied in many ways. At present, SOI has applied the Unified Sports concept to five team sports: basketball, bowling, soccer, softball, and volleyball. Bowling is considered a team sport in this program because it is structured by team rosters with a minimum of four players (two retarded, two nonretarded) per team.

Two principles guide Unified Sports: (a) age grouping and (b) ability grouping. Team members are matched as closely as possible on chronological age, and teams compete with other teams composed of members of the same age. Within a team, the sport abilities of players with and without mental retardation are matched so that the nonretarded peers do not dominate or assume peer tutor relationships. Persons with disabilities other than mental retardation can be members of Unified Sports teams, but they must be counted as nonretarded. At all times, 50% of the players on the floor or field must be mentally retarded.

The Unified Sports program has been tried in public schools in New York City and in Massachusetts and several other states. Although Unified Sports teams primarily play other Unified Sports teams, innovators envision competition with groups of varied composition as long as general ability level is matched. In fairness, the term *Unified Sports* should be used only in relation to Special Olympics and mental retardation. When the idea is applied to other disabilities, an alternative name for the model, such as integrated or mainstream sports, should be used.

Integrated Cooperative Sports

Illustrative of integrated cooperative sports is a study of 13- to 15-year-olds in bowling (Rynders, Johnson, Johnson, & Schmidt, 1980). Each bowling group was comprised of four students with Down syndrome and six without disabilities. Group members were told that they would be bowling together for 8 weeks (1 hr a week) and would be rewarded with prizes for improvement in performance.

In the cooperative condition, the students were instructed to increase their group bowling score by over 50 points from the previous week and to offer each other verbal encouragement, reinforcement, and help in ball handling. In the competitive condition, the students were instructed to outperform the other students in their group by maximizing their own scores. In the individualistic condition, the students were told to increase their own score by 10 points over the previous week.

FIGURE 8.5

Chart showing the analysis of traditional game (softball) into six components.

Players	Equipment	Movements	Organization Pattern	Limitations (Rules)	Purpose
9 per team	Ball Bats Four bases Gloves Backstop	Throw Catch Field Pitch Bat Tag Run Slide	Offense at bat, Defense in field, each covering designated areas	Diamond, run bases counterclockwise, Defense pitches ball, three strikes equals out, three outs per team each inning, seven innings, out-of-bounds rules, fly ball rule, etc.	Win, or practice skills, or have fun! Which is priority?

The findings favored the cooperative condition, showing it produced significantly more positive interactions than the other conditions. The implication, of course, is that physical education conducted to promote mainstreaming and peer acceptance must utilize a cooperative class structure rather than the traditional games that encourage individual skill development and competition.

Inclusive Regular Physical Education Models

In inclusive or Model B designs (see Figure 8.3), the teaching style, content, and orientation have been purposely designed to meet the needs of all students. Several variations of this type of model follow.

Games Design Model

The games design model is a systematic approach to changing established games and developing new games that (a) are inclusive in nature, (b) meet individual needs, and (c) promote cooperative problem solving and creativity among students and teacher. G.S. Don Morris of California State Polytechnic University in Pomona first described games design pedagogy in 1976; his classic book (Morris & Stiehl, 1989) has undergone several revisions and it is recommended as a supplementary text for adapted physical education courses.

Although many elementary school physical education textbooks discuss ways of changing games, Morris was the first to suggest a model. Three steps are required in designing games:

1. Understanding the basic structure underlying all games
2. Modifying the basic game structure
3. Managing the game's degree of difficulty

If a regulation game is to be changed, the first procedure is to analyze the game's components and develop a chart like that in Figure 8.5. All games can be broken down into six components: (a) number and function of players, (b) equipment and space requirements, (c) movements (what, who, when, where, how), (d) organization (game formation), (e) limitations or rules, and (f) purposes(s). Games design begins with reviewing these components with students on a chalkboard or poster board.

The next procedure, when working with students who are beginners at games design, is to select one category in which to make a change. In kickball and softball, for example, two bases might be used instead of four. Under limitations, the out-of-bounds rule might be eliminated so there are no foul balls—the batter runs on everything. Or the method of putting the ball in play might be changed, with each batter choosing his or her own way. It is important that students choose the change, not the teacher. Much of the value in the games design model is practice in problem solving and creative thinking.

Once the majority agree on a change, students try it out. As they become increasingly adept at implementing change, several components can be altered simultaneously. An important role of the teacher is to provide guidance about degree of difficulty. Tell students that they can change anything as long as (a) all students get to play all the time (i.e., there is no elimination) and (b) all students have an equal opportunity of success.

The games design model is an excellent way to enhance students' understanding of the many purposes of physical education, the need to use class time wisely and get as much physical activity as possible, and the importance of caring about and including everyone. A common criticism of many games like softball and kickball is that half the students are sitting and watching all the time. Students offer great solutions when posed a problem like this.

One variation that Sherrill's students devised was *Everyone-in-Action Softball.* Each time the ball was put into play (batted, thrown, kicked), everyone on the batting team had to do one of three things (sit-ups, rope jump, stair stepping) until the batter rounded all the bases. The defensive team had to run to whoever fielded the ball, form a file behind him or her, and pass the ball backward and then forward so everyone touched the ball two times before the original fielder could yell "fisheye." This word permitted the batter to cease running and the batting team members to quit their respective fitness activities. The score was the number of bases run. The students changed this game hundreds of ways and never seemed to tire of it.

Two research studies have been published on the games design model. Marlowe, Algozzine, Lerch, and Welch (1978) reported the success of the model in decreasing "sissy" games choices of emotionally disturbed boys whose play interests were too "feminine" for social acceptance. Marlowe (1980) reported a second study in which the games design model was effective in increasing peer acceptance of socially isolated children.

Cooperative or New Games

The cooperative or new games model has been explained and promoted by Terry Orlick (1978) of Canada and colleagues (Mender, Kerr, & Orlick, 1982). Orlick points out that games are played cooperatively in many cultures (e.g., Eskimos, Chinese, New Guineans) but that in North America, few games are designed specifically so that everyone works toward one common, mutually desirable goal. Alternatives to the competitive games and sports that currently dominate physical education are needed. Cooperation, according to Orlick (1978),

is directly related to communication, cohesiveness, trust, and the development of positive social-interaction skills. Through cooperative ventures, children learn to share, to empathize with others, to be concerned with others' feelings, and to work to get along better. (pp. 6–7)

Mender et al. (1982) also showed that cooperative games significantly increase the motor skills of children with learning disabilities.

Four criteria must be met for an activity to be considered cooperative: (a) all players help each other to achieve a common goal, (b) everyone's efforts are accepted, (c) everyone is involved, and (d) everyone has fun. Orlick's books describe many such games and offer suggestions for creating others.

Illustrative of a cooperative game is devising as many ways as possible for a small group (three to six people) to keep a beach ball in the air. One way, of course, is volleying, but another way is to permit use of any body parts. Try everyone assuming a sitting or shoulder-lying position and the rule that only feet or legs can touch the ball. Or try a blanket, parachute, or tablecloth series of tosses with everyone holding on. Each group tries to better its best time in the air. Groups never compete with one another to see who can keep the ball in the air the longest (see Figure 8.6).

Another example is nonelimination musical chairs (or hoops or towels). In the beginning, each student has one chair. The object is to keep everyone in the game, even though a chair is removed every time the music stops. As more and more chairs are removed, persons must share. Orlick reports that 20 children can perch on one chair and/or sit on top of each other so that at least one body part of everyone touches some part of the chair.

Numerous partner activities and stunts can be devised, such as three-legged runs and three-armed target tosses. Sometimes, the variation is one person blindfolded and one sighted. Carrying stunts also are fun: How many ways can three people cooperate to carry another person or some object like a tumbling mat or chair?

Adventure Activities

Adventure activities are challenges that involve ropes courses, jumps, climbs, and swings, with several persons helping one another (see Figure 8.7). Sometimes called risk recreation, the idea is to successfully cope with fears and anxieties and/or to develop trust and other social behaviors. The ropes to be traversed can be any distance from the ground. This is true also of various kinds of beams to be walked and jumped from. There are also walls to be climbed, rope ladders to be mastered, and map and compass orienteering activities.

Teachers need special training about safety aspects, and a budget is needed to underwrite ropes courses and other equipment. The adventure concept and activities have been particularly successful with students with behavior disorders, low self-esteem, and/or relationships problems (Rohnke, 1977). Information can be obtained from Project ADVENTURE, P.O. Box 100, Hamilton, MA 01936.

Movement Education

Movement education was described in Chapter 3 as an approach that permits many students to work simultaneously on the same skill but at their own level of difficulty. In movement education, the teacher does not demonstrate or ask students to do so. Instead, lessons are built around problems that are solved through movement and have no right or wrong answers. Often, a series of questions is used to guide discovery of the body, effort, space, and relationships. Mosston and Ashworth (1986) designated this general approach a "guided discovery teaching style."

The idea of movement education was first proposed by Rudolph Laban, a Hungarian who spent most of his adult life in England and greatly influenced the teaching of dance and movement both there and abroad. His two classic books, *Modern Educational Dance* (1975) and *The Mastery of Movement* (1960), are the primary sources for movement education pedagogy.

Both regular and adapted physical educators should learn to use the movement education model. This model is described in many elementary school physical education methods texts, often under the headings of educational gymnastics, dance, and games (Holt/Hale, 1988; Kirchner, 1985; Logsdon et al., 1984; Sherborne, 1987, 1990).

Creative dance, educational gymnastics, and *developmental movement* are other terms used when prescribing a teaching style that stresses fluency, originality, and imagination (components of motor creativity). This approach not only guides exploration of what the body can do but teaches students how to relate to each other in partner and small-group problem solving and choreography.

Other Models

Classes that center on individual and dual activities also offer success for differently abled students. Among the units that work especially well are recreational games (e.g., darts, horseshoes, shuffleboard, croquet, table tennis), dance, individual sports (archery, bowling, rifle shooting), and swimming.

FIGURE   8.6

Cooperative games.

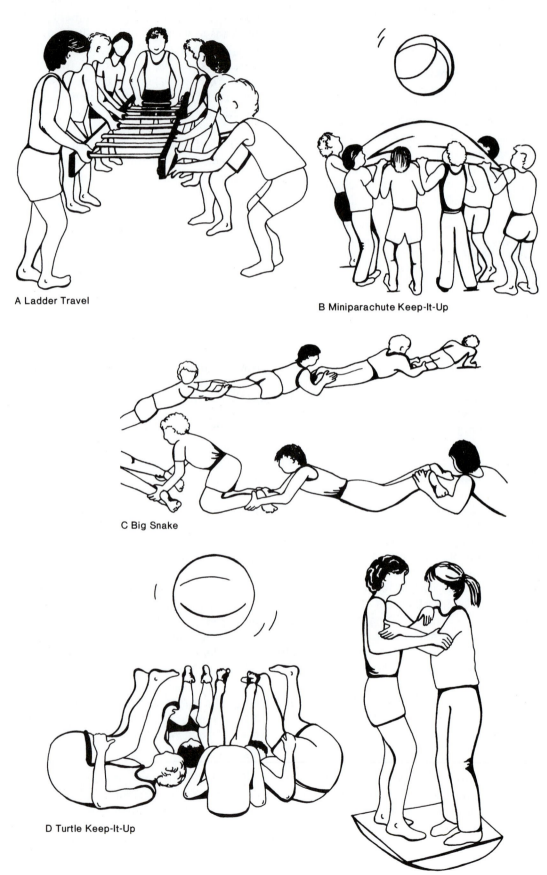

A Ladder Travel

B Miniparachute Keep-It-Up

C Big Snake

D Turtle Keep-It-Up

E Partner Balance

FIGURE 8.7

Adventure activities to overcome fears.

A. Jump forward from various distances to grab horizontal bar.

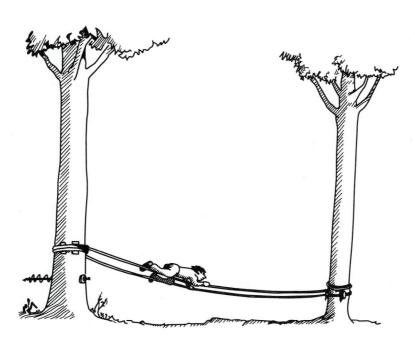

B. Traverse parallel ropes at various distances from ground.

FIGURE 8.7 (continued)

C. Move from swing to swing at various distances from ground.

Prescription in the IEP

Figure 8.8 offers an example of how the services part of the IEP is written. Note the importance of prescribing number of minutes per week in each type of setting, the maximum student/teacher ratio, and the type of teacher. Federal legislation does not designate that physical education must be taught by a physical educator. The only way to ensure this is to write it into the IEP. Teaching or management styles, explained in greater detail in Chapter 9, need to be prescribed also.

Prescription in Lesson Plans

Whereas the IEP is the broad prescription designed to guide several weeks of instruction, the concept of prescription also pertains to the writing of daily lesson plans. Lesson plans should include three parts: introductory activity, lesson body, and summary. Figure 8.9 gives the outline for a 30-min elementary school lesson plan designed to achieve goals in running skills, self-concept, social interactions, and play and game concepts.

The introductory activity (about 5 min) is usually an obstacle course, game, or dance activity in which everyone is involved. Physiologically, this is warm-up time, but instruction should be directed toward self-concept and social interactions by stressing that warm-ups are the way we show respect and appreciation for our bodies and prevent injury. Also during this time, we get in touch with our body and establish a mental attitude favorable to learning. The first 5 min are also a time for partner interactions, particularly in the transitional mainstream and inclusion class structures.

The lesson body (21 min) is specific to the individual. It is divided between self-testing and game activities for achieving functional competence. Note that a group game usually requires at least 8 min (2 of teacher talk, 1 to get into formation, and 5 of actual activity). Every minute must be carefully used. Waste during transitions from one activity to another can be eliminated by the rule that everyone must be in place within 60 sec. The transition time is structured by counting, a timer that buzzes, or tape-recorded music.

FIGURE 8.8

Example of services part of the individualized education program (IEP).

A. Placement Variables

		Adapted PE	Regular PE Model B
1.	Placement in minutes per week	60	90
2.	Projected dates	9/15–12/21	9/15–12/21
3.	Teacher/pupil ratio	1:5 or less	1:20 or less
4.	Taught by whom	PE teacher with 12 credits in adapted PE	Teacher with PE degree

B. Services to Be Delivered

1. Instruction in skills of creative movement, ball handling, and swimming following task analysis sequences of selected curriculum guide or book
2. Instruction in games using these skills following the game progression sequences of selected curriculum guide or book

C. Teaching Management Style

_____ Command		_____ 1:1 behavior management	
_____ Traditional		__X__ Individualized token or point system	
__X__ Guided discovery			
_____ Motor creativity		__X__ Group contingency system	
		_____ Traditional	

D. Adaptations and/or Special Equipment

1. Availability of sport wheelchair for at least 900 min during semester
2. Videotape equipment for student to view his or her movement patterns
3. Clubs for throwing instruction that meet specifications of the U.S. Cerebral Palsy Athletic Association

E. Transition

1. Field trip once a month to neighborhood community center
2. Home-school-community family nights

FIGURE 8.9

Lesson plan for running skills.

I. Introductory Activities	**5 min**
a. A 1-min or less attendance-taking protocol	
b. Obstacle or challenge course *or*	
c. Group aerobics with music	
II. Body	**21 min**
a. Self-testing (state number of trials)	5 min
b. Two games (8 min each)	16 min
2 min—instructions	
1 min—get into formation	
5 min—actual activity	
III. Summary/Evaluation/Cool-down	**4 min**
a. Group or partner discussion *or*	
b. Individual counseling	
Total	**30 min**

Self-testing is usually done in stations and guided by task cards. These state what skill is to be practiced, under what conditions (i.e., size, weight, and color of ball; distance from target; type of target), and number of trials. Task cards are kept at stations, stored in individual mailboxes or in files containing clipboards. Or they may be made of heavy cardboard with string attached for wearing around the neck. Development of task cards is described in more detail in Chapter 11.

The summary (4 min) can be activity or talk time or both. Physiologically, this is cool-down and relaxation time. In terms of self-concept, this is evaluation and cooperative goal-setting time. Emphasis should be on (a) "How are we going to use what we learned today?" (b) "When can we show our parents?" (c) "How much can we practice this at home?" and (d) "Who can we practice with?" Students need this kind of reinforcement to internalize that they have learned something, met their goals, and so on.

Each part of the lesson plan should be directly linked to terminal objectives. Some of these require time of their own, whereas others are embedded in activities that teach motor skills and practice. There are not enough minutes of instructional time in a semester to permit free play. When free time is awarded as part of a behavior management approach, the freedom should be to choose from among established activities that reinforce learning of objectives, not the freedom to engage in social dance, card games, and other activities that are unrelated to physical education objectives.

Figure 8.10 shows specifically how class activities contribute to four objectives for running games. Motor skills and patterns are broken down into two terminal objectives, and most of class time is spent on these. Skill time, however, is task analyzed into listening, getting into formation, and actual learning or practice. Self-concept is broken down into two terminal objectives and allotted 10 min, the parts of the lesson designated as introduction and summary. Social interactions and play and game behaviors are broken down into two and three objectives, respectively, and allocated no time because their achievement is embedded in other activities.

Teaching/Counseling/Coaching

Teaching/counseling/coaching is the process of facilitating learning while building and/or preserving ego strength. It requires special skills in listening and communicating as well as in instruction and management. Humanistic philosophy requires that teaching, counseling, and coaching be integrated processes. Within this context, counseling can be thought of as any communication that is helpful rather than

FIGURE   8.10

Daily plan showing how terminal objectives direct use of time.

Goal	Terminal Objectives	Minutes Per Day

Motor skills and patterns	1. To run 50-m dash in 9.9 sec or less
	
	Activity—Self-testing: Race against best time
	
	  a. Listen to instructions.
	  b. Get into formations.
	  c. Stay on task.
	
	2. To demonstrate functional competence in 10 running games
	
	Activity—Running games
	
	  a. Listen to instructions.
	  b. Get into formations.
	  c. Stay on task.
		20

Self-concept	1. To feel good about self in running activities
	
	Activity—Embedded
	Activity—Discussions
	
	  a. Pregame visual imagery: "I am good at running"
	  b. Prompts and praise
	  c. Postgame evaluation: Tell things you did well
	  d. Ask others what you did well.
	
	2. To respect self and body
	
	Activity—Embedded
	Activity—Warm-up and cool-down
	
	  a. Listen to instructions.
	  b. Stay on task.
	  c. Discuss why this is good for body.
	  d. Praise and prompts.
		10

Social interactions	1. To say hello and goodbye to relevant persons 2. To praise at least one person during every 5 min of game time Activity—Embedded, but may need prompts	0
Play and game behaviors	1. To listen to 2 min of teacher talk (game instructions) without interruption 2. To stay on-task during a 5-min game 3. To get into designated formations within 60-sec count Activity—Embedded, but may need prompts	0

Note. Social interactions and play and game behaviors are not assigned minutes of their own because their achievement is embedded in other activities.

neutral or hurtful. Most counseling is based on cognitive psychology and incorporates tenets of attitude, self-concept, and motivation theory. This section is short because counseling techniques are woven throughout the text.

Characteristics of a healthy counseling relationship are active listening, understanding the other's point of view, acceptance, willingness to become committed and involved, and genuineness (Adams & Younger, 1988). There is a difference between hearing what is being said and understanding what is being felt. You need both skills. Taking the time to *actively listen* is a challenge that many busy teachers find difficult, but persons with disabilities need to be able to talk through problems related to movement and fitness, use of leisure time, and barriers that limit self-actualization through sport.

Techniques associated with active listening are (a) establishing and maintaining eye contact, (b) squarely facing the person who is talking, (c) maintaining an open posture (i.e., not crossing the arms or legs because these gestures suggest disagreement or closing out the speaker), (d) leaning slightly forward to show interest and involvement, and (e) appearing relaxed and comfortable. In counseling, the person being helped (the helpee) does most of the talking.

The following are three roles associated with active listening:

1. **Encourager.** During pauses, the listener says "uh-huh," "go on," "yes," and "then what happened?" This enables the student who is upset to calm down and gain perspective as he or she hears self and considers reasons and alternatives.

2. **Interpreter.** In this role, the teacher attempts to clarify and objectify the student's feelings by restating the student's words in a different way, more clearly and objectively. For example:

    Student: I know that everyone is always laughing at me because I am so clumsy and awkward. No one wants me on the team. I don't have many friends.

    Teacher: You resent the fact that your classmates seem to judge you on the basis of your athletic ability and not for who you are.

3. **Reflector.** The teacher responds with reflective statements that convey an understanding and acceptance. The role moves beyond paraphrasing into reflecting the feelings of the student and indicating that it is OK or normal to have such feelings. The teacher asks questions to help guide the student into positive thinking and problem solving. For example:

    Student: I hate being fat. I hate myself because I can't take control and do something about it.

    Teacher: Yes, lots of people feel that way. Have you considered asking a friend to help you? Who are some people who might tackle this problem with you?

During a counseling session, the teacher's attitude and responses should make it easier for a student to listen to himself or herself. When the student perceives that the teacher thinks that he or she is worth listening to, self-respect is heightened. When another self (the teacher) can look upon the student's obesity, awkwardness, or lack of fitness without shame or emotion, the student's capacity to look at himself or herself grows. Realization that whatever attitude the student expresses is understood and accepted leads to a feeling of safety and the subsequent courage to test new ideas and try different methods of improving self.

Conferences with students should be held in a quiet setting where the teacher is free from interruption. Students should be assured that information will be kept in confidence. Two feelings are most important for optimal growth and positive change: (a) "I exist; therefore, I am lovable" and (b) "I am competent." Early conferences may be devoted to getting acquainted, finding common interests and values, and sharing ideas. An invitation to go fishing, take a walk, or eat out may contribute to the establishment of rapport more readily than formal interviews or conferences. Only when the student feels lovable and competent is he or she ready for preplanned regular counseling sessions.

Every word spoken by a teacher carries some meaning to the student. Likewise, shifts in postures, hand gestures, slight changes in tone, pauses, and silences convey acceptance or nonacceptance. Over 50% of the teacher's responses in a counseling session should fall into the reflection category. The teacher sets the limits on how long a session may last, but the student determines how short it can be. In other words, a student should feel free to terminate a session whenever he or she wishes.

Successes and failures in the gymnasium are accepted with equanimity. Neither praise nor blame is offered. The teacher uses words primarily to reflect what the student is feeling in a manner similar to that employed in the counseling session. On some occasions, the teacher may imitate the movement of the student, using this technique to reflect how the student looks to another and to reinforce the belief that others can accept the student and his or her movement as the best of which he or she is capable at the moment. Imitation of movements, performed without words, shows willingness to suffer what the student is suffering, to feel as he or she feels, to perform through his or her body, and to walk in his or her shoes.

Success in counseling is dependent upon the skill of the teacher in the following functions: (a) seeing the student as a coworker on a common problem, (b) treating the student as an equal, (c) understanding the student's feelings, (d) following the student's line of thought, (e) commenting in line with what the student is trying to convey, and (f) participating completely in the student's communication. The teacher's tone of voice is extremely important in conveying willingness and ability to share a student's feelings.

As counseling proceeds, the student should grow in self-acceptance. The following criteria may serve as one basis for evaluation: (a) the student perceives self as a person of worth, worthy of respect rather than criticism; (b) the student perceives his or her abilities with more objectivity and greater comfort; (c) the student perceives self as more independent and more able to cope with problems; (d) the student perceives self as more able to be spontaneous and genuine; and (e) the student perceives self as more integrated, less divided.

Leisure counseling is particularly important in helping persons with disabilities generalize skills learned at school to the community setting (Bender, Brannan, & Verhoven, 1984; Dowd, 1984; Taylor, 1987). This entails asking persons what they want to do during free time and helping them overcome environmental and personal constraints. Often, it is necessary to provide information about opportunities and resources; this can be done through field trips written into the IEP under transitional services and conducted as part of school physical education.

Counseling is very time consuming. Teachers need to know when and how to refer students for additional help. Support or empowerment groups are often as facilitative as one-to-one counseling (Chesler & Chesney, 1988).

Weaving counseling into teaching/coaching functions assures that students are actively involved in goal setting and maximizing learning conditions. Indicators of effective teaching, stated in Chapter 3, emphasize the importance of a warm, positive learning environment and high rates of on-task behaviors. Preplanning, or teacher preparation, is especially important (Brophy, 1983; Rosenshine, 1983). This is why planning is considered a function in its own right.

Teaching and coaching are broken down into six job functions: (a) reviewing, assessing mastery of previous material, and retraining, if necessary; (b) presenting new material; (c) structuring and supervising initial practice; (d) matching feedback and correctives to individual needs; (e) motivating and rewarding on-task behavior during independent practice of newly learned material; and (f) conducting weekly and monthly reviews to assure retention and generalization (Rosenshine, 1983). Success in these functions depends on adaptation, individualization, creativity, and motor-learning principles, all of which are covered in Chapter 9.

Evaluation

Program evaluation can entail examination of a class, a school, or a school district. Because employment policies, and consequently, the physical education placement options for students with disabilities are often determined by school districts, it is good to have available checklists for evaluation at this level. The following is such an instrument, modified from a research tool called Survey of Adapted Physical Education Needs (Sherrill & Megginson, 1984).

Checklist For Evaluating School District Adapted Physical Education

Instructions: First, check yes or no to indicate school district practices. Then, rate the item in order of its importance to you. *The highest rating is 5*. Do not give all items an equal rating. Use the rating procedure to help you decide on the relative importance of each item.

Assessment, Placement, and the IEP Process

Yes	No	Importance	
___	___	5 4 3 2 1	1. The school district has an effective screening program for the identification of students with motor and physical problems that need attention.
___	___	5 4 3 2 1	2. The school district has specific eligibility standards for placement of students in adapted physical education.
___	___	5 4 3 2 1	3. Adapted physical education placement/ instruction is made available for all students with medical excuses that exempt them from *regular* physical education.
___	___	5 4 3 2 1	4. The school district provides for a continuum of placements, including separate adapted physical education, partial integration in mainstream physical education, and full integration.
___	___	5 4 3 2 1	5. Motor and physical ability assessment in the IEP process is done by a physical educator specially trained in motor evaluation who utilizes appropriate assessment tools.
___	___	5 4 3 2 1	6. Specially trained physical education personnel participate in the IEP process and/or other interdisciplinary planning sessions concerning education of students with disabilities.
___	___	5 4 3 2 1	7. Appropriate physical education placement is agreed upon by school personnel and parents at the initial IEP meeting and at each program review thereafter.
___	___	5 4 3 2 1	8. Students with medical excuses to exempt them from regular physical education classes have these medical excuses reevaluated/renewed annually.
___	___	5 4 3 2 1	9. IEPs include present level of motor and physical performance, physical education goals and short-term objectives, and specific physical education services to be provided.

Instruction and Programming

Yes	No	Importance		
___	___	5 4 3 2 1	1.	The school district provides evaluative criteria to guide administrators in monitoring the quality of adapted physical education service delivery.
___	___	5 4 3 2 1	2.	A curriculum manual describing physical education instruction/services for students with disabilities is available.
___	___	5 4 3 2 1	3.	When students with disabilities are integrated into regular physical education classes, the student-staff ratio is 30 to 1 or less.
___	___	5 4 3 2 1	4.	Adapted physical education classes designed specially for students with severe disabilities have a student-staff ratio of 5 to 1 or less.
___	___	5 4 3 2 1	5.	The content of adapted physical education classes is diversified and includes opportunities to learn movement patterns, games, sports, dance, and aquatics adapted to individual abilities.
___	___	5 4 3 2 1	6.	Physical education programming is based on IEPs, which include present levels of motor performance, long-range goals, and short-term objectives.
___	___	5 4 3 2 1	7.	Students with disabilities in regular physical education classes receive comparable attention and instruction as peers.

Yes	No	Importance		
___	___	5 4 3 2 1	8.	Students with disabilities are adequately prepared for optimal leisure and lifetime sports through school physical education programs.
___	___	5 4 3 2 1	9.	Physical education teachers have as an education goal strengthening the self-concept of students with disabilities.
___	___	5 4 3 2 1	10.	The physical education curriculum for grades K–12 creates positive attitudes toward people who "differ" from the norm.

Personnel

Yes	No	Importance		
___	___	5 4 3 2 1	1.	The local school district employs at least one adapted physical education specialist *full-time* to provide assessment, IEP, and instructional services for students with disabilities and/or to assist regular educators in these tasks.
___	___	5 4 3 2 1	2.	Sufficient numbers of qualified personnel to meet the physical education requirements in federal legislation are available in the school district.
___	___	5 4 3 2 1	3.	Certified physical education teachers and/or adapted physical education specialists deliver physical education instruction/services to students who are disabled.

Yes	No	Importance	
____	____	5 4 3 2 1	4. Administrators understand the competencies that adapted physical education specialists should possess and know who to contact for additional consultant and/or in-service training assistance.
____	____	5 4 3 2 1	5. Teachers of students with disabilities possess the necessary adapted physical education competencies and knowledges.
____	____	5 4 3 2 1	6. Regular physical education personnel are provided at least one in-service training session each year on adapted physical education by specialists in this area.
____	____	5 4 3 2 1	7. Teacher aides are provided at least one session of in-service training each year by an adapted physical education specialist on instructional techniques.
____	____	5 4 3 2 1	8. Peer and crossage tutors are used to *supplement* service delivery by regular and adapted physical education teachers.
____	____	5 4 3 2 1	9. Administrators encourage persons who teach physical education to attend professional meetings, workshops, and seminars in order to strengthen adapted physical education competencies.

Yes	No	Importance	
____	____	5 4 3 2 1	10. Persons with disabilities who have achieved success in sports, dance, or aquatics are employed as consultants, teachers, or aides and serve as role models for students with disabilities.
____	____	5 4 3 2 1	11. Persons who teach physical education are knowledgeable about federal and state legislation/policies/guidelines regarding physical education for students with disabilities.

Time Allocation, Equipment, and Facilities

Yes	No	Importance	
____	____	5 4 3 2 1	1. Secondary school students with disabilities receive at least 200 min of physical education instruction each week.
____	____	5 4 3 2 1	2. Elementary school students with disabilities receive at least 150 min of physical education instruction each week.
____	____	5 4 3 2 1	3. Kindergarten students with disabilities receive at least 100 min of physical education/ motor development instruction each week.
____	____	5 4 3 2 1	4. Early childhood students with disabilities receive at least 100 min of physical education/ motor development instruction each week.
____	____	5 4 3 2 1	5. Students with disabilities receive the same number of minutes of physical education/motor development instruction each week as nondisabled students.

Yes	No	Importance	
___	___	5 4 3 2 1	6. Program resources (instructional materials, equipment, and media) are available for effective physical education instruction of students with disabilities.
___	___	5 4 3 2 1	7. Facilities used in physical education for students with disabilities are architecturally accessible.
___	___	5 4 3 2 1	8. Comparable facilities and equipment are allocated for instruction of physical education for students with and without disabilities.
___	___	5 4 3 2 1	9. School districts with an enrollment of 500 or more students have at least two sport wheelchairs as part of their permanent physical education equipment.
___	___	5 4 3 2 1	10. Community sport and recreation facilities and resources are used in joint school-community programs to promote transition goals.
___	___	5 4 3 2 1	11. Home sport and recreation facilities and resources are used in joint home-school programs to reinforce skills and fitness.

Ecological and Administrative Perspectives

Yes	No	Importance	
___	___	5 4 3 2 1	1. Administrators are knowledgeable about federal and state legislation/policies/guidelines regarding physical education for students with disabilities.

Yes	No	Importance	
___	___	5 4 3 2 1	2. Administrative personnel understand that adapted physical education services are separate and different from those provided by a physical, occupational, or recreational therapist.
___	___	5 4 3 2 1	3. Administrators are utilizing funding alternatives for hiring adapted physical education specialists.
___	___	5 4 3 2 1	4. Administrators in physical education and special education work together effectively in promotion of physical education for students with disabilities.
___	___	5 4 3 2 1	5. Special educators and physical educators work together to develop optimal physical education programs for students with disabilities.
___	___	5 4 3 2 1	6. Physical education teachers of students with disabilities seek cooperation from and maintain communication with parents.
___	___	5 4 3 2 1	7. Parents of students with disabilities are made aware of adapted physical education services through a variety of techniques, including special meetings.
___	___	5 4 3 2 1	8. Physical educators provide special counseling on fitness, weight control, and use of leisure time for students and their families to facilitate increased involvement in home and community activities.

Yes	No	Importance		
___	___	5 4 3 2 1	9.	Students with disabilities who can succeed in regular interscholastic athletics are given the opportunity to do so.
___	___	5 4 3 2 1	10.	The school district works with parents and other groups in promoting Special Olympics and other afterschool sport programs.
___	___	5 4 3 2 1	11.	Students with disabilities take field trips to recreation and health/fitness facilities in the community as part of their school physical education instruction.

References

Adams, G., & Younger, T. (1988). Counseling in adapted physical education. In C. Sherrill (Ed.), *Leadership training in adapted physical education* (pp. 257–264). Champaign, IL: Human Kinetics.

Aufsesser, P. M. (1991). Mainstreaming and the least restrictive environment: How do they differ? *Palaestra, 7* (2) 31–34.

Bender, M., Brannan, S., & Verhoven, P. (1984). *Leisure education for the handicapped.* San Diego: College Hill Press.

Block, M., & Krebs, P. (1992). An alternative to the continuum of least restrictive environments: A continuum of *support* to regular physical education. *Adapted Physical Activity Quarterly, 9* (2), 97–113.

Brophy, J. E. (1983). Classroom organization and management. *The Elementary School Journal, 83* (4), 265–285.

Chesler, M., & Chesney, B. (1988). Self-help groups: Empowerment attitudes and behaviors of disabled or chronically ill persons. In H. E. Yuker (Ed.), *Attitudes toward persons with disabilities* (pp. 230–245). New York: Springer.

Davis, W. E. (1989). The regular education initiative debate: Its promises and problems. *Exceptional Children, 55* (5), 440–446.

DePaepe, J. L. (1985). The influence of three least restrictive environments on the content motor ALT and performance of moderately mentally retarded students. *Journal of Teaching in Physical Education, 3,* 34–41.

Dowd, E. (Ed.). (1984). *Leisure counseling.* Springfield, IL: Charles C. Thomas.

Folio, M. R., & Norman, A. (1981). Toward more success in mainstreaming: A peer teacher approach to physical education. *Teaching Exceptional Children, 13,* 110–114.

Gartner, A., & Lipsky, D. K. (1987). Beyond special education: Toward a quality system for all students. *Harvard Educational Review, 57,* 367–395.

Holt/Hale, S. A. (1988). *On the move.* Mountain View, CA: Mayfield Publishing.

Jenkins, J., & Jenkins, L. (1981). *Cross-age and peer tutoring: Help for children with learning problems.* Reston, VA: Council for Exceptional Children.

Jenkins, J., Pious, C., & Jewell, M. (1990). Special education and the regular education initiative: Basic assumptions. *Exceptional Children, 56* (6), 479–491.

Johnson, D. W., & Johnson, R. (1975). *Learning together and alone: Cooperation, competition, and individualization.* Englewood Cliffs, NJ: Prentice-Hall.

Johnson, D. W., Johnson, R., Holubec, E., & Roy, P. (1984). *Circles of learning: Cooperation in the classroom.* Alexandria, VA: Association for Supervision and Curriculum Development.

Karper, W. B., & Martinek, T. J. (1985). The integration of handicapped and nonhandicapped children in elementary physical education. *Adapted Physical Activity Quarterly, 2* (4), 314–319.

Karper, W. B., Martinek, T. J., & Wilkerson, J. D. (1985). Effects of competitive vs. noncompetitive learning environments on motor skill performance among handicapped and nonhandicapped children in mainstreamed physical education classes. *American Corrective Therapy Journal, 39,* (1), 10–15.

Kirchner, G. (1985). *Physical education for elementary school children.* Dubuque, IA: Wm. C. Brown.

Krebs, P. (1990). Mental retardation. In J. Winnick (Ed.), *Adapted physical education and sport* (pp. 153–176). Champaign, IL: Human Kinetics.

Laban, R. (1960). *The mastery of movement* (2nd ed.). London: MacDonald & Evans.

Laban, R. (1975). *Modern educational dance.* London: MacDonald & Evans.

Lilly, M. S. (1988). The regular education initiative: A force for change in general and special education. *Education and Training in Mental Retardation, 23,* 253–260.

Logsdon, B. J., Barrett, K. R., Ammons, M. P., Broer, M. R., Halverson, L. E., McGee, R., & Roberton, M. A. (1984). *Physical education for children: A focus on the teaching process* (2nd ed.). Philadelphia: Lea & Febiger.

Long, E., Irmer, L., Burkett, L., Glasenapp, G., & Odenkirk, B. (1980). PEOPEL. *Journal of Physical Education and Recreation, 51,* 28–29.

Marlowe, M. (1980). Games analysis intervention: A procedure to increase peer acceptance of socially isolated children. *Research Quarterly for Exercise and Sport, 51,* 422–426.

Marlowe, M., Algozzine, G., Lerch, H. A., & Welch, P. D. (1978). Games analysis intervention: A procedure to decrease the feminine play patterns of emotionally disturbed boys. *Research Quarterly, 49,* 484–490.

Mender, J., Kerr, R., & Orlick, T. (1982). A cooperative games program for learning disabled children. *International Journal of Sports Psychology, 13,* 222–233.

Morris, G. S. D., & Stiehl, J. (1989). *Changing kids' games.* Champaign, IL: Human Kinetics.

Mosston, M. (1992). Tug-O-War, No more: Meeting teaching-learning objectives using the spectrum of teaching styles. *Journal of Physical Education, Recreation, and Dance, 63* (1), 27–31, 56.

Mosston, M., & Ashworth, S. (1986). *Teaching physical education* (3d ed.). Columbus, OH: Merrill.

Mosston, M., & Ashworth, S. (1990). *The spectrum of teaching styles: From command to discovery.* White Plains, NY: Longman.

Orlick, T. (1978). *The cooperative sports and games book.* New York: Pantheon.

Rarick, G. L., & Beuter, A. (1985). The effect of mainstreaming on the motor performance of mentally retarded and nonhandicapped students. *Adapted Physical Activity Quarterly, 2,* 277–282.

Rohnke, K. (1977). *Cowstails and cobras: A guide to ropes courses, initiative games, and other adventure activities.* Hamilton, MA: Project ADVENTURE.

Rosenshine, B. (1983). Teaching functions in instructional programs. *The Elementary School Journal, 83* (4), 335–351.

Rynders, J., Johnson, R., Johnson, D. W., and Schmidt, B. (1980). Producing positive interaction among Down syndrome and nonhandicapped teenagers through cooperative goal structuring. *American Journal of Mental Deficiency, 85,* 268–273.

Sherborne, V. (1987). Movement observation and practice. In M. Berridge & G. R. Ward (Eds.), *International perspectives on adapted physical activity* (pp. 3–10). Champaign, IL: Human Kinetics.

Sherborne, V. (1990). *Developmental movement for children: Mainstream, special needs, and preschool.* Cambridge, England: Cambridge University Press.

Sherrill, C., & Megginson, N. (1984). A needs assessment instrument for local school district use in adapted physical education. *Adapted Physical Activity Quarterly, 1,* 147–157.

Special Olympics International. (1989). *Special Olympics Unified Sports handbook.* Washington, DC: Author.

Stainback, W., & Stainback, S. (1984). A rationale for the merger of special and regular education. *Exceptional Children, 51* (2), 102–111.

Strain, P. (1981). *The utilization of classroom peers as behavior change agents.* New York: Plenum.

Taylor, M. J. (1987). Leisure counseling as an integral part of program development. *CAHPER Journal, 53,* 21–25.

Titus, J. A., & Watkinson, E. J. (1987). Effects of segregated and integrated programs on the participation and social interaction of moderately mentally handicapped children in play. *Adapted Physical Activity Quarterly, 4,* 204–219.

Vodola, T. (1976). *Project ACTIVE maxi-model: Nine training manuals.* Oakhurst, NJ: Project ACTIVE.

Watkinson, E. J. (1987). The development and evaluation of integrated programs. *CAHPER Journal, 53,* 13–20.

Watkinson, E. J., & Titus, J. A. (1986). Integrating the mentally handicapped in physical activity: A review and discussion. *Canadian Journal for Exceptional Children, 2* (2), 48–53.

Watkinson, E. J., & Wall, A. E. (1982). *PREP: Play skill instruction for mentally handicapped children.* Ottawa: Canadian Association for Health, Physical Education, and Recreation.

Webster, G. E. (1987). Influence of peer tutors upon academic learning time—physical education of mentally handicapped students. *Journal of Teaching in Physical Education, 6,* 393–403.

Wessel, J. (1976). *I CAN—Primary skills.* Northbrook, IL: H. Hubbard. (Now available from Pro•Ed, Austin, TX.)

Wessel, J. (1977). *Planning individualized education programs in special education with examples from I CAN physical education.* Northbrook, IL: H. Hubbard. (Now available from Pro•Ed, Austin, TX.)

Wessel, J., & Kelly, L. (1986). *Achievement-based curriculum development in physical education.* Philadelphia: Lea & Febiger.

CHAPTER
9
Adapting Instruction and Behavior Management

FIGURE 9.1

Peer teacher demonstrates hitting piñata for classmate with Down syndrome.

After you have studied this chapter, you should be able to:

1. Identify four cognitive behaviors in the creative process and discuss each in relation to adapting instruction to meet individual needs, interests, and abilities. How can these behaviors be assessed and developed in teachers as well as in students?

2. Discuss different methods of individualizing instruction and cite examples of each.

3. Explain the concept of *developmental sequences* and apply it to the acquisition of (a) locomotor skills, (b) object skills, and (c) running game concepts. List the components of each in chronological order and/or from easiest to most difficult.

4. Differentiate between task analysis and activity analysis and apply each to the individualization of instruction.

5. Explain the use of different levels of assistance in teaching: physical, visual, verbal, or a combination of all.

6. Analyze four teaching styles from most to least restrictive and describe each in relation to (a) learning environment, (b) starting routine, (c) presentation of new learning activities, and (d) execution. Relate teaching styles to behaviors that students with various disabling conditions might exhibit.

7. Discuss behavior management concepts in relation to teaching and describe specific techniques useful in various situations.

8. State illustrative procedures for adapting instruction to problems of (a) strength and endurance, (b) balance and agility, and (c) coordination and accuracy.

9. Discuss application of motor learning, exercise physiology, and biomechanics to the individualization of instruction.

10. Identify 16 variables that affect the physical education teaching-learning process and discuss their manipulation in adapting instruction.

Good physical education implies *adapting* instruction to the individual needs, interests, and abilities of all students. An important part of adapting is helping students to manage their behaviors so that the teaching-learning environment affords as much time-on-task as possible. The ability to adapt is dependent upon personal creativity and a knowledge of the principles of motor development, biomechanics, exercise physiology, and motor learning. Figure 9.1 depicts a creative instructional approach planned by a physical educator and implemented by a peer teacher. Important, also, is a good self-concept and a high level of aspiration for all students (i.e., teachers must believe in themselves, their ability to teach, and the ability of their students to learn).

Creativity

Behaviors in the creative process are presented in Table 9.1. Teachers should periodically assess themselves on the different behaviors that comprise creativity (Runco & Albert, 1990). Among the standardized instruments that can be used for this purpose are *Thinking Creatively with Pictures* and *Thinking Creatively With Words* by E. Paul Torrance (1974). Both can be ordered from Scholastic Testing Service, Incorporated, 480 Meyer Road, Bensenville, IL 60106.

Each inventory includes several subscales. The best known of the pictorial instruments is probably the circles task, in which each person is given a page containing 40 circles, each of which is about the size of a quarter. The task is to create as many different objects or pictures out of these circles as possible in 10 min. Responses are scored, not only for number of different objects, but for originality or uniqueness of drawings. The best known of the verbal instruments is to

Table 9.1
Cognitive behaviors in the creative process.

Behavior	Meaning
1. Fluent thinking: to think of the *most*	Generation of a quantity, flow of thought, number of relevant responses
2. Flexible thinking: to take *different* approaches	Variety of kinds of ideas, ability to shift categories, detours in direction of thought
3. Original thinking: to think in *novel* or unique ways	Unusual responses, clever ideas, production away from the obvious
4. Elaborative thinking: to *add on* to	Embellishing upon an idea, embroidering upon a simple idea or response to make it more elegant, stretching or expanding upon things or ideas.

Note. Adapted from the *Total Creativity Program,* by Frank E. Williams. Educational Technology Publications, 140 Sylvan Avenue, Englewood Cliffs, NJ 07632

take a word with multiple meanings (like *head* or *ball*) and think of as many uses as possible. Head, for instance, can refer to a body part, the foam on beer, the position one holds in class, the bathroom, the boss or supervisor, and several other things.

Table 9.2
How creative are you?

Regulation Round Balls That Vary in Size, Weight, Texture	Homemade Projectiles	Projectiles of Varying Shapes
Baseballs	Beanbags: 3 × 3-inch, small;	Airplanes (paper, cloth)
Basketballs	5 × 5-inch, jumbo	Arrows
Bocce balls	Clay	Balloons
Bowling balls	Cork	Beans
Cage balls: 18, 24, 30, 36, 48, 60, and	Felt	Beanbags (soft shots)
72-inch	Foam	Clubs
Croquet balls	Leather	Coffee can lids (plastic)
Golf balls	Nerf ball	Coins
Field hockey balls	Nylon sock stuffed	Darts
Lacrosse balls	Paper crumpled into ball	Discs
Marbles	Plastic: Ping-Pong, scoop balls, whiffle	Footballs
Medicine balls: 4–5 lb, 6–7 lb, 8–9 lb,	balls	Frisbees
11–12 lb, 14–15 lb	Rubber	Hoops
Playground balls: 5, 6, 7, 8½, 10, 13,	Snowballs	Horseshoes
and 16-inch	Sponge	Javelins
Racket balls	Velcro-covered yarnballs	Lemmi sticks
Rhythm balls: 3¼-inch		Paper plate Frisbees
Soccer balls		Peas
Softballs: 9, 10, and 12-inch		Pucks: shuffleboard, ice hockey
Table tennis (Ping-Pong)		Rings (quoits): plastic game rings,
Tennis ball		embroidery hoops, canning rubbers
Tetherball		Rocks (pebbles)
Volleyball		Shots: iron or plastic
Water polo ball		Shuttlecocks
		Yardsticks

Measures of motor creativity (Wyrick, 1968) also have been developed for use with prospective teachers. Illustrative of the kinds of challenges these present are

1. How many ways can you put a paper cup in a wastebasket?
2. How many ways can you move a ball, by striking or hitting only, to a wall?
3. How many ways can you move from one end of a low balance beam to another so that at some time in the moving the hips are higher than the head? The floor and beam may be used in combination.
4. How many different ways can you pick up a hoop or beanbag from the floor?

By engaging in this kind of problem-solving behavior, educators can brainstorm ideas for teaching students who cannot learn or perform in expected ways. Try each of these movement challenges, for instance, while pretending to be blind or to have an amputation or a severe balance problem. The essence of teaching children who are clumsy and/or disabled is to *try another way.* Success-oriented physical education depends on the teacher trying alternative pedagogies as well as different ways of changing games, equipment, and environment until one works.

Fluency and Flexibility

Two traits of creativity—fluency and flexibility—are important in adapting instruction, particularly in schools where teaching supplies and equipment are limited. Conceptualize a movement education session in which you want every student to have a ball or projectile of some kind. They do not all have to have the same kind. How many different kinds can you think of? *Fluency* is your ability to generate a large number of relevant responses. When you thought of different kinds, did you vary your ideas with respect to size, weight, shape, color, texture, and composition? *Flexibility* is your ability to shift categories and think of different kinds. Table 9.2 gives a sampling of the fluent and flexible responses you might have made.

Having thought of numerous alternatives, the next step is to match balls and projectiles with the students' abilities. A student who has coordination problems needs something big and soft. One with grasp and release problems (cerebral palsy) might do best with a yarn or Nerf (sponge rubber) ball. A student who is blind needs an object with a bell or noisemaker in it, whereas a student who is visually impaired simply needs a bright color like yellow. Someone in a wheelchair can profit from a string attached to the ball to facilitate recovery, whereas a hyperactive or high-energy student can enjoy a "crazy ball" with unpredictable bounces and great distance capacity.

Next, pretend that you have a class of 10 students, each with a different disability, but all needing to work on objectives pertaining to throwing. Your assessment records reveal that the students represent all the different stages of throwing ability. Specific objectives to be worked on have been circled on each student's assessment form. In this kind of setting, the more projectiles the students experiment with, the more likely that their skills will generalize from one game or sport to another. The important thing is that the students do not get bored, that each has a maximum number of trials to practice, and that each experiences some success.

Developing throwing skills often takes 5 or 10 min of every class period for several weeks. How many different targets can you think of, and how will you organize your space for the different kinds of projectiles and targets? Appropriate degree of difficulty is essential to both success and motivation. How can you change projectiles and/or targets to organize stations for students needing easy, medium, or difficult learning progressions? The number of different kinds of targets you conceptualize is a measure of fluency. If your targets are of different colors, sizes, shapes, heights, widths, and materials, you have demonstrated good flexibility (the ability to think of different categories). If some of your targets make noise or fall down when they are hit, you are more likely to maximize on-task practice time. Have you devised moving as well as stationary targets? Targets that integrate story, television, or movie themes are a measure of originality. If these have a lot of detail, lending themselves to different scoring systems, you have demonstrated elaboration.

So now you have targets! How many different kinds of games can you devise for teaching and practicing throwing? How many different scoring systems can you think of? How many ways can a student experience success? Try applying this process to teaching other motor skills. Will it work in the development of specific play and/or social skills?

Individualization

Creative teaching and/or adapting pedagogy, content, and environment to specific needs lead to individualization of instruction. The individualized education program (IEP) required by law is based on the belief that teachers are creative. Individualization does not mean teaching one-to-one, but changing classroom organization and pedagogical approaches to meet the needs of individuals.

Integration of students with disabilities into regular physical education tends to make classes more *heterogeneous* (encompassing wide individual differences). Integration does not necessarily increase heterogeneity with regard to psychomotor abilities, however, since students of normal intelligence have always displayed a wide range of motor abilities. Some students with disabilities are better in motor ability than their nondisabled peers. Mental retardation (MR), learning disabilities (LD), and emotional disturbances (ED) primarily affect heterogeneity in cognitive and affective behaviors (i.e., actual game behaviors like rules, strategies, sportsmanship). Sensory impairments primarily affect mode of presentation and enhancement of environmental stimuli.

All in all, integration within the gymnasium setting affects group dynamics and interpersonal relationships more than actual motor teaching and learning. Individual differences generally intensify problems of classroom management, motivation, and discipline. *Teachers of mainstream physical education must be excellent—more competent in every respect than regular physical educators with students of same or similar ability levels.*

No longer is good physical education a teacher standing in front of the entire class and instructing all students simultaneously on the same skill. With the trend away from ability grouping in all educational settings (not just physical education), the role of teaching is changing from information giver to learning facilitator. Most mainstream physical education seems to function best in classes organized as *learning stations* with an adult teacher aide, a peer or crossage tutor responsible for each station (Jenkins & Jenkins, 1981).

The mainstream physical educator then moves from station to station, giving attention and assistance as needed. Much of the mainstream teacher's work must be completed before class: reviewing assessment data; developing *task cards* for individuals, pairs, and triads and *learning plans* for stations; and teaching (in-servicing) aides and student leaders. Unless teachers are allowed planning periods for such management tasks, mainstreaming is apt to function less than smoothly.

Learning Stations

Learning stations may vary according to number of students assigned, permanency of assignment, nature of learning tasks, and type of teaching style. In an elementary school unit on games, for instance, the largest station may be the playing area for the game itself. Additionally, there should be two or three smaller learning stations (two to six persons in each) with different instructional objectives being implemented at each. A student who experiences a problem pertaining to a skill, rule, strategy, or interpersonal relationship (sportsmanship) during the game goes to the appropriate learning station for help (Figure 9.2). One station may be for motorically gifted students who do not need the game for skill practice as do their peers. Such athletes should have the opportunity for *new learning* of alternative skills/sports. Physical education should be primarily a time of *learning for everyone,* with practice (repetition) and competition occurring mainly after school and during weekends.

In an alternative gymnasium/playing field arrangement, the student might elect (or be assigned) to the same station for several days or weeks. A different sport, dance, or movement education activity is taught at each station. Peers and crossage tutors can serve as teachers at the stations. Occasionally, an adult athlete with a disability from the community can be recruited to teach a unit at a particular station, thereby serving as a model for students and facilitating positive attitude change.

Still another classroom arrangement is rotation of students from station to station for learning different skills during the same period. Not all students have to rotate around

FIGURE 9.2

A student who exhibits jumping difficulties during a basketball game rotates out of the game to a *learning station,* where he receives individualized help with vertical jumping. Dr. Joanne Rowe assists.

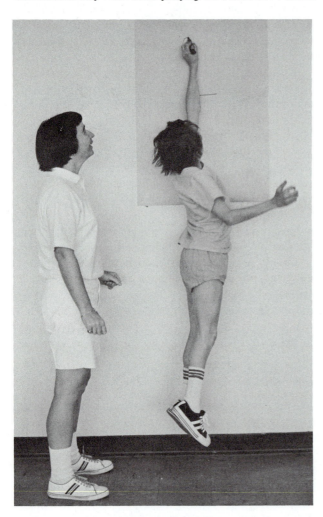

all stations. The *direction* of rotation (counterclockwise), however, should be the same for everyone to avoid confusion. The *time* for changing stations can be the same for everyone (on a set signal) or can vary according to individual differences in learning and completing task cards. For students for whom changing stations may be confusing or impossible without help, *buddies* can volunteer (or be assigned) as partners for the day or the unit.

Task Cards and Learning Materials

Predeveloped learning materials are necessary for individualized and personalized physical education. These may be task cards that the student picks up as he or she enters class, audiovisuals as individualized learning packages or modules that the student can carry along, or an infinite variety of materials. Computers are already within the price range of some school districts and increasingly will be used to store IEPs, behavioral objectives, and progressive, day-by-day achievements of students. Videotapes can capture trial-by-trial performance and provide immediate, personalized feedback for the student as well as assessment data that can be used later by teachers.

Table 9.3
Developmental sequence for acquiring locomotor skills.

Skill	Approximate Age in Years
Rolling from side to side	.50
Crawling (on belly)	.60
Creeping (hands and knees)	.75
Walk	1.50
Run	1.75
Step (leap) downward	2.00
Vertical jump	2.33
Long jump	3.00
Forward roll	3.00
Hop forward five times	3.50
Gallop with correct rhythm	4.50
Skip	5.00
Slide (step, close, step)	5.25
Backward roll	6.00

Note. Fall-bend-roll should be taught and practiced before the jump. Teach that falling can be a game.

Table 9.4
Developmental sequence for acquiring beginning object skills.

Skill	Approximate Age in Years
Grasping	.50
Pounding	.55
Pushing pellets off table	.65
Releasing	1.00
Throwing[a]	2.00
Striking, downward	3.00
Striking, horizontal	4.00
Catching/trapping large balls	4.00
Catching small balls	6.00

[a]For students with cerebral palsy and others who have problems with release, throwing should be moved to the end of the sequence and considered the hardest skill.

Developmental Sequences

A knowledge of developmental sequences guides lesson planning. A *developmental sequence* is a list of movement patterns presented in the chronological order in which they are acquired by most children. Most elementary school physical educators have these lists memorized since the lists are used continuously in determining readiness of a child to learn new skills. The lists also enable a teacher to decide whether motor development is normal, delayed, or abnormal.

Developmental sequences specify the order in which movement patterns should be taught. Table 9.3, for instance, indicates that hopping should be taught before skipping and that vertical jumping should be taught before horizontal jumping. The sequence is more important to remember than

Table 9.5
Developmental progression I for teaching running game concepts.

Step	Illustrative Games
1	*Easiest (one concept)*
	Flying Dutchman
	Concept: Run home on cue.
	Formation: Line of children holding hands. Start with circle and then break into line.
	Instructions: Leader pulls line in any direction around the gymnasium. On the cue "Flying Dutchman," all children run to wall or mat designated as home (safety). The term *floor spaces* may be substituted in movement education variations of this game.
2	*Medium (two concepts)*
	Huntsman
	Concepts: Follow leader; run home on cue.
	Formation: File, one student behind the other.
	Instructions: Teacher moves around the room and says, "I'm going to hunt the monster. Who wants to go on a hunt with me? Get in the file and follow!" This continues, with students joining file and following the leader until the cue "bang." On it, all students run independently to safety zone. Theme can be varied, as "I am a police officer. Who wants to chase robbers with me?"
3	*Harder (four concepts)*
	Chickens and Fox (Run, Children, Run)
	Concepts: Follow leader; run home on cue; avoid being tagged; penalty.
	Formation: Scattered, with safety and danger zones clearly marked.
	Instructions: All children (chickens, rabbits, or whatever) are at home safe with leader. Outside safety zone is a fox or bad person either walking back and forth or pretending to be asleep. Leader says to group, "Let's take a walk" and all walk around danger zone while fox sleeps. Leader or fox can give cue to run home: "Run, chickens, run." Fox tries to tag children before they get home. Fox makes persons who are tagged sit in prison (this introduces penalty concept).
4	*Very Hard (five or more concepts)*
	Simple One-to-One Tag Games
	See activity analysis in Table 9.6.

Note. In writing lesson plans, refer to Game Progression 1, step 1, 2, 3, or 4.

the approximate age, since children exhibit wide individual differences in age of learning. The order of the hop and the gallop in Table 9.3 is controversial and depends on the level of maturity required. Table 9.4 shows that children should be taught to roll a ball before learning to throw and that striking skills should be introduced before catching skills.

Many children have acquired the basic movement patterns described in Tables 9.3 and 9.4 before entering school. The goal, then, is to help these children refine movement patterns and use the patterns in games and sports. In contrast, children eligible for adapted physical activity services usually lag 2 to 3 years behind normal peers in acquisition of motor skills. The older the student, the larger the lag, with sometimes as much as 6 to 9 years difference in motor functioning of students with severe disability. Along with motor performance lags are deficits in fitness, play, and social functioning.

A developmental sequence can also be a list of play behaviors listed in the chronological order in which they evolve in most children (see Chapter 18). Little research has been conducted on the chronological order in which game concepts are mastered, but these, too, should be organized into developmental sequences; then they can be taught sequentially, one at a time, the way motor patterns are taught.

The following is a hypothesized developmental sequence for play concepts:

1. Peek-a-boo and similar hide/seek games
2. Follow the leader
3. Start-stop on cues like *Red Light, Green Light*
4. Run-to-change-places games like *Under the Parachute* and *Squirrels in Trees*
5. Run to safety (safe vs. not safe places or people) like *Huntsman*
6. Flee (avoiding being tagged) like *Chickens and Fox*
7. Tag (learning to tag another)
8. Chase (learning to chase another)
9. Flee-tag-chase combinations with a penalty (like going to prison) for being tagged
10. Flee-tag-chase combinations involving changing roles (when tagged, you become a chaser)

Table 9.5 presents a developmental progression (sequence) for teaching and practicing game concepts. Go through elementary school methods textbooks and try putting games in developmental sequences, as in Table 9.5. Think of how many ways the theme of each game can be varied without changing the number of concepts.

Forward and Backward Chaining

Individual steps within a developmental sequence or task analysis are taught by a technique called *chaining*. This refers to mastery of a task or concept and then linking it to a task or several tasks previously learned, thereby performing a chain of tasks. Sometimes, a movement pattern can best be taught by *forward chaining,* the traditional approach of moving from Step 1 forward through Step 8. Other times, *backward chaining* (i.e., starting with the last step in the chain and moving backward to Step 1) is more efficient. Backward chaining is particularly effective in movement patterns like throwing and striking, in which the last step is dramatic and constitutes a reward within itself (i.e., the noise of a ball hitting a target or striking a bat).

Once the tasks comprising a movement pattern are mastered, new learning progressions can be developed that focus on increasing the height, distance, or speed of the movement. For instance, a second learning progression for jumping might read

1. Jump down from 8-inch step.
2. Jump down from 12-inch step.
3. Jump down from 18-inch bench.
4. Jump down from 24-inch bench.

A third learning progression might read

1. Jump forward 6 inches.
2. Jump forward 12 inches.
3. Jump forward 18 inches.

A fourth learning progression might read

1. Jump over a rope 3 inches high.
2. Jump over a rope 6 inches high.
3. Jump over a rope 12 inches high.

Levels of Assistance

In performing a task or sequence of tasks, students require different levels of assistance: physical, visual, verbal, or a combination of these (Figure 9.3). Evaluation and record keeping entail writing next to the task the type of assistance needed. A student might progress, for instance, through the following levels of assistance:

1. **P**—Performs overarm throw with *physical* and verbal assistance.
2. **D**—Performs overarm throw with visual and verbal assistance (i.e., a *demonstration* accompanied by explanation).
3. **C5**—Performs overarm throw with much verbal assistance (i.e., *cues* throughout the sequence).
4. **C1**—Performs overarm throw with minimal verbal assistance (i.e., one or two *cues* only).
5. **I**—Performs overarm throw with no assistance (i.e., *independently*).

FIGURE 9.3

Physical and verbal assistance are almost always needed in teaching children with severe disabilities to bat. Note that the target is waist high to make the skill easier. A ball on top of a coffee can is an excellent target because noise is reinforcing.

These five levels of assistance can be applied to a single step within a task analysis or to a movement pattern or a sequence of movement patterns (i.e., folk dance). Use of initials to represent levels facilitates ease of record keeping and lesson writing.

Physical assistance should always be accompanied by verbal cues. These cues can be spoken, chanted, or sung. Physical assistance should never be called physical manipulation (a medical term often used in therapy and orthopedics). Several learning theorists have created good synonyms for physical assistance. Sherrill likes the term *coactive movement,* taken from the Van Dijk (1966) approach from Holland, now widely used throughout the world in working with individuals who are deaf-blind (Leuw, 1972). In coactive movement, the bodies of the teacher and student move as one, closely touching, in activities like rolling, seat scooting, creeping, knee walking, and upright walking. As the student gets the feel of the task, the distance between the two bodies is gradually increased. The emphasis is then on *mirroring* (i.e., imitating the teacher's movements).

Table 9.6
Behavioral requirements of simple tag game: An activity analysis showing teaching progression.

Cognitive

1. Responds to name
2. Follows simple directions:
   a. Sit down
   b. Stay
   c. Stand up
   d. Run
3. Responds appropriately to cues:
   a. Stop, start
   b. Good, bad
4. Attends to teacher long enough to grasp game structure and rules:
   a. Visually
   b. Auditorially
5. Understands fleeing role:
   a. "You (Amy) have a beanbag, squeaky toy, orange, make-believe tail."
   b. "Someone (Bob) wants it."
   c. "You (Amy) do not want Bob to have object."
   d. "You (Amy) run away from Bob when I give cue."
6. Understands chasing role:
   a. "Bob chases you when I give cue."
   b. "Bob chases you until
      (1) you touch safety base or
      (2) he tags you."

7. Understands concept of safety base
8. Understands concepts of tagging, penalty, and changing roles
   a. "When tagged, the penalty is you must give Bob the object."
   b. "You change roles because you want the object (i.e., you chase Bob or someone else who has object)."

Affective

1. Has fun
   a. Is not frightened by being chased
   b. Is sufficiently involved that attention does not wander
   c. Smiles and/or makes joyous sounds
2. Shows awareness of others
3. Displays competitive spirit
4. Tags other person gently

Psychomotor

1. Performs motor skills
   a. Runs
   b. Dodges/ducks
   c. Tags
2. Demonstrates sufficient fitness
   a. Does not become breathless
   b. Does not develop muscle cramps

Generalization

The learning of a task sequence is relatively meaningless if generalization does not occur. Generalization refers to the transfer of learning from one piece of equipment to another and from one setting to another. In students with intact intelligence, generalization usually occurs without specific training. When teaching students with MR, however, generalization should be built into task sequences. For example, a learning progression might read

Roll 10-inch rubber ball toward milk cartons.

Roll 10-inch rubber ball toward bowling pins.

Roll bowling ball toward bowling pins.

Roll bocce ball toward target ball.

Roll 10-inch rubber ball toward persons inside a circle (as in dodgeball).

Such tasks should be practiced on different surfaces (grass, dirt, floor) and in different environments (gymnasium, outdoors, bowling alley). Use generalization training to develop creativity in students. Repeatedly ask, "How many things can we make roll? How many places can we go to roll things? At how many targets can we roll things?"

Activity Analysis

Activity analysis is the process of breaking down an activity into the behavioral components requisite for success. In physical education and recreation, the activity to be analyzed is usually a game, sport, or exercise. The process can, however, be directed toward activities of daily living, leisure, or work. Whereas special educators and physical educators commonly use the terms *task analysis* and *activity analysis* interchangeably, therapeutic recreation specialists and occupational therapists prefer *activity analysis*. This is because they are concerned with the total activity, not just the motor skill and fitness requisites.

Activity analysis typically entails consideration of the three educational domains: cognitive, psychomotor, and affective. Table 9.6 presents an activity analysis for a simple tag game. This type of detailed analysis is needed in teaching games to students with severe disabilities. Note the use of a beanbag, squeaky toy, orange, or make-believe tail; a prop is usually necessary with children deficient in pretending skills; otherwise, they simply cannot understand the point of chasing and fleeing.

Prior to being taught the simple tag game described in Table 9.6, children should have learned games involving only one or two concepts: *stop-start,* as in *Red Light, Green Light* and *Musical Chairs* and *follow the leader* and *safety-not safety,* as in *Flying Dutchman* and *Huntsman* (see Table 9.5). In developmental progressions for teaching games, tag is relatively difficult. Tag involves eight concepts: start-stop, safety-not safety, chasing, tagging, fleeing, dodging, penalty, and changing roles. When MR is severe, each concept must be taught and practiced separately; then, chains of concepts must be practiced. Task and activity analyses are essential processes in the assessment and instruction of students with disabilities.

FIGURE 9.4

Sherrill spectrum of teaching styles, based on concepts of Muska Mosston (1966, 1981). The variables that the teacher manipulates to create different teaching styles are learning environment, starting and stopping routine, presentation mode, and practice of execution mode. See Table 9.7 for suggestions.

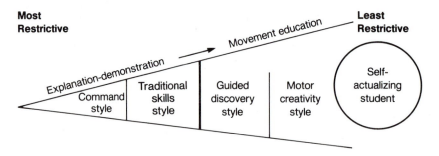

Teaching Styles

Important to the learning success of all students is the teaching style used. Muska Mosston, in 1966, revolutionized physical education pedagogy by describing a spectrum of seven alternative teaching styles and suggesting that teachers master all styles. Today, Mosston (1992) posits 11 teaching styles, and spectrum theory guides pedagogy (Goldberger, 1992). Mosston emphasizes that teaching style should match the needs of students and, thus, vary from group to group. The ultimate goal, however, is to progressively increase the student's responsibility for his or her learning by moving from the command and practice styles to learner-initiated and self-teaching styles. Mosston's concept provided the stimulus for Figure 9.4, which is Sherrill's attempt to create a simplified spectrum of teaching styles appropriate for adapted physical activity.

The command teaching style is usually prescribed for students with severe mental retardation, severe learning disabilities, severe emotional disturbance, autism, severe hyperactivity or distractibility, and inner or receptive language deficits. Four basic principles guide the creation of a learning environment for the command teaching style:

1. Use optimal structure.
2. Reduce space.
3. Eliminate irrelevant stimuli.
4. Enhance the stimulus value of specific equipment or materials.

Table 9.7 summarizes the characteristics of most and least restrictive teaching styles for normal students. Remember that what is most restrictive for the normal student may be least restrictive for students with disabilities.

Table 9.8 describes in detail the optimal teaching procedures within each style. Particular attention is given to the learning environment itself and to starting and stopping protocol. In the mainstream setting, different teaching styles may be in operation at the various learning stations. The same teaching style the child experiences in other subject areas should be used in physical education. Especially for students with severe disabilities, such *consistency* is imperative.

Table 9.7
Characteristics of teaching styles.

Least Freedom	Most Freedom
Teacher Dominated	*Student Dominated*
Assisted Movement	*Independent Movement*
Coactive/enactive	Self-initiated
Shaping/chaining	Exploring/creating
Homogeneous Grouping	*Heterogenous Grouping*
Much structure	Little structure
Assigned floor spots	Free choice
Move on cue	Free choice
Drum or musical accompaniment	Own rhythm
Sameness	Role differentiation
Reduced Space	*Increased Space*
Decreased Stimuli	*Increased Stimuli*
One instruction	Several instructions
No equipment	Lots of balls/props
One "it"	Several "its"
One base	Several bases
Indoors	Outdoors
Enhanced Stimulus Intensity	*Weakened Stimulus Intensity*
Bright lights	Normal lighting
Loud signals	Soft, quiet signals
Colorful equipment	Regulation colors
Increased size balls, bases	Regulation size
Memorable texture	Regulation texture
Exaggerated teacher gestures and facial expressions	Normal teacher gestures and facial expressions
External Motivation	*Intrinsic Motivation*
Rewards/awards	No external rewards
Praise	Facilitating/accepting
Consistency of teacher	Flexibility of teacher

Table 9.8
Four teaching styles, reflecting increasing freedom for learners.

Situation	Least Freedom		Most Freedom	
	Command Style	*Traditional Skills Style*	*Guided Discovery Style*	*Motor Creativity Style*
Learning Environment	Small space/ Clearly defined boundaries/ Floor spots/ Circles and lines painted on floor/ Equipment always set up in same location/ Cubicles available	Normal play space/ Clearly defined boundaries/ No floor spots/ Regulation sport markings painted on floor/ Equipment in different locations	Space varies/ Boundaries clearly defined, but space changes with each problem/ Imaginary floor markings/ Equipment varies	Determined by student within the limits imposed by school rules and regulations about use of space and equipment
Starting Routine	Student goes to assigned floor spot and sits/ Waits for teacher to give *start* cue	Student goes to space of own choice and warms up Warm-ups may be prescribed as a set routine for each piece of equipment *or* Warm-ups may be created or chosen freely by student	Same as traditional skills approach except that student assumes responsibility for own warm-ups, explores alternative ways of warming up, discovers best warm-ups for self	Determined by student within the limits imposed by school rules and regulations about use of time
Presentation of New Learning Activities	Teacher states objectives/ Teacher designates student leaders/ Teacher puts students into formation/ Teacher gives directions: One task presented at a time, accompanied by demonstrations	Teacher states objectives/ Students choose own leaders/ Teacher puts students into formation/ Teacher gives directions: Several tasks presented at a time, accompanied by demonstrations	Teacher states objectives/ Teacher establishes structure in form of questions designed to elicit movement/ Teacher offers *no* demonstration; stresses that there is no one correct answer, and reassures pupils that no one can fail	Student states objectives/ Student establishes own structure, poses original movement or game questions
Execution	*Student* Practices in formation prescribed by teacher/ Waits turn and follows set routine for going to end of file/ Starts on signal/ Moves in unison with peers to verbal cues, drum, or music/ Stops on signal/ Rotates or changes activity on signal; in same direction (CCW)	*Student* Chooses own space or formation for practice/ Waits turn but chooses own space and own activity while waiting/ Chooses own time to start/ Moves in own rhythm/ Chooses own time to stop/ Rotates or changes activity when chooses in same direction (CCW)	*Student* Finds own space/ Chooses own time to start and stop/ Moves in own rhythm/ Finds movement responses to teacher's questions/ Considers movement alternatives/ Discovers movement patterns most efficient for self/ Changes activity when teacher poses new question	*Student* Finds own space/ Chooses own time to start and stop/ Moves in own rhythm/ Finds movement responses to own questions through creative processes (see Table 9.1)
Feedback	*Teacher* Moves about room/ Offers individual praise/ Identifies and corrects movement errors by verbal *cues* and modeling	*Teacher* Moves about room/ Offers individual praise/ Identifies and corrects movement errors by *questions* that evoke answers from students	*Teacher* Moves about room/ Offers words and phrases of acceptance/ Poses additional questions to individuals/ Acquaints students with names of their movement discoveries	*Teacher* Moves about room/ Offers words and phrases of acceptance/ Mostly observes and shows interest/ Reinforces initiative

Note. CCW means counterclockwise

Teaching styles to a large extent determine educational environment (Mosston & Ashworth, 1986, 1990). The IEP should prescribe the teaching style for which the student is ready. The guiding principle is to facilitate progress from the teaching style and environment that are most restrictive (command style) to the one that is least restrictive (motor creativity). Some children, who need *optimal structure* and lack the ability to cope with freedom (manage their own behaviors), may remain at the command or traditional skills level throughout their schooling. Others, who have no cognitive, perceptual, or behavior problems, may enter the spectrum at the guided discovery level.

Behavior management is a pedagogy specific to the command teaching style. Because of its effectiveness in working with students with severe MR and ED problems, it is presented separately.

Behavior Management

Behavior management is a precisely planned, systematic application of cues and consequences to guide students through tasks or activities that are ordered from easy to difficult. It is used in the functional teaching approach and comes from a philosophy and body of knowledge called *behaviorism.*

All humanistic teachers are, to some extent, behaviorists. This is because contemporary teacher education stresses such practices as (a) breaking goals down into behavioral objectives, (b) assessing students on observable behaviors, (c) task-analyzing activities to be taught and ordering them into easy-to-hard sequences, (d) matching instruction to specific assessed needs, and (e) carefully managing the learning environment to maximize desired behavior changes. These practices are important in humanistic teaching.

There are many forms of behaviorism. Followers of B. F. Skinner, who created operant reinforcement theory in the 1940s, today are called radical behaviorists (Bandura, 1986). These theorists believe that behavior is cued by the stimuli that precede it and shaped and controlled by the reinforcing stimuli that follow it. Originally, behaviorism did not recognize thought or cognition as a mediating variable. Neither did it consider self-concept or the affective domain. The theory had only three components: (a) a stimulus or situational cue, (b) a response or behavior, and (c) a consequence. Behavior management, based only on these three components, was mechanistic and presumably wholly dependent upon managing the environment.

In the 1950s, cognitive psychology or cognitivism began to replace stimulus-response psychology (Bell-Gredler, 1986; Hoover & Wade, 1985). As its name indicates, cognitivism centers on the mental processes involved in learning new skills and demonstrating appropriate behavior. The predominant cognitive model since the early 1970s has been information processing and the development of strategies to improve attention, memory, perception, and cognition. Most behaviorists today are cognitive behaviorists in that they recognize the role of thought in interpreting a stimulus and deciding on a response. A continuum thus exists between educators who focus on cues, consequences, and observable behaviors and those who concentrate on cognitive and/or affective processes.

Whereas cognitivism emphasizes attention, memory, perception, and cognition, behaviorism is concerned with the development and application of learning theories to weaken, strengthen, or maintain a specific behavior. In the real world of teaching, there is considerable overlap between use of instructional strategies to improve information processing and the application of behavior management principles to weaken, strengthen, or maintain specific strategies.

General Procedures

General behavior management procedures include (a) specify the desired behavior, (b) establish baseline performance by graphing the number of times the behavior normally occurs, (c) apply the intervention, and (d) continue graphing the number of times the behavior occurs to see if the intervention is effective—that is, the desired behavior increases in frequency.

Figure 9.5 illustrates the kind of graphing procedure used to record changes in play behaviors with toys and social interactions as the result of an *educational intervention.* The intervention in such programs is generally social reinforcement, attention, and praise for showing the desired behavior and no attention otherwise. While such graphing and recording of frequency of behavior is time consuming, the technique is used in many settings (Tawney & Gast, 1984; Watkinson & Wasson, 1984).

In Figure 9.5, one person was observed for 10 sessions to determine baseline interactions with peers and toys. On the IEP, this student's present level of performance, derived from the graph's baseline, was written as follows: (a) Joe usually has no interactions with peers during play sessions (i.e., he is in the parallel play stage), and (b) Joe interacts with toys for about 20 sec out of every 5-min play period; the remainder of the time he stares into space, rocks, or watches others.

Using this baseline information, the teacher described Joe's desired behaviors in the form of short-term objectives, as depicted in Table 9.9. Then, during 20 sessions of intervention, Joe was given 10-min, specific lessons on how to interact with peers and toys, followed by 5 min of free play. Behaviors tallied and graphed during the free-play period (see Figure 9.5) show that Joe's peer interactions varied from 0 to 50, with an average of 7.75; Joe, therefore, achieved the first objective. With regard to the second objective, Joe's toy interactions improved tremendously, but not quite enough to meet the criterion level.

Cues and Consequences

Behavior management is based on the concepts of *cues* and *consequences,* the actions used by a teacher to change student behavior. Behavior management, in its strictest and most effective sense, demands a one-to-one relationship so that virtually every response of the student can have an immediate consequence. Nothing the student says or does is unnoticed.

FIGURE 9.5

Frequency of social interactions with peers and appropriate play behaviors with toys for child over a 6-week period (30 sessions).

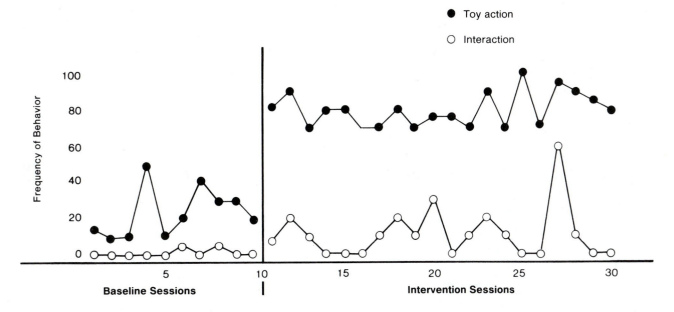

Table 9.9
Illustrative short-term objectives derived from baseline observations.

Condition	Behavior	Criterion Level
While playing in a room with five to seven other children,	Joe will interact positively by initiating conversation, sharing a toy, or coactively using toys in episodes of at least 3 sec duration	for an average of 6 episodes per 5-min observation over 20 sessions.
While playing in a room with tricycle, jungle gym, slide, drums, balls, dolls, and toy cars/ trucks,	Joe will interact with toys	for an average of 90 sec out of each 5-min observation session over 20 sessions.

Cue is the behavioral management term for a command or instruction telling a student what to do. Three rules should be followed in giving cues:

1. Make the cue as brief as possible in the beginning (i.e., "sit" or "stay" or "ready, run").

2. Use the same cue each time.

3. Never repeat a cue until the student makes some kind of response. If correct response is made, reinforce. If no response or wrong one is made, use a correction procedure.

The correction procedure is to say, "No, that is not correct; do it this way," and then demonstrate again and /or take the student through the task coactively.

Consequence is the immediate feedback to a behavior that increases or decreases its occurrence (see Figure 9.6). For instance, for aggressive behavior (hitting, kicking, biting, and the like), the consequence should be punishment. For noncompliant behavior ("I don't want to;" "I can't;" "I don't have to"), the consequences should be ignoring the student's words or actions and, if appropriate, coactively taking him or her through the activity.

A consequence can be *reinforcement* (causing a behavior to increase), *punishment* (causing a behavior to decrease), or *time-out* (ignoring inappropriate behavior, removal from a reinforcing environment, or withholding of reinforcers). Rules to be followed in enacting consequences are:

1. Give immediate feedback to every response the student makes.

2. Accompany nonverbal reinforcement (food, tokens, hugs) with words or, for deaf students, signs.

3. Reinforce within 2 sec after a student responds correctly.

4. Ignore inappropriate behavior that affects only the student.

5. Punish inappropriate behavior that hurts others.

Use of consequences to teach or manage behavior is also called *contingency management*. A *contingency* is the relationship between a behavior and the events following the behavior. Giving *tokens* (or points) for correct responses or good behavior is a method of contingency management, providing the tokens are meaningful to the students and can be traded in on things or privileges of real value.

FIGURE   9.6

A basic principle of behavior management is *Catch 'em being Good!* Authorities recommend a five-to-one praise/criticism ratio. When teachers issue a criticism or correct a motor skill, they should offer at least five praises around the class before criticizing anyone again.

To encourage practice of motor skills, tokens are sometimes given for a set number of minutes or practice trials in which an individual, a team, or an entire class exhibits on-task behavior. *Response cost* is another method of contingency management. In it, points, tokens, or privileges are taken away when students fail to show appropriate behaviors.

Behavior management is data based. In addition to graphing behaviors, teachers keep records of number of trials required to learn each step and the pass or fail performance for each trial. This system has been called a data-based gymnasium by Dr. John Dunn at Oregon State University and colleagues (Dunn, Morehouse, & Fredericks, 1986). Dunn is one of the foremost authorities in applying behavior management to teaching motor skills to students with severe MR. His book includes numerous task analysis sequences for use in teaching motor skills.

In summary, behavior management pedagogy is based on four general concepts: *cues, consequences, task analysis,* and a *data-based gymnasium.* Most authorities consider behavior management the best pedagogical approach for instructing students with severe mental retardation, autism, and emotional disturbance. In the continuum of most to least restrictive teaching styles and environments, behavior management is least restrictive for students with severe problems, but, strictly applied in its entirety, is most restrictive for most students.

Specific Behavior Management Techniques

Although few physical educators have the student-teacher ratio necessary for using behavior management in its entirety, all good teachers use some behavior management techniques. Teaching a complex motor skill to normal students, for instance, requires the techniques of shaping, chaining, and fading. Reinforcement and punishment are integral parts of the structure of every classroom. Table 9.10 presents specific behavior management techniques commonly used in physical education.

Academic Learning Time

Also important is academic learning time (ALT), also called on-task time. Research shows that individualizing instruction leads to increased ALT (Aufderheide, 1983; DePaepe, 1985; Vogler, Van der Mars, Darst, & Cusimano, 1990). The more practice trials a student completes, assuming he or she is paying attention and trying his or her best, the more likely the student is to learn. Increased competence leads to improved self-concept when the competence is acquired in an environment of praise and encouragement rather than criticism and correction.

Principles of Motor Learning/Teaching

Good teaching involves application of the principles of motor learning/teaching. Illustrative of these are the following principles:

1. **Individual differences.** Learners differ in rate of learning, amount of learning, method of learning, and response to external motivation and/or stress. Children with disabilities demonstrate more variability than do normal children; thus, *individualization* is especially important.

2. **Developmental stages.** Children's thought, play, and movement patterns evolve through the same stages but at different speeds. Assessment and IEP tasks are facilitated by determining stages and levels. See Chapter 5.

3. **Readiness.** Learning proceeds in accordance with neurological maturation. Critical learning periods exist.

4. **Progression.** Motor learning proceeds from simple to complex, large to small, and gross to fine. Learners should be introduced to progressively more difficult tasks. The teacher's ability to task-analyze activities as well as motor skills largely determines the success.

5. **Effect.** Learning, for the most part, occurs best when the effect is pleasurable. Success leads to success. Not at all pleasurable are such physical education practices as elimination games, choosing up sides (for the last to be chosen), and competition (for children who generally lose). Reward is a stronger learning reinforcement than punishment.

Table 9.10
Specific behavior management techniques.

Technique	Description
Shaping	Refers to reinforcing small steps or approximations of a desired behavior; an analogy might be the praise "You're getting warmer" in the old game of finding a hidden object. Inappropriate or undesired behaviors are ignored.
Chaining	Leading a person through a sequence of responses, as is done in a task-analyzed progression of skills from easy to hard. The sequential mastery of a folk dance with many parts might also be considered chaining.
Backward chaining	Entails starting with the last step in the chain first. For instance, in an overarm throw, the backward chain would begin with the release of the ball; then the forward swing of arm and release are practiced; and then the backswing, the foreswing, and the release are practiced. Usually, manual guidance is used in backward chaining.
Prompting	The cue or stimulus that makes a behavior occur. It can be physical, verbal, visual, or some combination of sensory stimuli. In physical education, prompting is usually the behavior management term for physical guidance of the body or limb through a skill.
Fading	The gradual removal of the physical guidance as the person gains the ability to perform the skill unassisted. It can be gradual reduction in any reinforcement that is designed to help the student become increasingly independent.
Modeling	The behavior management term for demonstrating.
Positive reinforcement	An increase in the frequency of a behavior when followed by an event or stimulus the student finds pleasurable. This term should not be confused with *reward*. Although a reward is pleasurable, it does not necessarily increase behavior.
Negative reinforcement	An increase in the frequency of a behavior as a result of removing or terminating something the student perceives as unpleasant, such as being ignored, scolded, or punished by teachers or peers or hearing a loud buzz every time a postural slouch occurs. Negative reinforcement is when students exhibit good behavior because they are intimidated or frightened by the consequence. In contrast, positive reinforcement is when students exhibit good behavior because they look forward to the consequence.
Punishment	The opposite of both positive and negative reinforcement. Punishment is anything that decreases the frequency of a behavior. A spanking, in the behavioral management context, is not punishment unless it decreases undesired behavior.
Extinction	Failure to reinforce (i.e., ignoring a response or behavior). It is a method of decreasing the frequency of a behavior. It can occur unintentionally, as when teachers are too busy or too insensitive to reinforce, or it may be done purposely to eliminate a previously reinforced response to make way for the teaching of a new behavior.
Premack technique	A method of reinforcement that involves pairing something a student likes with something the teacher wants him or her to learn or do. The promise of free play when work is done illustrates this technique. It is based on the Premack principle.
Contract teaching	A method of assuring understanding and agreement between student and teacher concerning what is to be learned. A contract is a written document signed by all parties concerned. It lists what is to be learned and the possible consequences of learning and not learning.
Time-out	Withholding of reinforcers, ignoring inappropriate behaviors, or removal from a reinforcing environment. When a game or activity becomes so stimulating to a student that he or she cannot control negative behaviors, there should be a quiet place to go. Time-out can be either required by a teacher or opted by a student.
Good behavior game	Refers to use of a group contingency approach in which all students are affected by the behaviors of each individual. Rules governing good behavior are in writing. The goal of the game is to accumulate points that can be used in buying a pleasant consequence (like free time or a field trip) agreed upon by majority vote. Points are gained by adhering to rules and are subtracted for breaking rules.

6. **Maximum involvement.** Learning occurs best when the child is actively and totally involved. Games and movement education activities should be selected on the criterion that every child is moving all (or most) of the time.

7. **Specificity/transfer.** Motor skills should be practiced in gamelike settings under the same space/time factors in which they will be used. For example, softball throws and dashes are more effective when practiced in a diamond formation than in parallel lines (back-and-forth throwing/running patterns). *Splinter skills* (the ability to perform a motor task in one setting but not in others) often occur in children with MR or LD; these can be avoided by practicing motor skills in a variety of settings with varied equipment; each practice is *specific* and will transfer only to the extent that the next setting is similar.

8. **Attention to relevant cues.** Learning occurs more effectively when the student can attend to relevant cues. This involves not only length of attention span, but also knowledge/understanding of cues. Many cues are *sensory* rather than verbal. Children with MR seem to benefit more from visual and kinesthetic cues (demonstrations or manual assistance through a movement) than verbal cues. Specific, precise, and near cues are easier to understand than general, vague, and distant ones.

9. **Goal direction.** Learning occurs best when the student knows and understands the goal or objective. This is related to attending, since knowledge of specific goals allows students to attend to them. Precisely written, measurable behavioral objectives implement this principle in that they clarify learning goals for both student and teacher.

10. **Significant others.** Learning occurs in a social context and is influenced by the presence/absence of spectators, peers, and teacher; by the sex, age, and personalities of these persons; and by the extent they are perceived to care. Considerable evidence exists that motor skills and activities are better learned at some ages when taught by a peer than by an adult. Evidence also substantiates the importance of the values, leisure patterns, and lifestyle of the home and family setting to what is learned in school.

11. **Motivation.** Learning occurs best when motivation is present. Considerable evidence exists, however, that response to motivation is highly individualized. The physical educator must determine the *conditions* under which each student learns best, the *trial* (when repeated trials are given) during which the child is likely to perform best, and the *reinforcers* that are most effective. Motivation is highly related to the *principle of effect* (i.e., students are more likely to have high motivation when they are succeeding than otherwise).

12. **Knowledge of results.** Learning is more effective when performance is reinforced with *immediate* and *specific* feedback. Knowledge of results is a type of motivation.

13. **Reward.** Reward is a form of reinforcement and motivation that facilitates learning. In initial skill learning, *continuous* reinforcement may be necessary. In later stages of learning, *random* reinforcement seems more effective. Rewards may be *external* (praise, hugs, candy, tokens, points, ribbons) or *internal* (simply feeling good about oneself).

14. **Exercise/practice.** *Practice,* done in "good form," with attention to relevant cues, and a high level of motivation leads to improvement. Practice without the presence of these conditions seldom facilitates learning or improves motor performance. "Good form" refers to the form best for the individual and encompasses specificity; the practice must be specific to the speed, distance, force, and rhythm for which the end product is to be used. Some evidence exists that *overlearning* is the preferred approach to facilitate motor learning for persons with MR.

15. **Drill versus problem solving.** *Drill* appears to be a faster, more efficient way of learning motor skills that are performed in stable, predictable environments; some examples are individual tasks (not dependent upon another) like volleyball and softball serves, pitching, and bowling. *Problem solving* (movement education tasks) appears better for learning motor skills that are used in changing, unpredictable environments like team games. *Drill* is best with children whose cognitive disorders limit problem-solving abilities.

16. **Whole versus part learning.** Simple motor tasks and skills are believed to be learned best by the *whole method*—that is, a demonstration of the skill and the challenge, "Can you do this?" Complex skills are believed to be learned best by the *part method.* In using the part method, apply a whole-part-whole approach so that students can conceptualize where the mastery of parts is leading them. In mastery of complex skills, some evidence indicates that cognitive mode (holistic or sequential) is specific to the individual. Learning efficiency is increased when method is individualized according to cognitive mode.

17. **Mass versus distributed practice.** In initial motor learning stages, *distributed* (intermittent) practice is better than massed (continuous), *short* practices are better than long, and *frequent* practices are better than infrequent.

18. **Order of learning.** Initial learnings are retained best, final learnings next best, and middle learnings worst. This appears to be related to attention theory in that the first parts of a lesson are generally attended to better than later ones. Since physical educators have traditionally placed review and warm-up first and new skill presentation and practice second, this principle warrants experimentation. *Serial order* is particularly important with children who fatigue easily. Time of day, as related to blood sugar levels, affects learning of some children.

Table 9.11
Illustrative Chart for Tabulating Teacher and Student Behaviors in a Small-Group Instructional Setting.

Teacher's Name _____L. Barnes_____ Setting _Gymnasium_

Date ___2/14_____ Time ___9 – 9:30 AM Class___

Place a tally mark for every 3 sec. of the same behavior and for every change of behavior, regardless of its duration.

Teacher Behaviors	Student Behaviors	Ann	Joe	Amy
Directions /	Rote response	//	/	//
Information giving LHT /	Analytic response	/		
Questions //	Questions		/	//
Acceptance of students' ideas ///	Acceptance of others' ideas	/	/	
Praise, encouragement LHT LHT /	Praise, encouragement	//	/	
Criticism /	Criticism	/		
Anger, confusion	Silence, confusion			///
Other	Initiating new idea	///	/	
	Other			

Signature of Recorder ____L. Gilstrap_____

Number of Minutes Behaviors Were Recorded ____5_____

19. **Rate of learning.** Beginners make more progress in mastering a motor skill than intermediate or advanced learners. After initial learning, improvement levels off and plateaus may occur. Scores on many trials should be plotted on graphs to show learning curve and document rate and amount of learning during an instructional unit. Much patience and encouragement are needed during plateaus.

20. **Retention.** The more meaningful the skill (or material), the longer it will be retained (remembered). In general, gross motor skills are retained longer than fine motor skills and other types of material. Overlearning of a skill seems to improve retention. Often, the activities that occur immediately before and after a lesson influence retention as well as learning itself.

Research in motor learning applied to persons with disabilities is just beginning to appear (Reid, 1990). Scan the *Adapted Physical Activity Quarterly* and other journals for articles related to each of these principles. In which areas of motor learning is research most needed? What can you do?

Student-Teacher Interaction Analysis

How teachers interact verbally and nonverbally with students can either help or hinder learning and personal commitment to exercise (Rich, Wuest, & Mancini, 1988). Table 9.11 presents an illustrative form for recording and studying interactions. In the humanistic gymnasium, students are taught to praise, encourage, and accept each other. This is achieved largely by modeling the teacher's behaviors.

Scientific Foundations of Adapting Activity

Students with problems of strength, endurance, balance, agility, coordination, and accuracy require adaptations that are based on principles of exercise physiology and biomechanics. Illustrative adaptations follow.

FIGURE 9.7

Students with cerebral palsy and other conditions of low muscle strength need a lowered basket for optimal success.

Problems of Strength and Endurance

1. Lower the net or basketball goal (Figure 9.7).
2. Reduce the distance the ball must be thrown or served (a) between bases, (b) between serving line and net, (c) between partners.
3. Reduce the weight and/or the size of the ball or projectile. Balloons are probably lightest, whereas medicine balls are heaviest (Figure 9.8).
4. Reduce the weight of the bat or striking implement. Shorten the length of the striking implement or choke up on the bat.
5. Lower the center of gravity. Games played in a lying or sitting position demand less fitness than those in a standing/running position.

FIGURE   9.8

In a task analysis, the manipulation of light balls (like balloons) comes before heavy balls. This teenager has so little arm and shoulder strength that shaking a balloon on a string is the first ball-handling activity he is able to master.

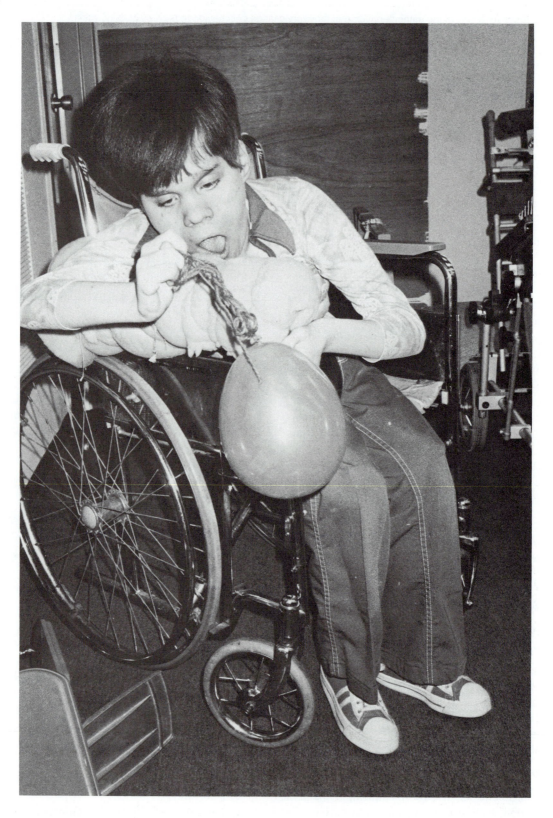

6. Deflate air from the ball or select one that will not get away so fast in case the student misses a catch and has to chase the ball.

7. Decrease activity time. Reduce the number of points needed to win.

8. Increase rest periods during activity.

9. Utilize frequent rotation in and out of the game or a system for substitution when needed.

10. Reduce the speed of the game. Walk rather than run through movements.

11. Consider ambulation alternatives—one inning on scooterboards, one inning on feet.

Problems of Balance and Agility

1. Lower the center of gravity. On a trampoline, for instance, practice logrolls, creeping, and four-point bounces before trying activities in a standing position. Stress bending the knees (or landing low) when jumping or coming to quick stops.

2. Keep as much of the body in contact with the surface as possible. Flat-footed ambulation is more stable than on tiptoe. Balancing on four or five body parts is more stable than on one.

3. Widen the base of support (distance between feet).

4. Increase the width of lines, rails, or beams to be walked. Note that straight lines are easier to walk than curved ones.

5. Use extended arms for balance. Holding a fishing pole while walking the beam facilitates balance.

6. Use carpeted rather than slick surfaces. Modify surfaces to increase friction. Select footwear (rubber soles) to reduce falls.

7. Learn to fall; practice different kinds of falls; make falls into games and creative dramatics.

8. Provide a barre to assist with stability during exercises or have a table or chair to hold on to.

9. Understand the role of visual perception in balance; learn to use eyes optimally.

10. Determine whether balance problems are related to prescribed medications. If there appears to be a relationship, confer with the physician.

Problems of Coordination and Accuracy

1. For catching and striking activities, use larger, lighter, softer balls. Balls thrown to midline are easier to catch and strike than those thrown to the right or left. Decrease the distance the ball is thrown and reduce speed.

2. For throwing activities, use smaller (tennis-size) balls. If grasp and release is a problem, try yarn or Nerf balls and beanbags.

3. Distance throwing is an easier progression than throwing for accuracy.

FIGURE 9.9

Adapting equipment (like attaching a string to the ball) and using backstops increase easy recovery of ball and maximize time devoted to practicing a skill.

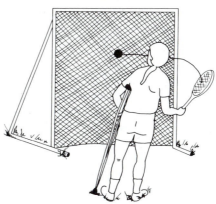

4. In striking and kicking activities, succeed with a stationary ball before trying a moving one. Increase the surface of the striking implement; choke up on the bat for greater control.

5. Reduce frustration when balls are missed by using backdrops, backstops, nets, and rebounder frame sets. Or attach a string to the ball for ease of recovery (Figure 9.9).

6. Increase the size of the target or goal cage to be hit, the circumference of the basket to be made. Give points for nearness (like hitting backboard) to avoid feeling failure until basket is actually made.

7. In bowling-type games, use lighter, less stable pins. Milk cartons are good.

8. Optimize safety by more attention than normal to glasses protectors, shin guards, helmets, and face masks. Do not remove the child's glasses!

Exercise Physiology Principles in Adaptation

Decreasing the physiological demands of an activity to make it easier for a student has its roots in the *principle of overload*. This principle states that strength and endurance result when the work load is greater than that to which the student is accustomed. Whereas all students should be pushed to increase their physiological limits once a motor pattern has been acquired, some students may take much longer than their peers to learn skills.

Exercise physiology principles are further discussed in relation to assessment and teaching in Chapter 13 on fitness. Many students, if properly motivated, can develop the same levels of fitness as their peers. If, however, they do not possess the movement patterns and play skills for participation in sports, their fitness needs are more health-related than physical or motor.

Biomechanical Principles in Adaptation

Most of the adaptations made for problems of strength, endurance, balance, agility, coordination, and accuracy have their roots in biomechanics. Principles of leverage, force production, and stability and the laws of motion explain adaptations, particularly those that pertain to degree of difficulty.

Leverage

Levers are rigid bars used to impart force or speed. The shorter the lever, the easier it is to move and control. In biomechanics, levers are implements for striking or batting, body parts, or the entire body. Difficulty in using a lever is reduced by shortening the length of rackets and bats or teaching students to choke up on the grip.

Applied to body position in exercise, the shorter the lever being moved, the easier the movement. In sit-ups, for example, the body length is shortened by placing arms on thighs or chest, making the exercise easier than the traditional placement of arms behind or over the head (Figure 9.10). Likewise, in push-ups, the shortened body position afforded by bending the knees makes bent-knee push-ups easier than regulation push-ups. In rotation movements like forward rolls, the tuck position is the shortest lever the body can become and, thus, the easiest for control.

Principles of Force Production

Magnitude of force can be changed by altering (a) leverage, (b) mass of object, (c) weight of object, (d) surface on which object is moving, (e) direction in which object is moving (with or against gravity), and (f) resistance of air or water. In

FIGURE 9.10

Two ways of shortening body length in accordance with the principle of leverage to make abdominal strength exercises easier.

Sit-ups   **Leg-lifts**

A. Exercises appropriate for weak students

B. Exercises appropriate for strong students

adapted physical education, the concern is often slowing an object so that students will have more success in fielding, catching, trapping, or striking it. *Mass* of object refers to its total body surface. In general, the larger the ball or projectile, the slower it moves because there is more surface to be affected by gravity (friction) or air resistance. The heavier an object, the slower it moves, but the more strength is needed to control it. Relationships between force, speed, and distance are discussed more fully in the upcoming "Laws of Motion" section.

Clumsy students often have difficulty in getting objects to move in the intended direction. This problem relates either to angle of release or point of application of force. Both are matters of timing or rhythm. Sometimes, painting a mark on the center of gravity (CG) of an object helps students to understand where the implement should hit the ball. Force applied in line with an objects's CG results in straight movement unless the object is acted upon by another force, such as the wind. Force applied not in line with an object's CG results in crooked or rotatory movement.

Principles of Stability

Principles of stability are important in helping to maintain balance against the force of gravity. They also can be used to alter the nature of objects to be knocked down or moved in bowling and target games.

1. The lower the CG, the more stable the position. Bending the knees lowers the CG. To make bowling-type games easier, devise objects to be knocked over that are top heavy (i.e., CG is high).

2. The larger the base of support, the more stable the position. Increasing the distance between the feet widens the base. Walking on soles of feet uses a larger base of support than walking on tiptoes or heels. To make bowling-type games easier, devise objects to be knocked over that have a narrow base.

FIGURE   9.11

When teaching students with missing limbs, apply biomechanical principles.

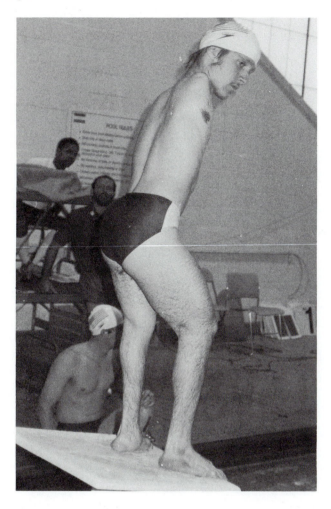

3. The more nearly centered the line of gravity is to the base of support, the more stable the position. Good body alignment thus facilitates balance. Carrying objects anywhere except on the head affects the line of gravity and tends to throw the body off balance. When holding or carrying heavy objects like bowling balls, keep them as close as possible to the body's CG.

4. The larger the mass of a body, the greater is its stability. To make hockey- and shuffleboard-type games easier, reduce the mass of the object to be hit. If tipping over is a problem while sitting, increase the mass of the chair, scooterboard, or tricycle by adding weight to it and making it larger.

5. To maintain body balance on a surface that is accelerating or decelerating, widen the stance in the direction the vehicle is moving. Lean opposite the direction of movement. Keep the body weight centered above the base of support. Persons with severe disability may need to be strapped in a wheelchair to keep weight centered properly.

Laws of Motion

Sir Isaac Newton's three laws of motion explain all adaptations that relate to starting and stopping, accelerating and decelerating, and reacting of surfaces.

Law of Inertia

A body will not move until a force sufficient to overcome ground, water, or air resistance is applied to it. Likewise, a body will move forever if not acted upon by an external force (presence of a barrier that stops it or friction of surface, water, or air).

The law of inertia refers to starting and stopping the movement of objects, including the human body. How, for instance, can sprint starts (on foot or in a wheelchair) be made most efficient? How does obesity affect starting and stopping? How does the absence of a limb affect starting and stopping (see Figure 9.11)?

How does muscle strength affect giving impetus to an external object? How do short arms and legs compare with those of average or long dimensions in force production? With students who lack muscle strength (e.g., have muscular dystrophy, cerebral palsy), the teacher makes adaptations in relation to several variables: (a) leverage, (b) mass (amount of surface) of object, (c) weight of object, (d) surface on which object is moving, and (e) resistance of air or water that the object is moving through. Concurrently, the teacher motivates students to increase the strength of their muscles as much as possible and introduces them to strength exercises. Weight reduction programs are initiated for fat students because weak muscles are less able to move heavy limbs than muscles of normal strength.

Law of Acceleration

Velocity of a moving body will remain constant unless acted upon by an external force. Change in speed is inversely proportional to the mass of an object and directly proportional to the amount of force or resistance causing the change. For clumsy children in games requiring retrieval, fielding, catching, or dodging of balls, teachers apply this principle to reduce the speed of the object and make it easier to handle.

Law of Reaction

To every action, there is an equal and opposite reaction. This law applies primarily to the surface one pushes or throws against in order to start or stop an object, to increase or decrease its speed, or to determine its direction of movement.

Effective application of force, whether against the floor (as in locomotor movement) or against an external object (as in pushing, lifting, or pulling), is easier on a nonslippery, stationary surface. A balance beam is easier to walk across than a trampoline, bed mattress, or water bed. A floor or a hard dirt surface is easier to walk or run on than sand or grass. This is because to move the body forward, the feet must exert most of their force backward. In swimming, to move forward in the front crawl, the arms apply force backward.

Cooperative Planning

In cooperatively working out adaptations with students, encourage honest appraisal of what they can and cannot do, but *stress abilities in making the adaptations.* Consider adaptations temporary, and plan teaching progressions that facilitate growth from the easy stage toward the more difficult. Utilize motivation and reinforcement techniques, showing that you *care* and that you *believe* in the individual's potential to improve.

Variables to Be Manipulated

Adapting involves manipulating the variables that affect the teaching/learning process. Some of these factors are

1. **Teaching style** (as discussed earlier in this chapter).
2. **Verbal instructions.** Length of command or verbal challenge, depending upon language development of group; bilingual or unilingual; accompanied by sign language or gesture; loud, soft, or varied; pleasant or stern facial expression and body language; use of certain cue or action words; continuous or intermittent; distance from pupil(s) while talking.

FIGURE 9.12

Physical guidance through a movement is called the *enactive* or *coactive* method of teaching.

3. **Demonstrations.** By teacher or peers? One person or several simultaneously? How many demonstrations? How often? How long? Best location for demonstrating?
4. **Level of methodology.** Physical guidance through a movement (enactive, coactive) (Figure 9.12); demonstration or follow the leader (iconic); verbal instructions (symbolic); or some combination.
5. **Starting and stopping signals.** Discover which works best: voice, whistle, gesture (raising arm), flicker of lights, drumbeat, some combination.
6. **Time.** Time of day, season of year.
7. **Duration.** Fixed or variable at each station? For each skill? For taking a test? Number of weeks in instructional period; number of days; number of minutes each day. Amount of activity versus amount of rest. Massed versus distributed practices.
8. **Order of learning or trials.** What comes first, middle, and last? What type of rest periods between trials? What type of reinforcements?

9. **Student-teacher ratios.** One-to-one or one-to-sixty? Variable or fixed? Remember that teachers can be peers, volunteers, aides.

10. **Size of group.** At each station? In particular games, drills, movement education activities?

11. **Nature of group.** Same or variable for a given period? Ratio of students with and without disability? Homogeneous or heterogeneous in ability level, age, and sex, among others? Predetermined on basis of criteria or random?

12. **Instructional setting.** Indoors or outdoors; temperature; allergen-free; humidity; wind; dust; lighting; acoustics/noise; large versus small; open versus partitioned; carpeted versus wooden floors; concrete versus abstract (imaginary) boundaries; amount of wall space; availability of mirrors?

13. **Equipment.** A lot or a little; movable or stationary; storage space; safe (good repair) or otherwise; variations in terms of size, shape, texture, and weight?

14. **Architectural barriers and distance of playing area from classrooms.** How difficult is it for a person with a physical disability to travel to and from the gymnasium; to get a drink of water; to use dressing and bathroom facilities?

15. **Level of difficulty/complexity.** Skill; formation; game rules; game strategies.

16. **Motivation.** Fixed or variable; random or consistent; what kind works best?

Decisions about these variables largely determine the student's success. Go back over the list and consider how each can be manipulated to provide optimal learning conditions for various disabilities, body compositions, age groups, personality types (shy vs. assertive), and ability levels (beginners vs. advanced).

References

Aufderheide, S. (1983). ALT-PE in mainstreamed physical education classes. *Journal of Teaching in Physical Education, 1,* 22–26.

Bandura, A. (1986). *Social foundations of thought and action: A social cognitive theory.* Englewood Cliffs, NJ: Prentice-Hall.

Bell-Gredler, M. (1986). *Learning and instruction: Theory into practice.* New York: Macmillan.

DePaepe, J. L. (1985). The influence of three least restrictive environments on the content motor ALT and performance of moderately mentally retarded students. *Journal of Teaching in Physical Education, 3,* 34–41.

Dunn, J., Morehouse, J., & Fredericks, H. (1986). *Physical education for the severely handicapped: A systematic approach to a data based gymnasium* (2nd ed.). Austin, TX: Pro·Ed.

Goldberger, M. (1992). The spectrum of teaching styles: A perspective for research on teaching physical education. *Journal of Physical Education, Recreation, and Dance, 63* (1), 42–46.

Hoover, J., & Wade, M. (1985). Motor learning theory and mentally retarded individuals: A historical review. *Adapted Physical Activity Quarterly, 2,* 228–252.

Jenkins, J. R., & Jenkins, L. M. (1981). *Crossage and peer tutoring: Help for children with learning problems.* Reston, VA: Council for Exceptional Children.

Leuw, L. (1972). Co-active movement with deaf-blind children: The Van Dijk model. Videotape made at Michigan School for Blind. (Available through many regional centers for deaf-blind.)

Mosston, M. (1966). *Teaching physical education.* Columbus, OH: Charles E. Merrill.

Mosston, M., & Ashworth, S. (1986). *Teaching physical education* (3rd ed.). Columbus, OH: Charles E. Merrill.

Mosston, M., & Ashworth, S. (1990). *The spectrum of teaching styles: From command to discovery.* White Plains, NY: Longman.

Reid, G. (Ed.). (1990). *Problems in movement control.* Amsterdam: North-Holland.

Rich, S., Wuest, D. A., & Mancini, V. (1986). CAFIAS: A systematic tool to improve teaching behaviors. In C. Sherrill (Ed.), *Leadership training in adapted physical education.* Champaign, IL: Human Kinetics.

Runco, M. A., & Albert, R. S. (Eds.). (1990). *Theories of creativity.* Newbury Park, CA: Sage.

Tawney, J. W., & Gast, D. L. (1984). *Single subject research in special education.* Columbus, OH: Merrill.

Torrance, E. P. (1974). *Torrance tests of creative thinking.* Bensenville, IL: Scholastic Testing Service.

Van Dijk, J. (1966). The first steps of the deaf-blind child towards language. *International Journal for the Education of the Blind, 15* (1), 112–115.

Vogler, E. W., van der Mars, H., Darst, P., & Cusimano, B. (1990). Relationship of presage, context, and process variables to ALT-PE of elementary level mainstreamed students. *Adapted Physical Activity Quarterly, 7* (4), 298–313.

Watkinson, E. J., & Wasson, D. L. (1984). The use of single-subject time-series designs in adapted physical activity. *Adapted Physical Activity Quarterly, 1* (1), 19–29.

Wyrick, W. (1968). The development of a test of motor creativity. *Research Quarterly, 39,* 756–765.

PART

II

Generic Service Delivery

Note that Sport is highlighted in Part III.
Note also that neurological bases of clumsiness is in Chapter 10.

CHAPTER

10

Motor Learning, Sensorimotor Integration, and Reflexes

FIGURE   10.1

Children with developmental delays need teachers who understand all of the systems of the body, as well as environmental interactions and constraints. Of particular importance is knowledge of (*A*) postural and balance reactions and (*B*) reflexes that interfere with body control.

A

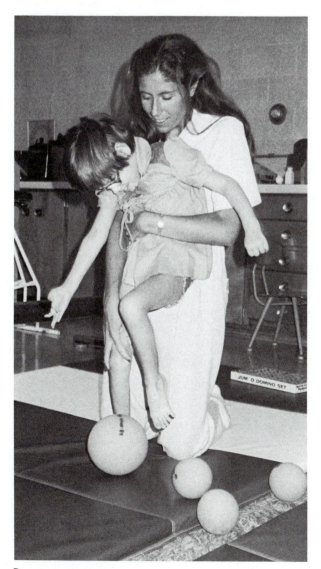

B

After you have studied this chapter, you should be able to:

1. Discuss motor-learning models that guide assessment and remediation and explain how dynamic action theory can be woven into each.

2. Explain why *sensorimotor integration* is a better term than *sensory integration*.

3. Identify 10 sense modalities and discuss four sensory systems that are especially important in motor learning. Explain common developmental problems in each and techniques used for remediation.

4. Define three types of motor output or action patterns and discuss two basic principles used in relation to motor output.

5. Describe 10 reflex patterns of most importance to physical educators and discuss contribution of reflexes in early infant development and problems caused by abnormal retention.

6. Discuss pedagogy in working with persons whose reflexes are interfering with motor learning and performance. Identify four principles that guide pedagogy.

7. Identify and discuss reactions: (a) righting, (b) parachute, and (c) equilibrium. Discuss how these relate to balance and how they can be strengthened and reinforced.

8. Use the Milani-Comparetti system to assess 9 motor milestones, 5 primitive reflexes, and 13 postural reactions.

9. Demonstrate understanding of the neurological bases of motor development. Know how each part of the central nervous system (CNS) develops. Be able to (a) identify parts of the nerve cell and the CNS; (b) describe their structure, location, and function; and (c) discuss how delayed and abnormal development affect motor learning and control.

10. Discuss the functions of the pyramidal and extrapyramidal systems in motor control. Relate these functions to (a) reciprocal innervation and muscle tone disorders, (b) upper and lower neuron disorders, and (c) praxis disorders.

11. Discuss the neurological bases of clumsiness. Include in your discussion the seven characteristics of a mature, intact CNS.

12. Identify some theories that guide teaching practices in this chapter. Go to the library and read more about these theories.

Teaching persons with problems is obviously more complex and difficult than working with students who learn spontaneously and easily and have all body systems intact and functioning in predictable ways (see Figure 10.1). The challenge in adapted physical activity is to be both a generalist and a specialist. The specialization is individual differences—specifically, everything that relates to resolving psychomotor problems. To achieve this goal, we must be able to synthesize and apply information from many disciplines and areas of knowledge: anatomy, physiology, neurology, psychology, motor learning, and the like. Much of what we need to know has not yet been discovered, so we must also be creative, innovative, and research oriented.

Pedagogical Challenges in Adapted Physical Activity

This chapter discusses motor learning and performance in relation to developmental delays and disability. In regular physical education, the emphasis is on teaching and learning voluntary movement. The assumptions are that the reflex and postural reaction systems are intact, that muscle tone is normal, that sensory input is organized efficiently, that abilities (perceptual, cognitive, memory, attention, motor) are within expected ranges for a specific age group, and that all body systems (nervous, skeletal, muscular, sensory, endocrine, respiratory, cardiovascular, and the like) are intact and normal in structure and function.

FIGURE 10.2

Major parts of the brain. Regular educators direct teaching at the cortical level (cerebrum), whereas adapted physical educators often focus on subcortical function (the structures below the cerebrum).

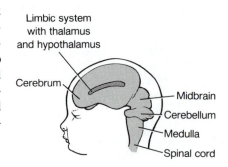

When these assumptions are met, learning proceeds smoothly. There are ups and downs, and certainly individual differences in learning and performance, but no major psychomotor problems. *Learning* traditionally is defined as a permanent change in behavior at the cortical or conscious level. In adapted physical education, this concept is extended to include permanent changes in behavior at the subconscious or subcortical levels like the brain stem, midbrain, and cerebellum (see Figure 10.2).

FIGURE   10.3

Three learning models that emphasize different areas of breakdown.
Adapted physical educators use all three models.

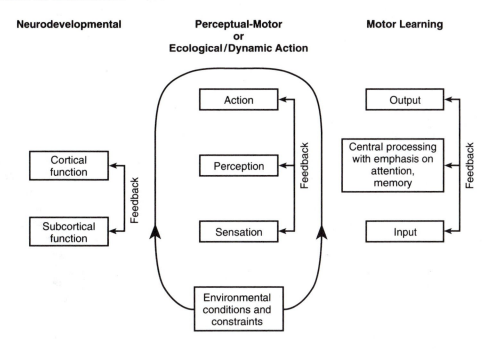

Persons who are clumsy or disabled have special needs at these levels. The relationships between voluntary (cortical-directed movement) and nonvoluntary movement are not entirely understood, but the resolution of motor-learning problems is clearly dependent upon many processes not under conscious control. Like occupational and physical therapists, adapted physical educators work with both voluntary and nonvoluntary movement. Often, this work is concurrent. Adapted physical educators do not necessarily assume hierarchical learning. They simply emphasize the whole child and use all body and environmental resources.

Whereas regular educators assume that students are ambulatory and focus therefore on locomotor patterns and ball-handling skills from standing or running postures, adapted physical educators often work with individuals who are nonambulatory. These may be (a) young children with delayed motor development who need help in learning to roll, sit, creep, stand, and walk or (b) individuals in wheelchairs for whom walking will never be functional. Adapted physical educators use mat activities and work with students in lying, sitting, all-fours, and kneeling postures more than do regular physical educators.

Motor-Learning Models

Three models guide pedagogical beliefs about assessment and remediation (see Figure 10.3). Each model emphasizes different areas of breakdown (dysfunction) in learning.

The neurodevelopmental (or sensory integration) model has typically been applied to children who manifest problems at the reflex and reaction levels (i.e., those who cannot perform age-appropriate locomotor and object control skills or who demonstrate general clumsiness). Jean Ayres (1972) supports the neurodevelopmental approach:

The educators' error has been in the direction of considering all sensation, perception, and cognition as exclusively cortical, overlooking the probability that some subcortical function may still be critical. . . . Perhaps to err in the direction of stressing the subcortical will balance the matter. (p. 8)

Thus, over the years, therapists have developed motor-learning models that address both subcortical and cortical functions. Today, many adapted physical educators are following this trend.

Perceptual-motor models have been used by both special educators and physical educators. From the 1930s through the 1960s, special educators used the perceptual-motor model more than any other pedagogy (Hallahan & Cruickshank, 1973). The assumptions that guided special education and early perceptual-motor theorists were (a) perception is dependent upon movement abilities, (b) academic performance is dependent upon perceptual ability, and (c) perceptual-motor training can improve academic performance. However, systematic research did not support these assumptions (Kavale & Mattson, 1983). Special educators became disenchanted with perceptual-motor remediation as an approach to cognitive learning and soundly rejected the perceptual-motor model.

Physical educators continue to use the perceptual-motor model as an approach to motor learning and control (Burton, 1987; Sherrill & Montelione, 1990). The assumptions that guide contemporary physical educators, however, are different from those in the 1930 to 1980 era. *Physical educators believe that (a) movement success is partly dependent on perception and (b) perceptual-motor training can improve motor performance.* The perceptual-motor model in Figure 10.3 presents the physical education, not the special education, philosophy. Perhaps the name of this model should be changed because it holds different meanings for special and physical educators. Special educators in individualized education program (IEP) meetings often are not supportive of perceptual-motor training simply because of the term's negative connotations.

A proposed name change that is gradually gaining acceptance is the ecological model. This name emphasizes that all learning occurs in response to interactions between the person and the environment. Common sense and creativity have led adapted physical educators to vary the environment in as many ways as possible when remediating perception and movement problems, but theories are now available to support an ecological approach (Barnes, Crutchfield, Heriza, & Herdman, 1990; Bronfenbrenner, 1979; Burton, 1990a, b; Davis, 1983; Davis & Rizzo, 1991; Gibson, 1979). Proponents of ecological theory always include a component labeled "environment" or "ecology" in their learning models (see Figure 10.3).

The motor-learning model, which emphasizes central processing (i.e., attention, memory, and executive function) rather than input, has typically been used in regular physical education (Thomas, 1984), where interest focuses on children age 5 years or older and the assumption is that the sensory input system is properly functioning. Jerry Thomas, perhaps the best known of the motor-learning researchers whose work has centered on children, observed that the sensory registers (kinesthetic, visual, auditory) do not change much after age 5. Thomas (1984, p. 94) stated, ". . . equivalent levels of initial information are available to children and adults. Thus, the functions of the sensory registers are not the source of the increase in motor performance seen as children grow and develop."

Motor-learning theory primarily emphasizes the keenness of perceptual judgments (i.e., increases in sensitivity to movement feedback that occur with age), rather than input inadequacy of the perceptual mechanism. Regular educators assume that maturation will proceed normally and that motor control problems related to perception will resolve themselves. Thomas noted, therefore, that the main interest in the motor-learning model is on attention and memory.

The adapted physical educator, as a specialist especially responsible for ameliorating difficult psychomotor problems, relies on all three learning models. The typical clumsy student demonstrates learning breakdowns in all of the areas highlighted in the different models (Sugden & Keogh, 1990). These breakdowns must be considered, of course, in relation to the environment.

Sensorimotor Integration

Learning is influenced first and foremost by the environment because it affords the stimuli for sensory input. We take in far more than the central nervous system (CNS) can process,

and past experience (attention and memory processes) enables us to attach meaning to some stimuli and learn from interactions with them. In spontaneous learning, we are dependent on our own resources. In directed learning, the teacher carefully shapes the environment and provides specific sensory input to elicit desired behaviors. In both kinds of learning, the neural processes are not well understood.

Sensory integration is a term widely used to describe these neural processes in persons with developmental delays. Jean Ayres, an occupational therapist, is credited with evolution of the term and a system of therapy (Ayres, 1972, 1980). Ayres defined *sensory integration* as the organization of sensory input for use. Some occupational therapists feel strongly that this term belongs to their profession, but this is naive inasmuch as many kinesiologists refer to sensory integration (Bard, Fleury, & Hay, 1990; Sage, 1977; Williams, 1983).

Sensorimotor integration (Brooks, 1986) is, perhaps, a more accurate term for the organization of sensory input for movement. In this text, *sensorimotor integration* and *sensory integration* are used synonymously to denote the CNS processing that occurs bidirectionally between sensory input and motor output. If this processing is cortical, involving perception and cognition, then *perceptual-motor integration* may be the preferred term. This chapter focuses on subcortical processes, and Chapter 12 emphasizes all neural systems working together in perceptual-motor function.

Development of Sensory Systems

Ten modalities provide sensory input that must be organized and processed. These are (a) touch and pressure, (b) kinesthesis, (c) vestibular system, (d) temperature, (e) pain, (f) smell, (g) taste, (h) vision, (i) audition, and (j) common chemical sense. With the exception of the last one, these senses are familiar to all of us. The common chemical sense controls the complex reaction to such activities as peeling an onion (eyes burning, nose sneezing) or eating a hot pepper. Each modality has a special type of end organ (sensory receptor) that is sensitive only to certain stimuli, and each has a separate pathway from the sensory receptor up the spinal cord to the brain. Figure 10.4 depicts some of these sensory receptors.

Sensory systems especially important to motor learning are tactile and deep pressure, kinesthetic, vestibular, and visual. When these systems exhibit delayed or abnormal functioning, motor development and/or learning is affected.

Tactile System

The tactile system is probably the most fully developed sensory apparatus at birth, as is evidenced by the infant's cries signifying discomfort with wet diapers. The tactile system includes many different receptors in the skin that provide sensory input regarding touch, deep pressure, pain, heat, and cold.

FIGURE 10.4

Sensory receptors. Each sensory input system has distinctly different receptors.

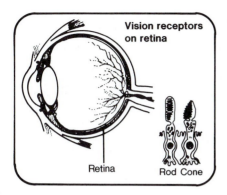

Vision receptors on retina

Retina

Rod Cone

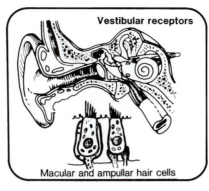

Vestibular receptors

Macular and ampullar hair cells

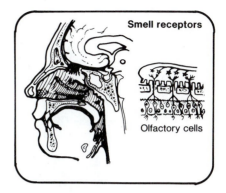

Smell receptors

Olfactory cells

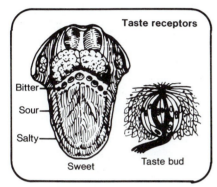

Taste receptors

Bitter

Sour

Salty

Sweet

Taste bud

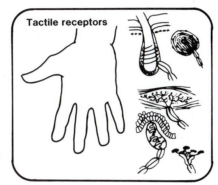

Tactile receptors

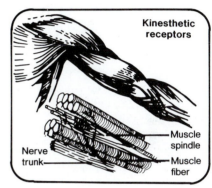

Kinesthetic receptors

Nerve trunk

Muscle spindle

Muscle fiber

Tactile Craving and Defensiveness

Need for tactile stimulation varies widely among human beings. Some persons seem impulse-driven to touch everything: They are particularly obvious in stores and museums; among children, they are often the ones who get in trouble for poking at others or pulling pigtails. At the opposite end of the individual differences spectrum are persons who dislike and avoid touch; if someone accidently brushes against them, a fight may ensue. Persons exhibiting these extremes have disorders of tactile reception/perception called *tactile craving* or *tactile defensiveness*. Such disorders are commonly associated with learning disabilities, autistic-like behaviors, mental retardation, and severe emotional disturbances.

Using Tactile Stimulation

Tactile stimulation is recommended for persons with severe disability and for infants with delays. Swimming or aquatic play, with a variety of water temperatures, is especially stimulating; cold water assists in arousal, whereas warm water has a relaxing effect. Massage, either by hand or vibrator, is used to activate the deep pressure receptors, whereas stroking the skin with the hand or cloths of various textures (silk, velvet, denim, corduroy, terry) stimulates touch receptors. Deep pressure receptors are also stimulated by locomotion, movement exploration, and gymnastic activities in which the weight of the body is taken on different parts. Almost all children learn body control better when they are barefooted

than when wearing shoes. Rolling on mats or surfaces with different textures is an excellent tactile stimulation activity. Partner stunts and tumbling increase tolerance for touch in tactile defensiveness.

Research shows that infants need stroking and cuddling to survive. Tactile stimulation associated with love and affection is extremely important, and parents and/or caretakers must be encouraged to use touch and become aware of the approach/avoidance behaviors it evokes. Tactile defensiveness is usually treated by pairing touch with rewards and gradually increasing the amount that can be tolerated.

Kinesthetic System

The kinesthetic system encompasses all of the sensory receptors in the muscles, tendons, and joints that provide CNS input regarding changes in tension within fibers. Neural impulses travel to various parts of the brain and, when interpreted, allow us to know (a) the position of the body and its parts in space, (b) whether or not we are moving, and (c) what the qualities (time, space, force, flow) of the movements are. The kinesthetic system works closely with the vestibular apparatus in the inner ear to tell us everything we know (without the use of vision) about position and movement.

The kinesthetic system is responsible for the tonic neck reflexes (both asymmetrical and symmetrical) and other reflexes (see Figure 10.5). As the kinesthetic system matures, these reflexes are integrated, and movement becomes increasingly coordinated.

FIGURE 10.5

Immature kinesthetic system allows reflexes to interfere with voluntary movement. (*A*) Asymmetrical tonic neck reflex. (*B*) and (*C*) Symmetrical tonic neck reflexes.

A. Head rotation causes arm and leg to extend.

B. Head flexion causes legs to extend.

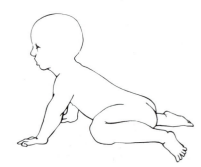

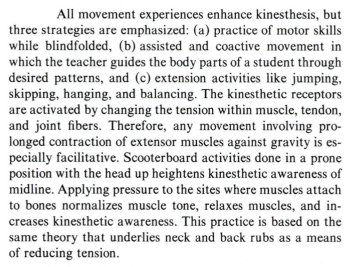

C. Head extension/hyperextension causes legs to flex.

All movement experiences enhance kinesthesis, but three strategies are emphasized: (a) practice of motor skills while blindfolded, (b) assisted and coactive movement in which the teacher guides the body parts of a student through desired patterns, and (c) extension activities like jumping, skipping, hanging, and balancing. The kinesthetic receptors are activated by changing the tension within muscle, tendon, and joint fibers. Therefore, any movement involving prolonged contraction of extensor muscles against gravity is especially facilitative. Scooterboard activities done in a prone position with the head up heightens kinesthetic awareness of midline. Applying pressure to the sites where muscles attach to bones normalizes muscle tone, relaxes muscles, and increases kinesthetic awareness. This practice is based on the same theory that underlies neck and back rubs as a means of reducing tension.

Vestibular System

The vestibular system originates in the inner ear area of the temporal lobe, where hair cell receptors take in information about the position of the head and all of its movements, however subtle (see Figure 10.6). This information, when interpreted and acted upon by other parts of the brain, helps to maintain static and dynamic balance. The vestibular system is the most important structure in the regulation of body postures. It prevents falling, keeps body parts properly aligned, and contributes to graceful, coordinated movement.

Equilibrium and balance, once used as synonyms, are now defined separately. *Equilibrium* is a biomechanical term denoting equal forces acting upon an object. In the human body, the forces exerted by muscles must equal external forces like gravity to keep the body upright. *Balance* is a more global term, referring to the control processes that maintain body parts in the specific alignments necessary to achieve different kinds of mobility and stability. Most persons with psychomotor problems have difficulty with balance. Four sensory systems (vestibular, kinesthetic, tactile, and visual) interact with environmental variables to enable balance. These, especially the vestibular system, are of considerable interest in adapted physical activity.

The vestibular apparatus is named for the hollow, bony vestibule (chamber) within the inner ear. This vestibule contains a labyrinth (maze) of interconnecting membranous tubes and sacs filled with fluid. The tubes are three semicircular canals arranged at right angles to each other. Two are vertical, and one is horizontal (see Figure 10.7). They are named superior, inferior, and horizontal (or anterior, posterior, and lateral). The sacs are the utricle and saccule. When the head is upright, the utricle is in a more superior position.

The two types of structures (canals and sacs) take in different kinds of sensory information about head movement. The semicircular canals are responsive to *angular movements,* especially rotation of the head to the left or right and diagonal movements forward and backward toward the

FIGURE   10.6

The vestibular system. The *sensory component* consists of the semicircular canals (rotatory input) and sacs (linear input). *The motor component* consists of the four vestibular nuclei and the vestibulo-spinal tract. The vestibular nuclei relay information about the position of the head to many parts of the brain.

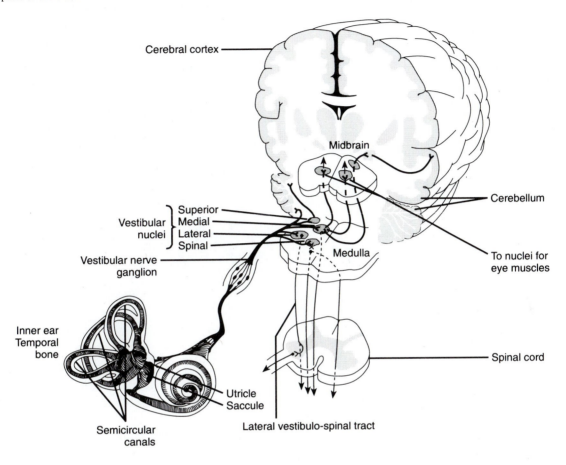

FIGURE   10.7

Close-up of semicircular canals and sacs (utricle and saccule).

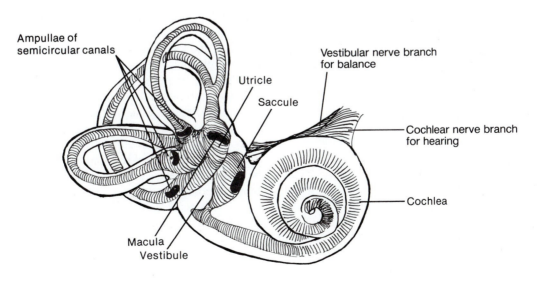

floor. The sacs are responsive to *linear* or straight plane movements, like side to side, up and down, or forward and backward in the same plane (Barnes et al., 1990).

The sensory receptors of the canals and sacs have different names. The hair cells of the canals are called *ampullae, cristae,* or *ampullary cristae* and are located in the bulbous enlargements of the canals at the point where they join the utricle. The hair cells of the sacs are called *maculae* or *otoliths.* To help remember, visualize Big Macs from McDonalds in sacs. Thinking of the sacs in straight lines on the counter correctly associates the maculae with linear movements of the head.

Static and Dynamic Balance

Outdated references associate the semicircular canals with dynamic balance and the sacs with static balance. This division is not accurate. Input from both structures is needed in all kinds of balance. This is because the head moves in many ways during both static and dynamic balances. The principle of specificity tells us that there are many kinds of static and dynamic balances, and a test of balance in one position will not yield data that are generalizable to other positions.

The maintenance of balance involves both sensory input and motor output. *Vestibular apparatus* refers to the structures that provide sensory information, whereas *vestibular system* refers to both sensory and motor components (see Figure 10.6). Vestibular impulses are carried via the vestibular nerve (eighth cranial) to four vestibular nuclei (clumps of gray matter) in the medulla (brain stem). Here, many motor impulses are generated to control balance. Some go directly to muscles that activate reflexes and/or reactions, some go to the cerebellum, and some go to midbrain nuclei of cranial nerves that innervate the eye muscles.

This process is very complicated because vestibular impulses are modified, reorganized, and integrated by tactile, kinesthetic, and visual input. Balance in young children is heavily influenced by vision, whereas adults rely more on tactile and kinesthetic input (Barnes et al., 1990; Woollacott & Shumway-Cook, 1989). This explains why children and persons with developmental delays are encouraged to focus their eyes on a designated point during balance activities. It also explains why blindfolds are often used in testing and remediating balance.

Enhancing Vestibular Development

The vestibular system is well developed at birth, as is evidenced by the calming effect of cradling or rocking the infant in arms, crib, or rocking chair. Swings, seesaws, merry-go-rounds, and other playground apparatus owe their popularity to children's natural craving for vestibular stimulation. The use of balance boards, various kinds of balance beams, swinging bridges, and trampolines (all of which have unstable surfaces) in early childhood physical education is based

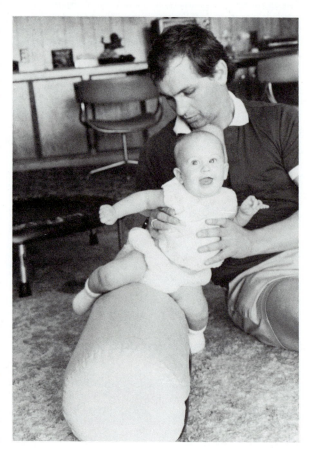

FIGURE 10.8

Use of unstable surfaces in early childhood play promotes development of the vestibular system.

largely on theory that posits that the vestibular system is a coordinating mechanism for all sensory function (see Figure 10.8).

The goal in enhancing vestibular development is to cause momentary losses of balance (perturbations) that change head position. This activates compensatory postural adjustments and reinforces balance reactions. The more practice the vestibular system is given, the more it improves. Regular physical educators typically focus on balance in standing and locomotor patterns and do not realize that head position changes are the key. Adapted physical activity personnel focus on perturbations in all positions. They also pay particular attention to vision.

Whereas physical educators call apparatus that causes perturbations balance boards or swings, therapists refer to them as vestibular apparatus. Adapted physical educators use both sets of terminology. They also use vestibular boards, hammocks, and large balls that permit vestibular input in prone and supine positions.

Persons certified in sensory integration remediation (contact an occupational therapy department for further information) also use spinning and other rapid rotary movements for vestibular stimulation. Special training is needed for use of spinning as remediation.

Nystagmus and Motion Sickness

Anatomical interrelationships between vestibular, visual, and visceral systems help to explain why, after rapid spinning, the eyes normally exhibit *nystagmus* (rapid movements) and the student feels nauseous or dizzy. There are many individual differences in this response. Some persons feel dizzy after a single forward roll. Vestibular testing is done by rapid spinning of a student sitting on a stool; 20 sec of spinning normally results in 9 to 11 sec of nystagmus, an automatic midbrain response. A longer or shorter duration of nystagmus, nausea, or prolonged dizziness are signs of vestibular dysfunction. Motion sickness, which originates in the vestibular system, also involves vision and viscera.

Remediation for vestibular-induced discomfort is short practice periods paired with rewards. If a short-duration activity makes us feel dizzy, it is probably good for us (Barnes et al., 1990). Physical educators should refer persons who continue to complain of dizziness to physicians.

Visual System

The visual system is comprised of many subsystems, some reflex and some voluntary. All are important in postural control and motor performance. The many subsystems can be organized into two types of vision: (a) refractive and (b) orthoptic.

Refractive Vision (Acuity)

Refractive vision refers to visual acuity, the product of light rays bending and reaching the receptor cells (rods and cones) of the retina. Visual impulses are transmitted via the optic nerve (second cranial) to many parts of the brain for interpretation. Refractive problems include myopia (nearsightedness), hyperopia (farsightedness), and astigmatism (blurring and distortion). Refraction is influenced by the size and shape of the eyeball, which changes with age. At birth, the eyeball is short (about three-fourths of adult length), which explains why young children tend to focus more easily on middle-distance items than near ones.

Orthoptic Vision (Coordination)

Orthoptic vision refers to activity of the six external muscles of the eyeball, which are innervated by cranial nerves 3, 4, and 6. These muscles move the eyeballs up, down, in, out, and in diagonal directions. Of particular importance is *binocular coordination,* the ability of the two eyes to work in unison. Physiologically, because of their separate locations, each eye receives slightly different sensory stimuli and thus forms a different image. The two eyes must work together to fuse these separate images into one which, when interpreted by the brain, is seen as a solid with height, width, and depth dimensions and interpreted in relation to distance. The closer something is to the eyes, the greater the disparity between the images and the harder it is to fuse them into one. Likewise, the farther away the two eyes are set from one another, the more difficult the fusion (see Figure 10.9).

FIGURE   10.9

Eye problems affect vision and perceptual-motor function. (*A*) Eyes set abnormally far apart interfere with binocular coordination. (*B*) Strabismus in Down syndrome interferes with depth perception.

A

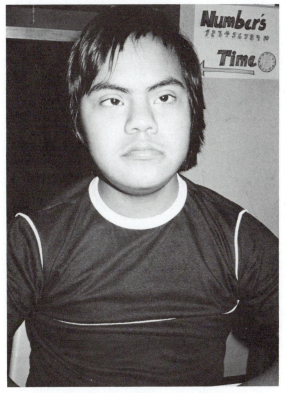

B

Binocular coordination is closely linked with balance and postural reactions. We take for granted the subcortical processing of three dimensions of space and the automatic adjustment of body parts to avoid bumping into things, falling, and other inappropriate movements.

Depth perception is often used as a synonym for binocular coordination, but this oversimplification is inaccurate (Guyton, 1981). Depth perception is the mental process of deriving meaning from visual space-time relationships, as in judging the distance of a balance beam from the ground or the speed/distance of a moving object. It is dependent upon three complex mechanisms, one of which is binocular coordination. Simplified, depth perception is problem solving about near/far relationships. Abilities can be classified as static (near/far judgments about stationary things) and dynamic (near/far judgments about moving things). Developmentally, we refine static perception abilities first. By age 12, depth perception is usually mature.

Eye muscle coordination problems are common among persons with disabilities. These include (a) developmental delays in binocular coordination and depth perception, (b) strabismus (squint or crossed eyes), and (c) pathological nystagmus (constant, involuntary movement of the eyeballs). Strabismus is associated with cerebral palsy, Down syndrome, and fetal alcohol syndrome (see Figure 10.9). Nystagmus has a high prevalence among visually impaired persons with albinism (blond, blue eyes, pale skin).

Enhancing Vision

When vision problems are suspected, an eye specialist should be consulted (Herman & Retish, 1989). Refractive problems are treated by prescriptive glasses or surgery. Some orthoptic problems like strabismus can also be treated with surgery. Teachers can administer screening tests, but most of these relate to vision for reading rather than for body control. Findings regarding binocular control in near-vision tasks (30 inches or closer) do not generalize to the depth perception demands in dodgeball, catching, and striking activities.

The best way to enhance vision for body control is to provide lots of practice in many and varied movement tasks. The breakdown in vision typically is not exclusively a problem of the eyes but rather the complex process of integrating inputs from several sensory modalities and translating them into appropriate motor outputs.

Head position and movement (vestibular input) is so important in sensory integration that object manipulation (e.g., beanbags, balloons) and ball handling should be systematically practiced from many positions: midline and looking up, down, and sideways. This includes prone-, supine-, and side-lying on mats as well as on apparatus of different heights and tilts to give looking downward new perspectives. Practice should be with (a) the body stationary, (b) the body in locomotion, and (c) the body moved by external forces like swings, balance boards, scooterboards, merry-go-rounds, escalators, treadmills, and the like. Only the creativity of the professional limits the ways vision can be practiced and enhanced.

Intersensory Integration

Intersensory integration refers to the ability to use and integrate input from several sensory modalities simultaneously. Remediating one sensory system independent of others is impossible. Adapted physical educators, however, give more attention to tactile, kinesthetic, and vestibular (TKV) input than regular educators.

Because these three modalities are so interrelated, they are sometimes referred to as somatosensory, haptic, or proprioceptive. Sources differ on the exact definitions of these terms. Guyton (1981, p. 105) stated: "*Proprioceptive sensations* are those having to do with the physical state of the body, including position sensations, tendon and muscle sensations, pressure sensations from the bottom of the feet, and even the sensation of equilibrium."

Vision is important in body control at all ages, but especially in childhood. *Until about age 7 or 8, most children develop skills most efficiently through movement exploration and trial and error.* During the primary grades, they gradually become better at processing visual and auditory input from external sources (demonstrations, videotapes, films, and verbal instructions). Age 7 to 8 is the time of shifting from self-input to other-input. In persons with severe problems, this shift may be delayed considerably. It may also be complicated by some persons becoming primarily visual or auditory learners, and thus unable to profit equally from visual and auditory instruction.

Motor Output or Action

Motor output or action occurs in three types of patterns: (a) reflex, (b) reaction or automatic response, and (c) skill. These are present in all age groups. Some persons associate reflexes only with infants, but contemporary sources emphasize that reflexes are *recognizable synergies that span many body segments and affect coordination at all ages* (Barnes et al., 1990, p. 350). Knowledge about reflexes is changing as research leads to new theories but, for practical purposes, various reflexes can be thought of as normal in infancy and as pathological when they interfere with voluntary patterns at older ages.

Adapted physical educators follow two basic principles in relation to motor output: (a) inhibit, suppress, or integrate patterns that cause clumsiness or loss of balance and (b) facilitate patterns that contribute to success. In general, reflexes are inhibited, and reactions are facilitated. The section that follows provides help in working with persons who are nonambulatory or clumsy because of developmental delays.

Reflexes

Primitive reflexes are involuntary, predictable changes in muscle tone in response to sensory input. These changes may be movements of body parts or as subtle as shifting of muscle tone (i.e., a tightening up or tensing). You need to understand reflexes for many reasons. The most common orthopedic impairment in the public schools is cerebral palsy; this condition is characterized by retention of primitive reflexes into late childhood and sometimes throughout life.

Table 10.1
Reflexes of most importance to physical educators.

Reflex	Age of Dominance	Muscle Tone	Body Part	Distribution
1. Tonic labyrinthine-prone	0–4 months	Flexion	Total body	Total
2. Tonic labyrinthine-supine	0–4 months	Extension	Total body	Total
3. Asymmetrical tonic neck	0–4 months	Flexion-extension	Arms	Asymmetrical
4. Symmetrical tonic neck	6–8 months	Flexion-extension	Arms-legs	Symmetrical
5. Moro	0–4 months	Extension	Arms-hands	Symmetrical
6. Hand grasp	0–4 months	Flexion	Hands-arms	Symmetrical
7. Foot grasp	0–9 months	Flexion	Toes, feet	Symmetrical
8. Extensor thrust	0–3 months	Extension	Legs	Symmetrical
9. Crossed extension	0–3 months	Flexion-extension	Legs	Symmetrical
10. Positive supporting-legs	3–8 months	Extension	Legs-trunk	Symmetrical

Note. Content for table was taken from Fiorentino (1981) and the *Milani-Comparetti Motor Development Screening Text Manual* (1987). Age range in which reflex is considered normal varies considerably, with some sources adding 1 to 2 months to those cited above.

Many persons with learning disabilities, mental retardation, autism, and developmental delays also exhibit reflex problems.

Approximately 30 primitive reflexes dominate infants' motor behavior. Some assessment approaches include all of these reflexes (Barnes et al., 1990; Fiorentino, 1963). In extensive observation of clumsy students, Sherrill has found that only about 10 primitive reflexes affect physical education performance (see Table 10.1). Only these reflexes are covered in this text, and they are presented in a special format so that you can copy the information on each one and paste it on a 5-inch-by-7-inch study card.

Table 10.1 states the average age range during which each reflex dominates in normal development and indicates that most reflexes are integrated by 4 months of age, and all are integrated by 9 months of age. *Integration, however, is never total or complete.* Abnormal reflex activity is recognized in clumsy movements at all ages. The muscle tone of body parts shifts in predictable ways when new activities are tried and/or we are tired or anxious. Although primitive reflex responses are layered over and thus suppressed by increasingly refined movement patterns, the layering or integration varies greatly from individual to individual. The reflexes are always there, ready to burst forth.

Table 10.1 shows the muscle tone that becomes dominant in each pattern, thereby interrupting the balance that should characterize the relationship between opposing muscle groups. When the predominant tone is flexion, more tension is seen on the anterior surface of the body than the posterior. Usually, the affected body parts are bent. When the predominant tone is extension, the opposite is true. The posterior surface shows tenseness, and the body parts are straightened and sometimes stiff. The exception to this generalization about the relationship between body surface and prime mover is knee joint actions.

Table 10.1 also summarizes the body parts affected by the reflexes and the nature of the muscle tone distribution (total, symmetrical, or asymmetrical). The two reflexes affecting the total body are the most serious. Reflexes affecting the legs interfere with locomotor activities, while those affecting the arms and hands make ball-handling patterns look awkward.

The following explanations of each reflex include three parts: (a) description, (b) contributions during the time the reflex is normal, and (c) problems caused by abnormal retention of the reflexes. In infancy, all reflexes are good and serve a definite purpose. Normal motor development cannot proceed until the purpose is achieved. If, however, a reflex outlasts its time, it becomes a liability, preventing the emergence of the motor milestones that are programmed to emerge after its integration.

Reflex Integration in Teaching

If not integrated, the primitive reflexes discussed in the preceding section affect physical education instruction. First, they explain why some students continue to make movement errors in spite of corrective feedback. Good examples are students who continue bending the elbow in tennis strokes, who fail to follow through across midline in throwing, and who cannot get the total body to work together smoothly in a forward roll or jump. Such students often say, "I know what I'm supposed to do. I can visualize every part. I just can't make my body do what my mind says." In essence, these students are saying that they do not have the cortical control to override reflex patterns. Visual and auditory instructions (their own self-talk or the teacher's input) are not effective when used alone because they are directed toward the thinking parts of the brain when the problem is at the lower levels.

Tonic Labyrinthine Reflex (TLR)-Prone

Description

Increased flexor tone in response to any change in the position of head. Figure 10.10A shows an infant in prone; the TLR is responsible for this position. Figure 10.10B shows an older child who is severely delayed.

Contributions

Stimulates flexor tone of total body.

Problems

Results in abnormal distribution of muscle tone and inability of body segments to move independently of one another. Prevents raising head, which, in turn, prevents development of symmetrical tonic neck reflex, righting reactions, and Landau extensor reaction. Characteristic shoulder protraction (abduction) results in inability to move arms from under body (see Figure 10.10B). Infant or person with severe disabilities dominated by TLR is virtually helpless. Compromises any activity done against gravity from a prone position.

FIGURE 10.10

Two examples of tonic labyrinthine reflex–prone.

A

B

Tonic Labyrinthine Reflex (TLR)-Supine

Description

Increased extensor tone in response to any change in position of head.

Contributions

Helps create a balance between extensor and flexor muscles.

FIGURE 10.11

Two examples of tonic labyrinthine reflex–supine. (*A*) Older adult showing opisthotonic or windswept position, spasticity in which head and heels are bent backward. (*B*) Six-year-old with severe cerebral palsy.

Problems

Domination by extensor tone, which holds shoulders in retraction (adduction) and prevents or compromises head raising, bringing limbs to midline, and rotation (turning) of body. In persons with severe disability, may contribute to windswept (opisthotonic) position (see Figure 10.11A).

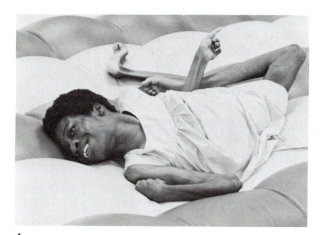

A

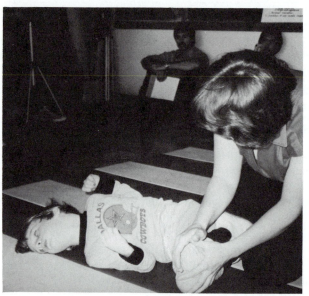

B

Description

On-guard, fencing position activated by rotation or lateral flexion (tilt) of head. Increased extensor tonus of limbs on chin side and increased flexor tonus in limbs on head side.

Contributions

Helps break up flexor and extensor pattern dominance so that each side of body can function separately.

Problems

1. Prevents learning to roll from supine to prone and vice versa since extended arm gets in the way.
2. Interferes with limb movement, which, in turn, impairs normal hand-eye coordination development. Associated problem is loss of visual fixation.
3. Prevents independent flexing of limb to bring it toward midline, as in playing with object or feeding self. Helps explain why persons bend their elbow in tennis forehand drive; as head rotates to left to see ball, right elbow flexes.
4. Causes one arm to bend or collapse in the beginning forward roll position if head tilts or rotates even slightly.
5. In sport positions that involve a rotated head, such as softball batting or tennis stance, prevents or compromises the bat or racquet crossing midline and, thus, properly following through.
6. In severe conditions, may contribute to scoliosis, subluxed or dislocated hips, or windswept lying position.

FIGURE 10.12

Adolescent with cerebral palsy exhibiting asymmetrical tonic neck reflex.

Failure of this reflex to become integrated explains much of the clumsiness physical educators observe, especially in relation to ball activities (see Figure 10.12). Many of the verbal cues that physical educators give ("Keep your eye on the ball." "Don't bend your elbow." "Remember to follow through.") are not commands that can be entirely consciously implemented. Thus, bright, but clumsy, students often think and sometimes respond, "I know what I'm doing wrong, but my body won't do what my mind tells it."

Description

Flexion and extension movements of the head influence muscle tone distribution in relation to upper and lower body. Head flexion increases flexor tone of upper body and extensor tone of lower body; head extension does the opposite (see Figure 10.13). Predominant upper-body muscle tone is always that of the head and neck.

Contributions

Contributes to such important motor milestones as lifting and supporting upper body on arms and rising to four-point creeping position.

Problems

1. Prevents reciprocal flexion and extension movement of legs needed in creeping (i.e., with head up, child is frozen in bunny-hop position).
2. Compromises ability to do certain stunts, exercises, and animal walks with head up. Makes holding legs extended difficult in regulation push-up position, in prone scooterboard activities, and in wheelbarrow races.
3. Compromises ability to do exercises, stunts, gymnastics, and synchronized swimming that require head held down in tucked position with knees simultaneously tucked to chest. Explains why "tuck position" is difficult to maintain as head changes position from flexion to extension (i.e., why persons come out of their tuck too soon).
4. Compromises sitting position. Head down helps activate extensor thrust in lower extremities; increases high-guard position of arms. Head up contributes to good sitting posture

FIGURE 10.13

Two symmetrical tonic neck reflexes (STNR). (*A*) Flexion STNR. (*B*) Extension STNR. Child is in creeping or bunny-hop position.

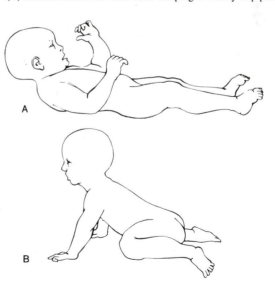

but increases difficulty of hand and arm activities that entail flexion, like lifting arm for overarm throw.

5. Looking down at ground or balance beam when walking compromises distribution of muscle tone; helps to explain gait of toddler with arms in high guard and abnormally stiff leg action and/or tendency to toe walk.

Description

The body stiffens and arms and legs involuntarily spread and close in response to unstable lying/sitting surface or falling movement (see Figure 10.14).

Contributions

Contributes to development of extensor and abductor strength of upper extremities, including fingers; serves as precursor to propping and parachute reactions.

Problems

Interferes with learning to sit and using the arms for balance. Prevents using one arm at a time.

FIGURE 10.14

Two phases of the Moro reflex. (*A*) Spread. (*B*) Close.

A

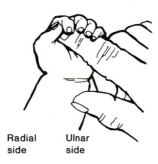

B

Description

Flexion of fingers in response to object being drawn across palm or hypertension of wrist (see Figure 10.15).

Contributions

Tactile stimulation by object in hand is the beginning of eye-hand coordination and visual body awareness.

Problems

Interferes with development of voluntary grasp; compromises tactile sensory input.

FIGURE 10.15

Hand grasp reflex.

Radial side   Ulnar side

Description

Flexion of toes (clawing motion) in response to deep pressure stimulation of soles of feet, as in standing or when object is pressed against toes (see Figure 10.16).

Contributions

Tactile stimulation enhances body awareness. The reflex also strengthens foot muscles.

Problems

Interferes with balance in walking and standing. Often seen in conjunction with positive supporting reflex (increased extensor tone that results in toe walking).

FIGURE   10.16

Foot grasp reflex.

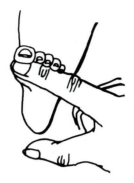

Description

Increased extensor tone throughout the body evoked by stimulus of sudden pressure to soles of feet. Most often mentioned in conjunction with sitting postures, a common problem in nonambulatory persons with cerebral palsy (see Figure 10.17). In first 2 months, sometimes mistaken for early standing ability.

Contributions

Strengthens extensors, thereby promoting balance between flexor and extensor postural tone.

Problems

Inability to maintain proper sitting position; entire body stiffens so that person slides out of wheelchair unless strapped into one that is specially made. Usually occurs in conjunction with positive supporting reflex of legs and/or tonic labyrinthine supine reflex or symmetrical tonic neck reflex. Often, the abnormal movement produced by one or both of these is called an *extensor thrust pattern* (i.e., the term is not limited to action of the extensor thrust reflex alone).

FIGURE   10.17

Extensor thrust reflex or pattern.

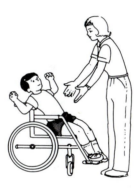

Description

Elicited by flexing or tapping medial surface of one leg. One leg reflexly affects the other (see Figure 10.18A). Evidenced when one leg cannot flex (as in kicking a ball) without associated extension of the other leg. Also evidenced when medial surface of upper legs touches or rubs against one another; this stimulus contributes to scissoring. Correct positioning in a wheelchair, with bolster between thighs, prevents this.

Contributions

Helps to break up dominant symmetrical flexion and extension patterns. Facilitates development of extensor tone to stand on one leg while the other leg flexes (i.e., permits reciprocal leg movements needed for creeping and walking).

Problems

1. Prevents coordinated leg movements needed to crawl, creep, and walk.
2. Causes scissoring of legs (see Figure 10.18B).
3. Sometimes serves as substitute for absent positive support reflex in athetosis and ataxia. Child can stand only on stiffly extended legs and raises legs too high in walking.

Problems Combined With Positive Supporting Reflex

1. Affects kicking in a standing position. When leg is lifted to kick ball, a strong extensor spasm affects support leg and causes loss of balance. Child loses balance because he or she pushes reflexly against ground with ball of support foot (positive supporting reflex thereby reinforcing extensor spasm); this is accompanied by knee hyperextension and clawing of toes. To prevent falling backward, reflex activates flexion of trunk at hips and brings kicking leg down and forward, leaving weight-bearing foot, leg, hip, and shoulder behind. This rotary movement prevents straight follow-through in the kick.

FIGURE 10.18

Two examples of crossed extension reflex. (*A*) In testing position. (*B*) In scissors gait.

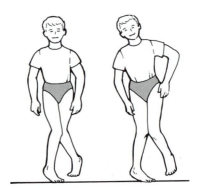

A

B

2. Affects walking pattern. Results in hyperextended knees, clawing of toes, and hip flexion in support leg to prevent falling. This is typically compensated for by forward flexion of head and lordosis.

Description

Increased extensor tone (plantar flexion at ankle joint) caused by soles of feet touching floor or footrests of wheelchair.

Contributions

Strengthens hip and leg extensors needed for straight-back sitting and standing.

Problems

1. When fully present, prevents independent standing and walking; creates difficulty (along with extensor thrust reflex) in wheelchair posture adjustments and/or wheelchair transfers because sensory input from foot plates stimulates soles of feet, which, in turn, increases extensor tone.
2. When partially present, affects walking gait by causing toe walking (prevents placing heel on floor), contributing (with crossed extension reflex) to scissoring, narrowing base of support, and producing backward thrust of trunk with compensatory lordosis and arm out to assist with balance (see Figure 10.19).
3. Also interferes with kicking a ball (see crossed extensor reflex).

FIGURE 10.19

Two examples of positive supporting reflex. (*A*) Toe-pointing and foot-stiffening response to foot touch in assisted jumping. (*B*) Toe walking, usually unstable.

A   B

FIGURE 10.20

Rood's developmental exercises that have stood the test of time. (See more about Rood on page 267.)

A. Body tuck. Helps normalize tonic labyrinthine reflexes.

B. Rollover with limbs on one side flexed. Helps normalize asymmetrical tonic neck reflex.

C. Pivot prone, swan, or wing lift. Helps normalize tonic labyrinthine and symmetrical tonic neck reflexes.

D. Head lift and hold neck co-contraction. Promotes strength.

E. Prone-on-elbows. Helps normalize symmetrical tonic neck reflex.

F. Four-point or creeping. Promotes strength.

G. Standing. With practice on stand-to-squat, stand-to-sit, stand-to-lie, and vice versa.

H. Walking. Arm opposition and trunk rotation begin at age 4 to 5 years.

Principles of Reflex Integration

In working with students with reflex problems, remember four principles:

1. Maximize tactile, kinesthetic, and vestibular (TKV) input.
2. Use total body movement patterns and games that inhibit reflexes.
3. Increase practice time and time-on-task for correctly executed patterns.
4. Intensify individual assistance so that patterns are performed correctly. Pay particular attention to head position.

TKV input is maximized mainly by four strategies. *Coactive movement* is the professional term for teacher and student moving together, bodies touching, so that the student receives input from all three modalities (TKV) concurrently. *Passive assistance* refers to the teacher moving only one body part of the student. *Tactile cueing* refers to tapping or rubbing a body part to reinforce memory. *Balancing activities* (both static and dynamic) give the CNS practice in processing input from TKV modalities as well as vision. Balancing should be interpreted as achieving and maintaining stability in all kinds of positions.

Many authorities recommend spending part of class time on total body management activities in prone and supine lying positions (see Figure 10.20). The body tuck, roll, and pivot prone are universally accepted as tasks that promote neurological integration (Pyfer, 1988; Stockmeyer, 1978). The tasks in Figure 10.20 were first proposed by Margaret Rood in the 1950s and called the Rood mobility-stability model. This model emphasizes many exercises and positions common to physical educators, such as the supine tuck and hold, modified logroll, swan, and creeping. Whereas regular physical educators have used these exercises primarily to develop abdominal and back extensor strength, therapists believe the exercises facilitate sensory integration and neurological maturation. Whatever the rationale, the tasks have stood the test of time and should be incorporated into programming for awkward students.

Creative teachers can devise many games and exercises that utilize these patterns. Of particular importance is practice in moving the head (up, down, right, left) alone or in combination with designated body parts while striving to inhibit undesired associated movements.

Overflow (Associated Movements)

A common indicator of clumsiness is associated movements, also called overflow. These are undesired reflex responses of body parts that should remain stationary. Examples are (a) facial grimaces when concentrating on a hand-eye or hand-foot motor task, (b) an increase in muscle tone or a mirroring action on the noninvolved side when trying to perform one-arm or one-leg acts, and (c) unnecessary, uncoordinated, or funny-looking movements of the arms during locomotion. Associated movements are caused by poorly integrated reflexes. They are remnants of the mass flexor and extensor patterns present at birth, when body parts cannot move independently of one another. As such, associated movements are normal in early childhood, diminish by ages 6 to 8 years, and generally disappear by adolescence.

Simply telling a student to stop an associated movement does not work because reflex mechanisms can be overridden only by many, many repetitions of the correct movement pattern. Programming should therefore include many activities like *Simon Says* that provide practice in moving one body part at a time. Such activities, which help the nervous system to organize sensorimotor processes and facilitate subcortical motor planning, are discussed further in Chapters 12, 16, and 17.

Four Most Troublesome Reflexes

Understanding of the cause-effect relationship between specific reflex mechanisms and associated movements helps teachers to be precise in planning remediation. Of the 10 reflexes, the four initiated by head movements are generally the most troublesome. These are the tonic labyrinthine reflex-prone (TLR-prone), tonic labyrinthine reflex-supine (TLR-supine), asymmetrical tonic neck reflex (ATNR), and symmetrical tonic neck reflex (STNR). In these four reflexes, the student cannot move the head without initiating associated movements or subtle muscle tone tensions of other body parts.

Remediation is thus directed toward practice in moving the head and (a) keeping everything else stationary or (b) simultaneously performing body part movements that are the opposites of what the reflex mechanisms enact. This is essentially the same as repeatedly performing a skill the *right way* as called for in the principle of specificity (i.e., practice the specific pattern in which you want skill). Achieving the *right way,* however, is often impossible without special focus on the head.

The tonic labyrinthine reflexes help explain coordination and control problems in exercises done from lying positions like, for example, sit-ups from supine, trunk lifts from prone, rolling over, and moving rapidly from lying to standing positions, as in recoveries from falls and dives in such sports as volleyball. The tonic labyrinthine reflexes also help to explain the abnormal standing, walking, and jumping postures seen in many persons with severe disability (see Figure 10.21). When gravity acts to pull the head downward and the total body responds by assuming a flexion posture, the reflex responsible is the TLR-prone. When the head, for

FIGURE 10.21

Many abnormal locomotor postures are caused by the tonic labyrinthine reflexes (TLR). (*A*) Posture caused by TLR–prone. (*B*) Posture caused by TLR–supine. In both, postural integration has not been achieved.

A   B

any reason, is thrown backward and the total body responds in an extension posture, the reflex responsible is the TLR-supine.

The ATNR and STNR are operative when only part of the body responds reflexively to head movements. The ATNR explains clumsiness in activities involving head and trunk rotation. Head turning causes obligatory extension patterns of limbs on the face side and simultaneous obligatory flexion patterns on the nonface side. Think how many sport patterns require turning the head to the right and left and how obligatory arm responses or subtle muscle tone shifts make movements look and feel awkward. In contrast, the STNR explains clumsiness in activities that involve the top and bottom parts of the body working together. When the STNR is operative, up and down head movements cause obligatory bilateral arm and leg responses.

The developmental sequence followed by most children in learning the long jump provides a good example of how the jump matures as the STNR is progressively better integrated (see Figure 10.22). In Level 1, as the head and trunk extend, the legs should be able to extend also to provide power for the jump. Instead, the legs stay flexed more than they should because the STNR pattern of *head up, arms extended, legs flexed* is not yet totally integrated. In Levels 2 and 3, the lower extremities are affected less and less by the head movement, and the legs and arms can extend simultaneously in the takeoff and flight and bend simultaneously in the landing.

Sometimes, several reflexes, rather than one, contribute to lack of coordination and control. This is often the case in the jump. In addition to the STNR, the jump may be affected by the four reflexes that act on the feet and legs: foot grasp, extensor thrust, crossed extension, and positive

FIGURE   10.22

Developmental levels in standing long jump. In Level 1, the symmetrical tonic neck reflex (STNR) has not yet been integrated. In Levels 2 and 3, as STNR integration is better achieved, the lower extremities are affected less and less by head movement.

Level 1

Level 2

Level 3

supporting-legs. Except for the foot grasp, these reflexes all cause extension of the lower extremities and interfere with the flexion needed to land smoothly and comfortably. These four reflexes also affect locomotion. Extreme pigeon-toed walking (hip adduction and inward rotation patterns) called *scissoring* is elicited by crossed extension and positive supporting reflexes.

In summary, the primitive reflexes become progressively better integrated in normally functioning children without external help. By 9 months of age, most reflexes have changed from gross body movement to subtle muscle tone shifts or associated movements. Ordinary everyday practice, coupled with normal development, continue to integrate the reflexes so that they are not a problem for most children. In contrast, individuals who evidence psychomotor problems need teachers who understand reflexes and can work to integrate them.

Reactions

Reactions are automatic responses to sensory input that act to keep body parts in alignment, maintain equilibrium, and prevent injury. Some reactions replace reflexes, but others emerge to perform unique functions. In normal development, reactions appear between the ages of 2 and 18 months. With a few exceptions (e.g., the Landau and body derotative), these reactions persist throughout life. Some authorities believe that delays in the appearance of postural reactions are more detrimental to motor success than reflex disorders, especially in severe mental retardation (Molnar, 1978). Many persons, of course, have both reflex and reaction problems.

This text describes only the most important reactions, the ones that physical educators need to be able to assess and facilitate. Like reflexes, these develop naturally and are taken for granted in regular physical education. Reactions are primarily important for their role in balance and help to explain why so many clumsy individuals have balance problems.

There are basically three categories of reactions: (a) righting, (b) parachute, and (c) equilibrium. Righting reactions are adjustments of the head or trunk. Parachute reactions are protective extension movements of the limbs. Equilibrium reactions are total body responses. Assessment and programming for clumsy students should include consideration of each type of reaction.

FIGURE 10.23

Four types of righting reactions. Optical righting reactions comprise the fifth type.

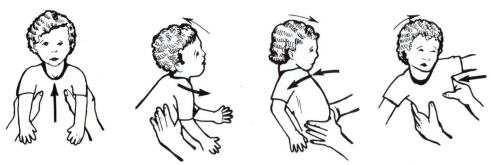

A. Head-in-space and optical righting reactions when held upright and tilted forward, backward, and sideward. Bottom arrow shows movement created by teacher's positioning or testing. Top arrow shows head movement that results if child has normal response.

Immature   Mature

B. Body righting in sagittal plane (Landau)

C. Body derotative (segmental rolling)

D. Body rotative (rise to sit or stand)

Righting Reactions

Righting reactions are the automatic postural responses elicited by sensory input that signals that the head or trunk is not in midline. The first three righting reactions (head-in-space, optical righting, and Landau) are up, down, and sideways compensatory actions, whereas the last two reactions (body derotative and body rotative) are rotational movements. Figure 10.23 illustrates the righting reactions.

Head-in-Space

The head-in-space righting reactions emerge at about 2 months of age and persist throughout life. They are elicited by holding the child vertically upright in the air and then slowly tilting him or her forward, backward, and sideward

(see Figure 10.23A). In each tilt, the head automatically moves in the direction opposite the tilt. Of course, the entire body follows the head, so this mechanism helps a person to return to an upright, midline position. *Midline* is defined as the position in which the nose is vertical and the mouth and eyes are horizontal. The head-in-space righting reactions are elicited by vestibular input. Hence, the head-in-space righting reactions are also called labyrinthine or vestibular patterns.

Optical Righting

The optical righting reactions are precisely the same as the head-in-space reactions except that the responses are elicited by visual input to the optic nerve instead of vestibular input. Optical righting develops soon after the head-in-space reactions appear and remains active throughout the lifespan.

Normally, both reactions work together. The optical righting reactions are, however, dependent upon the integrity of the head-in-space reactions and the integration of the primitive reflexes that act on the head. Persons with abnormal muscle tone distribution, like those with cerebral palsy, can use vision to know the head is not properly aligned. However, the optical reactions are not able to automatically correct the head alignment problem in cerebral palsy.

In young children and/or those with severe disability, no attempt should be made to assess or work with head-in-space and optical righting separately. With older students, however, a blindfold may be used in head-in-space work to eliminate visual input. In summary, the vestibular and visual systems work together to always return the head to midline. Body parts follow the head, and balance is preserved. These reactions must be overridden by higher CNS centers in activities requiring purposeful loss of balance (e.g., falls for fun, various activities in dance, gymnastics, and aquatics, and diving).

Landau

The Landau reaction, also called body in sagittal plane righting, is an extension response of the trunk, hips, knees, and ankles that occurs in prone position when the head is lifted (see Figure 10.23B). As the term *sagittal* indicates, the righting is in the up-and-down or flexion-extension plane. The Landau develops shortly after the head-in-space reactions are established. In essence, the Landau is a spreading of the extensor tone of the lifted head down the muscles of the back and legs.

The Landau is assessed from a prone position in the air or water, called ventral suspension. The Landau is one of the few reactions that is integrated instead of persisting throughout life. It serves a specific developmental function not needed after about 3 years of age. Specifically, the Landau facilitates the change from the flexion posture of infancy to the fully extended prone position with head up and back arched, called the pivot prone in therapy and the *swan, wing lift,* or *front rocker* in physical education. The Landau overrides the STNR pattern (head extended, arms extended, legs flexed) so that the legs can be fully extended at the same time the head and arms are extended. The ability to maintain a pivot prone position is one of the first milestones in mastering the one-handed reach and grasp from a prone position. Without the Landau, the pivot prone pattern cannot emerge.

Body Derotative and Rotative

Developmentally, the capacity to rotate the body develops after flexion, extension, abduction, and adduction patterns are established. At 2 months of age, infants reflexly roll from side to back or side to prone, but a full body roll is not possible because the lower arm is stiff and straight and will not get out of the way (i.e., the ATNR prevents rolling). This reflex must be integrated and the righting reactions must be

FIGURE 10.24

Infants are about 4 months old before they can roll over independently.

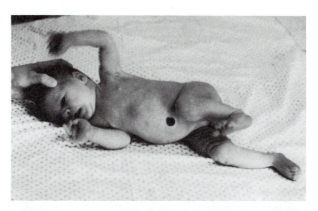

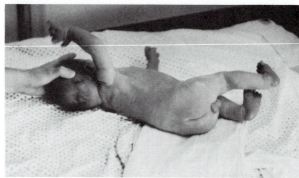

A. Logroll pattern, birth to 4 months

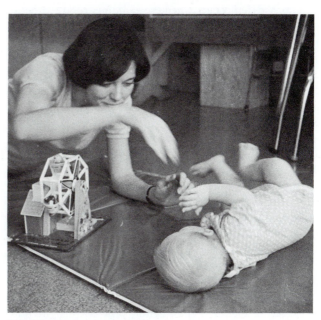

B. Independent segmental rolling.

FIGURE 10.25

Body rotative reaction in immature rise-to-stand that utilizes trunk rotation and arm assistance. Film tracings of a 17-year-old girl with cerebral palsy, who demonstrates body rotative pattern of normal 9-to-12-month-old infant. The mature rise-to-stand requires no trunk rotation and no arm assistance.

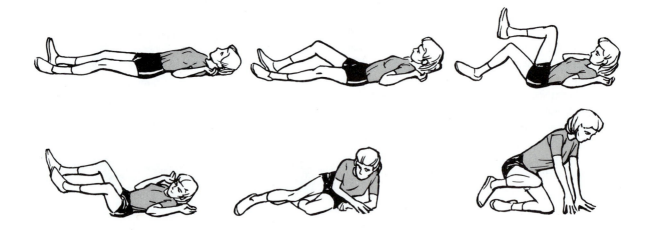

operative for independent rolling to be possible. Total body rotation patterns, like rolling over or rising from lie to sit or stand, thus require considerable nervous system integrity. The body derotative (segmental rolling) and body rotative (rise-to-sit or rise-to-stand) reactions are needed until about age 5 years to assist in rotatory actions (see Figure 10.23C, D).

The body derotative is an automatic segmental rolling response that occurs when the examiner rotates a body part. Until the age of 4 months, the infant does not have this reaction, and the body plops over as a rigid unit, called a logroll pattern (see Figure 10.24). From age 4 months until about 5 years, the normally functioning individual responds to external body part rotation by rolling over one segment at a time (head, then shoulders, then trunk, then hips, or vice versa).

The body rotative or rise-to-sit/rise-to-stand reaction is elicited by placing a wide-awake child in a supine lie. The body rotative is the ability to move segment by segment from a supine lie to some other position: a four-point, a sit, or a stand, depending on developmental level. If children have the coordination to rotate up to a more functional position, doing so is a normal response.

Rise-to-stand or scramble up, a widely used screening activity for all age groups, is derived from the body rotative reaction. Beginning in a supine lie, the person is challenged to rise to a stand as fast as he or she can. Observation of the efficiency of this action provides insight into overall coordination. The rise-to-stand (body rotative) is the righting reaction most often examined in school-age children (see Figure 10.25).

Parachute or Propping Reactions

The parachute or propping reactions are protective extension movements of the limbs used to break or prevent a fall. There are four such reactions, named for the direction in which the body is falling (downward, sideward, forward, and backward) (see Figure 10.26). The downward parachute, which refers to being dropped or falling feet first, is the only one that involves the legs. The other three reactions are the natural propping responses of both arms (falling forward or backward) or one arm (falling sideward).

The parachute reactions, like the reflexes that cause arm movements, are elicited by vestibular input, which signals a change in the movement of the head. The arm-propping reactions are generally tested from a sitting position, with the examiner gently pushing the child off balance. Developmentally, the downward parachute develops first (about 4 months); in it, the child extends and spreads the legs, thereby automatically preparing for a wide-based and therefore safe landing. The sideward parachute develops next, at 6 to 8 months, then the forward parachute at 7 to 8 months, and the backward parachute at 9 to 10 months. All of the parachute reactions remain throughout the lifespan. These reactions are often delayed or absent in persons with severe disability and thus constitute adapted physical education goals.

Equilibrium or Tilting Reactions

The equilibrium (or tilting) reactions are total body responses that, when mature, prevent falls. They appear between the ages of 5 and 18 months and remain the entire life. These reactions, initiated primarily by vestibular input, can

FIGURE 10.26

Four types of parachute or propping reactions (protective extensions). All responses are limb movements.

A. Downward. Normal response to downward thrust: abduction, wide base, 4 months on.

B. Sideward. Normal response to sideward thrust, 6 to 8 months.

C. Forward. Normal response to forward thrust, 7 to 8 months.

D. Backward. Normal response to backward thrust, 9 to 10 months.

be elicited in any position the body assumes, but testing is usually limited to five positions (see Figure 10.27). Listed developmentally in the order of their appearance, these are (a) prone equilibrium, 5 months; (b) supine equilibrium, 7 to 8 months; (c) sitting equilibrium, 8 months; (d) all-fours equilibrium, 8 to 12 months; and (e) standing equilibrium, 14 to 18 months. To assess these reactions, the teacher must have or be able to create an unstable surface that can be tipped about 15° in any direction. A mat or cushion can be moved from side to side, or a tilt board or large ball can be maneuvered to cause loss of equilibrium. These reactions can also be observed in trampoline work or in locomotor activities on unstable surfaces.

The equilibrium responses are all rotatory and can perhaps best be observed by focusing on the spinal curvature needed to maintain balance. Curves are described as convex (rounded like the back of a *C*) or concave (hollow like the front of a *C*). In mature equilibrium responses, the concavity of the spinal curve is always uphill. The face and trunk are rotated toward the uphill side. In some sources, the uphill side is called the stressed side (Ramm, 1988). In forward-backward tilts, the face and trunk bend or curve toward uphill. In side-to-side tilts, the face and trunk rotate toward the up side.

The position of the limbs also should be noted. Limbs on the uphill side are abducted (raised or held away from midline) and extended. Limbs on the downhill side tend

to be adducted (drawn in toward the body) and flexed. Forward-backward tilts elicit bilateral arm movements (i.e., both arms do the same thing). Sideward tilts cause the arms to do opposite things.

In normal development, this rhythmical shifting of the arm and leg positions with the up-and-down movement of the tilting surface is automatic and graceful. Absence or immaturity of these reactions results in balance problems. If the student's balance is disrupted to the extent that the reactions are not effective in recovering an upright posture, the arms will automatically move into the protective extension patterns of the parachute reactions to break the fall.

Standing equilibrium may involve steps as well as shifts in alignment of body parts. Stepping reactions (also called hopping, shifting, or staggering reactions) are the steps a person automatically takes to keep his or her balance in a standing posture. These are a more mature type of equilibrium reaction than those previously discussed. Stepping reactions are often seen when children try to maintain a one-foot balance.

Balance Assessment and Remediation

The balance problems that most clumsy individuals exhibit are directly related to righting and equilibrium reactions. These reactions are mediated by different parts of the brain that receive and coordinate various kinds of sensory input.

FIGURE 10.27

Five types of equilibrium reactions. Note the concavity of the spinal curve is always uphill in the mature response. Also, the face and trunk are rotated toward the uphill side.

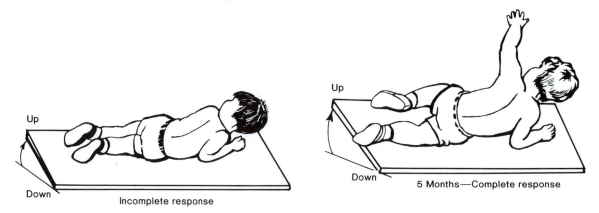

Up

Down — Incomplete response

Up

Down — 5 Months—Complete response

A. Prone equilibrium (5 months)

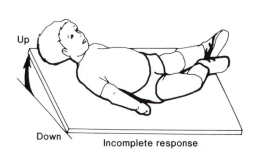

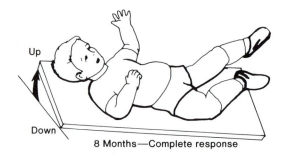

Up

Down — Incomplete response

Up

Down — 8 Months—Complete response

B. Supine equilibrium (7 to 8 months)

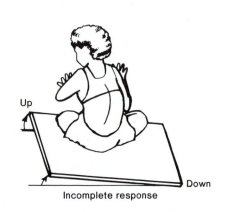

Up

Incomplete response — Down

Up

Complete response — Down

C. Sitting equilibrium (8 months)

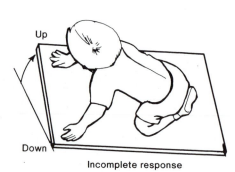

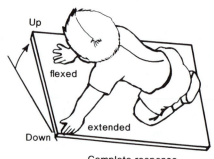

Up

Down — Incomplete response

Up

flexed

extended

Down — Complete response

D. All-fours equilibrium (8 to 12 months)

FIGURE   10.27 (continued)

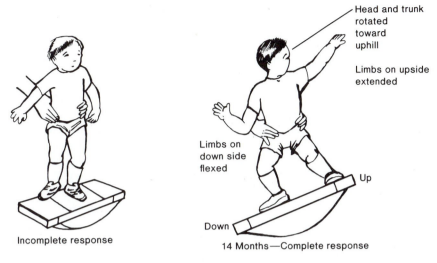

Head and trunk rotated toward uphill

Limbs on upside extended

Limbs on down side flexed

Up

Down

14 Months—Complete response

Incomplete response

E. Standing equilibrium (14 to 18 months)

FIGURE   10.28

Tilting reactions.

Backward tilt   Level   Forward tilt

Forward tilt should result in extension/hyperextension of head, neck, and trunk and in adduction of scapulae. *Backward tilt* should result in flexion of head, neck, and trunk and abduction of scapulae.

Backward tilt   Level   Forward tilt

Sideward tilt should result in rotation of the head and trunk toward the uptilting side. There is also flexion and abduction of the limbs on the uptilting side; the opposite characterizes limbs on the downtilting side.

Backward tilt   Level   Forward tilt

Forward tilt on all-fours results in symmetrical extension tonic neck reflex posture.

Traditionally, balance tests have focused only on time-on-balance. This chapter provides background information to extend assessment to include qualitative analysis of problems and classify performance as (a) no loss of balance, (b) success of equilibrium reactions in stopping a balance loss, (c) nonsuccess of equilibrium reactions, and (d) no evidence of equilibrium reactions.

Balance is considered both a perceptual-motor ability and a component of motor fitness. Assessment and remediation of standing and locomotor balance are further discussed in Chapter 12. Adapted physical educators, however, often work with lying, sitting, and all-fours balance, as indicated in Figure 10.28. In most cases, tilt or balance boards should be the first pieces of equipment the professional constructs or requests. Playground apparatus (e.g., swings, seesaws, slides) also affords opportunities for teaching lying, sitting, and all-fours balance. Think of games and rhythms that can be used to keep hundreds of practice trials interesting and fun. For older children, horseback riding, cycling, and scooterboard/wagon activities are used specifically to develop sitting balance (Biery & Kauffman, 1989).

Neurologically, balance is not well understood. It involves organization of tactile, kinesthetic, vestibular, and visual data at both subcortical and cortical levels. Research indicates that balance is related to cognition and academic success (Ayres, 1972; Gorman, 1983; Quiros & Schrager, 1978). This may be partly because sitting balance and head control are prerequisites for success in the average classroom. Reading and writing skills, like balance, are dependent upon intersensory integration. It makes sense that academic remediation should be *supplemented* by intensive practice of activities designed to help tactile, kinesthetic, vestibular, and visual integration.

Milani-Comparetti Assessment System

Of the many assessment systems that include reflexes and reactions, the Milani-Comparetti (MC) protocol is perhaps the easiest and most appropriate for physical educators (Milani-Comparetti & Gidoni, 1967). Figure 10.29 shows that the scoring chart is divided into two sections: spontaneous behavior and evoked responses. Spontaneous behavior encompasses motor milestones in nine areas: *four* head postures, *three* body postures, and *two* active movement sequences. The evoked responses section includes 5 primitive reflexes and 13 postural reactions (righting, parachute, and tilting). Months listed horizontally across the top of the chart show the ages at which responses are normal. Administration of this test requires about 5 min.

Although function on the MC can be scored numerically (Ellison, Browning, Lawson, & Denny (1983)), most teachers use letters to note absence (A) or presence (P) of motor milestones, reflexes, and reactions. Noting appearance of muscle tone—hypotonic, normal, hypertonic, or fluctuating—is also important. This chapter already has covered all of the items on the MC except spontaneous behavior, the easy part! Let's briefly consider head and body control and active movement.

Motor Milestones on MC Chart

Head Control

Head control is assessed in four positions. As early as 1 month of age, normal infants can hold the head upright when they are held vertically in the air or against someone's chest. The angular lines on the MC chart next to "body held vertical" denote growing control from a few seconds at 1 month of age to several minutes at 4 months of age. In contrast, many adults with cerebral palsy have difficulty with this task.

In "body lying prone," infants exhibit three distinct developmental stages:

1.5 months Momentary head raise
3.0 months Holds head up 45° to 90° with chest up
4.0 months Holds head up and props on extended arms

In "body lying supine," the normal infant lifts the head at about 5 months (note location of the word *lifts* on MC chart). Between 5 and 7 months, this head lifting is observed in conjunction with playing with feet.

In "body pulled up from supine," the stick figures on the MC indicate the amount of head lag normal at each age when the body is pulled upward by the arms. Figure 10.30 depicts the first two test positions in this category with a normal infant.

Body Control

Body control is assessed in three positions. Stick figures on the MC indicate normal performances. Five developmental stages are depicted for "sitting." These are based on amount of spinal curve and ability to fully extend legs. Independent sitting is achieved between 6 and 8 months. The L3 next to the second figure on the MC chart indicates that the pro-

gressive head-to-foot uncurving of the vertebral column has extended downward to the level of the third lumbar segment by the age of 4 months.

"All-fours" refers to three developmental stages. *Forearms/hands* denotes a propping position, with head and chest up and weight taken on the forearms. This propping behavior begins between the ages of 3.5 and 6 months. The *creeping position* is listed as 4-feet kneeling; it begins between the ages of 7 and 9 months. *Plantigrade* refers to a bear walk position; infants can assume it between 10 and 12 months of age (see Figure 10.31).

"Standing" also develops through several stages, the first of which is controlled subcortically by supporting reactions (really a reflex). When the infant loses this reflex, *astasia* occurs (see Figure 10.32). This is a condition in which weight is taken momentarily, after which the body collapses. When infants take weight on their feet at about age 5 months, this is finally voluntary movement under cortical control. Independent standing does not occur until about 10 months.

Active Movement

"Standing up from a supine (lying) position" is evaluated in terms of amount of trunk rotation and arm assistance. Note four levels on the MC chart, extending from 9 months of age until 5 years. The mature rise-to-stand requires no trunk rotation and no arm assistance. "*Locomotion*" emphasizes rolling over between 4 and 6 months of age, creeping at around 7 months of age, and walking at about 12 months of age. The terms *high, medium, no guard* refer to the position of the arms.

Application to a 9-Year-Old

Let's now apply our knowledge about motor milestones, reflexes, and reactions to Kay, a 9-year-old born with cerebral palsy (CP) affecting all four limbs (see Figure 10.33). Kay's intelligence quotient is about 90 (i.e., low average). She is in the fourth grade of a public school in which she is mainstreamed into first-grade spelling and mathematics classes. The rest of the school day, she is in a self-contained class for multidisabled students. Kay receives adapted physical education on a one-to-one basis three times a week, 30 min a day. She also receives physical, occupational, speech, and music therapy in 30-min sessions.

Kay needs special equipment to help her function independently. She lacks the arm strength and control to maneuver a manual wheelchair, so a motorized chair is required. Kay is nonverbal, so a head pointer is essential so that she can point out words on a Bliss symbol board, type, and do art work. Figure 10.29 shows that all five primitive reflexes are present: hand grasp, ATNR, Moro, STNR, and foot grasp. This knowledge guides the physical educator in selecting which throwing, striking, and kicking patterns to teach Kay.

Also present is the crossed extensor reflex (not covered by the MC chart). This reflex adversely affects kicking a ball from a standing position and other reciprocal leg movements. When one leg is lifted to kick the ball, a strong extensor spasm affects the support leg and causes loss of balance.

FIGURE 10.29

Milani-Comparetti evaluation for Kay, a 9-year-old girl with athetoid cerebral palsy affecting control of head and all four limbs. An *A* on the chart indicates absence of a response, and a *P* indicates presence of a response. Note that absence is interpreted as bad under spontaneous behaviors and under righting, parachute, and tilting reactions, but as good in relation to primitive reflexes. The circled areas indicate the body positions that were attained. To interpret, the "Spontaneous Behavior" section indicates the actions Kay could perform independently. She could lift her head from prone- or supine-lying and when being pulled up into a sit-up position. She could not, however, maintain the head in an upright position when her body was vertical. She could sit independently only if the arms and legs were placed in the proper support position. Four-point kneeling could be maintained only momentarily. Kay could do no independent standing or locomotor activities. The "Evoked Responses" section indicates that all five reflexes were still present and that all reactions except *body derotative* were absent (i.e., Kay could do mature segmental rolling but otherwise totally lacked head and neck control and body equilibrium).

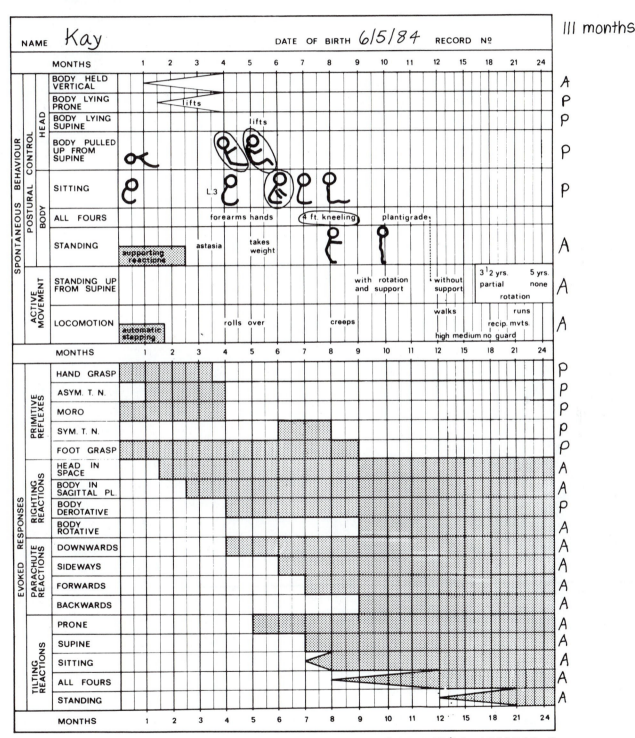

A. Milani Comparetti, E.A. Gidoni: Dev.Med.Child. Neurol. Vol. 9 No 5 Oct 67

255

FIGURE   10.30

Body pulled up from supine item on Milani-Comparetti chart.
(*A*) Normal infant at 1 month of age. (*B*) Normal infant at about 4
months.

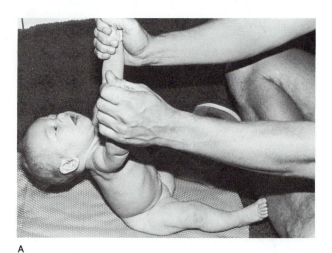
A

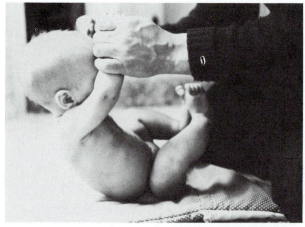
B

FIGURE   10.31

Plantigrade is a position in which the weight of the body is taken on the
hands and feet, but there is not yet enough neurological maturation for
reciprocal arm or leg creeping movements. Often, the infant rocks
forward and backward in plantigrade and appears to be playing or doing
tricks.

The crossed extensor reflex explains much of the awkwardness in young children learning to kick, as well as problems of students with CP.

In teaching object control to persons with tonic neck reflexes, position in relation to the target is very important. With the ATNR present, for instance, placing the throwing-arm side to the target, rather than facing it, is best. The best throwing pattern for Kay is arm extended sideward at shoulder height and pointed toward the target with most of the movement coming from wrist flexion. Because of the presence of the hand grasp reflex, release is very difficult. Therefore, beanbags are used rather than balls. Overall, striking activities offer Kay more success than throwing ones. Adaptations to pedagogy should be based on knowledge of which reflexes and reactions are present. Much research is needed in this area.

FIGURE   10.32

Earliest standing progression. (*A*) Supporting reaction elicited by top of foot rubbing against table. (*B*) Same infant in *astasia* as supporting reaction weakens and is lost.

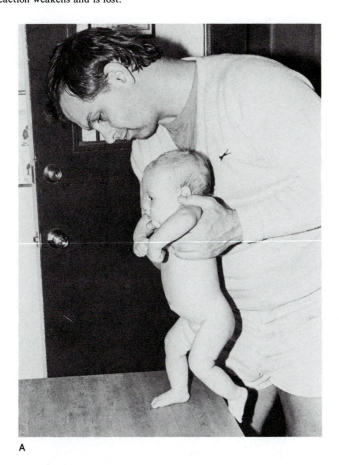

A

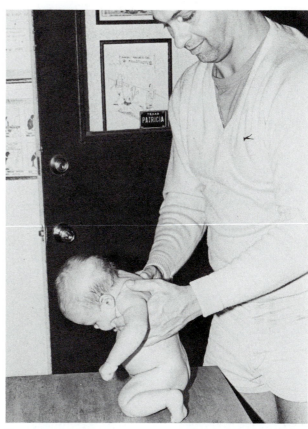

B

Pedagogy in Relation to Reflexes and Reactions

Physical education for young students with abnormal reflexes and balance problems is guided by the neurophysiological treatment approach of Bobath (1980). This approach rests on two principles:

1. Inhibition or suppression of abnormal reflex activity
2. Facilitation of righting, parachute, and equilibrium reactions in their proper developmental sequence

The first principle is achieved primarily through correct positioning and the proper selection of activities. With students who are severely disabled, correct positioning is achieved through specially designed wheelchairs and strapping of body parts. Maintaining the head in midline is especially important, since head rotation and flexion/extension elicit the ATNR and STNR, respectively. Velcro ties are often used to prevent undesirable head movement. Targets and/or balls to be hit off tees should be placed at eye level or, in the case of floor targets, far enough away so that the student does not drop the head to look downward. As long as therapists are striving to inhibit or suppress abnormal reflex activity, physical educators should cooperate. Often, however, this goal

is reevaluated at age 7 or 8 years, if it becomes evident that it may not be achievable. In this situation, the emphasis may change to finding ways the student can utilize reflex activity to his or her advantage. For instance, a side position to the target, with the head rotated to the right, thereby eliciting the ATNR, may make it easier to release objects with the right arm.

The second principle is achieved primarily through exercises, stunts, and games that follow the natural developmental sequence whereby students gain the strength and coordination needed to attain a proper balance between mobility and stability (i.e., voluntary control over purposeful movement as well as maintenance of a set posture against the pull of gravity). To understand students like Kay, we must know the neurological bases of movement.

Neurological Bases of Motor Development

Adapted physical activity specialists need to understand the neurological bases of motor development (Cowden & Eason, 1991; Sherrill, 1988). Regular educators also need to understand the neurological basis of clumsiness and some of the theories that guide teaching practices. The sections that follow introduce or review fundamentals.

FIGURE   **10.33**

Photos of the nine-year-old discussed on page 254 who has cerebral palsy. (*A*) Child with no arm/hand control using head pointer to touch symbols on a communication board. (*B*) Crossed extensor reflex interfering with kicking. This child should be taught kicking only from a sitting position. (*C*) One of several correct ways to position a child with cerebral palsy so head can be maintained in upright posture.

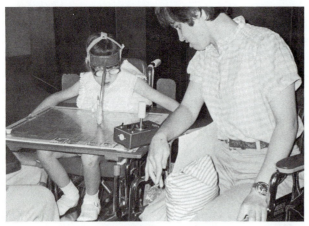

A

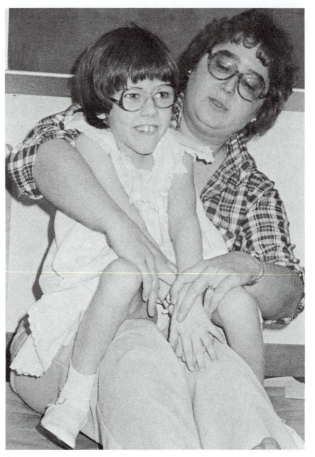

C

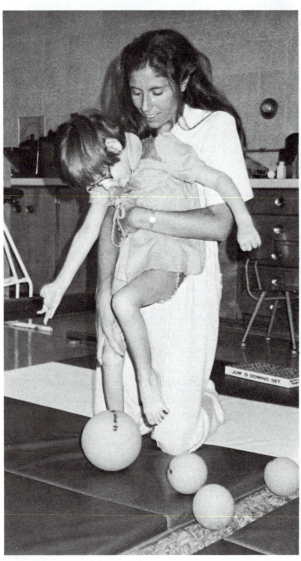

B

FIGURE 10.34

Growth of nerve cells (neurons) during infancy. Each nerve cell has three parts: cell body, dendrites, and axon. Cell bodies are located in the brain and spinal cord. Dendrites and axons are the nerve fibers that comprise nerves throughout the body and neural pathways (tracts) inside the spinal cord and brain.

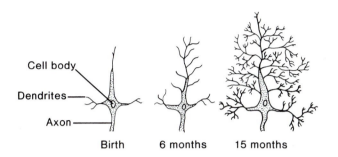

Organization of the Nervous System

The nervous system is organized as a *central nervous system* (brain and spinal cord) and as a *peripheral nervous system* (12 pairs of cranial nerves, 31 pairs of spinal nerves, and the autonomic nervous system). The central nervous system (CNS) and cranial nerves are of primary interest in working with individuals who are clumsy because of developmental delays or acquired head injuries. The spinal nerves, a primary concern in paralysis and paresis, are covered in Chapter 23. The autonomic nervous system, of special importance in fitness and cardiorespiratory function, is mentioned often in chapters pertaining to these concerns.

To understand clumsiness, you need to know the organization of the nervous system and understand nerve cells, myelination, the human brain, the development of the CNS, and at least 13 parts of the CNS. This background will help you to make sense of systems that classify disabilities as pyramidal and extrapyramidal or upper and lower neuron disorders.

Nerve Cells

The normal adult has approximately 100 billion nerve cells called *neurons*. Each has a cell body, one axon, and several dendrites. Figure 10.34 shows how the appearance of these cells changes from birth until about 15 months. During this time, in normal development, the *dendrites* rapidly form many treelike branches that receive impulses from other neurons. Through this *dendritization,* each neuron becomes interconnected with approximately 10,000 other neurons.

The *axon* conducts impulses away from the cell body (the executive part of the neuron). The speed and efficiency with which neurons transmit impulses determine, to a large extent, motor control. The junction between two neurons is a *synapse*. From the time that sensory input is received until a mental or motor response occurs, hundreds (and sometimes millions) of neurons are involved via synaptic linkups throughout the body.

There are many kinds of neurons. In general, their functions are described as (a) motor, (b) sensory, or (c) associative or internuncial. The location of the cell body and the pathway of its fibers (dendrites and axon) determine

function. Motor and associative neurons have their cell bodies in the gray matter of the spinal cord or brain (see Figure 10.35). They receive information via a dendrites-to-cell body pathway. The cell body then sends an action impulse to another part of the spinal cord or brain or to an effector organ (muscle) via its axon.

Sensory neurons, in contrast, have their cell bodies in the dorsal root ganglia of spinal nerves, close to where these nerves issue from the spinal cord (see Figure 10.35). Their cell bodies receive sensory information also via a dendrites-to-cell body pathway. The cell body then directs the axon to carry the sensory message to the dendrites of a motor or associative neuron.

Billions of different kinds of neurons are thus interacting or synapsing all of the time. Think, for instance, about movement when you have been sitting and decide to get up. The impulse to move originates in the thinking part of the brain (cerebral cortex), which generates thousands of action impulses that are transmitted from neuron to neuron down through the various parts of the brain to the spinal cord. Since getting up from a chair requires almost all of the body parts to move, motor neuron axons carrying the command to move must simultaneously exit at each level of the spinal cord via the 31 pairs of spinal nerves. The exit is always via the anterior or ventral root of the spinal nerve.

Thousands of individual nerve fibers are grouped together into bundles to make a nerve (see Figure 10.35). Note how the dorsal and ventral roots join together in the spinal nerve. Thus, inside every spinal nerve are (a) sensory fibers carrying messages from receptor organs in the skin, muscles, tendons, ligaments, and bones back to the spinal cord and (b) motor fibers carrying messages from the brain and spinal cord out to the muscles and other effector organs.

Myelination

The mature, healthy CNS is characterized by a multiplicity of synaptic connections and rich neuronal interactions. Approximately 5 months before birth, myelination begins. This is the development of the fatlike protein and lipid substance that forms the covering of axons and influences their ability to conduct impulses. At birth, some parts of the nervous system (optic tract, motor and sensory roots of the 31 pairs of spinal nerves) have a moderate amount of myelination, but others have none.

Myelination continues rapidly from birth until 3 to 4 years of age, when it is mostly complete except for the association areas of the brain. Myelination in these areas is finished between ages 20 to 30 years. Motor milestones, such as head lifting, sitting, creeping, standing, and walking, cannot be achieved until myelination in the related nerves and CNS parts is completed. Likewise, certain kinds of complex reasoning cannot occur until the association areas of the cerebral cortex are fully myelinated.

There appears to be no way to speed up myelination. A characteristic of nerve cell injury and/or disease is *demyelination* (the disintegration of the myelin covering of the nerve's fibers) and subsequent loss of motor coordination. Demyelination is the cause of multiple sclerosis, a CNS condition that mainly occurs in adults (see the "Index").

FIGURE   10.35

The peripheral nervous system. (*A*) Each of the 31 spinal nerves emerges from the spinal cord by a dorsal (posterior) root and a ventral (anterior) root. The dorsal root transmits sensory messages, whereas the ventral root transmits motor messages. (*B*) The roots merge after leaving the vertebral area to form a nerve. Nerves are made up of nerve fibers called dendrites and axons.

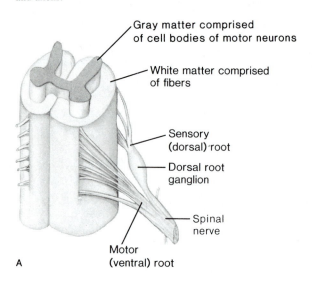

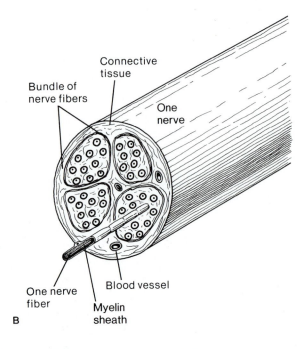

FIGURE   10.36

Lobes of the right cerebral hemisphere are separated by dotted lines.

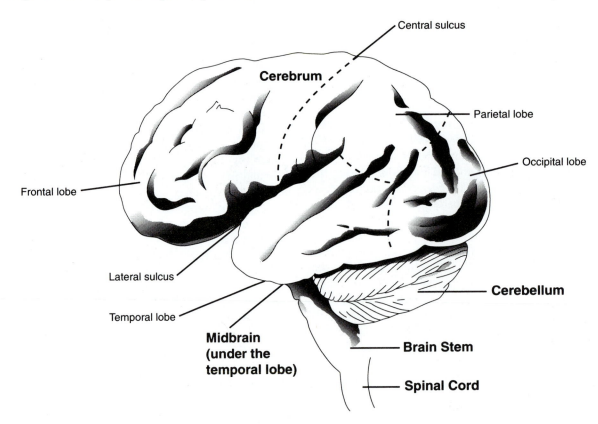

The Human Brain

The human brain, much simplified, can be thought of as white and gray matter. The white matter is comprised of all the nerve fibers. These are grouped together as tracts and given names (e.g., pyramidal and extrapyramidal). In the cerebrum, these tracts collectively are called the internal capsule. The gray matter, made up of concentrations of cell bodies, is (a) the cortex or outer covering of the cerebrum and cerebellum and (b) nuclei with specific names like thalamus, hypothalamus, and basal ganglia. The cerebral cortex performs all of the higher level mental functions (voluntary movement, perception, cognition, and memory). The cerebellar cortex is less well understood but plays an important part in regulating both voluntary and involuntary movements, especially during rapid changes in body position and equilibrium. The nuclei located within the white matter of the cerebrum perform or govern reflex or regulatory functions.

The cerebral cortex, which is smooth before birth, rapidly develops numerous *convolutions* (folds, hills, gyri) and *depressions* (grooves, sulci, fissures). Some of these, like the central sulcus that separates the frontal lobe from the parietal lobe, have names. The cerebral cortex is divided into right and left hemispheres. In right-handed persons, the right hemisphere governs spatial, artistic, and creative abilities. The left hemisphere governs analytical and verbal skills, like mathematics, reading, and writing.

Figure 10.36 shows that each hemisphere is divided into four lobes: frontal, parietal, occipital, and temporal. Each lobe performs different functions. *Simplified,* the occipital lobe governs vision and visual perception. The temporal lobe governs audition and provides memory storage for both auditory and visual experiences. The parietal lobe is responsible for the interpretation of skin and muscular sensations and for speech. The frontal lobe is the site of processes pertaining to cognition, personality, and voluntary movement. In reality, there is much overlapping of function.

Figure 10.36 also shows the brain stem, the cerebellum, and the midbrain, a small, distinct area between the brain stem and the cerebrum. Theorists on reflexes and postural reactions posit that the evolution of voluntary movement is related to the structure and function of (a) the brain stem, which governs reflexes; (b) the midbrain, which governs postural reactions; and (c) the cortex of the cerebrum and cerebellum, which governs equilibrium and voluntary movement.

Brain growth follows a specific pattern. The brain stem becomes functional first, then the midbrain, and last the cortical areas controlling voluntary movement. This explains why infants are born with reflexes, righting reactions begin at about 1.5 months of age, and voluntary movement is evident at about 4 months of age. In normal growth and development, this happens so fast we hardly notice. In delayed or abnormal development, teachers must devote much time and energy to reflexes and reactions.

Development of the Central Nervous System

Just as the body progresses through stages of development (embryo to fetus to infant), so also does the CNS. Beginning as cells called the ectoderm (see age 23 days in Figure 10.37), the CNS evolves into the neural tube that, 28 days after conception, has subdivided into four distinct parts: forebrain, midbrain, hindbrain, and neural tube (spinal cord). Long before birth, these structures evolve into the parts of the CNS with which we are familiar. The hindbrain separates into medulla and pons (the brain stem); the cerebellum develops later, in the ninth week. The midbrain expands in size, but its name does not change. The forebrain evolves into a cerebrum with several interdependent structures. The innermost of these are the thalamus, hypothalamus, basal ganglia (clumps of cell bodies), and limbic system. The outermost part is the cerebral cortex.

Parts of the Central Nervous System

Knowing the function of each part of the CNS is essential to understanding individual differences in motor functioning. The following is a simplified explanation of each:

1. **Spinal cord.** Comprised of numerous tracts (pathways), each of which contains nerve fibers carrying impulses to and from the brain. Each tract has a distinct name and function. The name typically indicates the direction in which impulses are carried and the two parts of the CNS connected by the pathway. Illustrative *ascending pathways* are spinocerebellar and spinothalamic. Illustrative *descending pathways* are corticospinal and vestibulospinal. The speed and efficiency with which impulses are carried up and down these tracts are major determinants of motor coordination and control. Spinal cord damage results in muscle weakness or paralysis and lack of sensation.

2. **Medulla.** The upper part of the spinal cord that regulates such vital functions as respiration, heart rate, and blood pressure. Contains nuclei (cell bodies) from which cranial nerves 9 to 12 emerge. These nerves pertain to swallowing, chewing, salivating, moving the tongue, and speaking.

3. **Pons (means "bridge").** Consists mainly of fibers forming a bridge between the medulla and the cerebellum. Contains nuclei from which cranial nerves 5 to 8 emerge. The *eighth cranial nerve* is the vestibulocochlear nerve. The vestibular branch is important in the reflex control of head, neck, and eyes and helps regulate coordination and posture. The cochlear branch is important in audition.

4. **Brain stem.** The bundle of nerve tissue that extends upward from the spinal cord to the base of the cerebrum. The brain stem regulates reflexes. It contains all of the centers for the 10 sense modalities except vision and smell. Some authorities say that it

FIGURE 10.37

Rapid growth of body and brain before birth.

Age	Length	Appearance
4 days		
23 days	2 mm	
28 days	4 mm	
45 days	17 mm	
7 weeks	2.8 cm	
12 weeks	8.8 cm	
28 weeks	38.5 cm	
First postnatal year+		

Embryo at 28 Days

Forebrain • Midbrain • Hindbrain • Neural tube

Embryo at 45 Days

Thalamus/Hypothalamus • Midbrain • Cerebellum • Medulla • Cerebrum • Limb bud

Infant at Birth

Limbic system with thalamus and hypothalamus • Cerebrum • Midbrain • Cerebellum • Medulla • Spinal cord

FIGURE 10.38

Side view of brain stem, midbrain, and lower cerebrum. This level of the brain governs the primitive reflexes and righting reactions.

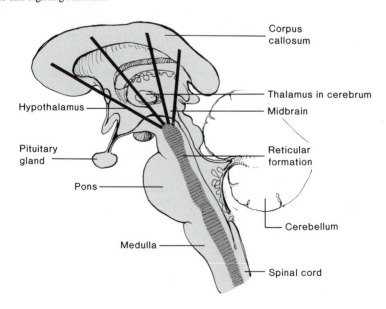

Corpus callosum

Thalamus in cerebrum

Midbrain

Reticular formation

Cerebellum

Spinal cord

Hypothalamus

Pituitary gland

Pons

Medulla

includes the medulla, pons, and midbrain. Others say that it includes only the medulla and that the pons and midbrain are independent structures. The primary reason for considering these three structures together is the presence in all of them of the *reticular formation,* also called the reticular activating system (see Figure 10.38).

5. **Reticular activating system (RAF).** A complex network of nerve fibers with tiny clumps of cell bodies that connects the brain stem with virtually all other parts of the brain. Its main functions pertain to reciprocal innervation, activation, wakefulness, and arousal; thus, it is important in attention, learning, and behavior deficits involving hyperactivity versus hypoactivity. The RAF filters incoming sensory impulses and prevents sensory bombardment of the cortex by selectively transferring some sensory impulses upward and inhibiting others. This permits the cortex to process significant stimuli, rather than coping with all neural impulses.

6. **Midbrain.** Short portion between pons and cerebral hemispheres or upper part of the brain stem. Contains nuclei for nerves pertaining to vision. These are in the red (rubro) nucleus. The midbrain is essentially a servomechanism (relay center) for transmitting impulses related to righting and postural reactions. The rubrospinal tract starts here.

7. **Cerebellum (means "little brain").** Essentially, a servomechanism (relay center) for transmitting nerve impulses from kinesthetic and vestibular input and for regulating postures and automatic movement. The cerebellum is important in excitation (activation) and inhibition of muscles, a major determinant in smooth versus jerky movements. It is especially important in the control of fast movements. It is also believed to be the structure that, after training and practice of a new motor skill, assumes responsibility for automatic rather than conscious control of motor performance. A major goal of physical education is to motivate students to practice a new skill until it no longer requires motor planning (i.e., conscious thought). At that point, performance becomes subcortical, or automatic, meaning that it can be executed at the cerebellar level.

8. **Thalamus (means "little chamber or anteroom").** A football-shaped cluster of nerve cells deep within the cerebrum, located immediately above the midbrain. One part acts as a servomechanism for relaying sensory impulses, and the other helps to regulate arousal in relation to activity. Except for smell, each of the senses relays its impulses through the thalamus.

9. **Hypothalamus.** Group of small nuclei underneath the thalamus and close to the pituitary gland. Integrates autonomic nervous system responses, thereby playing a key role in *homeostasis* (the regulation of balance in internal bodily functions). Among these are regulation of physical growth, heart rate, body temperature, sleep and wakefulness, hunger, dehydration, emotion, and control of stress. This regulation occurs primarily through stimulation of glands that release hormones.

10. **Basal ganglia.** Masses of subcortical gray matter (cell bodies) in the interior of the cerebrum, mainly in the corpus callosum area near the junction of right and left cerebral hemispheres. Some of the basal ganglia have specific names: globus pallidus, putamen, caudate nucleus, subthalamic nucleus, and substantia nigra. In general, the basal ganglia help to regulate posture and movement, particularly slow movement. Damage to basal ganglia results in such conditions as athetosis (involuntary, purposeless, slow, repeated motions), tremors of face and hands, and Huntington's chorea.

11. **Limbic system.** A ring of interconnecting pathways and centers in the cerebrum that includes the hypothalamus, thalamus, basal ganglia, and other subcortical nuclei that are important in control of emotional responses and activity levels (i.e., hyperactivity vs. hypoactivity). *Limbus* is Latin for "rim" or "border;" the limbic system forms the inner rim of structures that comprise the evolutionally old cortex. It is closely connected to the sense of smell in that the olfactory bulbs and tracts are nearby. Evolutionarily, the cerebrum is believed to have begun as a center for smell.

12. **Cerebral cortex (means "bark of tree").** Anatomically refers to six layers of gray matter (cell bodies) that comprise the outer part of the cerebrum. The cortex performs the higher level functions: voluntary movement, perception, thought, memory, and creativity. Cortical areas are named according to function: sensory, association, and motor. *Sensory areas* interpret impulses from 10 kinds of sensory receptors. *Association areas* link sensory and motor input and create associations essential to verbalization, memory, reasoning, judgment, and creativity. *Motor areas* control voluntary movement; damage to the motor cortex and/or its descending tracts results in spasticity.

13. **Corpus callosum.** Bridge of nerve fibers that connects right and left cerebral hemispheres, thus allowing them to keep in touch with one another. An important function is transfer of learning from one hemisphere to another.

Pyramidal and Extrapyramidal Systems

Pyramidal and *extrapyramidal* are terms used to describe the higher level motor control systems of the brain. The systems are named after large, pyramid-shaped cells of the cerebral cortex. The pyramidal system includes motor neurons that form the corticospinal or pyramidal tracts. The extrapyramidal system includes motor neurons not in the pyramidal system (i.e., those that are extra). Names of some of the extrapyramidal tracts are vestibulospinal, rubrospinal, and reticulospinal.

FIGURE   10.39

Developmental levels of central nervous system at which motor problems occur.

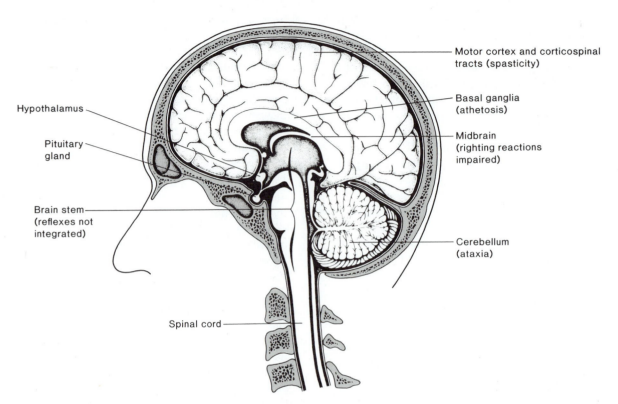

The pyramidal tracts are mostly concerned with the voluntary initiation of controlled movements. The extrapyramidal tracts are mainly responsible for automatic reactions and postural control.

Reciprocal Innervation and Muscle Tone

Muscle tone is the contractile tension within a muscle. Motor neurons have two functions: (a) excitation or facilitation, which increases muscle tone, and (b) inhibition, which decreases muscle tone. These two mechanisms innervate muscles (i.e., cause them to move). The pyramidal system is responsible for excitation, whereas the extrapyramidal system handles inhibition. For muscle tone to be normal and movements smooth, the pyramidal and extrapyramidal systems must work in perfect balance.

Normal muscle tone is explained by the *principle of reciprocal innervation*. Simply explained, reciprocal innervation is the phenomenon of muscles on one surface contracting (the agonists or prime movers), while muscles on the opposite side (the antagonists) are relaxing. When the principle of reciprocal innervation is violated and/or motor neurons in either the pyramidal or extrapyramidal systems are damaged, clumsiness results. Damage to the cerebellum, the midbrain, and the brain stem can also cause clumsiness.

Upper and Lower Motor Neuron Disorders

Figure 10.39 presents the names of disorders caused by damage to motor neurons in the brain. These conditions are often called upper motor neuron syndromes to distinguish them from motor problems that have their origin in the spinal cord (i.e., lower motor neuron syndromes). Most lower motor neuron problems are the result of spinal cord lesions that cause weakness or paralysis. The main upper motor neuron problems are spasticity and athetosis. *Spasticity,* caused by pyramidal system malfunction, is primarily a problem of overexcitation or too much tightness in muscles. *Athetosis,* caused by extrapyramidal breakdown, is a problem of excessive movement (i.e., inhibition is impaired). *Ataxia,* or general incoordination, may be either an upper motor neuron disorder (cerebellum) or a lower motor neuron problem. In the latter, degeneration of cell bodies in the posterior spinal cord interferes with kinesthesis.

Neurological Bases of Clumsiness

Clumsiness, the inability to perform culturally normative motor activities with acceptable proficiency, is caused by delayed or abnormal CNS development, musculoskeletal limitations, and other constraints. The severity of the CNS condition(s) typically determines whether the person is called clumsy or cerebral palsied. Without sophisticated laboratory equipment, determining the CNS site and other contributing factors is difficult. Always, the problem is complex; certainly, sound motor functioning cannot occur without intact sensory and central processing systems.

The following questions typically are used in searching for neurological reasons for clumsiness:

1. Is something wrong with the sense organs?
2. Is something wrong with the nerve fibers that carry sensory input?

3. Is something wrong with central processing (i.e., the servomechanisms that relay impulses, the reticular activating system that controls arousal, or the association areas of the cerebral cortex that translate impulses into meaning)?

4. Is something wrong with motor output (i.e., the motor areas of the CNS that activate movement; the nerve fibers that carry motor input to muscles, tendons, and joints; or the motor effectors [endings] within these structures)?

This approach, while interesting, seldom results in specific answers that help physical education programming.

Systems or Distributed Control Models

An alternative approach to explaining clumsiness, used in the therapies and in adapted physical education, entails assessing characteristics of a mature, intact CNS (see Table 10.2) and directing remediation at specific problems. Instead of concern with specific parts of the brain, *systems or distributed control models* recognize that sensorimotor integration is shared by several parts or is broadly distributed (Barnes et al., 1990; Woollacott & Shumway-Cook, 1989). Proponents of these models assert that there is no strict hierarchy of control from one part of the brain to another. Instead, requirements of the task and environmental conditions determine brain function. Biomechanics is also important in these models, with attention given to musculoskeletal constraints like overall shortness, limb lengths, and postural deviations.

The systems or distributed control models are relatively new and much more difficult to understand than models that associate motor problems with specific levels or parts of the brain. In the future, more intense study of neurology will permit understanding of individual CNS parts and the complex networking between parts and environmental variables. However, remediation clearly should be directed toward several CNS parts simultaneously, and practice should be variable, utilizing all resources. *Teaching the whole child, not the separate systems, means working simultaneously on reflexes, reactions, voluntary movement, and environmental constraints.*

Disorders of Muscle Tone

Several characteristics in Table 10.2 pertain to postural or muscle tone (tonus). Before the CNS matures sufficiently to permit voluntary action (i.e., at about 4 months of age), tonus shifts with body position. *Flexor tonus* refers to tension within muscles on the anterior surface of the body that, when mature, will cause flexion movements (i.e., bending, curling). *Extensor tonus* refers to tension within muscles on the posterior surface of the body that will cause extension movements (i.e., straightening, stretching).

In newborn infants, flexor tonus works with adductor tonus and inward rotator tonus to cause the characteristic curled posture with bent arms and legs. Consider the position in the womb: flexion, adduction (limbs drawn in toward the midline), and inward rotation of arms and legs. At birth, the muscle groups that cause these patterns are

---

Table 10.2
Characteristics of a mature, intact central nervous system.

1. **Reflex integration.** Primitive reflexes are involuntary motor responses to stimuli. Reflexes must be fully suppressed or integrated before coordinated, graceful, voluntary movement can occur.

2. **Optimal functioning of reactions.** Reactions are generalized involuntary responses that pertain to static and dynamic balance. Developmentally, reactions replace primitive reflexes.

3. **Freedom from ataxia.** Ataxia is incoordination characterized primarily by irregularity and lack of precision in voluntary motor acts. Ataxic behaviors include overshooting or undershooting the object when reaching for something or going through an obstacle course; problems include spilling, bumping into things, knocking things over, or stumbling for no apparent reason. In stepping over an object or climbing stairs, persons with ataxia tend to lift their feet too high. An ataxic gait is characterized by irregular steps.

4. **Freedom from athetosis.** Athetosis is involuntary, purposeless, relatively slow, repeated movement that interferes with steadiness, accuracy, and control of one or more body parts.

5. **Freedom from spasticity.** Spasticity is hypertonus (too much muscle tone) that results in reduced range of movement, overly active tonic reflex activity, and stiff, awkward-looking movements. Spasticity occurs only in relation to voluntary movement.

6. **Freedom from associated movements.** The ability to move one body part without associated movements of other parts. This problem is sometimes called *overflow.*

7. **Freedom from sensory input problems.** Visual and auditory problems affect the teaching/learning process in mastering new motor skills and patterns.

Note. The terms *ataxia, athetosis,* and *spasticity,* although used to specify types of cerebral palsy, are not limited to this group of conditions. They also describe clumsy movements and gaits with an infinite variety of etiologies (causes), including brain damage from vehicular accidents, drugs, alcohol, and disease. A person intoxicated with alcohol, for instance, is said to have an ataxic gait; likewise, the toddler just learning to walk evidences developmental ataxia, which disappears with neuromuscular maturation.

---

stronger than their antagonists (opposites). In normal development, the extensor, abductor, and outward rotator muscle groups gradually develop tonus, thereby allowing the trunk, arms, and legs to straighten out. An important principle is *emphasize strengthening the extensors.*

In severe cases of cerebral palsy and other conditions in which spasticity is developmental and widespread, the excessive tightness in the flexor, adductor, and inward rotator muscle groups does not disappear. Obviously, this severely limits range of motion. *Postural tone* refers to when the entire body is affected, as in quadriplegia. *Muscle tone* refers to when only some parts of the body are affected.

Disorders of muscle tone include (a) hypertonus, (b) hypotonus, and (c) fluctuating tonus. *Hypertonus* is excessive muscle tension, as in spasticity, rigidity, and muscle spasms. *Hypotonus* is too little tension, as in a muscle group characterized by paralysis or weakness (relaxed, flabby, flaccid). *Fluctuating tonus,* often seen in the athetoid type of cerebral palsy, refers to intermittent increases of postural tone in response to stimulation. Such persons exhibit both hypertonus and hypotonus.

Hypotonus (also called hypotonia and atonia) is so common among infants and children with disabilities that it has been designated the *floppy infant syndrome* (Dubowitz, 1969). Many infants with mental retardation, especially those with Down syndrome, are characterized by hypotonia. The main features associated with hypotonia are (a) bizarre and unusual postures and (b) increased range of movement in joints. Hypotonic infants and/or persons with severe CNS damage generally lie on their backs, with a froglike posture of the legs (abduction and outward rotation of hips).

Disorders of muscle tone can result from both developmental and acquired disorders. While spasticity is usually associated with cerebral palsy, it occurs also in relation to spinal cord paralysis and many *les autres* conditions.

Disorders of Praxis (Apraxia, Dyspraxia)

Praxis is the ability to plan and execute purposeful motion. It comes from the Greek word for action (*prassein,* meaning "to do") and is related to such words as *practice, practical,* and *pragmatic.* When movement problems cannot be linked with reflexes, reactions, sensory input, physical and motor fitness, comprehension, or inattention to commands, they are typically classified as apraxia or dyspraxia (Ayres, 1972; Cratty, 1986; Roy, 1978; Sugden & Keogh, 1990).

In instructional settings, apraxia and dyspraxia are usually called problems of motor planning or sequencing. Among the specific problems that are classified as apraxia are difficulties with (a) imitation, (b) initiating movement, (c) terminating movement, and (d) ordering or sequencing parts of a movement. Persons with these problems do not seem to benefit from instruction. The cortical functions that translate movement intention into action are impaired. Such persons say that they *see* the demonstration, they *know* what to do, but they cannot make the body do it.

Apraxia is believed to be cortical rather than subcortical dysfunction because the movement problems are executive in nature. In general, there are three types of movement errors: (a) selecting the wrong response, (b) misordering or omitting responses, and (c) incorrectly timing responses, delaying their initiation or prolonging them by too many repetitions (perseveration). These problems are often observed in persons with learning disabilities who are clumsy.

Movement problems of this type are linked to damage of the left hemisphere of the cerebral cortex, the part that also governs analytical and verbal skills like mathematics, reading, and writing. Major neural theories proposed to explain apraxia are (a) center or hemispheric localization and (b) disconnection (Roy, 1985; Sugden & Keogh, 1990).

In the first, apraxia is linked with certain centers within the left hemisphere where information is processed and movements are programmed. In the second, apraxia is explained as an interruption of transmission of sensory information to motor areas.

Obviously, understanding of the neurological bases of motor development and control helps adapted physical educators to devise appropriate pedagogy and/or evaluate intelligently the remediation procedures proposed by others. Ayres (1972), for example, recommends that reflex problems and apraxia be treated simultaneously with scooterboard and other activities that require motor planning. Cratty (1986) emphasizes imitation of limb movement sequences. Kowalski and Sherrill (1992) stress imitation and sequencing of total body postures or stunts, with and without verbal rehearsal.

Theories That Guide Practices

In the past, therapists and educators have tended to rely on different theories to explain and guide practices. Today, however, sources are synthesizing information from several disciplines and professions (Barnes et al., 1990; Burton, 1990a, b; Hoover & Wade, 1985; Reid, 1990). The following are brief descriptions of theories that are pertinent to adapted physical activity.

Maturation Theory

Arnold Gesell, a physician and director of the Yale University Clinic of Child Development from 1911 to 1948, is generally accredited with evolution of maturation theory (Clark & Whitall, 1989; Salkind, 1985). Maturation theory posits the orderly, sequential appearance of developmental milestones in accordance with an inborn biological timetable. Today's principles of motor development (see Chapter 18 on infant, toddler, and early childhood programming) are based on Gesell's *Infancy and Human Growth* (1928) and subsequent publications.

Gesell, like others of his time, did not use the term *theory.* His principles and developmental sequences, however, were tested and refined by followers, who subsequently organized them into maturation theory. Today, some of his principles are being challenged (Barnes et al, 1990), but his developmental sequences continue to guide developmental diagnosis and norm-based tests for children from birth to age 6 (Gesell & Amatruda, 1941; Knobloch & Pasamanick, 1974).

Theories Based on Levels of Function

Several developmental theories are based on hierarchical levels of CNS functioning. Among these are the neurophysiological theory of the Bobaths, the reflex-testing theory of Fiorentino, the sensorimotor theory of Rood, and the sensory integration theory of Jean Ayres. The three levels of reflex/reaction development that form the basis of these theories are presented in Table 10.3.

Table 10.3
Normal reflex/reaction development.

Level of Development	Level of CNS Maturation	Motor Behaviors
Primitive reflexes	Spinal cord and/ or brain stem	Prone-lying Supine-lying
Righting reactions	Midbrain	Right self, turn over, sit, crawl, creep
Equilibrium reactions	Cortical	Stand, walk

Neurodevelopmental/Neurophysiological

The origin of neurodevelopmental/neurophysiological theories is generally accredited to Karel Bobath, a physician, and his wife, Berta Bobath, a physical therapist (Huss, 1988). Their work began in England in the 1940s and is now known worldwide. Physical therapists, occupational therapists, and adapted physical educators all use the Bobath treatment approaches, especially with persons severely disabled by cerebral palsy or head injury. The Bobaths (1980, 1985) posited that (a) delayed or abnormal motor development is the result of interference with normal brain maturation, (b) this interference is manifested as an impairment of the postural reflex mechanism, (c) abnormal reflex activity produces abnormal degree and distribution of postural and muscle tone, and (d) righting and equilibrium reactions should be used to inhibit abnormal movements while simultaneously stimulating and facilitating normal postural responses.

The *normal postural reflex mechanism,* according to the Bobaths, is the product of interactions among three factors: (a) normal postural tone, (b) reciprocal innervation, and (c) the proper emergence of developmental sequences of postural reactions and voluntary movement. Interference with any of these factors requires treatment or therapy. The Bobaths thus stressed that all movement behavior is postural (we assume thousands of postures each day) and that the integration of reflexes and the emergence of righting and equilibrium reactions form the basis of normal movement.

Mary Fiorentino, an occupational therapist from Connecticut, built upon the ideas of the Bobaths and other developmentalists and synthesized existing knowledge about reflexes and reactions into reflex testing theory in the 1960s. Fiorentino (1963) described and illustrated 37 distinct reflexes and reactions, organized according to the scheme presented in Table 10.3. Later (1981), she wrote a comprehensive text on the influence of reflexes and reactions on normal and abnormal motor development.

Sensorimotor/Sensory Integration

Margaret Rood, who was certified in both occupational and physical therapy, evolved a sensorimotor theoretical approach to treatment in the 1950s based on three principles:

(a) motor output is dependent on sensory input, (b) activation of motor responses should follow the normal developmental sequence, and (c) stimuli used to remediate one sensory function will influence other functions (Huss, 1988). Rood posited that an eight-step developmental mobility-stability model (total flexion pattern, rolling, prone-lying with hyperextension of the entire spine, prone-lying with contraction of neck muscles, prone-lying with weight on elbows, hands and knees kneeling, standing, and walking) should be used in conjunction with sensory stimulation (icing, heating, brushing, exerting deep muscle pressure, and the like) (see Figure 10.20). Rood's work was the basis for much of Ayres's (1972) sensory integration theory.

Jean Ayres, an occupational therapist with a doctoral degree in neuropsychology, outlined sensory integration theory in the 1970s. A professor at the University of Southern California, Ayres focused most of her research on learning disabilities. Her ideas, however, have been widely applied, especially in infant and early childhood programs. Ayres's theory emphasizes that the nervous system must be integrated at the lower levels before cognitive approaches like watching demonstrations and listening to directions can be successful. Development is spiral, with the integrity of each system built on sound functioning of the level immediately below it. Sensory integration is defined by Ayres (1980) as:

the organization of sensory input for use. The "use" may be a perception of the body or the world, or an adaptive response or learning process, or the development of some neural function. Through sensory integration, the many parts of the nervous system work together so that a person can interact with the environment effectively and experience appropriate satisfaction. (p. 184)

By emphasizing organization, Ayres based her theory on central processing, what goes on in the brain after sensory impulses arrive. Ayres believes that movement therapy should be directed at six levels: spinal cord, brain stem with emphasis on reticular formation, cerebellum, basal ganglia, old cortex and/or limbic system, and neocortex. She cautions, however, that, in reality, several CNS levels function simultaneously in human motor behavior.

Therapy is based on several principles:

1. Since the brain stem is the lowest level of the brain, it receives the greatest focus of therapeutic attention. The brain stem regulates reflexes. Therefore, reflex inhibition and integration are important parts of therapy.

2. Tactile stimulation contributes to generalized neurological integration and enhances perception of other sensory modalities.

3. One approach to normalization of vestibular mechanisms is swinging and spinning activities. These can be initiated by the child or therapist, but extreme care should be taken to avoid overstimulation (nausea, dizziness).

FIGURE 10.40

Rhythmical stereotypies of the legs and arms. (*A*) Alternate leg kicking. (*B*) Foot rubbing. (*C* and *D*) Single leg kicking. (*E*) Single leg kicking in prone. (*F*) Both legs kicking. (*G*) Both legs kicking with back strongly arched. (*H*) Arm waving with object. (*I*) Arm banging against surface.

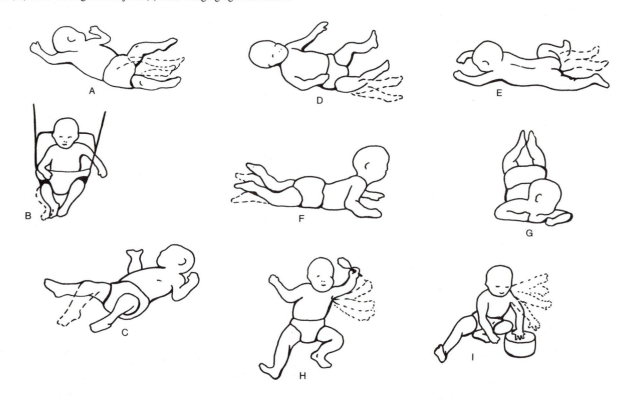

4. Activities involving extensor muscles should be emphasized. Prone-lying on a scooterboard with head held high is an illustrative extensor muscle activity. Among the many scooterboard tasks recommended are 30 ways to descend a ramp that is elevated at one end about 2 ft.

5. Body control activities should be emphasized. Some of these are (a) moving on all-fours through tunnels or obstacle courses, (b) jumping games, and (c) balancing tasks.

Parts of sensory integration theory have been challenged (Arendt, MacLean, & Baumeister, 1988) and defended (Cermak, 1988; Ottenbacher, 1988). Most of the activities recommended by Ayres, however, have been used in elementary physical education and in therapeutic settings for many years. The activities appear sound, but researchers are still trying to explain neurologically how and why they work.

Theories Based on Systems or Distributed Control Models

Many theories emphasize the dynamic interplay between environment and function and the complexity of the CNS (Barnes et al, 1990; Burton & Davis, 1992; Hoover & Wade, 1985; Woollacott & Shumway-Cook, 1989). Some of these reject early theories, whereas others emphasize that theories formulated before the 1980s are gross oversimplifications of the neurological bases of motor control. Sherrill agrees with oversimplification criticisms but believes that parts of the CNS must be understood before creative thinking about environment and function can be accurate. This text provides information that beginning teachers can link with pedagogy; graduate students are urged to study more advanced texts and to derive applications from discussions of theory.

Dynamic Action Theory

Dynamic action theory brings together the work of many researchers from the past two decades. A theoretical framework that stresses motor action from a systems perspective, it emphasizes that perception is driven by ecological interactions rather than by stimulus-response linkages. This chapter has woven dynamic action theory into the traditional input/central processing/output model by stressing that environmental input can be external (visual, auditory, tactile) or internal (vestibular, kinesthetic). Many systems are operative in reflexes, reactions, and voluntary movement patterns. Control of these actions is distributed and dynamic.

Linkages between systems are not linear but circular and many-faceted. Action influences sensation and perception, and vice versa. Movement can be initiated through either sensory input or dynamic action within the brain (e.g., the decision to rise from a chair and change to jogging clothes).

Sensorimotor integration, as described in this chapter, should be conceptualized as dynamic action within the brain that simultaneously involves many structures and functions. Sensory and motor are parallel, interactive processes.

Inborn Motor Pattern Generators

Much of the new literature refers to reflexes and reactions as patterns and to the spinal cord and lower levels of the brain as central pattern generators. Whereas early theorists only described specific stimuli that elicited reflexes, new sources discuss "specific patterns of muscular activity that result from particular sets of circumstances" (Barnes et al, 1990, p. 11). Milani-Comparetti (1981) stated that spontaneous movements of fetuses (thumb sucking, reaching, grasping, and position changes) have been documented through ultrasonography. Because no stimuli are evident as effectors of these movements, Milani-Comparetti concluded that motor actions can result from inborn pattern generators.

These and other research findings suggest that some spontaneous patterns occur without sensory input. Particularly supportive of this construct is animal research showing that, when sensory roots are cut, thereby eliminating sensory input, locomotion patterns can still be generated. Esther Thelen, a psychologist at Indiana University, is one of the pioneer researchers whose findings support pattern generators that are not dependent on sensory input (Thelen, 1979; Thelen, Kelso, & Fogel, 1987; Thelen, Ulrich, & Jensen, 1989). Thelen (1979) reported that, in infants, 47 rhythmical stereotypies of body parts emerge at specific times, persist for weeks, peak, and then decline. These include various kicking and arm patterns, as well as shaking and pounding object manipulations (see Figure 10.40). She and colleagues have also studied the emergence of locomotor patterns in infants, noting that their appearance is not dependent upon sensory input.

The implications of Thelen's work for pedagogy are receiving increasing attention, and Barnes et al. (1990) consider her a leader in dynamic action theory. Thelen emphasizes that many systems are operative in the development of infant locomotion and that the nervous system is only one. This is true of all motor patterns.

References

Arendt, R. E., MacLean, W., & Baumeister, A. (1988). Critique of sensory integration therapy and its application in mental retardation. *Mental Retardation, 92* (5), 401–411.

Ayres, A. J. (1972). *Sensory integration and learning disorders.* Los Angeles: Western Psychological Services.

Ayres, A. J. (1980). *Sensory integration and the child.* Los Angeles: Western Psychological Services.

Bard, C., Fleury, M., & Hay, L. (1990). *Development of eye-hand coordination across the lifespan.* Columbia, SC: University of South Carolina Press.

Barnes, M. R., Crutchfield, C., Heriza, C., & Herdman, S. (1990). *Reflex and vestibular aspects of motor control, motor development, and motor learning.* Atlanta, GA: Stokesville.

Biery, M. J., & Kauffman, N. (1989). The effects of therapeutic horseback riding on balance. *Adapted Physical Activity Quarterly, 6* (3), 221–229.

Bobath, K. (1980). *A neurophysiological basis for the treatment of cerebral palsy.* Philadelphia: J.B. Lippincott.

Bobath, B. (1985). *Abnormal postural reflex activity caused by brain lesions* (3rd ed.). Rockville, MD: Aspen Systems.

Bronfenbrenner, U. (1979). *The ecology of human movement.* Cambridge, MA: Harvard University Press.

Brooks, V. B. (1986). *The neural basis of motor control.* New York: Oxford University Press.

Burton, A. W. (1987). Confronting the interaction between perception and movement in adapted physical education. *Adapted Physical Activity Quarterly, 4,* 257–267.

Burton, A. W. (1990a). Applying principles of coordination in adapted physical education. *Adapted Physical Activity Quarterly, 7* (2), 126–142.

Burton, A. W. (1990b). Assessing the perceptual-motor interaction in developmentally disabled and nonhandicapped children. *Adapted Physical Activity Quarterly, 7* (4), 325–337.

Burton, A. W., & Davis, W. E. (1992). Assessing balance in adapted physical education: Fundamental concepts and applications. *Adapted Physical Activity Quarterly, 9* (1), 14–46.

Cermak, S. A. (1988). Sensible integration. *Mental Retardation, 92* (5), 413–414.

Clark, J. E., & Whitall, J. (1989). What is motor development? The lessons of history. *Quest, 41* (3), 183–202.

Cowden, J. E., & Eason, B. L. (1991). Pediatric adapted physical education for infants, toddlers, and preschoolers: Meeting IDEA-H and IDEA-B challenges. *Adapted Physical Activity Quarterly, 8* (4), 263–279.

Cratty, B. J. (1986). *Perceptual and motor development in infants and children* (3rd ed.). Englewood Cliffs, NJ: Prentice-Hall.

Davis, W. E. (1983). An ecological approach to perceptual-motor learning. In R. L. Eason, T. L. Smith, & F. Caron (Eds.), *Adapted physical activity: From theory to application* (pp. 162–171). Champaign, IL: Human Kinetics.

Davis, W. E., & Rizzo, T. L. (1991). Issues in the classification of motor disorders. *Adapted Physical Activity Quarterly, 8* (4), 280–304.

Dubowitz, V. (1969). *The floppy infant.* London: Spastics International Medical Publications.

Ellison, P., Browning, C., Larson, B., & Denny, J. (1983). Development of a scoring system for the Milani-Comparetti and Gidoni methods of assessing neurological abnormality in infancy. *Physical Therapy, 63* (9), 1414–1423.

Fiorentino, M. (1963). *Reflex testing methods for evaluating C.N.S. development.* Springfield, IL: Charles C. Thomas.

Fiorentino, M. (1981). *A basis for sensorimotor development— Normal and abnormal.* Springfield, IL: Charles C. Thomas.

Gesell, A. (1928). *Infancy and human growth.* New York: Macmillan.

Gesell, A., & Amatruda, C. S. (1941). *Developmental diagnosis: The evaluation and management of normal and abnormal neuropsychologic development in infant and early childhood.* New York: Hoeber.

Gibson, J. J. (1979). *The ecological approach to visual perception.* Boston: Houghton Mifflin.

Gorman, D. R. (1983). Balance ability and reflex maturation among normal, learning disabled, and emotionally handicapped populations. *American Corrective Therapy Journal, 37* (1), 18–22.

Guyton, A. (1981). *Basic human neurophysiology* (3rd ed.). Philadelphia: W.B. Saunders.

Hallahan, D., & Cruickshank, W. (1973). *Psychoeducational foundations of learning disabilities.* Englewood Cliffs, NJ: Prentice-Hall.

Herman, E., & Retish, P. (1989). Vision therapy—Hoax, hope, or homilies? A physical education perspective. *Adapted Physical Activity Quarterly, 6* (4), 299–306.

Hoover, J. H., & Wade, M. G. (1985). Motor learning theory and mentally retarded individuals: A historical review. *Adapted Physical Activity Quarterly, 2* (3), 228–252.

Huss, A. J. (1988). Sensorimotor and neurodevelopmental frames of reference. In H. Hopkins & H. Smith (Eds.), *Willard and Spackman's occupational therapy* (7th ed.) (pp. 114–127). Philadelphia: J.B. Lippincott.

Kavale, K., & Mattson, P. D. (1983). One jumped off the balance beam: Meta-analysis of perceptual motor training. *Journal of Learning Disabilities, 16,* 165–173.

Knobloch, H., & Pasamanick, B. (Eds.). (1974). *Gesell and Amatruda's developmental diagnosis.* New York: Harper & Row.

Kowalski, E., & Sherrill, C. (1992). Motor sequencing of learning disabled boys: Modeling and verbal rehearsal strategies. *Adapted Physical Activity Quarterly, 9* (3), 261–272.

Milani-Comparetti, A. (1981). The neurophysiologic and clinical implications of studies on fetal motor behavior. *Seminars in Perinatology, 5,* 183–189.

Milani-Comparetti Motor Development Screening Test Manual (1987). Available from Meyer Children's Rehabilitation Institute, University of Nebraska Medical Center, 444 South 44th Street, Omaha, Nebraska 68131–3795.

Milani-Comparetti, A., & Gidoni, E. (1967). Pattern analysis of motor development and its disorders. *Developmental Medicine and Child Neurology, 9,* 625–630.

Molnar, G. (1978). Analysis of motor disorder in retarded infants and young children. *American Journal of Mental Deficiency, 83,* 213–221.

Ottenbacher, K. J. (1988). Sensory integration—Myth, method, imperative. *Mental Retardation, 92* (5), 425–426.

Pyfer, J. (1988). Teachers, don't let your students grow up to be clumsy adults. *Journal of Physical Education, Recreation, and Dance, 59* (1), 38–42.

Quiros, J. B., & Schrager, O. L. (1978). *Neuropsychological fundamentals in learning disabilities.* San Rafael, CA: Academic Therapy Publications.

Ramm, P. (1988). Pediatric occupational therapy. In H. Hopkins & H. Smith (Eds.), *Willard and Spackman's occupational therapy* (7th ed.) (pp. 601–627). Philadelphia: J.B. Lippincott.

Reid, G. (Ed.). (1990). *Problems in movement control.* Amsterdam: North-Holland.

Roy, E. A. (1978). Apraxia: A new look at an old syndrome. *Journal of Human Movement Studies, 4,* 191–210.

Roy, E. A. (Ed.). (1985). *Neuropsychological studies of apraxia and related disorders.* Amsterdam: North-Holland.

Sage, G. H. (1977). *Introduction to motor behavior: A neuropsychological approach* (2nd ed.). Reading, MA: Addison-Wesley.

Salkind, J. T. (1985). *Theories of human development* (2nd ed.). New York: John Wiley & Sons.

Sherrill, C. (Ed.). (1988). *Leadership training in adapted physical education.* Champaign, IL: Human Kinetics.

Sherrill, C., & Montelione, T. (1990). Prioritizing adapted physical education goals: A pilot study. *Adapted Physical Activity Quarterly, 7* (4), 355–369.

Stockmeyer, S. A. (1978). A sensorimotor approach to treatment. In P.H. Pearson & C. E. Williams (Ed.), *Physical therapy services in the developmental disabilities* (pp. 186–217). Springfield, IL: Charles C. Thomas.

Sugden, D. A., & Keogh, J. (1990). *Problems in movement skill development.* Columbia, SC: University of South Carolina Press.

Thelen, E. (1979). Rhythmical stereotypies in normal human infants. *Animal Behavior, 27,* 699–715.

Thelen, E., Kelso, J. A. S., & Fogel, A. (1987). Self-organizing systems and infant motor development. *Developmental Review, 7,* 39–65.

Thelen, E., Ulrich, B. D., & Jensen, J. (1989). The developmental origins of locomotion. In M. H. Woollacott & A. Shumway-Cook (Eds.), *Development of posture and gait across the lifespan* (pp. 25–47). Columbia, SC: University of South Carolina Press.

Thomas, J. R. (1984). *Motor development during childhood and adolescence.* Minneapolis: Burgess.

Williams, H. G. (1983). *Perceptual and motor development.* Englewood Cliffs, NJ: Prentice-Hall.

Woollacott, M. H., & Shumway-Cook, A. (Eds.). (1989). *Development of posture and gait across the lifespan.* Columbia, SC: University of South Carolina Press.

CHAPTER
11
Motor Performance: Assessment and Instruction

FIGURE   11.1

Success should be achieved in batting a stationary ball before games with moving balls are introduced. Note how the batter is applying the *principle of leverage* by choking up on the bat, thereby making it shorter and easier to control.

After you have studied this chapter, you should be able to:

1. Identify basic locomotor and object control skills.

2. Discuss five basic questions in assessing and teaching motor skills: (a) performance, (b) functional competence, (c) performance standards, (d) constraints, and (e) developmental level.

3. Develop task sheets for use in clipboard assessment and teaching.

4. Identify different kinds of gaits used with and without crutches. Given a picture or videotape of a gait, discuss assessment and programming. State which motor skills are appropriate goals and discuss pedagogy.

5. Demonstrate understanding of biomechanical analysis. Given a motor skill, be able to analyze it into major parts or phases.

6. Discuss qualitative and quantitative assessment of each locomotor and object control skill. State evaluative criteria for mature form and be able to apply knowledge in assessing several children (live or videotaped).

7. List in correct developmental sequence locomotor skills and the approximate age when each should be mastered. Do the same for object control skills.

8. Identify problems associated with performance of selected locomotor and object control skills and suggest adaptations and strategies.

9. Assuming that motor skills and patterns is the priority goal, write an IEP for a selected child.

A primary goal of adapted physical education is *functional competence* in motor skills and patterns (see Figure 11.1). This chapter discusses assessment of and instruction in motor performance. Knowledge in these areas must extend beyond that of the regular physical educator to include all kinds of individual differences, including motor development delays, abnormal muscle tone (spasticity, athetosis, paralysis, and paresis), structural deviations, and learning problems caused by perceptual-motor deficits.

Motor skills and patterns is the term used in the federal definition of physical education. *Skills,* as defined in motor learning literature, are acts or tasks that must be *learned* in order to be correctly executed. *Patterns* is a broader term. It refers to acts or tasks that have a similar appearance. A pattern may be learned, or it may emerge naturally as the result of normal motor development.

Some theorists say that acts like walking and running are not skills, but patterns that occur without instruction. To qualify for adapted physical education, however, students typically do not evidence normal development. They have delays and/or abnormal structure and function that require careful instruction. In this text, the terms *skills* and *patterns* are therefore used interchangeably.

Basic Questions in Assessing and Teaching Motor Skills

Figure 11.2 lists basic locomotor and object control skills covered in this chapter. Instruction should begin by assessing present level of performance and setting goals and objectives that match assessment information. The five basic questions that guide assessment and instruction also appear in Figure 11.2. The sections that follow show that assessment and instruction proceed together. Hundreds of trials are required to learn a motor skill. Task sheets that guide instruction should provide space for recording success or failure on each trial.

FIGURE 11.2

Basic locomotor and object control skills and the five basic questions that guide assessment.

Locomotor Skills	Object Control Skills
1. Walk or use wheelchair	Roll/bowl
2. Run	Throw
3. Ascend/descend	Catch
4. Jump	Bounce/dribble
5. Hop	Strike
6. Leap	Kick
7. Gallop	Stop/trap
8. Skip	
9. Slide	

Basic Assessment Questions

1. Performance—Does student perform skill?

2. Functional competence—Does student use skill in activities for fun and/or fitness?

3. Performance standards—Does student meet form, distance, accuracy, speed, and function standards for age group?

4. Constraints—Does student have muscle tone, bone, or joint abnormalities that limit success and/or contraindications to be remembered?

5. Developmental level or form—Is form immature, mature, or adapted to accommodate pathology?

Performance

Assessment at the first level addresses whether the student can perform a skill (yes or no) in a particular context under designated conditions. Three *contexts* that are very different are (a) informal play, (b) structured games, and (c) formal command-response situations. Students may, for example, perform a skill in an informal play setting but be unable to do so in the other settings because of comprehension or motivation problems. Therefore, informal play (preferably in a small group) should be observed first.

If the student does not play spontaneously and/or try to imitate classmates, then one-to-one testing is initiated to determine the conditions needed for successful performance. The first condition to be considered is language comprehension, including what language (English, Spanish, sign) is being used and how many words are in the instructions (two to three, four to seven, eight or more). Often, the problem is simply communicating what needs to be done and how!

Some students do not comprehend and/or pay attention to words. For them, the next condition is assistance, including how much assistance is needed (maximal, many cues, three or fewer cues, no cues) and what kind of modeling/teacher talk (physical, verbal, visual, or a combination) should be used. *No assistance* means that the student understands and responds to verbal instructions. If this is not the case, then demonstrations and words are used in various combinations to find the type of modeling/teacher talk condition that works best (verbal, then visual; visual, then verbal; concurrent visual and verbal). On occasion, physical (kinesthetic) assistance may be needed. This is called *coactive* to emphasize that it is more than physical manipulation. Under this maximal input condition, the teacher uses both verbal and physical prompts. The student says or sings the key words in unison with the teacher. Levels of assistance thus range from none to maximal, which means a combination of physical-verbal-visual input.

In addition to these instructional conditions, environmental variables also influence success. Among these are size, weight, and texture of an object, as well as surface, slope, and stability of the movement area. Also important is number of persons at each station and whether or not the student can work independently or needs a helper. Footprints and floor markings can assure that every person at a station is in the right place and in his or her own space. The direction a student faces should also be controlled to block out irrelevant stimuli or to systematically teach coping skills in relation to multiple environmental input.

Conditions are important in both testing and practice. Figure 11.3 shows how conditions are prescribed. A common practice in adapted physical activity skill development is a clipboard for each student containing task sheets like Figure 11.3. During a 30-min class, for example, a student might work on different skills at three stations, each of which provides a rich choice of equipment so that level of difficulty can be matched with prescription on the task card. A separate task sheet for each station is on the clipboard.

The order of the sheets on the clipboard indicates the order in which the student should progress from station to station.

The task card provides spaces to indicate performance on 60 trials. After each set of 15 trials, an alternate activity may be used to break monotony and/or provide work on another objective, such as abdominal strength (sit-ups), cardiovascular endurance (bench stepping), or tension release (slow stretches). Sometimes, this alternative activity should be in one of the student's areas of strength so that it can serve as a reward. In general, however, the focus should be on completion of as many trials as possible before the signal to rotate to the next station. The greater the student's time on task, the better the learning outcome.

Reinforcers are not left to chance. Their inclusion on the task sheet signals their importance. *Other* under "Reinforcers" on Figure 11.3 recognizes what works best for each student. *Self-praise* is included as a reinforcer because students need to learn to tell themselves that they are good and to gradually rely on their own self-reinforcement more than that of an external source. The *same as nondisabled* reinforcer category implies use of informational and questioning feedback that requires problem solving. Reinforcement obviously can take many forms. The key is for the teacher or partner to respond in some way, thereby showing interest and support.

The *objective* that guides the task sheet can focus on quantitative or qualitative performance or both. Assessment and instruction should attend to each (Kelly, Reuschlein, & Haubenstricker, 1989; Ulrich, 1988).

Functional Competence

Functional competence refers to proficiency in performing life functions like locomotion, play, work, and self-care. It is not enough, for example, to run or throw a ball in response to demonstrations and prompts in the instructional setting. Students must be able to spontaneously use runs and throws in a variety of settings to achieve a number of purposes (e.g., safety, joy, fitness).

Functional competence also implies performance similar to that of others within the same chronological age range. This second part of the definition is important when the placement goal is integration because the student must have the skills to participate fully, safely, and successfully. For example, to benefit from the numerous third- and fourth-grade lead-up games that teach and reinforce softball skills, students must be able to stop a ball on the ground or in the air and to throw it accurately and quickly to a base or teammate. Functional competence thus involves chaining together several motor skills and decision making about where to throw the ball.

Performance Standards

Instruction in motor skills is directed toward meeting *performance standards* with respect to form, distance, speed, accuracy, and function. These task variables are not equally important for all skills, and time limitations usually force teachers to select two or three rather than all five. When an

FIGURE 11.3

Clipboard sheet indicating objective, context, and task conditions.

Task _____ Overarm throw _____ Date _____ 9/12 _____

Student name _____ J. Garza _____ Partner/aide name _____ CS _____

Objective _____ To throw 30 ft. using correct form _____

Context: C1 Informal play   (C2 Structured game)   C3 Formal drill or test

DIRECTIONS:

Go to station _____ #2 _____ . Work on objective under the circled task conditions. Record number of trials attempted and succeeded in boxes at bottom.

SIX TASK CONDITIONS

Object Size		**Texture/Weight**	
(O1)	Tennis ball	T1	Nerf or sponge
O2	Small softball	T2	Rubber
O3	Regular softball	(T3)	Regular

Assistance		**Instructions**	
A1	Maximal	(I1)	Short, two to three words
(A2)	Many cues	I2	Medium, four to seven words
A3	Three or fewer cues	I3	Long, eight or more words
A4	None		

Modeling/Teacher Talk		**Reinforcers**	
M1	Coactive	R1	Maximal: Token, hug/pat,(praise),(smile)
M2	Verbal, then visual	(R2)	Two or three of above
M3	Visual, then verbal	R3	Same as nondisabled
(M4)	Concurrent visual-verbal	R4	Self-praise
M5	Verbal only		Other _____

Trials (Tr)

1	2	3	4	5	6	7	8	9	10	11	12	13	14	15

integrated setting is the placement goal or the student is already integrated, assessment should focus on the skill levels expected of the grade or chronological age level.

Much of adapted physical education is devoted to initial-level skills teaching. Students with motor delays and/or pathology often do not have time to master all of the motor skills of normal children, ages 2 to 7 years. In this case, the walk, run, jump, throw, strike, and kick are usually emphasized. Norms for the run, jump, and throw appear in Appendix J.

To help plan the order in which basic skills should be taught, three teaching/testing progressions (TTPs) are included in this chapter: walk and run, jump and hop, and object control skills. Each TTP breaks skills into observable, measurable tasks that are ordered from easy to hard. By stating a criterion level and the average age at which normal children pass, the TTPs permit the teacher to determine the number of months of developmental delay. This information is often helpful in making placement decisions.

FIGURE   11.4

Overarm throw section of IEP for 9-year-old boy with motor delay.

Present Level of Performance
   Form: Mostly Level 3 (homolateral throw) with the following appearance. No muscle tone or reflex pathology.

   Distance: Throws softball 70 ft, best of 3 trials (15th percentile).
   Accuracy: Scores 3 on target overarm throw at distance of 50 ft, 10 trials (below school district average).
   Function: Cannot use throw in game setting.
   Long-Term Goal—Functional competence for placement with nondisabled 8- and 9-year-olds.

   Short-Term Objectives
      Form: 1. Pass TGMD #2, full trunk rotation.
                2. Pass TGMD #4, opposition of limbs.
      Distance: 3. Throw softball 79 ft, best of 3 trials.
      Accuracy: 4. Score 5 on accuracy test at 50 ft, 10 trials.
      Function: 5. Perform throw-and-run and field ball-and-throw sequences in softball lead-up games.

Constraints

Constraints, within an assessment context, refer to abnormalities of body structure and function that limit functional ability. These include short stature, obesity, posture problems, deviant sizes and shapes of body parts, amputations, and abnormalities of muscle tone. Little is known about good form, mechanical efficiency, and developmental levels when such constraints are present. Indicating pathology in assessment reports is therefore important.

Describing present level of performance for a person with spasticity, athetosis, or paralysis takes many, many words. Therefore, professionals describe abnormal patterns in terms of muscle tone.

Abnormalities of muscle tone are

1. **Spasticity or hypertonus.** Muscle tone is too tight; may be evidenced by contractures or spasms. Usually associated with cerebral palsy but can be caused by many conditions.

2. **Athetosis or fluctuating muscle tone.** Body parts in constant, purposeless motion. A type of cerebral palsy.

3. **Paralysis or atonus.** Common in spina bifida.

4. **Paresis or hypotonus.** Weakness caused by partial paralysis or muscle deterioration. Common in muscular dystrophy.

Problems like round shoulders, swayback, and pigeon toes (see Chapter 14) should be taken into consideration in assessment and instruction of basic movement patterns. Also important are neurological constraints like deficits of balance, coordination, and motor planning. Identification of constraints forces attention on adaptation, especially in regard to ideas about good form and procedures of qualitative analysis.

Developmental Level

Qualitative analysis of form sometimes focuses on *developmental level.* Normal children progress fairly rapidly from immature to mature patterns (McClenaghan & Gallahue, 1978; Wickstrom, 1983). Immature patterns, often broken down into initial and elementary levels, are called developmental in that they are normal for a particular chronological age. Children with disabilities and/or clumsiness typically display initial and elementary performance levels far longer than normal peers. This not only results in inefficient and energy-exhausting movement but often affects social acceptance and self-esteem. The sissy throw, seen in both girls and boys of elementary age, is an example of an immature movement. This movement pattern, however, is totally acceptable in early childhood, when it would be called developmental.

Mature movement patterns are mechanically efficient, a quality called good form. Although there are many individual differences in mature form, certain performance criteria must be met. Ulrich's (1985) Test of Gross Motor Development (TGMD) is recommended to assess form.

To assist teachers in visualizing different developmental levels and planning remediation for progress toward mature form, this chapter includes pictorial and checklist assessment instruments based on the concept of developmental levels. Use of these instruments simplifies writing the individualized education program (IEP) and other reports that require a description of present level of performance.

Figure 11.4 is a sample IEP format that illustrates how developmental level is described under form. When movement patterns are immature, the major goal is to assist students in progressing to the next developmental level. This is done by specifying objectives that pertain to form (e.g., demonstrate opposition of limbs).

Writing Goals and Objectives

Because of heavy workloads, teachers devise many shortcuts to writing goals and objectives. For students whose assessment data indicate that work is needed on basic motor skills, the goal is almost always: *To achieve functional competence in locomotor and object control skills.* Sometimes, specific skills are highlighted, as in Figure 11.2. Functional competence for each age or grade level is explained in school district curriculum guides. These explanations include performance standards that must be met and/or a minimal percentile (e.g., the 30th percentile) to be achieved on district norms. Also in curriculum guides are lists of games and sport activities that a student of a certain age or grade should be able to play in order to be in an integrated classroom.

Short-term objectives are often computerized or printed in list form in curriculum guides so that the teacher can use numbers or abbreviations when making out IEPs for large numbers of students. Objectives, remember, have three parts: (a) condition, (b) observable behavior, and (c) criterion level. The part of the objective that requires the most words is the condition, which typically includes many parts. Consider, for example, an objective pertaining to throwing:

1. Given these conditions,

   - A specified object (size, weight, texture)
   - A set number of trials
   - In a designated context (informal play, structured game, formal test)
   - With appropriate instructions (short, medium, long)
   - With needed assistance (physical, verbal, visual)
   - With necessary reinforcers (token, hug/pat, praise, smile)

2. the student will throw

3. at a designated criterion level (e.g., form, distance, accuracy, function).

Writing out all of these conditions for every objective takes too much time, so most teachers use an abbreviation system (see Figure 11.3). The objective might therefore look like this:

1. Given these conditions,
   O2, T2, Tr10, C3, I2, A3, R2

2. the student will throw

3. at a designated criterion level (state what it is).

Individualizing instruction requires considerable record keeping so that the teacher can remember the task conditions under which a student is most likely to succeed. This is often facilitated by creating a clipboard with mimeographed sheets like Figure 11.3 for each student. The clipboard system permits an aide, peer tutor, or partner to understand and work toward a designated objective.

As you progress through this chapter, consider the task conditions that can be altered in teaching and/or testing each skill. In locomotor skills, for instance, the surface slope (even, uphill, downhill, variable), surface texture (floor, short grass, long grass, sand), and surface stability (rigid, yielding, variable) might be altered. Likewise, tasks might be executed under a blindfold or a rhythm condition. Try developing your own sheets to show your understanding of task analysis.

Biomechanical Analysis of a Movement Pattern

An ability to break skills into their respective phases or parts aids observation, identification, and description of problems. Terms used for phases of locomotor skills are *heel strike, foot plant, midstance, swing, recovery, pushoff, takeoff, flight,* and *landing.* Terms used for most object control skills are *starting position* or *preparation, backswing, forward swing, release* or *contact,* and *follow-through.*

For each phase, the teacher must look carefully at the actions of individual body segments: head, trunk, arms/hands, legs/feet. In analysis of normal movement, criteria like those in Ulrich's (1985) Test of Gross Motor Development (TGMD) are used. When movement is abnormal or structural deviations are present, phases and segmental actions are analyzed in more detail.

Good teaching requires providing informational feedback. Since most students can attend only to one or two correctional cues at a time, prioritizing which body part should be worked on first is important. Often, head control is selected as the focus, and students are told to keep their eyes on a designated target. For informational feedback to be helpful, students must be taught a vocabulary of body parts and actions. Movement exploration helps them to match words with feedback from other sources (vestibular, kinesthetic, mirrors, sounds). Taps on shoes and noise-making equivalents in gloves are especially useful in reinforcing correct foot/ankle and hand/wrist positions. For example, children, especially those with mental retardation or learning disabilities, often do not know the meaning of such cues as "Land on the *balls* of your feet."

With average performers, detailed biomechanical analysis is not necessary. Adapted physical activity specialists, however, must become skilled observers to give useful feedback. Most important, they must know how much feedback to give, when, and how. Some students learn best by seeing wholes, others by seeing parts. Learning style determines the nature of both demonstration and verbal input.

Walking: The Foundation Skill

Walking is the first locomotor pattern to be performed in the upright position. In normal children, the onset of walking is between 9 and 18 months of age. In children with disabilities, this skill may be delayed for only a few months or up to 6 or 7 years. The average age of independent walking ranges from 20 to 36 months for children who are blind and from 12 to 65 months for youngsters with Down syndrome. Children with cerebral palsy on one side of the body (hemiplegia) usually walk before age 2, but those with all four limbs involved (quadriplegia) often do not walk until age 6 or 7. Many children with mental retardation have confounding neurological deficits that delay walking by several years.

FIGURE 11.5

Abnormal gaits associated with spasticity and ataxia.

Scissors gait. Associated with quadriplegic spastic cerebral palsy. The legs are flexed, inwardly rotated, and adducted at the hip joint, causing them to cross alternately in front of each other. There is excessive knee flexion. Toe walking causes a narrow base. Scissoring and toe walking may be caused also by the *positive supporting reflex*. The positive supporting reflex is an extension (plantar flexion) response of the feet to tactile stimuli.

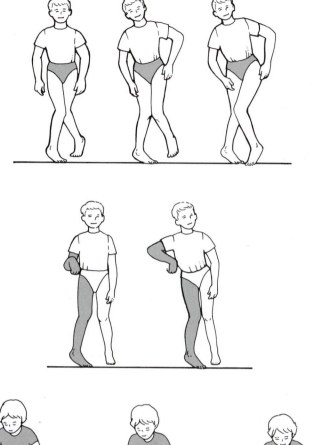

Hemiplegic gait. Associated with hemiplegic spastic cerebral palsy and stroke. Arm and leg on the same side are involved. Tends to occur with any disorder producing an immobile hip or knee. Individual leans to the affected side, and arm on that side is held in a rigid, semiflexed position.

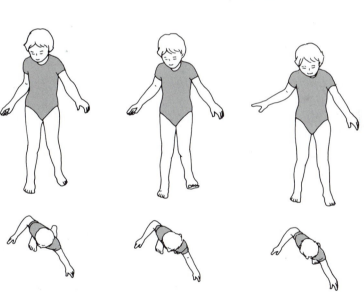

Ataxic or cerebellar gait. Associated with ataxic cerebral palsy, Friedreich's ataxia, and similar *les autres* conditions. Individual walks with a wide base, and there is irregularity of steps, unsteadiness, tendency to reel to one side. Individual seems to experience difficulty in judging how high to lift legs when climbing stairs. Problems are increased when the ground is uneven. Note the similarity between this and the immature walk of early childhood before the central nervous system has matured.

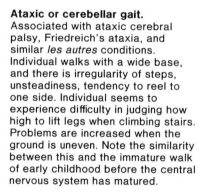

Typically, children who are slow to walk are provided physical therapy until age 7 or 8. If functional locomotion is not achieved by this time, experts agree that mobility goals should switch to wheelchair ambulation. Bleck (1982) states: "Physical therapy to improve a child's walking once he or she has reached 7 or 8 years is unlikely to be worth the time and effort expended, and other areas of function (like play and sports) should take precedence" (p. 79).

Adapted physical education typically focuses on the walk as an activity for improving dynamic balance, enhancing physical attractiveness via good postures, and increasing fitness. Beam walking is an important skill in perceptual-motor training and gymnastics. Walking in time to a drumbeat or music is a way of learning rhythm and relaxation. Walking across the swimming pool provides confidence for trying to float. Many persons with health impairments (e.g., obesity, asthma, heart conditions) walk for exercise, at least in the beginning sessions of a fitness or rehabilitation program. Walking can also be a competitive sport; race walking is a popular event among able-bodied persons and is an official track event for Special Olympians.

FIGURE 11.6

Gaits characterized primarily by shuffling or impairment in the heel-toe transfer of weight.

Shuffling gait. Associated with central nervous system immaturity (probably retention of tonic labyrinthine reflex-prone and symmetrical tonic neck reflex). Inability of lower body to move independently of upper body. Seen in severe mental retardation. Excessive flexion at hip, knee, and ankle joints, and the trunk is usually inclined forward. Contact with floor is flat-footed. Usually, there is no opposition of arms and legs.

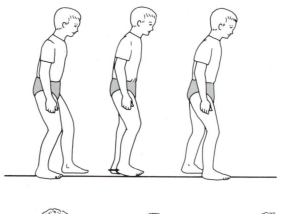

Propulsion or festination gait. Associated with Parkinson's disease, also called *paralysis agitans*. Individual walks with a forward leaning posture and short, shuffling steps that begin slowly and become progressively more rapid. This gait is seen also in very old persons with low fitness.

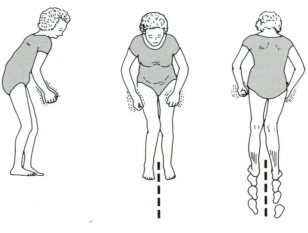

Steppage gait. Also called foot-drop gait and is associated with flopping of the foot on the floor. Knee action is higher than normal, but toes still tend to drag on floor. Caused by paralysis or weakness of the ankle dorsiflexors. Results in excessive hip and knee flexor work.

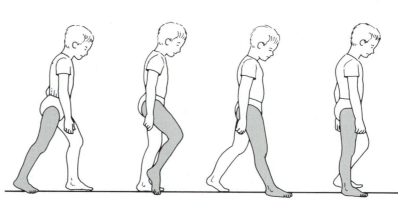

Among adults, walking is the most popular leisure-time physical activity. Walking or wheeling (the wheelchair equivalent) is something that everyone can do. Thus, physical educators strive to help persons of all ages to make their walking patterns efficient and fun.

Individual Differences in Gaits

One of the first assessment challenges in getting acquainted with a new student is determining whether the walk is normal or pathological and why. Physical educators should be able to recognize abnormal gaits and associate them with common conditions. Figures 11.5 to 11.7 present three groups of gaits categorized loosely by appearance. For each gait, there are many individual differences depending, in part, on whether the impairment is mild or severe. Persons with these gaits are often in mainstream physical education.

In studying these figures, remember that cerebral palsy, spina bifida, and muscular dystrophy are the three most common physical disabilities among school-age persons. These conditions are covered in Part 3 of this text, but the first knowledge acquired about each should be basic walking pattern.

FIGURE 11.7

Gaits characterized by waddling, lurching, or abnormal lateral movement.

Waddling gait. Main deviation from normal is a rolling movement from side to side. This is usually caused by structural problems like bowlegs (genu varum), hip problems and dislocations (coxa vara), knock-knees, or one leg longer than the other.

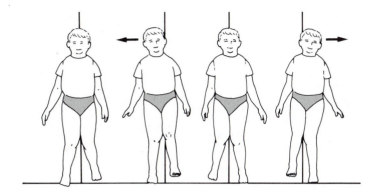

Muscular dystrophy gait. This is an awkward, side-to-side waddle, swayback (lordosis), arms held in backward position, and frequent falling. Shoulder girdle muscles are often badly atrophied. Calf muscles may be hypertrophied but weak because fat has replaced the muscle tissue.

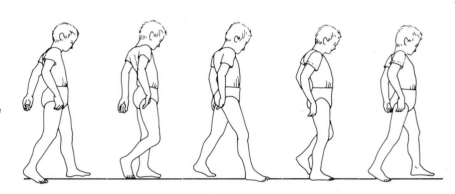

Gluteus maximus lurch. Associated with polio and other spinal paralysis conditions in which the paralyzed limb cannot shift the body weight forward onto the normal limb. To compensate, the trunk is thrust forward. The gait is thus associated with alternate sticking out of chest (salutation) and pulling back of shoulders.

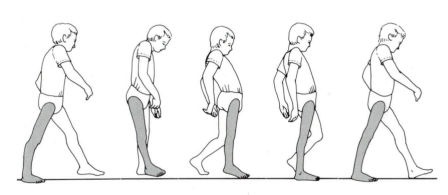

Trendelenburg gait. Limp caused by paralysis or weakness of gluteus medius. Pelvis is lower on nonaffected side. In walking, each time the weight is transferred, the body leans slightly in the direction of the weight transfer. Shifting the weight compensates for weak abductors.

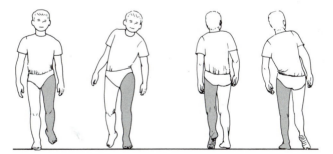

Gluteus medius

Major hip abductor

FIGURE 11.8

Crutch gaits used by persons with severe disabilities.

Step to, swing to, or drag to gait. This is used by persons with severe disability who have little or no control of legs. In public schools, the young child with spina bifida in long leg braces is the best example. In rehabilitation settings, this is the first gait taught to persons with lesions above T10. It is a staccato gait with no follow-through in front of the crutches. All the weight is taken by the arms, while the legs are lifted and swung or dragged forward. The pattern is lift and drop, lift and drop. The crutches shown are axillary crutches. Axillary refers to armpit area, and axillary crutches are those that fit under the arms. These should never be used for running because of possible damage to the brachial plexus (a network of nerves under the arm).

Four-point gait. This gait is used by persons with severe disability who can move each leg independently. The pattern is (1) advance left crutch, (2) advance right foot, (3) advance right crutch, and (4) advance left foot. The weaker leg is shaded. The crutches shown are Lofstrand (also called Canadian or forearm) crutches.

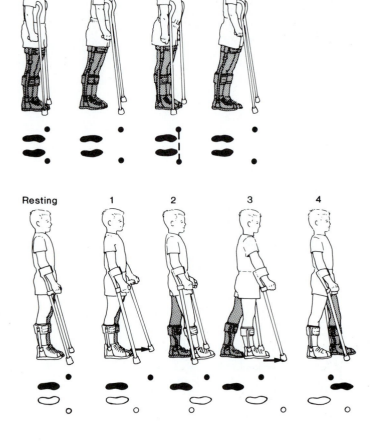

FIGURE 11.9

Crutch gait used with temporary disabilities or amputation.

Swing-through gait. The person leans into the crutches, lifting the body off the ground by extending the elbows. The body is swung through the crutches so that the good foot lands in *front* of the crutches. Then the crutches are brought forward, and the sequence is repeated.

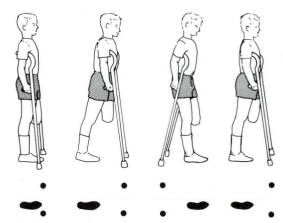

DO NOT CONFUSE SWING-THROUGH WITH SWING-TO.

FIGURE 11.10

Crutch gaits used by persons with mild to moderate impairments. The weaker leg is shaded.

Three-point gait. In this gait, both crutches move forward in unison as in the step-to and swing-through gaits, but the feet move separately. Unlike most gaits, the involved, or weaker, leg takes the first step up to and even with the crutches, so it bears only partial body weight as the good leg then steps out in front of the crutches. The pattern is (1) advance both crutches, (2) advance weak leg, and (3) advance strong leg.

Two-point gait. This gait is most like normal walking and running. It is the fastest of the gaits but requires the most balance because there are only two points of contact with the ground at any time. Whenever a crutch moves, the opposite leg moves in unison. The pattern is (1) advance left crutch and right leg simultaneously and (2) advance right crutch and left leg simultaneously.

Hemiplegic gait. This gait is similar to the three-point except that one cane is used instead of two crutches. The cane moves first, then the weak leg opposite the cane, then the strong leg. The steps taken with each leg should be equal in length, with emphasis placed on establishing a rhythmic gait. Although used by persons of all ages, this gait is most common in older persons who have had strokes.

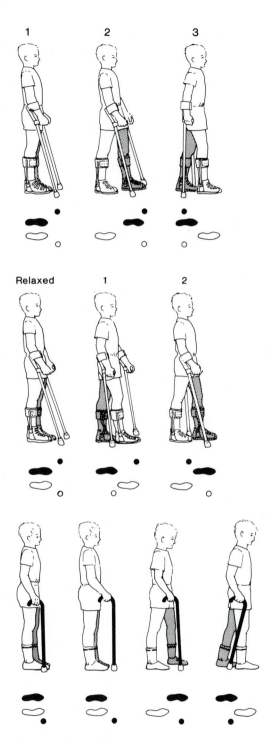

Many students ambulate with crutches or canes. To assess and describe present level of psychomotor performance, crutch gaits must be referred to by name (see Figures 11.8 to 11.10). Students who use crutches and canes can compete in track-and-field events like able-bodied peers. They are limited only by your ability to teach and coach.

Developmental Levels in Walking

Normal walking gait varies with age. Walking matures as the central nervous system (CNS) develops and myelination is completed. If maturation is delayed or frozen or brain damage occurs, a person may exhibit a gait similar to the pattern of a young child. Figure 11.11 depicts normal gaits

FIGURE   11.11

Normal gaits at different ages.

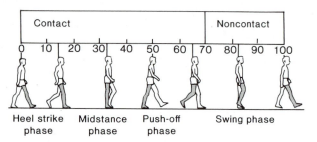

Normal, mature walking gait of children from ages 4 to 5 years and older. A gait cycle begins with the heel strike and ends when the heel of the same leg strikes again. Step and stride length relate to height.

Initial-Toddler

First walking pattern, showing high guard position of arms, rigid torso, excessive flexion of hip and knee joints, and flat-footed or toe-walking steps.

Early Childhood

Walking pattern of children until age 4 or 5. There is still no trunk rotation and, hence, no opposition of arm and leg movements. Hip and knee action is still excessive, but heel-toe transfer of weight is beginning to appear.

at different ages. Major changes in the transition from immature to mature walking pertain to (a) carriage of arms, (b) trunk rotation, (c) opposition of limbs, (d) hip and knee action, and (e) type of foot plant and pushoff. Especially important in the mature walk is the heel-toe transfer of weight.

Figure 11.12 shows illustrative children with walking problems and strategies that help. The girl with Down syndrome, who is still wobbly because of hypotonus, can push a cart filled with weights more easily than walking without something to hang onto. The use of creative dramatics helps to motivate time on task. For example, the teacher can make up a story about a little girl taking her doll for a walk and what she sees on the way. The boy with spina bifida needs lots of practice to gain arm and shoulder strength. Puppets are useful motivational devices in keeping a child moving back and forth across the room.

The shuffling gait is associated with developmental delays often seen in adapted physical education. Abnormal retention of several reflexes—tonic labyrinthine-prone, symmetrical tonic neck, positive support, and toe grasp—contributes to shuffling. With the tonic labyrinthine-prone reflex, flexor tone dominates, explaining why the person seems always to be looking at the feet. Flexion of the head is also nature's way of facilitating leg extension via the symmetrical tonic neck reflex. With the positive support and toe grasp reflexes, contact with the floor heightens extensor activity, making flexion to lift the leg difficult. Remediation of the shuffling gait should begin with activities in Chapter 10.

Also helpful are games that require reciprocal lifting of feet, as in stepping over bamboo poles, rungs of a ladder, tires, and other obstacles. Tap-dance games, in which the goal is to make noises with different parts of the foot (heel-toe, heel-toe, toe-toe-toe), also help. These can be done in a sitting position or while holding onto a bar for support. Hundreds of walking games, particularly when songs and creative dramatics are woven in, are helpful. Marching, for instance, is fun when children play that they are members of a band or participants in a parade. Walking, combined with carrying loads of different sizes and weights, generalizes to activities of daily living, such as carrying in the groceries and taking out the garbage.

Figure 11.13 provides checklists for evaluating immature and mature walking. The 11 criteria under the mature pattern can be used as objectives.

Table 11.1 ends this section with a developmentally sequenced teaching/test progression (TTP) to show walking and running activities. These should be done on many surfaces, with different degrees of incline and stability, with and without blindfolds. How many ways can you vary each activity?

Teaching the Run

Ability to analyze a walk carries over into the teaching of other locomotor skills. Many of the items for evaluation of walking are applicable to running (see Figure 11.14). The run is a locomotor pattern comprised of four phases: foot plant, recovery, pushoff, and flight. Unlike the walk, the run has no period of double support. Children pass through three distinct developmental levels in running. Normal children demonstrate Levels 1, 2, and 3 at about ages 2, 3, and 5, respectively. All of the components of a mature run, however, are not typically present until age 7 or 8. In adapted physical activity, you will see many developmental delays. Let's consider what to emphasize in teaching the run.

FIGURE **11.12**

Illustrative walking activities and motivational devices.

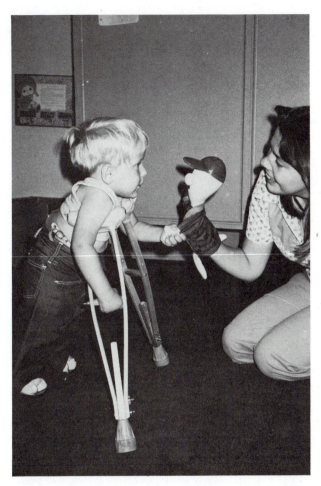

Leg Action

Foot plant, similar to the heel strike in the walk, marks the end of the forward leg swing. The foot plant in the sprint is on the metatarsals; the teacher stresses "Run on the balls of your feet." In the mature run (Level 3), the support foot contacts the floor approximately under the body's center of gravity (CG). In immature runs, the support foot lands in front of the CG. The body lean (line between support foot and CG) in the mature run is at 1 o'clock, whereas it is too far forward or backward in the immature pattern.

Recovery, similar to the midstance in the walk, is the best time to check the presence of a high heel kick. This mechanism readies the knee to spring forward with maximal propulsive thrust in the pushoff phase. In the immature run, the hip and knee may be outwardly rotated and cause a toe-out gait, but this problem ameliorates itself in normal development. Unless there are muscle imbalances, 6-year-olds can run straight, placing their feet on or near a designated line.

Pushoff, the same term as in the walk, demands excellent bilateral coordination inasmuch as the support leg pushes backward and downward while the swing leg lifts forward and upward. Focal points to be checked are the amount of extension in the pushoff leg and the height of the knee lift of the swing leg. At the end of the knee lift, the thigh is more-or-less horizontal to the ground.

Flight is the period of nonsupport, the time when both legs are in the air. As children mature, an increasing proportion of time is spent in flight. In addition, the elevation of the flight decreases, an indication that force is being properly directed forward and not upward.

Arm Movements

The coordination of proper arm movements with the leg actions is the hardest part of the run and the last to appear. Level 3 of Figure 11.14 shows the opposition of limbs and the use of a pumping action of the arms to increase forward momentum. The elbows are kept bent at about 90°. The hand

FIGURE 11.13

Checklist for evaluation of walking in persons of different ages.

Directions: Observe the student walking on several different terrains or surfaces (even or uneven), uphill, downhill, and on a level surface. Consider the 11 sets of alternate descriptions and check the one of each set that represents the student's level of performance. Until the child is about age 4 years, most checks will be in the left-hand column. After age 4, the normal child exhibits mature walking. Use findings to write specific behavioral objectives.

Check One	Developmental or Immature Walking	Check One	Mature Walking

	1. Forward lean
	   a. From ground
	   b. From waist and hips
			1. Good body alignment
			   a. Head up
			   b. Good extension of spine

	2. Wide base of support, with heels 5–8" from line of progression		2. Narrower base of support with heels 2–3" from line of progression
	3. Toes and knees pointed outward		3. Toes and knees pointed straight ahead
	4. Flat-footed gait		4. Heel-ball-toe transfer of weight
	5. Excessive flexion at knee and hip; no double knee lock		5. Strong pushoff from toes; double knee lock present
	6. Uneven, jerky steps[a]		6. Smooth and rhythmical shift of weight, with minimal up-and-down movement
	7. Little or no pelvic rotation until second or third year. Body sways from side to side.		7. Minimal rotatory action of pelvis (short persons will have more than tall ones)
	8. Rigidity of upper torso		8. Compensatory shoulder rotation inversely related to pelvic rotation
	9. Outstretched arms, also called high guard position		9. Arms swing freely and in opposition with legs
	10. Relatively short stride. In preschool children, the distance from heel to heel is 11–18"		10. Greater length of stride dependent upon length of leg
	11. Rate of walking stablilizes at about 170 steps per minute		11. Rate of walking decreases to about 115 to 145 steps per minute

[a]Jerkiness may be caused by a flat-footed or shuffle gait or by excessive stride length.

swings as high as the chin in the forward swing; the elbow reaches as high as the shoulder in the backswing. In the less mature runs, the arms' range of motion is very limited.

Assessment Ideas

Assessment of the run can be complex or simple, depending on the number of performance criteria. Ulrich (1985) in the Test of Gross Motor Development (TGMD) indicated that the four most important criteria are

1. Brief period where both feet are off the ground
2. Arms moving in opposition to legs, elbows bent
3. Foot placement near or on a line (not flat-footed)
4. Nonsupport leg bent approximately 90° (close to buttocks)

Runners should be observed at their fastest speed over a minimum distance of 50 ft in two or more trials. Devise game settings for examining the run. Challenges might be "How

fast can you run around the baseball diamond?" "How fast can you run to a designated goal line?" Low organized games, in which students chase and tag one another or run from place to place on cue, also can be used for assessment purposes.

Use both process and product assessment. When measuring speed, plan adaptations for poor reaction time and the problem of slowing down before reaching the finish line. Typically, both problems are resolved by having the student run further than the timed distance (see Figure 11.15). Regardless of the activity, teach students not to slow down until after they have crossed the finish line.

Teach runners start signals ("On your mark, get set, go") that are the same as those used in track meets. Conduct assessment and practice in a class setting in such a way that skills learned can be generalized to Special Olympics or other competitive events. The running task, the finish line, and the concept of personal best should all be clearly understood.

FIGURE   11.14

Pictorial checklist for assessing running.

Directions: Observe several 50-ft runs. Circle the level that best depicts the pattern you observe and underline the descriptors that can be used on the IEP to indicate present level of performance.

Phases	Foot plant	Recovery	Pushoff	Flight
Main Focal Points	Center of gravity (CG)	Heel kick	Straight-leg push High knee lift	Time

Level 1: Initial Usually age 2

Foot plant: Support foot in front of CG / Front leg stiff / Little knee flexion / Limited arm action does not help

Recovery: Outward rotation at hip and knee joints / Toes point out / Low rear heel kick

Pushoff: Minimal backward-downward thrust / Poor knee lift of swing leg

Flight: No flight or short flight

Level 2: Transitional Usually age 3

Foot plant: Support foot in front of CG / Some knee flexion / Bent arms begin to work in opposition to legs

Recovery: Minimal rotation / Toes point straight / Medium rear heel kick

Pushoff: Good backward-downward thrust / Some knee lift of swing leg

Flight: Longer flight / Sometimes, too much elevation

Level 3: Mature Usually age 5

Foot plant: Support foot under CG / Body lean at 1 o'clock / Bent arms (90° elbow flexion) provide forceful pumping action

Recovery: Minimal rotation / Toes point straight / High rear heel kick

Pushoff: Back leg straight / Excellent backward-downward thrust / Front thigh horizontal to ground

Flight: Very long flight / Little elevation / Force directed forward

Table 11.1
Walk and run skills listed from easy to hard: A developmentally sequenced teaching/testing progression.

Task	Criterion to Pass	Average Age (Months)
1. Walk, Level 1 pattern (see Figure 11.11)	4–5 steps	12–14
2. Walk, Level 2 pattern	10-ft distance	15–17
3. Walk backward	5 steps	15–17
4. Walk sideward	10-ft distance	15–17
5. Run, Level 1 pattern (see Figure 11.14)	10-ft distance	18–23
6. Walk on tiptoes	5 steps, hands on hips	24–29
7. Walk backward	10-ft distance	24–29
8. Walk 4-inch beam	3 steps forward	24–29
9. Walk 4-ft circular pattern	Fewer than 5 stepoffs	24–29
10. Walk line on tiptoes	8-ft distance	30–35
11. Walk backward, 4-ft circular pattern	Fewer than 2 stepoffs	42–47
12. Walk 4-inch beam	4 steps forward	48–53
13. Heel-toe walk backward, 4-inch beam	5 steps, toes touching heels	54–59
14. Walk 4-inch beam, hands on hips	8-ft distance	54–59
15. Walk on tiptoes, hands on hips	15-ft distance	60–71
16. Walk 4-inch beam, sideward	8-ft distance	60–71
17. Run/walk 1 mile as fast as possible	13 min for boys; 14 min for girls	60–71
18. Run/walk 1 mile as fast as possible	12 min for boys; 13 min for girls	72–83
19. Run 50 yd for speed	9.9 sec for boys; 10.2 for girls	72–83
20. Shuttle run for speed, 12 ft apart, 2 cans	Complete cycle of 2 cans in 12 sec	72–83

Note. Information for Items 1–16 and 20 was abstracted from the Peabody Developmental Motor Scales (Folio & Fewell, 1983). Items 17–19 come from AAHPERD (1988) and Hanson (1965).

Pedagogy

Children who lack the concept of running should be introduced to it by walks down hills steep enough to quicken the pace to a run. In early stages of learning, they may have a rope around the waist and be pulled into a running gait. Patient teaching is required also to convey the concepts of starting, stopping, and staying in a lane.

Less involved children need special instruction related to running on the balls of the feet, lifting the knees, and swinging the arms. To facilitate running on the balls of the feet, practice can be up steep hills or steps. Jumping and hopping activities also tend to emphasize staying on the balls of the feet. Possible solutions to inadequate knee lift include riding a bicycle, particularly uphill; running up steep hills or steps; and running in place with knee action exaggerated to touch the outstretched palms of hands. Corrections for swinging arms across the body or without vigor include practice in front of a mirror and running with a baton or small weight bar.

To understand the mechanics of running, children should be taught the meanings of such words as *forward lean, driving leg, recovery leg, center of gravity,* and *striding.* *Forward lean* is the line between foot contact and center of gravity. Forward lean is greatest early in the sprint, when the runner is accelerating rapidly, and levels off after the point of maximum speed is reached. The *driving leg* is the one that extends and pushes against the ground. The *recovery leg* is the one in which the high knee lift is important. The *center of gravity* is the point in the pelvis below which the recovery foot should try to land.

The rate of striding depends upon four factors: (a) speed of extension of driving leg, (b) speed with which recovery leg is brought through, (c) length of time body is in air, and (d) landing position of the recovery foot in relation to the center of gravity. Speed, of course, is dependent on range of motion.

Children may need help to understand the concept of speed. Any child with number concepts up to 15 can understand running a 50-yd dash in 9 versus 13 sec. In track meets, emphasis can be placed on self-competition by pinning cards with the children's best times on their backs. As they finish a dash, they are told whether or not they beat their own time. Ribbons can be awarded to children who beat their own times rather than (or in addition to) children who beat others. An alternative technique is recording the child's expressed level of aspiration and making awards for meeting or surpassing this estimate.

Types of Runs

The physical educator should be able to evaluate different kinds of runs: (a) sprinting; (b) middle-distance runs—880 yd and up; and (c) long-distance runs—mile and over for children. The 440-yd dash can be classified as either a sprint or a middle-distance run, depending upon cardiorespiratory

FIGURE   11.15

Adaptation when timing a 50-yd-dash for persons with developmental delay.

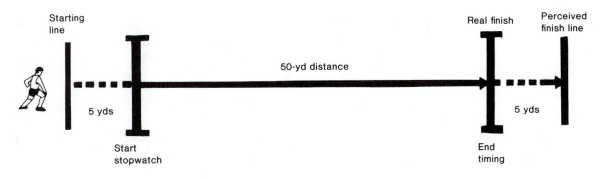

FIGURE   11.16

Comparison of three types of runs.

Phases	Sprint	Middle-Distance Run	Long-Distance Run
Foot plant	Land high on ball of foot; heel does not touch	Land lower on ball of foot than in sprint; heel does not touch	Land low on ball of foot, drop to heel
Knee action	Less rear kick than in other kinds of runs	More rear kick than in sprint	More rear kick than other runs
	Lift knee high and straight forward	Lift knee less high than in sprint	Lift knee slightly as compared to other runs
	Thigh should be more or less horizontal to ground at end of knee lift	Thigh should be less horizontal, about 70° to 80° at end of knee lift	Thigh is less horizontal at end of knee lift than in other runs
Forward body lean	Lean between 25° and 30°—about 1 o'clock	Lean between 15° and 18°—about halfway between 12 and 1 o'clock	Lean about 10°—about one-third of way between 12 and 1 o'clock
Arm action	Pump arms vigorously, with hands reaching chin level or higher	Use slightly less vigorous arm action	Swing arms naturally at about shoulder level

endurance. Jogging can be either a middle- or long-distance run. Figure 11.16 shows that each type of run varies with respect to foot plant, knee action, forward body lean, and arm action. These four components are generally the ones on which students need the most practice.

The shuttle run is traditionally used as a test of running speed and agility and should be practiced frequently. In this type of run, the goal is to shuttle back and forth between two end lines. On a signal, the student runs to a designated line and picks up an object (wooden block, eraser, sponge); then he or she returns to the starting line and deposits the object on the ground. The distance between lines and the number of objects vary. The American Alliance for Health, Physical Education, Recreation, and Dance (AAHPERD) uses a 30-ft distance and two blocks. The Bruininks-Oseretsky Test of Motor Proficiency (BOTMP) uses a 15-ft distance and one block.

Teaching Stair Skills

Functional locomotion in the community requires that children with developmental delays be given instruction and practice in the use of various kinds of stairsteps and ladders. Every school should have playground apparatus that motivates children to want to climb and affords opportunities for seeing the world at different heights (see Figure 11.17).

Ascending is much easier than descending and should be taught first. Slides are particularly good because they eliminate the problem of how to get the child down. Slides do not have to be slick. They can also be carpeted and made with a gentle slope that can be scooted or rolled down. Some apparatus should have only two or three steps, while others should offer more challenge.

Marking time and *alternate feet* are the terms used to assess developmental levels in ascending and descending. *Marking time* is a pattern in which the same foot always

FIGURE   11.17

Play apparatus should be designed so that children practice progressively more difficult kinds of climbing, balancing, and jumping.

FIGURE   11.18

Thirteen-year-old child with Down syndrome descends stairs in immature fashion, leading with the same foot and marking time on each rung. This pattern is exhibited in the normal child at about 23 months of age.

FIGURE   11.19

Comparison of jump, hop, and leap.

	Jump	**Hop**	**Leap**
Takeoff	May be either two-foot or one-foot takeoff	Always a one-foot takeoff	Always a one-foot takeoff
Flight	Weight always transferred to two feet	Weight never transferred	Weight always transferred from one foot to the other
Landing	Always a two-foot landing	Always a one-foot landing on same foot	Always a one-foot landing

Table 11.2
Averages ages (in months) for stair skills.

Developmental Patterns	Ascending	Descending
1. Marking time using handrail	18–23 months	18–23 months
2. Marking time without support	24–29 months	24–34 months
3. Alternate feet using handrail	29–31 months	30–50 months
4. Alternate feet without support	31–41 months	49–55 months

Note. These patterns should be assessed on staircases of variable height (2, 4, 6, 8 inches) and width.

leads. The name is derived from the lead foot marking time while the other foot steps up to create a period of double support on the one step. *Alternate feet* (also called a foot-over-foot pattern) is the mature pattern, in which left and right feet take turns leading, and only one foot is on a step at a time.

Table 11.2 shows four developmental levels of stair skills. Height and width of steps affect success, so assessment and goal setting should be specific to each piece of apparatus. Marking time skills occur at about the same age for ascending and descending, but the balance demands of the alternate feet pattern make descending more difficult. Typically, children cannot use the mature pattern in descending until about 15 months after it has been mastered in

Table 11.3
Jumping and hopping tasks listed from easy to hard: A developmentally sequenced teaching/testing progression.

Task	Criterion to Pass	Average Age (Months)
1. Step down from 8- to 10-inch height	One foot leads	18–23
2. Jump forward, two-foot takeoff	4 inches without falling	18–23
3. Jump up, two-foot takeoff	2 inches, both feet together	18–23
4. Jump down from 16- to 20-inch height	One foot leads	24–29
5. Jump over 2-inch high rope	Two foot takeoff	30–35
6. Jump down from 18- to 24-inch height	Two foot takeoff, land	30–35
7. Jump forward, two-foot takeoff	24 inches	30–35
8. Hop in place on one foot	3 times	30–35
9. Jump down from 24- to 30-inch height	Two-foot takeoff, land	36–41
10. Hop forward, one foot	5 times on one foot, then 3 times on other	36–41
11. Jump forward, two-foot takeoff	26 to 30 inches	36–41
12. Hop for distance	6 inches	42–47
13. Hop forward, one foot	8 times on one foot, then 8 times on other	42–47
14. Vertical jump for height	3 inches beyond normal reach	48–53
15. Jump down from 32-inch height	One foot leads	48–53
16. Hop for distance, preferred foot	16 inches	48–53
17. Hop for distance, nonpreferred foot	16 inches	48–53
18. Jump and turn 180°	Feet together, hands on hips	54–59
19. Jump sideways back and forth across line	3 times without stopping	54–59
20. Jump forward, two-foot takeoff	36 inches	54–59
21. Jump over 10-inch-high rope	Two-foot takeoff, land	60–71
22. Hop for speed, 20-ft distance	6 sec	60–71
23. Vertical jump for height	8 inches beyond normal reach	72–83

Note. The information in this table has been abstracted from the Peabody Developmental Motor Scales (Folio & Fewell, 1983).

ascending. Thus, most children do not exhibit alternate-step ascending and descending until age 4. Persons with disabilities show considerable delay and thus are often denied the opportunities for motor and social development afforded by playground apparatus (see Figure 11.18).

The mature pattern of stair climbing is an excellent cardiovascular fitness activity. The task can be made more demanding by adding weights (e.g., backpacks, books, stuffed animals).

Jump, Hop, Leap

Teachers must use the terms *jump, hop,* and *leap* correctly to communicate movement challenges to students. Figure 11.19 clarifies the meaning of these words. These patterns are similar in that they have three phases: a takeoff, flight, and landing. The jump for distance or height has an additional phase (the preliminary crouch) at the beginning of the sequence.

Average children learn to jump at about the same time they master the marking-time/ascending-stairs skills. Once a position of height has been attained, it makes sense to want to jump down. The earliest jumps, therefore, are usually step-downs in which one foot leads.

The ages at which children master jump, hop, and leap skills are of interest in planning assessment and de-

signing instruction. Table 11.3 presents information about the jump and the hop, and also a teaching progression, with tasks listed from easiest to hardest. In general, children begin to learn jumping skills at about 18 months, hopping at about 30 months, and leaping after they are in kindergarten or first grade.

In the jump, hop, and leap, students must know kinesthetically what the flight phase feels like. Figure 11.20 presents one approach to facilitating a kinesthetic awareness of up and down. The trampoline is another way. Manually lifting the student into the air while saying *up* may be necessary. Think of how many ways this can be done, alone and with a partner.

Teaching the Jump

Jumping is an extremely difficult skill for persons with neurological deficits because of its demand for good balance and bilateral integration. Many persons with severe mental retardation (MR) never learn to jump. Persons with mild MR conditions usually learn to jump, but their movement patterns may be immature compared to those of peers (Di-Rocco, Clark, & Phillips, 1987; Ersing, Loovis, & Ryan, 1982; Hemmert, 1978). Likewise, distance jumped lags 2 to 3 years behind nondisabled peers.

FIGURE 11.20

Three-year-old improves kinesthetic awareness of up and down as a lead-up to jumping.

Jumping is a popular field event, however, in meets for athletes with disabilities. Attending these meets enables prospective teachers to see persons with amputations, blindness, cerebral palsy, and other conditions excelling in jump events. There is widespread agreement that persons can learn to jump if physical educators make this a major goal.

Once you have ascertained the task or step that should be the focus, the next protocol is assessment to determine how to improve the quality of the jump. For the long jump, Ulrich (1985) suggested the following performance criteria:

1. Preparatory movement, including flexion of both knees with arms extended behind the body
2. Arms extended forcefully forward and upward, reaching full extension above head
3. Takeoff and landing on both feet simultaneously
4. Arms brought downward during landing

Of these criteria, the arm movements are the most difficult to master. Ulrich (1985) reported that 60% of nondisabled children do not master Criterion 2 until age 9. DiRocco et al. (1987) reported that arm actions were more of a problem than leg actions in children with mild MR.

Because many children with disabilities exhibit delays in jumping, different developmental levels must be recognized (see Figure 11.21). Persons exhibiting a Level 1 pattern probably have not yet sufficiently integrated the symmetrical tonic neck reflex; they obviously have deficits in bilateral coordination (see Chapter 10). Figure 11.22 provides a checklist for evaluation.

Developmental Sport Training

A developmental gymnastics or track-and-field program is recommended to provide practice in jumping. This approach supports the normalization principle and gives older students who still need work on basic skills the self-esteem of having a sport and of training to be an athlete. By using terms like *dismount, vault,* and *mount,* you can lend dignity to basic skill practice.

Jump Used As a Dismount

The gymnastics term *dismount* is a jump from a piece of apparatus down to the floor. Dismounts are used to end routines on the balance beam, the even parallel bars, the uneven parallel bars, the horse, and the buck. Judged for their aesthetic appearance and mechanical efficiency, dismounts may involve difficult movements, such as handsprings and cartwheels, or simple jumps downward using a two-foot takeoff and land.

Children need to know how to get off a piece of gymnastic apparatus or play equipment safely. The first skill that should be taught on a balance beam is the *jump-off dismount.* Children who feel secure about their jumping ability will no longer fear falling. Only then should locomotor movements (walks, runs, skips) on the balance beam be introduced.

Vault

Jumping becomes a sport skill when it is used in gymnastics as a means of getting over a piece of apparatus. Students can *vault* over many different kinds of apparatus: (a) a low beam about thigh or hip height, (b) a tumbling bench, (c) a vaulting box, (d) a horse, or (e) a buck.

Instead of demonstrating standard vaults and expecting the student to imitate, observe the different movement approaches explored by the student in attempts to get over the apparatus. Which of the following movement patterns offer the student the most success?

1. *Squat vault.* Weight taken equally on both arms, knees are pulled upward, tucked to chest, and then continue forward. Body passes over box in a squat position.
2. *Straddle vault.* Weight taken equally on both arms, and legs are abducted in wide-stride semi-sitting position. Hands are on inside and legs on the outside. Body passes over box in this straddle position.

FIGURE 11.21

Pictorial checklist for assessing standing long jump.

Directions. Circle the level that best depicts the pattern you observe and underline the descriptors that can be used on the IEP to indicate present level of performance.

Level 1: Initial

Descriptors: (1) Incomplete crouch, (2) difficulty in using both feet and arms simultaneously, (3) arms used for balance during flight but not contributing to forward momentum, (4) feet leading in flight and landing phases rather than arms.

Level 2: Transitional

Descriptors: (1) Forward body lean, (2) arms initiating takeoff, (3) body not fully straightening out during flight, (4) insufficient trunk flexion during flight downward, (5) unsteady landing.

Level 3: Mature

Descriptors: (1) Trunk parallel to ground in preliminary crouch, (2) angle of takeoff being 45°, (3) body fully extended during upward flight with arms stretched upward, (4) full trunk flexion during flight downward, (5) steady landing with arms forward.

3. *Flank vault.* Initially done with both arms on the box. Standard flank vault is performed with one arm. While arms support weight of body, both legs are lifted simultaneously over the box. The side of the body passes over the box. Sometimes called a side vault.

4. *Front vault.* Same as flank vault except that the front of the body passes over the box.

The beginning vault is often a combined side-front vault with both hands on the box and the knees bent as the legs pass over. Most elementary school textbooks recommend that the squat vault be taught first. The law of individual differences rules that *all* children should not be introduced

to the same progression of vaults nor tested on a single movement pattern selected by the teacher. When allowed to discover their own ways of getting over, first-grade children can succeed at vaulting. A beatboard or springboard is necessary to attain the height necessary for propulsion of the body over the box.

Movement Patterns for Jumping on a Springboard or Beatboard

The movement patterns used on the springboard, beatboard, minitramp, and diving board are similar. For better transfer of learning, the child should have experience on all four pieces of apparatus. If the budget allows the purchase of only one, the beatboard is recommended.

FIGURE 11.22

Checklist for evaluation of standing long jump.

Directions: Observe the student performing several broad jumps. Consider the 18 sets of alternate descriptions and check the one of each set that represents the student's present level of performance. Most normal children exhibit mature jumps by ages 7 or 8 years. Use findings to write specific behavioral objectives.

	Check One	Developmental or Immature	Check One	Mature
Preliminary Crouch		1. Little or no crouch		1. Assume preparatory crouch with hips, knees, and ankles in deep flexion.
		2. Trunk not parallel to ground		2. Trunk is almost parallel to ground.
		3. No backward-upward swing of arms		3. Weight moves forward as arms swing backward-upward.
		4. No return movement of arms; no weight shift forward		4. Weight continues to move forward as arms swing forward-downward.
		5. Insufficient shoulder joint flexion—arms not lifted high enough		5. Crouch phase ends when arms are in line with trunk.
Takeoff		6. Takeoff begins with *simultaneous* extension at hip, knee, and ankle joints.		6. Takeoff begins with *successive* initiation of extension at hip, knee, and ankle joints.
		7. Takeoff angle is more than 45°.		7. Takeoff is approximately 45°.
		8. Arm swing not coordinated with leg movements		8. Arms swing forward-upward as heels are lifted.
Flight Upward		9. Incomplete body extension at takeoff		9. Body is in full extension at beginning of flight.
		10. Arms never fully flexed overhead to form single, long lever with trunk		10. Arms are flexed at shoulder joint and elbows extended. Arms are in line with trunk to form single, long lever.
		11. Knee and hip flexion occur simultaneously.		11. Lower legs flex first during flight.
Flight Downward		12. Incomplete hip flexion during flight		12. Hip joint flexion begins when knee flexion reaches 90°.
		13. Forward arm action not coordinated well with knee and hip extension		13. As knees come forward and knee joint extends, arms and trunk reach forward.
		14. Incomplete knee extension at end of flight		14. Knees are fully extended at end of flight.
Landing		15. Toes contact ground first.		15. Heels touch ground before toes.
		16. Incomplete spinal and hip flexion at moment of contact		16. Trunk and thighs are almost touching at moment of contact.
		17. Center of gravity too far backward at moment of contact, resulting in unsteady landing		17. Instantaneous flexion of knees when heels contact ground
		18. Hands touch the floor.		18. Arms reach forward-upward to help maintain balance.

The following questions serve as guides for observation and evaluation of the child's natural movement pattern when challenged to run up the board, jump once on the end of the board, and then land on the mat:

1. Does the child run slowly, with hesitancy, or at an appropriate speed?
2. How long is the child's approach—that is, how many steps does he or she take prior to reaching the beatboard?
3. Does the child run flat-footed or on the balls of the feet?
4. Does the child slow down or stop before executing the jump on the end of the board?
5. Does the child use a two-foot takeoff from the board?
6. Which foot is the last to push off before the two-foot takeoff is initiated?
7. Does the child gain maximum height in his or her jump?

8. Is the amount of forward lean mechanically efficient so that the child falls neither forward nor backward?

9. Does the child bend at hip, knee, and ankle joints upon landing in order to absorb the shock?

10. Does the child have trouble maintaining balance upon landing?

Specific tasks that the child can be asked to perform while jumping are

1. Clap hands overhead, behind back, in front of body.
2. Land beyond a certain line or marker on the mat.
3. Assume a tuck position in the air.
4. Assume a pike position in the air.
5. Assume a straddle position in the air.
6. Assume a hurdle position in the air.
7. Assume a laterally flexed position in the air.
8. Make a turn in the air.
9. Land with feet together, feet apart, one foot in front of the other.
10. Land with arms in various positions.
11. Land and immediately perform a forward roll.

Jump Used As a Mount

The gymnastics term *mount* is a jump from a beatboard, springboard, or minitramp onto a piece of apparatus. Mounts are used to begin routines on the balance beam, the even parallel bars, the uneven parallel bars, the horse, and the buck.

Children need practice jumping up onto things as well as jumping down. If no apparatus can be improvised, they may jump (two-foot takeoff) *up* the stairs, *up* on automobile tires, *up* on street curbs, *up* on rocks, and so on.

Jumping on a Trampoline

The trampoline is an excellent vehicle for improving balance. This objective is best achieved if the student is afforded many opportunities for movement exploration.

Emphasis should not be on the learning of such traditional skills as the seat drop during early lessons, but rather upon motor fluency and originality. The child may attempt rolls, animal walks, rope jumping, turns in the air, and other stunts. The teacher who is capable of maintaining silence, accepting a child as he or she is, and observing closely will find the trampoline an extremely valuable diagnostic aid. The problems that a child exhibits on the trampoline are the same as those the child has overcome and/or learned to compensate for when on the ground.

Teaching the Hop

Taking off and landing on the same foot requires both static and dynamic balance. To determine whether children are ready for hopping instruction, ask them to imitate you in a single-foot standing balance, free leg bent backward, and hands at hips. Given two trials, most normal children can hold this stance for 3 sec by age 30 to 35 months. Shortly thereafter, they can hop in place on one foot three times without losing balance (Folio & Fewell, 1983). Approxi-

mately 6 months later, they can hop forward on the preferred foot five times and the nonpreferred foot three times.

Some insist that hopping forward is an easier developmental progression than hopping in place, but no research seems to have addressed this. Individual differences in balance, strength, body weight, and limb positioning may explain why some children find it easier to hop moving forward. Hopscotch and other games using floor patterns require forward locomotion, so this skill may be practiced more.

Little research has been conducted on hopping and disability. Cratty (1967) reported that children with mild MR seem to improve significantly in their ability to balance between the ages of 8 and 14 years. Using a test that required hopping in circular and square patterns, Cratty reported that few children with Down syndrome (25%) and moderate MR (5%) were successful. The performance of children with mild MR approached that of normal peers, although games like hopscotch were decidedly difficult for about half of them. Hemmert (1978) reported that students with moderate MR did not exhibit mature hopping patterns until a mean age of 15 years.

Process evaluation of hopping can be guided by the four criteria that follow (Ulrich, 1985). The student should be asked to hop three times on preferred and nonpreferred foot.

1. Foot of nonsupport leg bent and carried in back of the body
2. Nonsupport leg swinging in pendular fashion to produce force
3. Arms bent at elbows and swinging forward on takeoff
4. Able to hop on the right and left foot.

Testing and games of hopping can also involve speed, distance, floor patterns, and rhythmic sequences. Cratty (1986) reported that most 5-year-olds can hop 50 ft in about 10 sec. The Purdue Perceptual Motor Survey (Roach & Kephart, 1966) emphasized the following bilateral coordinations:

Hop 1/1. The person is asked to stand with feet together, then to hop on the right foot, lifting the left, and next to alternate, hopping first on the right and then on the left.

Hop 2/2. This task is the same as the foregoing except that the person hops twice on the right foot, twice on the left, and so on.

Hop 2/1. The person is asked to hop twice on the right foot, once on the left, twice on the right, and so on.

Hop 1/2. The person is asked to hop once on the right foot, twice on the left, and so on.

Performance on these tasks is evaluated in accordance with the following 4-point scale:

4—Performs all tasks easily
3—Can alter sides symmetrically
2—Can hop on either foot at will; can alternate, but cannot maintain a rhythm
1—Can perform only symmetrically

Teaching the Leap

A leap is a special kind of run in which the upward and forward direction of the flight is increased as much as possible. Consequently, the period of nonsupport is greater than the run. Children usually describe the leap as "going way up in the air, stretching out from one leg to the other—like going over a big puddle." The leap is used mostly in crossing-the-brook type games (leap over an obstacle), gymnastics (stride leap on floor and beam), and creative dance.

The leap is not included in most tests of motor development; thus, little information is available on its emergence. When shown a leap across a pretend brook (narrow sheet of paper or cloth), many children as young as 3 years old can follow the leader. However, the leap is usually considered an elementary school skill.

For several leaps in succession, Ulrich (1985) recommended the following evaluation criteria:

1. Takeoff on one foot and landing on the opposite foot
2. A period when both feet are off the ground (longer than running)
3. Forward reach with arm opposite the lead foot

These criteria are similar to those used for the run. The main difference is the long flight period. Other criteria, usually emphasized with older children, are full extension of the back leg and pointed toes. The front leg may be fully extended during the entire leap, or bent and held high (deer leap) during the flight and then quickly extended for the landing. In general, the leap in the air is similar to splits on the ground by cheerleaders. Practicing the splits seems to have carryover value in improving leaps.

Teaching Rhythmic, Two-Part Motion

The gallop, skip, and slide are rhythmic two-part patterns derived from combinations of the walk, hop, and leap. They are called rhythmic patterns because the major challenge is to capture the long-short rhythm of each two-part combination. Each pattern has a short period when both feet are off the floor, so considerable balance is required for execution.

The order in which these patterns are learned is the gallop, skip, and slide (Clark & Whithall, 1989; Murray, 1963). This order is based on the criterion of consistency over several trials in performing 8 to 10 steps with the correct rhythmic pattern. Ordering of these rhythmic patterns according to time of first occurrence is difficult because of different criteria used.

Gallop

The gallop is a walk and leap pattern, with the same foot always leading, done in a forward or backward direction in a long-short rhythm. This is the first asymmetrical gait learned by the young child (Clark & Whithall, 1989). The front foot takes a step (walk), which is long in duration, while the back foot tries to catch up with a leap that is short in duration.

Performance criteria for judging the gallop (Ulrich, 1985) are as follows:

1. A step forward with the lead foot followed by a step with the trailing foot to a position adjacent to or behind the lead foot
2. Brief period when both feet are off the ground
3. Arms bent and lifted to waist level
4. Able to lead with the right and left foot

A fifth criterion might be consistency of the long-short rhythm. Children may demonstrate a primitive form of the gallop as early as age 3, but the correct rhythmic leg action does not generally appear until about age 5. Between 60 and 71 months, most children can gallop 8 to 10 steps with the same foot leading (Folio & Fewell, 1983).

Rhythmic accompaniment (voice, hand clapping, drum, music) helps in learning to gallop. The idea of moving like a horse or playing cowboys and Indians, together with a demonstration, elicits a gallop. You can then cue children to gallop higher and higher and to push with the arms to achieve height.

Skip

The skip is a walk and a hop, with alternate feet leading, in a long-short rhythm. The pattern is smooth and symmetrical, with each foot taking a long-in-duration walk step followed by a short-in-duration hop.

The following are performance criteria for judging the skip (Ulrich, 1985):

1. A rhythmical repetition of the step-hop on alternate feet
2. Foot of nonsupport leg carried near surface during hop phase
3. Arms alternately moving in opposition to legs at about waist level

Criterion 1 might be clearer if "rhythmical repetition" was changed to "a long-short rhythm" because approximately twice as much time must be spent on the step as on the hop.

The skip is difficult for many children. To assist with assessment, three levels can be identified:

Level 1—Shuffling or one-footed skipping
Level 2—Jerky and/or inconsistent skipping
Level 3—Mature, smooth, symmetrical, long-short foot action

At Level 1, children alternate a step-hop with a walk; usually, the preferred foot does the step-hop. These children simply lack the bilateral coordination to enable both sides of the body to perform the same way. At Level 2, children can do alternate step-hops, but they are not yet consistent in the long-short rhythm. Level 1 and 2 skipping characterizes most 3- and 4-year-olds. Level 3 emerges at about age 5.

Between 60 and 71 months, most children can skip 8 to 10 steps with mature foot action (Folio & Fewell, 1983). Coordination of the arms to move in opposition to the legs often does not appear until ages 8 or 9. Instruction in skipping, like galloping, is facilitated by rhythmic accompaniment. When students seem frozen at the one-footed skip level, skip with them in partner position, holding hands on the problem side.

Slide

The slide (a walk and a leap) is identical to the gallop except that it is performed sideward rather than forward and, hence, requires better balance. The importance of moving sideward as a means of improving laterality was emphasized by Kephart (1971), who noted that this is one of the few skills that teach lateral body control.

The following are performance criteria for judging the slide (Ulrich, 1985):

1. Body turned sideways to desired direction of travel
2. A step sideways, followed by a slide of the trailing foot to a point next to the lead foot
3. A short period where both feet are off the floor
4. Able to slide to the right and to the left side

In Criterion 2, the foot action must reflect a long-short rhythm. Ability to slide equally well on both sides is seldom seen, and most children perform a mature pattern to their preferred side before their nonpreferred side.

The slide is used in gymnastics (floor exercise and balance beam) and in all forms of dance. Often, the arms are extended sideward at shoulder height, and children should practice with different arm positions. In dances that use a single circle formation, the slide is one of the easiest and most popular steps. The pattern traditionally used is seven slides to the right with a transfer of weight to the opposite foot on the eighth count, followed by seven slides to the left and a transfer of weight. This sequence should be practiced early.

Teaching Object Control Skills

Object control skills may be gross or fine motor. *Gross motor* refers to use of large muscles (i.e., moving the hands, feet, or larger body parts), as in ball handling. *Fine motor* refers to use of small muscles (i.e., fingers) as in paper-pencil-scissors-blocks-shoelace activities. This chapter is delimited to gross motor object control.

The development of object control skills is dependent upon development of normal muscle tone, integration of primitive reflexes, maturation of perceptual-motor abilities, and CNS organizational and sequencing abilities. Research shows that perception and action are coordinated from birth (Bard, Fleury, & Hay, 1990); one does not precede the other, as some early theorists posited. Effective interaction with the environment, however, is not possible until voluntary grasping and holding behaviors appear at about 4 to 5 months of age.

Normal infants thus begin exhibiting pounding, shaking, striking, pushing, and pulling play behaviors during their first year. Many children with disabilities, however, need help in learning these initial object control skills. The ability to grasp is often absent or weak in persons with cerebral palsy, muscular dystrophy, and conditions that cause hypotonus, paresis, or paralysis.

Adaptations When Grasp Is Absent or Weak

When grasp is impaired, object control focuses on pushing or striking a light object with the hand or a head pointer. Games like wheelchair boccia, bowling, and shuffleboard typically permit use of ramps so that gravity can assist in moving the object (Jones, 1988). The games can be played on the floor or adapted to a tabletop with sideboards. Balloon tetherball is another game option (see Figure 11.23).

Two-handled paddles and other implements that can be held with two hands offer another alternative. These work well in balloon tetherball and tabletop games like shuffleboard and table tennis. If grasp is too weak, one or both hands can be strapped to the implement or special gloves worn with a Velcro surface that sticks to Velcro strips on the handles.

Use of Velcro or other kinds of straps to attach a paddle, racquet, mallet, or stick to one hand opens opportunities for many types of games for practicing striking skills. Creating oilcloth or plastic tablecloth shuffleboard or target patterns that can be moved easily from floor to tabletop increases game options.

Adaptations When Release Is Difficult

The ability to throw is dependent upon the emergence of voluntary release abilities at about 10 to 11 months. Although the hand grasp reflex is integrated at 3.5 to 4 months, the CNS does not permit voluntary object release until much later. In persons with brain injury that causes hypertonus (namely, cerebral palsy), voluntary grasp and release are impaired throughout the lifespan.

In such cases, the normal teaching progression must be altered and emphasis placed on striking activities rather than those requiring a release. Striking can be directed at objects in the air, on a table with sideboards, or on a ramp. Either the hand or an implement can be used. When success in striking games is achieved, instruction can begin to alternate between striking and throwing. A major adaptation for persons with grasp and release problems is use of yarn, sponge, or Nerf balls, a soft discus, or beanbags (called soft puts) when throwing. Floor targets are typically used. Experiment with wheelchair placement in relation to the target or partner. Determine which position is best for each student and record this information on the IEP.

FIGURE   11.23

Object control activities when grasp is weak.

A. Balloon tetherball

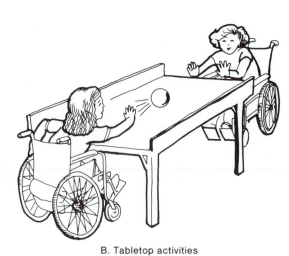

B. Tabletop activities

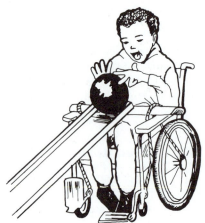

C. Bowling with ramp

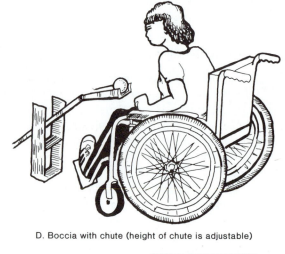

D. Boccia with chute (height of chute is adjustable)

E. Two-handed racket for tetherball

F. Table tennis with double-handle paddle suspended from frame

Table 11.4
Object control skills listed from easy to hard: A developmentally sequenced teaching/testing progression.

Task	Criterion to Pass	Average Age (Months)
1. First voluntary grasp	Grasps rattle	4–5
2. First voluntary release	Releases cube on command	10–11
3. Roll ball from sitting position	Moves ball 3 ft	12–14
4. Throw (cast) tennis ball	Level 1 pattern (see Figure 11.25)	12–14
5. Kick ball	Steps on or kicks into ball	15–17
6. Throw (hurl) tennis ball	Level 2 pattern (see Figure 11.25)	15–17
7. Throw (hurl) tennis ball	Travels 3 ft forward	18–23
8. Kick ball	Travels 3 ft forward	18–23
9. Throw (hurl) playground ball	Travels 5 ft forward	24–29
10. Throw (hurl) tennis ball	Travels 7 ft forward	24–29
11. Kick ball	Travels 6 ft forward	30–35
12. Catch large ball from 5-ft distance	2 of 3 trials; Level 1 (see Figure 11.26)	30–35
13. Bounce-throw tennis ball against wall 5 ft away	Ball hits floor once before wall contact	36–41
14. Catch large ball from 5-ft distance	1 of 2 trials; Level 2	36–41
15. Throw tennis ball	10 ft with trunk rotation and follow-through	42–47
16. Use underarm toss to hit wall target from 5 ft	Hits target 2 of 3 trials with tennis ball	42–47
17. Catch tennis ball from 5-ft distance	2 of 3 trials; Level 2	42–47
18. Use overarm throw to hit wall target from 5 ft	Hits target 2 of 3 trials with large ball	42–47
19. Throw playground ball	10 ft, 1 of 2 trials	48–53
20. Use overarm throw to hit wall target from 12 ft	Hits target 2 of 3 trials with tennis ball	54–59
21. Bounce and catch tennis ball two times	Two hands, successful 2 of 3 trials	60–71
22. Kick stationary ball into air	Travels 12 ft in air	60–71
23. Run and kick moving ball	Travels 8 ft	72–83
24. Drop-kick ball	Travels 5 ft, 2 of 3 trials	72–83
25. Wall pass and catch at 5-ft distance	Catches large ball on rebound after first bounce	72–83

Note. Large ball is 8 to 10 inches. Wall target is 2-ft-square and 2 ft above floor. A wall pass is like a basketball pass except that you throw at a wall and catch the rebound. The information in this table was abstracted from the Peabody Developmental Motor Scales (Folio & Fewell, 1983).

Adaptations for Slow Learners

Most children in adapted physical education are simply delayed in the emergence of grasp and release abilities and follow the developmental sequence of normal children, with skills mastered 1 to 3 years later than normal peers. Table 11.4 presents the order in which object control skills are learned by most students.

Adaptations for Throws While Seated

Many conditions prevent persons from throwing in a standing position. Roper (1988) is an excellent source for teaching the throw from a wheelchair. Particularly recommended is extensive practice in trunk rotation, with the ball held in a position just behind the head. The chair should be placed at an oblique angle to the direction of intended throw. The sides and back of the chair should be as low as possible.

Teaching Rolling or Bowling

The first ball-handling activity is usually rolling an 8- to 10-inch playground ball while sitting widestride on the floor. For children whose orthopedic impairment prohibits floor sitting,

a long table can be used, with partners sitting in chairs at either end. This adaptation allows a pushing rather than rolling pattern.

From rolling in the sitting position, children progress to rolling in the standing position. They also begin rolling balls toward wall targets, bowling pins, and similar targets. For persons with severe disability, a long cord on the ball facilitates recovery. Through rolling, children have their first visual tracking activities. Stress to the children that they should *watch the ball move*.

Teaching Throwing

Throws should be practiced with objects of many sizes, shapes, textures, and colors. Each lesson should involve hundreds of practice trials, with variety provided at different stations. Remember the creativity exercise in Chapter 9. Use lots of different objects and interesting targets set at varied heights (see Figure 11.24).

In teaching throwing, the first objective is an efficient throwing pattern. The cue used to obtain a good pattern is "Throw hard." The pedagogy is demonstration of the overarm throw. No verbal corrective feedback is given, other

FIGURE **11.24**

Targets recommended for accuracy throwing and kicking.

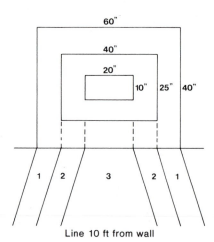

A. Project ACTIVE target for throwing and kicking assessment.

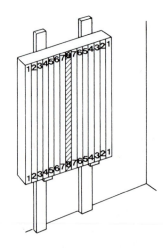

B. Rarick tennis ball toss target. May be used vertically or horizontally. Parallel divisions are 4.8 inches each.

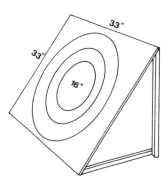

C. Rarick soccer ball accuracy toss from distances of 9, 12, 15, and 18 ft.

D. High-toss target for overarm throw.

E. Precision throw with seven scoring areas.

than "Nice try. Let's do it again. Throw hard." Table 11.4 shows that early throws are assessed in terms of distance achieved and developmental level.

Throwing is comprised of several phases: (a) starting position, (b) preparatory or backward swing, (c) forward swing, (d) release, and (e) follow-through. In relation to each of these, specific body parts should be observed: (a) feet, (b) trunk, and (c) arm (shoulder, elbow, wrist, fingers).

Figure 11.25 presents the four developmental levels through which average children, ages 1 to 7, progress. Use of names for each level (casting, hurling, homolateral, crosslateral) saves time when describing performance on the IEP. Many adults with severe/profound mental retardation use the casting pattern. Hurling and the homolateral patterns typically characterize clumsy persons of all ages.

Some persons, however, demonstrate components characteristic of more than one level. The performance descriptors in Figure 11.25 permit the teacher to check the movement components that best describe present performance level. Then, specific components that need work are listed when writing instructional objectives (e.g., Demonstrate Components 3, 4, and 6 of crosslateral pattern).

This assessment process can be simplified by using four performance criteria (Ulrich, 1985):

1. A downward arc of the throwing arm initiating the windup
2. Rotation of hip and shoulder to a point where the nondominant side faces an imaginary target
3. Weight transfer by stepping with the foot opposite the throwing hand
4. Follow-through beyond ball release diagonally across body toward side opposite throwing arm

In addition to task analysis and process assessment, the throw should be examined in terms of product. The usual measures are distance and accuracy. Throws from base to base on a softball diamond permit good assessment of distance and accuracy.

Teaching Catching

Catching entails a *reach, bend, pull* movement pattern. It also presupposes integrity of the visual tracking system. It is a more difficult task to master than throwing, and early learning of throwing and catching should probably occur separately at different stations.

The principle of specificity should guide the teaching of catching in that large balls demand movement patterns different from small balls. Catching lessons should involve practice with all sizes of balls coming in different flight patterns (horizontal vs. vertical) at different speeds. Little transfer of learning from one kind of catch to another occurs.

Visual acuity, which is poor in infants and improves up to age 8 or 9 years, affects catching. Many children with Down syndrome, for instance, are nearsighted (myopic).

Astigmatism causes blurring of the ball. Poor binocular fusion (*integration*) is manifested in double vision (*diplopia*) and functional blindness in one eye (*amblyopia*). Many persons with cerebral palsy and mental retardation have *strabismus* (cross-eyes), which also affects visual acuity and tracking.

Practice in visual tracking of a suspended ball is a good lead-up activity for catching as well as for striking and kicking skills. A tetherball apparatus or a homemade system of balls of different sizes, shapes, and colors suspended at different heights works well. Simply tracking a moving object is boring, so the activity should entail touching, striking, kicking, or catching the object being tracked. Developmentally, *horizontal tracking* occurs before vertical tracking, and near-to-far tracking is successful before far-to-near.

Visual tracking should be practiced with (a) *ground balls;* (b) *straight trajectory balls* coming to knee, waist, shoulder, and head; and (c) *fly balls* with curved trajectories. Research shows that, in far-to-near tracking for catching, young children attend to the thrower rather than to the flight of the ball. Developmentally, children next are able to attend both to the source of the flight and to their own motor response. Only with much practice do children achieve the ability to visually monitor the entire flight and make discriminatory judgments with respect to velocity.

Figure 11.26 presents levels in catching that can be used in describing present level of performance and writing objectives for the IEP. Remember that catching problems are *visuomotor,* and work with other team members in the development of comprehensive visual programs.

Performance criteria for evaluating a catch follow (Ulrich, 1985):

1. Preparation phase where elbows are flexed and hands are in front of body
2. Arms extended in preparation for ball contact
3. Ball caught and controlled by hands only
4. Elbows bent to absorb force

These criteria are for a 6- to 8-inch sponge ball tossed underhand with a slight arc from a 15-ft distance. The ball should arrive at a point between shoulders and waist, the easiest zone for catching.

Teaching Stationary Bounce/Dribble

Ability to dribble is an important factor in basketball success. Beginners can be assessed on this skill by the following performance criteria (Ulrich, 1985):

1. Ball contacted with one hand at about hip height
2. Ball pushed with fingers (not a slap)
3. Ball contacting floor in front of (or to the outside of) foot on the side of the hand being used

Once children can dribble the ball in place, they add a walk or run. This should be practiced in all directions.

FIGURE 11.25

Pictorial checklist for assessing overarm throw.

Directions. Circle the level that best depicts the pattern you observe and underline the descriptors that can be used on the IEP to indicate present level of performance.

Level 1: Casting

Descriptors: (1) feet remaining stationary, (2) no trunk or hip rotation, (3) ball thrown primarily by elbow extension.

Level 2: Hurling

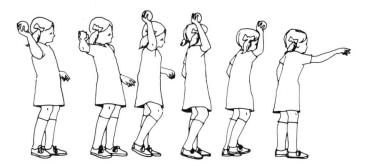

Descriptors: (1) feet remaining stationary, (2) preparatory movement involving a rotation of the trunk toward the throwing side, (3) outward rotation and abduction at shoulder joint resulting in cocking of hand slightly behind head, (4) trunk rotating back to starting position with forward arm swing, (5) angle of release usually 80 to 100°.

Level 3: Homolateral Throwing

Same descriptors as Level 2 except (1) child steps into throw (i.e., as right arm throws, right foot steps forward, (2) there is weight shift forward and more pronounced follow-through, (3) angle of release is more horizontal (forward).

Level 4: Crosslateral Throwing

Descriptors: (1) opposition (left foot forward as right arm throws), (2) weight transfer in forward-backward-forward pattern, (3) full rotation of trunk to left and right, (4) coordinated involvement of nonthrowing arm in maintaining balance, (5) abduction/outward rotation at shoulder joint in backswing changes to abduction/inward rotation in forward swing and follow-through, (6) angle of release about 45°.

FIGURE   11.26

Pictorial checklist for assessing catching skills.

Directions. Circle the level that best depicts the pattern you observe and underline the descriptors that can be used on the IEP to indicate present level of performance.

Level 2: Stiff-Arm Clapping

Level 1: Passive Arm Cradle

Descriptors: (1) making arm cradle, often with adult help, before ball is tossed; (2) rigid stationary position of feet and body; (3) no response until after ball has landed in cradle; (4) pulling toward chest.

Descriptors: (1) extending arms and spreading fingers, (2) rigid stationary position of feet and body, (3) clapping response when ball touches either hand, (4) gaining control by forearm pull toward chest.

Level 3: Initial Eye-Hand Control

Descriptors: (1) eyes tracking ball from far to near, with most attention given to the source of flight and own motor responses; (2) body moving to position self in line with trajectory of ball; (3) arms outstretched while running to meet the ball; (4) hands only contacting the ball; (5) ball pulled toward chest.

Level 4: Mature Basketball Catch

Descriptors: (1) eyes tracking ball continuously through entire flight; (2) body moving to position self in line with trajectory of ball; (3) arms, hands, and fingers relaxed until time to catch ball; (4) catch accomplished by simultaneously stepping toward ball, partially extending arms, and spreading fingers; (5) following through by a slight flexion at shoulder and elbow joints.

FIGURE 11.27

Variables to be altered in teaching striking skills.

Striking Implement	Trajectory of Object Being Struck	Size of Object Being Struck	Object Direction in Flight	Weight of Object Being Struck	Color of Object Being Struck	Anticipation Location	Speed Object Is Traveling
Hand ↓ Paddle ↓ Bat	Horizontal ↓ Vertical ↓ High arc	Large ↓ Small	Right ↓ Left ↓ Center	Light ↓ Heavy	Blue ↓ Yellow ↓ White	How far must the performer move before striking the object	Slow ↓ Fast

Hand

Paddle

Bat

Other bouncing/dribbling skills to be learned are (a) two-hand bounce and catch to self, (b) one-hand bounce and catch to self, and (c) propelling ball by means of a bounce throw or pass. This last activity is typically practiced against a wall and concurrently provides experience with rebounds. When this is the case, the task is called a *wall pass*. It can also be practiced with floor patterns and/or a partner.

Teaching Striking

Striking is any arm and hand movement pattern (sidearm, overarm, underarm) used to hit an object. Examples are skills used in tetherball, volleyball, handball, hockey, golf, shuffleboard, croquet, paddle and racquet sports, and activities involving batting (teeball, softball, cricket). In general, these movement patterns are analyzed like the throw. The phases are (a) starting position, (b) preparatory or backward swing, (c) forward swing, (d) contact, and (e) follow-through. In each, judgments are made about action of the (a) feet, (b) trunk, and (c) arm (shoulder, elbow, wrist, and fingers).

Provide opportunities for striking objects of different sizes, weights, and colors with all kinds of implements. Lighting conditions should be optimal, with the student never facing the sun. Carefully regulate the degree of difficulty, keeping in mind the variables in Figure 11.27.

Batting is probably the striking activity most popular in our culture, with children exhibiting skill directly proportional to their parents' interest and willingness to toss them balls. Often, 3-year-olds use implements with large heads (racquets, paddles, special bats) quite successfully. Almost universally, the first striking pattern is a downward, chopping action. As bilateral coordination and strength increase, the swing becomes increasingly horizontal. The following are performance criteria for evaluating batting (Ulrich, 1985):

1. Dominant hand gripping bat above nondominant hand
2. Nondominant side of body facing the tosser (feet parallel)
3. Hip and spine rotation
4. Weight transfer by stepping with front foot

A ball-tossing apparatus that can be regulated for speed is probably more important in adapted physical activity than for the tennis or softball team. If a sharing arrangement cannot be worked out, purchase is of high priority. Homemade systems of pulleys with suspended balls moving horizontally or vertically at different speeds also can be created. Learning to control the direction balls are sent is important. See Chapter 12 for ideas regarding timing and body positioning in relation to the arriving ball.

The principle of leverage (*the shorter the lever, the easier it is to achieve accuracy and control*) should be applied in selecting bats, rackets, and other striking implements. Hitting a balloon or yarn ball with the hand creates a shorter lever for beginners than use of an implement. Thus, balloon volleyball and movement exploration activities comprise an excellent first teaching progression.

Adapted games using field or ice hockey, croquet, and golf concepts, in which a ball or puck on the floor is given impetus, are sometimes easier for clumsy persons to master than throwing, catching, and striking games. This is particularly true of persons with grasp and release problems.

Teaching Kicking

Kicking is a striking activity using the feet and legs. The popularity of soccer and football give this skill prime importance. Kicking is analyzed in the same way as striking, using the same phases and body parts to guide observation. Likewise, the variables to be considered in planning teaching progressions are similar.

Table 11.4 indicates that children begin kicking balls between the ages of 15 and 17 months, shortly after they achieve stability in walking. Developmentally, they first kick a stationary ball forward along the ground and later propel it 12 ft in the air. Next, they learn to judge direction and speed and become successful at running and kicking a moving ball.

The following are performance criteria for kicking an 8- to 10-inch stationary playground ball (Ulrich, 1985):

1. Rapid, continuous approach to the ball
2. The trunk inclined backward during ball contact
3. Forward swing of the arm opposite kicking leg
4. Follow-through by hopping on nonkicking foot

Verbal instructions are "Kick the ball *hard* toward the wall." Many persons who are clumsy in hand-eye coordination activities seem to do well in kicking games. Try experimenting with kicking at various targets. Children also profit from kicking rocks, cans, and other objects as they walk or run. Soccer is the preferred sport in many private schools for students with learning disabilities.

References

American Alliance for Health, Physical Education, Recreation, and Dance (1988). *Physical best: A physical fitness education & assessment program.* Reston, VA: Author.

Bard, C., Fleury, M., & Hay, L. (1990). *Eye-hand coordination across the life span.* Columbia, SC: University of South Carolina Press.

Bleck, E. (1982). Cerebral palsy. In E. Bleck & D. Nagel (Eds.), *Physically handicapped children: A medical atlas* (2nd ed.) (pp. 59–132). New York: Grune & Stratton.

Clark, J. E., & Whithall, J. (1989). Changing patterns of locomotion: From walking to skipping. In M. H. Woollacott & A. Shumway-Cook (Eds.), *Development of posture and gait across the lifespan.* Columbia: University of South Carolina Press.

Cratty, B. J. (1967). *Developmental sequences of perceptual motor tasks.* Long Island, NY: Educational Activities.

Cratty, B. J. (1986). *Perceptual and motor development in infants and children* (3rd ed.). Englewood Cliffs, NJ: Prentice-Hall.

DiRocco, P., Clark, J., & Phillips, S. (1987). Jumping coordination patterns of mentally retarded children. *Adapted Physical Activity Quarterly, 4* (3), 178–191.

Ersing, W., Loovis, E. M., & Ryan, T. (1982). On the nature of motor development in special populations. *Exceptional Education Quarterly, 3* (1), 64–72.

Folio, M. R., & Fewell, R. (1983). *Peabody developmental motor scales.* Allen, TX: DLM Teaching Resources.

Hanson, M. (1965). *Motor performance testing of elementary schoolchildren.* Unpublished doctoral dissertation, University of Washington, Pullman.

Hemmert, T. J. (1978). *An investigation of basic gross motor skill development of moderately retarded children and youth.* Unpublished doctoral dissertation, Ohio State University.

Jones, J. A. (Ed.). (1988). *Training guide to cerebral palsy sports* (3rd ed.). Champaign, IL: Human Kinetics.

Kelly, L., Reuschlein, P., & Haubenstricker, J. (1989). Qualitative analysis of overhand throwing and catching skills: Implications for assessing and teaching. *Journal of the International Council for Health, Physical Education, and Recreation, 25,* 14–17.

Kephart, N. (1971). *Slow learner in the classroom* (2nd ed.). Columbus, OH: Charles E. Merrill.

McClenaghan, B., & Gallahue, D. (1978). *Fundamental movement patterns: A developmental and remedial approach.* Philadelphia: Saunders.

Morris, G. S. D. (1980). *How to change the games children play* (2nd ed.). Minneapolis: Burgess.

Murray, R. L. (1963). *Dance in elementary education* (2nd ed.). New York: Harper & Row.

Roach, E., & Kephart, N. (1966). *The Purdue perceptual-motor survey.* Columbus, OH: Charles E. Merrill.

Roper, P. (1988). Throwing patterns of individuals with cerebral palsy. *Palaestra, 4* (4), 9–11, 51.

Ulrich, D. A. (1985). *The test of gross motor development.* Austin, TX: Pro•Ed.

Ulrich, D. A. (1988). Children with special needs—Assessing the quality of movement competence. *Journal of Physical Education, Recreation, and Dance, 59* (91), 43–47.

Wickstrom, R. (1983). *Fundamental motor patterns* (3rd ed.). Philadelphia: Lea & Febiger.

CHAPTER
12

Perceptual-Motor Learning: An Ecological Approach

FIGURE 12.1

Movement exploration uses kinesthetic, vestibular, and visual sensory input to increase body awareness.

After you have studied this chapter, you should be able to:

1. Give a contemporary physical education definition of perceptual-motor training and explain the ecological theory and model that guide training.

2. Explain and discuss the perceptual-motor assessment model in this chapter and/or make up your own. Include all of the basic abilities requisite to learning and refining motor skills and patterns.

3. Discuss learning or performance breakdowns. Identify common breakdowns under (a) sensorimotor integration disorders, (b) perceptual disorders, and (c) perceptual-motor disorders. Recommend activities for remediation of each.

4. Differentiate among and discuss ataxia, apraxia, and aphasia.

5. Discuss the evolution of perceptual-motor theory and implications for practice. Contrast the approaches of special educators and physical educators.

6. Identify and discuss perceptual-motor tests that can be used for comprehensive testing.

7. Use concepts in Figure 12.11 to plan task cards and lessons. Apply ecological task analysis to expand learning opportunities.

8. Explain how practice in basic game and dance formations contributes to perceptual-motor abilities.

9. Describe how perceptual-motor learning occurs in sports and everyday game and play activities (see Figure 12.1).

Perceptual-motor function and sensory integration comprise a high-priority goal in adapted physical education (Sherrill & Montelione, 1990). This goal is defined as *to increase visual, auditory, tactile, vestibular, and kinesthetic functions; to simultaneously improve cognition, language, and motor abilities through large muscle play and game activities.*

Perceptual-motor function and sensory integration are linked in the same goal to stress their developmental interrelatedness. Some persons favor one term over the other, but this text follows the Piagetian model of development. The terms *sensorimotor* and *sensory integration* are associated primarily with function from birth to age 2, before the child has expressive language. *Sensory integration* is typically the goal when movement is constrained by reflex and equilibrium reaction problems. After age 2, however, sensory integration is embedded in perceptual-motor processes. Ages 2 to 7, when preoperational mental functions dominate, are the years when movement, cognition, and language work together to give meaning to self and the ecosystem.

Perception is functionally inseparable from movement, cognition, and language. Voluntary, conscious thought and action are rooted in meanings derived from the environment. In normal development, perceptual-motor learning is spontaneous. Abilities like balance, coordination, and imitation mature into specific motor skills and patterns that emerge in a predictable sequence.

Perceptual-motor function is the goal when persons capable of cognition at the 2-year-old level or higher cannot perform age-appropriate motor skills and patterns. In the perceptual-motor approach, we try to identify the underlying abilities that are acting as constraints. Concurrently, we analyze the environment to determine variables that affect these abilities. Perceptual-motor function is similar to *motor fitness* in that both are concerned with balance, coordination, and basic abilities.

Perceptual-motor training in physical education refers to the systematic use of person-environment relationships in *large muscle activities* to improve balance, coordination, motor planning/sequencing, imitation, following directions, and metacognition. The pedagogy that guides perceptual-motor training is largely ecological task analysis (see Chapter 3). Large muscle activities can be play and game oriented or built around dance and aquatics (see Chapters 16 and 17).

Ecological Perceptual-Motor Theory

Perceptual-motor training is guided by ecological theory (see Figure 12.2). Both assessment and remediation begin with consideration of environmental conditions. Theorists divide these into affordances (opportunities) and constraints (limitations). During assessment, the environment is changed in various ways to determine which set of conditions affords the most success. When the student is consistently successful across several trials, the environmental conditions that contributed to success are noted and considered the baseline condition. From this point, training consists of manipulating one or two variables at a time, so practice is in many environments.

The circle around the model in Figure 12.2 emphasizes that the networking between sensation, perception, and action is multilevel and multidirectional, rather than linear. Each process affects every other process, and all systems are activated. Brief definitions of terms follow.

Sensation

Sensation is the process by which sensory receptors pick up and transmit information to the sensory areas of the cerebral cortex (Kolb & Whishaw, 1985). Information can originate outside the body (exteroception) or inside the body (interoception). Sensation, properly defined, is feeling, seeing,

FIGURE   12.2

Model of ecological perceptual-motor theory.

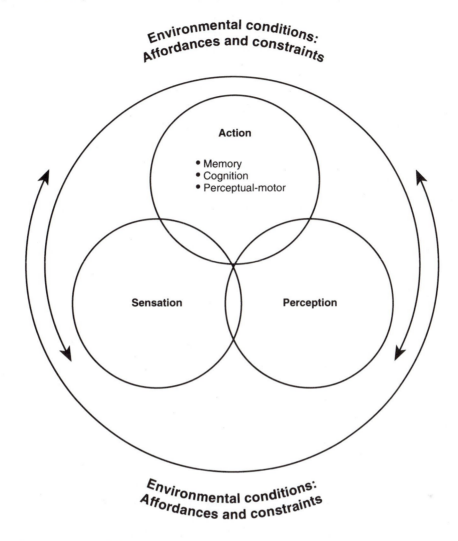

Environmental conditions:
Affordances and constraints

Action

- Memory
- Cognition
- Perceptual-motor

Sensation

Perception

Environmental conditions:
Affordances and constraints

hearing, and the like without meaning. These are physiological processes that occur below the awareness level. Kinesthesis, vision, and audition, in contrast, denote awareness and ability to derive meaning; these are perceptual abilities. An impulse is sensation until it reaches the cerebral cortex. When it integrates with other impulses and acquires meaning, it becomes perception.

Perception

Perception is variously defined as (a) decoding the environment, (b) the process by which information is interpreted within the cortical areas of the brain, or (c) the process of obtaining meaning from sensation and thus having knowledge of the environment. Many games center around perception. One that is fun for all ages is *I See Something You Don't See* or *I Hear Something You Don't Hear.* The environment is a room or outside area rich with either visual or auditory stimuli. The leader picks out some object or sound (the degree of obviousness dependent upon players' abilities) and tells players whether they are hot (close) or cold (dis-

tant) as they guess the right answer. This game can also be played with a picture that has lots of hidden or embedded objects or a piece of music like "Peter and the Wolf," in which the challenge is to identify different sounds or instruments. Hide-and-seek games and scavenger hunts also call on perceptual abilities; they can involve objects, people, or sounds. Seeking usually involves moving around a large area so that big muscle exercise is assured as well as practice in perception. How many games like this do you remember? What did you learn by playing them?

Games like *I See* and *I Hear* provide clues about visual and hearing impairments and whether or not persons are decoding and learning to name things at age-appropriate developmental levels. One measure of perception is the amount of time needed to process a sensation and derive meaning. Another is the amount of sensory information that can be simultaneously converted into meaning. To study problems of duration and capacity, teachers break perception into several subprocesses: (a) awareness, (b) discrimination, and (c) organization.

Awareness, typically the first level of perception assessed, is consciousness at the *there* or *not there* levels. There is light or no light, sound or no sound, smell or no smell, touch sensation or no feeling. Lack of awareness can be caused by a breakdown at the sensory receptor area (e.g., injury to the eye), during the information transmission process (nerve fibers), at the sensory integration level (noncortical area of brain), or at the perceptual level (cortical areas). Obviously, determining the site of breakdown is important for planning remediation.

Discrimination is multilevel, higher order awareness or the ability to differentiate between many levels of some variable (e.g., colors, sizes, shapes, identities, similarities, movements, weights, speeds). For example, children first learn to distinguish between colors (red, blue, green) and then hues or shades of the same color. They first learn to imitate up-and-down movements, as in bye-bye and pounding and shaking tasks, and then learn to discriminate between qualities and can be taught to vary up-and-down movements by making them big and little, fast and slow, straight and curved. Discrimination obviously follows a developmental sequence, with ability to discriminate between two things coming before three things and so on. Discrimination is typically measured by matching, classification, and imitation games and tasks (e.g., *Can You Do What I Do?* and *Follow the Leader*).

Organization is the ability to synthesize stimuli into meaningful, conceptual wholes (e.g., trees into a forest or body parts into a person) and to disassemble the parts of a whole (e.g., the separate trees that make up the forest). Organization, for assessment and remediation purposes, is broken down into such subabilities as

1. **Whole/Part/Whole Relationships.** "Can you identify this figure even though some parts are missing?" "Can you assemble parts of a puzzle to make a whole?"

2. **Figure/Background Relationships.** "Can you find hidden or embedded figures?"

3. **Object Constancy.** "Can you find all of the balls and bats in this room regardless of color, size, background, and tilt?"

4. **Object Position.** "Can you identify which object is rotated or reversed, near or far?"

5. **Sequences.** "Can you put several things in correct sequence or recognize when sequences are faulty?"

Attention, or cue selection, was once considered a subcomponent of perception. Today, attention is acknowledged as a separate entity that influences all aspects of information processing, not just perception.

Action

Action in the model of ecological perceptual-motor theory is thought and movement. In educational jargon, action is behavior. Clearly, action cannot be functionally separated from perception and sensation. Deficits in behavior are therefore traced back through the neurological chain of action, perception, and sensation to determine the breakdown site and/or processes of most consequence. Breakdowns, like sensory input, can be internal or external. Often, the breakdown is not within the student but rather the environment. If no one teaches a student the meaning of what he or she sees, hears, or feels, sensations will likely remain undifferentiated, unlabeled, unorganized, and useless. Action can be spontaneous and random, or directed and learned. For learning to occur, movement, cognition, and memory are integrated.

Perceptual-Motor Assessment Model

Figure 12.3 presents an assessment model to guide perceptual-motor programming. Skilled movement in this model is depicted as the outcome of a five-dip ice-cream cone. The cone or foundation represents attention processes because formal learning cannot occur without attention. Each dip of ice cream is analogous to a set of processes requisite to motor learning and performance. Perceptual-motor abilities, although represented by only one circle, are not viable without the other abilities. Hence, perceptual-motor training begins with consideration of each set of abilities and the environmental conditions that influence them.

Attention Processes

Individual differences in attention affect both performance and learning. There are many kinds of attention, each of which may be specific to a sense modality. Let us consider (a) selective attention, (b) attention span or duration, and (c) limited attention capacity.

Selective attention is the process of blocking nonpertinent information from entering short-term memory. Because what is pertinent varies from second to second, this is an adaptive mechanism that switches attention from one input to another. This process is related to cue selection (knowing what cues to attend to).

Attention span or duration refers to the amount of time an individual can attend to the same task. This varies by sense modality, interest level, motivation, meaningfulness of the material, and many other factors (Krupski, 1987; Samuels, 1987).

Attention capacity refers to the number of items or chunks that can be assimilated at one time. For most adults, this is between five and nine. An *item* is a letter, musical note, fact, or movement. A *chunk* is a word, phrase, or series of facts or movements. Attention capacity also denotes number of sense modalities that can be attended to simultaneously. Some persons, for example, can read a book and listen to music at the same time. When motor skills are taught by providing a visual demonstration concurrent with a verbal explanation, the teacher assumes that students can attend to simultaneous input from both sense modalities or successfully block out one. When this is not the case, *interference* is said to be occurring.

Memory Processes

Motor learning specialists are more likely than therapists to conceptualize disorders as problems of memory rather than perception. This is probably because learning is defined as a permanent change in behavior, and permanency is measured by retention or memory. *In actuality, memory and perception are linked because meaning cannot occur without*

FIGURE 12.3

Perceptual-motor assessment model: The five-dip ice-cream cone. Central processing includes everything that happens inside the brain. Like a five-dip ice-cream cone, the overlapping areas melt and blend together to constitute central processing. Everything is influenced by environmental conditions.

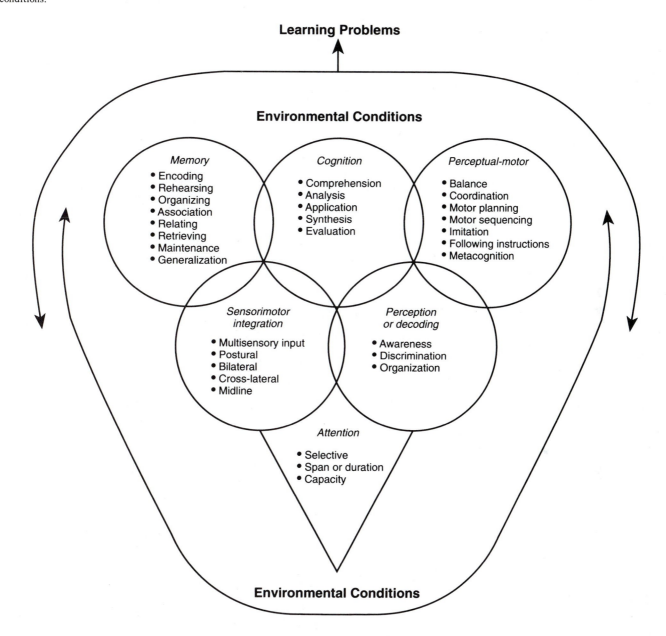

memory. Both processes (a) depend upon the integrity of input systems, (b) result in output, and (c) have duration and capacity deficiencies.

There are two kinds of memory: (a) short-term and (b) long-term. The short-term memory is a perceptual mechanism in that it is associated with central processing. It is also the source of cognitive, affective, and motor outputs. According to Schmidt (1988), data can be held in the short-term memory store only about 60 sec before decay or loss occurs. Thus, when trying to learn something new, we must immediately use an effective rehearsal (practice) strategy. We have only about 1 min to get the new information or motor pattern into long-term memory. Long-term memory is essen-

tially a storage mechanism; schemas and representations of past actions are organized so that they can be retrieved and linked with new ideas and experiences.

Memory subprocesses have names to help teachers and researchers (see Figure 12.3). Assessment is directed toward determining which processes need specific help. *Encoding* is screening and assimilating new data into short-term memory, a task that requires both attention and memory. Encoding success is evaluated by asking people to immediately imitate a pattern that they have just seen or been coactively moved through. The discrepancy between the model and the imitation reveals the extent of encoding problems. Timing is very important when assessing encoding. Check what a learner can do 15 sec after a demonstration, 30 sec after, and so on. Consider also whether there is *contextual interference* between the time instructions are given and the task is performed. This is the term given to irrelevant stimuli, detractors, or interpolated activity.

Rehearsal refers to practice strategies, whereas *organization* describes planning strategies. Associating, relating, and retrieving can be considered either rehearsal or organization. All of these emphasize the importance of *active learning*. Thus, students are taught (a) self-cueing by talking aloud, (b) repeating aloud cues or labels stated by others, (c) associating or relating with something already known, and (d) imagery (Gallagher & Thomas, 1984; Hoover & Horgan, 1990; Kowalski & Sherrill, 1992; Rose, Cundick, & Higbee, 1983; Surburg, 1989; Weiss & Klint, 1987). Holding the endpoint of a movement for about 10 sec and concentrating on its feel before beginning another repetition is also emphasized (Reid, 1980; Hoover & Horgan, 1990). *Associating* or *relating* with something already known involves *retrieval*, pulling things from long-term memory and organizing them in new and different ways. *Maintenance* refers to periodically pulling something out of long-term memory and using it so the ability is not lost. *Generalization* refers to ability to apply newly learned tasks to many and varied situations.

Memory does not necessarily imply understanding. Memorizing a list or paragraph is easier than trying to understand it. Dustin Hoffman, in the Oscar winning movie *Rainman,* portrayed a person with phenomenal memory abilities who could not care for himself and live independently. Persons who have impaired mental processes but show genius in recalling dates, performing mathematical calculations, or playing musical instruments by ear are called *idiot-savants,* an unkind term dating back to the use of the words *idiot, imbecile,* and *moron* to designate types of mental retardation.

Memory function (as well as attention, perception, and cognition) is directly related to age. The memory system operates much more slowly in children than adults. This is probably because children do not yet know efficient rehearsal strategies. When watching demonstrations and hearing instructions, they do not know what cues to attend to unless carefully taught. Thus, cue selection is often a breakdown targeted for remediation in perceptual-motor training. Children also do not use error information unless taught to do so. The younger they are, the more impulsive and less reflective. While still in the preoperative mental stage, children are motivated to have fun simply by doing. They do not try to analyze and improve performance unless systematically taught how to do so. Persons with developmental delays obviously need much help with higher order cortical functions like analysis.

There appear to be no standardized tests or protocols for assessment of memory functions and processes related to learning large muscle physical education activities. You can, however, identify duration and capability deficiencies by experimenting with the number of words you use in giving instructions. You can also probe periodically by asking students to recall and perform a task that has not been practiced for several days. Later, you should repeatedly ask, "How do you remember? What strategies do you use?"

Cognitive Processes

Perceptual-motor learning cannot occur without cognition. As shown in Figure 12.3, comprehension, analysis, application, synthesis, and evaluation are all needed. *Comprehension* refers to understanding of instructions. *Analysis* is ability to break a task down into parts and relationships, to consider variables and conditions, and to plan new combinations or orders. Think, for example, of the body parts and time-space-force-flow elements being assembled and ordered each time a new balance, coordination, or motor-sequencing task is learned. *Application* is analogous to generalization; persons apply new learning when task and environmental demands are varied. *Synthesis* and *evaluation* are higher order cortical tasks that entail the development of products (movement sequence, choreographed dance or aquatics composition, sport performance demonstrating game strategies) and the ability to judge these products according to standards or criteria. These processes are associated with metacognition.

Cognitive development was discussed in Chapter 5, and the acronym CAASE was introduced as a memory device for comprehension-analysis-application-synthesis-evaluation. Assessment of perceptual-motor abilities involves creating tasks that require different types and levels of cognition.

Motor Processes: Subcortical and Cortical

Subcortical and cortical movement processes are the special concern of adapted physical educators. Subcortical processes (i.e., sensorimotor integration) were emphasized in Chapter 10. The sections that follow review these and emphasize perception and perceptual-motor abilities. These demand higher level central nervous system (CNS) functioning until learned, at which time they become automatic and largely subcortical. Several screening inventories enable teachers to identify persons with perceptual-motor problems.

Perceptual-Motor Screening

The adapted physical educator must assume initiative in preparing materials to help colleagues identify children who may benefit from perceptual-motor training. The Sherrill Perceptual-Motor Screening Checklist, developed specifically for use by classroom teachers, lists behaviors commonly exhibited by children with learning disabilities and/or mild neurological damage and has proven successful as a screening device for identifying perceptual-motor awkwardness (see Figure 12.4). This checklist should be filled out for each child early in the year. The Purdue Perceptual Motor Survey is also a helpful screening instrument (see Figure 12.5).

Learning or Performance Breakdowns

Writing behavioral objectives to guide instruction requires identifying areas of breakdown. Figure 12.6 shows areas that physical educators should assess and use in programming. It also identifies output problems: (a) agnosias, (b) ataxias, (c) apraxias, and (d) aphasias. When assessing breakdowns,

FIGURE 12.4

Sherrill Perceptual-Motor Screening Checklist.

_____ 1. Fails to show opposition of limbs in walking, sitting, throwing.
_____ 2. Sits or stands with poor posture.
_____ 3. Does not transfer weight from one foot to the other when throwing.
_____ 4. Cannot name body parts or move them on command.
_____ 5. Has poor muscle tone (tense or flaccid).
_____ 6. Uses one extremity much more often than the other.
_____ 7. Cannot use arm without "overflow" movements from other body parts.
_____ 8. Cannot jump rope.
_____ 9. Cannot clap out a rhythm with both hands or stamp rhythm with feet.
_____ 10. Has trouble crossing the midline of the body.
_____ 11. Often confuses right and left sides.
_____ 12. Confuses vertical, horizontal, up, down directions.
_____ 13. Cannot hop or maintain balance in squatting.
_____ 14. Has trouble getting in and out of seat.
_____ 15. Approaches new tasks with excessive clumsiness.
_____ 16. Fails to plan movements before initiating task.
_____ 17. Walks or runs with awkward gait.
_____ 18. Cannot tie shoes, use scissors, manipulate small objects.
_____ 19. Cannot identify fingers as they are touched without vision.
_____ 20. Has messy handwriting.
_____ 21. Has difficulty tracing over line or staying between lines.
_____ 22. Cannot discriminate tactually between different coins or fabrics.
_____ 23. Cannot imitate body postures and movements.
_____ 24. Demonstrates poor ocular control; unable to maintain eye contact with moving objects; loses place while reading.
_____ 25. Lacks body awareness; bumps into things; spills and drops objects.
_____ 26. Appears tense and anxious; cries or angers easily.
_____ 27. Responds negatively to physical contact; avoids touch.
_____ 28. Craves to be touched or held.
_____ 29. Overreacts to high-frequency noise, bright lights, odors.
_____ 30. Exhibits difficulty in concentrating.
_____ 31. Shows tendency to fight when standing in line or in crowds.
_____ 32. Avoids group games; spends most of time alone.
_____ 33. Complains of clothes irritating skin; avoids wearing coat.
_____ 34. Does not stay in assigned place; moves about excessively.
_____ 35. Uses either hand in motor activities.
_____ 36. Avoids using the left side of body.
_____ 37. Cannot walk sideways on balance beam.
_____ 38. Holds one shoulder lower than the other.
_____ 39. Cannot hold a paper in place with one hand while writing with the other.
_____ 40. Avoids turning to the left whenever possible.
_____ 41. Cannot assemble puzzles that offer no difficulty to peers.
_____ 42. Cannot match basic geometric shapes to each other.
_____ 43. Cannot recognize letters and numbers.
_____ 44. Cannot differentiate background from foreground in a picture.
_____ 45. Cannot identify hidden figures in a picture.
_____ 46. Cannot catch balls.

Note. Students with 10 or more items checked should be referred for comprehensive examination.

FIGURE 12.5

Purdue Perceptual Motor Survey.

Purpose

To identify children, ages 6 to 10 years, who do not possess perceptual-motor abilities necessary for acquiring academic skills by the usual instructional methods (i.e., this was designed to be a screening instrument, not a test).

Description

Thirty items organized under five headings: balance and postural flexibility, body image and differentiation, perceptual-motor match, ocular control, and form perception. Of these, only the first two sections include physical education type movements. These are

Balance and Postural Flexibility
1. Walking board forward.
2. Walking board backward.
3. Walking board sideward.
4. Jumping (including jump, hop forward, skip, hop in place 1/1, 2/2, 2/1, and 1/2).

Body Image and Differentiation
1. Identification of nine body parts: shoulders, hips, head, ankles, ears, feet, eyes, elbows, mouth.
2. Imitation of 17 arm movements categorized as unilateral, bilateral, and crosslateral.
3. Obstacle course (chair and 3-ft broomstick) entailing three tasks: going over, going under, and going between.
4. Strength tests in prone position from Kraus-Weber: (a) raise chest and hold 10 sec and (b) raise legs and hold 10 sec.
5. Angels-in-the-snow sequence including 10 tasks (R arm only, R leg only, L arm only, L leg only, both arms, both legs, L arm and L leg, R arm and R leg, R arm and L leg, L arm and R leg).

Scoring

See test manual. Different system used for each of 30 items, but score ranges from 1 to 4 on each.

Validity

Criterion-related against teachers' ratings of 297 children; coefficient was .65.

Reliability

Test-retest r of .95 on 30 children (Seaman & DePauw, 1982). For 88 mildly mentally retarded children, ages 8 to 10 years, test-retest coefficients for specific items were identification of body parts, .75; imitation of movement, .51; obstacle course, .64; and angels-in-the-snow; .35 (Sherrill, 1985).

Primary Sources

Roach, E., & Kephart, N. (1966). _The Purdue perceptual-motor survey._ Columbus, OH: Charles C. Merrill.
Seaman, J., & DePauw, K. (1982). _The new adapted physical education._ Palo Alto, CA: Mayfield Publishing Co.
Sherrill, C. (1985). _Reliability coefficients for selected body image items performed by mentally retarded children._ Unpublished manuscript, Texas Woman's University, Denton.

Address for Ordering

Charles E. Merrill Publishing Co., 1300 Alum Creek Drive, Columbus, OH 43216.

FIGURE 12.6

Model for identifying specific areas of breakdown.

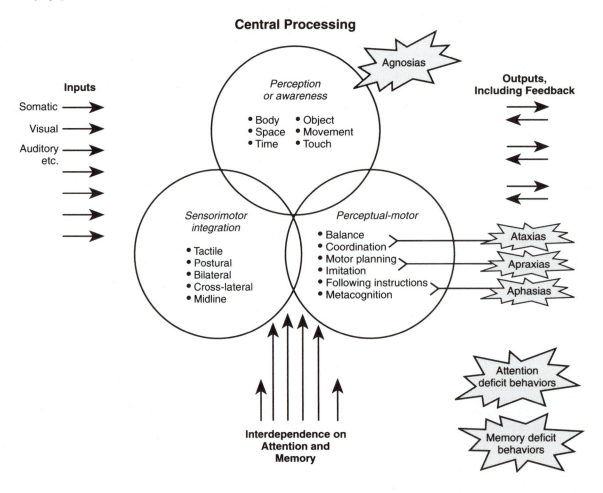

Central Processing

Inputs

Somatic →

Visual →

Auditory
etc. →

*Perception
or awareness*

- Body   • Object
- Space • Movement
- Time   • Touch

Agnosias

Outputs,
Including Feedback

*Sensorimotor
integration*

- Tactile
- Postural
- Bilateral
- Cross-lateral
- Midline

Perceptual-motor

- Balance
- Coordination
- Motor planning
- Imitation
- Following instructions
- Metacognition

Ataxias

Apraxias

Aphasias

**Interdependence on
Attention and
Memory**

Attention
deficit behaviors

Memory deficit
behaviors

remember the ecological model and the importance of manipulating environmental variables to find the baseline level at which each person can succeed.

Sensorimotor Integration Disorders

Major breakdown areas of interest to physical educators are (a) tactile integration; (b) postural or bilateral integration; (c) laterality, verticality, and directionality; and (d) crossing the midline. These areas can be assessed before the child can understand and use language. Visual and auditory integration, also important, is not usually assessed until some kind of language system has developed.

Tactile Integration

Several different types of sensory receptors, each sensitive to different stimuli, are located in the skin: (a) light touch and pressure, (b) pain, (c) cold, and (d) heat. Tactile integration refers to the ability to (a) increasingly differentiate between types of stimuli and localize the exact point where a stimulus occurs; (b) generate protective mechanisms like shivering, sweating, and reflex withdrawal from pain; and (c) make appropriate approach and withdrawal responses. Approach responses are *general,* such as the total body action involved in

cuddling, and *specific,* such as the mouth rooting for food or the eyes signaling interest. Withdrawal responses are also both general and specific.

Tactile integration disorders include (a) inability to feel and/or localize certain sensations, (b) absence of protective responses, (c) exaggerated reflex responses, (d) tactile defensiveness (i.e., touch results in generalized discomfort and irritability), and (e) tactile craving or aggressiveness (i.e., greater than average need to touch and be touched). In each of these disorders, the sensory apparatus is intact; the problem occurs within the brain at the subcortical processing level.

Activities for remediation include the following:

1. Use exercise, stunts, and games in water (see Chapter 17). Stress the feel of *in* and *out* of the water; jump in and climb out again and again.

2. Use lots of rolling activities on different kinds of surfaces. Also use crawling and similar activities that keep most of the body in contact with a surface.

3. Use coactive activities in which two bodies touch and move in unison. For infants, riding in a chest pack or backpack is a coactive activity.

4. Use rolling activities on unstable surfaces, such as balls, that elicit protective arm extension.

5. Use barefoot activities on sand, carpet, grass, and interesting textures. Create obstacle courses that require moving across different textures.

6. Use games and relays that require putting on, taking off, and playing in clothes, blankets, or sacks of various textures. Tubular jersey is good for this purpose (see Figure 12.7).

7. Let children body-paint or sponge each other, wrestle in mud, or run in and out of showers from a garden hose. Activities that alternate getting dirty and getting clean are helpful in some kinds of tactile defensiveness.

Postural or Bilateral Integration

Postural or bilateral integration refers to (a) the inhibition of primitive reflexes and the normalizing of muscle tone so that body parts can move separately (unilateral) or together (bilateral), (b) the smooth working together of both sides of the body and of the top and bottom halves, and (c) the absence of overflow. The smooth assembly of body part actions occurs according to an inborn timetable, beginning with head lifting from a prone position at about 2 months and progressing through a locomotor sequence (crawling, creeping, walking, running) and an object control sequence (grasping, pounding, throwing, striking, and catching) that dominate motor skill learning during the first 6 years of life.

Bilateral integration problems indicate that the two sides (left and right) are not functioning together as a unit. This is tested by activities in which both arms and/or both legs move simultaneously. Examples are rolling, seat scooting, bunny or frog hop stunts, and using both arms simultaneously in crawling and propelling scooterboards. Developmentally, this is the first level that children achieve. Later, bilateral patterns are two-handed throws, jumping patterns, and the breaststroke in swimming.

Some persons refer to bilateral integration problems as *laterality deficits* because it is not known whether the breakdown is at the perception or action level. Ecological theory posits that perception and action are functionally inseparable. Therefore, either diagnostic term can be used.

Laterality is internal or vestibular-kinesthetic awareness of the two sides of the body, a dimension of body image that evolves through experimenting with the two sides of the body and their relationship to each other. According to Kephart (1971, p. 87), "The primary pattern out of which this differentiation develops is that of balance." Laterality is well established by age 3 in most children. Kephart (1971, p. 88) clarifies that laterality is not handedness or the ability to name right and left. Laterality is a subcortical and nonverbal ability.

Integration of the top and bottom halves of the body implies postural control for stationary and locomotor activities. Problems in this area are sometimes referred to as verticality deficits. *Verticality* is internal or vestibular-kinesthetic awareness of up and down that evolves as the infant gains

FIGURE   12.7

Activities inside stretchable, tubular jersey help remediate tactile integration disorders.

the body control to move from horizontal to upright positions. Some children do not seem aware of forward and backward alignments in postures. Others, when asked to raise or lower limbs a certain distance, do not have the kinesthetic feel to enable success. Problems in rise-to-stand positions and jumping relate to verticality because top and bottom halves of the body must work together. Problems with these kinds of activities often indicate inadequate integration of the symmetrical tonic neck reflex.

Unilateral integration or coordination problems indicate that a body part cannot move independently without causing overflow in other parts. Drawing and handwriting are fine muscle unilateral activities in which some students have to be taught to use the free hand to hold the paper down. One-limb throwing and kicking activities require that students be taught how to use free limbs.

Test creators distinguish between integration and coordination. *Integration* is a first-level activity that usually refers to infant and toddler function. *Coordination* is a higher level function that implies ability to imitate and to learn by incidental and formal modeling. Children with delays that interfere with modeling are diagnosed as having integration problems, regardless of their age.

FIGURE 12.8

Teacher moves the barrel in unexpected ways to help students with bilateral integration.

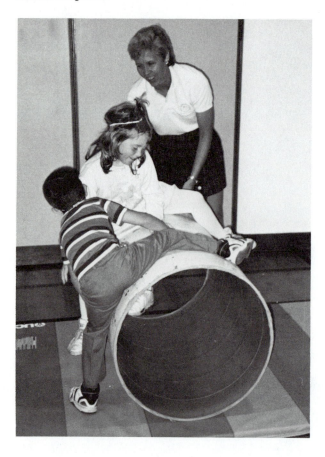

Activities for remediation include the following:

1. Use activities that activate and promote tactile, kinesthetic, vestibular, and visual systems working together—tiltboards and balance boards, barrels, and balls controlled by you because integration deficits are characterized by inadequate balance for independent control of such apparatus (see Figure 12.8).

2. Use hammock activities (see Chapter 16 on dance therapy).

3. Use traditional playground swings for sitting and standing or specially constructed ones for lying and four-point.

4. Use slides, seesaws, merry-go-rounds, and other playground apparatus that can accommodate nonambulatory children.

5. Use surfaces that respond in unpredictable ways to locomotor movements (rolling, crawling, creeping, walking). These include moon walks, mattresses, trampolines, and changing-consistency balance boards and beams.

6. Lift children into the air and play airplane in various directions.

7. Use wheel toys and vehicles to move children across variable surfaces and inclinations.

8. Passively or coactively move children through several trials of up-and-down and side-to-side patterns. (This activity is used when the children cannot move themselves through these patterns.)

9. Create reach-and-grasp and reach-and-strike activities that can be done from all positions (prone, supine, sit, four-point, stand) while stationary or moving.

10. With good personal flotation devices (PFDs) and individual monitoring, use water activities. Bilateral arm patterns usually happen spontaneously.

11. Use therapeutic horseback riding conducted by persons certified in this area (Biery & Kauffman, 1989).

Crosslateral and Midline Problems

Crosslateral integration, the most mature limb pattern, refers to right arm and left leg (contralateral limbs) working in opposition to each other as in a mature locomotor, throwing, or kicking pattern. Age 6 or 7 is when failure to exhibit crosslateral patterns is diagnosed as a problem. Crosslateral integration cannot really be distinguished from coordination because crosslateral patterns emerge long after children acquire imitation and modeling abilities.

The ability to move a limb across the body's midline is a special kind of crosslateral integration. Problems in this area are evidenced in ball-handling activities, such as failure to follow-through in the direction of a throw or a racquet swing and difficulty in reaching across the body to field balls coming to the left or right. Standing at a chalkboard and reaching the right hand across the board to the far left to draw a long horizontal line is also a good test. Individuals with problems will walk or take steps as they draw to avoid crossing midline. The mature pattern requires keeping the feet stationary. Many midline problems reflect inadequate integration of the asymmetrical tonic neck reflex.

Activities for remediation include the following:

1. Use the previously mentioned activities that reinforce bilateral and unilateral integration. Many authorities believe that these build the foundation on which crosslateral efficiency is built.

2. Use agility locomotor activities that require moving as fast as possible around curves and obstacles.

3. Use exercises and games (supine, four-point, sitting, standing) that require the right hand to touch the left leg or body parts and vice versa. Sit-ups and toe touches with trunk twists are good. Integrate these into *Simon Says* games.

4. Use games that require crossing midline to pick up stationary and moving objects of all sizes and shapes.

5. Use games that require crossing midline to block or trap objects rolled or tossed. This can be done with hands, broom, hockey stick, or other implement.

6. Use a variety of objects in games that require crossing midline when throwing and striking.

7. Use games that require crossing midline, such as catch the snake (a rope carried by a runner), catch the stick (a broomstick released from vertical), catch the hoop, and catch the soft discus, beanbag, or ball.

8. Use games that require students to leap brooks or barriers.

Perceptual Disorders

The ability to derive meaning from what we see, hear, and feel is perception. Abilities begin to develop shortly after birth, but assessment often is not accurate until language is acquired. Perception builds schema about the body, movement, space, objects, and time. Major breakdown areas of interest to physical educators are visual and auditory perception, body awareness, bilateral and directional awareness, spatial and object awareness, temporal awareness, and tactile awareness. Breakdowns in these areas (perceptual deficits) are called *agnosias*.

Visual and Auditory Perception

Visual and auditory perception includes the use of vision and audition to make sense of both the external and internal environment. It can best be assessed by (a) guessing games ("What do you see? What do you hear?"), (b) hide-and-seek games ("Can you find a hidden object? Can you locate the hidden source of a sound?"), and (c) tracking games ("Can you use your eyes to follow a moving object? Can you use your ears to follow a hidden sound?"). Games should be devised for assessment at each level of perception: (a) awareness, (b) discrimination, and (c) organization.

Visual and auditory perception are dependent upon acuity, bilateral eye coordination, depth perception, and various reflex mechanisms (see Chapter 10). If you suspect that acuity or depth perception problems are interfering with learning, refer the student to the appropriate specialist (e.g., optometrist, audiologist, ophthalmologist).

Body Awareness

Body awareness is the ability to derive meaning from the body. Illustrative assessment questions are (a) What body parts is the student aware of? (b) What body surfaces is the student aware of? (c) What body positions (upside down vs. erect; leans in various directions; tucked vs. straight) is the student aware of? and (d) What movements is the student aware of? For each of these, determine whether awareness is primarily tactile, kinesthetic, and vestibular (TKV); visual; or auditory. The ideal is good awareness of each type of sensation. Clumsy students, however, often have good visual and auditory awareness and can verbally identify body parts, surfaces, and shapes but are limited by deficits in kinesthesis, equilibrium sense, and tactile perception.

Body awareness is almost always in relation to the elements of space and time. These, in turn, are perceived differently under various environmental conditions (light, dark; loud, quiet; soft, hard; stable, unstable; hot, cold) and in various states of motion (externally imposed, self-initiated; fast, slow; airborne, one-, two-, or three-part contact with a surface; linear, rotary; in balance, out of balance). In relation to movement, body awareness is largely dependent on bilateral and directional awareness. These, then, are assessed separately.

Bilateral and Directional Awareness

When the TKV sensations of bilaterality and verticality are fused with visual and auditory sensation and the child develops language to communicate that he or she is deriving meaning from this intersensory input, bilateral and directional awareness can be assessed and remediated. *Bilateral awareness* is, first, the ability to initiate unilateral movements (awareness that only one part of the pair should be moved) and, later, the verbal ability to understand and make right-left discriminations. *Directional awareness* denotes ability to respond to many directional commands: right-left, up-down, north-south, in-out, forward-backward.

Directional awareness becomes progressively keener between ages 2 and 8 years, with up-down typically the first direction learned and right-left the last. Sometimes, these abilities are called discriminations to indicate a more advanced level than general awareness.

Spatial and Object Awareness

Spatial awareness occurs after bilateral and directional awareness. First, the child understands directional concepts as they relate to his or her own body, then as they relate to other persons and objects. Awareness also expands from stationary to moving objects. In the well-integrated child, this awareness is both cognitive and somatic. In some children, however, there is a split. The mind may know what is happening in space, but the body does not, or vice versa.

Spatial awareness is linked to many perceptual abilities (TKV, visual, or auditory). These abilities may enable *discrimination* (color, form, size, or identity; pitch, intensity, tone or sound localization) or *organization* (wholes/parts; figure/background; two- or three-dimensional recognition like depth parameters).

Temporal Awareness

Temporal or time awareness is the ability to derive meaning in relation to such qualities as fast and slow, now and later, long and short, continuous and intermittent, even and uneven, and set variations in rhythm like 4/4, 3/4, or 6/8. This kind of awareness is needed to succeed in reaction-time tasks and ball-handling activities that require judgments about how fast a ball is moving. Temporal awareness is intersensory, primarily visual-auditory, and very complex. Matching of visual and auditory input, as in judging speeds and distances, usually occurs by chance rather than ability until about age 7. Thereafter, temporal awareness slowly matures, progressing from discrimination to perceptual organization and cognition.

Tactile Awareness

The ability to feel and interpret sensations of touch, pressure, pain, and temperature varies widely but obviously provides much information, especially to the young child. Disorders include finger agnosia (inability, when blindfolded, to recognize which finger has been touched), one-point discrimination and/or tactile location (like finger agnosia but refers to anywhere in body), multiple-point tactile discrimination (inability to identify two or more points touched simultaneously), inability to reproduce designs drawn on a body part like back of hand, and stereoagnosia (inability to identify shapes, textures, and weights of three-dimensional objects by touch).

Agnosias

Agnosia, a diagnostic term for perceptual deficits, is inability to recognize sensory stimuli when there is no known structural or physiological damage. The word *agnosia* is derived from *a* ("without") and *gnosis* (meaning "knowledge"). A way to remember agnosia and to distinguish it from all of the conditions beginning with *a* is to associate the pronunciation (ag-nō-zē-a) with *knows* (*noze*), a word that sounds the same while reminding us of its derivation. Agnosias can affect any part of the body or a particular sense (e.g., visual and auditory agnosias). Agnosias for sounds and music are commonly called tone and melody deafness.

Activities for Remediation

Within the physical education context, perception should be combined with big muscle action for remediation. Games, movement exploration, and drills in a variety of environments should emphasize *awareness* (there, not there), *discrimination* (different intensities, qualities, and sources), and *organization* (parts/wholes, assembly/disassembly, similarities/differences, correct/incorrect, sequencing).

1. Use follow-the-leader games in moving (visual perception) and in making noises or rhythm patterns (auditory perception).

2. Emphasize follow-the-leader games that entail space and time judgments, like squeezing through narrow openings, climbing over and under barriers, jumping over moving ropes or poles, and navigating surfaces that respond in unpredictable ways.

3. Use blindfolds for locomotor, ball-handling, and object manipulation games. Hitting a piñata or paper sack filled with goodies is fun. *Blindperson's Bluff* is an age-old favorite.

4. Use discover-and-gather games in which cardboard cutouts of different colors, sizes, and shapes are taped to a distant wall or floor. Challenge, "How many times can you run to the wall and bring back something red? Bring back only one thing each time."

5. Scatter parts of broken dolls all over the room and challenge, "Who can find a head, trunk, two arms, and two legs and build a doll?" Repeat with other three-dimensional objects.

FIGURE 12.9

Imitating animals while learning names of stunts like the dog walk enhances perception.

6. Scatter letters all over the room and challenge children to run about finding the letters to match the word you are showing or to form words and sentences of their own choice.

7. Cut pictures or greeting cards into several pieces and scatter all but one piece of each. Give students the one piece and challenge them to find the others to make a whole.

8. Sound different notes on musical instruments and have students respond with a preestablished stunt for each sound.

9. Bring pets to class and have students imitate animals while learning names for stunts like the dog walk (see Figure 12.9). Animals can also be used to increase awareness of others and how they use time and space.

10. Keep creating. There are hundreds of activities. Be sure that each uses the entire body and thus reinforces motor skills and patterns and builds fitness.

Perceptual-Motor Disorders

Perceptual-motor processing varies with respect to amount of time that elapses between perceiving and moving. Task difficulty and novelty obviously affect delays. Much depends on whether the movement impulse or idea occurs within the student (i.e., spontaneous movement exploration) or is externally prompted by a visual demonstration and/or verbal input.

Balance

Balance is to body control what information processing is to cognition. As such, balance is the process of integrating sensory input from multiple sources (vestibular, kinesthetic, tactile, and visual) so as to plan and execute static and dynamic postures. Balance is a conscious state and thus capable of some regulation by the cerebral cortex. It is largely determined,

FIGURE   12.10

Tiltboards, like the homemade one pictured, are used to improve dynamic balance and thereby enhance vestibular functioning.

however, by various automatic righting and equilibrium re-actions. Dynamic balance has a very low correlation with static balance and should be assessed and remediated separately. Balance is extremely task specific, so success on one balancing task cannot be generalized to other tasks, even those of the same type.

Activities for remediation include the following:

1. Use the activities described under sensorimotor integration disorders.
2. Use activities in which the student, rather than the teacher, controls apparatus like tiltboards and balance boards and beams.
3. Challenge students to discover how many ways they can perform static balances. For example, (a) use one, two, or three body parts; (b) use different surfaces; (c) alter positions of body parts at different speeds while balancing.
4. Ask students to imitate various static balances (see Figure 12.10). The best known of these is the stork or single-leg stand with sole of nonsupport leg on the inner surface of the support knee; arms are folded across the chest, or hands are placed on hips. Two others are (a) tip-toe balance stand, with heels lifted

and hands on hips, and (b) tandem stand on beam (also called heel-to-toe stance).

5. Perform static balances under various visual conditions: eyes open, eyes closed, and eyes focused on targets set at various heights and distances. Try looking at moving targets while balancing.
6. Try static balances while holding different weights in one or both arms or on the head. Use Velcro to attach weights to legs or other body parts.
7. Try holding static balances while raising and lowering the center of gravity.
8. Try dynamic balances under various conditions.
9. Combine creative dramatics with beam walking so that students portray characters as a story is read. Have these characters move at different speeds and levels and do lots of turns.
10. Teach gymnastics routines that combine various kinds of balances.

Coordination

Coordination is the CNS processing needed to assemble body parts into a skilled movement. For coordination to occur, there must already be body, object, space, time, and movement schemes stored in long-term memory from past experience.

Of particular importance are postural, bilateral, and cross-lateral integration and freedom from midline problems. Coordination is thus the cortical activity of short- and long-term memory interacting to refine schema pertaining to the body parts working together.

Coordination, like balance, is specific to the task. Thus, fine motor coordination (use of fingers or toes in manipulative activities) is not much related to gross or large muscle motor coordination (locomotor and object control patterns). This is recognized in standardized motor proficiency tests that have separate batteries or subtests to measure (a) *bilateral coordination* (tapping feet alternately while making circles with fingers, jumping up and clapping hands); (b) *upper limb coordination* (catching a ball tossed from 10 ft, throwing a ball at a target); (c) *visual-motor control* (paper-pencil and scissors activities); and (d) *upper limb speed and dexterity* (sorting shape cards, displacing pegs, making dots in a small circle).

Coordination is often assessed by speed, accuracy, and distance measures. Each of these can be considered a subtype of task-specific coordination and calls for a different kind of CNS processing. Little research has been conducted, however, on the motor-learning processes through which children learn speed, accuracy, and the production of force necessary to achieve specific physical education goals (e.g., distance).

Coordination is interwoven with body composition and fitness attributes like body weight, strength, and range of motion. These can act as constraints or affordances. It is also dependent upon static and dynamic balances in the many postures the task demands.

Burton (1990) suggested two basic principles to guide remediation of coordination problems: (a) movement coordination must be developed before movement control, and (b) movement coordination and control should be developed in hierarchical sequences. The *first principle* emphasizes that persons with disabilities often perform a coordination in a stereotypical pattern. For example, they can do the jumping jacks exercise only under certain conditions. If environmental variables are changed, they cannot adapt or generalize. Coordination is developed best by ameliorating this problem. The teacher therefore changes the jumping jacks task in many ways: (a) altering the surface by tilting it or making it soft or slick, (b) changing from land to chest-high water, (c) adding a drumbeat or music to guide the speed or rhythm, and (d) adding weights to limbs or having the person hold streamers.

The *second principle* emphasizes the use of hierarchical sequences in teaching; this refers to task-analyzing the body part assembly. The easiest assembly is movement of arms or legs only in a bilateral pattern. Next might be movements of limbs on right side only and left side only (a lateral pattern). Then come combinations: (a) right and left sides together or (b) top and bottom parts together. Practice at each hierarchical level should include different body positions, speeds, rhythms, ranges of motion, and visual conditions.

Activities for remediation include the following:

1. Teach various coordinations in prone- and supine-lying to eliminate balance constraints of working against gravity.
2. Teach students to say verbal cues aloud as they move (e.g., "in-out" or "apart-together" for jumping jacks). Use words as cues rather than numbers.
3. Teach students to use visual imagery before attempting new coordinations.
4. Teach students to hold the endpoint of a coordination 7 to 10 sec and to concentrate on remembering its feel.
5. Alter practice conditions in many ways.
6. For standing and locomotion coordinations, supply bars or apparatus to hold on to if balance is a constraint.
7. Supply videotaped and other kinds of feedback.
8. Make available time-out environments where students can go to practice in private or with a peer tutor.
9. Reward lots of trials and self-initiated efforts.

Motor Planning (Praxis)

Motor planning or *programming* is a global term used in physical education to denote the organizational activity of the neural systems that command coordinated movement patterns. Sports and games, for example, do not require individual coordinations but many kinds linked together in appropriate sequences.

There are many kinds of motor-planning problems. In one kind, persons can see a sequence of body actions and state correctly what they have seen (e.g., "Run to red line, duck under bar, climb up ladder, and then jump down"), but they cannot execute the sequence. The inability to imitate or follow visual and verbal directions in executing a series of actions is called *apraxia* or *dyspraxia*. The ability to sequence develops with age, and inability to sequence should not be considered a dyspraxia until age 6 or 7. Motor sequencing is sometimes used as a synonym for motor planning because both abilities denote cortical command systems that activate patterns or chunk responses, rather than initiate single actions like running, jumping, and throwing.

Of concern in motor planning is whether skills are closed or open. *Closed skills* are repetitive activities in a predictable environment. Examples are bowling, archery, and similar activities in which the target does not change. *Open skills* are those in a multiplayer game setting in which movements of the ball are unpredictable. Obviously, open skills require quick motor planning for success. Planning errors in such cases can be selection or executive. *Selection errors* are mismatches between the expected condition and what really happens. Examples are readiness for a straight ball when a curved one arrives or readiness for a smooth running surface when a hole suddenly appears. *Executive errors* occur when the CNS program is correct but the muscles do not do what they are told because of fatigue or other constraints.

Little is known about remediating apraxia (Sugden & Keogh, 1990). This term is just beginning to be used in adapted physical activity, although it has been part of the vocabulary of occupational therapists since the 1970s (Ayres, 1972).

Activities for remediation include the following:

1. Practice increasingly longer sequences. Start with combining two things and then gradually add more.
2. Find out the conditions under which persons best learn sequences: (a) visual demonstration only, (b) verbal instructions only, (c) simultaneous visual demonstration and verbal instructions, (d) visual first followed by verbal, or (e) verbal first followed by visual.
3. Find out if background music helps with motor planning. Experiment with different kinds of music.
4. Provide lots of practice in game settings that require open skill proficiency. Vary these settings to match perceptual-motor decision making with greater and lesser demands.

Imitation

Imitation (also called modeling) of a motor act, depending on how many parts are involved, is a complex perceptual-motor ability. Imitation of single hand movements (bye-bye) begins around 10 months of age. As children become aware of other body parts, imitation becomes increasingly sophisticated visual reproduction. Breakdowns in imitation are hard to trace. The origin can be input, sensory integration, one of the perceptual processes (awareness, discrimination, organization), or one of the perceptual-motor processes (balance, coordination, motor planning, and the like). The problem can also be attention or memory.

Following Instructions

Assuming that there is no behavioral disorder, following instructions is a perceptual-motor ability. Breakdown sites for this ability are the same as for imitation except that audition is the modality used. The breakdown is often in the complexity of the command. At age 5 or 6 years, most normal children can follow only three or four commands in sequence. The more words in a command, the harder to follow. Auditory processing improves rapidly from ages 5 to 8. The ceiling most persons eventually reach for remembering sequences is seven commands or tasks plus or minus two.

Ataxia, Apraxia, and Aphasia

Ataxia, apraxia, and aphasia are output problems that can be traced to perceptual-motor origins. Each denotes deficits in central processing caused by brain damage. The etiology is often unknown and undifferentiated.

Ataxia, from the Greek word meaning "lack of order," is defective muscular coordination, especially in relation to reaching and walking. There are many kinds of

ataxia. Different parts of the CNS cause the condition (cerebellar damage in cerebral palsy; degeneration of ascending spinal cord tracts in alcoholism, syphilis, and Friedreich's ataxia). In each of these, the vestibular-kinesthetic-tactile sensations are impaired. Both balance and coordination are affected. Reaching problems are manifested primarily in overshooting or undershooting objects. Walking problems are evidenced by balance deficits and a peculiar reeling or wide-based staggering gait. To help you remember, think about a*tax*ia as very energy-*tax*ing.

Apraxia, essentially the same as dyspraxia, was discussed under motor planning. These three words (*apraxia, dyspraxia, motor planning*) each include a *p*, the key for keeping apraxia (the *p* word) separate from ataxia (the *t* word) in your mind.

Aphasia, derived from *a* ("not") and *phasis* ("speaking"), can be sensory or motor or both. It refers to all kinds of language and communication deficits caused by brain injury, not just speaking problems. The brain injury can be developmental or acquired, as in the case of a stroke or trauma.

Common aphasias are dyslexia or alexia (reading disorders), dysgraphia or agraphia (writing disorders), and word-finding problems in speech, like the inability to name an object or action even though we know what it is. Aphasias can encompass any kind of language system, concrete or abstract.

In educational diagnoses, aphasias are often grouped together as language and learning disorders. They have no relationship to intelligence and are not caused by sensory deficits. Diagnosis of an aphasia first requires ruling out mental retardation, inability to see and hear, and lack of learning opportunity or motivation. Aphasia relates only to central processing in the association parts of the cerebral cortex. It is possible, of course, to have both aphasias and sensory input deficits, especially in persons with widespread CNS damage who are severely disabled.

Perceptual-Motor Training: Past and Present

The beginning of perceptual-motor training is often traced back to 1800, when Jean-Marc Itard, a physician in France, created a system for educating a nonverbal child, now called the Wild Boy of Aveyron, who was found wandering the forest. Itard's student, Edouard Seguin, brought Itard's ideas to America in the 1860s, where they were applied in residential schools for persons with mental retardation.

Another innovator of perceptual-motor training was Maria Montessori, a physician in Italy, who wrote classic books about the education of the senses in 1912 and 1917. Her works, however, did not stimulate much interest in America until the 1940s and 1950s. Then her ideas were used more in early childhood than in special education.

Hallahan and Cruickshank (1973) point out that, between 1936 and 1970, perceptual-motor training was the most popular method of education of children with learning disabilities (LD). It was also used widely in teaching persons with mental retardation (MR). Hallahan and Cruickshank trace the origins of perceptual-motor theory in America to Alfred A. Strauss and Heinz Werner, German psychologists who migrated to the United States in the 1930s to escape Hitler. Both eventually settled in Michigan, where they conducted the pioneer research on children with brain injury and/or MR that formed the basis for almost all early LD practices.

Some of the people influenced by Strauss and Werner were William Cruickshank, a special educator who applied their research specifically to persons with cerebral palsy (CP) and traumatic brain injury; Newell C. Kephart, an educational psychologist, whose 1960 classic *The Slow Learner in the Classroom* (2nd ed., 1971) still serves as the guide for some perceptual-motor practitioners; and Gerald Getman, an optometrist, who popularized the importance of vision in learning. Marianne Frostig, a developmental psychologist in Los Angeles, whose *Test of Developmental Vision* and prolific writing/speaking on perceptual-motor remediation dominated the 1950s and 1960s, also regards the works of Strauss and Werner as important to her orientation.

Individually, these perceptual-motor theorists who all believed that perceptual-motor activities led to improved reading skills and cognition might not have made a great impact on education. In 1964, however, they all (with the exception of Getman) became part of the Professional Advisory Board of the newly formed Association for Children with Learning Disabilities. Collectively, they exerted tremendous influence on teaching practices. Parents especially came to believe in their theories. This enthusiasm attracted the attention of many physical educators, who were supportive of movement and games as strategies for enhancing academic learning.

By the early 1980s, however, special educators rejected perceptual-motor training because research showed that it did not significantly change academic performance (Kavale & Mattson, 1983). This stance had little influence on physical educators, who primarily used perceptual-motor training to improve motor abilities rather than reading and math. The activities associated with perceptual-motor training have always been part of elementary school physical education.

Of the many perceptual-motor theorists, let's consider the contributions of one special educator—Newell Kephart—and one physical educator—Bryant Cratty. Each wrote classic books that are well worth reading.

Contributions of Kephart

Newell C. Kephart's theory is presented in *The Slow Learner in the Classroom,* published in 1960 and revised in 1971. Kephart, like Piaget, is a developmentalist. Whereas Piaget established the sensorimotor stage as 0 to 2 years of age, Kephart emphasized that movement is the basis of the intellect, without clarifying an age span for which the assumption is most true. Under the motor bases of achievement, Kephart (1971) discussed infant motor explorations, reflex

FIGURE   12.11

Balance beam work was popularized by Kephart as an integral part of perceptual-motor training.

and postural adjustments, laterality, directionality, body image, motor generalization, and motor learning. The terms *laterality* (internal awareness of two sides of the body) and *directionality* (understanding of directional concepts in relation to self and space) were coined by Kephart and continue to influence theory and practice.

Kephart taught at Purdue University in Indiana during most of his career. There, he and a colleague developed the well-known screening instrument called the Purdue Perceptual-Motor Survey (Roach & Kephart, 1966). Most of the items contained in the Purdue Perceptual-Motor Survey are presented in *The Slow Learner in the Classroom* as training activities. Kephart used the term *slow learner* to denote clumsy children, not mentally retarded ones. His greatest emphasis in perceptual-motor training was on balance. To improve balance, Kephart emphasized that students must be exposed to many and varied activities that make them lose balance. Only by struggling to regain balance does a child improve. Hence, Kephart recommended locomotor activities and stunts on walking boards (i.e., low balance beam) (see Figure 12.11), balance boards, trampolines, and bedsprings and mattresses. Kephart believed that laterality was largely a matter of balance (i.e., without internal awareness of two sides of the body, one can hardly balance), so these activities are now widely accepted as contributing to the development of laterality.

In regard to body image and the ability to move one or more body parts without overflow (i.e., differentiation), Kephart recommended use of an angels-in-the-snow sequence, including unilateral, bilateral, and crosslateral movements. He also stressed the importance of follow-the-leader activities in which the teacher performed an arm movement and then the students imitated it from memory. In such imitations, students were taught not to mirror activities, but to use the same body parts (right and left) as the demonstrator. Kephart's idea of an obstacle course was two chairs and a broomstick; with these, he created problem-solving situations that required squeezing through, stepping over, and ducking under.

Kephart believed that stunts and games entailing forward, backward, and sideward movements also were important to body image development. Specifically, he recommended the duck walk, rabbit hop, crab walk, measuring worm, and elephant walk. Today, physical educators continue to emphasize all of these except the duck walk, which is believed injurious to knee joints.

Kephart stressed the practice of rhythmic patterns as important in remediating kinesthetic and tactual problems. In this regard, he recommended the use of bongo drums and the child learning to imitate even and uneven rhythms, first using one side of the body and then alternating right and left sides. Theorists later named this *bilateral motor coordination* because it combines ability to make right-left discriminations with ability to imitate rhythmic patterns and gestures.

In regard to hand-eye coordination, Kephart focused most of his attention on perceptual-motor match, ocular control, and form perception. This part of his theory was primarily visual motor. It emphasized use of chalkboard activities like drawing circles simultaneously with both arms and drawing lines to connect dots. Also important were tasks that required that the student fixate eyes on a small object and then follow its movement. Most of today's striking activities that use a ball suspended on a string come from Kephart's marsden ball tasks.

The marsden ball, named after the optometrist who conceived the idea in the 1950s, is a soft object about the size of a tennis ball, suspended by a string from overhead. The child stands about an arm's length from the ball and tries to touch it as the teacher swings it from side to side and forward and backward. Physical educators tend to conceptualize this activity as individual, dual, or team tetherball and to vary the size of the balls in accordance with students' skill levels.

Work on form perception was primarily tracing and copying crosses, circles, rectangles, diamonds, and other shapes. Whereas Kephart conceived this as a paper-pencil activity, physical educators have generalized it to large shapes and patterns on the floor that form paths to be followed in practicing locomotor activities. Likewise, various shapes are used on walls so that form perception is taught concurrently with target throwing. The copying tasks on the Purdue Perceptual-Motor Test come directly from the Bender-Gestalt Test (Bender, 1938).

Contributions of Cratty

Although many physical educators have subscribed to perceptual-motor training at one time or another, few have contributed to theory and practice through writing or research. Bryant J. Cratty, a physical education professor at the University of California at Los Angeles, thus stands out as the major contributor. Throughout the 1960s and 1970s, Cratty published about 30 books on this topic (Cratty, 1969a, b; 1971). He also developed a test (the Six-Category Gross Motor Test, 1969) to measure body image and perceptual-motor function (Knapczyk & Liemohn, 1976).

In his books, Cratty described games that incorporated concepts of perceptual-motor match, ocular control, and form perception. He stressed that academic learning would not improve as the result of Kephart-like activities unless numbers, letters of the alphabet, and words were woven into floor and wall grids (patterns) and emphasized. Thus, Cratty called attention to the principle of specificity. He emphasized that movement is not the sole basis of the intellect. If properly planned and conducted, however, movement can contribute to problem-solving skills and academic learning (see Figure 12.12).

The New Perceptual-Motor Emphasis

In the 1980s, physical educators continued to affirm their belief in perceptual-motor learning as a means of enhancing motor performance. Walter Davis of Kent State University in Ohio applied the ecological approach of James J. Gibson (1979) to perceptual-motor learning (Davis, 1983) and worked with Allen Burton of the University of Minnesota to establish ecological task analysis as important pedagogy (Davis & Burton, 1991). Burton (1990) showed how perceptual-motor interactions can be assessed in children and recommended that future research be directed toward ways that motor behavior is limited by perceptual problems.

Also in the 1980s, many physical educators became serious scholars of perception and perceptual development. In most instances, their primary sources were the works of Eleanor and James Gibson (husband and wife) of Cornell University, who independently have published much research (E. J. Gibson, 1969, 1987; J. J. Gibson, 1966, 1979; Pick, 1979).

New books on the development of eye-hand coordination (Bard, Fleury, & Hay, 1990), postural control and balance (Woollacott & Shumway-Cook, 1989), and movement skill development (Sugden & Keogh, 1990) cite the Gibsons and many researchers who have followed their lead.

Most experts agree that understanding and teaching movement is impossible without a strong background in perception and neurology. This belief particularly relates to the remediation of balance deficits (Shumway-Cook, 1989; Woollacott, Shumway-Cook, & Williams, 1989).

FIGURE   12.12

Perceptual-motor training, as advocated by Cratty, emphasized the integration of problem solving with movement tasks. Here, Dr. Gail Webster challenges a child to find New Mexico and do a forward roll on top of it.

Comprehensive Perceptual-Motor Testing

When the goal is to teach or improve motor skills and patterns, professionals must decide whether to focus objectives on skills or on the abilities underlying the skills. The profession is divided about half and half on which approach to take. Chapter 11 described the skill approach. The remainder of this chapter explains the abilities approach.

Perceptual-motor screening is followed by comprehensive testing to identify areas of breakdown. Table 12.1 presents perceptual-motor abilities measured by some of the better-known tests. The Bruininks-Oseretsky Test of Motor Proficiency (BOTMP) (1978) was discussed extensively in Chapter 7 on assessment because it is widely used in making placement decisions. It generates data for writing objectives and selecting remediation activities in six gross motor areas and two fine motor areas. The tests created by Roach and Kephart (1966), Ayres (1965), and Sherrill (1976) include similar areas and items.

The Sherrill Perceptual-Motor Tasks Test is the only one that is criterion-based rather than normative (see Figures 12.13 and 12.14). It is designed for both testing and teaching. Items in the 10 test areas are written as behavioral objectives that can be reproduced on task cards to guide practice at stations or made into checklists. The test's strength

is that many items are sport-specific. The checklist can be filled in by child, peer tutor, or teacher over a period of several lessons. Some teachers may wish to write in dates when each task is accomplished or indicate levels of assistance (types of prompts) needed. Regardless of approach, the 10 perceptual-motor areas should be covered in instruction.

Ideas for Lesson Plans

The behavioral objective approach to perceptual-motor appraisal results in a concrete list of things the student can and cannot do that should serve as the basis for developing lesson plans. When developing lessons or task cards, state the number of trials and progressively change variables and conditions so that tasks become more challenging. Identify the sense modality through which the child seems to learn best: visual, auditory, or haptic (tactile and proprioceptive input). Also note deficits, since they are sometimes as disabling as real blindness or deafness.

Teaching Game Formations

Getting students into game formations is a difficult task. This is because persons with disabilities often cannot visually image what they are supposed to do when the teacher says, "Form a circle" or "Everyone stand in two-deep formation on the line." Getting into various game formations is thus important

Table 12.1
Perceptual-motor factors that widely used tests purport to measure.

Roach-Kephart Purdue Perceptual-Motor Survey (1966)	Ayres Southern California Perceptual-Motor Tests (1965–69)	Sherrill Perceptual-Motor Tasks for Physical Education (1976)	Bruininks-Oseretsky Test of Motor Proficiency (1978) (Ages 4.6 to 14.6)

1. Balance and posture
   a. Walking board
   b. Hopping and jumping
2. Body image and right-left discrimination
   a. Identification of body parts
   b. Imitation of movement
   c. Obstacle course
   d. Kraus-Weber
   e. Angels-in-the-snow
3. Perceptual-motor match
   a. Chalkboard activities
   b. Rhythmic writing
4. Ocular control; ocular pursuits
5. Form reproduction; drawing simple geometric figures on blank paper
	1. Imitation of postures; reproduction of 12 arm and hand movements
	2. Crossing midline of body; using right or left hand to touch designated ear or eye
	3. Bilateral motor coordination; rhythmic tapping, using palms of hands on thighs
	4. Right-left discrimination; identification of right and left dimensions of various objects
	5. Standing balance, eyes open
	6. Standing balance, eyes closed
		1. Identification of body parts
		2. Right-left discriminations
		3. Changing positions in space
		4. Crossing the midline
		5. Imitation of movements
		6. Imitation of sport movements
		7. Visual tracking
		8. Static balances
		9. Dynamic balances
		10. Lateral dominance
			1. Running speed and agility—a 30-yd shuttle run
			2. Balance, static and dynamic
			3. Bilateral coordination—tapping and jumping tasks
			4. Strength—long jump, sit-ups, push-ups
			5. Upper-limb coordination, mostly ball handling
			6. Response speed
			7. Visual-motor control—Hand-eye activities like cutting, drawing, and copying
			8. Upper-limb speed and dexterity—Hand-eye activities like sorting shape cards and making dots

FIGURE 12.13

Arm positions that children should be able to imitate in Sherrill Perceptual-Motor Tasks Test. The top seven positions are used in the Purdue Perceptual-Motor Survey. These positions should be incorporated into follow-the-leader activities with dramatic themes like imitating airplanes or robots.

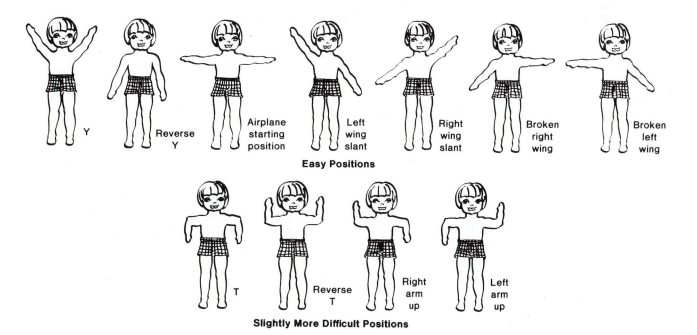

FIGURE 12.14

Sherrill Perceptual-Motor Tasks Test.

CHECKLIST FOR TEACHING-TESTING PERCEPTUAL-MOTOR TASKS

Name _____ Date _____

I. Major Task: Identification of Body Parts.
Other tasks: Auditory discrimination, memory, and sequencing.
  A. Given opportunities to touch body parts and surfaces after the teacher has called his or her name, the student can:
_____ 1. Touch body parts one by one in response to one-word directions:

_____ Mouth	_____ Ankles
_____ Elbow	_____ Head
_____ Eyes	_____ Hips
_____ Feet	_____ Shoulders
_____ Ears	_____ Chin
_____ Wrist	_____ Waist

_____ 2. Touch two body parts simultaneously.
_____ 3. Touch five body parts in the same sequence as they are named by the teacher.
_____ 4. Do all of the above with eyes closed.

II. Major Task: Right-Left Discriminations with Body Parts.
Other tasks: Auditory discrimination, memory, and sequencing.
  A. Given opportunities to touch body parts and surfaces after the teacher has called out the instructions, the student can:
_____ 1. Use the right hand to touch parts named on right side.
_____ 2. Use the right hand to touch parts named on left side (this involves crossing the midline and is more difficult than item 1).
_____ 3. Use the left hand to touch parts named on the left side.
_____ 4. Use the left hand to touch parts named on the right side.
  B. Given opportunities to position a beanbag or large cardboard letter shaped like a *b*, the student can make *p, q, b,* and *d.*
  C. Given opportunities to touch body parts of a facing partner, the student can follow verbal instructions without demonstrations. The student can:
_____ 1. Use the right hand to touch body parts on the right side of partner.
_____ 2. Use the right hand to touch body parts on the left side of partner.

III. Major Task: Changing Positions in Space.
Other tasks: Auditory discrimination, memory, and sequencing.
  A. Given opportunities to identify his or her body position in relation to fixed objects, the student can:
_____ 1. Stand in front of, in back of, to the right of, and to the left of a chair or a softball base.
_____ 2. Run to first base on a softball diamond.
_____ 3. Demonstrate where the right fielder, the left fielder, and the center fielder stand on a softball diamond.
_____ 4. Put specified body parts on top of diamonds, squares, circles, and other shapes on the floor.
_____ 5. Climb over a rope or horizontal bar and duck under it in obstacle course.

  B. Given opportunities to follow verbal directions in warm-ups without the benefit of demonstration, the student can:
_____ 1. Assume the following basic exercise positions: supine lying, hook lying, prone lying, long sitting, hook sitting, cross-legged sitting, kneel, half-kneel, squat, half-squat.
_____ 2. Demonstrate the following different foot positions in response to commands: wide base, narrow base, forward-backward stance, square stance, closed stance, open stance.
_____ 3. Perform a specific exercise seven times, use the eighth count to return to starting position, and stop precisely on the stop signal.
  _____ Seven walks and stop
  _____ Seven stretches and stop
  _____ Seven jumps and stop

IV. Major Task: Crossing the Midline.
Other tasks: Auditory discrimination, memory, and sequencing.
  A. Given opportunities to move the right arm across the midline in response to verbal instructions with no demonstration, the student can:
_____ 1. Throw a ball diagonally to a target on the far left.
_____ 2. Field a ball on the ground that is approaching the left foot.
_____ 3. Perform a backhand drive in tennis.
_____ 4. Catch a ball that rebounds off the wall to the left.
_____ 5. Toss a tennis ball vertically upward in front of left shoulder.

V. Major Task: Imitation of Movements; Motor Planning.
Other tasks: Visual discrimination, memory, and sequencing.
  A. Given opportunities to imitate the arm and leg movements of the teacher in an **Angel-in-the-Snow** sequence, the student can:
  1. Imitate bilateral movements.
_____ a. Move both arms apart and together while legs remain stationary.
_____ b. Move both legs apart and together while arms remain stationary.
_____ c. Move all four limbs apart and together simultaneously.
_____ d. Move any three limbs apart and together simultaneously while the fourth limb remains stationary.
  2. Imitate unilateral movements.
_____ a. Move the right arm and right leg apart and together simultaneously while the left limbs remain stationary.
_____ b. Move the left arm and left leg apart and together simultaneously while the right limbs remain stationary.
  3. Imitate cross-lateral movements.
_____ a. Move the right arm and left leg apart and together simultaneously while the other limbs remain stationary.
_____ b. Move the left arm and right leg apart and together simultaneously while the other limbs remain stationary.

FIGURE 12.14 (continued)

B. Given opportunities to imitate the arm movements of the teacher as depicted in Figure 12.13, without verbal instructions, the student will not mirror movements and can:

_____ 1. Start and stop both arms simultaneously.

_____ 2. Correctly imitate six of nine arm movements.

C. Given opportunities to imitate the arm movements of the teacher who is holding a racquet, the student can correctly imitate, while holding a racquet, 6 out of 11 arm movements in Figure 12.13.

D. Given instructions to play the **Copy Cat Game,** student will watch teacher perform a sequence of stunts, wait 30 sec, and then perform the sequence in correct order.

_____ a. Three stunts (tiptoe walk, dog walk, sit-up)

_____ b. Four stunts

_____ c. Five stunts

VI. Major Task: Imitation of Sport Movements
Other tasks: Visual discrimination, memory, and sequencing.

A. Given opportunities to imitate the movements of the teacher, without verbal instructions, the student with a tennis ball can:

_____ 1. Imitate the teacher's movements precisely, using the right arm when the teacher does.

_____ 2. Toss the ball into the air to exactly the same height as the teacher tosses the ball. Stand under a rope to help assess height.

_____ 3. Bounce the ball so it lands on the floor in precisely the same place as does the teacher's (in front of right foot, to the left side of left foot, and so on).

_____ 4. Bounce the ball so that it rises to the same height as the teacher's before it is caught.

_____ 5. Throw the ball so that it touches a wall target in a designated place.

VII. Major Task: Visual Tracking.
Other tasks: Visual discrimination, memory, and sequencing.

A. Given opportunities to track beanbags (easier than flying balls) thrown by teacher or partner, the student can:

_____ 1. Run or move the body so that the beanbag hits some part of him or her as it falls.

_____ 2. Run or move the body so that he or she catches 7 of 10 beanbags before they fall.

_____ 3. Run or move the body so that he or she strikes the beanbag with some kind of a racquet, paddle, or bat before it falls.

B. Given opportunities to track 30 ground balls being rolled toward him or her from a 15-ft distance, the student can

_____ 1. Stop 8 of 10 balls coming to the right.

_____ 2. Stop 8 of 10 balls coming to the midline.

_____ 3. Stop 8 of 10 balls coming to the left.

VIII. Major Task: Static Balance.
Other tasks: Visual or auditory.

A. Given opportunities to explore static balance, the student can:

_____ 1. Balance on one foot with eyes open for 10 sec.

_____ 2. Balance on tiptoes with eyes open for 10 sec.

_____ 3. Balance on a stick, a rock, or a log with one foot.

_____ 4. Perform a knee scale.

_____ 5. Balance while maintaining a squatting position.

_____ 6. Assume a tripod balance or head stand.

_____ 7. Repeat each of the above with eyes closed.

IX. Major Task: Dynamic Balance
Other tasks: Visual or auditory.

A. Given opportunities to explore dynamic balance, the student can:

_____ 1. Walk a straight line in heel-to-toe fashion for six steps.

_____ 2. Jump backward five times and stop without losing balance.

_____ 3. Walk six steps on a balance beam while holding a 10-lb weight in one arm.

_____ 4. Alternate walking and squatting on a balance beam. Use a step-step-step-squat sequence and repeat three times.

_____ 5. Turn completely around three times while walking a beam.

_____ 6. Do six kangaroo jumps with a rubber playground ball held securely between the legs.

_____ 7. Maintain balance on a tiltboard or stabilometer for 20 sec.

X. Major Tasks: Lateral Dominance.
Other tasks: Visual or auditory.

A. Given opportunities to explore movement possibilities with beanbags, balls, ropes, bats, pencils, and other implements, the student can:

_____ 1. Demonstrate more skill with the preferred hand than the nonpreferred hand.

_____ 10 balls tossed from 10 ft
Record whether caught by R or L hand

_____ 5 kinds of striking apparatus
Record whether held by R or L hand

_____ 10 target throws, beanbags on floor
Record whether thrown with R or L hand

_____ 2. Exhibit a consistent preference for one hand over the other.

Table 12.2
Basic game and dance formations (easiest).

Formation	Drills or Movement Exploration	Games	Dances
Single circle	Facing in	Parachute activities	Farmer in the Dell
	Facing out	Hot Potato	Hokey-Pokey
	Facing counterclockwise (CCW)	Cat and Rat	Loopty Loo
	Facing clockwise (CW)	Duck, Duck, Goose	Did You Ever See a Lassie?
	With "It" in the middle	Mickey Mouse (Spaceman)	Go In and Out the Windows
	With "It" as part of the circle	With "It" in middle, Circle Call-	Captain Jinks
	When part of the circle, "It" may	Ball, Catch the Cane	Cshebogar
	be described as at a 1 o'clock,		
	3 o'clock, 6 o'clock position		
Double circle or two-deep	Both facing in (also called two-deep)	Two-Deep	How D'Ye Do, My Partner
	Both facing out	Caboose Dodgeball	Seven Steps
	Facing partner	Run for Your Supper	Hot Cross Buns
	Facing in, side by side		Pop Goes the Weasel
	Facing out, side by side		Skip to My Lou
	Facing CCW, side by side		Bleking
	Facing CW, side by side		American Schottische
	Boy rotates CCW, girl remains stationary		Patticake Polka
	Girl rotates CCW, boy remains stationary		
	Grand right and left, girl rotates CCW while boy rotates CW		
Single line or row XXXXX	Side by side	Mother, May I?	Technique classes in modern dance, ballet, tap dance
	Straight versus crooked	Red Light, Green Light	
	Curved	Fire Engine (Beef Steak)	
	Staggered	Midnight	
		Old Mother Witch	
Double line or two-deep XXXXX XXXXX	Side by side	Brownies and Fairies	Crested Hen (three pupils)
	Two-deep, all facing front	Crows and Cranes	I See You (any number)
	Two-deep, all facing back	Steal the Bacon	Troika (three pupils)
	Two-deep, facing partner	Line Dodgeball	
	Two-deep, back to back	Volleyball	
		Newcomb	

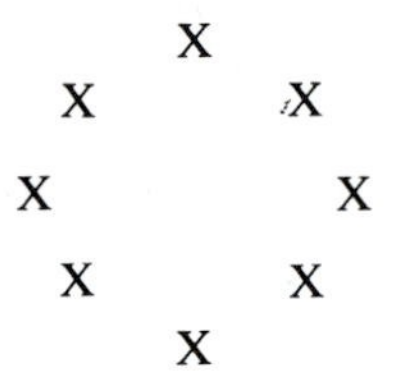

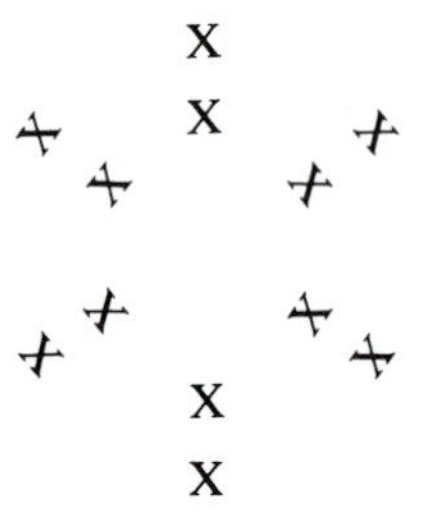

perceptual-motor learning. Likewise, responding correctly to instructions like "Move to the left" and "Go counterclockwise" requires careful teaching.

Design lessons that teach students the names of formations and provide practice for getting into formations with increasingly larger numbers. This practice results not only in perceptual-motor learning but also in improved social awareness and cooperation. Begin with groups of three or four. Give the same verbal cues each time, followed by a count from 1 to 10. Teach students that they must be in the new formation by the count of 10 and that they should help anyone having trouble.

Circles and lines on the floor help beginners, but eventually, form or shape perception should be good enough to enable success without floor cues. Tables 12.2 and 12.3 present the basic game and dance formations that students should learn. The drills or movement exploration column contains the verbal cues that initiate movement. Children enjoy fast-paced drills to these cues, and various routines can be developed. For example:

Single circle 1–2–3–4–5–6–7–8–9–10

Facing in

Facing out

Facing in, walk forward

Facing out, jump to place

Facing in, clap-clap-clap-clap

Single line 1–2–3–4–5–6–7–8–9–10

Run to the wall

Single circle 1–2–3–4–5–6–7–8–9–10

Table 12.3
Basic game and dance formations (hardest).

Formation	Drills or Movement Exploration	Games	Dances
Single file or column	Each child behind the other	Basketball shooting games	
X	Straight versus crooked	H–O–R–S–E	
X	"It" in front of file	Twenty-one	
X	Everyone in file facing forward	Over and under relay	
X	Everyone in file facing backward	Running relays	
X	Everyone in file facing alternately forward and backward	Ball-handling relays	
	Everyone in file facing diagonally right or left		
Double file or	Each child and a partner behind	Three-legged relay	A Hunting We Will Go
longways set	the leading couple	Partner relay	London Bridge
XX	Girl traditionally on the right	Tandem relays	Bumps-a-Daisy
XX	Lead or head couple move		Paw Paw Patch
XX	Last or rear couple move		Virginia Reel
XX	All couples facing forward		
XX	All couples facing backward		
Shuttle formation	Two files, facing one another	Throw object and shuttle to end of own file *or* to end of the other file	Good use of space in continuous practice of locomotor skills
drill and relays:			
XXXXX XXXXX			
Target shooting	Two files, diagonally facing same goal, like a basket or wall target	Throw and shuttle to end of other file	
O			
X X			
X X			
X X			
Square or quadrille,	Facing partner		Most square dances, such as:
comprised of four	Facing opposite		Arkansas Traveler
couples	First couple out to the right		Texas Star
OX	(CCW)		Dive for the Oyster
X O	Circle all		Red River Valley
O X	Swing partner		Take a Little Peek
XO	Swing opposite		

Easy to Hard Formations

The scattered or random formation is the easiest because it permits persons to stand wherever they wish as long as they do not touch anyone else. This structure avoids discipline problems and teaches respect for each other's space. The verbal cue is "Find your own space. Good, now stretch in all directions to show that you cannot touch anyone. Great, you each have your own space."

To play games, however, structured formations must be learned. Circles and lines are easiest, and most primary school games use these (see Table 12.2). Files, shuttles, and target-shooting and square dance formations are progressively harder (see Table 12.3). When girls and boys are partners, the girls traditionally stand on the right.

Two-Deep: Beginning Partner Work

The "two-deep" verbal cue is especially useful and can be used with a circle or line. It comes from the game *Two-Deep,* in which a circle is formed by twosomes, standing one behind the other and facing in. On the outside of the circle is an "It" (person who is chasing) and a target person who is fleeing. To avoid being tagged, the target person can duck inside the circle and stand in front of any twosome. Since there can only be two people in two-deep, the one on the outside becomes the new runner who is chased. The game can also be played as three- or four-deep. It is fun, but the value lies in being able to use the cue "two-deep" whenever you want to structure a partner activity. This also serves as a lead-up to teaching the file or column formation.

Counterclockwise Direction Dominates

Telling children to move right and left often results in bedlam, particularly in activities in which partners are facing. Most experienced teachers therefore use clockwise (CW) and counterclockwise (CCW) terminology. This avoids right-left discrimination problems and also reinforces clock-reading skills.

The counterclockwise direction should be emphasized because this is the traditional direction for running laps around a field, performing partner folk dances, and moving around bases in softball. CCW rotation from station to station helps students to internalize and generalize this. Students typically need lots of practice and structure in moving from one place to another because this skill requires much perceptual-motor processing.

Novel Floor Patterns

Adhesive-paper shapes (circles, triangles, squares) on the floor reinforce form perception and permit lots of games that teach CW, CCW, right-left, and north-south-east-west directions. Maps of states and countries on the floor create similar opportunities. Some gymnasiums have the alphabet in cursive writing on the floor, with all letters 5 to 8 ft high. Various games entail running the letters of the alphabet with the same self-talk used as when learning to write at a desk (e.g., *up, down, up,* and *horizontal* for a cursive *b*).

Activities for Form Perception

The following activities teach or reinforce perceptions of forms and shapes:

1. Give each group a deck of specially made cards that depict different formations. The leader shuffles the deck, someone draws, and the group makes the designated formation. The shuffling and drawing continue until all the cards are used.

2. Project formations or shapes onto the wall with an opaque or slide projector. The group makes the formation that appears on the wall. Words can be projected, rather than diagrams and pictures.

3. Hold up an artificial fruit or vegetable, such as an apple, orange, grape, banana, ear of corn, or hot red pepper. The group then forms a large or small circle or rectangle in keeping with the shape of the object being shown.

4. Give each child a stretch rope (see Figure 12.15). Then show a cardboard shape and/or name a shape and have the child make this shape with the stretch rope.

5. Organize class so each child has one hand holding a long, continuous stretch rope shared by the group. When you call out the name of a formation, the children stretch the rope into the correct shape.

6. Give each group a list or diagram of four or five shapes that have duplicates hidden about the play area. The rules of a scavenger hunt are followed. When all the duplicate cards are found, the group carries them to you and demonstrates ability to get into each formation.

7. Give each group a long and a short bamboo pole representing the hands of a clock. On command, the poles are moved to show different times of day. Bodies lying on the floor can be substituted for the hands of a clock or made into the arrow on a compass.

Perception Learned in Volleyball

The lead-up games to volleyball, which are begun at about the third-grade level, can be used to reinforce right-left discriminations and to provide practice in visual pursuit and/or tracking. For most children, these lead-up games represent their initial experience in tracking large objects that move through a predictable low-high-low arc and in catching and/or striking balls that *descend* rather than ascend (like a bouncing ball) or approach horizontally (like a thrown ball).

Newcomb, the best-know lead-up game to volleyball, substitutes throwing and catching various objects over a net for volleying. It is based on the assumption that tracking and catching a descending ball are prerequisites to tracking and striking (volleying). Certainly, catching and throwing are more familiar skills than volleying and serving. *Visual tracking* is an important contribution of volleyball at the elementary grade level. Children should not be rushed into mastery of the relatively difficult skills of volleying and serving. Nor should individual differences be ignored and all children forced to use the same skills in a game setting. When a volleyball approaches, each child should have options: to catch the ball and return it across the net with a throw or to volley it across. Likewise, the child whose turn it is to serve may choose to put the ball into play with a throw from behind the baseline or a serve from any place on the right-hand side of the court. Thus, in the early stages of learning the serve,

FIGURE   12.15

Making shapes with stretch rope is part of perceptual-motor training in physical education.

some children may be only three giant steps behind the net, while others may have the coordination and arm and shoulder strength to achieve success from behind the baseline. *Balloons* can be substituted for volleyballs with the very young or very weak.

Visual Pursuit and Space Perception

Badminton, tennis, and deck tennis also emphasize visual pursuit skills; they should be introduced at the same time as other net games. Any kind of racquet can be used; the shorter the handle, the better for beginning players. *Large yarn balls* can be substituted for shuttlecocks.

Team games teach spatial awareness through *position play.* Playing a particular position on the court and rotating from position to position reinforces the concepts of right, center, and left and of front and back. Starting with a small number of children on a team and gradually increasing the number of team members is educationally sound, whereas assigning 8 to 10 elementary school children to a team is not. Socially, children must learn to relate to and work with one or two friends before being thrown into larger, impersonal game settings. The average class needs a net for every six beginning players; this is not a budgetary problem for the creative teacher, who uses strings with crepe paper (or rag) streamers as substitutes.

Rotation in volleyball depends upon the child's ability to make right-left discriminations; ability to walk or move sideward, backward, and forward; and comprehension of clockwise as a direction. Teachers who care about transfer of learning and wish to save children with directional deficits embarrassment on the playground use the concept of rotation in the classroom. They have the child sitting in the *RB* (right back) chair stand, recite, and then allow everyone to rotate in a clockwise position so that a new child is *RB* and preparing to recite.

Perception Learned in Softball

A child's success or lack of success in softball, kickball, and baseball may be an excellent indicator of perceptual-motor efficiency, especially with respect to right-left discriminations, crossing the midline, and visual pursuits. No other physical activity offers richer opportunities for perceptual-motor training.

First, the understanding of the diamond and the positions of the players on the field requires the ability to make right-left discriminations. The concept of infield versus outfield offers a new dimension of spatial awareness. The expectation that each player *cover* a particular area of the field and *back up* other players is based upon spatial awareness. Bases are run in a *counterclockwise* direction. Pitches are

FIGURE 12.16

Variations in batting that should be practiced in the classroom with a yarn or paper ball.

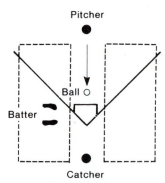

Swinging too early: ball has not yet arrived at the plate; if hit, it will probably go to the left.

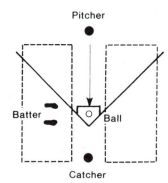

Correct timing of swing: ball is directly over plate; when hit, it will probably go toward the shortstop.

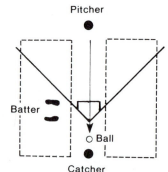

Swinging too late: ball has already passed over the plate; if hit, it will probably go to the right.

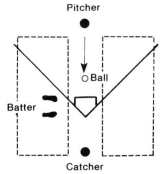

Square stance: best for beginners.

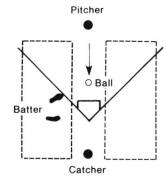

Open stance: if hit, the ball will probably go to the left.

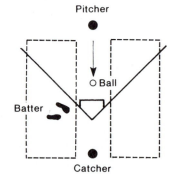

Closed stance: if hit, the ball will probably go to the right.

described as inside, outside, high, low, and curved to the right or left. A batter who misses the ball is told that he or she swung too early or too late. Decision making by a fielder as to where to throw the ball is based upon visual memory of sequences. Is there a player on third base? On first and third? On all of the bases? Where should the ball be thrown first? The batter must make decisions with respect to directions also. If there is a runner on third base, where should the batter hit the ball? If there are runners on first and second base, where should the ball be hit? And *ad infinitum.*

Figure 12.16 offers suggestions for teaching children three sets of terms that are applicable to any sport that entails use of a bat or racquet—square stance, open stance, and closed stance. The different types of stances are seen in golf also. Opportunities for practicing each of the situations depicted should be provided within the structure of the classroom, where distractions are minimal. Knowledge gained in the classroom can be applied later in problem solving during a game situation. For instance, when the ball goes to the right instead of over the net in a tennis game, can the child reason why? When the golf ball goes to the left into a sand trap instead of straight down the fairway, does the student know what caused the directional deviation?

References

Ayres, A. J. (1965). Patterns of perceptual-motor dysfunction in children: A factor analytic study. *Perceptual and Motor Skills, 20,* 335–368.

Ayres, A. J. (1972). *Sensory integration and learning disorders.* Los Angeles: Western Psychological Services.

Bard, C., Fleury, M., & Hay, L. (Eds.). (1990). *Development of eye-hand coordination across the life span.* Columbia, SC: University of South Carolina Press.

Bender, L. (1938). *Bender gestalt test.* New York: American Orthopsychiatric Association.

Biery, M. J., & Kauffman, N. (1989). The effects of therapeutic horseback riding on balance. *Adapted Physical Activity Quarterly, 6* (3), 221–229.

Bruininks, R. H. (1978). *Bruininks-Oseretsky test of motor proficiency: Examiner's manual.* Circle Pines, MN: American Guidance Service.

Burton, A. W. (1990). Assessing the perceptual-motor interaction in developmentally disabled and nonhandicapped children. *Adapted Physical Activity Quarterly, 7,* 325–337.

Cratty, B. J. (1969a). Cratty six-category gross motor test. In B. J. Cratty, *Perceptual-motor behavior and educational processes* (pp. 220–241). Springfield, IL: Charles C. Thomas.

Cratty, B. J. (1969b). *Motor activity and the education of retardates.* Philadelphia: Lea & Febiger.

Cratty, B. J. (1971). *Active learning*. Englewood Cliffs, NJ: Prentice-Hall.

Davis, W. E. (1983). An ecological approach to perceptual-motor learning. In R. L. Eason, T. L. Smith, & F. Caron (Eds.), *Adapted physical activity: From theory to application*. Champaign, IL: Human Kinetics.

Davis, W. E., & Burton, A. W. (1991). Ecological task analysis: Translating movement behavior theory into practice. *Adapted Physical Activity Quarterly, 8,* 154–177.

Gallagher, J., & Thomas, J. (1984). Rehearsal strategy effects on developmental differences for recall of a movement series. *Research Quarterly for Exercise and Sport, 55* (2), 123–128.

Gibson, E. J. (1969). *Principles of perceptual learning and development*. Englewood Cliffs, NJ: Prentice-Hall.

Gibson, E. J. (1987). What does infant perception tell us about theories of perception? *Journal of Experimental Psychology: Human Perception and Performance, 13,* 515–523.

Gibson, J. J. (1966). *The senses considered as perceptual systems*. Boston: Houghton Mifflin.

Gibson, J. J. (1979). *The ecological approach to visual perception*. Boston: Houghton Mifflin.

Hallahan, D., & Cruickshank, W. (1973). *Psychoeducational foundations of learning disabilities*. Englewood Cliffs, NJ: Prentice-Hall.

Hoover, J. H., & Horgan, J. S. (1990). Short-term memory for motor skills in mentally retarded persons: Training and research issues. In G. Reid (Ed.), *Problems in movement control* (pp. 217–239). Amsterdam: North-Holland.

Kavale, K., & Mattson, P. D. (1983). One jumped off the balance beam: Meta-analysis of perceptual-motor training. *Journal of Learning Disabilities, 16,* 165–173.

Kephart, N. C. (1971). *The slow learner in the classroom* (2nd ed.). Columbus, OH: Charles E. Merrill.

Knapczyk, D., & Liemohn, W. (1976). A factor study of Cratty's body perception test. *Research Quarterly, 47,* 678–682.

Kolb, B., & Whishaw, I.Q. (1985). *Fundamentals of human neuropsychology* (2nd ed.). New York: W.H. Freeman.

Kowalski, E., & Sherrill, C. (1992). Motor sequencing of learning disabled boys: Modeling and verbal rehearsal strategies. *Adapted Physical Activity Quarterly, 9* (3), 261–272.

Krupski, A. (1987). Attention: The verbal phantom strikes again in response to Samuels. *Exceptional Children, 54* (1), 62–65.

Pick, A. D. (1979). *Perception and its development: A tribute to Eleanor J. Gibson*. Hillsdale, NJ: Lawrence Erlbaum.

Reid, G. (1980). The effects of memory strategy instruction in the short-term memory of the mentally retarded. *Journal of Motor Behavior, 12,* 221–227.

Roach, E., & Kephart, N. (1966). *The Purdue perceptual-motor survey*. Columbus, OH: Charles E. Merrill.

Rose, M., Cundick, B., & Higbee, K. (1983). Verbal rehearsal and verbal imagery: Mnemonic aids for learning disabled children. *Journal of Learning Disabilities, 16* (6), 352–354.

Samuels, S. J. (1987). Why it is difficult to characterize the underlying cognitive deficits in special education populations? *Exceptional Children, 54,* 60–62.

Schmidt, R. A. (1988). *Motor control and learning* (2nd ed.). Champaign, IL: Human Kinetics.

Sherrill, C. (1976). *Adapted physical education and recreation*. Dubuque, IA: Wm. C. Brown.

Sherrill, C., & Montelione, T. (1990). Prioritizing adapted physical education goals: A pilot study. *Adapted Physical Activity Quarterly, 7,* 355–369.

Shumway-Cook, A. (1989). Equilibrium defects in children. In M. H. Woollacott & A. Shumway-Cook (Eds.), *Development of posture and gait across the life span* (pp. 230–252). Columbia, SC: University of South Carolina Press.

Sugden, D. A., & Keogh, J. F. (1990). *Problems in movement skill development*. Columbia, SC: University of South Carolina Press.

Surburg, P. (1989). Application of imagery techniques to special populations. *Adapted Physical Activity Quarterly, 6* (4), 328–337.

Weiss, M., & Klint, K. (1987). "Show and tell" in the gymnasium: An investigation of developmental differences in modeling and verbal rehearsal of motor skills. *Research Quarterly for Exercise and Sport, 58* (2), 234–241.

Woollacott, M. H., & Shumway-Cook, A. (Eds.). (1989). *Development of posture and gait across the life span*. Columbia, SC: University of South Carolina.

Woollacott, M. H., Shumway-Cook, A., & Williams, H. G. (1989). The development of posture and balance control in children. In M. H. Woollacott & A. Shumway-Cook (Eds.), *Development of posture and gait across the life span* (pp. 77–96). Columbia, SC: University of South Carolina Press.

CHAPTER

13

Fitness and Healthy Lifestyle

FIGURE   13.1

The AAHPERD Physical Best fitness test item to assess the flexibility of the lower back and hamstrings entails one slow maximal reach and stretch.

After you have studied this chapter, you should be able to:

1. Differentiate between health, wellness, and fitness. What are the five components of fitness? Discuss lifestyles and special fitness needs in disability.

2. Differentiate between physical and motor fitness and discuss trends and issues in fitness testing. Explain items used in the current AAHPERD fitness test (or the equivalent in your country) and demonstrate ability to administer them.

3. Identify and explain the five components of an exercise prescription. Discuss how the meaning of fitness varies with the nature and severity of disability.

4. Discuss assessment and programming for cardiorespiratory endurance, body composition, muscle strength and endurance, range of motion and flexibility, and beliefs, attitudes, and practices.

5. Explain adaptations and exercise contraindications that are especially important for (a) severe developmental disabilities, (b) spinal paralysis, (c) other health impairments, (d) limited mental function, and (e) limited sensory function. Relate this to exercise prescription guidelines and fitness components.

6. Describe some models for enhancing fitness beliefs, attitudes, and practices. Discuss new assessment approaches that can be used in conjunction with these models.

7. Discuss weather, temperature, space, and equipment in assessment and programming for fitness.

8. Select and describe a disability, and develop several lesson plans that focus on fitness. What five parts should a fitness lesson include?

9. Critique the 16 principles recommended to guide fitness teaching. Which are most and least important? Discuss applications and cite anecdotes from your experience.

10. Explain and discuss exercise conditioning methods: (a) interval, (b) circuits, (c) continuous, and (d) combinations.

Exercise can be directed toward health, wellness, or fitness (see Figure 13.1). *Health,* according to the World Health Organization (1947), is a state of complete physical, mental, and social well-being and not merely the absence of disease or infirmity. *Wellness* is the integration of all parts of health (physical, mental, social, emotional, and spiritual) that results in feeling good about life and functioning effectively (Corbin & Lindsey, 1990). *Fitness,* broadly defined, includes the same components as wellness.

Definitions of Physical Fitness

How do we know when we are physically fit? The President's Council on Physical Fitness and Sports (1987) stated:

Being physically fit means having the energy and strength to perform daily activities vigorously and alertly without getting "run down" and having energy left over to enjoy leisure-time activities and meet emergency demands. When you are physically fit, your heart, lungs, and muscles are strong and your body is firm and flexible. Your weight and percent body fat are within a desirable range. (p. 6)

Since the 1980s, physical fitness has been conceptualized as a health-related state associated with a lifestyle that minimizes risk of disease and maximizes wellness. Of particular concern is prevention of hypokinetic conditions like obesity, heart disease, high blood pressure, low back pain, adult-onset diabetes, stress, and bone degeneration (osteoporosis). *Hypokinetic* means insufficient movement or exercise. Although often not manifested until middle age, hypokinetic disease begins in childhood (Berenson, 1986) and is aggravated by bed rest and/or activity restrictions imposed by injury, illness, or environmental barriers.

Like self-concept, physical fitness is multidimensional. The American College of Sports Medicine (ACSM, 1991) recommended that physical fitness be defined operationally as the separate components that one intends to assess, target, and develop. ACSM stated: "Health-related physical fitness is typically operationally defined as including cardiorespiratory endurance, body composition, muscular strength and endurance, and flexibility" (p. 35). This four-component definition guides most fitness programs. Among schoolchildren, fitness is almost universally associated with the tests used to measure these four components (see Figure 13.2). A fifth component is the composite of beliefs, attitudes, and intentions that lead to fitness. Thus, in this text, five components are addressed, rather than the traditional four.

Lifestyle Problems

Only about 20% of adults meet the ACSM exercise guidelines; about 40% exercise at low frequency and intensity levels; and about 40% report no physical activity during leisure (Dishman, 1988; Stephens, Jacobs, & White, 1985). Persons with health problems and/or disabilities tend to exercise less than able-bodied peers (Canada Fitness Survey, 1986). Sedentary lifestyle is the main behavior that must be targeted for change if fitness is to improve. The average adult watches television nearly 4 hr a day. This use of leisure is negatively related to fitness, mental health, and life satisfaction (Iso-Ahola, 1980; Tucker, 1990).

Sedentary lifestyle begins in childhood. From about age 3 on, duration and intensity of daily physical activity decline. Boys tend to be more active than girls, but both sexes engage in far less vigorous activity than experts recommend

FIGURE 13.2

AAHPERD test items used to measure fitness. See page 159 for criterion-referenced standards.

1. **Aerobic or Cardiorespiratory Endurance:**
   One mile completed in 10–14 min, depending on age.

2. **Body Composition:** Sum of triceps and calf skinfolds should be no more than 36 mm for girls and 25 mm for boys.

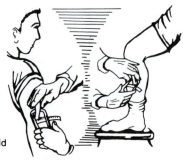

3. **Muscular Strength/Endurance:**
   a. Bent-knee sit-ups for 60 secs. Number depends on age.

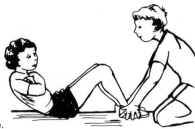

   b. Pull-ups, using palms-outward grasp. One for girls and 1–5 for boys, depending on age.

4. **Lower-Back/Hamstrings Flexibility:** One slow, maximal reach of at least 25 cm.

(Rowland, 1990). For example, the average schoolchild watches television about 20 hours a week. Fewer than 50% of U.S. youth participate in nonschool sport. Only about 11% of high school students compete in school-sponsored sports. Among youth who do participate, the dropout rate from sport each year is about 35%.

About half of everyone who sets exercise goals fails to follow through (Dishman, 1988). Even in supervised programs established for persons at medical risk, about 50% drop out within 6 months to a year. The best dropout predictors for adults are body weight, percent body fat, and self-motivation. For children and youth, the best predictors are fun, enjoyment, and the desire to please significant others. In general, exercise dropouts tend to be those who need exercise the most. *An important goal of adapted physical education is to persuade persons with low fitness that regular exercise can ameliorate problems and increase the richness of life.*

Fitness and Disability

Fitness is a family or sociocultural phenomenon. Societal expectations partly determine fitness aspirations for self and others. Adapted physical education takes an ecological approach to fitness, stressing lifestyle and involving parents, siblings, and significant others in support groups. Persons with disabilities and health impairments obviously have to work harder at fitness than more fortunate peers. Because this process often takes far longer than average and demands considerable perseverance, the benefits of fitness training must be clear.

Fitness is a special concern in adapted physical activity for many reasons:

1. Poor body alignment and inefficient movement patterns increase energy expenditure beyond normal ranges and result in fatigue that reduces job efficiency, leisure-time activities, and overall quality of life (Shephard, 1990).
2. Mechanical efficiency, and thus energy level, is negatively affected by (a) reduced or altered sensory input, as in blindness, deafness, and perceptual deficits (Kobberling, Jankowski, & Leger, 1989); (b) spasticity and abnormal reflex activity (Skrotsky, 1983); (c) use of crutches and prostheses (Fisher & Gullickson, 1978); and (d) loss of functional muscle mass, as in paresis/paralysis (Wells & Hooker, 1990). These and other problems place heavy burdens on the cardiorespiratory and neuromuscular systems.
3. Coping with architectural, attitudinal, and aspirational barriers requires extra energy. Architectural barriers alone increase the energy expenditure of persons with physical disabilities 15-fold over that of able-bodied peers (Miller, Merritt, Merkel, & Westbrook, 1984).
4. Persons with cognitive and/or language disabilities are more likely to be employed in manual labor than desk jobs and thus need high levels of fitness. Fitness training promotes on-the-job success for persons with mental retardation (Beasley, 1982).

5. Persons with disabilities need the best possible physiques and exemplary fitness to overcome discrimination and obtain social acceptance. Physical appearance is an important factor in finding employment.
6. Chronic depression and other mental health problems that plague some persons with disabilities can be ameliorated by fitness programs (Morgan & O'Connor, 1988). Active disabled persons typically rate their emotional well-being and total health higher than do sedentary persons (Canada Fitness Survey, 1986).
7. Many persons with disabilities have never been socialized into sport and/or physically active lifestyles and thus have weight problems and other health concerns associated with sedentary living.
8. Clumsy persons whose body image and self-concept have been negatively affected by balance-coordination-timing problems often find success in walking, jogging, cycling, swimming, and weight lifting. This success can be the springboard for better attitudes toward self.

Types of Fitness: Physical and Motor

Two types of fitness are recognized: (a) physical and (b) motor. *Physical fitness* is health-related and includes five components, as already discussed. *Motor fitness* is skill-related and includes agility, balance, coordination, speed, power, and reaction time. Since 1980, regular physical educators have given little attention to motor fitness. In adapted physical education, however, motor fitness components are helpful in diagnosing problem areas. In this text, motor fitness is associated with perceptual-motor function (see Chapters 10 and 12). The Individuals with Disabilities Education Act includes the term *physical and motor fitness* in its definition of physical education.

Trends and Issues in Fitness

Adapted physical activity personnel must be knowledgeable about fitness tests and exercises. Opinions about many of these have changed and can best be understood from a historical perspective.

Fitness as a physical education goal gained recognition in the 1950s, when Dwight Eisenhower was president and the world was impressed by Russia's shooting of Sputnik into space. The 1950s is the decade of the Kraus-Weber research findings (Kraus & Hirschland, 1954), the founding of the American College of Sports Medicine (ACSM), the establishment of the President's Council on Youth and Fitness (now called the President's Council on Physical Fitness and Sports), and the creation of the first AAHPER Youth Physical Fitness Test. The Kraus-Weber research indicated that American children were less fit than those in several European countries. This research included testing in six items: straight- and bent-knee sit-ups, double-leg lift and hold from supine and prone, trunk lift from prone, and toe touch from stand.

AAHPERD Tests

Of the six Kraus-Weber tests, only the bent-knee sit-up endured. It was incorporated in the first AAHPER(D) fitness battery and not modified until the 1980s. The correct way to administer the sit-up is shown in Figure 13.2. Note that the heels are not more than 12 inches from the buttocks, the angle of knee flexion is less than 90°, and the arms are crossed over the chest.

The AAHPERD test has undergone several revisions since its first administration in the 1950s (AAHPER, 1976, 1980; AAHPERD, 1988). This battery originally included seven items, four to measure motor fitness (standing broad jump, 50-yd dash, 30-ft shuttle run, and overarm throw for distance) and three to measure physical fitness (a distance run, bent-knee sit-ups, and pull-ups or flexed arm hang). The overarm throw was eliminated in the first revision because improper warm-up was causing injuries. The distance run also was subject to much debate. Some authorities accepted the 600-yd walk-run as a measure of cardiorespiratory function, but most supported the 9- or 12-min runs.

The 1980 and 1988 revisions of the AAHPERD test included only health-related items. The 1980 battery included (a) 1- or 1.5-mi run, (b) skin caliper measures of body fat, (c) bent-knee sit-ups, and (d) a sit-and-reach flexibility item. This test was normative, with norms published for each gender by age. The 1988 revision included the same items, except for changes in body fat measurement sites and the addition of pull-ups (see Figure 13.2). The major change in 1988 was philosophical: AAHPERD's 1988 Physical Best Test was recommended for use by all populations, including those with disabilities. Instead of norms, the criterion level necessary for good health was stated for each item. Current AAHPERD philosophy is that the same minimal health standards apply to everyone and that fitness pedagogy should be individualized, with each student striving for a physical best. This philosophy promotes least restrictive environment and inclusion concepts.

Other Tests

Everyone, of course, does not agree with the AAHPERD Physical Best philosophy. Also, many fitness tests are available. Each country has its own test (Government of Canada, 1987), norms, and minimal standards. The President's Council on Physical Fitness and Sports (1987) includes five items: 1-mi run/walk, curl-ups, V-sit reach, shuttle run, and pull-ups. The 30-ft shuttle run is used to evaluate leg strength/endurance/power/agility, and skinfold measures are not taken. The President's Council supports the use of norms and offers awards to individuals who score at the 85th percentile on all five of its items. The YMCA has its own test battery (one of the few with norms for adults) and is used worldwide (Franks, 1989; Golding, Myers, & Sinning, 1989). In addition to these batteries, many tests have been validated as measures of a single fitness component. These are fully described in tests and measurements texts.

Testing and Disability

Test batteries and sets of norms for individuals with disabilities also exist. These mirror the philosophy of the decade in which they were published and contain items similar to those used for able-bodied peers. Frank Hayden (1964) of Canada and Julian Stein of AAHPERD (1968) were the pioneers in the adaptation of fitness tests for youth with mental retardation (see Figure 13.3). Charles Buell (1973) developed norms and recommendations for youth who were blind or visually impaired. The AAHPERD tests for the educable mentally retarded (1968), the trainable mentally retarded (1976), and the visually impaired (1973) are no longer in print because of the AAHPERD philosophy that the minimal standards for health-related fitness in its Physical Best Test are applicable to everyone. Norms for tests published in the 1960s and 1970s are no longer valid.

The U.S. government has funded several large studies of fitness that relate to adapted physical activity. Among these is work in mental retardation by senior researchers G. Lawrence Rarick (1980), John Dunn (Dunn, Morehouse, & Fredericks, 1986), and Paul Jansma (Jansma, Decker, Ersing, McCubbin, & Combs, 1988). Rarick's research centered on mild and moderate mental retardation (MR), whereas Dunn and Jansma focused on severe and profound MR. Rarick was concerned only with testing, but Dunn and Jansma each developed curriculum models based on task analysis and prompting. These models are called Data-Based Gymnasium and Project Transition, respectively.

Rarick's finding that students with MR performed 2 to 4 years behind peers was a major factor in the enactment of federal laws pertaining to physical education and recreation for this population. His work began in the 1950s (Francis & Rarick, 1959) and continued until his retirement in the late 1970s. About 50 test items were administered to hundreds of subjects to determine the factor structure of fitness for educable and trainable MR (Rarick, 1980). Rarick concluded that persons with MR should be tested with the same items as peers but that separate sets of norms were needed. His work created the foundation for other researchers.

Fitness for persons who are blind, deaf, or orthopedically impaired (cerebral palsy, amputations, spinal cord injuries, etc.) has been researched extensively by Joseph Winnick and Francis Short (1984, 1985) through Project Unique. These leaders have developed norms and test adaptations for each sensory and physically impaired population. Winnick and Short recommend the same tests for special populations (adapted as needed) as used in AAHPERD's Physical Best. Additionally, they suggest dynamometer grip strength measures, the softball throw for distance, and the 50-yd/m dash (ambulatory or wheelchair) to evaluate muscular strength and endurance.

Holistic Approaches

In the 1990s, holistic approaches to fitness are becoming popular, with some persons preferring the term *wellness*. Increasing attention is being given to self-esteem, self-

FIGURE 13.3

Leaders in physical education and recreation: (*A*) Dr. Julian Stein,
Director of Programs for the Handicapped from 1966 to 1981,
AAHPERD Headquarters in Reston, VA. (*B*) Dr. Lawrence Rarick,
renowned researcher in motor performance from the University of
California at Berkeley. (*C*) Dr. Frank Hayden, first director of Special
Olympics.

A   B   C

Table 13.1
Responses of persons with disabilities concerning active lifestyles.

Reasons for Being Active		Changes That Would Encourage More Activity	
To feel better	59%	More leisure time	29%
To improve flexibility	43	Better or closer facilities	22
To control weight	39	People with whom to participate	22
To relax, reduce stress	38	Common interest of family	19
For pleasure and fun	37	Less expensive facilities	18
Doctor's advice	35	Common interest of friends	15
For companionship	26	Organized fitness classes	11
Fitness leader's advice	21	A fitness test and program	11
To challenge abilities	18	Information on benefits	7
To learn new things	17		

Note. Forty-seven percent responded that nothing would increase activity. Percentages do not add up to 100% because persons could
check any number of items.
Note. From *Physical Activity Among Activity-Limited and Disabled Adults in Canada* by permission of the Canadian Fitness and
Lifestyle Research Institute, Ontario, Canada.

motivation, and other psychological parameters (Dishman,
1988). Models and theories are being developed that include
beliefs, attitudes, and intentions. Particularly recommended
are the social cognitive (efficacy) and reasoned action models
presented in this text (see Chapters 2 and 6). Instead of
merely describing fitness, researchers are now trying to explain and/or predict its development (Dzewaltowski, Noble,
& Shaw, 1990).

Canada in the 1980s surveyed both its able-bodied
and disabled populations (Canada Fitness Survey, 1986), applying a holistic model to determine patterns of physical activity and related beliefs and attitudes (see Table 13.1).
Responses of persons with disabilities were similar to those
of able-bodied Canadians except that the able-bodied ranked
"for pleasure and fun" as the second most important reason.

Perhaps, persons with disabilities are not socialized early in
life to perceive physical activity as fun; often, their first regular exercise is physical therapy. Clearly, more emphasis
needs to be placed on enjoyment. Note in Table 13.1 that
47% indicated that nothing would make them exercise more.
Counseling is needed on time management, assertiveness in
locating facilities and friends, and ways to increase family
support and involvement.

In summary, fitness practices are changing. Many
of the old tests and exercises are no longer considered safe.
Normative tests are not as popular as in the early years. Instead, seeking one's physical best is emphasized. Adapted
physical activity is assuming a lifespan, ecological approach
and serving persons of all ages (Rimmer, 1993).

Exercise Prescription: Five Components

Exercise prescription is a process of recommending activity for health, fitness, or wellness in an individualized and systematic manner. It is analogous to the individualized education program (IEP) process in that implementation requires (a) assessment, (b) goal setting, (c) decision making about training, (d) establishment of dates and program duration, and (e) evaluation to determine if goals are being achieved.

Components of an exercise prescription are frequency, intensity, time, modality, and rate of progression. These can be remembered by the acronym *FIT-MR.* Guidelines for aerobic fitness for ablebodied persons are

F Frequency—Daily
I Intensity—70 to 90% of maximal heart rate
T Time—At least 30 min
M Modality—A rhythmic, large muscle activity like walking, jogging, cycling, aerobic dance, swimming
R Rate of progression—Gradual increase in intensity

Intensity (how hard) refers to amount of exertion. For *muscle strength/endurance,* intensity refers to number of pounds (the weight or resistance) to be lifted, pushed, pulled, or propelled. For *flexibility,* intensity refers to the distance a muscle group is stretched beyond normal length. For *body composition,* intensity refers to caloric expenditure in relation to caloric intake. For *cardiorespiratory fitness,* intensity refers to distance and speed.

Modality refers to the type of exercise. For *muscle strength/endurance,* modality refers to isotonic, isometric, or isokinetic. For *flexibility,* modality refers to a specific slow, static stretch and whether it is independent (active) or assisted (passive). For *body composition,* modality refers to combination of diet, aerobic exercise, and counseling. For *cardiorespiratory endurance,* modality refers to type of rhythmic, large muscle activity and whether it is continuous or discontinuous (intermittent).

Rate of progression is analogous to dates and program duration on the IEP. Exercise prescription theory recognizes three stages of progression: (a) initial conditioning (usually 4 to 6 weeks), (b) improvement conditioning (the next 5 or 6 months), and (c) maintenance.

For most persons with poor fitness, change is slow during the first few weeks. This is the critical time in regard to attitude formation, injury prevention, and weight loss. ACSM (1991) recommended that exercise intensity during this stage be at a step lower than functional ability. For example, if a person's best effort is a mile in 18 min, then the targeted goal for the first week might be a 20-min mi done daily. Table 13.2 presents an illustrative walking program for a person classified as having poor fitness (i.e., unable to perform a 20-min mi). Awarding points is a good incentive, especially when everyone understands that the goal is to work up to the maintenance level of 30 points a week.

Improvement should be targeted mostly for the 5 to 6 months after the initial conditioning stage and will occur only if intensity and time are progressively increased. The

Table 13.2
A 14-week run walk aerobics program.

Week	Distance in Miles	Time Goal in Minutes	Points
1	1	20:00	3
2	1	18:00	5
3	1	16:00	5
4	1	15:00	5
5	1½	27:00	7½
6	1½	26:00	7½
7	1½	25:00	7½
8	1	14:25	10
9	2	33:00	10
10	2	32:00	10
11	1½	21:40	15
12	2	28:50	20
13	2	28:30	20
14	2½	36:00	25

Note. The goal is 30 points a week. This point system is used only for conditioning, not maintenance.

rate of this progression depends on the physical and mental state. Whenever there are performance plateaus and/or persons indicate a desire to slow down, the maintenance phase begins. At this point, a decision must be made about the minimum frequency, intensity, and time (FIT) required to maintain the training effect. If regular exercise is stopped or decreased too much, *detraining* occurs. This term refers to the gradual loss of all that was gained.

Exercise prescription theory constitutes a large body of knowledge. It is not attributed to one person, as are many theories, but is often associated with ACSM, the organization that publishes *Guidelines for Exercise Testing and Prescription* (1991) and offers certification for various levels of fitness expertise. Exercise prescription theory can be broken down into specific theories and/or practices associated with pioneers like Cooper (1968) (aerobic fitness), Lange (1919) and Hellebrandt and Houtz (1956) (the overload principle), DeLorme and Watkins (1948) (progressive resistance exercise), and Hettinger and Müller (1953) (isometric exercise). There is much to be learned. This chapter presents only beginning level essentials.

Continuum of Abilities and Goals

Adapted physical activity specialists must be able to program for a continuum of fitness abilities. The meaning of fitness varies with the nature and severity of disability. Let's consider the needs of some of the populations served and a hierarchy of goals to guide training.

Severe Developmental Disabilities

In nonambulatory persons with severe developmental disabilities, physical fitness is dependent upon adequacy of the postural reflex mechanism and muscle tone to perform basic movements like lift head, roll over, sit, and crawl/creep. These persons are extremely limited in both mental and physical

FIGURE   13.4

(*A*) With severe developmental disabilities, the emphasis should be on functional ability to perform movement patterns. (*B*) Nonambulatory persons need to develop strength to move their bodies from place to place.

A

B

capacities. They do not play spontaneously and do not initiate movement. Their muscle tone is hypertonic (spastic) or hypotonic (flaccid). A major concern is *contractures,* the permanent shortening and distortion of muscle groups caused by hypertonicity. Problems are not strength and endurance but rather related to basic central nervous system (CNS) function, especially sensorimotor integration. Major goals for such persons are (a) range of motion (ROM) to prevent contractures and stimulate CNS integration, (b) functional ability to perform movement patterns used in fitness tasks, and (c) exercise capacity tolerance. These goals, strictly speaking, are prerequisites to fitness training (see Figure 13.4). Emphasis is on increasing the time dimension of prescription (i.e., the number of minutes or trials the person will persist or tolerate).

Many individuals with severe disability, however, have limited physical capacities but good intelligence. They are able to use motorized wheelchairs at an early age and to independently exercise. ROM to prevent contractures is their primary fitness goal. As slow, static stretches increase ROM on one surface, the opposite surface is automatically strengthened. Thus, ROM and strength are developed concurrently, and muscle imbalances caused by pathology are corrected. Chapter 14 on postures and muscle imbalances is particularly applicable to this group. The breathing exercises described under asthma in Chapter 19 on other health impaired conditions are also important.

When persons are not at risk for contractures and muscle imbalances, equal attention is given to ROM and strength goals. Free weights, pulleys, and Nautilus- or Universal-type machines are used in ways similar to those in able-bodied programs, but more emphasis is placed on concurrent ROM exercises (Holland & Steadward, 1990; Jones, 1988). Weight control and cardiorespiratory endurance goals depend upon mobility options and aspirations to be athletes and/or maintain active, healthy lifestyles.

Spinal Paralysis and Injury Rehabilitation

Strength is a special concern of persons with paralysis, paresis (muscle weakness), or injury that has required surgery. Physical therapy and physical medicine are professions particularly known for work in strength rehabilitation. In paralysis, strength is associated with ROM (i.e., is there enough strength to move the body part?). Residual strength is tested manually (Daniels & Worthingham, 1986) and graded on a 5 (normal) to 0 (complete paralysis) scale as follows:

Grade 5   Normal strength. Full ROM against gravity and full resistance applied by the examiner.
Grade 4   Good strength. Full ROM against gravity with only moderate resistance applied by the examiner.
Grade 3   Fair strength. Full ROM against gravity only.
Grade 2   Poor strength. Full ROM only if the part is positioned so that the force of gravity is negated.
Grade 1   Trace strength. Muscle contraction can be seen or palpated, but strength is insufficient to produce motion even with gravity eliminated.
Grade 0   Zero strength. Complete paralysis. No visible or palpable contraction.

This system of strength testing is used in sport classification of athletes with spinal cord injury, polio, and related disabilities (see Chapter 23). Volunteer work with a wheelchair team and/or persons in a rehabilitation center is perhaps the best way to learn about strength from a paralysis/paresis perspective.

Strength and flexibility in adapted physical activity are often approached as components of *postural fitness.* Imbalances in strength and flexibility, whether developmental or acquired, cause postural deviations, low mechanical efficiency, and problems of coordination, control, and balance. Chapter 14 on postures presents exercises for developing strength and flexibility in specific muscle groups.

FIGURE   13.5

Different methods of classifying fitness. (METS—Metabolic Equivalents.)

Functional Class	Clinical Status			VO₂ max ml • kg • min	METS	Walk/Run Profile	
						Miles per hour	Minutes per mile
Normal and I	Healthy, dependent on age, activity			56.0	16	9	6.5
				52.5	15		
				49.0	14	8	7.5
				45.5	13		
				42.0	12	7	8.5
				38.5	11		
		Sedentary healthy		35.0	10	6	10
				31.5	9		
				28.0	8	5	12
				24.5	7		
II			Limited	21.0	6	4	15
				17.5	5		
III			Symptomatic	14.0	4	3	20
				10.5	3		
				7.0	2	2	30
IV				3.5	1	Bed rest	

Weight control and aerobic endurance are also very important to persons with paralysis/paresis. Persons with quadriplegia and paraplegia have run marathons and are capable of high levels of aerobic endurance.

Other Health Impairments

Persons with other health impairments (OHI) are typically more interested in weight loss and aerobic endurance than strength and flexibility. Sedentary lifestyle may have contributed to their disability or vice versa. Often, these persons are coping concurrently with several conditions: heart disease, hypertension, obesity, asthma, diabetes, cancer, and the like. These may have been present since birth or a young age, distorting their perceptions of what feeling good is like. More than likely, however, the onset has been slow and insidious. They do not realize how poor their condition is until challenged to take a fitness test or advised to exercise by their physicians.

Most persons with OHI fall within the symptomatic clinical status in Figure 13.5. This means that they (a) have a maximum oxygen uptake (VO₂max) of 21 milliliters· kilograms·minutes (ml·kg·min) or less, (b) have a MET (metabolic equivalent) classification of 6 or less, and (c) need 15 or more min to walk/run a mile. (Both maximum oxygen uptake and MET classifications are discussed in detail later in the chapter.) By American College of Sports Medicine (ACSM) standards, they have low or poor fitness that inter-feres with activities of daily living. For example, 5 METs is the criterion level associated with walking up hills and stairs, carrying groceries, and having sexual intercourse. From 3 to 5 MET capacity is needed to take a quick shower, make a bed, scrub the floor, push a power mower, and garden.

Limited Mental Function

Persons with mental retardation (MR) typically have the same fitness needs and capacities as the general population. In the hierarchy of possible goals, weight loss and cardiorespiratory endurance usually rank highest. Of major concern in assessment and programming is the individual's ability to understand speed and distance (i.e., "Run as fast as you can for a mile"). Adaptations like a partner or role model to set the pace are often required (Reid, Seidl, & Montgomery, 1989). Additionally, more care is needed in programming because 20 to 60% of infants born with chromosomal defects like Down syndrome have congenital heart disease. When MR is severe or profound, the autonomic nervous system that regulates heartbeat may be affected. In such cases, the heart rate response to strenuous exercise is not normal, and traditional methods of monitoring exertion are not valid.

A consideration in severe retardation is whether goals like play and game behaviors, social competency/acceptance, and perceptual-motor function should take precedence over fitness. These persons have so many needs that

Table 13.3
Summary of exercise prescription guidelines for fit and unfit people.

Fitness Component	Frequency	Intensity	Time
Cardiorespiratory endurance			
Fit	3–5 times a week	70 to 90% of maximal heart rate	15–60 min
Unfit	Several times daily	55 to 70% of maximal heart rate or whatever is possible	5–15 min
Body composition			
Fit	Usual	Calorie expenditure *equals* calorie intake	Usual
Unfit	Daily or several times daily	Calorie expenditure *greater* than calorie intake in low-intensity/low-impact exercise	Long duration
Flexibility			
Fit	3 times a week	Slow, static stretch held 10–30 sec	3–5 repetitions
Unfit	Daily or several times daily	Slow, static stretch held 5–10 sec	3–5 repetitions
Muscle strength			
Fit	2–3 times a week	Maximal weight that can be moved 5–7 times *or* Isometrics	3 sets, 5–7 repetitions per set
Unfit	Daily	Maximal weight that can be moved 3–5 times *or* Isometrics	Whatever is possible, but aim for 3 sets
Muscle endurance			
Fit	2–3 times a week	Light weight that can be moved 9–25 times, usually 40–70% maximal weight	2–5 sets, 5–7 repetitions each
Unfit	Daily	Light weight that can be moved easily, usually 20–30% maximal weight	2–5 sets, 9–25 repetitions each

Note. Fit refers to the average person wanting to improve or maintain fitness. *Unfit* refers to persons functioning at the 1 to 6 MET level (i.e., unable to walk a 12-min mile and/or meet AAHPERD's Physical Best standards for their age).

deciding which are most important is difficult. In most cases, however, play and game behaviors are necessary to make fitness training ecologically valid.

Limited Sensory Function

Persons with visual and hearing impairments also have the same fitness needs and capabilities as the general population. Many senior citizens fall into this category and need help with cardiorespiratory fitness.

Summary

The hierarchy of fitness goals is determined by the nature and severity of disability. Table 13.3 presents a summary of exercise prescription guidelines for fit and unfit persons.

Achievement of fitness goals is much more time consuming for unfit than average fit persons, and adapted pedagogy is needed to enhance exercise adherence and compliance. The remainder of this chapter focuses on development of competencies to work with people who have low fitness.

Cardiorespiratory or Aerobic Endurance

Four principles guide cardiorespiratory or aerobic endurance work with low-fit people: (a) use low-impact activities; (b) match frequency, intensity, and time to ability; (c) pay attention to self-concept and motivation; and (d) teach acceptance that rate of progression will be slower than for average people. Low- and high-impact activities refer to modality choices. *Low-impact* includes (a) nonweight-bearing activities like swimming, cycling, and rowing and (b) exercises that put minimal stress on joints, like walking, cross-country skiing, and slow stair climbing. *High-impact* includes any activity with a running or jumping component.

Assessment of Aerobic Function

Laboratory testing (treadmill, bicycle ergometer, and arm-cranking devices) or field tests (distance/speed measures and step tests) can be used to assess aerobic function. Adapted physical activity specialists need to understand lab-test findings and be able to use them in exercise programs.

Maximum Oxygen Uptake

Maximum oxygen uptake (VO_2max), the best measure of cardiorespiratory endurance, is the maximum rate that oxygen is consumed by cells in the final seconds prior to total exhaustion and cessation of exercise. Synonyms for VO_2max are maximum oxygen intake or consumption, maximum aerobic power, physical working capacity (PWC), cardiovascular endurance capacity, and peak power output.

VO_2max values are reported in either absolute (liters per minute) or weight-relative units (milliliters·kilograms·minute or ml·kl·min). In adapted physical activity, weight-relative units are preferred. Values typically range from 3.5 ml·kg·min at rest to 56 ml·kg·min during exercise. When best speed is 9 mph or a 6.5–min mile, the amount of oxygen consumed is 56 ml·kg·min. The highest values reported for males and females are 94 and 77 ml·kg·min, respectively (Wilmore & Costill, 1988).

An understanding of VO_2max concepts is necessary to make sense of lab-test findings. For example, average values for individuals with spinal cord injuries range from 17 to 20 ml·kg·min for quadriplegia (Ward & Fraser, 1984) and from 31 to 40 ml·kg·min for paraplegia (Shephard, 1990). Average values for young adults with MR range around 25 to 30 ml·kg·min (Fernhall & Tymeson, 1987; Schurrer, Weltman, & Brammerl, 1985). There are, of course, many problems in measuring VO_2max among persons who do not understand the concept of all-out effort and/or are so unfit that breathing discomfort and muscle pain limit achievement.

Age and gender affect VO_2max. Compared to adults, children have high values. VO_2max ranges from 40 to 60 ml·kg·min for boys and 35 to 50 ml·kg·min for girls. VO_2max peaks between ages 17 and 25 and then declines approximately 9% per decade. Average values for males are 10 to 20% higher than for females (ACSM, 1991), probably because men have less body fat, higher hemoglobin concentrations, and more active lifestyles. Hemoglobin concentration refers to the amount of oxygen in the red blood cells. Sex differences in VO_2max are not generally significant and meaningful until puberty.

VO_2max values are obtained by protocols in which work load is progressively increased until exhaustion sets in. Exercise modalities most frequency used in laboratory testing are the treadmill and cycle ergometer (see Figure 13.6). Per-

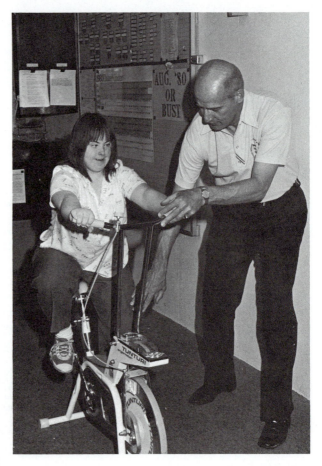

FIGURE 13.6

Work on the bicycle ergometer is one of the best ways to increase aerobic fitness. Here, Dr. Lane Goodwin of the University of Wisconsin at LaCrosse works with an adolescent with Down syndrome.

sons with lower limb disabilities are tested with wheelchair ergometers and arm-cranking devices (Shephard, 1990).

While laboratory measurement is common in university, hospital, and rehabilitation settings, most adapted physical activity specialists use field tests to estimate VO_2max: (a) step tests, (b) distance runs, and (c) walking tests. Distance runs (12-min or 1 to 1.5 mi) at fastest possible speeds are popular, but fast walking may be maximal effort for many unfit persons. ACSM recognizes the Rockport Fitness Walking Test (Kline et al., 1987; Rippe & Ward, 1989) as a valid aerobic fitness measure. The goal of this test is to walk 1 mi as fast as possible.

Roy Shephard, a Canadian physician, is a leader in applying fitness concepts to special populations. In an excellent text (Shephard, 1990), he describes a 12-min wheelchair distance field test. VO_2max on this test ranged from below 12 to above 36, showing that the decreased muscle mass of paralyzed persons lowers their endurance. Individual differences in height, weight, usable body parts, and coordination-control parameters make accurate measurement of VO_2max a challenge. Field test results are only estimates of ability.

Table 13.4
Energy requirements of various activities for persons weighing 154 lb.

Activity or Exercise	METs[a]	Cal Per Hr[b]	Activity or Exercise	METs[a]	Cal Per Hr[b]
Archery	2–3	150–250	Karate/Judo	6–10+	450–800+
Backpacking	3–8	250–600	Kayaking (see canoeing)		
Badminton			Mountain climbing	6–8	450–800
Social doubles	3–4	250–300	Mowing		
Social singles	6	450	Pushing power	3–4	250–300
Competitive singles	8–10	600–750	Pushing hand	6–8	450–600
Baseball or softball			Paddleball/Platform tennis	4–8	300–600
Except pitcher	2–3	150–250	Ping-Pong (table tennis)	4–6	300–450
Pitcher	6	450	Racquetball	6–10	450–750
Basketball	4–10	300–750	Raking leaves	3–5	250–400
Bicycling (on level)			Rope skipping	8–12	600–900
5 mph or 8 km	3	250	Rowing	3–12	250–900
10 mph or 16.1 km	6	450	Rugby	6–8	450–600
13 mph or 20.9 km	9	650	Running and jogging		
Boardsailing	3–8	250–600	5 mph	7–8	500–600
Bowling	1½–3	100–225	7 mph	12	800
Calisthenics	2–8	150–600	9 mph	15	1,100
Canoeing			Sailing		
Flat water	2–8	150–600	Crew	2–4	150–300
White water	5–10	400–750	Skipper	1–3	75–200
Dancing			Sexual intercourse	5–8	400–600
Ballet and modern	4–9+	300–700+	Shoveling	5–9	400–700
Vigorous ballroom	3–8+	250–600	Skating	4–10+	300–800+
Folk and square	3–8+	250–600+	Skiing		
"Aerobic"	5–9	300–700	Cross-country	5–12+	400–900+
Driving car	2	170–200	Downhill	4–10+	300–800+
Fencing	6–9	450–700	Scuba diving	6–10	450–750
Fishing			Soccer	8–10+	600–750+
Casting	2–3	150–250	Squash	8–10+	600–750
Walking with waders	4–6	300–500	Surfing	4–7	300–500
Football (while active)	6–9	450–700	Swimming	4–10+	300–750
Gardening	2–8	150–600	Tennis	4–10	300–750
Golf	2–4	150–300	Volleyball	4–7	300–500
Gymnastics	3–5	250–400	Walking (on level)		
Handball	6–10	450–750	2 mph/3 kph	2	150
Hockey			3 mph/5 kph	3+	250
Field	8–10	600–750	4 mph/6.5 kph	5–6	400–500
Ice	8–10	600–750	Walking stairs/hills	7–12+	500–900
Horseback riding	6–8	480–600	Waterskiing	4–8	300–600
Isometrics	2–5	150–400	Weight lifting	3–6	250–450
Isotonics	2–10+	150–800	Woodsplitting	2–6+	150–500
Jogging (see running)			Yoga	1–4	75–300

[a]METs. The range reflects the varying intensity, from the leisurely or recreational pace to the competitive or frenetic.
[b]Calories per hour—based on a weight of 70 kg (154 lbs). A 10% increase or decrease should be applied for each 7 kg (15 lb) over or under 70 kg, respectively.
Data based largely on a paper by Samuel M. Fox, M.D., Preventive Cardiology Program, Georgetown University Medical Center, and presented by W. L. Haskell at N.I.M.H. meeting, Washington, D.C., April 1984.

Metabolic Equivalents

*M*etabolic *equivalents* (METs) of VO$_2$max are increasingly used in exercise settings. One MET is the equivalent of 3.5 ml·kg·min, the amount of energy expended at rest. Table 13.4 presents approximate energy requirements in METs and cal-ories for leisure and fitness activities. The range of METs is typically 1 to 16. Persons find it easier to understand that their functional exercise capacity is only three times greater than at rest (3 METs) than to conceptualize a maximum ex-penditure of 10.5 ml·kg·min. METs are used in exercise pre-scriptions as well as in assessment.

FIGURE 13.7

Maximal heart rate and target zone for use in aerobic exercise training
programs.

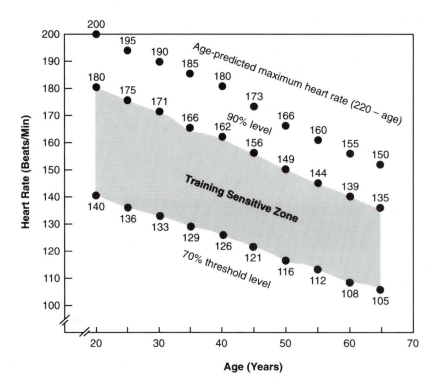

Figure 13.5 shows how VO$_2$max is converted to
METs. Ability to perform at an 11 MET level is needed to
achieve a classification of good fitness. Adapted physical activity typically serves persons functioning at 7 METs or less.

The MET concept originally was created by the
American Heart Association and applied mainly in cardiac
rehabilitation settings. Today, it is used as often in weight
control as in endurance because remembering an energy expenditure scale of 1 to 16 is far easier than thinking in units
of 100, as in calorie counting.

Resting and Exercise Recovery Heart Rates

Resting heart rate is a good indicator of fitness. Ranges considered normal for each age group (Bates, 1983) are

Newborns	110–200
1–24 months	100–200
2–12 years	80–150
13 years and older	60–100

Highly trained adult athletes may have rates as low as 40
beats a minute. In general, however, resting rates outside these
ranges indicate serious problems. Slow rates are associated
with an active lifestyle and fast rates with sedentary habits.

Recovery time after aerobic exercise helps determine whether exercise demands are appropriate or excessive.
Heart rate should decrease to below 120 after 5 min of rest
and to below 100 after 10 min of rest (Cooper, 1982). The
faster this recovery, of course, the better. The pulse rates of
most persons decrease to under 100 during the first minute

of rest. Generally, the heart rate decreases during the first 2
to 3 min after exercise at about the same rate that it increased during activity.

Recovery rates determine the amount of time needed
for cool-down. For healthy young persons, cool-down should
last until the heart rate is about 120. For middle-aged and
older adults, respectively, rates for ending cool-down are 110
and 100.

Recovery breathing rate is also a concern. At rest,
normal respiration is 12 to 16 breaths a minute. Recovery to
this rate should require less than 10 min.

Prescribing Aerobic Exercise

Continuous, low-impact exercise is recommended for persons
with low fitness. *Continuous* means that the activity lasts
more than 3 min. This marks the approximate point at which
contracting skeletal muscle shifts to aerobic metabolism to
produce energy. Intensity of exercise training can be prescribed by several methods: (a) VO$_2$max, (b) rating of perceived exertion (RPE), (c) METs, (d) calories, or
(e) maximal heart rate. The easiest method, when the heart
responds normally to exercise, is maximal heart rate.

Maximal Heart Rate and Target Zone

Maximal heart rate (MHR) is the fastest speed (beats per
minute) a heart can attain during exhaustive exercise without
compromising or endangering life. Figure 13.7 shows estimated MHRs (150 when over 65; 200 when under 20) and
recommended target zones to guide exercise intensity (i.e.,

70 to 90% of MHR). For average persons, the 70% level allows conversation during exercise and is considered a moderate energy expenditure.

Laboratory protocols can be used to determine MHR, but usually it is estimated by formula: 220 − age in years. Thus, a 40-year-old has a MHR of about 180, and a 10-year-old has a MHR of about 210. This formula has a prediction error of about ± 15 beats a minute (e.g., the MHR of 10-year-olds ranges between 195 and 225). There is little or no difference in MHR between sexes.

For persons of low fitness, the lower level of the MHR threshold range is adapted. ACSM (1991) indicated that a 55 to 70% threshold level is appropriate for sedentary or health impaired persons; 55% of a MHR of 200 is 110. This is an appropriate target heart rate for starting the initial 4-to-6 week conditioning stage. Starting too low is better than starting too high. The goal is to gradually increase intensity until the 70 to 90% range can be tolerated.

During aerobic training, persons should be taught to take pulse rate frequently. For hearts that respond normally to exercise, there is a rapid increase during the first 3 to 5 min, after which a steady state or plateau occurs. In children, the steady state occurs earlier, after about 2 min. A good way to check whether intensity is appropriate is to exercise moderately (as hard as possible while maintaining a conversation) for 3 to 5 min, take an immediate 10-sec pulse, and multiply by 6. The result should be within the heart rate target zone.

Factors Affecting Heart Rate Response

Many factors affect heart rate response and must be taken into account. Among these are hot temperatures, high humidity, emotional stress, and medications. Overweight conditions cause hearts to beat faster than average. Infections with fever increase heart rate response so much that elevated body temperature is an exercise contraindication.

The information in Figure 13.7 is not applicable to all persons. When active muscle mass is limited by paralysis, amputations, and muscular dystrophies/atrophies, persons have lower MHRs. Several heart conditions are characterized by lower than normal MHR. Brain stem and autonomic nervous system damage can cause low MHRs. Medications like the beta blockers used to manage high blood pressure and heart conditions suppress both MHR and exercise response. In cases like this, intensity is generally prescribed by rating of perceived exertion (RPE) or METs rather than by heart rate.

Perceived Exertion, Pain, and Dyspnea

Creating a regimen light enough for persons with low fitness requires much experimentation. It is important to provide instruction on intensity and to help exercisers get in touch with their bodies and develop a vocabulary for describing perceived exertion, pain/discomfort, and breathlessness. Table 13.5 presents the RPE scales commonly used in exercise assessment, prescription, and communication (ACSM, 1991; Arnhold, Ng, and Pechar, 1992; Borg, 1982; Ward & Bar-

Table 13.5
Rating of perceived effort (RPE) scales.

Original Category RPE Scale	Revised Category-Ratio RPE Scale
6	0 Nothing at all
7 Very, very light	0.5 Very, very weak
8	1 Very weak
9 Very light	2 Weak
10	3 Moderate
11 Fairly light	4 Somewhat strong
12	5 Strong
13 Somewhat hard	6
14	7 Very strong
15 Hard	8
16	9
17 Very hard	10 Very, very strong
18	+ Maximal
19 Very, very hard	
20	

Note. From *Medicine and Science in Sports and Exercise,* vol. 14, pp. 377–387h, "Rating of Perceived Effort (RPE) Scales." © The American College of Sports Medicine.

Or, 1990). The original scale (6 to 20) is preferred in the field setting because adding a 0 to each number provides a rough estimate of heart rate per minute. *Somewhat hard,* for example, corresponds with a heart rate of 130. *Hard* and *very hard,* respectively, are comparable to heart rates of 150 and 170. The typical intensity range for training is 11 to 16. RPEs of 18 and over describe fatigue so great that exercise must be stopped. In general, warm-ups and cool-downs range between 7 and 11.

Children from age 7 onward give RPEs that correlate highly with heart rate (Bar-Or, 1983). Overweight persons tend to overestimate RPE (Ward & Bar-Or, 1990) but can be taught accurate perceptions. RPEs eliminate the nuisance of counting pulse rate during aerobic activities. The RPE is also recommended for people whose hearts do not respond properly to exercise. Charts with RPE adjectives in large print are hung on walls to teach about intensity and increase awareness of its importance.

If persons are unable to sustain large muscle exercise at 55 to 90% of maximal heart rate for 15 min, the goal should be exercise tolerance or functional capacity rather than cardiorespiratory endurance. Tolerance is influenced mainly by (a) cognition/motivation; (b) muscle pain caused by lactic acid accumulation, oxygen deprivation, or tissue swelling; (c) chest pain or stitch in side caused by insufficient oxygen supply; and (d) breathing discomfort, called *dyspnea.*

Everyone experiences some discomfort as intensity of exercise increases, but persons with low fitness often perceive real pain. Asthma and obesity particularly challenge pain threshold. Persons who cannot get enough oxygen into the blood may experience severe hip, leg, or foot pain called *claudication.* The calf is most commonly affected, and the intense pain occurs after only a short distance (half a block to quarter mile) has been covered. Claudication should not be confused with ordinary muscle cramps. It is rare in the general population but relatively common in persons with oxygen deficiency conditions.

The challenge in adapted physical activity is to increase intensity so gradually that discomfort is minimal. Otherwise, persons tend to drop out. Also, coping with or ignoring discomfort may need to be taught. Athletes and physical education majors take "No pain, no gain" for granted. In contrast, sedentary persons have no experience in judging exercise-induced discomfort.

Numerical scales are used to objectify ratings of pain and dyspnea (see Table 13.6). An objective for a person with asthma, for example, might be to reduce dyspnea from 3 to 2 during a 1-mi walk for speed. The scales in Table 13.6 should be incorporated into assessment systems that urge all-out effort. Fitness training for health should be adapted (slower, lighter than training for sports) so that activity is associated with pleasure, not pain and dyspnea.

Body Composition

Body composition refers to the individual components that constitute the total body mass. The relative percentages are shown in Table 13.7. Females have more fat, and males have more muscle tissue. Differences between genders are minimal until puberty, when sex hormones become active and promote development of male and female characteristics. In general, children have less body fat than adults (10 to 15% compared to 15 to 27%). Body composition is largely genetically determined, as evidenced by similarities in fat distribution and body shapes/sizes/builds within families. Genetic predisposition, however, can be tempered by exercise and nutrition. Some disabilities affect body composition. Spinal cord injuries, for example, increase body fat percentage and decrease lean body mass.

Body fat percentages, rather than body weight, are the major fitness concern. Healthy body fat standards depend on whether or not an individual wants to excel in sports. For nonathletes, desirable percentages of fat are 18 to 30% for women and 10 to 25% for men. For athletes, less fat is desirable: 12 to 22% for women and 5 to 13% for men. Fat reduction goals thus depend on leisure interests.

Assessment of Body Fat

Percentage of body fat can be determined by laboratory protocols and formulae (ACSM, 1988; Lohman, Boileau, & Slaughter, 1984) or estimated by skinfold caliper measures. Calipers provide a measure of the amount of fat that can be pinched away from a body part at a particular landmark (see Figure 13.8).

When time is so limited that only one measure can be taken, the triceps skinfold is recommended. To assure accuracy, measurements are taken three times, and the middle value is recorded. Care must be taken to pinch the skin at precisely the point indicated in test directions. Measurements are usually taken on the right side only.

Table 13.6
Scales for objectifying ratings of pain and dyspnea.

Pain Scale

1+	Light, barely noticeable
2+	Moderate, bothersome
3+	Severe, very uncomfortable
4+	Most severe pain ever experienced

Dyspnea Scale

1+	Mild, noticeable to exerciser but not observer
2+	Mild, some difficulty, noticeable to observer
3+	Moderate difficulty, but can continue
4+	Severe difficulty, cannot continue

Table 13.7
Relative percentages of components of total body mass.

Component	Average Male	Average Female
Muscle	45%	36%
Bone	15%	12%
Fat	15%	27%
Remainder	25%	25%

When possible, several skinfold measures are used. The best combination of skinfold measures is controversial. The 1988 AAHPERD Physical Best Test recommends a triceps and calf skinfolds combination. For girls, ages 5 to 18, the criterion for good health is 16 to 36. For boys of the same age, the criterion is 12 to 25. The 1980 AAHPERD Health-Related Fitness Test used the sum of triceps and subscapular skinfolds. The 1987 Canadian Standardized Test of Fitness recommends the sum of triceps, biceps, subscapular, and suprailiac skinfolds. Figure 13.9 presents various skinfold measures.

Body Mass Index: Substitute Measure

Body mass index (BMI) refers to height, weight, and anthropometric measures and is accepted by AAHPERD as a substitute for body fat measures when skinfold calipers are not available. The BMI is the ratio of body weight to the square of body height:

$$\text{BMI} = \frac{\text{Body weight}}{\text{Height}^2}$$

Health fitness standards for BMI vary with age and gender (see Chapter 7 on assessment).

Physical and motor fitness scores should be interpreted in relation to height, weight, and skinfolds. The classic research of Dobbins, Garron, and Rarick (1981) showed that many statistically significant differences between persons with and without MR disappear when adjustments are made for differences in body size.

FIGURE 13.8

(*A*) Triceps skinfold measure of body fat is part of AAHPERD fitness test. (*B*) The midpoint of the back upper arm is the standard place to make the measurement. (*C*) Minimum triceps skinfold thickness indicating obesity (in millimeters).

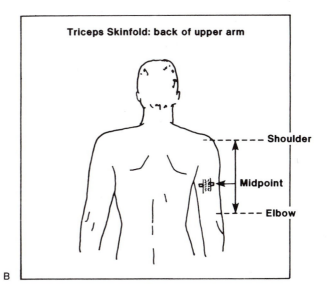

B

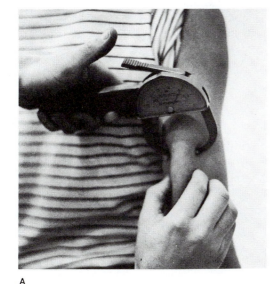

A

Age (Years)	Males	Females
5	12	14
6	12	15
7	13	16
8	14	17
9	15	18
10	16	20
11	17	21
12	18	22
13	18	23
14	17	23
15	16	24
16	15	25
17	14	26
18	15	27
19	15	27
20	16	28
21	17	28
22	18	28
23	18	28
24	19	28
25	20	29
26	20	29
27	21	29
28	22	29
29	23	29
30	23	30

C

FIGURE   13.9

The triceps skinfold is used with one or more of the following skinfolds:
(*A*) Calf skinfold. (*B*) Biceps skinfold. (*C*) Suprailiac skinfold.
(*D*) Subscapular skinfold.

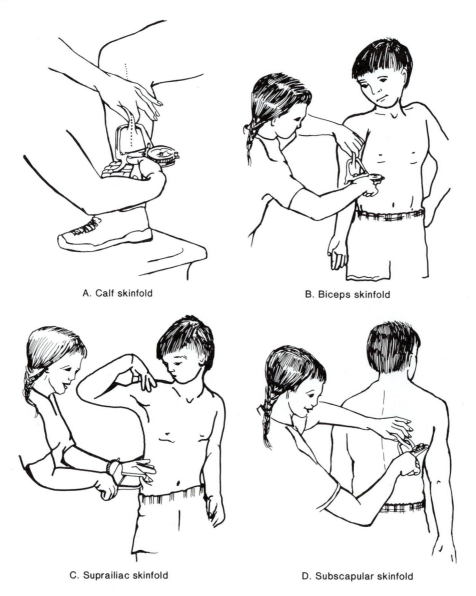

A. Calf skinfold

B. Biceps skinfold

C. Suprailiac skinfold

D. Subscapular skinfold

Height-weight tables heighten motivation for lifestyle changes because they are easily understood. However, the correlation between weight and percent body fat is about .67. Thus, weight is not a reliable predictor of body fat. Nevertheless, height and weight are important indicators of normal growth. Most youth reach the final 2% of their height by age 18 (females) and age 20 (males). After about age 45, height begins to decrease, probably because of loss of bone mass and related degeneration of the spinal column. Bone loss (osteoporosis) in old age proceeds faster in women than men. Osteoporosis is a major body composition problem.

Exercise for Fat Loss

Body fat can best be reduced by assuring that large muscle activity uses more calories than daily intake. This is achieved through change of lifestyle (both exercise and nutrition) and generally requires counseling as well as participation in a support group. Exercise should be aerobic at whatever intensity is possible. Table 13.4 shows the calories expended per hour in various activities for a person weighing 154 lb. The heavier a person, the more calories are expended. Tables like this must therefore be adjusted for individual differences. A good formula for this purpose is to increase or decrease the calories by 10% for each 15 lb (7 kg) over or under 154 lb (70 kg).

One pound of fat equals 3,500 calories. No more than 2.2 lb (1 kg) should be lost each week (ACSM, 1991). To achieve this goal, exercise should be increased by at least 300 calories a day. For a 154-lb person whose highest intensity level is 2 mph (one 30-min mi), 2 hr a day must be spent walking to expend 300 calories. Obviously, the more fit a person is, the less time per day is needed to expend calories.

Obesity is addressed in Chapter 19 on other health impairments because it is a medical problem as serious as asthma, diabetes, and the like. Obese persons need to be assured that long-duration activity at low intensity is as effective as short-duration/high-intensity activity. Time management counseling is a high-priority need because most persons have a difficult time finding an extra 1 to 2 hr a day in their schedules to use for exercise. Counseling and support group involvement should continue after weight loss to assure maintenance of target weight.

Muscle Strength/Endurance

Muscle strength and endurance are developed concurrently in childhood through vigorous activities of daily living. *Strength* is developed every time that muscle exertion is near maximum, as in lifting, pushing, pulling, holding, or carrying a heavy object. Jumping as far as possible, for example, requires a maximal lift of body weight. Pull-ups and rope climbing also demand lifting body weight. *Endurance* is developed whenever a muscular activity continues for several seconds, as in sit-ups, push-ups, running in place, continuous jumps, or short-distance sprints.

Age and gender differences in strength parallel changes in muscle mass. Females tend to show a steady increase in strength until about age 30. Males likewise increase steadily but demonstrate a sudden, rapid increase at puberty (ages 13 to 14), which is associated with testosterone, the sex hormone that stimulates muscle growth. At all ages, the average male is stronger than the average female. After adolescence, muscle bulk (the result of muscle fiber hypertrophy) characterizes males who engage in strength training. Women in equivalent programs increase in strength but do not develop comparable bulk because of their lack of testosterone. After age 30, strength plateaus and then begins to gradually decline. The rate of this decline is largely dependent on amount of physical activity.

Assessment of Muscle Strength/Endurance

The principle of specificity must be remembered when assessing muscle function. There is no such thing as total body strength/endurance, so choices must be made about which muscle groups are most important to test. Generally, the groups selected are abdominal (bent-knee sit-ups), upper arm and shoulder (pull-ups, push-ups), and hip and thigh (distance jump or sprint).

Strength/endurance is specific to the joint angle at which a movement is done. Following starting position directions precisely is therefore important. Pull-ups, for example, use different muscle groups when palms are facing in (an easier progression) than when palms are facing out. Sit-ups should be performed with heels from 12 to 18 inches from buttocks and with the feet held down because research shows that this is the best position for measuring abdominal function.

When physical disability results in paralysis or paresis, assessment is more comprehensive. In such cases, movement capacity may be graded on a 0 to 5 scale or number of repetitions recorded for objects of different weights being taken through specific ranges of motion.

Exercise for Muscle Strength/Endurance

A muscle can be strong and lack endurance or vice versa. Therefore, daily living must include activities for both strength and endurance. Children and youth who participate year-round in a variety of game, sport, dance, and aquatic activities do not need special exercises unless they aspire to high-level sports performance. In contrast, serious athletes of all ages engage in weight training and individualized systems of exercise.

Sedentary persons should take all their major muscle groups through both strength and endurance exercises at least 2 days a week (ACSM, 1991). Adapted physical activity for young people uses animal walks, stunts, games, self-testing activities, and movement education to achieve this purpose (see Figure 13.10). For example, arm and shoulder strength/endurance can be increased by crab walk, dog walk, lame-dog walk, inchworm, and coffee grinder. Any activity in which the arms support, propel, or lift body weight develops muscles. Hanging, rope or apparatus climbing, and overarm travel on a horizontal ladder are especially good. Abdominal strength/endurance is developed by hands and knees creeping and by lifting body parts (trunk or legs) from a supine position. Back strength is developed by lifting body parts from a prone position. Swimming is often considered the best all-round muscle developer, and exercises/games can be devised that use arm and leg movements from the various strokes.

Central to the development of muscles is the principle of overload, which refers to progressively increasing the demands made on a muscle group. Strength/endurance can be developed by three types of activity: (a) isotonic, (b) isometric, and (c) isokinetic (see Figure 13.11).

Isotonic Exercise

Isotonic exercise is categorized according to equipment needed: (a) no equipment, as in animal walks, push-ups, and sit-ups; (b) stationary bars for pull-ups; (c) wall, floor, or ceiling pulleys; (d) free weights, and (e) variable resistance machines like the Universal and Nautilus. Free weights are divided into dumbbells for one-hand lifts, barbells for two-hand lifts, and cuff weights that are attached to body parts via Velcro. Machines offer multiple stations for pushing, pulling, and lifting and provide either constant or variable resistance.

Creative teachers devise all kinds of free weights and color-code or mark them to indicate number of pounds. Examples are

1. Stuffed animals filled with 7, 10, and 15 lb of sand
2. Fireplace logs, bricks, or rocks
3. Sacks of potatoes, cat sand, dry dog food, or flour found in grocery stores
4. Plastic bottles filled with sand
5. Backpacks, such as those used on hiking and camping trips
6. Buckets, chairs, and other daily living objects
7. Handmade weights from tin cans, cement, and broomsticks

FIGURE   13.10

Fun activities for developing arm and shoulder strength.

1. Can you do a dog walk? Note that knees are bent.

2. Can you lift one leg and do a lame-dog walk?

3. Can you do a bear walk? Note that legs are straight.

| Push-up position | Bear walk | Push-up position |

4. Can you do the inchworm walk? Start in push-up position, then inch forward using only your feet to the bear walk position, then inch forward, using only your hands, to the push-up position again.

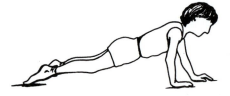

5. Can you do a seal (walrus) crawl? Only your arms can move.

6. Can you touch your chin to the mat and come back up? This is called *dumping sand*. Can you do the wheelbarrow walk?

7. Can you do the crab walk?

FIGURE **13.10** (continued)

8. Can you hold a bridge?

9. Can you hold a one-arm side stretch?

10. Can you do the coffee grinder?

11. Can you do a rabbit jump? Knees stay bent.

12. Can you do a mule kick? Knees straighten out.

13. Can you do an elephant walk with a partner?

14. Can you do a centipede walk with one or two partners?

FIGURE 13.11

Three types of strength training.

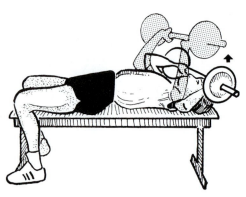

A. Isotonic

B. Isometric

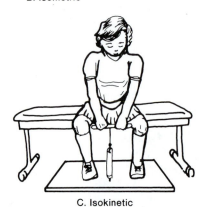

C. Isokinetic

Most isotonic exercise for adolescents and adults is weight training. Prescriptions are stated in terms of sets and the repetition maximum (RM). One set is the number of repetitions done consecutively without resting. RM is the maximal weight that can be lifted in one set. Strength is best developed when the resistance (weight) allows no more than 5 to 7 repetitions and three sets are performed two or three times a week (ACSM, 1991). This guideline varies, however, with disability and purpose of training. In general, training for muscle endurance requires use of lighter weights (one half or three fourths of maximum), with greater number of repetitions. In contrast, training for strength uses heavier weights with fewer repetitions.

Progressive resistance exercise (PRE) is a popular rehabilitation technique used to ameliorate weakness and atrophy after surgery. Often called the DeLorme method after one of its founders (DeLorme & Watkins, 1948), PRE is based on maximal resistance that pain tolerance permits to be lifted 10 times (10RM) and a lifting program of 30 repetitions executed several times each week as follows:

1 set of 10 repetitions at one-half 10RM

1 set of 10 repetitions at three-fourths 10RM

1 set of 10 repetitions at full 10RM

Much research indicates that fewer repetitions (four to eight) may be effective.

Safety is a concern when using free weights. Persons should not lift alone for obvious reasons. Lifts should be slow, smooth, and continuous to avoid injury, and breathing should be natural. Strength training should be coordinated with a good flexibility routine.

Isometric Exercise

Isometric exercise is a maximum or near-maximum muscle contraction that is held for 6 sec and repeated several times during the day. This exercise is highly specific, strengthening muscles only for work at the same angle as the training. Squeezing a dynamometer or tennis ball to develop hand grip strength is an example; the isometric part of the exercise begins after movement has ceased. Persons with low back pain use the gluteal pinch and pelvic tilt. Almost everyone occasionally pulls inward on abdominal muscles and holds to improve appearance. Straining during bowel movements is another example of isometric exercise. Arm and leg exercises entail pressing against doorways and walls and pulling against towels, ropes, or tire strips that permit no movement and hence no change in muscle length.

Isometric exercise is the only form of strength training that is not based on the overload principle. Founded by Hettinger and Müller (1953) of Germany, isometrics are especially recommended for persons bedridden or limited in movement for reasons other than cardiorespiratory disease. Because of associated breath holding, isometrics is the worst form of strength training for individuals with heart disease and high blood pressure.

Isokinetic Exercise

Isokinetic exercise is associated with constant resistance machines. These keep velocity of a movement constant and match the resistance to the effort of the exerciser. This allows maximal tension to be exerted throughout the range of motion. Illustrative machines of this type are Cybex II, Apollo, Exer-Genie, and Hydra-Fitness. Isokinetics is the newest type of weight training and, theoretically, should lead to the greatest improvement.

Cybex machines provide data on both joint position and peak torque (the turning or rotary force). The torque produced on a body segment by a muscle group is dependent on the angle of muscle attachments to the bone, the length-tension properties of the muscle, and the speed of shortening. Isokinetic machines can be set at many speeds (e.g., fast, 108° per second; slow, 36° per second). Training velocity determines strength. Thus, training should be at speeds approxi-

FIGURE 13.12

Two types of goniometers with their respective measurement systems. The movable bar indicates the number of degrees a body part can be moved.

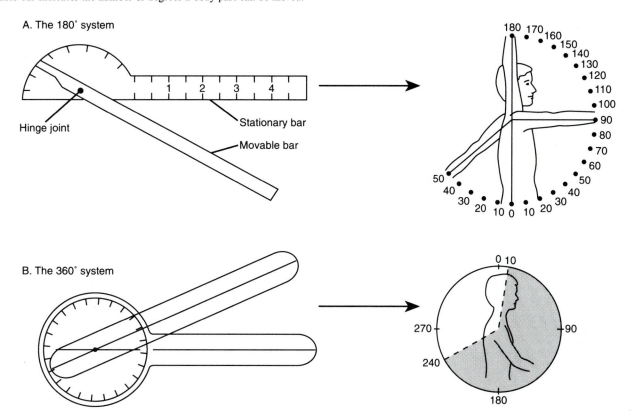

A. The 180° system

Hinge joint

Stationary bar

Movable bar

B. The 360° system

mating or exceeding those desired. Isokinetic machines take body parts through their entire range of movement. Some adapted physical activity researchers who have used the Cybex are Holland and Steadward (1990) and McCubbin and Shasby (1985).

Valsalva Effect and Contraindications

The *Valsalva effect* is an increase in intraabdominal and intrathoracic pressure that results when breath is held, as in straining to lift a heavy object or to exert maximal force. Increased pressure causes slowing of heart rate, decreased return of blood to the heart, and elevated blood pressure. Heavy strength training is generally contraindicated in high blood pressure conditions and heart disease. Breath holding during exercise can also rupture tissues, especially in the abdominal region (hernias) and in the eyes when pathology already is present, such as increased internal pressure (glaucoma) and torn or detached retina.

Range of Motion and Flexibility

The range of motion and flexibility component refers to ability to move body segments through the actions and planes designated as normal for each joint. For example, movements in three planes are possible at the shoulder and hip joints: (a) sagittal plane—flexion and extension; (b) frontal plane—abduction, adduction; and (c) horizontal plane—rotation. In contrast, the elbow and ankle joints permit movement in only one plane.

Range of motion (ROM) is the term used when the movement capacity at a joint is measured in degrees through use of a goniometer (a protractor-type device) or a flexometer (a 360° dial with pointer that is strapped to the body part). These devices can be purchased through equipment companies like J. A. Preston (see Appendix E). A knowledge of goniometry is necessary when the goal is increased ROM at designated joints (see Figure 13.12). In pathological conditions that require therapeutic exercise to prevent contractures or to rehabilitate a body part after surgery, ROM is the accepted term. Conditions like cerebral palsy, muscular dystrophy, arthritis, spina bifida, and paralysis require daily ROM exercises. These are typically prescribed by physicians and therapists and carried out by parents, teachers, and aides (Kottke, 1990; Surburg, 1986; Tecklin, 1989).

Flexibility is the term used in physical education and sport settings to specify functional stretching ability (i.e., ability to stretch well enough to perform activities of daily living and to achieve personal sport and dance goals without injury). Flexibility tests measure simultaneous function of several joints in performing a function like reaching. When movement is limited by illness, disability, or sedentary lifestyle, flexibility is the first fitness parameter to suffer. Thus, activity programs for convalescing or sedentary persons often focus on gentle stretching exercises during the first weeks.

Gender, age, occupation, and musculoskeletal differences affect flexibility. At all ages and most joints, females demonstrate more flexibility than males. This difference widens with age. Flexibility seems to improve from childhood through adolescence. Thereafter, it declines steadily. Persons in occupations demanding much physical activity are more flexible than those in sedentary jobs. Flexibility is affected by bony structure or configuration of joints, muscles, tendons, ligaments, and skin. Arthritis, dwarfism, muscular dystrophy, paralysis, cerebral palsy, and burns are examples of conditions that limit flexibility. In contrast, some disabilities like Down syndrome are associated with excessive flexibility.

Assessment of ROM/Flexibility

Flexibility is specific to each muscle group. Since testing all muscle groups is not feasible in large-scale fitness tests, AAHPERD and its Canadian counterpart include the sit-and-reach test as a combined estimate of hamstring, hip, and spine flexibility. These muscle groups, when tight, contribute to injury and/or chronic lower back problems. Tightness is associated with excessive sitting, and the sit-and-reach test is a good predictor of sedentary lifestyle.

Measurement of ROM begins with the body part in anatomical position, which is designated as 0 in the 180° system (see Figure 13.12). The hinge joint of the goniometer is placed over the joint so that both bars point to 0. The movable bar moves with the body part, and its pointer marks the angle of motion achieved. Two or three measures of each movement are taken to assure reliability. Either the maximum (Shephard, Berridge, & Montelpare, 1990) or the average (Holland & Steadward, 1990) is recorded. Measurements are often taken from a supine position to eliminate balance and gravity problems.

Stretching Exercises

The nature of stretching depends on its purpose: (a) to maintain elasticity, (b) to warm-up and cool-down, or (c) to correct pathological tightness. Stretches that take body parts to their movement extremes should be done after warm-ups, not before. If done incorrectly, stretches can cause injury or worsen disability. Chapter 14 on postures and muscle imbalance covers stretches for specific body parts and contraindications. Overall body stretching for maintenance is described in Chapter 15 on relaxation, where Yoga and Tai Chi are emphasized. These are particularly good for older populations.

Regardless of nature, stretches should be only slow and static. Ballistic movements (i.e., bobbing and bounces) are no longer considered as stretching exercises and are, in fact, contraindicated when the purpose is flexibility. Modalities used in stretching are (a) active, (b) passive, and (c) combinations. When stretches are directed toward correcting specific tightness, they should slowly move the body part to the extreme of its range of motion, where it remains for several seconds. Sport references recommend 10 to 30 sec (ACSM, 1991; Anderson, 1980; Curtis, 1981; Kennedy, 1988), whereas therapeutic exercise references suggest 5 to 10 sec (Basmajian & Wolf, 1990; Surburg, 1986; Tecklin, 1989).

Beliefs, Attitudes, and Practices

Several theories presented in Chapters 2 and 6 can be applied to help persons develop fitness and change lifestyle. Statements of goals and objectives should always include targeted beliefs, attitudes, and practices.

According to *reasoned action attitude theory* (see Chapter 2), persons will change their lifestyles to include regular exercise if they are helped to reason out the probable outcomes/consequences and perceive the support of significant others. They are asked to write a personal exercise goal, list the possible good and bad consequences, and then predict the likelihood of these consequences coming true. This becomes their attitude toward behavior score. Next, they identify four or five significant others and what these people think they should do. A subjective norm score is derived by multiplying this with a rating of personal motivation to comply. Together, attitude toward behavior and subjective norm determine intention to implement the exercise goal and exercise behaviors.

According to *self-efficacy* or *social cognitive theory* (see Chapter 6), one must perceive self as capable of carrying out a desired behavior and expect to succeed. Efficacy expectations result when certain antecedents are planned and implemented: (a) reminders of past mastery, (b) role models to provide vicarious learning opportunities, (c) verbal persuasion by self and others, and (d) cognitive control of anxiety, fear, and related negative emotions. These four antecedents represent the most important variables that shape social cognitive behaviors. This comprehensive model works well if the person has been fit in the past and has memories to pull from.

According to *perceived competence theory* (see Chapter 6), three variables affect achievement: (a) perceived competence, (b) perceived control (self, others, unknown), and (c) motivation orientation (challenge, curiosity, mastery, judgment, criteria). Attention to these variables will enhance fitness programming, especially if the person has had little fitness success in the past.

New assessment approaches include self-reports of motivation, food intake, physical activity, and attitudes about the body and exercise. Illustrative is the Self-Motivation Inventory (Dishman & Ickes, 1981; Dishman, Ickes, & Morgan, 1980). This 40-item instrument includes items like the following that are rated on a 5-point scale ("very unlike me" to "very much like me"):

1. I get discouraged easily.
2. Sometimes, I push myself harder than I should.
3. I can persevere at stressful tasks, even when they are physically tiring or painful.

Research indicates that the self-motivation score combined with body weight and percent fat is an excellent predictor of exercise adherence. Information yielded by instruments like the Self-Motivation Inventory helps in counseling and individualized teaching.

Diaries or logs of food intake (Block et al., 1986) and physical activity (Baranowski, 1988) help structure goal setting. They focus attention on goals and provide concrete facts; 24-hr recalls tend to be more accurate than 3- or 7-day recalls. Illustrative of an interview format to assess activity is the following:

Teacher: In order to set goals for after-school and weekend physical activity for the next month, let's think about what you did this past week. Let's start with yesterday, and you list everything you did that was of moderate, hard, or very hard intensity. *Moderate* things are activities that make you feel like you are taking a brisk walk. *Very hard* activities make you feel like you are running. *Hard* activities are those that fall between brisk walking and running. Ready? Let's start.

Client/Student: OK, yesterday was Sunday. I got up about 7 A.M., messed around, took a shower, and went to church.

Teacher: What kind of transportation did you take to church? It is important that you tell me about transportation so that we can determine how much energy you spent. Did you walk, and was the pace slow, medium, or fast? Or did you cycle or take a car?

Client/Student: Dad drove the car, but after church, I went with my friends, and we walked about 12 blocks to Bill's house. We messed around a while and then took the bus to a movie.

Teacher: Then what did you do in the evening?

Client/Student: Shot baskets for about an hour with some friends, watched TV a couple of hours, and studied an hour or so. Went to bed about 11 P.M.

Teacher: So your main exercise for the day was basketball shooting. Can you think of any other activities?

Client/Student: No, it rained most of the day.

Teacher: Then let's go back to Saturday. Tell me about your day. You don't need to tell me everything, just the activities that you consider moderate, hard, or very hard.

Interview continues until the past 7 days are covered.

Weather and Temperature Concerns

Weather and temperature are important in all aspects of fitness testing and training. Persons with disabilities tend to be more vulnerable to extremes of hot and cold than able-bodied peers. This is particularly true in spinal paralysis, cerebral palsy, and the widespread nervous system damage associated with severe MR. The hypothalamus in the brain (temperature regulation center) and the autonomic nervous system must be intact for sweat glands, skeletal muscles, and blood vessels to function properly in temperature regulation. Nervous system damage above T8 (the eighth thoracic segment of the spinal cord) renders the body incapable of maintaining normal temperature (98.6°F or 37°C).

Anyone with damage above T8 should be closely watched for *poikilothermy,* a condition in which the body assumes the same temperature as the surrounding environment. Such persons are entirely dependent upon clothing, external heating and cooling systems, and ingestion of warm or cool fluids. Temperature regulation problems do not contraindicate heavy exercise; they simply require appropriate adaptations.

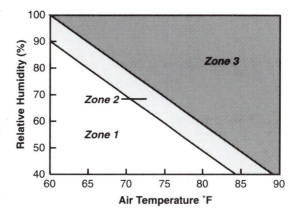

FIGURE 13.13

Weather guide for prevention of heat illness. Zone 1 is safe; for Zone 2, use caution; for Zone 3, use extreme caution.

Regardless of whether temperature regulation problems are present, persons should not be expected to exert all-out effort when temperatures are above 90° or below 50° or when temperature plus humidity exceed 175°. Figure 13.13 presents a simple system for determining when caution and extreme caution are essential. Whereas humidity is the greatest problem in hot weather, wind-chill factor should be considered in cold weather.

Generic terms for body temperature responses are hypothermia (absence of heat) and hyperthermia (excessive heat). *Hypothermia* is associated with frostbite, frozen parts, progressive loss of consciousness, and death. *Hyperthermia* results in heat cramps, heat exhaustion (headache, sweating, dizziness, awkwardness, goose bumps with cold sensation, paleness of face and lips), and heat stroke (diminished sweating, loss of consciousness, life threatening when oral temperature reaches 105°F or about 40°C). Obesity and fluid depletion increase the risk of heat-related disorders.

Dehydration, a normal exercise response, is intensified in persons with autonomic nervous system dysfunction. Several prescribed medications also increase thirst. Water and other fluids should be taken at regular intervals during exercise, whether or not the person is thirsty.

Space and Equipment

Schools should have several exercise areas to supplement gymnasium and sport field space. The more equipment available, the more likely people are to use it. Figure 13.14 shows some homemade, inexpensive equipment appropriate for indoor or outdoor use in schools, homes, and community centers. Selection of equipment is typically based on muscle groups weakest in the individuals served. For most children and youth, these are the abdominal and arm and shoulder muscles. Persons in wheelchairs or on crutches also have a special need for strong arm and shoulder muscles. Therefore,

FIGURE 13.14

Homemade fitness equipment developed by Bill Price, University of South Florida at Tampa. Each shows ways to adapt for individual differences.

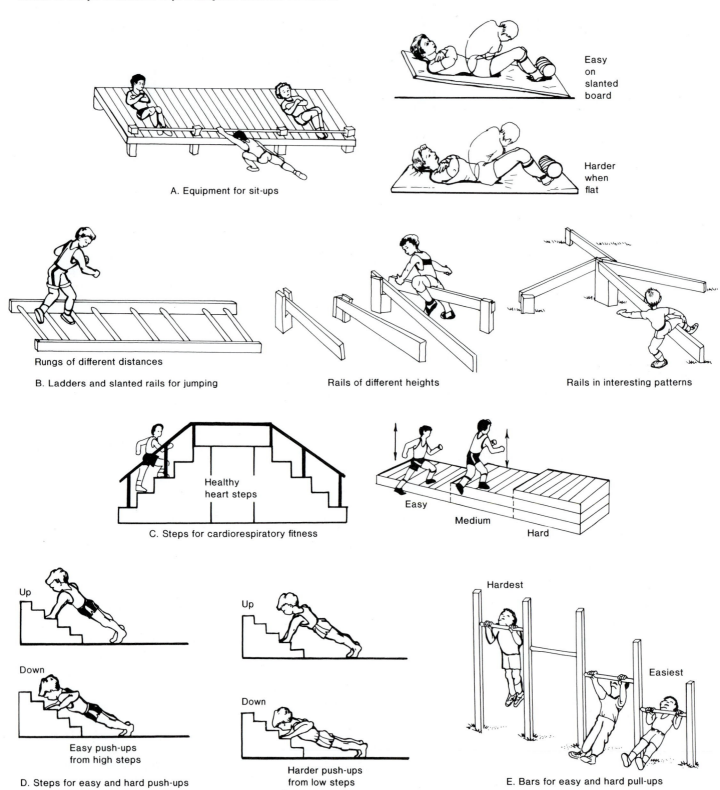

A. Equipment for sit-ups

Easy on slanted board

Harder when flat

Rungs of different distances

B. Ladders and slanted rails for jumping

Rails of different heights

Rails in interesting patterns

Healthy heart steps

C. Steps for cardiorespiratory fitness

Easy

Medium

Hard

Up

Down

Easy push-ups from high steps

D. Steps for easy and hard push-ups

Up

Down

Harder push-ups from low steps

Hardest

Easiest

E. Bars for easy and hard pull-ups

equipment for sit-ups, pull-ups, push-ups, and arm hangs/travel is of first priority. Equally important is equipment for aerobic endurance. When space is limited, the equipment of choice is stationary cycles, jump ropes and/or obstacles, stairs for climbing, and benches or steps for continuous stepping. Tracks and jog/walk/cycle paths with distances clearly marked should be available in schools, parks, and neighborhoods. These require no equipment other than signs.

Lifestyle change requires that schools, homes, and other facilities budget for equipment, plan for space, and provide incentives for use. Equipment should be available in self-contained classrooms, hallways, restrooms, and the like, as well as special exercise stations. Schools should also provide instruction and experience in use of community health and exercise centers to assure carryover when school facilities are not available.

Equipment design should take into account easy, medium, and hard progressions so that individual differences can be met. Inclined boards, for example, can be used to make sit-ups easier or harder. Persons with low abdominal strength should have head higher than feet; many persons in wheelchairs need this adaptation. A bar to tuck feet under provides needed stability and frees partners to do their own exercise. Different heights of pull-up bars, stair steps, ladders, and rails/ropes allow concurrent work by persons of various heights, weights, and abilities.

Organization of the Lesson

Ideally, each fitness session includes five parts: (a) warm-up, (b) endurance conditioning, (c) flexibility exercises for each major muscle group, (d) muscle strength/endurance exercises, and (e) cool-down. For the average person, sessions last 30 to 45 min because the endurance component requires only 15 to 30 min. For persons with low fitness, however, considerably more time is needed. Often, exercise tolerance is so poor that exercise time must be distributed throughout the day.

Regardless of the fitness components chosen for emphasis, every session should include a 5- to 10-min warm-up and cool-down. During this time, the same muscles and movements should be used as in the regular workout, except at a lower intensity. Typically, 2 or 3 min are spent in walking or slow running, and the remaining time is devoted to slow, static stretches, rhythmical circling of body parts, and gentle calisthenics. Obstacle courses and follow-the-leader activities work well with children. In persons with very low fitness, the warm-up may be all the exercise that can be endured.

Teaching for Fitness: A Review of Principles

A common misconception is that physical activities automatically develop fitness. Two laps around the field or 3 min of calisthenics seldom have the effect desired. The same amount of exercise executed faithfully each day contributes to the maintenance of whatever level fitness already exists, but it does *not improve* fitness.

Fitness lessons should include scientifically planned warm-up, training, and cool-down activities conducted in accordance with the following principles of fitness training:

1. **Individual differences.** Every exercise prescription and/or IEP should be different, based on specific assessment of data, motivation level, and activity preferences. Remember the acronym FIT when making exercise prescriptions:

   F Frequency
   I Intensity or resistance
   T Time or duration
   Let individuals choose their own modality!

2. **Overload/intensity.** Increases in fitness result when the *work load* is greater than usual. Overload is associated with muscle strength/endurance. Intensity relates more to cardiorespiratory endurance. *Progressive resistance* refers to increasing overload gradually but consistently over time. Overload/intensity can be achieved in the following ways:

   a. Increase the number of pounds being lifted, pushed, or pulled. This results in progressive resistance exercises.
   b. Increase the number of repetitions, sets, or types of exercise performed.
   c. Increase the distance covered.
   d. Increase the speed.
   e. Increase the number of minutes of continuous all-out effort.
   f. Decrease the rest interval between active sessions.
   g. Increase the intensity/type of activity during rest/relaxation phases.
   h. Use any combination of the above.

3. **Frequency.** Training sessions (particularly those of all-out effort) should be scientifically spaced so that there is time for physiological homeostasis to occur (i.e., for muscles to rest). Too frequent practices tend to result in chronic fatigue, muscle stress, and motivation problems.

4. **Specificity/transfer.** Values gained from exercises done in one position or at one speed will not transfer or benefit the person in other positions or at alternative speeds. Exercises are highly specific; thus, strength exercises particularly need to be done at many joint angles and many intensities. Warm-ups should use the same movements and positions that will be used later in the game or training exercise.

5. **Active/voluntary movement.** Outcome is most effective when the exercise is *active* (done by the student) rather than passive (done by a therapist or teacher). In the case of persons with severe disability with little or no movement capacity of a particular body part,

encourage an all-out effort to initiate the movement, which then can be assisted by the teacher. The student should be actively concentrating and assisting in coactive movement.

6. **Correct breathing.** Breath holding should be avoided because of the Valsalva effect.

7. **Recovery/cool-down.** Persons should not lie or sit down immediately after high-intensity exercise. This tends to subvert the return of blood to the heart and causes dizziness. *Cool-down* should entail continued slow walking or mild activity.

8. **Warm-up.** Warm-ups using movements specific to the game or training to follow should precede high-intensity activity. Warm-up is particularly important for persons with chronic respiratory or cardiorespiratory conditions.

9. **Static stretch.** Slow, static stretches are effective in increasing range of motion and flexibility. Note that ballistic exercises are contraindicated when the goal is to stretch. In spastic cerebral palsy, ballistic exercise elicits an exaggerated stretch reflex.

10. **Contraindication.** If correct postural alignment cannot be maintained during execution of an exercise, it is usually too difficult a progression and is therefore contraindicated.

11. **Adaptation.** Exercises should be analyzed into easy, medium, and difficult progressions so that each person is doing the adaptation best for him or her. A biomechanical principle often used in adapting exercises is *leverage;* the shorter the lever, the easier the exercise. For instance, straight-leg lifts from a supine position to develop or assess abdominal strength are very difficult since the body (as a lever) is in its longest position. By doing bent-knee leg lifts, the body lever is shortened and the exercise is made easier.

12. **Motivation.** Persons who wish to be physically fit must be willing to pay the price. They must be motivated to tolerate boredom, fatigue, and discomfort. Fitness does not come easily.

13. **Maintenance.** Lifespan fitness requires lifespan activity. Instruction should emphasize maintenance.

14. **Nutrition.** Food and liquid intake should be balanced with activity. Instruction on eating and exercise should be integrated.

15. **Environmental factors.** Activity should be safe and pleasurable. Give particular attention to temperature, humidity, windchill, and pollution.

16. **Ecological or social validity.** Fitness activity should make sense and have carryover value. For example, to persons with severe MR, lifting chairs or sacks of groceries may make more sense than lifting bars and dumbbells.

Exercise Conditioning Methods

This chapter concludes with methods that can be applied to more than one fitness component: (a) interval or intermittent, (b) circuits, (c) continuous, and (d) combinations. ACSM (1991) specified these four methods and recommended that they be considered in writing exercise prescriptions. For adults, these methods are often built around one modality (weight lifting, running, cycling, swimming). With children, animal walks, stunts, calisthenics, and locomotor activities that are known to develop specific muscle groups are fun. Any large muscle activity done long enough at the right intensity develops cardiorespiratory endurance.

Interval or Intermittent Training

Developed originally to condition long-distance runners and swimmers, interval training can be adapted to any physical activity. It is especially beneficial for persons with asthma and/or low fitness. The basic objective is to exercise for short periods of time with rest intervals between.

The interval training prescription (ITP) should be planned for each person individually or for small, homogeneous groups, rather than for the class as a whole. After the first 2 weeks, training only twice weekly will result in significant gains in cardiorespiratory endurance.

ITPs require an understanding of the following terms:

1. **Set.** Term that encompasses both the work interval and the rest interval. An ITP may have any number of sets.

2. **Work interval.** Also called a bout. A prescribed number of repetitions of the same activity under identical conditions. Traditionally, the work has been walking, running, or swimming a prescribed number of yards at optimum or near-optimum speed *in an effort to raise the heart rate to a prescribed level.* For variety, work intervals may entail performing an optimum number of squat thrusts, sit-ups, or push-ups within a prescribed number of seconds.

3. **Rest interval.** The number of seconds or minutes between work intervals. During rest, persons should walk rather than sit, lie, or stand. A light activity like walking, arm circles, or toe touches may be psychologically beneficial in that it keeps the mind off exhaustion. The number of seconds comprising the rest interval depends on individual heart recovery rate. *The next repetition should not begin until the heart rate drops to 120 beats per minute or lower, depending on age and fitness status.* If taking the pulse rate is not feasible, the time of the rest interval initially should be approximately twice the amount of time consumed by the work interval.

Table 13.8
Sample ITP card for pupils of similar ability.

Day 5	Repetitions (reps)	Activity	Rest Interval	Self-Evaluation		
				Easy	Medium	Hard
Set 1	4 reps	Runs 220 yd	Walk for 60 sec between sprints			
Set 2	6 reps	Squat thrusts for 10 sec	Head circling for 20 sec between bouts			
Set 3	4 reps	Crab walk for 10 sec	Movement of choice for 20 sec between bouts			
Set 4	8 reps	Run 100 yd	Walk for 30 sec between sprints			

4. **Repetitions.** The number of times the work is repeated under identical conditions. The amount of effort exerted in each repetition should be more or less constant.

5. **Target time.** The best score that a person can make on the prescribed activity. Target times are generally not set until after the first 2 weeks and are then used as a motivational device to encourage all-out performance.

6. **Level of aspiration.** A statement made by the exerciser indicating expected score or level. This is also a motivational device.

All-out effort is often motivated after the first few weeks by prescribing the speed of the sprint as follows:

One repetition of 660 yd in 2:03

Six repetitions of 220 yd in 0:33

Six repetitions of 110 yd in 0:15

Persons may be guided in developing individualized exercise sessions comprised of sets that reflect their own levels of aspiration. Presumably, this is more motivating than trying to accomplish goals set by others.

In keeping with the overload/intensity principle, the exercise sessions become increasingly more demanding each week. As training progresses, the long, slow runs are gradually replaced with shorter, faster sprints. *For healthy adolescents and adults, a total workout distance of over 1.5 mi must eventually be achieved for maximum benefits.*

The following list of procedures may help you in planning each ITP:

1. Test each person individually to determine his or her maximum running time for 110, 220, and 440 yd. If a track is not available, adjust these distances in accordance with the space available.

2. On the basis of these preliminary scores, organize persons into small, homogeneous groups. If the group is small, each person may work with a single partner of like ability.

3. Develop specific objectives for each small group. Whenever possible, let the group participate in the development of objectives. Give each person a written copy of the objectives.

4. Explain the principle of interval training and establish a card file where persons may pick up their individualized ITPs at the beginning of each session. This procedure serves as a substitute for roll call and enables everyone to begin exercise immediately upon entering the room.

5. An ITP card for three persons of similar ability appears in Table 13.8. On the right-hand side of the card, the individuals check whether each set was easy, medium, or difficult. These checks help you to determine the extent to which the degree of difficulty (strenuousness) should be changed on the next ITP. On the back of the card, the students may record their individual scores or write comments.

6. Apply the principle of overload in developing new cards for each session or let persons develop their own ITPs.

7. Retest periodically to determine if goals are being met and to regroup persons if necessary.

Circuit Training

Circuit training is a method that involves moving from station to station. Ideally, the task performed at each station uses different groups of muscles. For adolescents and adults, from 6 to 10 stations are recommended, depending upon available space and equipment. For elementary school children and persons with mental limitations, from two to six stations may be attempted.

The amount of time at each station varies, but initially is relatively brief. Thirty seconds at each station, with 10 sec for rotation, is satisfactory. Thus, a four-station circuit can be completed in approximately 2 1/2 min. As training progresses, the amount of time at each station can be extended or the number of circuits increased. The intensity of the work demanded should be increased gradually in keeping with the overload principle.

Procedures to be followed are

1. Ascertain that everyone knows how to perform the fitness tasks.
2. Divide the group into squads of two to six persons, and assign each squad to a different starting point on the circuit.
3. Practice rotating in a counterclockwise direction from station to station.
4. Develop an individualized circuit-training plan for each student:
   a. Determine the best score on each task during a set time limit like 30 sec. Base future work at each station on one half to three fourths of the student's best score.
   b. Determine the best time in completing the circuit and challenge the person to better this time on the next test, which is scheduled after several days of practice.

An alternative or adapted method for young children and persons with mental limitations who cannot work independently is to have a leader at each station who keeps people exercising until the whistle blows. Persons then join hands or form a file and follow the leader to the next station. This procedure works best if someone calls out, "Rotate, 1–2–3–4–5–6–7–8–9–10," and everyone knows that he or she must be at a new station by the count of 10. To implement the overload/intensity principle, time at each station is periodically increased and/or number of circuits is increased. For this adapted method to work, squads must be homogeneous in fitness level.

Continuous Conditioning

Continuous conditioning refers to exercise that imposes a consistent submaximal energy requirement throughout the training session. Examples are aerobics and rope jumping.

Aerobics

Aerobics is a progressive physical conditioning program that stimulates cardiorespiratory activity for a time period sufficiently long to produce benefits. The originator of aerobics is Kenneth H. Cooper, a physician and major in the U.S. Air Force Medical Corps, who directs The Aerobics Center at 12100 Preston Road in Dallas, Texas. In a longitudinal study of the fitness of over 5,000 adult male subjects, Cooper (1968) stressed two principles: (a) If the exercise is vigorous enough to provide a sustained heart rate of 150 beats per minute or more, the benefits begin about 5 min after the exercise starts and continue as long as the exercise is performed; and (b) if

the exercise is not vigorous enough to provide a sustained heart rate of 150 beats per minute, but is still demanding oxygen, the exercise must be continued for a longer duration.

The aerobics exercise program can be divided into three phases: (a) evaluation of cardiorespiratory fitness, (b) a period of progressive conditioning that extends over several weeks, and (c) maintenance of optimal fitness by earning a specific number of points for exercise each week.

Prior to undertaking an aerobics program, individuals are assessed on distance covered in 12 min in the modality of their choice (walking, running, swimming, cycling). They are then assigned to one of six fitness categories based on gender and age. For males under age 50, a good classification hovers around 1.5 mi in 12 min (see Table 13.9). For females, it is slightly less. Aerobic fitness peaks at ages 20 to 29 and then slowly drops.

The fitness classification determines the number of weeks of conditioning required to work up to the maintenance phase of 30 points per week. Use the following guidelines: (a) very poor category—16 weeks, (b) poor category—13 weeks, and (c) fair category—10 weeks. An illustrative 14-week program is presented earlier in the chapter in Table 13.2. Points are awarded to determine the frequency of walks per week. Persons who score in the "good," "excellent," or "superior" fitness categories do not participate in the program of progressive conditioning. They go directly to the maintenance phase, earning 30 points each week.

The most efficient way to earn 30 points is to jog 1.5 mi in 12 min (for which, 7.5 points are awarded) four times a week. The following activities, each worth 5 points, create a basis for developing an individualized maintenance program:

Bicycling 5 mi in less than 20 min

Running 1 mi in less than 8 min

Swimming 600 yd in less than 15 min

Handball played for a total of 35 min

Stationary running for a total of 12.5 min

For individual sports enthusiasts, one set of singles tennis earns 1.5 points, nine holes of golf earn 1.5 points, waterskiing or snow skiing for 30 min earns 3 points, and ice or roller skating for 15 min earns 1 point. For the bicycle rider who enjoys leisurely pedaling, at least 30 min of cycling is required to earn 1 point.

Aerobic dancing (Sorensen 1979) and water exercise, called hydro-aerobics or hydrorobics (deVarona, 1984; Krasevec & Grimes, 1984) are popular applications of aerobic theory. Many persons with lower limb disabilities can walk or run laps in chest-high water even though they cannot walk on land. Continuous calisthenics produce lower heart rates in water than on land and are particularly recommended for low fitness, obesity, and heart disease.

Rope Jumping, Continuous

Individual rope jumping and long-rope jumping done to chants or music of different speeds and duration provide excellent exercise, especially for maintenance. The usual ca-

Table 13.9
Twelve-minute walking/running test (distance [miles] covered in 12 min).

Fitness Category	Sex	Age (Years)					
		13–19	20–29	30–39	40–49	50–59	60+
I. Very poor	M	<1.30	<1.22	<1.18	<1.14	<1.03	< .87
	F	<1.0	< .96	< .94	< .88	< .84	< .78
II. Poor	M	1.30–1.37	1.22–1.31	1.18–1.30	1.14–1.24	1.03–1.16	.87–1.02
	F	1.00–1.18	.96–1.11	.95–1.05	.88– .98	.84– .93	.78– .86
III. Fair	M	1.38–1.56	1.32–1.49	1.31–1.45	1.25–1.39	1.17–1.30	1.03–1.20
	F	1.19–1.29	1.12–1.22	1.06–1.18	.99–1.11	.94–1.05	.87– .98
IV. Good	M	1.57–1.72	1.50–1.64	1.46–1.56	1.40–1.53	1.31–1.44	1.21–1.32
	F	1.30–1.43	1.23–1.34	1.19–1.29	1.12–1.24	1.06–1.18	.99–1.09
V. Excellent	M	1.73–1.86	1.65–1.76	1.57–1.69	1.54–1.65	1.45–1.58	1.33–1.55
	F	1.44–1.51	1.35–1.45	1.30–1.39	1.25–1.34	1.19–1.30	1.10–1.18
VI. Superior	M	>1.87	>1.77	>1.70	>1.66	>1.59	>1.56
	F	>1.52	>1.46	>1.40	>1.35	>1.31	>1.19

Note. From *The Aerobics Program for Total Well-Being* by Kenneth H. Cooper M.D., M.P.H. Copyright © 1982 by Kenneth H. Cooper. Used by permission of Bantam Books, a division of Bantam Doubleday Dell Publishing Group, Inc.

Table 13.10
Illustrative rope-jumping sequences individualized to meet capabilities.

Easy Sequence	Medium Sequence	Difficult Sequence
1. Rope jump 1 min	1. Rope jump 3 min	1. Rope jump 4 min
2. Rest 60 sec	2. Rest 30 sec	2. Rest 20 sec
3. Rope jump 30 sec	3. Rope jump 1 1/2 min	3. Rope jump 2 min

dence of 60 to 80 jumps a minute requires 9 METs, about the equivalent of running a 11-min mile. This high metabolic demand may make rope jumping inappropriate for sedentary persons, especially those who are obese or have heart disease (ACSM, 1991). Rope jumping is a high-impact exercise and particularly stresses joints in obesity, so weight loss is a prerequisite.

Individual rope jumping has been promoted by AAHPERD and the American Heart Association, and an adapted physical education goal may be developing fitness to participate in school "jump for heart" programs (Lavay & Horvat, 1991). Ropes of different lengths should be available. Ropes should be long enough so that the ends reach the armpits or slightly higher when the jumper stands on the rope's center. Wrists should supply the force to turn the rope so that energy is not wasted with unnecessary arm motions.

Combination Conditioning

Combination methods use both continuous and intermittent activity. Rope jumping, for example, can use the protocol in Table 13.10 until students build up the fitness for aerobic-level jumping. The goal is to be able to jump 60 to 80 times a minute. During the rest, students should walk or do stretches.

Astronaut or Football Drills

Astronaut or football drills are continuous exercise routines done in response to one-word cues that require changes of body position. The correct response to each cue follows:

1. **Go.** Run in place with vigorous high-knee action. Maintain top speed.
2. **Front.** Drop to prone lying position and assume a ready position to ensure quick response to the next cue.
3. **Back.** Drop to supine lying position and assume a ready position to ensure quick response to the next cue.

These cues are given in various orders, challenging the student to persist in continuous motion. The principle of overload is applied by progressively increasing the duration of time spent in the "go" position. After students have mastered these cues, others might be added: right side lie, left side lie, squat, long sit, and so on. Astronaut drills teach and reinforce concepts and vocabulary concerning body parts and body positions.

Jogging, Hiking, and Cycling

Long walks are called hikes and can be combined with map reading, nature study, scavenger hunts, and other themes. Hiking, jogging, and cycling are particularly successful when correlated with social studies and/or related to a trip across the state, the United States, or another continent. Students can update individual mileage sheets, superimposed upon maps. Merit badges or achievement certificates may be awarded for the completion of every 50-mi distance.

The *scout's pace* can be used in early stages of training as follows: jog 110 yd, walk 55 yd, jog 110 yd, walk 55 yd, ad infinitum. The scout's pace can also be interpreted

FIGURE   13.15

Cycles must be adjusted to body size. Arrows indicate correct seat height and handlebar position. The knee should be slightly bent when the toes are on the lower pedal. The body should be relaxed and leaning slightly forward. (Reproduced with permission. © *American Heart Association Heartbook,* 1980. Copyright American Heart Association.)

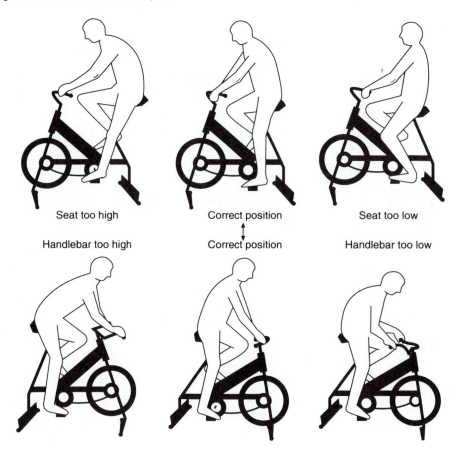

| Seat too high | Correct position | Seat too low |
| Handlebar too high | Correct position | Handlebar too low |

as meaning run as far as you can, then walk until breath is restored, after which running is resumed. Wheelchair activities are conducted like walks and jogs.

Cycling can be done on two- or three-wheeled vehicles and be stationary or moving. Persons with cerebral palsy or other balance impairments may use special adult-size tricycles available through Sears and similar stores. Cycles must be adjustable to body size (see Figure 13.15). Seat height should permit the knee to be slightly bent when toes are on the lower pedal. Handlebar height should encourage good posture, with slight body lean.

Obstacle or Challenge Courses

Perhaps no activity is as popular with elementary school students as following a leader through an obstacle course. Apparatus for these courses can be purchased commercially or constructed by teachers and parents. Homemade obstacle courses are often built around a theme. Assigning pieces of equipment novel names creates the mood for activity built around space travel, a jungle trek, a western outpost, or an Indian village.

Seldom is a class small enough that all students can move through an obstacle course simultaneously. Congestion and confusion are prevented by assigning not more than two

students to each piece of apparatus and by having them stand at their assigned apparatus while awaiting the signal "go," rather than all standing in a file behind the leader. Thus, only 14 students can move efficiently through a seven-piece obstacle course at any given time. Flexible teachers post time schedules listing each student's name and stating the time at which he or she is excused from regular class activities to go through the obstacle course.

References

American Alliance for Health, Physical Education, and Recreation. (1976). *Special fitness test manual for the mildly mentally retarded.* Washington, DC: Author. (First edition, 1968.)

American Alliance for Health, Physical Education, and Recreation (1976). *AAHPER youth fitness test manual* (2nd ed.). Washington, DC: Author. (First edition, 1965.)

American Alliance for Health, Physical Education, and Recreation. (1980). *Health-related physical fitness test manual.* Washington, DC: Author.

American Alliance for Health, Physical Education, Recreation, and Dance. (1988). *Physical best.* Reston, VA: Author.

American College of Sports Medicine. (1988). *Resource manual for guidelines for exercise testing and prescription.* Philadelphia: Lea & Febiger.

American College of Sports Medicine. (1991). *Guidelines for exercise testing and prescription* (4th ed.). Philadelphia: Lea & Febiger.

Anderson, B. (1980). *Stretching*. Bolinas, CA: Shelter Publications.

Arnhold, R., Ng, N., & Pechar, G. (1992). Relationship of rated perceived exertion to heart rate and workload in mentally retarded young adults. *Adapted Physical Activity Quarterly, 9* (1), 47–53.

Baranowski, T. (1988). Validity and reliability of self-report measures of physical activity: An information processing perspective. *Research Quarterly for Exercise and Sport, 59,* 4, 314–327.

Bar-Or, O. (1983). *Pediatric sports medicine for the practitioner.* New York: Springer-Verlag.

Basmajian, J., & Wolf, S. (Eds.). (1990). *Therapeutic exercise* (5th ed.). Baltimore: Williams & Wilkins.

Bates, B. (1983). *A guide to physical examination* (3rd ed.). Philadelphia: J. B. Lippincott.

Beasley, C. R. (1982). Effects of a jogging program on cardiovascular fitness and work performance of mentally retarded persons. *American Journal of Mental Deficiency, 6,* 609–613.

Berenson, G. S. (1986). Evolution of cardiovascular risk factors in early life: Perspectives on causation. In G. S. Berenson (Ed.), *Causation of cardiovascular risk factors in children* (pp. 1–26). New York: Raven.

Block, G., Hartman, A., Dresser, C., Carroll, M., Gannon, J., & Gardner, L. (1986). A data-based approach to diet questionnaire design and testing. *American Journal of Epidemiology, 124* (3), 453–469.

Borg, G. A. (1982). Psychophysical bases of perceived exertion. *Medicine and Science in Sports and Exercise, 14,* 377–381.

Buell, C. (1973). *Physical education and recreation for the visually handicapped.* Washington, DC: American Alliance for Health, Physical Education, and Recreation.

Canada Fitness Survey. (1986). *Physical activity among activity-limited and disabled adults in Canada.* Ontario, Canada: Author.

Cooper, K. H. (1968). *Aerobics.* New York: M. Evans.

Cooper, K. H. (1982). *The aerobics program for total well-being.* New York: Bantam Books.

Corbin, C., & Lindsey, R. (1990). *Concepts of physical fitness* (7th ed.). Dubuque, IA: Wm. C. Brown.

Curtis, K. (1981). Stretching routines. *Sports 'N Spokes, 7* (3), 16–18.

Daniels, L., & Worthingham, C. (1986). *Muscle testing: Techniques of manual examination* (5th ed.). Philadelphia: W. B. Saunders.

DeLorme, T., & Watkins, A. (1948). Techniques of progressive resistance exercise. *Archives of Physical and Medical Rehabilitation, 29,* 263–273.

deVarona, D. (1984). *Hydro-aerobics.* New York: Macmillan.

Dishman, R. K. (Ed.). (1988). *Exercise adherence: Its impact on public health.* Champaign, IL: Human Kinetics.

Dishman, R. K., & Ickes, W. (1981). Self-motivation and adherence to therapeutic exercise. *Journal of Behavioral Medicine, 4,* 421–438.

Dishman, R. K., Ickes, W., & Morgan, W. (1980). Self-motivation and adherence to habitual physical activity. *Journal of Applied Social Psychology, 10,* 115–132.

Dobbins, D., Garron, R., & Rarick, G. S. (1981). The motor performance of EMR and intellectually normal boys after covariate control for differences in body size. *Research Quarterly for Exercise and Sport, 52* (1), 1–8.

Dunn, J., Morehouse, J., & Fredericks, H. (1986). *Physical education for the severely handicapped: A systematic approach to a data-based gymnasium.* Austin, TX: Pro·Ed.

Dzewaltowski, D., Noble, J., & Shaw, J. (1990). Physical activity participation: Social-cognitive theory versus the theories of reasoned action and planned behavior. *Journal of Sport and Exercise Psychology, 12,* 388–405.

Fernhall, B., & Tymeson, G. (1987). Graded exercise testing of mentally retarded adults: A study of feasibility. *Archives of Physical Medicine and Rehabilitation, 68,* 363–365.

Fisher, S. V., & Gullickson, G. (1978). Energy cost of ambulation in health and disability: A literature review. *Archives of Physical Medicine and Rehabilitation, 59,* 124–132.

Francis, R. J., & Rarick, G. L. (1959). Motor characteristics of the mentally retarded. *American Journal of Mental Deficiency, 63,* 792–811.

Franks, B. D. (1989). *YMCA youth fitness manual.* Champaign, IL: Human Kinetics.

Golding, L. A., Myers, C. R., & Sinning, W. (1989). *Y's way to physical fitness.* Champaign, IL: Human Kinetics.

Government of Canada. (1987). *Canadian standardized test of fitness, interpretation, and counseling manual.* Ottawa: Fitness Canada.

Hayden, F. J. (1964). *Physical fitness for the mentally retarded.* Ontario: Toronto Association for Retarded Children.

Hellebrandt, F., & Houtz, S. (1956). Mechanisms of muscle training in man: Experimental demonstration of the overload principle. *Physical Therapy Review, 36,* 371–383.

Hettinger, T., & Müller, E. (1953). Muskelleistung und muskeltraining. *Arbeitphysiologie, 15,* 111–126.

Holland, L., & Steadward, D. (1990). Effects of resistance and flexibility training on strength, spasticity/muscle tone, and range of motion of elite athletes with cerebral palsy. *Palaestra, 6* (4), 27–31.

Iso-Ahola, S. (1980). *The social psychology of leisure and recreation.* Dubuque, IA: Wm. C. Brown.

Jansma, J., Decker, J., Ersing, W., McCubbin, J., & Combs, S. (1988). A fitness assessment system for individuals with severe mental retardation. *Adapted Physical Activity Quarterly, 5* (3), 223–232.

Jones, J. A. (1988). *Training guide to cerebral palsy sports* (3rd ed.). Champaign, IL: Human Kinetics.

Kennedy, S. O. (1988). Flexibility training for wheelchair athletes. *Sports 'N Spokes, 13* (5), 43–46.

Kline, G. M., Porcari, P., Hintermeister, R., Freedson, P., Ward, A., McCarron, R., Ross, J., & Rippe, J. (1987). Estimation of VO_2max from a one-mile track walk, gender, age, and body weight. *Medicine and Science in Sports and Exercise, 19,* 253–259.

Kobberling, G., Jankowski, L., & Leger, L. (1989). Energy cost of locomotion in blind adolescents. *Adapted Physical Activity Quarterly, 6* (1), 58–67.

Kottke, F. (1990). Therapeutic exercise to maintain mobility. In F. Kottke & J. Lehmann (Eds.), *Krusen's handbook of physical medicine and rehabilitation* (4th ed.) (pp. 436–451). Philadelphia: W. B. Saunders.

Krasevec, J., & Grimes, D. (1984). *Hydrorobics.* Champaign, IL: Leisure Press.

Kraus, H., & Hirschland, R. (1954). Minimum muscular fitness tests in schoolchildren. *Research Quarterly, 25* (2), 177–188.

Lange, L. (1919). *Uber funktionelle anpassurig.* Berlin: Springer-Verlag.

Lavay, B., & Horvat, M. (1991). Jump rope for heart for special populations. *Journal of Physical Education, Recreation, and Dance, 62* (3), 74–78.

Lohman, T., Boileau, R., & Slaughter, M. (1984). Body composition in children and youth. In R. Boileau (Ed.), *Advances in pediatric sport sciences, Vol. 1, Biological issues* (pp. 29–57). Champaign, IL: Human Kinetics.

McCubbin, J., & Shasby, G. (1985). Effects of isokinetic exercise on adolescents with cerebral palsy. *Adapted Physical Activity Quarterly, 2,* 56–64.

Miller, N., Merritt, J., Merkel, K., & Westbrook, P. (1984). Paraplegic energy expenditure during negotiation of architectural barriers. *Archives of Physical Medicine and Rehabilitation, 65,* 778–779.

Morgan, W. P., & O'Connor, P. (1988). Exercise and mental health. In R. Dishman. (Ed.), *Exercise adherence: Its impact on public health* (pp. 91–121). Champaign, IL: Human Kinetics.

President's Council on Physical Fitness and Sports. (1987). *Get fit: A handbook for youth ages 6–17.* Washington, DC: Author.

Rarick, G. L. (1980). Cognitive-motor relationships in the growing years. *Research Quarterly for Exercise and Sport, 51* (1), 174–192.

Reid, G., Seidl, C., & Montgomery, D. (1989). Fitness tests for retarded adults: Tips for test selection, subject familiarization, administration, and interpretation. *Journal of Physical Education, Recreation, and Dance, 60* (6), 76–78.

Rimmer, J. H. (1993). *Fitness and rehabilitation programs for special populations.* Dubuque, IA: Brown and Benchmark.

Rippe, J. M., & Ward, A. (1989). *The Rockport walking program.* New York: Prentice-Hall.

Rowland, T. W. (1990). *Exercise and children's health.* Champaign, IL: Human Kinetics.

Schurrer, R., Weltman, A., & Brammerl, H. (1985). Effects of physical training on cardiovascular fitness and behavior patterns of mentally retarded adults. *American Journal of Mental Deficiency, 90,* 167–170.

Shephard, R. (1990). *Fitness in special populations.* Champaign, IL: Human Kinetics.

Shephard, R., Berridge, M., & Montelpare, W. (1990). On the generality of the sit-and-reach test: An analysis of flexibility data for an aging population. *Research Quarterly for Exercise and Sport, 61* (4), 326–330.

Skrotsky, K. (1983). Gait analysis in cerebral palsied and nonhandicapped children. *Archives of Physical Medicine and Rehabilitation, 64,* 291–295.

Sorensen, J. (1979). *Aerobic dancing.* New York: Rawson Wade.

Stephens, T., Jacobs, D. R., Jr., & White, C. C. (1985). A descriptive epidemiology of leisure-time activity. *Public Health Reports, 100,* 147–158.

Surburg, P. R. (1986). New perspectives for developing range of motion and flexibility for special populations. *Adapted Physical Activity Quarterly, 3* (3), 227–235.

Tecklin, J. (1989). *Pediatric physical therapy.* Philadelphia: J. B. Lippincott.

Tucker, L. (1990). Television viewing and physical fitness in adults. *Research Quarterly for Exercise and Sport, 61* (4), 315–320.

Ward, D. S., & Bar-Or, O. (1990). Use of the Borg scale in exercise prescription for overweight youth. *Canadian Journal of Sport Science, 15* (2), 120–125.

Ward, G. R., & Fraser, L. N. (1984). Fitness characteristics of Canadian national wheelchair athletes. *Medicine and Science in Sports and Exercise, 16,* 142.

Wells, C., & Hooker, S. (1990). The spinal injured athlete. *Adapted Physical Activity Quarterly, 7* (3), 265–285.

Wilmore, J. H., & Costill, D. L. (1988). *Training for sport and activity* (3rd ed.). Dubuque, IA: Wm. C. Brown.

Winnick, J., & Short, F. (1984). Test item selection for the Project UNIQUE physical fitness test. *Adapted Physical Activity Quarterly 1* (4), 296–314.

Winnick, J., & Short, F. (1985). *Physical fitness testing of the disabled: Project UNIQUE.* Champaign, IL: Human Kinetics.

World Health Organization. (1947). Constitution of the World Health Organization. *Chronicle of WHO, 1,* 1–2.

CHAPTER

14

Postures, Appearance, and Muscle Imbalance

FIGURE   14.1

Mirror work to increase body awareness.

After you have studied this chapter, you should be able to:

1. Discuss assessment techniques for postures and body typing.
2. Explain normal postural development with implications for strength and flexibility training at different ages.
3. State posture training guidelines and contrast old and new approaches to ameliorating posture problems.
4. Identify the most common postural problems and explain which muscle groups (extensors, flexors, abductors, and adductors) are abnormally weak or tight in relation to each. Apply this to activity selection.
5. Discuss kyphosis and scoliosis as orthopedic problems that require cooperative program planning among physician, teacher, and family. State the procedures for initiating and/or facilitating this cooperation.

Improvement of postures and overall physical appearance is an important objective within the fitness/wellness goal domain. Physical attractiveness is strongly related to global self-esteem (Harter, 1988) and socialization (Zakahi & Duran, 1988). Many persons are not in tune with their bodies and lack awareness of how they look. Yet, we often form lasting first impressions on the basis of appearance.

Normalization philosophy challenges physical educators to make persons aware of movement patterns and to give them opportunities for developing the postures most likely to help them make friends, win social acceptance, and obtain jobs (Sherrill, 1980). This includes living, learning, and working in environments where significant others model good postures.

Persons with physical disabilities and/or clumsiness particularly need help with postures (see Figure 14.1). Skeletal anomalies and imbalances in muscle strength and flexibility require careful attention. Often, an objective of postures training is acceptance of limitations and learning to make the best of potential. Efficient postures also prevent injury, minimize fatigue, and enable the development of fitness.

Many Postures: Plural

Each person possesses not one but many postures. Any position is a posture, and we assume thousands of static and dynamic postures each day—standing, walking, running, sitting, sleeping, stooping, climbing, and on ad infinitum. Josephine Rathbone, a pioneer in postures education and physical disabilities, emphasized that postures is a plural concept (Rathbone & Hunt, 1965). Head postures cannot be considered without shoulder postures; shoulder postures cannot be taught without back postures; and so on. Reference is thus made to *postures* training; the word is not used in a singular format.

Muscle Imbalances and Postures

Good postures are efficient movement patterns. This is because postures are the product of muscle balance or imbalance. An erect, attractive position is possible only when muscles on all the body surfaces are in perfect balance with just the right amount of strength and flexibility. Muscles on the anterior surface (flexors) must be in balance with muscles on the posterior surface (extensors). Muscles on the lateral surface (abductors) must be in balance with muscles on the medial surface (adductors). In general the names of muscle groups (flexors, extensors, abductors, adductors, inward and outward rotators) are used when instructing persons about their bodies.

The powerful force of gravity tends to pull body parts downward, thereby tightening and strengthening the flexors. This causes an imbalance between flexors and extensors that underlies the major principle of postures training: *Strengthen the extensors!* The extensors of the neck and back, called the antigravity muscles, are the target of most work in people without specific disabilities.

Infants are born with muscle imbalance. Specifically, the flexors, adductors, and inward rotators are tighter than their antagonists (the extensors, abductors, and outward rotators). This is obvious from the postures that babies assume. In normal development, this imbalance corrects itself. In developmental delays, the basic principle is *Focus on strengthening extensor-abductor-outward rotation patterns to promote muscle balance.*

Body Alignment

Body alignment is the concept of body parts being perfectly balanced, one on top of another, and all properly aligned over the feet when standing or over the buttocks when sitting (commonly referred to as the base of support). Alignment is primarily a matter of muscle balance. Muscles on the right and left sides of the spine, for example, must be of equal strength, or the spine will be pulled out of alignment by the stronger group. Unequal muscle pulls, in time, distort the shape of bones, as well as their position.

Persons with paralysis and spasticity are particularly vulnerable to severe alignment problems. Muscle imbalance is minimized by strapping, bracing, casting, and surgery. Proper positioning when sitting or lying for long periods is obviously important because muscle groups adapt their size and shape to the position in which they spend the most time.

Thus, another important principle of postures training is *Keep body parts in correct alignment.* This typically means as close to symmetrical as possible, with weight equally distributed on both sides of midline.

Instructional Themes

Physical education is the only subject in the curriculum that focuses on the body. Instruction in making self as attractive as possible is relevant to all age groups. Many persons think that appearance is enhanced mainly by clothing, makeup, and weight reduction. That understanding needs to be extended to include postures. Clothes do not make much of an impression if postures are slouched and body parts are out of alignment. Interest in clothes, however, can be used as an instructional theme. Fashion shows are an excellent device for exploration of different postures. Interdisciplinary units with home economics, clothing design, and marketing specialists can focus attention on the interrelationships between clothing selection, moving well, and physical attractiveness.

Understanding that postures are expressions of thoughts, feelings, and moods helps us to better understand ourselves and others. How often do we think a person doesn't feel well or vice versa simply on the basis of postures! Movement exploration based on the theme of postures promotes understanding and acceptance. For example, physical educators can challenge: (a) "Show me how we move when we are angry. How do people know we are angry?" (b) "How do very, very old persons move? How can we help such persons?" (c) "Show me how you plan to walk into the room for your job interview. How will you sit?"

Postures are affected by body type, height, weight, fitness, disability, age, clothing, shoes, occupation, and body image/self-concept. Units on postures provide opportunities for individual and small-group counseling on these and other factors. Why persons think that they and others are or are not physically attractive falls within this domain. Counseling focuses on accepting what cannot be changed and taking the initiative in shaping the rest according to goals.

Body image refers to all of the opinions, attitudes, and beliefs a person holds about his or her body and its capacities. In young children, beliefs begin with matching skills (like me, unlike me) and expand to include function of body parts and ability to describe appearance. Opinion/attitude dimensions emerge with feelings of good/bad, pretty/ugly, and clumsy/graceful. Understandings about alignment and balance often do not develop without help.

Body Types and Sport Selection

A good way to begin units on postures is to focus on body types and identify strengths and weaknesses in relation to sports. Assessment should center on ability to identify body types (both own and those of parents and siblings) and to understand implications in relation to probable success in selected sports. Figure 14.2 shows the seven pictures that are often used in body-type assessment. The pictures are presented as a group or separately, in random order. The student is asked to select the one that most resembles self and various family members. Then he or she is asked, "What picture would you rather be like?" (Rowe & Caldwell, 1963). This approach helps to establish rapport for other kinds of assessment (e.g., "Rate your satisfaction with each of the following body parts." or "Tell me what body part you would most like to change."). Cooperative goal setting follows.

Classification of persons with respect to body build or type is called *somatotyping.* William H. Sheldon (1954) is accredited with describing three basic body types (endomorph, mesomorph, and ectomorph) and creating a system whereby how much of each type is present in any given individual can be specified. A somatotype classification is comprised of three numbers, such as 236 or 171. Each digit ranges from 1 (lowest) to 7 (highest). Students are helped to see these ratings as strengths and weaknesses and as indicators of probable sport success.

The first digit in the series indicates what degree of *endomorph* body build characteristics are present. These characteristics are roundness and softness of the body; breasts and buttocks well developed; high, square shoulders and short neck; and predominance of abdomen over thorax.

The second digit indicates what degree of *mesomorph* body build characteristics are present. These characteristics are solid, well-developed musculature; bones usually large and covered with thick muscle; forearm thickness and relative largeness of wrist, hand, and fingers; large thorax and relatively slender waist; broad shoulders and well-developed trapezius and deltoid; buttocks exhibiting muscular dimpling; and abdominal muscles prominent and thick.

The third digit indicates what degree of *ectomorph* body build characteristics are present. These characteristics are small bones and thin muscles; linearity, fragility, and delicacy of body; limbs relatively long, trunk short, and shoulders narrow; shoulders drooping and predisposed toward winged scapulae; abdomen and lumbar curve flat; thoracic curve relatively sharp and elevated; and no bulging of muscle at any point.

A predominantly endomorphic person commonly has a somatotype of 721, 731, or 631. For such persons, physical education should emphasize the management of obesity. Strenuous activities, such as contact sports, weight lifting, and pyramid building, are contraindicated, particularly during periods of rapid growth. Their joints are more subject to trauma than those of other students, either from cumulative daily gravitational stresses or sudden traumas. Almost always, during childhood and adolescence, physiological age is not commensurate with chronological age. The endomorph is predisposed to such postural deviations as knock-knees, pronated feet, flat feet, sagging abdomen, round shoulders, and round back. Physical education for obese youngsters is discussed in Chapter 19.

A predominantly mesomorphic person commonly has a somatotype of 171, 172, 272, or even 372. For success in contact sports, the student requires a certain amount of cushioning by fat. A 2, 3, or 4 rating in endomorphy is therefore desirable for athletes. Football players typically have somatotypes of 273, 371, or 471; baseball players tend to have 262, 263, or 462; while tennis players and long-distance runners may be classified as 153 or 154. Mesomorphs are better

FIGURE   14.2

(*A*) Instructor requests student to select the body-type picture that most
closely resembles his own as part of posture counseling. (*B*) Seven body
types differing on somatotype dimensions. (See Rowe & Caldwell, 1963,
in the references.)

A

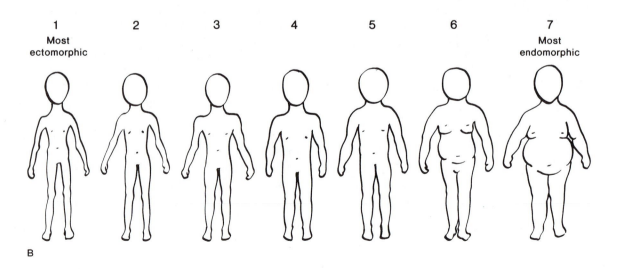

B

adapted structurally, organically, and neurologically to meet stress than other body types. They seldom exhibit severe postural deviations. Their major problem seems to be a substantial gain in weight after age 30.

A predominantly ectomorphic person commonly has a somatotype of 217, 227, or 236. The 217 extreme seldom succeeds in athletic endeavors; such a person is characterized by muscle flaccidity, a floppiness of movement, and looseness at joints that predisposes him or her to many postural problems that do not respond to exercise. A predominantly ectomorphic person simply lacks potential to persist in movement long enough for the principle of overload to be operative; he or she fatigues easily and is sometimes described as having *asthenia,* which means "without strength." He or she can be helped best by a program that provides instruction in relaxation, dance, and individual sports. Less extreme ectomorph types often excel in activities like cross-country running, in which they set their own pace. They tend to have too little body padding to engage safely in contact sports. Likewise, they chill easily and require shorter swimming periods and outdoor play sessions than their peers.

Group Screening

Screening for postural deviations and movement problems should be completed early in the semester. Whenever possible, students should not be aware that they are being screened. Instead, they may think they are practicing selected locomotor skills or engaging in movement exploration. Ideally, they are moving in a circle and responding to changes in direction while you observe from the center of the circle. Their movements should be natural, spontaneous, and relaxed.

One of the most efficient procedures is to group the students into quartiles. First, identify the 25% of the class who have the best postures and the 25% who have the worst postures. Then place the remaining students in the upper and lower middle quartiles. Approximately 1 week later, repeat the screening procedures without reviewing your notes. Compare the names of the students assigned to each quartile with those assigned previously. Schedule individual posture examinations for those students who fell into the lowest quartile during both screening sessions.

Identical procedures may be used in the classroom when the students are unaware that their sitting postures are being evaluated. The way a student sits at a desk, the tilt of the head, the distance of eyes from paper, and whether or not the feet touch the floor—all have significance in determining postural fitness. Postures, like movement patterns, are unique to the individual. Family similarities appear in postures as well as in faces. Genetic predispositions toward body build, weight, height, and energy level have as great an influence on postures as do environmental factors.

Individual Examination

Schedule students identified as needing special guidance and counseling with respect to postures for an individual examination. The whole person must be considered, including anxiety about being singled out as different, and thoughts and feelings about physical self. The general procedures used in posture counseling parallel those described under fitness counseling. Unless you plan to schedule relatively frequent follow-up conferences, the individual examination should not be conducted.

Figure 14.3 presents one of the many forms that can be filled out during the examination. The form is identical to that used in the New York Posture Test with the exception of three omissions: feet, side view of shoulders, and side view of chest. The New York State Fitness Test, which includes the Posture Test, can be obtained by writing to the State Education Department, Division of Health, Physical Education, and Recreation, Albany, NY 12224.

Posture Grid

The room in which the posture examination is administered should have a wall grid comprised of 2-inch squares (see Figure 14.4). The vertical lines are at right angles to the horizontal lines and extend all the way to the floor. These lines provide reference points for ascertaining the correct alignment of body parts. Footprints should be painted on the floor in front of the grid to facilitate correct standing positions.

Some individuals prefer a posture screen comprised of vertical and horizontal strings hooked onto a frame so as to make 2-, 4-, or 6-inch squares that serve as reference points. The student stands behind the screen and is viewed through it.

Posture Photographs and Videotapes

Photographs and videotapes of students whose postural fitness warrants individual examination are recommended for the following reasons:

1. To enable students to see themselves as others see them and to serve as a motivational device toward positive change
2. To orient parents and the public to the broad objectives of physical education
3. To serve as a measure against which postural change can be estimated
4. To supplement school files, thereby improving the permanent record of the whole child

The following procedures are recommended for filming postures:

1. Two students standing in front of the grid can be photographed simultaneously and the resulting snapshot divided. In videotapes, two friends of similar body types on the same tape permit partner discussion.
2. Only back and side views of the student are essential.
3. The students should be barefoot. Swimming trunks or shorts are recommended for boys. Pants and bra or a two-piece swimming suit are recommended for girls. Long hair should be pulled back to reveal the earlobe.
4. The back should be bare, with a black-marker dot placed on each spinous process. Dots should be made with the student standing. Position changes during the procedure should be avoided.

FIGURE 14.3

Posture score sheet.

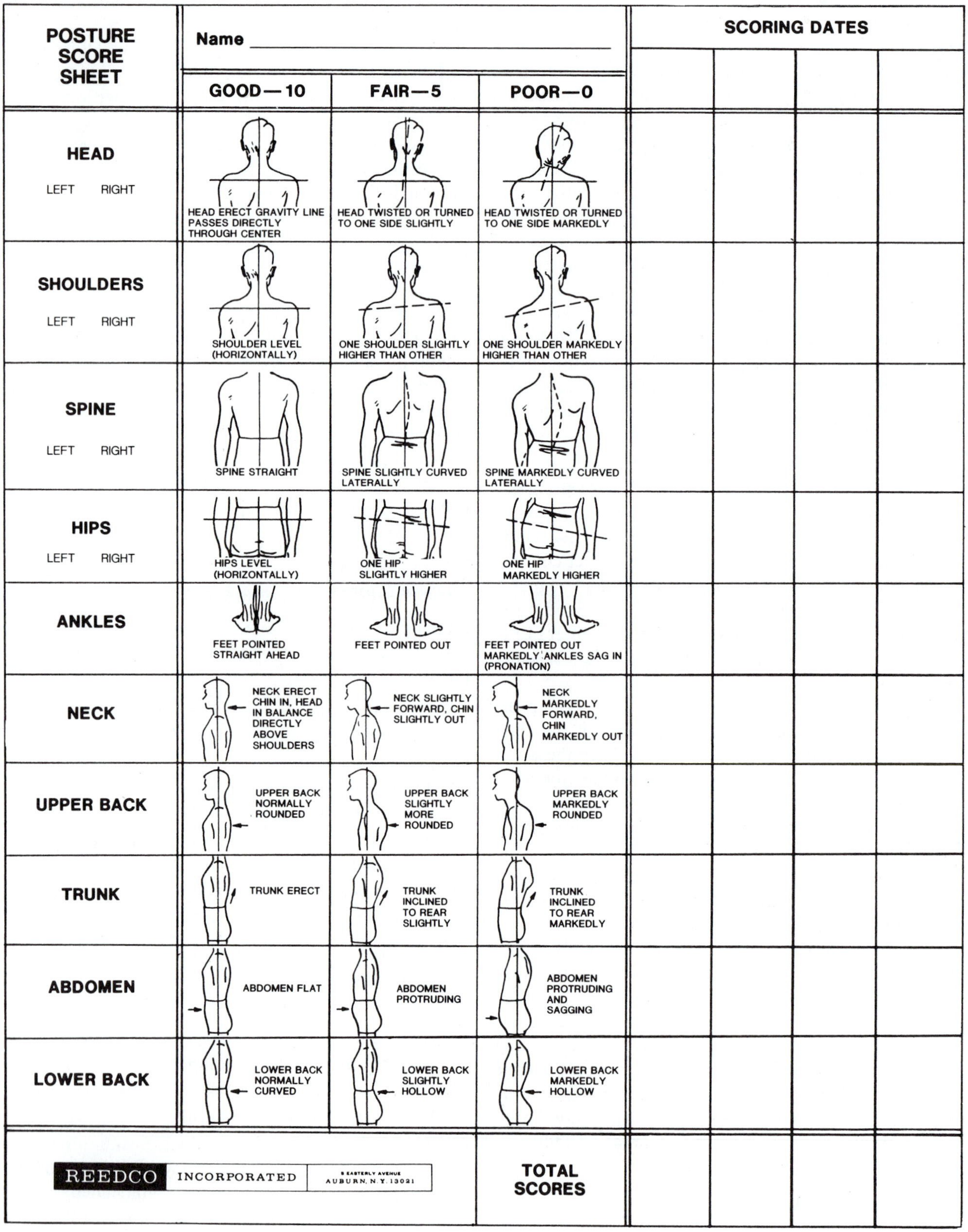

POSTURE SCORE SHEET	Name _____			SCORING DATES			
	GOOD—10	FAIR—5	POOR—0				
HEAD LEFT RIGHT	HEAD ERECT GRAVITY LINE PASSES DIRECTLY THROUGH CENTER	HEAD TWISTED OR TURNED TO ONE SIDE SLIGHTLY	HEAD TWISTED OR TURNED TO ONE SIDE MARKEDLY				
SHOULDERS LEFT RIGHT	SHOULDER LEVEL (HORIZONTALLY)	ONE SHOULDER SLIGHTLY HIGHER THAN OTHER	ONE SHOULDER MARKEDLY HIGHER THAN OTHER				
SPINE LEFT RIGHT	SPINE STRAIGHT	SPINE SLIGHTLY CURVED LATERALLY	SPINE MARKEDLY CURVED LATERALLY				
HIPS LEFT RIGHT	HIPS LEVEL (HORIZONTALLY)	ONE HIP SLIGHTLY HIGHER	ONE HIP MARKEDLY HIGHER				
ANKLES	FEET POINTED STRAIGHT AHEAD	FEET POINTED OUT	FEET POINTED OUT MARKEDLY ANKLES SAG IN (PRONATION)				
NECK	NECK ERECT CHIN IN, HEAD IN BALANCE DIRECTLY ABOVE SHOULDERS	NECK SLIGHTLY FORWARD, CHIN SLIGHTLY OUT	NECK MARKEDLY FORWARD, CHIN MARKEDLY OUT				
UPPER BACK	UPPER BACK NORMALLY ROUNDED	UPPER BACK SLIGHTLY MORE ROUNDED	UPPER BACK MARKEDLY ROUNDED				
TRUNK	TRUNK ERECT	TRUNK INCLINED TO REAR SLIGHTLY	TRUNK INCLINED TO REAR MARKEDLY				
ABDOMEN	ABDOMEN FLAT	ABDOMEN PROTRUDING	ABDOMEN PROTRUDING AND SAGGING				
LOWER BACK	LOWER BACK NORMALLY CURVED	LOWER BACK SLIGHTLY HOLLOW	LOWER BACK MARKEDLY HOLLOW				
REEDCO INCORPORATED 8 EASTERLY AVENUE AUBURN, N.Y. 13021			**TOTAL SCORES**				

FIGURE 14.4

Two-year-old stands in front of posture grid. His posture is normal for his age.

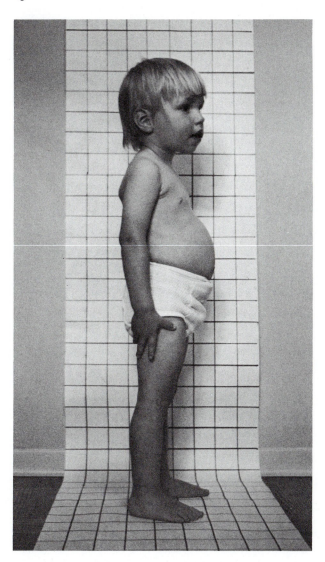

5. Polaroid cameras have the advantage of instantaneous film development. If the snapshot is not good, a second one can be taken immediately.

6. Students must be assured that pictures will be held in confidence. Often, giving the pictures to the student for further study is more valuable than filing them.

Spinal Column Curves

From about age 7 or 8 on, four curves are readily discernible in the spinal column. Viewed from the side, these are

1. **Concave.** Cervical spine comprised of 7 vertebrae.
2. **Convex.** Thoracic spine comprised of 12 vertebrae.
3. **Concave.** Lumbar spine comprised of 5 vertebrae.
4. **Convex.** Sacral spine comprised of 5 sacral vertebrae fused in adulthood and called the sacrum.

Erect, extended carriage results when the thoracic and sacral flexion curves are in balance with the cervical and lumbar hyperextension curves. Whenever one curve increases, the other curves also tend to increase to compensate for the imbalance.

Analysis of Muscle Imbalance

When a posture problem is evident, analyze the imbalance of the muscle groups by considering these questions:

1. Muscles on which surface are too tight—that is, stronger than their antagonists? Which stretching exercises are indicated?
2. Muscles on which surface are too loose—that is, weaker than their antagonists? Which strengthening exercises are indicated?
3. What role is gravity playing in the muscle imbalance?

Usually, strength exercises are chosen for amelioration of posture problems. Remember the principle of *reciprocal innervation:* When muscles on one surface are being strengthened, muscles on the antagonistic surface are being stretched simultaneously. Regardless of the type of exercise selected, both surfaces are affected (Lowman & Young, 1960).

Normal Postural Development

Figure 14.5 depicts nine stages in the development of normal postures. At birth, the entire spinal column of the infant is flexed in a single C curve. Only when the extensor muscles of the neck and back are sufficiently strengthened by random kicking and wiggling do the cervical and lumbar curves begin to appear. The cervical curve develops at about 4 to 5 months of age, while the lumbar curve begins to develop sometime after the child learns to walk. Toddlers and young children with disabilities that prevent upright locomotion characteristically have *flat backs.* This condition is normal during the months when the child is gaining confidence in walking and running activities. Flat back that persists beyond the toddler stage is considered a postural deviation.

The normal preschool child tends to develop an exaggerated lumbar curve, which may persist throughout elementary school. This condition is caused by the imbalance in the strength of the abdominal muscles and the hip flexors. The abdominal musculature of the preschool child normally is too weak to maintain the pelvis in a neutral position.

The resulting lordosis (swayback) characterizes the young child's postures until sufficient abdominal strength is developed to counteract the downward pull of the hip flexors. Lordosis, therefore, is normal in a young child and should not be labeled as a postural deviation until adolescence. The degree of lumbar curvature should, however, lessen from year to year.

Posture Training Guidelines

Once the present level of postural fitness is assessed and annual goals written to include posture training, short-term objectives are developed. These objectives can be broken down

FIGURE   14.5

Normal postural development from infancy through age 2.

A. Spinal column is flexed in single C curve; arms and legs are flexed—birth to 2 months.

B. Reflex stretching out of arms (Moro) until about 6 months, at which time protective extensor (parachute) reaction appears.

C. Extensor tone increases, reinforced by random limb movements, and cervical curve begins to appear.

D. Early sitting with head control shows strong cervical extensor muscles—about 6 months.

E. Prone-on-elbows crawling position, combined with labyrinthine and optical righting reflexes, reinforces development of cervical curve.

F. Creeping further strengthens abdominal and lumbar spine muscles—8 months.

G. Early standing with support shows flat back posture.

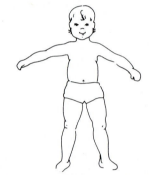

H. Lumbar curve appears as back muscles are further strengthened by walking, with wide base stance—about 14 months.

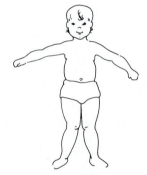

I. Knock-knees is normal in early walking, especially in endomorphic body types.

into behaviors. Illustrative target behaviors for improving walking postures are (a) keeps head and trunk erect with eyes generally focused straight ahead; (b) swings arms in opposition with normal range of motion; (c) uses regular, rhythmic, heel-ball-toe transfer of weight; and (d) maintains normal support base—that is, heels, 2 to 3 inches from line of progression.

For many years, individualized, prescribed exercises were the accepted practice in posture training and body mechanics activities. These exercises were often boring and, if not rigidly adhered to, ineffective. Moreover, if performed incorrectly, such exercises could actually injure the child. The trend now is away from isolated exercises and toward game-like activities that utilize muscle groups in therapeutically sound ways. This chapter, therefore, includes only a few exercises for each condition.

General physical education programming designed to achieve posture training objectives emphasizes use of the kinesthetic, vestibular, and visual sense modalities in such activities as body awareness or proprioceptive training, body image work, static and dynamic balance tasks, and body alignment activities in front of mirrors. Whenever possible, videotape feedback is provided. Sports, dance, and aquatics activities that demand full extension of the trunk, head, neck, and limbs—that is, reaching toward the sky, lifting the chest, stretching upward—are emphasized. Dance, gymnastics (free exercise and balance beam routines), trampolining, and swimming typically reinforce extension, correct body alignment, and good balance. Relaxation training is used to teach and/or reinforce understanding of tightness/tension in muscle groups versus looseness/nontension.

FIGURE   14.6

Exercises that are contraindicated when certain posture problems are present.

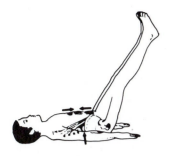

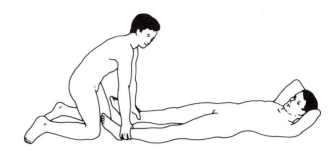

A. Straight leg lift and hold should not be used when persons have weak abdominal muscles and/or lordosis.

B. Straight leg sit-ups should not be used when persons have weak abdominal muscles.

C. Push-ups should not be used when persons have round shoulders.

D. The swan should not be used when persons have lordosis.

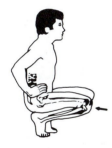

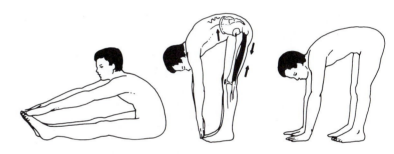

E. Deep knee bends and the duck walk are contraindicated for most students because of the strain put on the knee joints.

F. Straight leg toe touch and bear walk should not be used when persons have hyperextended knees.

Contraindicated Exercises

Figure 14.6 depicts exercises that students with certain kinds of posture problems should not do. *Contraindicated* is a medical term meaning that there is an indication against (*contra*) prescription of such exercises. The exercises shown may make tight muscles even tighter, as in push-ups and the swan, or they may lead to stretching and tearing of a tight muscle group, as in straight-leg toe touches.

Behavior Management and Postures

Posture problems can be corrected by behavior management techniques. The types of behavior management apparatus used for correcting postures include:

1. A portable apparatus worn on the back at about the level of the second thoracic vertebra that emits a 550-cps (cycles per second) tone at an intensity of 55 decibels whenever the wearer slouches (Rubin,

O'Brien, Ayllon, & Roll, 1968). Twenty-five adults, ages 18 to 49 years, showed a mean 86% reduction in slouching.

2. A vibrotactile posture harness designed to detect slouching and energize a vibrotactile stimulator on the shoulder whenever slouching occurs. There is no auditory signal, just tactile; the harness is not detectable by others (O'Brien & Azrin, 1970). Eight adults showed a mean 35% reduction in slouching.

3. Foam helmet training device with a mercury switch and buzzer that emits noise whenever the head deviates from the upright position, used in conjunction with a vest containing a buzzer system that makes noise whenever the torso inclines abnormally (Tiller, Stygar, Hess, & Reimer, 1982). Used with one moderately retarded female, age 20 years, in 4 months of training (200 steps each session).

FIGURE 14.7

Severe degree of forward head and neck causes compensatory dorsal and lumbar curves.

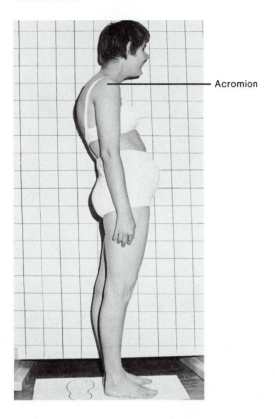

Acromion

FIGURE 14.8

Cervical extensors adaptively shorten and tighten as forward head and neck becomes severe. (*A*) Splenius capitis and cervicis. (*B*) Trapezius.

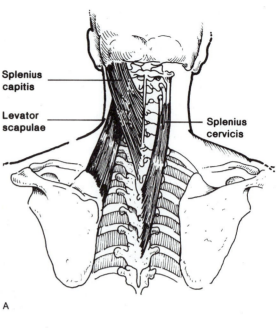

Splenius capitis

Levator scapulae

Splenius cervicis

A

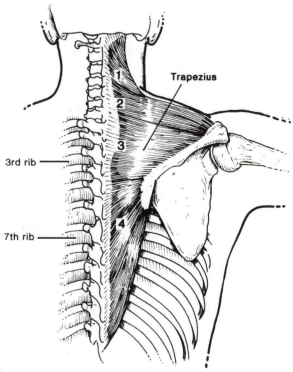

Trapezius

3rd rib

7th rib

B

4. Music played during the duration of appropriate posture for 9-year-old boy with cerebral palsy and mental retardation who needed physical support of orthopedic chair and straps for good posture. Johnson, Catherman, and Spiro (1981) reported that response-contingent music is more effective than physical support alone in teaching a child with multiple disabilities good posture.

Forward Head and Neck

Normally, the head is balanced above the cervical vertebrae in such a way that minimal muscle effort is required to resist the pull of gravity. When the earlobe is no longer in alignment with the tip of the shoulder (acromion process), forward head and neck is diagnosed.

In its *mildest form,* the head tends to droop forward. The cervical spine curve increases so slowly that most persons are unaware that forward head and neck is developing. In the mild stage, the best ameliorative exercise is practice in discriminating between good and poor alignment.

In more *severe cases,* usually accompanied by round back, the cervical spine hyperextends to whatever degree is necessary to compensate for the forward droop of the head and the increasing dorsal convexity of the thoracic spine (Figure 14.7). This results in adaptive shortening and tightening of the cervical extensors, mainly the upper trapezius and splenius capitis and cervicis (Figure 14.8). This tight-

ness is accentuated in the area of the seventh cervical vertebra, where a layer of fat tends to accumulate. The combined prominence of the seventh cervical vertebra and excess adipose tissue is called a *dowager's hump.* The neck flexors tend to stretch, sag, and become functionally worthless. This hyperextension of the neck is sometimes called cervical lordosis.

In mild forward head and neck, the extensors primarily need strengthening exercises. Flexibility is not a problem. As the condition becomes progressively severe, the muscles may feel stiff, tense, and sore. The emphasis in exercise shifts to flexibility, particularly stretching the cervical extensors.

Ameliorative Exercises

1. **Chin to shoulder touch.** Attempt to align the head and neck with other segments of the body. Rotate slowly to the left until the chin touches the shoulder. Repeat to the opposite side.
2. **Lateral flex with ear touch.** Attempt to align the head and neck with other segments of the body. Laterally flex to the left until the ear touches the shoulder. Repeat to the opposite side.
3. **Head lift.** Lying prone, with arms at side, palms up, raise the head only and hold.
4. **Halo push.** Stand or sit with fingers interlaced above the head. Extend the head upward toward the "halo."
5. **Object on head walk.** Walk, race, or play games with different objects on the head. Experiment with different head and trunk positions.

Contraindicated Exercises

1. Circling the head
2. Neck hyperextension
3. Activities related to atlantoaxial instability when working with individuals with Down syndrome (see Chapter 21 on mental retardation)

Excessive Head Tilt

The top of the head tilting toward the right is called a right tilt (RT). The symbol LT is used for the opposite condition. A head habitually held in a tilted position is often symptomatic of vision or hearing impairments. Almost always, the individual is unaware of the tilt and needs exercises for improving proprioception.

Over a long time, head tilt causes an adaptive shortening and tightening of the neck muscles on the side of the tilt. Tight muscles on the right side may be stretched by lateral flexion exercises to the left, and vice versa. A slow, static stretch and hold is more effective than rhythmic exercises.

Kyphosis

Translated literally, *kyphos* means a sharp angulation. Increasing backward convexity in the thoracic region results in the condition commonly known as humpback, hunchback, Pott's curvature, or round upper back. The condition is rare among normal children in the public school setting.

True kyphosis is associated with disease of the intervertebral disks or of the epiphyseal area of the vertebrae. The intervertebral disk is the fibrocartilage padding between vertebral bodies (see Figure 14.9). The disk is comprised of two parts: the outer annulus fibrosus, known for its strength and elasticity, and the inner nucleus pulposus, which contains

FIGURE 14.9

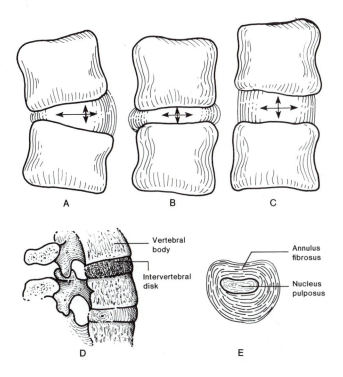

The intervertebral disk. (*A*) Flexion of the spine permitted by shift of fluid. (*B*) Compression of the disk occurs when noncompressible fluid of nucleus expands the elastic annulus. (*C*) Normal extended position with annulus fibers held taut; internal pressure is indicated by arrows. (*D*) Section of vertebrae. (*E*) Cross section of intervertebral disk.

fluid that absorbs shock in locomotor movements and maintains the separation of the vertebral bodies. The nucleus pulposus has all the characteristics of a hydraulic system.

Any degenerative disease of the intervertebral disk is characterized by changes in pressure that cause pain. *Scheuermann's disease,* described in Chapter 24 on les autres, is a kyphosis condition affecting adolescents. *Ostereoporosis* is a common cause of kyphosis in older adults, especially women. In old age, the fluid content of the nucleus pulposus decreases, and the annulus fibrosus becomes progressively less elastic. These changes limit motion of the back. Any prolonged inactivity seems to contribute to degeneration of the intervertebral disks. Individuals with severe or profound mental retardation whose mobility is limited often exhibit kyphosis at a young age.

Lordosis

Lordosis, also called swayback or hollow back, is an exaggeration of the normal posterior concave curve in the lumbar region. It not only affects the five lumbar vertebrae but also throws the pelvis out of correct alignment (see Figure 14.10).

Lordosis has many possible causes: genetic predisposition; weak abdominal muscles, which allow the pelvis to tilt downward anteriorly; weak gluteal muscles and hamstrings, which cannot counteract this anterior tilt; overly tight lumbar extensors, which contribute to an anterior tilt; overdeveloped hip flexors, which cause anterior tilt; and, on rare occasions, occupations like professional dance.

FIGURE   14.10

Pelvic tilts. (*A*) Normal pelvic tilt (neutral position). The buttocks are tucked in. Anterior and posterior muscles are equal in strength. (*B*) Anterior pelvic tilt causes lordosis and protruding abdomen. The anterior iliac spines are rotated downward by tight hip flexors. The posterior sacrum is rotated upward by tight lumbar extensors.

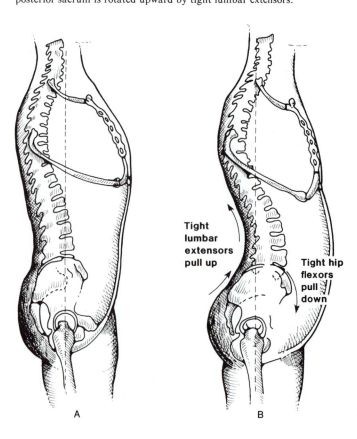

FIGURE   14.11

Good posture for a normal preschooler includes a protruding abdomen.

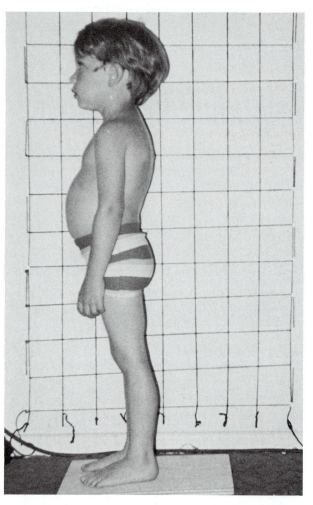

True lordosis usually has the following characteristics:

1. Anterior tilt of pelvis.
2. Tight lower back muscles, tight lumbodorsal fascia, tight hip flexors, tight iliofemoral (Y) ligaments, weak abdominals, weak hamstrings, and weak gluteals.
3. Knees may be hyperextended.
4. Compensatory kyphosis may develop to balance the increased concavity; if so, the pectorals and anterior intercostals may be tight also.
5. Upper body tends to shift backward as a compensatory measure. This shifts the weight of the body from the vertebral bodies onto the neural arches, bringing the spinous processes closer together than normal and sometimes pinching the nerves.
6. Lower back pain.
7. Faulty functioning of internal organs, including those of digestion, elimination, and reproduction.
8. Predisposition toward dysmenorrhea and menstrual pain.
9. Increased incidence of back strain and back injuries.

Correction of lordosis, at least in the early stages, is largely a matter of increasing proprioceptive awareness so that the student can feel the difference between an anterior and a posterior tilt. Alternate anterior and posterior pelvic tilts should be practiced while lying supine, kneeling, sitting, standing, and performing various locomotor activities. Helpful exercise cues are "Tuck your buttocks in" and "Pinch the gluteals together." Activities like the backbend, which emphasize hyperextension of the lumbar spine, are contraindicated.

Weak abdominals almost universally accompany lordosis. For this reason, strength exercises for the abdominals should be undertaken along with stretching exercises for the tight lumbar extensors. This dual purpose is accomplished to some extent without special effort in accordance with the principle of reciprocal innervation.

Abdominal Weakness

Abdominal weakness is classified as mild, moderate, or severe or as first, second, and third degree. Abdominal protrusion is normal in the young child and usually accompanied by lordosis (see Figure 14.11). This posture defect is almost always present in adolescents and adults who lead sedentary lifestyles, especially if they are overweight. The protruding abdomen also characterizes paralysis or muscle weakness that results from spinal cord injuries.

When a lifestyle changes from active to sedentary, regardless of the reason, abdominal exercises should become part of the daily routine. In middle and old age, the upper abdominal wall may become slightly rounded, but the musculature below the umbilicus should remain flat and taut.

The *lower part of the abdomen* contracts reflexly whenever the body is in complete extension, as in most locomotor activities. The emphasis upon extension in modern dance and ballet contributes particularly to abdominal strength, as does swimming the front crawl and other strokes executed from an extended position. The *upper part of the abdomen* works in conjunction with the diaphragm, gaining strength each time breathlessness in endurance-type activities forces the diaphragm to contract vigorously in inhalation. Abdominal exercises in a physical education class are a poor substitute for natural play activities. They are not recommended as long as the child derives pleasure from running, jumping, climbing, hanging, and skipping.

Because the child's abdominal wall normally protrudes, evaluating strength on the basis of performance tests rather than on appearance alone is important. Bent-knee sit-ups are generally used for this purpose.

Visceroptosis is the term used when an abdominal protrusion is severe and the viscera (internal organs) drop down into a new position. The stomach, liver, spleen, kidneys, and intestines may all be displaced, resulting in adverse effects upon their various functions. This condition occurs mainly in adults.

Exercise Principles for Abdomen and Lower Back

1. Teach abdominal exercises that will simultaneously stretch the tight lumbar extensors and hip flexors (psoas and iliacus).
2. Use the bent-knee sit-up position rather than the straight-leg lying position to eliminate the action of the strong hip flexors.
3. Avoid hyperextension of the spine. For most persons, this means avoid the double-leg lift and hold.
4. Avoid prone-lying exercises like the swan and the rocking chair.
5. Eliminate breath holding during exercise by requesting the students to count, sing, whistle, hum, or exhale. Incorrect breathing tends to build up intraabdominal pressure, which may result in a hernia. This is called the Valsalva effect.
6. Include lots of twisting movements of the trunk to strengthen oblique abdominal muscles.
7. Gradually build tolerance for endurance-type exercises that cause vigorous breathing, which in turn, strengthens the upper abdominal wall.

8. Use locomotor activities that emphasize extension of the spine. Skipping and swimming are especially good.
9. Take advantage of the extensor reflex elicited in the creeping position.
10. Use the upside-down positions in yoga for training the extensor muscles. The neck stand is preferred to the head stand.
11. If there is a history of back problems, avoid sit-ups and exercises using trunk lift from supine.

Exercises in the Creeping Position

For these exercises, always wear knee pads or move across mats. Make these into games. Also use music and create routines.

1. Crosslateral creeping. As the right arm moves forward, the left knee should move forward.
2. Crosslateral creeping combined with blowing a Ping-Pong ball across the floor.
3. Crosslateral creeping combined with pushing an object like a bottle cap or toy automobile with the nose.
4. Angry cat. Alternate (a) humping the back and letting the head hang down with (b) extending the spine with the head held high.
5. In static creeping position, move the hips from side to side. For fun, pin tail on and play wag the tail.

Exercises in Supine or Bent-knee Sit-up Position

1. Abdominal pumping (Mosher exercise). Arms in reverse T to prevent lumbar hyperextension. Reverse T means arms outstretched above head. Put book or weight on abdomen. Forcefully push abdomen up and down and feel the weight move.
2. Curl down or reverse trunk curl. Knees and hips are flexed, and knees are drawn toward chest, so curl commences at the lower spinal levels. Obliques are more active in reverse curls than in regular trunk curls. First third of curl is most valuable.
3. Sit-up with trunk twist for maximal activity of oblique abdominals. Feet should not be held down because holding them activates the unwanted hip flexors.
4. Double-knee raise and patticake. Keep the knees bent.
5. Alternate ballet legs. From bent-knee position, raise knees to chest and then lift legs alternately, as done in the synchronized swimming stunt by the same name. To make this more difficult, legs can be adducted and abducted in this position.
6. Double knee circling. Keep heels close to thighs, arms in reverse T. Flex the hips until the thighs are vertical. Keeping the shoulders flat, make circles with the knees.

    More difficult variation: Flex knees toward the chest, straighten legs to vertical, and make circles with both feet. Keep the shoulders flat and the heels together.

7. Alternate leg circling. Retract the abdominal wall and flex both knees to chest. Extend one leg and then the other in reciprocal leg circling or bicycle motion. Return the flexed legs to the chest and then lower to the floor.

8. Leg circling games. Vary the difficulty by changing the size of the circles, the number completed before resting, and the speed of the performance. The most difficult is making small circles at slow speed just above the floor. The right foot makes clockwise circles, while the left foot makes counterclockwise circles. Both legs make clockwise circles. Both legs make counterclockwise circles. Describe a figure eight with one foot or both together.

9. Drumming. Feet are used like drumsticks, alternately beating the floor.

10. Alternate knee and elbow touch in opposition. Hands behind neck. Each time, try to reach farther with the elbow and less far with the opposite knee.

11. Supine bent-knee lower trunk twist. Arms in reverse T. Raise both knees until the thighs are vertical. Keep the shoulders flat, and lower the knees toward the mat on one side; return to a vertical position. Repeat to the other side and return. Legs should not be allowed to fall; must be controlled throughout the movement.

Values of Abdominal Exercises

Abdominal exercises

1. Relieve congestion in the abdominal or pelvic cavities; this includes expelling gas and improving local circulation.

2. Retrain the upper abdominal wall to increase its efficiency in respiration.

3. Retrain the lower abdominal wall to improve its efficiency with respect to holding the viscera in place.

4. Relieve menstrual pain.

5. Strengthen muscles needed for coughing in asthma and respiratory diseases.

Flat Back

Flat back is a decrease or absence of the normal anteroposterior curves. It is the opposite condition from lordosis. The posterior concavity of the lumbar curve is decreased—that is, the normal posterior concavity is gradually changing toward convexity.

Characteristics of flat back include

1. The pelvic inclination is less than normal, with the pelvis held in posterior tilt.

2. The back appears too flat, with little or no protrusion of the buttocks.

3. Lower back muscles are weak.

4. Hip flexors, especially the psoas major, are weak and elongated.

5. Hamstrings are abnormally tight.

FIGURE 14.12

Right total scoliosis with 80° curve in 16-year-old. Curve was first noticed at age 6.

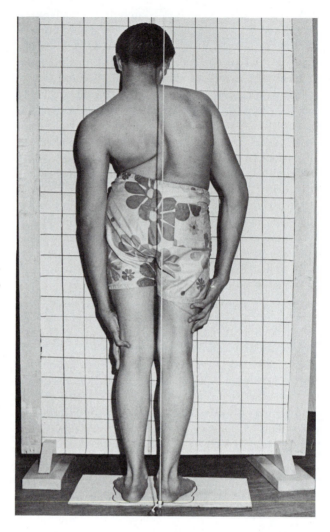

Flat back is associated with the debutante slouch, seen so often in fashion magazines, in which young women pose languidly with hips thrust forward and upper back rounded. Such models are usually flat chested and so thin that the abdomen cannot protrude. It is sad that the fashion world sometimes chooses to present this image to the American public, rather than one of good body alignment with normal busts, hips, and buttocks in gracefully curved balance. Flat back is also characteristic of the body build of young toddlers who have not been walking long enough to develop the lumbar curve.

Ameliorative exercises include

1. Alternate anterior and posterior pelvic tilts from a hook lying position to increase proprioceptive awareness.

2. Hyperextension of the lumbar spine to strengthen back muscles.

3. Most exercises in supine or bent-knee sit-up position from the previous section.

FIGURE 14.13

In right total scoliosis, the right shoulder is high and carried forward.

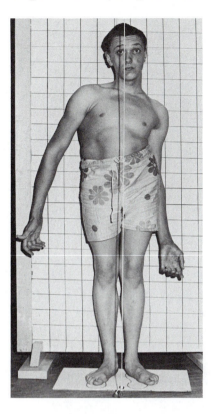

FIGURE 14.15

Left (concave) side of right total scoliosis reveals muscles that need stretching.

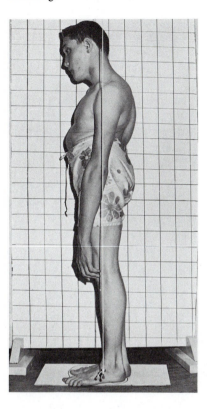

FIGURE 14.14

Right (convex) side of right total scoliosis shows back hump and bulging rib cage. Muscles on this side require strengthening.

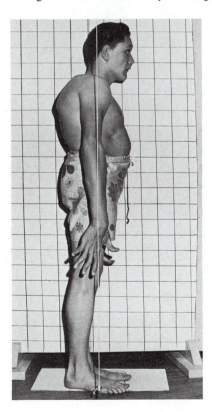

Scoliosis

Scoliosis is a lateral curvature of the spine (see Figures 14.12 to 14.15). Although the condition begins with a single curve, it usually consists of a primary curve and a compensatory curve in the opposite direction.

Keynote Positions

When certain *keynote positions* are assumed, the functional curve straightens out for the duration the position is held (see Figures 14.16 and 14.17). A functional curve can be ameliorated by therapeutic exercise, and most physicians choose to combine prescribed exercises with bracing and/or surgery (Keim, 1972).

Keynote positions may be used as diagnostic devices or as corrective exercise. Among the most common keynote positions are the following:

1. Adam's position—relaxed forward bending held for several seconds from a standing posture (see Figures 14.16 and 14.17). The knees are straight so that the flexion occurs from the hips and spinal column.

2. Hanging with both arms from a horizontal bar.

3. Symmetrical arm raise from a standing position. The individual with a total left curve flexes the right arm at the shoulder joint to whatever height is necessary to straighten the spine. The other arm is maintained in a position of abduction. In some cases, raising both arms and/or raising one leg sideways may help the curve to disappear.

FIGURE   14.16

FIGURE   14.17

Sixteen-year-old with right total scoliosis in Adam's position. If the curve were not structural, it would disappear in this keynote position.

Permanent scoliotic hump prominent in Adam's position. Boy lacks lumbar flexibility to touch toes without bending knees.

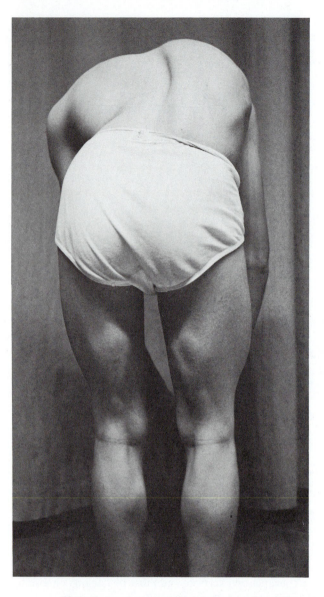

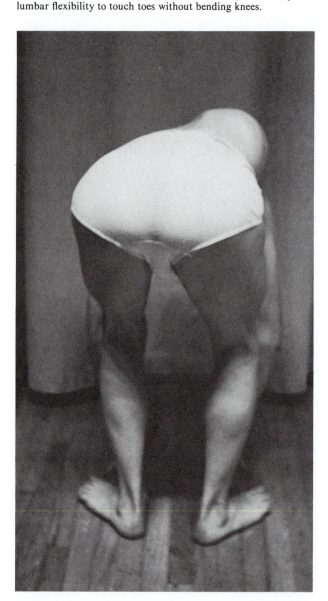

If the lateral curve is not temporarily obliterated by any of these positions, it can be assumed that scoliosis is in a transitional or structural stage. In such instances, the physical educator should insist that the child be examined by a physician. No corrective exercises should be undertaken without a permission slip from the parents and a medical clearance from the physician. Ideally, the physician will prescribe specific exercises to be practiced under the supervision of adapted physical education personnel.

Lateral curves are named in terms of the direction of their convexity. Among right-handed persons, the most common type of scoliosis is the *total left curve*.

Rotation in Normal and Lateral Curvatures

Kinesiologically, rotation of the trunk is defined in the direction that the *anterior vertebral bodies* move. If the trunk rotates to the right, the vertebral bodies are turned to the right. Normally, any rotation of the trunk to the right is ac-

companied by a slight amount of lateral flexion to the right. In scoliosis, the rule with respect to the normal rotation of vertebral bodies reverses itself. *Thus, scoliosis is a condition in which the vertebral bodies rotate toward the convexity of the curve and the spinous processes toward the concavity.* This occurs partly because the bodies are less firmly bound together by strong ligaments than the spinous processes.

Characteristics of Left Curve

In the total left lumbar curve to the convex side, the following characteristics may be observed:

1. Spinous processes deviate from midline, rotating toward the concavity of the curve.
2. The left shoulder is higher than the other shoulder and may also be carried forward. In appraisal of the asymmetry of the shoulders, check the inferior angles of the scapula to see if one is carried lower than the

other, abducted further away from the spinal column, or winged away from the rib cage. Also check the angle between the neck and the shoulder on both sides of the body.

3. The head may be tilted to one side.

4. There is a lateral displacement of the trunk toward the side of convexity since the thorax is no longer balanced directly over the pelvis.

5. Posteriorly, the ribs usually bulge out on the convex side of the curve; the rib cage tends to lose its flexibility.

6. The right hip is usually higher than the other and the right iliac crest more prominent. Said in another way, when there is a lateral pelvic tilt, the convexity of the spine is toward the lower hip.

7. The contour of the waistline is affected, with the notch on the concave side greater than that on the convex.

8. The right leg may be longer than the left. In other words, a long leg will push the hip to a higher level and contribute to curvature on the opposite side.

9. Side bending tends to be freer to the right (concave side) than to the left.

10. Forward flexibility of the spine may be limited as a natural protective mechanism of the body against further deformity.

11. Muscles on the concave side become increasingly tight, while those on the convex side are stretched and weakened.

Ameliorative Exercises

Principles for planning ameliorative exercises for a child with functional scoliosis include

1. Work on improvement of body alignment in front of a mirror before undertaking specific exercises for scoliosis.

2. Use keynote positions (with exception of Adam's position) as corrective exercises. When a position is identified in which the curve is temporarily obliterated, spend as many seconds as comfortable in it; rest and repeat.

3. Emphasize swimming and other activities that encourage development of the trunk without placing weight-bearing strain on the spine.

4. Avoid forward flexibility of spine unless prescribed by a physician.

5. Use breathing and chest expansion exercises to maintain flexibility of chest and prevent further distortion of thorax.

6. If you tend to be conservative and wish to avoid controversial practices, use only symmetrical exercises that develop left and right sides equally. Exercises for strengthening the back extensors are recommended.

7. If you are willing to use activities that authorities are about equally divided on, try such *asymmetrical* exercises as

   a. Hang facing outward from stall bars and swing legs in.

   b. Hang from stall bars with right hand only (for left total curve). Right side is to the stall bars, and left hand is used whenever needed for balance.

   c. Kneel on right knee, with leg extended to side, right arm curved above head. Laterally flex trunk several times to the left. *The purpose of most asymmetrical exercises is to stretch muscles on the concave side and/or to strengthen muscles on the convex side.* Generally, exercises prescribed by physicians are asymmetrical in nature.

8. Encourage the student with scoliosis to participate in regular physical education classes and athletic competition.

Scoliosis is more prevalent in girls and among ectomorphic body types, but it is not confined to either. About 75% of the known cases are idiopathic, about 12.5% are congenital anomalies, and the other 12.5% result from paralysis or paresis of muscles on one side of the spinal column. Many persons with poliomyelitis have scoliosis.

Among the kinds of treatments used are the Milwaukee brace, Harrington instrumentation and spinal fusion, and various kinds of body casts (see Figures 14.18 and 14.19). Students with severe scoliosis or kyphosis in the Milwaukee brace should have a well-rounded physical activity program rather than exercise alone. Cailliet (1975) stated in this regard:

Just as exercises alone are of limited value in either correcting or controlling scoliosis, applying a Milwaukee brace without exercises is of limited value. . . . The brace permits almost unlimited activities, excluding only contact sports for the safety of other children and very active sports, such as tumbling on a trampoline, horseback riding, and strenuous gymnastics. . . . (pp. 72, 75)

Uneven Shoulder Height

When the two shoulders are of unequal height, the higher one is recorded as LH (left high) or RH (right high). Shoulder unevenness is best ascertained by using a horizontal line on the wall behind the student. Other techniques include

1. If the head is not tilted, comparing the distance between the shoulders and earlobes on the right and left side.

2. Comparing the level of the inferior angles of the scapulae. The inferior angles are at about the level of the seventh thoracic spinous process.

3. Comparing the level of the two clavicles.

Whenever a high shoulder is recorded, a lateral spinal curve convex on the same side should be suspected (see Figures 14.19 and 14.20). If scoliosis is not found, shoulder asymmetries are not a problem. *In normal development, the dominant side of the body has a slightly depressed shoulder and slightly higher hip.* This should not be confused with scoliosis.

FIGURE   14.18

Milwaukee brace fitted to a right thoracic, left lumbar scoliotic curve. Developed in 1945 by Blount and Schmidt of Milwaukee, this brace is successful in preventing further curvatures in about 70% of the cases. It is generally worn 23 hours a day over a long undershirt, and children can run and play in it with few restrictions.

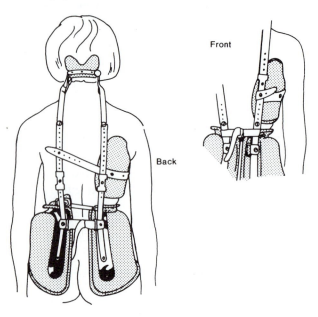

FIGURE   14.19

Right dorsal scoliosis with 65° curve. This 18-year-old has worn a Milwaukee brace and had Harrington instrumentation and spinal fusion. Further correction is not feasible.

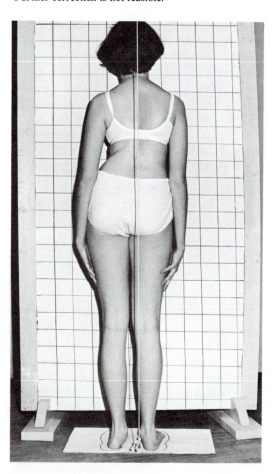

FIGURE   14.20

Left shoulder high and some evidence of a beginning left scoliotic curve. Note unevenness of waistline notches.

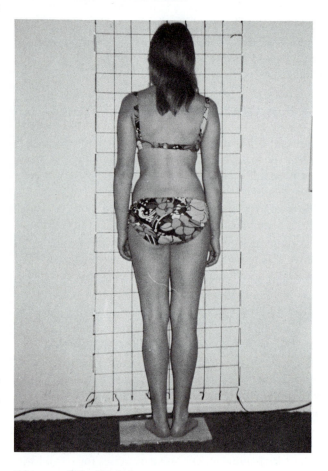

Uneven Hip Height

When two hips are of unequal height, the higher one is recorded as LH or RH. Traditionally, the anterior superior iliac spines serve as the anatomical landmarks for judging asymmetry. A string may be stretched between these two points.

Differences in hip height may be caused by scoliosis, uneven leg length, or the habit of standing on one leg for long periods of time. To determine leg lengths, the student lies in a supine position. The length of each leg is recorded as the distance from the anterior superior iliac spine to the medial ankle bone.

Round Shoulders

Round shoulders is a forward deviation of the shoulder girdle in which the scapulae are abducted with a slight lateral tilt. This brings the acromion processes (shoulder tips) in front of the normal gravitational line. Round shoulders should not be confused with round back (kyphosis). They are distinctly different problems.

Synonyms for round shoulders are abducted scapulae, forward deviation of the shoulder girdle, protraction of scapulae, and separation of scapulae. Kinesiologically, the condition results when the strength of the shoulder girdle abductors (pectoralis minor and serratus anterior) becomes greater than that of the adductors (rhomboids and trapezius III). To determine the extent of the forward deviation, the distance between the vertebral borders of the scapulae is measured. In the adult, the normal spread is 4 to 5 inches, depending on the breadth of the shoulders.

The incidence of round shoulders is high among persons who work at desk jobs and, hence, spend much of their time with the shoulders abducted. Athletes often exhibit round shoulders because of overdevelopment of the anterior arm, shoulder, and chest muscles resulting from sports and aquatics activities, which stress forward movements of the arms. This tendency may be counteracted by engaging in an exercise program designed specifically to keep the posterior muscles equal in strength to their antagonists. Perhaps the easiest way to do this is to swim a few laps of the back crawl each day. Certainly, the well-rounded athlete who enjoys many different activities is less likely to develop round shoulders than is one who specializes almost exclusively in tennis, basketball, or volleyball.

Changes in Body Alignment from Round Shoulders

The following segmental analysis demonstrates the compensatory changes in alignment of body parts that result from round shoulders:

1. **Head and neck.** Out of alignment and displaced forward.
2. **Thoracic spine.** Increasing convexity that tends to negate the effectiveness of the upward pull of the sternocleidomastoid and scaleni muscles, which normally maintain the upper ribs and sternum in a high position. The weak back muscles are elongated by the increased convexity of the spine.
3. **Chest.** Lowered position. Whereas persons with good postures lead with the chest, this individual leads with the shoulders. The failure of the anterior muscles to exert their usual effect on the sternum and ribs results in a lowered position of the diaphragm, which, in turn, affects breathing.
4. **Shoulder girdle.** Scapula abducted. Anterior muscles need to be stretched, and posterior muscles need to be strengthened.
5. **Shoulder joint.** Increased inward rotation of the humeral head.
6. **Arms.** Arms are carried more forward than usual, with palms facing toward the rear, whereas normally, only the little finger of the hand can be seen from the rear (see Figure 14.21). The elbows may be held out close to the body.
7. **Lumbar spine.** Lordosis may develop to compensate for increased convexity of thoracic spine.
8. **Knees.** Knees may hyperextend to compensate for the change in the lumbar curve.

With the alignment of almost all the body segments altered, the entire body slumps, creating the impression of general fatigue. This posture is assumed temporarily in times of extreme mental depression or bereavement, revealing the unity of mind and body. Mentally ill persons who have been institutionalized several years often assume the round-shouldered postures of defeat.

FIGURE 14.21

Round shoulders can be detected from a rear view by the palms of the hands. This child also has mild scoliosis, knock-knees, and pronated feet.

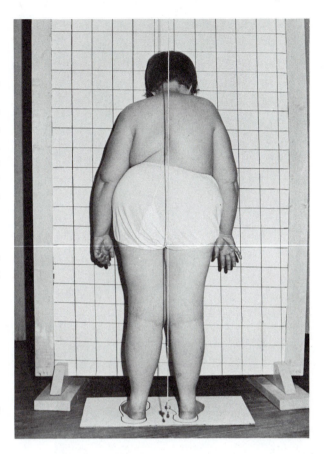

Ameliorative Exercises

Exercises for round shoulders are directed toward the shoulder girdle (scapular) abductors and adductors. *They should simultaneously stretch the tightened anterior muscles and strengthen trapezius III and the rhomboids.* So many exercises for round shoulders are recommended in textbooks that it is difficult to evaluate their respective effectiveness in accomplishing these goals. The four that appear to be most effective, in rank order from best to good, are

1. **Pull resistance.** Sit on chair facing the wall with pulleys, with the arms extended sideward at shoulder height and the hands grasping the handles. Slowly move the arms backward, keeping them at shoulder height.
2. **Prone lateral raise of weights.** Assume a prone position on a bench. The hands grasp dumbbells on the floor to each side of the body. The weights are lifted toward the ceiling as far as possible, keeping the arms straight. Hold. (Chin should remain on the bench.)
3. **Push against wall.** Sit cross-legged with the head and back flat against the wall. The arms are bent at shoulder height with the palms facing the chest, fingertips touching, and elbows against the wall. Keeping the head and spine against the wall, press the elbows back with as much force as possible.

FIGURE   14.22

Winged scapulae are normal in preschool children. Atrophied right leg has not yet affected shoulder height.

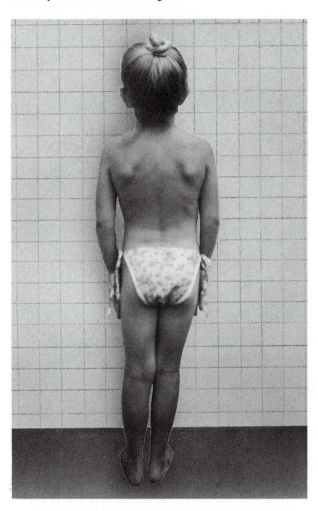

FIGURE   14.23

Winged scapulae in predominantly ectomorphic preadolescent.

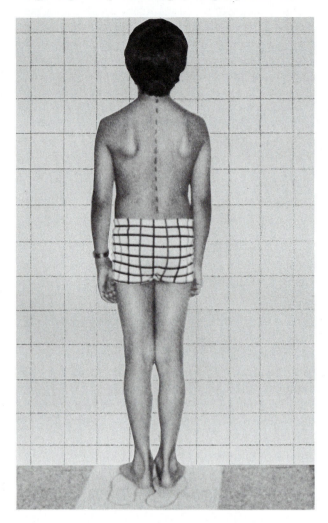

4. **Head resistance.** Lie on back, arms out to side, palms down, knees flexed, and feet spread. Raise hips and arch back so that shoulders are off mat, supporting weight on feet, hands, and back of head in a modified wrestler's bridge.

Winged Scapulae

Also called projected scapulae, the term *winged scapulae* refers to a prominence of the inferior angles of the scapulae. The scapulae are pulled away from the rib cage, and the vertebral borders are lifted. The serratus anterior, the muscle that normally holds the inferior angle of the scapula close to the rib cage, is believed to be weak when winging occurs.

Winged scapulae are normal in preschool and elementary school children since the serratus is slower in developing than its antagonists (see Figures 14.22 and 14.23). Since the serratus anterior is a prime mover for upward rotation and abduction, it is strengthened by hanging, climbing, and other activities executed above the head. Many girls in our society do not outgrow winged scapulae as do boys. This postural deviation is often a part of the debutante slouch de-

scribed earlier. Winged scapulae often accompany round shoulders. They are associated also with congenital anomalies and postural conditions in which the ribs protrude.

Deviations of the Chest

Asthma, other chronic upper respiratory disorders, and rickets may cause changes in the rib cage with resulting limitations in chest flexibility and improper breathing practices. These changes are designated as functional, transitional, and structural, depending upon their degree of severity. Congenital anomalies, of course, do account for some chest deviations.

Hollow Chest

The most common of the chest deviations, hollow chest denotes the depression of the anterior thorax that normally accompanies round shoulders and/or kyphosis. Specific characteristics of hollow chest are concave or flattened appearance of anterior thoracic wall, depressed (lowered) ribs, low sternum, tight intercostal and pectoral muscles, limited chest flexibility, and habitually lowered diaphragm that limits breathing.

Hollow chest can be traced to the failure of the neck and pectoral muscles to exert their usual lifting effect on the ribs and sternum. The neck muscles are elongated and weak. The pectoral muscles are excessively tight and strong.

Barrel Chest

The barrel chest is characteristic of persons with severe, chronic asthma who become hyperventilated because of their inability to exhale properly. Over a period of years, the excess air retained in the lungs tends to expand the anteroposterior dimensions of the thorax so that it takes on a rounded appearance similar to that of full inspiration.

Specific characteristics of barrel chest are

1. The thoracic spine extends.
2. The sternum is pushed forward and upward.
3. The upper ribs (second through the seventh) are elevated and everted. Eversion of the ribs is defined as the inner surfaces rotating to face downward. This occurs when the lower border of the rib turns forward.
4. The costal cartilages tend to straighten out when the ribs elevate.
5. The lower ribs (8th through the 10th) move laterally, thus opening the chest and widening the subcostal angle.
6. The floating ribs are depressed and spread.
7. The diaphragm is habitually depressed, which, in turn, displaces the internal organs in the direction of the abdominal wall.
8. The abdomen protrudes in response to organs pressed against the weakened abdominal wall.

Barrel chest is normal for infants and preschool children. The lateral widening of the thorax from side to side so that it no longer resembles a barrel occurs normally as a result of the vigorous play activities of young children. Individuals with severe disabilities who cannot engage in physical activities often have chests that remain infantile and underdeveloped.

Funnel Chest

The opposite of barrel chest, funnel chest is an abnormal increase in the lateral diameter of the chest with a marked depression of the sternum and anterior thorax. The sternum and adjacent costal cartilages appear to have been sucked inward.

Funnel chest, also called *pectus excavatum,* is usually a congenital anomaly. It appears in many persons with severe mental retardation. It also may be caused by rickets or severe nasal obstruction—that is, enlarged adenoids—and characterizes syndromes like Turner and Noonan caused by sex chromosome aberrations.

Pigeon Chest

Also called chicken breast, or *pectus carinatum,* pigeon chest takes its name from the abnormal prominence of the sternum. The anteroposterior diameter of the thorax is increased as a

FIGURE 14.24

Mild to moderate bowlegs is normal in infancy and corrects itself, usually by 2 years of age. Children then tend to develop knock-knees, which is most obvious at ages 3 to 4. This condition also corrects itself.

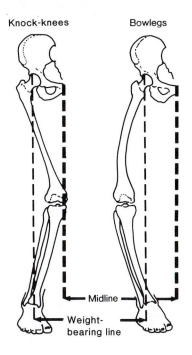

result of the forward displacement of the sternum. The deviation is rare, caused by rickets during the early growth period. It may also be congenital or caused by les autres conditions like osteogenesis imperfecta.

Alignment of Lower Extremities

A quick screening device to judge the overall alignment of the legs is the game known as *Four Coins.* The challenge is, "Can you put a coin between your thighs, your knees, your calves, and your ankles and simultaneously hold all the coins in place?" If the body parts are well proportioned and correctly aligned, this task should present no problem. When the student stands with feet together and parallel, the medial aspects of the knees and ankles should be touching their opposites. Figure 14.24 depicts developmental changes in hip and leg alignment. It is normal for infants and toddlers to have bowlegs and for preschool children to have knock-knees. These conditions generally correct themselves.

Individual differences in leg alignment and in locomotor patterns are largely dependent upon the hip joint. Students who toe inward or outward in their normal walking gait, for instance, usually have nothing wrong with their feet. The problem's origin usually can be traced to a strength imbalance in the muscles that rotate the femur at the hip joint.

Hip Joint Problems

The hip joint is formed by the articulation between the head of the femur and the acetabulum of the pelvis. Figure 14.25 depicts its anatomy. How the head fits into the acetabulum determines function and stability. Important to the understanding of several problems is the angulation of the neck of

FIGURE 14.25

Anatomy of the hip joint. The acetabulum is a cup-shaped hollow socket that is formed medially by the pubis, above by the ilium, and laterally and behind by the ischium. Around the circumference of the hip socket is a fibrocartilaginous ring that serves to deepen the socket and assure stability of the joint. Three ligaments reinforce the joint. Of these, the most often injured is the iliofemoral (Y) ligaments. These are the ligaments that are stretched when students do splits or turn the legs outward in ballet positions.

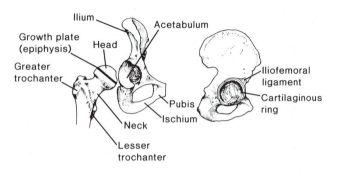

FIGURE 14.26

Angulation of the neck of the femur helps to explain coxa valga and vara. (*A*) Decreased neck-shaft angle shortens leg. (*B*) Normal for adolescents and adults. (*C*) Increased neck-shaft angle lengthens leg. Normal for infants.

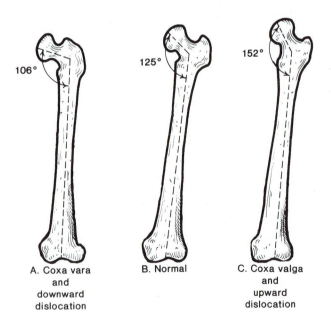

the femur, depicted in Figure 14.26. Hip joint problems affect leg alignment and gait. Several of these are discussed in Chapter 24 on les autres conditions.

Abnormal positioning of the femoral head within the acetabulum is called *coxa vara* (decreased angulation) or *coxa valga* (increased angulation). Both cause waddling gaits. Neither condition can be corrected by exercise. Casting, bracing, and surgery are used.

FIGURE 14.27

Bowlegs in early childhood are almost always accompanied by coxa vara. (*A*) The horizontalization of the femoral neck limits the action of the gluteus medius, the abductor responsible for maintaining hip joint stability during locomotion. (*B*) The result is a waddling gait in which the shoulders incline toward the weight-bearing foot. Exercise cannot correct this gait because it is caused by a structural abnormality.

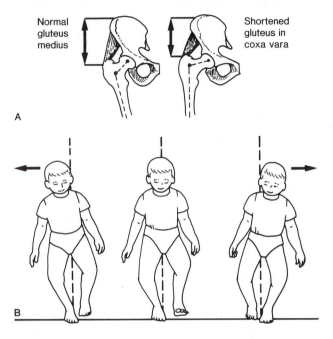

Coxa Vara

The decreased angulation in coxa vara may result in the affected leg becoming shorter. Inward rotation and abduction are limited. Bowlegs in early childhood is associated with coxa vara (see Figure 14.27). Coxa vara also often appears in adolescence. It may be called either *slipped femoral epiphysis* or adolescent coxa vara and is more common in males than females. The epiphysis (growth center) of the femoral head slips down and backward, making the angulation of the femoral neck more horizontal.

Coxa Valga

In contrast, coxa valga malpositions in normal children are associated with upward, anterior dislocations of the hip. The condition is almost always congenital and is often called *congenital dislocation of the hip* (CDH), rather than coxa valga. This is the fourth most common orthopedic birth defect. The affected leg is longer, and both inward and outward rotation are limited. Adductors are very tight. Many severely disabled nonambulatory persons develop coxa valga between ages 2 and 10; in this condition, the head of the femur is usually displaced upward (like CDH) and posteriorly (unlike CDH).

Knee Joint Problems

Knee joint problems include (a) bowlegs, (b) knock-knees, (c) hyperextended knees, and (d) tibial torsion. These problems may be congenital or acquired through injury. Malalignment increases the risk of osteoarthritis in middle and old age. Obesity, over time, injures the knee joint. This is why weight-bearing exercises are often contraindicated for obese persons.

Bowlegs (Genu Varum)

Although the Latin term *genu,* meaning "knee," emphasizes the capacity for knees and ankles to touch simultaneously, bowing can occur in the shaft of the femur as well as the tibia. *Varum* refers to inward bowing. One or both legs may be affected.

The legs of infants are often bowed. The natural pull of the peroneal muscles on the shaft of the tibia during the first months of walking tends to straighten out the bow. In this instance, an imbalance in strength between two muscle groups works to the toddler's advantage. By the age of 2 years or so, the tibials have gained sufficient strength to offset the pull of the peroneals, and any bowing that remains may become structural.

Persistent or late-appearing bowlegs may be caused by such pathological conditions as renal or vitamin D resistant rickets and growth disorders that affect the epiphyseal plates. Illustrative of the latter is *Blount's disease,* or *tibia vara,* an outward bowing of the tibia caused by retardation of growth of the medial epiphyseal plate at the top of the tibia. Blount's disease usually occurs between 1 and 3 years of age and is corrected by surgery. Pathological conditions that are often complicated by bowed legs include *arthrogryposis, dwarfism,* and *osteogenesis imperfecta* (check the "Index" at the back of the book for specific discussions).

In adulthood, bowing is structural, and exercises are not beneficial. Many individuals with mild to moderate conditions have strong muscles and are not impaired noticeably by this deviation. Bowlegs tends to shift the weight toward the lateral border of the foot and to maintain the foot in a supinated position.

Functional bowlegs is sometimes confused with the structural condition. In functional bowlegs, the curve appears as a result of hyperextending the knees and inwardly rotating the femurs. If the patellae face inward, the apparent bowlegs is likely a functional adaptation that can be eliminated by strengthening the outward rotators of the hips and relaxing the knees so that correct leg and thigh alignment is possible.

Knock-Knees (Genu Valga)

The Latin word *valgum* can mean either knock-knees or bowlegs but is used in most adapted physical education references as knock-knees, referring specifically to the bending outward of the lower legs so that the knees touch, but the ankles do not.

Knock-knees occurs almost universally in obese persons. In the standing position, the gravitational line passes lateral to the center of the knee rather than directly through the patella, as is normal. This deviation in the weight-bearing line predisposes the knee joint to injury. Knock-knees is usually accompanied by weakness in the longitudinal arch and pronation of the feet (see Figure 14.28).

No treatment or exercises are recommended for knock-knees in children younger than age 7 because, developmentally, this is a normal condition. In severe knock-knees, physicians often prescribe a 1/8-inch heel-raise on the medial border and/or use of a night splint. Severe cases that persist are treated with surgery (osteotomy).

The gait is altered by *increased lateral sway* to position the body weight directly over the weight-bearing foot and by *inward rotation at the hip* to prevent the knees from striking each other while passing.

Ameliorative exercises include

1. Stretch the muscles on the lateral aspect of the leg (peroneal group) by doing supination exercises (inversion and adduction of the foot).
2. Strengthen the tibials by doing supination exercises; this also helps to strengthen longitudinal arch.
3. Strengthen the outward rotators of the hip joint by doing activities that stress outward rotation.

Hyperextended Knees

Also called back knees or *genu recurvatum,* hyperextended knees is a deviation in which the knees are pulled backward beyond their normal position. This posture problem can be identified best from a side view (see Figure 14.29). Hyperextension of the knees tends to tilt the pelvis forward and contribute to lordosis, thereby throwing all of the body segments out of alignment.

This condition is usually caused by knee extensor weakness or muscle imbalance. When the quadriceps muscles are too weak to hold the knee in correct alignment, it is stabilized by the posterior ligamentous capsule, which, not being designed for this purpose, gradually yields. Back knees can also be caused by tight calf muscles, Achilles tendon contractures, and bony abnormalities that fix the foot in a plantar flexion (equinus) position and consequently affect stance and gait. In cerebral palsy, back knees often result from surgical overcorrection of knee flexion deformities. In spinal cord injuries and polio, the knees are sometimes surgically placed in recurvatum to permit independent walking as an alternative to wheelchair locomotion (see the information on gaits in Chapter 11).

Severe cases of back knees are usually treated by prescription of a knee-ankle brace that holds the foot in slight dorsiflexion and the knee in flexion. Specific exercises should not be done in physical education unless medically prescribed. *Contraindicated activities include touching the toes from a standing position, deep-knee squats, and duck and bear walks.* Standing with knees in hyperextension should always be discouraged by telling people to relax or bend at the knees.

Tibial Torsion

With tibial torsion, the tibia is twisted and the weight-bearing line is shifted to the medial aspect of the foot. The deviation is often more marked in one leg than in the other, with the affected foot toeing inward and pronating. Tibial torsion often

FIGURE 14.28

Knock-knees elongates tendons on the medial side and tightens tendons on the lateral side. Lateral muscles of the lower leg tighten, pulling the outer border of the foot upward and forcing weight onto the inner border.

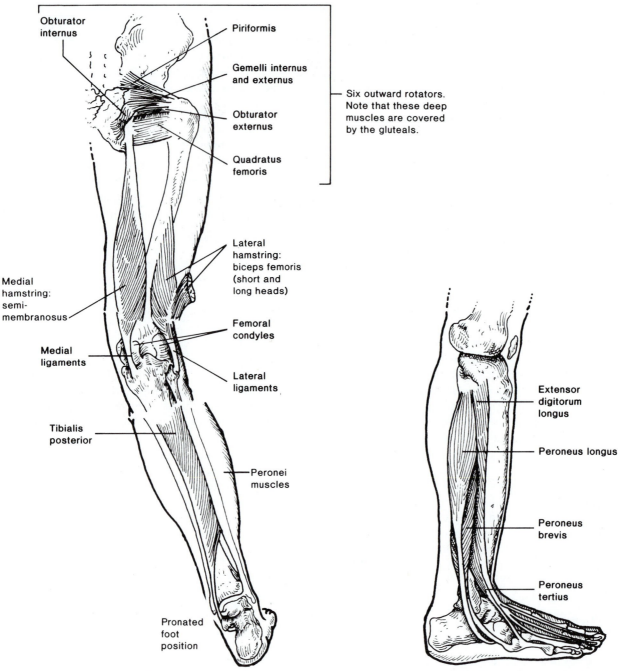

A. Posterior muscles need strengthening.

B. Lateral muscles need stretching.

accompanies knock-knees, flat feet, and pronated feet (see Figure 14.30). Congenital anomalies of the foot may be accompanied by twisting of the lower end of the tibia. Congenital tibial torsion is usually corrected in infancy by plaster casts, braces, splints, and/or surgery.

Deviations of the Feet

Poor alignment in any part of the body affects the weight-bearing function of the feet. Obesity increases the stress on the joints. Abnormal formation of bones, as in clubfoot (see foot in Figure 14.30), also affects alignment, as does weak or paralyzed leg and foot muscles resulting from spinal cord injury or neuromuscular conditions like cerebral palsy. Figure 14.31 depicts foot bones that often get out of alignment.

Toeing Inward

Toeing inward (pigeon toes) is usually caused by a strength imbalance in the hip joint muscles. When the inward rotators—*gluteus minimus* and *gluteus medius*—are stronger

FIGURE   14.29

Right knee in hyperextension after knee surgery following an automobile accident. Malalignment of legs contributes to lordosis.

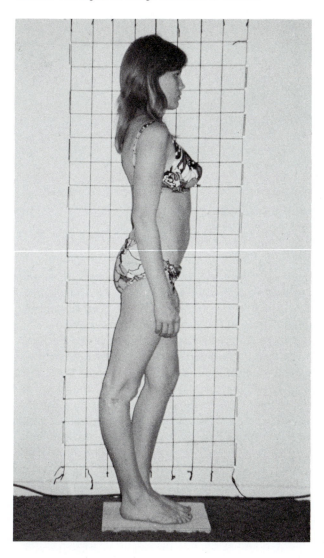

FIGURE   14.30

Medial torsion of left tibia in young adolescent with surgically corrected clubfoot.

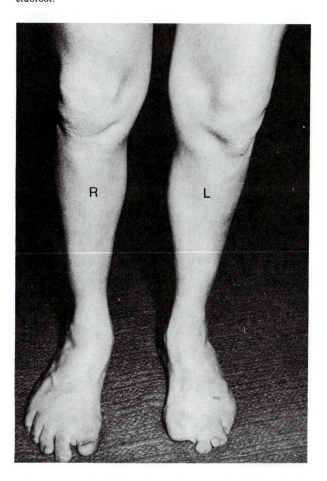

than the outward rotators, the student toes inward. This problem is also associated with the scissors gait in cerebral palsy.

Ameliorative exercises include

1. Develop proprioceptive awareness of the different foot positions through movement exploration on all kinds of surfaces.
2. Stretch the tight inward rotators by doing activities that emphasize outward rotation. Ballet techniques are especially effective.
3. Strengthen the weak outward rotators by doing activities that emphasize outward rotation.
4. Avoid inward rotation movements.

Toeing Outward

Toeing outward occurs when the posterior group of muscles on the sacrum, called "the six outward rotators," is stronger than the prime movers for inward rotation (see Figure 14.28).

Since toeing outward is a way of widening the stance and improving the balance, it may be observed in toddlers just learning to walk, the aged, persons who are blind, and others who are unsure of their footing. *Ameliorative exercises are the opposite of those done for toeing inward.*

Supination and Pronation

The two joints of the foot where most of the movements occur—and subsequently, the deviations—are the *talonavicular* and *talocalcaneal* joints (see Figure 14.31). In the former, the talus is transferring the weight of the body to the forward part of the foot, and in the latter, it is transferring the weight to the back part of the foot. How this weight is transferred determines the presence or absence of foot problems.

Normally, the weight of the body in locomotor activities is taken on the outer border of the foot and then transferred via the metatarsal area to the big toe, which provides the push-off force for forward movement. During this sequence, the foot is maintained in *slight supination,* which is considered the foot's "strong position." All locomotor activities should be performed in this slightly supinated position, which forces the weight of the body to taken on the foot's outer border.

14   Postures, Appearance, and Muscle Imbalance   **389**

FIGURE 14.31

Normal bone structures affect alignment of the leg and foot and determine capacity for correct foot placement during gait. Joints are named for the two bones that touch. Thus, the ankle joint is the talotibial joint. The talocalcaneal and talonavicular joints are the sites of varus (inward) and valgus (outward) foot deformities.

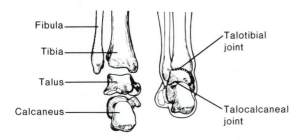

FIGURE 14.32

Thomas heel shoes used to correct flatfoot and other alignment problems. The medial border of the shoe is extended forward and raised.

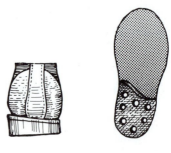

Pronation is the most common and the most debilitating of foot problems. It is defined variously as taking the weight of the body on the inner border of the foot, rolling inward on the ankles, and combined eversion and abduction. Eversion, which is the kinesiological term for turning the sole of the foot outward, occurs when the lateral muscles of the lower leg (peroneals) are tighter than the tibials. This deviation occurs mainly in the talonavicular and talocalcaneal joints.

Pronation causes a stretching of the bowstring ligaments and the subsequent dropping of the tarsals so that flatfoot is a related disorder. The student tends to toe outward and to complain of pain in the longitudinal arch and in the calf muscles (gastrocnemius and soleus). The Feiss line and the Helbing's sign (described under flatfoot) are also used for diagnosis of pronation.

Pronation may occur in early childhood as well as other growth periods. In affluent areas, well over 10 to 20% of the children may wear corrective shoes designed to ameliorate pronation (see Figure 14.32). In these shoes, the medial border is built up in such a way as to force the weight of the body to be taken on the foot's outer border. The shoes are prescribed by physicians. Children who wear corrective shoes should not change to tennis shoes for physical education activity; nor should they go barefooted without the permission of their orthopedist.

Ameliorative exercises include

1. Begin with nonweight-bearing exercises and do not add weight-bearing exercises until indicated by orthopedist.
2. Emphasize toe-curling exercises to strengthen the flexors of the toes.
3. Emphasize plantar flexion and inversion.
4. Avoid dorsiflexion exercises and maintenance of foot in dorsiflexion for long periods of time.
5. Avoid eversion movements.
6. In picking up marbles and other objects with the toes, stress a position of inversion, such as:
   a. Pick up marbles with toes.
   b. Deposit into box across the midline, which forces the foot into inversion.

7. In relay activities for correction of pronation, make sure objects held by toes of right foot are passed to the left to ensure inversion.

Flatfoot (Pes Planus)

Flatfoot may be congenital or postural. The black race is predisposed to congenital flatfoot. If the muscles of the legs and feet are strong and flexible and the body is in good alignment, congenital flatfoot is not considered a postural deviation.

Infants are born with varying degrees of flatfoot. Strong arches develop as the natural consequence of vigorous kicking and strenuous locomotor activities.

Faulty body mechanics and improper alignment of the foot and leg may create an imbalance in muscle strength, which, in turn, prevents maintenance of the longitudinal arch in the correct position. The result is an orthopedic problem, rather than one that can be corrected by exercise alone. The physician often prescribes special shoes.

The *Feiss line* method evaluates the severity of flatfoot (see Figure 14.33). This entails drawing an imaginary line from the knee joint to the metatarsophalangeal joint of the big toe. The distance that the navicular (scaphoid) is from the Feiss line determines whether the condition is first, second, or third degree as follows:

First degree—navicular 1 inch below line

Second degree—navicular 2 inches below line

Third degree—navicular 3 inches below line

The *Helbing's sign* may also be used to evaluate the severity of flatfoot (see Figure 14.33). It is defined as a medial turning inward of the Achilles tendon as viewed from behind.

Ameliorative exercises include

1. Strengthen the tibials by supination exercises like patticake, with feet together, apart.
2. Strengthen and tighten other muscles, ligaments, and tendons on the medial aspect of the foot by inversion exercises.
3. Stretch the tight muscles, ligaments, and tendons on the lateral aspect of the foot.

FIGURE 14.33

Assessment of severity of flatfoot. (*A*) *Feiss line method:* Arrow shows approximate location of navicular bone in normal foot on left and third-degree flatfoot on right. (*B*) *Helbing's sign method:* Arrow denoting straight Achilles tendon on left shows normal foot; arrow denoting Achilles tendon flaring inward on right shows flatfoot. Note that in both (*A*) and (*B*) flatfoot is accompanied by pronation.

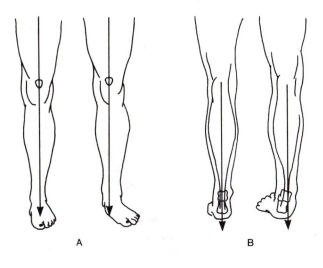

FIGURE 14.34

Medial view of foot illustrating pain centers and structures that support the longitudinal arch. Pain centers are (*A*) under metatarsal-phalangeal joints, (*B*) where the plantar ligaments are attached to the calcaneus, (*C*) under navicular, and (*D*) middorsum, where shoelaces tie.

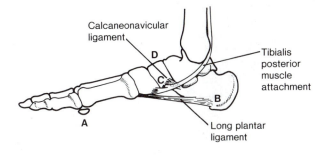

Fallen Arches

Fallen or broken arches, in the layperson's language, are sprains of the ligaments that normally provide support for the longitudinal arch (see Figure 14.34). These sprains are classified as traumatic or static. *Traumatic arch sprain* is caused by violent stretching of one or more ligaments. *Static sprain* is the term given to arches that are more or less permanently lowered because the ligaments are too elongated to maintain the tarsals and metatarsals in their respective positions. The condition cannot be traced to a particular injury. Instead, it is the result of continuous stress on the longitudinal arch like, for instance, that imposed by obesity. For persons with these problems, arch supports and adequate strapping should be prerequisites for participation in physical education. In addition, the student should practice prescribed foot exercises daily for strengthening the tibials and improving foot alignment.

FIGURE 14.35

Absence of big toe affects balance and locomotor efficiency.

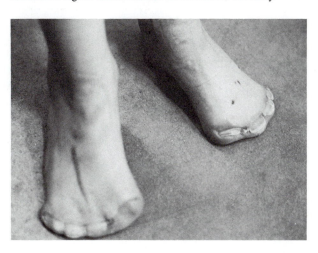

Pain Centers

Examinations of the feet should include questions concerning pain or discomfort in the following five "pain centers" of the foot: sole of the foot under the metatarsal-phalangeal joints; sole of the foot close to the heel where the plantar ligaments attach to the calcaneus; under the surface of the navicular; middorsum, where shoelaces tie; and the outer surface of the sole of the foot, where most of the weight is borne (see Figure 14.34). These areas should be inspected closely for thicknesses and other abnormalities.

Syndactylism

Extra toes, the absence of toes, or the webbing of toes all affect mechanical efficiency in locomotor activities (see Figure 14.35), but a child with good coordination can learn to compensate well enough to achieve recognition as an outstanding athlete. An example is Tom Dempsey, stellar kicker for the Philadelphia Eagles of the National Football Conference, who has part of his kicking foot missing.

Webbing of toes is usually corrected surgically, and extra toes may be removed to facilitate purchase of shoes. The most debilitating defect is absence of the big toe, which plays a major role in static balance and in the push-off phase of locomotor activities.

Hallux Valgus (Bunion)

Hallux is the Latin word for "big toe" and *valgus* is a descriptive adjective meaning "bent outward." Hence, *hallux valgus* is a marked deviation of the big toe toward the four lesser toes. This adduction at the first metatarsophalangeal joint causes shoes to exert undue pressure against the medial aspect of the head of the first metatarsal, where a bursa (sac of synovial fluid) is present in the joint. This bursa may change as a result of the pressure exerted by the shoe. If the bursa enlarges, it is called a *bunion,* the Greek word for "turnip" (see Figure 14.36). This phenomenon happens so often that the terms *bunion* and *hallux valgus* are used as

FIGURE 14.36

Bunion limits flexion of big toe.

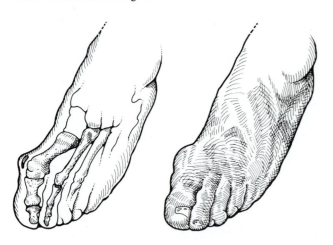

synonyms. If the bursa becomes inflamed, it is called *bursitis*. If the irritation results in a deposit of additional calcium on the first metatarsal head, this new growth is called an *exostosis*.

References

Cailliet, R. (1975). *Scoliosis: Diagnosis and management*. Philadelphia: F. A. Davis.

Harter, S. (1988). *Manual for the Self-Perception Profile for Adolescents*. Denver, CO: Author.

Johnson, C. M., Catherman, G. D., & Spiro, S. H. (1981). Improving posture in a cerebral palsied child with response-contingent music. *Education and Treatment of Children, 4* (3), 243–251.

Keim, H. (1972). *Scoliosis*. Summit, NJ: Ciba Pharmaceutical.

Lowman, C. L., & Young, C. H. (1960). *Postural fitness*. Philadelphia: Lea & Febiger.

O'Brien, F., & Azrin, N. H. (1970). Behavioral engineering: Control of posture by informational feedback. *Journal of Applied Behavior Analysis, 3*, 235–240.

Rathbone, J., & Hunt, V. V. (1965). *Corrective physical education* (7th ed.). Philadelphia: W. B. Saunders.

Rowe, A. S., & Caldwell, W. E. (1963). The somatic apperception test. *Journal of General Psychology, 68*, 59–69.

Rubin, H., O'Brien, T., Ayllon, T., & Roll, D. (1968). Behavioral engineering: Postural control by a portable operant apparatus. *Journal of Applied Behavior Analysis, 1*, 99–108.

Sheldon, W. H. (1954). *Atlas of man: A guide for somatotyping of adult males at all ages*. New York: Harper & Row.

Sherrill, C. (1980). Posture training as a means of normalization. *Mental Retardation, 18*, 135–138.

Tiller, J., Stygar, M. K., Hess, C., & Reimer, L. (1982). Treatment of functional chronic stooped posture using a training device and behavior therapy. *Physical Therapy, 11*, 1597–1600.

Zakahi, W., & Duran, R. (1988). Physical attractiveness as a contributing factor to loneliness. *Psychological Reports, 63*, 747–751.

CHAPTER

15

Relaxation and Reduction of Hyperactivity

FIGURE   15.1

Concentrating on body parts.

After you have studied this chapter, you should be able to:

1. State behavioral objectives for relaxation training and indicate a method of evaluating whether these objectives are being met.
2. Describe assessment techniques for determining hypertension.
3. Demonstrate ability to use the following approaches to teaching relaxation: imagery, deep body awareness, Jacobson techniques, static stretching exercises, yoga, and Tai Chi.
4. List and discuss suggestions for reducing hyperactivity.

Instruction and practice in relaxation are integral parts of comprehensive adapted physical activity. One of the nine goals of adapted physical activity is *fun/tension release*. Work in this area focuses on improvement of mental health through activity involvement and reduction of stress and hyperactivity through relaxation techniques, counseling, and behavior management.

Relaxation instruction is sometimes combined with body image training, particularly with young students (see Figure 15.1). Children must be able to recognize body parts before relaxation of body parts can be learned. Relaxation, defined physiologically, is a neuromuscular accomplishment that results in a reduction of muscular tension. Tension is the amount of electrical activity present in a muscle. The shortening of muscle fibers is attended by an increase of electrical voltage. *Shortening, contracting,* and *tightening* are synonyms in the sense that each implies increased muscle tension. The release of tension within a muscle is attended by a decrease of electrical voltage, which is expressed in microvolts or millivolts. Complete muscle relaxation is characterized by electrical silence—that is, zero action potentials.

Neuromuscular tension is a positive attribute. No movement can occur without the development of tension in the appropriate muscle groups. Unfortunately, however, many persons maintain more muscles in a state of tension than is necessary for the accomplishment of motor tasks. Such excessive neuromuscular tension is known as *hypertension,* not to be confused with arterial hypertension. The purpose of relaxation training is to prevent or reduce hypertension.

Not all persons need relaxation training. Individual differences in tension should be assessed, and only students who exhibit abnormal signs should be assigned to relaxation and slowing-down activities in lieu of the vigorous activities that traditionally comprise the physical education program.

Signs of Hypertension

Knowledge of the signs of hypertension enables you to assess, write specific behavioral objectives, and plan remediation. The following are signs of hypertension that should be assessed and included in the objectives you write.

1. **Hyperactivity.** Inability to remain motionless for set period of time; wriggles in chair; shifts arm or leg; plays with hair; scratches, rubs or picks at skin; makes noises with feet; drums fingers on desktop or doodles with pen; chews gum, pencil, or fingernails; fails to keep place in line or any set formation.

2. **Facial expression.** Lines in face seldom disappear; eyes frequently shift focus; lips quiver or seem abnormally tight; cheek muscles show tension; immobile expression, such as frozen smile or incessant frown; eye tic.

3. **Breathing.** Unconscious breath holding; shallow, irregular breaths; hyperventilation.

4. **Skin.** Nervous perspiration; irritations caused by picking; hives, eczema.

5. **Voice.** Two opposite patterns, the more common of which is talking too much, louder than usual, faster than usual, and with higher pitch; deep sighs indicating excessive respiratory tension; crying.

6. **Sadness.** Manifested by slouched postures, slowness in thought and action, difficulty with concentration, inability to cope, failure to laugh and enjoy activities that are designed to be fun and relaxing.

7. **Muscle tightness.** Tension and sometimes pain, usually most prevalent in face, neck, and back.

These signs are characteristic of persons on the verge of emotional breakdowns, but they also appear in times of great stress, such as final examination periods, death or severe illness in family, impending divorce of parents, and/or incessant bickering among family members. Certain prescribed drugs, such as diet pills, and also those consumed illegally, result in overt signs of hyperactivity. Constant physical pain or discomfort is sometimes evidenced in signs of hypertension.

When the problems causing hypertension are not resolved over long periods of time, the sufferers slip into a state of *chronic fatigue.* They often experience insomnia. When they do sleep, they typically awaken unrested. Symptoms of chronic fatigue are (a) increase of tendon reflexes, (b) increase of muscle excitability, (c) spastic condition of smooth muscles exhibited in diarrhea and stomach upsets, (d) abnormal excitability of heart and respiratory apparatus, (e) tremors, (f) restlessness, and (g) irritability. In this stage, many persons seek the help of a physician; generally, they complain of feeling tired all of the time. They know they are not really sick, but neither do they feel well.

Hypertension in Children

In the past, hypertension has been associated more with adults than children. Now, however, many hyperactive youngsters, especially those with learning disabilities, are recognized as

FIGURE 15.2

Imagery as a relaxation technique is often enhanced by giving the children props like scarves, ribbons, or towels.

exhibiting signs of neuromuscular hypertension that can be ameliorated through relaxation training (Brandon, Eason, & Smith, 1986; Cautela & Groden, 1978). Likewise, may essentially *normal* persons are simply high-strung, just as others are slow moving and easygoing. Levels of hypertension seem to be largely determined by heredity and reinforced by the environment.

Children who need training in tension reduction may feel guilty about the hypertension, particularly if they have been led to believe that they are different from others in the household. Many children deny that they feel tense. Others, accustomed to hypertension, do not realize that conditions of less tension exist.

Testing for Excess Tension

Awareness of residual hypertension can be developed by instructing students to lie on their backs and release all tensions. Then you lift one body part at a time and let go. Record the degree of hypertonus present as *negative, slight, medium,* or *marked* on the right and left sides for the muscles of the wrist, elbow, shoulder, ankle, knee, hip, and neck. Hypertonus is detected by such *unconscious* muscular responses as

1. **Assistance.** Student assists you in lifting the body part.
2. **Posturing or set.** Student resists gravity when you remove support.
3. **Resistance.** Student tenses or resists your lifting the body part.
4. **Perseveration.** Student continues a movement after you start it.

The presence of residual hypertension can be assessed also through electromyography. It is now being used in several programs of relaxation therapy for children with learning disabilities. The electromyometer, like any electromyographical apparatus, records the amount of electrical activity present in the muscle fibers. Biofeedback in the form of sound and a digital readout reinforces attempts to reduce tension, making the apparatus effective both as a teaching and an evaluation device.

Teaching Relaxation

Techniques of teaching relaxation vary with the age group, the nature of the disability, and the number of class sessions to be spent. Each of the techniques described in this section aims at lowering the tension—that is, the electrical activity of skeletal muscles. With the exception of the Jacobson techniques, few have been subjected to scientific research. Although their effectiveness may not be substantiated statistically, each of the various techniques has strong proponents and is worthy of exploration. Imagery, deep body awareness, the Jacobson techniques, static stretching exercises, yoga, and Tai Chi are considered. Breathing exercises are also important in relaxation training.

Imagery

The *imagery* or ideational approach is well received in the primary grades (see Figure 15.2). Poems and short stories are excellent to help children become rag dolls flopping, ice cream melting, merry-go-rounds stopping, balloons slowly deflating, icicles melting, faucets dripping, salt pouring from

FIGURE 15.3

Two girls with Down syndrome participate in a deep body awareness relaxation activity at the close of their physical education class. This constitutes a "cool-down" time to help them make the transition from strenuous motor work to quiet academic learning.

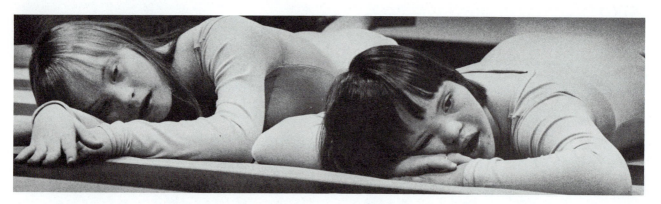

a shaker, bubbles getting smaller, and snowflakes drifting downward. For greatest effectiveness, draw the children into discussions of what relaxes them and encourage them to make up their own stories and poems. Asking children to develop lists of their favorite *quiet* things and *slow* activities is also enlightening. Focus on enacting things that start out fast, gradually decrease in speed, and eventually become motionless.

Some ideational approaches used to elicit relaxed movements follow:

You are a soft calico kitten lying in front of the warm fireplace. The fire is warm. You feel so-o-o good. First, you stretch your right arm—oh, that feels good. Then you stretch your left arm. Then you stretch both legs. Now you are relaxed all over. The fire is so warm and your body feels so relaxed. This must be the best place in the whole world—your own little blanket in front of your own fire. You are so-o-o relaxed that you could fall asleep right now. You are getting sleepy now—maybe you will fall asleep now.

You are the tail of a kite that is sailing gently high, oh so-o-o high in the light blue sky. The kite goes higher and so do you—very slowly and very gently in the soft breeze. Now you are going to the right. Oh, the breeze is warm and ooh so soft—it is blowing so gently that you can feel it only if you think real hard. Can you feel the soft, warm breeze blowing you to the left? It is so-o-o gentle and so-o-o soft.

You are becoming a puppet. The change starts in your feet. Slowly, each part of your body becomes lifeless and is completely relaxed, as if it were detached from you.

Let's make believe we are a bowl full of jello! Someone has left us out of the refrigerator, and we begin to dissolve slowly away. Our arms float down, and our body sinks slowly into the bowl.

Older children, no longer able to assume magically the feeling/tone of an animal or object, continue to find relaxation in the mood of certain poems and stories read aloud. They may lie in comfortable positions in a semidarkened room while listening and attempt to capture the essence of the words through consciously releasing tensions. Instrumental music may be substituted for reading if the group desires. Surburg (1989) discusses imagery techniques for special populations.

Deep Body Awareness

To facilitate deep body awareness, begin the class with everyone in a comfortable supine position (see Figure 15.3). Then direct everyone's attention to specific parts of the body, asking them to analyze and verbalize the sensations they are experiencing. If students seem reluctant to share aloud their feelings, offer such additional guidance as

1. Which parts of your arm are touching the floor? Is the floor warm or cool, smooth or rough, clean or dirty?
2. How long is your arm from the tip of the middle finger to the shoulder joint? From the tip of the middle finger to the elbow? From the tip of the middle finger to the wrist crease? How heavy is your arm? How heavy is each of its parts?
3. Can you feel the muscles loosening? If you measured the circumference of your upper arm, how many inches would you get?
4. Can you feel the blood pulsating in veins and arteries?
5. Can you feel the hairs on your arm? The creases in your wrist? Your fingernails? The cuticles? Any scars?
6. What other words come to mind when you think about *arm*?

The underlying premise in deep body awareness is that students must increase kinesthetic sensitivity before they can consciously control it. They must differentiate among parts of a whole and be able to describe these parts accurately. As deep body awareness is developed, each student discovers which thoughts and methods of releasing tension work best for him or her personally.

Deep body awareness should progress from other-directed to self-directed states. The latter is called autogenesis (self-generating). The activities described in this section are often called *autogenic training.*

Jacobson Techniques

Most widely known of the techniques of neuromuscular relaxation are those of Edmund Jacobson, a physician and physiologist who began his research in tension control at

Harvard University in 1918. His first two books, *Progressive Relaxation* and *You Must Relax,* were published in 1920 and 1934, respectively. Jacobson's work had a profound influence on Josephine Rathbone, the foremost pioneer in corrective physical education, who taught relaxation as an integral part of correctives. Rathbone's books (1969; Rathbone & Hunt, 1965) continue to be excellent primary sources.

Jacobson's techniques, known originally as a system of *progressive conscious neuromuscular relaxation,* are referred to as *self-operations control* in his later books (Jacobson, 1970). The progression of activities is essentially the same. He suggests three steps for learning to recognize the sensations of *doing* and *not doing* in any specific muscle group: (a) tension followed by relaxation against an outside resistance, such as the teacher pushing downward on a limb that the student is trying to lift; (b) tension within the muscle group when no outside resistance is offered, followed by release of the tension; and (c) release of tension in a resting muscle group that has not been contracted.

Jacobson recommends that relaxation training begin in a supine position with arms at the sides, palms facing downward. The mastery of *differential control* of one muscle group at a time begins with hyperextension at the wrist joint only. All other joints in the body remain relaxed while the student concentrates on bending the hand backward. The resulting tension is felt in the back upper part of the forearm.

Self-operations control outlined by Jacobson is a slow procedure. Each class session is 1 hr long. During that time, a particular tension, like hyperextension of the wrist, is practiced only three times. The tension (also called the control sensation) is held 1 to 2 min, after which the student is told to *go negative* or completely relax for 3 to 4 min. After the completion of three of these tension and relaxation sequences, the student lies quietly with eyes closed for the remainder of the hour. Session 2 follows the same pattern except that the tension practiced is bending the wrist forward so as to tense the anterior muscles of the forearm. Every third session is called a zero period in that no tension is practiced. The entire body is relaxed the whole time.

In all, seven sessions are recommended for learning to relax the left arm. During the fourth session, the tension created by bending the elbow about 35° is practiced. During the fifth session, the tension created in the back part of the upper arm when the palm presses downward against a stack of books is practiced. The sixth session is a zero period. The seventh session calls for progressive tension and relaxation of the whole arm.

Detailed instructions are given for proceeding from one muscle group to the next. The completion of an entire course in relaxation in the supine position requires the following amount of time: left arm, 7 days; right arm, 7 days; left leg, 10 days; right leg, 10 days; trunk, 10 days; neck, 6 days; eye region, 12 days; visualization, 9 days; and speech region, 19 days. Then the same order and same duration of practices are followed in the sitting position. While Jacobson indicates that the course can be speeded up, he emphasizes that less thoroughness results in reduced ability to recognize tension signals and turn them off. Almost all textbooks on stress reduction describe Jacobson techniques (Girdano, Everly, & Dusek, 1990; Greenberg, 1990).

Static Stretching Exercises

To illustrate the efficacy of static stretching, try these experiments, holding each position for 60 sec or longer:

1. Let the head drop forward as far as it will go. Hold this position and feel the stretch on the neck extensors.
2. Let the body bend at the waist, as in touching the toes. When the fingertips touch the floor, hold, and feel the stretch in the back extensors and hamstrings.
3. Do a side bend to the left and hold.
4. Lie supine on a narrow bench and let your head hang over the edge.
5. Lie on a narrow bench and let the arms hang down motionless in space. They should not be able to touch the ground.

When students learn to release tension in these static positions, relaxation is achieved. Yoga, because it is based upon such static stretching, is often included in instructional units on relaxation.

Yoga

Yoga is a system of physical, mental, and spiritual development that comes from India, where it dates back several centuries before Christ (Hittleman, 1983; Isaacson, 1990). The word *yoga* is derived from the Sanskrit root *yuji,* which means "to join or bind together." Scholars recognize several branches of yoga, but in the United States, the term is used popularly to refer to a system of exercises built upon held positions or postures and breath control. More correctly, you should say *Hatha Yoga* rather than yoga when teaching aspects of this system to your students. In the word *Hatha,* the *ha* represents the sun (expression of energy) and the *tha* represents the moon (conservation of energy). In yoga exercises, these two are always interacting.

Hatha Yoga offers exercises particularly effective in teaching relaxation and slowing down the hyperactive child (Hopkins & Hopkins, 1976). The emphasis upon correct breathing in Hatha Yoga makes it especially valuable in the reconditioning of persons with asthma and other respiratory problems. Moreover, the nature of Hatha Yoga is such that it appeals to individuals whose health status prohibits participation in vigorous, strenuous physical activities.

Hatha Yoga, hereafter referred to as yoga, can be subdivided into two types of exercises: *asanas* and *pranayanas.* Asanas are held positions or postures like the lotus, the locust, and cobra poses. Pranayanas are breathing exercises. In actuality, asanas and pranayanas are interrelated since correct breathing is emphasized throughout the assumption of a particular pose. Several of the asanas are identical or similar to stunts taught in elementary school physical education. The yoga *bent bow* is the same as the human rocker. The *cobra* is similar to the swan and/or the trunk lift from a prone position to test back strength. The *plough pose* resembles the paint-the-rainbow stunt.

Differences between yoga and physical exercise as it is ordinarily taught are

1. Exercise sessions traditionally emphasize movement. *Yoga is exercise without movement.*

2. Exercises usually involve several bounces or stretches, with emphasis upon how many can be done. Yoga stresses a *single, slow* contraction of certain muscles followed by a general relaxation. Generally, an asana is not repeated. At the very most, it might be attempted two or three times.

3. Exercises usually entail some pain and discomfort since the teaching progression conforms to the overload principle. In yoga, the number of repetitions is not increased. The duration of time for which the asana is held increases in accordance with ease of performance.

4. Exercises ordinarily stress the development of strength, flexibility, and endurance. Yoga stresses relaxation, balance, and self-control.

In summary,

The gymnast's object is to make his body strong and healthy, with well-developed muscles, a broad chest, and powerful arms. The yogi will get more or less the same results; but they are not what he is looking for.

He is looking for calm, peace, the remedy for fatigue; or, better still, a certain immunity to fatigue.

He wants to quiet some inclination or other of his, his tendency to anger, or impatience—signs of disturbance in his organic or psychical life. He wants a full life, a more abundant life, but a life of which he is the master. (Dechanet, 1965, p. 18)

Tai Chi

T'ai Chi Ch'uan, pronounced *tie jee chwahn* and called Tai Chi for short, is one of the many slowing-down activities found to be successful with hyperactive children (Kuo, 1991; Maisel, 1972). An increasing number of U.S. adults also practice this ancient Chinese system of exercise. In large metropolitan areas on the East and West coasts, instruction from masters, usually listed in the telephone directory, is available. Tai Chi is used by many dance therapists.

Tai Chi is a series of 108 specific learned patterns of movements called *forms* that provide exercise for every part of the body. The forms have colorful names that tend to captivate children: Grasp Bird's Tail Right, Stork Spreads Wings, Carry Tiger to Mountain, Step Back and Repulse Monkey, Needle at Sea Bottom, High Pat on Horse, Parting with Wild Horse's Mane Right. The 108 forms are based upon 37 basic movements; thus, there is much repetition in the execution of a series of forms.

Tai Chi is characterized by extreme slowness, a concentrated awareness of what one is doing, and absolute continuity of movement from one form to another. The same tempo is maintained throughout, but no musical accompaniment is provided. All movements contain circles, reinforcing the concepts of uninterrupted flow and quiet continuity. All body parts are gently curved or bent, allowing the body to give into gravity rather than working against it, as is the usual practice in western culture. No posture or pose is ever held. As each form is approximately completed, its movement begins to melt and blend into the next form. This has been likened to the cycle of seasons, when summer blends into autumn and autumn into winter.

Although instruction by a master is desirable, Tai Chi is simple enough that it can be learned from a pictorial text. Movements can be memorized by repeatedly performing forms 1 to 20 in the same order without interruption. One form should never be practiced in isolation from others. Later, forms 21 to 57 are learned as a unity, as well as forms 58 to 108. This approach is especially beneficial for children who need practice in visual perception, matching, and sequencing. Its greatest strength, however, lies in the principle of slowness. Each time the sequence of forms is done, day after day, year after year, the goal is to perform it more slowly than before.

For persons who feel disinclined to memorize and teach preestablished forms, the essence of Tai Chi can be captured by restructuring class calisthenics as a follow-the-leader experience in which flowing, circular movements are reproduced as slowly as possible without breaking the continuity of the sequence. For real relaxation to occur, the same sequence must be repeated daily.

Suggestions for Reducing Hyperactivity

The etiology of hyperactivity is generally unknown. One has only to observe a new litter of kittens or puppies to note substantial differences in levels of activity, energy, and aggressiveness. What keeps children keyed up? How can hyperactivity be channeled into productivity? How can hyperactivity be reduced?

A common misconception is the belief that regular physical education provides an outlet for releasing excessive nervous tensions and letting off steam. This may be true on some days for a few of the better coordinated youngsters who find satisfaction in large motor activities. It is not a valid supposition, however, when physical education is an instructional setting in which students are introduced daily to new learning activities. Hyperactive children have just as much trouble listening to the physical educator and conforming to the structure of the play setting as they experience in the classroom. The mastery of a new motor skill, or even the practice of an old one, is no more relaxing than reading or learning to play the piano.

Once a skill is refined and is performed without conscious thought, it can become a channel for releasing tensions. Simple repetitive activities like jogging and swimming laps may serve this purpose for some individuals, just as knitting, gardening, or playing the piano is soothing to others. A good physical education program, however, devotes little of its time allotment to such repetitive activities. *Letting off steam* simply is not an objective of the regular physical education program.

Hyperactive children need vigorous physical activity, as do all students. Whereas normal children typically make the transition from play to classroom work without special help, hyperactive children require a longer period of time and assistance in making the adjustment. *This is not a reason for excusing them from physical education.* It does call for recognition of individual differences and the availability of a quiet, semidark area where children can lie down and practice relaxation techniques before returning to the classroom. Large cardboard boxes that children can creep into and hide are recommended for the primary grades. When a place free from noise cannot be found, earphones with music or a soothing voice giving relaxation instruction can be used to block out distractions. The use of this quiet space should not be limited to a particular time of day or to certain children. All persons, at one time or another, need a retreat where they can go of their own accord, relax, and regain self-control.

If several children appear to be especially hyperactive during a physical education period, end the vigorous activity early and devote the last 10 min or so to relaxation training. Changes of weather—particularly the onset of rain—seem to heighten neuromuscular tensions. Examinations, special events, and crises carried by the news media may have students so keyed up that the best physical education for the entire class is rest and relaxation. Certainly, physical educators should ask themselves at the beginning of each period, "Do the students need slowing down or speeding up? Is any one child especially keyed up? Which activity can that child be guided into before a discipline problem occurs?"

Hyperactivity can be reduced only if the causes are eliminated. The following adaptations seem to help the hyperactive child retain self-control in the activity setting:

1. Decrease the space. If outdoors, rope off boundaries. If indoors, use partitions.

2. Decrease the noise by arranging for smaller classes and using yarn balls and beanbags rather than rubber balls. Use verbal stop and start signals instead of a whistle. Do not tell the children to be quiet; inhibiting their natural inclination to shout, run, jump, and throw only raises tension levels.

3. Structure the activities so that the children do not have to wait in lines and take turns. Good physical education implies maximal involvement of all the children all the time. Each pupil should have his or her own ball, rope, or piece of apparatus.

4. Designate certain spaces such as learning stations and use the same direction of rotation each period. If necessary, rope or partition off these stations to minimize distractions.

5. Deemphasize speed by stressing accuracy and self-control.

6. Avoid speed tests. This approach necessitates a whole new look at measurement and evaluation in physical education. On a paper-pencil test, do not count questions that are not answered as wrong. Instead, send the child home with a similar test and instruction to repeatedly practice taking it until he or she can answer all questions accurately within a set time limit. This may require 10 trials for some children and 50 for others. Learning to cope with speed tests, however, should take place in a nonthreatening situation.

7. Avoid relays based upon the team or individual who can finish the fastest. Instead, experiment with different concepts: Who can go the slowest? Who can use the most interesting movement pattern? Who can be the most graceful? Who can be the most original? Who can create the funniest movement pattern?

8. Build in success. Even a hyperactive child will remain motionless to hear himself or herself praised. Much of the residual neuromuscular tension that characterizes certain children stems from failure and fear of failure. After success in a new motor skill has been achieved, stop the student while he or she feels positive about the effort and direct attention to something new.

References

Brandon, J. E., Eason, R. L., & Smith, T. J. (1986). Behavioral relaxation training and motor performance of learning disabled children with hyperactive behaviors. *Adapted Physical Activity Quarterly, 3,* 67–79.

Cautela, J., & Groden, J. (1978). *Relaxation: A comprehensive manual for adults, children, and children with special needs.* Champaign, IL: Research Press.

Dechanet, J.M. (1965). *Yoga in ten lessons.* New York: Cornerstone Library.

Girdano, D., Everly, G., & Dusek, D. (1990). *Controlling stress and tension: A holistic approach* (3rd ed.). Englewood Cliffs, NJ: Prentice-Hall.

Greenberg, J. (1990). *Comprehensive stress management* (3rd ed.). Dubuque, IA: Wm. C. Brown.

Hittleman, R. (1983). *Yoga for health.* New York: Ballantine.

Hopkins, L. J., & Hopkins, J. T. (1976). Yoga in psychomotor training. *Academic Therapy, 11,* 461–464.

Isaacson, C. (1990). *Yoga step by step.* London: Butler and Tanner.

Jacobson, E. (1920). *Progressive relaxation.* Chicago: University of Chicago Press. (Second edition in 1938.)

Jacobson, E. (1934). *You must relax.* New York: McGraw-Hill. (Second edition in 1970.)

Jacobson, E. (1970). *Modern treatment of tense patients.* Springfield, IL: Charles C. Thomas.

Kuo, S. (1991). *Long life, good health through Tai Chi Chuan.* Berkeley, CA: North Atlantic Books.

Maisel, E. (1972). *Tai Chi for health.* New York: Holt, Rinehart, & Winston.

Rathbone, J. (1969). *Relaxation.* Philadelphia: Lea & Febiger.

Rathbone, J., & Hunt, V. (1965). *Corrective physical education* (7th ed.). Philadelphia: W.B. Saunders.

Surburg, P. R. (1989). Application of imagery techniques to special populations. *Adapted Physical Activity Quarterly, 6* (4), 328–337.

CHAPTER

16

Adapted Dance and Dance Therapy

with coauthor Wynelle Delaney, DTR

FIGURE   16.1

Anne Riordan of the University of Utah demonstrates modern dance
skills and choreography to adolescents with disabilities.

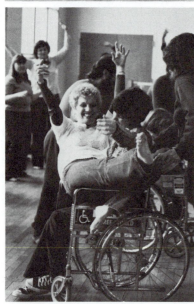

After you have studied this chapter, you should be able to:

1. Discuss the similarities and differences between adapted dance and dance therapy.

2. Identify two broad pedagogical approaches and discuss the types of dance associated with each. Evaluate your experience with each type and develop a personal learning plan for enhancing knowledge and skill.

3. Explain why creative dance is recommended as a first form of movement education for children and discuss the movement and rhythm elements associated with creative dance.

4. Discuss the assessment and teaching of rhythmic patterns when persons have temporal perception problems. Design and try out activities for teaching even and uneven rhythmic patterns.

5. Identify and discuss activities especially recommended for (a) increasing body awareness, (b) improving relationships, and (c) expressing feelings. Relate your ideas to emotional disturbance and behavioral disorders.

6. Explain how dance therapy materials, principles, and tools can be used in adapted physical activity teaching and counseling. Give concrete examples.

It is beautifully apparent that dance and the child are natural companions. If, as Merleau Ponty suggests, our bodies are our way of having a world, the child is busily at home in his own body forming and shaping his own world, its inner and outer hemispheres. He is making himself up as he goes along.
—*Nancy W. Smith*

Perhaps no part of the physical education curriculum is as important to students with disabilities as creative rhythmic movement boldly and imaginatively taught. It can be enjoyed by the nonambulatory in beds and wheelchairs, by other health impaired persons who need mild range-of-motion exercise, and by the thousands of youngsters who find greater fulfillment in individual and dual activities than in team sports. Whereas much of physical education focuses upon cooperation, competition, and leadership-followership, creative dance offers opportunities for self-discovery and self-expression.

Children must understand and appreciate their bodies and their capacities for movement before they can cope with the world's external demands. The additional barriers to self-understanding and self-acceptance imposed by a disability intensify the need for carefully guided nonthreatening movement experiences designed to preserve ego strength, increase trust, and encourage positive human relationships. Gesture, pantomime, dance, and dance-drama can substitute for verbal communication when children lack or mistrust words to express their feelings. *Dance programming is particularly important for people with emotional disturbances, behavioral disorders, and learning disabilities.*

Distinction Between Adapted Dance and Dance Therapy

It is important to differentiate between dance as a therapeutic experience, dance therapy as a profession, and adapted dance. Prior to the formation of the American Dance Therapy Association, Inc. (ADTA), in 1966, little distinction between terms was made. Dance conducted with persons with disabilities was typically called dance therapy. Today, the term *dance therapy* is used for dance/movement conducted by persons registered as dance therapists with the ADTA. In this sense, dance therapy is like physical therapy and occupational therapy. Dance specialists and others who are not registered therapists may use dance with populations who are disabled and/or for therapeutic purposes, but they may not ethically describe their work as dance therapy. So what do we call dance designed to meet the educational and artistic needs of persons with special needs?

Adapted Dance

Adapted dance is a term appropriate to denote rhythmic movement instruction and/or experiences that are modified to meet the needs of persons who have significant learning, behavioral, or psychomotor problems that interfere with successful participation in programs of regular dance in education and art. *Adapt* means to make suitable, to adjust, to accommodate, or to modify in accordance with needs. These needs may be developmental or environmental. Dance specialists may *adapt* curriculum content, instructional pedagogy, assessment and evaluation approaches, and physical environment; the essence of this process of adapting is personal creativity.

Adapted dance focuses on the identification and remediation of problems within the psychomotor domain in individuals who need assistance in mainstream dance instruction and/or specially designed educational and artistic experiences. The use of adapted dance is not limited to persons with disabilities, but encompasses such special populations as the aged, juvenile delinquents and criminals, substance abusers, pregnant women, and our nation's many obese and/or unfit citizens. It also provides specialized help for clumsy persons, for whom dance instruction, in the presence of the graceful and the beautiful, is often a nightmare.

Adapted dance, like adapted physical education, is first and foremost an attitude that refuses to categorize human beings into special populations, such as the aged or the mentally retarded, and instead celebrates individual differences.

Adapted dance is conceptualized especially for persons who are not comfortable and/or successful (for whatever reason) in the regular dance setting. The purpose of adapted dance, like adapted physical education, is to facilitate self-actualization, particularly as it relates to understanding and appreciation of the body and its capacity for movement. The resulting changes in psychomotor behavior eventually permit full or partial integration in regular dance as a joyous, fulfilling experience.

Adapted dance can be used to achieve any of the nine goals of adapted physical activity. A job of the specialist is to determine whether dance, sports, or aquatics is more personally meaningful to the student.

Adapted dance can be education, art, or recreation. It can also be therapeutic, but it is not therapy. The foremost pioneer in adapted dance, particularly in exploring its potential as a performing art, is Anne Riordan (see Figure 16.1), in the Modern Dance Department at the University of Utah (Fitt & Riordan, 1980). In a film titled *A Very Special Dance*, marketed by the National Dance Association, Riordan demonstrates dance as both education and art with persons who have disabilities and are members of the performing group called SUNRISE.

Dance Therapy

The official ADTA (circa 1975) definition of *dance therapy* is as follows:

Dance therapy is the psychotherapeutic use of movement as a process which furthers the emotional and physical integration of the individual. Dance therapy is distinguished from other utilizations of dance (for example, dance education) by its focus on the nonverbal aspects of behavior and its use of movement as the process for intervention. Adaptive, expressive, and communicative behaviors are all considered in treatment, with the expressed goal of integrating these behaviors with psychological aspects of the person. Dance therapy can function as a primary treatment modality or as an integral part of an overall treatment program.

This explanation stresses the use of dance/movement as nonverbal psychotherapy requiring a therapeutic contract between therapist and client. Thus, dance therapy is a specific treatment modality used in mental illness and emotional and behavioral problems. Dance therapy is not prescribed for other disabilities (like mental retardation and orthopedic impairment) unless the individual has emotional problems that require nonverbal psychotherapy.

Similarities of Adapted Dance and Dance Therapy

Both the dance educator and the dance therapist rely heavily on the medium of creative dance to accomplish certain objectives. Dance education can be therapeutic, just as dance therapy can be educational. Certainly, the adapted physical educator who uses creative dance as a means of helping children with disabilities to understand and appreciate their bodies and their movement capabilities is engaged in a therapeutic endeavor. But the work should not be considered dance therapy anymore than physical therapy or occupational therapy. Since the incorporation of the ADTA in May of 1966, dance therapy has gained increasing recognition as an independent profession.

Table 16.1
Two Pedagogical Approaches and Types of Dance.

Guided Discovery	Explanation-Demonstration-Drill
Creative or modern dance with emphasis on	*Many types of dance including*
• Space (shape, level, size, path, focus)	Singing games
	Marching/clapping
• Time or rhythm (beat, accent pattern, phrasing)	Tap and clog
	Folk and square
• Force, effort, or weight	Social and ballroom
Heavy → Light	Aerobic
Strong → Weak	Ballet
• Flow	
Free → Bound	
Fluent → Inhibited	

Adapted Dance in the Curriculum

Dance is an integral part of physical education. As such, it must be given the same amount of time and emphasis in the curriculum as other program areas. Table 16.1 groups types of dance according to teaching style. Each type teaches a set body of knowledge and skills that enrich living. Students with disabilities need exposure to dance both as a participant and observer (Boswell, 1989; Jay, 1991; Roswal, Sherrill, and Roswal, 1988; Schmitz, 1989). Field trips to dance events broaden horizons on use of leisure time and make school-based instruction more meaningful.

The method of teaching (guided discovery or explanation-demonstration-drill) determines outcomes. Guided discovery, linked with creative and modern dance, is similar to movement education (Laban, 1960; Sherborne, 1987). One goal is to develop understanding of *movement elements* (space, time, force, and flow) and ways they can be used to create compositions depicting ideas, feelings, or themes. A second goal is to develop motor skills and fitness to create and perform. Other goals (self-concept, social competence, etc.) parallel those of adapted physical activity. Creative dance is recommended as the first form of movement education for children (Fleming, 1973; Jay, 1991; Joyce, 1984). It is appropriate for children ages 3 and up who understand language. In middle school and high school, terminology changes from *creative dance* to *modern dance*.

With exploration-demonstration-drill pedagogy, dance can be a medium for perceptual-motor training, learning about cultural heritage, and achieving artistic excellence. It is particularly valuable in teaching relaxation, ameliorating rhythm and timing problems, and enhancing body image. Folk and square dance, properly conducted, can help slow learners with social studies. Singing games and rhythmic chants also help with academic learning (Bitcon, 1976; Sherrill, 1979).

Movement Elements

Both creative and modern dance focus upon the movement elements of space, time, force, and flow. Sally Fitt (Fitt & Riordan, 1980) proposed an excellent model for relating

FIGURE 16.2

Movement improvisation in which the teacher contributes to individualized education program (IEP) goals of improving both body image and balance.

movement elements to dance instruction for students with disabilities (see Figure 16.2). The *element of space* can be broken down into several factors:

1. **Direction and shape.** Right, left, forward, backward, sideward, up, down, in, out, over, under.
2. **Level of movement or of body position.** High, low, medium; lie, sit, squat, kneel, stand.
3. **Dimension or size.** Large, small, wide, narrow, tall, short.
4. **Path of movement.** Direct (straight) or indirect (curved, zigzag, twisted, crooked).
5. **Focus of eyes.** Constant, wandering, near, far, up, down, inward, outward.

The elements of time, force, and flow are explained in Table 16.1. Excellent videotapes on how to teach the movement elements to children with disabilities are available from Dr. Boni Boswell, Physical Education Department, East Carolina University, Greenville, NC 27834.

Rhythm Elements

Rhythmic structure in dance has four aspects:

1. **Pulse beat.** The underlying beat of all rhythmic structure. Can be taught as the sounds of walk or run; the ticking of a clock, watch, or metronome; the tapping of a finger; the clapping of hands; or the stamping of feet. The beats can occur in fast, medium, or slow tempos and in constant or changing rates of speed.

2. **Accent.** An emphasis—that is, an extra loud sound or extra hard movement. Syllables of words are accented, and beats of measures are accented.

3. **Rhythmic pattern.** A short series of sounds or movements superimposed on the underlying beat and described as even or uneven. Illustrative of *even* rhythmic patterns are the walk, run, hop, jump, leap, step-hop, schottische, and waltz. Illustrative of *uneven* rhythmic patterns are the gallop, slide, skip, two-step, polka, and bleking. Remember that the polka is a hop, step-close-step and the bleking is a heel, heel (slow), followed by heel-heel-heel-heel (fast). In rhythmic patterns, the duration of time between beats varies. The simplest patterns for children are as follows:

   a. *Uneven* long-short patterns, as in the gallop, skip, and slide in 6/8 tempo:

   b. *Even* twice-as-fast or twice-as-slow walking patterns in 4/4 tempo:

   Walk, ♩ ♩ ♩ ♩ 4 steps to a measure.

   Run, ♫ ♫ ♫ ♫ 8 steps to a measure.

   Slow walk, ♩ ♩ 2 steps to a measure.

4. **Musical phrasing.** The natural grouping of measures to give a temporary feeling of completion. A phrase must be at least two measures long and is the expression of a complete thought or idea in music. Phrasing may help to determine the *form* of a modern dance composition, and children should be guided in the recognition of identical phrases within a piece of music. One movement sequence is created for each musical phrase; identical phrases may suggest identical movement sequences.

Rhythm Skills

Many persons with disabilities have difficulty with rhythm. Initial lessons should focus on creative movement with the teacher beating a drum to the tempo established by the student. Make an effort to determine the child's natural rhythm—whether fast, slow, or medium tempo; whether 4/4 or 3/4 phrases; whether there is a rhythmic pattern or underlying beat; whether the child responds to accents; and whether transitions from one tempo to another are made. During this period of observation, encourage the child to make up his or her own accompaniment: with a song, a nursery rhyme, a verse, hand clapping, foot stamping, or a tambourine, drum, or jingle bells. Only after the child has given evidence of moving in time to his or her own accompaniment should you introduce the next stage—conforming to an externally imposed rhythm.

Teaching Dance and Rhythm

Some children require no special help in movement to music. They do not need adapted dance. Others, who have grown up in homes without music or who have central nervous system (CNS) deficits affecting temporal perception, must be provided a carefully designed progression of experiences broken down into parts so small that success is ensured. Wearing taps on shoes is a good reinforcer. Likewise, rhythmic instruments, used as part of a dance, promote goal mastery. Music therapists often are available to help. A succession of units might include

1. Creative movement without accompaniment in which an idea, feeling, or mood is expressed.

2. Creative movement, with the child encouraged to add sound effects.

3. Creative movement interspersed with discovery activities in which the child can beat a drum, clash cymbals, or use other rhythmic instruments as part of a dance-making process. No instructions are given on how to use the instruments. They are simply made available, along with the freedom to incorporate sounds as the child wishes.

4. Creative movement accompanied by the teacher or another student using a variety of interesting sounds that fit the child's dance making.

5. Discussions concerning what kind of accompaniment best supports the theme or idea of different movement sequences. Through problem solving, the child tells the teacher what kind of accompaniment he or she wants, the idea is tried, and the child evaluates whether or not it worked.

6. Introduction of the concept that a dance can be repeated over and over again. A dance has some kind of *form*—at least a beginning and an end—and both movements and accompaniment must be remembered so that they can be reproduced.

At this point, students learn the difference between dancing—that is, moving for pleasure—and making a dance. They are helped to see their creation as an art product that may endure like a painting or a musical composition. They take pride in organizing their movement sequences into an integrated whole and comparing their dance-making process and products with those of dance artists on the various films that can be rented. Since children with disabilities typically become adults with an abundance of leisure, spectator appreciation of modern dance and ballet should be developed concurrently with their first attempts at dance making. Perhaps a performing group from a local high school or college can be invited to demonstrate dance compositions. Expecting children to retain excitement about dance making (choreography) is futile unless they are exposed to the art products of others and led to believe that dance is a significant part of the cultural-entertainment world.

Only when dance experiences in which movement is primary and accompaniment is secondary prove successful should you introduce the study of rhythmic skills to children

known to be weak in temporal perception. These students typically will be off the beat as often as on it. They are likely to accent the wrong beat of a measure. And they may find the recognition of musical phrases hopelessly frustrating. Dance researchers have not yet designed studies to investigate the learning problems of these students. Some dance educators seem to believe that any child can keep in time with the music if he or she tries hard enough. Such is not the case! Just as reading specialists seek alternative approaches to teaching their subject, dance educators must devise ways in which the child who is rhythmically disabled or mentally retarded can find success. Murray (1953) stressed that calling attention to inaccurate response and creating tensions through continuous drill do not solve the problem. Nothing is sadder than a child concentrating so hard on tempo that the joy of movement is lost. The child who does not keep time to the music truly may be hearing a different drumbeat.

Dance Therapy in Schools and Hospitals

The pages that follow, written by a registered dance therapist, offer specific ideas that the adapted physical educator can test in the school setting. In those parts of the country where dance therapists are available, they may be employed to work cooperatively with the adapted physical educator or to provide consultant services. Remember that people who use dance therapeutically are not dance therapists unless they have received the special extensive training that qualifies them to meet the registry standards of the ADTA.

Through the therapeutic use of rhythmic and expressive movements, children gain better perspective about themselves, their ideas, and their feelings. They come to know their bodies better. They gain skill and control as they move through space. They find ways to use body action constructively, insight is gained into the meanings implied in their body action, and a more accepting body image develops.

Therapeutic dance encourages and fosters children's faith in their own ideas and in their own ways of expressing these ideas. A sense of personal worth begins to emerge. Children begin to like themselves better as they realize that their ideas do count, are worth listening to and watching, and can be shared. Positive group relationships develop through sharing and experimenting with ideas. Children gain appreciative understanding of other people's ideas and their ways of expressing them.

The expression of feelings is interwoven in various ways into dance, both indirectly in body action at the nonverbal level and directly with words and action at a conscious level (Eddy, 1982; Riordan, 1989). It is usually characteristic of dance therapy techniques that emotional tensions are worked with indirectly by centering attention on how the muscles can be used—such as hard or fast, or slow or easy ways—rather than by speaking directly to the children's feeling-states. When children express their tensions in forceful moving-out behavior, activities are centered around aggressive-moving circle dances or controlled, slow-motion, aggressive pantomime. At other times, fast running, challenging ways of jumping-falling-rolling-pushing-spinning, or tug-of-war can reduce tensions. When tensions seem high, and forceful moving-out action seems contraindicated be-

FIGURE 16.3

Reflecting the movement patterns of others.

cause the children's behaviors are expressed in depressed, turned-in movements, the action moves into gently paced rocking, swaying, swinging, controlled slow rolling, or tension-relaxation muscle isolation movements. On other occasions, when the children's tension levels are not high, activities focus on feelings directly at a conscious level. Only then do the children experiment with the different ways that feelings can be expressed through movement.

Activities to Achieve Objectives

Persons with mental health problems typically need help with three objectives: (a) increasing body awareness, (b) improving relationships and making friends, and (c) expressing feelings.

Some of the activities used in helping people become aware of their bodies and how their muscles work include

1. **Stretches, contractions, relaxations.** Individually, with partners, and in moving circle-dance action.

2. **Opposites movements.** Experimenting with such movements as tall-short, wide-narrow, fast-slow, stiff-floppy, open-closed, heavy-light, high-low.

3. **Feeling the floor different ways with bodies.** By rolling across the floor stretched out full length at varying speeds and levels of muscle tension; rolling around in tight curled-up balls; doing front and back somersaults; crumpling body movements to effect collapsing to the floor; free-falls sideward-forward-backward.

4. **Exploring movement through space.** Making different shapes and patterns; creating geometric patterns, writing imaginary letters and numbers with their bodies stationary and/or traveling.

5. **Using different traveling styles across the floor.** Running, jumping, walking, and creeping; variations within each style; working individually, with partners, and with groups of different sizes.

6. **Muscle isolation.** Using specific parts of the body in movement patterns while the rest of the body remains immobile, or following the action of the specific set of muscles leading a movement pattern; immobilization of body parts by playing *freeze* and *statue* games that stop movement in midaction; continuing on in movement retaining the *frozen* or *statue* position; having partners arrange each other's bodies into shapes or statues.

7. **Reflection movement patterns of others** (see Figure 16.3). Moving in synchrony with a partner's movements as though looking in a mirror; moving on phrase-pattern behind a partner as though echoing his or her movements; moving in opposite patterns to partner's; reflecting similar or complementary movement patterns, yet different.

Encourage individuals' ideas to emerge in a variety of ways. At times, emphasis is on verbalization of abstract ideas, and at other times, the focus is on body movement expression. Many times, verbal and physical expression are combined. The following activities are some of the experiments and experiences that children seem to enjoy:

1. **Single-word or object stimulus.**
   a. "How many different ideas does the word *beach* remind you of?" "What kinds of ideas come to you when you hear the word *beach*?"
   b. "How many different ways can you pretend to use a popsicle stick?"

2. **Imaginary props.** "Without telling us what it is, think of one particular thing or object you could use in three different ways. Show us how you would use it. After you have finished using it three different ways, call on us and we will try to guess what object you were using." Sometimes, after the person has completed his or her turn, and the object has been guessed, the others contribute ideas orally on how the object could also be used. Stress being creatively supportive of each other's ideas.

3. **Word cues.** Words written on slips of paper are drawn in turn; the person translates the word into pantomime or dance movement. As the others think they recognize the word cue, they join in with the movement in their own ways and within their own framework of understanding. When the action is stopped, verbal comparison is made of the meanings given to the movement interpretations. Observations and comments are shared about the different ways used to express the same word-meaning in movement. Movement can then resume with everyone sharing each other's movement styles. The word cues are usually presented in categories:
   a. *Doing*—chopping, hiding, twisting, carrying, hurrying, touching, dropping, sniffing, bouncing, flying, planting, pushing
   b. *People*—old person, mailcarrier, maid, nurse, airplane pilot, cook, police officer, doctor, hunted criminal, firefighter, mother, baby
   c. *Muscle isolation dances*—shoulder, head, knee, hip, hand, elbow, foot, leg, back, finger dances
   d. *Feelings*—ashamed, surprised, sad, stuck-up, angry, worried, greedy, jealous, happy, excited, in love, afraid, disgusted
   e. *Animals*—bee, horse, alligator, lion, snake, spider, elephant, crab, butterfly, worm, monkey, gorilla, mouse
   f. *Mime dramas*—underwater adventure, a scary time, at the beach, at a bus stop, going on a picnic, climbing a mountain, a visit to the zoo, on a hike outdoors, an afternoon in the park, a baseball game
   g. *A happening story*—a siren blowing, red light flashing, thick fog, whistle blowing, fire burning, animal sounds, gun firing, child crying, dream happening, rushing water

4. **Different ways over and under a rope.** As a rope is gradually raised or lowered, everyone moves over or under it without touching it in as many ways as they can.

5. **Idea box.** Everyone puts various objects they find or like—for example, leaves, crayon bits, combs, brushes, tiny statues, clothespins, buttons, pictures, paper clips, rubber discs—into the group's idea box. Periodically, an object is taken from the box to play around with. The different ideas individuals think up about the object can be translated into creative movement, creative storytelling, or creative dramatics.

6. **Stories.** Stories are read to the children so that they can make up their own endings and/or think about the possible alternative endings. The stories and the possible endings can be translated into dramatic action, either in part or total.

When feelings are focused on directly and at a conscious level, children can experiment with different ways feelings can be expressed through movement. The following activities illustrate some of the ways children can purposefully work with feelings or feeling-tones:

1. Descriptive mime or dance movements to a stimulus word indicating a specific feeling—for example, see item 5, "Idea box," in the preceding list.

2. Descriptive mime, dance, or story reflecting the feeling-tone of a spontaneous sound made by the child.

3. Feeling-tones in music. As music is played, the children respond in their own movement styles to the feeling-quality they *hear* in the music. When the action is finished, the children compare their responses, noting difference in responses to the same music. They also *try on* each other's feeling responses or movement styles as the music is played again.

4. Stories *danced* to feeling-quality of the music. Individuals, pairs, or several children take turns as they dance a story they have planned around the feeling-quality in the music. Sometimes, the same music is chosen for all the children; other times, the different groups of children choose different music. When the danced story is finished, the children who watched attempt to relate their observations and interpretations of the story to the dancers. After everyone has had a chance to interpret, the performer(s) describe their own story. When it seems appropriate, children share some of the movement qualities presented in the stories.

5. Feeling-tones in colors. Lightweight fabrics of different colors are placed around the floor in order of child's color preference; talk about what a specific color "makes you think about;" list ideas on paper; try on some of the ideas in movement. List ideas about what kinds of feelings might be reflected in a specific color. Experiment and show through movement how one can move to express the feelings listed, in pairs, groups, or individually. Continue on from one color fabric to

another. The single feeling-action can be enlarged into pantomime or dramatizations of a story idea woven around the feeling.

6. Baseball game (or alternate sport) in different movement styles. All players work together to reflect a specific feeling in their movement styles as they "play" the game.

a. *Sad*—The batter waits sadly for the ball to be thrown; the pitcher sadly throws the ball; the batter sadly hits at the ball. If the batter misses, everyone is sad and says so or makes sounds accordingly. The ball is sadly put back into play. If the ball is hit, the batter sadly runs to the base as the pitcher or players sadly go after the ball and try to throw the runner out. Such mood continues throughout the play around the bases until the runner sadly makes a run or is thrown out.

b. *Happy*—Follows the same format as above. The batter is happy when he or she misses the ball or strikes out. The pitcher is happy when the batter makes a base run or a home run.

c. *Laughing-angry*—This type of contradictory expressive behavior becomes challenging and hilarious. Different combinations of contradictory feelings/sounds demand special awareness of how one uses expressive action. This also comes close to the reality of the mixed communication many people use in less exaggerated fashion in everyday life.

Materials Used in Dance Therapy

Soft materials are used in all three of the areas discussed in the previous section for stimulating a variety of safe activities that are imaginative and self-structuring. Two-and-a-half-yard lengths of nylon fabrics of different hues aid in reducing tension and hyperactivity and in relaxing tight muscles (see Figure 16.4). In response to the floating, smooth quality of the colorful nylon, children move rhythmically—stretching, turning, reaching, and covering themselves in various ways. Their actions seem to reflect a sensuous enjoyment and an aesthetic awareness as the fabrics float and move across their bodies.

Paradoxically, the soft fabrics can become a factor in spatial structuring as well (see Figure 16.5). At times, when children feel extremely tense and seem to have a need for containment, being wrapped completely immobile in the full width of the fabric by either turning when standing or rolling when lying down has a relaxing and quieting effect. Without speaking directly to such needs, children will ask for this kind of containment by suggesting familiar activities that have included it in other movement contexts.

Nylon fabrics also provide an intermediary focus for children who find it difficult to relate directly to other persons. Spin-arounds, with partners holding opposite ends of the fabric, aid in keeping distance yet staying together. Wrap-up spin-outs allow a moment's closeness with access to quick and immediate freedom from nearness.

FIGURE 16.4

Soft nylon has a relaxing and quieting effect.

FIGURE 16.5

Experiencing the spatial structure of soft, floating fabric.

Imaginative play and imagery are stimulated by using the fabric as clothing, costumes, bedding, housing, or light-shields to put a color glow in a darkened room. Aggressiveness is accommodated by wrapping a soft yarn ball inside one end of the fabric and throwing it as if it were a comet streaming through space. *Dodge fabric* has aggressive moments of fun and beauty combined when one or several fabrics are loosely wadded into a ball and thrown at a moving human target. The floating open of the fabric(s) while traveling in space sometimes creates unusual beauty. Children also like to lie down and be covered completely with one fabric at a time in layering fashion. As the layers of fabric increase, children typically comment on the constant change of color and the increasing dimness.

Soft, stretchy, tubular-knit fabrics approximately 3 yd long have soothing, protecting properties. The tubular fabrics make excellent *hammocks* on which to lie and be swung (see Figures 16.6 and 16.7). When persons alternate in lifting ends of the fabric, causing the body to roll from side

FIGURE   16.6

Experiencing the sensation of directional change in a different way.

FIGURE   16.7

Learning trust as the hammock descends.

FIGURE 16.8

Yarn balls permit safe release of aggressive tensions.

to side, the child feels a special sensation of being moved in space. An interesting sensation of directional change is experienced when running and bouncing forward into a tautly stretched fabric that *gives* and then bounces the person off backward.

Stretch-tube fabrics also lend themselves well to nondirected dramatic play and fantasy-action. They become roads, rivers, roofs, ghosts, hooded persons, Roman togas, stuffed sausages, pickles, grass, tunnels. Playing inside stretch-tube fabrics is a way for children to shield themselves from direct observation and physical touch contact with other persons, while at the same time being able to look out through the fabric and see other persons. When working inside, the fabrics can become an open-ended tunnel to explore, or a closed and safe haven for being swung, rolled, dragged gently around the floor, or for pretending all alone in fantasy-action. Inside the fabrics can also become a place to experiment with making different shapes and forms by bending and extending body parts against the softly resilient material.

When lying outside on the fabric and being swung gently, spontaneous pantomimes of *dreams* are easily evoked. These dreams come from children's unconscious urges and needs, and the expressive body action accompanying the

dream fantasies allows for safe catharsis and emotional release of tensions reflected in the dream content. The fabrics offer opportunity for rocking and swaying when children need comforting and relaxing, without those needs being openly or directly addressed. Games experienced earlier, when the children were simply exploring the use of the fabrics, can be repeated when the need for comforting arises.

Yarn balls about 6 inches in diameter permit many varieties of throwing activities for imaginative play as well as for safe release of aggressive tensions (Figure 16.8). The teacher's imaginative thinking about different ways to throw, jump with, and bat the ball stimulates alternative ways of thinking and also encourages children to risk expressing their own ideas. Warm-up stretches are executed by using different body positions to transfer the ball to the next recipient. One-to-one synchronization of full body action occurs when partners try to support a ball between them with various parts of their bodies while traveling across the room. Yarn balls can be used aggressively for bowling or dodgeball. They also can be vigorously hand-batted back and forth across the floor. More structured and functionally demanding activities are done with rhythmically synchronized toss, catch, and rolling games. Isolation of body parts can be experienced by bouncing the ball off different parts of the body or by contacting the ball with a specific body part before releasing and passing it on to another person. In dramatic play and fantasy-action, the balls become various kinds of foods, jewels, rocks, rockets, bombs, and the equipment for pretend games of baseball, kickball, touch football, and bowling.

Dance Therapy Principles

With modification, dance therapy techniques are applicable to persons of most ages and with most disabilities because dance therapy focuses on qualities of nonverbal communication in everyday life. Marian Chace (n.d.), one of the pioneers in the evolution of dance therapy as a profession, was influential in obtaining acceptance of principles that she felt were basic to dance therapy and common to all forms of therapy. These principles relate specifically to patients in a clinical setting but are applicable to students with mental health needs. Chace believed that the dance therapist should keep things simple by leading out from what is happening inside the patient, rather than imposing the action from the outside. The therapist should allow time for things to happen within the ongoing action rather than trying to *do* a lot.

Chace recommended that the dance therapist work toward enriching experiences in a nonjudgmental, neutral way, without moralizing. This is best accomplished by working *with* the patient rather than *on* him or her. The dance therapist must be secure and able to listen to what is going on at the verbal level and yet see subtle, nonverbal cues. The therapist should emanate friendliness, yet remain neutral and resist being caught up in his or her need to be liked by the patient. Patients need to relate to persons who are genuine and truthfully warm. They need relationship space that allows them to give back warmth without feeling threatened by the therapist's needs.

Therapeutic Tools

The *therapeutic tools* used by the dance therapist could be thought of as rhythm, touch, verbalization, space, and people. Activities are simply the media for the use of therapeutic tools.

The *movement of the patient,* rather than that of the therapist, is used as a means of establishing the therapeutic relationship. By tuning in and sharing a patient's movements, the therapist can very clearly and quickly relate to the patient. They can *speak* to each other in movement. The therapist then works toward transcribing patients' movements into reality-oriented and functional expressions since patients are unable to do this for themselves. The therapist also tries to influence change in patients' distorted body images through muscular action.

Basically, the *rhythmical* quality of expressive movement is what enables the patient to use body action in safe ways that hurt no one. Open use of aggressive movements has less therapeutic value than rhythmic action that

focuses on body awareness. For optimal results, expressive movement must be under the patient's conscious rather than unconscious control. Rhythmic action also affords an area for relating that is outside both the patient and the dance therapist. It offers the satisfaction of sharing movement and minimizes destructiveness of action. The patient does not feel a need for the movement to be realized in its destructive form. This leaves him or her free to go on to other things, with pathological urges released rhythmically, constructively, and safely, for the moment.

All therapeutic body movement is geared toward getting in *touch* with as much of the skin's surface as possible. Tactile stimulation and muscular contraction allow the patient to regain contact with his or her body surface and to come to understand its boundaries. Direct touch by the therapist reinforces the patient's growing ability to distinguish between himself or herself and others.

Verbalization between the therapist and patient is geared to the meaning of muscular action, rather than the feeling-tone behind the action. The patient comes to realize that his or her movement qualities are reality based and that he or she is capable of purposive movement. Verbalization is not for telling the patient what to do, but for helping him or her to know where he or she is going and why.

Space is an extension and reflection of body image, so the use of space is important. A patient who is manic and hyperactive perceives his or her own space zone as wide and scattered and as having tremendous force and power. The dance therapist then uses movements far away from the patient, coming in only tentatively as the patient will allow. The patient already feels that they are *together,* even though they are actually far apart. If a patient is frozen or constricted in movement, the space zone is small and constricted. The dance therapist then moves in quite closely, but with care and awareness, because a constricted space is generally a supercharged zone. The dance therapist also uses space to encourage a *coming forward.* Such dance movements can provide safe areas for hostile body action that might have been used out of control. *Going forward* movements can provide safe areas for a withdrawn person to learn that he or she can come out and not be hurt nor hurt anybody else.

The dance therapist's ultimate goal is for patients to work in a group. Group work reduces one-to-one identifications and increases opportunities for patients to assume responsibility for their own growth and not stay dependent upon the therapist.

References

American Dance Therapy Association. (circa 1975). Annual proceedings and other materials available through the national office.

Bitcon, C. H. (1976). *Alike and different: The clinical and educational use of Orff-Schulwerk.* Santa Ana, CA: Rosha.

Boswell, B. (1989). Dance as creative expression for the disabled. *Palaestra, 6* (1), 28–30.

Chace, M. (n.d.). *Dance alone is not enough.* From mimeographed materials distributed by St. Elizabeth's Hospital and Chestnut Lodge in Washington, DC.

Eddy, J. (1982). *The music came from deep inside: Professional artists and severely handicapped children.* New York: McGraw-Hill.

Fitt, S., & Riordan, A. (Eds.). (1980). *Dance for the handicapped—focus on dance IX.* Reston, VA: American Alliance for Health, Physical Education, Recreation, and Dance.

Fleming, G. A. (Ed.). (1973). *Children's dance.* Washington, DC: American Alliance for Health, Physical Education, Recreation, and Dance.

Jay, D. (1991). Effect of a dance program on the creativity of preschool handicapped children. *Adapted Physical Activity Quarterly, 8,* 305–316.

Joyce, M. (1984). *Dance technique for children.* Palo Alto, CA: Mayfield.

Laban, R. (1960). *The mastery of movement* (2nd ed.). London: MacDonald & Evans.

Murray, R. L. (1953). *Dance in elementary education.* New York: Harper & Row.

Riordan, A. (1989). Sunrise Wheels. *Journal of Physical Education, Recreation, and Dance, 60* (9), 62–64.

Roswal, P. M., Sherrill, C., & Roswal, G. M. (1988). A comparison of data-based and creative dance pedagogies in teaching mentally retarded youth. *Adapted Physical Activity Quarterly, 5,* 212–222.

Schmitz, N. B. (1989). Children with learning disabilities and the dance/movement class. *Journal of Physical Education, Recreation, and Dance, 60* (9), 59–61.

Sherborne, V. (1987). Movement observation and practice. In M. Berridge & G. R. Ward (Eds.), *International perspectives on adapted physical activity* (pp. 3–10). Champaign, IL: Human Kinetics.

Sherrill, C. (Ed.). (1979). *Creative arts for the severely handicapped.* Springfield, IL: Charles C. Thomas.

CHAPTER

17

Adapted Aquatics

FIGURE   17.1

Although this child is orthopedically impaired, he is not disabled in the
water. (Photos by Judy Newman.)

After you have studied this chapter, you should be able to:

1. Discuss the benefits of water activity for persons with different disabilities and identify adaptations that will contribute to success. List conditions for which swimming is contraindicated.

2. Discuss resources, goals, and practices for hydrotherapy, adapted aquatics, and competitive swimming.

3. Discuss similarities and differences between the Halliwick and Sherrill models and regular teaching approaches.

4. Describe activities appropriate for the explorer, advanced explorer, and floater levels. Test these activities with beginners and share your experiences.

5. Explain how different conditions affect buoyancy and describe adaptations.

6. Explain how synchronized swimming stunts and routines can be used for fun and success before stroke proficiency is achieved.

7. Discuss administrative aspects of an aquatics program for persons who are differently abled.

A mother speaks of her dyslexic son in a poignant account of learning to cope with learning disabilities:

He might not be able to manage a tricycle, but he had the freedom of a large, safe beach, where he could run for a mile if he felt inclined. Beach balls eluded him—he could neither throw nor catch—but there was the warm sand to mess with, and the water itself. The big moment of Mike's young life came at three-and-a-half, when he learned to swim. . . . The beach baby turned into a water rat. By five, he could safely swim out of his depth, and by six, he not only had a crawl stroke, but was so at home in the water that he literally did not seem to know if he was on it or under it. (Clarke, 1973, p.9)

When Mike grew up, he graduated from Harvard University with a doctoral degree. He still could not "read, write, nor talk too good either," but he had learned to compensate for his weaknesses and to utilize fully his strengths. Like other boys, he longed for athletic success, tried out for teams, failed. He was especially awkward in baseball and handball. As an adult, he recalled the pleasure derived from swimming and its contribution to the maintenance of some ego strength throughout a childhood characterized by very few successes.

Water can be used for physical and mental rehabilitation, fitness, relaxation, perceptual-motor remediation, self-concept enhancement, fun, and competition (see Figure 17.1). Exercises, stunts, and games traditionally done on land achieve the same goals when executed in the water.

Water activity, while beneficial for everyone, may be the program of choice for persons who are nonambulatory, unfit, obese, asthmatic, or arthritic. Because water minimizes the force of gravity, persons can often move with greater ease in a pool than on land. Water also eliminates the risk of joint damage associated with weight-bearing exercise in obesity and certain types of arthritis (Sheldahl, 1986). Swimming strokes, whether done on land or water, have long been recognized as one of the best systems of exercise.

Water also can be used to manage behaviors and change mental states. Warm water—96–98° Fahrenheit (F), 35.5–36.5° Celsius (C)—reduces hyperactivity, stress, and tension, whereas water of normal pool temperature—78–86°

F, 26–30° C—increases alertness and promotes a state of "feeling good." Cold water is often used in mental health programs to snap persons out of depression and help them act out anger.

Hydrotherapy and Adapted Aquatics

Hydrotherapy (water exercise for therapeutic purposes) was systematized in the 1930s by Charles Lowman, an orthopedic physician, who today is recognized as the father of hydrotherapy (Lowman, 1937; Lowman & Roen, 1952). Although originally used primarily for persons with physical disabilities, water exercise is now recommended for everyone (Campion, 1985; Krasevec, 1989; Mayse, 1991). Water exercise may be a supplement to land exercise or an alternative.

Adapted aquatics (activities adapted to individual differences) evolved in the 1960s and 1970s as awareness increased that all persons should have opportunities to learn basic swimming skills. Leaders in this movement were Judy Newman (1976), Louise Priest, who was employed by the American Red Cross (Priest, 1979, 1987, 1990), Grace Reynolds (1973) of the YMCA, and Sue Grosse of the Milwaukee, Wisconsin, public schools (Grosse, 1985, 1987, 1993; Grosse & Gildersleeve, 1984; Grosse & McGill, 1989). In 1977, the American Red Cross published *Adapted Aquatics,* a comprehensive source available until the 1990s when the American Red Cross (1992a, 1992b) decided to include information on disability in its regular programs rather than continuing separate adapted aquatics certification. Special Olympics International (1981) and the YMCA of the USA (1986, 1987) publish excellent adapted aquatics materials, and the Council for National Cooperation in Aquatics (CNCA), under the leadership of Louise Priest, offers consultant services.

Today, adapted aquatics philosophy has been expanded to include boating (British Sports Association for the Disabled, 1983), infant/preschool swimming (Kochen & McCabe, 1986; Langendorfer, 1989, 1990), swimming for seniors (Shea, 1986), and scuba diving (Green & Miles, 1987; Robinson, 1986).

Several instructional models are available for teaching persons who are extremely fearful of water and/or who are slow learners. This chapter describes two models: (a) the Sherrill water fun and success model and (b) the Halliwick water confidence model, named for the Halliwick School for Crippled Girls in England, where James McMillan (creator of the model) taught. Both models were created in the 1950s and 1960s.

Competitive Swimming and Disability

Local, national, and international swimming competition is available for persons with disabilities through affiliation with sport organizations governed by the International Paralympic Committee and Special Olympics International (see Appendix D). Meets are conducted in the same way as for nondisabled swimmers, and similar distances are used.

Various classification systems group swimmers either by functional ability or medical status to ensure fair competition and to permit persons with severe disability the opportunity to achieve personal bests (Gehlsen & Karpuk, 1992; Richter, Adams-Mushett, Ferrara, & McCann, 1992). Competitive swimming for people with and without disabilities is governed by United States Swimming, Inc. (U.S. Swim), 1750 East Boulder Street, Colorado Springs, CO 80909. Many swimmers with disabilities train with nondisabled teams, and some compete in regular venues (Andersen, 1989).

Instructional Models for Beginners

Many persons with disabilities learn swimming through regular Red Cross and YMCA programs. The Halliwick and Sherrill models are for persons who need more help and longer time than regular programs provide. These models are similar in that both recommend (a) a one-to-one teaching ratio until swimmers gain confidence for small-group instruction; (b) teachers in the water, stimulating and supporting their swimmers; (c) learning through play and games; (d) emphasis on body awareness, movement exploration, and breathing games; (e) consideration of buoyancy principles; and (f) no use of personal flotation devices (PFDs) except for persons with severe nonambulatory conditions.

PFDs are inner tubes, arm and head floats, vests, and inflatable swimsuits that aid buoyancy. PFDs should never take the place of a one-to-one teaching ratio. Experts vary in their support of PFDs (Andersen, 1986; Grosse, 1987; Jones, 1986), but there is consensus that some persons with severe cerebral palsy need PFDs and that these devices should be carefully selected. Persons using PFDs should never be left unsupervised.

Halliwick Water Confidence Model

The *Halliwick water confidence model* is described by Kahrs (1974) and Bull et al. (1985) of Norway, by Grosse and Gildersleeve (1984) of the United States, and by Campion (1985) of Australia. The purpose of the model is to teach water buoyancy and confidence through various kinds of body rotations, floats, glides, and games. Once persons are comfortable with the buoyancy force of the water, they can learn swimming strokes by traditional methods. The Halliwick model is based on 10 points:

1. **Mental Preparation.** Emphasis is on getting to know the instructor, the pool, and the dressing rooms. This is achieved through walking, talking, and showing. The goal is to have fun while learning to feel at ease in the water. Familiar land activities (games, dances, and rhythms) are adapted to water.

2. **Self-Sufficiency.** Instruction begins with the teacher and student touching: (a) holding hands during locomotor activities; (b) holding hands, waist, or shoulders in face-to-face and face-to-back movement explorations; and (c) holding hands while being pulled in a horizontal position. *The head is never held because emphasis is on learning to alter body position and regulate balance through independent head movements.* As confidence is achieved, the distance between teacher and student is gradually increased by such devices as a washcloth, floatboard, and towel. Finally, there is no contact, and the teacher moves a little further away each lesson. PFDs are not sanctioned because they lessen self-sufficiency.

3. **Vertical Rotation.** Mastery is achieved by learning to change from vertical to horizontal positions and vice versa. Somersaults are advanced vertical rotations.

4. **Horizontal or Lateral Rotation.** Mastery is achieved by learning to rotate from back to front and vice versa while in a horizontal position. Logrolls are advanced horizontal rotations.

5. **Combined Rotation.** Many games that include both vertical and horizontal rotations are played.

6. **Application of Buoyancy.** Games like trying to sit on the pool bottom without floating up are used to develop trust of the water's buoyancy force.

7. **Floating Positions.** Movement exploration challenges are used to find different body shapes for floating.

8. **Turbulence Floating and Gliding.** Students learn to cope with increasing amounts of turbulence. First, confidence is gained in calm water. Then the teacher creates small, medium, and large turbulence conditions by swirling his or her hands in the water near the student's head.

9. **Simple Propulsion.** Underwater, symmetrical arm movements (finning, sculling, breaststroke) are added to the back and front glides to promote simple propulsion.

10. **Development of Strokes.** Swimming strokes are introduced by traditional methods after Halliwick points 1 to 9 have resulted in complete water confidence.

Table 17.1
Beginning competency levels of swimming for Sherrill model.

Level I, Explorer Movement Exploration in Water	Level II, Advanced Explorer Movement Exploration in Water	Level III, Floater Prebeginning Swimming
1. Enter and leave water alone	1. Put face in water	1. Blow bubbles (10 sec)
2. Walk across pool holding rail	2. Blow bubbles (5 sec)	2. Bracketing on front with kick
3. Walk across pool holding teacher's hand	3. Touch bottom or toes with hands	3. Change of position: stand; front-lying with support; stand
4. Stand alone	4. Retrieve objects from bottom	4. Prone float
5. Walk across pool pushing kickboard	5. Assume horizontal position with teacher's help	5. Change of position: stand; back-lying with support; stand
6. Jump or hop several steps alone	6. Hold onto kickboard pulled by teacher	6. Back float
7. Walk and do breaststroke arm movements	7. Jump into water without help	7. Flutter kick using board
8. Do various locomotor movements across the pool	8. Take rides in back-lying position	8. Jellyfish float
9. Blow bubbles through plastic tube	9. Change of level: squat to stand; stand to squat	9. Perform breaststroke arm movements
10. Blow Ping-Pong ball across pool	10. Play follow-the-leader type water games	10. Swim one-half width any style
	11. Demonstrate bracketing on back with kick (see Figure 17.5)	11. Perform at least one stunt like stand or walk on hands, front somersault, back somersault, tub, surface dive

Sherrill Water Fun and Success Model

The *Sherrill water fun and success model* began as part of a Texas Woman's University practicum program in which university students teach children with developmental disabilities to swim. Over the years, three prebeginner swimming certificates have evolved. Initially, the levels of competency that the certificates represent were named after fish: minnows, crappies, and dolphins. The children were not as enamored of these appellations as were the adults who created them. First of all, many of them had never seen real fish, alive or dead, and to them, the names were meaningless. Some of the pupils did report firsthand knowledge of fish but remembered the unpleasant odor more than the beauty of movement. Said one, "I don't want to be a fish—ugh—they stink." Still another problem arose with respect to self-concept; heavily muscled boys, particularly from economically deprived areas, had no intention of being "sissy minnows," regardless of their dependence upon the teacher in the water.

The three certificates subsequently were designated as Explorer, Advanced Explorer, and Floater in accordance with the levels of competency achieved. These certificates were printed on cards of the same size and shape as the standard Red Cross certificates. Originally, they came in different colors, but after the year that a girl with Down syndrome sobbed all through the awards ceremony because her card was not white like her boyfriend's, it was decided to make the cards uniform in color as well as size, shape, and format.

The motor tasks required for passing each certificate are listed in Table 17.1. The major achievement at the Explorer level is to release the teacher's hand and perform basic locomotor movement patterns independently at a distance several feet away from the side of the pool. Putting the face in the water is not necessary to earn Explorer status. Many youngsters initially are so terrified of the water that several lessons are required before they will loosen their deathlike grips on the teachers. Many additional lessons pass before enough courage is developed to let go of the side of the pool and walk independently. Nevertheless, *all* students who earn the Explorer certificate take as much pride in it as their peers do in the Red Cross achievement cards.

The Advanced Explorer certificate represents two major accomplishments: putting the face in the water and willingness to lift the feet from the pool bottom, thereby assuming a horizontal position with the help of the teacher. Also at this level, the child begins experimenting with somersaults, standing on his or her head, walking on hands, and other stunts that are not based on the ability to float.

Earning the third and final prebeginner Floater certificate is dependent upon the ability to relax sufficiently to float for several seconds. At this level, children usually begin to swim. Navigation is more often under the water than on top, and underwater swimming can be used to fulfill the requirement of one-half width. Long before the pupils learn to swim recognizable strokes, they become proficient in many basic stunts of synchronized swimming. They develop creative routines to music that are weird combinations of walks, runs, jumps, hops, standing in place and stroking with arms, and regulation synchronized swimming stunts.

Goals of Adapted Aquatics

The water can be viewed as simply another medium for refining movement patterns and exploring time-space-self relationships. The Texas Woman's University aquatics program is coordinated with lessons in movement exploration conducted in the gymnasium. Virtually every activity learned out of water is attempted also in the swimming pool. The movement exploration teaching style described in Chapter 9 (guided discovery and motor creativity) establishes the framework in which learning occurs. The three most important goals of the program are (a) to improve self-concept, (b) to increase self-confidence, and (c) to develop courage. Secondary to these goals, the teacher concentrates on dimensions of body image: (a) identification of body parts, (b) improvement of proprioception, and (c) development of such inner language concepts as bent versus straight, vertical versus horizontal, pike versus tuck, back layout versus front layout, and pull phase (application of force) versus recovery phase. As a technique for enhancing self-concept, children are drilled on the *names* of the stunts and skills they learn to perform. As they acquire a vocabulary that enables them to share their successes with others, children seem to demonstrate increased motivation for undertaking new aquatic adventures. Moreover, this emphasis on vocabulary in the swimming setting reinforces words learned in the classroom and the gymnasium, thereby contributing to transfer of learning and reducing development of splinter skills.

Adapted Aquatics Principles

Some of the differences between an adapted aquatics program and regular swimming instruction are explicit in the following principles for teachers:

1. Be in the water with the children rather than on deck (see Figure 17.2). Physical contact between teacher and student is based on the student's needs for security and affection. Although independence in the water is the ultimate goal, do not rush it.

2. Avoid saying "Put your face underwater," a task that students tend to interpret as unpleasant. Instead, introduce gamelike situations that induce the child to attempt the task without conscious realization of what he or she is doing. The following anecdote demonstrates teaching:

I had been in the water with Charles for about 20 min and had had no success with anything I had tried to teach him. I was particularly concerned with getting him to put his entire face and head in the water. I finally decided to make a game out of it, so I borrowed the small inner tube from one of the other instructors. Without any type of explanation, I placed the inner tube between Charles and myself and ducked under water and came up with it around my neck. Charles was delighted and asked me to do it again. After repeating it I asked him if he would like to put his head through the inner tube. Without answering my question, he completely submerged his body and came up with the inner tube around his neck. I was more than pleased and had him repeat it five or six times. Then I asked him to submerge without coming up under the inner tube. I

FIGURE   17.2

A one-to-one relationship in the water facilitates learning.

received a very blunt "no." He told me he could not put his head under water, and he did not wish to try. We continued using the inner tube for the remainder of the hour.

3. Use as few words as possible in teaching. Cues like "up," "down," "pull," "recover," and "kick 2-3-4" are substituted for sentences. A well-modulated voice helps to convey the meaning of instructions. Use a *high* voice for *up* movements and a *low* (pitch) voice for *down* movements. Use a loud and forceful voice during the pull phase and a soft and gentle voice during the recovery phase.

4. Move the child's limbs through the desired pattern of movement rather than using the explanation-demonstration technique. Some persons refer to this as the *kinesthetic* method of teaching since such input is proprioceptive.

5. Show acceptance of the child through frequent mirroring of his or her movements. Take turns *following the leader* with precise imitation of postures, arm movements, and kicks.

6. Introduce synchronized swimming, jumping, and diving much earlier than usual in swimming instruction. Emphasize the combination of stunts and locomotor movements—that is, creating sequences (routines) and remembering and executing sequences developed by others.

7. Modify requirements in accordance with individual differences. Plan testing on the basis of the individual's strengths, not preestablished competences that are thought to meet the needs of all beginner swimmers.

8. Encourage bilateral, unilateral, and crosslateral movement patterns, in that order, which reflects an understanding of child growth and development. Thus,

FIGURE   17.3

Comparison of bilateral and crosslateral strokes.

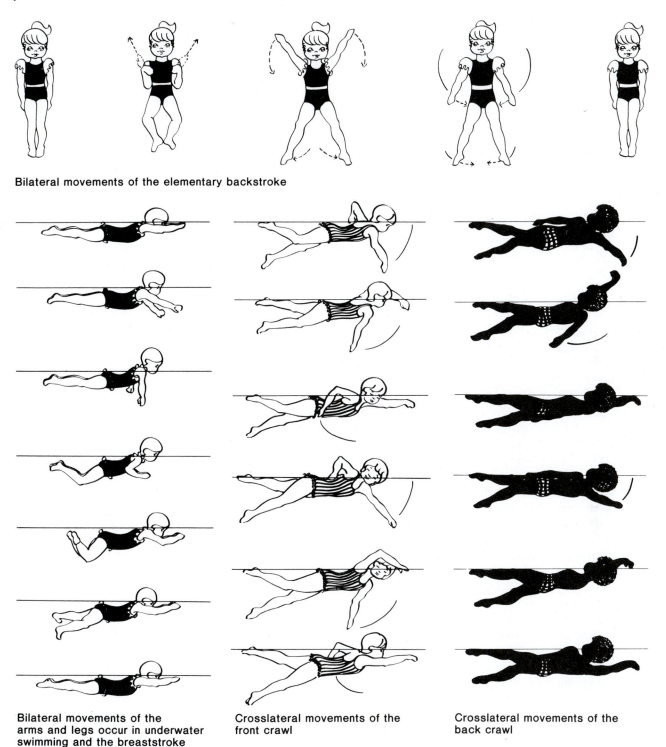

Bilateral movements of the elementary backstroke

Bilateral movements of the
arms and legs occur in underwater
swimming and the breaststroke

Crosslateral movements of the
front crawl

Crosslateral movements of the
back crawl

the breaststroke and the elementary backstroke are
the first real swimming strokes introduced. The
bilateral movements of the breaststroke usually appear
in underwater swimming without the benefit of
instruction. Figure 17.3 compares the simplicity of
bilateral strokes with the relative complexity of
crosslateral strokes.

The bilateral movements of the elementary backstroke are similar to those in angels-in-the-snow and jumping
jacks. Land drill is used before the children shower or after
they dry and dress to ensure transfer of learning. Drill in the
water can be facilitated by suspending a hammock from the
ceiling, using flotation devices, and lying on a table under the
water.

Figure 17.3 shows bilateral movements of the arms and legs in underwater swimming and the breaststroke and in the elementary backstroke, as well as the more difficult crosslateral swimming strokes. Six kicks of each leg are coordinated with every cycle of arm movements. As the right arm pulls, for instance, the right leg kicks *up*, down, *up*. The emphasis in the flutter kick is on the *up* beat! Arm strokes and leg kicks must be practiced in a horizontal rather than a standing position. Equally important, the teacher should demonstrate new skills in the horizontal position.

No stroke is more difficult to master than the front crawl. Although the rhythm of the flutter kick may come naturally to a few students, it is a nightmare for many others. Land drills to music in 3/4 time with a strong accent on the first beat in every measure may contribute to relaxed, effective kicking in the water; if not, the practice can be justified for its contribution to abdominal strength. Both in land drills and in the water, there is a tendency to collaborate with the force of gravity and accentuate the downbeat; this error must be avoided. Devising some kind of contraption 12 to 18 inches above the floor to be kicked on each upbeat may focus the student's attention on the desired accent.

The flutter kick warm-up exercise should begin in the position depicted in Figure 17.4 rather than with both legs on the floor, since at no time during the crawl stroke are the legs motionless and in the same plane. With poorly coordinated students, it is best to leave the arms motionless in the starting position until the rhythm of the kick is mastered. The verbal cues *right-arm-pull* or *left-arm-pull* can be substituted for *kick-2-3* even though the arms do not move. The first progression for this exercise is lying on the floor; the next progression is lying on a bench with arms and legs hanging over.

When a student demonstrates no progress in the flutter kick over a period of weeks, it can be safely assumed that the desired movement is not *natural* for him or her and that an alternate method of kicking should be substituted. In such instances, the front crawl can be modified into the *trudgeon stroke* by substituting the scissors kick for the flutter kick.

The American Red Cross teaches many basic strokes. The student's ability to perform one or two of these strokes really well is the criterion for success in a program for persons with disabilities. Which stroke(s) the child chooses is not important as long as he or she feels safe in the water and enjoys swimming. One of the purposes of movement exploration is to guide the student toward personal discovery of this stroke.

Activities for the Explorer

Washcloth Games

Give each child a washcloth, and compare the swimming pool with the bathtub at home. Your relaxed patter of questions usually elicits the desired water exploration:

1. "What do you do with a washcloth? Don't tell me; show me!"

FIGURE   17.4

Ready position for flutter kick warm-up.

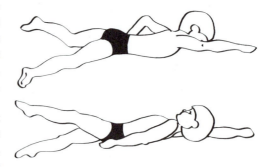

2. "What part do you wash first? Did you wring the cloth out before you started to wash? Don't you wring it out first at home?"
3. "Did you wash behind your ears? The back of your neck? Your elbows? Your knees? Your ankles? What about the soles of your feet? Are they clean?"
4. "Do you like to have someone wash your back? If you do, find a partner and take turns washing each other's back."
5. "Can you play throw and catch with your partner by using the washcloth as a ball?"
6. "What happens if you miss the catch? Can you pick the washcloth off the bottom of the pool with your toes? With some other part of your body?"
7. "Let's play steal each other's washcloth. To begin, each of you must fold your washcloth and put it neatly over your shoulder or on top of your head. When I say 'go,' move around stealing as many washcloths as you can but don't forget to protect your own. When I say 'stop,' everyone must have one hand on the railing before I count to 10; then, we will determine who is the winner."

Sponge Games

Give each child a sponge.

1. "Do you see something at the bottom of the pool? That's correct! There are plates, saucers, bowls, glasses, and cups. Guess what your job is? That's correct! Recover the dishes any way you wish, wash them with your sponge, and set the table on the deck. Whoever finishes the most place settings wins."
2. "Have you ever scrubbed down walls? Each of you find your very own space on the wall and let's see you scrub! Have you ever washed a car? Let's pretend the wall is a car! What else can we pretend the wall is? Does anyone know how to scrub the floor? Let's see!"
3. "See this big inner tube? Let's use it to shoot baskets with our sponges. Can you make your sponge land inside the inner tube?"
4. "What other target games can we invent with the sponges?"

5. *Dodge or Catch.* This game is played like dodgeball except that the child has the option of dodging or catching. Occasionally, someone may get hit full in the face with a wet sponge. Although a sponge cannot hurt, some children feel threatened by this activity; hence, the participants should be volunteers.

The children put their sponges in the water.

1. "Who can get his or her bucket filled with water first? The only way to get water in the bucket is by squeezing out sponges."
   a. *Individual game.* "Who can recover the most sponges, squeeze them out, and toss them back in the water?"
   b. *Partner game.* One student remains in the water recovering sponges and handing them to his or her partner on deck, who squeezes the sponges and tosses them back into the water.
2. Sponges of different colors are floating in the water. Children all have one hand on the pool railing. On the signal "go," they respond to the question,"Who can recover a blue sponge and put it on the deck first? A yellow sponge? A pink sponge?"
3. Sponges of different shapes or sizes are floating in the water. [Same instructions as before.]
4. "Who can recover two sponges and put one under each of his or her feet? How many of you are standing on sponges? Can you walk across the pool on the sponges?"

Parachute Games

In the water, a large sheet of clear plastic makes the best parachute; round tablecloths and sheets can also be used. All of the parachute activities played on land can be adapted to the water. "Who can run under the parachute?" invariably gets the face in the water. "Who can climb over the parachute?" leads to taking turns riding on the magic carpet that is pulled through the water by classmates.

Blowing Games

Blowing games can be played either in or out of the water; they are important lead-up activities to rhythmic breathing.

1. Give each child a clear plastic tube 12 to 18 inches long. Plastic tubing can be purchased in any hardware store. "Who can walk along with the plastic tube in a *vertical* position and blow bubbles in the water? Who can walk along with the plastic tube in a *horizontal* position and blow bubbles in the water?"
2. "Who can blow a Ping-Pong ball across the water? A toy sailboat? A small sponge?"
3. "On the side of the pool are many balloons that need blowing up. The object is to blow up a balloon while you walk or run across the pool. Who can make the most trips back and forth and thus blow up the most balloons? You may take only one balloon each trip."

4. Inflatable air mattresses and rafts provide ample practice in blowing for several children. Teams of three or four children may cooperate in blowing up a mattress with the promise that they may play on it in the water after it has been sufficiently inflated.
5. Give each child a yarn ball or Ping-Pong ball suspended from a string. "Who can keep the ball in motion the longest by blowing?"

Self-Testing Activities for the Explorer

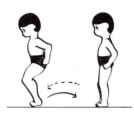

Horizontal or long jump

1. "Who can jump forward across the pool? Who can jump backward? Sideward? How many different ways can you jump? Can you carry something heavy as you jump?"

Vertical jump and reach

2. "How high can you jump?" A pole with flags of various colors provides incentive for progressively increasing the height of the jump. "Which flag did you touch when you jumped?"

Cable jump

3. "Can you jump over a stick, a scarf, or a rope? In which nursery rhyme does someone jump over a candlestick?"

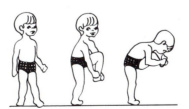

Greet the toe

4. "Can you greet your toe? Can you hop while holding one foot?"

Jump and tuck

Airplane or single-
foot balance

5. "Can you jump up and touch your knees? Can you jump up and touch your toes?"

Straight arm support
lean

6. "Stand in the water facing the side of the pool with both hands on deck. How many times can you lift your body up almost out of the water with your arms alone? This is like a push-up on land. Can you lift your body upward and maintain a straight-arm support?"

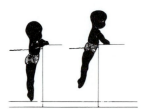

Aquatic sprint

7. "How many seconds does it take you to run across the pool? How many widths of the pool can you run in 3 min?"

Bracketing with back
lean

8. "Can you hang on the pool railing (gutter) and arch your back? Can you do this with the soles of your feet on the wall instead of the floor? Can you do this with only one arm?"

Matching locomotor movements
to lines and forms

9. "Can you walk a straight line drawn on the floor of the pool? A circular line? A zigzag line? Can you march on the line? Can you hop on it? Can you do these movements backward? Sideward?"

10. "How many different ways can you balance on one foot? Can you do an arabesque? A pirouette?"

Activities for the Advanced Explorer

Advanced explorers are learning to put their heads under water and to change level from up to down and vice versa. They are also experimenting with all of the possible ways to enter the water. They are not yet secure about a horizontal position in the water but will assume it when your hand is in contact with some part of their bodies.

Towel Games

1. **Taking rides.** A child who trusts you enough to hold his or her hands and allow the feet to rise from the bottom, thereby assuming a horizontal position in the water, can be taken on *rides*. These rides can be as dramatic as the child's (or your) imagination, with sound effects for a train, rocket ship, or whatever. Talk to the child, continuously maintaining eye contact and pulling him or her along while walking backward. The next step in the development of trust is to convince the child to hang onto a towel or kickboard while you pull on the other end. Thus, the rides across the pool continue, but the child is progressively farther away from you.

2. **Individual tug-of-war.** Every two children share one towel, each holding onto one end. A line on the bottom of the pool separates the two children, and the object is to see who can pull the other over the line first. As balance and body control in the water improve, teammates can be added until group tug-of-war is played. Only one teammate should be added to each side at a time.

3. **Catch the snake.** A rope about 6 ft long has a towel tied onto the end. You or an agile child pulls the rope around the pool. The object is to see who can *catch the snake* first. The winner then becomes the runner who pulls the snake around the pool.

4. **Beater goes round.** Children stand in a single circle, facing inward. The *beater* stands on the outside of the circle, facing counterclockwise and holding a small hand towel (one not big enough to hurt when a child is hit with it). A second child is running counterclockwise in front of the *beater*, trying to avoid being hit by the towel. He or she can be safe by ducking in front of any player in the circle after he or she has run around at least one-half of the circle. The player whom he or she ducked in front of must now run to avoid being beaten.

5. **Tag.** Towels on the pool bottom are safety rests.

6. **Over and under relay.** Use towels instead of a ball.

Body Shapes Used in Aquatics

The terms *tuck, pike,* and *layout* are used in synchronized swimming, diving, and gymnastics. The Advanced Explorer learns to assume these shapes on land, in shallow water, and in the air. Movement exploration on the trampoline and the springboard in the gymnasium reinforce learning in the pool area. This aspect of aquatics training is designed specifically to improve proprioceptive awareness. The following questions elicit desired responses:

Tuck positions

1. "In how many different ways can you assume a tuck position on land? In the water? In the air?"

Pike positions

2. "In how many different ways can you assume a pike position on land? In the water? In the air?"

Layout positions

3. "How many ways can you assume a layout position on land? In the water? In the air? Can you do back layouts? Front layouts? Side layouts?"

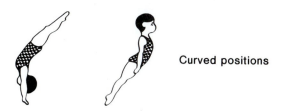

Curved positions

4. "In how many ways can you make your body curved on land? In the water? In the air? Can you combine a front layout with a curve? A back layout with a curve? A side layout with a curve?"

Early attempts at assuming tuck, pike, and layout positions in the water often result in sinking to the bottom. Many children accidentally discover floating while concentrating on body shapes. Those who do not discover floating gain valuable practice in breath control and balance.

Ways to Enter the Water

Many children prefer a session of jumping and/or diving to swimming. In the beginning, they may wish to have you hold one or both hands and jump with them. Others prefer you to be standing or treading water and awaiting their descent with outstretched arms. Participation in some kind of creative dramatics that demands a jump into the water often subtly evokes the desired response in children who have previously demonstrated fear and reluctance. Themes that have been particularly successful in motivating children to enter the water are (a) playing firefighter and sliding down the fire pole, (b) carrying lighted candles through a dark cave or perhaps the ancient Roman catacombs, (c) going on an African safari, (d) imitating Mary Poppins by opening an umbrella in flight, and, of course, (e) emulating space travelers through various trials and tribulations.

In response to "How many different ways can you enter the water feetfirst?" children may demonstrate the following:

1. Climb down the ladder. Most efficient method is facing ladder with back to water.
2. Sitting on edge of pool, scoot off into water: (a) freestyle (any way you wish), (b) in tuck position, (c) in pike position, and (d) with one leg straight, one bent.
3. Kneeling or half-kneeling, facing water.
4. Kneeling or half-kneeling, back to the water.
5. Squatting, facing water.
6. Squatting, back to water.
7. Standing, facing water using (a) stepoff, (b) jump and kneel in air before contacting water, (c) jump and tuck in air, (d) jump and clap hands, (e) jump and turn, (f) jump and touch toes, (g) hop, (h) leap, (i) arabesque, and (j) pike drop forward (camel walk position).
8. Standing, back to water, using: (a) stepoff, (b) jump, (c) hop, and (d) pike drop backward.

Stages in learning to dive

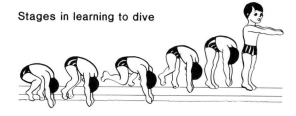

In response to "How many different ways can you enter the water headfirst?" children discover the various stages in learning to dive. They may also lie on the side and do a logroll into the water or accidently perform a front somersault.

Frog jump

1. "Can you jump like a frog under the water?"

Jack-in-the-box

2. "Can you squat in water over your head and then jump up and yell 'boo' like a jack-in-the-box?"

Dog walk when four limbs touch pool bottom; lame dog walk when three limbs touch bottom.

3. "Can you do a dog walk with your head under the water? A lame-dog walk?"

Mule kick

4. "Can you do a mule kick in the water?"

Seal walk

5. "Can you do a seal walk under the water?"

Camel walk

6. "Can you do a camel walk under the water? This is also called a wicket walk."

Egg sit followed by V sit

7. "Can you do an egg sit at the bottom of the pool? Can you do an egg sit near the surface and sink downward?"

Human ball bounce

8. "Can you do five bent-knee bounces at the bottom of the pool? Pretend that you are a ball being dribbled."

Coffee grinder

9. "Can you do the coffee grinder stunt at the bottom of the pool?"

Knee scale

10. "Can you do a balancing stunt under the water with one knee and both hands touching the bottom? Can you lift your arms and do a single-knee balance?"

FIGURE 17.5

Bracketing on the front and back.

Bracketing

Bracketing is the term for holding onto the gutter (rail) of the pool with one or both hands and allowing the feet to rise from the bottom of the pool so that the body is in a horizontal position (see Figure 17.5).

Retrieving Objects from the Bottom of the Pool

Advanced Explorers learn about spatial relationships within a new context as they open their eyes under water and see objects *through* the water. In the earliest stages of underwater exploration, they may hold both of your hands and

FIGURE 17.6

Simple sequencing.

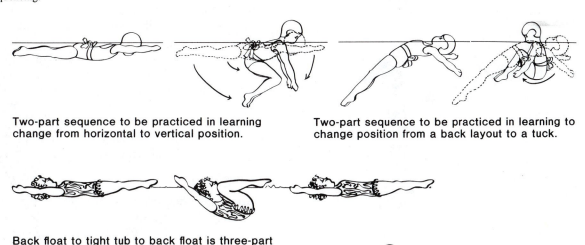

Two-part sequence to be practiced in learning
change from horizontal to vertical position.

Two-part sequence to be practiced in learning to
change position from a back layout to a tuck.

Back float to tight tub to back float is three-part
sequence in learning to change positions.

A five-part sequence in changing position.

submerge with you. Under water, you and the student may establish eye contact, shake hands, and mirror each other's hand and arm movements. Later, you can challenge the student to retrieve all sorts of things from the bottom. Practice in form, size, weight, and color discrimination can be integrated with the instructions for retrieval of objects.

Activities for the Floater

The Floater is comfortable in the water and can do almost anything but swim a coordinated stroke for 20 yd to qualify for the Red Cross Beginner card. The Floater is probably more competent in underwater swimming than in performing strokes near the surface. This is the period during which the following tasks are mastered: (a) horizontal to vertical positioning, (b) floating, (c) bobbing, (d) front-to-back positioning and vice versa, and (e) simple stunts in synchronized swimming.

Horizontal to Vertical Positioning

Floaters demonstrate ease in moving from a horizontal position to a vertical one. The degree of difficulty of this task varies with amount of buoyancy, specific gravity, and absence or paralysis of limbs. Simple sequencing is introduced, as depicted in Figure 17.6.

Floating

To teach floating to persons with varying body builds and/ or amputations of one type or another, you must have some understanding of the following terms: *buoyancy, specific gravity,* and *center of buoyance.*

Buoyancy is the quality of being able to float. The buoyancy of a human being depends upon the amount of water that each body part is able to displace and the weight of the body part itself. The larger the surface of the body part, the more water it will displace. For instance, the typical woman with wide pelvis and well-rounded buttocks displaces more water than the average man with his narrow hips and flat buttocks. The lighter the weight of the body part, the less upward force is required to buoy it up. Thus, if a cork and a marble of the same surface area are dropped into water, the cork will float and the marble will sink. Adipose tissue (fat) weighs less than muscle and bone tissue. Thus, if two persons of equal surface areas try to float and one individual is fat while the other is heavily muscled, the fat person will be buoyed upward more easily than the person with well-developed musculature. Buoyancy is explained by *Archimedes' principle,* which states: A body submerged in a liquid is buoyed up by a force equal to the weight of the displaced liquid.

The *specific gravity* of a human being is his or her weight compared to the weight of an equal amount of water, as shown in this formula:

$$\text{Specific gravity} = \frac{\text{Weight of body}}{\text{Weight of equal amount of water}}$$

After full inspiration, the specific gravity of most adult human beings is slightly less than 1. This means that most adults can float with their head above the surface of the water when their lungs are filled with air. After exhalation, the specific gravity of most adults is approximately 1.02. Only when the specific gravity is above 1.02 do individuals experience difficulty in floating.

FIGURE 17.7

Effects of buoyancy on floating explain why there are many correct ways. (CB=Center of buoyancy; CG=Center of gravity.)

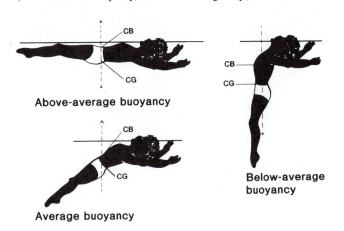

Above-average buoyancy

Average buoyancy

Below-average buoyancy

The *center of buoyance* (CB) of a human being in water is similar in function to the center of gravity (CG) when the body is not immersed in fluid. Both are areas where weight is concentrated; both serve as fulcrums about which the body rotates.

The CB, for most persons, is located in the thoracic cavity. The more obese an individual is, the lower his or her CB is. The CB is defined as the center of gravity of the volume of the displaced water before its displacement. If an object were of uniform density, its CB and CG would coincide; this is not the case with living creatures, human or fish.

In the water, the body can be likened to a first-class lever, which, like a seesaw, totters back and forth around its fulcrum (CB) until balance is achieved. Only when the CB and the CG are in the same vertical line can a person float without motion.

Figure 17.7 shows that there is no one correct way to float. Each person must experiment until he or she discovers the position in which CB and CG are aligned vertically. The hints that follow may help students cope with problems of buoyancy.

Below-Average Buoyancy

Men, as a whole, have less buoyancy than women. Black students have less buoyancy than white students. Buoyancy can be increased by raising the CG and hence the CB. This can be done by extending the arms overhead, by bending the knees so that heels almost touch the buttocks, or by assuming a tuck or jellyfish floating position. Hyperventilating—keeping the lungs filled with air and exhaling as seldom as possible—also helps.

Students should not attempt to lift the feet and legs and attain a horizontal position since the feet and legs will only drop downward again, building up enough momentum as they do so to pull the entire body under. Many persons who believe themselves to be *sinkers* could float if they started in the vertical rather than the horizontal position.

Above-Average Buoyancy

The obese person experiences many balance problems in the water for which he or she must learn to compensate. The alternate-arm stroke on the back crawl, for instance, must be performed twice as fast as normal to prevent the body from rolling over. The hips, legs, and feet are often above water level so that no kick is possible.

The most anxiety-ridden experience, however, for the obese beginning swimmer is changing from a horizontal position to a vertical stand. Try as he or she may, it is not easy to make the legs drop and the shoulders and trunk come forward so that the CG and CB are aligned over the feet.

Amputations

Amputations affect the location of the CG and the CB, which, in turn, affects buoyancy and balance. The loss of a limb causes displacement of the CG and CB to the opposite side. Thus, a student who has lost a right leg or arm has a tendency to roll to the left, where the weight of the body is centered. Most persons with amputations, whether congenital or acquired, can become excellent swimmers.

Extensive movement exploration is recommended to enable each person to discover the floating position and swimming strokes that best serve his or her needs. Most students with severe orthopedic disabilities seem to prefer swimming on the back. Specifically, the following strokes are suggested:

1. Loss of both legs—Back crawl or breaststroke.
2. Loss of one leg—Back crawl, elementary backstroke, or sidestroke.
3. Loss of both arms—Any kick that can be done on the back. This person has exceptional difficulty in changing from horizontal layout position to a stand.
4. Loss of one arm—Sidestroke or swimming on back with legs providing most of the power and the one arm finning.
5. Loss of one leg and one arm—Sidestroke with leg on the bottom; arm will create its own effective finning action.

Spasticity and Asymmetric Strength

Persons with spasticity or paralytic asymmetries tend to spin or rotate in the horizontal water position. To stabilize a float, swimmers should turn the head in the opposite direction of the body rotation. Backstrokes should be taught before front strokes, and symmetric strokes should be mastered before asymmetric strokes.

Bobbing

Bobbing is similar to several vertical jumps in place except that all the power comes from the arms. It can be done in either shallow or deep water, but traditionally is associated with water over the head.

Down phase in bobbing   Up phase in bobbing

Bobbing consists of two phases. In the *down phase,* both arms are raised simultaneously upward, causing the body to descend. The breath is exhaled. When the feet touch the bottom of the pool, the arm movement ends. The *up phase* is then initiated by both arms pressing simultaneously downward. This action pushes the body upward. The arm movements in bobbing are different from all others the child has encountered. The concept of displacing water—that is, pushing in the direction opposite from that which you wish to go—should be explained.

Bobbing accomplishes several goals: (a) improves rhythmic breathing, (b) increases vital breathing capacity—that is, tends to hyperventilate the swimmer, (c) heightens proprioceptive awareness, and (d) serves as a warm-up activity. Bobbing is recommended especially for asthmatic children. Variations of bobbing are

1. **Progressive bobbing.** The down phase is identical to that of bobbing in place. The up phase, however, is modified by using the legs to push the body off the pool bottom at approximately a 65° angle. The arm movement is basically the same. Progressive bobbing is a survival skill in that it can be used as a means of locomotion from the deep end of the pool to the shallow.

2. **Bobbing on one leg.**

3. **Bobbing in a tuck position.** Down phase: Arms pull upward, legs extend so that feet touch the bottom. Up phase: Arms press downward, tuck knees to chest so that full tuck is achieved at height of up phase.

4. **Seesaw bobbing with a partner.** To begin, partners face each other and hold hands. Then a rhythm is established in which one person is up while the other is down, as in partner-jumping on a trampoline.

Finning and Sculling

After students master a float, several sessions in movement exploration should focus on the arms and hands. Such problems as the following can be posed for the back layout, front layout, tuck, and pike positions:

1. "In the back layout position, how many different ways can you place your arms?"

2. "Which positions of the arms make floating easier? More difficult?"

3. "How many different kinds of movements can you perform with your arms in each position?"

4. "Which of these movements seem to make you sink? If you do sink, which of these movements can help your body rise to the surface of the water?"

5. "Which arm movements propel the body through the water headfirst?"

6. "Which arm movements enable you to execute the following position changes: (a) prone float to stand, (b) prone float to back float, (c) back float to stand, and (d) back float to prone float?"

7. "If you move only one arm, what happens? Can you propel the body directly to the right by using one arm only? Directly to the left?"

8. "In what other ways can you propel the body directly to the left? Directly to the right?"

9. "In how many different ways can you *push* the water away from you? *Pull* the water toward you?"

Ideally, creative dramatics should be combined with movement exploration so that the child can tell you and/or peers which emotions are being expressed by particular arm and hand movements: Variations of charades can be played in the water, and/or students may *act out* the feeling that a particular musical composition conveys.

Given sufficient time and encouragement, students eventually discover *finning* and *sculling* for themselves. Introduce the names of these movements and explain their usefulness in changing positions in the water. Movement exploration can then focus on how many different ways students can fin or scull.

Finning

Finning is a series of short pushes with the palms of the hands against the water in the *opposite* direction to the one in which the student wishes to move. Each push is followed by a quick, bent-arm recovery under the surface of the water.

Sculling

Many different types of *sculling* are recognized. In the standard scull, the hands are at the hips, close to the body. Movement at the shoulder joints is limited to inward and outward rotation of the arms that seems to be initiated by the hands in their execution of tiny figure-eight motions close to the water surface.

The motion of the hands and wrists consists of an inward and outward phase, each of which is performed with equal force. The palms move toward midline during the inward phase and away from midline during the outward phase so that the water is alternately scooped toward the hips and then pushed away. The thumbs are up during the inward phase and down during the outward phase. If students do not discover sculling for themselves, the movement should be introduced in the classroom and mastered before it is attempted in water. Sculling, for many swimmers, is a difficult pattern to learn through imitation.

Synchronized Swimming

The regulation stunts usually taught in units on synchronized swimming are similar to those performed in tumbling and gymnastics. Executing stunts in the water improves proprioception, enhances body awareness, and provides practice in movement imitation. The stunts described on the following pages can be mastered early in beginning swimming. The primary prerequisites are a feeling of ease in the water, the ability to scull while floating, and a keen sense of where the body is in space. Research at the Texas Woman's University has demonstrated that many slow learners can be taught to execute simple synchronized swimming stunts long before they achieve skill and endurance in regulation strokes. All stunts are begun from either the front layout position or the back layout position, as depicted below and in Figures 17.8 and 17.9.

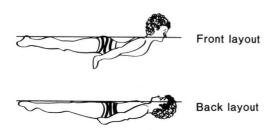

Front layout

Back layout

Whereas skilled performers are concerned with the aesthetic appearance of a stunt, the adapted physical educator does not worry about *good form*. The stunts are introduced in a manner similar to other tasks in movement exploration. Very few verbal directions are posed; on some occasions, a casual demonstration motivates the student to attempt new positions in the water. The stunts that follow are listed in order of difficulty under their respective starting positions. *Stunts in which the body is carried in a tuck position are easier than those executed in the pike or layout positions.*

Stunts That Begin in a Back Layout Position

1. **Tub.** "Can you change from a back layout position to a tuck position with the thighs perpendicular to the surface of the water? In this position, can you use sculling to revolve the body around in a circle?"

2. **Log Rolling.** "Can you roll the extended body over and over while keeping the legs motionless? This is identical to the stunt by the same name on land."

3. **Back Tuck Somersault.** "Can you perform a backward roll in a tuck position?"

4. **Oyster, Clam, or Pike up.** "Can you drop your hips as you simultaneously hyperextend and inwardly rotate the arms at the shoulder joints? When you are touching your toes in a pike position, can you sink to the bottom?"

5. **Back Pike Somersault.** "Can you assume a pike position with trunk under the water but parallel to the surface? Can you perform a backward roll in this pike position? Which part of this stunt is like the oyster?"

6. **Torpedo.** "Can you scull with your hands overhead so that your body is propelled in the direction of your feet? Submergence of the head and shoulders is optional."

7. **Back Dolphin.** "Can you maintain a back layout position as your head leads your body around in a circle under the surface of the water? Can you perform this same stunt with one knee bent?"

8. **Single Ballet Leg.** "Can you scull across the pool with one leg perpendicular to the surface of the water and the other leg extended on the surface of the water?"

9. **Submarine.** "While performing a single ballet leg, can you submerge the entire body up to the ankle of the perpendicular leg and then rise to the surface?"

10. **Back Walkover.** "Can you start a back dolphin but do *the splits* with the legs while they are above the surface of the water? This stunt ends in a front layout."

Stunts That Begin in a Front Layout Position

1. **Front Tuck Somersault.** "Can you perform a forward roll in a tuck position?"

2. **Flying Porpoise.** "Can you stand on the bottom, push off, and do a surface dive that looks like a flying porpoise?"

3. **Porpoise.** "Can you bend at the waist so that the trunk is almost perpendicular to the bottom, while the thighs remain parallel to the water? From this position, can you raise both legs until the entire body is vertical and then submerge?"

4. **Front Pike Somersault.** "Can you assume a pike position identical to the beginning of a porpoise? From this position, can you do a forward roll?"

5. **Front Walkover.** "Can you assume a pike position identical to the beginning of a porpoise? As the legs come out of the water, they do *the splits* so that you finish in a back layout position."

Rolling in the Water

Methods of rolling from back to front and vice versa in the water each have names within synchronized swimming circles. Use these terms to teach children names for the stunts that they can perform, thereby improving their communication skills.

1. **Half Log Roll.** "Can you change from back to front float or from front to back float?"

2. **Log Roll.** "Beginning from a back layout position with arms overhead, can you execute the log roll by reaching your arm across your body, by crossing one arm over the other, or by crossing one leg over the other?"

3. **Corkscrew.** "Can you log roll from a sidestroke position to prone float or to same side on which you started? If the sidestroke is on the left, a complete roll to the left is executed."

FIGURE   17.8

Stunts that begin in a back layout position.

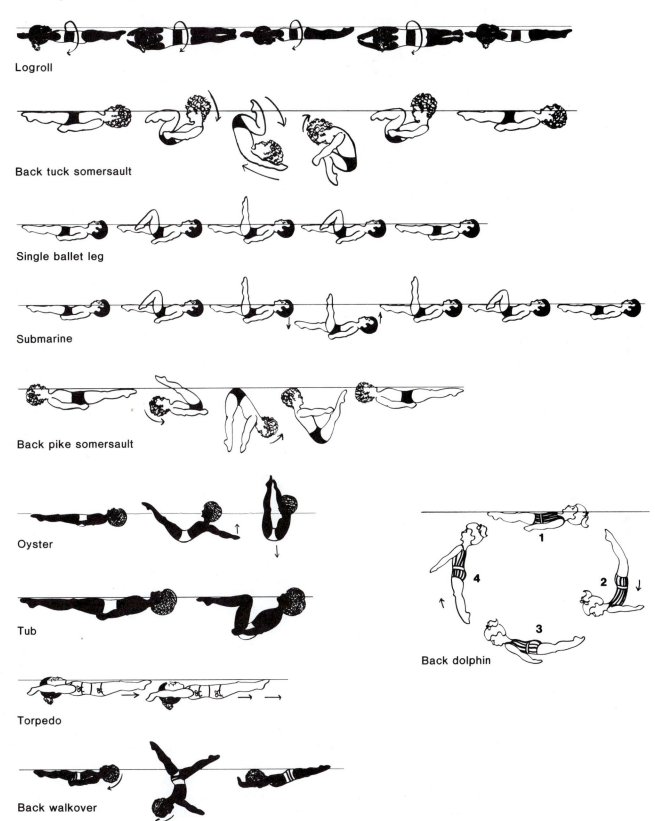

Logroll

Back tuck somersault

Single ballet leg

Submarine

Back pike somersault

Oyster

Tub

Torpedo

Back walkover

Back dolphin

FIGURE   17.9

Stunts that begin in a front layout position.

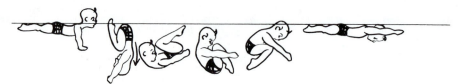

Front tuck somersault

Flying porpoise

Porpoise

Front pike somersault

Front walkover

4. **Reverse Corkscrew.** "If the sidestroke is on the left, can you execute a complete roll to the *right?*"

5. **Marlin.** "Can you (a) start in a *back layout* position, arms in T position, palms down; (b) roll onto right side, moving right arm to a sidestroke position and left arm to side for a *side layout* position; (c) continue roll onto a front layout position, with both arms in T position; (d) roll onto left side, moving left arm to a sidestroke position and right arm to side for a *side layout* position; and (e) finish in a *back layout* position with arms in T position?"

Administrative Aspects of an Aquatics Program

Pool Recommendations

Few teachers of students with disabilities have the opportunity to design their own pool, but a community or school committed to serving *all* persons will implement adaptations recommended by a specialist. These may include construction or purchase of the following:

1. Nonskid surface for floors and decks.
2. Handrails in the shower room.

3. Several ways to turn the water off and on in the shower room, such as a button on the floor as an alternative for persons who have no use of their arms. Ideally, the water in the shower room should turn itself off automatically.

4. Doors into the locker room and the pool wide enough to allow wheelchairs through.

5. Ramps as well as stairsteps; a movable ramp for entrance into the swimming pool; ladders that telescope up and down (see Figure 17.10).

6. Flashing red and green lights at the deep and shallow ends, respectively; a metronome or radio playing at the shallow end.

7. Floating buoys extended across the pool to warn of deep water; a change in the texture (feel) of the tile along the gutter in the deep end; the depth of the pool written in braille in the tile every several feet.

8. A horizontal line on the wall that is the same height as the depth of the water below it. This line allows children to compare their heights with the line on the wall to ascertain that the water will not be over their heads if they jump into the pool at a certain point. The line on the wall or the wall itself may be color-coded in terms of water depth.

9. A large storage cabinet with good ventilation to house the sponges, candles, rubber toys, Ping-Pong balls, and other accessories to movement exploration not used in ordinary swimming.

10. Hooks on the wall or plans for storage of inner tubes and other flotation devices needed in adapted physical activity.

The depth of the pool determines its expense in large part. The Olympic-size pool that provides for progressively deeper water is not recommended when instruction is the primary purpose. There is a definite trend toward building two or three separate pools rather than the multipurpose structure of the past. The instructional pool needs a depth of only 3 1/2 to 4 ft of water. Separate pools are constructed for diving, advanced synchronized swimming, and scuba diving.

Several public schools are now purchasing the porta-pool, which can be moved from school to school every several weeks. At the end of the day's instruction, a roof is pulled over the pool and securely locked in lieu of having to provide fencing and other safety measures. Nursery schools and special education units would do well to purchase the aluminum tank type pool sold by Sears and other commercial companies. Such pools are less expensive than trampolines and other pieces of playground apparatus.

The temperature of a swimming pool is normally maintained between 78° and 86° F, 26° and 30° C. While this temperature is invigorating, it is not geared to the needs of the beginning swimmer, who is partially out of the water when not in a horizontal position. Moreover, cold water tends to produce hypertonus and to heighten the spasticity of children with cerebral palsy.

FIGURE 17.10

Use of chairlift for student with multiple disabilities.

To facilitate relaxation of muscles in the water and ensure an optimum learning environment, the water temperature for adapted physical activity should be in the low 90°s. Increasing the temperature of the water causes two problems in pool management: (a) the chlorine evaporates in 90° water, and (b) the windows in the pool steam up from the evaporated water. Increasing the chlorine count is easy enough, but swimmers' complaints about the chlorine hurting their eyes appear unavoidable. Sunlamps or infrared lamps built into the ceiling tend to control evaporation.

Health Examination

Written approval of both the student's physician and parents should be on file prior to the beginning of swimming instruction. Most physicians prefer to use their own form but are willing to fill out supplementary information sheets (see Figure 17.11).

Close rapport with local physicians is essential to good adapted physical education. Mail a thank-you to the physician after receipt of the supplementary sheet and also send a list of the similarities and differences between swimming in the adapted physical education setting and the regular class. Explain such adaptations as increased pool temperature, availability of ramps and flotation devices, and individualized or small-group instruction.

FIGURE   17.11

Sample information sheet to be filled in by physician.

Name _____

Medical Diagnosis _____

Diagnosis in laymen's terms _____

_____

Which part of the body, if any, is involved:

____ Right arm   ____ Left arm   ____ Neck

____ Right leg   ____ Left leg   ____ Trunk

Other_____

What specific exercises or movements do you recommend for the involved parts?

_____

Do you recommend learning to float or swim in any particular position?

____ Front   ____ Right side   ____ Head out of water

____ Back   ____ Left side   ____ Head used normally in rhythmic
                                                  breathing

Should any special precautions be taken?

____ Needs to wear nose clip   ____ Should *not* dive

____ Needs to wear ear plug   ____ Needs to wear glasses

____ Should *not* hold breath   ____ Should *not* hyperventilate

____ Should *not* put head under water

   I recommend that this person participate in regularly scheduled swimming lessons adapted to his special needs as indicated on this sheet.

_____   _____
Date   Name of Physician

Contraindications and Swimming

Swimming is universally recommended for individuals with all kinds of disabilities, with the exception of the following conditions: infectious diseases in the active stage—that is, the person still has an elevated temperature; chronic ear infections and also the months during which tubes are in the ears; chronic sinusitis; allergies to chlorine or water; skin conditions such as eczema and ringworm; open wounds and sores; osteomyelitis in the active stage; and severe cardiac conditions. Physicians will sometimes prescribe hydrotherapy for individuals with some of these conditions.

Girls who wear internal tampons should be encouraged to participate fully in regularly scheduled instruction during their menstrual periods. Pregnant women generally swim until the sixth or seventh month, depending upon the philosophy of the obstetrician.

Diving may be contraindicated for individuals with arrested hydrocephalus, hemophilia, or anomalies of the face or head that affect normal breathing. Children with spastic cerebral palsy should not be taught to dive unless instruction is requested specifically by the parents and endorsed by the physician.

Time of Day for Swimming Instruction

The practice of waiting 1 or 2 hr after eating before engaging in swimming instruction is no longer viewed as valid except in the case of training for competitive swimming. Hence, swimming may be scheduled whenever it is convenient. However, conducting instruction after lunch may be better than immediately before, when the level of blood sugar characteristically reaches its daily low.

Classroom teachers report that swimming early in the day tends to exert a quieting influence upon hyperactive children. A procedure should be created whereby a student may request a pass to report to the swimming teacher in lieu of a regularly scheduled class when the child feels exceedingly aggravated or in special need of *letting off steam*.

Undressing, Showering, and Dressing

Assisting young children and individuals with severe disabilities with dressing procedures is an integral part of adapted aquatics. Be extremely careful to dry the skin and hair of children with Down syndrome since they are especially susceptible to upper respiratory infections.

Apply moisturizing cream or oil to dry skin immediately after swimming. The dry, rough skin of many children can be softened by regular applications of cream.

If land drill is planned prior to entrance in the water, eliminate the preliminary shower. At no time should a child in a wet suit be out of the pool for more than a few seconds.

Observe swimmers closely for blueness of lips, teeth chattering, goose bumps, and other evidence of chilling. Children tend to chill more quickly than adults; the thinner

the child, the shorter the time in the water he or she can endure. In accordance with the principle of individual differences, *all* students should not be scheduled for instructional periods of identical lengths. Children in wet suits should *not* be allowed to sit on the edge of the pool with a towel draped about them in the hope that they will magically warm up and return for additional instruction. A child who professes to be too cold to remain in the pool should be expected to dry off and dress fully. Activities should be planned for individuals who leave the pool early, and the dressing room should be supervised at all times.

References

American Red Cross. (1977). *Adapted aquatics*. Garden City, NY: Doubleday.

American Red Cross. (1992a). *American Red Cross swimming and diving*. St. Louis: Mosby-Year Book.

American Red Cross. (1992b). *Water safety instructor manual*. St. Louis: Mosby-Year Book.

Andersen, L. (1986). Swimming to win. In J. A. Jones (Ed.), *Training guide to cerebral palsy sports* (3rd ed.) (pp. 161–166). Champaign, IL: Human Kinetics.

Andersen, L. (1989). *Handbook for adapted competitive swimming* (3rd ed.). Colorado Springs, CO: United States Swimming, Inc.

British Sports Association for the Disabled. (1983). *Water sports for the disabled*. West Yorkshire, England: EP Publishing.

Bull, E., Haldorsen, J., Kahrs, N., Mathiesen, G., Mogensen, I., Torheim, A., & Uldal, M. (1985). *In the pool: Swimming instruction for the disabled*. Oslo, Norway: Ungdoms-Og Idrettsavdelingen. (Distributed in the United States by American Alliance for Health, Physical Education, Recreation, and Dance.)

Campion, M. (1985). *Hydrotherapy in pediatrics*. Rockville, MD: Aspen Systems.

Clarke, L. (1973). *Can't read, can't write, can't takl too good either*. New York: Walker & Company.

Gehlsen, G., & Karpuk, J. (1992). Analysis of the NWAA swimming classification system. *Adapted Physical Activity Quarterly, 9* (2), 141–147.

Green, J. S., & Miles, B. (1987). Use of mask, fins, snorkel, and scuba equipment in aquatics for the disabled. *Palaestra, 3* (4), 12–17.

Grosse, S. (1985). It's a wet and wonderful world. *Palaestra, 2* (1), 14–17, 40.

Grosse, S. (1987). Use and misuse of flotation devices in adapted aquatics. *Palaestra, 4* (1), 31–33, 56.

Grosse, S. (1993). *Computer information retrieval system in adapted aquatics (CIRSA): A comprehensive reference list*. Available from S. Grosse, 7252 Wabash Ave., Milwaukee, WI 53223.

Grosse, S., & Gildersleeve, L. (1984). *The Halliwick method: Water freedom for the handicapped*. Unpublished material available from S. Grosse, 7252 Wabash Ave., Milwaukee, WI 53223.

Grosse, S., & McGill, C. (1989). Independent swimming for children with severe physical impairments. In AAHPERD (Ed.), *The best of practical pointers I* (pp. 227–240). Reston, VA: American Alliance for Health, Physical Education, Recreation, and Dance.

Jones, J. A. (1986). *Training guide to cerebral palsy sports* (3rd ed.). Champaign, IL: Human Kinetics.

Kahrs, N. (1974). *Swimming teaching for the handicapped.* Oslo, Norway: Statens ungdoms- og idrettskontor.

Kochen, C., & McCabe, J. (1986). *The baby swim book.* Champaign, IL: Human Kinetics.

Krasevec, J. (1989). *Y's way to water exercise instructor's guide.* Champaign, IL: Human Kinetics.

Langendorfer, S. (1989). Aquatics for young children with handicapping conditions. *Palaestra, 5* (3), 17–19, 37–40.

Langendorfer, S. (1990). Contemporary trends in infant/preschool aquatics. *Journal of Physical Education, Recreation, and Dance, 61* (5), 36–39.

Lowman, C. L. (1937). *Techniques of underwater gymnastics.* Los Angeles: American Publications.

Lowman, C. L., & Roen, S. (1952). *Therapeutic use of pools and tanks.* Philadelphia: W. B. Saunders.

Mayse, J. (1991). Aquacise and aquafitness for adapted aquatics. *Palaestra, 7* (2), 54–56.

Newman, J. (1976). *Swimming for children with physical and sensory impairments.* Springfield, IL: Charles C. Thomas.

Priest, L. (1979). Integrating the disabled into aquatics programs. *Journal of Physical Education, Recreation, and Dance, 50* (2), 57–59.

Priest, L. (1987). Adapted aquatics—education and training. *Palaestra, 4* (1), 26–30.

Priest, L. (1990). Aquatics. In J. Winnick (Ed.), *Adapted physical education and sport* (pp. 391–408). Champaign, IL: Human Kinetics.

Reynolds, G. (Ed.). (1973). *A swimming program for the handicapped.* New York: Association Press.

Richter, K., Adams-Mushett, C., Ferrara, M., & McCann, B. C. (1992). Integrated swimming classification: A faulted system. *Adapted Physical Activity Quarterly, 9* (1), 5–13.

Robinson, J. (1986). *Scuba diving with disabilities.* Champaign, IL: Human Kinetics.

Shea, E. J. (1986). *Swimming for seniors.* Champaign, IL: Human Kinetics.

Sheldahl, L. M. (1986). Special ergometric techniques and weight reduction. *Medicine and Science in Sports and Exercise, 18* (1), 25–30.

Special Olympics International. (1981). *Special Olympics swimming and diving sports skills instructional program manual.* Washington, DC: Author.

YMCA of the USA. (1986). *YMCA progressive swimming instructor's guide.* Champaign, IL: Human Kinetics.

YMCA of the USA. (1987). *Aquatics for special populations.* Champaign, IL: Human Kinetics.

PART

III

Individual Differences, with Emphasis on Sport

CHAPTER
18

Infants, Toddlers, and Young Children: The New Emphasis

FIGURE 18.1

The individualized family service plan (IFSP) goal of crawling to a desired toy is implemented for a motorically delayed 2-year-old infant with Down syndrome. The cold, slick mirror provides tactile stimulation to the bare skin, as well as visual input. The infant's primary locomotor pattern will continue to be belly crawling and/or a bunny-hop movement until he loses the symmetrical tonic neck reflex. Then the IFSP goal will be changed to creeping.

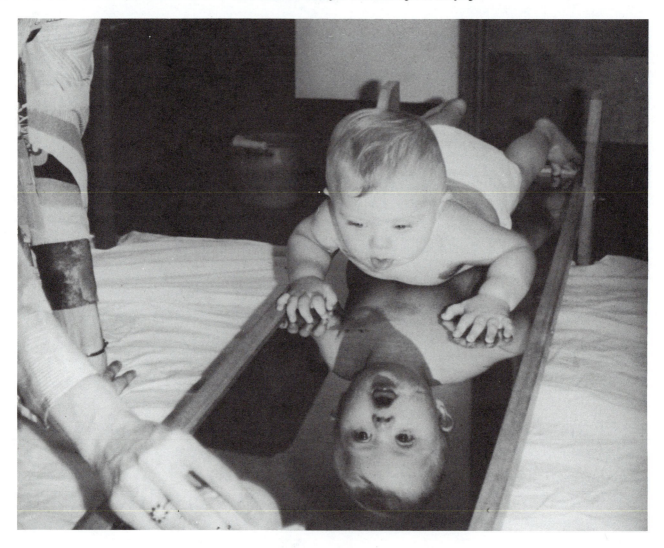

After you have studied this chapter, you should be able to:

1. Discuss the legal bases for special education programming (including adapted physical education) of infants, toddlers, and young children.

2. Discuss diagnostic terms, assessment approaches, and eligibility for special services.

3. Discuss the neurological bases of motor development for infants, toddlers and young children, with special emphasis on reflexes, reactions, developmental milestones, and application of motor development principles. For help, review Chapter 10.

4. Identify adapted physical activity goals and objectives of most importance for infants, toddlers, and young children and discuss programming in relation to each. For help, see Chapters 11 and 12.

5. Explain the IFSP and IEP, associate them with correct age groups, and contrast the two approaches.

6. Discuss placement and programming in relation to (a) social acceptance and integration and (b) sport socialization.

7. Describe the Language-Arts-Movement Programming (LAMP) model and create some play activities that promote integrated motor-language-cognitive development.

The newest emphasis in adapted physical activity is on infants, toddlers, and children ages 8 years and under (Cowden, 1991; Cowden & Eason, 1991; Eason, 1991). Federal law defines *infants and toddlers with disabilities* as individuals from birth to age 2. Children ages 3 to 8 are designated as *young* rather than *preschool,* because most are in some kind of early education school-based program. Impetus for this new area is found in the Individuals with Disabilities Education Act (IDEA) of 1990. Subchapter III (Part C) describes outreach preschool and early intervention programs for children with disabilities from birth through age 8. Subchapter VIII (Part H) describes infant and toddler services that were created by PL 99–457 of 1986. Regulations for PL 99–457 were published in the *Federal Register* of June 22, 1989.

Federal law emphasizes that assessment and programming shall be in five areas of development: (a) physical, (b) cognitive, (c) psychosocial, (d) self-help, and (e) language and speech. These are the areas highlighted in this chapter (see Figure 18.1). Body image and play and game behaviors are primarily cognitive at this age; self-concept is psychosocial. Everything should relate to language, speech, and self-help.

Three Diagnostic Terms

Infants, toddlers, and young children eligible for special services are classified as (a) disabled, (b) developmentally delayed, or (c) at risk for developmental delays (see Figure 18.2). This shows the recent trend away from use of the word *handicapped.*

Disabled is the term used to describe children who fit into established diagnostic categories (e.g., speech and language impaired, learning disabled, mentally retarded). About 75% of young children with diagnosed disabilities fall into the speech and language impaired category.

Developmentally delayed is a generic term that permits states to establish their own criteria as to what consti-

tutes performance significantly below average. Federal legislation indicates that developmental delays can occur in five areas: (a) cognitive, (b) physical, (c) language and speech, (d) psychosocial or emotional, and (e) self-help skills. Statistical criteria are usually established for diagnosis—for example, (a) functions at 75% or less of his or her chronological age in two or more areas, (b) scores at least 1.5 standard deviations below the mean, or (c) scores below the 30th percentile. Two or more tests, with good validity and reliability, are used to make a diagnosis. Other diagnostic procedures include documented, systematic observation by a qualified professional, parental reports, developmental checklists, and criterion-referenced instruments.

At risk for developmental delays refers to those who "have been subjected to certain adverse genetic, prenatal, perinatal, postnatal, or environmental conditions that are known to cause defects or are highly correlated with the appearance of later abnormalities" (Peterson, 1987, p. 138). Poor development often is not noticeable during the first several months of life. Many children do not evidence clear delays until the end of the second year (Peterson, 1987).

Among the many factors contributing to risk are low socioeconomic environments, prematurity and low birth weight, difficult or traumatic delivery, maternal age of under 15 or over 40, a family history of genetic disorders and/or problem pregnancies, and mothers with substance abuse or chronic health problems (Cratty, 1990; Diamond, 1989; Peterson, 1987; Thurman & Widerstrom, 1985). Young children with HIV infections and AIDS are discussed in Chapter 19.

Reflexes and Reactions

Work with infants and toddlers demands an understanding of reflexes and reactions. *Reflexes* are involuntary changes in muscle tone elicited by certain stimuli or conditions. These changes range from barely noticeable, subtle shifts in muscle

FIGURE 18.2

Illustrative children in early childhood programs.

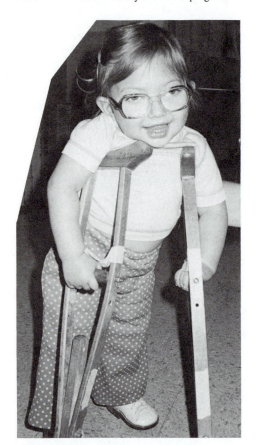
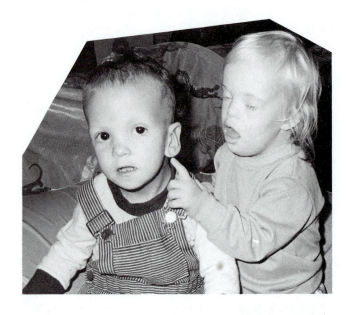
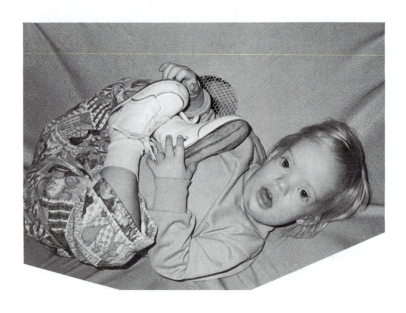
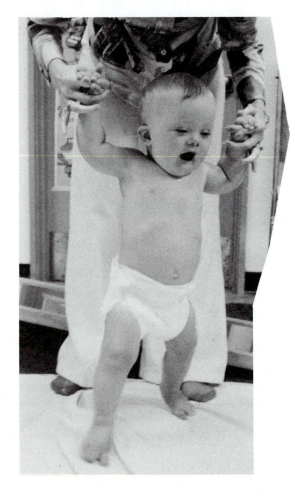

FIGURE   18.3

Domination of flexor tone in prone position is seen in infant from birth
until about 4 weeks old.

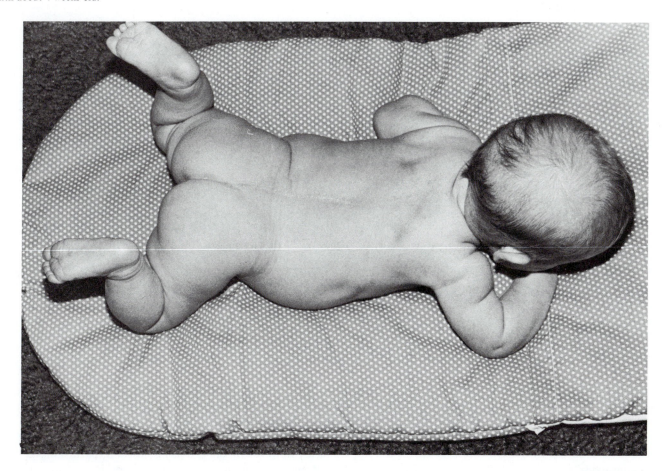

tension to big muscle movements that force limbs into undesired positions. *Reactions* are automatic movement patterns that replace reflexes in accordance with an inborn
timetable. Most reactions are lifelong and act to protect the
body and/or help it maintain equilibrium.

Newborn infants have no motor control because
every position change elicits reflexes. When in prone position, they are in a flexed fetal posture referred to as *flexor
tone dominance* because the anterior surface muscles contract in response to the tactile stimuli from the surface (see
Figure 18.3). Movement to a supine position causes the extensor muscles on the posterior surface to automatically contract. This is called *extensor tone dominance*. Any movement
of the head likewise causes associated movements of other
body parts. Until infants are 4 months of age, they seldom
initiate voluntary, purposeful movement (see Figure 18.4).

As the central nervous system (CNS) matures, automatic reactions and voluntary movement patterns emerge
to override reflex control of muscle tone. This process is
analogous to layering; it is continuous and lifelong. The
more a specific voluntary act is practiced, the more the reflex activity that could have interfered is layered over or
suppressed.

Children with developmental delays and movement
problems need help with reflex integration and reaction
emergence. This information is presented in Chapter 10 because reflex abnormalities are not associated only with infancy and early childhood. They are lifespan problems in
many disabilities.

Principles of Motor Development

Principles of motor development help explain normal function in young children and thus serve as guides to assessment
and programming. When one or more of the principles in
Table 18.1 are violated, an infant or child cannot perform at
age-level expectations.

Assessment often focuses on how many motor development principles are violated and for how long. Some
children's development is delayed and can be facilitated by
activities based on motor development principles. Other children, especially those with cerebral palsy (CP), are plagued
by abnormalities that remediation can ameliorate but not
eliminate.

The motor development principle of *continuity* is violated in infants and children who, because of a disability,
remain frozen at a particular level and/or are unable to

FIGURE 18.4

Same infant as in Figure 18.3 at about 6 months of age, when no longer dominated by flexor tone. Note ability to reach with one arm, while the other arm remains motionless. Arms and legs can fully extend.

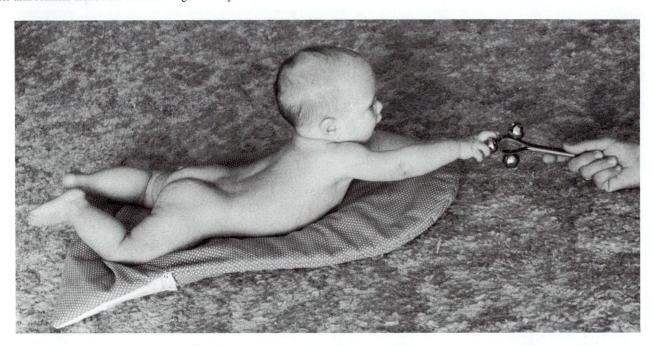

master motor tasks appropriate to chronological age. For example, infants and children with severe CP have CNS dysfunction that does not permit the primitive reflexes to be suppressed according to the normal timeline. As a result, they are unable to progress through the continuum of developmental milestones for achieving locomotion (see Figure 18.5).

The principle of *uniform sequence* is violated when tasks are not mastered in the order that developmentalists have indicated is normal. Research on thousands of infants, toddlers, and children has established normal developmental sequences like that presented in Figure 18.5. Deviance from uniform sequence, however, has been reported in infants who are blind or multiply disabled (deJong, 1990) and others who exhibit clumsiness in later years.

With respect to programming, the principles of continuity and uniform sequence provide the rationale for using developmental sequences to guide decisions about the order in which tasks should be taught. They also provide the rationale for *patterning,* taking the body parts through prescribed movements over and over again, a technique used when persons are too severely disabled to move themselves.

The principle of *neurological maturation* is violated whenever continuity and uniform sequence are affected. Growth and maturation within the brain and spinal cord determine rate of motor development. Foremost among problems is *myelination,* the process of forming a protective covering (myelin) around nerve fibers. Myelination begins approximately 5 months before birth and continues into young adulthood. Parts of the CNS are myelinated in a specific order, which explains why control of body parts occurs in a specific, predictable sequence. Until nerve fibers are myelinated, they cannot carry messages back and forth between the CNS and the muscles.

Myelination cannot be speeded up in normal infants. In developmental delays, however, patterning and independent practice of age-appropriate tasks provide stimulation to the nervous system that supports progressive myelination. The amount of myelination determines the nature of motor responses. Simplified, responses occur at three levels (reflex, reaction, and voluntary movement), each governed by progressively higher centers of the brain. Damage or delay in the development of any part affects all other parts.

The principle of *reflex integration and reaction emergence* emphasizes that reflexes and reactions are the foundation of movement coordination and control. Physical awkwardness is explained by this principle. Difficulty with balance relates to failure of the equilibrium reactions to fully function. Problems with coordination and control stem partly from inability to move a specific body part without undesired associated shifts of muscle tone in other parts; this occurs because reflexes have not been sufficiently integrated. Likewise, smooth, reciprocal contraction and relaxation of muscles is determined by reflex mechanisms.

The principle of *general-to-specific activity* explains reflex integration and motor control. The newborn responds to stimuli with generalized mass activity. With CNS maturation, children are progressively able to move specific body parts without associated overflow movement. This principle explains why early childhood physical education stresses movement exploration and imitation of total body actions

Table 18.1
Principles of normal motor development.

1. **Continuity.** Development is a continuous process, from conception to death.

2. **Uniform sequence.** The sequence of development is the same in all children, but the rate of development varies from child to child.

3. **Neurological maturation.** Development is intricately related to the maturation of the nervous system. No amount of practice can enable a child to perform a motor task until myelination has occurred.

4. **Reflex integration and reaction emergence.** An inborn timetable is followed, whereby reflexes are suppressed and righting, protective extension, and equilibrium reactions emerge. These developments enable voluntary movement patterns to unfold and coordination and control to be acquired.

5. **General-to-specific activity.** Generalized mass activity is replaced by specific responses of individual body parts. The child learns to assemble the parts of a general pattern before altering the parts to meet specific environmental demands.

6. **Cephalocaudal direction.** Gross motor development begins with head control (strength in neck muscles) and proceeds downward.

7. **Proximodistal coordination.** Muscle groups near (proximo) midline become functional before those farther away (distal) from midline do. For example, a child learns to catch with shoulders, upper arms, and forearms before catching with fingers. Movements performed at midline (in front of body) are easier than those that entail crossing midline (to left or right of body—i.e., more distant from midline).

8. **Bilateral-to-crosslateral motor coordination.** *Bilateral* movement patterns (both limbs moving simultaneously, as in arm movements of the breaststroke or reaching for an object at midline) are the first to occur in the human infant, followed by *unilateral* movement patterns (right arm and right leg moving simultaneously or vice versa), followed by *crosslateral* patterns (right arm and left leg moving simultaneously).

Note. Primary sources for these principles are Gesell and Ames (1940) and Illingsworth (1983).

(e.g., animal walks, rolls, jumps) rather than activities that require specific body parts to be used in accordance with visual and auditory input. This supports *whole-part-whole pedagogy.* General or whole body challenges are the focus until reasonable control of body parts is achieved.

The principle of *cephalocaudal direction* explains why emphasis is placed on head control in remediation. The infant achieves control of head (*cephalus*) before control of the lower spine (generalized to *caudo,* meaning "tail"). This principle is violated by persons dominated by reflexes who learn to sit, crawl, and creep but cannot hold the head erect and motionless.

FIGURE 18.5

Developmental milestones in achieving normal walking gait. Note correct terminology for *crawl* (on belly) versus *creep* (on hands and knees). Ages given are *average* time of appearance.

Fetal posture — 0 month
Chin up — 1 month
Chest up — 2 months
Reach and miss — 3 months
Sit with support — 4 months
Sit on lap, grasp object — 5 months
Crawl — 6-8 months
Sit alone — 7 months
Stand with help — 8 months
Stand holding furniture — 9 months
Creep — 10 months
Walk when led — 11 months
Pull to stand by furniture — 12 months
Climb stair steps — 13 months
Stand alone — 14 months
Walk alone — 15 months

The principle of *proximodistal coordination* explains the emphasis on midline activities. The nervous system matures from the midline (spinal column) outward. Thus, muscles closer (proximo) to the midline have mature innervation before those farther (distal) from midline. Muscles moving the head, neck, scapula, and trunk become coordinated to permit sitting, crawling, creeping, and standing before muscles of the arms and legs become coordinated enough for throwing, catching, and kicking. Likewise, large muscles of the shoulders and hips become coordinated before the small muscles of the hands and feet that move the digits.

The principle of *bilateral-to-crosslateral motor coordination* explains progress through three levels of limb movement. Bilateral movements are arms or legs simultaneously reaching, spreading, or closing. At about 4 months of age, when voluntary movement control begins, infants bring both hands to midline and begin looking intently at them. This seems to be the beginning of awareness of body parts and cognition that parts can do something. Shortly thereafter, infants in supine or propped sitting positions reach and grasp with both hands. They also learn to hold the bottle with both hands.

By age 6 or 7 months, infants can succeed in purposeful unilateral movements, usually the reaching of one arm to grasp a toy. Some children with disabilities, however, cannot perform unilateral movements without undesired overflow activity in the opposite limb. Games like waving bye-bye are often used to assess early unilateral development. Imitations of single arm or leg movements are used as remediation for children who appear to be frozen at the bilateral level.

Crosslateral movements are those in which the limbs work in opposition (e.g., the left leg moves forward with the right arm). These evolve naturally in walking patterns but are typically not exhibited in throwing and kicking patterns until age 5 or 6. Many adults who are clumsy still do not consistently use opposition. Crosslateral coordination is essential to good balance, and the emphasis on balancing activities in early childhood is partly to support neural maturation that will lead naturally to opposition.

Body Image: A Major Goal

Body image is all of the feelings, attitudes, beliefs, and knowledge that a person has about his or her body and its capacity for movement. These include psychomotor, affective, and cognitive understandings that begin in infancy. Development of body image is fundamental to shaping a good self-concept, especially in early childhood, when most feelings about the global self stem from movement and language experiences. Consider, for example, the first praise that infants receive. This is typically directed toward physical appearance ("such a pretty baby") or achievement of motor milestones (first grasp, first steps, first playfulness).

Body image development in early childhood is synonymous with sensorimotor development. Table 18.2 shows that different terms are applied to body image constructs at different ages. Body image objectives are (a) to develop body awareness, (b) to develop pride in the body and self-confidence in using it, and (c) to develop self-initiative in moving in new and different ways. Normal children often achieve these objectives without help, but in adapted physical education, these objectives are major challenges.

Body schema is the diagram of the body that evolves in the brain in response to sensorimotor input. The body schema enables the infant to feel body boundaries, identify body parts, plan and execute movements, and know where the body is in space. Figure 18.6 depicts an adult brain, showing developed potential. The motor projection areas of the brain are topographically organized, with each part controlling specific muscles that, in turn, control body movement. At birth, this capacity to control movement is not yet developed. Remember the motor development principle of general-to-specific activity (i.e., generalized mass activity is replaced by specific responses of individual body parts). Each

Table 18.2
Terms used in different stages of body image development.

Developmental Stage	Body Image Construct
Sensorimotor (0 to 2 years)	Body schema
Preoperational (2 to 7 years)	Body awareness
	Self-awareness
Concrete operational (7 to 11 years)	Body image
	Self-concept

FIGURE   18.6

(*A*) Lateral view of adult brain depicts premotor and motor cortex strips on the frontal lobe. (*B*) Diagram of the body that evolves in the brain in response to sensorimotor input. Each voluntary movement is controlled in the same place on the motor strip of every human being.

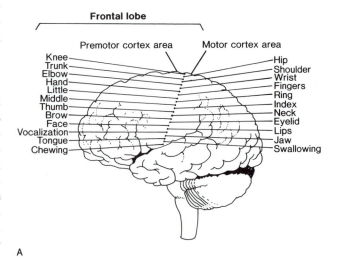

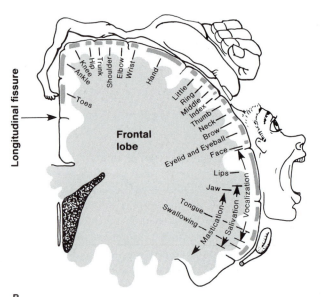

FIGURE 18.7

First stages in the development of body image.

4 weeks
or
1 month

Proprioceptive and tactile input from movement of another. First proprioceptive input initiated by self: head and neck muscles.

16 weeks
or
4 months

First awareness of hands. Can voluntarily bring hands to midline. Rolls over, providing proprioceptive input regarding total body in space.

28 weeks
or
7 months

First interest in mirror play.
First awareness of feet.

40 weeks
or
10 months

Laterality is reinforced when balance is maintained in sitting, creeping.
Imitation of movements begins, usually with bye-bye and shaking head yes and no.

movement of the body or its parts by the infant or another provides sensorimotor input (kinesthetic, vestibular) to the brain, which causes the body schema to evolve.

Sensory input from the skin, muscles, and joints (touch, pressure, temperature, pain) also contributes to the early development of body schema. Figure 18.6 shows that the body schema develops in a cephalocaudal direction, with the infant first becoming aware of eating/drinking and then of seeing. Later, the infant gains control of head/neck muscles (turning head from side to side, lifting head), then the hand/finger muscles (grasping/holding toys), then the upper extremities, and finally, the lower extremities. Figure 18.6 shows also that a disproportionately large cortical area is devoted to muscle groups responsible for fine muscle control, such as that required for lips and fingers.

Visual input is important in the evolution of body schema. At birth, infants have the ability to briefly fixate on stable objects and to track slow-moving objects through short arcs. From birth to 1 month of age, infants have Snellen vision of 20/150 to 20/400. This means that they see at 20 ft what persons with mature vision and normal acuity see at 150 ft. Near vision, however, is better than far vision, and infants begin to visually fixate very early on body parts, especially their hands and feet. Even before their random, generalized movements are brought under control, infants are adding visual images of self to their body schemas.

Body schema continues to develop and change throughout the lifespan. As the child matures, cognitive and affective dimensions are added to the psychomotor parameters. If problems occur, the body schema is affected, motor planning is damaged, and faulty movements occur. The sequence of body image development seems to parallel Piaget's stages in cognitive development.

Sensorimotor Stage of Development

During the sensorimotor stage (ages 0 to 2 in children without disabilities), infants become aware of their bodies and their capacities for movement (see Figure 18.7). Input from the 10 sensory modalities creates and then reinforces awareness of body boundaries (self/not-self), two sides of the body (laterality), space (verticality and directionality), time (synchrony, rhythm), force, and flow.

During the sensorimotor period, children also learn to imitate facial expressions, limb movements, and body positions. Visual input is the most important sense modality in imitation, since seeing others motivates the child to locomotion. Needing or wanting an object (food/toy) within the visual field is another reinforcer of imitation. These facts help explain why sensorimotor development is delayed in children who are congenitally blind.

Motor planning (praxis) also emerges during the sensorimotor period as cognition develops and the child wants to manipulate objects/toys and to move from place to place. Early voluntary movement can leave the child feeling competent and loved or clumsy, scorned, and pitied. Thus, body image components in the affective domain begin to interweave with those in the psychomotor domain.

From birth until 2 years of age, children normally acquire a speaking vocabulary of about 300 words. Among these are names of common body parts, like hands, feet, face, tummy, nose, eyes, ears, and mouth. Self-awareness develops in a definite order: hands, feet, face, and trunk (see Figure 18.8). The emergence of language for body parts and movements reinforces the growing understanding and appreciation of the body.

FIGURE   18.8

Self-awareness develops in a definite order: hands, feet, face, and trunk. Infants learn about the body parts they see. Mirrors are needed to learn about the face.

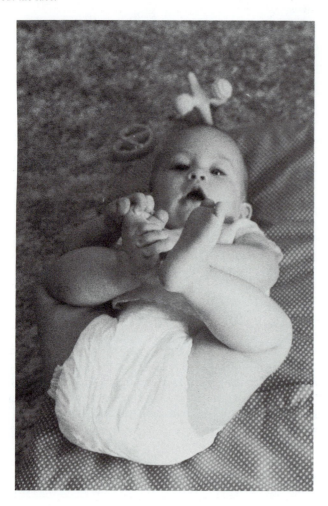

Preoperational Stage of Development

In the preoperational stage, speech develops rapidly (from 300 words at age 2 to several thousand words at age 7) and gradually takes precedence over movement as a means of expression. During this time span, children also begin to perceive themselves as competent and lovable, or the opposite. The way they look and move has much to do with such perceptions (see Figure 18.9). Thus, body image development is primarily in the cognitive and affective domains.

Play and Game Behaviors: A Major Goal

Children with severe delays/disabilities do not play spontaneously. Neither do they laugh and show evidence of having fun. Thus, a major goal of early childhood adapted physical activity is learning the concept of fun and responding appropriately to social and/or sensory stimulation. Normal infants smile and laugh spontaneously in response to pleasurable sights and sounds between 1 and 4 months of age. They begin reaching for objects at about 3 to 5 months and, as soon as they develop coordination, spend considerable energy working for a toy out of reach and exploring what body parts can do.

Peek-a-boo, typically learned between 5 and 10 months of age, is the beginning of social game behaviors. Thereafter, normal infants seem to know instinctively how to imitate and respond to play activities initiated by significant others. Moreover, when left alone, they move about, explore the environment, and engage in solitary play. Gradually, without much help, they develop body control, object control, and basic movement patterns. Placed in an environment with play apparatus and equipment, nondisabled preschoolers seem self-motivated to run, jump, climb, hang, slide, and balance. Movement is obviously fun, intrinsically rewarding, and inseparable from play.

In children with severe delays/disabilities, this spontaneity is often diminished or absent. Compared with nondisabled peers, they engage in fewer activities and spend much of their time sitting and lying (Burstein, 1986). Assessment of such children should begin with structured observations of their spontaneous interactions with the environment. Do they initiate contact with people and objects, and is their contact appropriate? How long do they sustain contact? Do they demonstrate preferences for some

FIGURE 18.9

Later stages in development of body image.

1 year
or
12 months

2 years
or
24 months

Proprioceptive input from walking and changing positions from up to down. Competence feeling from casting balls / objects that others must retrieve. Feelings about body as good / bad from toilet training.

Has about 300 words in vocabulary.
Can name body parts of doll.
Understands on-off concepts, then in-out, turn around.
Beginning imitative play with dolls, projects feeling about self into doll play.

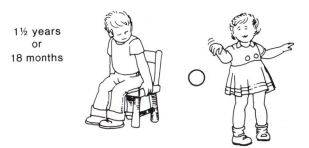

1½ years
or
18 months

3 years
or
36 months

Understands and can say up, down (first movement concepts).
Is learning names of body parts.
Increased competence from hurling balls / objects.
Retrieves balls for self.

Understands over-under, front-back, big-little, short-tall / long, high-low.
Copies circles, crosses on paper, but cannot yet draw a person.
Balances on one foot.
Rides tricycle.

objects and people? If so, these preferences can guide the selection of reinforcement strategies in shaping behavior management plans.

Table 18.3 presents an inventory developed to assess play and game behaviors and guide programming. The play and game behaviors goal encompasses the following:

to learn to play spontaneously; to progress through developmental play stages from solitary and parallel play behaviors up through cooperative and competitive play; to promote contact and interaction behaviors with toys, play apparatus, and persons; to learn basic game formations and mental operations needed for play.

No child is too severely disabled to benefit from physical education instruction. The goals, objectives, and pedagogy, however, differ from those used with nondisabled children. The major emphasis should be on the development of play and game behaviors that are movement oriented and result in good feelings about the self.

Motor skills should not be taught or practiced separate from function and/or play, as sometimes occurs in therapy. This is because special education children, unlike nondisabled peers, tend not to generalize motor skills. They do not know how to use motor skills unless direct instruction and practice in many different settings are provided.

Thus, physical education for children with disabilities/delays is often conceptualized as developmental play instruction. Objectives focus on appropriateness and duration of interactions with toys, sport objects and implements, play apparatus, and people (Cowden & Torrey, 1990; Evans, 1980; Loovis, 1985; Wasson & Watkinson, 1981; Watkinson & Wall, 1982).

Motor Skills and Patterns: A Major Goal

Most, but not all, children with delays/disabilities have motor skill problems. Typically, patterns like sitting, crawling, creeping, standing, and walking emerge later than in normal children. Whereas patterns occur without instruction in normal infants and toddlers, they must be carefully taught to most special education children (see Figure 18.10). Mastery of motor skills is compromised by retention of primitive reflexes and the presence of abnormal muscle tone, which is manifested as spasticity or the opposite condition, floppy baby syndrome (hypotonia, atonia). Moreover, the appearance of righting, protective extension, and equilibrium reactions is often delayed or impaired, causing difficulty with balance and body control.

Table 18.3
Sherrill social play behaviors inventory.

	Mary	Jim	Juan
Autistic/Unoccupied			
Shows no spontaneous play. _____			
Makes no response to stimuli. _____			
Shows no object or person preference. _____			
Makes stereotyped/repetitive movements. _____			
Pounds/shakes/mouths objects without purpose. _____			
Self-stimulates. _____			
Wanders about aimlessly. _____			
Self-mutilates. _____			
Solitary/Exploratory			
Reacts to stimuli (approach/avoid). _____			
Reacts to persons/objects. _____			
Understands object permanence (peek-a-boo, hide-and-seek). _____			
Explores body parts. _____			
Explores objects/toys. _____			
Shows object preference. _____			
Shows person preference. _____			
Parallel			
Establishes play space near others. _____			
Shows awareness of others but doesn't interact. _____			
Plays independently with own things. _____			
Plays on same playground apparatus as others. _____			
Follows leader in imitation games and obstacle course. _____			
Associative/Interactive			
Initiates contact/play with others. _____			
Talks, signs, or gestures to others. _____			
Imitates others. _____			
Rolls/hands toy or ball to another without being asked. _____			
Retrieves objects for another without being asked. _____			
Offers to share objects/toys. _____			
Engages in make-believe play with others. _____			
Takes turns talking/listening. _____			
Cooperative			
Participates in small-group games. _____			
Sustains play in group of three or more for 5 min. _____			
Follows simple game rules. _____			
Understands stop/go. _____			
Understands safety zone, boundary line, base. _____			
Understands "It"/not "It." _____			
Understands game formations (circle, line, file, scattered). _____			
Plays games demanding one role (fleeing). _____			
Switches roles to achieve game goals: hide/seek, chase/flee, tag/dodge. _____			

Adapted physical educators in good teacher training programs are given instruction and practice with reflexes, reactions, and muscle tone similar to that received by occupational and physical therapists. It is important to lift, move, and position children in ways that do not elicit abnormal reflexes. When children are delayed in learning to walk, teachers must provide rich, full, developmental play activities in lying and sitting positions. Scooterboards, slides, and surfaces for body rolls become important. Because ability to retrieve thrown and kicked objects is impaired, balls and balloons are often suspended from the ceiling or attached to the wheelchair.

Ball-handling activities may require considerable instructional creativity when grasp and release mechanisms are affected by spasticity, muscle weakness, or generalized clumsiness. Emphasis is often placed on striking, kicking,

FIGURE   18.10

Young children and infants with delays need careful, systematic
instruction in many environments.

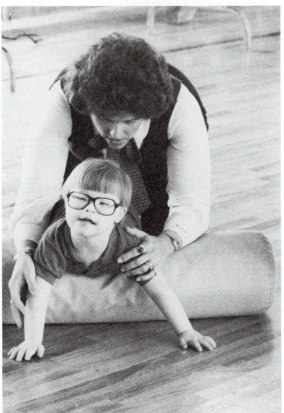

Table 18.4
Developmental levels in toy or object play.

Level	Activity	Level	Activity
1	**Repetitive manual manipulation.** Usually an up-and-down shaking movement of rattles and other noisemakers. May be an autistic behavior or blindism. All repetitive movements of this nature are described as *stereotypic behaviors.*	7	**Personalized toy play.** Occurs first as imitation, usually in conjunction with toy dishes, dolls, and stuffed animals. Pretending to feed toy or rocking it to sleep are early play behaviors. Riding a broomstick horse or using wheel-toys to get from place to place is another example. Child can respond, with gesture, to question, "What is this toy for?" These abilities emerge between ages 1 and 2 years.
2	**Oral contacts.** Mouthing of objects. Also considered stereotypic behaviors.	8	**Manipulation of moveable toy parts.** This includes all the commercial toys (dolls and trucks, for example) with parts that can be turned, pushed, or pulled without coming apart. This manipulation is purposeful, often combined with dramatic play. Also includes doorknobs, zippers, Velcro fasteners, horns, and bells. These abilities emerge between ages 1.5 and 2.5 years.
3	**Pounding.** Developmentally, the first purposeful play movement to appear. It cannot occur until voluntary, one-handed grasp appears, usually at about 5 months of age, and child can sit upright with support so that at least one hand is free.		
4	**Striking, raking a stationary object.** At about 7 months of age, normal children enjoy raking food pellets or other objects off of a table surface. An ulnar (toward ulna and little finger) raking movement occurs developmentally before the more mature radial (toward radius and thumb) movement. With older students who are severely disabled (especially those with cerebral palsy), striking is easier than throwing.	9	**Separation of toy parts.** This includes putting puzzles (large parts) together and taking them apart, dressing and undressing dolls, connecting and disconnecting cars of a train, building towers with blocks, and pinning tail on donkey and body parts on drawing of a person. These skills emerge between ages 2 and 3 years.
5	**Pulling or pushing.** This includes pulling toys by strings and pushing toys on wheels. In normal development, it occurs at about 10 months of age after evolution of pincer grasp (i.e., use of thumb and index finger). In older students with severe disabilities, pushing skills include box hockey and shuffleboard-type games in which a stick is used to push the object. Rolling balls back and forth to a partner is classified as a pushing activity.	10	**Combinational uses of toys.** This refers to dramatic play like tea parties, doctor/nurse, cowboys/Indians in which toys, costumes, and props are used in various combinations. Well developed by ages 3 to 4 years, at which time fine motor activities (drawing, printing, coloring, cutting) begin to assume dominance.
6	**Throwing.** The first two levels, according to child development theory, are called casting and hurling. Casting and hurling are often done from a sitting position. This skill cannot evolve until the child can voluntarily *release* objects—a motor milestone that occurs at about 12 months of age.	11	**Cards and table games.** These activities involve fine motor coordinations (i.e., moving checkers from place to place, handling dice, holding cards). These skills become functional at about age 5.

trapping, and stopping skills, rather than throwing and catching. These can be executed equally well from wheelchair or standing positions. Early intervention aims at discovering what children can do best and then building potentials into strengths.

Chapter 11 on motor performance presents developmental sequences for teaching locomotor and ball-handling skills to children ages 1 to 8. The pedagogy described in Chapter 11 is also developmental and applies to toddlers and early childhood.

Object control and toy play is an important learning objective. Children with developmental delays need instruction and practice with many kinds of objects before ball-handling skills are introduced.

Table 18.4 depicts levels in learning to manipulate play objects. Toy play is largely dependent on normal evolution of voluntary grip (about 5 months) and voluntary re-

lease (about 12 months); these abilities are often impaired in children with CP and others slow to integrate reflexes. Toy play is also dependent on visual integrity. Children who are blind are usually delayed in developing object manipulation skills. Throwing a ball is not as motivational for children who cannot see as for those reinforced by visual input.

Table 18.4 is recommended as a checklist for assessing what infants, toddlers, and young children do with objects. It can help determine amount of delay and guide program planning. Assessment should be conducted in both free-play and imitation settings. Often, children with disabilities learn to imitate before they show initiative in free play.

If a child shows no interest and/or ability in manipulating objects, the developmental sequence in Table 18.4 may be useful in writing lesson plans. Starting with up-and-down movements, like shaking a balloon tied to the wrist or a rhythm instrument (try sewing tiny bells into gloves), may

FIGURE   18.11

Pounding movements are the first object control skills developed. They are easily integrated into running and language activities.

be easiest. Pounding movements, as in using a drum or hammer, come early in the developmental sequence (see Figure 18.11). Children should be taught to tap the bat on home base, release the bat, and run before batting is introduced. Remember: All children can learn if professionals use appropriate task analyses based on an awareness of which activities are developmentally the easiest to learn.

Self-Concept: A Major Goal

The early years are a critical period in the formation of self-concept (Wright, 1983). By ages 4 to 5 years, feelings about the self can be measured in four domains—cognitive competence, physical competence, peer acceptance, and maternal acceptance (Harter & Pike, 1984)—using an interview technique with a pictorial instrument. The child is shown two pictures at a time; the teacher interprets each picture (e.g., "This boy isn't very good at running." "This boy is pretty good at running."); and then the child is asked to point to the picture most like him or her. This and other assessment approaches show that preschoolers have begun to form definite concepts about both their acceptance and competence.

Children with orthopedic disabilities become gradually aware that they are different and/or have a disability between the ages of 3 and 7 (Dunn, McCartan, & Fuqua, 1988; Wright, 1983). However, even when aware that arms or legs are different, they tend to deny difficulty in running or problems in doing things that others do (Teplin, Howard, & O'Connor, 1981). Most children do not begin to compare themselves with others until ages 7 or 8. Self-evaluation of physical appearance and abilities thus is strongly rooted in what persons tell them. Much research is needed on how young children with disabilities perceive themselves, what shapes their beliefs, and what influences their behaviors.

Growing awareness of self as a person with differences, disabilities, or limitations should not be left to chance, which is often both traumatic and cruel. Parents should begin providing general information to young children about their disability at age 3 or 4 (Dunn et al., 1988; Wright, 1983). Typically, children ask questions that initiate discussions or

become involved in interactions with siblings or peers that require mediation. Responses should be matter-of-fact and stress assets rather than comparisons.

Wright (1983, p. 240) offers examples of good and bad answers to the question: "Do you think I'll ever be able to walk like everyone else?"

Good: "Probably not, but you are learning to walk better, and that is good. And do you know that there are lots of other things you can do? Let's name some of them."
Bad: "Probably not. But even if you can't walk as well as some people, there are other things that you can do better than some people."

Young children thus should be helped to understand their limitations in a friendly and caring atmosphere. As younger and younger children receive special education services, caretakers outside the family circle may have to answer first questions about being different and cope with interpersonal situations in which peers point out shortcomings.

Most children with severe disabilities/delays are inevitably exposed to discrimination and prejudice (Wright, 1983). They should therefore be prepared for difficult social encounters. Story-telling, role-playing, and discussion help with learning appropriate responses to others' thoughtless and inconsiderate behavior. A number of books are now available that feature children coping with disabilities. Among these is the "Kids on the Block" book series, available from Twenty-First Century Books, 38 South Market Street, Frederick, Maryland 21701. Each "Kids on the Block" book describes a child with a different disability (e.g., cerebral palsy, asthma, diabetes, AIDS) who copes in appropriate ways, feels good about self, and interacts with nondisabled children.

The "Kids on the Block" are also available as puppets, although somewhat expensive. Scripts and discussion guidelines come with the puppets, and over 900 community-based organizations are using these materials to increase awareness and improve attitudes (Aiello, 1988).

Young children with disabilities need access to dolls and stuffed animals with and without disabilities. This permits imaginative play comparable to real-life situations. "Hal's Pals" is a line of cabbagepatch-type dolls with different disabilities (e.g., a skier with one leg, an athlete in a wheelchair, a dancer with hearing aids) available through Jesana Ltd., P.O. Box 17, Irvington, NY 10533.

Language Development: A Concomitant Goal

Language development is so important that it is integrated into all learning activities. Authorities generally identify three areas of language development: (a) inner, (b) receptive, and (c) expressive. Physical education can contribute to each.

Inner Language

Inner language refers to thought, the ability to transform experience into meaning. Consider the infant who cries and receives attention or the toddler who touches something hot and is burned. In both cases, there may be no words, but the average infant and toddler makes a cause-and-effect linkage. Likewise, good and bad feelings derived through movement are translated into approach and avoidance thoughts.

Receptive Language

Receptive language is comprehension of gestures, postures, facial expressions, and spoken words. It is also understanding of the symbols or signs used to represent words. Receptive language presupposes integrity of memory, including the ability to remember sequences. Memory may be primarily auditory, visual, or proprioceptive, or a blending of all three.

Receptive language skills are dependent upon inner language, and vice versa. The following passage describes the interrelationship between the development of receptive language and inner language skills in Helen Keller at age 7, who was both deaf and blind:

My teacher placed my hand under the spout. As the cool stream gushed over one hand, she spelled into the other the word water, *first slowly, then rapidly. I stood still, my whole attention fixed upon the motions of her fingers. Suddenly, I felt a misty consciousness, as of something forgotten—a thrill of returning thought; and knew somehow the mystery of language was revealed to me. I knew then that "w-a-t-e-r" meant the wonderful cool something that was flowing over my hand. That living word awakened my soul, gave it light, hope, joy, set it free! There were barriers still, it is true, but barriers that could in time be swept away.*

I left the well-house eager to learn. Everything had a name, and each name gave birth to a new thought. (Keller, 1965, p. 14)

Until age 7, Helen Keller had neither inner language nor receptive language in the ordinary sense. The following passage, however, does show that inner language can develop without vision and audition if the child possesses sufficient intelligence to capitalize upon proprioceptive cues:

I cannot recall what happened during the first months after my illness. I only know that I sat in my mother's lap or clung to her dress as she went about her household duties. My hands felt every object and observed every motion, and in this way, I learned to know many things. Soon, I felt the need of some communication with others and began to make crude signs. A shake of the head meant "No" and a nod, "Yes," a pull meant "Come" and a push, "Go." Was it bread that I wanted? Then I would imitate the acts of cutting the slices and buttering them. If I wanted my mother to make ice cream for dinner, I made the sign for working the freezer and shivered, indicating cold. (Keller, 1965, p. 14)

Children vary widely with respect to receptive language skills. The emphasis placed on *learning to follow directions* reveals that many teachers are not satisfied with the receptive language of their pupils. Physical educators should cooperate with classroom teachers in designing movement experiences that reinforce the meanings of words (see Table 18.5). Children should be taught the names of the things they can do, the pieces of apparatus and equipment used, and the games played.

Expressive Language

Expressive language can be verbal or nonverbal. It presupposes integrity of both receptive and inner language. The way a child speaks and writes reveals his or her memory of words, sequences, and syntactic structures. It also lends insight into the child's ability to discriminate between words and letters that sound or look alike. Nonverbal language includes sign, gesture, and facial expression. Young children with disability often rely on nonverbal language. Chapter 16 on adapted dance and dance therapy will help you learn to teach expressive language.

Perceptual-Motor Training

Chapter 12 on perceptual-motor functioning offers ideas for weaving language development into movement. Children must first develop perceptions in relation to the concepts presented in Table 18.5. In early childhood, imitation and "Show me" behaviors are emphasized. Teachers should use the same action words over and over to ensure understanding.

Assessing Young Children

The best way to assess young children is to observe them several times in an informal play setting with multipurpose apparatus that encourages exploration of locomotor and object control skills (see Figure 18.12). Swimming and wading pools also make good assessment settings. Same-age or slightly older peers without disabilities make excellent models, and much follow-the-leader type activity typically occurs. These observations can be used to set specific objectives for improvement of both qualitative and quantitative performance.

Developmental inventories are also used, especially in making placement decisions. These instruments are criterion-referenced in that they state developmental milestones and the examiner simply indicates pass, fail, or no opportunity to observe. Some, like the Denver II, are both criterion- and norm-referenced (see Chapter 7). The ages at which children perform these milestones vary from instrument to instrument but, overall, are about the same.

The Individualized Family Service Plan

The individualized family service plan (IFSP) is used with infants and toddlers in place of an individualized education program (IEP). The IFSP includes seven parts:

1. **Information on Child Status** (physical development, cognitive development, psychosocial development, self-help development, and language and speech development)
2. **Family Information** (family strengths and needs)
3. **Outcomes** (procedures, criteria, timelines)
4. **Early Intervention Services** (description, intensity, frequency, location, and method of service delivery)
5. **Dates** (initiation and duration of services)
6. **Case Manager** (from the profession most closely related to the child's and family's needs)
7. **Transition Plan at Age 3** (parental consent, transfer of information, future placement, and transfer preparation procedures)

This written plan is based on family/professional collaboration. Services can be delivered anywhere, including the home. Service delivery personnel work with families as well

Table 18.5
Words representing language concepts that can be acquired through movement lessons.

Self	Space	Time	Force[a]	Flow
Body parts	*Directions*	*Speed*	*Force*	*Qualities*
Fingers	Forward	Fast	Strong	Hyperactive
Elbow	Backward	Medium	Medium	Uncontrolled
Shoulders	Sideward	Slow	Weak	Free
Knee	Inside	Accelerating	Heavy	Abandoned
Body surfaces	Outside	Decelerating	Light	Exaggerated
Front	Up	*Quantity*	*Qualities*	Fluent
Back	Down	A lot (long)	Sudden, explosive	Inhibited
Top	Left	A little (short)	Sustained, smooth	Restrained
Bottom	Right	Variable	*Creating force*	Bound
Inside	*Levels*	*Rhythm*	Quick starts	Repressed
Outside	High	Pulse beats	Sustained, powerful	Tied up
Body movements	Medium	Accents	movements	Overcautious
Bend/flex/curl	Low	Rhythmic patterns	Static balances	*Movement*
Straighten/extend	*Size/dimensions*	Even	*Absorbing force*	Smooth, graceful
Spread/abduct	Large	Uneven	Sudden stops on balance	Rough, awkard
Close/adduct	Medium	Phrases	Gradual absorption,	Continuous
Turn/rotate	Small	Numbers	"give" as in catching	Staccato
Circle	Wide	Concepts	*Imparting force*	
	Narrow	Sequences	Rolling	
	Planes	Processes	Bouncing	
	Sagittal		Throwing	
	Frontal/vertical		Kicking	
	Horizontal		Striking	
	Pathways (floor or air)			
	Slanted			
	Straight			
	Curved			
	Zigzag			

[a]Some persons prefer "Effort" or "Weight."

FIGURE 18.12

Multipurpose apparatus encourages exploration of what the body can do.

as infants and toddlers. This has implications for increased emphasis on home-based programs of adapted physical activity that are developed and monitored by professionals.

Placement and Programming

For children ages 3 to 8, the IEP is used. The trend is toward placement of infants, toddlers, and children with delays/disabilities in integrated classrooms and play settings. When children cannot safely or successfully participate in an integrated environment without assistance, several options are possible. Typically, an aide is provided to assist the regular educator in meeting the child's special needs, and/or a consultant or resource teacher helps with environmental and instructional adaptations. Sometimes, a pull-out arrangement is used in which the child leaves the regular classroom for a few hours each week for special tutoring and/or therapy. Every attempt is made to keep children in integrated settings so that they can be afforded the same socializing and learning experiences as normal peers.

Special education thus no longer means instruction in a separate setting. Today, special education, as well as adapted physical activity, connotes a comprehensive service delivery system in which performance is assessed, goals and objectives are established, and instruction is designed and implemented in environments that are considered least restrictive in that services, equipment, and supplies are matched to needs. Appropriate matching eliminates restrictions to learning and development.

When an infant or child is assessed and found eligible for special education, the community and/or school district must find the money to provide the special assistance or adaptations needed to achieve the child's educational goals. The multidisciplinary diagnostic team, with the parents' assistance, makes decisions about which services can best be delivered in integrated settings and which require alternative arrangements (Lerner, Mardell-Czudnowski, & Goldenberg, 1987; Thurman & Widerstrom, 1985).

Social Acceptance and Integration

Social rejection and avoidance of children who are different begins at about age 4, unless there is intervention to promote interaction and acceptance (Siller, 1984; Weinberg, 1978). Research suggests that nondisabled children do not automatically include slow and/or different children in their activities (Jenkins, Speltz, & Odom, 1985). Early childhood educators must therefore devise curriculums that systematically involve preschoolers in cooperative activities and promote caring, nurturing attitudes.

Experts favor open discussion of disabilities/differences in front of children and recommend inclusion of units covering individual differences in preschool curricula (Dunn et al., 1988). Emphasis should be on each human being's uniqueness and the importance of supporting and helping one another. Children should be helped to see that being different is not bad but simply a chance occurrence. Discussion can center on differences in eye, hair, and skin color; height and weight; the ways people walk, talk, and think; and expressions of individuality in work, play, hobbies, and leisure pursuits. Movement education and creativity training in which emphasis is on "Find another way" or "Show me all the different ways you can do something" are excellent approaches to understanding and appreciating individual differences. Likewise, good teachers stress not being afraid of people, places, foods, and other things that are different, but approaching them, assessing them, and getting acquainted.

Stories like the princess who kissed the frog and turned him into a prince can teach sensitivity. Emphasizing that appearances can be deceiving is also important. Too often, Halloween witches and storybook monsters are characterized as physically ugly or disfigured; small wonder that young children without special training begin equating being different with being bad. To counteract these influences, movement activities should feature creatures who look different but are kind, loving, and lovable. Examples are television and movie characters like Vincent in "Beauty and the Beast," Alf, ET, and the casts in *Star Wars* and *Return of the Jedi*.

FIGURE 18.13

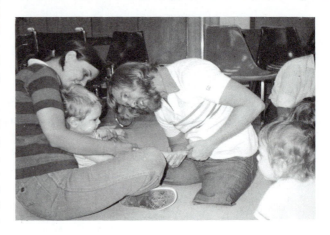

Young children need to see persons with disabilities in leadership roles.

Preschoolers, both with and without disabilities, need exposure to older persons with disabilities (see Figure 18.13). Research shows that children in the 3- to 6-year-old age range tend to make no verbal references to the missing leg of an interviewer; this suggests that inhibiting responses to a physical disability occurs in the early years and limits opportunities for direct learning (Somervill, Cordoba, Abbott, & Brown, 1982). Thus, when speakers with disabilities are invited to the early childhood setting, they should explain how they are similar to and different from other people and encourage questions.

Sport Socialization

Children with disabilities should have the same opportunities for sport socialization as peers. This means that they must see persons with conditions similar to their own in athletic roles both in integrated and nonintegrated sport settings. For attitude development, nondisabled preschoolers should also be exposed to athletes with disabilities. All young children should thus be taken to sport events like Special Olympics, wheelchair basketball and tennis, and cerebral palsy handball and boccia. Real-life experiences of this kind should be supplemented with films and videotapes (Sunderlin, 1988) and magazines like *Sports 'N Spokes* and *Palaestra* that feature athletes with disabilities. Several sport organizations that serve people with disabilities are establishing "Futures Teams" by providing recreational activities for children ages 3 and up in the same setting and at the same time that older athletes practice.

The Language-Arts-Movement Programming Model

Many curriculum models are available in early childhood education, but little attention has been given to movement training designed to concurrently teach language. The Language-Arts-Movement Programming (LAMP) model was designed to achieve this purpose. The acronym LAMP is intended to conjure up the vision of Aladdin's lamp and the magic of wishes that can come true (i.e., all children can learn when teachers believe in themselves and creatively use all of their resources). In this model, arts (creative drama and dance, music, story-telling, puppets, painting, drawing, and constructing) are the medium for unifying movement and language, and vice versa (Eddy, 1982; Sherrill, 1979; Sherrill & McBride, 1984).

Language, in this model, is operationally defined as speaking, singing, chanting, or signing. It may come from the teacher only, the teacher and child in unison, or the child only. Language is used to express the intent to move and/or to plan and rehearse a desired movement sequence, to describe movement as it occurs, and to praise once the action is completed. The combining of language and movement to teach concepts and develop schemas is powerful because the whole child is involved in active learning. The use of self-talk (also called verbal rehearsal) is well documented as a sound pedagogical device (Kowalski & Sherrill, 1992; Luria, 1961; Weiss & Klint, 1987). Learning words/labels for what they are doing enhances recall. Self-talk also facilitates time-on-task because it keeps attention focused on the movement goal.

A useful strategy is to create action songs or chants to familiar tunes like "Mulberry Bush," "Farmer in the Dell," and "Looby Loo" or nursery rhyme rhythms. The words must teach the name of the movement, associated body parts, or concepts about space, time, and effort (i.e., be relevant to the action). For example, beam walking on a low, wide beam might inspire a "Row, Row, Row Your Boat" chant like this:

Walk, walk, walk your feet
Gently down the beam
Merrily, merrily, merrily, merrily
It is fun to walk a beam!

Or a simple repetitive chant like this:

I am walking, I am walking
You walk, too, You walk, too
Walk, Walk, Walk; Walk, Walk, Walk
And Stop, Freeze . . . Quiet, shh. . .

Young children with disabilities/delays need more repetition than normal peers. For repetition to provide the needed reinforcement, however, the child must be paying attention and receiving the kind of teacher input (eye contact, smiles, praise, pats) that makes him or her feel competent and good about self. Question and answer chants in unison with movement help to achieve this goal:

Teacher: "Can you kick? Can you kick?"
Child: "I can kick. I can kick."
Teacher: "What did you kick? What did you kick?"
Child: "A ball. I kicked a ball."
Teacher: "Good, now go get the ball. Bring it here."

The same words are used over and over so that children develop vocabulary and improve memory for sequences. Rhythmically synchronous background music can also help young children remember movement sequences (Staum, 1988).

LAMP begins with much structure in that the goal is to simultaneously teach motor skills, language, and play concepts so that the child, in turn, develops the capacity for solitary play. When he or she begins interacting sponta- neously with the environment (objects, playground apparatus, or people) in appropriate ways, this initiative is praised and reinforced. Emphasis then is on helping the child progress from solitary to parallel to interactive/cooperative play. Young children need language (both receptive and expressive) to engage in cooperative play and to benefit from small-group movement and game instruction. The LAMP model promotes integrated motor-language-cognitive development.

References

Aiello, B. (1988). The Kids on the Block and attitude change: A 10-year perspective. In H.E. Yuker (Ed.), *Attitudes toward persons with disabilities* (pp. 223–229). New York: Springer Publishing.

Burstein, N. (1986). The effects of classroom organization on mainstreamed preschool children. *Exceptional Children, 52* (5), 425–434.

Cowden, J. E. (1991). Critical components of the individualized family service plan. *Journal of Physical Education, Recreation, and Dance, 62* (6), 38–40.

Cowden, J. E., & Eason, R. L. (1991). Pediatric adapted physical education services for infants, toddlers, and preschoolers: Meeting IDEA-H and IDEA-B challenges. *Adapted Physical Activity Quarterly, 8* (4), 263–279.

Cowden, J. E., & Torrey, C. (1990). A comparison of isolate and social toys on play behaviors of handicapped preschoolers. *Adapted Physical Activity Quarterly, 7,* 170–182.

Cratty, B. J. (1990). Motor development of infants subject to maternal drug use: Current evidence and future research strategies. *Adapted Physical Activity Quarterly, 1,* 110–125.

deJong, C. G. A. (1990). The development of mobility in blind and multiply handicapped infants. In A. Vermeer (Ed.), *Motor development, adapted physical activity, and mental retardation* (pp. 56–66). Basel, Switzerland: Karger.

Diamond, G. W. (1989). Developmental problems in children with HIV infection. *Mental Retardation, 27* (4), 213–217.

Dunn, L., McCartan, K., & Fuqua, R. (1988). Young children with orthopedic handicaps: Self-knowledge about disability. *Exceptional Children, 55* (3), 249–252.

Eason, R. L. (1991). Adapted physical education delivery model for infants and toddlers with disabilities. *Journal of Physical Education, Recreation, and Dance, 62* (6), 41–43, 47–48.

Eddy, J. (1982). *The music came from deep inside: Professional artists and severely handicapped children.* New York: McGraw-Hill.

Evans, J. (1980). *They have to be carefully taught.* Reston, VA: American Alliance for Health, Physical Education, Recreation, and Dance.

Gesell, A., & Ames, L. B. (1940). The ontogenetic organization of prone behavior in human infancy. *Journal of Genetic Psychology, 56,* 247–263.

Harter, S., & Pike, R. (1984). The pictorial scale of perceived competence and social acceptance for young children. *Child Development, 55,* 1969–1982.

Illingsworth, R. S. (1983). *The development of the infant and young child* (8th ed.). Baltimore: Williams & Wilkins.

Jenkins, J., Speltz, M., & Odom, S. (1985). Integrating normal and handicapped preschoolers: Effects on child development and social interaction. *Exceptional Children, 52* (1), 7–17.

Keller, H. (1965). *The story of my life.* New York: Airmont Publishing.

Kowalski, E., & Sherrill, C. (1992). Motor sequencing of learning disabled boys: Modeling and verbal rehearsal strategies. *Adapted Physical Activity Quarterly, 9* (3), 261–272.

Lerner, J., Mardell-Czudnowski, C., & Goldenberg, D. (1987). *Special education for the early childhood years* (2nd ed.). Englewood Cliffs, NJ: Prentice-Hall.

Loovis, E. M. (1985). Evaluation of toy preference and associated movement behaviors of preschool orthopedically handicapped children. *Adapted Physical Activity Quarterly, 2,* 117–126.

Luria, A. (1961). *The role of speech in the regulation of normal and abnormal behavior.* New York: Liveright.

Peterson, N. L. (1987). *Early intervention for handicapped and at-risk children.* Denver: Love.

Sherrill, C. (Ed.). (1979). *Creative arts for the severely handicapped* (2nd ed.). Springfield, IL: Charles C Thomas.

Sherrill, C., & McBride, H. (1984). An arts infusion intervention model for severely handicapped children. *Mental Retardation, 22* (6), 316–320.

Siller, J. (1984). Attitudes toward the physically disabled. In R. L. Jones (Ed.), *Attitudes and attitude change in special education: Theory and practice* (pp. 184–205). Reston, VA: Council for Exceptional Children.

Somervill, J., Cordoba, O., Abbott, R., & Brown, P. F. (1982). The origins of stigma: Reactions by male and female preschool children to a leg amputation. *American Corrective Therapy Journal, 36* (1), 14–17.

Staum, M. (1988). The effect of background music on the motor performance recall of preschool children. *Journal of Human Movement Studies, 15,* 27–35.

Sunderlin, A. (1988). Film festival: Sports and recreation videos and films, from aerobics to wilderness access. *Sports 'N Spokes, 14* (2), 51–57.

Teplin, S. W., Howard, J. A., & O'Connor, M. J. (1981). Self-concept of young children with cerebral palsy. *Developmental Medicine and Child Neurology, 23,* 730–738.

Thurman, S. K., & Widerstrom, A. H. (1985). *Young children with special needs: A developmental and ecological approach.* Boston: Allyn & Bacon.

Wasson, D. L., & Watkinson, E. J. (1981). The effect of an instructional program on the social behavior of young moderately mentally handicapped children in play. *Canadian Association for Health, Physical Education and Recreation Journal, 48,* 9–24.

Watkinson, E. J., & Wall, A. E. (1982). *The PREP play program: Play skill instruction for mentally handicapped children.* Ottawa: Canadian Association for Health, Physical Education, and Recreation.

Weinberg, N. (1978). Preschool children's perceptions of orthopedic disability. *Rehabilitation Counseling Bulletin, 21,* 183–189.

Weiss, M., & Klint, K. (1987). "Show and tell" in the gymnasium: An investigation of developmental differences in modeling and verbal rehearsal of motor skills. *Research Quarterly for Exercise and Sport, 58* (2), 234–241.

Wright, B. A. (1983). *Physical disability—A psychosocial approach* (2nd ed.). New York: Harper & Row.

C H A P T E R

19

Other Health Impaired Conditions

FIGURE 19.1

Students classified as *other health impaired* (OHI) generally look normal but have chronic or acute health problems that adversely affect their educational performance.

After you have studied this chapter, you should be able to:

1. Define each of the conditions in Table 19.1, discuss causes and/or biochemical bases, and state symptoms, signs, and behaviors. Relate your discussion to persons you have known, seen on television or film, or read about.

2. Discuss the role of exercise, diet, and lifestyle in managing each condition and summarize principles/guidelines relevant to each. Refer to Chapters 15 and 16 for information on stress management.

3. Given any condition in Table 19.1, be able to write a physical education IEP. State age, gender, and other relevant information you used in developing the IEP. Include environmental variables to be altered.

4. Discuss the role of medication in managing OHI conditions and identify major drugs related to each. State side effects that affect exercise programming.

5. Identify and discuss contraindicated practices, activities, and environmental variables associated with OHI conditions.

6. Discuss prevention of OHI conditions. Describe some creative approaches to prevention that would be appropriate for different age groups.

Other health impairments (OHI) is a broad diagnostic term created by the U.S. Department of Education to include all conditions not encompassed by specific disability categories (e.g., mental retardation, orthopedic impairments). Legislation defines OHI as limited strength, vitality, or alertness due to chronic or acute health problems that adversely affect educational performance. In a lifespan approach, OHI encompasses the health problems that anyone can develop, at any age, that interfere with work productivity, leisure activities, and life satisfaction. This chapter is thus an extension of Chapter 13, "Fitness and Healthy Lifestyle."

Overcoming exercise limitations caused by poor health requires help. Aerobic fitness is a particular challenge, and many persons give up, exacerbating their conditions by developing negative feelings about themselves and physical activity, becoming increasingly sedentary, and gaining weight. Adapted physical activity services in school and community settings are needed to create support groups for working toward common goals (e.g., weight loss, improved breathing, a 12-min mile) and to teach ways that exercise can develop self-confidence and manage stress (see Figure 19.1). These services should supplement rather than replace regular activity programs.

Common OHI Conditions

OHI conditions covered in this chapter are listed in Table 19.1. The incidence of these and other conditions is presented in Appendix A. OHI conditions may be chronic or acute. *Chronic* means that they are present over long periods of time, often causing no problem as long as lifestyle is healthy, no new or excessive stressors appear, and medication is taken as prescribed. *Acute* refers to episodes that have a rapid onset and require medical attention. Acute episodes typically last a few hours, sometimes a few days, but never more than several weeks.

Table 19.1
OHI conditions covered in this chapter.

Condition	Page
1. Overweight/obesity syndrome	456
2. Cholesterol problems	460
3. Diabetes mellitus	461
4. Cardiovascular problems	465
Atherosclerosis	466
Heart attack	467
Stroke	467
Congestive heart disease	467
Conduction abnormalities	468
Chronotrophic incompetence	470
Sick sinus syndrome	470
Fibrillations and flutters	470
Tachycardias	470
Bradycardias	470
Heart block	470
Inflammation of the heart wall	471
Valve defects and heart murmurs	471
Rheumatic fever	473
Congenital heart defects	473
5. Hypertension	477
6. Asthma	481
7. Chronic obstructive pulmonary diseases	487
8. Bronchitis and emphysema	487
9. Cystic fibrosis	487
10. Hemophilia	489
11. Sickle-cell disease (anemia)	489
12. Anemia	489
13. Menstrual problems	490
14. Cancer	490
15. Kidney and urinary tract disorders	491
16. Convulsive disorders	491
17. Environmental disorders	496
18. Tuberculosis	496
19. AIDS (acquired immune deficiency syndrome)	497

Medications and OHI Conditions

Medications are emphasized in this chapter because most serious OHI conditions are managed by drugs. Adherence to prescribed doses is essential to wellness, and physical educators must be able to discuss side effects and exercise indications and contraindications. The *Physician's Desk Reference* (PDR), which is revised annually, is the primary source of choice, but many reference books are available (e.g., Griffith, 1992; Long, 1992). Medications can be identified by family names (e.g., diuretics or thiazides), generic names (chlorothiazide), and trade or brand names (Diuril). Generally, generic names are needed to find drugs in reference books.

For ease of reading, this and subsequent chapters primarily use family names. Appendix B presents several categories of drugs and provides illustrative generic and trade names. Some drugs are listed under two or more family names because they have multiple functions.

Diuretics, for example, are used to manage obesity, heart disease, high blood pressure, and several other conditions. *Diuretics* are water pills that stimulate urination in order to rid the body of excess fluids and to reduce edema (swelling caused by a fluid accumulation). When exercisers take diuretics, professionals must allow frequent bathroom breaks and check periodically for dehydration. Diuretics, when combined with vigorous exercise and hot weather conditions, can cause adverse side effects like *hypovolemia* (excessive fluid loss) and *hypokalemia* (excessive potassium loss), both life-threatening conditions. Early danger signs are dizziness, weakness, and muscle cramps. These side effects can be prevented by drinking water and eating foods high in potassium (e.g., fresh fruits and vegetables). Persons taking diuretics should maintain regular fluid-intake levels.

Drugs that lower blood pressure affect both heart and peripheral vascular function and have similar side effects. The most common side effect is *hypotension* (dizziness or lightheadedness when changing from sitting to standing positions). Hypotension frequently causes falls and injuries in persons who are medically fragile. To minimize hypotension, teach slow pacing of position changes.

Some drugs that manage heart, lung, and blood vessel conditions interact in complex ways because they work on the receptor cells of the sympathetic nervous system (SNS). These receptor cells are named *adrenergenic* and designated as alpha (mostly in vessel linings), beta 1 (in heart and vessels), and beta 2 (in lungs). Drugs that increase SNS action are called adrenergic agonists or sympatho*mimetic* agents because they mimic natural activity. Illustrative of these are the asthma drugs that dilate (widen) the bronchial tubes in the lungs. An adverse side effect of these beta 2 adrenergic agonists is increased heart rate.

Drugs that decrease the action of the SNS are called alpha- and beta-adrenergic blockers or antagonists (commonly shortened to alpha blockers and beta blockers). These drugs lower blood pressure and heart rates but are contraindicated in asthma and diabetes because of side effects (i.e., blockers depress functions needed to keep bronchial tubes open and to signal blood sugar changes associated with diabetes crises). Beta blockers are frequently mentioned in exercise literature because they mask the intensity of physical activity and complicate heart rate monitoring. Hearts of persons taking beta blockers do not respond normally to exercise; the heart rate remains low, giving the false impression that exercise effort is not maximum.

The side effects of most drugs do not affect exercise performance as directly as do the beta blockers. Nevertheless, professionals must be responsive to behavior and attitude changes that may be drug related. Every person responds to medications differently, and responses vary from day to day. Discipline problems, mood swings, and undesirable activity levels often can be traced to medication.

Of particular importance are the *steroids*, drugs that mimic the action of the sex hormones and the adrenal gland hormones. Almost everyone has heard of the illegal sex steroids (anabolic or androgenic) because of the publicity given athletes who take them, but few people know about the *adrenal gland steroids*, the miracle drugs prescribed to manage many OHI conditions. When persons with OHI indicate they are "on steroids," physical educators should understand that these are the *adrenocorticosteroids*, not the sex steroids.

The adrenocorticosteroids (usually shortened to corticosteroids or steroids) mimic the hormones (glucocorticoids and mineralocorticoids) secreted by the cortex (outer covering) of the adrenal gland located above each kidney. These hormones are *systemic*, meaning that they influence the biochemistry of all body systems. When natural endocrine functions are inadequate, corticosteroids (e.g., cortisone, prednisone) are administered to suppress inflammation (swelling, redness, itching) and manage cellular pathology. Unfortunately, the systemic action of the corticosteroids also causes side effects. These are described later, in the section on obesity.

Most persons with chronic OHI must take medication every day at approximately the same time. Physicians prescribe medication because benefits outweigh adverse side effects.

Risk Factors in OHI

The risk factors in all or most of OHI conditions are the same as those popularized in relation to cardiovascular disease. Four of these (heredity, age, sex, and race) cannot be changed. Yet, by understanding the role of heredity, we can predict our probable health problems and plan a lifestyle conducive to wellness. Each person's ecosystem influences implementation of this plan and the extent to which lifetime wellness can be achieved.

Stress, exercise, diet, smoking, and drugs are the risk factors that persons can be taught to manage. All of these play major roles in *homeostasis* (wellness at the cellular level; a state of internal equilibrium). Persons with OHI must work especially hard to maintain a balance between exercise and eating. Both overweight and underweight intensify OHI and

Table 19.2
Old and new guidelines for healthy weight.

The U.S. government has revised its guidelines for weight according to age and height. In reading the weight range on the new chart, higher weights generally apply to men, who have more muscle and bone; lower weights apply to women.

	Old (1985)			New (1990)	
Height Without Shoes	*Weight Without Clothes*		*Height Without Shoes*	*Weight Without Clothes*	
	Men (Pounds)	Women (Pounds)		19–34 Years	35 Years and Over
4′10″		92–121			
4′11″		95–124	5′	97–128	108–138
5′		98–127	5′1″	101–132	111–143
5′1″	105–134	101–130	5′2″	104–137	115–148
5′2″	108–137	104–134	5′3″	107–141	119–152
5′3″	111–141	107–138	5′4″	111–146	122–157
5′4″	114–145	110–142	5′5″	114–150	126–162
5′5″	117–149	114–146	5′6″	118–155	130–167
5′6″	121–154	118–150	5′7″	121–160	134–172
5′7′	125–159	122–154	5′8″	125–164	138–178
5′8″	129–163	126–159	5′9″	129–169	142–183
5′9″	133–167	130–164	5′10″	132–174	146–188
5′10″	137–172	134–169	5′11″	136–179	151–194
5′11″	141–177		6′	140–184	155–199
6′	145–182		6′1″	144–189	159–205
6′1″	149–187		6′2″	148–195	164–210
6′2″	153–192		6′3″	152–200	168–216
6′3″	157–197		6′4″	156–205	173–222
			6′5″	160–211	177–228
			6′6″	164–216	182–234

Note. From 1992 news release from U.S. Agriculture Department and Health and Human Services Department.

affect mental as well as physical health. Weight, therefore, is often the first concern in OHI assessment and programming.

Ideal weight depends on sex, age, body type, ethnic or cultural expectations, athletic goals, and work demands. Governments issue guidelines for healthy weight, based on averages within the population (see Table 19.2). The 1990 standards of the U.S. Department of Health and Human Services, for example, reflect research that older people can grow a little heavier without added health risks. The main concern is with fat distribution.

Fat distribution varies by age and sex. Infants and young children have a continuous layer of adipose tissue beneath the skin, often called baby fat. The amount is fairly small, 10 to 15%. As children age, the subcutaneous fat becomes thicker in some areas than others (e.g., triceps, abdomen, calf). These are the sites used in skinfold fat measurement. Hormones associated with the adolescent growth spurt cause thickening of fat deposits in different areas for females than males. In general, females have larger fat cells in the buttocks and hips, whereas the fat of males centers around the upper body. These fat distributions are popularly referred to as apple and pear shapes. *The apple shape,*

more common in males than females, carries more health risk. In general, hormones and genes influence fat distribution more than diet and exercise.

Overweight/Obesity Syndrome

Definition of the overweight/obesity syndrome depends on assessment approach. Criteria for obesity, based on use of skinfold calipers to determine percent body fat, are percentage of body fat greater than 25% for males and greater than 30% for females. With height-weight tables, the traditional criterion for *overweight* is 10 to 20% above ideal weight for sex and age. The criterion for *obesity* is 20% above ideal weight. Persons over 50% of their ideal weight are considered *super obese*. Height-weight guidelines for ages 5 to 19 appear in Appendix C. Although not as accurate as skinfold measures, these tables are easily understood and valuable in assessment and goal setting.

Incidence and Prevalence

Obesity affects 5 to 25% of school-age children and youth, depending on criteria used, and an even higher percentage of adults (Kien, 1990). Nearly 34 million Americans weigh 20% or more above their ideal weight, and about one third of these are severely obese. With the 10 to 20% criterion, 60 to 70 million adults and 10 to 12 million teenagers are overweight.

Causes of Obesity

Causes of obesity are endocrine, medication-induced, or nonendocrine. Typically, the physician rules out endocrine and medication-induced etiologies before delving into other possible causes.

Endocrine obesity is caused by malfunction of glands that secrete hormones: (a) the hypothalamus, pituitary, and thyroid in the brain and (b) the adrenal cortex located above the kidneys. In the resulting syndromes, the fat is typically concentrated about the breasts, hips, and abdomen, and the face is moon-shaped and ruddy. *Cushing's syndrome* or cushingoid obesity, the most common form, is caused by excessive production of the glucocorticoids by either the pituitary or adrenal glands. Other indicators of Cushing's syndrome are (a) *hirsutism* or excessive hair growth, (b) menstrual irregularities, (c) a buffalo hump (kyphosis condition) that progressively worsens because of related osteoporosis (bone degeneration), and (d) diabetes. Overall, less than 10% of obesity is caused by endocrine disorders.

Medication-induced obesity is caused by synthetic hormones like the corticosteroids and has the same appearance as Cushing's syndrome. The most common of these—prednisone and cortisone—are used to reduce inflammation and manage such severe chronic conditions as arthritis, asthma, cancer, leukemia, and kidney disease. Corticosteroids, even when taken for short periods, cause many side effects like edema (excessive fluid retention), hyperactivity, increased appetite, insatiable hunger for sweets, and mood swings. Withdrawal results in depression, even when daily dosages are progressively decreased. Long-term prescription of the corticosteroids has such side effects as growth retardation, diabetes, high blood pressure, and osteoporosis. Corticosteroids are used when no other medication is effective, so persons must learn to accept and manage side effects.

Side effects of medications often complicate weight management and contribute to multidisability. Another problem is that many medications must be taken with food to offset undesirable side effects like stomach cramps, nausea, and nervousness. Alteration of food intake and metabolism, as in dieting and exercising, may require reassessment of medications. Sometimes healthy lifestyle reduces the amount of medication that must be taken.

Nonendocrine obesity, the most common condition, is caused by interacting hereditary and environmental factors that result in an imbalance between caloric intake and output. Studies show that, when parents have normal weight, only 8 to 9% of the children are obese. When one parent is obese, 40% of the children are likewise. When both parents are obese, this percentage doubles. Eating patterns learned early in childhood and passed down from generation to generation seem to be as much a factor as genetic predisposition. The leisure-time attitudes, interests, and practices of family and neighborhood also affect the balance between food intake and energy expenditure.

Long-Term Management of Obesity

Long-term management of obesity has been likened to that of alcoholism and drug abuse. The problem can be solved temporarily, but never cured. Of the many persons who diet, only 10% achieve lifetime weight control. Clearly, new strategies must be tried, with physical educators playing a leading role in cooperative home-school-community programming. Lifestyle prescriptions must focus jointly on food intake and exercise output, and self-responsibility for monitoring behaviors and seeking help must be taught.

ACSM Guidelines

Three guidelines structure program planning (ACSM, 1991):

1. Maintain a minimum intake of about 1,200 calories a day.
2. Engage in a daily exercise program that uses 300 or more calories a day. For weight-loss goals, exercise of long duration/low intensity is generally best.
3. Lose only about 2.2 lb (1 kg) a week. Gradual weight loss prevents metabolic imbalances.

Lifestyle Prescription and Caloric Balance

The FIT acronym introduced in Chapter 13 on fitness can be modified to include both exercise and eating:

F Frequency (Three to five small meals a day at set times and places with no snacking in between; daily exercise)

I Intensity (1,200 cal distributed among the four food groups; exercise intensity great enough to expend 300 cal a day)

T Time (Each meal of long duration, with food eaten slowly, chewed well, and supplemented with pleasant conversation; exercise duration long enough to expend 300 cal a day)

The *principle of caloric balance* is extremely important in lifestyle prescription. This principle specifies that, for weight loss to occur, exercise expenditure calories must exceed food intake calories. Implementation of caloric balance requires knowledge to guide food and exercise selection and self-discipline to apply this knowledge and to change lifestyle.

Principles Guiding Food Selection

The easiest way to control caloric intake is to use a system of food servings or exchanges (see Table 19.3). Several principles guide food selection:

1. **Four Foods Principle.** Eating right requires a knowledge of the four food groups and the amounts that constitute servings. To lose weight, reduce the size or number of portions but keep all meals approximately the same size. Inclusion of these food groups in every meal assures that the six nutrients necessary for wellness are ingested. *These nutrients are carbohydrates, proteins, fats, minerals, vitamins, and water.* Only the first three generate calories.

Table 19.3
Four food groups to guide daily intake (1300 to 1650 calories).

Food Group	Nutrient Value	Number of Daily Servings	Calorie Average Each Serving
Bread/Cereal/Grain Group 1 slice or equivalent 1/2 cup cooked cereal, pasta, rice 3/4 cup cold cereal	Carbohydrates, iron, thiamine, riboflavin, niacin	4–6	100
Fruit and Vegetable Group 1 medium size, raw 1 cup, raw 1/2 cup cooked or juice	Carbohydrates, iron, calcium, vitamins A, C, potassium	4–5	75
Milk and Dairy Products 8 oz milk or yogurt 1 oz cheese 1/2 cup cottage cheese 1/2 cup ice cream	Protein, fats, calcium, vitamin A, riboflavin	2	150
Meat or Protein Equivalent 2 oz lean meat 2 eggs, boiled 1/2 cup cottage cheese 1 cup cooked beans, peas 4 tbsp peanut butter 1 tbsp salad dressing	Protein, fats, iron, calcium, thiamin, riboflavin, potassium	2	150

Note. Children and adolescents need twice the amount in the milk and dairy product group; otherwise, recommended servings are the same. Liquid oils and margarine should be substituted for meat fats and butter in cooking.

2. **The 2:1 Food Group Principle.** This principle states that the number of servings in the bread/cereal/grain group and the fruit and vegetable group should be twice that of the other two groups. This ratio assures that the correct proportions of nutrients are eaten. The recommended daily dietary intake is 55% or more carbohydrates, 30% or less fats, and 15% or less proteins. Table 19.3 shows that the first two food groups provide carbohydrates, whereas the last two are the source of proteins and fats.

3. **Dietary Fat Reduction Principle.** Reducing dietary fat is especially important for weight loss. This is because 1 gram of fat is 9 cal whereas 1 gram of carbohdrates or protein is only 4.5 cal. Major sources of fat are mayonnaise, salad dressing, cooking oils, meat fats, butter, and cheese. Reducing fats also helps to control blood pressure and cholesterol problems.

Principles Guiding Exercise Selection

1. **Nonweight-bearing Activities Principle.** Nonweight-bearing activities minimize stress on joints and feet. Exercise modalities of choice for most obese persons are water-based exercises, cycling, and mat activities in lying and sitting positions (Sheldahl, 1986). Water-based exercises include swimming, treading water, locomotor and stationary activities in waist-deep water, and pedaling a cycle ergometer placed in the water so that only the head and shoulders are out. Obese persons can typically perform for longer durations at higher intensities in water than on land. Heart response to exercise in water is different from that on land. Therefore, if exercise prescription is based on heart rate, assess target intensity range in the water.

2. **Walking for Long Duration Principle.** When walking is the preferred exercise, it should be done only on a level surface to minimize joint stresses. A temperature-controlled environment is recommended to keep perspiration under control. Long-duration, low-intensity walking causes weight loss more effectively than traditional aerobic exercise. *Research shows that most obese persons do not lose weight until walking time is at least 30 min a day. Two hours daily is recommended* (Sheldahl, 1986). Remember that heavy persons spend more energy per minute than light persons. An exercise leader of normal weight should perhaps wear waist or ankle weights or carry a backpack to get the feel of exertion and learn to empathize.

3. **Exercise for Enjoyment Principle.** Alternate exercise modalities and use stimulating music to reduce boredom and enhance enjoyment. Use Table 13.4 in the fitness chapter to determine amount of exercise needed to burn 300 cal. Adapt this table to individual weights as explained in the footnote. Regardless of modality chosen, remember that the emphasis is on attitude change and on developing the habit of daily exercise.

4. **Partner and Support Group Principle.** One day of not exercising for an obese person is like falling off the wagon for an alcoholic. Teach persons how to ask for help with motivation. A buddy system generally helps. If this is not possible, create a telephone help-line that persons can call for assistance. Emphasize praising and reinforcing each other.

5. **Time Management Counseling Principle.** Help persons who are obese with time management. Weight loss is not typically achieved in a physical education or exercise class because obese persons lack the fitness to exercise at high intensity. Additional time must be committed. Teach and reinforce realistic expectations. If time cannot be found, the individual will have to settle for losing fewer pounds each week.

6. **Teach Exercise Fallacies Principle.** Teach that spot reduction is an exercise fallacy. Fat distribution depends on genetic code. Exercise may decrease the circumference of a body part by firming up the muscle, but number of fat cells remains constant. The size of fat cells is reduced only when overall energy expenditure is greater than food intake. Fat-cell size reduction seems to follow a pattern from top to bottom. Most persons notice weight loss in the face and neck first.

Implications for Physical Education

Physical educators who wish to introduce a weight reduction program into their schools must be conscious of working not only with the child, but with the entire family and ethnic group. The most successful weight reduction programs are cooperative school/community endeavors that involve the entire family.

Programs should be engaged in voluntarily and supported by sympathetic counseling. The approach must be nonthreatening and nonchastising. Fat persons often have emotional problems that perpetuate habits of overeating. Many psychologists believe that eating is a form of oral gratification to which persons unconsciously regress when they feel unloved or insecure. Such persons tend to nibble continuously, not because they are hungry, but to meet hidden needs and drives.

Persons must be reassured that they are loved and accepted. The self, however, is not easily separated from the body. Criticism of excessive body weight thus is often internalized as criticism of self. Many obese persons have built up elaborate defense mechanisms to preserve ego strength. Do not assume that they will be receptive to offers to help with weight loss or that they will admit openly to dissatisfaction with their bodies.

The well-proportioned physical educator often does not realize how unpleasant vigorous exercise can be for obese persons. Realistic program planning results from a consideration of the physical characteristics of obesity:

1. **Distended Abdomen.** This results in anatomical differences in the position of the stomach and in the length of the intestinal tract, thereby affecting vital processes. It also creates excessive pressure on the diaphragm, which leads to difficulty in breathing and the consequent accumulation of carbon dioxide, which helps to explain patterns of drowsiness. The distended abdomen makes forward bending exercises difficult or impossible.

2. **Mobility of Rolls of Fat.** The bobbing up and down of breasts, abdomen, and other areas where excessive fat is deposited is uncomfortable and often painful during locomotor activities.

3. **Excessive Perspiration.** Layers of fat serve as insulation, and the obese person more quickly becomes hot and sweaty than the nonobese.

4. **Galling Between the Thighs and Other Skin Areas that Rub Together.** After perspiration begins, continued locomotion causes painful galling or chafing somewhat similar to an abrasion. Such areas heal slowly because of continuous irritation and sometimes become inflamed.

5. **Postural Faults.** Obese children are particularly vulnerable to knock-knees, pronation, flatfoot, sagging abdomen, drooped shoulders, and round back. These postural deviations all affect mechanical efficiency in even simple locomotor activities.

6. **Skeletal Immaturity.** The growth centers in the long bones of obese adolescents are particularly susceptible to injury, either from cumulative daily gravitational stress or sudden traumas from such strenuous or heavy activities as contact sports, weight lifting, and pyramid building.

7. **Edema.** Obese persons seem to retain fluids more readily than nonobese. Ankles, breasts, and wrists swell, particularly during the menstrual period. Diuretics are often prescribed.

8. **Broad Base in Locomotor Activities.** The combination of knock-knees, tendency toward galling between thighs, and pronation results in a slow, awkward gait with feet often shoulder-width apart.

9. **Fear of Falling.** Added weight makes falling from heights both painful and dangerous (see Figure 19.2).

10. **Excessive Buoyancy in Water.** The inability to keep most of the body submerged makes the mastery of standard swimming strokes difficult.

The need for socialization through sports and games is the same for obese students as for others. Walking and exercising done in conjunction with a special weight reduction program should not substitute for physical education activities with peers, even though participation may be limited. Others must learn to accept the obese person just as they would a person with a missing limb. Allow persons with weight problems privacy in dressing and showering if requested. Standard gymnasium clothes may be impossible to find, and long pants may be more appropriate than shorts.

The heavier a person is, the more important it is that certain activities be avoided. These activities include tasks that involve lifting his or her own weight, such as chinning

FIGURE 19.2

Obesity, when classified as either an *other health impaired* condition or an *orthopedic impairment,* is eligible for special education funding. Such children often need adapted physical activity more than students who are mentally retarded, blind, or deaf.

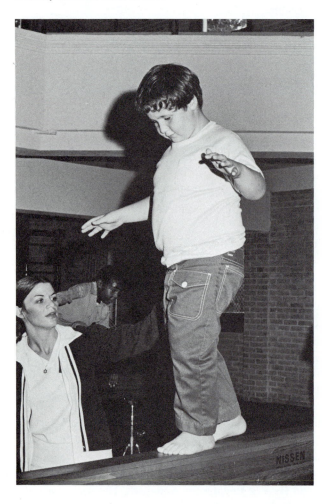

and rope climbing, and those that entail lifting external weights, such as weight training, serving as the base of a pyramid, and partner tumbling stunts. The sympathetic teacher can devise many adaptations to draw the student into the group and to foster the development of favorable attitudes toward fitness.

The use of successive contracts, specifying specific goals and rewards after the loss of each 5 or 10 lb, is an effective motivational technique in weight reduction. The student is free at all times to revise the contract to allow more food and less exercise, but few take advantage of this option. Group contracts, in which several persons pledge weight losses, are particularly effective.

Cholesterol Problems

There is much concern today about cholesterol, a fatlike substance that is manufactured by the liver and plays a vital role in the formation of hormones and metabolic products. Total blood cholesterol levels above 180 milligrams per deciliter (mg/dl) signal borderline or high-risk status for high blood pressure and heart disease (Cooper, 1988; Corbin & Lindsey, 1990). See Table 19.4.

Table 19.4
Cholesterol goals in mg/100 ml.[a]

	Total Cholesterol	LDL-C	TC/HDL-C
Goal	<180	<130	3.5
Borderline	180–219	130–159	[b]
High risk	220+	160+	[b]

[a]Total cholesterol values can be adjusted by 2 mg/100 ml for each year of age over 30 until age 50.
[b]Suggested values not yet established.
Note. Data from H. R. Superko, "The Role of Diet, Exercise, and Medication in Blood Lipid Management of Cardiac Patients," in *Physician and Sportsmedicine,* 1988, 16:67.

High cholesterol is caused by (a) the liver producing excessive amounts, (b) eating too many animal fats, or (c) a combination. Foods containing the most cholesterol (egg yolk, liver, brain, whole milk, butter, cheese, red meats) should be avoided. Dietary cholesterol intake should be less than 300 mg a day for the average person and reduced further, as needed, by persons with problems. Many books on cholesterol (Cooper, 1988; Kowalski, 1987) give information for counting milligrams. For example, one egg yolk contains 252 mg; 3 oz of shrimp contain 115 mg; and 3 oz of lean, broiled sirloin contain 77 mg.

Obesity is associated with high cholesterol, so a concurrent treatment is daily long-duration/low-intensity exercise to lose weight. Blood testing provides separate measures for three components of cholesterol: (a) low-density-lipoprotein cholesterol (LDL-C), (b) very-low-density-lipoprotein cholesterol (VLDL-C), and (c) high-density-lipoprotein cholesterol (HDL-C). The first two of these are bad, and the third is good. See Table 19.4 for goals. The term *lipoprotein* reminds us that fats are insoluble in water and must combine with proteins or some other substance to travel through body fluids.

LDL-C and VLDL-C are the bad components of cholesterol. LDL-C is the worst because the excess amounts attach themselves to artery walls, build up plaque, and clog passageways. LDL-C levels above 130 are borderline or risk. VLDL-C is the substance used by the liver to manufacture and transport LDL-C, so its bad effects are indirect. To remember whether LDL-C or HDL-C is bad, it helps to think: *Lousy, Lethargic, Lazy Living is Linked with LDL-C that Likes to attach to artery walls.* LDL-C can be lowered in most persons by weight loss. However, 75% of the body's cholesterol is manufactured by the liver, and only 25% comes from food. Genes and cholesterol problems appear to be strongly linked.

HDL-C, the good cholesterol, draws fats away from artery walls, serving to counterbalance LDL-C activity. The higher the HDL-C, the better. Aerobic exercise raises HDL-C activity. The ratio between total cholesterol (TC) and HDL-C should be about 3.5. Most blood tests give this information.

Medication can lower cholesterols when caloric balance, weight loss, and exercise are not effective. Common medications are colestipol (Colestid), gembibrozil (Lopid), lovastatin (Melacor), and niacin (also called vitamin B₃ or nicotinic acid). Each has minor side effects that do not affect exercising: Illustrative side effects are constipation, increases in blood sugar, reduced absorption of vitamins, and interference with fat absorption. Certain foods, most notably oat bran, are used also but are controversial.

Diabetes Mellitus: Major Metabolic Disorder

Diabetes (meaning passing through) is a general term for conditions characterized by excessive urination. The most common is diabetes mellitus, which derives its name from high sugar (glucose) content in the blood and urine. In common usage, diabetes mellitus is shortened to diabetes. This condition is a disorder of carbohydrate, protein, and fat metabolism that affects vital functions, especially the conversion of foods into energy.

Diabetes is a high-incidence condition that affects from 2 to 4% of the population. Infants have a one in five chance of becoming diabetic. At least 1 of every 600 school-age children has diabetes. According to the American Diabetes Association, for every 10,000 persons, there will be 1 with diabetes under age 20, 10 between ages 20 and 40, 100 between ages 50 and 60, and 1,000 over age 60. Diabetes ranks among the leading 10 causes of death for all age groups over 14 years.

Diabetes increases the risk of blindness, coronary heart disease, amputations, and kidney and urinary conditions. Within 10 years of onset, 50% have pathological changes in the retina of the eye, called diabetic retinopathy. Between the ages of 20 and 65, diabetes is the leading cause of blindness. Diabetes is a contributing factor in 50% of all heart attacks and 75% of all strokes (Duda, 1985).

Causes of Diabetes

The cause of diabetes remains unknown. Several theories, however, have been proposed to explain insulin deficiency and pancreatic cell dysfunction. The genetic or hereditary theory is based on the fact that many persons with diabetes have relatives with the same condition. The autoimmune theory posits that the body's immune system attacks its own cells, treating them like viruses or bacteria. The virus theory suggests that an unidentified virus attacks or that diabetes is a side effect of viral infections like measles and mumps.

Types of Diabetes

The two major types of diabetes are Type I and Type II. Type I is insulin-dependent diabetes mellitus (IDDM) or juvenile-onset diabetes (JOD). This condition has the same incidence for males and females. Its onset is usually before age 25, and the condition is serious because the pancreatic beta cells are capable of producing little or no insulin. Type II, which occurs mainly in adults, is noninsulin-dependent diabetes mellitus (NIDDM).

Only about 10% of diabetes is Type I. Rapid weight loss, frequent urination, drowsiness, and fatigue are the classic symptoms. Type I is managed by daily insulin injections, careful monitoring of glucose, and disciplined balancing of food intake and exercise. Even with treatment, Type I persons typically are underweight or slender (Berg, 1986). Type I cannot be cured; it is a lifelong condition.

Type II is associated with overweight or obesity and sedentary lifestyle. More women have Type II diabetes than men. Diagnostic symptoms are the same as Type I except for rapid weight loss. Type II may be treated with insulin, but usually the emphasis is on diet and exercise. Often, when weight is lost and regular physical activity becomes a part of leisure, diabetic symptoms disappear. This is easier said than done, however, and most persons simply try to cope. When Type II cannot be managed by diet and exercise, sulfonylurea therapy (oral tablets) is often used.

Role of Glucose and Glycogen

Glucose is a simple sugar that, through carbohydrate metabolism, is converted either to (a) cellular energy, (b) glycogen, or (c) fat. Desired concentration of glucose in the blood is 80–120 mg/dl (milligrams per deciliter). The glucose level rises slightly after meals and falls as the stomach becomes empty. The level also falls during aerobic exercise, which enhances cellular glucose intake.

Glycogen is a converted form of glucose that is stored in liver and muscle cells. When blood glucose is high, it is converted into glycogen. When blood glucose is low, glycogen is changed back to glucose.

Hormones: Insulin and Glucagon

Figure 19.3 shows how the two pancreatic hormones (insulin and glucagon) function together to maintain a relatively stable blood glucose level. These hormones are secreted by different kinds of pancreatic cells and have opposite functions. *Insulin,* secreted by beta cells, prevents blood glucose from rising too high and is most active during full stomach and after emotional stress conditions. *Glucagon,* secreted by alpha cells, prevents blood glucose from sinking too low and is most active during empty stomach and exercise conditions. Diabetes occurs when this cyclical action is inefficient. One of the first signs is frequent urination, a reaction of the kidneys to the stress of having to extract glucose from the blood.

Protein and Fat Metabolism

When glucose is not properly absorbed, cells begin to starve, causing the body to use protein as an alternative energy source. This results in protein deficiency, which is manifested by skin problems, slow healing, and infections that sometimes lead to amputations. The body also uses its stored fat to meet energy demands. In Type I diabetes, weight is lost. The person feels hungry all the time, eats more and more with no weight gain, and begins to complain of tiredness and weakness. In Type II diabetes, persons typically remain overweight because their condition is directly related to low energy and lack of exercise.

Ketone Bodies and Ketosis

Ketone bodies are the waste products that result from fat metabolism. They accumulate in the blood and urine and rely on the kidneys for disposal. When the kidneys cannot handle this extra load, the intensified spillover of ketone bodies into the blood causes *ketosis.*

FIGURE   19.3

Two pancreatic hormones (insulin and glucagon) work together to
maintain relatively stable blood glucose.

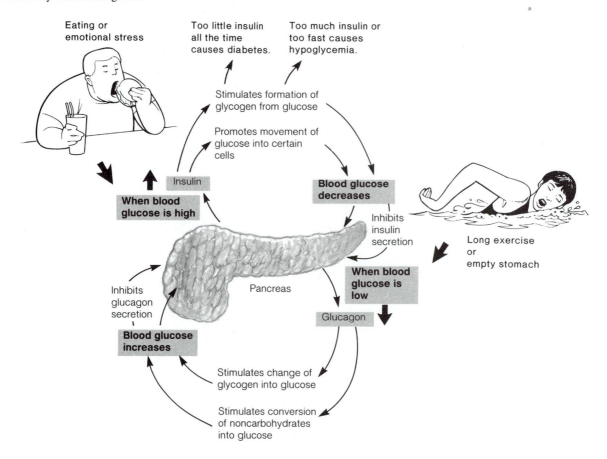

Ketosis and *ketoacidosis* are terms that describe an imbalance between the body's acids and alkalites caused by excess ketone bodies. *Ketosis,* which results from high-fat diets as well as diabetes, affects the body in many ways: (a) muscle cramps during exercise, (b) decreased ability to fight infections, and (c) increased loss of electrolytes (sodium, potassium, calcium, and magnesium) through excess urination. As the resulting electrolyte imbalance becomes more pronounced, *ketoacidosis* ensues.

Ketoacidosis progresses from lethargy to drowsiness to diabetic coma. Signs include excessive urination, thirst, dehydration, hunger, fatigue, nausea, vomiting, and abdominal pain. Respiration becomes rapid, deep, and labored in a last effort to get rid of acids. The skin becomes dry, flushed, and hot. The breath takes on a fruity (acetone) odor, and the urine smells more and more like ammonia. Blood pressure drops.

In Type I diabetes, ketoacidosis (also called hyperglycemia) is always a threat. Crisis proportions are reached in only a few hours, and immediate hospitalization is required. Any condition that raises ketone levels increases the risk of ketoacidosis. Among these are (a) infection or illness; (b) diarrhea, vomiting, and stomach upsets; (c) overeating or excessive alcoholic intake; (d) emotional stress; and (e) failure to take enough insulin to offset exercise demands.

Whenever blood glucose tests show that glucose has risen to 300 mg/dl, urine should be checked for ketone bodies. A drop of urine is placed on an acetone tablet (or equivalent), and the color change caused by the presence of ketone bodies is compared against a color chart supplied with the tablets. When ketone bodies are present, adjustments are made in insulin, food intake, and diet. Most physicians want to be contacted immediately when ketones are found in the urine (Berg, 1986).

Insulin Reaction (Hypoglycemia)

Table 19.5 shows that the opposite condition of hyperglycemia/ketoacidosis is hypoglycemia. Of the two conditions, hypoglycemia is the more common. It is the reaction that persons continuously work to avoid as they carefully monitor blood glucose and balance food intake with exercise. The movie *Steel Magnolias* showed a hypoglycemic attack. The behaviors and symptoms are in Table 19.5. Not all persons manifest all of these, and attacks vary.

Hypoglycemic reactions are most likely to occur before meals and during strenuous exercise. Many of the behaviors, symptoms, and signs are normal outcomes of exercise (excitement, perspiration, rapid heartbeat). Physical educators and coaches must monitor these especially carefully during the hour before lunch and dinner. Despite good

Table 19.5
Information about crisis situations.

Focal Points	Hyperglycemia and Ketoacidosis	Hypoglycemia: An Insulin Reaction
Situation	*Unmanaged Diabetes* *Crisis Response to Stress, Infection*	*Reaction to Delayed Food,* *Insufficient Food*
Imbalance	Low insulin, high glucose	High insulin, low glucose
Onset	Within hours	Within minutes
Behavior	Lethargic to drowsy	Nervous, restless, excited, argumentative
	Sitting, lying	Moving about
	Weak, tired all day	Sudden weakness, fainting
Symptoms, signs	Excessive urination	Normal urination
	Excessive thirst, hunger	Thirst, hunger varies
	Abdominal pain	Headache
	Dry skin	Lots of perspiration
	Weak pulse	Rapid heartbeat, palpitations
	Deep, labored breathing	Normal to shallow, rapid breathing
Treatment	Insulin shot	Glucose tabs, candy, juice
	If severe, hospitalization	Glucagon shot
If No Treatment	Coma, death	Coma, death

management, everyone with diabetes has an occasional hypoglycemic episode. The following are some accounts:

Bill Talbert, who has had diabetes since age 10, tells of having an insulin reaction during a finals tennis match with Pancho Gonzalez, then the amateur champion:

I took the first set from the fiery Californian but lost the next two. In the fourth set, my game collapsed completely as I double-faulted, sprayed shots wildly out of court, and stumbled about. My old doubles partner, Gar Mulloy, rushed out on the court after I had lost three games in succession to Pancho.

"Drink this, Willie," Gar commanded. He put a glass of sugared water into my hand, and I downed it greedily. It was the answer. Gar had realized that I was losing control of my functions and going into insulin reaction through rapid burning of sugar. In a reversal of form that baffled Pancho and the gallery, I took twelve of the next fourteen games to win the match and the Southampton trophy. (Talbert, 1971, p. 27)

Another description of an insulin reaction comes from the parents of a 6-year-old boy:

I found him sobbing on the edge of his bed at five in the morning. I thought he was having a nightmare. He couldn't tell me what was wrong. He lay looking at his hands like someone on an LSD trip finding minuscule meanings in the texture of his skin. Then I noticed that he was unsteady when he went for a drink of water, and I knew. It was insulin reaction.

We were frantic—preparing orange juice, jelly on bread, cookies, ice cream—but he cried hysterically and pushed away the food. We tried to force him; he fell and bumped his head. We panicked. We felt the insulin reaction was too far gone. We injected glucagon—a hormone that rapidly raises the blood sugar level.

In a few minutes, his head was clear, and he began to eat some of the sweets. But none of us was ever the same again. (Brandt, 1973, p. 36)

Monitoring of Glucose

Glucose levels should be checked several times each day. Target blood glucose levels are 60–130 mg/dl before meals, 140–180 mg/dl 1 hr after meals, 120–150 mg/dl 2 hr after

meals, and 80–120 mg/dl at other times (Berg, 1986). If glucose is below target level, a carbohydrate snack is eaten. If it is above, additional insulin or sulfonylurea is taken. *Values above 240 mg/dl contraindicate aerobic exercise, and values above 300 mg/dl contraindicate all kinds of exercise.*

Glucose levels are determined by either blood or urine tests. Today, most persons use a pen-size, battery-operated device called a *glucometer*. A drop of capillary blood is obtained by pricking the side of a fingertip. The blood is placed on a paper strip that is inserted into the glucometer, which gives a precise electronic readout. This is far more accurate than the urine test, in which specially treated paper is dipped in urine and then evaluated for color change.

Management of Diabetes

Good diabetic control is based on proper diet, exercise, and insulin. A change in any one of these necessitates adjustment in the others. All persons with Type I take daily insulin injections and must acquire knowledge about insulin use and reactions that may occur if insulin dosage is miscalculated. Type II management is not as complicated. Therefore, this section focuses primarily on Type I.

Multiple Daily Insulin Shots

Insulin shots are subcutaneous—that is, under the skin but above muscle tissue. Children are taught to administer their own shots at an early age. Common injection sites are buttocks, upper arms, outer sides of thighs, and lower part of the abdomen. The injection site should be changed frequently to minimize tissue breakdown. Adjusting the injection site according to anticipated activity is also important. When the exercise is primarily lower limb, as in track, insulin should be injected into the arm. When both upper and lower extremities are involved, the preferred injection site is the abdomen.

Types of insulin vary with respect to time elapse before peak effect (2–20 hr) and duration of effect (6–36 hr). Rapid-acting insulins begin to work in about 1/2 hr, although peak effect is at 2 hr. Most persons take several injections daily that are mixtures of rapid- and intermediate-acting types and provide overlapping protection.

Insulin is injected before meals, with the largest dose taken before breakfast. It may not be needed before all meals. Persons learn to adjust dosages when corrective measures are needed because of unplanned changes in eating and exercising. The major principle followed for both meals and exercise, however, is consistency in time of day, duration, and amount.

Illness, infection, and emotional stress may make diabetes worse and require extra insulin injections. Medications taken for other conditions also affect insulin dosage. Among those that increase blood glucose are diuretics (water pills that promote loss of fluids), prednisone (anti-inflammatory corticosteroid medication), beta blockers (used to manage heart and blood pressure conditions), and decongestants (for colds and sinus infections). Birth control pills inhibit insulin action and thus indirectly raise blood glucose.

Diet

Persons with diabetes typically know a lot about diet but may need support and companionship in eating correctly. The following guidelines should be emphasized:

1. Follow the consistency principle: Eat meals at the same time every day and exercise likewise.
2. Eat several small meals (about five) instead of three big ones.
3. Keep caloric intake about the same from meal to meal and day to day.
4. Identify foods that cause rapid glucose rise (have high glycemic index) and avoid them.
5. Emphasize fibers and starches (complex carbohydrates).
6. Avoid food and liquid intake when feeling nervous or anxious.
7. Balance food intake with exercise.
8. Keep glucose tablets, hard candy, or fruit juice available in case low glucose precipitates an insulin reaction.
9. Eat a carbohydrate snack about every 30 min during heavy, prolonged exercise.
10. Coordinate time and amount of food intake with exercise.

Exercise

Regular exercise is extremely important in diabetes management and may be prescribed just like medication. The prescription is typically what is good for everyone: aerobic exercise at least three times a week on alternate days, with each session lasting 45–60 min. The intensity and duration depend on initial level of fitness. Nonexercisers begin with progressive distance and speed walking programs to start at-

FIGURE 19.4

Dr. Bruce Ogilvie, the father of sport psychology, confers with athlete who is blind. Many persons who are blind also have diabetes and need lifelong leisure and fitness counseling.

titude and habit changes. Leisure counseling helps persons to discover what is fun for them and to learn new sports (see Figure 19.4).

Blood glucose is not affected the same way by all types of exercise. Aerobic exercise lowers blood glucose and is the activity of choice if the glucose level is under 240 mg/dl. When blood glucose goes above this safety criterion, the opposite is true, and aerobics are contraindicated. Anaerobic exercises like push ups and weight lifting do not lower glucose and should be used in moderation. They are important for strength development, but a person with diabetes should not select weight lifting as a major sport.

Persons with diabetes typically utilize protein and fat for energy during exercise more extensively than nondiabetics (Berg, 1986). Extra protein and carbohydrates should be eaten 15 to 30 min before exercise when planned intensity exceeds 300 cal an hour. During exercise of this intensity or greater, carbohydrate snacks are recommended every 30 min. Persons with diabetes often lose weight by exercise more quickly than nondiabetic peers.

If blood sugar is above 300 mg/dl or ketone bodies are in the urine, exercise is contraindicated. Other conditions that indicate exercise should be stopped or not initiated include (a) infection anywhere in the body, (b) high resting blood pressure, (c) severe pain in calf muscles, and (d) signs of hypoglycemia. These are all temporary problems. As soon as they are resolved, exercise programs should be resumed. For advanced reading on contraindications, see Coram and Mangum (1986).

On the day after strenuous exercise, persons with diabetes may need to decrease insulin and eat more because of a tendency toward low blood glucose. This is because muscle and liver glycogen have been depleted, and several hours are required to build up normal storage levels.

Implications for Physical Education

Emphasis should be on students with diabetes developing healthy attitudes toward exercise and body care. Students need models who have been excellent athletes despite diabetes. Among these are Kris Berg, a physical education professor at the University of Nebraska at Omaha; Jackie Robinson, Catfish Hunter, and Ron Santo, baseball star; Bill Talbert and Ham Richardson, tennis stars; and Coby O'Brien, football star.

Recommendations for teaching follow:

1. Ask the school nurse or appropriate person for the names of all students with diabetes and keep information readily accessible on emergency protocol, type of diabetes and medication, and special diet and snack needs. This is especially important for after-school practices and trips.

2. Meet with the school counselor or appropriate person and arrange to have students with diabetes scheduled for physical education after breakfast or lunch. Explain the importance of not exercising when blood glucose is low.

3. Create a prearranged signal that students with diabetes can use to call for a substitute or to be excused from class to respond to warning signs (i.e., to eat something or to monitor glucose because of feeling funny).

4. Provide breaks for fluid every 15 min during strenuous activity and give special attention to dehydration in hot weather.

5. Insist that students with diabetes protect themselves against sunburn, falls, blows, and the like that damage skin. This includes avoiding contact sports like boxing and football (Coram & Mangum, 1986).

6. Pay extra attention to clean, dry socks and proper shoes. Athlete's foot, blisters, and corns can become major problems for students with diabetes.

7. Treat students with diabetes with dignity and expect them to have glucose tablets, candy, or juice on hand at all times, in case of reactions. Keep a backup supply in case a student forgets. Remember that diet soda does not have enough glucose to work.

8. Do not give untrained persons with diabetes physical fitness tests that are concentrated in short time periods (Coram & Mangum, 1986). Evaluate fitness over several sessions in which duration and intensity are gradually increased.

FIGURE   19.5

The coronary arteries branch downward from the aorta and encircle the heart like a crown encircles the head. Disease of these arteries is the number one cause of death in persons ages 25 and over. (From *American Heart Association Heartbook.* New York: E. P. Dutton, p. 176. Reproduced with permission. © *American Heart Association Heartbook,* 1980. Copyright American Heart Association.)

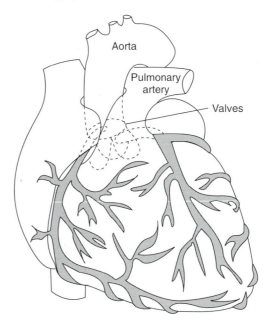

9. Teach students with diabetes to exercise with partners who understand diabetes. Pairing persons with diabetes with those who want to lose weight is a good idea because of common interest in food and exercise.

10. Be understanding of mood swings, good and bad days, and behaviors associated with insulin reaction. Let students talk out embarrassment, frustrations, and concerns.

Cardiovascular Problems

The two causes of cardiovascular disease are acquired and congenital. Acquired conditions, the number one cause of death in persons aged 25 and over, primarily affect the arteries that supply oxygen to the heart and brain. In contrast, congenital conditions are typically defects in the structure of the heart walls and valves.

Statistics for acquired and congenital conditions are startling. Approximately 10% of the world's population has acquired cardiovascular disease. This is typically diagnosed after age 50 or 60, but pathology begins in youth. By age 60, one out of every five American males has coronary artery disease (CAD), the most common disorder (see Figure 19.5). Women also have CAD, but the prevalence is about six times greater in males than females. With respect to congenital heart disease, about 1% of all newborns have a heart disorder, but 20 to 60% of infants born with chromosomal defects are affected. Alcohol, tobacco, drugs, and viruses like AIDS and rubella are also associated with congenital heart disease.

Table 19.6
Risk factors in cardiovascular disease.

Factors That Can Be Altered
1. Hypertension (high blood pressure)
2. Elevated low-density-lipoprotein cholesterol (LDL-C) and triglycerides
3. Cigarette smoking
4. Diet
5. Physical inactivity
6. Body fatness
7. Diabetes
8. Emotional stress

Factors That Cannot Be Altered
1. Heredity
2. Age
3. Sex
4. Race

A lifespan approach to adapted physical activity emphasizes prevention of both acquired and congenital disorders. Surgery is so successful in correcting congenital disorders that regular physical educators seldom are confronted with defects of the heart walls and valves. The school years, however, are the critical time for developing an active, healthy lifestyle that will minimize heart attacks, strokes, and the like. Family education and exercise programs are probably the best approach. The adapted physical activity expert initiates and coordinates home/school/community programs to meet the needs of persons of all ages. This education emphasizes reduction of risk factors (see Table 19.6).

Atherosclerosis

Atherosclerosis and arteriosclerosis are the degenerative processes that lead to heart attacks, strokes, and circulatory problems. Both cause *sclerosis* (hardening of the arteries). Understanding of the derivation of the first half of these words helps with correct usage. *Athero* is the Greek word for "gruel" (porridge or cereal) and refers to accumulation of fatty substances resembling gruel inside the arteries. This is a lifespan process, beginning as early as age 3. In contrast, *arterio* means artery. *Arteriosclerosis* is the broader term, encompassing all of the pathological conditions (hardening, thickening, loss of elasticity) that slow or block blood circulation.

Today, atherosclerosis is the more common diagnosis. It is the specific form of arteriosclerosis that begins in childhood as fat streak deposits (see Figure 19.6). These are found in the aorta as early as age 3. Fat deposits subsequently appear in the coronary and peripheral arteries in late childhood and adolescence. The exact age depends on many factors. The coronary arteries are the heart's only source of oxygen. They branch downward from the aorta and encircle the heart like a crown encircles the head. Coronary is derived from the word *corona,* meaning "crown". Consider how the coronary arteries are as important to the heart as a crown is to royalty. All arteries outside of the heart are called peripheral, meaning "away from the center" (i.e., the heart).

By early adulthood, enough fatty substances have accumulated to be called plaque (see Figure 19.6). This ath-

FIGURE 19.6

Atherosclerosis is a lifespan degenerative process that is related to known risk factors. Note how the arteries change from decade to decade when risk factors are ignored.

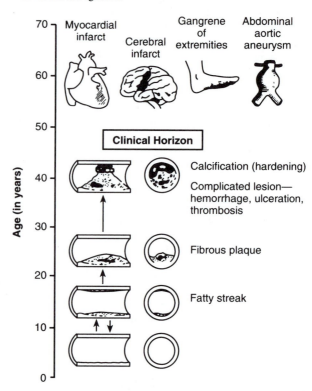

erosclerotic process can be happening anywhere in the body but is most dangerous in the heart and brain. Unlike soft, fatty streaks, plaque is hard with rough edges. The slow progressive buildup of plaque during the adult years not only narrows passageways but also damages surrounding cells, causing hemorrhage, ulceration, and blood clots known as thrombi (singular: *thrombus*) and emboli (singular: *embolus*). A *thrombus* is a blood clot that remains at its point of origin. An *embolus* is a traveling obstruction; it may be a blood clot or a bubble of gas.

The ages between 40 and 60 represent the clinical horizon for most persons when symptoms of atherosclerosis begin to be noticed (see Figure 19.6). Among the most common indicators are (a) high blood pressure, (b) discomfort or pain during strenuous exercise, and (c) blood analysis that shows high levels of triglycerides, low-density-lipoprotein cholesterol (LDL-C), and very-low-density-lipoprotein cholesterol (VLDL-C). Most persons at risk try to change their lifestyles during these years, and adapted physical activity becomes high priority.

If lifestyle change is ineffective or genetic predisposition to cardiovascular disease is overpowering, pathology is manifested in the form of heart attacks, strokes, circulatory dysfunctions, and aneurysms (see Figure 19.6). The heart, brain, and extremities are primarily damaged by *ischemia*, meaning inadequate oxygen to cells. The resulting cell death is called *infarcts* or *infarction* in the heart and brain and *gangrene* in the extremities. Thus, atherosclerosis is an *ischemic disease.*

Aneurysms are deformities of blood vessels, usually the arteries, caused by progressive, long-term weakening of the walls by atherosclerosis and/or high blood pressure. The most common site is the aorta in the abdominal region, but aneurysms can occur anywhere. The most serious aneurysms, of course, are those in the heart and brain. There are several types. Most aneurysms are blood-filled pouches that balloon out from the inner vessel wall and obstruct blood flow. If not removed by surgery, they may rupture. A *dissecting aneurysm,* one of the ACSM exercise contraindications, is an anomaly that affects all three layers of the artery wall. A tear in one layer permits blood to leak out and separate (dissect) the layers from one another, thereby causing cell death.

The atherosclerotic process results in over 1 million deaths in the United States each year. About 60% of these come from heart attacks associated with coronary artery disease (CAD), 20% from strokes, and 20% from overall system failure related to heart muscle degeneration and high blood pressure. Heart attack and stroke usually are not fatal on first occurrence. They are, however, costly in terms of time, money, and mental health.

Heart Attack

Heart attack, called *myocardial infarction* (MI) because cells are dying, is a life-threatening crisis that occurs when the oxygen demand of the heart muscle cells is greater than the coronary arteries can supply. Stress or heavy exertion when coronary arteries are occluded by advanced atherosclerosis or a blood clot (thrombus or embolus) is the cause. Inadequate oxygen is signaled by chest pain (angina) in the area behind the breast bone. This pain may radiate to the jaw, neck, shoulder, or arms. The pain is felt as a continuous, heavy, squeezing pressure lasting 2 or more minutes, rather than sharp or stabbing twinges. Sweating, shortness of breath, general weakness, nausea, and vomiting may also be present.

Persons of all ages have heart attacks, but most often, infarction strikes males ages 50 and above with high-risk profiles. The first 48 to 72 hr after a heart attack are critical because death of heart muscle cells and their replacement with scar tissue disrupt the rhythm of the heartbeat. This dysrhythmia often brings on a second attack. The section "Cardiac Rehabilitation for Adults," later in the chapter, discusses adapted physical activity.

Stroke

Stroke, also called cerebrovascular accident (CVA) or apoplexy, is a sudden loss of function (awareness, motor, speech, perception, memory, cognition) caused by ischemia or hemorrhage affecting brain cells. Consciousness is sometimes but not always lost. Recovery of function depends on the site and extent of brain cell death. Strokes can be massive, causing much damage, or small episodes, called transient ischemic attacks (TIAs), that are hardly noticed. TIAs result in muscle weakness, speech difficulty, or other mild problems that last only a few hours. These are warnings of cerebral atherosclerosis and impending major strokes.

Strokes are more common in males until about age 75, after which the incidence is equal for both sexes. Strokes can occur at any age but are most frequent after age 60. Blacks and orientals are more prone to strokes than whites. *Cerebral thrombosis related to atherosclerotic degeneration is the most common cause.* Visualize the four main arteries and many small branches that supply oxygen to the brain. Clogging kills brain cells by denying them oxygen, whereas hemorrhage destroys cells by issuing blood into the wrong places. Approximately one-third of stroke victims die. Others recover slowly. Additional information about stroke appears in Chapter 25 on cerebral palsy and traumatic brain injury. Stroke results in disabilities similar to these conditions.

Problems of the Extremities

Atherosclerosis can also affect arteries of the arms and legs, reducing the supply of oxygen to muscles, skin, and nails. This is one reason why the fingernails and toenails of many elderly people become abnormally thick and hard to cut. It also explains why older persons often have cold feet and hands and more frequent bruising and skin breakdown.

Legs and feet are more commonly affected by atherosclerosis than upper extremities. The first indication of an inadequate supply of oxygen to muscle is pain, aching, and cramping in the calf caused by walking short distances (e.g., half a block to a quarter mile). This pain is called *claudication,* a term derived from Emperor Claudius of ancient Rome, who walked with a limp. Claudication can be felt in any part of the hip, leg, and foot, depending on the site of arterial blockage, but the calf is most commonly affected. Pain is severe but disappears within a minute or two of rest. When walking is resumed, the pain recurs after about the same distance as before. As atherosclerosis becomes progressively worse, pain is felt even during inactivity, especially during bed rest. This is because a horizontal position prevents gravity from assisting the blood to flow down to the legs.

In advanced stages of arterial insufficiency, the extremities become increasingly susceptible to injury, disease, and temperature extremes. Open sores do not heal properly, infection sets in, and tissue death may be so great that gangrene requires amputation of affected body parts. This pathology is associated with old age; however, persons with diabetes are at high risk at all ages.

Congestive Heart Disease

A weak heart muscle can result from (a) cell death (ischemia) caused by heart attack, (b) work overload caused by structural defects, and/or (c) a sedentary lifestyle. Like other muscles, the myocardium must be used vigorously a few minutes each day to stay strong. Progressive weakness of the heart is characterized by accumulation of fluid in body parts. This is called congestion or edema.

A brief review of the parts of the heart and the direction of normal blood circulation enhances understanding of what is happening during congestive heart disease (Table 19.7 and Figure 19.7). *Systemic circulation,* initiated by contraction of the left ventricle, carries oxygenated blood to all systems of the body and returns waste-laden, oxygen-depleted blood. Weakness of the left ventricle is manifested

Table 19.7
Review of parts of heart and direction of blood flow.

Function	Pumping Chamber	Upward-Flow Valves	Artery	Circulation Capillary Exchange	Venous Return	Collecting Chamber	Downward-Flow Valves
Left heart systemic circulation	Left ventricle	Aortic	Aortic	Total body	Superior and inferior vena cava	Right atrium	Tricuspid
Right heart pulmonary circulation	Right ventricle	Pulmonary	Pulmonary	Lungs	Pulmonary veins	Left atrium	Mitral or Bicuspid

Note. All blood goes through both a systemic and pulmonary circuit. To trace blood flow, read from left to right.

FIGURE 19.7

Four chambers of the normal heart and physiology of pulmonary and systemic circulation. Systemic circulation is shaded.

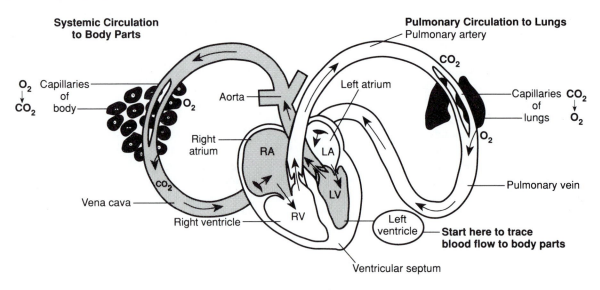

by inability to pump hard enough to empty the chamber, and fluids begin to back up in the left atrium and lungs. *Pulmonary circulation,* initiated by contraction of the right ventricle, carries the deoxygenated blood to the lungs, where wastes are exchanged for oxygen. Insufficiency of right ventricle function causes blood to back up in the right atrium and the veins of body parts.

The left and right sides of the heart react differently to congestion. *Left heart congestion,* the most common, is characterized by fluid in the lungs, shortness of breath, wheezing, and coughing. This condition makes persons particularly susceptible to death by pneumonia (lung inflammation caused by bacteria, viruses, and chemical irritants). *Right heart congestion* causes fluid retention in the liver, legs, and feet. Edema anywhere in the body is an indication of dysfunction that is increasing blood volume and making the heart muscle work harder than normal.

Congestive heart disease may progress slowly, with no discomfort felt for years. The weak ventricular muscle, unable to squeeze strongly, simply wears out, and the blood flows too slowly to meet oxygen needs. Persons become less and less fit, eventually dying in their sleep. This problem is particularly acute among nonambulatory persons with severe mental retardation, brain damage, or physical disabilities, who are dependent upon others to get them out of bed and provide exercise. The primary cause of death for this population is pneumonia/heart congestion, whereas the primary cause of death for all other adult populations is coronary artery disease. Persons in nursing homes (especially the ill elderly) are at particular risk because the staff is often not able to meet their exercise needs. Congestive heart disease can be ameliorated simply by sitting upright a few hours each day so that fluids can drain, but some persons are too weak to manage this without help. Breathing exercises and games (described later in the chapter discussion of asthma) are recommended also, along with gentle exercise (passive, if necessary) of all body parts.

Conduction Abnormalities and Heart Rate

Electrical impulses are what makes the heart beat. Abnormalities in the heart's electrical conduction system result in various kinds of *dysrhythmias* (fast, slow, or irregular heart-

FIGURE 19.8

The electrocardiogram indicates the conduction of electrical impulses through the heart and records both the intensity of this electrical activity (in millivolts) and the time intervals involved. (*A*) Heart showing parts related to electrical impulses. (*B*) Computer printout of intensity and time interval of an electrical impulse. (*C*) Section of an electrocardiogram.

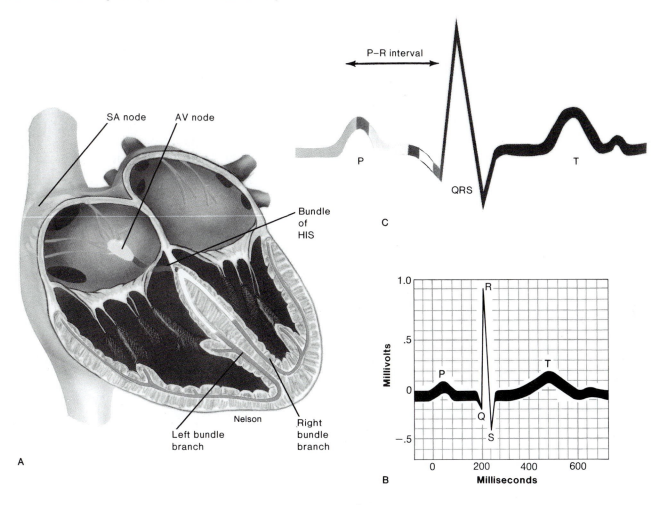

beats) and *blocks* (interruptions or delays in conduction). Many of these are important in endurance testing and exercise prescription.

The electrocardiogram (ECG) is used by physicians to identify conduction abnormalities (see Figure 19.8). Roy Shephard (1990) and ACSM literature (1991) note that lists of exercise contraindications commonly include *ST depression* and *T-wave inversion,* two ECG readings that indicate conduction abnormalities. The waves of electrical activity recorded on the ECG are designated by letters (*P, QRS, T*), which are used in describing heart function. The letters are not abbreviations for words; they were arbitrarily selected to denote up-and-down changes in the waves. Normal heartbeats display a characteristic ECG pattern with ventricular contraction beginning near the end of the *QRS*. The *T* wave represents systole (contraction) and the *P* wave represents diastole (relaxation). Figure 19.8 shows the electrical activity of one normal heartbeat.

The structure within the heart that normally initiates the electrical impulses is the sinus or sinoatrial (SA) node (see Figure 19.8). This is the heart's natural pacemaker. Im-

pulses travel from the sinus node to the atrioventricular (AV) node and then to the ventricles via neural pathways called the bundle of HIS, the left bundle branch, and the right bundle branch. Anything that alters these impulses affects heart function.

Sometimes, cardiac tissue other than the sinus node produces electrical impulses. When this happens, the heartbeats are called *ectopic,* meaning that they are displaced or in an abnormal position. Extra or skipped beats, also called premature ventricular contractions (PVC), are examples. These may indicate cardiac dysfunction but often are responses to stress or anxiety. *Repetitive or frequent ventricular ectopic activity is an exercise contraindication.*

The function of the sinus node is regulated by the hypothalamus and the autonomic nervous system. The parasympathetic system, through the vagus nerve, can lower the heart rate between 20 and 30 beats. The sympathetic system, in contrast, can speed the heart up so that it beats well over 200 times a minute. Disorders in heart rate that originate from autonomic system dysfunction are called *chronotropic* (Ellestad, 1986). These may be congenital or acquired.

Chronotropic Incompetence

Chronotropic dysfunction or incompetence is suspected when response to aerobic exercise is not normal. A slow heartbeat that fails to rise normally in response to strenuous activity makes knowing when to stop exercise difficult. This condition is relatively common in severe developmental disabilities and postoperative congenital heart defects. *Endurance activities may be contraindicated or need to be adapted to a lower-than-normal target heart rate range.*

Before birth, the parasympathetic and sympathetic systems develop at different rates, with the parasympathetic (vagal) maturing first. In premature births, chronotropic incompetence sometimes occurs because the sympathetic system is not yet mature and the heart rate is too slow (i.e., less than 100). In some persons with severe brain damage, the sympathetic system does not mature properly, and heart function remains chronotropic.

Sick Sinus Syndrome

Sick sinus syndrome (SSS) is a generic term for dysrhythmias that stem from problems of the sinus node, autonomic nervous system, and hypothalamus. This term, sometimes a synonym for chronotropic incompetence, is applied to persons with widespread, though not necessarily serious, abnormalities of rhythm (e.g., too fast or slow, or alternating fast and slow). Chronic fastness or slowness may not be noticed because the condition develops slowly or is congenital. Some sources say that SSS is most common among the elderly (NurseReview, 1987), but recently, the condition is mentioned in exercise literature pertaining to disabilities (Fernhall & Tymeson, 1987; Pitetti & Tan, 1991; Rimmer, 1993; Shephard, 1990). Fatigue, dizziness, and syncope (temporary unconsciousness) are exercise responses associated with SSS.

Fibrillations and Flutters

Fibrillations (rapid quivers) are incomplete contractions of heart fibers caused by conduction disturbances. *Flutters* are similar but less severe disturbances. While in fibrillation, the heart is unable to pump blood.

Ventricular fibrillation is the cause of most cardiac arrests and deaths in adults (Wilmore & Costill, 1988) and is commonly associated with coronary heart attack, electrical shock, and excess amounts of digitalis or chloroform. Electrical devices called *defibrillators* counteract fibrillation and save lives.

Atrial fibrillation also requires immediate treatment because it compromises ventricular filling. Among children and adolescents, the most common cause of atrial fibrillation is Wolff-Parkinson-White (WPW) syndrome, a condition precipitated by congenital anomalies of some of the conduction pathways. This is one of the ACSM exercise testing contraindications.

Tachycardias

Tachycardia is diagnosed when the resting heart rate in adolescents and adults is faster than 100 beats per minute. In infants and children, the criterion is much higher. There are many types of tachycardias, all caused by conduction disorders. Fast rhythms originating in the sinus node, typically between 100 to 150 beats per minute, are called *sinus tachycardias*. Alcohol, caffeine, and nicotine can trigger sinus tachycardia in healthy persons. Other causes include infection and/or disease with fever, dehydration, anemia, blood loss, hyperthyroidism, anoxia, and certain drugs used to manage asthma (theophylline) and hyperactivity (epinephrine). A fast sinus rhythm may be benign, with no exercise restrictions, or it may signal medical problems.

Fast rhythms (resting rates above 150) caused by problems arising outside the sinus node (i.e., ectopic) typically contraindicate aerobic exercise and endurance testing. In *ventricular tachycardia,* the fast rhythm originates in the ventricles, is usually associated with heart disease, and may herald ventricular fibrillation and sudden death. In *supraventricular tachycardia* (also called atrial or nodal), the abnormality is in the atria. This results in episodes of fast heartbeat (paroxysms), rather than continuous speeding, and may occur in persons with no other evidence of heart disease.

Bradycardias

Slow heartbeat can indicate either cardiovascular wellness or pathology. Chronic, slow heartbeat (sinus bradycardia) in athletes is an indication of excellent cardiorespiratory fitness. Resting heart rates as low as 28 beats per minute have been observed in world-class long-distance runners (Wilmore & Costill, 1988). Pathology-related causes of bradycardia are the sick sinus syndrome, acute myocardial infarction, hypothermia (prolonged coldness or freezing), hypothyroidism, complete heart blocks, anorexia nervosa, residual effects of congenital heart defects after surgery, and medications like digitalis and beta blockers designed specifically to slow heartbeats. Slow heartbeat, as long as there is energy to complete desired tasks, is not a problem because persons generally self-select only activities that are comfortable. *Aerobic activities are contraindicated unless prescribed by a physician.*

For adults, a heart rate less than 40 beats per minute, unless the person is a trained athlete, is an indication for medication and/or an artificial pacemaker (NurseReview, 1987, p. 113). Less than 60 beats per minute is the diagnostic criterion for prepubertal persons.

Heart Block

Heart block is a pathologic interruption or delay in electrical impulse conduction that alters the rhythm of the heartbeat. Blocks may be congenital or acquired through disease or injury. There are many kinds, but only two are ACSM exercise contraindications: complete atrioventricular (AV) block and left bundle branch block.

AV blocks are interruptions between the atria and ventricles that disturb the synchrony of atrial and ventricular beats. These blocks are classified as first, second, and third degree. The third-degree condition is the complete heart block (CHB). In most persons, the atrial rate is normal, but the ventricular rate (the one monitored by taking a pulse) is abnormally slow during both rest and exercise. Even during all-out exercise, the heart rate does not rise beyond 100 to 120 beats per minute (Bar-Or, 1983). There are many individual differences in exercise response, but fatigue and breathing difficulty are common. *In assessment of maximal aerobic power, heart rate response to standardized exercise cannot be used because it is not a valid indicator of exertion. Some persons with AV blocks can exercise normally, but physician clearance is important.*

Left bundle branch blocks (see Figure 19.8) disrupt the normal left-to-right ventricular conduction pattern, causing the ventricles to beat out of rhythm with each other. This problem is associated with myocardiac infarction but may accompany numerous other conditions.

Cardiovascular Medications

The best-known heart medications are the *nitrates* (e.g., nitroglycerin) for angina conditions and the *digitalis preparations* (e.g., digoxin) for congestive heart failure and some conduction abnormalities. Nitrates relax and dilate smooth muscles, thereby increasing heart rate and oxygen supply and decreasing blood pressure. Digitalis preparations lower heart rate but do not affect blood pressure.

Heart rhythm regulators include drugs that block or depress the sympathetic nervous system (e.g., the beta blockers) and the transmembrane calcium flow in cardiac smooth muscle tissue (e.g., the calcium channel blockers). These drugs have variable effects on heart rates, depending on whether they manage tachycardia or bradycardia. Both beta blockers and calcium channel blockers lower blood pressure. Alpha blockers, also prescribed to lower blood pressure, are not heart rhythm regulators because they do not affect heart rate.

Beta blockers lower heart rate and mask exercise effects, making the pulse an invalid indicator of effort. The main side effects of beta blockers are early exercise fatigue and lowered maximum oxygen uptake. Some new beta blockers have built-in sympathomimetic agents to lessen side effects. Overall, the blockers are extremely complex. Only professionals with special training should work with conditions that require SNS blockers.

When heart disease is complicated by high blood pressure, vasodilators and diuretics are typically prescribed. *Vasodilators* are drugs that lower blood pressure by increasing the size of vessels. Some vasodilators work specifically on arteries, while others work on veins. The effect of vasodilators on heart rate is therefore variable. Several cause tachycardia.

Diuretics, discussed earlier, decrease blood pressure by reducing fluid volume through urination. None of the many kinds of diuretics affect heart rate. Remember—drugs that lower blood pressure often cause hypotension.

Persons taking cardiovascular drugs can and should exercise. Graded exercise and cardiac rehabilitation programs are discussed later in this chapter. Weight loss is often the first exercise priority.

FIGURE 19.9

(*A*) The wall of the heart consists of three layers: an endocardium, a myocardium, and an epicardium. (*B*) Close-up of middle layer, showing cardiac muscle that contracts and relaxes.

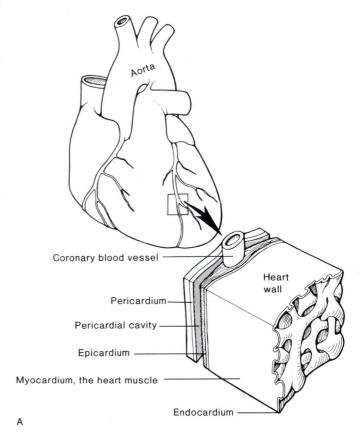

Aorta

Coronary blood vessel

Pericardium

Pericardial cavity

Epicardium

Myocardium, the heart muscle

Heart wall

Endocardium

A

Myocardium

B

Inflammation of the Heart Wall

Figure 19.9 shows the pericardium (fibrous sac that surrounds the heart and great vessels) and the three layers that comprise the heart wall. Inflammation of these structures results in conditions called *pericarditis, myocarditis, and endocarditis.* Inflammation is caused by a variety of viral, bacterial, and unknown agents. Often, these are introduced into

FIGURE 19.10

Four valves open and close to regulate blood entering and leaving chambers. (*A*) Close-up of valves. (*B*) Relationship of valves to other parts of heart. (19.10 B from *American Heart Association Heartbook*. New York: E. P. Dutton, p. 266. Reproduced with permission. © *American Heart Association Heartbook*, 1980. Copyright American Heart Association.)

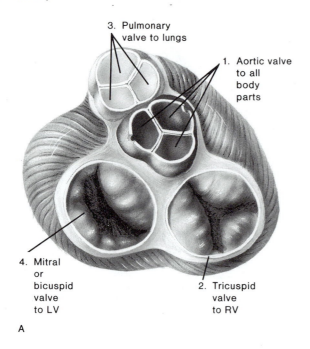

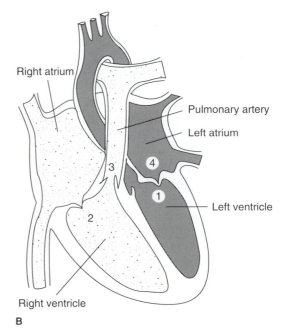

A   B

the bloodstream during corrective surgery. Anything inserted into the body (e.g., tubes, shunts, or catheters) can carry a virus or bacteria. Intravenous drug users are particularly at high risk. Inflammation can also be caused by viral and bacterial diseases like influenza, diphtheria, measles, and chicken pox. Inflammation is treated by several families of anti-infective drugs (e.g., antibiotics, antimicrobials) and by corticosteroids. Exercise is contraindicated until inflammation is under control.

Valve Defects and Heart Murmurs

Valves are the membranous structures that rhythmically open and close to force the blood within the heart to flow in the right direction (see Figure 19.10). For simplicity, the mitral and tricuspid valves are called the atrioventricular (AV) valves because they open at the same instant to permit blood to flow downward from atria to ventricles. The closing of the AV valves is what makes the "lubb" sound in the "lubb-dupp" of the heartbeat and is the mechanism that starts constriction. Shortly thereafter, the aortic and pulmonary valves (called the semilunar valves for brevity) open to permit blood to be squeezed upward into the aorta and pulmonary artery. The closing of the semilunar valves marks the beginning of the rest period during which all four valves are closed.

Valvular defects typically cause heart murmurs that are heard with a stethoscope. In spite of their weird sounds, most valvular defects are mild, and some even heal themselves. About 80% of young children have a heart murmur. Most of these disappear during adolescence.

Most persons with valvular disease have few or no exercise restrictions. Ordinary physical activity does not cause shortness of breath, undue fatigue, palpitation, or chest pain. Ability to excel in vigorous activity like aerobic fitness tests and lengthy competitive games may be limited, depending on the nature and severity of the defect.

Valvular defects are of three types: (a) regurgitation, (b) stenosis, and (c) prolapse. *Regurgitation* is the backward leakage that occurs when damaged valves are unable to close tightly. This leakage places extra stress on the heart, causing the left ventricle to enlarge and the muscle wall to thicken. The ventricle gradually loses its ability to completely empty the chamber with each contraction. This results in shortness of breath and reduced exercise tolerance. *Stenosis,* or narrowing of the valves, compromises the valves' ability to open widely and permit blood to flow freely. Stenosis of the pulmonary valve causes right heart congestion. Stenosis of the aortic valve causes left heart congestion. Valvular stenosis progresses slowly and may not cause discomfort for years. *Prolapse* is the slipping or falling out of place of an organ.

The most common is mitral valve prolapse (MVP), in which the valve leaflets flop backward into the left atrium during the heart's squeezing action (systole). The main symptoms are arrhythmias and chest pain. MVP occurs mostly in adults and more often in Down syndrome (14% prevalence) than in the nondisabled population (Goldhaber, Brown, & St. John Sutton, 1987). It is also common in connective tissue disorders like osteogenesis imperfecta, Marfan syndrome, and Ehlers-Danlos syndrome (see Chapter 24 on les autres conditions).

Some heart valve disease is diagnosed at birth and corrected in early childhood, but most is not identified until late childhood or adolescence. The cause is typically unknown unless symptoms can be traced back to an infection. Among the childhood diseases most likely to cause valvular defects is rheumatic fever.

Rheumatic Fever

Rheumatic fever is the most common cause of acquired heart disease in children and adolescents. In the United States, this disease is steadily declining, but in Third World countries, rheumatic fever continues to be a major cause of illness and death. Some developing countries report an almost equal incidence of congenital and rheumatic heart disease. In sharp contrast, rheumatic fever accounts for only 1 to 3% of children's heart disease in the United States.

Rheumatic fever is an autoimmune disease in which antibodies attack tissues and cause various kinds of inflammation. The disease typically follows inadequately treated childhood streptococcal infections (e.g., strep throat or scarlet fever). Therefore, sore throats must be properly diagnosed and cared for. Fortunately, the most common sore throat is viral and does not cause rheumatic fever. A viral sore throat is characterized by a runny nose and cough; in contrast, a strep throat is very sore without these symptoms. Streptococcus is a bacteria that infects most school-age children about once every 3 to 5 years. The sore throat can be suppressed after 1 or 2 days of antibiotic (e.g., penicillin) treatment, but drugs must be taken for about 10 days to kill the strep bacteria and prevent the possibility of rheumatic fever or a strep reoccurrence.

The onset of rheumatic fever averages about 18 days after recovery from a strep throat. Symptoms are variable. Fever and sore, swollen joints (polyarthritis) are the most common. The pain typically migrates from joint to joint, with the knees, ankles, elbows, and wrists affected most often. Shortness of breath, chest pains, and exercise intolerance are indications of inflammation of the heart (carditis), a common manifestation. *Carditis* is the term used when two or more of the heart wall layers are affected. Skin rash and/or nodules under the skin and an involuntary twitching of muscles called chorea or St. Vitus Dance are indications of skin and central nervous system involvement. The clinical picture varies with each individual, but acute inflammation is always present in one or more of the body systems. Chorea appears much later than other symptoms, often 2 to 6 months after the strep infection.

Initial treatment is usually hospitalization and medications like aspirin and the corticosteroids to reduce inflammation, thereby relieving symptoms. The duration of this anti-inflammatory treatment varies from a few days to 3 or 4 months, depending on the tissues involved. Bed rest is recommended until symptoms disappear because inflammation anywhere in the body places extra stress on the heart. Children without carditis may return to school in 2 or 3 weeks with no restrictions other than common sense in gradually increasing exercise duration and intensity.

When carditis is present, activity is increased a little at a time, and tests are administered to assure that there is no residual heart damage. Chorea, which occurs in only 8 to 10% of patients, is managed by sedatives and tranquilizers. Usually 4 to 6 weeks are required for abnormal movement to subside. Most children recover completely from rheumatic fever. They are, however, highly susceptible to recurrent attacks for about 5 years and therefore take penicillin by oral or intramuscular injection at regular intervals until adulthood. Prior to dental work and surgery, additional penicillin may be prescribed because they remain at risk to bacterial infections that affect the heart.

The heart is permanently damaged in about 60% of the children who have rheumatic fever (Maurer, 1983). The mitral and aortic valves are the parts of the heart most frequently affected (see Figure 19.10).

Congenital Heart Defects

Whereas adult heart problems are mostly of an acquired etiology, the problems of children are mostly congenital. The incidence of congenital heart defects is 6 to 10 per 1,000 live births. While some of these infants die during their first year, most are kept alive by surgery, often during the first few weeks of life. Ideally, this surgery is undertaken before age 6 so that the child can start school with a normal or near-normal heart and few exercise restrictions. Physical educators should be familiar with the most prevalent congenital heart defects (see Figure 19.11).

Once a congenital defect has been surgically corrected, the chances are good that the child will have no exercise restriction. Many participate in strenuous, high-level, competitive sports. The student should be allowed the freedom to decide how hard to play, since sensations are usually a reliable guide to exercise tolerance. The psychological problems stemming from parental overprotection and preoperative anxieties and fears are generally greater than residual physiological limitations.

Definitions of Terms

A review of the basic terms used in heart disease helps to make sense of the congenital disorders:

Septal—refers to septum, meaning a dividing wall between two chambers. In the heart, there is an atrial septum and a ventricular septum.

Patent—is from the Latin word *patens,* meaning "wide open" or "accessible."

Ductus arteriosus—is a tubelike passageway in the fetus between the aorta and the main pulmonary artery.

Tetralogy—is a group or series of four.

Great vessels—are the aorta and pulmonary artery.

Stenosis—means constriction or narrowing of a passageway.

Coarctation—means tightening or shriveling of the walls of a vessel; compression.

Atresia—means pathological closure of a normal anatomical opening or congenital absence of the opening.

FIGURE 19.11

Common congenital heart defects grouped according to impairment.
(From *American Heart Association Heartbook*. New York: E. P. Dutton,
pp. 243–246. Reproduced with permission. © *American Heart Association
Heartbook,* 1980. Copyright American Heart Association.)

Left to Right Shunts

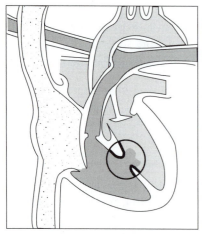

Ventricular septal defect (VSD)

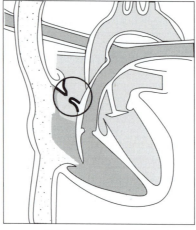

Atrial septal defect (ASD)

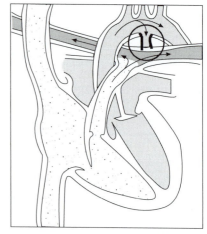

Patent ductus arteriosus (PDA)

Obstructive Lesions (Impaired Blood Flow)

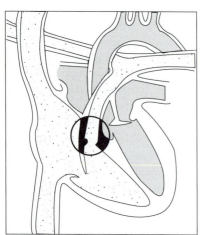

Pulmonic stenosis, valvular (PSV)

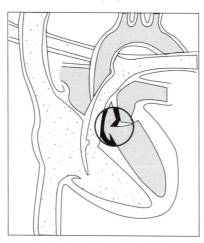

Aortic stenosis, valvular (ASV)

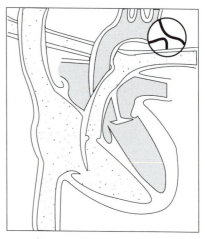

Coarctation of the aorta (COA)

Right to Left Shunts

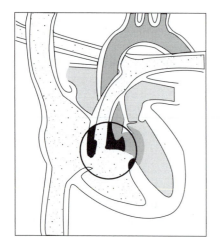

Tetralogy of fallot (TOF)

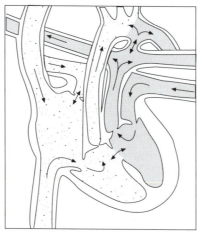

Transposition of the great vessels (TGV)

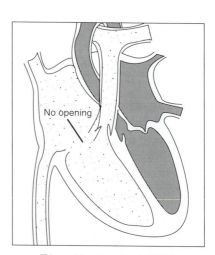

Tricuspid valve atresia (TVA)

Shunt—is a hole in the septum between the atria or the ventricles that permits blood from the systemic circulation to mix with that of the pulmonary circulation or vice versa.

Cyanosis—is blueness resulting from oxygen deficiency in the blood.

Types of Congenital Heart Defects

Figure 19.11 shows that congenital heart defects fall into three categories: (a) left-to-right shunts, (b) obstructive lesions, and (c) right-to-left shunts, The *left-to-right shunts* are the most common, the easiest to understand, and generally the least serious. Two are septal defects, and one is a duct that fails to close. In each, oxygenated blood from the arteries seeps through a hole in the heart wall (septum) into the waste-filled blood in the right chambers. This causes a volume overload on the right ventricle and raises blood pressure, but these effects are minimal when holes are small.

Obstructive lesions narrow (a) the valves that govern upward flow of blood or (b) the aorta itself. The most serious is aortic stenosis valvular (ASV), which leads to left heart congestion and has been linked with sudden death syndrome. This is the only congenital heart defect in which physical exertion is considered detrimental to health (Bar-Or, 1983). The effects of coarctation of the aorta depend on the location of the narrowing, but high blood pressure is the greatest problem. Pulmonary stenosis valvular (PSV) leads to right heart congestion.

The *right-to-left shunts* are caused by complicated conditions, as indicated by their names. In each of these, poorly oxygenated venous blood somehow gets into the aorta, thereby reducing the oxygen being carried to all body parts. The low oxygen content causes skin, lips, and nail beds to take on a bluish tint, a characteristic known as *cyanosis*. Obviously, low oxygen limits energy and endurance. The volume overload on the left ventricle also raises blood pressure.

The nine congenital heart defects shown in Figure 19.11 comprise 90% of all congenital heart defects. Ventricular septal defect (VSD) and patent ductus arteriosus (PDA) rank first and second, respectively, in prevalence estimates. Pulmonic stenosis valvular (PSV) and Tetralogy of Fallot (TOF) tie for third place, each affecting about 10% (Maurer, 1983). Together, these four defects comprise about 70% of the total.

A brief discussion of the four most common conditions follows. Other defects can best be remembered by visualization and grouping them by type (see Figure 19.11).

Ventricular Septal Defect

The severity of VSD depends on whether the hole in the ventricular septum is small or large. Small holes often close spontaneously in early childhood. Many small- and medium-sized openings that do not close are harmless. Large holes must be surgically repaired. VSD is the most common congenital heart defect (Maurer, 1983). Before surgery, respiratory infections and slow physical growth are particular problems.

VSD, complicated by a defect of the adjacent endocardial cushion lining, occurs in about 40% of the infants born with Down syndrome. Unlike VSD in the normal population, the hole is typically large and causes breathing difficulty, early fatigability, profuse sweating, feeding problems, and poor growth. About 30% of infants with Down syndrome have multiple cardiac defects (Spicer, 1984). The most common defects accompanying VSD are patent ductus arteriosus (5 to 15%) and pulmonic stenosis (9%). Early surgery ameliorates these problems.

Patent Ductus Arteriosus

Before birth, there is no need for blood to circulate through the lungs because the placenta takes care of oxygen needs. Therefore, the fetus has a tubelike passageway (the ductus arteriosus) between the aorta and the pulmonary artery that enables the blood to bypass the lungs. At birth, when breathing starts, reflex muscle contractions in the wall of the ductus arteriosus causes this bypass to close within a few days. When this fails to take place, normal circulation cannot be established. Part of the oxygenated blood in the aorta that should be flowing to other body parts leaks into the pulmonary artery via the open duct.

When this seepage is large, the symptoms and treatment are the same as for severe VSD. PDA occurs in about 20% of premature infants and 5% of full-term infants, making it the second most common congenital heart defect (Maurer, 1983).

Tetralogy of Fallot

Tetralogy (meaning "four symptoms") is characterized by (a) VSD, (b) PSV, (c) an enlarged right ventricle, and (d) a malpositioned aorta that receives blood from both ventricles. This combination of abnormalities was discovered by a man named Fallot and thus is known as Tetralogy of Fallot. The resulting shunt is unoxygenated blood from the right ventricle leaking into the left ventricle, which pumps it throughout the body. The unoxygenated blood, bluish in color, causes the condition known as *blue baby* or cyanosis.

TOF is usually severe, requiring surgery in infancy. Without surgery, spells of breathlessness, increased cyanosis, and loss of consciousness may occur. Breathing can be made easier by holding the child upright against an adult's shoulder, with the knees tucked up to the chest.

TOF is the most common cause of cyanosis in young children. Surgical repair may be either palliative (partial to relieve symptoms) or total. Naturally, there are more residual deficiencies in the former than the latter. The main residual is reduced maximal aerobic capability.

Pulmonic Stenosis Valvular

PSV, although relatively common, is usually mild. If blood pressure remains more-or-less normal, surgery is typically not required. In such cases, aerobic capacity is slightly reduced. The less common ASV is the valvular defect that contraindicates vigorous exercise.

Exercise and Congenital Heart Defects

For almost all moderate to severe heart conditions, corrective surgery is performed in early childhood. A healthy, active lifestyle is emphasized thereafter, with walking recommended 3 days after surgery. Children return to school within 2 to 3 weeks of surgery and soon begin a graded exercise

Table 19.8
Graded exercise program.

Week	Graded Exercise
1	Walk 10 min, try not to stop
2	Walk 5 min, jog 1 min
3	Walk 5 min, jog 3 min
4	Walk 4 min, jog 5 min
	Walk 4 min, jog 4 min
5	Walk 4 min, jog 5 min
6	Walk 4 min, jog 6 min
7	Walk 4 min, jog 7 min
8	Walk 4 min, jog 8 min
9	Walk 4 min, jog 9 min
10	Walk 4 min, jog 13 min
11	Walk 4 min, jog 17 min
12	Walk 4 min, jog 17 min
13	Walk 2 min, jog slowly 2 min, jog 17 min
14	Walk 1 min, jog slowly 3 min, jog 17 min
15	Jog slowly 3 min, jog 17 min

Note. Warm-up should consist of stretching and limbering exercises for 5 min, while cool-down should involve 3 min of walking slowly and 2 min of stretching. Check your pulse periodically to see if you are exercising within your target zone. As you become more fit, try exercising within the upper range of your target zone.

Note. From W. B. Strong and B. S. Alpert (1982). The child with heart disease: Play, recreation, and sports, *Current Problems in Pediatrics, 13* (2), 1–34.

Table 19.9
Classification of sports used by physicians.

Strenuous Contact	Moderately Strenuous
Body surfing	Badminton
Diving	Baseball
Football	Curling
Ice hockey	Golf
Lacrosse (boys)	Horseback riding
Rugby	Table tennis
Surfing	**Nonstrenuous**
Wrestling	Bowling
Strenuous Limited Contact	Riflery
Basketball	**Primarily Isometric**
Field hockey	Archery
Lacrosse (girls)	Waterskiing
Skiing	Weight lifting
Soccer	Wrestling
Volleyball	
Water polo	
Strenuous Noncontact	
Climbing	
Crew	
Cross-country	
Fencing	
Gymnastics	
Swimming	
Tennis	
Track and field	

Note. From W. B. Strong and B. S. Alpert (1982). The child with heart disease: Play, recreation, and sports, *Current Problems in Pediatrics, 13* (2), 1–34.

program of walking, swimming, or cycling. Within 4 months of surgery, most children can participate in regular physical education with no restrictions (Cumming, 1987).

Table 19.8 is an example of the type of graded exercise program begun 3 days after surgery. See the *Note* for a description of proper warm-ups and cool-downs. While parents are encouraged to perform this program with their children (Strong & Alpert, 1982), school or agency personnel often are relegated responsibility. The ultimate goal is ability to exercise 30 min at least three times a week within the upper limit of the target heart rate zone recommended by the physician. See Chapter 13 (Figure 13.7) for target heart rate zones.

The target heart rate zone after surgery depends on whether correction was total or partial. In many postoperative persons, the maximal heart rate is and always will be slightly lower than normal (see the sections "Chronotropic Incompetence" and "Sick Sinus Syndrome" earlier in the chapter). A lowered maximal heart rate seldom affects class participation because activities, with the exception of occasional aerobic testing, do not demand total exertion. Persons with postoperative conditions have a lifelong tendency to fatigue more quickly than peers. The general consensus is that

teachers and coaches should allow these individuals to impose their own exercise restrictions during vigorous activity.

Most physicians recommend participation in sports. Table 19.9 presents the classifications typically used in recommending sport involvement. After completion of their graded exercise program, most postoperative persons have no restrictions except for a caution against primarily isometric activities. Isometrics increase blood pressure and risk of heart attack (Freed, 1984) because blood vessels reflexly contract during static muscle contraction.

Mild Defects and Delayed Surgery
Often, no surgery is recommended for mild heart conditions because normal activity, including sport involvement, is not seriously limited. In moderate to severe defects, surgery is sometimes delayed until overall health status is improved or a certain age is reached. In the case of delayed surgery, physicians are likely to restrict children to moderately strenuous or nonstrenuous sports (see Table 19.9). Children with mild heart conditions typically can engage in strenuous sports in an instructional or recreational setting, but high-intensity, competitive sports may be restricted.

Implications for Physical Education

Many students from low socioeconomic backgrounds have mild heart defects that go undetected. Follow the ABCDEF plan in making physician referrals when symptoms are observed during vigorous activity:

A Angina, severe chest pain
B Breathing difficulty
C Color changed, bluish or pale
D Dizziness
E Edema, fluid retention and swelling of extremities
F Fatigue

Persons with disabilities, especially the various syndromes caused by chromosomal and inborn metabolic disorders, are more prone to cardiac disorders than others. The prevalence rate of heart disease for various syndromes ranges from 20 to 60%. Many of these conditions are mild and go undetected unless a teacher or coach urges vigorous activity. Particular care therefore should be taken in fitness testing and programming.

Use graded exercise programs like that in Table 19.8 before fitness testing, rather than the pretest-posttest models favored in research. Emphasize activities described in Chapters 13 and 15 on fitness and relaxation. Programming is similar to that for other OHI conditions in that exercise progressions are slower, and better motivation is needed because discomfort is greater and/or the persons do not yet understand their bodies and the meaning of true exertion. Guidelines for working with obese/overweight and asthmatic persons are particularly applicable because of shared cardiorespiratory fitness problems.

Cardiac Rehabilitation for Adults

Cardiac rehabilitation programs begin with a medical examination, including an exercise stress test administered or supervised by a physician. Many physical educators learn to give stress tests in exercise physiology courses. In the case of cardiovascular disease, however, electrocardiographic monitoring capacity and emergency equipment like the DC cardiac defibrillator must be available. Cardiovascular rehabilitative training should not begin until a signed release from the physician and the patient (or client) is on file.

The aerobic exercise phase of cardiac rehabilitation begins about 8 to 12 weeks after a heart attack or coronary bypass surgery. With regard to intensity and duration of prescribed exercise:

The usual procedure is to recommend that the patient maintain his or her highest conditioning heart rate at 80 to 85 percent of the measured maximal or symptomatic heart rate on the exercise test for 15 to 20 min 3 times a week . . . preliminary data on patients with coronary atherosclerotic heart disease indicate that this level of intensity, duration, and time of conditioning does provide measurable benefits in 6 to 12 weeks. (Gilbert, 1978, p. 559)

Table 19.10
Unsupervised walking program.

Exercise tolerance test information: A patient is stopped by 3+ angina (heart rate, 130) after 2.5 min at 3 mph on a 10% upgrade on the treadmill. Angina and ST segment depression began at 2.5 mph at a heart rate of 120.

First exercise prescription: 2.5 mph at 10% upgrade = 6 METs = 21 ml·kg·min. This is the angina threshold. Train at 75% of 6 METs = 4.5 METs = walking at 3.0–3.5 mph on level ground, daily.

Period	Intensity (METs)	Intensity (ml·kg·min)	Equivalent Exercise
Warm-up	2–3	7–11	Walk 1/4 mi in 7.5 min (2 mph)
Training	4–5	14–18	Walk 1 mi in 20 min (3 mph)
Cool-down	2–3	7–11	Walk 1/4 mi in 7.5 min (2 mph)

Subsequent exercise prescriptions: Using the same warm-up and cool-down patterns, alter the training period as follows:
1. Walk 2 mi in 40 min daily for 3 weeks (4.5 METs for twice the duration).
2. Walk 2 mi in 35 min daily for 3 weeks (approximately 7 METs for nearly the same duration).
3. Retest. If the patient completes the 4 mph stage at 10% grade on the treadmill with 3 mm ST depression (28 ml·kg·min, 8 METs) and develops 1+ angina at the 3.5 mph stage, the patient should then:
4. Walk 2 mi in 35 min, increasing to 3 mi in 51 min within 3 weeks.
5. Increase to 3 mi in 45 min for 3 weeks.

Note. Reproduced with permission. American Heart Association.

Stress testing is repeated periodically and the exercise prescription revised accordingly. Persons in cardiac rehabilitation programs demonstrate achievement at the 6 MET capacity before transferring from an individualized program involving continuous heart monitoring to a group program. Table 19.10 illustrates how MET capacity is used in an exercise prescription. Refer to Chapter 13 on fitness for further information on METs and other activities appropriate in cardiac rehabilitation.

Hypertension

Hypertension, or high blood pressure, is a cardiovascular problem in which the blood exerts a greater than normal force against the inner walls of the blood vessels. This excess force, in time, permanently damages organs, most often the heart, brain, kidneys, and eyes. Hypertension can be caused by atherosclerosis; certainly, anything that obstructs blood flow increases pressure. However, there are many other causes, and hypertension can exist separate from atherosclerosis.

FIGURE   19.12

(A) A sphygmomanometer provides two measures of blood pressure.
(B) For the upper measure, visualize valentine shape and ventricles squeezing blood upward, causing arterial pressure to surge or soar.
(C) For the lower measure, visualize pressure dropping during diastole. Can you find the valves that open and close to permit heart action?

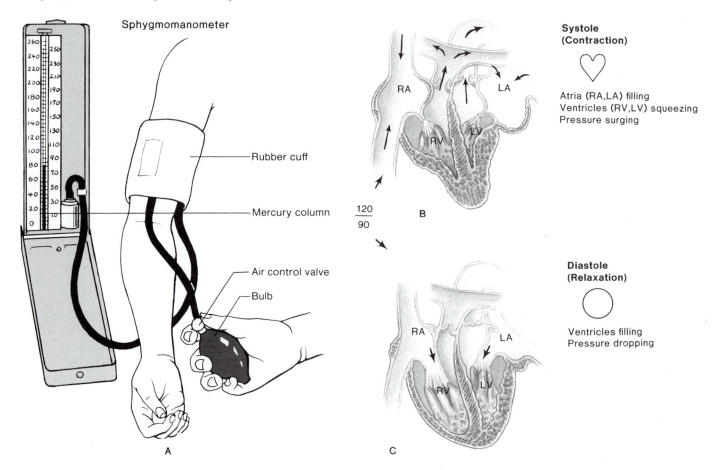

For the population as a whole, hypertension is the leading reason for taking prescription drugs (Kaplan, 1990). Approximately 58 million persons in the United States (or about 25% of the general population) have hypertension. Of these, about 3 million are under age 17. The prevalence is greater for males than females and for blacks than other races. Prevalence increases decade by decade until about age 65 and then levels off. At this age, approximately 50% of whites and 60% of blacks have high blood pressure.

Hypertension places persons at high risk for organ damage until the golden 70s and 80s. After ages 75 and 85 for men and women, respectively, death rate tends to be lower when blood pressure is higher. Across the lifespan, however, hypertension is a major risk factor for death by heart attack or stroke.

One reason hypertension is dangerous is that rises in blood pressure typically cause no pain or discomfort. Persons who do not have routine medical checkups are unaware of blood pressure abnormalities. When hypertension progresses to a severe stage, strenuous exercise and other forms of stress may cause headache, visual disturbances, vomiting, and/or convulsions. On the other hand, the condition may continue to be asymptomatic. There are many individual differences.

Blood Pressure Measurement

With sophisticated laboratory equipment, pressure can be measured in any blood vessel anywhere in the body, but arterial blood pressure in the upper arm is the common measure, usually taken with a sphygmomanometer. Normal blood pressure for adults is 120/90 millimeters of mercury (mm Hg) or less. A pressure of 120 mm Hg causes the mercury column of the sphygmomanometer to shoot upward a distance of 120 mm (see Figure 19.12).

A value like 120/90 indicates the pressure inside the aorta and pulmonary arteries when the ventricles of the heart contract and relax. The upper number indicates systolic or contraction pressure. The lower number indicates diastolic or relaxation pressure. Systolic and diastolic pressure are equal in importance. Elevation of either one is cause for concern, but high blood pressure is not diagnosed until after several readings on different days. In research and clinical settings, systolic pressure can be monitored reliably during exercise on a treadmill or bicycle ergometer, but diastolic pressure cannot (Bar-Or, 1983).

Systolic and Diastolic Pressures

The heart looks like a valentine during systole, the time of greatest pressure, when the ventricles are squeezing all of their blood upward into the arteries and the atria are bulging because the atrioventricular (AV) valves have closed (see Figure 19.12). Systole is the beginning of the heartbeat, the loud "lubb" sound in the "lubb-dupp" heard by a stethoscope. To remember, *v*isualize *V*alentine's Day and *v*entricles (the 3 *V*s) with *s*queezing the blood out during *s*ystole, causing the arterial pressure to *s*urge (the 3 *S*s).

Diastole is easy to remember because the overall heart shape is a relaxed oval. Word derivation helps us to visualize *di* (two chambers), *a* (without), *systole* (contraction). The pressure is at its lowest point when the ventricles are relaxed, the AV valves are open, and blood is filling the lower chambers. Duration of this low blood pressure phase depends upon rate of heartbeat. The slower the rate, the more relaxation and filling time.

Causes of Hypertension

For simplicity, causes of hypertension are classified in two ways: (a) primary or essential (cause unknown) and (b) secondary (cause can be linked with specific disorders or pregnancy). Among adults, 90% of all hypertension is primary.

Pregnancy is a time of particular risk. Blood volume increases to about 30% above normal during pregnancy, and many compensatory mechanisms must operate to keep blood pressure normal. *Preeclampsia,* a toxemia of pregnancy condition characterized by hypertension and edema, occurs in 5 to 7% of pregnancies.

Primary hypertension is diagnosed when unknown factors are increasing cardiac output and/or peripheral resistance. *Cardiac output* is the amount of blood pumped by the heart per minute. *Peripheral resistance* is the vascular system's reflex response to blood pressing against its walls. This response can be (a) vasodilation (widening), which lowers pressure, or (b) vasoconstriction (narrowing), which raises pressure. The sympathetic nervous system controls these reflex changes in vessel diameter, which are influenced by the condition of the vessel walls (elastic or nonelastic) and of the blood (thick and slow moving or thin and fast moving). Elasticity depends on age and disease. Relative blood thickness, called *viscosity,* depends on composition (i.e., the proportion of cells and platelets to plasma).

High blood pressure is usually associated with increased blood volume and consequent edema. The many reasons for this pathology are too complicated to explain here. The blood volume increase can begin centrally (inside the heart) or peripherally (anywhere in the vascular system, called a systemic problem).

Central origin is associated with a weak heart muscle or defective valves that interfere with effective emptying of the cardiac chambers; this increases blood volume and, consequently, the pressure inside the heart. Central pressure also builds up when a diseased aorta cannot widen enough to let blood enter at normal speed.

In contrast, *peripheral origin* is associated with sympathetic nervous system and endocrine action at the capillary level. Fluids are continuously moving in and out of the capillaries by hydrostatic pressure (causing outward movement) and osmotic pressure (causing inward movement), and many factors operate to maintain correct blood volume. Principal among these factors are the many salts in the body (e.g., chlorides, carbonates, bicarbonates, sulfates, and phosphates) and the ways they combine with sodium, potassium, calcium, and magnesium. Any imbalance in these minerals affects blood composition and, hence, volume. Sodium chloride (common table salt) particularly causes water retention. This makes the kidneys work harder and, in time, can cause kidney damage.

Most severe childhood hypertension is associated with kidney disease, obesity, or coarctation of the aorta (a congenital heart defect that narrows the aorta). Unlike adults, the classification is seldom primary. This may be partly because hypertension is asymptomatic and cases go undiagnosed. In the 1990s, the early identification of children at risk for cardiovascular disease is being emphasized. Therefore, physicians are now diagnosing primary hypertension in children whose blood pressure readings over time exceed the 95th percentile for their age and sex. Those with weight that exceeds the 95th percentile and a family history of hypertension are at greatest risk. Regardless of classification, research on children indicates that the single best correlate of hypertension is large body mass (Kaplan, 1990). The best treatment for primary hypertension in children is loss of excess weight.

Classification by Severity

According to ACSM (1991), adult hypertension can be classified in four categories: borderline to mild (140/90), mild to moderate (150/95), moderate to severe (160/100), and uncontrolled (170/110). *Medically supervised exercise testing is contraindicated when resting values exceed 200/ 120.* Nonsupervised physical activity, even of low intensity, should be discontinued whenever resting rates evidence a change from normal pattern. This usually means that medication is no longer effective and that a physician needs to reassess management of the disease.

Table 19.11 shows that different criteria are used in diagnosing and classifying hypertension in children. Blood pressure in healthy persons gradually increases from infancy through adulthood. This change results from size rather than age differences. The largest increase occurs in conjunction with the adolescent growth spurt. Because blood pressure is correlated strongly with body mass, height and weight are considered in making a diagnosis.

Typically, when systolic blood pressure is elevated, the diastolic is also, and vice versa. The exception is old age, when isolated systolic hypertension (ISH) often occurs because atherosclerosis has decreased the elasticity of major

Table 19.11
Classification of hypertension by age group.

Age (in Years)	Mild/Moderate	Moderate/Severe
Infants (<2)	112/74	118/82
Children (3–5)	116/76	124/84
Children (6–9)	122/78	130/86
Children (10–12)	126/82	134/90
Adolescents (13–15)	136/86	144/92
Adolescents (16–18)	142/92	150/98
Adults	150/95	160/100

Note. Modified from Kaplan (1990) and the Task Force on Blood Pressure Control in Children (1987).

FIGURE 19.13

Blood-pressure changes in response to vigorous big-muscle exercises in a healthy adult.

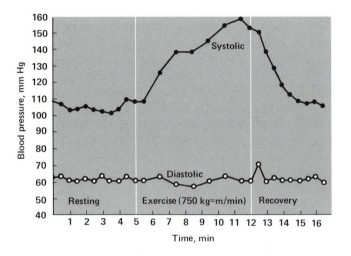

Blood Pressure Responses to Exercise

In healthy adults, systolic blood pressure rises by 30 to 60 mm Hg during strenuous isotonic exercise. Diastolic pressure rises little or not at all (see Figure 19.13). In aerobically trained persons, diastolic pressure may even fall. In hypertension, blood pressure response to exercise is exaggerated. Monitoring values before and after exercise is a good practice. In laboratories, where pressure readings during exercise are possible, the criterion for stopping exercise is a value exceeding 250/120. In field settings, exercise pressures of 225/90 are considered high risk.

Isometric exercise and activities involving a Valsalva maneuver like weight lifting are controversial because they increase both systolic and diastolic blood pressures to high rates. ACSM (1991) says that isometric exercise is not strictly contraindicated in hypertension but should be used with extreme caution. High repetitions and low resistances are recommended for weight training.

Management of Hypertension

Mild hypertension is managed by accepting responsibility for healthy diet and exercise practices and acting on environmental factors that cause emotional stress. Excess weight must be lost and proper weight maintained. Salt intake, for many persons, must be reduced. This means use of fresh or frozen foods rather than canned goods, which are high in sodium, and avoidance of high-salt items like bacon, cheese, and pickles. The recommended sodium intake is 1,100 to 3,300 mg daily.

Regular aerobic exercise is beneficial because it reduces blood pressure. This occurs over time, like weight loss. Training effects, however, do not last more than 3 to 6 weeks if exercise is discontinued.

Moderate to severe hypertension requires medication in addition to healthy lifestyle. Physical activity specialists need to understand these medications because of exercise side effects. Among the major classes of antihypertensive drugs are diuretics, vasodilators, and the blocking agents. Appendix B gives generic and trade names for some of these.

Antihypertension drugs affect the validity of heart rate monitoring during exercise. There is no way to separate the heart's natural response to exercise from drug-induced slowness or fastness. Therefore, collect data on medications and discuss side effects before helping persons to start exercise programs.

Respiratory Problems

Most of us take breathing for granted. We squeeze air out of our lungs 20,000 times a day and seldom think about the phenomenon of respiration. Yet respiratory diseases are the fastest rising causes of death in the United States. This section is about persons who struggle to breathe. They may have *asthma, chronic obstructive pulmonary diseases,* or *cystic fibrosis.* The symptoms are similar in all conditions, and exercise is vital for the maintenance of respiratory fitness. Almost half of the chronic diseases suffered by children under age 17 are respiratory in nature. Asthma, hayfever, and other allergies account for approximately 33% of all chronic diseases in this age group. Bronchitis, sinusitis, and related conditions cause 15.1%. Cystic fibrosis, although rare, results in death from chronic lung disorders. The physical activities for these children are the same as those for children with asthma.

Emphysema is primarily a disease of middle and old age, but its origins can often be traced to asthma and chronic bronchitis in earlier years. Over a million Americans lead restricted lives because of emphysema. The fastest growing cause of total disability in the United States, it is surpassed only by heart disease.

arteries. Cardiac output shows no associated change. The diseased aorta simply cannot distend to accommodate the amount of blood ejected with each ventricular contraction.

FIGURE   19.14

The lungs are filled with large and small bronchial tubes, called *bronchi* and *bronchioles,* respectively, that are lined with mucous membrane. Also shown is an alveolus or air cell.

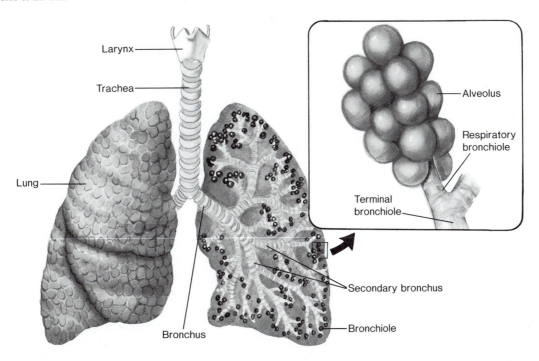

Asthma

Asthma is a chronic lung disease characterized by hyperactive airways. Management depends largely on medication and avoidance of stimuli that trigger attacks. Attacks are characterized by spasms of the bronchial tubes (see Figure 19.14), swelling of their linings, and excessive secretion of mucus, all of which cause coughing, wheezing, dyspnea (breathing difficulty), and a feeling of constriction in the chest.

Prevalence and Causes

In the United States, asthma is the leading chronic disease in the age group under 18. Approximately 6 million Americans have asthma, most of whom are under age 15. The incidence of asthma is slightly higher among boys than girls. Many children seem to *grow out of* asthma during puberty; thus, the greatest concentration of problems is in elementary school.

Persons with asthma tend to be multiply disabled in that they frequently suffer also from hayfever, allergies, sinus trouble, and upper respiratory infections. They are prone also to weight problems and low fitness.

Physicians classify asthma according to primary cause: (a) intrinsic, meaning the problem is homeostatic or inside the body, and (b) extrinsic, indicating that an allergen from the outside is needed to trigger an attack. Intrinsic asthma is treated by medications discussed later in this chapter, whereas extrinsic asthma is managed by desensitization shots and/or systematic avoidance of irritants. Both types of asthma seem to run in families, but the particular genes responsible have not yet been discovered.

Most asthma is intrinsic but complicated by various allergies, so the etiology is often mixed. The defective homeostatic function is at the cellular level—specifically, an abnormality in the beta adrenergic receptors of the lungs. These receptors maintain balance between the nerve fibers that release epinephrine (adrenalin) and those that liberate acetylcholine. Any alteration of this balance causes changes in the tonus of the bronchial tube linings, increasing irritability of the bronchi to all kinds of stimuli.

Persons with asthma may be hypersensitive to cigarette smoke, weather changes, changes in body temperature, air pollutants, and other stimuli too numerous to name. Because infection affects homeostasis, it is a major precipitator of asthmatic symptoms. Heavy exercise also affects homeostasis, and 60 to 90% of persons with asthma have breathing difficulty after 4 to 8 min of continuous, vigorous, aerobic exercise. This condition is called exercise-induced asthma (EIA).

Asthma Attacks

While asthma is chronic and always present, *attacks* occur only occasionally. Asthma attacks progress through three stages: (a) coughing, (b) dyspnea, and (c) severe bronchial obstruction.

Coughing warns of an impending attack. In this stage, the bronchial tubes are secreting mucus, which accumulates and obstructs the passage of air. Coughing is caused by the reflex action of the smooth, involuntary muscles of the bronchioles in an attempt to remove the accumulating mucus.

Dyspnea, meaning breathing difficulty, occurs when the linings of the bronchioles swell, thus narrowing the air passages and diminishing the flow of air. Wheezing is caused by the movement of the air in and out of the constricted bronchial tubes and through the accumulated mucus. During this stage, the pattern of breathing is markedly altered, with difficulty experienced in *exhalation* and resultant gasping for air. Fortunately, use of an inhalator usually brings relief within a few seconds. As the medication begins to dilate the bronchioles, the attack subsides, usually with much coughing and spitting of mucus.

If the inhalator does not bring relief, *severe bronchial obstruction* or *status asthmaticus* occurs. This labored breathing typically continues for hours or days, until the person gives up and goes to the hospital. No activity is possible. Even walking a few steps causes intense coughing. The onset of this stage can be sudden and demand immediate emergency room treatment, or it can be slow and progressive. Often, it is associated with a cold or illness.

A status asthmaticus condition leaves fluid in the lungs that may cause days of occasional coughing spasms. Physicians emphasize that this fluid must be coughed up and not swallowed. Part of hospital treatment is respiratory therapy to aid weak or exhausted muscles in coughing up mucus.

Ordinarily, however, persons do not go to the hospital and must struggle on their own to get mucus up. This becomes a psychological as well as a medical problem because of awareness of how unpleasant this coughing and spitting is for others. Often, upon return to school or work, persons with asthma try to stifle coughing. This is definitely contraindicated, so help should be given to facilitate understanding and acceptance of the cough-and-spit phenomenon.

Medication and Asthma

Almost everyone with asthma carries an inhalator that dispenses an aerosol to relieve sudden or acute asthma symptoms. The prescription for some persons is one or two puffs every 3 or 4 hr, whereas others take it only when needed. Most aerosols are also available in tablet, powder, or liquid form, but these take longer to act. By about age 6, most children can be taught to use aerosols.

The aerosols most frequently prescribed are *beta-adrenergic agents* that work on the defective receptors in lung cells and relax and dilate the smooth muscle lining of the bronchioles. These drugs are sympathomimetic in that they mimic the action of the sympathetic nervous system. Foremost among these are albuterol (Ventolin, Proventil) and metaproterenol (Alupent, Metaprel). These bronchodilators relieve asthma symptoms in 1 or 2 min and have no side effects for most persons unless overused. Aerosols can also be taken 15 to 20 min before exercise to reduce the possibility of an attack.

Sodium cromolyn (Intal) is the aerosol most frequently used in EIA to prevent attacks. Two puffs taken 15 to 20 min before starting exercise provides about 4 hr of protection. This has been hailed as a miracle drug because it allows persons with asthma to engage in any kind of exercise they wish. About 10% of the U.S. athletes in the Olympics each quadrennium have asthma and rely on sodium cromolyn (Hogshead & Couzens, 1990). Like the sympathomimetic agents, it has no side effects for most persons.

Many persons with severe chronic asthma take *theophylline* daily in liquid, tablet, or capsule form. Among its many brand names are Slophyllin, Slobid, Primatene, and Quibron. Theophylline works in two ways: (a) prevents the release of histamine from lung cells that overreact to allergens and (b) acts as a bronchodilator. This activity is needed when the theophylline level in the blood is low, a common deficiency in persons with asthma that requires periodic blood tests and considerable experimentation to find the right drug dosage. Theophylline does have side effects (insomnia, nervousness, diarrhea, stomach cramps) and can be most unpleasant until the physician determines the correct amount.

The medication of last resort, used only when the others fail and/or the body is fighting an infection, is the *corticosteroids* like prednisone (Deltasone) and flunisolide (AeroBid). These drugs have many side effects, but their powerful anti-inflammatory properties reduce bronchial tube swelling when nothing else will. They are typically taken for only a few days, but very severe asthma may demand regular dosage.

The four types of drugs described in this section are prescription medications and should be taken according to directions. All of the drugs mentioned, except for the corticosteroids, are approved by the International Olympic Committee (IOC) and similar athletic bodies. The corticosteroids are banned because they act as stimulants. They should not be confused with anabolic or sex steroids, the muscle-building drugs, which are also banned. Athletes taking prescribed drugs should report these to their coaches or have their physicians notify the sport governing body. An excellent book by an Olympic swimmer (Hogshead & Couzens, 1990) reports the importance of prescribed drugs in making sports a viable option for persons with asthma.

Overuse of Aerosols

Correct use of aerosols can prevent attacks, but persons often forget to use their inhalers 15 to 20 min before exercise or opt to try an activity without protection. Whatever the reason, when coughing and breathing difficulty occur, persons tend to overuse the inhaler and try to keep going.

Most inhalers carry warnings to take no more than two or three puffs every 3 hr. Overuse causes nervousness, increased heart rate, high blood pressure, and other symptoms. These side effects are often ignored because they do not seem bad compared to the oxygen deficit that is causing panic. Nevertheless, excessive use of inhalers and other asthma medications can cause death.

Persons with chronic asthma have good and bad days. Often, these are related to weather changes, high pollen counts, environmental pollutants, or an infection. A common cold, for example, usually causes the lungs to fill with fluid with a resultant mild status asthmaticus condition. On days when the lungs feel bad and breathing is harder than usual, persons with asthma must decide between slowing down and trying to keep going. Those who make the latter decision often overuse the inhaler, each time thinking that, somehow, another puff will help. It typically does not.

Implications for Physical Education

The Committee on Children with Handicaps of the American Academy of Pediatrics issued a formal statement on the asthmatic child and participation in physical education:

Physical activities are useful to asthmatic children. The majority of asthmatic children can participate in physical activities at school and in sports with minimal difficulty, provided the asthma is under satisfactory control. All sports should be encouraged, but should be evaluated on an individual basis for each asthmatic child, *depending on his tolerance for duration and intensity of effort. Fatigue and emotional upheaval in competitive athletic contests appear to be predisposing factors in precipitating asthmatic attacks in some instances. This may depend to some extent on the duration and severity of the disease. As a general rule, every effort should be made to* minimize restrictions and to invoke them only when the condition of the child makes it necessary. *(American Academy of Pediatrics, 1982)*

Students who experience breathing problems in physical education are not yet properly managing their asthma and need to be referred to a specialist for further study. Often, considerable time is required to determine the best medication; likewise, time is needed to learn to manage both the environment and stresses related to feeling different from peers. Should the student with asthma want to give up and resume a sedentary lifestyle, the physical educator must inspire the faith and courage to return to the physician once again and to keep trying alternatives.

Role models are particularly helpful. Among the many Olympic athletes who manage asthma with medication are track stars Jackie Joyner-Kersee and Jeannette Bolden; medal-winning cyclists Alexei Grawal, Bill Nitts, and Steve Hegg; swimmer Nancy Hogshead; and rowing medalist Ginnie Gilder. The new message is that persons with asthma can excel in competitive sports. For an excellent pamphlet on asthma and exercise, write to Exercise and Asthma, Asthma and Allergy Foundation of America, 1717 Massachusetts Avenue, Suite 305, Washington, DC 20036.

Persons with asthma can do low-intensity exercise for long periods without an attack. This type of exercise is good for losing weight but does not improve aerobic fitness. Once weight is lost and aerobic fitness is targeted, three basic principles should be followed to prevent attacks: (a) premedication, (b) long warm-up of mild intensity, and (c) intermittent or interval training. The last principle, when applied to EIA, is typically defined as no more than 5 min of vigorous exercise followed by 5 min or less of rest. This sequence can be repeated over and over. The 5-min criterion is based on the average amount of time that the nonmedicated person with EIA can engage in continuous vigorous exercise at target heart rate before the onset of an attack.

Various kinds of warm-up are used. A 15- to 30-min warm-up is typically needed rather than the 5 to 10 min recommended by ACSM. Wind sprints are also good. For example, seven 30-sec sprints, each 2.5 min apart, have a beneficial effect on a distance run performed 30 min later.

Although persons with asthma have excelled in practically every sport, some activities are less likely to trigger bronchospasm than others. This is probably because they are conducted in a warm, humid environment (e.g., water sports) or demand relatively short bursts of energy. Baseball, softball, volleyball, doubles tennis, weight training, and wrestling are particularly recommended. For persons who prefer to take little or no medicine, continuous-duration sports of high intensity, such as basketball, soccer, cross-country skiing, and marathons, are contraindicated for most, but not all. Swimming traditionally has been the sport of choice because it seems to interrupt homeostasis less than activities that cause perspiration and require breathing dry, cold, or pollen-laden air.

The greatest challenge to exercise specialists is helping persons with asthma overcome initial barriers. Many, in the beginning, are overweight and have very low fitness. The breathlessness and severe discomfort they experience thus are a combination of asthma and low fitness. The nature of their condition is such, however, that it takes longer to achieve fitness than nonasthmatic peers. There also is more discomfort. These persons need the same graded exercise programs as postoperative heart patients and obese/overweight individuals.

Diaphragmatic Breathing

Most persons with asthma breathe incorrectly all or most of the time, overworking the upper chest and intercostal muscles and underworking the diaphragm. A goal, therefore, is to teach them that there are two kinds of breathing and for them to feel the difference. The two kinds are (a) shallow or costal (meaning rib cage) and (b) deep or diaphragmatic. To teach this, the physiology of respiration must be explained and practice given in diaphragmatic breathing (see Figure 19.15). The ability to breathe deeply is dependent on the strength of the diaphragm during inhalation and its ability to relax during exhalation.

The diaphragm is the dome-shaped muscle that separates the thoracic and abdominal muscles. In inhalation, the diaphragm contracts, descends 1 to 7 cm, and creates space for the lungs to fill with air. Exhalation begins when fullness of the lungs triggers relaxation and upward recoil of the diaphragm. This squeezes the air up and out. No muscle action other than this recoiling is needed in exhalation except during vigorous exercise.

FIGURE   19.15

Phenomena of normal breathing.

Inhalation	Exhalation
Bronchial tubes widen.	Bronchial tubes narrow.
Diaphragm contracts and descends.	Diaphragm ascends as a result of its elastic recoil action when it relaxes.
Abdominal muscles relax (return to normal length).	Abdominal muscles shorten, particularly in forced exhalation.
Upper ribs are elevated.	Ribs are depressed.
Thoracic spine extends.	Thoracic spine tends to flex.

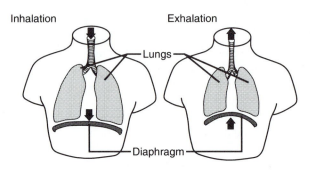

Persons with asthma have more difficulty with exhalation than inhalation. This is because the phrenic nerve that innervates the diaphragm is sensitive to anything that alters the breathing pattern (wheezing, coughing, tightness, exercise, nervous tension). All of these things interfere with relaxation of the diaphragm which, in turn, decreases the amount of air pushed out. During an attack, exhalations progressively let out less and less air. The chest distends and begins to feel heavy and ache. Learning correct breathing therefore is closely related to learning to relax.

Persons who take only shallow breaths allow the diaphragm to weaken. This may not be a problem in a sedentary lifestyle unless a cold, lung infection, or asthma creates mucus or phlegm that must be coughed up. Then the reflex respiratory mechanism is inadequate, and abdominal muscle action must supplement the recoil force of the diaphragm. This explains why the abdominal muscles, especially if they are weak, are so sore after heavy coughing.

Exercise, all kinds, is easier when breathing is diaphragmatic rather than costal. Intensity of the exercise, together with fitness of the diaphragm, determine the extent that abdominal muscles must assist with exhalation. In sedentary persons with asthma, even light exercise may require abdominal activity to expel air from the lungs, whereas in fit persons, the abdominals work only during heavy exercise.

Diaphragmatic breathing is often called abdominal because persons best understand deep breathing by watching and feeling the abdomen protruding in inhalation and flattening in exhalation. Slow abdominal pumping in a supine position reinforces new understandings. Various weights (books, sandbags, etc.) can be placed on the abdomen with

FIGURE   19.16

Child exhales into spirometer as test of pulmonary efficiency.

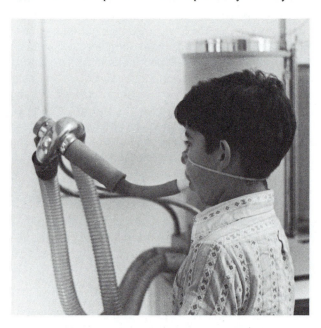

a challenge to watch or feel the weight go up and down. Persons may need to be reminded that normal breathing ranges from 12 to 14 breaths a minute at rest and from 40 to 50 during vigorous exercise.

Also of concern is making sure that persons with asthma breathe through the nose rather than the mouth. Many do not because of nasal congestion, but new prescription sprays eliminate this problem. Nasal breathing warms and moistens the air before it gets to the lungs, helping to maintain homeostasis. Mouth breathing does the opposite.

Changing overall pattern of breathing is as hard as permanently losing weight. Nevertheless, diaphragmatic breathing is an important goal. Activities like yoga (see Chapter 15 on relaxation) are a good way to improve breathing patterns (Nagarathna & Nagendra, 1985). During routine vigorous exercise, persons with asthma must be repeatedly reminded to breathe deeply and slowly.

Spirometers and Peak-Flow Meters

A spirometer test is periodically administered to determine status or improvement in pulmonary efficiency (see Figure 19.16). The test used most often is the FEV_1 (forced expiratory volume for 1 sec). To obtain a computer printout, the person inhales deeply and then blows air out of the mouth into the tube as hard and fast as possible.

The FEV_1 is the number of cubic centimeters of air forcefully exhaled in the first second after a deep inspiration. Normal FEV_1 values range from 500 to 4,500 cc (cubic centimeters) for boys and from 350 to 3,400 cc for girls. Any condition that causes bronchial obstruction and resistance in the airways reduces FEV_1.

The peak-flow meter is similar but less expensive, so persons can keep one at home and periodically test themselves. A scale indicating the velocity of air expelled in liters per second is on the gadget, so no computer is needed. A drop of more than 10% from one's normal reading indicates significant airflow resistance and signals the need to reevaluate one's management protocol with a physician.

Games to Improve Expiration

Breathing exercises are no longer considered a viable approach to the management of asthma. They may be used in chronic obstructive lung disease, cystic fibrosis, muscular dystrophy, and other very severe conditions that cannot be managed by medication and environmental controls. In such instances, they are commonly associated with hospitalization and inability to exercise in normal ways. Research, with one or two exceptions, has repeatedly indicated no significant values accruing from breathing exercises. Games are more effective in improving expiration and also help to clear mucus from passageways.

In ordinary expiration, no muscles are used. In vigorous exhalation, the following muscles contract: internal and external obliques, transversus abdominis, transversus thoracis, serratus posterior inferior, and posterior portions of the intercostals. Since the abdominal muscles participate vigorously in laughing, blowing, and singing, games based on these activities can be developed.

Games Using Abdominal Muscles

1. **Laugh-In.** Circle formation with "It" in center. "It" tosses a handkerchief high into the air. Everyone laughs as loudly as possible as it floats downward, but no laughter must be heard after the handkerchief contacts the floor. Anyone breaking this rule becomes the new "It." For variation, students can cough instead of laugh.

2. **Laugh Marathon.** Each student has a tape recorder. The object is to see who can make the longest-playing tape of continuous laughing.

3. **Guess Who's Laughing.** All students are blindfolded. One, who is designated as "It," laughs continuously until classmates guess who is laughing.

4. **Red Light, Green Light Laughing.** This game is played according to traditional rules except that laughing accompanies the running or is substituted for it.

All games designed to improve exhalation should be played in erect standing or running postures since the spine and pelvis must be stabilized by the lumbar extensors in order for the abdominal muscles to contract maximally.

Blowing Activities

Blowing activities are especially valuable in emphasizing the importance of reducing residual air in the lungs. Learning to play wind instruments is recommended strongly. Swimming offers a recreational setting for stressing correct exhalation. Games found to be especially popular follow:

1. **Snowflakes.** *Equipment:* A 1-inch square of tissue paper for each child. *Procedure:* Two teams with each child having one piece of paper. Each participant attempts to keep the paper above the floor after the whistle is blown. When the paper touches the floor, the participant is disqualified. The winner is the team in which a player keeps the tissue in the air for the longest time.

2. **Ping-Pong Relay.** *Equipment:* One Ping-Pong ball for each team. *Procedure:* Two teams with one-half of the players of each team behind lines 50 ft apart. A player blows the Ping-Pong ball across the floor to his or her team member, who blows the ball back to the starting line. The relay continues until each player has blown the ball. The team that finishes first is the winner.

3. **Under the Bridge.** *Equipment:* One Ping-Pong ball for each team. *Procedure:* Teams with players standing in single file with legs spread. The last player in the file blows the ball forward between the legs of his or her team members, with additional blowing provided by the other players to move the ball quickly to the front. If the ball rolls outside the legs of the players, the last player must retrieve the ball and blow it again. When the ball reaches the front, the first player in the file picks up the ball, runs to the end of the file, and blows the ball forward again. The team finishing first is the winner.

4. **Balloon Relay.** *Equipment:* One balloon for each player. One chair for each team placed on a line 95 ft from the starting line. *Procedure:* Children on the teams line up in single file behind the starting line. Upon the signal to start, the first player of each team runs to the opposite line, blows up his or her balloon, places it on the chair, and sits on the balloon until it breaks. He or she then returns to the starting line and tags the next player, who proceeds in the same manner.

5. **Blow Out the Candle.** *Equipment:* A candle is placed on the floor between every two children. *Procedure:* Opponents lie on the floor on opposite sides 8 ft from the candle. Players attempt to blow out the candle from the greatest distance possible. The child who blows out the candle at the greatest distance is the winner.

6. **Ping-Pong Croquet.** *Equipment:* Ping-Pong balls and hoops made of milk cartons taped to the floor. *Procedure:* Each player blows the Ping-Pong ball through the series of hoops, positioned on the floor in the same manner as in a game of croquet. The ball must be moved and controlled entirely by blowing. The hands may not touch the ball at any time. The players who finish first are the winners.

7. **Self-Competition in Candle Blowing.** *Equipment:* Movable candle behind a yardstick placed opposite the mouth (see Figure 19.17A). *Procedure:* Child attempts to blow out lighted candle set at gradually lengthened distances on the yardstick.

8. **Self-Competition in Bottle Blowing.** *Equipment:* Two half-gallon bottles, half filled with water and connected with three rubber hoses and two glass pipes (see Figure 19.17B). *Procedure:* Child attempts to blow water from one bottle to another, first from sitting position and then standing position.

FIGURE 19.17

Blowing exercises. (*A*) Self-competition in candle blowing. (*B*) Self-competition in bottle blowing.

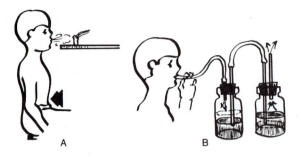

Pursed-Lip Breathing Contests

This can be competition against self or others. Emphasize a short inspiration through the nose and long expiration through gently pursed lips, making a whistling or hissing noise. This is called *pursed-lip breathing*. Try timing the expiration phase with a stopwatch or metronome. Expiration should be at least twice as long as inspiration.

The Physical Activity Environment

Since so many persons with asthma are sensitive to pollens and dust, physical activity should be indoors at least during the seasons of peak incidence of attacks. Ideally, the room should be air-conditioned and dust-free.

Changes in weather, particularly cold, dry air, predispose persons to attacks. Alterations in body temperature—specifically, becoming overheated—seem to cause wheezing. A cold, wet towel on the forehead and/or the back of the neck between activities helps to maintain uniform body temperature.

When the chalkboard is in use, students with asthma should be stationed as far away from it as possible. Nylon-covered, allergen-free mats containing foam rubber as filler are recommended.

Most persons with asthma are extremely sensitive to cigarette smoke. Even if a cigarette is not burning, residual fumes can trigger an attack.

Whereas all children become thirsty during vigorous physical activity, they are generally encouraged to wait until the end of the period to get a drink of water. *In contrast, forcing fluids is an essential part of the total exercise program for students with asthma.* As tissues become drier during exercise, the mucus thickens and is more difficult to cough up. More than three or four consecutive coughs should be avoided, since coughing itself dries out the mucous membranes. The only means of thinning this mucus is through fluids taken by mouth or intravenously. Four or five quarts of water a day are recommended. Cold drinks are contraindicated since they may cause spasms of the bronchial tubes; hence, fluids at room temperature are recommended.

Antihistamines are not desirable for persons with asthma because they tend to dry out the mucus in the airway. If, because of hay fever or other allergies, a person is taking antihistamines, it is even more important that fluid intake be increased.

Posture Problems

Chronic asthma may result in permanent deformities of the chest—kyphosis, barrel chest, pigeon chest—and Harrison's groove (a depression along the lower edge of the thorax). These defects can be traced to an actual shortening of the muscle fibers of the diaphragm and intercostals. When maintained in the lowered position characteristic of inspiration, the diaphragm affects the position and function of the viscera, which are pushed against the abdominal wall. The person with asthma typically experiences difficulty in flattening the abdomen, which, along with the chest, may become permanently distended.

Psychological Problems

In the past, some persons believed that psychological problems caused asthma. This etiology is not valid. Asthma is a chronic lung disease that, like all illnesses and disabilities, complicates life. Different persons cope with illnesses in different ways, and some handle stress better than others.

The psychological phenomenon known as a *reaction formation* is common among persons with asthma. To prove their worth to others, they tend to establish unrealistically high levels of aspiration and then totally exhaust themselves in all-out effort to accomplish such goals. When it appears that they cannot live up to their own or the perceived expectations of others, an asthmatic attack often occurs, thereby adding more stress. "I could have made the deadline if I hadn't gotten sick!" "I would have won the match if I hadn't started wheezing." The physical educator will find many children eager to play, despite parental restrictions, and unwilling to withdraw from a game even when they evidence asthmatic symptoms. Many do not impose limitations upon themselves, refusing to accept the inevitability of an attack. Like all children, they want to be *normal*. The following memories of adults lend some insight into the phenomenon of reaction formation.

I can remember going out to play with the kids in the neighborhood. I never thought about my asthma. I was highly competitive . . . loved to run . . . had to win. The asthma never came while I was playing. Oh, maybe a little wheezing, but I ignored that. But invariably in the middle of the night, after an unusually hard day of play, I would awake gasping . . . terrified . . . unable to breathe. Of course, this roused up the whole family, and we were all exhausted the next day.

My parents used to find me sitting and holding a neighborhood cat . . . stroking and loving it. My nose would be running and my eyes half swollen and filled with tears. It wasn't any special cat, just any animal I could find. They wouldn't let me have a pet at home because I was so allergic to them. The first thing I did after college was to buy a cat and start taking weekly injections to build up tolerance.

I never took a test in high school that I didn't stay up all night beforehand studying. By the time everyone else woke up, I'd have diarrhea, stomach cramps, a headache . . . and be literally convinced I didn't know enough to make an A. But I always made it to school. If I accidentally fell asleep or something prevented me from learning the material, I'd wake up with asthma and be in bed for a week. The whole time I was in bed, I'd worry about not taking the test, and this would make me sicker. Then my mouth and nose would break out with fever blisters, and I would be too ashamed of my appearance to return to school until it healed. I'd catch up on my studies and make As on the next round of tests. I always felt like the teachers wouldn't like me if I didn't make As.

The reaction formation creates a vicious circle in which stress precipitates coughing, wheezing, and dyspnea. The inability to breathe, particularly in a young child, results in helplessness, frustration, and anxiety which, in turn, intensifies the asthmatic problem. The child wants attention during an attack, yet experiences considerable emotional conflict about such dependency. Should an attack occur in physical education class, the child likewise has mixed feelings. The more the child worries about what others think, the worse the asthma becomes. Once an attack begins, the child cannot will it to stop. Nor can he or she *consciously* bring on an attack. The interplay of physiological and psychological etiological factors in asthma is so enigmatic that they remain little understood.

Occasionally, childhood asthma cannot be managed efficiently in the school and home environment. In such instances, the child is typically referred to such treatment centers as CARIH, the Children's Asthma Research Institute and Hospital, in Denver, Colorado. CARIH is the largest hospital in the Western Hemisphere that treats children with asthma and the only center whose staff conducts research exclusively on asthma and allergic diseases.

Special Asthma Exercise Programs

Many school systems, often with help from the local lung association, have started special exercise programs for children with asthma. These programs teach understanding of the respiratory system, stress breathing games, and attempt to build self-confidence in movement. They are intended as *supplements* to the regular physical education program.

The main value of special asthma exercise programs is the opportunity for persons with similar problems to talk together, share solutions, and reinforce each other. The teacher best qualified to conduct such programs is one who has had formal training in both physical education and counseling.

The trend of the 1990s, encouraged by the American Lung Association, is family exercise programs, camping trips, and other activities that permit sharing at all levels. School nurses are excellent resources in helping to locate the local branch of the American Lung Association. In most cities, this organization offers numerous activities. It also provides, usually at no cost, speakers and films.

Chronic Obstructive Pulmonary Diseases

Chronic obstructive pulmonary diseases (COPD), including chronic bronchitis and pulmonary emphysema, now constitute the fastest growing chronic disease problem in America. The death rate has doubled every 5 years over the past 20 years.

Chronic bronchitis is a recurrent cough characterized by excessive mucus secretion in the bronchi. The three stages are (a) *simple,* in which the chief characteristic is mucoid expectoration; (b) *mucopurulent,* in which the mucus

is intermittently or continuously filled with pus because of active infection; and (c) *obstruction,* in which there is narrowing of the airways in addition to expectoration. This is the stage at which the complications of emphysema and/or heart failure occur. The three stages may merge one into the other and span a period of 20 or more years.

Pulmonary emphysema is a destruction of the walls of the alveoli of the lungs. This destruction results in overdistention of the air sacs and loss of lung elasticity. *Emphysema* is a Greek word that means, literally, "to inflate or puff up." Persons with emphysema have difficulty expelling air. Whereas the normal person breathes 14 times a minute, the person with emphysema may breathe 20 to 30 times a minute and still not get enough oxygen into the bloodstream. The characteristic high carbon dioxide level in the blood causes sluggishness and irritability. The heart tries to compensate for lack of oxygen by pumping harder, and possible heart failure becomes an additional hazard.

Emphysema is more common among men than women. Over 10% of the middle-aged and elderly population in America have emphysema. The specific etiology is still under study, but smoking and air pollution are causal factors.

Persons with COPD tend to restrict their activities more and more because of their fear of wheezing and dyspnea. This inactivity results in muscle deterioration, increased shortness of breath, and increasing inactivity—a vicious cycle! The activities recommended for persons with asthma are suitable also for individuals with bronchitis and emphysema.

Cystic Fibrosis

Cystic fibrosis, a childhood disease that was not recognized as a separate entity from bronchopneumonia until 1936, is included in this section because 90% of persons with cystic fibrosis die from chronic lung disorders. The physical activity program for a person with cystic fibrosis is similar to that for asthma.

It is estimated that 1 child in every 1,000 is born with cystic fibrosis. The cause is a recessive gene. There are approximately 10 million carriers of this gene in the United States. If two carriers happen to bear offspring, there is a 1-in-4 chance that their infant will have cystic fibrosis and a 2-in-4 chance that the child will be a carrier.

Cystic fibrosis accounts for almost all the deaths in childhood from chronic nontuberculosis pulmonary disease. Although the lifespan in cystic fibrosis is increasing, many still succumb before age 10 and 80% before age 30.

The child with cystic fibrosis looks and acts essentially normal. In most cases, no one, save the parents and physician, is aware of the disease until the final stage. No cure is known, and treatment revolves around prevention and/or control of pulmonary infection, maintenance of proper nutrition, and prevention of abnormal salt loss. Many persons perform well above average in tests of muscle power, endurance, and agility despite moderately severe respiratory disease (Thompson, 1990).

The primary disorder of cystic fibrosis is the abnormal secretion of the membranes that line the internal organs. Normal mucus is thin, slippery, and clear. In cystic

FIGURE   19.18

Hospital treatment for persons with asthma, cystic fibrosis, and similar conditions consists largely of special medications via a bronchodilator, chest physiotherapy done by a respiratory therapist, and postural drainage. The major purpose is to facilitate coughing to clear mucus from the clogged bronchial tubes.

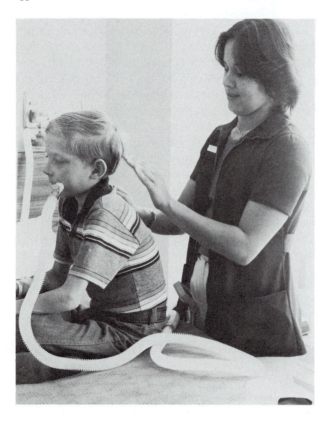 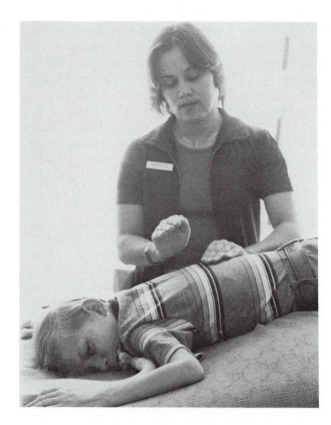

fibrosis, the mucus is thick and sticky, creating two major problems. First, it clogs the bronchial tubes, interfering with breathing, and it lodges in the branches of the windpipe, acting as an obstruction. The resulting symptoms resemble those in asthma, bronchitis, and emphysema. Second, it plugs up the pancreatic ducts, preventing digestive enzymes from reaching the small intestine, and causing malnutrition.

Commercially prepared pancreatic extracts must be taken to substitute for the enzymes no longer present in the digestive tract. In some severe cases, the intestinal tract is obstructed completely by an accumulation of the thick, puttylike material. The sweat glands also produce an unusually salty sweat. Excessive loss of sodium chloride in perspiration is an ever-present danger. Many persons take salt tablets regularly as part of their general management program.

In addition to regular breathing exercises, the child with cystic fibrosis undergoes daily aerosol therapy. A nebulizer or inhalator may be used to relieve bronchospasms.

Treatments for Severe Respiratory Conditions

Persons with severe asthma, chronic obstructive lung disease, and cystic fibrosis generally spend some time each year in the hospital or at home convalescing from attacks that were complicated by colds, flu, or other respiratory illness. Special treatment in hospitals includes postural drainage and thumping by a respiratory therapist, as well as intermittent, positive pressure breathing (IPPB).

Postural Drainage

Postural drainage entails lying in various positions that enable gravity to help the cough drain the bronchial tree of accumulated mucus. The bronchodilator is used before the person assumes 10 different positions. The teacher, therapist, or parent taps the upper torso with his or her fingers, as depicted in Figure 19.18. Each of the positions is designed to drain a specific area of the bronchial tree; hence, the benefit derived from the position depends upon the amount of congestion present. Not all positions are required each session.

Intermittent Positive Pressure Breathing

In IPPB, the person breathes into a plastic mouthpiece attached to a machine that forces a measured amount of medication through the lungs under a controlled level of pressure (see Figure 19.19). Bronchodilators and other kinds of medication can be put in the positive pressure machine. IPPB may be prescribed on a daily basis or used only in times of pulmonary crises.

FIGURE 19.19

Young adolescent with cystic fibrosis undergoes intermittent positive pressure breathing therapy several times each day during her frequent hospital confinements. Note characteristic stunting of physical growth caused by several years of drug therapy.

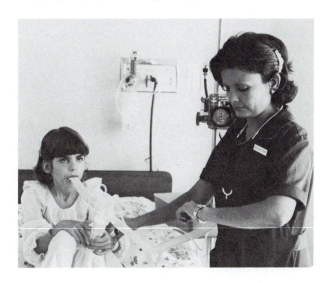

Similar effects are obtained through the use of an aerosol or hand nebulizer. Additional information about available equipment can be obtained through the local lung association.

Hemophilia

The term *hemophilia* encompasses at least eight different bleeding disorders caused by the lack of clotting factors in the blood. Although only 1 in 10,000 persons is afflicted in the United States, the physical educator who has one child with hemophilia is likely to have several since it is an inherited disorder. Historically, hemophilia has been said to appear only in males and to be transmitted through females. Recently, however, a type of hemophilia in women has been identified.

Contrary to popular belief, outward bleeding from a wound is not the major problem; rather, internal bleeding is. A stubbed toe, a bumped elbow, a violent sneeze, or a gentle tag game can be fatal. Each may cause internal bleeding that is manifested by discoloration, swelling, and other characteristics of a hematoma. The person with hemophilia tends to have many black and blue spots, swollen joints, and considerable limitation of movement. Minor internal bleeding may be present much of the time. When internal bleeding appears extensive, blood transfusions are administered.

Over a period of years, repeated hemorrhages into joints, if untreated, result in hemophilic arthritis. To minimize joint bleeding, the afflicted body part is frequently splinted. Pain is severe, and persons may avoid complete extension. This tendency, of course, results in such orthopedic complications as contractures.

Persons with hemophilia should be allowed to engage in regular physical education and should be expected to establish their own limitations. The problems of peer group acceptance, parental overprotection, and social isolation are more intense than the unpredictable episodes of bleeding that halt the usual routine of life. Swimming, creative dance, rhythmic exercises on heavily padded mats, and such individual sports as fishing, shuffleboard, and billiards or pool offer much satisfaction. Catching activities generally are contraindicated.

Sickle-Cell Disease (Anemia)

Although discovered by physician James Herrick in 1910, *sickle-cell disease* did not receive widespread attention until the early 1970s. At that time, 1 of every 400 black Americans was believed to have the disorder.

Sickle-cell disease is an inherited blood disorder that takes its name from the sickle shape the red blood cells assume when the blood's oxygen content is low. Persons with the disease are anemic, suffer crises of severe pain, are prone to infection, and often have slow-healing ulcers of the skin, especially around the ankles. Many do not live to adulthood.

Regular exercise should not be curtailed, *but tests and activities of cardiovascular endurance are contraindicated.* Under intense exercise stress, particularly at altitudes above 10,000 ft, where the air's oxygen content is decreased, persons with sickle-cell anemia may collapse. They should also avoid becoming overheated since the normal evaporation of perspiration cools the skin and may precipitate an attack.

The disease develops at the time of conception, but symptoms do not usually appear until the child is 6 months or older. The first symptoms are pallor, poor appetite, early fatigue, and complaints of pain in the back, abdomen, and extremities. The child may not evidence sickle-cell anemia until he or she catches a cold or has an attack of tonsillitis; then he or she reacts worse than the normal child.

The course of the disease is marked by a sequence of physiological crises and complications that can be recognized, predicted, and treated, but not prevented. The crisis results from spasms in key blood vessels. The child experiences agonizing pain in certain muscles and joints, particularly those of the rib cage, and may run a high fever. Some crises are severe enough to require hospitalization. As the child grows older and learns limitations, the attacks become less frequent.

Anemia

Anemia is a condition of reduced oxygen-carrying capacity of the blood caused by deficiency in either red blood cells or hemoglobin, the oxygen-carrying pigment within the red blood cells. Mild anemia is not easily recognizable, but more severe conditions are characterized by loss of color in cheeks, lips, and gums; lowered activity level because of limited amount of oxygen available to burn calories; and increased heart and breathing rates.

Anemia, often a characteristic of chronic debilitating conditions like leukemia, kidney disease, and lead poisoning, can also occur independently. *Cooley's anemia,* a genetic disorder most common in persons whose descendents are from Italy, Greece, Turkey, and surrounding areas, affects approximately 9 of every 10,000 U.S. citizens (i.e., it

FIGURE 19.20

Exercises for dysmenorrhea. (*A*) *Billig pelvic stretch*. Place forearm, elbow, and palm of hand against wall at shoulder height. Place other hand against posterolateral pelvis and push pelvis forward and sideward toward wall while strongly contracting gluteal and abdominal muscles. Relax and repeat eight times to each side. (*B*) *Knee-chest position*. Lie as indicated for several minutes with knees as close to chest as possible. For variation, combine with abdominal pumping or extend legs alternately backward very slowly. (*C*) *Mosher abdominal pumping*. Alternately contract and relax abdominal muscles slowly but forcefully enough that, on contraction, pelvis flattens against floor, and on relaxation, pelvis moves upward. Coordinate deep breathing with tensing and relaxing, and massage area if it seems to relieve pain. (*D*) *Golub stretch and bend*. Perform exercise in two parts as shown, lifting leg as high as possible on stretch phase while maintaining rest of body in good alignment. At end of each upward stretch, relax momentarily in good standing posture with arms extended at shoulder height. Repeat to opposite side.

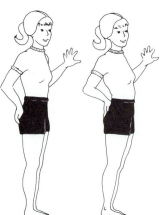
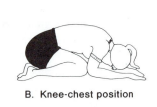

A. Bellig pelvic stretch   C. Mosher abdominal pumping   D. Golub stretch and bend

B. Knee-chest position

is almost twice as common as autism and Down syndrome). Symptoms begin to appear at 1 or 2 years of age, and medical treatments (blood transfusions and drug therapy) are needed throughout life.

Iron deficiency anemia, caused by insufficient daily intake of iron or excessive loss of iron through hemorrhaging, is even more common than Cooley's anemia. Persons with severe mental retardation, cerebral palsy, and disorders that affect chewing/swallowing processes or food intake are at particularly high risk.

Symptoms of anemia, regardless of the cause or type, include irritability, lethargy, and increased fatigability because of high cardiac output. Persons with anemia, however, can perform well at low and moderate exercise intensities. In spite of this, many adopt sedentary lifestyles. Hypoactivity contributes more to their lack of fitness than pathological limitations. Students with anemia should not be excused from regular physical education; rather, they should be encouraged to participate fully, with adaptations made in regard to fitness testing expectations and standards.

Menstrual Problems

Girls sometimes use menstrual problems as an excuse for not participating in physical education. A healthy approach to solving this problem is *modeling* by the female physical educator, who should point out that she always participates in physical education, regardless of her period, and that in the real world, women are expected to show up for work every day and to be optimally productive. Most girls (using internal tampons) swim during their periods and engage in normal or strenuous exercise. *Task cards* with special abdominal exercises designed to alleviate pain can be given to girls who prefer mild activity on these days (see abdominal exercises in Chapter 14 on postures).

Dysmenorrhea (painful menstruation) occurs in some girls early in the menstrual cycle, usually before the blood begins to flow freely. This pain is often partly caused by an accumulation of gas (flatus) or by constipation. Exercises that relieve flatus, such as the bent-knee creeping position/movement, and several yoga techniques also ameliorate menstrual pain (see Figure 19.20). Severe or continued pain that cannot be relieved by aspirin and exercise signals the need to see a physician. *Menorrhagia* (excessive flow) is not normal and contraindicates exercise. The student should lie in a supine position with legs propped up and should see a physician as soon as possible.

Cancer

Cancer, a condition of unknown etiology in which body cells multiply in an abnormal manner and cause tumors, is second only to accidents as a cause of death in children ages 1 to 15 years. Most children who develop cancer, however, do not die; they continue to attend school while undergoing treatment. The incidence in children under 15 years is approximately 13 per 100,000. Each year, about 7,000 new cases are diagnosed within this age range. Table 19.12 indicates the incidence of the various types of childhood cancer.

For the population as a whole, it is estimated that one in every four persons will have cancer. Cancer, the second greatest cause of death in adults, affects more persons in middle and old age than in youth. Research shows that sport activity is a factor in preventing cancer (Grossarth-Maticek et al., 1990).

Cancer is treated by chemotherapy (drugs), radiation therapy, and surgery. Illustrative anticancer drugs are chlorambucil (Leukeran) and methotrexate (Folex). Estimates are that of every six persons with cancer, two will be saved, one will die but could have been saved if proper treat-

Table 19.12
Incidence of various types of cancer in childhood.

Type	Relative Incidence (%)
Leukemias	33.8
Lymphomas, including Hodgkin's disease	10.6
Central nervous system tumors	19.2
Adrenal glands and sympathetic nervous system	7.7
Muscle, tendon, fat cancers	6.7
Kidney cancer (Wilms' tumor)	6.0
Bone cancer	4.5
Eye cancer	2.7
Other	1–2.0

Note. In contrast, cancer of the lung, breast, colon, and skin is most common in adults.

ment had been received, and three cannot be saved with current knowledge. These estimates are for the total population, not children and youth whose chances for recovery are considerably higher. Over half of the cancer fatalities are over age 65.

Side effects of treatment are sometimes more difficult to manage than cancer itself. Radiation treatments are painless, but the side effects may include hair loss, nausea, vomiting, and weight loss. The side effects of chemotherapy are similar, with additional problems like anemia and associated decreased exercise tolerance, easy fatigability, and heightened susceptibility to respiratory infections. Often, low blood cell counts caused by chemotherapy result in the need for periodic blood transfusions.

No physical education research has yet been published in relation to childhood cancer. The psychological effects of physical exercise and the importance of continued involvement in peer activities form the major rationale for keeping students with cancer in regular physical education, adapting instruction as needed.

Kidney and Urinary Tract Disorders

Approximately 3% of American schoolchildren have some history of a kidney or urinary tract disorder. Moreover, urinary-genital malformations account for 300,000 of the common birth defects in the United States, sharing second place in prevalence with congenital blindness and congenital deafness. Only mental retardation afflicts more newborn infants. *Vigorous exercise is contraindicated when kidney infection is present,* and the physician who has not been oriented to the possibilities of an adapted program often excuses the child from physical education.

Biochemical Explanation

Normal functioning of the kidneys is required to excrete urine and to help regulate the water, electrolyte, and acid base content of the blood (i.e., to maintain homeostasis within the body). Problems of fluid retention (edema) and fluid deple-

tion (dehydration) relate largely to the ability of the kidneys to alter the acidity of urine. Urination gets rid of body wastes like urea (an end product of protein metabolism). Renal failure often results in death by uremic poisoning.

Kidney and urinary disorders are many and varied. When both the kidneys and the urinary tract are involved (see Figure 19.21A), problems are often referred to as *renal disorders.* Federal law lists *nephritis* as one of its 11 examples of other health impairments. Nephritis (also called Bright's disease) is inflammation of the kidneys. The name is derived from *nephron,* the functional unit within the kidneys (see Figure 19.21B). Each kidney is comprised of about 1 million nephrons, each of which helps to filtrate substances from the blood and, subsequently, changes some of the resulting filtrate into urine and reabsorbs the remainder. This process results in about 45 gal (180 liters) of filtrate every 24 hr; only about 3 liters of this is voided as urine. The ability of the renal system to reabsorb the rest and maintain the balance between all its contents is obviously vital to life. The many possible disorders are too numerous to name and discuss. Approximately 55,000 deaths are kidney-related each year.

Kidney diseases often involve reduced blood flow to the kidneys. This problem, in turn, elevates blood pressure. The mechanism causing this is release of an enzyme called *renin* that stimulates production of the hormone *aldosterone* (a mineralosteroid). This hormone causes the kidneys to retain salts and water, increasing blood volume, which, in time, may overload the arterial walls and heart because of increased peripheral pressure causing elevated blood pressure.

Management of Renal Disorders

As last-resort treatments, dialysis and kidney transplants are becoming increasingly successful and affordable. Many congenital disorders are corrected through surgery, as are kidney stones and urinary tract obstructions. Routine management of less severe conditions includes antibiotics to treat infections, drugs to control hypertension, low-salt and other modified diets, and iron supplementation to control anemia.

Persons with spina bifida, spinal cord injuries, and amputations are particularly susceptible to renal disorders. Further detail on management of urinary problems appears in Chapters 23 and 24, which cover these disabilities.

Implications for Physical Education

Students with nephritis are in and out of the hospital many times. Each time they return to school, the fitness level is low. Most physicians concur that persons with kidney and urinary tract disease need moderate exercise. They are adamant, however, that such persons should not be subjected to physical fitness tests nor to actual physical stress of any kind.

Convulsive Disorders

The terms *epilepsy, seizure disorders,* and *convulsive disorders* are used interchangeably to denote a chronic condition of the central nervous system that is characterized by

FIGURE   19.21

The kidneys are located in the posterior abdomen at the junction of the thoracic and lumbar vertebrae. (*A*) The urinary tract consists of the ureter (the tube connecting kidneys with bladder), the bladder, and the urethra. The kidneys and urinary tract together are often called the *renal tract* or *renal system.* (*B*) One of the million nephrons inside the kidneys.

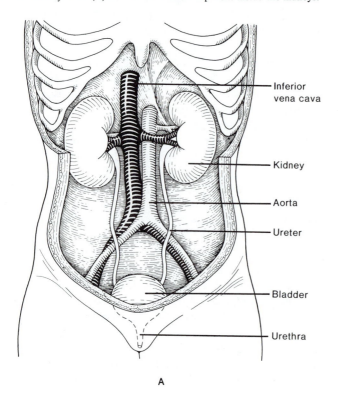

Inferior
vena cava

Kidney

Aorta

Ureter

Bladder

Urethra

A

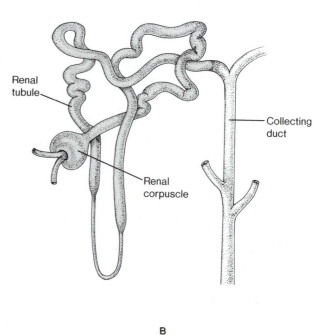

Renal
tubule

Renal
corpuscle

Collecting
duct

B

FIGURE   19.22

Muscle contractions during seizures are tonic or clonic. They may affect all parts of the body.

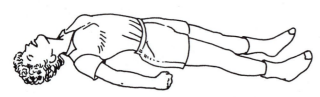

Tonic stage

Clonic stage

recurrent seizures. This condition is not a disease, but rather an upset in the electrical activity of neurons within the cerebral cortex.

Seizures may or may not be accompanied by *convulsions* (fits), defined as sudden, uncontrolled, and unpredictable muscle contractions and relaxations. Muscle activity in convulsions may be *clonic* (jerky or intermittent), *tonic* (continuous, stiff, or rigid), or both (tonic-clonic) (see Figure 19.22).

Most persons with epilepsy take daily medication that is 100% effective in preventing seizures. They live normal lives, and friends seldom know about their condition. A few, however, have periods of short- or long-term uncontrolled seizure activity that require restrictions on driving and exercise.

Biochemical Explanation

Seizures are caused by abnormalities in cell membrane stability. Normally, the cell membrane maintains equilibrium between sodium outside the cell and potassium inside the cell (see Figure 19.23). The balance controls *depolarization,* the cellular process that permits electrical current to be transmitted down the nerve fiber and carry messages to other nerve

FIGURE 19.23

Neurons within the cerebral cortex have synaptic knobs that release neurotransmitters that cause an increase in membrane permeability to sodium and thus trigger nerve impulses. Problems in synaptic transmission sometimes result in seizures.

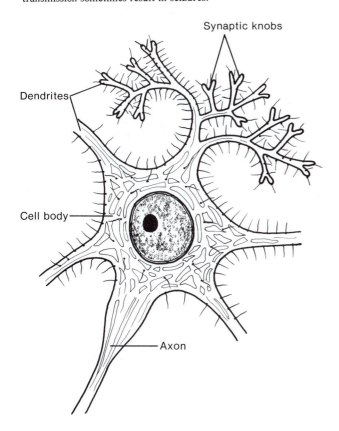

FIGURE 19.24

Ages at which various seizure types occur most often.

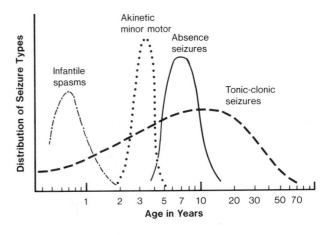

Table 19.13

Two commonly used classification systems in epilepsy: A comparison of terms.

International Classification System (Gastaut, 1970)	Traditional Clinical Classification System
I. Partial seizures	Focal epilepsy
A. Without impairment of consciousness	Motor (Jacksonian) or sensory
B. With impairment of consciousness	Psychomotor or temporal lobe epilepsy
II. Generalized seizures	
A. Absence	Petit mal
B. Tonic-clonic	Grand mal
C. Tonic only	Limited grand mal
D. Clonic only	
E. Myoclonic	Atypical petit mal *or* minor
F. Atonic	seizures *or* Lennox-Gastaut
G. Akinetic	syndrome
H. Infantile spasms	Jackknife or Salaam seizure
III. Unilateral seizures	
IV. Unclassified seizures	

fibers. Epileptic cells are unable to maintain the normal balance; therefore, depolarization occurs too easily and too frequently. The resulting abnormal discharge of electrical activity spreads to the normal neurons, causing them to discharge also so that, soon, an entire area of the brain is involved.

Seizures are designated as *focal* or *generalized,* depending on how much of the brain is involved. *Focal* seizures are focused, or localized, in one specific area of the brain, such as, for instance, the motor strip of the right frontal lobe. The synonym for focal is *partial. Generalized seizures* involve the entire cerebral cortex (both hemispheres).

Prevalence

Prevalence of epilepsy varies from 3 to 7 per 1,000 in the nondisabled population. Among persons with brain injury, either congenital or acquired, the incidence is much greater. From 25 to 50% of the population with cerebral palsy has seizures. About one third of everyone with severe mental retardation has seizures. Seizures are also relatively frequent in extreme old age.

Age at Time of First Seizure

The age of onset of the first seizure helps to explain why so many physical educators must cope with this problem. Twenty percent of all persons with epilepsy have their first

seizure before age 10 (see Figure 19.24). These are usually children with known or suspected neurological damage. Thirty percent of persons with epilepsy have their first seizure in the second decade, while 20% convulse initially in the third decade. The final 30% have their first seizure after age 40.

Types of Seizures

Classification of seizures varies according to whether traditional clinical symptomology serves as its basis or the international classification system adopted by the World Health Organization in 1970. The Epilepsy Foundation of America favors the latter (Gastaut, 1970), but textbooks have been slow to embrace the new system. Table 19.13 presents a comparison of the two systems. A nationwide effort is underway to educate physicians to the new terms and to convince them to discard such words as *grand mal, petit mal,* and *Jacksonian.* Different types of seizures have their first incidence at certain ages (see Figure 19.24).

Partial Seizures

Of the many kinds of partial seizures, the Jacksonian is most common. Clonic (jerky) contractions begin in one part of the body, usually a hand or foot, and from that point spread up the limb until all of the muscles are involved. This is sometimes called *march epilepsy* because the contractions march up the limb. The individual usually does not lose consciousness, although speech and other responses may be impaired.

Psychomotor epilepsy (sometimes called *automatism*) is characterized by unexplainable short-term changes in behavior that later are not remembered. Automatic activity is carried on while in a state of impaired consciousness. One person may have temper tantrums, suddenly exploding for no reason, hitting another, provoking a fight, or throwing things. Another may have spells involving incoherent chatter, repetition of meaningless phrases, and inability to answer simple questions. Still another has episodes of sleepwalking or wakes the family at night with hysterical, unexplainable sobbing. Psychomotor attacks also may be confused with daydreaming or not paying attention in class.

Generalized Seizures

Absence seizures (previously called petit mal) account for about 8% of all epilepsy. Their symptoms are so subtle that the inexperienced observer seldom notices the seizure. There is an impairment of consciousness, never more than 30 sec, in which the individual seems dazed. The eyes may roll upward. If the person is talking at the time, there is a momentary silence and then continuation, with no loss of unity in thought. These seizures are rare before age 3 and often disappear after puberty. They are more common in females than males.

Tonic-clonic seizures (previously called grand mal) are the most dramatic and easily recognized. They have three or four stages.

1. **Aura.** This is a warning or premonition of the attack that is always the same for a particular person. An aura may be a certain smell, flashing of lights, vague feeling of apprehension, sinking feeling in the abdomen, or feeling of extraordinary rapture. Only about 50% of persons have auras.

2. **Tonic Phase.** *Tonic* means constant, referring to the continuous contraction of muscles. The person straightens out, becomes stiff, utters a cry, and loses consciousness. If there is a tonic contraction of respiratory muscles, the person becomes cyanotic. Fortunately, this phase seldom lasts more than 30 sec.

3. **Clonic Phase.** *Clonic* refers to intermittent contraction and relaxation of muscles. The clonic phase persists from a few seconds up to 2 or 3 min. The tongue may be bitten as the jaws work up and down. The

sphincters around the rectum and urinary tracts relax, causing the person to urinate or defecate.

4. **Sleep or Coma Phase.** After a period of brief consciousness or semiconsciousness, during which the person complains of being very tired, he or she lapses into a sleep that may last several hours. Upon awakening, the person is either very clear or is dazed and confused. Usually, there is no memory of the seizure.

Occasionally, seizures occur that are entirely clonic or tonic.

Myoclonic seizures are brief, sudden, violent contractions of muscles in some part or the entire body. Often, these are manifested by a sudden head jerk, followed by jerking of arms and legs, and the trunk bending in upon itself. The individual may lose consciousness, but the duration of a myoclonic seizure is much briefer than that of tonic-clonic or tonic- or clonic-only types.

Atonic seizures are similar to absence seizures except that there is momentary diminution or abolition of postural tone. The individual tends to sag or collapse.

Akinetic seizures (also called sudden drop attacks) cause the individual to suddenly lose muscle tone and plummet to the ground, momentarily unconscious. These seizures may be sometimes purposely aborted. Sudden falling asleep (narcolepsy) may be a form of akinetic seizure.

Infantile spasms (also called jackknife seizures) are usually characterized by a "doubling up" motion of the entire body, although they may be less generalized and manifested only by head dropping and arms flexing. Infantile spasms typically occur between 3 and 9 months of age, after which other types of seizures may replace them. This problem is associated with severe mental retardation. Infantile spasms should not be confused with the generalized seizures that many normal infants and children (5 to 10%) have in conjunction with illness and high fever; these are called *febrile seizures* and typically are a once-in-a-lifetime happening.

Unilateral seizures involve only one side of the brain and, therefore, only one side of the body. These may be of any type.

Unclassified seizures are those that do not meet the criteria for any one type or those that are mixed types. About 35 to 40% of epilepsy is a combination of absence and tonic-clonic seizures.

Etiology

The etiology of epilepsy falls within two broad classifications: (a) idiopathic (genetic or endogenous) and (b) acquired (symptomatic or exogenous). *Idiopathic* means that the cause is unknown, and 80% of all epilepsy remains unexplainable. There appears to be a genetic predisposition toward epilepsy, but this is controversial. In general, the parent with epilepsy has 1 chance in 40 of giving birth to a child with epilepsy. The incidence is increased if both parents are epileptic. *Acquired* epilepsy can be traced directly to birth injuries, brain tumors, oxygen deprivation, lead poisoning, cerebral abscesses, and penetrating injuries to the brain.

FIGURE   19.25

Most factors that aggravate seizures relate to electrolyte balance in the cellular fluids, especially the balance between acidosis and alkalosis in the pH of arterial blood. pH, an abbreviation for potential of hydrogen, is a measure used to express relative degree of acidity and alkalosis.

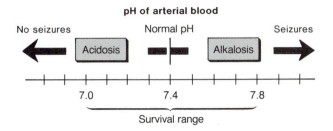

Factors That Aggravate Seizures

1. Increases in alkalinity of the blood (see Figure 19.25). These changes are very subtle and minute. High alkalosis favors seizures. High acidity inhibits seizures. Diet therapy is used frequently. Acid-producing diets, high in fat content—such as cream, butter, eggs, and meat—have successfully produced a quieting effect. This kind of diet is called a *ketogenic diet* (high in fat). The accumulation of acid products in the blood as a result of exercise is also believed to help prevent seizures.

2. Hyperventilation (overbreathing) that leads to respiratory alkalosis, especially when exercise causing hyperventilation is suddenly interrupted (Linschoten, Backx, Mulder, & Meinardi, 1990). Holding the breath as long as possible, as in distance underwater swimming, is a common form of hyperventilation that is contraindicated. Breath-holding lowers the carbon dioxide content of the blood, which increases alkalosis. Sports that commonly induce hyperventilation are scuba diving and high-altitude climbing. Taking a deep breath and jumping into water sometimes triggers hyperventilation.

3. Hyperhydration (ingestion of too much water). This can occur during swimming, especially in beginners.

4. Hyperthermia (too much body heat) as sometimes occurs in marathons and triathlons in high temperatures under humid conditions.

5. Hypoglycemia in diabetes or in persons exercising vigorously over a long duration with no food or liquid.

6. Fatigue, especially sleep deprivation and disturbances of nocturnal rhythms.

7. Sudden emotional stress or excitement like bad news, fright, or anger.

8. Excessive alcohol and caffeine.

9. In women, menstrual periods. Many girls and women have seizures only around their periods. Edema aggravates the onset of seizures.

Seizures and Exercise

Seizures seldom, if ever, occur during vigorous physical activity. Convulsions are most likely during the cool-down after exercise and during late-night hours.

There is no evidence that intense sport competition increases the likelihood of seizures. Seizure-prone persons must, however, be conscientious in taking their medication, eating properly, and getting enough sleep. Obviously, they must minimize the factors that aggravate seizures. Within the disabled sport movement, many athletes take medication to control epilepsy. Occasionally, a seizure occurs, necessitating rest for a few hours. Thereafter, training and competition are resumed. The overall philosophy is that an isolated seizure is no big deal.

Social Problems

The social problems in epilepsy are greater than the medical ones. The person regaining consciousness after a first seizure does not remember anything that happened. He or she is self-conscious and embarrassed. Who wouldn't be? First seizures in adolescence are a particular concern.

Adolescence in our culture is a time of particular sensitivity, and most teenagers with convulsive disorders confess that their greatest hang-up is what friends think. On the other hand, the peer group that has witnessed the seizure has undergone a terrifying, traumatic experience. It is probably the first seizure they have seen, and they are eager to talk about it and share perceptions. Individual responses are as variable as human beings themselves, but many persons are reluctant to continue dating or even socializing with a person who has seizures. Driver's licenses, if issued, have restrictions. Employment opportunities are reduced, and insurability under workmen's compensation may be a problem.

Medication

Phenobarbital (Luminal) and phenytoin (Dilantin), the drugs used most often in controlling *tonic-clonic seizures,* were not introduced until 1912 and 1938, respectively. Teachers who work with children from low-income families see many seizures, almost always caused because a prescription is not filled on time. Often, the problem is carelessness or ignorance rather than lack of money. When taken regularly according to directions, modern medications are almost completely effective in preventing seizures.

Epilepsy medications have a number of adverse side effects. Among these are reduced coordination and concentration, poor reaction time, drowsiness, blurred vision, and irritability. Dilantin, in particular, causes gum and teeth problems.

Management of a Seizure

Should a seizure occur, clear the area around the individual. Do not attempt to hold the body down or restrain limbs. Ascertain that the mouth and nose are clear and permit breathing. Lying in a prone or side position is best. The seizure should be allowed to run its normal course, with everyone remaining calm and accepting.

Implications for Physical Education

The American Medical Association (AMA, 1983) recommends that students with epilepsy participate fully in school physical education and athletics. Reversing its initial stand, the AMA now indicates that collision (football, ice hockey, lacrosse) sports and contact (basketball, soccer, wrestling) sports can be played by the medically balanced student. Boxing should be avoided. Activities like heading the ball in soccer, which involve repeated insults to the head, are controversial.

Activities that might result in a fall (cycling, horseback riding, rope- or tree-climbing, parallel bars, trampoline, balance beam, mountain climbing) should always be done with a partner or group. Likewise, individuals with epilepsy should not swim or engage in other water sports alone. In some students, a specific activity, for unknown reasons, may precipitate seizures. If this occurs *repeatedly,* then that one activity should be restricted.

S. Livingston, a physician at Johns Hopkins Hospital, points out that the emotional disturbances of children excluded from the sports of their peers are more difficult to handle than medical problems. He allows his patients to participate in all sports but diving, prohibiting it not because of the possibility of head injuries but because of the obvious complications associated with a seizure underwater. Livingston states,

Over the past 33 years, I have observed at least 15,000 young children with epilepsy, many of whom have been under my personal care during their entire scholastic careers. Hundreds of these patients have played tackle football; some have participated in boxing, lacrosse, wrestling, and other physical activities which render the participant prone to head injuries. I am not cognizant of a single instance of recurrence of epileptic seizures related to head injury in any of these athletes. (Livingston, 1969, p. 1917)

Students whose seizures are under control are no different from their peers. They need good supervision when enrolled in beginning swimming, but so do all children! Likewise, they need a gymnastics teacher who is competent in spotting techniques. Again, this does not make them different from their peers, who also need a good spotter when undertaking activities on the high balance beam, parallel bars, and trampoline. Most important, persons with epilepsy need the acceptance and belonging that team membership ensures.

Environmental Disorders

The three most common environmental hazards to children's health are metal pollution (lead, mercury, zinc), air pollution (including cigarette smoke), and low-level radiation. Of these, the most research has been done on lead.

Lead poisoning is a leading cause of health impairments in children ages 1 to 4 years. Elevations in blood/lead concentration are associated with cognitive and behavioral difficulties. Approximately 600,000 children under 6 years of age have elevated blood/lead levels; this has been estimated at 5 to 8% of all preschool children.

Approximately 600,000 tons of lead are released by the smelting industry into the environment annually, much of which is carried by winds and deposited in soil where children play. This lead fallout, as well as that caused by lead gasoline, is now the leading cause of lead poisoning. In earlier decades, the main routes of exposure were ingestion of paint or paint dust, milk formulas from improperly soldered cans, and tainted drinking water. The federal Lead Poisoning Prevention Act of 1971 permits large-scale screening of preschool children to identify those at risk, but little else has been done (except in individual communities) to cope with this problem.

Physical educators working in blighted urban areas can expect as many as 40% of their students to carry significant lead burdens, which cause subtle health and behavior problems. Indicators of mild lead poisoning are listlessness, lethargy, irritability, clumsiness, and anemia, all of which contribute to developmental delay. Severe or persistent lead poisoning, without treatment, results in seizures, coma, and eventual death. Even with treatment, mental retardation and epilepsy often occur. Lead poisoning is treated by such drugs as edetate calcium disodium and penicillamine, which can be taken either orally or by intramuscular injection. Most important, however, is removal of students from lead-tainted environments.

Tuberculosis

Tuberculosis, although no longer a common cause of death, still ranks within the top 10 reportable diseases. The incidence of reported tuberculosis is about the same as that of infectious hepatitis, measles, and rubella. Among causes of death, tuberculosis ranks 19th. A vaccine is about 80% effective in disease prevention. This vaccine, however, often is not used in poverty areas, especially those devastated by drug use and acquired immune deficiency syndrome (AIDS). In the 1990s, tuberculosis often occurs as a complication of AIDS.

Tuberculosis, although often conceptualized as a lung disease, can affect any tissue in the body. Tuberculosis is an infectious disease caused by bacteria (i.e., the tubercle bacillus) and characterized by the formation of tubercles (little swellings). In this country, bone and joint tuberculosis is more likely to come to the attention of physical educators than the other types. Of the skeletal sites of tuberculosis, the most common is the spine, followed by hip and knee.

Pott's disease, or tuberculosis of the spine, is a disorder that often results in kyphosis (round upper back). This inflammation of the vertebral bodies occurs most often in children and young adults. Pott's disease is characterized by the formation of little tubercles on the vertebral bodies. Destruction and compression of the vertebral bodies affects the spinal cord and adjacent nerves to the extent that movement becomes extremely painful. The characteristic kyphotic curvature is called a *gibbus,* meaning hump. The condition of having a humpback is *gibbosity.* A medical synonym for Pott's disease is *tuberculous spondylitis.*

FIGURE 19.26

Tuberculosis remains a common cause of meningitis (infection of covering of brain) during early childhood. The consequences of this disease, even with the best treatment, are severe, with some degree of intellectual deficit occurring in about 20% of children, as well as hearing and vestibular defects. Seizures, hydrocephalus, spasticity, ataxia, and incoordination are common outcomes also.

Acquired Immune Deficiency Syndrome

Acquired Immune Deficiency Syndrome (AIDS) is a group of virus-caused conditions that weaken or destroy the immune system so that it cannot fight certain infections, malignancies, and neurological diseases. The first cases of AIDS were reported in 1981, but the virus that causes it was not identified until 1984. Over the last few years, there have been many changes in terminology, prognosis, acceptance, and high-risk populations (see Figure 19.26). There is still, however, no cure or immunization. About 50% of persons with AIDS die within 18 months of diagnosis. Very few live longer than 5 years.

Human immunodeficiency virus (HIV) causes AIDS. HIV is different from most other viruses because it lives only in body fluids and cannot survive long outside of the body. Contact with three body fluids (blood, semen, and vaginal secretions) results in HIV infections. This knowledge is rapidly changing attitudes and practices in regard to sex, intravenous drug usage, and first-aid measures.

HIV infections are transmitted in four ways: (a) sex involving the anus, penis, or vagina; (b) contaminated needles; (c) infected blood products; and (d) newborn infant HIV carriers (Landry, 1989). Persons with HIV infections do not look different from anyone else. The average latency period between infection and the onset of symptoms is 7 to 8 years. During this time, infected persons are carriers. They may not be aware that they are infected. We never know, therefore, when we are in contact with blood, semen, or vaginal secretion that is carrying the virus.

Safe Practices for the 1990s

AIDS is most often transmitted through sex without condoms and/or with multiple partners. Risk is high under these conditions, whether the relationship is heterosexual or homosexual. Condoms are not 100% safe. The best practice is obviously having sex with one mutually faithful, uninfected partner. Most teenagers and adults have control over their sex and can be safe. Children who are victims of sex abuse and/or who learn about sex from the streets or television are special risk groups. Persons with mental retardation and other disabilities who are not provided prevention education are also at risk.

Another safe practice is to use only sterile needles or syringes. Never share a needle with another, regardless of the fluid being injected. Intravenous drug abusers are a high-risk group because so many have neither the money nor the inclination to purchase sterile needles.

Infected blood products can be avoided in several ways. Because we never know when an emergency blood transfusion may be needed, it is a good practice to have blood drawn and stored for later personal use. Care of hemophilia requires frequent transfusions, and hospitals today are accountable for using only uninfected blood. Before knowledge about the HIV virus was commonplace, however, hemophilia was a high-risk condition.

First-aid and emergency care that involves blood should be rendered with rubber gloves. Even when gloves are used, hands should be washed with soap and water. If nosebleeds or injuries result in blood on the floor or equipment, wash the surface clean with a household bleach solution of 1 part bleach to 10 parts water. Towels and clothing with blood contamination are safe after hot-water/detergent washing but should be stored in tied plastic bags until laundered or trashed. These first-aid guidelines come from the U.S. Public Health Service, Centers for Disease Control (CDC).

Wounds that might seep blood should be kept covered during sport activity. Bandages not only protect the injured site but minimize the chance of blood contact by others. Care givers and teachers should maximize their own skin care and realize that they are at most risk for accidental infection when there is a skin breakdown.

AIDS prevention, especially in relation to injury and skin care, should be a part of physical education and sports. Persons should be taught to take care of their own blood spills when possible. Students often care for one another and should know safe practices.

Types of HIV Infections

While AIDS will continue to be the layperson's term, professionals now refer to HIV infections (Diamond, 1989; Gray, 1989). All persons with these infections test seropositive, meaning that the virus is found in their blood serum. There are three types:

1. **AIDS.** This term refers to the advanced stage when opportunistic infections, malignancies, and neurological diseases predominate. This stage is characterized by acute medical crises requiring hospital and/or bed care, followed by periods of remission in which life is more or less normal. Colds, flu, and respiratory infections are the most life threatening. Most persons with AIDS take a medication called AZT or zidovudine (Retrovir).

2. **Symptomatic HIV Infection (formerly referred to as AIDS-related complex or ARC).** This is the earlier, milder stage. Signs/symptoms are unexplained weight loss greater than 10%, chronic diarrhea, swollen lymph nodes (neck, armpit, groin), fever, skin rashes, and increased susceptibility to infections. In the congenital form of this, additional signs are developmental delay, central nervous system disorders, and failure to thrive.

3. **Asymptomatic HIV Infection.** This includes everyone who tests seropositive but exhibits no symptoms. In children and adults, this is the latency period. In newborn infants, the diagnosis is more complex because only half of the babies born to HIV-infected mothers become ill. All such newborns, however, test seropositive and are carriers until about age 2 years. This is because infants live off the antibodies passed on from their mothers and do not begin to develop their own immune system for several months.

Incidence/Prevalence

AIDS statistics are changing so fast that they should be checked every year. The disease spread during the 1980s was considered an epidemic. The incidence of infection rates among all age groups is about 4 to 7 per 1,000. In 1990, cases in the United States numbered 115,000, of which about 2,000 were under age 13. Most authorities believe that these official CDC figures underrepresent the problem, especially in children. Probably 5 to 10 times more children have HIV infections than are reported.

The greatest problem of the 1990s is anticipated to be congenital infections in infants born of mothers who are intravenous drug users. This is obviously greatest in communities where drug abuse is rampant. In New York City, for example, 5% of all pregnant women coming to public hospitals are HIV positive (Gray, 1989).

Implications for Physical Education

As the number of HIV-infected children increase, more will obviously be attending public schools (Surburg, 1988). Likewise, more teachers and coworkers will have the syndrome. Lawsuits of the 1980s assure these persons the same education and employment rights as everyone else. HIV-infected students fall under the other health impairments category of federal legislation, and their physical education should be conducted accordingly.

Their physical education adaptations are similar to those of other OHI children with weight loss, easy fatigue, and increased susceptibility to infections. They miss more school, which creates social and learning problems. As the condition becomes more severe, children may need to carry portable oxygen tanks with them (see Figure 19.27). An excellent children's book and teacher's guide is available from Prickly Pair Publishing and Consulting Company, 9628 W. Oregon Place, Denver, CO 80236 (Schilling, 1990). Other teacher resources are by Hubbard (1990) and Yarber (1989).

Students like Ryan White who have AIDS prefer to tell classmates about their condition and solicit their support (White & Cunningham, 1991). They want to be treated like normal persons in physical education and to be included in after-school sports. Ryan White contracted AIDS through a blood transfusion for hemophilia; he was diagnosed in 1984 and lived 6 years, during which time his battle against discrimination in an Indiana school district became national news. Several videotapes tell his story.

Ignorance, fear, hysteria, and discrimination are probably the greatest problems to be resolved in physical education as well as in other school subjects. The American Coaching Effectiveness Program emphasizes that AIDS is *not* transmitted by

1. Competing in sports
2. Coming in contact with sweat
3. Having casual contact, such as handshaking or hugging
4. Living with someone who has AIDS and sharing eating utensils, towels, and toilets
5. Kissing
6. Swimming in a pool with someone who has AIDS (Landry, 1989, p. 22)

HIV infections cause many of the same fitness problems as asthma. Recovery after respiratory illness is slow, and aerobic fitness especially suffers.

Congenital HIV

The characteristics of HIV-infected infants are different from those of older persons. Congenital etiology results in 78 to 90% of infants having central nervous system involvement, as compared to 39 to 60% incidence in adults (Diamond, 1989). The involvements most common in early childhood are variously called mental retardation, cerebral palsy, developmental delays, and motor abnormalities. Meningitis and encephalitis occur more often in adults.

FIGURE 19.27

Jonathan, a first-grader, tells classmates how he contracted AIDS from a blood transfusion during infancy. The machine in front of Jonathan is a portable oxygen tank, an adaptation used for a few months to make breathing easier, but later abandoned. Courtesy of Sharon Schilling, Author of *My Name is Jonathan, (and I Have AIDS)*.

Whereas there is a 7- to 8-year latency period for many adults, HIV-infected infants seem to follow three patterns. About 50% are not infected but test seropositive until about 2 years old because of the mother's antibodies. The other 50% appear healthy until 6 to 9 months of age. Then the disease appears in either a progressive or static form. In the progressive form, the infant is almost always ill and rapidly deteriorates. The median survival time is 8 months. In the static form, there are long plateau periods, and median survival time is 24 months (Diamond, 1989).

Current estimates are that about 60% of the infants in these latter two patterns survive until at least age 5. As advances occur, more and more will live. Adapted physical educators in early childhood programs will thus need to know a lot about cerebral palsy and other indications of brain damage (e.g., attention deficits, hyperactivity).

Motor development problems result from both HIV infection and drug-related damage. Separating what causes what is not yet possible. Spasticity, persistence of primitive reflexes, and visuomotor perceptual and organizational problems are frequently noted (Cratty, 1990; Diamond, 1989). Several kinds of cerebral palsy (spasticity, athetosis, ataxia) have been reported. The most severe viral-caused neurological changes are in the basal ganglia and pyramidal tracts of the white matter (Epstein & Sharer, 1988).

Children With AIDS, a newsletter published six times annually, is an excellent source for staying abreast of new developments. It is published by The Foundation for Children With AIDS, Inc., 77B Warren Street, Brighton, MA 02135.

References

American Academy of Pediatrics, Committee on Sports Medicine. (1982, August). *The asthmatic child and his participation in sports and physical education.* Mimeographed.

American College of Sports Medicine. (1988). *Resource manual for guidelines for exercise testing and prescription.* Philadelphia: Lea & Febiger.

American College of Sports Medicine. (1991). *Guidelines for exercise testing and prescription* (4th ed.). Philadelphia: Lea & Febiger.

American Medical Association. (1983). Sports and children with epilepsy. *Pediatrics, 72,* 884–885.

Bar-Or, O. (1983). *Pediatric sports medicine for the practitioner.* New York: Springer-Verlag.

Berg, K. (1986). *Diabetic's guide to health and fitness.* Champaign, IL: Life Enhancement Publications.

Brandt, N. (1973). Your son and diabetes. *Today's Health, 51* (6), 34–37, 69–71.

Cooper, K. H. (1988). *Controlling cholesterol.* New York: Bantam Books.

Coram, S., & Mangum, M. (1986). Exercise risks and benefits for diabetic individuals: A review. *Adapted Physical Activity Quarterly, 3,* 35–37.

Corbin, C. B., & Lindsey, R. (1990). *Concepts of physical fitness* (7th ed.). Dubuque, IA: Wm. C. Brown.

Cratty, B. J. (1990). Motor development of infants subject to maternal drug use: Current evidence and future research strategies. *Adapted Physical Activity Quarterly, 1,* 110–125.

Cumming, G. R. (1987). Children with heart disease. In J. S. Skinner (Ed.), *Exercise testing and exercise prescription for special cases* (pp. 241–260). Philadelphia: Lea & Febiger.

Diamond, G. W. (1989). Developmental problems in children with HIV infection. *Mental Retardation, 27* (4), 213–217.

Duda, M. (1985). The role of exercise in managing diabetes. *The Physician and Sports Medicine, 13,* 164–170.

Ellestad, M. H. (1986). *Stress testing: Principles and practices* (3rd ed.). Philadelphia: F. A. Davis.

Epstein, L. G., & Sharer, L. R. (1988). Neurology of human immunodeficiency virus infection in children. In. M. L. Rosenblum, R. M. Levy, & D. E. Bredesen (Eds.), *AIDS and the nervous system* (pp. 79–101). New York: Raven Press.

Fernhall, B., & Tymeson, G. (1987). Graded exercise testing of mentally retarded adults: A study of feasibility. *Archives of Physical Medicine and Rehabilitation, 68,* 363–365.

Freed, M. D. (1984). Recreational and sports recommendations for the child with heart disease. *Pediatric Clinics of North America, 31,* 1307–1320.

Gastaut, H. (1970). Clinical and electroencephalographic classification of epileptic seizures. *Epilepsia, 11,* 102–113.

Gilbert, C. A. (1978). Exercise and the heart. In J. Basmajian (Ed.), *Therapeutic exercise* (3rd ed.) (pp. 548–564). Baltimore: Williams & Wilkins.

Goldhaber, S., Brown, W. D., & St. John Sutton, M. (1987). High frequency of mitral valve prolapse and aortic regurgitation among asymptomatic adults with Down syndrome. *Journal of American Medical Association, 258,* 1793–1795.

Gray, C. D. (1989). Opening comments on the conference on developmental disabilities and HIV infection. *Mental Retardation, 27* (4), 199–200.

Griffith, H. W. (1992). *Complete guide to prescription and nonprescription drugs.* New York: The Body Press/Perigee.

Grossarth-Maticek, R., Eyesenck, H. J., Uhlenbruck, G., Rieder, H., Freesemann, C., Rakic, L., Gallasch, G., Kanazir, D., & Liesen, H. (1990). Sport activity and personality as elements in preventing cancer and coronary heart disease. *Perceptual and Motor Skills, 71,* 199–209.

Hogshead, N., & Couzens, G. S. (1990). *Asthma and exercise.* New York: Henry Holt & Company.

Hubbard, B. M. (1990). *A disease called AIDS: For grades 5 through 7—Instructor's guide.* Reston, VA: American Alliance for Health, Physical Education, Recreation, and Dance.

Kaplan, N. M. (1990). *Clinical hypertension* (5th ed.). Baltimore: Williams & Wilkins.

Kien, C. L. (1990). Current controversies in nutrition. *Current Problems in Pediatrics, 20* (7), 355–408.

Kowalski, R. E. (1987). *The 8-week cholesterol cure.* New York: Harper & Row.

Landry, G. (1989). *AIDS in sport.* Champaign, IL: Leisure Press.

Linschoten, R., Backx, F., Mulder, O., & Meinardi, H. (1990). Epilepsy and sports. *Sports Medicine, 10* (1), 9–19.

Livingston, S. (1969). Letter to the editor. *Journal of American Medical Association, 207,* 1917.

Long, J. W. (1992). *The essential guide to prescription drugs.* New York: Harper Perennial.

Maurer, H. M. (1983). *Pediatrics.* New York: Churchill Livingstone.

Nagarathna, R., & Nagendra, H. R. (1985). Yoga for bronchial asthma: A controlled study. *British Medical Journal, 291,* 1077–1079.

NurseReview. (1987). *Cardiac problems.* Springhouse, PA: Springhouse Corporation.

Physician's Desk Reference. (published annually). Oradell, NJ: Medical Economics Company.

Pitetti, K. H., & Tan, D. M. (1991). Effects of a minimally supervised exercise program for mentally retarded adults. *Medicine and Science in Sports and Exercise, 23,* 594–601.

Rimmer, J. (1993). *Fitness and rehabilitation programs for special populations.* Dubuque, IA: Brown & Benchmark.

Schilling, S. (1990). *My name is Jonathan (and I have AIDS): Teacher's edition.* Denver, CO: Prickly Pair.

Sheldahl, L. M. (1986). Special ergometric techniques and weight reduction. *Medicine and Science in Sports and Exercise, 18* (1), 25–30.

Shephard, R. J. (1990). *Fitness in special populations.* Champaign, IL: Human Kinetics.

Spicer, R. L. (1984). Cardiovascular disease in Down syndrome. *Pediatric Clinics of North America, 31* (6), 1331–1344.

Strong, W. B., & Alpert, B. S. (1982). The child with heart disease: Play, recreation, and sports. *Current Problems in Pediatrics, 13* (2), 1–34.

Surburg, P. R. (1988). Are adapted physical educators ready for students with AIDS? *Adapted Physical Activity Quarterly, 5* (4), 259–263.

Talbert, W. F. (1971, February–March). Double challenge for a champion. *World Health,* 25–27.

Task Force on Blood Pressure Control in Children. (1987). Report of the task force. *Pediatrics, 79,* 271.

Thompson, K. (1990). Cystic fibrosis—Update on exercise. *Physician & Sportsmedicine, 18* (5), 103–106.

White, R., & Cunningham, A. M. (1991). *Ryan White: My own story.* New York: Dial Books.

Wilmore, J. H., & Costill, D. L. (1988). *Training for sport and activity* (3rd ed.). Dubuque, IA: Wm. C. Brown.

Yarber, W. L. (1989). *AIDS: What young adults should know: Instructor's guide* (2nd ed.). Reston, VA: American Alliance for Health, Physical Education, Recreation, and Dance.

CHAPTER

20

Learning Disabilities, Attention Deficits, and Hyperactivity

FIGURE   20.1

An alternative to beam walking is a Cratty floor grid on which every letter of the alphabet and every number can be found. Here a boy with learning disabilities leads his teacher in walking out the number 8.

After you have studied this chapter, you should be
able to:

1. Differentiate between learning disabilities and mental
   retardation. See Chapter 21, and contrast behaviors.

2. Discuss the prevalence and educational placements
   of individuals with learning disabilities.

3. Discuss the evolution of pedagogy for learning
   disabilities and the dilemma of perceptual-motor
   training. Differentiate between beliefs of physical and
   special educators.

4. Define soft signs and give examples of behavioral,
   perceptual, and motor soft signs. Identify tests used
   to elicit motor soft signs.

5. Discuss remediation for (a) perceptual-motor
   problems and (b) clumsiness and apraxia. Identify or
   create some games, dance, and aquatics activities
   that would be helpful for each and explain possible
   adaptations.

6. Discuss instructional strategies. Make up dialogue
   that might occur between students and teacher
   when these strategies are used. Weave these
   together into a play that is presented to the class or
   try role-playing.

7. Describe illustrative behaviors and remediation for
   (a) inattention, (b) impulsivity, (c) hyperactivity,
   (d) social imperception, and (e) perseveration.

8. State and discuss four principles for managing the
   learning environment of children with LD.

9. Describe behaviors and present level of performance
   and develop a physical education IEP for a student
   with LD.

10. Discuss available and needed research on physical
    education-recreation for persons with LD. Document
    with research published during the last 3 years.

---

*L**earning disability is not mental retardation.* Thomas
Edison, Winston Churchill, Albert Einstein, Walt Disney, and
Mickey Mantle all manifested learning disabilities (LD).
Each at one time or another was labeled a failure because of
specific deficits in language or mathematical processes. Each
had a discrepancy between estimated intellectual potential
and actual academic achievement.

Definition of Learning Disabilities

Specific learning disabilities (SLD) is defined by federal legislation as follows:

a disorder in one or more of the basic psychological processes
involved in understanding or in using language, spoken or
written, which disorder may manifest itself in an imperfect
ability to listen, think, speak, read, write, spell, or do
mathematical calculations. Such disorders include such
conditions as perceptual disabilities, brain injury, minimal brain
dysfunction, dyslexia, and developmental aphasia. Such term
does not include children who have learning problems which are
primarily the result of visual, hearing, or motor disabilities, of
mental retardation, of emotional disturbance, or of
environmental, cultural, or economic disadvantage. (Individuals
with Disabilities Education Act of 1990, Section 1401)

This definition assumes that readers are familiar with such
terms as *dyslexia* (a severe reading disorder presumed to be
of neurological origin) and *aphasia* (impairment of ability to
communicate presumed to be of neurological origin). Other
types of aphasias are *dysgraphia* (writing disorder), *dyscal-*
culia (math disorder), and *amnesia* (memory disorder). The
most common disorders are reading and spelling, but any
combination of aphasias may result in SLD.

The federal definition of SLD is purposely broad so
as to accommodate a variety of philosophical stances about
who should qualify for special education services. A second
part of this definition states that eligibility for special education depends on two criteria: (a) failure to achieve at proper

age and ability levels when provided with appropriate learning
experiences and (b) a severe discrepancy between achievement and intellectual ability in one or more areas.

A number of other definitions have been proposed,
but all have five common elements: (a) neurological dysfunction, (b) uneven growth pattern, (c) difficulty in academic and learning tasks, (d) discrepancy between
achievement and potential, and (e) clear distinction between
LD and concomitant conditions (Lerner, 1988). The neurological dysfunction is presumed to be biological (i.e., a central processing disorder within the brain) but usually is not
confirmable by electroencephalogy (EEG).

LD is not a homogeneous disorder. Distinct
subgroups identified by Lazarus (1990) are (a) language impaired with subtle motor difficulties, mainly in information
processing, and (b) visual-spatial-motor impaired with obvious perceptual-motor problems and clumsiness (see Figure
20.1). The latter may have language-related problems, especially in pronunciation and comprehension, but academic
deficits also include math. The language impaired subgroup
tends to prefer information processing through a visual modality, whereas the visual-spatial-motor impaired subgroup
prefers auditory input (Lazarus, 1990). Many persons with
LD, however, have problems with both visual and auditory
learning.

Since the early 1980s, LD has been emphasized as
a condition distinct from attention deficit disorder (ADD)
and hyperactivity (American Psychiatric Association, 1980).
These disorders are described in the second half of the chapter
because they often complicate LD.

Prevalence

Approximately 2 million students in the United States are
classified as LD and receive special education services. This
represents about 47% of all students in special education and

4 to 5% of the total school-age population. The number of students served under the LD label has been growing by 1 to 2% each year.

Educators are reluctant to assign disability classifications to young children. Therefore, infants, toddlers, and children served under IDEA-Part C and H are typically called developmentally or language delayed. Many of these children later are classified as LD.

Definite gender differences are evident in LD. Approximately three times as many boys as girls receive special education services for LD. Many students with other disabilities also have LD. Chief among these are individuals with cerebral palsy or severe hearing impairments.

Educational Placements

Most students with LD (about 60%) receive their special education services in resource rooms. Of the remaining 40%, half are served primarily in the regular classroom, and half are served in self-contained classrooms. Placement practices vary widely by state and community; these figures reflect the national average.

Almost all students with LD (even those in self-contained classrooms) spend some time each day in the regular education program. The average is 2.1 hr a day or 35% of their time (U.S. Department of Education, 1989). Although statistics are not available concerning physical education placement, most students with LD are integrated into regular physical education. The rationale for integrated placements is often not well documented. Physical and special educators seem to have widely different perceptions of what happens in a gymnasium and whether the regular class placement is least restrictive.

Historical Perspectives

Historically, LD has been linked with reading and speaking difficulties caused by brain damage. Accounts of individuals with congenital word blindness appear in the literature of the 1800s, but specific pedagogy was not proposed until the landmark publication of *Psychopathology and Education of the Brain-Injured Child* in 1947 by Alfred Strauss and Laura Lehtinen. This book described problems of learning, attention, and hyperactivity that subsequently became known as the *Strauss syndrome.* Four principles for managing the learning environment were stressed: (a) use optimal structure, (b) reduce space, (c) eliminate irrelevant stimuli, and (d) enhance the stimulus value of equipment or instructional material. These principles remain sound.

In addition, early theorists stressed perceptual-motor training as a means of remediating perceptual problems and teaching language. This thrust can be traced back to the sensory-motor techniques used in the early 1800s by Jean Marc Itard, a French physician, with Victor, a 12-year-old mute found wandering naked in the forest. Victor, now often known as the Wild Boy of Aveyron, is recognized in special education texts as the first recipient of systematic sensory or perceptual-motor training. Until 1970, perceptual-motor training was widely accepted as appropriate pedagogy for remediating language and learning problems (Hallahan & Cruickshank, 1973).

Until the 1960s, no professional organization or official nomenclature existed for LD. Dr. Samuel Kirk, a special educator at the University of Illinois, proposed the term *learning disabilities* in 1963, and a parent-professional organization called the Association for Children with Learning Disabilities (ACLD) was founded in 1964. This group was largely responsible for the recognition of LD in federal legislation and subsequent progress in theory and practice. In 1990, ACLD changed its name to Learning Disability Association of America (LDA).

Physical educators became aware of LD in the 1970s. Sherrill (1972) was the first to write a chapter on LD for an adapted physical education text; it appeared in Hollis Fait's *Special Physical Education.* Sherrill, mentored by ACLD parents and professionals, relied heavily on the works of followers of Strauss: William Cruickshank's *The Brain-Injured Child in Home, School, and Community* (1967) and Newell Kephart's *The Slow Learner in the Classroom* (1971). From Cruickshank, she learned Strauss's principles for managing the learning environment and applied them to the gymnasium setting. From Kephart, she stressed balance activities and imitation of movement games to remediate clumsiness. From association with ACLD parents and children, however, Sherrill formed the self-concept beliefs underlying her adapted physical education pedagogy.

Byrant J. Cratty, at the University of California at Los Angeles, also contributed substantially to perceptual-motor pedagogy (Cratty, 1971, 1972; Cratty & Martin, 1969). Cratty rejected the theory that movement attributes are the basis of perceptual and intellectual development (e.g., Kephart, Getman, Frostig). Instead, he stressed the use of highly structured movement experiences to remediate clumsiness and improve self-control and self-concept. Cratty believed that academic abilities would be enhanced by movement only if games were developed to teach specific academic skills. He recommended that games be used to supplement classroom instruction, not to substitute for it.

The Perceptual-Motor Training Dilemma

Since the 1970s, most physical educators have believed that perceptual-motor training is valuable in developing motor and game skills, remediating clumsiness, and enhancing body image. The physical education philosophy and approach, however, have been different from that of special education, which posited that perceptual-motor training was a direct route to academic improvement. Likewise, physical educators have defined perceptual-motor training differently. Auxter and Pyfer (1989), for example, define *perceptual-motor programming* as "use of activities believed to promote the development of balance, body image, spatial awareness, laterality, and directionality" (p. 484). In essence, most physical educators believe that teaching movement without simultaneously enhancing perception is impossible (see Figure 20.2). To them, movement and perceptual-motor activity often mean the same thing.

This is not true in special education, where the term *perceptual-motor training* has traditionally been defined as the use of motor activities to promote academic learning and/or improve cognitive and language function. By the 1980s, it

FIGURE 20.2

A movement lesson designed to improve hopping and jumping enhances perception of space and time.

was evident that research findings failed to support perceptual-motor pedagogy in special education (Kavale & Mattson, 1983). The American Academy of Pediatrics Committee on Children with Learning Disabilities (Cohen et al., 1985) and the Board of Trustees, Council for Learning Disabilities (1986) were among the several groups that issued formal statements opposing perceptual-motor training.

Current Beliefs About Pedagogy

Special educators today focus primarily on attention, memory, and cognition and direct their instruction toward specific reading, writing, spelling, and math disabilities. Physical educators also are concerned with attention, memory, and cognition because these processes obviously are important in learning motor skills, rules, and strategies. Listening, thinking, and speaking are central to success in a gymnasium as well as to safety.

Perceptual-motor training and its noncortical counterpart, sensorimotor integration, remain important physical education goals. Their purpose, however, is to improve movement abilities, not to remediate specific learning disabilities.

Most students with LD require adapted physical education services to self-actualize their motor, fitness, and leisure potential. These services can be delivered in the mainstream, but the individualized education program (IEP) should specify maximum class size, a consultant arrangement between regular and adapted physical educators, and a class structure that emphasizes cooperative behaviors, social competence, and self-esteem.

Neurological Soft Signs

Neurological soft signs is the term given to behavioral, perceptual, and motor indicators of central nervous system (CNS) dysfunction that cannot be substantiated through hardware technology (e.g., electroencephalogy or EEG). Research repeatedly shows that students with LD evidence neurological soft signs not present in the general population; this is why all definitions of LD emphasize its biological origin. *Behavioral soft signs* pertain to attention deficits, hyperac-

tivity, conceptual rigidity, inappropriate reactions, emotional lability (instability), and the like. *Perceptual soft signs* include defective visual discrimination of letters (confusion of *b* and *d; p* and *q; u* and *n; b* and *h*) and words (reversals like *saw* for *was, dog* for *god*), auditory discrimination problems, and deficits in organizing, remembering, and repeating sequences. (See Chapter 12 for a review of perceptual and perceptual-motor deficits.) *Motor soft signs* include static and dynamic balance deficits, associated and choreiform movements, awkwardness, and agnosias.

Many of the neurological tests that physicians administer are used by adapted physical educators. Table 20.1 presents tests commonly used to identify soft signs and introduces terms used in medical records. Educators often consider motor soft signs to be perceptual-motor difficulties.

Not all students exhibit soft signs, but enough do that assessment in the areas specified in Table 20.1 should be thorough. These soft signs have obvious implications for physical education performance. Research shows, however, that soft signs do not correlate highly with academic performance.

Perceptual-Motor Strengths and Weaknesses

Not all students with LD have perceptual-motor problems; many are fine athletes. But most do! One of the few prevalence studies of such problems among children diagnosed by school psychologists as LD indicated that 12% demonstrated no problems, 75% scored average on some tests but below average on others, and 13% scored 2 to 3 years below normative standards for their age group on all tests (Sherrill & Pyfer, 1985).

Many students with LD have difficulty decoding or making sense out of their bodies and space (Haubenstricker, 1983). Assessment should identify the level at which each problem is most pronounced: (a) awareness, (b) discrimination, or (c) organization. Remember, in LD, the primary cause is neurological, but problems are often confounded by environmental conditions. Therefore, remediation must address both.

Immature Body Image and Agnosias

As normal children mature, they become conscious of their bodies, internalize their perceptions, and acquire a *body image*. Children with LD, however, manifest many problems: (a) finger agnosia, (b) inability to identify body parts and surfaces, (c) inability to make right-left discriminations, and (d) difficulty in making judgments about body size, shape, and proportions. These deficits are thought to stem from brain damage.

Of the many body image deficits, *finger agnosia* has received the most attention. Table 20.1 describes the test commonly used to identify finger agnosia. This body image deficit is also evidenced in drawing, handwriting, and other fine motor tasks. The following description of a 6-year-old with high average intelligence is typical:

He made the drawing after being instructed to draw a picture of himself and quickly drew all of the figure except the fingers. When he came to the point of wanting to put on fingers, he became confused, looked at the examiner's hands and then at his

Table 20.1
Examples of tests used to elicit neurological soft signs and verify neurological dysfunction.

Sign	Description	Assessment Questions
Romberg	Student stands erect with both feet together, with eyes open and then closed.	Does student sway or lose balance? In unilateral cerebellar damage, falls are toward side of lesion.
Choreiform movements	Student stands in Romberg position, but with arms held straight out in front, eyes closed, and tongue stuck out as far as possible.	Are there rotary or twitching movements of the fingers, tongue, or head?
Motor impersistence	Same as for choreiform movements.	Can student maintain this position for at least 30 sec?
Tandem stand, walk (also called Mann test sign)	Student stands in heel-toe posture, with eyes open, then closed. Also walks heel-to-toe at least six steps.	What is performance discrepancy between eyes open and eyes closed? Eyes open compensates for ataxia caused by cerebellum or sensory nerve, root, and posterior spinal lesions.
Heel walking	Student walks on heels at least six steps.	Are anterior foot and toes off the floor and the body in good control?
Stork or one-foot stand (also called one-foot Romberg) Shallow one-leg squat and rise	Student stands on one foot, with eyes open and then closed. If successful, student is asked to squat and rise (one time only), bearing the entire weight on one leg.	Can student stand on preferred leg at least 10 sec and do squat and rise with good control?
Associated movements (also called synkinesia—*syn* [without] and *kinesia* [movement]) Dysdiadochokinesia (dis-di-ad-o-ko-ki-ne-se-a) from *dys* (bad) + *diadochos* (succeeding) + *kinesis* (movement) (also called alternating motion rate [AMR])	Student touches thumb to index finger of same hand as rapidly as possible, at a rate of about 3 per second. Student alternates pronation and supination movements of one hand as rapidly as possible, with arm bent at 90° angle. If successful, student is asked to do same movement with both hands, beginning with one palm up and one palm down. This is usually done in sitting position, with hands resting on knees.	Can student keep the other hand motionless, or does it mirror the moving hand? Can student maintain a 90° angle with arms close to body while doing this, or do arms begin to flail wildly? Can student maintain rapid alternating movements with hands moving in opposite directions?
Finger dexterity: Touching thumb to fingertips (also tests alternating motion rate [AMR])	Student uses thumb to rapidly touch each finger in succession, moving from little finger to index finger and then from index finger to little finger. Eyes open, then closed.	Can student perform this task in 90 sec? Alternative tests are buttoning and unbuttoning, using safety pins, and other finger patterns like pivoting thumb and index finger.
Dyssynergia or dyskinesthesia: Touching nose with index finger or touching two index fingers	From erect stand, arms extended sideward, student touches tip of index finger to tip of nose; also can bend elbows and touch tips of index fingers in front of chest.	Can the student touch precisely the place desired with eyes open, then closed? Are the movements smooth, with no tremor?
Finger agnosia: Failure to discriminate touch	With eyes closed or hands hidden from sight, the student can identify which finger or part of the finger is being touched. Sometimes, touches are simultaneously to two or three fingers or to parts of the same finger.	Can student recognize and label touches?
Right-left discriminations	Student, on command, touches right and left parts of body as well as external objects.	Can student perform both unilateral (right hand to right ear) and cross-lateral (right hand to left ear) tasks?

FIGURE 20.3

Body image work with a real skeleton is exciting. Here, the child and the skeleton are taking turns leading a *Simon Says* type game (i.e., the skeleton says," Lean to the left!").

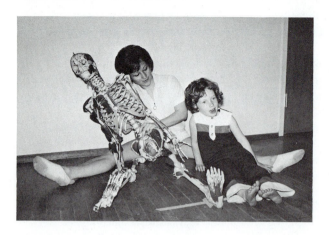

Motor Proficiency

Students with LD exhibit wide individual differences in motor proficiency. Most research is based on the Bruininks-Oseretsky Test of Motor Proficiency (BOTMP). Findings generally indicate a significant difference between students with LD and nondisabled peers, especially in the areas of balance, bilateral coordination, and fine motor visual-control (Bruininks & Bruininks, 1977; Sherrill & Pyfer, 1985). Balance is typically measured by single-leg stands and heel-toe walking. Bilateral coordination is appraised by tasks that require the upper and lower limbs to work together. Examples are (a) jumping up and clapping hands, (b) jumping up and touching heels with hands, (c) tapping feet alternately while making circles with hands, and (d) maintaining the same rhythm while simultaneously tapping with foot and index finger. Fine motor visual-control is assessed by scissors and paper-pencil tasks, with emphasis on the ability to copy circles, overlapping pencils, and other shapes.

These motor proficiency deficits have a cerebellar-vestibular basis. Levinson (1988), after a study of 4,000 individuals with LD, reported that over half (52 to 67%, depending on age group) demonstrated static balance problems, 25 to 87% had dynamic balance difficulties, and 60 to 87% failed the finger-to-finger test of kinesthesis. Levinson generalized that the greatest motor problems were balance, coordination, and rhythm.

Many authorities stress the cerebellar-vestibular basis of LD motor problems (Ayres, 1972; Quiros & Schrager, 1979; Sherrill & Pyfer, 1985). Such beliefs provide the foundation for sensorimotor-integration and perceptual-motor training. IEPs should emphasize balance, coordination, and rhythm activities and cooperative home-school programming.

Clumsiness and Apraxia

Clumsiness, the inability to perform culturally normative motor activities with age-expected proficiency, is a problem for many individuals with LD. The more complex an activity, game, or sport, the more likely that performance will be clumsy because of information processing and motor planning difficulties. These are called praxis (singular) or praxes (plural) and pertain to remembering, planning, organizing, and sequencing. These deficits can be at either the noncortical or cortical levels. Apraxia is to movement what dyslexia is to reading. There are many kinds, and none is well understood.

Louise Clarke, the mother of a boy with LD, devoted several passages to this difficulty in her excellent book:

There was a new area of incompetence too. Mike's school was very big on athletics. All the men teachers directed at least one sport, and starting in the second grade, there was a great deal of talk about who made what team.
Mike did not make any.

own mittens in an attempt to adapt them to the situation. Finally, in a mood of desperation, he placed his hand on the paper in the appropriate position and traced around two of his fingers; he repeated this procedure on the other side, thus putting fingers at the end of both arms. From this performance and on the basis of other evidence, we concluded that this boy had a finger agnosia. He was unable, except by highly devious routes, to visualize his own fingers. (Johnson & Myklebust, 1967, p. 237)

Remediation of immature body image problems through physical education involves the use of action songs, dances, games, and exercises that refer to body parts (see Figure 20.3). Provide opportunities for children to see themselves in the mirror, on videotape, and on film. Many body image activities are presented in Chapters 12, 15, 16, and 17 on perceptual-motor learning, relaxation, dance, and aquatics. Obstacle courses that require problem solving about body size and shape in order to squeeze under or through are especially excellent.

Poor Spatial Orientation

Closely allied to body image deficits are disturbances in spatial orientation. Children with LD are described as *lost in space.* They typically lose their way enroute to a destination and show confusion when given north-south-east-west and right-left directions. Moreover, they experience difficulty in estimating distance, height, width, and the other coordinates of space. As a result, they are forever bumping into things and misjudging the space requirements in such tasks as stepping through geometric forms, ducking under a low rope, and squeezing through a narrow opening. To remediate, games must involve obstacle courses, mazes, and maps. Orienteering and treasure hunts are good. Risk recreation and adventure activities in an outdoor setting give meaning to this type of programming. Instruction in cue detection is important, as well as self-talk and rehearsal, both visual and verbal.

Mr. Klein, the athletic director, was openly contemptuous, and the best Mike got from any of the male staff was amused tolerance. He wanted very much to make a team, and during vacations he and his father threw balls back and forth, or his father would throw them for him to bat. It was an endless exercise. . . .

Mike never did get the knack of it. He would miss catches by fractions of inches, but near-misses do not count in games. His batting was so erratic that his father . . . could not field them half the time. (Clarke, 1973, p. 20)

Mike, like most other children with LD, seemed to have trouble primarily in hand-eye coordination and balance. He was an excellent swimmer, winning many ribbons in competitive events from grade school on. Moreover, his strength, cardiorespiratory endurance, and running speed enabled him to perform well on fitness tests. Having completed a PhD in science at Harvard University in his 20s, Mike recalled his physical education experiences and stated,

My hand-eye coordination was never very good, and it still isn't. But I wouldn't tell dyslexics to stay away from sports, just the competitive sports that put a premium on hand-eye coordination, like baseball or handball. Anything where the margin of error is small. Tennis and squash allow for a margin of error. They demand coordination, but you can get away with it; you don't have to hit the ball every time at dead center of the racquet. (Clarke, 1973, p. 132)

From a remediation standpoint, problems can be broken down into (a) dissociation (problems in perceiving and organizing parts into wholes), (b) motor planning and sequencing (problems in organizing parts into logical or correct order), (c) motor timing and rhythm, and (d) other executive functions involved in making the body do what the mind wills. Clumsiness, the combination of apraxia and specific motor deficits like balance and incoordination, can be devastating, affecting self-efficacy, self-concept, and other dimensions of life.

Dissociation and Figure-Background

Dissociation refers to problems in perceiving and organizing parts into wholes. This ability is age-related, with young children able to make sense only of wholes. Awareness that parts make up wholes develops at about age 7 (onset of concrete mental operations), but many children do not fully grasp relationships between parts and wholes until about age 9. The ability to shift back and forth between wholes and parts is prerequisite to success in tasks that require copying or imitating a model. Delays cause frustrations in integrating and coordinating movements in response to a demonstration. They also cause problems in fine motor copying, constructing, and assembly tasks that require a finished product to look like the model.

We often say that *persons do not see whole* or that *they can't see the forest for the trees*. This ability is also related to game sense, intuitively knowing where to be and what to do. The ability to process and act on several bits of information at one time is dependent on whole-part perceptions.

Dissociation is a consideration in selecting teaching method. Problems with whole-part synthesizing and integrating generally indicate the need for whole teaching methods rather than whole-part-whole or part. Whole methodology refers to demonstration of the total pattern with no verbalization other than "Watch me." The child on the trampoline for the first time, for instance, must get the *feel* of the whole before he or she cares much about using the arms properly and landing in shoulder-width stride. Beginning instruction in throwing and striking activities should focus on the target to be hit, not on the stance, grip, backswing, release, and follow-through.

During warm-up, locomotor activities that demand the integrated working together of the whole body tend to be better than calisthenics that emphasize the movement of parts. Thus, runs, hops, jumps, animal walks, log rolls, and tumbling activities are preferable to arm flinging, side bending, toe touching, and head circling.

When students evidence success with whole methodology, instructional strategies that teach and reinforce whole-part-whole learning can be introduced. Demonstrations can include one wrong part that students are helped to identify. Emphasis can be placed also on creative movement: "Show me everything you can do with a ball; now show me one thing you like to do best; now show me three things." Another approach is, "Show me something you can do with your whole body; now show me something you can do with one body part."

Practice in getting into different game and dance formations teaches students to see themselves as parts of a whole. Creative dance, swimming, and gymnastics in which individuals or partners devise an original stunt or movement sequence and then combine it with those of others reinforce understandings of parts versus wholes. Even a pyramid formation can be taught as a whole comprised of parts.

Figure-background and depth-perception problems are part of dissociation. *Figure-background constancy* is the ability to pick one object or figure out of a complex background. For some children, however, balls and classmates blend together or float in and out of focus. Confusions pertaining to near-far, front-back, and high-low are common.

To minimize such problems, equipment and apparatus should be brightly colored to contrast with the background. Balance beams and mats should be a different color from the floor. Masking tape figures on walls and floors should utilize reds and blues, colors that have been shown to be children's favorites (see Figure 20.4). Basketball backdrops and goal cages should stand out boldly against less relevant stimuli.

Visual and auditory games that stress the locations of objects and sounds may be directed toward remediation of figure-background problems. Illustrative of these are such guessing games as *I Bet You Can't See What I See, Who's Got My Bone?, Huckleberry Beanstalk,* and *Hot and Cold*. Scavenger hunts also demand the ability to isolate relevant stimuli from the background.

FIGURE 20.4

Masking tape figures on wall help children with figure-background problems.

FIGURE 20.5

Children with rhythm problems need to gain success in moving to their own rhythm before trying to follow an externally imposed one.

Motor Planning and Sequencing

Motor planning and sequencing is an organizational ability that includes thought and action in relation to (a) initiating movement, (b) terminating movement, and (c) putting parts in correct order. Problems typically occur when attempting to imitate something that has been seen or heard. Remediation involves games, dance, water play, and gymnastic routines in which an increasing number of movements must be remembered and chained together into sequences. Movement games like *I'm Going to Grandmother's House, Copy Cat,* and *Who Can Remember How Ted Got to the Moon?* simultaneously provide practice in movement and memory.

Temporal Organization, Rhythm, and Force

Some individuals can organize parts into wholes and get them in the right order but cannot cope with rhythm. It is difficult to know whether the underlying problem is perception, organization, or a combination. In order to look right, virtually all body movements must be timed correctly. This is especially true when accuracy, speed, and force are involved.

Another manifestation of this cluster of disorders is the inability to move or dance in time with music or externally imposed rhythms. When other adolescents are developing social and romantic relationships through dance, many youth with LD miss these experiences because rhythm does not come naturally to them, and they have received no compensatory instruction.

Bilateral coordination items in the Bruininks-Oseretsky Test of Motor Proficiency (BOTMP) measure timing. This is done by synchronized, rhythmical tapping of two body parts and imitations of hands-to-thighs rhythmical patterns. This is one of the three areas in which students with LD are weakest.

Pedagogy to remediate these problems includes early instruction in music, rhythm, and dance with teachers especially trained to understand problems (see Figure 20.5). Many students with LD profit from the use of background

music or a strong percussive beat (i.e., drum or metronome) as accompaniment. The music, of course, should be carefully selected to reinforce the natural rhythm of the skill and the desired performance speed. Videotaping pairs of students (one strong, one weak) doing movement to music enables the student with LD to make visual comparisons and to develop compensatory strategies since the auditory-kinesthetic feedback circuits obviously are not working properly. Many students with LD, when dancing, do not know they are out of rhythm.

Other Executive Functions

Labeling, rehearsal, elaboration, association, organization, and chunking are among the information-processing strategies that affect academic learning, but little is known about the comparable functions in motor performance and learning (Reid, 1986, 1987). Many persons with LD say that their problem is not perception: They see, hear, and know what to do but cannot make the body perform as the mind wills.

Adults with LD, when asked to discuss motor executive functions, describe different patterns. Many say that they do not learn effectively from either demonstration or listening to instructions. Instead, they learn new motor skills best by trial and error, helped occasionally by specific, individual, corrective feedback. These people say that being labeled as impulsive or described as having attention deficits is unfair because it is natural to want the teacher to stop explaining when the words and demonstration have little meaning. The only way such individuals can achieve skill is to dig in and find out what, kinesthetically, feels right or works. Other adults with LD indicate that they think they are grasping the explanation, but something seems to happen in short-term memory. The visual and auditory input do not get encoded. Many adults with LD describe extreme difficulty with visualization of motor skills. Others insist that they learn best when one modality (visual or auditory) is used, and only one or two points are made at a time.

Instructional Strategies

Whereas adults with LD have generally given much thought to their clumsiness, children become frustrated and often give up. Spontaneous instructional strategies are not typically applied until about age 7 or 8. Children with LD show delays or absence of these strategies. Instruction must focus on how to learn (Bouffard & Wall, 1990; Vallerand & Reid, 1990; Wall, McClements, Bouffard, Finlay, & Taylor, 1986).

Metacognitive Strategy Instruction

Metacognitive strategy instruction is effective in improving academic skills of persons with LD (Harris & Pressley, 1991; Palincsar, 1986) and offers promise in motor learning. *Metacognition* is personal knowledge about the ways we think, move, and learn. Individual and small-group sessions create an atmosphere in which students with LD talk freely about their motor-learning problems. Only through such sharing can the teacher come to know how students learn and provide meaningful input about learning strategies. Students with LD have little insight into visualization, self-talk, spontaneous rehearsal, and the like. Once made aware of these processes, they need gentle and persistent help in making them workable.

Use of new strategies may be tiring and fraught with uncertainty and anxiety. Thus, class instruction should offer a balance between traditional learning (imitation and following verbal instruction) and movement exploration. Originality in responding to movement challenges may be a strength of children with LD (Holguin & Sherrill, 1989). Movement education, creative dance, and games that utilize original ideas and dramatic themes are especially recommended (i.e., sometimes, it is good to teach toward strengths instead of weaknesses). Instruction in relaxation is also important.

Modality-Based Instruction

Modality-based instruction is an approach for students who learn better when information is presented through one modality (visual or auditory) rather than both, as is the tradition in physical education. Research shows that most persons are mixed-modality learners by age 7 or 8. About 20 to 25% of children with LD, however, are visual preference learners,

and about 10% are auditory preference learners. For these children, presenting information in the preferred modality may be better. Clinicians typically support preferred modality teaching (Dunn, 1990; Guild & Garger, 1985), whereas researchers question it (Kavale & Forness, 1987, 1990). Sherrill supports modality-based instruction.

Cognitive Style Matching

Cognitive style refers to the individual's approach to analyzing and responding to stimuli. When the student's style matches that of the teacher, there are few problems. If styles are widely divergent, however, both persons must learn tolerance. Cognitive styles are designated by bipolar adjectives: (a) field dependent, field independent, (b) global, analytical, and (c) impulsive, reflective. Field-dependent (FD) people are strongly influenced by the visual field. They see wholes and have trouble finding embedded figures and coping with details. Moreover, they tend to have a fast conceptual tempo, spend little time planning, and need external structure. Field-independent (FI) people exhibit the opposite behaviors (Guild & Garger, 1985).

Either extreme is associated with learning disabilities. The younger persons are, the more likely they are to be field dependent. This helps to explain why children typically are not much interested in details. Persons with LD are more likely to be FD than FI (Lazarus, 1990). Awareness of cognitive styles helps teachers to match instructional demands to strengths. Then, gradually, they can remediate weaknesses.

Self-Talk and Verbal Rehearsal

A self-talk and verbal rehearsal strategy is successful in helping children to learn motor sequences, improve game performance, and control impulsivity (Kowalski & Sherrill, 1992). *Self-talk* usually refers to talking oneself through an activity or sequence. It is simultaneous talking and moving. When the student does jumping jacks, for instance, he or she says *out* as the limbs spread and *in* as they return to midline. When a locomotor pattern is performed, the child says aloud *jump, jump, step, step, step, hop-2–3-4.*

Verbal rehearsal is saying aloud the parts of a planned movement before execution. This is often in response to the teacher's request, "Tell me the three things you are going to do." With guidance, students learn to ask and answer their own questions.

Motivation and Self-Concept Enhancement

Students with LD typically have lower self-concepts and more external locus of control than nondisabled peers (Sherrill & Pyfer, 1985; Switzky & Schultz, 1988; Tarnowski & Nay, 1989). The reason for this seems to be the accumulation of failure after failure and the inability of parents and teachers to help students build areas of competence that offset acknowledged weaknesses and deficits. External locus of control is manifested by low motivation and passivity. Such responses are easily understood if one considers how it must feel to visualize failure before starting each day.

Not all students with LD manifest these problems. Scores on self-concept inventories depend on reference groups. When students with LD attend private schools and/or use peers with LD for their social, academic, and motor comparisons, the self-concept seems to be higher than most research indicates. Only about 1% of all students with LD attend private schools, however.

Teams and partners in the integrated gymnasium should be assigned with great care, rather than left to chance. These become the new reference groups and significant others for persons with LD. Games and sports should be adapted to emphasize cooperation rather than competition. For example, volleyball can be changed to a "How long can you keep the ball in the air?" theme. Basketball can be changed to give points for number of passes completed before shooting.

Enhancement of self-concept through success-oriented movement experiences and concomitant individual and small-group counseling is the most important physical education goal for students with LD. Closely related to this goal is helping students with LD gain peer acceptance and make one or two really close friendships that carry over into leisure-time activities. Curriculum models with particular promise are cooperative games (Mender, Kerr, & Orlick, 1982), motor creativity (Sherrill, 1986), games design (Morris & Stiehl, 1989), and social-personal development (Hellison, 1985; Johnson & Johnson, 1986). See Chapters 6 and 8 for a review of these models and techniques for enhancing self-concept.

Fitness and Leisure Concerns

Students with LD must be helped to find one or two lifetime physical activities that they can do well enough to feel the satisfaction needed to maintain an active, healthy lifestyle. Although research indicates that individuals with LD are inferior to nondisabled peers on fitness tasks, such findings probably reflect differences in experience and motivation rather than capacity deficits. Students with LD in private schools that employ physical education specialists and provide daily physical education instruction score average or better on standardized fitness tests. There is no neurological reason why individuals with LD cannot excel in strength, cardiorespiratory endurance, and flexibility.

Teachers in LD private schools report that many of their students do well in soccer. There appear to be fewer coordination problems in foot-eye than in hand-eye ball activities. Students with LD need exposure to competitive sport in accordance with the principle of normalization. Much can be learned from carefully structured teamwork that emphasizes cooperation, sharing, and sportsmanship. Review Chapter 5 in regard to age-appropriate programming, competition, and sport socialization. Remember that children with LD are often delayed in social competence. Private schools in the Dallas-Fort Worth area have developed a soccer league for students with LD so that initial competitive sport experience is against peers with similar skills in a carefully monitored, success-oriented environment.

The play and leisure activities of individuals with LD tend to be different from that of nondisabled peers.

Children with LD engage in significantly more solitary play and hold inferior sociometric status compared to others (Gottlieb, Gottlieb, Berkell, & Levy, 1986). Their leisure activities tend to be passive and accompanied by feelings of loneliness (Margalit, 1984). Many demonstrate a kind of learned helplessness in regard to initiating activities with others and depend on their parents and siblings for recreational activities.

The game choices of children with LD have been studied by Cratty, Ikeda, Martin, Jennett, and Morris (1970), who concluded that clumsy children tend to avoid vigorous, active games, particularly those involving direct contact, such as football, wrestling, and boxing. Boys with movement problems seemed to prefer some type of fantasy play in which "pretend" bravery could be evidenced (spaceman, cowboy, cops and robbers). This was not true of boys of the same age representing the normal population.

Although research on the play and leisure of students with LD is sparse, there is strong indication that leisure education and counseling should be integrated into physical education instruction. School-community partnerships should utilize the expertise of therapeutic recreation specialists and foster generalization of school learning to use of community resources.

Separation of LD From Attention Deficits and Hyperactivity

Since 1980, LD, attention deficit disorders (ADD), and hyperactivity (H) have been recognized as distinctly separate conditions that can occur independently or in combination with other conditions. Three distinct subtypes are recognized: LD only, LD-ADD, and LD-ADDH. Physical education programming obviously differs for each of these groups. Diagnoses of only ADD or ADD-H also are possible, or these diagnoses can be made in conjunction with other conditions.

Hyperkinesis and *hyperactivity* are often used as synonyms. According to the American Psychiatric Association (1980), this is no longer appropriate. *Hyperkinesis,* or hyperkinetic syndrome, is a combination of attention problems, impulsivity, and hyperactivity (ADD-H). In contrast, *hyperactivity* is comprised of two or more specific excessive movement behaviors (see Table 20.2). Many children meet the diagnostic criteria for inattention and impulsivity (see Table 20.2) but not for hyperactivity. Churton (1989) provided an excellent review of literature on hyperkinesis or ADD-H, concluding that there is no definitive consensus on nomenclature, etiology, treatment, and symptomology. Churton (1989) noted that various authors report prevalence rates of 3 to 25%.

Attention Deficit Disorder With Hyperactivity

Inattention, impulsivity, and hyperactivity obviously affect physical education programming. Remediation should be directed toward the specific indicators in Table 20.2, and physical educators should work closely with classroom teachers in implementing behavior management programs. Physical educators should also be aware of students who are taking medication for ADD-H or are on special diets.

Table 20.2
Diagnostic criteria for ADD-H used by physicians.

A. **Inattention.** At least three of the following:
1. Often fails to finish things he or she starts
2. Often doesn't seem to listen
3. Is easily distracted
4. Has difficulty concentrating on schoolwork or other tasks requiring sustained attention
5. Has difficulty sticking to a play activity

B. **Impulsivity.** At least three of the following:
1. Often acts before thinking
2. Shifts excessively from one activity to another
3. Has difficulty organizing work (this not being due to cognitive impairment)
4. Needs a lot of supervision
5. Frequently calls out in class
6. Has difficulty awaiting turn in games or group situations

C. **Hyperactivity.** At least two of the following:
1. Runs about or climbs on things excessively
2. Has difficulty sitting still or fidgets excessively
3. Has difficulty staying seated
4. Moves about excessively during sleep
5. Is always "on the go" or acts as if "driven by a motor"

D. **Onset** before the age of 7 years

E. **Duration** of at least 6 months

F. **Not due to** schizophrenia, affective disorder, or severe or profound mental retardation

Note. From American Psychiatric Association: *Diagnostic and Statistical Manual of Mental Disorders,* Third Edition, Revised, Washington, DC, American Psychiatric Association, 1987.

Inattention

Inattention encompasses many separate processes. Among these are *selective attention* (the ability to pick up and attend to the central or desired stimulus), *concentration* (the ability to sustain attention, presumably in an environment conducive to learning), *narrow focusing* (the ability to narrow attention to a particular task in spite of distractions), and *broad focusing* (the ability to effectively attend to many stimuli at one time). Time-on-task is often the way attention is measured.

Attention is affected by many variables. Among these are age (the younger the child, the less able to block out irrelevant detail), degree of difficulty (the harder the task, the shorter the duration of concentration), the number and intensity of distractors in the environment, the novelty and/or interest and fun features of the activity, changes in weather and humidity, and the like. Moreover, definite attentional styles appear to be related to external and internal locus of control, motivation, and incentive (Nideffer, 1977). Some persons attend well to external stimuli, whereas others concentrate better on ideas and tasks that come from within.

Stimuli overload seems to be a particular factor in ADD. Students cannot block out irrelevant stimuli and thus seem driven to react to everything. Admonishing such pupils to *pay attention* is useless. They would if they could. Instead, such a pupil reacts to

the grinding of the pencil sharpener, to the colors of dozens of shirts and dresses which surround him, to the movement of the child next to him across the aisle, to an announcement on the intercommunication system, to the leaves on the tree blowing in the wind outside the room, to the movement of the goldfish in the aquarium, to another child who just sneezed, to the teacher's whispers to yet a third child, to the footsteps of a group of children walking past his room in the hall, to the crack at the top of his desk into which his pencil point will just fit, to the American flag hanging in the front of the room, to the Thanksgiving Day decorations on the walls, to dozens and dozens of other unessential things in the room which prevent him from writing his name on the top line! It isn't that he refuses to cooperate with the teacher's request to "start here." It is that he simply cannot refrain from reacting to the unessential stimuli in his environment. This is, we think, the result of a neurological impairment. (Cruickshank, 1967, p. 33)

Inattention consists mainly of errors of omission rather than commission. The main problem is failure to finish tasks.

Impulsivity or Disinhibition

In contrast, impulsivity results from errors of commission. *Impulsivity* is the tendency to move without carefully considering alternatives. It is the opposite of reflectivity. Impulsive individuals finish tasks quickly, often with lots of errors. They are typically the first ones done, demanding "What do we do next?" Because they do not consider alternatives, they are sometimes perceived as conceptually rigid.

Impulsivity is also associated with *field dependence,* a perceptual-cognitive-behavioral style descriptive of persons who are dependent upon the environment (i.e., the field) rather than their own ideas and internal motivation (Lazarus, 1990). Field dependence is a lack of inhibitory control, a *forced responsiveness* to the field that leads persons to try to please significant others. Impulsivity, or field dependence, is characteristic of young children. As youth mature, they become increasingly reflective or field independent.

Impulsive children may display *catastrophic reactions* to unexpected stimuli like a sharp noise, a scary incident in a movie, or a playful jab from a teammate. They tend to fall apart, to sob uncontrollably, to scream, or to display sudden outbursts of anger or physical aggression.

Hyperactivity

The hyperactive child manifests disorders of listening, thinking, reading, writing, spelling, or arithmetic primarily because he or she cannot sit still long enough to complete a task. Such children are forever wiggling, shuffling their feet, swinging their legs, doodling, pinching, chewing gum, gritting their teeth, and talking to themselves or others. They seem never to tire and require unbelievably little sleep. They have been described as

being up by 5:05 A.M., into the kitchen by 5:08 A.M., having the pans out of the cupboard by 5:09 A.M., mixing the flour and sugar on the floor by 5:11 A.M., walking through it in bare feet by 5:15 A.M., turning attention to the living room drapes by 5:18 A.M., and inadvertently knocking over a table lamp at 5:20 A.M. This wakens all members of the family, who individually and collectively descend on the first-floor scene, and thus begins another day of tension, discipline, and frustration. (Cruickshank, 1967, p. 34)

Hyperactivity may be worse on some days than others. Classroom teachers have been known to send the child to the playground on such days: "You take him. . . . I can't teach him a thing in the classroom."

Hyperactivity should not be confused with individual differences in energy, impulse control, and enthusiasm. All toddlers exhibit problems with impulse control. This is evidenced when children of different ages are asked: "How slowly can you draw a line from this point to that point?" or, "How slowly can you walk across the room?" or, "How slowly can you do tasks in the Bruininks-Oseretsky tests?" The older the child is, the more easily he or she can slow down the pace and consciously determine the tempo. Impulse control may be related to hyperactive behavior, but it is not the same thing.

Other Behavioral Problems

Other behavioral problems are associated with neurological soft signs (e.g., conceptual rigidity, inappropriate reactions, perseveration) and misunderstandings that stem from deficits in listening, thinking, and speaking skills.

Social Imperception

Inadequacies of social perception—namely, the inability to recognize the meaning and significance of the behavior of others—contribute to poor social adjustment. Problems in this area occur concomitantly with both LD and ADD-H.

Children with LD often have difficulty in making and keeping friends of their own age. Attention deficits, impulsivity, and hyperactivity are complicated further by their inability to deal with abstractions and double meanings. They become the butt of jokes when they cannot share the multiple meanings of such words as *screw, ball, grass, pot,* and *head.* Moreover, much of the humor in our society is abstract and entirely lost on them. Because they fail to comprehend the subtleties of facial expression, tone of voice, and body language, they do not realize that they are angering, antagonizing, or boring others until some kind of explosion erupts. They retreat with hurt feelings, wondering why the others *blew up all of a sudden* or told them *to get out and leave them alone.*

With severely involved children, play should seldom, if ever, be left unstructured. It is far better to delimit the activity with "You may play cowboys and Indians with John and Chris in Room 121 for 20 min" than to allow the group interaction to continue indefinitely, ultimately ending with a fight of some kind. In schools that have daily recess, the teacher should specify ahead of time names of persons who have permission to play together, the space on the playground they may occupy, and the equipment they may use. Children with social imperception are given freedom only in small degrees, as they demonstrate increasing ability to cope in social situations.

Perseveration

Often interpreted as stubbornness, perseveration is the inability to shift easily from one idea or activity to another. Perseveration is present when a pupil

1. Continues to grind on and on long after a pencil is sharpened.
2. Continues to bounce the ball after the signal for stopping has been given.
3. Continues to laugh or giggle after everyone else stops.
4. Repeats the same phrase over and over or gets hung up on one topic of conversation.

Perseveration is the opposite of distractibility. It contributes to a behavioral rigidity, which is evidenced in games when the student refuses to adapt rules or to test a new strategy. One approach to remediation is creativity training with emphasis on fluency and flexibility.

Another approach is to plan activities that are distinctly different from each other in formation, starting position, basic skills, rules, and strategies. A circle game, for instance, might be followed by a relay in files. In circuit training, a station stressing arm and shoulder strength might be followed by one emphasizing jumping activities. Games based upon stop-and-go concepts reinforce the ability to make transitions from one activity to another. Illustrative of these are *Red Light, Green Light, Musical Chairs, Cakewalks, Statues,* and *Squirrels in the Trees.*

Principles for Managing Environment

The concepts of Cruickshank (1967) and Strauss and Lehtinen (1947) continue to shape the educational prescriptions of students with behavioral problems. A good teaching environment is based upon four principles:

1. Establishment of a highly structured program
2. Reduction of environmental space
3. Elimination of irrelevant auditory and visual stimuli
4. Enhancement of the stimulus value of the instructional materials

Structure

The principle of *structure,* as applied to the physical education setting, requires the establishment of a routine that is repeated day after day and leaves nothing to chance. For instance, the pattern of activities should follow the same sequence each period: sitting on prescribed floor spots while waiting for class to begin, warm-ups always done in the same area and facing the same direction, introduction and practice of new skills, participation in games or dances, return to floor spots, and sitting during *cool-down* period of relaxation and discussion.

If instructional stations are used, a certain piece of apparatus should always be located in the same space and the students should always mount it from the same direction. Rotation from station to station should always be in the same direction, traditionally counterclockwise. Characteristically, after warm-ups, each student goes to his or her assigned station to start instruction, and rotation always proceeds from the same spot. Identical start, stop, and rotation signals also contribute to structure since the child knows precisely which response is appropriate for each signal.

Moreover, the composition of each squad or team should be structured in much the same fashion as are groups for play therapy or psychotherapy. A balance is maintained between the number of hyperactive and sluggish children so that one behavioral extreme tends to neutralize the other. The proportion of aggressors and nonaggressors is weighted, as are natural leaders and followers.

Structure also denotes a carefully planned system of behavior management in operation. Cues and consequences are consistent. See Chapter 9 for a review of behavior management.

Space Reduction

The principle of *space reduction* suggests the use of lane markers and partitions to delimit the vast expanse of play area considered desirable for normal children. Special emphasis must be given to boundaries and the penalties incumbent upon stepping out-of-bounds. The major value of low organized games may be learning about boundaries, baselines, and space utilization.

Space reduction necessarily limits the size of the squads, which rotate from station to station. Most elementary school children function well in groups of six to eight; children with LD often require smaller groups.

Extraneous Stimuli Control

The principle of *extraneous stimuli control* demands the maintenance of a neat, clean, well-ordered play area. No balls or equipment are in sight unless they are required for the game in progress. When several squads are each practicing different motor tasks, often on different pieces of apparatus, the student's attention may be diverted by persons at other stations. Partitions to eliminate the extraneous visual stimuli from other stations prevent problems. Similar distractions are present when physical education is held outdoors: Cars in the nearby street, neighborhood animals, leaves rustling on the trees, birds flying overhead, weeds among the grass where the ball is rolling, even the wind and sun command the child's attention. The student with severe hyperactivity should be scheduled only for indoor physical education, where environmental variables can be more easily controlled.

Instructional Stimulus Enhancement

The principle of *instructional stimulus enhancement,* as applied to the physical education setting, implies the extensive and concentrated use of color to focus and hold the student's attention on a particular piece of apparatus, a target, or a ball. Sound may be used similarly. Wall-to-wall mirrors in which students can see and learn to evaluate their motor performance also seem to increase concentration (see Figure 20.6).

The principles of structure, space reduction, stimuli control, and instructional stimulus enhancement form the basis of a sound physical education program for students with LD. Freedom is increased gradually in accordance with the student's ability to cope.

FIGURE 20.6

Mirrors are extremely important in learning disabilities because visual input enhances kinesthetic and vestibular feedback.

Modifying Physical Education Content

Students with ADD-H obviously need a different kind of physical education content than that which exists in most regular physical education settings. Emphasis should be on learning relaxation techniques (see Chapter 15), impulse control, and sport, dance, and aquatic activities that encourage reflectivity and attention to detail. Individual and small-group counseling helps students to set personal goals for managing their behavior in school and community facilities where fitness and leisure skills are pursued.

The goal, of course, is to learn self-control and self-responsibility requisite to social acceptance in afterschool and weekend youth sport. This can be achieved when teachers systematically apply the content in this chapter and related literature (Decker & Voege, 1992).

Medication

ADD-H is a medical problem. Most physicians use medication only as a last resort. Nevertheless, a large number of youngsters with ADD-H are so uncontrollable that drugs are prescribed: *ritalin* (methyiphenidate), *dexedrine, benzedrine, methedrine,* and *cylert,* all of which are stimulants. These stimulants slow down the child, increase the attention span, and help with concentration (Forness & Kavale, 1988). Use of stimulants in hyperactivity is analogous to prescription of insulin for diabetes. Both conditions involve deficits in body chemistry for which drugs compensate.

Children do not become addicted to the drugs used in ADD-H, and there are no withdrawal problems. The main side effects are depressed appetite and sleeplessness, according to medical sources. Physical educators note, however, that these medications sometimes affect balance and coordination.

References

American Psychiatric Association. (1980). *Diagnostic and statistical manual of mental disorders* (3rd ed.). Washington, DC: Author.

Auxter, D., & Pyfer, P. (1989). *Principles and methods of adapted physical education and recreation.* St. Louis: Times Mirror/Mosby College.

Ayres, A. J. (1972). *Sensory integration and learning disorders.* Los Angeles: Western Psychological Services.

Board of Trustees, Council for Learning Disabilities. (1986). Measurement and training of perceptual and perceptual-motor functions. *Learning Disabilities Quarterly, 9* (3), 247.

Bouffard, M, & Wall, A. E. (1990). A problem-solving approach to movement skill acquisition: Implications for special populations. In G. Reid (Ed.), *Problems in movement control* (pp. 107–131). Amsterdam: North-Holland.

Bruininks, V., & Bruininks, R. (1977). Motor proficiency of learning disabled and nondisabled students. *Perceptual and Motor Skills, 44,* 1131–1137.

Churton, M. (1989). Hyperkinesis: A review of literature. *Adapted Physical Activity Quarterly, 6* (4), 313–327.

Clarke, L. (1973). *Can't read, can't write, can't takl too good either.* New York: Walker & Company.

Cohen, H. J., Coker, J. W., Crain, L. S., Healy, A., Katcher, A., Openheimer, S. G., & Weisskopf, B. (1985). School-aged children with motor disabilities, *Pediatrics, 76* (4), 648–649.

Cratty, B. J. (1971). *Active learning.* Englewood Cliffs, NJ: Prentice-Hall.

Cratty, B. J. (1972). *Physical expressions of intelligence.* Englewood Cliffs, NJ: Prentice-Hall.

Cratty, B. J., Ikeda, N., Martin, M., Jennett, C., & Morris, M. (1970). Game choices of children with movement problems. In B. J. Cratty (Ed.), *Movement abilities, motor ability, and the education of children* (pp. 45–85). Springfield, IL: Charles C. Thomas.

Cratty, B. J., & Martin, M. M. (1969). *Perceptual-motor efficiency in children.* Philadelphia: Lea & Febiger.

Cruickshank, W. (1967). *The brain-injured child in home, school, and community.* Syracuse: Syracuse University Press.

Decker, J., & Voege, D. (1992). Integrating children with attention deficit disorder with hyperactivity into youth sport. *Palaestra, 8*(4), 16–20.

Dunn, R. (1990). Bias over substance: A critical analysis of Kavale and Forness' report on modality-based instruction. *Exceptional Children, 56* (4), 357–361.

Forness, S., & Kavale, K. (1988). Psychopharmacological treatment: A note on classroom effects. *Journal of Learning Disabilities, 21* (3), 144–147.

Gottlieb, B. W., Gottlieb, J., Berkell, D., & Levy, L. (1986). Sociometric status and solitary play of LD boys and girls. *Journal of Learning Disabilities, 19* (10), 619–622.

Guild, P., & Garger, S. (1985). *Marching to different drummers.* Alexandria, VA: Association for Supervision and Curriculum Development.

Hallahan, D., & Cruickshank, W. (1973). *Psychoeducational foundations of learning disabilities.* Englewood Cliffs, NJ: Prentice-Hall.

Harris, K. R., & Pressley, M. (1991). The nature of cognitive strategy instruction: Interactive strategy construction. *Exceptional Children, 57* (5), 392–404.

Haubenstricker, J. L. (1983). Motor development in children with learning disabilities. *Journal of Physical Education, Recreation, and Dance, 53,* 41–43.

Hellison, D. R. (1985). *Goals and strategies for teaching physical education.* Champaign, IL: Human Kinetics.

Holguin, O., & Sherrill, C. (1989). Use of a motor creativity test with young learning disabled boys. *Perceptual and Motor Skills, 69,* 1315–1318.

Johnson, D. J., & Myklebust, H. R. (1967). *Learning disabilities.* New York: Grune & Stratton.

Johnson, D. W., & Johnson, R. T. (1986). Mainstreaming and cooperative learning strategies. *Exceptional Children, 52* (6), 553–561.

Kavale, K. A., & Forness, S. R. (1987). Substance over style: Assessing the efficacy of modality testing and teaching. *Exceptional Children, 54* (3), 228–239.

Kavale, K. A., & Forness, S. R. (1990). Substance over style: A rejoinder to Dunn's animadversions. *Exceptional Children, 56* (4), 357–361.

Kavale, K., & Mattson, P. D. (1983). One jumped off the balance beam: Meta-analysis of perceptual motor training. *Journal of Learning Disabilities, 16,* 165–173.

Kephart, N. C. (1971). *The slow learner in the classroom* (2nd ed.). Columbus, OH: Charles E. Merrill.

Kowalski, E., & Sherrill, C. (1992). Modeling and motor sequencing strategies of learning-disabled boys. *Adapted Physical Activity Quarterly, 9* (3), 261–272.

Lazarus, J. A. (1990). Factors underlying inefficient movement in learning-disabled children. In G. Reid (Ed.), *Problems in motor control: Advances in psychology series* (pp. 241–282). Amsterdam: North-Holland.

Lerner, J. (1988). *Learning disabilities* (5th ed.). Boston: Houghton Mifflin.

Levinson, H. N. (1988). The cerebellar-vestibular basis of learning disabilities in children, adolescents, and adults: Hypothesis and study. *Perceptual and Motor Skills, 67,* 983–1006.

Margalit, M. (1984). Leisure activities of learning disabled children as a reflection of their passive lifestyle and prolonged dependency. *Child Psychiatry and Human Development, 15* (2), 133–141.

Mender, J., Kerr, R., & Orlick, T. (1982). A cooperative games program for learning disabled children. *International Journal of Sport Psychology, 13,* 222–233.

Morris, G. S. D., & Stiehl, D. (1989). *Changing kids' games.* Champaign, IL: Human Kinetics.

Nideffer, R. M. (1977). *Test of attentional and interpersonal style.* San Diego, CA: Enhanced Performance Associates.

Palincsar, A. S. (1986). Metacognitive strategy instruction. *Exceptional Children, 53* (2), 118–124.

Quiros, J. B., & Schrager, O.L. (1979). *Neuropsychological fundamentals in learning disabilities.* Novato, CA: Academic Therapy.

Reid, G. (1986). The trainability of motor processing strategies with developmentally delayed performers. In H. A. Whiting & M. Wade (Eds.), *Themes in motor development* (pp. 93–107). Hingham, MA: Kluwer-Academic Publishers.

Reid, G. (1987). Motor behavior and psychosocial correlates in young handicapped performers. In D. Gould & M. R. Weiss (Eds.), *Advances in pediatric sport sciences, Volume 2* (pp. 235–258). Champaign, IL: Human Kinetics.

Sherrill, C. (1972). Learning disabilities. In H. Fait, *Special physical education* (3rd ed.) (pp. 168–182). Philadelphia: W. B. Saunders.

Sherrill, C. (1986). Fostering creativity in handicapped children. *Adapted Physical Activity Quarterly, 3,* 236–249.

Sherrill, C., & Pyfer, J. (1985). Learning disabled students in physical education. *Adapted Physical Activity Quarterly, 2* (4), 283–291.

Strauss, A. A., & Lehtinen, L. (1947). *Psychopathology and education of the brain-injured child.* New York: Grune & Stratton.

Switzky, H. N., & Schultz, G. F. (1988). Intrinsic motivation and learning performance: Implications for individual education programming for learners with mild handicaps. *Remedial and Special Education, 9* (4), 7–14.

Tarnowski, K. J., & Nay, S. M. (1989). Locus of control in children with learning disabilities and hyperactivity: A subgroup analysis. *Journal of Learning Disabilities, 22* (6), 381–383, 391.

U.S. Department of Education. (1989). *Eleventh annual report to Congress on the implementation of the Education of the Handicapped Act.* Washington, DC: Author.

Vallerand, R. J., & Reid, G. (1990). Motivation and special populations: Theory, research, and implications regarding motor behavior (pp. 159–197). In G. Reid (Ed.), *Problems in movement control.* Amsterdam: North-Holland.

Wall, A., McClements, J., Bouffard, M., Findlay, H., & Taylor, M. (1986). A knowledge-based approach to motor development: Implications for the physically awkward. *Adapted Physical Activity Quarterly, 2,* 21–42.

CHAPTER

21

Mental Retardation and Special Olympics

FIGURE   21.1

Special Olympics has demonstrated the potential of persons with mental retardation to the world. (*A*) Eunice Kennedy Shriver, the founder of Special Olympics, provides encouragement. (*B*) Action from the Little Stanley Cup game, a feature event of the International Special Olympics floor hockey tournament in Toronto, Ontario.

A

B

After you have studied this chapter, you should be able to:

1. State four criteria for educational diagnosis of mental retardation and discuss each part in relation to programming.

2. Summarize concepts that relate to normal curve theory, including the natural genetic distribution of IQs.

3. Discuss medical etiologies of MR, including syndromes. What percentage of persons with MR have medical etiologies?

4. Identify the three most frequently occurring syndromes associated with MR and discuss each.

5. Discuss motor and cognitive abilities of persons with MR. What are some implications for assessment and programming?

6. Explain how programming differs according to level of MR and give examples of models appropriate to guide programming.

7. Develop some task analyses and state cues, feedback, and reinforcement for each step.

8. Contrast and critique different programming models. See example by Greenwood, Silliman, and French (1990). Also read Krebs and Block (1992).

9. Describe Special Olympics programming and discuss how you would organize and implement a year-round program.

10. Given profiles of persons with MR, write IEPs and lesson plans.

Mental retardation (MR) is perhaps the best known of all disabilities because Special Olympics has given it so much visibility (see Figure 21.1). Definitions of MR, however, vary throughout the world. In the United States, mental retardation is distinguished from learning disabilities by federal law that specifies different diagnostic and funding categories. In contrast, Great Britain uses the terms *learning difficulty* and *special educational needs* instead of mental retardation (Sugden & Keogh, 1990). Much of the world prefers the term *mental handicap* over *mental retardation* and uses a broader diagnostic approach than the United States. In recognition of this, Special Olympics has changed its eligibility criteria to

persons at least 8 years old who are identified as having mental retardation, or who have handicapping conditions because of cognitive delays and have significant learning or vocational problems (to the extent that, if of school age, they are receiving specially designed instruction for at least 50% of their instructional day) . . . cognitive delays refer to significantly lower intellectual functioning or performance. (Special Olympics International, 1989a, p. 6)

Recognition of cognitive delays as an essential indicator of MR requires review of Chapter 5, which emphasizes age-appropriate programming. Cognitive delays affect many areas of function. Environmental constraints and affordances, however, often determine the extent that delays are limiting. The challenge is to afford opportunities for living and learning that are appropriate to chronological age and that facilitate social and community acceptance. This means being guided by the principle of normalization. Also important is the principle of ecological or social validity (i.e., meaningfulness and generalizability).

Changing Definitions

In 1992, the diagnostic criteria for mental retardation in the United States were broadened by the American Association on Mental Retardation to create a four-part definition (Luckasson et al., 1992). *Mental retardation*

1. Refers to substantial limitations in certain personal capabilities.

2. Is manifested as significantly subaverage intellectual functioning.

3. Exists concurrently with related disabilities in two or more of the following *adaptive skill areas:*

—Communications	—Self-care
—Home living	—Social skills
—Community use	—Self-direction
—Health and safety	—Functional academics
—Work	—Leisure

4. Begins before age 18.

This definition is similar to one used by the American Association on Mental Retardation (AAMR) in the 1970s and 1980s and in federal law. The older definition states that MR refers to "significantly subaverage general intellectual functioning existing concurrently with deficits in adaptive behaviors and manifested during the developmental period" (Grossman, 1983, p. 1). The problem with this definition was that many persons did not understand the meaning of *adaptive behaviors* and *developmental period*. The new definition makes meanings clear by specifying what the adaptive skill areas are and indicating age 18 as the ceiling for identification. The 1992 AAMR reference book by Ruth Luckasson and colleagues replaces the Grossman (1983) text as the definitive source for all background information on MR.

Intelligence Tests

The personal capabilities that are most limited in MR are abstract thinking, concept formation, generalization, problem solving, and evaluation. Significant subaverage intellectual functioning is defined as an IQ lower than 70 to 75, based on assessment that includes one or more individually administered intelligence tests (AAMR, 1992). Earlier references

FIGURE 21.2

Theoretical distribution of IQ scores based on normal curve with 10
standard deviations to show mentally retarded, normal, and gifted
classifications assigned on basis of Wechsler and Stanford Binet test
scores.

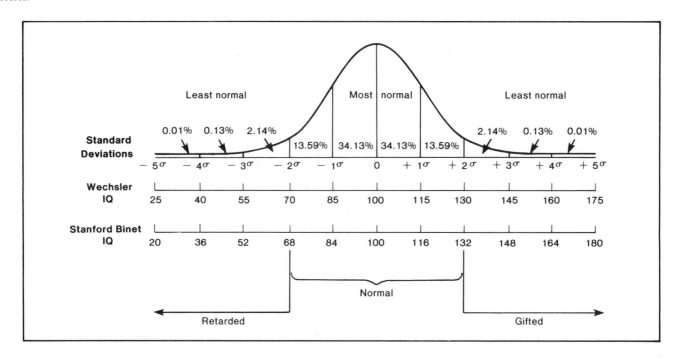

defined subaverage as any IQ that fell two or more standard
deviations below the mean (see Figure 21.2). This concept
continues to be accepted, although the 70 to 75 criterion is
less rigid, recognizing that IQs may vary a few points from
test to test.

Many standardized tests are used to assess IQ. The
oldest is the Stanford-Binet Intelligence Scale (also known
as the Terman-Merrill Scale), which has a mean of 100 and
a standard deviation of 16. Figure 21.2 shows markers of 84,
68, 52, and so on when 16 is subtracted from 100 and each
subsequent marker. Newer tests like the Wechsler Intelligence Scale for Children-Revised (WISC-R), the Kaufman
Assessment Battery for Children, and the Slosson Intelligence Test all have a mean of 100 and a standard deviation
of 15. Subtracting this standard deviation from 100 and subsequent markers yields 85, 70, 55, and so on. A 70 on the
Wechsler is thus equivalent to a 68 on the Stanford-Binet;
both IQs are 2 standard deviations below the mean and indicate that general intellectual function is lower than that of
97% of the population.

Level of Severity

Prior to the 1990s, IQs were specified for four levels of MR
function: (a) mild, 52–70; (b) moderate, 36–51; (c) severe,
20–35; and (d) profound, 19 and lower. About 90% of persons with MR fell into the mild classification, 5% into the
moderate, and 3.5% and 1.5%, respectively, into the severe
and profound.

The 1992 policy revision recognizes only two classifications of MR: (a) mild and (b) severe. These are not
based on IQ but on level of function within adaptive skill
levels. Thus, IQ, if correctly used, will be relevant only in the
first stage of a multidimensional classification system. The
emphasis will be on assessment of disability (mild or severe)
in communications, home living, community use, health and
safety, work, self-care, social skills, self-direction, and functional academics, and leisure.

The use of only two severity classifications is controversial. Block (1992), for example, emphasizes the need
to distinguish between severe and profound function levels.
Severe sometimes refers to persons with good levels of awareness and adequate resources to respond, learn, and function
in integrated community settings when extensive support is
provided. In contrast, *profound* denotes persons with very
limited awareness and response repertoires.

Prevalence

Prevalence of MR is generally estimated as 3% of the total
population, a figure based partly on normal curve theory. This
theory posits that 2.28% of the population will be born with
low intelligence and that an equal percentage will be born
gifted. To understand how the estimated 2.28% is derived,
look at Figure 21.2 and note the percentage of the population
that falls into the third, fourth, and fifth standard deviation
areas (2.14 + .13 + .01 = 2.28). Most MR is the result of

this natural genetic distribution of intelligence. The remaining MR (less than 1% of the total population) has an organic (medical) etiology.

The 1990 U.S. Census figure of 250 million U.S. citizens can be used to infer that the United States now has approximately 7.5 million citizens with MR. The varying criteria in different countries make estimates of mild MR especially difficult. Severe MR (generally defined as IQ under 50) has an incidence of about 3 to 5 per 1,000 in developed countries (Sugden & Keogh, 1990).

Persons with MR comprise the third largest disability group receiving special education in the United States. Almost 600,000 students in the age range from 6 to 21 years receive services. The placement distribution of these is regular class, 6%; resource room, 22%; separate class, 59%; separate school, 11%; residential facilities, 1.5%; and homebound/hospital, 0.5%. Children younger than 6 are not typically categorized by disability, so data are not available on them.

In striking contrast to the past, few persons with MR live in large residential facilities. Among the 6- to 21-year-old group, only 1.5% are in residential facilities. These are usually children with multiple disabilities, IQs of less than 35, from dysfunctional or nonexistent families. Adults with MR who used to live in institutions now mostly reside in the community in small-group homes accommodating six or fewer persons. They still receive mental health/mental retardation (MH/MR) services from a central agency, but living and learning arrangements are as close to those of nondisabled persons as possible. An adult counselor may live with them or visit regularly. Federal legislation and the Accreditation Council for Facilities for the Mentally Retarded (ACFMR) are largely responsible for these changes.

Etiology and Medical Classification

Etiology of MR is generally specified as *organic* (known medical causes) and *nonorganic* (unknown or familial/environmental causes). Most sources agree that about 75% of all MR is nonorganic. Within this category, about half have retarded parents (Zigler & Hodapp, 1986). However, a trend toward greater organic etiology, partly because of alcohol and drug abuse and the increasing incidence of traumatic brain injury from vehicular accidents, appears to be developing.

In general, persons with unknown or familial/environmental etiologies tend to have mild MR, whereas those with medical etiologies are more severely involved. There are exceptions, of course, but medical etiologies often cause multiple disabilities (see Figure 21.3).

Medical etiologies identified by AAMR (Grossman, 1983) include the following:

1. Infections and intoxications
2. Trauma or physical agent
3. Metabolism or nutrition
4. Unknown prenatal influence—cranial
5. Chromosomal anomalies
6. Perinatal (birth weight, failure to thrive)
7. Gross brain disease (postnatal)
8. Following psychiatric disorders
9. Environmental deprivation or abuse
10. Other

These 10 etiological classifications can be further broken down by time of onset: (a) prenatal, (b) perinatal, and (c) postnatal. *Peri* means around or about and includes the period extending from the 28th week of pregnancy to the 28th day following birth. Of particular concern are low birth weight (2,500 gm or 5 lb, 8 oz), premature birth, and postmature birth (exceeding normal time by 7 days).

Infections, Toxins, and Traumas

Infections, chemical toxins, and traumas can injure the brain before, during, and after birth. Sexually transmitted diseases, including AIDS, are the main maternal infections that cause risk today, whereas rubella (measles) was a major factor before immunizations were developed. Childhood infection of the brain (encephalitis, meningitis) can result from common diseases like mumps, measles, and scarlet fever. Alcohol, drugs, and tobacco heighten risk, and most physicians advise total abstention, especially during the first 3 months of pregnancy. Traumas include all physical injuries and accidents that injure the brain directly or through oxygen deprivation (anoxia, hypoxia, asphyxia).

Fetal alcohol syndrome (FAS) is the most common condition within the infection, toxin, and trauma etiologies (Abel, 1987). Among pregnant women who drink heavily, the incidence of FAS is about 35%. FAS is also associated with male alcoholism. From 10 to 20% of mild MR in developed countries can be traced directly to parents' drinking. *The Broken Cord* by Dorris (1989), available as a book or videotape, chronicles growth of a child with FAS and provides an excellent bibliography.

Indicators of FAS are (a) significant growth retardation before and after birth, (b) mild to moderate microcephalus (smaller than normal head), (c) altered facial features, (d) other physical and behavioral problems, and (e) diagnosis of MR, usually in the mild range. Altered facial features include almond-shaped, slanted eyes; short palpebral fissures (i.e., the opening between the eyelids); low or sunken nasal bridge; short nose; maxillary hypoplasia (small, flattened midface); thin, smooth upper lip; and indistinct philtrum (the groove between nose and upper lip). Often, there is also ptosis (dropping) of the eyelid. Most common physical and behavioral problems are fine motor incoordination, hyperactivity, stubbornness, seizures, ventricular septal defects, and mild cerebral palsy.

Crack or cocaine maternal use results in smaller than normal infants who require immediate treatment for addiction. These crack-babies exhibit combined MR-cerebral palsy patterns as they grow. Over 10% of infants born in the United States test positive for cocaine or alcohol the first time their blood is drawn (Dorris, 1989).

FIGURE 21.3

Faces of mental retardation. All of the children shown here have severe
MR except Child E. Make up a psychomotor profile for each.

A. Nonambulatory, alert

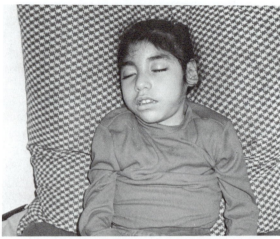

B. Microcephalus—nonambulatory,
mostly sleeps

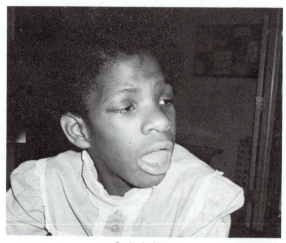

C. Ambulatory

D. Ambulatory

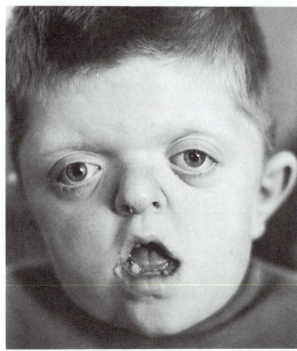

E. Apert syndrome

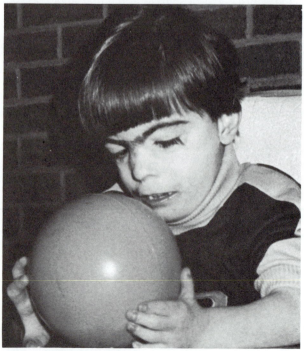

F. Cornelia de Lange syndrome

FIGURE 21.4

Unknown prenatal influences cause (*A*) abnormally small head (microcephalus) and (*B*) accumulation of fluid in the skull (hydrocephalus). Microcephalus is the more severe condition.

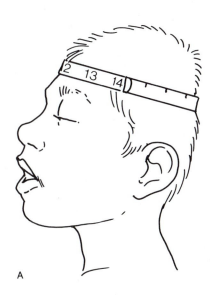

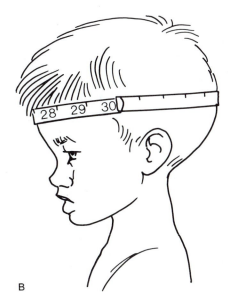

A

B

Metabolism and Unknown Influences

The metabolism or nutrition category mostly includes inborn errors that cause enzyme deficiencies that interfere with food metabolism. Infants look normal at birth but, within several months, evidence changes in appearance and function. Fair-skinned, fair-haired, and blue-eyed infants who begin persistent vomiting can be treated by diet therapy to manage *phenylketonuria* (PKU). If untreated, brain damage is severe. Other inborn errors of metabolism include galactosemia, Hurler's syndrome, and Tay-Sachs disease. Each is rare.

Unknown prenatal influences cause some infants to look abnormal at birth because of size and shape anomalies of the head (see Figure 21.4). Among these anomalies are *anencephaly* (partial or complete absence of the brain), *microcephalus* (abnormally small brain), *hydrocephalus* (large head caused by a cerebrospinal fluid problem), and *craniostenosis* (narrowed or flat cranium). Generally, microcephalus is associated with severe MR; it is also an indicator of specific conditions like fetal alcohol syndrome.

Syndromes are named for persons who first discovered them (e.g., Apert) or for the causative agent (fetal alcohol). Most are rare but can be easily remembered by cranial features. *Apert syndrome* is indicated by flat head appearance, microcephalus, defective formation of facial bones, bulging eyes, and malformed hands and feet (see Figure 21.3E). *Cornelia de Lange syndrome* is characterized by bushy eyebrows, long and curly eyelashes, lots of body hair, and small stature (see Figure 21.3F). *Amount of MR cannot be estimated by appearance. Occasionally, a person with these syndromes has normal intelligence.*

Hydrocephalus is described in detail in Chapter 23 because it often accompanies spina bifida. Usually, shunting procedures return head size to normal, but shunting does not always work. Hydrocephalus does not cause MR immediately. When treatment is ineffective, retardation develops slowly, as increased pressure within the cranium damages the brain.

Chromosomal Abnormalities

Chromosomal abnormalities affect about 7 in every 1,000 births (Gerber, 1990). These disorders usually result from chance errors in cell division shortly after an egg and sperm unite. With each cell division, 23 pairs of chromosomes should be passed on, each carrying the full DNA and genes to mastermind further development. Of the 23 pairs in each cell, 22 are *autosomes* (important for specific genetic markers), and one is the *sex chromosome,* designated as XX (female) or XY (male), which determines gender.

Abnormalities may occur in either autosomes or sex chromosomes. The most common autosomal chromosome disorder is *Down syndrome* (a short-stature MR condition, with distinguishing facial and other features). A common sex-linked chromosome disorder is *Turner syndrome,* caused by a division failure that results in only one X instead of the XX or XY pair in normal cells. Turner is also called XO syndrome. Some chromosomal disorders result in mental retardation (e.g., Down syndrome), but others may not (e.g., Turner syndrome). Turner syndrome, which occurs only in females, results in short stature (less than 5 ft), appearance of short neck because of low posterior hairline and/or cervical webbing, broad chest with widely spaced nipples, and failure to menstruate and mature sexually. A comparable condition in males is called *Noonan syndrome.*

Sex chromosome disorders occur more frequently than autosome ones and cause less severe conditions. Most sex chromosome disorders are primarily characterized by height abnormalities (extra short or tall) and underdeveloped or overdeveloped genitalia. Any syndrome that has X or O in its name is a sex chromosome disorder. There are multiple X female (XXX, XXXX) and multiple X male (XXXY, XXXXY) syndromes; these cause short heights. Two syndromes that occur in males only (XYY and XXY) cause abnormal tallness. XXY is also called Klinefelter syndrome (Jones, 1988).

Of particular interest is *Fragile X syndrome*, a condition that is inherited rather than occurring by chance. Discovered in 1969, it could not be accurately and consistently diagnosed until the 1980s (Chudley & Hagerman, 1987; Scharfenaker, 1990). Fragile refers to a gap or break in the long arm of the X chromosome. This occurs in 1 of 1,000 males and 1 of 2,000 females, but frequently goes undiagnosed. Mental function varies from severe MR to normal, with MR more common in males than females. Behaviors are often autistic, hyperactive, and impulsive. Physical indicators are large, narrow face, prominent ears, and large testicles.

Incidence of various syndromes (chromosomal and other) is given in Appendix A, Table A.2. The most frequently occurring syndromes are Down, fetal alcohol, and Fragile X. The specific etiology of Down syndrome is discussed later in this chapter.

Gross Brain Disease

Gross brain disease (postnatal) is a major AAMR etiological category, but it often does not result in MR. *Neurofibromatosis* (von Recklinghausen's disease) can best be remembered by the book, play, and movie about the elephant man (Montagu, 1971). It is the most common of the group of inherited disorders that affect both brain and skin. Indicators are (a) multiple fibromas (fibrous tumors that look like nodules) on the skin and in the central nervous system (CNS), (b) scoliosis, and (c) brown spots that look like coffee with cream (cafe au lait) stains. Neurofibromatosis usually does not become a problem until adolescence or adulthood.

In contrast, the less common *tuberous sclerosis* and *Sturge-Weber disease* are primarily neurologic disorders of infancy and childhood. To visualize tuberous sclerosis, remember that *tuber* means swelling and *sclerosis* means a hardening; the condition is characterized by hard little bumps on the nose and cheeks that resemble acne. These bumps are also scattered through the brain, heart, and other organs. Sturge-Weber disease is characterized by a large port-wine stain on parts of the face. Both conditions may cause seizures and muscle weakness (hemiparesis), and MR is common.

In summary, the individual differences in MR are obvious from the different etiologies (Netter, 1986). Degree of MR cannot be inferred from physical appearance. Most persons with MR look entirely normal if they have been taught proper grooming and postures.

Down Syndrome

Down syndrome (DS) is a unique chromosomal condition characterized by short stature, distinct facial features, and physical and cognitive differences that separate it from other manifestations of MR (see Figure 21.5). Intellectual function varies widely. Chris Burke as Corky on the popular ABC series "Life Goes On" demonstrates mild MR. He attends high school classes with nondisabled peers and is successful, with lots of effort, in regular education academics.

In the past, DS was associated with moderate-level function. This is now considered a misconception (Rynders & Horrobin, 1990), and parents are encouraged to advocate for regular education placement. Function in DS, like that in other kinds of MR, is largely related to infant and early childhood intervention and richness of opportunity to learn in home, school, and community partnership programs. Health and freedom from severe organ defects are also important factors.

Types of Down Syndrome

Chromosomal anomalies, because they occur near the time of conception, affect growth and development of all organs. Early literature described development as delayed; now it is considered abnormal because patterns are unique to DS (Dyer, Gunn, Rauh, & Berry, 1990; Henderson, 1986). Etiologically, there are three types of DS: (a) trisomy 21, (b) translocation, and (c) mosaicism.

Trisomy 21 explains about 95% of DS. It is caused by *nondisjunction*, failure of chromosome pair 21 to separate properly before or during fertilization. The result is three chromosomes instead of two like all the others and cells that have 47 chromosomes instead of the normal 46 (see Figure 21.5B). The overall incidence is about 1 in 800 live births, but this varies with maternal age. For instance, at age 25, the risk is 1 in 1,000; over age 35, the risk is 1 in 400; over age 45, the risk is 1 in 35. Fathers are also genetically linked to occurrence of DS, but the actual cause of chromosomal nondisjunctions remains uncertain.

Translocation DS occurs when a portion of the 21st chromosome is transferred to and fused with another chromosome (usually number 14, 15, or 22). This condition has a normal chromosome count, but the extra material causes problems. About 4% of DS is of this type (Blackman, 1983).

Mosaicism is very rare, accounting for less than 2% of DS. It results from a chance error in nondisjunction *after fertilization.* This causes the infant to have both normal and trisomic cells. The proportion of normal to trisomic cells varies, causing physical appearance and cognitive function to range from almost normal to classic DS (Fishler & Koch, 1991).

Physical Appearance

Persons with DS look like family members but also have many unique clinical features. Some of these are

- Short stature, seldom taller than 5 ft as adults.
- Short limbs, with short, broad hands and feet.
- Almond-shaped slanting eyes, often strabismic (crossed) and myopic (nearsighted).
- Flattened facial features, including bridge of nose.
- Flattened back of skull, short neck, with excess skin at nape of neck.

FIGURE 21.5

(A) The chromosomal abnormality most common is Down syndrome, in which every cell has 47 chromosomes instead of 46. (B) The karyotype was made by photographing a cell nucleus under an electron microscope. Then, the chromosomes were cut out of the photograph, matched up in pairs, and numbered. Although there are several kinds of Down syndrome, the usual problem is in chromosome 21. This affects all aspects of development and function.

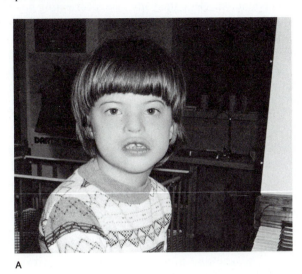

A

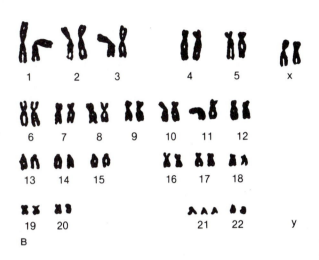

B

- Small oral cavity that contributes to mouth breathing and tongue protrusion.
- Hypotonic muscle tone in infancy that can be normalized in childhood through regular exercise.
- Joint looseness manifested by abnormal range of motion; this is caused by hypotonicity and lax ligaments. This looseness can be an advantage in gymnastics and activities requiring flexibility if muscles are strong enough to provide stability and prevent dislocation.

Sources indicate over 100 differences in physical features between people with and without DS (Sugden & Keogh, 1990). Shortness of stature, limbs, and feet and strength deficits related to hypotonia specifically limit balance (Burton & Davis, 1992) which, in turn, negatively affects other movement parameters. The mean age for walking of children with DS is 4.2 years.

Strengths and Weaknesses

Balance is one of the abilities in which persons with DS are most deficient (see Figure 21.6). In this area, they tend to perform 1 to 3 years behind other persons with the same level of retardation. Many persons with DS cannot balance on one foot for more than a few seconds, and most cannot maintain balance at all with eyes closed. In general, basic movements are awkward. Deficits in balance and coordination can be explained not only by physical constraints but by CNS dysfunction.

Children with DS demonstrate substantial delays in reflex integration and emergence of postural reactions and motor milestones. Moreover, the developmental sequence is somewhat different, probably because of hypotonic muscle

FIGURE 21.6

Preadolescent with Down syndrome exhibits balance deficits.

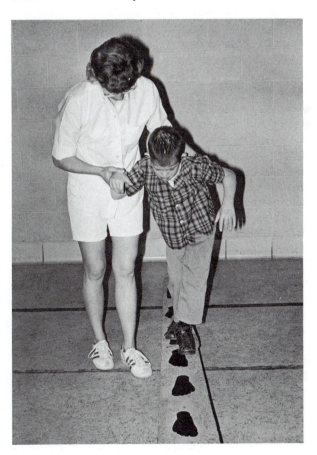

tone. Research on 229 children with DS in three countries showed that the rank order in which motor milestones are passed differs from that of normal babies (Dyer et al., 1990). Items passed later than expected involved balance and strength (e.g., standing, walking, throwing a ball). Items passed relatively earlier were reaching, grasping, and object manipulation. Findings like these allow programming for both strengths and weaknesses, but performance from child to child is extremely variable. Careful individual assessment is the only reliable approach.

Newborn infants with Down syndrome, like most severely neurologically involved babies, exhibit an extreme degree of *muscular hypotonia*. This fact has led to coinage of the term *floppy babies*. The muscular flabbiness decreases with age, if large-muscle exercise is stressed. The abdomen of the adolescent and the adult generally protrudes like that of a small child. Almost 90% have umbilical hernias in early childhood, but the condition often corrects itself. This finding suggests that abdominal exercises be selected and administered with extreme care. Straight-leg lifts and holds are contraindicated. Other postural and/or orthopedic problems commonly associated with Down syndrome are lordosis, kyphosis, dislocated hips, funnel-shaped or pigeon-breasted chest, and clubfoot.

The lax ligaments and apparent looseness of the joints lead some authors to describe persons with Down syndrome as "double-jointed." The structural weakness of ligaments perhaps affects the function of the foot most. Many children with DS have badly pronated and/or flat feet and walk with a shuffling gait. Chapter 11 describes strategies for correcting a shuffling gait.

Several excellent reviews of literature summarize research on DS that relates to motor development, learning, and control (Block, 1991; Henderson, 1986; Sugden & Keogh, 1990). In general, persons with DS tend to function motorically lower than most other persons with MR. They do benefit, however, from infant and early childhood sensorimotor programming and intensive training in sports. International Special Olympics events provide strong empirical evidence that some persons with DS can perform sports like gymnastics and swimming at high levels of proficiency.

An area in which persons with DS seem to function higher than others with MR is rhythm (Stratford & Ching, 1983). Music and other forms of rhythmic accompaniment, imaginatively used, seem to facilitate motor learning and practice. Most persons with DS can excel in dance and rhythmic movement. Aerobic dance thus is an excellent strategy for improving fitness because it builds on this strength.

Fitness of children and youth with DS has been studied extensively in Illinois, where a team of researchers led by Carl Eichstaedt collected data on over 1,000 persons with DS. Comparisons with same- or larger-sized samples of students with mild and moderate MR revealed that subjects with DS performed the poorest on all motor and physical fitness tests except the sit-and-reach test for flexibility (Eichstaedt, Wang, Polacek, & Dohrmann, 1991). Students with DS also weighed more, in spite of shorter heights, and had

larger triceps and subscapular skinfolds. Girls with DS also had larger calf skinfolds. These and other findings appear in an excellent book by Eichstaedt and Lavay (1992).

DS is associated with obesity and high blood cholesterol (Chad, Jobling, & Frail, 1990; Cronk, Chumlea, & Roche, 1985; Rimmer, Braddock, & Fujiura, 1992). This physical profile complicates health and impacts on all aspects of motor function. Sedentary lifestyle, poor eating habits, and lack of family nutritional awareness no doubt contribute to weight problems, but research also indicates that resting metabolism rate of individuals with DS is depressed (Chad et al., 1990). Implications are that combined exercise-nutrition programs should receive high priority in school and community programming.

Congenital heart disease complicates fitness programming and life expectancy for about 40% of the population with DS (Eyman, Call, & White, 1991; Spicer, 1984). The most common problem is ventricular septal defect (VSD) (see Chapter 19). Unlike VSD in the normal population, the holes in the heart wall are usually large and require surgical repair. Many infants with DS have multiple cardiac defects. Depending on severity, residual effects may be present after surgery.

The average lifespan of individuals with DS has changed from 9 years old in 1929 to over 50 in the 1990s (Eyman et al., 1991). Most closely correlated with early death are major mobility and eating problems (severe cerebral palsy). About 75% of nonambulatory persons with DS die of pneumonia. All persons with DS seem highly susceptible to upper respiratory infections. They must be protected against exposure to viruses and temperature extremes.

Self-care and cognitive abilities of adults with DS decline with age to a much greater extent than those of other people (Zigman, Schupf, Lubin, & Silverman, 1987). This is linked with early-onset Alzheimer-type neuropathology, which is present from about age 40 on. Substantial regression, however, is not observed until about 50. Only 15 to 40% of older DS adults show Alzheimer behaviors. IQ and general motor skills of children and adolescents with DS plateau in a puzzling manner (Henderson, 1986). Children placed in regular education typically need more and more resource help as they grow older.

In general, people with DS are friendly, cheerful, mannerly, and responsible. Their social competence is much higher than would be expected. Although usually cooperative, on occasion, they exhibit extreme stubbornness. When they say, "No," professionals experience a real challenge! This occasional stubbornness appears to be a CNS deficit similar to the conceptual rigidity and perseveration associated with brain damage. Persons with DS tend to like routine; professionals need to plan strategy carefully before changing routine. On the other hand, routine can be the key to regular inclusion and practice of needed motor and game skills.

Atlantoaxial Instability

Atlantoaxial instability is an orthopedic problem present in approximately 17% of persons with DS. *Atlantoaxial* refers to the joint between the first two cervical vertebrae, known

FIGURE 21.7

Atlantoaxial instability may contribute to a dislocation of the atlas, which may injure the spinal cord. It may be caused by either forceful forward or backward bending of the head.

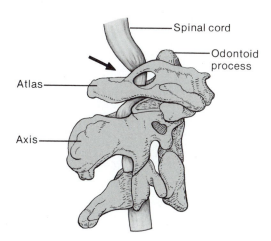

as atlas and axis, respectively. Instability indicates that the ligaments and muscles surrounding this joint are lax and that the vertebrae can slip out of alignment easily. Forceful forward or backward bending of the neck, which occurs in gymnastics, swimming, and other sport events, may dislocate the atlas, causing damage to the spinal cord (Figure 21.7).

Since 1983, Special Olympics has required a physician's statement that indicates absence of this condition in persons with DS as a prerequisite for unrestricted participation in Special Olympics. This statement must be based on X rays, the cost of which is typically covered by health insurance or Medicaid. Enforcement of this requirement by school administrators would be prudent also, since contemporary physical education practice favors vigorous activity for children with DS. If this medical clearance is not on file, physical educators should restrict students from participation in gymnastics, diving, butterfly stroke and diving start in swimming, high jump, pentathlon, soccer, and any warm-up exercise placing pressure on the head and neck muscles. This restriction should be temporary, with a time limit set for obtaining the X rays. If students with DS are diagnosed as having atlantoaxial syndrome, they are permanently restricted from these activities; there are, however, many other physical education activities in which they can safely engage.

Motor Ability and Performance

Most infants and young children with MR are developmentally delayed. Those with severe retardation tend to be *multidisabled* by such conditions as cerebral palsy, hydrocephalus/spina bifida, or sensory impairments. When physical disability is not present, the delayed motor development seems related to a *subtle but specific disturbance in the evolution of postural adjustment reactions* (*propping and equilibrium*).

Physical educators in early childhood units may have several children who do not yet walk. The mean age of walking in children with MR is 3.2 years; for DS, it is 4.2 years. For such children, physical education should empha-

size vestibular stimulation and balancing activities (adjustment to changing equilibrium while being held or while on a water bed, moon walk, tiltboard, and therapy ball, for example). Almost no physical education research is available to assist in curriculum planning for nonambulatory children under age 6. For ambulatory preschoolers, two excellent programs have come out of Canada (Evans, 1980; Watkinson & Wall, 1982). There is also a preprimary I CAN program (Wessel, 1980).

Summary of Knowledge Base

The major researcher in physical education for children with MR ages 6 and up is Lawrence Rarick, professor emeritus at the University of California at Berkeley. His works form the knowledge base with regard to motor ability. Among the most important facts are

1. The factor structure of motor ability is similar for children, ages 6 to 10 years, regardless of whether they have a normal IQ or score in the mild or moderate MR range. This means that differences come from constraints that affect performance, not from underlying motor abilities.

2. The greater the intellectual deficit, the more pronounced is the motor deficiency. One does not cause the other, but they go together.

3. Children with mild MR are 2 to 4 years behind normal peers on most measures of motor performance. With increasing age, the problem becomes greater. Whether this motor discrepancy is the result of inequitable instruction and experience or reflects limited learning capabilities and body build constraints is unknown. Rarick (1980) found that boys with mild MR were .96 standard deviation below the average motor performance of normal peers, meaning that 87% of the normal boys were better. Girls with mild MR were 1.83 standard deviations below the average performance of normal peers, meaning that 95% of the normal girls were better.

4. The greatest difficulty in teaching motor tasks lies in *attention and comprehension* rather than execution, once the task is understood. This implies that demonstrations should accompany verbal instructions, and careful attention should be given to task analysis in introducing new skills.

5. The relationship between motor performance and intelligence in persons with MR generally ranges between .10 and .30. The motor tasks that correlate highest with intelligence are balance items and tests of fine visual-motor coordination.

6. Motor development programs should provide great variability in the practice of skills. For instance, an overarm throw should be practiced with many different projectiles of varying size, weight, shape, and color in many different places, with varied targets, distances, and wind conditions. Such variable practice results in development of a motor schema that facilitates transfer to a similar but unfamiliar task.

FIGURE   21.8

Example of how deviation from average performance varies when scores of boys with mental retardation are statistically adjusted for height, hip width, and body fat.

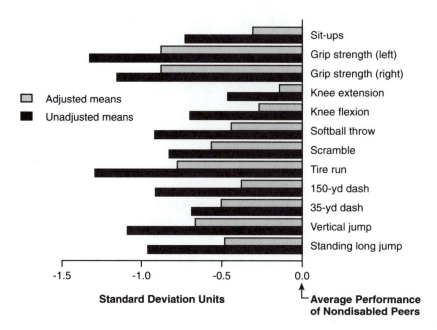

Influence of Physical Constraints

Some differences in motor performance between persons with MR and those with average IQs can be explained by height and body composition. Figure 21.8 shows, for example, that boys, ages 6 to 10 with a mean IQ of 67, perform from .50 to about 1.50 standard deviations below the norm (see unadjusted means). When a statistical procedure is used to equate boys with and without MR on height and body composition measures, these differences become much less (see adjusted means). In fact, the boys with MR are no longer significantly different from peers on 5 of the 12 tests (sit-ups, knee extension, knee flexion, 150-yd dash, and 35-yd dash).

The research reporting these findings indicated that boys with and without MR differ significantly on height, width of hips, and skinfold measures. Boys with MR are shorter and have wider hips and more body fat (Dobbins, Garron, & Rarick, 1981). No comparable research has been conducted on girls. The implications are, however, that reducing body fat will improve motor performance.

Numerous researchers have reported that persons with MR tend to be overweight or obese (Fox & Rotatori, 1982; Kelly, Rimmer, & Ness, 1986; Reid, Montgomery, & Seidl, 1985). The range of obesity for adult populations is 30 to 74%, with an average of 45% for men and 51% for women. Given these facts, it is surprising that no research reports success in reducing fat through combined exercise and nutrition protocols.

Prader-Willi syndrome is a condition of gross overweight and unmanageable eating behaviors that seem to be of biological origin (Goldman, 1988). Although rare, many teachers eventually are confronted with this disorder, which is associated with mild to moderate MR.

Physical Fitness

Studies of physical fitness of persons with MR indicate that this is a problem area that should be addressed. Even when persons are actively involved in sport programs, fitness is lower than that of peers without MR (Pitetti, Jackson, Stubbs, Campbell, & Battar, 1989; Roswal, Roswal, & Dunleavy, 1986). Eichstaedt et al. (1991) reported low fitness levels for students with MR, ages 6 to 21, tested in 1980 and 1990 (N over 1,000 in both years). This cross-sectional research showed that fitness scores were lower in 1990 on all tests except abdominal and hip flexor strength.

Research thus far has focused primarily on validity and reliability of fitness test protocols (Fernhall, Tymeson, & Webster, 1988; Kelly & Rimmer, 1987; Pizarro, 1990; Seidl, Reid, & Montgomery, 1987). In general, most attention centers on measurement of cardiovascular fitness. The lower the IQ, the less able persons are to understand the purpose of a distance run, concepts of speed, and discomfort like breathlessness associated with cardiovascular testing. In general, valid measures can be obtained from persons with mild MR but not from those with severe MR.

Chapters 13 and 19 on fitness and OHI (other health impairments) present several concerns about attempts to apply traditional test protocols to persons with severe MR. One is the increased likelihood that the heart will not respond normally to exercise because of autonomic nervous system damage; this condition is called *chronotropic incompetence* or *sick sinus syndrome* and is characterized by a slower-than-expected heartbeat. Another concern is that 20 to 60% of infants born with chromosomal defects have congenital heart disease. Others also may have undetected cardiac defects that require sophisticated technology for identification.

If persons with severe MR are overweight, this problem should be ameliorated before work on endurance running is begun. Chapter 19 emphasizes that low-intensity, long-duration activities achieve this goal. Walking, dance, and water activities are particularly recommended. Most persons with severe MR do not have the cognition and coordination to use regulation cycling apparatus. Apparatus can be adapted, however, so that they can pedal from a supine position.

The goal in severe MR should be *increased exercise tolerance* instead of cardiorespiratory endurance. Consideration also should be given to whether a person with severe MR will ever need the capacity to sustain a 1- or 1.5-mi run. If family members and significant others regularly run, then this may be an ecologically valid goal. Otherwise, it is probably not. Targeted cardiovascular levels should be matched to game and leisure skills. If the person with an IQ under 50 has few or no physical activity leisure competencies, then developing these competencies should, perhaps, be the primary goal.

Tests marketed by AAHPERD specifically for persons with MR in the 1970s and 1980s are no longer available. The AAHPERD Physical Best Test is recommended for everyone. The fitness standards established for this test are generally agreed to be applicable to all populations. See Chapter 13.

The emphasis for individuals with MR, however, should be on active lifestyle, not on fitness for the sake of fitness. In most cases, this depends on developing transition-type programs that involve the home and community.

Cognitive Ability Related to Motor Learning

Historically, defective mental functioning has been explained by two theories: (a) the structural difference or deficit theory (Ellis, 1963) and (b) the production deficiency or inappropriate strategy theory (Brown, 1974). The first theory, which posited a defective neural structure, has received little attention since the 1970s. The second theory drives efforts to find strategies that will help persons with MR learn more efficiently. Several physical educators have reviewed work in this area (Bouffard & Wall, 1990; Dummer, 1988; Hoover & Horgan, 1990; Reid, 1986; Thomas, 1984).

Attention

Many persons with MR exhibit delays in maturation of attention processes. Problems may be primarily overexclusive or overinclusive attention. *Overexclusive,* normal until about age 6, is focusing on one aspect of a task with restricted visual scanning and incidental learning. *Overinclusive,* normal from about age 6 to 12 years, is responsiveness to everything, rather than attending only to relevant cues. Either way, the attentional resources are inefficiently allocated.

In one-to-one task analysis protocol, this problem is largely ameliorated by shaping the environment so that there are no irrelevant cues (see Figure 21.9). The teacher then uses one particular cue to elicit the desired response (e.g., "Watch me. I roll the ball. Now you roll the ball"). The same cue is used every time, and appropriate behavior is reinforced. This approach is used when teaching persons with

FIGURE   21.9

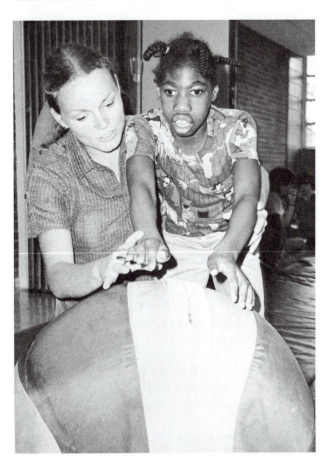

The one-to-one task analysis condition works best for persons with severe mental retardation.

severe MR but does not usually generalize to ordinary settings, where many environmental stimuli compete for attention. *Eventually, the student taught in this way must be given practice under conditions with progressively more irrelevant stimuli until such time that the instructional setting is normalized.* For example, whenever other students share a room, their presence creates stimuli that must be blocked out.

For most students, therefore, the emphasis is dually on recognizing relevant cues and blocking out irrelevant ones. Teachers begin by highlighting one cue and gradually adding two or three more. Level of cognition determines the number of cues that can be attended to simultaneously. Professionals typically teach *wholes* rather than parts by starting a lesson with a demonstration. As instruction progresses, however, corrective feedback necessarily focuses on parts, and specific cues and strategies are used as attentional-getters. Attention-getters that help persons focus are

U	Unexpectedness (surprise)
S	Size
I	Intensity (loud, bright, heavy)
N	Novelty (new or original)
G	Glorious color
N	Name (call person by name)
E	Eye contact (a long stare)
T	Touch

Remember these attention-getters by the concept "USING NET to capture attention." Some applications are (a) having a student wear a colorful elbow band to remember to keep the elbow straight in racket sports; (b) shouting a key word in the middle of a quietly stated sentence; (c) showing a large flash card with the body part or action to be remembered. The "Surprise Symphony" of Hayden reminds us of how effective an unexpected change can be. Consider how the eight attention-getters can be applied to sights and sounds associated with observing and imitating a new motor skill or sequence.

Memory or Retention

Persons with MR have long-term memory equal to that of peers (Hoover & Horgan, 1990). However, they have many problems with short-term memory (i.e., the encoding of new information into the long-term memory store). Research indicates that we have only 30 to 60 sec to make this happen. Whereas nonretarded persons use spontaneous rehearsal strategies, persons with MR are unlikely to do so. Research shows that they can use rehearsal strategies, when carefully taught, but even then, they lag behind peers in spontaneity of application and generalization. Memory strategies from trial to trial tend to vary considerably.

Implications are that teachers should focus on rehearsal strategies and provide many, many trials. Modeling, verbal rehearsal, self-talk, and mental practice are strategies commonly used. Modeling can be passive, with the student watching and then imitating; the imitation should occur, however, within 30 sec with no intervening, confounding stimuli between visual input and imitation. Or the modeling can be active, with the student playing follow the leader or copycat. Teachers should experiment to determine whether a student does better with a silent or talking model. With talking models, much attention should be given to how much talk and when.

Model talk and supplementary verbal instruction should focus on actions or body parts rather than numbers. For example, it is better to say, "Jumping jacks, out-in, out-in, out-in, out-in, walk-walk-walk-walk" than "Jumping jacks, 1–2–3–4, walk, 1–2–3–4." Research documents that persons with MR perform less well with alphanumeric stimuli than with action words and pictures (Stanovich, 1978). When models do self-talk as they perform, students are likely to imitate this strategy and incorporate it into their unique learning style.

Verbal rehearsal and *self-talk* sometimes refer to the same thing, but a distinction is often made. Verbal rehearsal is talking through what we plan to do. Self-talk is the strategy of talking while moving. *Mental practice* involves visualization as well as verbal rehearsal before beginning an activity.

After several trials of imitating a model, students may profit from questioning that focuses attention on problem areas. For example, the teacher may ask, "What was I thinking when I moved? What was I saying? Where was I looking? Were my feet far apart or close together?" Students working as partners should also learn to ask such questions. Ultimately, students learn to ask these questions of themselves and thus begin to provide self-feedback.

Persons with MR do not use feedback as fully as peers. Also, teachers often give lots of praise or motivational feedback but not enough informational feedback. *Feedback should include questioning about process as well as product.* Illustrative questions on *process* are "Did the movement *feel* good?" "Did you *tuck your head* when you did the forward roll?" "Did you *watch* the ball?" "Was your *elbow* straight?" Illustrative questions on *product* are "Did you hit the target?" "How far did you throw?" "What was your score?" Questioning is the type of feedback that involves the learner most actively, but feedback can also be passive, with the teacher telling and directing. Regardless of approach, more feedback (providing it is meaningful) leads to more success. This is the rationale for small class sizes, use of peer teachers, and availability of videotaped feedback technology.

Feedback, like input, is dependent on short-term memory. To be effective, it must be received immediately before new stimuli divert the mind from the task just completed. *A general rule is within 5 sec of task completion.* When feedback is delayed, students often need help in linking it with the antecedent. Too often, teachers move around the room saying, "Good!" without taking the time to ascertain that students understand what they are good at and why.

Production and Generalization

Persons with MR need more trials than peers and instruction in smaller chunks. This is the rationale underlying task analysis. The use of many trials is supported by research on overlearning and extended practice (Chasey, 1977; Kerr & Blais, 1987). Little is known about number of successes that should be required before stopping a practice and moving on to something else.

Persons with MR have more difficulty in chaining parts into sequences than peers. Therefore, much attention should be given to practicing progressively longer sequences. Games like *Copy Cat* and *I'm Going to Grandmother's House* (see Chapter 12) can make learning chains of gross motor activities fun (e.g., three walks, two jumps, one bend-and-reach, and sit).

Once a movement is learned, periodic practice ensures that it is remembered. This practice should be in variable environments to teach and reinforce generalization. Persons with MR have more difficulty in generalizing than peers.

Persons with MR need explicit directions. Whereas nondisabled peers learn incidentally and spontaneously, persons with MR learn best when instruction is direct, specific, and brief. The teacher should frequently ask, "What are we learning? What are we practicing? When are we going to use this"?

Crucial to generalization are field trips to parks and recreation centers where leisure skills can be practiced. Instruction must include use of public transportation, how to pay fees, and how to communicate with others who are using the facility.

Programming for Mild Mental Retardation

Approximately 90% of all MR conditions are mild. Persons with mild MR learn more slowly than peers but, with good programming, can function academically at the third-grade level or higher by adulthood. Most marry, rear children, and work full-time like everyone else at jobs in the community. Cognitively, their greatest problems are in short-term memory, concept formation, problem solving, evaluative activity, generalization, and abstract thinking. These weaknesses, of course, affect motor learning and game performance.

Programming for persons with mild MR is typically directed toward enhancing cognition. These persons are generally in regular physical education or a resource setting designed to prepare them for the mainstream. Strategies described in the preceding section are used to help them keep up with classmates, develop some physical activity strengths, remediate weaknesses, and accept limitations. Several models described in Chapter 8 are helpful in promoting integration and inclusion. The following are additional models that have been developed specifically for persons with cognitive delays or slowness. These are presented to stimulate creative thinking and to motivate development of your own models.

The Knowledge-Based Model

The knowledge-based model, which focuses on movement problem solving, was developed by Marcel Bouffard, University of Alberta; Ted Wall, McGill University; and colleagues (Bouffard, 1990; Bouffard & Wall, 1990; Wall, Bouffard, McClements, Findlay, & Taylor, 1985). It is based on observations that movement skill lag in persons with mild MR is related to five major sources: (a) deficiencies in the knowledge base or lack of access to it, (b) failure to use spontaneous strategies, (c) inadequate metacognitive knowledge and understanding, (d) executive control and motor planning weaknesses, and (e) low motivation and inadequate practice.

The knowledge-based model emphasizes instructional process rather than activities. To improve sport, dance, and aquatics performance, instruction is directed toward three components (see Figure 21.10). *Procedural knowledge* refers to understandings about process; it is information about how to do things. *Declarative knowledge* refers to factual information; it is knowledge about the body, environmental variables, and mechanical laws. *Affective knowledge* refers to feelings about the self and ecosystem that evolve through use of procedural and declarative knowledge.

Metacognition is knowledge about what we know and do not know. For example, metacognition tells us when to stop studying or practicing. Metacognition also allows us to analyze emotion and determine what we are afraid of or angry about. Persons with MR and/or low motor skills have less metacognition than peers. They do not accurately assess abilities and therefore practice either too little or too much.

Use of the knowledge-based model to guide instruction implies careful teaching of facts and processes, with emphasis on problem solving so learners are actively involved, not just listening to someone else. Persons with MR can be

FIGURE 21.10

Types of knowledge targeted in the knowledge-based model.

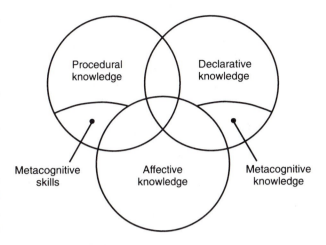

successful in problem solving but require more trial-and-error opportunities than peers. Ecological task analysis is one approach to teaching problem solving; movement education is another. Any question-answer teaching style will increase knowledge. Answers can be verbal, gestural, or movement.

Steps in problem solving that should be explicitly taught and practiced are

1. Identify the game or movement function—state what, who, where, why, and how.
2. Assess self and environmental variables. Make changes necessary for safety, comfort, and ease of motion. For instance, if facing the sun, then change position. If too hot, take off jacket. If there is an obstacle in pathway, move it.
3. Engage in motor planning. Use visual imagery, verbal rehearsal, and other strategies.
4. Monitor execution for feedback from all sensory modalities as well as external sources. Use self-checking routines to regulate and oversee learning and to determine when practice should be terminated.
5. Evaluate process, product, and feeling and redefine task at set intervals like every 10 trials.

Special Olympics Sports Skills Program

Developed in the 1980s by staff at Special Olympics International (SOI) headquarters, the Special Olympics Sports Skills Program is based on an illustrated guide for each sport, mandatory training for instructors, and the rule that athletes must complete at least 8 weeks of training in a particular sport before entering competition. Each guide presents a detailed 8-week training program (3 days a week), long-term goal and short-term objectives, a criterion-referenced skills test for pretraining and posttraining assessment, and a task analysis to direct the teaching of each skill.

FIGURE   21.11

Examples from the Special Olympics Sports Skills Program.

Long-Term Goal for Track and Field

The athlete will acquire basic track-and-field skills, appropriate social behavior, and functional knowledge of the rules necessary to participate successfully in athletics competitions.

Short-Term Objectives for Track and Field

1.0 Given demonstration and practice, the athlete will warm up properly before a track-and-field practice or meet.

2.0 Given demonstration and practice, the athlete will successfully perform track skills.

3.0 Given demonstration and practice, the athlete will successfully perform field skills.

4.0 Given verbal and written instruction, the athlete will comply with official athletics competition rules while participating in athletics competition.

5.0 Given an athletics practice or meet, the athlete will exhibit sportsmanship with teammates and opponents at all times.

Illustrative Assessment Checklist for Relay Race

Pre Score	Post Score	Test Item #3 Relays
☐	☐	Attempts to participate in a relay race.
☐	☐	Assumes a receiving position for a visual pass.
☐	☐	Receives the baton in a visual pass.
☐	☐	Performs an underhand baton pass.
☐	☐	Performs baton pass in exchange zone.
☐	☐	Runs designated leg of relay race in proper manner.
☐	☐	Participates in relay race competition.
☐	☐	1–2 Beginner
☐	☐	3–5 Intermediate
☐	☐	6–7 Advanced

_____ Approximate training time (hours)

Illustrative Task Analysis: Receive the Baton in a Visual Pass

Task Analysis

a. Assume proper receive position in front part of exchange zone.

b. Look back over inside shoulder for teammate (incoming runner).

c. Begin running forward when incoming runner reaches a point 4 to 5 m from exchange zone.

d. Keep left hand back with fingers pointing to the left, thumb pointing down and palm down.

e. Watch the incoming runner pass the baton underhanded into your left hand.

f. Turn to look forward, switch the baton immediately to the right hand, and continue relay.

Although Special Olympics is usually associated with competition, *the Sports Skills program is purely instructional.* As such, it is appropriate for use in schools, homes, and after-school programs. The task analyses are as helpful in teaching regular as adapted physical education. The quality of the instruction depends, of course, on the knowledge, skills, and integrity of the teachers. Although Special Olympics attracts millions of volunteers, there are still too few professionals involved.

A basic tenet of the instructional program is that skill development is not an end in itself but rather a vehicle to an active lifestyle and access to the same sport opportunities as able-bodied peers. This is the rationale for holding local and state competitions. These are designed to enable persons to generalize skills to real-life situations and to receive intensive positive feedback for effort as well as success. Competitions are also a way of involving family members and neighbors, thereby achieving some hidden agendas relative to awareness and attitude.

Sport skills guides are available for nine summer sports and six winter sports (SOI, 1980s):

Summer	Winter
Aquatics	Alpine skiing
Athletics (track and field)	Nordic skiing
Basketball	Figure skating
Bowling	Speed skating
Gymnastics	Floor hockey
Roller skating	Poly hockey
Soccer	
Softball	
Volleyball	

Figure 21.11 presents the long-term goal and short-term objectives for the track-and-field sports training program, an example of criterion-referenced assessment, and an illustrative task analysis. Under assessment, note that *relays* is broken down into seven tasks. The guide provides a separate task analysis for each of these.

The goal and objectives encompass three aspects of sports: skills, social behavior, and functional knowledge of rules. Social behavior is operationally defined as good sportsmanship and is taught via task analyses for (a) exhibiting competitive effort and (b) exhibiting fair play at all times. The Special Olympics oath reinforces the concept of competitive effort:

Let me win
But if I cannot win
Let me be brave in the attempt.

Special Olympics Sports Skills Program guides are available from Special Olympics International, 1350 New York Avenue NW, Suite 500, Washington, DC 20005. They represent only part of a broad-based technical assistance program available through SOI.

Special Olympics Competition and Unified Sports

Special Olympics competition was begun in 1968 by Eunice Kennedy Shriver as a vehicle for awareness, attitude change, and equal opportunity. There have been many changes in policies and practices, but the underlying philosophy has remained the same:

The mission of Special Olympics is to provide year-round sports training and athletic competition in a variety of Olympic-type sports for all children and adults with mental retardation, giving them continuing opportunities to develop physical fitness, demonstrate courage, experience joy, and participate in a sharing of gifts, skills, and friendship with their families, other Special Olympics athletes, and the community. (SOI, 1989a, p. 1)

Special Olympics is increasingly community based, with coaches encouraged to use community facilities and to attract volunteers of all ages. Many programs use a reverse mainstreaming approach, with peer tutors interacting with Special Olympians. The official rules book specifically states that athletes may participate in other organized sport programs while participating in Special Olympics. Rules that govern SOI sports are the same as those for regular sports, with only a few adaptations, so generalization from one setting to another is facilitated. All that is needed is a regular education teacher or coach who is open and receptive.

To further encourage integration, SOI created the unified sports model in 1989. This model, which requires an equal number of persons with and without MR on the floor or field at all times, is explained in Chapter 8.

SOI has been a major force in creating a body of knowledge about curriculum planning for persons with MR. It has provided evidence that they can succeed in both team and individual sports (see issues of *Palaestra* that feature Special Olympics). In addition to official sports, SOI sponsors demonstration sports, while concurrently conducting research on their appropriateness for persons with MR. Demonstration sports currently under study are canoeing, cycling, table tennis, team handball, tennis, and power lifting.

SOI also has a list of prohibited sports that authorities believe are not appropriate for competition. These sports are

1. Javelin	7. All martial arts	11. Wrestling
2. Discus	8. Fencing	12. Judo
3. Hammer throw	9. Shooting	13. Karate
4. Pole vault	10. All types of contact sports (i.e., rugby, American football)	14. Nordic jumping
5. Boxing		15. Trampoline
6. Platform dives		

SOI believes that competitive experiences are not appropriate until age 8. From this age on, all persons with MR are welcome to engage in competition. There is a Masters' Division for ages 30 and over, and occasionally, persons in their 60s and 70s participate. Competition can be serious or recreational. The important objective is active lifestyle for everyone.

Special Olympics does not use medical or functional classification to equalize abilities of persons competing against each other. Instead, it uses a system called *divisioning,* in which athletes are categorized according to their age, sex, and ability. Divisions must have at least three but no more than eight competitors or teams. The 10% rule is followed in ability grouping. This rule states that, within any division, the top and bottom scores may not exceed each other by more than 10%. Before individuals are placed in heats or events, they must submit their best times or distances to be used in the divisioning procedure.

In team sports, divisioning is achieved by administering a battery of four or five sport-specific skills to every team member. These scores are added to create a team score that is used in divisioning.

The Medallion Program in Manitoba, Canada, and the Kansas State University track-and-field program are illustrative of a *generic sport model* based on Special Olympics philosophy (Dahlgren, Boreskie, Dowds, Mactavish, & Watkinson, 1991; Johnson, Sundheim, & Santos, 1989). Sport clubs for athletes with MR that emphasize intensive training and the achievement of personal bests are increasing.

In Europe, an International Sports Federation for Persons With Mental Handicaps was established in 1988. This organization is also advancing the concept of sport clubs.

Stepping Out for Fitness Model

The Stepping Out for Fitness model was developed for adolescents and adults with mild to moderate MR who need programming specifically for fitness. It is described in a book (1990) by three Canadians: Greg Reid and David Montgomery of McGill University and Christine Seidl of Summit School. This book includes 48 lessons, each 40 min long, with graded intensity designed to enable persons to reach targeted heart rates. Sessions are to be conducted two to three times a week.

A unique feature of the model is its use of music in all lessons. Several exercise sequences are presented for popular works like Michael Jackson's "Bad" and George Michael's "Faith." Lessons are built around six themes: (a) calisthenics to music, (b) exercise break package, (c) ball activities, (d) hoop and rope activities, (e) circuit training, and (f) 20-km club. The latter is a challenge for groups of 8 to collectively run 20 km within the time span of 6 lessons. During these lessons, two 10-min periods are allocated for running laps.

The instructional model includes five components: (a) assessment, (b) objectives, (c) task analysis, (d) implementation, and (e) postevaluation. Effectiveness of the model is based on a 4-month experimental study conducted by Montgomery, Reid, and Seidl (1988) with 53 subjects. The assessment used is the Canadian Standardized Test of Fitness, although any comparable test is appropriate. The model is dually based on exercise physiology principles and behavior management theory.

Each lesson includes warm-up, conditioning, and cool-down, with activities specifically for flexibility, cardiovascular improvement, and muscular endurance. Behavioral management is applied primarily in the specification of teaching cues (prompts) on lesson plans (see Figure 21.12). The code for understanding cues is

D Demonstrate
MP Manipulative prompt
VC Verbal cue
MG Minimal guidance
M Manipulate

The book *Stepping Out for Fitness* is published by CAHPER/ACSEPL, Place R. Tait McKenzie, 1600 James Naismith Dr., Gloucester, Ontario K1B 5N4. It is appropriate for adapted or regular settings and can be followed exactly or used as an example for creating a similar program.

Programming for Young Children With MR

Children with developmental disabilities are eligible for public school intervention programs from birth on. Because children learn through play, physical educators should use play to full advantage. Many models are available for teaching motor skills. The PREP program, however, is highlighted here because it focuses on functional competence.

PREP Play Model

The PREP Play Program, used widely in Canada, was developed to guide the physical education of children with mental handicaps, ages 3 to 12 (Watkinson & Wall, 1982). This diagnostic-prescriptive model is applicable, however, to any child who needs individualized instruction in (a) locomotion, (b) large play equipment, (c) small play equipment, and (d) play vehicles. These four areas are divided into 40 specific gross motor play skills (see Figure 21.13).

A task analysis with recommended physical prompts is provided for each skill, as well as group activities for practicing and reinforcing the skills. For example, jumping down is analyzed into four steps:

1. Step down from shin height, one foot to the other foot.
2. Jump down from shin height, with a two-foot takeoff and landing.
3. Jump down from knee height, using the same pattern.
4. Jump down from hip height, using the same pattern.

Figure 21.13 also presents a sample from an instructional episode in which the teacher uses verbal and physical prompts to teach the jump-down skill. Execution is followed by both reinforcement and information feedback. A central feature of PREP is that instruction is carried out while children are at play.

Teachers interact with one child at a time for a 1- to 5-min intervention, so that everyone receives individual attention. Brief group-teaching episodes provide practice of new skills in a group context. The length of the group session is 3 to 5 min early in the year and progresses to 15 min.

FIGURE 21.12

Examples from the Stepping Out for Fitness Model. (D=Demonstrate;
MP=Manipulative prompt; VC=Verbal cue; MG=Minimal guidance.)

STEPPING OUT FOR FITNESS PROGRAM (Parts of Sample Lesson)

Lesson: 1

Major feature: Calisthenics to music
Time: 40 min

Equipment: Cassettes
Tape recorder
Mat or blanket

Activity	Teaching Cues

Introduce program:

5 min
 – Value of REGULAR EXERCISE
 – Proper clothing for exercising

Warm-up—Flexibility exercises:

10 min

1. 6 toe touches

D – Include demonstrations for all the following:
MP – Stand at side of person and move down
      together, partly manipulating at start.
VC – "Bend down SLOWLY."
      "Reach as far as you can."
      "Touch the floor."
      "Don't bounce."

2. 12 alternate-knee raises

MG – Tap the appropriate knee to lift.
VC – "Raise (lift) your knees."
      "Right, left,...."
      "One, two,...."

[Warm-ups continued but not included here.]

Cardiovascular activity:

5 min

1. Jog on the spot for 30 sec

VC – "Run on the same spot."
      "Faster....slower."

2. Walk one lap of the exercise area (briskly).

VC – "Now walk; breathe deeply." "Faster."

3. 10 floor jumps.

MG – Tap knees to bend prior to jump.

[Activity continued but not included here.]

Assessment is structured through use of a free-play inventory (checklist), an individual student profile, and a daily record-monitoring form. The profile permits recording of which step in the task sequence has been completed and the type of prompt (physical, visual, verbal, none) needed.

The PREP manual includes many activities for using locomotor skills in relation to play equipment. In conjunction with each of these, children work on their knowledge base by learning names of body parts and body actions. Prior to playing a jumping game, for example, children sit on a mat and identify body parts to be used. Then they stand and review body actions, like *bend knees* and *swing arms*.

FIGURE 21.13

Examples from PREP play program.

Skills for Locomotion	**Skills for Large Play Equipment**	**Skills for Small Play Equipment**	**Skills for Play Vehicles**
Running	Ascending an inclined bench on stomach	Throwing	Riding a scooter (sitting)
Ascending stairs	Ascending an inclined bench on hands and knees	Kicking	Riding a scooter down an incline (sitting)
Descending stairs		Catching	
Jumping down	Walking up an inclined bench	Bouncing	Tummy riding on a scooter
Jumping over	Jumping on a trampoline	Hitting with a baseball bat	Tummy riding down an incline on a scooter
Hopping on one foot	Seat drop on a trampoline	Striking with a hockey stick	
Forward roll	Swivel hips on a trampoline	Stopping a puck with a hockey stick	Pulling a wagon
Backward roll	Sliding down a slide	Passing a puck with a hockey stick	Riding a wagon
	Climbing on a box		Riding a tricycle
	Swinging on a rope	Jumping a rope turned by two people	Riding the back of a tricycle
	Swinging on a bar		
	Swinging on a swing		
	Hanging from knees on a horizontal ladder		
	Rolling around a bar		
	Ascending a ladder		
	Descending a ladder		

Sample Instructional Episode

Teacher behavior	Child behavior	Teacher behavior
1. Teacher says, "Look at me." (PROMPT)	Child looks at teacher. (ATTENTION)	Teacher smiles. (REINFORCEMENT)
2. Teacher says, "Jump down," and holds child's hands. (VERBAL AND PHYSICAL PROMPTS)	Child jumps down onto two feet. (CORRECT EXECUTION)	Teacher says, "Good, let's try again." (REINFORCEMENT)
3. Teacher says, "Jump down like this," and jumps, landing on two feet. (VERBAL AND VISUAL PROMPTS)	Child steps down onto one foot, then other. (INCOMPLETE EXECUTION)	Teacher says, "Land on both feet," and touches both feet. (INFORMATION FEEDBACK)
4. Teacher says, "Try again. Jump," and holds one hand of child. (VERBAL AND PHYSICAL PROMPTS)	Child jumps down onto two feet. (CORRECT EXECUTION)	Teacher says, "Good jump. You landed on two feet." (REINFORCEMENT AND INFORMATION FEEDBACK)

Other Models for Young Children

I CAN: Preprimary emphasizes six skill areas: (a) locomotion, (b) body control, (c) object control, (d) play equipment, (e) play participation, and (f) health-fitness (Wessel, 1980). The I CAN acronym created by Janet Wessel refers to teacher competencies:

I   Individualize instruction
C   Create social leisure competence
A   Associate all learning
N   Narrow the gap between teaching and practice

Like PREP, I CAN is a diagnostic-prescriptive model that recognizes play as a vehicle for learning. Children are helped to associate preacademic skills (colors, numbers, action words) with games and activities of daily living; this narrows the gap between school and home. A home activities program is an integral part of I CAN, and professionals teach parents how to implement specific learning objectives.

Chapter 18 described the Language-Arts-Movement Programming (LAMP) model, which is highly recommended for young children with MR because it

FIGURE   21.13 (continued)

What prompts are being used? What reinforcement? What information feedback?

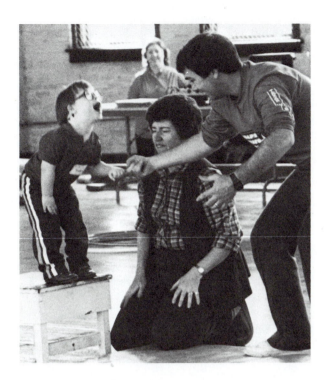

concurrently teaches language and movement through play activities based in the arts (e.g., dance, music, drama). From infancy on, rhythm and music are strong aids in motor learning.

Programming for Severe Mental Retardation

Approximately 10% of people with MR fall into the severe category, which encompasses the moderate, severe, and profound levels of the old AAMR classification system. IQs associated with severe MR range from 0 to 50, but a better descriptor is low functional ability in the nine adaptive skill areas mentioned in the "Changing Definitions" section earlier in the chapter. Typically, these persons have multiple disabilities. Their mental function may be frozen somewhere between infancy and 7 years old, or it may improve slowly up to a ceiling of about age 7.

There are many individual differences, depending on level of severity. Most individuals with severe MR, however, need a teacher-student ratio between one-to-one and one-to-three because they have little self-direction. If no one tells them what to do, they are likely to just sit or lie. Physical educators must therefore create, train, and supervise helper corps of peer tutors, teacher aides, and community volunteers. Novel approaches to this are use of older students with a higher level of MR who are training for jobs in child care and involvement of senior citizens who enjoy a foster grandparent role.

Excellent resources to help with programming are the journal and newsletter of TASH: The Association of Persons With Severe Handicaps, 11201 Greenwood Avenue N,

Seattle, WA 98133. TASH also holds an annual conference. *The Journal of the Association for Persons With Severe Handicaps* includes many articles on leisure skill training.

Persons with severe MR mature slowly motorically as well as cognitively. Most do not learn to walk before age 3. Many learn ambulation between ages 3 and 9. Physical education in the early years thus focuses on nonambulatory locomotor activities and object control (see Chapters 10, 11, and 12). Hundreds of activities can be invented on land and in the water that use lying, sitting, and four-point positions.

Social skills and communication are major goals because they are prerequisite to game play. Persons with severe MR will typically remain in the solitary or parallel play stage unless taught to play. With good teaching, they should move into the associative and cooperative play stages between ages 9 and 12 and be able to learn simple games.

Flying Dutchman, Musical Chairs, and *Catch My Tail* are examples of beginning-level games. In *Flying Dutchman,* a line of students holding hands is walked in any direction. When the verbal cue "Flying Dutchman" is called out by the teacher, the students drop hands and run back to a mat that has been established as home base. *Musical Chairs* can be played without modification, but the students may need help in finding their chairs. In *Catch My Tail,* one corner of a scarf is tucked into the back of the belt of one student, who runs about the room, with the others trying to grab the scarf.

Examples of games not usually successful are *Chicken, Come Home; Cat and Rat;* dodgeball; and relays. In *Chicken, Come Home* and similar activities, the students

FIGURE 21.14

Techniques of sensorimotor training for persons with severe mental retardation.

Goal	Action	Materials Required
Increasing awareness by stimulating sense modalities	1. Toweling, brushing, icing, stroking, tapping, contact with textures	1. Towels, brushes (light), ice bags, textured fabrics
	2. Applying restraints for short periods, promoting body awareness by cuddling and holding tightly	2. Sandbags; splint jackets; strong, gentle arms
	3. Following flashlight, hanging ball, colored toys, camera flashes	3. Flashlight, ball hanging from ceiling, blocks, balls, dolls, camera with flash
	4. Calling name of child; naming objects used, nearby persons, and actions; shaking ball, rattle; presenting music and commands	4. Wrist and ankle bells; noisemakers; tape recorders; nursery rhymes and records with varying loudness, pitch, and tempo
	5. Exposing child to extreme tastes	5. Sweet, sour, bitter, salty substances (honey, lemon, alum, salt)
	6. Exposing child to extreme odors	6. Pungent substances (coffee, cinnamon, vinegar), scented candles, incense, aerosol sprays
	7. Exposing child to extreme temperatures	7. Two basins with warm and cold water, ice bags, heating pads
	8. Mirror play	8. Full mirror, small mirrors that can be moved horizontally
	9. Wind movements	9. Fans to create wind tunnels, blowing air, fanning
	10. Vibration	10. Hand vibrators, mattress vibrators
Improving movement	1. Rolling	1. Mats with rough, smooth, hard, soft surfaces
	2. Rocking	2. Rocking chairs and horses, large beach balls
	3. Bouncing	3. Air mattress, trampoline, jump-up seat
	4. Swinging	4. Hammocks, suspended seats
	5. Coactive movements	5. Physical guidance of body or limbs (Chapter 9)
Improving manipulation	1. Reaching	1. Toys with various textures, colors, and sounds; water play; sticky clay; sand; finger paint; punching balls
	2. Grasping	2. Same as 1, yarn balls, Nerf balls
	3. Holding	3. Same as 1 and 2
	4. Releasing	4. Small balls
	5. Throwing	5. Balls, praise, food treats, affection
	6. Responding to social cues	6. Same as 5
	7. Developing relationship to one person	7. Individual teacher
Developing posture and locomotion	1. Lifting head while prone	1. Chest support
	2. Sitting	2. Rubber tube
	3. Crawling and creeping	3. Crawler, scooterboard, creep up padded stairs, inclined mats
	4. Standing	4. Standing tables, human support
	5. Riding tricycle	5. Tricycle with or without seat support and feet straps
	6. Walking	6. Parallel bars, human support, pushing weighted cart, coactive movement
	7. Stair climbing	7. Practice stairs

cannot remember which role they are playing or which direction to run. Only a few seem to understand the concepts of tagging, dodging, and catching. In *Cat and Rat,* there seems to be no idea about who is chasing whom, that one should get away, or that the circle should either help or hinder the players. In dodgeball, they fail to grasp the idea of the game and wander away from the circle. These students can be forced through the motions of a relay but have no idea of its purpose, of winning and losing, or of belonging to a team.

By adolescence, many persons with severe MR are interested in the opposite sex and activities that support romantic interests. Although mental age is delayed, social and recreational interests tend to parallel those they see on television and in the world around them. Many learn individual sports, although they seldom can handle the rules and strategies of unmodified team sports.

Criteria to guide programming include (a) valid and reliable assessment procedures, (b) clearly identified goals and objectives, and (c) activities that are specialized, practical, age-appropriate, developmental and functional (Greenwood, Silliman, & French, 1990). Underlying these criteria are the principles of normalization and ecological or social validity. Block (1992) favors the term *life-skills curriculum* to emphasize that age-appropriate, functional activities should be taught in natural environments and based on students' preferences. The following are curriculum models recommended for persons with severe MR. Goals and objectives vary widely, but pedagogy almost always incorporates behavior management with careful analysis, consistent cues and reinforcements, good correction protocols, and variable practice to aid generalization.

Sensorimotor Models

Among the earliest sensorimotor models developed specifically for persons with severe MR is the one by Ruth Webb and associates at Glenwood State Hospital-School in Iowa (Webb, 1969; Webb & Koller, 1979). Figure 21.14 summarizes this model, which focuses on four goals. The actions can be easily stated as objectives (e.g., *Show awareness of tactile stimulation by smile and/or approach-type body movements that last 3 or more sec; Reach for an attractive object and sustain reaching behavior for at least 5 sec*).

The first two goal areas in Figure 21.14 are directed toward persons who are nonambulatory, have no language, and seem to be unaware of their environment. They represent the lowest level of function. Only a small percentage of persons with MR fit this description, but under law, they must receive some kind of physical education. The last two goal areas are applicable to many persons with severe MR.

Teacher Problem Solving, Situation A

Given a 30-min class period three times a week and five non-ambulatory students, ages 5 to 10, use the activities in Figure 21.14 to guide development of some lesson plans. Visualize the students arriving in wheelchairs; some can talk and some cannot. All need as much gross motor activity as possible. Before developing lesson plans, remember to describe present level of psychomotor performance and write goals and objectives. Chapters 10, 11, and 12 will help.

Teacher Problem Solving, Situation B

Figure 21.15 presents differences in responses of persons whose mental ages are 0 to 2 as compared to 2 to 5. Although a description of real-life teaching, a class size of 25 to 30 is too large even with three energetic teachers. Consider how you would change the structure of the class. Write some lesson plans. Consider ways to enhance normalization and community integration.

Data-Based Gymnasium Model

The data-based gymnasium model is the application of special education technology developed by a group called Teaching Research in Monmouth, Oregon, to physical education. The model is fully described in a book by John Dunn, physical education professor at Oregon State University, and colleagues (Dunn, Morehouse, & Fredericks, 1986). Behavior management techniques emphasized are cueing, consequating (reinforcers, punishers, time-out), shaping, fading, and chaining. The teaching approach is task analysis with skills broken down into phases and steps.

A unique aspect of this model is the development of a clipboard of programming management for each student. This clipboard includes

1. **Weekly Cover Sheet.** Lists three or four motor programs to be practiced daily and spaces for a volunteer to check that the program was done.

2. **Language and Consequence File Sheet.** Lists student's preferred reinforcers and describes receptive and expressive language.

3. **Placement Form.** Lists about 10 specific tasks, states verbal cue for each task, and presents number of recommended trials. The teacher then records number of trials correctly done.

4. **Motor Skill Sequence Sheet.** Provides task analysis for a terminal objective like *The student will slide down the slide.* The task analysis is presented as a series of phases. Some phases are further broken down into steps.

5. **Program Cover Sheet.** Includes summary information on date the motor sequence was begun, verbal cue, materials needed, instructional setting, reinforcement procedure, correction protocol, and criterion.

6. **Data Sheet.** Provides space to record X or O for 10 trials on each phase and step of the motor skill sequence. Also requires that the reinforcers used be recorded.

7. **Maintenance File.** Summarizes the programs already learned, the cues used at the terminal phase and/or step, and the dates the skill is to be probed.

These seven pages on every clipboard enable anyone trained in the data-based pedagogy to work with and keep a student on task. For every additional skill sequence targeted, there are 4 additional pages (i.e., motor task sequence sheet, program cover sheet, data sheet, and maintenance file). Thus, some persons' clipboards have 15 or 20 pages.

FIGURE 21.15

Comparison of motor responses of persons with severe mental retardation.

Activities/Tasks	Responses of Males, Ages 10–32 (Mental Age 0–2)	Responses of Males, Ages 14–20 (Mental Age 2–5)
Beanbag: Free play; carry on head; step and hop over one bag; toss beanbag into container; toss beanbag to instructor.	This group preferred to chew or eat the beanbags. The free play consisted primarily of releasing the bag as soon as it was placed in the hand. The students were manually manipulated through each movement on a one-to-one basis. The shape of the beanbag appeared to make little difference, but occasionally, a student would reach for a certain color. Pleasure was derived mainly from attention of the teacher rather than the activity itself.	This group was more creative with the beanbags than those with lower IQs. There was less tendency to chew the bag and a better concept of throwing. Free play consisted of the students bringing the bag to the teacher to play with them on a one-to-one basis. Several observed the demonstrations and attempted to imitate. Coordination was more highly developed than in the other group, but much manual assistance was required in the footwork.
Rope and yarn: Hop on one or both legs; hop over rope; crouch down and stretch tall with rope in hand; curl up on floor and stretch long; grip rope and follow instructor.	The group did not follow instructions. Individuals were manipulated through the movements by two instructors. Curling and crouching were accepted far more readily than stretching. Walking out floor patterns seemed to be simply a matter of follow-the-leader with no real awareness of the patterns.	The group copied demonstrations, often adapting them to their own abilities. Although most attempted to hop, there was little success. This group had some concept of what was beneath their feet and enjoyed being led through and around objects. They preferred to hold the instructor's hand rather than a rope.
Cage ball: Roll ball to students on a one-to-one basis; small-group activities in a circle—sit and kick ball to each other, sit and push ball to each other; repeat from a standing position.	The ball appeared to be irritating. Group members turned away from it or attempted to push it away. Others grinned as they pushed it away, indicating that they recognized the teacher's pleasure at their correct response. None of the students used their feet to kick the ball without constant reminders. The students remained in the circle, but did not interact with their peers. Essentially, the activity was a one-to-one exchange with the teacher.	The students performed the activities with little effort. Their attention span, however, was short. The teacher had to repeatedly call out names to get responses to the ball and to close gaps in the circular formation. The group appeared to grasp the concept of the circle and playmates but preferred to roll the ball to the teacher rather than their peers. Compared to other daily lessons, the cage ball activities were especially successful.
Universal gym and mat: Press weights with legs; push and pull weights with arms; sit up on inclined board; logroll; forward roll; creeping activities on mat.	On a one-to-one basis, approximately half the group would perform what was requested to some degree. They enjoyed raising the weights and letting them drop with a loud bang. The noise appeared to be exciting to them and the center of the entire activity. The heights and weights of the students made mat work extremely fatiguing for the instructors. Many of the students were so large that they could not be safely manipulated by the two instructors. Four of the 30 pupils could do the mat activities. The group was too large for implementation of goals.	With a few exceptions, all of the students learned to perform simple presses and pulls on the universal gym. These students also enjoyed making loud noises with the weights but would lower them slowly and quietly when under the direct surveillance of the instructor. About half of the 25 pupils performed all the mat activities with the teacher's help. Others attempted the activities only after repeated urging. Most of the pupils expressed more fear and distress than enjoyment of the mat activities.

Note: Barbara Ross, an adapted physical educator, wrote these descriptions of group activities, comparing the responses of males with profound and severe retardation. Activities for the two groups were conducted separately. The sizes of the groups were 30 and 25, respectively. Two or three teachers worked together in handling groups of this size.

Another unique feature of the data-based model is its systematic plan for training and using volunteers and parents. The same protocol is used at home as at school, and the data sheet is passed back and forth daily to keep everyone informed of progress.

The data-based model offers task analyses in four areas: (a) movement concepts, (b) motor skills, (c) physical fitness, and (d) leisure skills. It is designed for one-to-one teaching and testing and is appropriate for all age groups. Task analyses focus on ambulatory persons. To use this model, formal training must be completed. Its value, however, is great in stimulating professionals to apply data-based protocol when creating their own models.

Project Transition Model

The project transition behavior management model encompasses task-analyzed sequences for teaching and testing five hygiene areas (face washing, teeth brushing, hand washing, deodorant use, and overall appearance) and five fitness areas (upper body strength, cardiovascular endurance, abdominal strength, trunk flexibility, and grip strength). Tests used to measure the latter are bench press, 300-yd run/walk, bent-knee sit-ups for 60 sec, sit-and-reach, and dynamometer. This model was created by Paul Jansma, a physical education professor at Ohio State University, and colleagues (Jansma, Decker, Ersing, McCubbin, & Combs, 1988).

A particular strength of this model is an assessment system that yields both qualitative and quantitative data. The qualitative data pertain to level of independence, and the quantitative data are traditional performance scores. Independence levels are

• UO	Unobserved. Person will not attempt, even with verbal, visual, and physical prompting.
• HI PHY+	Performs only with modeling and constant physical and verbal prompting.
• MIN PHY+	Requires physical prompt to start action and verbal prompting and modeling to finish it.
• HI V/M	Needs constant verbal prompting and modeling.
• MIN V	Needs no modeling but some verbal prompting.
• IND	Independent. No help needed except verbal prompt to start.

Knowledge about this model reinforces the importance of recording the amount of assistance needed when teaching persons with severe MR. The fitness tests used in this model provide insights into problems relative to cardiovascular endurance. Valid scores could not be obtained on distances greater than 300 yd. This means that exercise tolerance is being measured, not fitness of the heart and lungs.

FIGURE   21.16

Activities included in the Special Olympics Motor Activities Training program for persons with severe mental retardation.

1.0   Warm-up Activities
1.1   Breathing
1.2   Tactile stimulation
1.3   Relaxation activities
1.4   Range of motion

2.0   Strength and Conditioning Activities
2.1   Exercise bands
2.2   Continuous walking
2.3   Toe touches
2.4   Sit-ups
2.5   Aerobic dance

3.0   Sensory-motor Awareness Activities
3.1   Visual stimulation
3.2   Auditory stimulation
3.3   Tactile stimulation

4.0   Motor Activities
4.1   Mobility leading to gymnastics
4.2   Dexterity leading to athletics
4.3   Striking leading to softball
4.4   Kicking leading to soccer
4.5   Manual wheelchair leading to athletics
4.6   Electric wheelchair leading to athletics
4.7   Aquatics

Special Olympics Motor Activities Training Program

The Special Olympics Motor Activities Training Program (MATP) was instituted in 1989 as a replacement for the Special Olympics Developmental Program that previously served persons with severe MR (SOI, 1989b). The excellent *MATP Guide* focuses on four types of activities, so there is something for everyone, regardless of severity of condition (see Figure 21.16). Information is provided so that the MATP fits into the IEP model. The long-range goal is:

The participant will demonstrate motor and sensory-motor skills, appropriate behavior, and an understanding of the skills and rules of the MATP that will enable him/her to successfully take part in Training Day activities and official Special Olympics sports. (SOI, 1989b, p. 6)

Twelve illustrative short-term objectives are stated with the recommendation that volunteers select two to four of the objectives to guide an 8- to 16-week training program. The MATP is designed to supplement (not replace) existing programs and curricula used by parents, teachers, and therapists.

The MATP philosophy encompasses seven points:

1. Training should be fun and teach participants to ultimately self-initiate and choose these activities during their leisure time.
2. Activities should be age-appropriate.
3. Training, not competition, is the emphasis. This training may lead to competition, but 8 to 16 weeks of training should come first.

FIGURE 21.17

Special Olympics Sports Skills competitive events for persons with severe mental retardation.

Aquatics
- 10-m assisted swim
- 15-m walk
- 15-m flotation race
- 15-m unassisted swim

Athletics (Track and Field)
- 10-m assisted walk
- 25-m walk
- 10-m wheelchair event
- 25-m wheelchair race
- 30-m motorized wheelchair slalom
- 25-m motorized wheelchair obstacle race
- Ball throw for distance (tennis ball)

Basketball
- 10-m basketball dribble
- Speed dribble
- Target pass
- Spot shot
- Team skills basketball

Bowling
- Section B, rules of competition (see use of ramps)
- Target bowl
- Frame bowl

Gymnastics
- Level A wide beam
- Level A floor exercise
- Level A tumbling
- Level A all-around

Soccer (called football in many countries)
- Kick and score
- Dribble, turn, and shoot
- Team skills soccer

Softball
- Bat for distance
- Base race
- Team skills softball

Volleyball
- Volleyball pass

Team Handball
- Spot shot
- Team skills handball

Weight Lifting
- Bench press
- Modified push-ups
- Sit-ups
- Exercycle
- One-arm curl
- Chin-ups

4. After completion of MATP, every person should have the opportunity to show new skills to significant others in a Training Day program.

5. Functionality should guide activity selection. Criteria to be used are (a) high probability of opportunity to use skills in home, school, and community environments and (b) skills will increase self-sufficiency and acceptance.

6. The principle of partial participation shall be followed. This means that persons with severe MR who lack capability for independent function are given whatever assistance and adapted equipment are needed (i.e., their partial participation is supplemented to permit full inclusion). See Block (1992) and Krebs and Block (1992) for further explanation.

7. Volunteers should be creative in providing community-based sports and recreational opportunities. They should think integration first, rather than isolation.

The MATP begins with assessment of present level of performance. A task analysis assessment sheet is provided for each of the seven motor activities, with directions to chart the amount of assistance needed for 15 weeks. Codes used are *P,* for physical; *G,* for gestural; *V,* for verbal or visual; and *I,* for independent.

Training techniques emphasize setting objectives that match assessment data, utilizing behavior management techniques like shaping and reinforcing, and charting performance. Several task analyses are presented to guide teaching of each motor activity. For example, kicking is broken down into three subtasks:

1. Participant will touch ball with foot.
2. Participant will push ball forward with foot.
3. Participant will kick ball forward.

A separate task analysis is provided for each subtask, as well as general teaching suggestions that emphasize variability of practice conditions and application of skills in lead-up games.

SOI believes that competition, properly conducted and individualized, should be available to everyone who can meet three criteria:

1. Cognitively demonstrate awareness of competing against other athletes
2. Physically demonstrate the ability to perform the movements required by a particular event
3. Adhere to the rules and regulations of the particular sport

This belief is based largely on the principle of normalization (i.e., that persons with MR should have available the same opportunities as normal peers). Competition, when every participant is made to feel like a winner, provides conditions conducive to building good self-concepts (Gibbons & Bushakra, 1989; Wright & Cowden, 1986). The number of persons who watch, applaud, and praise are important aspects of the self-concept effect. Also important is the emphasis on personal best rather than social comparison.

Figure 21.17 lists official Special Olympics events designed specifically for persons with severe MR and multiple disabilities. These are conducted as individual skill tests and should be practiced many times in the school setting before being administered in the competitive milieu. Often, Special Olympics meets are the only time that the general public sees persons with severe MR. Philosophy supports the right of these persons to be seen and heard. This is a first step toward societal acceptance and toward inclusion of sport events for persons with severe MR in regular school and community track meets.

References

Abel, E. L. (1987). *Fetal alcohol syndrome and fetal alcohol effects.* New York: Plenum Press.

Blackman, J. A. (1983). *Medical aspects of developmental disabilities in children from birth to three.* Iowa City, IA: University of Iowa.

Block, M. E. (1991). Motor development in children with Down syndrome: A review of the literature. *Adapted Physical Activity Quarterly, 8* (3), 179–209.

Block, M. E. (1992). What is appropriate physical education for students with profound disabilities? *Adapted Physical Activity Quarterly, 9* (3), 197–213.

Bouffard, M. (1990). Movement problem solutions for educable mentally handicapped individuals. *Adapted Physical Activity Quarterly, 7,* 183–197.

Bouffard, M., & Wall, A. E. (1990). A problem-solving approach to movement skill acquisition: Implications for special populations. In G. Reid (Ed.), *Problems in movement control* (pp. 107–131). Amsterdam: North-Holland.

Brown, A. L. (1974). The role of strategic behavior in retarded memory. In N. R. Ellis (Ed.), *International review of research in mental retardation, Volume 7* (pp. 55–111). New York: Academic Press.

Burton, A. W., & Davis, W. E. (1992). Assessing balance in adapted physical education: Fundamental concepts and applications. *Adapted Physical Activity Quarterly, 9* (1), 14–46.

Chad, K., Jobling, A., & Frail, H. (1990). Metabolic rate: A factor in developing obesity in children with Down syndrome. *American Journal on Mental Retardation, 95* (2), 228–235.

Chasey, W. C. (1977). Motor skill overlearning effects on retention and relearning by retarded boys. *Research Quarterly, 48,* 41–46.

Chudley, A. W., & Hagerman, R. J. (1987). Fragile X syndrome. *Journal of Pediatrics, 110,* 821–831.

Cronk, C. E., Chumlea, W. C., & Roche, A. F. (1985). Assessment of overweight children with trisomy 21. *American Journal of Mental Deficiency, 89,* 433–436.

Dahlgren, W., Boreskie, S., Dowds, M., Mactavish, J., & Watkinson, E. J. (1991). The Medallion program: Using the generic sport model to train athletes with mental disabilities. *Journal of Physical Education, Recreation, and Dance, 62* (9), 67–73.

Dobbins, D. A., Garron, R., & Rarick, G. L. (1981). The motor performance of educable mentally retarded and intellectually normal boys after covariate control for differences in body size. *Research Quarterly for Exercise and Sport, 52,* 1–8.

Dorris, M. (1989). *The broken cord.* New York: Harper & Row.

Dummer, G. (1988). Teacher training to enhance motor learning by mentally retarded individuals. In C. Sherrill (Ed.), *Leadership training in adapted physical activity* (pp. 350–359). Champaign, IL: Human Kinetics.

Dunn, J. M., Morehouse, J., & Fredericks, H. (1986). *Physical education for the severely handicapped: A systematic approach to a data-based gymnasium.* Austin, TX: Pro•Ed.

Dyer, S., Gunn, P., Rauh, H., & Berry, P. (1990). Motor development in Down syndrome children: An analysis of the motor scale of the Bayley Scales of Infant Development. In A. Vermeer (Ed.), *Motor development, adapted physical activity, and mental retardation,* (pp. 7–20). Basel, Switzerland: Karger.

Eichstaedt, C., & Lavay, B. (1992). *Physical activity for individuals with mental retardation: Infant to adult.* Champaign, IL: Human Kinetics.

Eichstaedt, C., Wang, P., Polacek, J., & Dohrmann, P. (1991). *Physical fitness and motor skill levels of individuals with mental retardation, ages 6–21.* Normal, IL: Illinois State University.

Ellis, N. R. (1963). The stimulus trace and behavioral adequacy. In N. R. Ellis (Ed.), *Handbook of mental deficiency* (pp. 134–158). New York: McGraw-Hill.

Evans, J. (1980). *They have to be carefully taught: A handbook for parents and teachers of young children with handicapping conditions.* Reston, VA: American Alliance for Health, Physical Education, Recreation, and Dance.

Eyman, R. K., Call, T., & White, J. F. (1991). Life expectancy of persons with Down syndrome. *American Journal on Mental Retardation, 95* (6), 603–612.

Fernhall, B., Tymeson, G., & Webster, G. (1988). Cardiovascular fitness of mentally retarded individuals. *Adapted Physical Activity Quarterly, 5,* 12–18.

Fishler, K., & Koch, R. (1991). Mental development in Down syndrome mosaicism. *American Journal on Mental Retardation, 96* (3), 345–351.

Fox, R., & Rotatori, A. (1982). Prevalence of obesity among mentally retarded adults. *American Journal of Mental Deficiency, 87,* 228–230.

Gerber, S. E. (1990). Chromosomes and chromosomal disorders. *American Speech-Language-Hearing Association, 32,* 39–41, 47.

Gibbons, S. L., & Bushakra, F. (1989). Effects of Special Olympics participation on the perceived competence and social acceptance of mentally retarded children. *Adapted Physical Activity Quarterly, 6* (1), 40–51.

Goldman, J. J. (1988). Prader-Willi syndrome in two institutionalized older adults. *Mental Retardation, 26* (2), 97–102.

Greenwood, M., Silliman, L. M., & French, R. (1990). Comparisons of physical activity programs for severely/profoundly mentally retarded persons. *Palaestra, 6* (4), 38–47.

Grossman, H. J. (Ed.). (1983). *Classification in mental retardation.* Washington, DC: American Association on Mental Deficiency.

Henderson, S. E. (1986). Some aspects of the development of motor control in Down's syndrome. In H. T. A. Whiting & M. G. Wade (Eds.), *Themes in motor development* (pp. 69–92). Boston: Martinus Nijhoff.

Hoover, J. H., & Horgan, J. S. (1990). Short-term memory for motor skills in mentally retarded persons: Training and research issues. In G. Reid (Ed.), *Problems in movement control* (pp. 217–239). Amsterdam: North Holland.

Jansma, P., Decker, J., Ersing, W., McCubbin, J., & Combs, S. (1988). A fitness assessment system for individuals with severe mental retardation. *Adapted Physical Activity Quarterly, 5,* 223–232.

Johnson, R. E., Sundheim, R., & Santos, J. (1989). An outcome study of Special Olympics training techniques on athletes in track and field. *Palaestra, 5* (4), 9–11, 62.

Jones, K. L. (1988). *Smith's recognizable patterns of human malformation* (4th ed.). Philadelphia: W. B. Saunders.

Kelly, L. E., & Rimmer, J. (1987). A practical method for estimating percent body fat of adult mentally retarded males. *Adapted Physical Activity Quarterly, 4,* 117–125.

Kelly, L. E., Rimmer, J., & Ness, R. (1986). Obesity levels in institutionalized mentally retarded adults. *Adapted Physical Activity Quarterly, 3,* 167–176.

Kerr, R., & Blais, C. (1987). Down syndrome and extended practices of a complex motor task. *American Journal of Mental Deficiency, 91,* 591–597.

Krebs, P., & Block, M. E. (1992). Transition of students with disabilities into community recreation: The role of the adapted physical educator. *Adapted Physical Activity Quarterly, 9* (4), 305–315.

Luckasson, R., Coulter, D., Polloway, E., Deiss, S., Schalock, R., Snell, M., Spitalnik, D., & Stark, J. (1992). *Mental retardation: Definition, classification, and systems of supports* (9th ed.). Washington, DC: American Association on Mental Retardation.

Montagu, A. (1971). *The elephant man.* New York: Ballantine.

Montgomery, D. L., Reid, G., & Seidl, C. (1988). The effects of two physical fitness programs designed for mentally retarded adults. *Canadian Journal of Sport Sciences, 13* (1), 73–78.

Netter, F. H. (1986). *The CIBA collection of medical illustrations. Volume 1, Nervous system, Part II, Neurologic and neuromuscular disorders.* West Caldwell, NJ: CIBA Pharmaceutical.

Pitetti, K., Jackson, J., Stubbs, N., Campbell, K., & Battar, S. (1989). Fitness levels of adult Special Olympics participants. *Adapted Physical Activity Quarterly, 6,* 354–370.

Pizarro, D. (1990). Reliability of the health-related fitness test for mainstreamed educable and trainable mentally handicapped adolescents. *Adapted Physical Activity Quarterly, 7,* 240–248.

Rarick, G. L. (1980). Cognitive-motor relationships in the growing years. *Research Quarterly for Exercise and Sport, 51,* 174–192.

Reid, G. (1986). The trainability of motor processing strategies with developmentally delayed performers. In H. T. A. Whiting & M. G. Wade (Eds.), *Themes in motor development* (pp. 93–107). Dordrecht, Holland: Martinus Nijhoff.

Reid, G., Montgomery, D. L., & Seidl, C. (1985). Performance of mentally retarded adults on the Canadian standardized test of fitness. *Canadian Journal of Public Health, 76,* 187–190.

Reid, G., Montgomery, D. L., & Seidl, C. (1990). *Stepping out for fitness: A program for adults who are intellectually handicapped.* Ontario, Canada: Canadian Association for Health, Physical Education, and Recreation.

Rimmer, J., Braddock, D., & Fujiura, G. (1992). Blood lipid and percent body fat levels in Down syndrome versus non-DS persons with mental retardation. *Adapted Physical Activity Quarterly, 9,* 123–129.

Roswal, G. M., Roswal, P. M., & Dunleavy, A. (1986). Normative health-related fitness data for Special Olympians. In C. Sherrill (Ed.), *Sport and disabled athletes* (pp. 231–238). Champaign, IL: Human Kinetics.

Rynders, J. E., & Horrobin, J. M. (1990). Always trainable? Never educable? Updating educational expectations concerning children with Down syndrome. *American Journal on Mental Retardation, 95* (1), 77–83.

Scharfenaker, S. K. (1990). The Fragile X syndrome. *American Speech-Language-Hearing Association, 32,* 45–47.

Seidl, C., Reid, G., & Montgomery, D.L. (1987). A critique of cardiovascular fitness testing with mentally retarded persons. *Adapted Physical Activity Quarterly, 2,* 106–116.

Special Olympics International. (1980s, dates vary). *Sports skills program guides.* Washington, DC: Author. (There are 16 books, one for each official sport.)

Special Olympics International. (1989a). *Official Special Olympics summer sports rules.* Washington, DC: Author.

Special Olympics International. (1989b). *Special Olympics motor activities training guide.* Washington, DC: Author.

Spicer, R. L. (1984). Cardiovascular disease in Down Syndrome. *Pediatric Clinics of North America, 31* (6), 1331–1344.

Stanovich, K. E. (1978). Information processing in mentally retarded individuals. In N. R. Ellis (Ed.), *International review of research in mental retardation, Volume 9* (pp. 29–60). New York: Academic Press.

Stratford, B., & Ching, E. (1983). Rhythm and time in the perception of Down's syndrome children. *Journal of Mental Deficiency Research, 27,* 23–38.

Sugden, D. A., & Keogh, J. F. (1990). *Problems in movement skill development.* Columbia, SC: University of South Carolina Press.

Thomas, K. T. (1984). Applying knowledge of motor development to mentally retarded children. In J. R. Thomas (Ed.), *Motor development during childhood and adolescence* (pp. 174–184). Minneapolis: Burgess.

Wall, A. E., Bouffard, M., McClements, J., Findlay, H., & Taylor, M. J. (1985). A knowledge-based approach to motor development: Implications for the physically awkward. *Adapted Physical Activity Quarterly, 2* (1), 21–43.

Watkinson, E. J., & Wall, A. E. (1982). *PREP: The PREP play program: Play skill instruction for mentally handicapped children.* Ontario: Canadian Association for Health, Physical Education, and Recreation.

Webb, R. (1969). Sensory-motor training of the profoundly retarded. *American Journal of Mental Deficiency, 74,* 283–295.

Webb, R., & Koller, J. (1979). Effects of sensorimotor training on intellectual and adaptive skills of profoundly retarded adults. *American Journal of Mental Deficiency, 83,* 490–496.

Wessel, J. (1980). *I CAN implementation guide for preprimary motor and play skills.* East Lansing, MI: Michigan State University Marketing Division Instructional Media Center.

Wright, J., & Cowden, J. (1986). Changes in self-concept and cardiovascular endurance of mentally retarded youth in a Special Olympics swimming program. *Adapted Physical Activity Quarterly, 3,* 177–184.

Zigler, E., & Hodapp, R. (1986). *Understanding mental retardation.* Cambridge, England: Cambridge University Press.

Zigman, W. G., Schupf, N., Lubin, R., & Silverman, W. (1987). Premature regression of adults with Down syndrome. *American Journal of Mental Deficiency, 92* (2), 161–168.

CHAPTER

22

Serious Emotional Disturbance and Autism

FIGURE 22.1

The child with serious emotional disturbance must be taught how to channel aggression. Behavior disorders are a common problem in public schools.

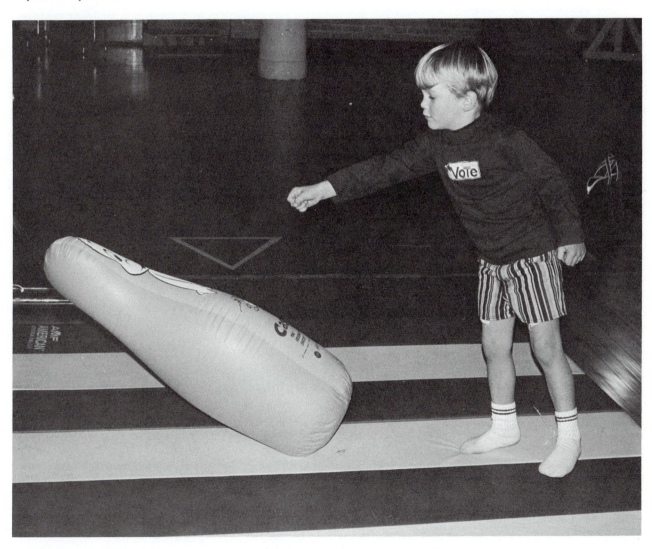

After you have studied this chapter, you should be able to:

1. Contrast the terminology and definitions of severe emotional disturbance used by federal law, the Council for Exceptional Children (CEC), and the American Psychiatric Association (APA). What is the major application and value of each?

2. Discuss changes in the diagnosis and treatment of emotional disturbance during the past decade. How have these affected attitudes toward persons with mental disorders?

3. Explain each of the following: (a) organic mental disorders, (b) substance use disorders, (c) schizophrenic disorders, (d) affective disorders, (e) personality disorders, and (f) the diagnostic categories specific to childhood and adolescence. Indicate behaviors that teachers should call to the attention of school counselors.

4. Differentiate between anorexia nervosa and bulimia and discuss each in relation to eating habits, exercise, and body image disturbances.

5. Differentiate between movement disorders associated with mental disorders and those not so associated.

6. Discuss the use of sports, dance, and aquatics as vehicles for the amelioration of different kinds of behavior and mental disorders.

7. Offer suggestions for working with students who are (a) schizophrenic and (b) depressed.

8. Discuss models and strategies like the *Good Behavior Game,* Hellison's social responsibility model, and the talking-bench strategies. Create some new approaches.

9. Discuss autism and strategies for teaching physical education to students with autism (see Figure 22.1).

The monkey bars, crisscrossing up and down, forward and backward, intrigued him. There was no question that his jiggler pointed in their direction. But what if he got caught in the middle of all that iron? What if he couldn't get out?

He walked over cautiously and touched the closest bar. It was cold. A sinister chill ran through him. But the jiggler pointed in that direction again. This time he touched a bar warmed by the sun. This felt different, more inviting, but he was still afraid. It looked like a wonderful toy to climb over and swing from. And it looked like an awful monster that could tangle you up, crush you, and kill you. (Rubin, 1962)

Playground and gymnasium settings can be terrifying to a child, as depicted so well by Theodore Isaac Rubin, a practicing psychiatrist in Brooklyn, whose book should be read by all teachers interested in childhood schizophrenia. In the preceding passage, he describes Jordi, an 8-year-old boy with a diagnosis of schizophrenic reaction-type, mixed, undifferentiated, chronic. Like most children with emotional disturbance (ED), Jordi lives at home and attends a day school. Jordi is afraid of almost everything and carries a jiggler (a doorknob tied to a string) for security. Only when he learns to play stoop ball does he give up the jiggler. Later, his skill in stoop ball gives him enough confidence to respond affirmatively to an invitation to participate in a handball game—one of his first efforts to relate to the peer group.

Prevalence of Emotional Disorders

Prevalence of severe emotional disorders varies widely because of differing definitions and diagnostic criteria. In the U.S. adult population, one of six persons at some time in life will have problems severe enough to require professional help.

The diagnosis of mental disorders is difficult, and most psychiatrists prefer not to attach a label. The prevalence of behavior disorders in the school population ranges from 2 to 22%, depending upon the criterion of behavior disorders used. The ratio of boys to girls with mental disorders is approximately 4 to 1. The U.S. Department of Education estimates very conservatively that approximately 2% of the school-age population is so severely emotionally disturbed that special education provisions are required. This includes over 1 million students between ages 5 and 19.

Suicide increasingly is a problem of childhood and adolescence, ranking third as the leading cause of death in the 15 to 24 age bracket. Statistics for all age groups combined reveal over 25,000 suicides each year. Approximately 2 million Americans have made one or more attempts at suicide.

Delinquency, a legal term reserved for youngsters whose behavior results in arrest and court action, is another manifestation of emotional problems. The crime rate among young persons has increased steadily during the past decade. Youthful offenders are estimated to account for 61% of all auto thefts, 54% of larcenies, 55% of burglaries, and 33% of robberies. Long before their initial arrest, many delinquents are described by classroom teachers as defiant, impertinent, uncooperative, irritable, bullying, attention seeking, negative, and restless. Other delinquents are seen as shy, lacking in self-confidence, hypersensitive, fearful, and excessively anxious.

Definitions of Emotional Disturbance

Definitions of severe emotional disturbance come from several sources. The three most frequently used are federal law, the Council for Exceptional Children (CEC), and the American Psychiatric Association (APA).

Federal Law Terminology

The federal term used in determining eligibility for special education services is *seriously emotionally disturbed*. This term means

a condition exhibiting one or more of the following characteristics over a long period of time and to a marked degree, which adversely affects educational performance:

(A) *An inability to learn which cannot be explained by intellectual, sensory, or health factors;*

(B) *An inability to build or maintain satisfactory interpersonal relationships with peers and teachers;*

(C) *Inappropriate types of behavior or feelings under normal circumstances;*

(D) *A general pervasive mood of unhappiness or depression; or*

(E) *A tendency to develop physical symptoms or fears associated with personal or school problems.* (Federal Register, *August 23, 1977, p. 42478*)

Originally, this definition included *autism*. In 1981, however, students with autism were included instead in the official definition of *other health impaired*. Finally, in 1990, autism was recognized as an independent diagnostic category. Autism is discussed at the end of this chapter.

CEC Terminology

Many special educators use the term *behavior disorders* rather than emotional or mental illness. In 1962, the CEC formed the Council for Children with Behavioral Disorders (CCBD). This organization publishes a quarterly journal called *Behavioral Disorders* and influences special education practices.

APA Terminology

The nomenclature of mental disorders is established by the APA in a book entitled *Diagnostic and Statistical Manual of Mental Disorders (DSM-III)*, which is published approximately every 10 years. The third edition (APA, 1980) made drastic changes in terminology that rendered many textbooks out of date. For example, the age-old classification of mental disorders into neuroses, psychoses, and personality or character disorders was discarded. The first two of these terms no longer appear in its glossary.

DSM-III identifies and discusses 16 diagnostic categories and states criteria for medical diagnosis. Among these are (a) disorders usually first evident in infancy, childhood, or adolescence; (b) organic mental disorders; (c) substance use disorders; (d) schizophrenic disorders; (e) affective disorders; (f) psychosexual disorders; and (g)personality disorders. Conditions previously lumped together as psychoses and neuroses now each have their own specific categories. Readers who still feel they must lump together conditions are told to use the terms *psychotic disorders* and *neurotic disorders;* lumping, however, is strongly discouraged. This new official recognition of the specificity of mental disorders reflects the knowledge explosion of the last decades, specifically in regard to diagnosis and treatment.

All of the disciplines that adhere to the medical rather than the educational model use *DSM-III* as their primary source. This includes therapeutic recreation personnel, occupational and physical therapists, and many others with whom adapted physical educators work. Within the multidisciplinary context, familiarity with at least some of the content of *DSM-III* is therefore important. New knowledge, published as research, also typically appears under specific rather than general classifications.

DSM-III also serves as the primary source for differentiating between sanity and insanity in court cases and for labeling certain behaviors as normal versus abnormal. Most state laws are consistent with theory evolved by the APA; this theory changes, of course, as knowledge about human behavior expands. For instance, masturbation and homosexuality were once considered evil and abnormal behaviors that would lead to insanity. *DSM-III* does not mention masturbation among psychosexual disorders. It states that homosexuality itself is not a mental disorder, but that homosexual feelings and practices that lead to persistent distress are a psychosexual disorder (p. 282).

Classic Mental Disorders

Of the 16 *DSM-III* diagnostic categories, the most common ones are described in this section. Children and youth, as well as adults, may be diagnosed as having these disorders. The behaviors are essentially the same, regardless of age.

Organic Mental Disorders

Organic mental disorders encompass psychological abnormalities associated with transient or permanent brain dysfunction. By tradition, disorders related to aging of the brain or damage to the brain from injuries (war, vehicle, and the like) or from drugs, alcohol, and other substances fall into this category. Alzheimer's disease (degeneration of the brain that results in premature aging) is illustrative of aging disorders, as is dementia senility. Substance-related damage is differentiated from substance use disorders that have not yet resulted in actual brain damage.

Substance Use Disorders

DSM-III states that use of substances like coffee, tobacco, alcohol, and caffeine soft drinks to modify mood or behavior under certain circumstances is generally considered normal and appropriate (p. 163). There are, however, widespread cultural and religious variations in what is considered appropriate.

When more or less regular substance use results in behavioral changes that negatively affect work and leisure productivity, social functioning, or happiness and welfare of family or friends, substance use is labeled a mental disorder. *Substance use disorders* may be manifested as either *abuse* or *dependence*. Substances may be either legal (coffee, tobacco) or illegal (marijuana, cocaine, amphetamines). Likewise, they may be medically prescribed to control a chronic

Table 22.1
Types of schizophrenic disorders specified in *DSM-III*.

1. **Disordered Type.** Characterized by marked incoherence and dull, silly, or inappropriate affect, but no delusions.
2. **Catatonic Type.** Characterized by marked psychomotor disturbance that may range from stupor to purposeless hyperactivity. Catatonic rigidity is the maintenance of a rigid posture against efforts to be moved. Catatonic posturing refers to assumption of inappropriate or bizarre postures.
3. **Paranoid Type.** Characterized by delusions and/or hallucinations.
4. **Undifferentiated Type.** Characterized by prominent delusions, hallucinations, incoherence, or grossly disorganized behavior. Meets criteria for more than one type of schizophrenia or for none.
5. **Residual Type.** Characterized by such chronic signs as social withdrawal, eccentric behavior, dull affect, and illogical thinking, but without prominence of delusions or hallucinations.

Table 22.2
Mental disorders usually first evident in infancy, childhood, or adolescence.

1. Mental retardation
2. Attention deficit disorders
3. Conduct disorders
4. Anxiety disorders
5. Attachment, schizoid, identity, and other disorders
6. Eating disorders, including anorexia nervosa
7. Stereotyped movement disorders
8. Stuttering, bed-wetting, sleep terror, and other disorders
9. Pervasive developmental disorders, including autism
10. Specific developmental disorders pertaining to learning and academic success (e.g., reading)

health problem or available on the open market. The nature of the substance is not relevant; the diagnostic criteria include inability to reduce or stop use and episodes of overuse.

Schizophrenic Disorders

The category of *schizophrenic disorders* includes numerous conditions, all characterized by deterioration from previous level of functioning and psychotic features and episodes. *DSM-III* defines *psychotic* as indicating gross impairment in reality testing. Psychotic features vary from person to person but include disturbances in thought processes, perception, and affect (i.e., emotions or feelings). The person tends to withdraw from and/or distort reality. Distortions include *hallucinations* (perceiving things that do not exist) and *delusions* (interpreting ideas and events in unrealistic, inappropriate ways).

Although the word *schizophrenia* is derived from *schizein* ("to split") and *phren* ("mind"), schizophrenic disorders are no longer described as split personalities. Table 22.1 summarizes the five types of schizophrenia described in *DSM-III*.

Of the mental conditions that require hospitalization, schizophrenic disorders are the most common. Half of all mental patients are schizophrenic. Moreover, 1 of every 100 persons in the world suffers from schizophrenia at some time or another. In the United States, more than a quarter of all hospital beds are filled with patients who have schizophrenia.

DSM-III states that the onset of schizophrenia is usually adolescence or adulthood. Nevertheless, estimates of childhood schizophrenia range from 100,000 to 500,000. There are approximately 4,000 children with psychotic disorders in state hospitals, close to 2,500 in residential treatment and day-care centers, and at least 3,000 children with schizophrenia in day-care clinics.

Affective Disorders

Affective disorders encompass the manic and depressive syndromes and thus are disturbances of mood. They may be bipolar disorders (i.e., characterized by mood shifts from mania to depression and vice versa) or unipolar (usually characterized by episodes of extreme depression). *Manic episodes* are defined as presence (for at least 1 week) of such behaviors as hyperactivity and restlessness; decreased need for sleep; unusual talkativeness; distractibility manifested as abrupt, rapid changes in activity or topics of speech; inflated self-esteem; and excessive involvement in such high-risk activity as reckless driving, buying sprees, sexual indiscretions, and quick business investments. *Depressive episodes* include loss of interest or pleasure in all or almost all usual activities; too much sleep or insomnia; poor appetite and significant weight loss; low self-esteem; chronic fatigue; diminished ability to think, concentrate, and make decisions; and recurrent thoughts of death and suicide.

Personality Disorders

Personality disorders is a broad category that characterizes persons whose personality traits are inflexible and maladaptive and significantly impair social, leisure, or vocational functioning. Individuals with personality disorders are grouped into three clusters: (a) persons who appear odd or eccentric; (b) persons who appear antisocial, erratic, or narcissistic; and (c) persons who appear anxious or fearful, as manifested by compulsive, dependent, or passive-aggressive behaviors.

Many children, as well as juvenile delinquents, fall into this diagnostic category. The term *personality disorders,* however, is not typically assigned until adolescence or adulthood because of the plasticity of childhood behavior.

Disorders in Students

DSM-III separates mental disorders first evident in infancy, childhood, or adolescence from the other 15 diagnostic categories. Table 22.2 lists the conditions included. Although such problems as substance use and schizophrenia often appear in childhood, they are excluded from this diagnostic category because symptoms are the same, regardless of age. This section describes disorders common in childhood and adolescence.

Attention Deficit Disorders

Signs of *attention deficit disorders* (*ADD*) are developmentally inappropriate inattention, impulsivity, and hyperactivity. Onset is about 3 years of age, but the disorder is often not diagnosed until problems occur at school. ADD is 10 times more common in boys than girls and seem to appear more often in some families than others (i.e., there appears to be a genetic predisposition). Other predisposing factors are mental retardation, convulsive disorders, and some forms of cerebral palsy and other neurological disorders. Children with learning disabilities have a high prevalence of ADD. *DSM-III* estimates that 3% of prepubertal U.S. children exhibit this disorder. ADD is described in detail in Chapter 20.

Conduct Disorders

Conduct disorders are characterized by repetitive and persistent behaviors that violate the basic rights of others and/or the norms and rules of society. Children in this category are divided into four subtypes. *Undersocialized* children are unable to establish a normal degree of affection, empathy, or bond with others; typically display a lack of concern for anyone but self; and feel little or no guilt. *Socialized* children show social attachment to some persons but are unduly callous or manipulative toward individuals to whom they are not attached. *Aggressive* types are those who exhibit any kind of physical violence; this includes theft, property damage, and intimidation or harm of persons and/or animals. *Nonaggressive* types are characterized by absence of violence. Nonaggressive behaviors include lying, truancy, running away, and substance use.

Conduct disorders are more prevalent in children of adults who have mental disorders, particularly those in the substance user category. With the exception of the undersocialized type, conduct disorders are more common in males than females, with the prevalence ratios ranging from 4 to 1 to 12 to 1.

Anxiety Disorders

The *anxiety disorders* category includes students who exhibit abnormal and persistent fears and/or unrealistic worries. After 18 years of age, this condition is called *agoraphobia*. It also includes students who persistently shrink from contact with strangers (avoidant disorders). Initial learning in swimming, gymnastics, and other physical education activities causes some students considerable anxiety. Determining whether these behaviors are specific to the gymnasium or part of a generalized pattern is important.

Attachment Disorders

The broad category of attachment disorders includes behaviors of immature emotional functioning and poorly developed social responsiveness that are not due to autism, mental retardation, or physical disabilities. The several types of attachment disorders include schizoid and identity dysfunctions. *Schizoid* should not be confused with *schizophrenia*. Schizoid disorders are defects in the ability to form social relationships, accompanied by lack of concern about social isolation; the condition is relatively rare and should be differentiated from normal individual differences in social reticence. *Identity disorders* (which are associated mostly with adolescence) pertain primarily to self-concept, friendship patterns, and gender orientation.

Eating Disorders

The eating disorders category includes gross disturbances in eating behaviors. Most common are anorexia nervosa and bulimia. Although these may occur at any age, their first manifestation is almost always in childhood or adolescence.

Anorexia nervosa is a condition characterized by significant weight loss, refusal to maintain normal body weight, disturbance of body image, and intense fear of becoming obese. In females, it is accompanied by amenorrhea (cessation of menstrual periods). The disorder occurs primarily in females (95%). The prevalence rate for females in the 12- to 18-year-old age range is about 1 of every 250. This condition leads to death by starvation in about 15 to 21% of the treated cases. Hospitalization is generally required to prevent starvation. The major diagnostic criterion is permanent weight loss of at least 25% of original body weight.

Bulimia is characterized by recurrent episodes of binge eating (the consumption of huge quantities in 2 hr or less), awareness that the eating pattern is abnormal, fear of being unable to stop eating voluntarily, and depressed mood following eating binges. The disorder is more common in females than males and typically begins in adolescence or early adulthood. Persons with bulimia are usually within a normal weight range, but they exhibit frequent weight fluctuations because of alternating binges and fasts. They try to control weight by dieting, self-induced vomiting, or the use of laxatives and medicines. Bulimia is seldom totally incapacitating, although it may affect social, leisure, and vocational functioning. Unlike anorexia nervosa, it does not result in death when untreated. It is, in fact, very much like alcohol and substance abuse.

Stereotyped Movement Disorders

The *stereotyped movement disorders* category includes persons with tics, stereotypic movement patterns (often called blindisms or autistic-like movements), and Tourette's syndrome. They may be independent disorders or coexist with such disabilities as deaf-blindness, blindness, autism, and severe mental retardation.

Tics are defined by *DSM-III* as involuntary, rapid movements of related skeletal muscles or involuntary production of noises or words. Tics should be differentiated from other kinds of movement disorders (choreiform, dystonic, athetoid, myoclonic, spastic) that are not encompassed by this diagnostic category (see Table 22.3).

Table 22.3
Movement disorders not associated with mental illness.

1. **Choreiform.** Random, irregular, nonrepetitive, dancelike movements.
2. **Dystonic.** Slow, twisting movements interspersed with prolonged states of muscular tension.
3. **Athetoid.** Slow, irregular, writhing movements.
4. **Myoclonic.** Brief, shocklike muscle contractions that affect one muscle or its parts, but not entire muscle groups.
5. **Spasms.** Stereotypic movements that affect groups of muscle. Slower and more prolonged than tics.

Stereotypic movement refers to voluntary habits or mannerisms that appear to be pleasurable. This category includes rocking, head banging, repetitive hand movements, bizarre posturing, and other movements.

Tourette's syndrome is a condition characterized by multiple vocal tics and the presence of involuntary, repetitive, rapid, purposeless movements of multiple muscle groups. Its onset is typically between 2 and 13 years of age, and its duration is usually lifelong, although there may be periods of remission.

Prevalence of Tourette's syndrome varies from 1 to 5 per 10,000 (i.e., about the same as Down syndrome or autism). The disorder affects three times as many males as females.

Vocalizations in Tourette's syndrome include clicks, grunts, yelps, barks, sniffs, coughs, and words. About 60% of persons with this condition experience an irresistible urge to utter obscenities. The symptoms are heightened by stress but disappear during sleep and sometimes during daytime activities that are particularly absorbing.

Implications for Physical Education

Sports, dance, and aquatics are vehicles for the amelioration of behavior disorders. Team membership can be made meaningful enough that a youngster will curb unsocialized behaviors. The physical educator soon learns to help aggressive students express hostility in socially acceptable ways (see Figure 22.2): punching a bag, jumping, leaping, throwing, pushing, and pulling. Offensive skills like the smash and volleyball spike can be practiced when tension is especially great. It sometimes helps to paint faces on the balls and punching bags. The teacher can join in stomping empty food cans, paper cups turned upside down, and balloons. The making of noise itself relieves tension.

Persons must learn that it is acceptable to take out aggressions on things but never on persons or animals. Thus, boxing or wrestling is contraindicated for some students with severe ED. Aggressive persons often can be developed into good squad leaders. Always, they demand special attention—a personal "Hello, John" at the *first* of the period and the frequent use of their names throughout class instruction.

Most difficult to cope with are withdrawing and overanxious behaviors. Most authorities concur that students should not be forced to participate in activities that they fear or intensely dislike. Swimming, tumbling, and apparatus seem to evoke withdrawal reactions more often than do other physical education activities. In normal persons, these fears gradually subside when it becomes obvious that the peer group is having fun. Coaxing, cajoling, and reasoning accomplish little other than giving the extra attention that the student is seeking. In the case of actual behavior disorders, psychotherapy and other specialized techniques are generally needed. The physical educator should work cooperatively with the school psychologist in strengthening the student's self-confidence and feelings of worth.

Placement of Students With Emotional Disturbances

Although most students with severe ED live at home and are educated in public schools, some (especially within the 16- to 21-year-old age range) are hospitalized and receive treatment similar to adult mental patients. An excellent hospital education and treatment program is described by Northcutt and Tipton (1978), who emphasize the importance of structure. At the time of initial hospital placement, adolescents with ED are typically confused, anxious, delusional, and angry. Hospitalization is a last resort, generally indicating the need for vigorous use of antipsychotic drugs (see Appendix B) and, for perhaps 5% of the patients, electroshock therapy.

During this initial stage, formal education is typically limited to recreation classes. These provide a wide range or activities, including rhythmic exercise, dance, yoga, and arts and crafts. Emphasis is upon success and immediate reward. These classes are mostly taught by therapeutic recreation or physical activity personnel with strong backgrounds in psychology. During the first weeks in the hospital, however, the major thrust is determining which medications should be prescribed and how much; equally important is control of medication side effects that may include drowsiness, listlessness, muscle stiffness, nausea, blurred vision, and others.

When students can concentrate on simple structured tasks and are no longer dangerous to themselves or others, they are moved to the intermediate unit, which offers more freedom. Additionally, the intermediate unit provides small-group instruction (8 to 10 students) in academic subjects, including physical education, art, and music. Emphasis at this stage is more on learning to assume responsibility for behavior (attending classes on time, managing anger and aggression, and acting appropriately) than on subject matter. A token economy and other behavior management techniques are used.

Within a few months, the student moves to the day school, which is as much as possible like a regular public school. The major difference is that classes are individualized and self-paced by the students. Emphasis is placed on their independently setting and achieving goals. Most adolescents are hospitalized for less than 1 year.

Successful mainstream reentry is obviously dependent upon public school personnel adhering to the same education principles as hospital personnel. Chief among these

FIGURE 22.2

Tetherball is a group activity in which hostility can be released in socially acceptable ways.

are minimizing stress and ensuring success. The techniques that follow are appropriate for either hospital or school personnel. The disciplines of therapeutic recreation and dance therapy emphasize working with mental disorders more than does physical education. Thus, persons from these fields make excellent consultants.

Techniques for Working With Schizophrenia

Four principles guide work with schizophrenia: (a) graded reversal of deterioration, (b) constructive progress, (c) education toward reality, and (d) directive guidance (Wolman, 1970). The first principle emphasizes *not removing, taking apart, or taking away whatever neurotic defenses the person possesses, but instead building on what is found.* The person must not feel disapproval and should not be criticized for acting like a baby. The growth process is likened to the normal child's transition from a nipple to a cup. The nipple is not taken away, but the cup is made as attractive as possible. For a while, the child uses both and then gradually rejects the nipple.

The *principle of constructive progress* implies the addition of new, more mature, and tempting elements to life. Since the student with schizophrenia is afraid of growing up, he or she must be lured and/or bribed into accepting adolescence and adulthood.

Students with schizophrenia typically are trying to escape reality through withdrawal. *Education toward reality* necessitates shifting attention from the inner world of fantasy toward the real world of happenings. When a student tries to attribute monsterlike qualities to playground apparatus or magical powers to a jiggler or ball, as Jordi does in this chapter's opening paragraph, the physical educator must convince him or her of the true nature of reality. It is wrong to *play along* with the fantasy of persons with ED. Likewise, the educator should not *play along* with hallucinations or ask questions pertaining to them, thereby appearing to be interested. Recommended responses to hallucinations are, "You know that is not true" or "That doesn't make sense."

Directive guidance, the fourth principle, emphasizes the importance of telling students the difference between right and wrong, rather than hoping that they will learn for themselves in a laissez-faire environment. Students with schizophrenia, to become whole, must become well-adjusted adults in a *given* society. They must believe in the value of rules and laws and be capable of accepting society's power figures: umpires, police officers, teachers, and administrators. Helping students to understand the structure of games and the importance of rules and penalties in facilitating good play is often a first step toward wellness.

Students with schizophrenia do not respond well to firm discipline. They are terrified by external power, both real and imagined.

A schizophrenic child becomes more paranoid when treated with firmness. He considers it proof of his paranoid ideas. But a loving, soothing attitude of a familiar, affectionate adult will bring him back to normal behavior. (Wolman, 1970, p.20)

Whereas normal students may feel hostile to authority figures, they can do so without acting out and without excessive guilt. In students with schizophrenia, even small bits of criticism may elicit destructive behavior. The physical educator should understand that hostility is basically a protective reaction. Some students feel endangered by criticism and/or even helpful suggestions. Yet, such students must be given firm limits. They must also learn that there are adults who do not get angry when they misbehave. The physical educator must combine friendliness and warmth with consistent enforcement of limits. Should a temper tantrum occur, it is better not to try to talk over the noise. A student driven by panic or rage is out of contact with reality, and reasoning will not help. Sometimes, the only alternative for stopping aggressive behavior is physical restraint.

The following suggestions may help:

1. Avoid conflict that might cause temper tantrums. Overlook minor transgressions. Each temper tantrum is a step backward.

2. If the person becomes aggressive, try to distract him or her. Introduce some new toy or game.

3. Should a person strike or bite you, do not become ruffled or angry. In a cool, calculated manner, say something like,"Ouch, that hurt! What in the world did I do to cause you to bite me?"

4. Do not show fear or confusion about a behavior. Students with schizophrenia tend to be extrasensitive to the feelings of teachers and may use such information to manipulate the adult. Never say, for instance, "I just don't understand you" or "I don't know what to do with you."

5. Do not use threats or physical violence or abandonment. Do not punish the students since punishment reinforces paranoid beliefs.

6. Reward good behavior and structure the situation so as to avoid bad behavior.

7. Create situations for learning to relate socially to others in movement exploration (see Figure 22.3), dance, and individual and dual sports before pushing the student into the complex human relationships of team sport strategy.

FIGURE 22.3

Sharing a piece of tubular jersey during a guided movement exploration lesson helps two children to begin to relate to each other socially in a nonthreatening setting.

8. Structure play groups and/or class squads very carefully, maintaining a balance between the number of aggressive and the number of passive persons. The school psychologist may help with this endeavor.

Techniques for Working With Depression

Extreme depression can characterize any age group. Depressive symptoms are present in approximately 40% of the adolescent suicide attempts. The incidence of suicide is rising among young children as well as teenagers, where it is already the third leading cause of death in the United States.

Depression is manifested by social withdrawal (Figure 22.4), loss of initiative, a decrease in appetite, and difficulty in sleeping. Persons with depression generally have a self-depreciating attitude, believe that they are bad, and wish to punish themselves. Suicide, truancy, self-destructive behaviors like head banging, and disobedience may all be behavioral equivalents of depression.

More than anything else, persons who are depressed need to be kept active. Yet, they often refuse to participate in physical activity. They have no desire to learn new skills since life is not worth living and they intend to kill themselves anyway. Some persons will sit for days, crying and thinking of methods of suicide. Whereas most of us are inclined to sympathize with anyone who cries, displaying a rough, noncommittal exterior to individuals who are depressed is best. For instance, the person may be asked,"Do you play golf?" The typical response is a self-depreciating,

FIGURE   22.4

Depression is associated with withdrawal. Here, Dr. Karen DePauw guides a rhythmic activity and encourages involvement.

"I'm not any good" or "I'm not good enough to play with so-and-so." Instead of trying to build up the person's ego, as a teacher might do with a well person, it is best to agree and make a statement like "That's probably true!" In other words, the teacher should mirror or restate the person's thoughts rather than contradict him or her. Psychologists concur that praise and compliments only make persons who are depressed feel more unworthy. They feel guilty when others say good things about them and/or are nice to them.

Severe depression is often treated by electric shock therapy (EST) and antidepressant medications (see Appendix B). The teacher or therapist cooperates with the psychiatric staff by maintaining a full schedule of physical activities. Persons who are depressed generally follow instructions but will not engage in activities voluntarily. They should be helped to recognize and cope with the anger that they turn inward toward themselves, thereby causing the state of depression. A goal is to get them angry and then help them express this anger outwardly instead of repressing it. Situations must be devised to make them angry enough to risk standing up for themselves, a first step back to self-respect and self-love.

In one situation, this was accomplished by awaking five patients with severe depression before dawn and insisting that they were scheduled for a 6 A.M. swimming class. Without breakfast, they were ushered into an ice-cold outdoor pool and told that they must stay in the water. In addition to these unpleasantries, the therapist scolded and ridiculed them. Typically, the person who is depressed sub-

mits to such a program, but if the unpleasantries are intense enough, there may be mild protests. When these are autocratically ignored, real anger can sometimes be evoked. Whatever techniques are used, the teacher or therapist must work closely with the psychiatric staff.

Each person with depression is unique and no single approach can be recommended. Physical education and recreation personnel should remember, however, that their primary role is to engage persons in activity, not to listen to sad stories and self-criticism. Other staff members are employed specifically to listen and conduct verbal therapy.

Adapting the Public School Program

Students whose problems are so severe that they meet federal law eligibility requirements for special services need separate, adapted physical education instruction in a class not larger than 12 students. Within special education, the average student-teacher ratio across the United States varies from 12 to 1 to 21 to 1, depending upon the nature of the disability. The special education average student-teacher ratio is lower for ED classes (12 to 1) than for any other disability except for students with severe or multiple disabilities. Small class size in physical education, as in special education, is probably the single most important criterion for success.

Behavior management techniques comprise the major pedagogy in most schools. Research by Vogler and French (1983) explains in detail the use of a behavior management strategy called the *Good Behavior Game.* This technique primarily focuses on helping students understand and conform to on-task behavior. Tokens in the form of frowny faces are given to class squads (six students in size) for each student who is not on task. Squads with the fewest tokens are rewarded with free time. The *Good Behavior Game* involves everyone on a squad helping and monitoring each other so as to achieve a desired reward; thus, it teaches caring behaviors.

The social development or social responsibility model of Don Hellison (1978, 1984) is also highly recommended. Use of this model begins with assessment to determine level of social development; the goal then is to provide curriculum that will enable students to advance from level to level (DeBusk & Hellison, 1989).

Hellison posits six levels of social development. Level 0, *Irresponsibility,* is characterized by disruptive behaviors, abuse, and refusal to participate and cooperate. Level 1, *Self-Control,* is beginning awareness of the importance of accepting responsibility for one's actions; the student is no longer disruptive, but neither is he or she prepared, productive, or fully participating. Level 2, *Involvement,* is characterized by genuine efforts to follow instructions and to cooperate with others; behavior is inconsistent, however, and students need frequent prompts and rewards. Level 3, *Self-Responsibility,* is evidenced by ability to work independently, set personal goals, and stay on task with minimal or no assistance. Level 4, *Caring,* is characterized by self-initiative in helping and supporting others; students are able to empathize and sustain caring relationships. Level 5, *Going Beyond,* is the social maturity to accept leadership responsibilities.

Curriculum to advance movement toward self-responsibility and leadership is built on humanistic philosophy and pedagogy. Emphasis is on students learning to make choices and accept responsibility. First, the teacher develops contracts that students sign. Gradually, students assume responsibility for their own contracts. Initially, contracts are for short periods, like 5 or 10 min, but later, they may structure several days or weeks.

In addition to contracting, students are taught social skills like negotiation and compromise. The *talking-bench strategy* is used when two persons get into an argument. The individuals go to a designated area, remain seated until differences are resolved, and then report the outcome to the teacher. Time missed from physical activity is made up.

In general, instruction of students with ED involves learning to cope with disruptive behaviors (Rimmer, 1989; Vogler & Bishop, 1990). The more strategies that teachers know, the more likely they will cope effectively (Johns, MacNaughton, & Karabinus, 1989). Effective teaching of students with ED requires courses in psychology and counseling. Research shows that children with ED have low self-concepts and poor attitudes toward physical activity involvement (Politino & Smith, 1989). Underlying problems like these must be addressed.

Autism

Autism is a severe, chronic developmental disability that occurs before age 3 and is manifested by lack of responsiveness to other people, gross impairment in communication, and bizarre, stereotypic behaviors. About one third of persons with autism are able to live and work fairly independently by adulthood; the other two thirds remain severely disabled. The 1988 movie *Rain Man* did much to sensitize the public to autism. Dustin Hoffman portrayed Raymond, an autistic savant, who was a genius with numbers but unable to live independently and to relate meaningfully to his brother. Viewing *Rain Man* is a recommended activity.

Autism is a moderate-incidence condition (see Appendix A). The range of incidence is 5 to 15 per 10,000 births, depending on the diagnostic criteria used. Autism is four times more common in males than females (Autism Society of America, 1987).

Diagnosis can be either *autism* (also called infantile autism and Kanner's syndrome) or *autistic-like behaviors*. Many persons, with and without disabilities, exhibit autistic-like behaviors. Autism comes from the Greek word *autos,* meaning "self," and refers specifically to self-absorption and withdrawal (i.e., lack of responsiveness to other people). Leo Kanner (1943) was the first to describe autism as a syndrome.

Autism was considered a form of emotional disturbance until 1981, when federal law reclassified it under *other health impairments.* In 1990, the Individuals With Disabilities Education Act (IDEA) recognized autism as a separate diagnostic category. In school settings, however, students with autism are generally placed with students who have ED because of common problems that require behavior management.

Autism is also associated with mental retardation, epilepsy, and other disorders that affect brain function. About 20% of people with autism have IQs above 70; 20% have IQs between 50 and 70; and 60% have IQs below 50 (Autism Society of America, 1987). Determining intellectual function is difficult because people with autism tend to score low on tasks demanding verbal skills and abstract reasoning but high on tasks requiring memory and visual-spatial or manipulative skills. From 20 to 40% of children with autism have seizures before age 10. Of these, 75% have psychomotor seizures.

The etiology of autism, although still unknown, is linked with metabolic and nutritional imbalances, chemical exposure during pregnancy, and untreated phenylketonuria (PKU, see Chapter 21 on mental retardation), rubella, and intestinal malabsorption syndrome (i.e., celiac disease). Research show structural defects in the brains of people with autism, and any embryonic insult (environmental or genetic) may contribute to autism. Fragile X syndrome, for example, is associated with autism, as are certain kinds of congenital blindness. Early hypotheses that autism is related to psychological environment, maternal behaviors, and child-rearing practices have not been supported by research. A good resource for staying abreast of etiologies is the *Autism Research Review International,* a quarterly publication of the Institute for Child Behavior Research, Bernard Rimland, 4182 Adams Ave., San Diego, CA 92116.

Criteria for Diagnosing Autism

The American Psychological Association lists six criteria for diagnosing autism:

1. Onset before 30 months of age
2. Pervasive lack of responsiveness to other people
3. Gross deficits in language development, including muteness
4. Peculiar speech patterns if speech is present
5. Bizarre responses to various aspects of the environment (e.g., resistance to change, peculiar interest in or attachments to animate or inanimate objects)
6. Absence of delusions, hallucinations, and other indicators of schizophrenia (APA, 1980, pp. 89–90)

These behaviors are manifested in many ways, each of which has implications for teaching. Lack of responsiveness to people means difficulty in getting and keeping the students's attention. There is little eye contact, and the student often seems not to hear. Social motivators and reinforcements (smiles, praise, pats, hugs) are relatively useless.

Delays in inner, receptive, and expressive language create problems similar to those in mental retardation. Among higher functioning people with autism, communication idiosyncracies like the "Who's on base" scenario in *Rain Man* are common. Speech is used essentially to talk to oneself, not to others. When individuals with autism are capable of relating to others through language, echolalia and pronominal reversal are common. *Echolalia* is involuntary repetition of words spoken by others. *Pronominal reversal* is generally avoidance of "I" by saying "you." For example, the teacher might say, "Do you want to jump on the trampoline?" The person with pronominal reversal would answer, "You want to jump," meaning "I want to jump." The avoidance of "I" is either a denial of selfhood or an absence of awareness of self, while the substitution of "you" shows some awareness of others.

Bizarre responses include unusual reactions to objects, persons, events, and stimuli. Persons with autism show excessive preoccupation with certain objects without regard for appropriate use. They may carry these objects about or constantly tap, twiddle, or spin them. Such behaviors are called *self-stimulations*. Many people with autism are mechanically gifted and enjoy alternate disassembly and assembly of parts. Inability to relate to people and objects in appropriate ways means they do not learn to play spontaneously by modeling others.

Pathological resistance to change is another manifestation of bizarre responses. Emotional outbursts are common when sameness of environment is threatened. Persons with autism want to do the same things every day in precisely the same way. Since the purpose of education is to change behaviors, teachers often feel thwarted. Physically guiding a person with autism through a new movement pattern has traditionally been the pedagogy of choice, but comparison of verbal/visual and verbal/physical teaching models shows equivalent results (Reid, Collier, & Cauchon, 1991). Many persons with autism are tactile defensive and thus respond better to verbal/visual input than to verbal/physical.

Abnormally limited attentional scope, often called *stimulus overselectivity* or overselective attention, is the basis of much bizarre behavior. Inability to select relevant cues and to see whole naturally results in learning problems. An example of stimulus overselectivity is discriminating between two people solely on the basis of shoe color or a piece of jewelry. Much research has focused on the nature and number of prompts that learners with autism can handle. Two instructional models that address stimulus overselectivity are (a) the extra-stimulus prompt model that uses extensive physical, visual, and verbal prompts and (b) the within-stimulus prompt model that minimizes the use of prompts. Physical education research favors the use of lots of prompts (Collier & Reid, 1987), whereas classroom research supports minimizing prompts.

For about 3% of persons with autism, bizarre behaviors are self-injurious and repetitive (e.g., head banging, finger chewing). Whereas the acronym SIBS commonly refers to *siblings,* it means *self-injurious behavior stimulations* in special education circles and signals the need for carefully planned behavior management.

Motor Behavior and Physical Activity Programming

Some persons with autism are graceful and coordinated, but most exhibit motor delays. Research indicates that students with autism are within normal ranges of height and weight but score below norms on physical fitness measures (Reid,

Collier, & Morin, 1983). In general, adolescents with autism perform motorically about the same as peers with mental retardation (Morin & Reid, 1985).

Most persons with autism are eligible for Special Olympics training and competition (see Chapter 21 on mental retardation). The estimated 80% of people with autism who have IQs under 70 can profit from the same kinds of programming as people with mental retardation. Preoccupation with sameness is a strength in fitness and sport training, and persons with autism often become models of schedule adherence and hard work.

Also important in programming are the behavior management techniques explained in Chapter 9 and the strategies discussed in this chapter under schizophrenia. The Premack principle (pairing something liked with something disliked) is the best approach to reinforcement since praise and other social rewards are seldom effective. Application of the Premack principle allows students to earn the right to a certain number of minutes of noninjurious self-stimulations. The graded reversal of deterioration principle that emphasizes not taking away neurotic defenses without providing viable substitutes is embraced by experts on autism, who stress using self-stimulations as rewards and as the basis for individualized programming. For example, if a person likes to spin objects, find him or her objects that are appropriate to spin. If a person likes to twiddle pieces of string, teach him or her to do it in a pocket.

Specific teaching suggestions recommended by Connor (1990) include (a) teach to the preferred modality, (b) minimize unnecessary external stimuli, (c) limit the amount of relevant stimuli presented at one time, (d) limit the use of prompts, and (e) teach in a gamelike environment to facilitate generalization. Research by Collier and Reid (1987) does not support limiting prompts. Reinforcement, task analysis, and physical prompting are the three keys to motor skill improvement for most persons with autism according to Reid et al. (1991). Sensory stimulation like that provided by music, dance, and water activities is especially successful in broadening attentional scope and providing substitutes and alternatives for self-stimulations. Children with autism proceed through the same aquatic skill levels of water orientation as nondisabled peers (Killian, Joyce-Petrovich, Menna, & Arena, 1984).

Dance Therapy and Autism

Dance and movement therapists particularly recommend mirroring self-stimulatory behaviors as a means of showing acceptance and getting attention. A goal of therapy is to help people improve on idiosyncracies rather than drop them. For example, the therapist imitates the child for a number of sessions and then gradually adds on to or modifies the movement. Adler, a pioneer dance therapist, describes the mirroring technique as follows:

I am deeply invested in providing an opportunity for a disturbed child to BE—to BE herself literally, with all of her "bizarre" and "crazy" mannerisms and expressions, I begin there, by reflecting her world, primarily on a body level. I try to "speak"

her language by moving with her, as she moves in space. In the beginning, there is much direct imitation, which by definition means delayed response on my part. However, as she permits my presence, and as the trust develops, I find that the one-sidedness falls away and a more mutual dialogue begins to creep into being; we become synchronous. (1968, p. 43)

The progress of children with autism is very slow. Kalish (1968), for instance, describes sessions with a child over a period of 3 years. Several months of this time were spent in establishing rapport and building trust. Initially, the 5-year-old tolerated little or no physical contact. She hovered in one corner of the room and occupied herself with perseverative head movements. Occasionally, she would burst out of her corner, jump up and down three or four times in a stylized ritual, and then return to the corner. Never did she stray more than a few feet from this spot. Kalish described her method of establishing contact as follows:

My first approach to her was to make use of the diagonal spatial path from the opposite corner of the room. Moving tentatively and in an indirect line, but toward Laura, I tried to incorporate her finger and hand rhythms into my feet and body movements. I did not venture past "her" side of the center of the room. Taking my cues from her, I would suddenly jump up and down, using her timing, and return to the corner.

For many sessions, she gave only a fleeting glance, but as she seemed to get "used" to my presence, her glance was more sustained looking, at a distance. I moved closer to her corner, than back to my own, until now we shared all the space in the room, sometimes together and sometimes separately. (Kalish, 1968, p. 56)

Approximately 2 years later, after sessions were increased to three or four times a week, Laura was willing to sit on the therapist's lap and able to concentrate on movement patterns in a mirror. She was still unable to imitate movements but was making definite progress toward this end. One of the most significant changes was her interest in the mirror. It seemed as though Laura was discovering her body for the first time.

Persons with autism can benefit from both therapeutic and educational programming. The dance and swimming activities described in Chapters 16 and 17 are particularly recommended.

References

Adler, J. (1968). The study of an autistic child. *American Dance Therapy Association Proceedings* (Third Annual Conference). Baltimore: ADTA.

American Psychiatric Association. (1980). *Diagnostic and statistical manual of mental disorders* (3rd ed.). Washington, DC: Author.

Autism Society of America. (1987). *Fact sheet*. Available from Autism Society of America, 1234 Massachusetts Ave. NW, Suite 1017, Washington, DC 20005.

Collier, D., & Reid, G. (1987). A comparison of two models designed to teach autistic children a motor task. *Adapted Physical Activity Quarterly, 4*, 226–236.

Connor, F. (1990). Physical education for children with autism. *Teaching Exceptional Children, 23*, 30–33.

DeBusk, M., & Hellison, D. (1989). Implementing a physical education self-responsibility model for delinquency-prone youth. *Journal of Teaching Physical Education, 8*, 104–112.

Hellison, D. (1978). *Beyond balls and bats: Alienated youth in the gym.* Washington, DC: American Alliance for Health, Physical Education, and Recreation.

Hellison, D. (1984). *Goals and strategies for teaching physical education.* Champaign, IL: Human Kinetics.

Johns, F. A., MacNaughton, R. H. & Karabinus, N. G. (1989). *School discipline guidebook: Theory into practice.* Boston: Allyn & Bacon.

Kalish, B. (1968). Body movement therapy for autistic children. *American Dance Therapy Association Proceedings* (Third Annual Conference). Baltimore: ADTA.

Kanner, L. (1943). Autistic disturbances of affective contact. *Nervous Child, 2*, 217–250.

Killian, K., Joyce-Petrovich, R., Menna, L., & Arena, S. (1984). Measuring water orientation and beginner swim skills of autistic individuals. *Adapted Physical Activity Quarterly, 1*(4), 287–295.

Morin, B., & Reid, G. (1985). A quantitative and qualitative assessment of autistic individuals on selected motor tasks. *Adapted Physical Activity Quarterly, 2*(1), 43–55.

Northcutt, J., & Tipton, G. (1978). Teaching severely mentally ill and emotionally disturbed adolescents. *Exceptional Children, 45*(1), 18–23.

Politino, V., & Smith, S. L. (1989). Attitude toward physical activity and self-concept of emotionally disturbed and normal children. *Adapted Physical Activity Quarterly, 6*, 371–378.

Reid, G., Collier, D., & Cauchon, M. (1991). Skill acquisition by children with autism: Influence of prompts. *Adapted Physical Activity Quarterly, 8*, 357–366.

Reid, G., Collier, D., & Morin, B. (1983). The motor performance of autistic individuals. In R. Eason, T. Smith, & F. Caron (Eds.), *Adapted physical activity* (pp. 201–218). Champaign, IL: Human Kinetics.

Rimmer, J. H. (1989). Confrontation in the gym: A systematic solution for behavior problems. *Journal of Physical Education, Recreation, and Dance, 60*(5), 63–65.

Rubin, T. I. (1962). *Jordi, Lisa, and David.* New York: Macmillian.

Vogler, E. W. & Bishop, P. (1990). Management of disruptive behavior in physical education. *The Physical Educator, 47*, 16–26.

Vogler, E. W. & French, R. (1983). The effects of a group contingency strategy on behaviorally disordered students in physical education. *Research Quarterly for Exercise and Sport, 54*(3), 273–277.

Wolman, B. B. (1970). *Children without childhood.* New York: Grune & Stratton.

CHAPTER
23

Wheelchair Sports and Orthopedic Impairments

FIGURE   23.1

Schools should provide opportunities to learn wheelchair sports. (Photo courtesy of Candy Jackson, Courage Center, Golden Valley, MN.)

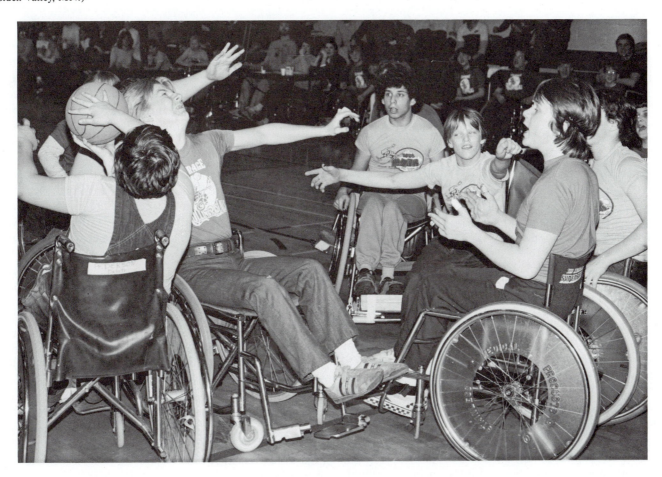

After you have studied this chapter, you should be able to:

1. Define orthopedic impairments, identify sport organizations associated with each, and discuss how these organizations can be used by public school personnel.

2. Discuss wheelchair sport philosophy and the inclusion of wheelchair sports in school and community programs, both integrated and separate.

3. Explain how nerves emerge from the spinal cord and how lesion levels determine severity of condition, walking potential, and physical activity programming.

4. Describe and discuss the three conditions featured in this chapter: (a) spina bifida, (b) spinal cord injury, and (c) poliomyelitis and postpolio syndrome. Include physical activity recommendations for each.

5. Identify common concerns in paralysis and discuss their implications for teaching and coaching.

6. Discuss assessment to guide programming in locomotor and ball-handling activities.

7. Given age, gender, lesion level, and condition, be able to write a physical education IEP and substantiate physical education placement.

8. Differentiate between types of wheelchairs and explain similarities and differences in parts.

9. Discuss wheelchair sports, rules and chair adaptations, and resources for learning more.

10. Know names and background on several famous wheelchair athletes and discuss how this information can be used in teaching, coaching, and advocacy.

Orthopedic impairments are so diverse that separate sport organizations have evolved to meet different needs. Because a major goal of physical education is to develop lifetime leisure sport skills, the next three chapters are organized around the clusters of disability served by major sport organizations in the United States. (See Chapter 3 for international equivalents.)

The following definition of *orthopedically impaired* (OI) appears in federal legislation:

Orthopedically impaired means a severe orthopedic impairment which adversely affects a child's educational performance. The term includes impairments caused by congenital anomaly (e.g., clubfoot, absence of some member, etc.), impairments caused by disease (e.g., poliomyelitis, bone tuberculosis, etc.), and impairments from other causes (e.g., cerebral palsy, amputations, and fractures or burns which cause contractures). (*Federal Register,* August 23, 1977, p. 42478).

Most orthopedic impairments do not adversely affect academic classroom performance. They do, however, require adaptations for safe and successful integrated physical education. Moreover, to learn wheelchair sports, students need some instruction each year built around their specific needs (see Figure 23.1). Wheelchair sport instruction, practice, and competition should be written into the individualized education programs (IEPs) of individuals eligible to play in wheelchairs.

This chapter focuses on spinal paralysis (spina bifida, spinal cord injuries, and poliomyelitis/postpolio syndrome). These impairments historically have been grouped together and are served respectively by two multisport organizations: the National Wheelchair Athletic Association (NWAA) and National Handicapped Sports (NHS). The publication *Sports 'N Spokes* is the best resource for this chapter because it focuses specifically on these impairments.

Chapters 24 and 25 are also about orthopedic impairments. Chapter 24 focuses on people served by the U.S. Les Autres Sports Association (USLASA) and NHS. *Les autres* is the French term for "the others" and refers to all physical disabilities not governed by NWAA and the U.S. Cerebral Palsy Athletic Association (USCPAA). Chapter 25 focuses on people served by the USCPAA. *Palaestra* is the journal that provides coverage of all of these disabilities.

Sport Organizations

Sport organizations are the best source of help in planning and conducting activities for persons with orthopedic impairments. Table 23.1 summarizes the disabilities associated with each of the five multisport organizations. NWAA requires that all sports be played in wheelchairs. In contrast, NHS, USCPAA, and USLASA offer both wheelchair and ambulatory sports.

In addition to the five multisport organizations are many single-sport organizations like the National Wheelchair Basketball Association (NWBA), the U.S. Quad Rugby Association (USQRA), and the National Foundation of Wheelchair Tennis (NFWT). These organizations, unlike the multisport structures, are open to people with all kinds of orthopedic impairments. This includes people who are ambulatory in activities of daily living (ADL) but who use wheelchairs for sport recreation and competition.

National Wheelchair Athletic Association

First organized in 1956, the NWAA used to be associated primarily with track and field. It now is the umbrella organization for several national governing bodies (NGBs). Among these are Wheelchair Athletics of the USA (track and field), U.S. Wheelchair Swimming, U.S. Wheelchair Weightlifting Federation, American Wheelchair Table Tennis Organization, National Wheelchair Shooting Federation, and Archery Sports Section. These are the main Paralympics sports for persons with spinal paralysis. Addresses of these and other sport organizations appear in Appendix D.

Table 23.1
Orthopedic impairments served by major multisport organizations.

National Wheelchair Athletic Association (NWAA)
Spinal cord injuries
Spina bifida
Poliomyelitis and postpolio syndrome
National Handicapped Sports (NHS)
Winter sports for everyone
Summer sports for amputees
Paralympic competition for les autres
U.S. Cerebral Palsy Athletic Association (USCPAA)
Cerebral palsy
Stroke
Closed head injuries
U.S. Les Autres Sports Association (USLASA)
Muscular dystrophies
Arthritis
Multiple sclerosis
Arthrogyposis
Osteogenesis imperfecta
Muscle weakness conditions
Burns
Nonparalytic skeletal disorders
    Congenital disorders (e.g., clubfoot)
    Acquired disorders (e.g., hip degeneration)
Dwarf Athletic Association of America
Achondroplasia
Other short stature syndromes

Note. Prior to 1991, sports for persons with amputations were governed by the U.S. Amputee Athletic Association. This organization dissolved in 1990.

Persons, age 16 and over, compete with adults in most wheelchair sports. Junior competition is increasingly available for ages 5 to 15. Several large cities, usually through the cooperation of sport organizations, school systems, and municipal parks and recreation associations, offer youth sport competitions. Illustrative of these are the Junior Orange Bowl Sports Ability Games in Coral Gables, Florida, begun in 1982. The first national junior wheelchair championship conducted by NWAA was held at the University of Delaware in July 1984.

Internationally, the NWAA is associated with the International Stoke Mandeville Wheelchair Sports Federation (ISMWSF), named for the famous Stoke Mandeville Sport Centre near London, England, and the International Paralympic Committee (IPC), which has its office in the Rick Hansen Centre in Canada. Thus, NWAA sport rules and classifications are similar to (but not always identical with) those of ISMGF and IPC. World sport politics are constantly changing, and the relationship between IPC and ISMGF is not yet clear.

National Handicapped Sports

NHS (originally named the National Handicapped Sports and Recreation Association) governs winter sports and facilitates fitness for everyone, regardless of type of OI con-

dition. *Sports 'N Spokes* and *Palaestra* include many articles on winter sports (Axelson, 1984, 1988). NHS is the governing body for athletes with amputations. In the 1992 Paralympics in Barcelona, it also served les autres athletes.

Normal Mental Function and Wheelchair Sports

The term *wheelchair sports* should be preceded by NWAA, USCPAA, or NHS to denote the population served. These organizations limit their sports to persons with normal intellectual functioning. Special Olympics offers wheelchair activities for persons with mental handicaps. The widespread association of the word *special* with mental retardation makes this word unacceptable to most persons with other disabilities. Terminology like *Special Physical Education* or *Special Events Day* should therefore be avoided.

Anatomy of Spinal Paralysis

Spinal paralysis is a broad term for conditions caused by injury or disease to the spinal cord and/or spinal nerves. Paralysis can be complete (total) or incomplete (partial). *Paresis* is muscle weakness in incomplete paralysis.

Spinal paralysis involves both the central and autonomic nervous systems. The central nervous system (spinal cord and nerves) governs movement and sensation. The autonomic nervous system governs vital functions like heart rate, blood pressure, temperature control, and bladder, bowel, and sexual activity.

Figure 23.2 shows how 31 pairs of spinal nerves issue from segments of the spinal cord and exit from the spinal column. The nerves are named, not for the segment of the cord they come from, but for their associated vertebrae. The exception is the eighth cervical nerve (C8); there are only seven cervical vertebrae.

Nerves are specified by stating region first (cervical, thoracic, lumbar, sacral) and number second. Thus, Figure 23.2 shows that the diaphragm (muscle that enables breathing) is innervated by C3 to C5, the upper arm is innervated by C5 to C8, and so on. Persons with spinal paralysis typically know their lesion level(s)—for example, C5/6 or T12/L1.

Physical activity personnel should be familiar with the body parts innervated by various nerve groups. In general, cervical nerve dysfunction affects arm and hand movements. Thoracic nerve dysfunction affects ability to (a) maintain balance in a sitting position and (b) breathe forcefully in aerobic endurance activities that cause respiratory distress. Lumbar nerve dysfunction affects leg and foot movements. Sacral nerve dysfunction affects bladder, bowel, and sexual function.

Severity of Condition

Severity of spinal paralysis depends on (a) the level of the lesion and (b) whether it is complete or incomplete. The higher the lesion, the more loss of function. *Quadriplegia* and *paraplegia* are terms used in many medical conditions to indicate level of severity.

Quadriplegia (also called tetraplegia) means involvement of all four limbs and the trunk. About half of the persons with quadriplegia have incomplete lesions, meaning

FIGURE 23.2

Thirty-one pairs of spinal nerves issue from the spinal cord and innervate groups of muscles as shown. (C=Cervical; T=Thoracic; L=Lumbar; Coc.1=Coccyx 1.)

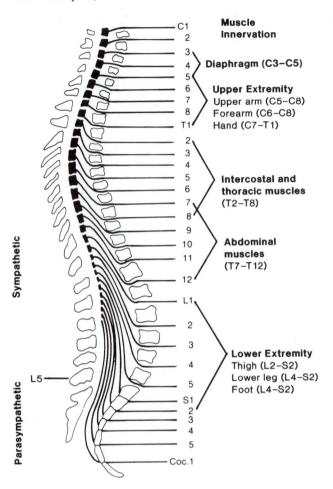

FIGURE 23.3

T₃ to T₁₁ ambulators wear long leg braces and primarily use parallel bars.

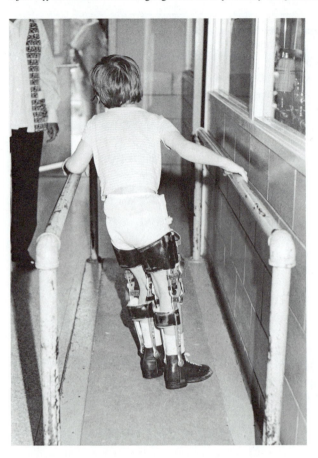

that they are able to walk. The disability caused by incomplete lesions is difficult to predict. Schack (1991) presents an excellent case study of a college-age male with an incomplete C1/2 lesion who is ambulatory and jogs. High-level quads are those with complete C1 to C4 lesions. These persons are dependent upon motorized chairs for ambulation. They are not eligible for NWAA sports because NWAA offers activities only for manual chairs. C1 to C4 quads and some C5 quads are encouraged to affiliate with the USLASA. Persons with complete lesions at C3 and above cannot breathe independently and must carry portable oxygen tanks.

Paraplegia means involvement of the legs but often includes trunk balance as well. *Para* comes from the Latin *par,* meaning "equal" or "a pair." For sport programming, trunk balance is the most useful criterion in determining level of severity. Persons with complete T1 to T6 lesions have no useful sitting balance and must be strapped in their chairs. A complete T7 to L1 lesion allows some useful sitting balance, whereas from L2 on there is normal trunk control. Persons with low-level lesions can walk without assistance (except for braces) but are still classified as paraplegics.

Walking Potential

Many persons judge severity of disability in terms of walking potential. Four classifications, based on complete lesions, are used:

T2 and above—Nonambulators
T3 to T11—Walking used only as therapy
T12 to L1—Household ambulators
L2 and below—Community ambulators

A community ambulator is defined as someone who can walk 1,000 yd nonstop, ascend and descend stairs, and function independently, with or without braces, in activities of daily living (ADL).

Except for persons with very low lesions, walking requires braces. T3 to T11 ambulators primarily use parallel bars for walking exercise; they wear long leg braces, and persons with the lower lesions can take a few steps with crutches (see Figure 23.3). Most household ambulators wear long leg braces and use crutches. In contrast, community ambulators usually have knee joint control (the quadriceps work) and wear only short leg braces. Persons with ankle joint control (the tibialis anterior and posterior work) may or may not use short leg braces (Basmajian & Wolf, 1990).

Regardless of ambulation classification, people with spinal paralysis are not able to engage in integrated competitive sports safely and successfully from a standing position. This is why the NWAA promotes only wheelchair sports. Community ambulators may be able to perform some of the skills and exercises in an integrated class (i.e., upper extremity activities) but require adaptations and support services for full integration.

Functional Electrical Stimulation

Technological advances offer the promise of more people walking in the future, but electrically stimulated walking ability is not likely to affect sport potential. Functional electrical stimulation (FES) is the computerized application of electrical current to paralyzed muscles to enhance functions like walking, stationary cycling, and hand control. FES machines can be used in physical therapy settings or purchased for home use. This rehabilitation modality, however, continues to be quite expensive.

Particularly exciting is the work of Dr. Jerrold Petrofsky, whose work was made famous by a television movie in 1983 that showed the rehabilitation of Nan Davis, who, aided by FES, walked across the stage to get her graduation diploma from Wright State. Petrofsky says the best candidates for FES gaiting systems are persons with C6 to T10 lesions with no contractures or skin breakdowns. Two Petrofsky Centers, in California and Pennsylvania, have been advertised in *Sports 'N Spokes* since the late 1980s. FES is heralded as rebuilding paralyzed muscles, providing neuromuscular re-education, and helping regain functions like bladder control, hand use, and walking (Petrofsky, Brown, & Cerrel-Bazo, 1992).

Transfers

Transfers is the generic term for how persons in wheelchairs or on crutches move from one position to another. Ability to transfer back and forth between chair, bed, toilet, automobile, swimming pool, and the like obviously influences capacity for independent living. Transfers are largely dependent on arm and shoulder strength and trunk control. They are categorized broadly as independent and assisted. Persons with complete lesions above C6 typically need assistance. C6 function (characterized by almost all shoulder movement, elbow flexion, and wrist extension) makes many independent transfers possible.

Efficient transfers are facilitated by weight management and disciplined development of residual muscle ability. Persons who need assistance with transfers are vulnerable to injury when unskilled persons try to help. Particularly at risk are the four rotator cuff muscles that stabilize the shoulder joint. These are known by the acronym SITS, referring to the first letter of each muscle (supraspinatus, infraspinatus, teres minor, and subscapularis). The SITS muscles are often injured when persons are lifted by their arms, as in downward transfers to a mat or swimming pool. Learning correct ways to assist is usually a part of orienta-

tion or on-the-job in-service. The best approach is always to ask people if they want help. If they say "yes," then ask for a description of how to provide it.

Congenital and Acquired Paralysis

Time of onset, of course, is an important factor in physical activity programming. Two types of spinal paralysis—congenital and acquired—have vastly different impacts on development. The child born with paralysis is shaped by life events very different from those that surround disability in later life by accident, disease, or war.

The hurt and disappointment of parents coping with a birth defect are often passed onto the child, influencing self-concept and personality development. Overprotection tends to lower self-expectation and achievement motivation. Children with congenital paralysis generally are not socialized into sport unless parents are athletes or adapted physical activity is provided early in life.

Acquired paralysis is associated more with sport success than congenital paralysis. This is because many persons with acquired disabilities have already been socialized into sport. Age of onset in acquired disability is extremely important in this regard. Research shows that acquired disability does not change personality and self-concept in adults (Sherrill, 1990). Less is known about children and adolescents.

In general, physical education and recreation programming is the same for congenital and acquired conditions. Problems to be resolved and pedagogy depend mainly on age, level of lesion, and complete or incomplete paralysis. The sections that follow describe the three most common spinal paralysis conditions. Thereafter, the content of the chapter is applicable to each.

Spina Bifida

Spina bifida is a congenital defect of the spinal column caused by failure of the neural arch of a vertebra to properly develop and enclose the spinal cord (see Figure 23.4). This developmental anomaly occurs between the fourth and sixth week of pregnancy, when the embryo is less than an inch long. Bifida comes from the Latin word *bifid,* meaning "cleft" or "split into two parts." As yet, there is no understanding of why this anomaly occurs.

Gender, race, geographical location, and socioeconomic status all relate significantly to spina bifida. More girls than boys are affected. Whites have higher rates of spina bifida than other races. In Great Britain and Ireland, about 4 of every 1,000 newborns have spina bifida. In the United States, the incidence is 1 to 2 per 1,000 (about 11,000 newborns each year). Poverty is associated with many of these births, but not all. Families with one spina bifida child have a 1 in 20 (5%) risk of reoccurrence in subsequent births.

Next to cerebral palsy, spina bifida is the cause of more orthopedic defects in school-age children than any other condition. Whereas the survival rate of spina bifida used to be less than 50%, it is now 90% with aggressive treatment

FIGURE   23.4

(*A*) Parts of a single vertebra viewed from the top. (*B*) Spina bifida in a newborn infant.

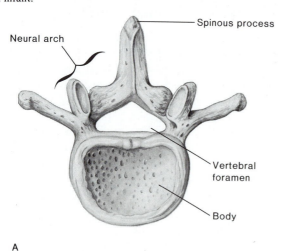

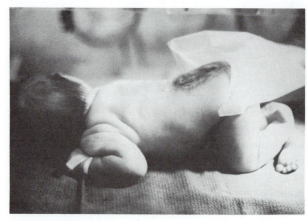

A

B

FIGURE   23.5

Three types of spina bifida. (*A*) Meningomyelocele. (*B*) Meningocele. (*C*) Spina bifida occulta.

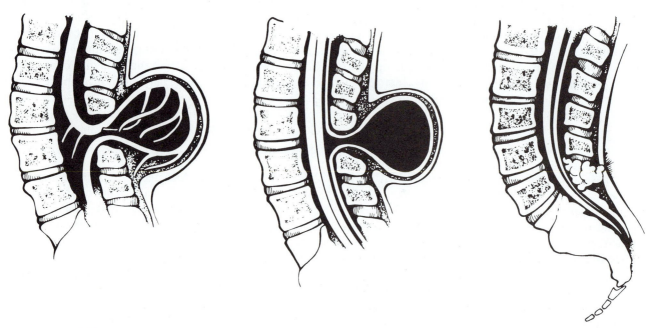

A. Meningomyelocele   B. Meningocele   C. Spina bifida occulta

(Tecklin, 1989). Corrective surgery is generally undertaken within 24 hr of birth, although some physicians prefer to wait 9 or 10 days.

Types of Spina Bifida

From most to least severe, the types of spina bifida are (a) meningomyelocele, (b) meningocele, and (c) spina bifida occulta (see Figure 23.5). The first condition (often shortened to MM) is by far the most common, and incidence rates (1 to 2 in 1,000) typically refer to it. The derivation of this word is *meningo-* (referring to membrane or covering of spinal

cord), *myelo* (denoting involvement of the cord), and *cele* (meaning "tumor"). Figure 23.5A shows how the spinal cord and nerve roots exit through a vertebral cleft and fill a tumorous sac in MM. In meningocele, only the spinal cord covering (meninges) pooches out into the sac; the cord and nerves are not displaced. In both conditions, the spinal cord fluid leaks into the sac. Both must be corrected by surgery.

Spina bifida occulta is so named because the condition is concealed under the skin. The occult, as in magic, astrology, and the supernatural, is hidden or secret. The occulta condition does not cause paralysis or muscle weakness, although it is associated with adult back problems. On some people, a tuft of hair, birthmark, or dimple mark the occulta, but most are not diagnosed unless X rays are taken for other problems.

Nonprogressive Condition

The type of spina bifida is nonprogressive—that is, it remains the same, never becoming worse. As explained in the section "Anatomy of Spinal Paralysis," the higher the location of MM on the spinal column, the more nerves are affected. Most MM occurs from T12 downward.

As with other types of paralysis, there is no cure. After surgery, MM is managed by passive range-of-motion (ROM) exercises done twice daily by family (Tecklin, 1989) until the child learns to creep/crawl and engages in enough activity that ROM therapy is not needed. Also important in infancy and early childhood is lots of handling and activity in the prone, side, and upright positions. The emphasis is on establishing equilibrium reactions and normalizing, as much as possible, visual and other kinds of input. This is to counteract the tendency of parents to leave babies in supine.

Developmental Activities

Development of head, trunk, shoulder, arm, and hand control is obviously important for persons with spina bifida. Pushing, pulling, and lifting with the arms are major goals because upper extremity strength must compensate for leg paralysis. Push-and-pull toys, scooterboards, parachute and towel activities, apparatus climbing and hanging, and weight lifting are high priority (see Figure 23.6).

Orthotics (splinting and bracing) is begun in infancy to facilitate upright positioning as close to the normal age as possible. Brief periods of supported standing from infancy onward aid blood circulation and other functions. Many preambulation devices help children learn to stand and walk at about the same age as peers. Crutches are introduced as early as age 2 or 3. See Chapter 11 for different kinds of crutchwalking and gaits. Whereas physical therapists focus on walking, educators teach play and game skills, creative expression, and fitness.

Appraisal of nonlocomotor movement capabilities lends insight into program planning. The following are questions to guide movement exploration. They can lead to games on land and in the water.

1. What body parts can you bend and straighten? What *combination* of body parts can you bend and straighten? What body parts can you swing?

2. What body parts can you stretch? In which directions can you stretch?

3. What body parts can you twist? What *combination* of body parts can you twist? Can you twist at different rates of speed? Can you combine twists with other basic movements?

4. What body parts can you circle? What *combination* of body parts can you circle?

FIGURE 23.6

Scooterboard activities offer young children with spina bifida easy mobility while building arm and shoulder strength.

5. Can you rock forward in the wheelchair and bend over to recover an object on the floor? If lying or curled up on a mat, can you rock backward and forward? Can this rocking movement provide impetus for changing positions? For instance, when sitting on a mat, can you rock over to a four-point creeping position?

6. Do you have enough arm strength to lift and replace the body in the wheelchair in a bouncing action? Can you relax and bounce on a mattress, a trampoline, or a moon walk?

7. What body parts can you shake? What combination of body parts? Can you shake rhythm instruments?

8. Can you sway from side to side? Can you sway back and forth while hanging onto a rope or maintaining contact with a piece of apparatus?

9. Can you push objects away from the body? Do you have the potential to succeed in games based on pushing skills, like box hockey and shuffleboard? Can you maneuver a scooterboard? A tricycle? A wagon? Can you walk while holding onto or pushing a wheelchair? Can you push off from the side of the swimming pool? Can some part of your body push off from a mat?

10. Can you pull objects toward yourself? In which directions can you pull? Can you use a hand-over-hand motion to pull yourself along a rope, bar, or ladder? Can you manipulate weighted pulleys?

11. Can you change levels? For instance, can you move from a lying position to a sitting, squatting, or kneeling position or vice versa? How do you get from a bed, sofa, chair, or toilet to the wheelchair and vice versa?

12. Can you demonstrate safe techniques for falling? When you lose balance, in which direction do you usually fall?

Table 23.2
Relationship between location of spina bifida, loss of muscle control, and type of ambulation.

Approximate Location of Vertebral Defect	Point Below Which Control is Lost	Prognosis for Ambulation	Equipment Used for Ambulation	NWAA Classification
12th thoracic	Trunk	Nonambulatory	Wheelchair, standing brace	Probable Class IV
1st lumbar	Pelvis	Exercise ambulation	Wheelchair, long leg braces, and crutches	
3rd lumbar	Hip	Household ambulation	Long leg braces and crutches	Probable Class V
5th lumbar	Knee	Community ambulation	Short leg braces and crutches	

Note. Table supplied by Dennis Brunt, who has his doctoral degree in adapted physical education and is certified also in physical therapy. (NWAA-National Wheelchair Athletic Association.)

Table 23.2 reviews ambulation goals for persons with spina bifida. Most children with high-level lesions are fitted with wheelchairs before age 5 because long leg braces are too cumbersome for easy walking. Thus, physical education emphasizes wheelchair games and sports and activities performed in sitting or lying positions. Most of these can be done in an integrated setting. Swimming is particularly good, although some persons are hesitant about exposing withered limbs.

Hydrocephalus

Approximately 90% of infants with MM have hydrocephalus (increased cerebrospinal fluid in ventricles of brain). About 25% are born with this condition, and the rest develop it shortly after surgery for spina bifida. Closure of the spinal lesion means that there is no longer an outlet for excessive fluid, which subsequently backs up in the ventricles and causes intracranial pressure and increased head circumference.

Hydrocephalus is surgically relieved by a shunting procedure (see Figure 23.7). Persons with shunts typically have no activity restrictions except avoidance of trauma to head (e.g., soccer heading, boxing, headstands, forward rolls). Diving is controversial. The only visible evidence of a shunt is a small scar behind the ear.

Shunts (also called tubes or catheters) sometimes become clogged or malfunction and must be replaced. Common symptoms of shunt problems are frequent headaches, vomiting, seizures, lethargy, irritability, swelling, redness along the shunt tract, and changes in personality or school performance.

Hydrocephalus in spina bifida is associated with the Arnold-Chiari malformation, also called Chiari II. This is a congenital defect of the hindbrain in which the posterior cerebellum herniates downward, displacing the medulla into the cervical spinal canal and obstructing the normal flow of cerebral spinal fluid. Chiari II varies in severity and is managed by shunting. There are many causes of hydrocephalus, but in MM, the Chiari II is the most common.

Cognitive Function and Strabismus

The IQs of most persons with spina bifida are average. However, a large percentage have perceptual-motor deficits, specific learning disabilities, and attention deficits. Content presented in Chapter 20 on learning disabilities therefore applies. Strabismus (cross-eyes) is relatively common and may partially explain visual perception problems. The restricted mobility lifestyle in early childhood no doubt limits spontaneous learning about space and figure-ground relationships, so sensorimotor deprivation is another explanation.

Cognitive function may be damaged before birth or before shunting is undertaken. In the past, complications arising from shunt-related infections caused subtle brain damage, but improved medical technology is reducing this problem.

Posture and Orthopedic Defects

Paralysis causes an imbalance between muscle groups that further complicates the orthopedic problems of growing children. Incorrect positioning and/or inadequate splinting and bracing create additional defects. For example, plantar flexion deformities often occur because, without movement, the ankle joint freezes in the toes-pointed-downward position. This makes fitting shoes and braces difficult. In high lumbar paralysis, the hip flexors and abductors are normal, but the extensors and abductors are weak or paralyzed. This imbalance often leads to hip dislocation. For children who can crutchwalk, this imbalance causes toeing inward (pigeon toes).

Posture problems vary with lesion level. Persons with T12 to L3 involvement often develop scoliosis. Also, the lower extremities of these persons fail to grow properly, so legs are small and frail. In contrast, children with L4 to L5 paralysis tend to develop hyperlordosis as they learn to walk. Without crutches, their gait is a side-to-side gluteus medius lurch (see walking gaits in Chapter 11). Persons with sacral-level paralysis walk unassisted but may develop a hip-and-knee flexion crouched gait because of weak ankle plantar flexors.

FIGURE 23.7

Sometimes, hydrocephalus can be corrected through a surgical procedure called *shunting*. The ventriculo-peritoneal (VP) shunt involves inserting a tube into the ventricles. This tube has a one-way valve that lets fluid flow out of the brain and into another tube that is threaded just under the skin down to the abdomen, where it is reabsorbed by the blood vessels in the membranes surrounding internal organs. A less-often used procedure is to thread the tube into the heart instead of the abdomen. Children with shunts typically have no activity restrictions except avoidance of blows to the head.

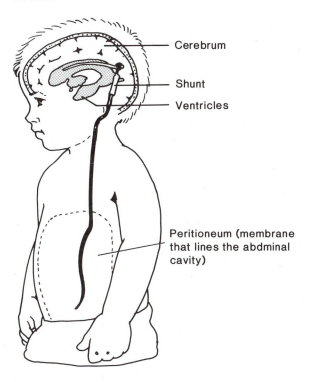

The activities presented in Chapter 14 on postures are helpful for these conditions. In most cases, however, problems are aggressively treated by splinting, bracing, casting, and surgery. These modalities remove children from normal movement and play for weeks at a time and further explain skill, fitness, and perceptual-motor problems associated with spina bifida. Adapted physical activity programming must be aggressive also in teaching these children to appreciate and use their motor strengths and to maintain body parts in good alignment.

Other Problems

Persons with spina bifida experience many problems common to all forms of spinal paralysis. These include bladder and bowel function, sexuality concerns, skin lesions, and obesity, all of which are discussed later in the chapter. Problems are greater for children—especially young ones who lack cause-and-effect understandings—than adults. Children, for example, often play with abandon, disregarding bruises and blows. Without sensation in the lower limbs, children with MM may not notice and report skin breakdown until serious infection sets in. Children also are more likely to be wearing splints and braces than adults, and many skin problems result from poorly fitted orthoses.

Sport and Active Lifestyle Socialization

Persons with spina bifida have the potential to become fine wheelchair athletes. They are not likely to be able to compete safely and successfully in ambulatory sports without adaptations. Integrated physical education should be supplemented with intensive training in wheelchair sports so that lifetime leisure options are available.

Models are especially important because children who frequent medical clinics and have a history of surgery and orthotics often perceive themselves as sickly and unathletic. Attitudes about self and sports are formed early, usually before age 8, so early adapted physical education should emphasize self-concept and active lifestyle socialization goals.

Spinal Cord Injuries

Spinal cord injuries (*SCI*) are quadriplegia and paraplegia acquired through some kind of trauma. Estimated causes of SCI are 48% motor vehicles, 21% falls, 14% violence (including war), 14% sport injuries, and 3% other. Diving causes 10 times more SCI than any other sport. Next highest in risk are football and snow skiing.

Industrialized countries report an incidence of 13 to 50 per million (Netter, 1986). Approximately 10,000 persons in the United States sustain SCI each year. About 80% are males, and most range in age between 16 and 30 years. Age of onset for about half of all SCI persons is under 25.

With improved roadside emergency service and medical technology, incomplete lesions are increasingly the trend. Of the estimated 200,000 to 500,000 Americans with SCI, the division between complete and incomplete lesions is about equal. Incomplete lesions, of course, are more conducive to sport success than complete lesions. This is particularly true in quadriplegia. In the sport world, these athletes are called *walking quads*. The first question to be asked when programming for SCI is whether the lesion is complete or incomplete. If incomplete, the potential is unpredictable and can be learned only by trial and error.

Most Common Injuries

The most common injury is quadriplegia—specifically, the middle-to-low lesion (C5 to C6). The individual with a C5/6 injury has little or no hand control without adaptive devices, an absence or great weakness of the triceps (elbow extensors), and almost no trunk control and mobility. Without good triceps, a person cannot effectively push a manual wheelchair. Therefore, this person is likely to use a motorized chair in activities of daily living.

In sports, however, a properly fitted high-back manual wheelchair permits competition in many activities, especially if the lesion is incomplete. Success in quad rugby is more realistic than in wheelchair basketball, where teams prefer lower level quads with more functional ability. Achievement depends largely on a properly designed chair and motivation. Some persons with quadriplegia have completed marathons (26.2 mi). In relearning how to swim, they initially need flotation devices but have the ability to swim independently.

FIGURE 23.8

In quad rugby, points are scored by carrying the ball over the opponents' goal line. This sport is played on a regulation basketball court with a four-person team. Quad rugby combines elements of football, ice hockey, and basketball.

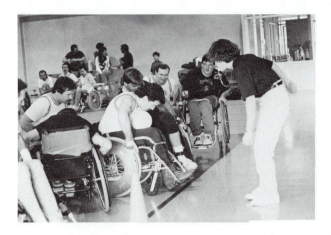

The second most common site of injury is the thoracolumbar junction (T12/L1). Persons with this injury can learn all gaits and typically use Lofstrand (forearm) crutches for activities of daily living. They can learn almost any wheelchair sport and, with special apparatus, can stand while snow skiing.

Learning About SCI

The best way to learn about SCI is to attend a wheelchair basketball or quad rugby game or watch wheelchair track and field and other sports (see Figure 23.8). Almost all marathons include some racers in wheelchairs. Films also increase awareness, particularly in regard to rehabilitation and emotional growth. Films about war veterans usually depict paraplegia, as in *Coming Home* and *Born on the Fourth of July,* both of which illustrate T11 to L2 injuries. Quadriplegia is shown in *Whose Life Is It Anyway* (depicting an architect with a C4/5-level injury caused by an automobile accident) and *The Other Side of The Mountain* (depicting an athlete with a C5/6-level injury caused by a skiing accident). The books and plays on which these films are based, as well as many excellent autobiographies, also may be read. Especially recommended are those of Brooklyn Dodger Roy Campanella (1959) and marathoner Rick Hansen (Hansen & Taylor, 1987).

Adapted Physical Activity for Individuals With SCI

Physical activity for individuals with SCI generally centers on strengthening and using the upper extremities. Concurrently, the person must learn to use and care for a wheelchair. The best approach with a school-age person is to introduce him or her to models who are wheelchair athletes and to affiliate the individual with a team. These persons also should be instructed in upper extremity activities that can be done in an integrated setting.

Students with SCI should be *asked* what they can do and encouraged to help plan their own physical education and recreation activities. Most important is motivation, optimal involvement with peers, and group problem solving about architectural barriers and transportation. Their problems are similar to those of other persons confined to wheelchairs: a tendency for the hip, knee, and ankle flexors to become too tight, with resulting contractures (abnormal shortening of muscles) from extended sitting; ulcers or pressure sores from remaining in one position too long; bruises and friction burns from rubbing body parts that lack sensation and give no pain warnings; and tendency toward obesity because of low energy expenditure.

Poliomyelitis and Postpolio Syndrome

Poliomyelitis is a viral infection that causes quadriplegia or paraplegia. The name is derived from the part of the spine attacked by the virus. *Polio* means "gray," referring to the color of the nerve cell bodies it attacks. *Myelitis* indicates infection of the protective covering around the nerve fibers. Specifically, the polio virus destroys only motor nerve cells, which are found in the anterior part of the spinal cord and in the brain. Polio is similar to SCI and spina bifida in that muscles are paralyzed. It is dissimilar in that sensation is intact because the virus does not attack sensory nerve fibers. For this reason, athletes with polio are often perceived to have an advantage when playing wheelchair sports.

Polio epidemics from 1915 through the 1950s left thousands paralyzed. Degree of disability varied according to whether the medulla or upper or lower spinal cord was affected. There are three types of polio virus: bulbar, spinal, and bulbarspinal. The bulbar types affected the breathing centers in the medulla, leaving survivors dependent upon iron lungs (now called ventilators) for respiration.

Two types of vaccine now provide immunization. The needle injection of inactivated poliovirus vaccine (Salk) was made available in 1955, and an oral live poliovirus vaccine (Sabin) was introduced in 1960. On rare occasions, the live virus vaccine results in vaccine-induced polio. Today, in industrial countries, polio is almost entirely eradicated. In Third World countries, however, it continues to cause paralysis. Worldwide, about 5 million new cases appear each year.

In the United States, there are approximately 300,000 polio survivors with some degree of disability. In the 1980s, about 25% of these persons began to experience new joint and muscle pain, muscle weakness at old and new sites, severe fatigue, profound sensitivity to cold, and new respiratory problems. This combination of symptoms has been named the *postpolio syndrome.* Its cause is not yet understood (Basmajian & Wolf, 1990). The postpolio weakness progresses very slowly over many years, requiring gradual lifestyle adjustments.

Franklin D. Roosevelt, U.S. president from 1932 to 1945, is the most famous person to have had polio. Paralyzed early in his political career, Roosevelt could stand and walk

FIGURE   23.9

Spinal nerve dermatones, showing innervation of sensation.

CUTANEOUS DISTRIBUTION OF SPINAL NERVES

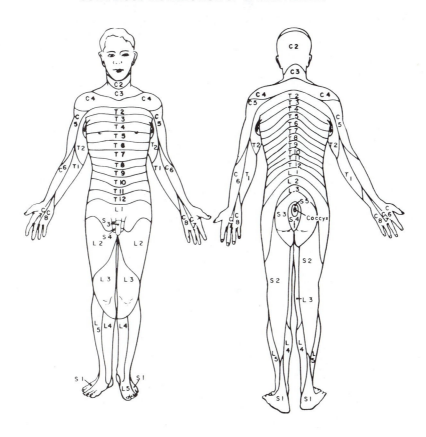

only with long leg braces and crutches. A 1960 movie, *Sunrise at Campobello,* chronicles Roosevelt's battle with polio prior to election; it is available on video and well worth seeing. In 1938, Roosevelt organized the National Foundation for Infantile Paralysis and the Memorable March of Dimes campaign. Until the 1950s, polio was the leading cause of orthopedic impairments in the United States.

Activity adaptations for polio are similar to those of other types of spinal paralysis. However, paralysis is often incomplete, and judging level of lesion is difficult. Because people with polio have sensation, pain is a concern. Muscle and joint pain are particularly aggravated by cold temperature and excessive exercise. *Overuse syndrome* describes pain and muscle weakness associated with diminished function after strenuous use.

Common Concerns in Paralysis

Concerns common to all types of spinal paralysis include (a) sensation and skin breakdown, (b) temperature control, (c) contractures and injury prevention, (d) spasms, (e) atrophy of limbs, (f) urination and defecation, (g) sexuality, (h) heart and circulatory function, (i) blood pressure and autonomic dysreflexia, and (j) weight manage-

ment and osteoporosis. The exception to this generalization is polio, which affects only motor nerve fibers and leaves sensation intact. In polio, paralysis is usually incomplete, and no assumptions should be made. Polio does not impair genitourinary function, so all body elimination processes and sexual activity are unaffected. Each of these concerns has implications for physical activity programming.

Sensation and Skin Breakdown

Feelings of touch, pressure, heat, cold, and pain are impaired by spinal cord lesions. In complete lesions, all sensation below the injury is lost. In incomplete lesions, there is no rhyme or reason to the pattern. Spinal nerve dermatomes are used to enable persons to point to areas of lost sensation or pain (see Figure 23.9). Whereas movement is innervated by impulses that travel the anterior part of the spinal cord, sensation is innervated by impulses that travel the posterior part of the spinal cord.

A person can have motor paralysis and no loss of sensation or vice versa. Usually, however, both are present. The exception is polio. Figure 23.9 shows which nerves innervate sensation of different body segments. Touch, pressure (light and deep), heat, cold, and pain each have different sensory receptors and their own specific tracts in the spinal cord. It is therefore possible to lose some sensations but not others.

Inability to feel sensation makes persons particularly vulnerable to injury and skin breakdown. Wrinkles in socks and poorly fitted shoes or braces cause blisters that become infected. Scooting across the floor on buttocks (ambulation often used by children) and crawling/creeping may cause scuff burns and bruises that go undetected. Lack of cleanliness in relation to urination, defecation, and menstruation causes itching in able-bodied (AB) persons but, when itching cannot be felt, rashes and infection result.

Persons with spinal paralysis should be taught to inspect their body parts regularly to see that all sores, however minor, are cared for. Skin should be kept dry also, with care given to remove perspiration after heavy exercise and to towel properly after swimming and bathing. Circulation problems related to paralysis increase the danger of infection and make healing slow. Infection can cause severe problems (see the section on autonomic dysreflexia later in the chapter).

Of particular concern are pressure sores caused by sitting or lying in one position for a long time. Pressure sores (also called decubitus or ischemic ulcers) often result in hospitalization. They heal very slowly. To prevent pressure sores, seat cushions are used and persons are taught to frequently change positions.

Sunburn is a special problem because persons with spinal paralysis cannot feel discomfort caused by sun on skin when there is no sensation. Clothes with long sleeves and pants are recommended.

Temperature Control

Spinal paralysis above T8 renders the body incapable of adapting to temperature changes. *Poikilothermy* is the name for the condition in which the body assumes the same temperature as the environment. To prevent poikilothermy, special attention must be given to appropriate clothing, heating, and air-conditioning. Whereas AB persons often do some vigorous movements to warm up, paralyzed individuals cannot. Teachers must be sensitive to signs of overexposure, especially in swimming pools and during weather extremes.

Fluid intake is closely related to temperature regulation. Hot and cold drinks are recommended aids. Additionally, persons engaging in activity and/or sitting in the sun should be encouraged to drink water about every 30 min.

Contractures and Injury Prevention

A *contracture* is a permanent shortening and tightening of a muscle or muscle group caused by spasticity, paralysis, or disuse. It is felt as a stiffened joint that impairs normal range of motion (ROM). Contractures should be prevented by ROM exercises twice daily. Once a contracture occurs, the treatment is typically splinting, casting, or surgery. Among persons who spend most of their time in wheelchairs, hip, knee, and ankle flexors tend to become too tight. This is true also of AB people who sit a lot.

Stretches should slowly move the body part to the extreme of its ROM, where it is held 10 to 30 sec (Curtis, 1981). These can be done by self, family, or friends. A physical therapist usually teaches technique, after which others assume responsibility (Tecklin, 1989). Gentle warm-up exercises should be done before ROM stretches. Stretching is also important prior to sport and dance activity to prevent injury. The same stretches are used as in AB sports.

Spasms

Paralyzed muscles in people with lesions above L1 often jerk involuntarily. This is caused by excessive reflex activity below the lesion level. Ordinarily, reflex activity is coordinated by the brain, but in spinal paralysis, impulse transmission is impaired. The stimuli causing spasms vary by person but include sensory input (touch, hot, cold) and pathology (bladder infections, skin breakdown).

Spasms are frustrating and sometimes embarrassing because they draw attention. They can be dangerous during transfers and interfere with activities of daily living. The teacher or coach should ignore spasms because they are normal. Moreover, occasional spasms are good for circulation and help with retention of muscle shape. When spasms are too severe, several treatment options are available: (a) physical therapy, mainly stretching; (b) drug therapy (baclofen, dantrolene, valium, diazepine), (c) nerve blocks, and (d) surgery.

Atrophy of Limbs

Over time, paralyzed limbs decrease in size and lose the attractive shapes associated with good muscle tone. This withering is called *atrophy*. Many persons with lower limb paralysis are self-conscious about this and do not like to wear shorts and swimsuits around AB peers. Trousers should be accepted as sport and dance attire until these individuals are able to accept and appreciate the body as it is.

Persons do tend to stare at atrophied limbs unless sensitized. Prospective teachers should visit rehabilitation and sport settings to see limbs of all sizes and shapes. Contact theory posits that repeated contact, combined with attitudinal guidance, decreases discomfort.

Urination and Defecation

All persons with spinal paralysis above S2 (except those with polio) have some kind of bladder dysfunction, requiring that they urinate in a different way. The most common alternative is *intermittent catheterization,* a procedure of inserting a tube into the urethra for a few seconds and draining urine into a small, disposable plastic bag (see Figure 23.10). Intermittent catheterization is performed several times a day on a rigid

FIGURE   23.10

Catheterization as a means of withdrawing urine from the bladder is used by persons with spina bifida, spinal cord injuries, and other conditions that cause urinary incontinence. The catheter is lubricated and then inserted into the penis about 6 inches or into the female opening about 3 inches. Parents can generally instruct teachers in the correct procedure.

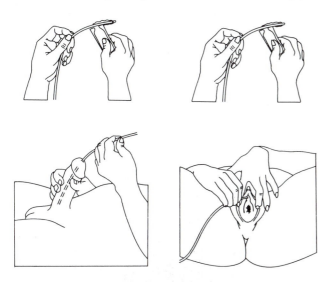

schedule to keep the bladder empty and prevent accidents. Persons with incomplete lesions may feel sensation and use catheterization only in response to need. Many of these persons have hyperactive bladders and urinate more frequently than AB peers. *Holding urine is contraindicated.* Architecturally accessible restrooms should be located near activity areas, and time planned for use.

In early childhood, catheterization must be done by the teacher or an aide, but later, persons learn to perform this simple, nonsterile procedure for themselves. Alternatives to catheterization are the *Crede maneuver* (exerting manual pressure on the lower abdomen to initiate urination), the wearing of urinary leg bags, and the use of an indwelling internal catheter (Foley) that remains inside the urethra.

Whatever the procedure, frequent emptying of the bladder is important. Retention of urine leads to urinary and kidney infections, a major cause of illness and death among persons with spinal paralysis. Should signs of infection (flushed face, elevated temperature) be noted, no exercise should be allowed without physician clearance. Any changes in urination frequency or in other practices related to urination should be noted.

Defecation is managed by scheduling time and amount of eating as well as by regulating time of bowel movements. If defecation becomes too great a problem, surgical procedures (ileostomy or colostomy) create an opening (stoma) in the abdomen. A tube inserted in this opening connects the intestine with a bag that fills up with fecal matter and must be emptied and cleaned periodically. These bags are not worn during swimming; the stoma is covered with a watertight bandage.

Sexuality

Sexual function is innervated by the same nerves as urinary function (S2 to S4). Lesions above the sacral region (except in polio) may make it necessary to alter roles, methods, and positions for lovemaking, depending on whether the lesions are complete or incomplete. Capacity for erection, ejaculation, and orgasm must be evaluated individually because both parasympathetic stimulation and reflex patterns are involved. Women with spinal paralysis can bear children. Menstruation is not affected.

Heart and Circulatory Concerns

Persons with quadriplegia and high-level paraplegia have abnormally low resting heart rates (Shephard, 1990). This condition is called *chronotropic incompetence* or sick sinus syndrome. Likewise, their heart rate response to aerobic exercise is sluggish because of sympathetic nervous system impairment. Lesions at or above T5 affect heart rate response to arm exercise, whereas lesions at or below T10 affect cardiac responses to leg exercises.

Obviously, maximum heart rates and target zones used in aerobic exercise programs for AB persons are not appropriate in high-level spinal paralysis. Instead, baseline data are collected and individual goals set.

A major circulatory problem is the pooling of blood in the veins of paralyzed body parts. This is called *venous pooling* or venous insufficiency and is caused mainly by sympathetic nervous system dysfunction. Specifically, the vasoconstrictor function is impaired, meaning that the vessels cannot constrict and force the blood through the venous valves and back to the heart. Two problems result. First, the sluggish return of blood to the heart lowers stroke volume which, in turn, limits the amount of blood available to carry oxygen to working body parts. Inadequate oxygen (also called arterial insufficiency) results in early fatigue and/or limited aerobic endurance. Second, venous pooling increases the cross-sectional area of the veins, creating stress on the vascular walls that is relieved by some of the fluid in the blood leaking into the surrounding tissue. This results in swelling (edema).

AB persons have similar problems in jobs that require motionless standing and during pregnancy. We all know the importance of shifting from foot to foot when standing for long periods. People in wheelchairs must use their arms to move paralyzed legs and/or must prop the legs up from time to time. Also recommended is the wearing of jobst pressure garments (sometimes called *jobsts*). Recently, many wheelchair racing clothes have been made of tight-fitting elastic fabric that presumably serves to ameliorate venous pooling. Excessive constriction about the abdomen and upper thighs should be avoided, however, because this is associated with the development of blood clots in the extremities.

FIGURE   23.11

Medical and functional classifications for wheelchair sports. NWBA refers to National Wheelchair Basketball Association.

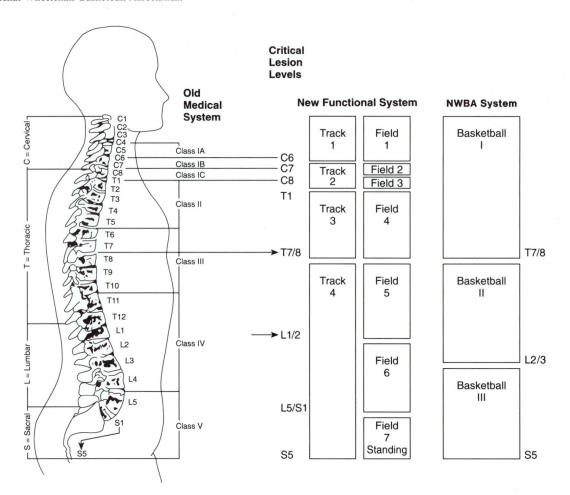

Blood Pressure and Autonomic Dysreflexia

The baseline blood pressure of persons with lesions above T6 is typically low. Whereas normal blood pressure for adults is 120/90 mm Hg (millimeters of mercury), the baseline in quadriplegia may be as low as 90/60 mm Hg. Blood pressure responses to exercise (see Chapter 13) must be interpreted in light of this fact.

Autonomic dysreflexia (AD), also called hyperreflexia, is a life-threatening pathology that sometimes occurs in lesions above T6. The pathology is characterized by sudden-onset high blood pressure/slowed heartbeat, sweating, severe headache, and goose bumps. AD is triggered by a stimulus within the body below the lesion level, usually by a distended bladder or colon because urination or defecation needs have been ignored.

In AB persons, the need to empty an organ is relayed up the spinal cord, but in individuals with spinal paralysis, the nerve impulses are blocked. This sets off a sympathetic nervous system reflex action that causes blood vessels below the lesion level to constrict, thereby raising blood pressure. Eventually and indirectly, the brain picks up sig-

nals and activates the parasympathetic system to bring the sympathetic system under control. It does this by dilating the blood vessels and slowing the heart rate but lacks capacity to act on the high blood pressure. This physiology is important to understand because many elite wheelchair athletes purposely induce AD states to maximize blood circulation during track and swimming events. Whereas AB persons normally void (urinate) before competition, these wheelchair athletes purposely keep the bladder full. This practice is obviously very dangerous and should be discouraged.

Anytime a person with a lesion above T6 vomits, loses consciousness, or appears sick during or after an athletic event, AD should be suspected. Usually, the cause is simply forgetfulness or carelessness about urine needs. AD may, however, be caused by infections or irritations like pressure sores, ingrown toenails, or burns below lesion level. First aid is simple. First, raise the head to a 90° angle or put the person in a sitting position; this helps lower the blood pressure. Next, drain the bladder or evacuate the fecal matter. If neither bladder nor colon are full, check for other causes. Obviously, there should be no physical activity until blood pressure is normalized. Typically, a physician is consulted.

Weight Management and Osteoporosis

Sedentary lifestyles usually lead to weight problems. Nonathletic persons in wheelchairs are at particular risk. Obesity is a health threat to all of us but is more dangerous to persons whose lean muscle mass is reduced by paralysis. Consider the size difference in leg and arm muscles. AB persons use the big muscles of the lower extremities to move their fat around, whereas persons in wheelchairs and on crutches are dependent on the strength of arm and shoulder muscles. These individuals also have less oxygen available to working muscles because of venous insufficiency. For many reasons, the hearts of persons with spinal paralysis are more stressed by obesity than those of AB peers.

Sedentary lifestyles also lead to *osteoporosis,* the gradual loss of calcium in bone tissue. This makes bones more vulnerable to fracture. The fatter one is, the more stress is placed on weight-bearing bones.

Sport Classification

Sport classification is an assessment system that (a) guides programming and (b) equalizes opportunity in competition. Each sport organization has its own classification system, and there is much controversy about medical versus functional classification (Curtis, 1991; Labanowich, 1988; McCann, 1987; Strohkendl, 1986; Thiboutot & Curtis, 1990; Weiss & Curtis, 1986).

The medical classification system, which developed in the 1940s when competitive sports were begun in England for people with spinal paralysis, dominated worldwide until recently. In this system, three quadriplegic classes (IA, IB, IC) and four paraplegic classes (II, III, IV, V) were assigned to track-and-field competitors on the basis of muscle strength tests and observations of trunk balance. In basketball, a similar system involved only three classes (see Figure 23.11).

Recently a sport-specific functional system has been adopted to guide international competition (Curtis, 1991). Whether the United States will adopt this system or continue with medical classification is not yet known. In a functional system, classifiers observe what persons can and cannot do in a particular sport. Assignment is based on a functional profile. The goal is to create classifications that are statistically significantly different from each other in range of scores, times, and distances. Several researchers have indicated that the medical classification system does not do this (Coutts & Schutz, 1988; Higgs, Babstock, Buck, Parsons, & Brewer, 1990).

Figure 23.11 shows the new functional classifications for the three sports most popular among people in wheelchairs. The number of functional profiles varies for each sport. For example, there are four for track, seven for field, and three for basketball. Each profile is matched with expected function when there is a *complete* lesion at a designated neurological level.

Considerable training is required to become a certified classifier. However, teachers, coaches and/or knowledgeable spectators, should understand this assessment system. Moreover, such understanding is useful in IEP meetings when describing present level of performance and justifying services needed.

Critical Lesion Levels for Sports

Of the 31 possible lesion levels, only eight are deemed critical for learning about sport potential. Simplified, each is associated with one or two performance criteria that describe highest function. Persons with complete quadriplegia have no trunk control or sitting balance. They use higher back chairs and are strapped in for safety. Progressive use of arm, hand, and finger muscles is what distinguishes between classes. The critical lesion levels are

C6—Have elbow flexion and wrist extension

C7—Have triceps (i.e., elbow extension)

C8—Have some finger control

T1—Have all arm, hand, and finger movement

Persons with paraplegia have full use of upper extremities but vary widely on trunk control and sitting balance. Those with lesions above T7/8 typically must hold onto the chair with one hand whenever they reach downward or sideward for a ball. They have some shoulder rotation that can be used in steering but lack the full trunk rotation needed in most sport activities. Progressive trunk control and balance are what distinguish between the first three paraplegic classes. The critical lesion levels are

T7/8—Have trunk rotation and fair-to-good sitting balance

L1/2—Have trunk extension from a bent-over position

L3—Have sideward bend and return capacity; trunk moves freely in all planes

L5/S1—Can throw while standing

Assessment of Sport Function and Skill

Few skill tests are available for people in wheelchairs (Brasile, 1984, 1986; Yilla, 1993). A good way for beginning teachers and coaches to become familiar with sport function is to learn to administer the basketball tests described in Figures 23.12 to 23.15. This assessment system was created in the early 1980s by Dr. Horst Strohkendl (1986) of the University of Cologne in Germany. Because everyone with permanent lower limb disability is allowed to play basketball, not just those with spinal paralysis, performance expectations are given for all disabilities. The Strohkendl system is an excellent method of describing present level of performance for IEP meetings. For school settings, it can be applied to all sports.

The *Strohkendl Basketball Function Tests,* which follow, serve as the basis for international classification in this sport. In the United States, three classes are assigned, but internationally, four are used.

FIGURE   23.12

Test 1. (*A*) Class I basketball athlete loses balance or leans back on chair
to prevent falling. Photo shows person with paraplegia caused by T5
lesion. (*B*) Class II basketball athlete shows no loss of balance,
demonstrates full range of arm motion, and good arm and shoulder
strength. Photo shows person with paraplegia caused by T11 lesion.

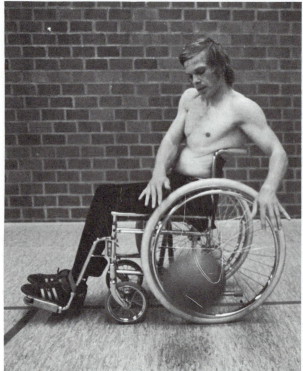

A. Fail Test 1   B. Pass Test 1

Test 1: Assessment of Sitting Stability and Rotation of the Trunk

Purpose
To differentiate between Class I and II basketball players.

Instructions
Sit as straight as possible in your chair. Bounce and catch the ball with both hands at the same time while changing the side of the
chair after each try. Rotate your trunk as far as possible to each side without losing your balance or leaning back in the chair.

Test Performance
See Figure 23.12A (failure of test) and 23.12B (passing of test).

Performance Expectations

Level of Lesion or Comparable Disability	Performance	Resulting Basketball Classification
T7 and above, CP classes 1–3	Fail	I
T8 to L2, CP classes 4–6, and bilateral hip amputees	Pass	II
L3 and below, CP classes 7–8, and lower extremity amputees	Pass	III

Functional Profile of Class I
In wheelchair with high back. Poor to nonexistent trunk control and sitting balance. Limited range of motion in arm movements;
cannot raise one or both arms above head. Functional limitations in pushing and steering chair; weak, short, choppy arm pushes.

FIGURE 23.13

Test 2. (*A*) Class II basketball athlete cannot perform sit-up by trunk strength alone; must use arm and shoulder thrust. Photo shows person with paraplegia caused by L1 lesion. (*B*) Class III basketball athlete does sit-up with trunk muscles alone; does not need arm and shoulder muscles. Photo shows person with paraplegia caused by L4 lesion.

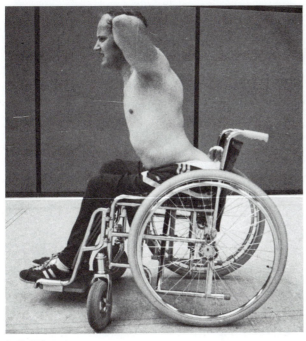

A. Fail Test 2

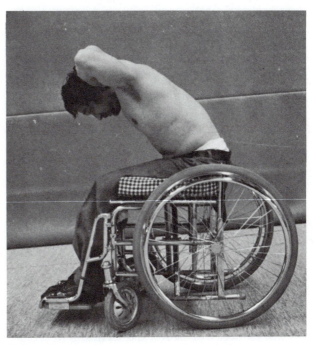

B. Pass Test 2

Test 2: Assessment of Forward/Backward Bending of Trunk

Purpose
To differentiate between Class II and III basketball players.

Instructions
Assume a forward bending position (trunk touching thighs) with hands behind neck. Now, raise your trunk to a normal sitting position without removing your hands from behind the neck.

Test Performance
See Figure 23.13A (failure of test) and 23.13B (passing of test).

Performance Expectations

Level of Lesion or Comparable Disability	Performance	Resulting Basketball Classification
T7 and above, CP classes 1–3	Fail	I
T8 to L2, CP classes 4–6, and bilateral hip amputees	Fail	II
L2 and below, CP classes 7–8, and lower extremity amputees	Pass	III

Functional Profile of Class II
In wheelchair with regular back height. Fair to good trunk control and sitting balance, but lacks ability to perform forward/backward trunk bending without holding onto wheelchair with one arm; may show some balance problems when lifting both arms over head with ball or shooting for goal. Normal hand, arm, and shoulder range of motion and strength.

FIGURE   23.14

Failure of Test 3. (*A*) Weak Class III basketball athlete in part 1 of test loses balance and leans the trunk and/or arms against wheel or lap for stability. (*B*) In part 2 of test, individual can do forward, but not sideward, raising of ball. Photos show person with paraplegia caused by L4 lesion.

A. Fail Part 1 of Test 3

B. Fail Part 2 of Test 3

Test 3: Assessment of Sideward Bending of Trunk (i.e., Lateral Flexion)

Purpose

To differentiate between functional abilities within Class III.

Instructions

A ball is lying to the side of your wheelchair. Pick up the ball with both hands simultaneously, using a sideward bend. Bring the ball over your head and place it on the floor to the other side of your wheelchair. Do this without bending your body forward. Repeat the test to the opposite side.

Test Performance

See Figures 23.14 (failure of test) and 23.15 (passing of test).

Performance Expectations

Level of Lesion or Comparable Disability	Performance	Resulting Basketball Classification
T7 and above, CP classes 1–3	Fail	I
T8 to L2, CP classes 4–6, and bilateral hip amputees	Fail	II
L3 and below, CP classes 7–8, and lower extremity amputees	Weak fails, strong passes	III

Functional Profile of Class III

In wheelchair with regular back height. Good to excellent control and balance in all trunk movements, except sideward bending, which varies among athletes. Can pick up ball from any position on floor and dribble with one hand, can steer chair by crossing free arm to grasp opposite wheel.

FIGURE 23.15

Passing of Test 3. Strong Class III basketball athlete performs (*A*) side bend and (*B*) overhead lift of ball with little difficulty. If the hip abductors and knee flexors are not completely paralyzed, some movements of the legs are available to help with balance. Photos show person with paraplegia caused by S1–S2 lesion.

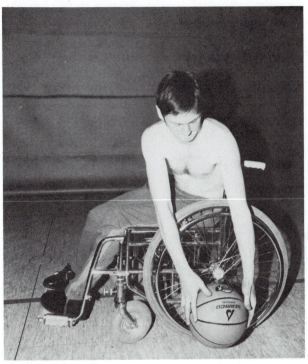

A. Pass Part 1 of Test 3

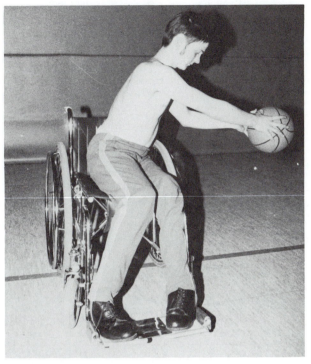

B. Pass Part 2 of Test 3

Programming for Paraplegia

Table 23.3 presents illustrative goals to guide programming for paraplegia. NWAA classes II to V are retained in this table because the United States is still using them, but research shows that track activities for people with paraplegia can be organized into two ability groups: (a) T1 to T7 and (b) T8 to S5 (see Figure 23.11). The major difference between groups is in the ability to use trunk movements (i.e., the abdominal muscles) for extra power and for improved balance, especially when negotiating curves. Both classes rely on a hand-flick or friction technique to propel the chair.

International rules break T1 to S5 down into four field classes (see Figure 23.11). Field Class 4 (F4) ends at the same lesion level as Basketball Class I. Both are characterized by no sitting balance and the need to hold onto part of the chair while throwing. Field Class 5 (F5) is roughly the equivalent of Basketball Class II, ending at L1 and L2, respectively. This means that athletes have full forward and backward trunk movements without holding onto the chair.

The major distinction between Field Classes 5 (F5) and 6 (F6) is the ability of F6 to lift the thighs off the chair (i.e., hip flexion), thereby imparting more force to the throw. F6 may also have leg function, such as pressing the knees together (hip adduction), straightening the knees, and bending the knees. Field Class 7 (F7) permits people who are able to stand and throw to do so; this is a major change from previous rules that mandated that all sports be done in wheelchairs.

Every sport available to AB persons can be adapted with minor changes to paraplegia. Wheelchair basketball, however, remains the most popular, with teams sponsored by all kinds of facilities and agencies. The University of Illinois at Urbana/Champaign is the institution of higher learning best known for leadership in both men's and women's wheelchair sports. A trend of the future is to help sport-oriented youth in wheelchairs select universities and communities where sports are accessible.

Table 23.3
Goals for persons with paraplegia.

NWAA Class	Spinal Cord Level	OT Goals *Self-Care and ADL Skills*	PT Goals *Wheelchair and Ambulation Skills*	PE and R Goals *Sports, Dance, and Aquatics Skills*
II	T1 to T5	Trunk, leg, foot Vocational rehabilitation	Do wheelies (see Figure 23.17A) Transfer chair to floor Walk in bars or with walker	Same as IC (see Table 23.4), except: 3-k shot put 50-yd front and back freestyle, breast
III	T6 to T10	Same as above	Swing-to on crutches Transfer chair to crutches Use stairs	Same as II, except: 400- and 1600-m track relay 50-yd butterfly 400-yd distance freestyle Class 1 wheelchair basketball Snow skiing (upright with special apparatus)
IV	T11 to L2	——	All gaits on crutches All transfers	Same as III, except: 200-yd individual medley Wheelchair tennis, racquetball 500-yd distance freestyle Class 2 wheelchair basketball
V	L3 and below	——	Functional walking without crutches—may use cane, braces	Same as above, except: Class 3 wheelchair basketball

Note. OT = Occupational therapy; ADL = Activities of daily living; PT = Physical therapy; PE and R = Physical education and recreation; NWAA = National Wheelchair Athletic Association.

Programming for Quadriplegia

Programming for persons with quadriplegia should be cross-disciplinary. Table 23.4 presents illustrative goals to guide programming. Complete lesions above C6 require activities in motorized chairs, similar to those conducted for severe les autres and cerebral palsy conditions. Persons with lesions above C4 have no appreciable movement but can use mouth devices to propel their chairs. C4 function indicates head and neck movement, whereas C5 function brings shoulder movement and weak elbow flexion.

At C6, all kinds of opportunities open up because there is (a) sufficient elbow flexion to propel a manual chair and (b) enough wrist extension to enable a crude grasp. Propelling a chair with only elbow flexion is slow and awkward, but it works. The hands remain in contact with or close to the handrim. They are placed either (a) with the back of the wrist behind the handrim or (b) with the palm pushing down on top of the handrim in a forward direction. Obviously, gloves are worn. Some athletes have completed marathons, but realistic distances to be conquered in a physical education class appear in Table 23.4. The club is the easiest field event for C6 function, although some persons like the challenge of a discus.

A C7 lesion means that the triceps are intact, allowing elbow extension, a mechanically efficient way to push a chair and give impetus to field implements. Grasp and release is still a problem because there is little finger use.

C8 represents the breakthrough for throwing events. A good fist can be made, and the fingers can be spread. Hand and finger power is not normal but sufficient for fairly good distance with the shot, discus, and javelin.

T1 is the indicator that upper extremities are normal. This marks the beginning of Track Class 3 (T3) and Field Class 4 (F4). Most persons with quadriplegia, if lesions are complete, find little success in wheelchair basketball, although they can meet Class I eligibility. Teams usually give the most playing time to the highest functioning representative of a class. In most communities, this would be a T5, T6, or T7 for Class I.

Wheelchair Sports

Almost every sport can be played in a wheelchair (Adams & McCubbin, 1991; Kelley & Frieden, 1989; Paciorek & Jones, 1989). Some, like basketball, quad rugby, and tennis, are frequented by persons with all kinds of lower limb disabilities. Others, like wheelchair team handball (previously called wheelchair soccer), are official sports of one disability organization (i.e., U.S. Cerebral Palsy Athletic Association).

Wheelchair Basketball

Wheelchair basketball is the world's most popular team sport for persons with disabilities. It was popularized by war veterans in the late 1940s. In 1949, the National Wheelchair

Table 23.4
Goals for persons with quadriplegia.

NWAA Class	Spinal Cord Level	OT Goals *Self-Care and ADL Skills*	PT Goals *Wheelchair and Ambulation Skills*	PE and R Goals *Sports, Dance, and Aquatics Skills*
—	Incomplete C5	Type, feed self Use assistive devices	Push on flat surface Manipulate brakes Stand at tilt table	Power chair activities, games, dance Basic sport skills Swimming with flotation devices
IA	C6	Drink Wash, shave Brush hair Dress upper half Sit up/lie down in bed Write, draw Crafts, hobbies	Push on sloping surface Turn wheelchair Remove armrests/foot plates Transfer chair to bed, chair to car Stand in bars	Manual chair activities, games, and dance 60-, 100-, 200-, 400-, 800-m track events 400- and 800-m track relay Slalom Pentathlon Club throw, 2-k shot put, discus Weight lifting 25-yd front and back freestyle, breast, and butterfly—no flotation devices 75-yd individual medley (3 × 25) 100-yd distance freestyle Archery, air weapons, table tennis Sit-skiing (snow events) Marathon and road racing
IB	C7	Turn in bed Dress lower half Skin care Bladder and bowel control Crafts, hobbies	Wheel over uneven surface Bounce over small elevations Pick up objects from floor Negotiate curbs Perform almost all transfers Swing-to in bars Drive automobile with manual controls	Same as IA, except: 100-, 200-, 400-, 800-, 1500-m track events Shot put, discus, javelin (no club) Swimming same, except 100-yd individual medley (4 × 25), with butterfly as fourth stroke
IC	C8	Same as IB, except more finger control	Same as IB, except more finger control	Same as IB, except 200-yd distance freestyle

Note. OT = Occupational therapy; ADL = Activities of daily living; PT = Physical therapy; PE and R = Physical education and recreation; NWAA = National Wheelchair Athletic Association.

Basketball Association (NWBA) was founded. This governing body permits anyone with a permanent lower limb disability to play.

The classification system for equalizing team abilities was explained in Figure 23.11. The United States uses three classifications, whereas many other countries use four. A numerical value of 1, 2, or 3 points is assigned to each player, depending on classification. Players on the floor, according to U.S. rules, cannot total more than 12 points. The two combinations used most often in game play are five players with the following classifications:

3	3
3	3
3	2
2	2
1	2
12	12

Only a few rule modifications are made:

1. Five, rather than 3 sec, are allowed in the lane.
2. When dribbling or holding the ball in the lap, the player can only make two thrusts of the wheels, after which he or she must dribble, pass, or shoot.

3. There is no double-dribble rule in wheelchair basketball.

4. A player raising his or her buttocks off the chair is a physical advantage foul. This counts as a technical foul.

Several books are available on coaching wheelchair basketball (Hedrick, Byrnes, & Shaver, 1989; Owen, 1982; Shaver, 1981). Obviously, good performance is dependent upon learning wheelchair- and ball-handling skills. Quad rugby, although designed for persons with quadriplegia, can serve as a lead-up game to wheelchair basketball. Many of the same skills are used.

Quad Rugby

Quad rugby (also called murderball and wheelchair rugby) is the team game that most persons with lesions from C6 through T1 enjoy (Hooper, 1991). Played on a regulation basketball court with a four-person team and a volleyball, the game combines elements of basketball, football, and ice hockey. The object is to score points by carrying the ball over the opponents' goal line. The ball is passed from player to player and advanced down the floor by whatever movement patterns that individual abilities allow. There must be one bounce every 10 sec (Yilla, Mikkelson, Willard, & Dimsdale, 1988).

Wheelchair Tennis

With the exception of track, field, and swimming, wheelchair tennis is the most popular individual sport (see Figure 23.16). This sport also has few modifications. The main rule change is two bounces instead of one. Persons with limited grip strength can use elastic, tape, or special orthotic devices to bind the racquet to the hand. If an overarm serve is not possible, the player uses a bounce-drop serve. The back wheels of the chair must remain behind the service line until contact with the ball is made.

Instead of a classification system, division play is used to ensure fairness. There are five divisions for men and three for women. These are designated as Open (for the best players), A, B, C, and D. Players move from division to division by winning in regional and then national tournaments; each knows his or her rank or standing within a division.

Wheelchair tennis officially began in 1976, with the founding of the National Foundation of Wheelchair Tennis (NFWT) by Brad Parks, a wheelchair user. Over 6,000 people worldwide play wheelchair tennis (Carhill, 1991). Many are children because Brad and his wife Wendy, a physical therapist, attach high priority to junior competition and sport camps. Many AB persons play doubles and singles with wheelchair athletes. Tennis uses community facilities and facilitates integration.

Racing, Slalom, and Cycling

Distance racing, track, and slalom are particularly popular wheelchair sports and should be begun as early as possible in school-based physical education. *Sports 'N Spokes* and *Palaestra* provide pictures and stories of models. Among these

FIGURE 23.16

Randy Snow, wheelchair tennis champ, conducts workshops around the country. See his life story in the January–February 1990 *Sports 'N Spokes* (Crase, 1990).

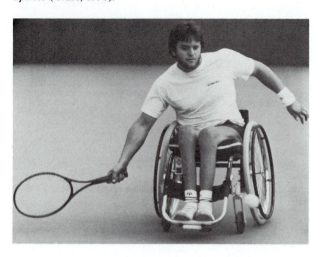

are Rick Hansen, who wheeled 24,901 mi on an around-the-world trip; Bob Hall, the first person to wheel in the Boston Marathon; George Murray, the first person to break the 4-min mi in a wheelchair; Candace Cable-Brooks, who has won the Boston Marathon five times; and Sharon Hedrick, star basketball player.

The slalom is a race against time in which persons follow an obstacle course that has been clearly marked to indicate required maneuvers (see Figure 23.17). This event can be done hundreds of ways to help children improve wheelchair techniques.

Cross-country and cross-world marathons have continued to be popular since George Murray and Phil Carpenter wheeled across the United States. Their "continental quest" was immortalized by an excellent book with this title (McBee & Ballinger, 1984).

The development of all terrain vehicles (ATVs) has contributed to this kind of sport, as well as to trail riding and other off-road adventures (Axelson & Castellano, 1990). ATVs typically have three or four wheels, low-set seats, and increased distance between front and back wheels.

On-the-road hand cycling is also becoming popular. David Cornelsen (1991), for example, reports that he regularly rides with members of an AB club. The rides are usually 35 to 55 mi of hilly terrain, averaging 15 mi an hour.

Wheelchair Technology and Basic Skills

Wheelchair technology is advancing so rapidly that readers should stay abreast of changes by consulting the review of chairs published annually by *Sports 'N Spokes*. This review includes hundreds of pictures, prices, and descriptions.

Chairs have come a long way since 1700, when King Philip V of Spain, the first wheelchair user, proudly displayed the wooden wheels and spokes of his vehicle. Historically, the first major change came in the 1930s, when H. A. Everest, one of the founders of the Everest & Jennings Wheelchair Company, designed the first compact, foldable

FIGURE 23.17

Learning to do wheelies (*A*) and to maneuver the chair over obstacles (*B*) are prerequisite to competing in NWAA obstacle courses, as well as to coping with street curbs and other architectural barriers.

A

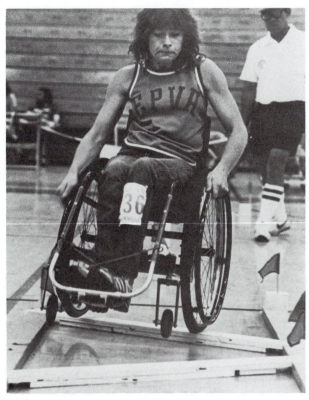

B

chair. In the 1950s, when wheelchair sports became a popular leisure-time option, improvements were swift. Today, there are many types of chairs, each designed for a specific purpose.

Success in sports depends largely on the appropriateness of the chair. Physical activity personnel must know about the different chair types and be assertive in offering guidance, especially to parents who may not know about the options.

A discussion of (a) the medical model, (b) the everyday chair, (c) the sport chair, (d) the motorized chair, and (e) the track or racing chair follows. Most persons who are serious about sports have several chairs. Elite athletes often use chairs given to them by commercial companies, but beginners typically buy their own or have a physician write a prescription that enables insurance payment.

The Medical Model

For persons with severe disabilities who cannot push their own chair or have minimal arm function, the *medical model* is typically prescribed (see Figure 23.19). This model is seen in residential facilities, nursing homes, rental agencies, schools, and recreation centers.

Figure 23.19A shows the parts of the chair that the teacher or recreator must understand in order to push the person about and/or teach basic sport skills. Note the two types of wheels: (a) main wheels, which contain the handrims and (b) casters, the smaller front wheels. The handrims are what the hands contact in self-propulsion activities. The following are skills the teacher should know.

Handling Brakes

Brakes are used to lock the main wheels, thereby immobilizing the chair and providing needed stability for making transfers, engaging in field events, and playing stationary games like shuffleboard. Brakes may be placed partially on to reduce acceleration in going down a steep ramp. Figure 23.19B depicts the most commonly used type of brake. Many sport and racing chairs do not have brakes.

Removing Armrests and Foot Plates

Armrests and foot plates should be removed before engaging in sport events and before transfers to and from the wheelchair. Armrests are removed by lifting the tubular frames of the arm out of the tubing on the wheelchair (see Figure 23.20). Removable foot plates are swinging or nonswinging. In the swinging type, the front rigging is released and swung to the side, after which it is removed. In nonswinging foot plates, a button-type or hook-in-place lock is released to permit removal.

FIGURE 23.18

(*A*) The medical model chair and the parts that are important when pushing and caring for a person who is severely disabled. (*B*) The toggle brake.

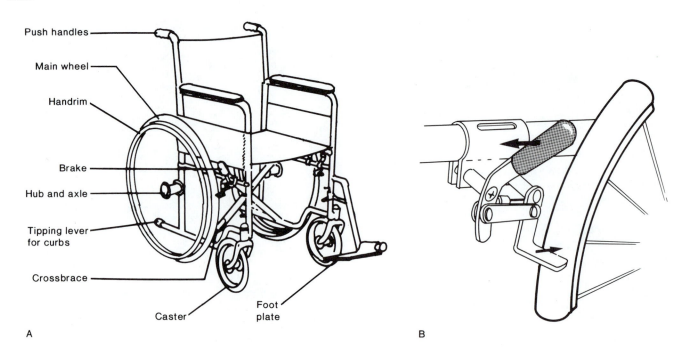

Push handles

Main wheel

Handrim

Brake

Hub and axle

Tipping lever for curbs

Crossbrace

Caster

Foot plate

A

B

Pushing Person in a Chair

When pushing an individual in a wheelchair the most important thing to remember is the safest direction for the rider to face. The rest (i.e., use of the tipping levers) is common sense. Guidelines include the following:

Descending curb or steep ramp: Turn self and wheelchair backward.

Descending stairs: Go down forward with chair tilted backward.

Ascending curb: Go forward.

Ascending stairs: Back up the stairs.

In managing stairs, two adults are best, one in back and one in front. The stronger adult should be in back since he or she has the heavier load. The person in back tilts the chair backward and lifts with the push handles. The person in front lifts the frame (never the foot plates, which might accidentally come off).

Opening and Closing the Chair

To open a wheelchair, *push down* on the two seat rails (outermost surfaces of seat). Do not try to open the chair by pulling it apart because this damages the telescoping parts of removable armrests.

To close the chair, lift up the foot plates. Then grasp the seat at its front and back and pull upward. If you intend to lift the folded chair into a vehicle, remove all detachable parts before closing it. *The best position to stand while opening or closing a chair is to the side (i.e., facing the wheel).*

Your First Time in a Chair?

Everyone should experience travel in a wheelchair, both self-propelled and pushed by a friend. Try wheeling about campus, checking buildings, sidewalks, and lawns for architectural barriers. Also, experiment with various track-and-field activities and make up some games, dances, and rhythmic exercises that can be done from a chair. When learning to maneuver a wheelchair, use gloves, since hands tend to blister from the vigorous push action. Try to achieve the following objectives:

1. Propel the wheelchair forward and backward and stop on command.
2. Cover 200 ft in 20 sec.
3. Perform a complete turn (360°) to the right in 1 min (Repeat to the left.)
4. Perform a complete turn to the right without touching the lines of a circle that has a diameter of 6 ft (Repeat to the left.)

For additional objectives, consult the qualifying times and distances published by sport organizations (e.g., see *Sports 'N Spokes*) and set goals for improving your skills.

Experience with the medical model wheelchair will make you a stronger advocate for the purchase of appropriate wheelchairs for school physical education. Medical model chairs are clumsy and slow in comparison with chairs manufactured specifically for sports. Because practice lags behind knowledge, however, finding anything but the medical model for use in developing beginning teaching competencies may be difficult in some communities.

FIGURE   23.19

Removing armrests and footplates is another important skill.
(*A*) Assistant removes armrest before transfer to mat. (*B*) Three types of
foot plates.

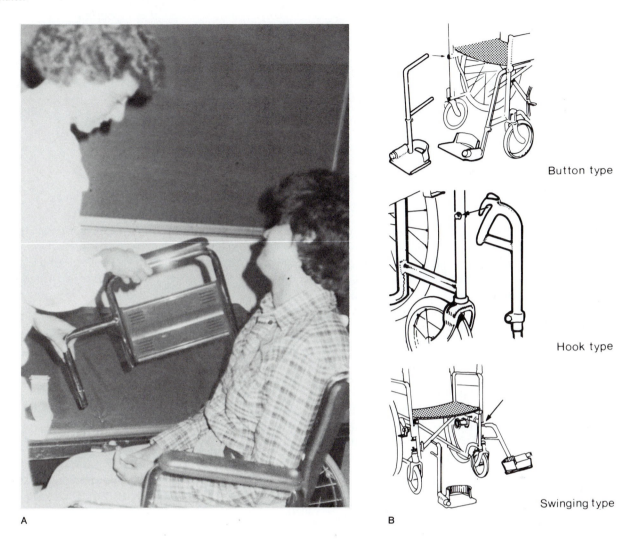

Button type

Hook type

Swinging type

A   B

Everyday and Sport Chairs

Originally, the term *sport chairs* referred to those wheel-chairs manufactured specifically for basketball. Now, with the proliferation of wheelchair sports (tennis, racquetball, soccer, football, softball), the term refers to any chair built to allow optimal maneuverability, quick turning, and rapid acceleration. Numerous manufacturers offer distinctly different models.

Most athletes use their sport chairs for everyday chairs, but nonathletes can purchase lightweight vehicles called *everyday chairs*. These typically weigh between 12 and 30 lb and are more like sport chairs than the medical model. Everyday chairs have many options (e.g., push handles, armrests, foot plates, brakes).

In contrast, sport chairs have no push handles, no armrests, and optional brakes that can be mounted either high or low on the frame. Instead of removable foot plates, there is a solid front bar for foot placement. Behind it, slightly lower,

is a *roll bar* that prevents the foot platform from damaging the floor. There are also optional *antitip casters* on a horizontal bar at the rear of the chair that decrease the possibility of tipping over.

Sport chairs have rigid frames and do not fold. They can, however, be disassembled easily and quickly for travel by pushing a quick-release button on the hub of the main wheel that disengages it. A similar device is used to disengage the casters. Some chair backs fold down.

Sport chairs also have different kinds of tires than medical models. The latter come with hard rubber tires, whereas sport chairs feature air-filled (pneumatic) tires like those on bicycles. This requires knowing how to fix flat tires. Athletes constantly debate the merits of two types of pneumatic tires: (a) the clincher, which has a separate tire and inner tube, and (b) the sew-up (also called continental or tubular), which has a tire sewn around the inner tube.

FIGURE **23.20**

(*A*) Axle plate mechanism on main wheel. (*B*) Bearings. (*C*) Hub of
wheel. (*D*) Wheelchair. All are important parts of wheelchair knowledge.

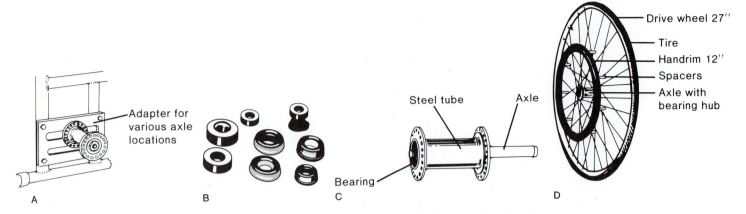

Drive wheel 27"
Tire
Handrim 12"
Spacers
Axle with
bearing hub

Steel tube   Axle

Adapter for
various axle
locations

Bearing

A   B   C   D

Axle plates on the main wheels are adjustable to
permit a wide variety of seat inclinations (see Figure
23.20). These mechanisms allow the player to sit taller during basketball, with the main wheels adjusted backward for greater
stability. In tennis, the player sits lower, with the main wheels
adjusted forward so that the chair can spin around faster and
be more maneuverable. Changing the axle position alters the
wheelchair's center of gravity, thereby adapting for all the
different sports.

A bearing is the outermost part of an axle (see Figure
23.20). Bearings affect the rolling resistance of a wheel (i.e.,
tightening the axle toward the frame makes wheel revolution
more difficult; loosening too much causes wheels to wobble).
Bearings may be sealed or not sealed. Teachers should know
how to adjust and/or lubricate bearings.

Handrims of sport and everyday chairs are about the
same size as those of the medical model. In general, their
diameters are about 2 inches smaller than the wheels. Handrims used by persons with minimal arm and hand function
have small handles (projections or spacers) on them that make
propulsion easier.

Motorized Chairs

Motorized chairs (sometimes incorrectly called electric
chairs) give persons with severe disabilities considerable independence. They move at high and low speeds and are generally capable of about 5 mi an hour. Most can climb inclines
of at least 10°. Families/agencies that can afford to do so
provide children who have little arm and shoulder strength
with motorized chairs at a very young age.

The battery-powered chair is the most common, with
two 12-volt batteries mounted on a carrier at the back of the
chair below seat level. These batteries must be recharged each
night to supply power for approximately 8 hr of continuous
use. Regular automobile batteries are used on most chairs.

Motorized chairs, which must have sturdy frames to
support the weight of batteries and other special equipment,
are very heavy. Without the batteries, a chair typically weighs
75 to 80 lb. Folding the chair is impossible without battery
removal. Problems in portability generally lead users of motorized chairs to purchase a second vehicle (manual) for
travel.

Track and Racing Chairs

Track and racing chairs differ from sport and everyday
models primarily in number of wheels, size of wheels (larger)
and handrims (smaller), lowered seat position, longer wheelbase (distance from front to back), and much camber (vertical angle of the main wheels). Figure 23.21 depicts these
characteristics.

Since 1975, when Bob Hall gained recognition as
the first wheelchair racer to enter the Boston Marathon,
chairs have changed drastically to permit greater efficiency
in 26.2-mi and even longer runs. Improved pneumatic tires,
often with over 100 lb of pressure, are used, with as little
surface on the ground as possible.

Camber, while built into some sport chairs, is a ne-
cessity in track. *Camber* is a characteristic of the main wheels,
describing a condition in which the bottoms are farther apart
than the tops. Camber typically ranges from 5 to 15°. It
makes pushing more efficient, lessens the chance that the arm
will bump against the wheel, and permits a natural, relaxed
position for the elbows.

Whereas the axle plate mechanisms of sport chairs
allow many adaptations, most racing chairs have a fixed/rigid
axle. This is because chairs are custom-built, and racers know
the one best seat position they want to maintain. Seats are
molded to fit the body and to keep it in an optimal position.
Typically, air resistance is minimized by forward bending so
that chest touches thighs. Knees are flexed as much as possible and held high.

Casters on racing chairs are generally larger than
on sport chairs. There are several types of caster or front end
mounts and these will no doubt continue to change. Most
racers prefer three-wheel racing chairs (Cooper, 1988).

FIGURE **23.21**

Chair style must be designed for the sport. (Photos courtesy of Top End Wheelchair Sports, Inc.).

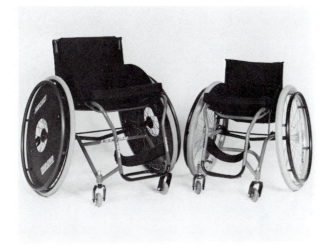

A. Sport chair for basketball, tennis, quad rugby, and everyday use

B. Aerodynamic kneel position racing chair

C. Racing chair showing long wheelbase

35 lbs.

D. Hand crank cycle

Triathlon racing or just cruising.

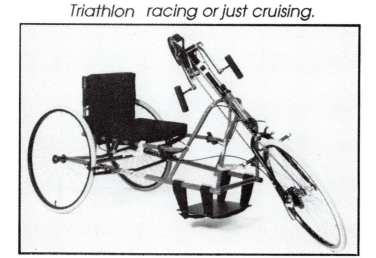

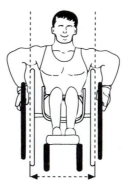

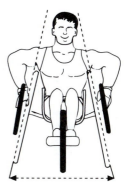

Everyday chair
- Narrow distance between main wheels
- No or little camber
- Vertical force applied to handrims
- Two casters

Track chair
- Wide distance between main wheels
- Much camber
- Diagonal force applied to handrims
- One front wheel

FIGURE   23.22

Characteristics of youth track chair. (Photo courtesy of Hall's Wheels.)

Wheelchair Sport Techniques

Technique varies according to sport, degree of disability, and type of wheelchair (Axelson & Castellano, 1990; Cooper, 1988; Hedrick, Wang, Moeinzadeh, & Adrian, 1990). The following are important points.

1. **Arm Propulsion.** The arm movement is different in track and marathon racing from that in most sports and activities of daily living (ADL). Figure 23.23 shows these differences. In athletes with good trunk control, the trunk alternately inclines forward and back during the thrust and recovery phases of the arm in all sports but track.

2. **High Knee Position.** Most athletes race with the knees as high as possible and the center of gravity as low as possible. This position permits optimal forward lean of the trunk, which, in turn, offers (a) lowered wind resistance, (b) better driving position for arms, and (c) increased trunk stability.

3. **Flexed Trunk Position.** Most athletes race with the trunk flexed and as close to the legs as possible. This position minimizes aerodynamic drag (Hedrick et al., 1990). Whereas in early racing history, persons with high-level lesions could not lean over because of trunk instability, new wheelchair technology enables them to assume desired positions. Increasing the sag in the seat and seat back is one way this is achieved.

Wheelchairs in Integrated School Physical Education

All schools with an enrollment of 300 or more should have at least two sport wheelchairs as part of their permanent physical education equipment. These chairs should be used in regular and separate physical education settings by both disabled and AB students. In team sport practice and competition, one chair can be assigned to each team; who is in the chair is relatively unimportant, since all students can benefit from exposure to wheelchair sports. The student with a physical disability, however, has no opportunity to develop locomotor sport skills generalizable to adulthood unless wheelchairs are provided. Wheelchairs can be integrated into all physical education instruction: dance, individual sport relays, challenge courses, and adventure activities. Equal learning opportunity for orthopedically impaired and AB students can be ensured only through the provision of wheelchairs (Brasile, 1992). This aspect of instruction should therefore be written into the IEP.

FIGURE 23.23

Wheelchair arm techniques.

Short propulsion thrusts in ADL activities, basketball, tennis, and most sports except racing. In this technique, the athlete pushes forward and downward (ie., applies force from A to B) while simultaneously inclining the trunk forward. The handrims are released at point B, the trunk returns to its upright position, and the arms are lifted and repositioned for the next downward and forward push.

Forward, downward thrust

Beginning of recovery

End of recovery

Long-duration, circular-propulsion thrust in track and marathon racing. In this technique, which requires small-diameter handrims and correct positioning of the wheelchair seat and back, the athlete maintains hands in contact with the handrims through approximately three-fourths of a circle, applying force the entire time. The grip on the handrim is never released, only loosened to allow repositioning. Shoulder joint extension is especially important in providing final propulsive thrust. The lower the seat, the more important the ability of the arms to lift backward.

Forward, downward thrust

Force continues

Beginning of recovery

The alternative to providing wheelchair instruction is to limit the physical education curriculum to upper extremity activities done from a stationary position (archery, riflery, table tennis, horseshoes, bowling), swimming, and horseback riding. No student should be forced to sit on the sidelines or serve as scorekeeper or official because an activity in which he or she cannot participate fully is being taught. During such units as basketball, football, and soccer, if wheelchair integration is not deemed appropriate, students with orthopedic problems should be rotated into separate, adapted physical education.

Winter Sports

Persons in wheelchairs enjoy winter sports like everyone else. For mobility on the snow, special apparatus called sit-skis and mono-skis have been invented (Axelson, 1984, 1986a, 1988). The sit-ski, similar to a sled with a bucket seat affixed, was invented first and is still used for learning basic skills and playing games like ice and sledge hockey. The sit-ski is propelled by poles or picks (special short sticks for pushing). To learn downhill skiing, the beginner practices direction and control while the sit-ski is tethered to an AB skier who stays behind, pulling on the tether to assist with control.

In the 1980s, mono-skis were invented for use in downhill skiing, especially racing. Whereas the sit-ski is close to the snow, the mono-ski is essentially a trunk-seat-leg orthosis suspended via a linkage system about 10 to 18 inches above a single ski (see Figure 23.24). Hand-held outriggers (forearm crutches with short ski tips attached to the ends) are used for control, including braking.

Sledge and pulk sports for persons with disabilities can be traced to Norway in the 1960s. *Sledge* means fishermen's sleigh, and the first racing was cross-country with dog teams and sledge toboggans. Shortly thereafter, special sledges with very thin metal runners were created. *Pulks* (originally, reindeer-drawn sleighs in Lapland) are similar to sit-skis; they have solid bottoms. Sledge and pulk events can be animal- or self-propelled, using poles or picks. Independent ambulation is often called *pulk poling* or *ice picking*.

Sledge or ice hockey is played on a regulation-size ice rink with a puck or small playground ball. Six players on each team play offense and defense similar to stand-up hockey, using picks that double as hockey sticks. Regulation padding, helmets, and gloves are important. A mask is optional. Persons with weak grips use Velcro strips on the gloves and picks (Paciorek & Jones, 1989).

Other popular winter sports that can be adapted for persons in wheelchairs are ice fishing, ice tubing, snowmobiling, snow camping, and cross-country sit-skiing. Just moving from place to place on snow- or ice-covered surfaces, like going out to get the mail, can be a challenge. Use of poles, called wheelchair poling, can be an activity of daily living (ADL) or an organized race for time and distance.

A major consideration in winter sports is appropriate warm clothing because of the temperature regulation problems in spinal paralysis above T6. Layered clothing and waterproof gloves are very important.

Winter sports are governed by NHS in affiliation with the U.S. Ski Association (USSA) and the International Ski Federation (ISF). Clinics are regularly held for learning to ski and for instructor training and certification. The Winter Park Handicapped Ski Association and Breckenridge Outdoor Education Center, both in Colorado, historically have pioneered training. Internationally, the famous Beitostølen Health Sports Center in Norway is best known. Addresses to write for further information follow:

Inge Morisbak
Beitostølen
 Helsesportsenter
2953 Beitostølen
Norway

Winter Park
Handicapped Ski
 Association
Box 36
Winter Park, CO 80482
(303) 726–4101

National Handicapped
 Sports
451 Hungerford Drive
Suite 100
Rockville, MD 20850
(301) 217–0960

Breckenridge Outdoor
 Education Center
P.O. Box 721
Breckenridge, CO 80424
(303) 453–6422

FIGURE   23.24

Winter sports. (*A*) Sit-ski or pulk used in downhill skiing in the 1970s and 1980s. Peter Axelson is shown in sled he designed. (*B*) Mono-ski developed by Enabling Technologies of Denver for downhill skiing in the 1990s. (*C*) Sledge hockey players from Beitostølen, Norway.

A

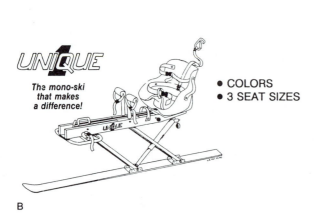

B

C

Fitness Programming

To date, the only published fitness research on youth with orthopedic impairments is that of Winnick and Short (1984) in conjunction with Project UNIQUE (see Chapter 13 on fitness). Their subjects included 141 youths, ages 10 to 17 years, with paraplegic spinoneuromuscular conditions classified into NWAA Classes II, III, IV, and V. Eleven tests (triceps, abdominal, and subscapular skinfolds; right and left hand-grip strength; arm hang; pull-ups; 50-yd dash; shuttle run; long-distance run; and softball distance throws) were administered.

Comparisons between AB students and students with disabilities showed that the latter were inferior on all measures. Moreover, the normally expected improvements from age to age did not appear in the youth with disabilities. Boys performed better than girls only on the softball throw. There were no significant test differences between NWAA classes. Norms, based on these subjects, and testing procedures appear in a Project UNIQUE manual (Winnick & Short, 1985). This research demonstrates the need for better fitness programming and more active lifestyles.

FIGURE   23.25

Hand-cranking apparatus must be available to develop cardiorespiratory endurance. (Photos courtesy of Saratoga Access & Fitness, Inc.)

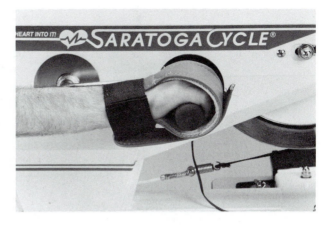

Research on adults with spinal paralysis also indicates the need for increased fitness. Excellent reviews of literature and training programs appear periodically (Shephard, 1990; Wells & Hooker, 1990). Athletically active persons in wheelchairs have fewer kidney infections, skin breakdowns, and other medical complications than sedentary persons (Stotts, 1986). They tend also to be self-actualized and happy (Sherrill, 1990; Sherrill, Silliman, Gench, & Hinson, 1990; Silliman & Sherrill, 1989). In general, it is not disability that affects wellness but, rather, poor attitudes toward exercise and lack of discipline.

Activity specialists should focus on making exercise fun, changing lifestyles, and promoting social support networks. One approach is to develop community-based programs in which wheelchair users can exercise with family, spouse, and friends (Lasko-McCarthey & Aufsesser, 1990). Another is to plan attractive risk recreation and/or strenuous outdoor ventures that motivate persons to develop the fitness levels needed for participation (Axelson, 1986b). For example, wanting to ride a horse is motivation for developing the arm and shoulder strength to mount and dismount. Likewise, sailboat racing, kayaking, canoeing, rock climbing, and the like require a commitment to strength and endurance training.

Fun means different things to different people. Often, it is associated with inclusion, friendship, and respect. Fitness activities done with partners or in small support groups help meet this need, especially if incentives are provided for out-of-class cooperative work toward shared goals. Points, rewards, or recognition should be given for both process (effort/time spent) and product (improved scores). A shared cooperative goal in weight management might be three people losing a grand total of 30 lb rather than each individual losing a certain amount. The same principle can be applied to pull-ups, grip strength, and other upper extremity goals.

Disability tends to isolate people. Children and youth, in particular, do not need further isolation at hand-cranking and arm-cycling machines. Partners can be assigned to face each other and talk while doing distinctly different fitness activities. Unless some kind of positive contact/sharing is assigned and reinforced, it may not happen.

Facilities that serve people with physical disabilities (integrated and other) need specialized equipment for assessment and training. Among these are various kinds of arm exercise machines (DeGraff, 1989; Glaser, 1989) and hand cycles (Cornelsen, 1991). Different kinds of handgrip designs must be available and/or support personnel to help people with quadriplegia (see Figure 23.25). Electronic, digital readouts help with motivation. Instead of floor mats, there must be raised, padded exercise areas about hip high that make transfers from a wheelchair easy.

Heart and circulatory limitations discussed earlier affect training protocol and outcomes. Additionally, the smaller muscle mass of the arms cannot produce the training effects associated with leg work. Goals should be individualized and comparisons with others avoided. Arm exercise done in an upright, sitting position may be so limited by blood pooling in the leg veins that apparatus must be adapted to allow hand-cranking from a supine position (Glaser, 1989).

When the purpose of fitness training is to prepare for athletic excellence, the principle of specificity is important. Rollers are to wheelchair users what treadmills are to ambulatory runners (see Figure 23.26). Hedrick and Morse (1991), coaches at the University of Illinois, describe roller training and the importance of a fan for ventilation and periodic fluid intake to prevent dehydration.

Reliance on upper extremities for fitness training makes wheelchair users especially vulnerable to shoulder joint injury (Millikan, Morse, & Hedrick, 1991). Pushing activities tend to overdevelop anterior arm and shoulder muscles and cause an imbalance in strength between anterior and posterior musculature. Characteristics of this are round shoulders, decreased flexibility, discomfort in the muscles between the shoulder blades, and increased risk of straining the rotator-cuff muscle group and/or dislocating the joint. Prevention focuses on stretching the anterior muscles and strengthening the posterior ones. For further information, see Chapters 13 and 14 on fitness and postures.

FIGURE   23.26

Rollers are to wheelchair users what treadmills are to ambulatory runners. (© The State Journal Register, Springfield, IL.)

References

Adams, R. C., & McCubbin, J. (1991). *Games, sports, and exercises for the physically disabled* (4th ed.). Philadelphia: Lea & Febiger.

Axelson, P. (1984). Sit-skiing: Part II. *Sports 'N Spokes, 9* (6), 34–40.

Axelson, P. (1986a). Adaptive technology for skiing. *Palaestra, 2* (2), 45–50.

Axelson, P. (1986b). Facilitation of integrated recreation. In C. Sherrill (Ed.), *Sport and disabled athletes* (pp. 81–89). Champaign, IL: Human Kinetics.

Axelson, P. (1988). Hitting the slopes . . . Everything you ever wanted to know about mono-skis and mono-skiing. *Sports 'N Spokes, 14* (4), 22–34.

Axelson, P., & Castellano, J. (1990). Take to the trail . . . Everything you ever wanted to know about off-road wheelchairs. *Sports 'N Spokes, 16* (2), 20–24.

Basmajian, J. V., & Wolf, S. (Eds.). (1990). *Therapeutic exercise* (5th ed.). Baltimore: Williams & Wilkins.

Brasile, F. (1984). A wheelchair basketball skills test. *Sports 'N Spokes, 9* (7), 36–40.

Brasile, F. (1986). Do you measure up? *Sports 'N Spokes, 12* (4), 42–47.

Brasile, F. (1992). Inclusion: A developmental perspective. A rejoinder to "Examining the Concept of Reverse Integration." *Adapted Physical Activity Quarterly, 9* (4), 293–304.

Campanella, R. (1959). *It's good to be alive.* New York: Little, Brown.

Carhill, M. E. (1991). People in sports: Brad and Wendy Parks— Making the dream come true. *Sports 'N Spokes, 17* (1), 42–45.

Cooper, R. (1988). Racing chair lingo . . . or how to order a racing wheelchair. *Sports 'N Spokes, 13* (6), 29–32.

Cornelsen, D. (1991). The wonderful world of hand cycling. *Sports 'N Spokes, 17* (2), 10–12.

Coutts, K. D., & Schutz, R. W. (1988). Analysis of wheelchair track performances. *Medicine and Science in Sport and Exercise, 20,* 188–194.

Crase, N. (1990). Winning: Randy Snow. *Sports 'N Spokes, 15* (5), 8–12.

Curtis, K. A. (1981). Stretching routines. *Sports 'N Spokes, 7* (3), 16–18.

Curtis, K. A. (1991). Sport-specific functional classification for wheelchair athletes. *Sports 'N Spokes, 17* (2), 45–48.

DeGraff, A. H. (1989). Accessible aerobic exercise: The Saratoga cycle. *Palaestra, 5* (3), 30–33.

Glaser, R. (1989). Arm exercise training for wheelchair users. *Medicine and Science in Sports and Exercise, 21* (5), Supplement, S149–S153.

Hansen, R., & Taylor, J. (1987). *Rick Hansen: Man in motion.* Vancouver, British Columbia: Douglas & McIntyre.

Hedrick, B., Byrnes, D, & Shaver, L. (1989). *Wheelchair basketball.* Washington, DC: Paralyzed Veterans of America.

Hedrick, B., & Morse, M. (1991). Getting the most from roller training. *Sports 'N Spokes, 16* (6), 81–83.

Hedrick, B., Wang, Y. T., Moeinzadeh, M., & Adrian, M. (1990). Aerodynamic positioning and performance in wheelchair racing. *Adapted Physical Activity Quarterly, 7,* 41–51.

Higgs, C., Babstock, P., Buck, J., Parsons, C., & Brewer, J. (1990). Wheelchair classification for track and field events: A performance approach. *Adapted Physical Activity Quarterly, 7,* 22–40.

Hooper, E. (1991). Quad rugby: The chance to compete. *Sports 'N Spokes, 16* (6), 70–71.

Kelley, J. D., & Frieden, L. (1989). *Go for it! A book on sport and recreation for persons with disabilities.* Orlando, FL: Harcourt Brace Jovanovich.

Labanowich, S. (1988). Wheelchair basketball classification: National and international perspective. *Palaestra, 4* (3), 14–54.

Lasko-McCarthey, P., & Aufsesser, P. (1990). Guidelines for a community-based physical fitness program for adults with physical disabilities. *Palaestra, 6* (5), 18–29.

McBee, F., & Ballinger, J. (1984). *The continental quest.* Tampa, FL: Overland Press.

McCann, C. (1987). The structure and future of sport for the disabled: The Arnheim seminar. *Palaestra, 3* (4), 9–40.

Millikan, T., Morse, M., & Hedrick, B. (1991). Prevention of shoulder injuries. *Sports 'N Spokes, 17* (2), 35–38.

Netter, F. (1986). *The Ciba collection of medical illustrations. Volume 1. Nervous system. Part 2. Neurologic and neuromuscular disorders.* West Caldwell, NJ: CIBA Medical Education Division.

Owen, E. (1982). *Playing and coaching wheelchair basketball.* Champaign, IL: University of Illinois Press.

Paciorek, M., & Jones, J. A. (1989). *Sports and recreation for the disabled: A resource manual.* Indianapolis: Benchmark Press.

Petrofsky, J. S., Brown, S. W., Cerrel-Bazo, H. (1992). Active physical therapy and its benefits in rehabilitation. *Palaestra, 8* (3), 23–27, 61–62.

Schack, F. (1991). Effects of exercise on selected physical fitness components of an ambulatory quadriplegic. *Palaestra, 7* (3), 18–23.

Shaver, L. (1981). *Wheelchair basketball: Concepts and techniques.* Marshall, MN: Southwest State University Press.

Shephard, R. J. (1990). *Fitness in special populations.* Champaign, IL: Human Kinetics.

Sherrill, C. (1990). Psychosocial status of disabled athletes. In G. Reid (Ed.), *Problems in motor control* (pp. 339–364). Amsterdam: North-Holland.

Sherrill, C., Silliman, L., Gench, B., & Hinson, M. (1990). Self-actualization of elite wheelchair athletes. *Paraplegia, 28,* 252–260.

Silliman, L., & Sherrill, C. (1989). Self-actualization of wheelchair athletes. *Clinical Kinesiology, 43* (3), 77–82.

Stotts, K. M. (1986). Health maintenance: Paraplegic athletes and nonathletes. *Archives of Physical Medicine Rehabilitation, 67,* 109–114.

Strohkendl, H. (1986). The new classification system for wheelchair basketball. In C. Sherrill (Ed.), *Sport and disabled athletes* (pp. 101–112). Champaign, IL: Human Kinetics.

Tecklin, J. S. (1989). *Pediatric physical therapy.* Philadelphia: J. B. Lippincott.

Thiboutot, T., & Curtis, K. (1990). NWBA classification: The player, coach, and classifier perspectives. *Sports 'N Spokes, 16* (1), 46–47.

Weiss, M., & Curtis, K. (1986). Controversies in medical classification of wheelchair athletes. In C. Sherrill (Ed.), *Sport and disabled athletes* (pp. 93–100). Champaign, IL: Human Kinetics.

Wells, C., & Hooker, S. (1990). The spinal injured athlete. *Adapted Physical Activity Quarterly, 7,* 265–285.

Winnick, J., & Short, F. (1984). Test item selection for the Project UNIQUE physical fitness test. *Adapted Physical Activity Quarterly, 1* (4), 296–314.

Winnick, J., & Short, F. (1985). *Physical fitness testing of the disabled: Project UNIQUE.* Champaign, IL: Human Kinetics.

Yilla, A. (1993). *Development of a quad rugby skill test.* Unpublished thesis, Texas Woman's University, Denton.

Yilla, A., Mikkelson, B., Willard, T., & Dimsdale, A. (1988). Quad rugby . . . what is it? *Sports 'N Spokes, 14* (2), 29–38.

CHAPTER

24

Les Autres Conditions and Amputations

FIGURE 24.1

Les autres, meaning "the others," is a sport term referring to all persons with physical disabilities who are not eligible to compete with persons who have spinal paralysis, cerebral palsy, stroke, or traumatic brain injury.

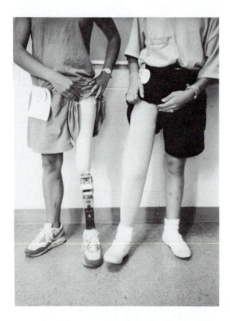

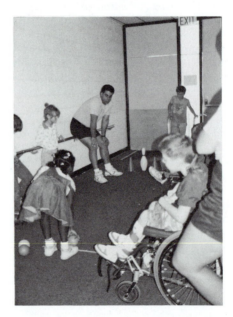

After you have studied this chapter, you should be able to:

1. Discuss sports for les autres conditions and amputations. Include governing bodies, recommended activities, and your personal experience with these conditions.

2. Describe assessment to guide programming in locomotor and ball handling activities for les autres conditions and amputations.

3. Describe and discuss each condition in this chapter (see Table 24.1). Include physical activity recommendations for each.

4. Be able to spell names of conditions and on a test to match descriptions with names. Be able also to classify each condition as mostly muscular or mostly skeletal.

5. Be able to recognize and name these conditions in real life or when shown films, videotapes, and slides.

6. Given age, gender, and condition, be able to write a physical education IEP. Substantiate physical education placement. Be sure to include contraindications and to consider inclusion.

Les autres conditions and amputations are grouped together in this chapter because, historically, they have been governed by the International Sports Organization for the Disabled (ISOD). *Les autres,* the French term for *the others,* is used in sport to denote the *other locomotor disabilities,* namely those not eligible to compete as spinally paralyzed or cerebral palsied (see Figure 24.1). Les autres conditions covered in this chapter are listed in Table 24.1.

This chapter builds on knowledge of wheelchair sports and fitness programming gained from Chapter 23. The medical diagnoses are different, but functioning is similar, especially in conditions that affect muscles. The chapter begins with conditions of progressive muscle weakness. Some of these, like the muscular dystrophies, have an unknown cause. Others can be classified as neuromuscular in that they are caused by degeneration of motor and/or sensory nerves. The chapter continues with thermal injuries (burns), a high incidence condition, that often results in contractures or amputations. Burns limit range of motion (ROM) and can be linked with both the muscular and skeletal systems.

The second half of the chapter presents conditions that affect bones and joints. First, conditions that can involve any body part or the entire body are described. These include arthritis, osteomyelitis, arthrogryposis, dwarfism, and osteogenesis imperfecta. Next, congenital and growth disorders that affect only one body part are described. The chapter concludes with a discussion of limb deficiencies and amputations.

Sport Governing Bodies

The disabled sports organizations (DSOs) in the United States that govern amputations and les autres conditions have changed within the past decade. From 1981 to 1990, the U.S. Amputee Athletic Association (USAAA) conducted sport activities. Now amputees are the responsibility of National Handicapped Sports (NHS). Originally, the cerebral palsy sport organization conducted les autres events, but the U.S. Les Autres Sports Association (USLASA) was organized in

1986 and continues to serve all conditions except dwarfism. The Dwarf Athletic Association of America (DAAA), also founded in 1986, sponsors its own events. For the Paralympics in 1992, the NHS served as the coordinating body for all disabilities in this chapter.

Originally, each organization held national meets at different sites and times. Since 1991, they have cooperated in conducting multidisability meets. DSOs for athletes with other disabilities (e.g., blind, cerebral palsied, spinally paralyzed) are also involved in this cooperative movement. One impetus for cooperation is the changing international approach to sport classification. Whereas classifications used to be disability-specific, the trend now is toward integration of some of the different disabilities.

ISOD has always stressed the philosophy of integration because the les autres conditions each have small numbers. Ways of combining these diverse conditions had to be devised to create enough competitors to run an interesting meet. This makes sense locally also. The new emphasis is on function, not the name of the medical condition.

Teachers, recreators, and coaches are expected, however, to know both medical conditions and probable levels of function. The conditions in this chapter each span the full range of individual differences. Many, like the muscular dystrophies, are progressively disabling. It is impossible to know the function of any given individual without careful assessment.

Les Autres Sport Assessment System

The first step in les autres physical education-recreation programming is to determine whether the person can best benefit from activity in a wheelchair, on crutches, or unassisted. The les autres system provides separate classifications for track and field. These are designated by abbreviations: LAT (les autres track) and LAF (les autres field). The one LAT and LAF profile that best describes a person should be written into his or her individualized education program (IEP). These profiles can then guide programming in all physical activities.

LAT Profiles (Les Autres Track Assessment)

LAT 1. Requires wheelchair. Has reduced function of muscle strength, mobility, and/or spasticity in one or both arms.

LAT 2. Requires wheelchair. Has normal function in both arms.

LAT 3. Ambulant with moderately reduced function in one or both legs.

LAT 4. Normal function in both legs. Disabilities in trunk and/or upper limbs affect movement success.

LAF Profiles (Les Autres Field Assessment)

LAF 1. Requires wheelchair. Has reduced function of muscle strength, mobility, and/or spasticity in throwing arm. Poor sitting balance.

LAF 2. Requires wheelchair. Has (a) normal function in throwing arm and poor to moderate sitting balance *or* (b) reduced function in throwing arm but good sitting balance.

LAF 3. Requires wheelchair. Has normal arm function and good balance.

LAF 4. Ambulant with severe problems when walking, *or* has problems with balance together with reduced function in throwing arm. Crutches allowed.

LAF 5. Ambulant with normal function in throwing arm. Reduced function in lower limbs or balance problem.

LAF 6. Ambulant with normal upper limb function in throwing arm. Has minimal trunk or leg disability. Reduced function in nonthrowing arm or some other minimal disability.

Motorized Chairs

International competition for les autres conditions does not permit the use of motorized wheelchairs. However, USLASA encourages full sport participation by persons whose disability is so great that the motorized chair is the only option. Motorized chair events (slalom and short-distance sprints) should be taught in school physical education. The slalom is an excellent test of ability to control a motorized chair (see Figure 24.2). Assessment and IEP development should include a description of the type(s) of wheelchair that best meets needs.

Sitting Balance and Ball Handling

Sitting balance and ball handling in a wheelchair can be assessed several ways. One is to use the wheelchair basketball assessment system described in Chapter 23. Another is to use the wheelchair basketball test positions but substitute various field implements and racquet swings. Most important, can the nonthrowing arm be free, or must it hold onto the chair during a throw or racquet swing to assist sitting balance?

For team sport assessment, the wheelchair basketball test in Chapter 23 yields findings generalizable to other sports. The skill tests of Brasile (1984) and Yilla (1993) are also appropriate.

Standing Balance and Ball Handling

Assessment of standing balance and ball handling first involves determining whether standing is assisted (e.g., crutches or holding on to a bar) or unassisted. Second, record whether best throws are from a stationary or a moving position. In regard to standing and moving balance, review the various crutchwalks and gaits described in Chapter 11 on motor performance. Describe gait in the IEP.

FIGURE 24.2

The slalom challenges persons to move through an obstacle course as fast as they can.

Crutches

Note the type of crutches used: (a) axillary, which fit under the armpits, or (b) forearm, also called Lofstrand or Canadian. Individuals with only axillary crutches cannot be programmed for ambulatory track because forceful pressure against the armpits, as in a race, cuts off circulation from the nerves and/or causes other kinds of nerve damage. An orthopedist should be consulted to see if the axillary crutches can be replaced with forearm ones.

Physical Activity Programming

If instruction in the regular physical education setting can be adapted so that students with disabilities can fully participate, they should be integrated part of the time with nondisabled peers. Part of their physical education, however, should be separate and focus on competence in wheelchair sports and/or activities in which they can compete equitably with persons having comparable disability. Regular exercise is more important for these students than for the able-bodied (AB).

Some les autres conditions may be complicated from time to time by respiratory and other infections. Persons running an elevated temperature and showing other signs of acute infection should not engage in vigorous exercise. Should students evidence chronic, long-term infection of any kind, the physical educator should confer with the physician concerning the best type of activity to prevent ROM loss and contractures.

When students are assigned to physical therapy, the exercises done in that setting should not be substituted for physical education and recreation activities that facilitate peer group involvement and social growth. Particular emphasis must be given to maintenance of good mental health, enjoyment of each day, and motivation to live life (however limited) to its fullest.

Muscular Dystrophies

The *muscular dystrophies* are a group of genetically determined conditions in which progressive muscular weakness is attributed to pathological, biochemical, and electrical changes that occur in the muscle fibers. The specific causes of these changes remain unknown. Several different types have been identified since 1850, many of which are rare. The three muscular dystrophies having the highest incidence are Duchenne, facio-scapular-humeral, and limb girdle types. Approximately 250,000 persons in the United States have

FIGURE   24.3

Walking posture and Gower's sign in muscular dystrophy. *Gower's sign* refers to the peculiar method of rise to stand.

muscular dystrophy. Of this number, 50,000 use a wheelchair. Most persons with muscular dystrophy fall between the ages of 3 and 13 and attend public school. Of these, few live beyond early adulthood. Specifically, 1 of every 500 U.S. children will get or has muscular dystrophy. Boys are affected five or six times more often than girls.

Muscular dystrophy in itself is not fatal, but the secondary complications of immobilization heighten the effects of respiratory disorders and heart disease. With the weakening of respiratory muscles and the reduction in vital capacity, the child may succumb to a simple respiratory infection. Dystrophic changes in cardiac muscle increase susceptibility to heart disease. The dilemma confronting the physical educator is how to increase and/or maintain cardiovascular fitness when muscle weakness makes running and other endurance-type activities increasingly difficult (Croce, 1987). Breathing exercises and games are recommended.

Duchenne Muscular Dystrophy

The *Duchenne type* of muscular dystrophy is the most common and most severe. Its onset is usually before age 3, but symptoms may appear as late as age 10 or 11. Males are affected more frequently than females. The condition is caused by a sex-linked trait that is transmitted through females to males. The sister of an affected male has a 50% chance of being a carrier and will pass the defective gene on to 50% of her sons. Persons with muscular dystrophy seldom live long enough to marry. Indicators of Duchenne muscular dystrophy include

1. Awkward side-to-side waddling gait.
2. Difficulty in running, tricycling, climbing stairs, and rising from chairs.

3. Tendency to fall frequently.
4. Peculiar way of rising from a fall. From a supine position, children turn onto their face, put hands and feet on the floor, and then climb up their legs with their hands. This means of rising is called the *Gower's sign* (see Figure 24.3).
5. Lordosis.
6. Hypertrophy of calf muscles and, occasionally, of deltoid, infraspinatus, and lateral quadriceps.

The hypertrophy (sometimes called pseudohypertrophy) occurs when quantities of fat and connective tissue replace degenerating muscle fibers, which progressively become smaller, fragment, and then disappear. The hypertrophy gives the mistaken impression of extremely well-developed healthy musculature. In actuality, the muscles are quite weak.

The initial areas of muscular weakness, however, are the gluteals, abdominals, erector spinae of the back, and anterior tibials. The first three of these explain lordosis and difficulty in rising, while the last explains the frequent falls. Weakness of the anterior tibials results in a foot drop (pes equinovarus), which causes children to trip over their own feet.

Within 7 to 10 years after the initial onset of symptoms, contractures begin to form in the ankle, knee, and hip joints. Contractures of the Achilles tendons force children to walk on their toes and increase still further the incidence of falling. Between ages 10 and 15, most children with dystrophy lose the capacity to walk, progressively spending more and more time in the wheelchair and/or bed. This enforced inactivity leads to severe distortions of the chest wall, kyphoscoliosis, and respiratory problems.

Facio-Scapular-Humeral Type

The *facio-scapular-humeral type* is the most common form of muscular dystrophy in adults. It affects both genders equally. Symptoms generally do not appear until adolescence and often are not recognized until adulthood. The prognosis is good, compared with that of the other dystrophies, and life span is normal. The condition may arrest itself at any stage. Indicators include

1. Progressive weakness of the shoulder muscles, beginning with the trapezius and pectoralis major and sequentially involving the biceps, triceps, deltoid, and erector spinae.
2. Progressive weakness of the face muscles, causing drooping cheeks, pouting lips, and inability to close the eyes completely. The face takes on an immobile quality, since muscles lack the strength to express emotion.
3. Hip and thigh muscles are affected less often. When involvement does occur, it is manifested by a waddling side-to-side gait and the tendency to fall easily.

Limb Girdle Type

The *limb girdle type* of muscular dystrophy may occur at any time from age 10 or after. The onset, however, is usually the second decade. Both genders are affected equally. The earliest symptom is usually difficulty in raising the arms above shoulder level or awkwardness in climbing stairs. Weakness manifests itself initially in either the shoulder girdle muscles or the hip and thigh muscles, but eventually, both the upper and lower extremities are involved. Muscle degeneration progresses slowly.

Progressive Muscle Weakness

Daily exercise slows the incapacitating aspects of muscular dystrophy. As long as the child is helped to stand upright a few minutes each day and to walk short distances, contractures do not appear. Once the individual is confined to the wheelchair, however, fitness deteriorates rapidly. Stretching exercises become imperative at this point, as do breathing games and exercises.

Eight stages of disability are delineated by the Muscular Dystrophy Associations of America, Inc.:

1. Ambulate with mild waddling gait and lordosis. Elevation activities adequate (climb stairs and curbs without assistance).
2. Ambulate with moderate waddling gait and lordosis. Elevation activities deficient (need support for curbs and stairs).
3. Ambulate with moderately severe waddling gait and lordosis. Cannot negotiate curbs or stairs but can achieve erect posture from standard-height chair.
4. Ambulate with severe waddling gait and lordosis. Unable to rise from a standard-height chair.
5. Wheelchair independence. Good posture in the chair; can perform all activities of daily living (ADL) from the chair.
6. Wheelchair with dependence. Can roll the chair but need assistance in bed and wheelchair activities.
7. Wheelchair with dependence and back support. Can roll the chair only a short distance but need back support for good chair position.
8. Bed patient. Can do no ADL without maximum assistance.

Even in Stage 8, some time each day is planned for standing upright by use of a tilt table or appropriate braces. Children should attend regular public school and engage in adapted physical education as long as possible, with emphasis upon the social values of individual and small-group games, dance, and aquatics. In the later stages, they may attend school only a small part of each day. Since they are not being educated for a future, they should be allowed to engage in school activities that give the most pleasure and allow the greatest socialization. The following illustrative case study describes a child in the early stages of muscular dystrophy (see Figure 24.3).

Case RS: Duchenne Muscular Dystrophy

RS's walk is characterized by a marked lordosis, with weight carried on the balls of the feet, arms slightly abducted for balance, and head held erect. RS is 9 years old and a member of a third-grade section in the regular wing of the school. He comes to the special education wing daily for mathematics and for physical therapy.

Medical Report

There is hypertrophy of the calf muscles, some shoulder involvement, winged scapulae, and a quadriceps weakness in addition to the hypertrophy of the gastrocsoleus group. The school physician has recommended a program of active exercise, muscle education, gait training, and hydrotherapy. RS has therapy sessions 5 days a week for 30 min each day with a group of three other boys. Four of these sessions are held in the pool and the other in individual activity. Additionally RS attends regular PE class 5 days a week.

Psychological and Social Status

Intellectually, RS ranks in the average group. In the classroom, RS is sometimes a leader and sometimes a follower. When working with others, he seems to resent correction. His general temperament is outgoing and his emotional outlook quite healthy. When faced with a frustrating situation, however, he angers easily, saying, "I can't," or quits trying.

RS is the second of three boys in his family. His brothers are 22 and 3 years old. The father is a building contractor and the mother a homemaker.

Physical Education Experience

RS's mobility is adequate for daily activities. He can walk and run, though somewhat more slowly than most of the boys in his class. He runs holding his head erect and swinging each leg out to the side as he moves it forward. He cannot squat or stoop well because of the difficulty of recovery from these positions. Arm movements are practically normal. He throws,

FIGURE 24.4

Boy in stage 5 of muscular dystrophy has such limited strength that bowling must be with a light ball and close to the pins.

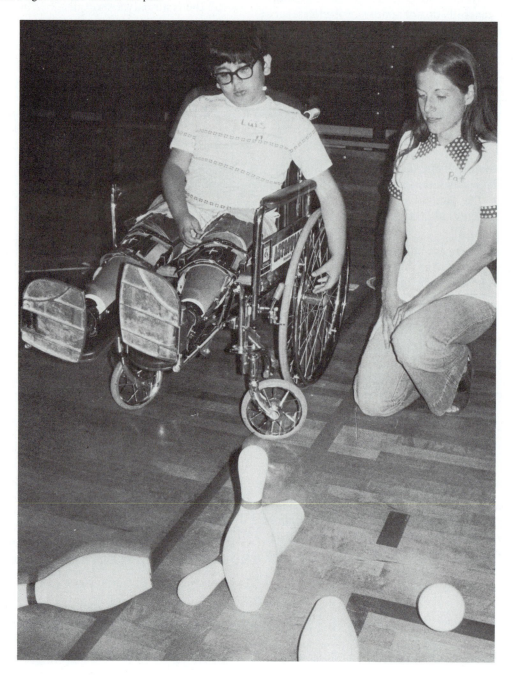

catches, and bats with average skill and enjoys hanging and swinging in the flying rings. His kicking is limited because of only fair balance. In kickball, a teammate kicks for him, and RS does his own running. He plays in the infield when his team is on the defense. School records indicate that RS participates in regular physical education classes. RS's mother indicates that she thought he needed more physical exercise. His teacher believes that he is carrying as full a schedule as is desirable for a child with progressive muscular dystrophy. While his program should be as active as possible, RS should also be developing sedentary recreational interests for the future (Spragens, 1964).

Program Implications

Until confined to a wheelchair, children with dystrophy should participate in regular physical education. They may fatigue more easily than their classmates, but specialists concur that they should be allowed to play as hard as they wish. Normal fatigue from vigorous physical activity is intrinsically good, and the child with dystrophy should be withdrawn from a game only when he or she appears totally exhausted. Should this occur, several *normal* children who are also showing signs of exhaustion should be excused at the same time. At no time should the child with dystrophy be sitting alone on the sidelines!

Full participation in games and athletics while the condition is in the early stages may enable the child to form close friends who will stick by as he or she becomes increasingly helpless. The child with muscular dystrophy and his or her friends also should receive instruction in some sedentary recreational activities that will carry over into the wheelchair years. Rifle shooting, dart throwing, archery, bowling, fishing, and other individual sports are recommended. The parents may wish to build a rifle or archery range in their basement or backyard to attract neighborhood children in for a visit as well as to provide recreation for their own child. Unusual pets, such as snakes, skunks, and raccoons, also have a way of attracting preadolescent children. Swimming is recommended, with emphasis upon developing powerful arm strokes to substitute for the increasing loss of leg strength.

Children with dystrophy are learning to adjust to life in a wheelchair just when their peers are experiencing the joys of competitive sports (see Figure 24.4). They are easily forgotten unless helped to develop skills like scorekeeping and umpiring, which keep them valued members of the group. The physical educator should not wait until disability sets in to build such skills, but should begin in the early grades, congratulating them on good visual acuity, knowledge of the rules, decision-making skills, and other competencies requisite to scorekeeping and umpiring. These integrated activities should not, however, substitute for adapted physical education.

Children with dystrophy tend to show lowered motivation for achievement, withdrawal of interest in their environment, emotional immaturity, and low frustration tolerance. These traits are not surprising when one considers that these children probably suspect their prognosis of early death, no matter how carefully guarded. Why should they study? Why should they consider different careers? Why should they care about dieting and personal appearance? Who wants to date them? The emphasis in academic studies, physical education, and social learnings must be upon the present, for they are not likely to have a tomorrow.

Multiple Sclerosis

Approximately 500,000 persons in the United States have *multiple sclerosis* (MS), a progressive neurological disorder. It is caused by *demyelination,* the disintegration of myelin covers of nerve fibers throughout the body. Its name is derived from the Greek word *sklerosis,* which means "hardening," and refers to the scar tissue that replaces the disintegrating myelin. The resulting lesions throughout the white matter of the brain and spinal cord vary from the size of a pinpoint to more than 1 cm in diameter. The cause of the demyelination is unknown.

Since MS characteristically affects persons between the ages of 20 and 40, the college physical educator may be called upon for counsel. Early symptoms of demyelination include numbness, general weakness, partial or incomplete paralysis, staggering, slurring of speech, and double vision. The disease is characterized by periods of relative incapacitation followed capriciously by periods of remission.

Case Study

The following description of MS over an 8-year period was written by Sherry Rogers, who developed MS while a junior physical education major in college:

Now with the diagnosis starts the story of the most demanding years of my life. The pain I experienced was tremendous. It was more localized now. It was mostly on my right side and the lower part of my back, especially the sciatic nerve of my right leg.

After about a month of getting one or two bottles of ACTH intravenously every day, I could see some improvement. Then the physician started me on cold showers to stimulate my circulation. All of this and my prayers worked for me. Physical therapy, mainly to exercise my legs, was given me also. I had not moved much of my body for about a year, and the therapy was designed to stimulate the muscles. I continued to progressively get better control of myself.

Then blindness, seeing only a narrow vision of light, appeared, lasting for about three weeks. Seeing double lasted for about another month. Then my vision progressively got better until it seems normal at present except that I now need glasses to read or do any close work.

I went to Gonzales Warm Springs for a short time, where I lost my voice for a while. I was told that the only thing to do for my disease was to rest and walk very much. Because of this, I rest each day for about an hour or more. I walk some distance each day, depending upon how I feel.

The effects of multiple sclerosis on me can best be described as weakening. There are days when I need crutches to walk and other days when I feel fine and can walk without any assistance. The muscle groups affected the most were all of the voluntary muscles of my right side. The most noticeable to me has been my right hand, which feels like it is asleep all of the time. I again was fortunate because I am left-handed. Endurance was the most noticeable change in fitness. I have to rest after any strenuous exercise. My strength is about one fourth of what it used to be before I was stricken. My posture has been very much affected. I bend forward from my waist some days when I stand. This is more apparent on some days than others, depending upon my strength. I was paralyzed for about a year. Gradually, I improved until now I walk almost normally.

My handwriting is not as legible as it was, and there are times when MS recurs slightly and affects portions of my right side. This sometimes lasts for days but always returns to what is now normal for me.

In spite of my disability, I returned to college and received my Bachelor of Science degree in physical education and was presented the most representative woman physical education major award from Delta Psi Kappa. All of this has impressed upon me the fact that the bodies of men are truly temples of God and should be cared for as such. If there is one thing I could tell you, it is that nothing is certain in this life and it is not to be taken for granted. Make certain that you live to the fullest because you never know what the future holds for you.

Course of the Disease

In the most advanced stages of MS, loss of bladder or bowel control occurs as well as difficulties of speech and swallowing. Progressively severe intention tremors interfere with writing, using eating utensils, and motor tasks. The prognosis for MS varies. Many patients have long periods of remission, during which their lives are essentially normal.

FIGURE   24.5

Ten-year-old boy with spinal muscular atrophy, Werdnig-Hoffman type. He has normal intelligence and attends a special school for children with orthopedic disabilities. Note how scoliosis limits breathing.

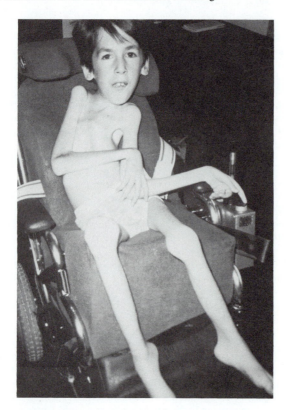

Program Implications

Most physicians recommend breathing exercises, gait retraining, gross coordination activities, stretching exercises, and hydrotherapy for individuals with MS. Swimming is helpful (Basmajian & Wolf, 1990). Therapeutic exercises, such as walking between two parallel bars, are easier in water than on land. College students with MS should engage in as normal a physical education program as possible. After graduation, they should find an exercise group to continue regular activity.

As MS progresses and ambulation is lost or becomes increasingly difficult, special therapeutic exercises are needed. The stationary bicycle is recommended.

Friedreich's Ataxia

Friedreich's ataxia is an inherited condition in which there is progressive degeneration of the sensory nerves of the limbs and trunk, which results in diminished kinesthetic input. The most common of the spinocerebellar degenerations, Friedreich's ataxia first occurs between ages 5 and 15 years. The primary indicators are ataxia (poor balance), clumsiness, and lack of agility. Many associated defects (slurred speech, diminished fine motor control, discoordination and tremor of the upper extremities, vision abnormalities, and skeletal deformities) may also develop and affect sport performance. Degeneration may be slow or rapid. Many persons become wheelchair users by their late teens; others manifest only one or two clinical signs and remain minimally affected throughout their life cycle. The incidence of Friedreich's ataxia is about 2 per 100,000.

Charcot-Marie-Tooth Syndrome

Also called peroneal muscular atrophy, *Charcot-Marie-Tooth syndrome* is a relatively common hereditary disorder that appears between ages 5 and 30 years. It begins as weakness in the peroneal muscles, which are on the anterolateral lower leg, and gradually spreads to the posterior leg and small muscles of the hand. Weakness and atrophy of the peroneal muscles causes foot drop, which characterizes the *steppage gait* (see Chapter 11). The condition, which is caused by demyelination of spinal nerves and motor neurons in the spinal cord, is progressive but sometimes arrests itself. Persons with Charcot-Marie-Tooth syndrome may be active for years, limited only by impaired gait and hand weakness.

Barre-Guillain Syndrome

A transient condition of muscle weakness, *Barre-Guillain syndrome* results from degeneration of approximately the same area as Charcot-Marie-Tooth syndrome. Its symptoms and progress are similar to polio except that there is usually complete recovery. Rehabilitation may require months of bracing and therapy. Some persons are left with muscle and respiratory weakness. The incidence of Barre-Guillain syndrome is 1 per 100,000.

Spinal Muscle Atrophies of Childhood

Several *spinal muscle atrophies* (SMA) have been identified: Werdnig-Hoffman disease (see Figure 24.5), Kugelberg-Welander disease, and Oppenheim's disease, among others. In school settings, however, these are usually called the floppy baby syndromes or congenital hypotonia since the major indicator is flaccid muscle tone. Most of these atrophies are present at birth or occur shortly thereafter. They are caused by progressive degeneration of the spinal cord's motor neurons.

The conditions vary in severity, with some leveling off, arresting themselves, and leaving the child with chronic, nonprogressive muscle weakness. Others are fatal within 2 or 3 years of onset. Typically, in severe cases, there is a loss of muscle strength, followed by tightening of muscles, then contractures, and finally nonuse. SMA is sometimes impossible to distinguish from muscular dystrophy. It can be differentiated from cerebral palsy because there is no spasticity, no ataxia, no seizures, and no associated dysfunctions. Sensation remains intact.

Deteriorations of Middle and Old Age

Several similar conditions in which the main indicator is progressive muscle weakness occur in adulthood. Among these are amyotrophic lateral sclerosis (ALS), also known as Lou Gehrig's disease; Huntington's disease, made famous by singer Arlo Guthrie; and Parkinson's disease.

Thermal Injuries

Approximately 300,000 Americans annually suffer disfiguring injuries from fires. Another 12,000 die each year. The mortality rate is greatest among persons under age 5 and over age 65. No other type of accident permanently affects as many school-age children. Many thermal injuries result in amputations. As more persons are kept alive, physical educators must become increasingly adept at coping with all aspects of thermal injuries.

During past decades, children with more than 60% of their skin destroyed seldom survived. Now, increasing numbers of individuals are returning to society scarred and disfigured. What kind of physical education should be provided for the young child with extensive scar tissue? How can we help such children find social acceptance? What are the effects of disfiguring thermal injuries upon self-concept? An account of a child with third-degree burns over 90% of his body helps to answer these questions (see Rothenberg & White, 1985).

Thermal injury can be caused by fire, chemicals, electricity, or prolonged contact with extreme degrees of hot or cold liquids. Children who have sustained disfiguring thermal injuries, upon entering school, frequently recognize for the first time that they are deviates from the *normal*. They have been known to describe themselves as monsters. Typically, they have no scalp hair and no eyebrows or eyelashes, and scar tissue covers the face.

FIGURE 24.6

Hypertrophic scarring of healed burn on lateral aspect of trunk 2 years after burn occurred.

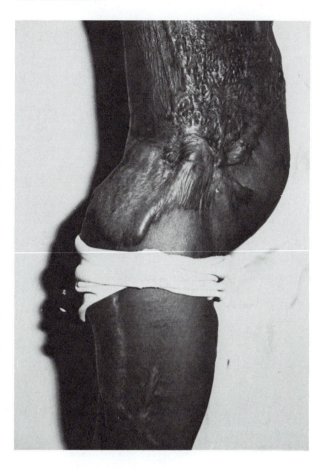

Scar Tissue

Scar tissue is an inevitable outcome of severe burns. Wound coverage is attained by the growth of scar tissue from the periphery to the center of the wound. Thick scar tissue forms *contractures* across joints, limits ROM, causes scoliosis of the spine, and shortens underlying muscles. The severity of hypertrophic scarring (see Figure 24.6) and scar contracture may be decreased by early splinting, pressure, and therapeutic exercise.

Jobsts, elastic supports made to fit a specified portion of the body, may be prescribed as a means of reducing scar hypertrophy (see Figure 24.7). The purpose of the jobst is to apply constant pressure to the healed areas that are presenting signs of thickening scar tissue. The elastic supports achieve the best results when worn 24 hr daily. Therefore, as the child is returned to the classroom, he or she is expected to wear these supports under clothing.

Isoprene splints or *braces* may be applied to areas where the jobsts do not provide adequate pressure to the scar tissue. The elastic face mask, although helpful, does not apply significant pressure to the junction of the nose and cheek, which frequently fills with scars (see Figure 24.8). Isoprene

FIGURE 24.7

Jobsts elastic support jackets applied to arm and hand.

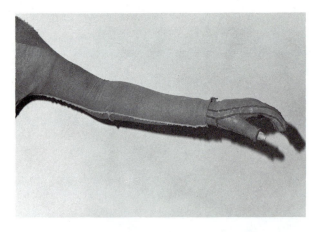

FIGURE 24.8

Jobsts elastic face mask and isoprene splint applied to the junction of the nose and cheek.

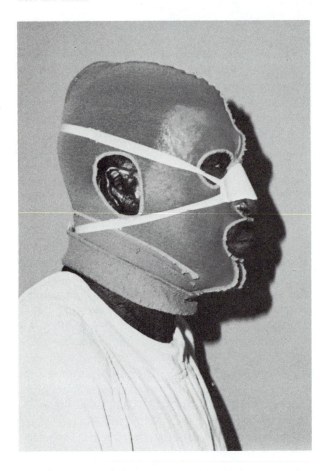

splints require frequent removal for cleansing of the splint and application of lotion to prevent skin dryness. A child may be required to wear one of various types of hand splints for abduction of the thumb during daily activities. The student wearing such splints should be encouraged to use the hands normally in physical education activities and should be given no restrictions. Hence, the student is encouraged to increase

pain tolerance. The physical educator may need to assist the child in proper cleaning and reapplication of the splint after vigorous exercise.

Program Implications

Several years of rehabilitation are required for persons with severe burns. They must not be excused from physical education because they are wearing jobsts, braces, or splints. Each student must learn the tolerance of new skin tissue to such elements as direct sunlight and chlorine in freshwater pools. They must expose themselves to the sun for a progressively longer period each day. PE-R personnel may wish to confer with a specialist in thermal injuries.

The young tissue of healed burns is delicate. It quickly becomes dry when exposed to sunlight for an extended period of time. Full thickness burns have a tendency to dry and irritate easily because of the absence or impairment of sweat ducts, hair follicles, and sebaceous glands. Itching occurs with drying and irritation of healed burn wounds. Frequent applications of a lanolin lotion are recommended.

Indoor physical education is preferable to activities in the direct sunlight. Since contractures are a major problem, emphasis should be upon flexibility or ROM exercises. Dance and aquatic activities are especially recommended. Many thermal injuries result in amputations, which are discussed later in the chapter.

Arthritis

Over 37 million Americans suffer from some form of arthritis and other rheumatic diseases (Samples, 1990). The terms *rheumatism* and *arthritis* are sometimes used synonymously, but technically, they are separate entities. *Rheumatism* refers to a whole group of disorders affecting muscles and joints. It includes all forms of arthritis, myositis, myalgia, bursitis, fibromyosis, and other conditions characterized by soreness, stiffness, and pain in joints and associated structures. *Arthritis* means, literally, inflammation of the joints. Rheumatoid arthritis is also completely different from rheumatic fever, although it is a side effect of rheumatic fever.

Adult Rheumatoid Arthritis and Osteoarthritis

Over 100 causes of joint inflammation have been identified, but the majority of cases fall within two categories: (a) rheumatoid arthritis and (b) osteoarthritis, often called degenerative joint disease. *Rheumatoid arthritis* affects all ages, with the usual onset between 20 and 50 years. It is three times more common in women than men until age 50, when the gender distribution becomes equal. *Osteoarthritis* mainly affects persons age 50 and over and has the same incidence in men and women. Osteoarthritis is the major cause of disability in the older population; advanced cases are aggressively treated with joint replacements that permit full range of motion (ROM) with no pain.

Joint problems in arthritis are pain, swelling, heat, redness (symptoms of inflammation), decreased ROM, and related muscle weakness. In advanced cases, the affected joint becomes unstable and deformed. Rheumatoid arthritis is most troublesome early in the day, and its characteristic aching and stiffness are relieved by gentle exercise. In contrast, pain in osteoarthritis is associated with use or weight bearing and worsens as the day goes on. Medication is prescribed to reduce inflammation and pain. Nonsteroidal anti-inflammatory drugs (NSAIDs) like aspirin and fenoprofere are favored.

Exercise is strongly recommended, with the *2-hr pain* principle serving as the guide to activity intensity. This principle states that any pain continuing 2 hr after exercise is an indicator that the exercise was too intense or inappropriate (Samples, 1990). Low-impact activities that are smooth and repetitive are recommended (e.g., swimming, walking, cycling, ice skating, cross country skiing). When osteoarthritis affects lower limbs, weight-bearing exercises may be contraindicated; swimming, water exercise, and cycling therefore are often the activities of choice.

The Arthritis Foundation YMCA Aquatic Program (AFYAP) is the best-known program for persons with arthritis. Recommended water temperature is 83° to 88° F. Information about AFYAP and other programs can be obtained from the Arthritis Foundation, Box 19000, Atlanta, GA 30326 and from YMCAs.

Juvenile Rheumatoid Arthritis

The average age of onset of juvenile rheumatoid arthritis is 6 years, with two peaks of incidence occurring between ages 2 and 4 and between ages 8 and 11. Rheumatoid arthritis affects three to five times as many girls as boys. The specific etiology is generally unknown. Because young children seldom complain of pain, a slight limp is often the only manifestation of the condition. Approximately 70,000 U.S. children and youth have juvenile rheumatoid arthritis.

Mode of Onset

The onset of juvenile rheumatoid arthritis is capricious, sometimes affecting only one joint and other times involving several joints. In about 30% of the initial episodes, only one joint, usually the knee, is involved, but within a few weeks or months, many more joints may swell. The onset of arthritis may be sudden, characterized by severe pain, or progressive, with symptoms appearing almost imperceptibly over a long period of time. In the latter situation, joint pain is not a major problem.

Systemic and Peripheral Effects

Rheumatoid arthritis may be *systemic,* affecting the entire body, or *peripheral,* affecting only the joints. When the disease is systemic, the joint inflammation is accompanied by such symptoms as fever, rash, malaise, pallor, enlargement of lymph nodes, enlargement of liver and/spleen, and pericarditis. Systemic rheumatoid arthritis in children is sometimes called *Still's disease,* deriving its name from George F. Still, a London physician who first described the condition in 1896.

Knee

The knee is involved more often than other joints, causing a slight limp as the child walks. The characteristic swelling gives the appearance of knock-knees. Swelling makes knee

FIGURE 24.9

Swollen fingers and hands require special attention.

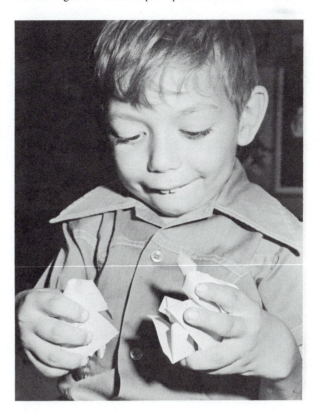

extension difficult or impossible. Knee flexion deteriorates from its normal range of 120° to 80 or 90°. Flexion contraction usually develops.

Ankle
Involvement of the ankle joint results in a ducklike, flat-footed gait similar to that of the toddler. Muscles of the lower leg tend to atrophy, and the Achilles tendon becomes excessively tight. Limitation of motion and pain occur most often in dorsiflexion.

Foot
Swelling within the foot joints makes wearing shoes uncomfortable. Characteristic arthritic defects are pronation, flatfoot, calcaneal valgus (outward bending), and a cock-up position of the metatarsal phalangeal joints, especially the big toe.

Wrist, Hand, and Arm
Wrist, hand, and arm extension is limited by many factors (see Figure 24.9). A common late manifestation is *ankylosis.* This is an abnormal union of bones whose surfaces come into contact because the interjacent cartilages have been destroyed. Normal grip strength is lessened by the combination of muscular atrophy, contracture, and pain on motion.

Hip
Over one third of the children with juvenile rheumatoid arthritis favor one hip over the other. All ROMs are limited, but the flexion contracture is most troublesome.

FIGURE 24.10

(*A*) First half of logroll demands all-out effort. (*B*) Second half shows characteristic flexion.

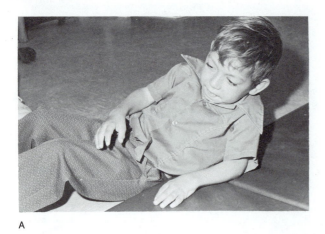

A

B

Spinal Column

Juvenile rheumatoid arthritis tends to limit motion in the cervical spine (see Figure 24.10). There may be spasms of the upper trapezius muscle and local tenderness along the spine. The thoracic and lumbar spine are seldom involved. In young males, a form of rheumatoid arthritis, classified as *rheumatoid spondylitis,* causes pain and stiffness in the back. This condition is also called *Marie-Strumpell disease.*

Course of the Disease

In spite of enlargement of the liver and spleen, pericarditis, and other side effects, rheumatoid arthritis is rarely fatal. It does cause severe disability in about 25% of the cases and mild to moderate disability in 30%. Complete functional recovery is reported in 30 to 70% of the cases. When the disease affects the entire body, the period of acute illness lasts from 1 week to several months. During this time, children may be confined to home. They require frequent rest periods and daily physical therapy. When joint swelling is significantly reduced and other symptoms disappear, the disease is said to be in partial or total remission. Unfortunately, periods of remission are interspersed with weeks of acute illness and maximum joint involvement.

Program Implications

The purposes of movement for the child with rheumatoid arthritis are (a) relief of pain and spasm, (b) prevention of flexion contractures and other deformities, (c) maintenance of normal ROMs for each joint, and (d) maintenance of strength, particularly in the extensor muscles (Tecklin, 1989). *Daily exercise* must begin as soon as the acute inflammation start to subside. At this time, even gentle, passive movement may be painful, but every day of inactivity increases joint stiffness and the probability of permanent deformity. Physical activity personnel should work with parents in establishing a home exercise program. In addition, children should participate in a school physical education program adapted to their needs.

Physical activity personnel must plan exercise sequences that will strengthen the extensors, the abductors, the internal rotators, and the pronators. *Most authorities agree that flexion exercises are contraindicated.* Activities of daily living (ADL) provide adequate flexion, and there is no danger that the joints will stiffen in flexion.

In the early stages of remission, most of the exercises should be performed in water or in a lying position to minimize the pull of gravity. When exercise tolerance is built up sufficiently, activities in a sitting position can be initiated. Riding a bicycle or tricycle affords a means of transportation as well as good exercise. Sitting for long periods of time, however, is contraindicated since it results in stiffness.

Some children, such as the 8-year-old boy depicted in Figure 24.11, are left so disabled that they cannot walk. The gait of the child with severe arthritis is slow and halting. The child has difficulty ascending and descending steps. Any accidental bumping or pushing in the hallway or while standing in lines is especially painful. Older students who change rooms should be released from each class early so that they can get to the next location before the bustle of activity begins. Occasionally, their schedule of courses must be adjusted so that all classrooms are on the same floor and/or in close proximity.

Physical activity personnel should know the normal ROM in degrees for each joint and be proficient in the use of the goniometer. The number of degrees through which each body part can move is recorded and serves as an index against which progress can be measured. Each body part, even the individual fingers and toes, should be taken through its full range of motion two or three times daily.

Contraindicated Activities

The following activities are contraindicated for individuals with arthritis because of trauma to the joints:

1. All jumping activities, including jump rope and trampoline work

2. Activities in which falls might be frequent, such as roller skating, skiing, and gymnastics

FIGURE 24.11

Cortisone and other drugs used in arthritis tend to inhibit normal growth. This 8-year-old boy is so disabled that he uses a quadricycle in lieu of walking.

3. Contact sports, particularly football, soccer, and volleyball
4. Hopping, leaping, and movement exploration activities in which the body leaves the floor
5. Diving
6. Horseback riding
7. Sitting for long periods

Recommended Activities

During periods of remission, persons with arthritis who can participate in an activity *without pain* should be allowed, but not forced, to do so. Because of the weeks and/or months of enforced rest during acute attacks, circulorespiratory endurance is likely to be subaverage. Hence, frequent rest periods are needed.

Swimming and creative or modern dance are among the best activities (Berson & Roy, 1982; Samples, 1990). The front crawl and other strokes that emphasize extension are especially recommended. Water must be maintained at as warm a temperature as is feasible. Creative dance also stresses extension in its many stretching techniques and affords opportunities for learning to relate to others. Group choreography and performance can provide as many positive experiences as the team sports that are denied youngsters with arthritis. Quiet recreational games include croquet, ring or ball tossing, miniature golf, horseshoes, shuffleboard, and pool. Throwing activities are better than striking and catching activities.

Medication Side Effects

Cortisone and other steroids are prescribed when NSAIDs like aspirin are not effective. Unfortunately, one of the major side effects of steroids is the inhibition of normal growth, causing children to look several years younger than they really are. Alterations in body growth occur as the direct result of severe rheumatoid arthritis. This stunting of growth, coupled with the overprotection of parents, may contribute to serious problems in peer adjustment. See Chapter 19 for other side effects of steroids.

Osteomyelitis

Osteomyelitis (inflammation of bone tissue) can occur at any age and is caused by staphylococcus, streptococcus, or pneumococcus organisms. Even with the best medical treatment, it may result in permanent disability. The bones most often affected are the tibia, femur, and humerus. The symptoms are similar to those of an infected wound: (a) pain and tenderness, particularly near the end of the bone in the metaphyseal region; (b) heat felt through the overlying skin; (c) overlying soft tissues feeling hard (indurated); and (d) neighboring joints possibly distended with clear fluid. Generally, a good range of joint movement is retained, although there may be a limp from the acute pain. Pus forms and finds its way to the surface of the bone, where it forms a *subperiosteal abscess.* If treatment is not begun, the abscess eventually works its way outward, causing a *sinus* (hole) in the skin over the affected bone, from which pus is discharged continuously or intermittently. This sinus is covered with a dressing that must be changed several times daily.

Although only a single limb is typically affected and the person appears otherwise healthy and energetic, we should remember that *exercise is always contraindicated when any kind of infection is active in the body.* The medical treatment is rest and intensive antibiotic therapy, often accompanied by surgery to scrape the infected bone and evacuate the pus.

In its early stages, osteomyelitis is described as *acute.* If the infection persists or reoccurs periodically, it is called *chronic.* Chronic osteomyelitis may linger for years.

Arthrogryposis

Approximately 500 infants are born with *arthrogryposis* (pronounced ar-throw-gry-pó-sis) each year in the United States. The incidence is 3 per 10,000 births. Arthrogryposis multiplex congenital (AMC) is a nonprogressive congenital contracture syndrome usually characterized by internal rotation at the shoulder joints, elbow extension, pronated forearms, radial flexion of wrists, flexion and outward rotation at the hip joint, and abnormal positions of knees and feet. This birth defect varies tremendously in severity, with some persons in wheelchairs and others only minimally affected.

FIGURE 24.12

FIGURE 24.13

Arthrogryposis, overweight, and poor fitness combine to make batting a real chore for this 11-year-old. Arms show the characteristic increase of subcutaneous fat and loss of skin flexion creases, which result in a tubular appearance sometimes described as wooden and doll-like. Despite the awkwardness of joint positions and mechanics, no pain is felt.

Lively 7-year-old with arthrogryposis demonstrates his best posture.

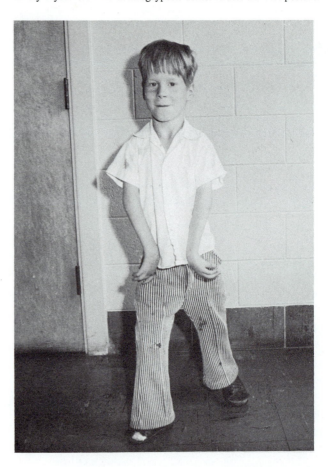

The contracture syndrome is characterized by dominance of fatty and connective tissue at joints in place of normal muscle tissue. Some or all joints may be involved.

The major disability is restricted ROM. Many persons with AMC have almost no arm and shoulder movement. They can, however, excel in track activities in a motorized chair. The opposite condition, only lower limb involvement, is illustrated by Ron Hernley, President of National Handicapped Sports, who participates in many wheelchair sports.

Figures 24.12 and 24.13 depict two boys, ages 11 and 7 and from the same school system, who have arthrogryposis. Although both boys have some limb involvement, their greatest problem is the fixed medial rotation of the shoulder joints (see Figure 24.14). Both have normal intelligence, as is almost always the case in arthrogryposis. Until recently, the older boy walked without the use of crutches. His present reliance on them is believed to be somewhat psychosomatic, although articular surfaces do tend to deteriorate with age.

Major physical education goals are to increase ROM (flexibility) and to teach sports and games for leisure use. Activities discussed under arthritis are appropriate in most cases, as are those in Chapter 25 on cerebral palsy. Programming depends, of course, upon sport classification. Swimming is particularly recommended in that it fulfills both goals. It teaches a leisure skill and stretches muscle groups.

Dr. Jo Cowden (1985), at the University of New Orleans, reported movement work with a 4-year-old AMC child over a 2-year period and emphasized the importance of early intervention (see Figure 24.15). Periodic videotapes show that levels of mobility have been obtained that were once not believed possible. When the child began the program, she used her chin to pull herself across the mat, rolled from place to place, or used a wheelchair. Now she can crawl and creep through obstacle courses and walk using reciprocal braces with a walker. Like many children with spina bifida, she was taught first to use a *parapodium* (standing apparatus) with a walker and then progressed to reciprocal braces. Surgery, casting, and bracing have characterized much of her early life. As a potential les autres athlete, this child can swim competitively with flotation devices and engage in slalom, track, and soccer activities in a wheelchair. As important as increasing ROM is developing attitudes and habits favorable to physical recreation.

Dwarfism and Short Stature Syndromes

Since 1986, the date of the founding of the Dwarf Athletic Association of America (DAAA), persons who meet the medical criteria for short stature syndrome have preferred to be called dwarfs. Earlier, the preferred terminology was "little

FIGURE 24.14

Medial rotation at the shoulder joints complicates fine muscle coordination.

FIGURE 24.15

Water activities provide range-of-motion exercises for young child with arthrogryposis.

FIGURE 24.16

Individual differences in stature and body proportions in three children, age 10 years. (*A*) Normal. (*B*) Achondroplasia. (*C*) Morquio syndrome.

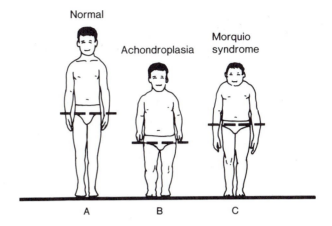

Normal

Achondroplasia

Morquio syndrome

A   B   C

people," as indicated by the formation of the Little People of America (LPA), an organization with about 5,000 members that meets annually. Today, both *dwarf* and *little people* are acceptable terms. The term *midget,* however, is offensive and should never be used. Dwarfs consider themselves normal and call nondwarfs *average-sized people* rather than normal.

The medical criteria for dwarfism varies. The height standard for membership in LPA is 4 ft, 10 inches or less, but DAAA uses a 5 ft or less criterion. In general, dwarfs are at least 3 standard deviations below the mean height of the general population and shorter than 98% of their peers (see Figure 24.16). Short stature in dwarfs is caused by a genetic condition or some kind of pathology.

Types of Dwarfism

Over 200 types of dwarfism affect about 100,000 persons (Ablon, 1988). In general, dwarfs are classified into two categories: disproportionate and proportionate (Scott, 1988). The disproportionate category is more common.

Disproportionate dwarfs typically have average-sized torsos but unusually short arms and legs. The major cause of disproportionate dwarfism is skeletal dysplasia or chondrodystrophy, the failure of cartilage (*chondro*) to develop into bone. This is either inherited or caused by spontaneous gene mutations.

Skeletal dysplasias are further divided according to spinal involvement. Conditions without spinal involvement' are achondroplasia (see Figure 24.17C) and hypoachondroplasia. *Hypo* indicates less achondroplasia and thus greater height. Conditions characterized by progressive kyphosis and/ or scoliosis and other spinal anomalies are spondyloepiphyseal dysplasia (SED) and diastrophic dysplasia (see Figure 24.17A and B). Good pictures of these are in several sources (Beighton, 1988; Jones, 1988; Scott, 1988). At a typical DAAA athletic event, these are the most common dwarf types seen.

FIGURE 24.17

Several types of dwarfism. Each individual is an excellent athlete.

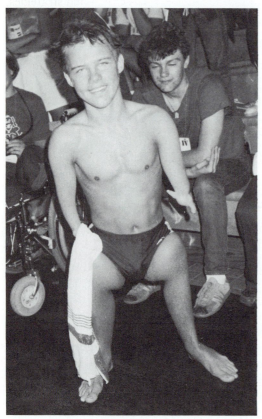

A. Diastrophic dysplasia
with bilateral hip
dislocation

B. Achondroplasia

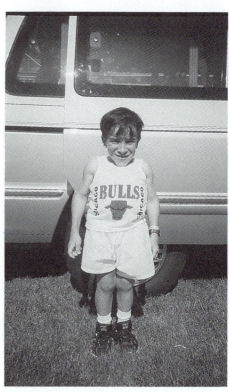

C. Spondyloepiphyseal dysplasia (SED)

Proportionate dwarfs are persons whose body parts are proportionate but abnormally short. The main cause of this is pituitary gland dysfunction, also known as growth hormone (GH) deficiency. In addition to endocrine etiologies, there are numerous other causes. Many of these conditions can now be treated so that prevalence within this category is decreasing.

Names of dwarf types are formidable but make sense when bone development and word derivations are reviewed. First of all, remember that skeletal bones begin as cartilage in the embryo. The Latin word for cartilage is *chondro* (pronounced kon-dro). Chondroplasia thus refers to normal formation of cartilage because *plasia* means "to mold or form." The most common form of dwarfism, *achondroplasia,* is simply the prefix *a* (meaning "without") attached to *chondroplasia.* Thus, growth failure begins before birth when initial cartilage development predetermines bone size.

The transition from cartilage into bone (i.e., ossification) extends from the third month of prenatal development until about age 25 years. Any pathology of this growth process is broadly categorized as a skeletal dysplasia or a chondrodystrophy. *Trophy* or *trophic* means nourishment, so *dystrophy* refers to failure of nerve centers that innervate

and/or failure of blood supply that carries nutrients. Diastrophic dysplasia refers to two (*di, dia*) problems: failure of nourishment and failure of initial bone formation.

Epiphysis (singular) and epiphyses (plural) refer to the bone-forming center or growth plate that is separated from the parent bone by cartilage until growth is complete. *Physis* means "growth," and its prefix *epi* means "upon," "over," or "in addition to." Epiphyseal closure occurs at different ages. Bones of the upper limbs and scapulae become completely ossified at ages 17 to 20 years. Bones of the lower limbs become completely ossified at 18 to 23 years. Bones of the vertebrae, sternum, and clavicle are the last to ossify (ages 23 to 25) and thus are the most vulnerable to growth disorders. The condition of SED is easy to figure out if we remember that *spondylo* refers to the vertebrae.

By far the most common type of dwarfism is *achondroplasia* (see Figure 24.17B). Incidence figures vary from 1 in 10,000 (Ablon, 1988) to 1 in 40,000 births (Scott, 1988). This disproportionate condition is characterized by average-sized trunk, short limbs, and often, a relatively large head. Associated problems are lumbar lordosis, waddling gait caused by abnormally short femoral head, restricted elbow extension, and bowed legs. The latter is generally corrected by surgery. Other than lordosis, there are no spinal problems. Aerobic fitness may be limited by small chest size and narrow nasal passages. In general, however, persons with achondroplasia can be excellent athletes.

Dwarf conditions with spinal involvement tend to limit athleticism. Nevertheless, swimming and other forms of exercise are needed for health and fitness. Diastrophic dysplasia is the most disabling, with bone deformities that often require crutches or wheelchairs for ambulation. It is characterized by clubfoot (talipes equinovarus), hand deformities, and frequent hip and knee dislocations. These anomalies, as well as the characteristic scoliosis, are resistant to corrective surgery. Figure 24.17A shows bilateral hip dislocation. SED is mainly abnormal development of the growth centers (epiphyses) within the vertebrae (spondylo)(see Figure 24.17C). This causes a disproportionately short trunk with various spinal and limb irregularities. The arms typically look abnormally long. The face and skull in SED are normal, but eye complications are common. Many persons with SED are excellent athletes.

Program Implications

Profound shortness is obviously a disadvantage in most sports. Moreover, disproportionately short limbs are a limitation in ball handling, racquet sports, and track. However, in some sports, such as powerlifting and tumbling, average trunk size and short limbs are advantageous.

DAAA promotes several sports. Especially popular are basketball, volleyball, powerlifting, track, field, swimming, bowling, and boccia. Basketball is played with baskets set at the standard height. The court size is regulation, and the ball size is that used by average-sized women. In volleyball, the net is lowered slightly so dwarfs can spike. Work is underway to create a sport classification system for track, field, and swimming so that competition among persons of different heights and proportions can be more fair (Low, 1992). Boccia is an accuracy sport in which players take turns throwing small balls toward a target ball.

In disproportionate dwarfism, several joint defects limit ROM and contribute to a high incidence of dislocations and trauma. Especially affected are the shoulder, elbow, hip, and knee joints (Knudsen, 1993). The inability to completely straighten the elbow causes difficulty with respect to the regulations that govern powerlifting. Thrusting the head forward to gain the advantage when crossing the finish line in track may cause muscle strain if the head is disproportionately large. Strenuous training in track and/or distance running may lead to hip and knee joint trauma. Swimming may be the best lifetime sport to promote because it does not stress joints.

Internationally, dwarfs compete with les autres. The classification system used is considered unfair by many dwarfs (Sawisch, 1990), and plans are underway to develop an international sport organization for dwarfs.

In school settings, adaptations are necessary for dwarfs as well as for nondwarf short people. Class teams, formed to practice basketball and volleyball skills, should be equated on heights or a system whereby the shorter team starts with a set number of points. No one likes to feel that he or she is a handicap to the team; the teacher's role is to prevent such feelings by adapting game rules and strategies.

Short Stature and Normal Intelligence

Intelligence and mental functioning of dwarfs are the same as in the average-sized population. Several other short stature conditions, in which intelligence is usually normal, warrant mention. Three conditions are characterized by a disproportionally short neck: (a) Turner syndrome (females only), (b) Noonan syndrome (males only), and (c) Morquio syndrome (both sexes).

The Turner and Noonan syndromes are chromosomal, whereas the Morquio syndrome is metabolic. Turner and Noonan syndromes have several common features: (a) necks often webbed as well as short, (b) broad chests with widely spaced nipples, (c) low posterior hairline, and (d) various other deviations. Most persons with Turner and Noonan syndromes are not sexually fertile; males have an abnormally small penis, whereas the ovaries in females fail to develop properly. In Morquio syndrome, the trunk and neck are abnormally short, causing the arms to look disproportionately long (see Figure 24.16C). Usually, severe kyphosis, knock-knees, and bone growth irregularity limit hip and joint flexibility.

Short Stature and Mental Retardation

Several mental retardation syndromes are characterized by short stature. These include Down syndrome (1 per 2,000 incidence), Cornelia de Lange syndrome (1 per 10,000 incidence), fetal alcohol syndrome (3 to 6 per 1,000 incidence), Hurler's syndrome (1 per 100,000 incidence), and rubella syndrome (1 per 10,000 incidence). These conditions obviously require physical education adaptations for short stature and short limbs. They are discussed more fully, however, in Chapter 21 on mental retardation since the primary adaptations relate to mental functioning (i.e., task analysis and behavior management).

Osteogenesis Imperfecta

Word derivation is also helpful in visualizing *osteogenesis imperfecta* (OI). *Os* and *osteo* refer to "bone." *Genesis,* like in the Bible, means "origin." *Imperfecta* clearly indicates that something is wrong with bone formation. The basic defect of OI (pronounced os-tee-oh-gen-e-sis im-per-fect'-ah) is in the collagen fibers (a type of protein) found in connective tissue (bone, ligaments, cartilage, and skin). The defect makes bone and cartilage soft and brittle, while causing skin and ligaments to be overly elastic and hyperextensible.

OI is an inherited condition that is present at birth. Bone breaks peak between 2 and 15 years of age, after which the incidence of fractures decreases. Indicators are short stature and small limbs that are bowed in various distortions from repetitive fractures. Joints are hyperextensible, with predisposition for dislocation. Most persons with OI are in wheelchairs.

FIGURE   24.18

Seventeen-year-old student with osteogenesis imperfecta (OI) awaiting his swimming competition at national games.

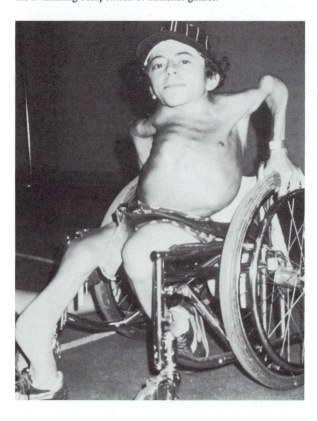

FIGURE   24.19

Wayne Washington, who has OI, is an international competitor in weight lifting. Here, he is visiting with a coach before a recreational swim.

FIGURE   24.20

Bill Lehr, international competitor with OI in swimming, with coach Kathi Rayborn.

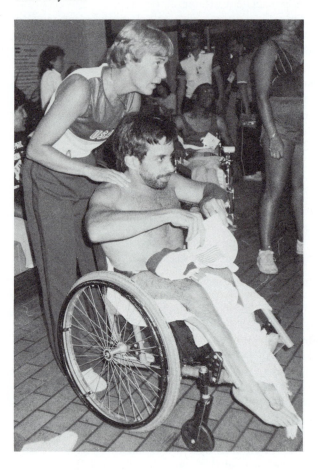

Chest defects (barrel and pigeon shapes) limit respiratory capacity and aerobic endurance, and spinal defects are common (see Figure 24.18). These are partly from osteoporosis (bone degeneration) caused by lack of exercise. Clearly, adapted physical activity, especially swimming and ROM games, is important. Until the condition arrests itself, usually in adolescence, motorized chairs permit the challenge and thrill of track and slalom events. Use of a 5-oz soft shot (beanbag) or discus seldom causes fractures, whereas regulation balls might. Shuffleboard and ramp bowling add variety.

After the condition arrests itself, the person can engage in almost any sport. Wayne Washington, who weighs 112 lb, is a world-class weight lifter with a 290-lb record; he began weight lifting at age 18(see Figure 24.19). Bill Lehr, a world-class track and swimming star, also plays wheelchair basketball and has completed the Boston Marathon in 2 hr and 50 min (see Figure 24.20). He has done the 100 m in 18.8, the 400 in 1:16.8, and the 800 in 2:34.

About his childhood, Bill says,

I was born with a broken collarbone, my knees were bent in a way a baby's knees aren't supposed to bend, and in the first 12 years of my life, I must have spent half the time in surgery. . . . When I was growing, I could walk and even run a few yards at a time. Then a bone would break in one of my legs, and they'd have to put a cast on me. I'd be laid up for a few weeks, get out of the cast, but that would only last a week or two before I'd break another bone and have to be put back in a cast again.

Before Bill's condition arrested itself, he had over 40 fractures. From age 7 onward, he was a wheelchair user; he began wheelchair basketball and track at age 12. Telling OI children about world class athletes like Bill Lehr and Wayne Washington and showing them photos and videotapes opens new horizons; this is an important part of the physical educator's job.

The incidence of OI is 1 in 50,000 births for congenital OI and 1 in 25,000 for a later appearing, less serious form called OI tarda. These medical statistics may be inaccurate in that OI students can easily be spotted in every large school system. OI makes persons eligible to compete either with the dwarf or les autres organizations.

Ehlers-Danlos Syndrome

Several collagen defects are similar to OI but do not cause bones to break. *Ehlers-Danlos syndrome* is an inherited condition characterized by hyperextensibility of joints, with predisposition for dislocation at shoulder girdle, shoulder, elbow, hip, and knee joints. Other features are loose and/or hyperextensible skin, slow wound healing with inadequate scar tissue, and fragility of blood vessel walls. Sports with a high risk of injury are therefore contraindicated. Special emphasis is given to blister prevention (e.g., properly fitted shoes) and hand protection (e.g., gloves). The best sport is probably swimming.

Childhood Growth Disorders

The physical educator working with junior high or middle school youngsters is confronted with a high incidence of *osteochondroses* or growth plate disorders. Such diagnoses as *Perthes' disease, Osgood-Schlatter disease, Kohler's disease, Calve's disease,* and *Scheuermann's disease* all fall within this category and demand adaptations in physical education.

An *osteochondrosis* is an abnormality of an *epiphysis* (growth plate) in which normal growth or ossification is disturbed. Disorders of the growth plate include premature closure, delayed closure, and interruption in the growth process. Bone growth and subsequent closure are affected by heredity, diet, hormones, general health status, and trauma. Ill health and malnutrition generally delay overall growth plate closure. Obese children are particularly susceptible to disorders of the growth plate.

Some of the most common sites of growth plate disorders are depicted in Figure 24.21 and listed in Table 24.2. Over 70% of the osteochondroses are found at the first four sites mentioned in Table 24.2. The pathology in all of the osteochondroses is similar. For unknown reasons, cells within the bony center of the epiphysis undergo partial *necrosis* (death), probably from interference with the blood supply. The *necrotic* tissue is removed by special cells called osteoclasts, and the bony center is temporarily softened and liable

FIGURE 24.21

Common sites of osteochondroses.

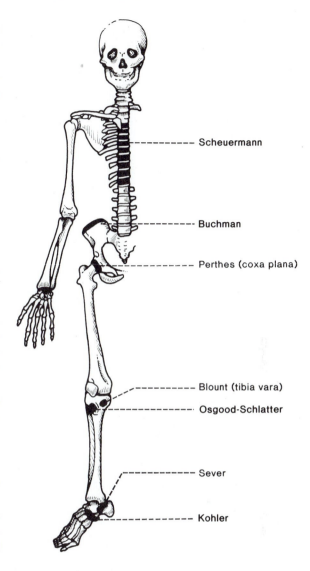

Table 24.2
Common sites of growth plate disorders.

Bony Part Affected	Name of Disorder
Tibial tuberosity	Osgood-Schlatter
Calcaneus	Sever
Vertebra	Scheuermann
Head of femur	Perthes (Less-Calve-Perthes)
Tibia	Blount
Tarsal, navicular	Kohler
Iliac crest	Buchman

to shape deformation, which may become permanent. In time, the condition arrests itself. New, healthy bone cells replace the dead tissue, and the bones return to normal.

This cycle of changes may take as long as 2 years, during which time the youngster must be kept off the affected limb. Enforcing this rule of no weight bearing on an

FIGURE   24.22

Site of Osgood-Schlatter disorder.

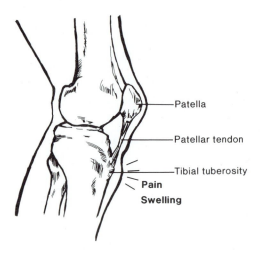

FIGURE   24.23

Common hip joint growth disorders.

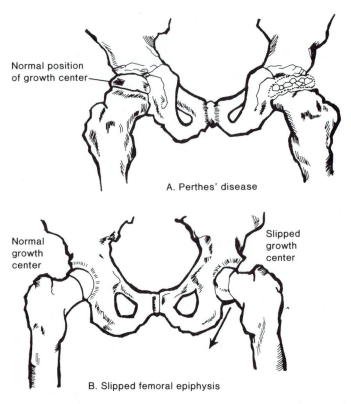

athletic child is not easy since the child experiences no symptoms of illness and only occasional pain. The primary danger in osteochondroses is not in the present, but rather in the deformity, limp, and predisposition to arthritis that may occur later if rules are not followed.

Osgood-Schlatter Condition

Osgood-Schlatter disease is a temporary degenerative condition of the tibial tuberosity that causes pain and swelling where the patellar tendon inserts on the tibia (see Figure 24.22). It is caused by a partial separation of the growth plate from the tibia, typically brought on by overuse or trauma. Adolescents who are active in strenuous sports involving the knee joint are the most vulnerable. Continuous rope jumping or kicking, for example, places much stress on the knee. Teachers who use contraindicated exercises like repeated squats and the duck walk may contribute to the onset of this condition.

Diagnosis is made by X ray, and treatment varies, depending on severity and the philosophy of the physician. The knee may be immobilized in a brace or cast for several weeks, after which activity is restricted for 3 to 6 months. *In most cases, students are told to avoid explosive knee extension or all knee extension.* Nonweight-bearing isometric exercises that strengthen the quadriceps and stretch the hamstrings may be prescribed.

Scheuermann's Disease

Juvenile kyphosis, or *Scheuermann's disease,* is a disturbance in growth of the thoracic vertebrae. It results from *epiphysitis* (inflammation of an epiphysis) and/or *osteochondritis* (inflammation of cartilage), either of which may cause fragmentation of vertebral bodies. One or several vertebrae are involved. The etiology is generally unknown. *During the active phase, forward flexion is contraindicated.* The student should be protected from all flexion movements by a hyperextension brace, which places the weight on the neural arches rather than on the defective vertebral bodies.

Although there is some discomfort, the pain is not great enough to impose limitation of natural movement; sometimes, the condition is pain-free. In such instances, convincing the student to refrain from activity may be difficult. Unfortunately, if bracing and nonactivity are not enforced, the resulting kyphotic hump may be both severe and persistent. When X rays reveal the healing of fragmented areas, class participation is resumed with no restrictions. Occasionally, the student will continue to wear a back brace, body jacket, or cast for a number of months after the disease is arrested.

Scoliosis and Chest Deformity

Lateral curvature of the spine is discussed fully in Chapter 14 on postures. Severe conditions are treated by surgery, casting, and braces. As in Scheuermann's disease, vigorous forward flexion of the trunk may be contraindicated. Otherwise, physical activity is seldom restricted unless the condition is caused by concurrent disabilities.

Many of the conditions in this chapter are associated with scoliosis and chest deformities that limit respiration and aerobic fitness. Breathing and ROM exercises and games are important.

Perthes' Condition

Perthes' condition, the destruction of the growth center of the hip joint, occurs between the ages of 4 and 8 (see Figure 24.23A). Its incidence is 1 per 18,000, and approximately four to five times more boys than girls are affected. Typically,

FIGURE   24.24

Hip joint dislocation and slippage.

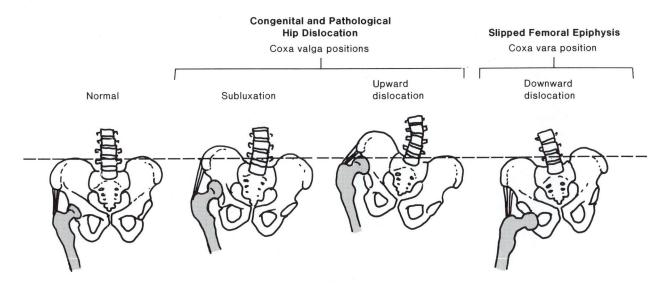

the condition lasts 2 to 4 years, during which the child may need adapted physical education—most likely in the mainstream setting. Adapting is needed in choice of activities that can be done while wearing a splint and/or using a wheelchair. If the hip joint is not protected (i.e., kept in nonweight-bearing status) during the body's natural repair process, the femoral head becomes flattened and irregular (*coxa plana*), which makes the joint surface incongruent and leads to hip joint degenerate arthritis.

Slipped Femoral Epiphysis

Also called adolescent coxa vara or epiphysiolysis, *slipped femoral epiphysis (SFE)* is a hip joint disorder diagnosed by a waddling gait or a limp that favors one leg. Typically, the head of the femur is outwardly rotated. This is caused by a downward-backward-medial slippage of the growth center on the femoral head (see Figure 24.23B). Attributed to trauma, stress, or overuse, the condition typically occurs in adolescence and is associated with obesity. The incidence is 2 to 13 per 100,000. SFE is more common in males (2.2 to 1) than females and in blacks than whites. It may also occur in younger children as a result of falls from great heights or abuse and in newborns as a result of difficult deliveries.

The groin, buttock, and lateral hip are the major pain centers. If the condition is not corrected, the affected leg becomes shorter, and adduction contractures result (Chung, 1981). These decrease the angulation of the neck of the femur, making it more horizontal, and causing an inward inclination (vara position) of the femur. During exercise, persons with SFE show limited hip joint inward rotation and abduction.

Once diagnosed, SFE is usually corrected surgically by pinning the epiphysis in place. More conservative treatment is use of short-leg casts with a crossbar to prevent weight bearing and to hold the femoral head in abduction and inward rotation. *Students are usually restricted from vigorous weight-bearing physical education for about a year.* Adaptation entails arranging for swimming and/or upper extremity sports and exercises in place of the regular curriculum.

Congenital Dislocation of the Hip

Congenital dislocation of the hip (CDH) encompasses various degrees of *dysplasia,* or abnormal development, of the hip socket (acetabulum) and/or head of the femur. This condition is the fourth most common congenital defect. It is more common among girls than boys and usually occurs in one hip rather than both. Its incidence is approximately 1 to 3 per 1,000 births.

Subluxation and *luxation* are synonyms for dislocation, describing the position of the femoral head in relation to a shallow, dysplasic acetabulum (see Figure 24.24). In subluxation, the femur is only partially displaced, whereas in luxation, the femoral head is completely dislocated above the acetabulum rim. These aberrations often are not recognized until the child begins to walk. Nonsurgical treatment involves repositioning, traction, and casting. In the majority of cases in which the child is over age 3, surgical reduction (repositioning) is used. After age 6, more complicated operative procedures, such as *osteotomy* (dividing a bone or cutting out a portion) and *arthroplasty* (reconstructing a joint), are applied.

Reference to congenital hip dislocation on a child's record usually means that he or she has undergone long periods of hospitalization and immobilization in splints or casts extending from waist to toes. Generally, the child has had fewer opportunities to learn social and motor skills through informal play than have normal peers. As in other congenital anomalies, any problems the child manifests are more likely to be psychological than physical.

FIGURE 24.25

(A) Surgically corrected clubfeet of preadolescent boy. (B) Corrective shoes. Note how the lateral side of the shoe heel is raised.

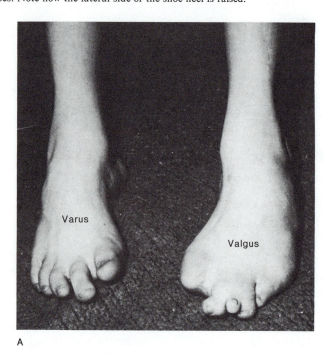

A

B

Pathological Dislocation of the Hip

Dislocation of the hip is a problem commonly associated with persons unable to stand because of severe paralytic or neurological conditions (polio, spina bifida, cerebral palsy). The incidence of dislocation in severely disabled nonambulatory persons is 25%. The average age of dislocation is 7 years, but the range of frequent occurrence varies from 2 to 10 years. Like CDH, the condition is corrected by surgery.

Pathological dislocation may occur at any age. In most cases, the head of the femur becomes displaced upward and anteriorly. Pathological dislocation appears mostly in persons with coxa valga (increased neck-shaft angle of femur) and hip adduction contracture. Coxa valga is present in most normal infants before weight bearing begins; the gradual change in neck-shaft femoral angle accompanies normal motor development. Childhood coxa valga and associated hip dislocation thus sometimes characterize delayed or abnormal motor development.

Clubfoot (Talipes)

Talipes equinovarus, or *congenital clubfoot,* is the most common of all orthopedic defects, with an incidence of 1 out of approximately 700 births. *Talipes* comes from two Latin words: *talus,* meaning "ankle" and *pes,* meaning "foot." *Equinovarus* (stemming from *equus,* meaning "horse," and *varus,* meaning "bent in") is an adjective specifying a position in which the entire foot is inverted, the heel is drawn up, and the forefoot is adducted. This forces the child to walk on the outer border of the foot. Although bracing, casting, and surgery may correct clubfoot, the child reverts to supinated walking when especially tired or upon first awakening.

Children who have undergone casting and splinting for clubfoot are generally required to wear *corrective shoes.* Extremely expensive, these shoes are often unattractive high-top, leather shoes with many laces (see Figure 24.25). Many children, sensitive about this prescription, refuse to wear their corrective shoes as they grow older. Or they may ask to wear tennis shoes, at least in physical education, in order to be like their friends. Permission should be tactfully denied unless written instructions from the physician indicate that the child need not wear the corrective shoes during physical education.

Types of Talipes

Talipes equinovarus varies in degree of severity. Changes in the tendons and ligaments result mostly from contractures. The Achilles and tibial tendons are always shortened, causing a tendency to walk on the toes or forefoot. Bony changes occur chiefly in the talus, calcaneus, navicular, and cuboid. Tibial torsion is usually present.

Several other types of talipes are recognized (see Figure 24.26):

1. **Talipes cavus.** Hollow foot or arch so high as to be disabling.
2. **Talipes calcaneus.** Contracture of foot in dorsiflexed position.
3. **Talipes equinus.** Contracture of foot in plantar-flexed position.
4. **Talipes varus.** Contracture of foot with toes and sole of foot turned inward. Associated with spastic hemiplegic cerebral palsy.

FIGURE 24.26

Abnormalities of foot alignment. Varus positions are frequently seen in hemiplegic spastic cerebral palsy and in uncorrected congenital bone and joint defects. Valgus positions are seen in association with flat and/or pronated feet. The cavus position is rare.

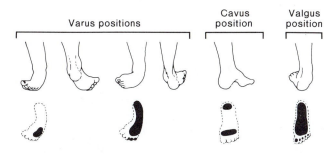

5. **Talipes valgus.** Contracture of foot with toes and sole of foot turned outward. Associated with athetoid cerebral palsy.

Just as *talipes equinovarus,* the most common form, is a combination of two types, so any two types can coexist as calcaneovarus, calcaneovalgus, or equinovalgus.

Program Implications

Figure 24.25A shows the clubfoot of a preadolescent boy who has undergone several operations and spent months in casts and braces. He is an enthusiastic athlete and in the starting lineup of his Little League baseball team. His slight limp is noticeably worse during cold winter days and rainy seasons, when he can hardly walk the first hour or so after awakening. As the day wears on, his gait becomes almost normal, enabling him to run fast enough to hold his own in athletic feats with peers.

Metatarsus varus is a frequent congenital defect similar to clubfoot except that only the forefoot or metatarsal area is affected. The treatment for talipes and metatarsus varus is similar, beginning preferably within the first 2 weeks of life with casting that may continue for many months. The weight of a cast prevents normal mobility of the infant and may delay the accomplishment of such motor tasks as rolling over, standing alone, and walking.

The Denis-Browne splint is used for correcting clubfoot and other defects (see Figure 24.27). It may be worn nights only or both day and night. Although it does not permit standing, the splint allows vigorous activities that utilize crawling, creeping, and scooterboards.

Congenital defects of the feet, legs, and hips are generally corrected by surgery, bracing, or casting in infancy or early childhood. In spite of the correction, the gait may continue to be impaired so that persons do not have a fair chance in competitive activities with peers. Such persons are eligible for wheelchair basketball and tennis. Swimming is also good.

Limb Deficiencies

International sport classifications distinguish between *limb deficiencies* (congenital amputations) and *acquired amputations.* Limb deficiencies are considered les autres conditions (see Figure 24.28).

FIGURE 24.27

The Denis-Browne splint used to correct clubfoot and other problems.

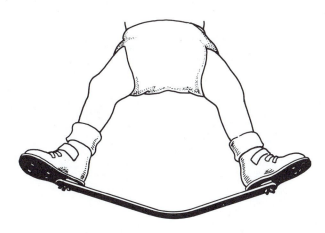

Types of Limb Deficiencies

There are two types of limb deficiencies: *dysmelia* (absence of arms or legs) and *phocomelia* (absence of middle segment of limb, but with intact proximal and distal portions). In the latter, hands or feet are attached directly to shoulders or hips, respectively. In phocomelia (*phoco* means "seal-like" and *melos* means "limb"), the hand or foot is often removed surgically within the first few months after birth. Absence of the fibula, with a congenitally deformed foot, is also a common condition that is corrected surgically.

Joey Lipski, world-class swimmer and track star, is illustrative of a person with dysmelia. Born without arms, he does not wear prostheses in competition. Joey learned to swim at age 8 and at age 15 set world records for his classification in the 100-m freestyle event (2:05.6) and in the 50-m backstroke (57.0). He runs the 100-m dash in 19.5 sec and the 200-m event in 41.42 sec.

Karen Farmer, world-class athlete in discus, javelin, and shot put, was born with a clubfoot and missing fibula. These were surgically removed when she was 18 months old, and a prosthesis was fitted soon afterward. Her shot put and discus records are 10.02 and 32.36 m, respectively. Almost all of Karen's competitive experience has been against AB athletes; she attended Washington State University on an athletic scholarship and says she has never found a sport she could not master.

Prostheses

A *prosthesis* (plural: *prostheses*) is a substitute for a missing body part. Age of prosthetic fitting is obviously very important in subsequent development of motor skills. Upper extremity prostheses are fitted when the child develops good sitting balance, usually between 8 and 10 months of age. Lower extremity prostheses are fitted when the child begins to pull up to a stand, usually between 10 and 15 months. As the child grows, the prostheses must be periodically replaced: every 15 to 18 months for an upper extremity prosthesis and about every 12 months for a lower extremity prosthesis.

FIGURE   24.28

Examples of limb deficiencies.

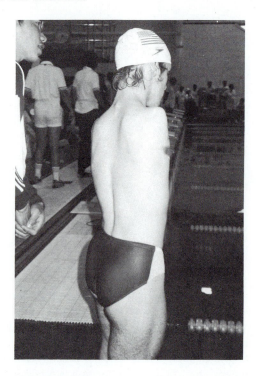

Acquired Amputations

Of the various disabilities that can result from trauma and disease, the *acquired amputation* is the most dramatic. Not only does the child suffer anxieties about no longer being *whole,* but efficient use of prosthetic devices demands much effort.

The etiologies of acquired amputations in children in order of incidence are trauma, cancer, infection, and vascular conditions like gangrene. Under trauma, the leading causes of amputation are farm and power tool accidents, vehicular accidents, and gunshot explosions. Most of these occur in the age group from 12 to 21. Children who lose limbs because of malignancy are also primarily within this age group.

Arnie Boldt, the one-legged world champion high jumper, is illustrative of a person with an acquired amputation (see Figure 24.29). Raised on a farm, he lost his lower leg in a farm accident at 3 years of age. Much of his competitive experience has been against AB athletes.

Prevalence of Amputations

Approximately 311,000 amputees reside in the United States. Of these, 7% are under age 21, 58% are between ages 21 and 65, and 35% are over 65 years. Among school-age persons, there are more upper extremity amputees than lower. This is reversed in the general population, probably because war injuries more commonly affect legs than arms.

Degree of Severity

The number of limbs missing and the level of the amputation determine, to a large extent, motor performance. Compared with other lower extremity disabilities, amputees are consid-

ered minimally disabled unless both femurs are amputated at the hip joint (bilateral hip amputee). With the exception of these persons, for instance, all amputees are in Class III (least disabled) in wheelchair basketball; this means that their abilities are equivalent to Class 7 and 8 athletes with cerebral palsy and Class V persons with spinal cord injuries who can walk, but with a limp.

Physical Education and Sports

Most school-age children and youths with amputations participate in regular physical education. With properly fitted prostheses, they typically can keep up with classmates, although supplementary adapted physical education may be needed (Kegel, 1985; Michael, 1989). Typically, there is only one student with an amputation in the school, and the extent of his or her participation depends largely on attitudes of parents, teachers, and classmates. Attitudes (and subsequently, participation) are affected by many factors, among which are time of occurrence (congenital or acquired) and degree of severity (number of limbs missing and level of amputation).

Amputee Sport Classifications

By the time children with amputations reach adolescence, many want opportunities for vigorous competition against others with comparable disabilities. To ensure fair competition, ISOD and NHS enforce a strict classification system, with nine classifications used for such sports as swimming (see Table 24.3). Some of these are presented in Figure 24.30 and 24.31. Note that the odd numbers (1, 3, 5, 7, 9) denote the greater disability.

FIGURE 24.29

Canadian Arnie Boldt, world champion high jumper.

Table 24.3
Nine general sport classifications for persons with amputations.

Class A1 = Double AK	Class A7 = Double BE
Class A2 = Single AK	Class A8 = Single BE
Class A3 = Double BK	Class A9 = Combined
Class A4 = Single BK	lower plus
Class A5 = Double AE	upper limb
Class A6 = Single AE	amputations

Note. AK = Above or through the knee joint; BK = Below the knee, but through or above the ankle joint; AE = Above or through the elbow joint; BE = Below the elbow, but through or above the wrist joint.

In track-and-field events, fewer classifications are used. In field, double arm amputees compete together in one class, whether the amputation is above or below the elbow, and single arm amputees likewise form one class. More severely involved lower extremity amputees use wheelchairs, whereas less involved ones throw from a standing position. A similar classification system is used in track.

In volleyball, a point system similar to that in wheelchair basketball is used to ensure equal distribution of abilities on opposing teams. Persons are assigned 1, 2, 3, or 4 points, depending upon two criteria: A1 to A9 classification and muscle strength score determined by certified testers. At all times, players on the floor must total 13 or more points. Like regular volleyball, six players comprise a team.

FIGURE   24.30

Amputee sports classifications. Classifications A1 to A4. How would you program for these persons?

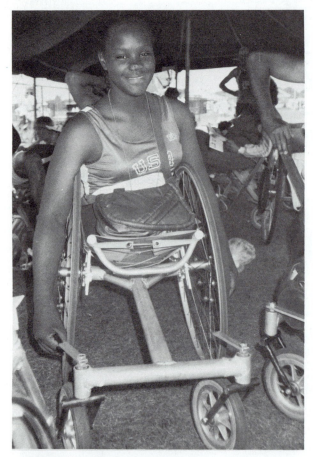

A. Classification A1

B. Classification A2

C. Classification A3

D. Classification A4

FIGURE   24.31

Amputee sports classifications. Classifications A6, A5, and A2. How would you program for these persons?

A. Classification A6

B. Classification A5 with girlfriend (A2).

Option of Sitting or Standing Rules

Lower limb amputees have the option in many sports of using a wheelchair or standing/walking/running/jumping. Some sports are organized primarily by sitting rather than standing rules. *Sitting volleyball* encompasses Classes A1 to A9, whereas only athletes in A2 to A4 and A6 to A9 are eligible for standing volleyball. Traditionally, basketball has been played in wheelchairs.

Whether track events should be in wheelchairs or ambulatory is highly controversial at this time, with the current rules mostly favoring wheelchair competition for lower limb amputees. In A4 events, which are ambulatory, competitors are required to wear prostheses and use both legs in running; hopping is not allowed.

Physical educators who permit students with lower limb amputations to compete in races against AB peers should study the pros and cons of this controversy carefully. Cinematographical research is helpful in the study of gaits (see Figure 24.32). Many physicians believe that ambulatory activities of this nature put too much stress on the good leg and predispose the athlete to eventual injury and/or degenerate arthritic disease.

Sport Rules on Prostheses and Orthoses

Use of prostheses and orthoses is regulated. In air pistol, air rifle, and swimming, for instance, prostheses and orthoses are not permitted. In archery, the draw may be made with a prosthesis or orthosis, and a releasing aid may be used by Classes A6, A8, and A9. These classes may also receive help with loading arrows into the bow. In field and most track events, the wearing of a prosthesis is optional. In volleyball, lower limb prostheses and orthoses are permitted, but not upper limb. In lawn bowling, Classes A5 and/or A7 may use prostheses or orthoses if they wish. In table tennis, however, these are not allowed. Persons who are unable to perform a regulation serve because of their disability are allowed to bounce the ball on the table and then smash it across the net. Obviously, physical educators need a lot of information to help students with amputations prepare for high-level competition.

Amputee Sport Governing Bodies

In the United States, NHS sponsors annual national as well as regional competitions in summer and winter sports. Every 4 years, as close to the Olympic Games as possible, international competition governed by ISOD is held. Amputees

FIGURE 24.32

(*A*) Running gait of A2 amputee. (*B*) Note that the structure and composition of a prosthesis is such that it is difficult to distinguish from a real leg. (From Dr. Bea Gordon and Dr. Sue Gavron.)

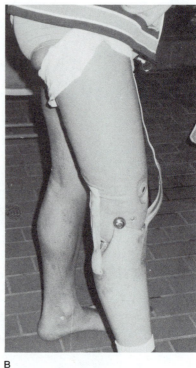

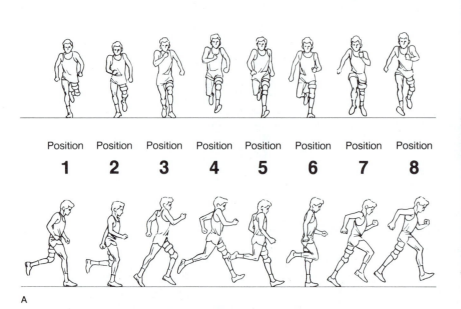

Position	Position	Position	Position	Position	Position	Position	Position
1	**2**	**3**	**4**	**5**	**6**	**7**	**8**

A

B

also compete in National Wheelchair Basketball Association (NWBA) games and in the open category of National Wheelchair Athletic Association (NWAA) events, such as track, field, swimming, table tennis, and archery. Persons with amputations are also becoming marathoners, tennis and racketball players, snow and water skiers, and competent participants in an ever-expanding variety of sports.

Fitting the Prosthesis

Since 1964, immediate postsurgical prosthetic fitting has gradually become the trend. In most cases, prostheses are fitted in less than 30 days after the amputation. This practice offers several advantages. First, particularly in a person with cancer, a prosthesis and early ambulation contributes to a positive psychological outlook. Second, amputation stumps in children do not usually shrink, and there is no physical reason for delaying fitting. Third, phantom pain has become almost nonexistent because of improved surgical techniques. Fourth, edema (swelling) is best controlled and wound healing facilitated by an immediate postsurgical socket.

In modern hospital settings, the patient is provided training in use of the prosthesis by physical therapists and occupational therapists. Ideally, this training includes exposure to playground equipment and recreational activities. If the child does not appear secure in class activities utilizing gymnastic and playground equipment, the adapted physical educator may need to supplement the hospital training.

Adaptations for Persons with Amputations

The only adaptations recommended pertain to dressing and shower rules. Girls and boys should be allowed to wear long pants or the type of clothing in which they feel most comfortable. Shower rules should be waived. The person who is sensitive about changing clothes in the locker room should be given a place of his or her own, and classmates should be encouraged to allow the desired privacy.

The general attitude among physicians is that persons with an amputation can do anything if the prostheses is well fitted.

Athletic activity is possible for the amputee, and there are numerous examples of those who have competed successfully in many sports—both as amateurs and as professionals. When strenuous activities are planned, it is recommended that the limb maker check the limb to make certain that the anticipated hard use can be tolerated. Special exercises are given to help the amputee acquire the balance, coordination, and ability to run rapidly that are prerequisites for sports. (Epps & Vaughn, 1972, p. 129)

Balance is probably the one aspect of motor performance that gives the most trouble. The sound limb is used for kicking balls while the prosthetic limb maintains the weight of the body. In ascending stairs, the child should be taught to lead with the sound limb; in descending, to lead with the prosthesis in the stable extended position. The bilateral above-knee amputee has more difficulty with steps and

FIGURE   24.33

FIGURE   24.34

The bilateral above-knee amputee may require months to learn use of prostheses.

Therapeutic horseback riding was initiated in England in the 1950s. The first established program in the United States began in 1968, when the Cheff Center in Augusta, Michigan, opened. This double-leg amputee was taught riding by a Cheff Center graduate. Note the specially made saddle.

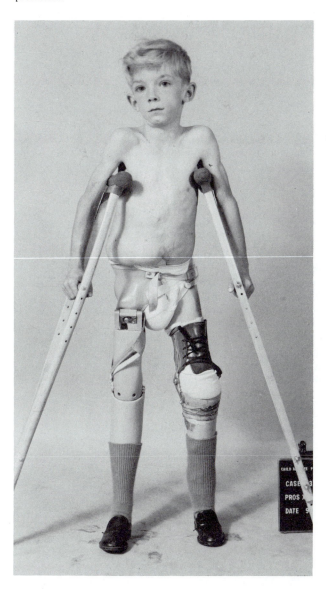

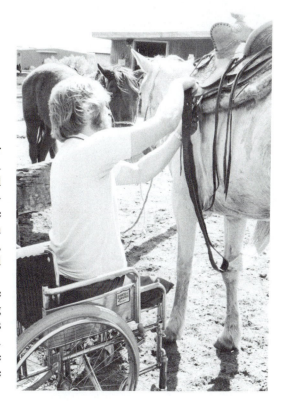

often requires a railing and crutch (see Figure 24.33). He or she typically climbs and descends stairs in a sideward manner. The weight of a bowling ball or tennis racquet in a unilateral upper-limb amputation often causes balance problems because the prosthetic arm may not compensate in accordance with the principle of opposition. This problem, at least in bowling, can be overcome by developing a scissors step, crossing the leg on the good arm side over the other, and taking the weight of the ball in stride.

Persons swim without their prostheses. Fins may be strapped to the arm or leg stumps as needed. For water skiing and/or activities in salt water, an old pair of artificial legs are used since salt water may cause the new ones to crack. Prostheses are not used in horseback riding. Specially made saddles and other equipment may be needed (see Figure 24.34).

The physical educator should recognize any gait deviations that may develop and refer the student back to the physical therapist and/or the prosthetist. Most gait deviations result from problems with the alignment or fit of the prosthesis.

References

Ablon, J. (1988). *Living with difference: Families with dwarf children.* New York: Praeger.

Basmajian, J. Y., & Wolf, S. (Eds.). (1990). *Therapeutic exercise* (5th ed.). Baltimore: Williams & Wilkins.

Beighton, P. (1988). *Inherited disorders of the skeleton* (2nd ed.). New York: Churchill Livingstone.

Berson, D., & Roy, S. (1982). *Pain-free arthritis.* Brooklyn, NY: S & J Books.

Brasile, F. (1984). A wheelchair basketball skills test. *Sports 'N Spokes, 9* (7), 34–40.

Chung, S. M. K. (1981). *Hip disorders in infants and children.* Philadelphia: Lea & Febiger.

Cowden, J. (1985). *Arthrogryposis: A case study approach for adapted physical education.* Unpublished manuscript, University of New Orleans.

Croce, R. (1987). Exercise and physical activity in managing progressive muscular dystrophy: A review for practitioners. *Palaestra, 3* (3), 9–14, 15.

Epps, C. H. Jr., & Vaughn, H. H. (1972). Training the child with an acquired lower limb amputation. In National Academy of Sciences (Ed.), *The child with an acquired amputation* (p. 129). Washington, DC: Author.

Jones, K. L. (1988). *Smith's recognizable patterns of human malformation* (4th ed.). Philadelphia: W.B. Saunders.

Kegel, B. (1985). Sports and recreation for those with lower limb amputation or impairment. *Journal of Rehabilitation and Research Development Clinical Supplement, No. 1.* Washington, DC.

Knudsen, M. (1993). *Flexibility and range of motion of dwarfs with achondroplasia.* Unpublished thesis, Texas Woman's University, Denton.

Low, L. (1992). *Prediction of selected track, field, and swimming performances of dwarf athletes by anthropometry.* Unpublished doctoral study, Texas Woman's University, Denton.

Michael, J. W. (1989). New developments in prosthetic feet for sports and recreation. *Palaestra, 5* (2), 21–22, 32–35.

Rothenberg, M., & White, M. (1985). *David: Severely burned by father.* Old Tappen, NJ: Fleming H. Revell.

Samples, P. (1990). Exercise encouraged for people with arthritis. *The Physician and Sportsmedicine, 18* (1), 122–127.

Sawisch, L. (1990). Strategic positioning in the disabled sports community: A perspective from the New Kids on the Block. *Palaestra, 6* (5), 52–54.

Scott, C. I. (1988). Dwarfism. *Clinical Symposia, 40* (1), 2–32.

Spragens, J. (1964). *A study of the physical education needs and interests of a selected group of orthopedically handicapped children with recommendations for planning and conducting physical activities.* Unpublished master's thesis, Texas Woman's University, Denton.

Tecklin, J. (1989). *Pediatric physical therapy.* Philadelphia: J.B. Lippincott.

Yilla, A. (1993). *Development of a quad rugby skill test.* Unpublished thesis, Texas Woman's University, Denton.

CHAPTER
25

Cerebral Palsy, Stroke, and Traumatic Brain Injury

FIGURE   25.1

Widespread individual differences exist within cerebral palsy. (*A*) Class 7 and 8 CP athletes play soccer. (*B*) Class 1 athlete, Mo Gayner, plays defense during team handball. (*C*) Class 1 athlete, Claude Prophete, cheering after the United States wins gold in team handball.

A

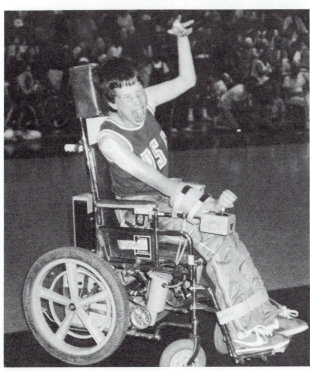

B

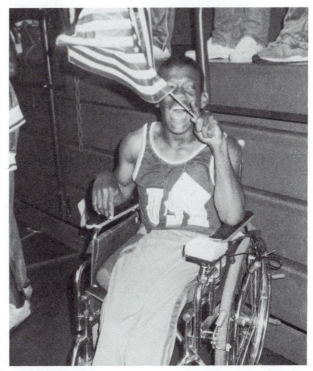

C

After you have studied this chapter, you should be able to:

1. Define and discuss etiology, prevalence, and incidence of (a) cerebral palsy (CP), (b) stroke, and (c) traumatic brain injury (TBI). Explain why they are grouped together in this chapter.

2. Contrast associated dysfunctions of the general CP population with U.S. Cerebral Palsy Athletic Association (USCPAA) athletes. Explain the importance of not making generalizations.

3. Explain four types of motor disorders: (a) spasticity, (b) athetosis, (c) ataxia, and (d) hypotonia. Discuss motor remediation for each.

4. Describe eight profiles that can be used for physical education-recreation assessment and programming for individuals with CP, stroke, and TBI. Given descriptions of functional ability, be able to correctly assign the profiles, discuss programming, and write IEPs.

5. Identify and discuss special problems that complicate programming for CP, stroke, and TBI.

6. Discuss USCPAA and other resources in terms of their roles in sport socialization and in lifelong sport interest and activity. Describe sports especially designed for CP.

This chapter is built on knowledge gained about reflexes in Chapter 10, neurological deficits and soft signs in Chapter 18, and wheelchair use in Chapter 23. Cerebral palsy, stroke, and traumatic brain injury are grouped together in this chapter because they are served by the U.S. Cerebral Palsy Athletic Association (USCPAA) and the Cerebral Palsy International Sports and Recreation Association (CP-ISRA). Obviously, for physical education, recreation, and sport programming, the disabilities present similar profiles (see Figure 25.1). Each results in varying degrees of sensory, perceptual, and cognitive impairment, as well as motor limitations, and each is an upper motor neuron disorder.

Definitions, Etiologies, and Incidence

Two conditions discussed in this chapter—cerebral palsy (CP) and stroke—are classified by the U.S. federal government as orthopedic impairments. The third condition—traumatic brain injury (TBI)—was recognized as a separate diagnostic category by PL 101-476, IDEA, enacted in 1990. Prior to this, TBI in children was associated with CP and learning disabilities. The federal definition of learning disabilities continues to include this sentence: "They include conditions which have been referred to as perceptual handicaps, brain injury, minimal brain dysfunction, dyslexia, developmental aphasias, etc." (IDEA, 1990, p. 4). CP has often been defined broadly as including congenital and acquired conditions (Bleck & Nagel, 1982; Thompson, Rubin, & Bilenker, 1983).

Controversy and confusion about these conditions, especially in regard to cognition and academic learning, will undoubtedly continue. Our concern here, however, is primarily with damage to motor portions of the brain. This is always present in CP but is variable in stroke and TBI.

Cerebral Palsy

Cerebral palsy (CP) is a chronic neurologic disorder of movement and posture caused by a defect or lesion of the immature brain and accompanied by associated dysfunctions (Sugden & Keogh, 1990; Tecklin, 1989; Thompson et al., 1983). It is not hereditary, contagious, or progressive. The disorder varies from mild (generalized clumsiness or a slight limp) to severe (dominated by reflexes, unable to ambulate except in motorized chair, inability to speak, and almost no control of motor function).

The etiology of CP is varied, including everything that can cause damage to the immature brain. About 90% of such brain damage occurs before or during birth. Common prenatal causes are maternal infections (e.g., AIDS, rubella, herpes), chemical toxins (e.g., alcohol, tobacco, prescribed and nonprescribed drugs), and injuries to the mother that affect fetal development. Maternal age is associated with CP, with the risk increased for mothers under age 20 or over age 34. Prematurity and low birth weight both increase the incidence of CP. Direct damage to the brain can occur during difficult deliveries or under conditions that cause oxygen deprivation (anoxia, hypoxia, asphyxia).

About 10% of CP occurs postnatally, with estimates ranging from 6 to 25% (Stanley & Blair, 1984). Sources vary with regard to definition of immature brain, with most requiring manifestation of a movement problem before age 2 years but some accepting age 5 as the diagnostic cutoff. Brain infections (encephalitis, meningitis), cranial traumas from accidents and child abuse, chemical toxins (airborne or ingested), and oxygen deprivation are the most common causes of acquired CP.

Because diagnostic criteria are controversial, CP incidence and prevalence rates vary. Thompson et al. (1983) reported an incidence of approximately 7 per 1,000 live births and a prevalence of 500 cases in every 100,000 persons. The 1990 census figures for the U.S. population (250 million) are the basis for the estimate that 1,250,000 Americans have CP. The condition is more common among males than females and also among firstborn. *CP is the orthopedic impairment most often found in the public schools.*

Stroke

Stroke, also called cerebrovascular accident (CVA) or disease, is the sudden onset of neurological impairment (awareness, motor, speech, perception, memory, cognition) caused by ischemia (blockage) or hemorrhage of blood vessels in or near the brain. Precipitating factors in adults are atherosclerosis, hypertension, and congenital arterial wall weakness (see Chapter 19). In children and adolescents, thrombotic and embolic strokes are associated with congenital and acquired heart disease, whereas intracranial hemorrhage is linked mostly with leukemia and weak or malformed arteriovenous structures.

Strokes are classified as complete or incomplete, depending on severity. Approximately one third of complete strokes result in death; strokes are the cause of 6 to 8% of all deaths. The other two thirds typically cause partial or total paralysis on either the right or left side (hemiplegia). There can be involvement of both sides, but this is less common.

Recovery of muscle function can progress through six or seven distinct stages (Basmajiian & Wolf, 1990; Brunnstrom, 1970) or stop abruptly. Simplified, the recovery process moves from a state of flaccidity, to spasticity, to flexor and extensor stereotypic patterns called synergies, to return of voluntary movement. The *synergies* look and act like primitive reflexes. Most persons with complete stroke have difficulty with both sitting and standing balance (Kottke & Lehmann, 1990), and postural reactions must be relearned. During the spasticity stage, contractures must be prevented by daily range of motion (ROM) exercises.

Over 2 million Americans are coping with the residual effects of stroke. This is about 1 of every 125 persons. Strokes occur most frequently after age 60. They are more common in males until about age 75, after which the incidence is equal for both sexes. The incidence of strokes in children is about 2.3 cases per 100,000 population per year (Roach, Garcia, & McLean, 1984), much more common than most people realize. In the past, early childhood strokes that resulted in motor impairment were often mistakenly considered CP and called infant hemiplegia. *The major difference is that stroke is followed by gradual improvement, whereas CP is nonprogressive.*

Children show more improvement after strokes than adults with similar-sized lesions, and young children show more recovery than older ones. Nevertheless, the *sequelae* (the conditions following or resulting from brain damage) often include hemiparesis (weakness on one side), seizure disorders, learning disabilities, visual perception problems, memory deficits, speech deficits, and mental retardation (Edwards & Hoffman, 1989; Isler, 1984; Roach et al., 1984). These children are prime candidates for adapted physical education and USCPAA sports.

Incomplete strokes, also called transient ischemic attacks (TIAs), occur in both children and adults. These strokes are characterized by total recovery (Kottke & Lehmann, 1990) but cause several hours of dysfunction in varied areas (e.g., muscle weakness, speech difficulty, memory and perception problems). Often, TIAs are warnings of severe cerebral pathology and impending major strokes.

Traumatic Brain Injury

Traumatic brain injury (*TBI*) refers to permanent damage caused by concussion, contusion, or hemorrhage sustained in vehicular accidents, assaults, falls, and other kinds of traumas. Most of these are *closed-head injuries* in that the skin is not broken. Collectively, these injuries are the leading cause of death and disability for persons under age 35. Each year, over 500,000 persons (about 1 out of 500) sustain TBI. Of these, approximately 100,000 die, 50,000 to 100,000 survive with severe impairments that prevent independent living, and the others learn to live with various sequelae that alter sensation, perception, emotion, cognition, and motor function.

Sequelae vary widely, depending on the site and extent of damage. The response of the brain to trauma also varies with age. Some research indicates that children recover more completely than adults, but this is controversial. Generally, recovery spans many years. Often, it appears to be complete, but professionals can detect minor deviations from normal, particularly in behaviors. Residual brain injury is also expressed by neurological *soft signs,* discussed in the next section.

Males sustain twice as many TBIs as females. Presumably, this is because males drive under the influence of alcohol more and are more involved in risk recreation and work activities than females. Over half of TBIs occur in motor vehicular accidents.

The major concern after injury is prediction of amount of recovery. Since 1974, the Glasgow Coma Scale (GCS) has been the major clinical assessment for this purpose (American Physical Therapy Association, 1983; Netter, 1986). Possible scores on this scale range from 3 to 15 points. Death or a vegetative state is the prognosis of over 50% of persons who score in the 5 to 7 range. The closer the score is to 15, the better the prognosis. The scale is based on three types of response: (a) eye opening, (b) motor, and (c) verbal. Patients who are conscious respond to commands ("Open your eyes." "Show me two fingers." "Tell me what day this is.") and obviously make the highest scores. The motor responses of unconscious persons to stimuli like pinpricks include withdrawal, abnormal flexion, abnormal extension or rigidity, and no reaction. Medical files almost always include a GCS score.

A GCS score of 8 or less indicates coma. The longer a person is comatose, the worse the prognosis. Research indicates that children in a coma for more than 24 hr are likely to have IQs less than 85 when tested 6 months after injury (Ylvisaker, 1985). Posttraumatic amnesia (PTA) is also a good predictor of future function. Recovery is better when PTA lasts only a few minutes. Often, PTA persists for many months. In fact, permanent memory deficits are common sequelae.

Attention, memory, and visuomotor difficulties are the predominant sequelae in school-age persons. Recovery from motor involvement is better than from cognitive and behavioral sequelae. Typically, however, over one half of children with TBI have some degree of permanent spasticity and/or ataxia. Percentages are somewhat higher for adults. The similarity of their motor profiles to those of persons with CP explains why USCPAA serves persons with TBI.

Soft Signs and Associated Dysfunctions

Persons described in this chapter are multidisabled. *Neurological soft signs* complicate behavioral, perceptual, and motor performance and interfere with learning. Soft signs

Table 25.1
Associated dysfunctions of general CP population as compared to USCPAA athletes.

Associated Dysfunctions	General CP Population %	USCPAA Athletes %
Mental retardation	30–70	10–20
Speech problems	35–75	25–35
Learning disabilities	80–90	45–55
Visual problems	55–60	20–30
Hearing problems	6–16	10–20
Perceptual deficits	25–50	60–70
Seizures	25–50	25–35
Reflex problems	80–90	65–75

Note. Estimates for the general population come from published sources (Bleck & Nagel, 1982; Thompson, Rubin, & Bilenker, 1983). Estimates for USCPAA athletes come from the author's research.

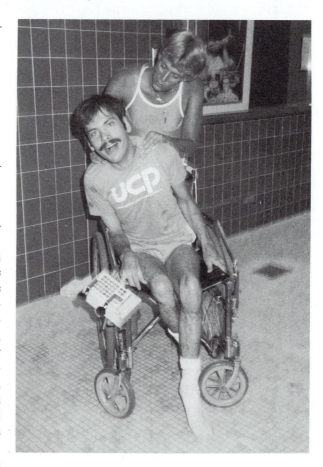

FIGURE 25.2

Bill Reilly, Class 2 international athlete with master's degree, often uses the Canon communicator instead of talking. Swim coach Kathi Rayborn notes absence of sideways parachute reaction as Bill loses balance during shoulder massage.

are indicators of central nervous system (CNS) dysfunction that cannot be substantiated by electroencephalogy (see Chapter 20). Common behavioral indicators of brain damage are attention deficits, hyperexcitability, perseveration, conceptual rigidity, emotional lability, and hyperactivity. Interpretation of sensory input is altered by brain damage, resulting in many kinds of perceptual problems (see Chapter 10). Particularly affected is sensorimotor integration of tactile, kinesthetic, vestibular, and visual input. Reflex, balance, and muscle-tone disorders are also considered soft signs. Soft signs and other diagnostic criteria indicate many associated dysfunctions in persons with upper motor neuron disorders (see Table 25.1).

In the remainder of this chapter, the abbreviation CP is used to encompass the motor sequelae and associated dysfunctions of stroke and TBI. Physical educators must assess carefully to determine whether students can best be served by a Special Olympics or a USCPAA sport-oriented curriculum. The major difference is in intellectual functioning. USCPAA specifies average or better intelligence as an eligibility criterion, although some athletes (5 to 15%) are perceived as borderline by coaches.

Table 25.1 describes differences between the general CP population and those served by USCPAA. Textbooks cite prevalence rates for coexisting CP and mental retardation (MR) as between 30 and 70%. Recognition that speech, language, and motor impairments make valid evaluation difficult is resulting in more learning disability (LD) diagnoses and less classification as MR. When associated dysfunctions make placement uncertain, it is better to assume LD and introduce the family to USCPAA activities. Many adults with CP describe lifetime academic achievement and self-concept problems that result from incorrect school placement and early exposure to curricula for MR rather than LD.

Electronic communication devices like the Canon communicator depicted in Figure 25.2 and the use of computers to teach language have demonstrated that many persons with CP, previously believed to be MR, have intact intelligence. The speech of many athletes who qualify for international competition cannot be understood without much practice. Interpreters are often used, just as with individuals who speak in sign or a foreign language. A person without intelligible speech should never be assumed to be MR.

Almost all children with CP need speech therapy. Even with intensive training, however, only about 50% improve to the degree that they communicate primarily by talking. Many use communication boards with words or symbols, as depicted in Figure 25.3. Others learn sign language. Teachers must take the time to listen to persons with CP, stroke, and TBI and to allow them to make as many of their own decisions as possible.

Inadequate communication skills lead to problems in socialization and delays in social development. Consider the leisure activities of able-bodied (AB) persons. Almost all require ability to use the hands (cards, board games, arts and crafts, cooking), to converse and/or sing, or to drive a car. About 50% of persons with upper motor neuron disorders do not have these abilities; their leisure and social functioning is therefore very different from that of peers. They can, however, excel in sports designed for their specific ability classification.

FIGURE 25.3

Different types of communication boards and pointing systems.

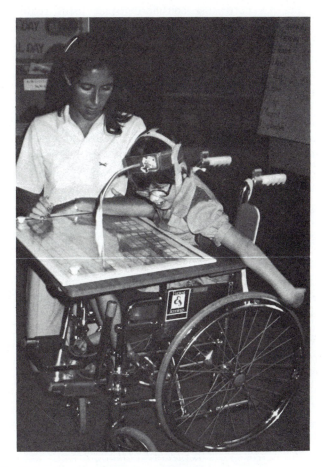

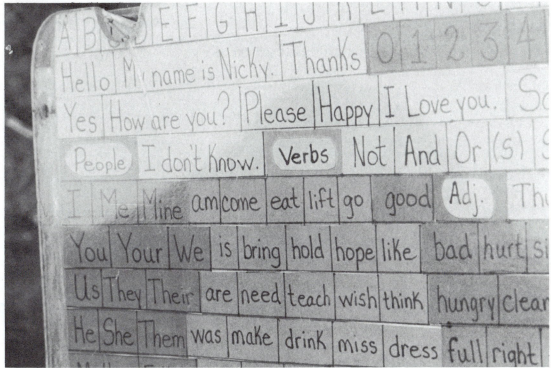

Visual defects affect over 50% of people with CP, stroke, and TBI. *Strabismus,* the inability to focus both eyes simultaneously on the same object, is the most common problem—not surprising considering that focus requires six pairs of muscles to move each eyeball. Imbalances in strength cause squinting, poor binocular vision, and inefficiencies in depth perception, pattern discriminations, and figure-background detection. These deficits naturally affect motor learning and success in sports.

Seizures are relatively common occurrences for individuals with upper motor neuron disorders but do not contraindicate sport participation. Over 25% of USCPAA athletes regularly take medication to control seizures. Travel and excitement inevitably result in some persons forgetting to take medication. An evening seizure, however, seldom prevents competition on the following day.

Of all the dysfunctions in Table 25.1, reflex problems concern physical educators the most. These prevent maturation of the balance reactions needed for stable sitting and for learning to walk. About half of USCPAA athletes are in wheelchairs because of reflex and reaction abnormalities. An additional 20 to 35% have coordination problems related to reflexes, even though the individuals are ambulatory.

In summary, associated dysfunctions explain why USCPAA needs a different sport classification system from that of other disabilities. Upper motor neuron disorders typically involve two or more limbs, causing abnormal muscle tone and postures that are worsened by perceptual and reflex problems. For example, few persons with CP are able to excel in wheelchair basketball. To compensate, USCPAA has devised alternative sports like *team handball,* formerly known as wheelchair soccer, and *boccia.*

Number of Limbs Involved

Number of limbs involved is typically specified on IEPs and other records to help with programming. The terms used, except for *paraplegia,* are the same as those in Chapters 23 and 24.

1. **Diplegia.** Lower extremities are much more involved than upper ones. This term is preferred over *paraplegia.*
2. **Quadriplegia.** All four extremities are involved. In international sports, a synonym is *tetraplegia.*
3. **Hemiplegia.** The entire right side or left side is involved.
4. **Triplegia.** Three extremities, usually both legs and one arm, are involved.

These terms permit description of and programming for functional abilities. Such terms as *mild* and *severe* indicate degree of involvement.

Types of Motor Disorders

Motor disorder in CP, stroke, and TBI is described in terms of abnormal muscle tone and postures (Bobath, 1980; Levitt, 1985; Sugden & Keogh, 1990; Thompson et al., 1983). The old (1956) neuromuscular classifications of the American Academy for Cerebral Palsy are no longer used. *Instead, three types of CP are recognized: (a) spasticity, (b) athetosis, and (c) ataxia.* Most persons have mixed types, and diagnosis indicates which is most prominent. Hypotonia is a temporary diagnosis associated with floppy baby syndrome and coma.

Spasticity

Spasticity, the most common type of motor disorder, is abnormal muscle tightness and stiffness characterized by *hypertonic* muscle tone during voluntary movement. About 65% of people with CP have this as their predominant type. Spasticity is mainly caused by damage to the motor cortex that results in an imbalance between pyramidal and extrapyramidal tract activity. Normally, the pyramidal tract causes continuous facilitation, which tends to increase muscle tone. The extrapyramidal tract counterbalances this with inhibitory signals. Extrapyramidal lesions are considered the basis of spasticity (Guyton, 1981). Damage to the basal ganglia, which also are responsible for inhibition, worsens spasticity. Likewise, the cerebellum, if damaged, exacerbates spasticity by failing to regulate the timing of excitatory and inhibitory messages, especially in rapid movements.

The resulting hypertonic state causes muscles to feel and look stiff (see fingers in Figure 25.4). Normally, muscles on one surface relax when those on the opposite surface contract (the reciprocal innervation principle), but hypertonicity results in *cocontraction* or stiffness. This, in turn, makes release of objects difficult or impossible, an obvious problem in learning to throw or to let go of the pool side when wanting to swim. It also interferes with ability to make precise movements.

Associated with spasticity is the exaggerated stretch or myotatic reflex. A *stretch reflex* is a spinal cord activated muscle contraction in response to a stretch detected by the spindle receptors inside muscle fibers. In normal function, this reflex serves a protective purpose because it instantaneously withdraws a body part from hurtful stimuli. In voluntary movement, the stretch reflex is operative also but regulated by a cerebellar component that dampens or smooths muscle contractions to prevent jerkiness and overshooting of limbs (i.e., it opposes sudden changes in muscle length). Malfunction results in exaggerated response (recoil, withdrawal, flexion) to stretch that ranges in intensity from a subtle timing problem to a violent recoil like a jackknife closing. All stretches do not activate exaggerated responses, and intensity varies from time to time. In some persons, the stretch reflex is so disruptive that limbs are strapped down (see Figure 25.4).

Among the abnormal postures associated with spasticity are the scissors gait (both legs involved) and the hemiplegic gait (arm and leg on same side involved). The *scissors gait* is a pigeon-toed walk caused by abnormal tightness of the hip joint flexors, adductors, and inward rotators that is associated with retention of the positive support and crossed extension reflexes. Also tight are the knee joint flexors (hamstrings) and ankle joint plantar flexors (calf muscles and

FIGURE   25.4

Spasticity in some persons may be so great that limbs need to be strapped down during physical activity. Here, Tom Cush, international Class 2 athlete with cerebral palsy, has both arms strapped to chair while he competes in team handball. In throwing and striking activities, only one arm is strapped down.

Achilles tendon) that keep knees bent and weight on toes (see Figure 25.5). If arms are involved, the tightness follows the same pattern (flexors, adductors, and inward rotators). The spastic arm is bent and pronated, carried close to the body, with a fisted hand. The *hemiplegic gait* is a limp caused by asymmetry in extension (see Figure 25.5).

Abnormal postures are also caused by retention of primitive reflexes and immaturity of postural reactions. Inability to move the head without associated muscle tension in the arms results in many abnormal postures. When reflex disturbances are severe, persons with spasticity remain nonambulatory.

Athetosis

Athetosis, the second most common type of motor disorder, is constant, unpredictable, and purposeless (CUP) movement caused by *fluctuating* muscle tone that is sometimes hypertonic and sometimes hypotonic. Damage to the basal ganglia in the cerebral white matter is the primary cause of this involuntary *overflow* disorder. Most persons with athetosis are quadriplegic. About 25% of CP is primarily athetosis.

Constant movement is most troublesome to the head and upper extremities. Facial expression, eating, and speaking are major problems. The head is usually drawn back but may roll unpredictably from side to side; the tongue may protrude and saliva drool down the chin. Lack of head control causes problems of visual pursuit and focus that impair ability to read and perform hand-eye accuracy tasks. Constant movement of the fingers and wrist render handwriting and fine muscle coordinations almost impossible.

Many persons with athetosis use wheelchairs, but some have enough motor control to walk. Their gait is typically unsteady or staggering. They walk with trunk and shoulder girdle leaning backward, reinforcing extensor tonus, to prevent collapsing (Bobath, 1980). Hips and knees tend to be hyperextended, the back in lordosis, and the feet kept dorsiflexed, pronated, and everted (a valgus position). Steps are short to help maintain balance. Falls are more often backward than forward. Persons with such gaits compete in track but wear knee and elbow pads and gloves.

There are many types of athetosis: (a) dystonia, with fluctuating muscle tone; (b) mixed with spasticity, in which muscle tone is mostly hypertonic; (c) mixed with floppy baby

FIGURE 25.5

Abnormal gaits associated with spasticity and ataxia.

Scissors gait. Characteristic of quadriplegic spastic cerebral palsy. The legs are flexed and adducted at the hip joint, causing them to cross alternately in front of each other with the knees scraping together. The knees may be flexed to a greater degree than normal, and the weight of the body may be taken primarily on the toes. The gait is characterized by a narrow walking base. Scissoring may be caused by retention of the positive supporting reflex. Toe walking may be caused also by the positive supporting reflex.

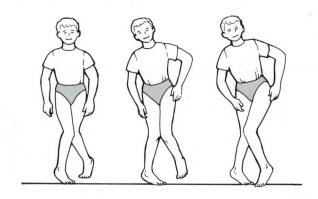

Hemiplegic gait. Characteristic of hemiplegic spastic cerebral palsy. Both arm and leg on the same side are involved. Tends to occur with any disorder producing an immobile hip or knee. Affected leg is rigid and swung from the hip joint in a semicircle by muscle action of the trunk. Individual leans to the affected side, and arm on that side is held in a rigid, semiflexed position.

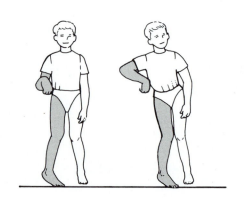

Cerebellar gait. Characteristic of ataxic cerebral palsy, Friedreich's ataxia, and similar les autres conditions. Irregularity of steps, unsteadiness, tendency to reel to one side. Individual seems to experience difficulty in judging how high to lift legs when climbing stairs. Problems are increased when the ground is uneven. Note the similarity between this and the immature walk of early childhood before CNS has matured.

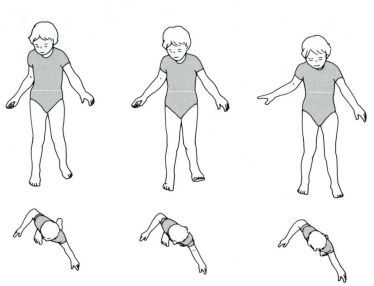

syndrome, in which muscle tone is primarily hypotonic; and (d) mixed with ataxia (Bobath, 1980). Changes from one type to another sometimes occur with age, particularly from floppy baby to dystonic children. Generally, *athetosis* and *dystonia* are synonyms.

Ataxia

Ataxia is a combined disturbance of balance and coordination generally characterized by hypotonia or low postural tone. Ataxia can result from disorders of the spinal cord as well as the brain. In CP, stroke, and TBI, however, the ataxia is of cerebellar-vestibular origin. Ataxia is diagnosed only in people who can walk unaided. To compensate for extreme unsteadiness of gait, the arms are typically overactive in balance-saving movements. Falls are frequent.

When persons can maintain balance with eyes open, but not closed, ataxia is usually the diagnosis. Voluntary movements are clumsy and uncoordinated with under-reaching and overreaching common. Uneven or unlevel ground, stairs, and stepping over objects are particular problems because of cerebellar-vestibular body awareness deficits.

Ataxia varies from mild to severe. A diagnosis of pure ataxia is made in only about 10% of CP. Many persons not diagnosed as disabled probably have ataxia. Combined disturbances of balance and coordination are common among low-skilled persons.

Flaccidity/Hypotonia

The terms *flaccidity* and *hypotonia* refer to low muscle tone. Infants and young children are sometimes assigned a diagnosis of flaccidity/hypotonia until type of CP (spasticity, athetosis, ataxia) becomes clear. Adults, however, can have this condition also. Persons in comas are hypotonic. After a severe stroke, the first stage in motor recovery is flaccidity.

Problems in persons with hypotonia are (a) poor head and trunk control, (b) absent postural and protective reactions, (c) shallow breathing, and (d) joint laxity or hypermobility. Hypotonia may be so severe that persons cannot sit or move unaided (i.e., they are in a vegetative state). Hypotonia is associated with damage of nuclei deep in the cerebellum that, in turn, affect motor cortex and brain stem action. In time, the motor cortex may compensate by increasing facilitatory impulses.

Profiles to Guide Assessment and Programming

USCPAA provides sport classifications that aid in visualizing the widespread individual differences in CP, stroke, and TBI. Virtually everyone fits into this classification system, which should be the assessment approach used to write individualized education programs (IEPs) and individualized family service plans (IFSPs). There are eight classes or profiles, four for the nonambulatory and four for the ambulatory. Classes 1, 2, 3, and 6 designate persons who are the most severely involved.

Assessment begins with determining whether a person is nonambulatory (Classes 1 to 4) or ambulatory (Classes 5 to 8). This requires careful questioning because many persons who use wheelchairs do not need them. This is particularly true of persons who (a) must navigate hills and other barriers in a school or work environment that demands speed in moving from place to place and (b) are overweight or have low fitness. Assessment for movement and sport programming places emphasis on abilities (i.e., how many steps can be taken without a wheelchair). Persons who cannot ambulate across the room, even with crutches or canes, are assigned to Classes 1 to 4. Those who need crutches or canes (called assistive devices) are placed in Class 5. All others are assigned to Classes 6 to 8.

Class 1—Motorized Chair

Class 1 includes everyone without the ROM and power to push a manual wheelchair. Such persons have severe involvement in all four limbs and little head and trunk control. They typically are dominated by reflexes, are unable to maintain body parts in good alignment without help, and have limited ROM. When placed in a lying position, they may be unable to initiate a roll, sit-up, or other voluntary movement. Usually, the motor disorder is primarily hypotonic (especially ages 0 to 7) or spastic.

Chapter 10 describes physical education programming for these persons in early childhood. Emphasis is on total body movement activities on mats, in the water, and in apparatus that can be pushed, pulled, or tilted by the teacher. Coactive movement is used to normalize muscle tone and prevent contractures. If the child is dominated by extensor muscle tone, then flexion activities are stressed as normalizers. If flexor tone dominates, then extensor activities are emphasized.

If the child has the mental function to learn use of a motorized chair, all kinds of activities are possible. By age 7 or 8, physical education goals should stress track and field. Whether the chair is powered by hand, foot, or mouth switch, speed and control must be learned. Racing for speed can be on straightaways or around obstacles like cones (see Figure 25.6). The child needs to learn how to weave around obstacles, make circles around them, and manage a ramp.

Appropriate field activities are those using soft implements that can be easily handled, like a soft shot or discus. Throws for distance and height should be practiced, as well as tosses at ground targets like those used in archery. If the hand grasp reflex is still present, release is difficult. It can, however, be overridden by higher cortical levels with much concentration and practice. Games should be devised that give points regardless of the direction the object flies.

Class 1 students can succeed in many game, sport, and aquatic activities if teachers are creative. Because release is so difficult, striking patterns are often emphasized. Inclined boards called *chutes* permit striking to activate a ball in bowling-type games. Suspended ball and tabletop activities are also good. Lying sideways or prone on mats, persons can use body parts to knock over strategically set bowling pins (Miller & Schaumberg, 1988) and hit or kick objects. In the motorized chair, a game goal may be moving around the room and knocking down pins with the hand. Similar games can be played in the water while lying on floating mats or being coactively moved in a vertical position. A personal flotation device (PFD) should be worn. Many water games should be played before swimming is introduced.

Class 1 persons often require one-on-one assistance. Principals may need to be convinced to supply aides. A record should be kept of each student's time on task (i.e., actual physical activity) or number of trials completed. No child is too disabled to benefit from physical education.

Class 2—Athetosis; 2L or 2U

Class 2 persons can propel a manual chair but have moderate to severe involvement in all four limbs and trunk. Individual differences at this level are so great that Class 2 is subdivided into uppers (U) and lowers (L), with the adjective denoting the limbs with greater functional ability. The 2L propels a chair with feet, with speed and control varying widely (see Figure 25.6). The 2L often is able to do everything with feet (i.e., eating, writing, turning pages) that ordinary people do with hands. Physical education for a 2L emphasizes kicking events and ball handling that is done with the feet. The toes can grasp a soft shot or discus and toss it in various ways. The 2L can learn to tricycle, swim, and do other activities that do not require upper extremities.

FIGURE   25.6

(*A,B*) Class 1 in track and swimming. Motorized chair is needed.
(*C,D*) Class 2l in track and 2U in swimming. Both Class 1 and 2 can use personal flotation devices in USCPAA swimming but not in international events. See Davis, Gehlsen, and Wilkerson (1990) for information on Class 1 foot pushing technique.

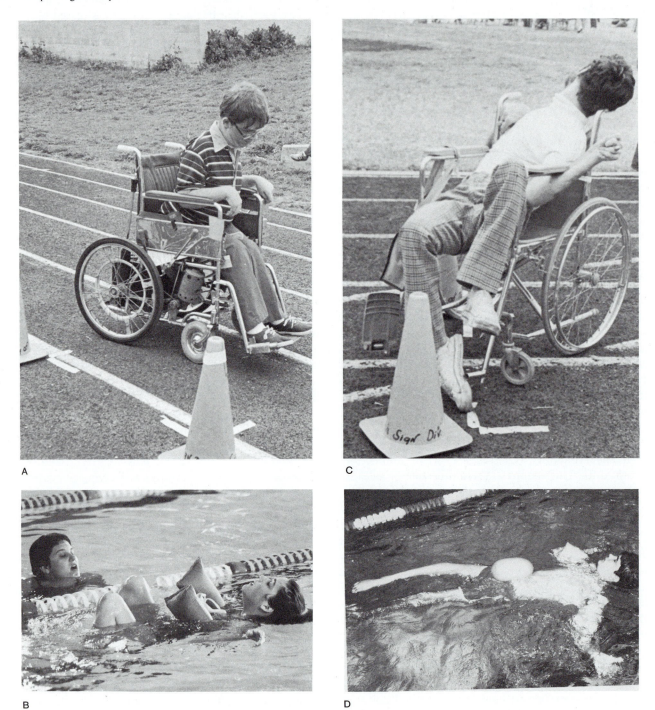

A

C

B

D

In contrast, the 2U relies on arms and learns traditional wheelchair track-and-field activities. Propulsion is weak and slow, however, so that even adult events require short distances (i.e., between 20 and 200 m). Early throwing activities may feature the soft discus and shot, but the 2U, as an adult, must use a regulation (but lightweight) club, shot, and discus. The sooner this equipment is introduced,

the better. The legs of a 2U are relatively useless, but the arm stroke can generate enough power for swimming success with and occasionally without a PFD (see Figure 25.6).

Class 2 persons typically have more athetosis than spasticity. Control in accuracy tasks is a challenge, but both 2L and 2U persons engage in bowling and other games similar to those played by Class 1 individuals. Bowling balls with retractable handles are available from several equipment companies (see Appendix F). Class 2 individuals also must cope with major reflex and postural reaction problems.

Class 3—Moderate Triplegic or Quadriplegic

Class 3 is similar to a 2U except that involvement is less and motor disorder is usually predominantly spastic. There is moderate involvement in three or four limbs and trunk. Class 3 individuals propel the chair with short, choppy arm pushes but generate fairly good speed. They can take a few steps with assistive devices, but this ambulatory mode is not functional. Some have enough leg control to learn tricycling events.

All wheelchair activities and swim strokes (except butterfly) are possible. Reflex and postural reaction problems affect performance, so wheelchair basketball and tennis are not games of choice because of their speed-distance-accuracy demands. Sports like team handball and quad rugby are better suited to abilities. In general, physical education should stress sports, dance, and aquatics, with as few adaptations as possible.

Class 4—Diplegic

Class 4 individuals use a wheelchair with the same skill, precision, and speed as people with spinal cord injury and spina bifida. They propel the chair with forceful, continuous pushes, have good strength in trunk and upper extremities, and minimal control problems. Some succeed at wheelchair basketball, but subtle associated dysfunctions like visual perception deficits often interfere with aspirations to be on the starting five. They are not eligible for quad rugby, so team handball is the game of choice. They can perform all swim strokes.

Class 4 persons are considered mildly disabled. Unlike others in wheelchairs, their associated dysfunctions are minimal and subtle. They are good candidates for integrated physical education but also need separate instruction in wheelchair sports.

Class 5—Assistive Devices

Class 5 is the only profile that includes persons who use crutches, canes, and walkers (see Figure 25.7). The motor disorder is primarily spastic, and involvement is either hemiplegic or diplegic. Spasticity is moderate to severe.

Many activities offer success. Track events include 100- to 400-m distances run on foot. The only contraindication is use of *axillary crutches* (those that touch armpits) because pressure in this area can cause nerve damage. In field events, the major problem is balance. Throws can be from either a standing or seated position. Some persons prefer the tricycle, but others use a bicycle. Class 5 persons are eligible to play team handball and need wheelchair skills to make the team. They are also eligible to play USCPAA soccer and are groomed particularly for goalkeeper and defensive positions.

In some countries, Class 5 people compete in wheelchairs. Although USCPAA rules do not encourage this type of skill development, Class 5 is eligible for wheelchair sports like tennis and handball that are sponsored by other organizations.

FIGURE 25.7

Class 5 persons use assistive devices.

Class 6—Athetosis, Ambulatory

Class 6 individuals are primarily affected by athetosis, and associated dysfunctions are severe. They have moderate to severe involvement of three or four limbs, with severe balance and coordination problems. These are less prominent when running and throwing than walking.

In terms of overall severity of condition, Class 6 is often grouped with Classes 1, 2, and 3. Unsteadiness of gait, balance, and reflex problems vary widely. All physical education, however, is ambulatory, with elbow and knee pads recommended because of frequent falls. When mainstreamed, these persons are helped by the presence of a bar or chair to provide support during calisthenics and other activities that require good balance. In USCPAA competition, Class 6 persons have a choice between tricycle and bicycle. Like Class 3 individuals, they can do all swim strokes except the butterfly.

Class 7—Hemiplegic

Class 7 includes only persons with hemiplegia. Spasticity ranges from mild to moderate. Class 7 persons ambulate with a slight limp and are able to pump effectively only with the noninvolved arm; the spastic arm is somewhat conspicuous because of its bent, pronated position (see Figure 25.8). The spastic leg is noticeably smaller than the normal one.

FIGURE 25.8

Class 7 athletes are hemiplegic and run with a slight limp.

Class 7 persons are typically in integrated physical education and able to do everything that peers do, except with more effort. Sue Moucha, an international Class 7 athlete, states:

I have biked 100 mi in one day, run a marathon, and have successfully completed an able-bodied Outward Bound course, which included rock climbing, rappelling, canoeing, and a mini-marathon. Sports acts as a benchmark. I enjoy physical activities and am eager to do something new. (Moucha, 1991, p. 38)

Class 8—Minimal Involvement

Class 8 persons run and jump freely without a noticeable limp (see Figure 25.9). Their gait is symmetrical in both walking and running. They demonstrate good balance but have noticeable (although minimal) coordination problems. This is usually seen in the hands or in a lack of power or coordination in one limb. Sometimes, associated dysfunctions are more disabling than the motor involvement.

Coping With Special Problems

Among the motor problems that require special attention are (a) delayed development, (b) reflex and postural reaction abnormalities, (c) abnormal muscle tone, (d) contractures, and (e) additional orthopedic defects. Attitudinal barriers constitute a major social problem.

FIGURE 25.9

Class 8 athletes run freely without a noticeable limp.

FIGURE   25.10

Different manifestations of tonic neck reflexes. (*A*) The ATNR causes increased extensor tone in the arm on the face side and increased flexor tone in the arm on the scalp side. (*B*) The STNR extends arms and flexes legs.

A

B

Delayed Motor Development

Children in Classes 7 and 8 often learn to walk by age 2, but others are delayed several years or never learn. All aspects of motor development are typically delayed, which limits the physical, mental, and emotional stimulation that children need. To compensate, early intervention should involve several hours of big muscle activity daily. Chapter 10 presents content to guide programming of nonambulatory children from birth until age 7.

The type of motor performance that a child with CP has at age 7 is predictive of performance as an adult (Bleck & Nagel, 1982). Most children who are going to learn to walk have done so by age 7. Bleck and Nagel (1982, p. 79) emphasize, "Physical therapy to improve the child's walking once he or she has reached 7 or 8 years is unlikely to be worth the time and effort expended, and other areas of function (like play and sports) should take precedence." These and other physicians agree that emphasis on integration of reflexes should change to instruction in sports, dance, and aquatics at about age 7. *Persons who have not lost reflexes by age 7 will probably have them forever and can be taught to compensate or to use reflexes to enhance performance.* Turning the head to the right, for example, can increase the power of a right-handed movement via the asymmetrical tonic neck reflex. Hyperextending the head can extend arms and flex legs, making the exit from a pool easier via the symmetrical tonic neck reflex (see Figure 25.10).

Postural Reactions

Sports, dance, and aquatics can be used to enhance postural reactions. Emphasis on protective extension of arms during falls (the parachute reactions) and on development of equilibrium should continue. Some sports should be selected for working on weaknesses (e.g., balance beam routines, horseback riding, gymnastics, roller and ice skating, dance, wrestling, and judo), whereas others should build on strengths and the desire to participate in the same activities as peers. Most sport skills, done in correct form, normalize muscle tone. The more difficult principle to implement is avoidance of abnormal postures and stereotyped patterns that may cause injury, contribute to posture deviations, and further social rejection. These are associated with reflexes and muscle tone abnormalities. Hence, work continues in these areas but for different reasons.

Reflexes and Abnormal Postures

Chapter 10 describes the 10 reflexes that are most troublesome, principles to guide integration, and activities. This section therefore focuses on proper holding, carrying, and positioning.

Holding and Carrying

Class 1 and 2 people, regardless of age, need help in making transfers. Unless body weight prohibits carrying children from place to place, it is both efficient and therapeutic to do

FIGURE   25.11

Correct ways to carry children with cerebral palsy.

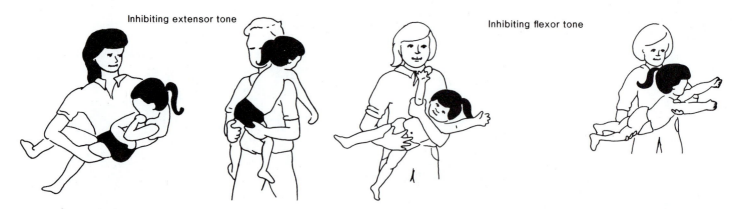

Inhibiting extensor tone   Inhibiting flexor tone

so. Figure 25.11 shows several correct ways for carrying on land and in water activities. Many games like airplane and Batman can be played from these positions. Children dominated by extensor tone (i.e., stiff all over) should be held close to the body in tucked positions that maintain their head and limbs in flexion. Children dominated by flexor tone (i.e., bent or curled) should be held in ways that maintain head and limbs in extension. Thus, the commonsense principle of keeping body parts in good alignment is followed.

When apparatus is used, much Velcro, padding, and cushioning is needed to achieve proper alignment. Often, each body part must be strapped in place. Many sources provide ideas for adapting equipment (Farber, 1982; Finnie, 1974; Robinault, 1973). Such equipment is also available from commercial companies like Preston (see Appendix F).

Strapping and Positioning

Good alignment in sitting requires that (a) the hips are at 90° flexion and in contact with the back of the chair, (b) thighs are slightly abducted and in contact with the seat, and (c) knees, ankles, and elbows are positioned at 90° flexion. There should be at least 1 inch of space between the knees and the seat to avoid pressure on the tender area behind the knees. The feet should be in contact with a firm, flat surface. The head and neck must be held in midline and kept in extension. Often, strapping is the only way to meet these criteria for a good sitting posture.

Strapping traditionally has been associated with occupational therapy and physical therapy, but the new emphasis on wheelchair sports in school physical education requires learning strapping techniques to assure safety and maximize performance (Burd & Grass, 1987). All-out effort in a wheelchair, without proper strapping, often elicits an extensor pattern that tends to pull the body down and out of the chair. This is characterized by spinal, hip, and knee extension and toe pointing (plantar flexion). In conjunction with this, scissoring is a problem.

To control the extensor pattern, a strap should come forward from the rear-underneath portion of the chair, where it is secured to the frame. The strap angle should be about 45°, with the fastening mechanism in front. This type of lap belt holds the hips in place much better than a traditional seat belt at waist level. Some persons, however, may need an H strap arrangement that holds both upper back and hips in place.

Knee flexion and the adduction/inward rotation pattern caused by scissoring are controlled by straps placed around each thigh and pulled tight. A single strap across the thighs may be sufficient. Experimentation is important.

The feet and lower legs may need to be strapped in similar fashion. Often, a strap is also placed beneath the feet as a means of elevating the footrests and increasing knee flexion. Regardless of body part strapped, wide, 2-inch Velcro or webbing should be used to reduce the possibility of circulation and irritation problems. If swelling or redness occurs or the athlete complains of discomfort, adjust the straps. Extremities should not be strapped for long periods. As soon as competition or the activity ends, straps should be loosened.

Figure 25.12 shows how strapping and positioning inhibit reflexes. A bolster between the thighs inhibits the crossed extension reflex that causes scissoring. The extensor pattern can be prevented by positioning self at eye level rather than forcing the student to look upward. Hyperextension of the head can elicit either the extension pattern or the symmetrical tonic neck reflex. In general, both should be avoided. This calls for proper placement of suspended balls and visual aids. Also depicted in Figure 25.12 is use of a bolster, wedge, and inclined board to correctly position a child in prone and inhibit flexor tone dominance.

During the time that no one is interacting with a severely involved person, positioning is very important. *For the person who cannot initiate voluntary movement, side-lying with the head propped up on a pillow is considered best.* Foam cushions maintain correct position. The individual should be facing the action, a television, or a source of stimulation. If a person can hold up the head and use arms, prone is better. Mirrors on the wall and floor reinforce voluntary movement. Supine-lying is avoided because of the helplessness it causes; propped sitting is better.

Severely involved persons spend so much time in wheelchairs that mat work is an important part of physical education. Ideally, the mat area should be an elevated plat-

FIGURE   25.12

Methods of inhibiting primitive reflexes. (*A*) Strapping the thighs and lower legs to wheelchair prevents extensor thrust. (*B*) A hard roll or bolster between the thighs maintains the legs in abduction and inhibits scissoring. (*C*) The position of the teacher influences extensor pattern. (*D–F*) Use of bolster, wedge, and inclined board for correct positioning in prone.

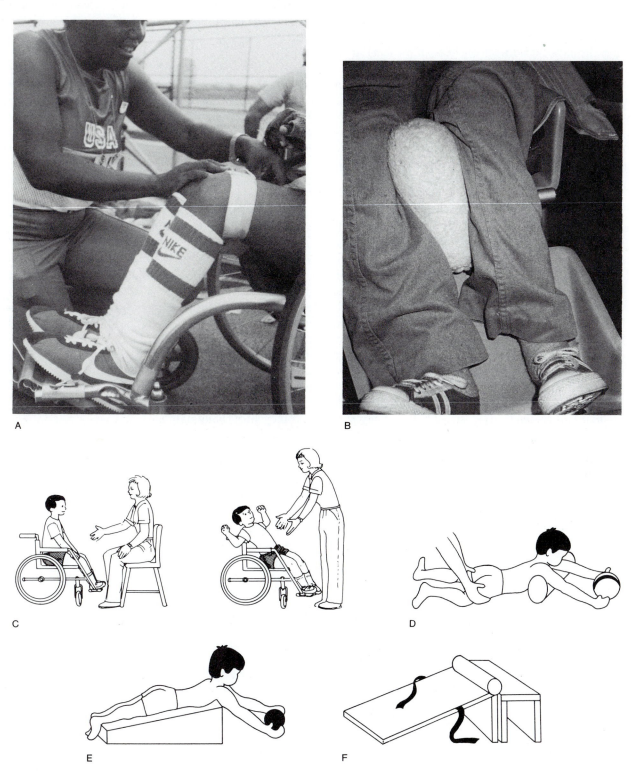

A

B

C

D

E

F

form about the same height as the wheelchair seat to facilitate transfers. Bolsters and wedges must be available if students wait turns.

Contraindicated Activities

Activities that elicit or reinforce abnormal movement patterns are contraindicated. Creeping on all-fours, for example, may be contraindicated in quadriplegia and diplegia if it increases flexor spasticity. The frog or W sitting position (resting on the buttocks between the heels of the feet) should be avoided because it worsens the hip joint adduction-inward rotation-flexion pattern that needs to be eliminated. Bridging in supine (pushing down with feet and lifting pelvis from mat), which often occurs in athetosis, should not be allowed because it worsens abnormal neck extension and scapulae retraction. Movement education challenges to walk on tiptoe or to point the toes are contraindicated for persons with tight calf muscles.

Spasticity Problems

Abnormal postures are often corrected manually, especially in young children. In particular, adduction-inward rotation-flexion patterns of the shoulder and hip joints must be corrected. In general, this is achieved by applying an inhibitory pattern that is the opposite of the spastic posture. To correct scissoring in supine, grasp the thighs and gently spread the legs while outwardly rotating and flexing the hip joint. This corrective pattern also decreases plantar flexion at the ankle joint and makes it easier to put on shoes and socks. To correct abnormal arm position, grasp the upper arm and lift it over the head while gently outwardly rotating.

Three principles underlie handling techniques. The first is to *maintain symmetry* (i.e., strive to keep body parts in midline). The second is to *use inhibitory actions that are the opposite of the undesired pattern.* The third is to *work from designated key points of central control* (i.e., grasp body parts as close to the joint as possible). Key points are (a) the shoulder joint for abnormal arm positions, (b) the hip joint for scissoring, and (c) the head and neck for the arched back extensor spasm.

The fisted hand, a common problem, is worsened by wrist hyperextension. When an activity calls for releasing an object or maintaining an open hand, use both shoulder joint and radioulnar rotation to relax the wrist and fingers. Do not try to pry fingers open.

Overall spasticity of the body is decreased by rotation of the trunk. This forms the rationale for rhythmic rolling activities on a stationary or moving surface (i.e., large therapy ball) and gentle rocking movements on lap, ball, or tiltboard. Horseback riding is also helpful, and many therapeutic programs are available. USCPAA can supply information on programs that serve nonambulatory as well as ambulatory persons. Rotation and rocking activities also create weight-shifting situations that promote development of equilibrium reactions.

Active exercises, for persons able to initiate independent movement, should follow the three principles of correct handling. Rotatory and rocking movements are important for warm-up and relaxation to minimize spasticity. Chapters 15, 16, and 17 on relaxation, dance, and swimming present many good activities. Water play and exercises in a warm pool (about 90°) are excellent. Swim fins are helpful in minimizing the stretch reflex.

Daily stretching exercises can help prevent contractures. These should be slow, static stretches as described in Chapter 13 on fitness.

Athetosis Problems

Class 2 and 6 persons exhibit more athetosis than spasticity, but both conditions are often present. Although constant, unpredictable, purposeless (CUP) movement would seem a hindrance in aiming activities, research shows that persons with athetosis can succeed in bowling, tennis, and golf (Hellebrandt & Waterland, 1961; Hellebrandt, Waterland, & Walters, 1961). USCPAA also has accumulated evidence that Class 2 people can excel in aiming activities and recommends bowling and boccia.

USCPAA promotes proper warm-up for persons with athetosis. Previous beliefs that athetoid movements provide a natural state of readiness have not been subjected to research and thus have no base for support.

Early childhood positioning and exercise goals are different for athetosis and spasticity. The main goal in athetosis is head and trunk control (proximal stability), which, in turn, tends to decrease undesired limb movement. To promote midline control, infants and toddlers are placed quite early in sitting, kneeling, and standing positions (see Figure 25.13). Upright rather than prone activities are stressed in mat work. Knee walking (wearing pads) is recommended, as well as walking using parallel bars for support. Tricycling and bicycling (both stationary and moving) reinforce midline control, as does horseback riding.

Surgery and Braces

Several surgical procedures correct or relieve problems caused by severe spasticity. A *tenotomy* is surgical sectioning of a tendon. It is primarily used to lengthen the Achilles tendon, thereby reducing toe-walking caused by abnormal tightness. In about 6 weeks, the cutout sections are filled in by new tendon growth. Tenotomy is also used to lengthen the iliopsoas tendon to relieve hip flexion contractures and to lengthen hamstring tendons to relieve knee flexion deformities. A *myotomy* is a similar procedure except it is applied to muscles, mainly the tight adductor muscles of the hip joint. A *neurectomy* is a cutting (partial or total) of nerves that supply spastic muscles. A *tendon transplant* is surgical relocation of the origin of a muscle, also a technique to ameliorate adduction and flexion deformities.

Arthrodesis is the surgical immobilization of a joint; it is sometimes done at the ankle joint to relieve severe *pes valgus* (combined eversion, plantar flexion, and adduction) caused by contractures. Valgus deformities occur most commonly in ambulatory spastic diplegia. Arthrodesis causes feet to remain in a fixed dorsiflexion position, which gives more stability than pathological plantar flexion.

FIGURE 25.13

Apparatus to help children with cerebral palsy stand is built with straps to keep body parts centered in midline and thus inhibit asymmetrical tonic neck reflex.

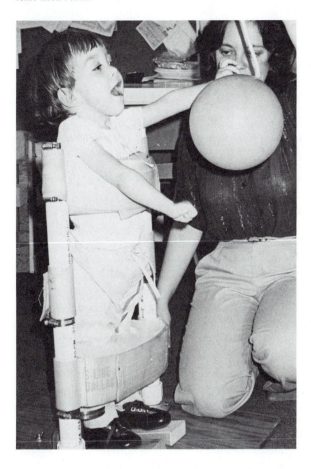

Braces (orthoses) are also used to control spasticity and to provide needed stability. Figure 25.14 shows some of these, which are typically referred to by their initials: AFOs (ankle-foot-orthoses), KAFOs (knee-ankle-foot orthoses), or HKAFOs (hip-knee-ankle-foot orthoses). Orthoses are not considered assistive devices and are allowed in all USCPAA events. The parapodium and other standing devices are primarily used in early childhood, before independent standing is possible.

Hip Dislocation, Scoliosis, and Foot Deformities

Nonambulatory children with CP are at high risk for hip dislocation (see pp. 609–610). In approximately 25%, the head of the femur becomes displaced in an upward direction. The average age of dislocation is 7 years. Correction is by surgery. This propensity for hip dislocation explains why learning to properly handle scissored legs is so important.

Abnormal muscle tone, reflex problems, and improper positioning result in a high percentage of scoliosis. Approximately one third have scoliosis and can benefit from the exercises and bracing described in Chapter 14 on postures. Nonambulatory persons are at greatest risk.

Foot deformities are common, presumably because insufficient attention is given to stretching the tight calf muscles and Achilles tendon (heel cord). *Equinovalgus* (abnormal plantar flexion, eversion, and pronation) is associated with ambulatory spastic diplegia, whereas *equinovarus* (abnormal plantar flexion, inversion, and supination) occurs most often in hemiplegia and nonambulatory persons with total involvement. *In both conditions, activities requiring toe pointing are contraindicated.* Dorsiflexion games like walking up (but not down) steep, inclined boards and hills should be devised. In contrast, ambulatory persons with athetosis tend to have a dorsiflexed valgus foot position.

Attitudinal Barriers

The multidisabled profiles of persons with CP result in attitudinal barriers that make social acceptance especially difficult. Research shows that persons with CP are ranked last or next to last as friendship choices when several disabilities are compared (Aufsesser, 1982; Tripp, 1988). This affects success in mainstream activities, self-concept, and motivation. Educational programming must therefore focus on attitudes and seek to ameliorate social delays and associated deficits in play and game knowledges and strategies (Brown, 1987).

Fitness and CP

Little is known about fitness of individuals with CP because widespread differences in Classes 1 to 8 tend to mask results when research is undertaken. As part of Project UNIQUE (see Chapter 13), Short and Winnick (1986) compared 309 individuals with CP to 1,192 AB adolescents, ages 10 to 17 years, and reported significant differences on all test items except skinfold measures. Items included sit-ups, leg raises, trunk raises, grip strength, flexed arm hang, pull-ups, standing broad jumps, and sit-and-reach. Interestingly, the subjects with CP generally did not improve with age, as is the expected developmental trend. Also, expected gender differences were not found on many of the items. Follow-up research, which compared persons with CP/MR dual diagnosis with CP-only diagnosis, indicated no significant difference (Winnick & Short, 1991).

Body build differences may affect fitness measures. Children with CP tend to be short for their age and to have reduced body cell mass and increased body water (Shephard, 1990). Allowance for these differences indicates that the aerobic power of well-trained persons with CP may be essentially normal, even though it is typically reported as 10 to 30% below normal standards.

Spasticity, athetosis, and exaggerated reflex action are associated with mechanical inefficiency and tremendous expenditure of energy, even on easy motor tasks. This helps to explain why weight is not typically a problem. Because persons with CP require more time than average to perform activities of daily living (ADL) and to travel to school or work, little time or energy is left at the end of the day for strenuous activities. When asked to prioritize physical education goals, many persons with CP select motor and leisure skills. Once

FIGURE   25.14

Illustrative orthoses.

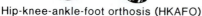

Hip-knee-ankle-foot orthosis (HKAFO)   Parapodium   Metal KAFO   Metal AFO   Plastic AFO

such skills are learned and people are socialized into sport, fitness training becomes more meaningful.

Flexibility has long been the most important fitness goal in CP, but athletes are interested also in strength and aerobic training (Jones, 1988). USCPAA sanctions power-lifting as one of its competitive sports and encourages weight training, especially free weights, Nautilus, and Universal (Cusimano & Davis, 1988). Research indicates that athletes can engage in a 10-week circuit-training strength program (2 to 3 days a week), supplemented by flexibility training, with no loss of ROM except at wrist and ankle joints, areas not given attention (Holland & Steadward, 1990). Muscle groups of every joint should be stretched daily in conjunction with strength training. This includes muscles not involved in strength training because spasticity is a total body response.

Sports and Aquatics

The first international games for persons with CP were held in 1968 in France. Sport groups have been testing activities and identifying those in which persons with CP have the most opportunity for success for almost 20 years. In general, persons with CP perform better in individual sports than in team activities.

Team Sports

Only three team sports are conducted by USCPAA: soccer, team handball, and boccia. Classes 6 to 8 are eligible to compete in *ambulatory soccer,* which is played (with only a few exceptions) according to the rules of AB soccer. The game is coed, with seven players on a team; these must include at least one Class 6 and no more than four Class 8 athletes. The game consists of two equal periods of 25 min each.

Team handball (a wheelchair sport) is a unique combination of soccer and basketball designed for Classes 1 to 6. Nine players are on each team; these must include four persons from Classes 1 to 3 and 6. The remaining players are made up of any combination of Classes 4 to 6. The game is played with a 10-inch playground ball and soccer-type goal that is 5 ft, 6 inches in height, 9 ft in width, and 4 ft in depth. Protective headgear is recommended. The playing area should be on a floor or concrete slab not smaller than a regulation basketball court. The game is coed, with all players required to stay in their chairs for the 25-min halves. Only Class 1 athletes can use motorized chairs.

Boccia, played with leather balls of about baseball size, can be either a team or an individual sport. Balls can be given impetus by throwing, rolling, kicking, or assistive device. Figure 25.15 illustrates this game. Although popular in Europe, boccia is just beginning to be known in the United States. Indoor adapted boccia sets, with game rules, can be ordered through USCPAA. All balls except the target ball (which is smaller) weigh 275 g and are 26.5 cm in diameter.

Individual Sports

Individual sports in which persons with CP do well include archery, bowling, bicycling and tricycling, track and field, horseback riding, swimming, rifle shooting, slalom, table tennis, and powerlifting (Jones, 1988). Tables 25.2 and 25.3 indicate distances that must be achieved in swimming, slalom, track, and cycling events before persons are eligible for USCPAA adult competition. School physical education should use these distances as goals. These tables also summarize events appropriate for the different classes.

Use of PFDs is permitted when teaching persons with CP to swim. Most Class 1 and 2 athletes, because of severe spasticity, need PFDs throughout their lives, regardless of how well they learn to swim. A few internationally ranked swimmers are exceptions to this generalization, but independence from PFDs is not a realistic goal for most Class 1 and 2 athletes. *Speed* is the goal rather than good form, although increasing ROM improves form as well as speed. Flippers are not allowed. Team relays are popular.

Tricycles, bicycles, and horses offer students a chance for freedom not possible in wheelchairs. Stationary tricycles and bicycles should be available in adapted physical education resource rooms and for winter use. Three-wheeled adult cycles are available through Sears and other popular chain stores. Like AB students, every child with CP should own his or her cycle and master this means of locomotion. Often, adaptations must be made to tricycles and bicycles; special seats can be used, and feet can be attached to pedals with Velcro straps.

FIGURE 25.15

Boccia is a bowling-type game specifically for Class 1 and 2 athletes. A team is comprised of three members, one of whom must be Class 1. The object is to give impetus to the ball so that it lands as close as possible to the white target ball. Each player has two balls per round. A team game is six rounds. (*A*) Class 1 athlete with no functional use of arms or legs uses head pointer to give impetus to the ball. (*B*) Class 2 athletes either kick or throw the ball into play, depending upon whether they are 2L or 2U.

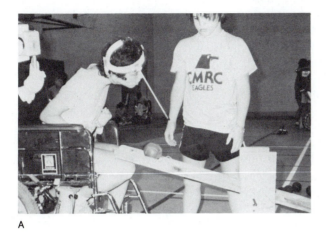

A

B

Table 25.2
Swimming events in USCPAA.

Event	Nonambulatory Classes				Ambulatory Classes			
	1	2	3	4	5	6	7	8
25-m freestyle	×	×						
25-m backstroke	×	×						
50-m freestyle	×	×	×	×	×	×	×	×
50-m backstroke	×	×	×	×	×	×	×	
50-m breaststroke			×	×	×	×	×	
50-m butterfly			×	×				
100-m freestyle			×	×	×	×	×	×
100-m backstroke			×	×	×	×	×	×
100-m breaststroke			×	×	×	×	×	×
100-m butterfly								×
200-m freestyle			×	×	×	×	×	×
200-m backstyle						×		×
400-m freestyle				×	×		×	×
800-m freestyle				×	×	×	×	×
1500-m freestyle				×	×	×	×	×
3 × 50 individual medley		×				×	×	
4 × 50 individual medley					×	×		×

Note. In the United States, Class 1 and 2 can compete with and without personal flotation devices (PFDs). International rules do not allow a PFD.

Table 25.3
Slalom, track, and cycling events for USCPAA.

Event	Nonambulatory Classes					Ambulatory Classes			
	1	2L	2U	3	4	5	6	7	8
Slalom	×	×	×	×	×				
60-m weave	×								
20-m			×						
60-m			×						
100-m		×	×	×	×	×	×	×	×
200-m		×	×	×	×	×	×	×	×
400-m		×		×	×	×	×	×	×
800-m		×			×		×	×	×
1,500-m					×			×	×
Cross country, 3,000-m							×	×	×
4 × 100		×	×	×	×		×	×	×
Tricycle									
1,500-m		×		×		×	×		
3,000-m						×	×		
5,000-m						×	×		
Bicycle									
1,500-m						×	×		
3,000-m						×	×		
5,000-m						×	×	×	×
10,000-m								×	×
20,000-m								×	×
Total	*2*	*7*	*6*	*6*	*7*	*9*	*12*	*10*	*10*

Note. All wheelchairs are manual except Class 1.

Table 25.4
Boccia, bowling, and field events for USCPAA.

| | Nonambulatory Classes | | | | Ambulatory Classes | | | |
Event	1	2	3	4	5	6	7	8
Boccia	×	×						
Chute bowling with assistant	×	×						
Chute bowling, no assistant			×			×		
Regulation bowling				×	×		×	×
Soft discus		×						
Precision throw		×						
Distance soft shot		×						
High toss		×						
Distance kick		×						
Thrust kick		×						
Shot put		×	×	×	×	×	×	×
Club throw		×	×	×	×	×		
Discus		×	×	×	×	×	×	×
Javelin				×	×	×	×	×
Long jump							×	×

Note. Class 2L do the two kicking events; 2U do the throws.

Table 25.5
Official equipment for sports for individuals with cerebral palsy.

Event	Implement	Weight or Design
Distance, precision, and high throws	Soft shot	5 oz (150 g)
Thrust kick	Medicine ball	6 lb (3 kg)
Distance kick	Playground ball	13 inches
Club throw	Club	1 lb, 14 inches long
Discus	Standard women's discus	2 lb (1 kg), 180 mm diameter
Shot put	Shot put	4, 6, or 8 lb, depending on classification
Javelin	Standard women's javelin except for Class 8 males	
Boccia	Leather-covered boccia ball	275 g, 26.5 cm diameter
Ambulatory soccer	Regulation soccer ball	14 to 16 oz
Team handball	Playground ball	10 inches
Weight lifting	Universal weight machine, nonprogressive bench	
Bowling	With or without retractable handle chute (ramp)	Varies; 10 lb for Classes 1 and 2

Note. The soft-shot *precision throw* uses a ground target with eight concentric rings. The athlete has six throws from a distance of 6 ft from the center of the bull's-eye. The bull's-eye counts 16 points. Each ring away from it counts 2 points less than the previous. The soft-shot *high throw* uses high-jump standards, with the bar set at 3 ft and raised 6 inches at a time. The competitor is at least 1 mm from the bar and has three throws per height. See chapter 11, page 298.

The slalom, a wheelchair race against time in which persons follow a clearly marked obstacle course, is a good school activity. Four components of the slalom course are (a) one 360° circle around a cone, (b) one 360° gate and three reverse gates, (c) one figure eight around three cones, and (d) one ramp. These components can be combined in various ways, or USCPAA can be contacted for a copy of official slalom courses.

Field events are more popular in USCPAA than any other activity. These also offer great promise in school physical education. In early childhood, beanbags are typically used. By age 7, terminology changes to soft shot. This is because of the normalization principle; beanbag activities are not appropriate for older children. Regulation-size soft shots are available through USCPAA. For Class 3 and above, instruction should focus on the club, shot put, and discus. The javelin is appropriate for Class 4 and above (see Figures 25.16 and 25.17). Of the official implements, the club is the easiest to handle.

Softball throwing and catching are deemphasized except for Classes 7 and 8 because these are not official events. Classes 7 and 8, when in integrated physical education instruction, may have limited success in softball games. In general, however, catching is difficult to teach (Rintala, Lytinen, & Dunn, 1990) and takes away time better spent on activities more suited to functional ability. Recreational sports that offer success are adaptations using clubs, sticks, and paddles.

Bowling, like field events, is a sport of choice because it permits many adaptations. The ball can be delivered from a sitting or standing position. Persons with fisted hands can use a ramp (also called a chute), with or without an assistant. The assistant does nothing but follow instructions (voice, gesture, head nod) on how to position the ramp or ball. Many bowlers use balls with retractable handles (see Appendix G).

Tables 25.4 and 25.5 summarize events that require equipment and describe adaptations. USCPAA sport clubs can help in obtaining equipment. Parents should be encouraged to begin taking children to USCPAA events at ages 3 to 4 because parents then learn about equipment and begin home programs. It also helps parents to understand differences in CP and MR and to socialize children into sports adapted to their special needs.

The national headquarters for USCPAA is in transition. Contact Jerry McCole at the Western Regional Office, 3810 W. NW Highway, #205, Dallas, TX 75220.

FIGURE   25.16

Throwing events for Classes 3–4 are the same as for Classes 5–8 except for the javelin, which is inappropriate for Class 3. (*A,B*) Class 3 athletes, Alfred Dore and Manyon Lyons, international competitors. Note that Class 3 athletes need waist and leg straps for support and hold onto their chairs during the release. (*C,D*) Class 4 athletes Rene Rivera and Joan Blalark, international competitors, do not need straps or arm support.

A

B

C

D

25   Cerebral Palsy, Stroke, and Traumatic Brain Injury   **639**

FIGURE 25.17

Class 6 athletes have more motor control problems than Classes 4–5.
Class 6 ambulates without assistive devices but typically has much
athetoid movement, which causes balance and accuracy problems.
(*A*) Class 6 athlete throwing discus. (*B*) Class 6 athlete putting shot.

A

B

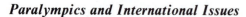

Paralympics and International Issues

Since 1978, athletes with CP have competed internationally
against each other, using a functional classification system
that assured equal opportunity. At the 1992 Paralympics in
Barcelona, however, the new integrated, functional classification system (see Chapter 23, page 568) required athletes
with CP to compete against athletes with spinal paralysis and
les autres conditions. Many experts believe that this new
system is unfair to people with CP because it does not adequately address associated dysfunctions that are unique to
upper neuron disorders (Richter, Adams-Muskett, Ferrara,
& McCann, 1992). Few athletes with CP won medals in
track, field, or swimming at the 1992 Paralympics. What are
possible solutions? Should we accept the new, integrated
system or seek to change it?

Another international issue is the social acceptance
of people with CP as elite athletes. Although the Paralympics movement began in 1960, athletes with CP were excluded until 1980, when ambulatory athletes were invited to
Arnhem, Holland. In 1984, nonambulatory athletes with CP
finally gained access to Paralympic competition. Many countries still do not enter athletes with CP into the Paralympics.
As a result women and nonambulatory athletes are severely
underrepresented.

To combat this problem, more efforts must be directed all over the world to socializing children with CP
into sport and providing lifespan opportunities for self-
actualization through both competitive and recreational sport
(Lugo, Sherrill, & Pizarro, 1992; Sherrill & Rainbolt, 1986;
1988). Also, more serious efforts must be directed toward
fitness training that generalizes to sport (Pitetti, Fernandez,
& Lanciault, 1991). How can you help?

References

American Physical Therapy Association. (1983). *Head injuries: Monograph.* Alexandria, VA: Author.

Aufsesser, P. M. (1982). Comparison of the attitudes of physical education, recreation, and special education majors toward the disabled. *American Corrective Therapy Journal, 36,* 35–41.

Basmajian, J. V., & Wolf, S. (1990). *Therapeutic exercise* (5th ed.). Baltimore: Williams & Wilkins.

Bleck, E., & Nagel, D. (Eds.). (1982). *Physically handicapped children: A medical atlas for teachers* (2nd ed.). New York: Grune & Stratton.

Bobath, K. (1980). *A neurophysiological basis for the treatment of cerebral palsy.* Philadelphia: J. B. Lippincott.

Brown, A. (1987). *Active games for children with movement problems.* London: Harper & Row.

Brunnstrom, S. (1970). *Movement therapy in hemiplegia: A neurophysiological approach.* New York: Harper & Row.

Burd, R., & Grass, K. (1987). Strapping to enhance athletic performance of wheelchair competitors with cerebral palsy. *Palaestra, 3* (2), 28–32.

Cusimano, S., & Davis, R. (1988). Weight training: The key to individual event success. In J. A. Jones (Ed.), *Training guide to cerebral palsy sports* (3rd ed.) (pp. 121–136). Champaign, IL: Human Kinetics.

Davis, R., Gehlsen, G., & Wilkerson, J. (1990). Biomechanical analysis of Class II cerebral palsied wheelchair athletes. *Adapted Physical Activity Quarterly, 1* (1), 52–61.

Edwards, M. S. B., & Hoffman, H. (Eds.). (1989). *Cerebral vascular disease in children and adults.* Baltimore: Williams & Wilkins.

Farber, S. D. (1982). *Neurorehabilitation: A multisensory approach.* Philadelphia: W. G. Saunders.

Finnie, N. R. (1974). *Handling the young cerebral palsied child at home* (2nd ed.). New York: E. P. Dutton.

Guyton, A. C. (1981). *Basic human neurophysiology* (3rd ed.). Philadelphia: W. B. Saunders.

Hellebrandt, F., & Waterland, J. C. (1961). The influence of athetoid cerebral palsy on the execution of sports skills: Tennis and golf. *Physical Therapy Review, 41,* 257–262.

Hellebrandt, F., Waterland, J. C., & Walters, C. E. (1961). The influence of athetoid cerebral palsy on the execution of sports skills: Bowling. *Physical Therapy Review, 41,* 106–113.

Holland, L. J., & Steadward, R. D. (1990). Effects of resistance and flexibility training on strength, spasticity/muscle tone, and range of motion of elite athletes with cerebral palsy. *Palaestra, 6* (4), 27–31.

Individuals with Disabilities Education Act (IDEA). (Enacted in 1990). Distributed through The National Association of State Directors of Special Education, Inc., P.O. Box 59105, Potomac, MD 20859–9105.

Isler, W. (1984). Stroke in childhood and adolescence. *European Neurology, 23,* 421–424.

Jones, J. A. (1988). *Training guide to cerebral palsy sports* (3rd ed.). Champaign, IL: Human Kinetics.

Kottke, F. J., & Lehmann, J. (1990). *Krusen's handbook of physical medicine and rehabilitation* (4th ed.). Philadelphia: W. B. Saunders.

Levitt, S. (1985). *Treatment of cerebral palsy and motor delay* (2nd ed.). Boston: Blackwell Scientific Publications.

Lugo, A. A., Sherrill, C., & Pizarro, A. L. (1992). Use of a sport socialization inventory with cerebral palsied youth. *Perceptual and Motor Skills, 74,* 203–208.

Miller, S. E., & Schaumberg, K. (1988). Physical education activities for children with severe cerebral palsy. *Teaching Exceptional Children, 20* (2), 9–11.

Moucha, S. (1991). The disabled female athlete as role model. *Journal of Physical Education, Recreation, and Dance, 62* (3), 37–38.

Netter, F. H. (1986). *The CIBA collection of medical illustrations: Volume 1, Nervous system.* West Caldwell, NJ: CIBA Pharmaceutical Company.

Pitetti, K., Fernandez, J., & Lanciault, M. (1991). Feasibility of an exercise program for adults with cerebral palsy: A pilot study. *Adapted Physical Activity Quarterly, 8* (4), 333–341.

Richter, K., Adams-Mushett, C., Ferrana, M., & McCann, B. C. (1992). Integrated swimming classification: A faulted system. *Adapted Physical Activity Quarterly, 9* (1), 5–13.

Rintala, P., Lytinen, H., & Dunn, J. M. (1990). Influence of a physical activity program on children with cerebral palsy: A single subject design. *Pediatric Exercise Science, 2,* 46–56.

Roach, E. S., Garcia, J. C., & McLean, W. (1984). Cerebrovascular disease in children. *American Family Physician, 30,* 215–227.

Robinault, I. (1973). *Functional aids for the multiply handicapped.* New York: Harper & Row.

Shephard, R. J. (1990). *Fitness in special populations.* Champaign, IL: Human Kinetics.

Sherrill, C., & Rainbolt, W. (1986). Sociological perspectives of cerebral palsy sports. *Palaestra, 2* (4), 20–26, 50.

Sherrill, C., & Rainbolt, W. (1988). Self-actualization profiles of male able-bodied and cerebral palsied athletes. *Adapted Physical Activity Quarterly, 5* (2), 108–119.

Short, F. X., & Winnick, J. P. (1986). The performance of adolescents with cerebral palsy on measures of physical fitness. In C. Sherrill (Ed.), *Sport and disabled athletes* (pp. 239–244). Champaign, IL: Human Kinetics.

Stanley, F., & Blair, E. (1984). Postnatal risk factors in the cerebral palsies. In F. Stanley & E. Alberman (Eds.), *The epidemiology of the cerebral palsies* (pp. 135–149). Philadelphia: J. B. Lippincott.

Sugden, D. A., & Keogh, J. (1990). *Problems in movement skill development.* Columbia, SC: University of South Carolina Press.

Tecklin, J. (1989). *Pediatric physical therapy.* Philadelphia: J. B. Lippincott.

Thompson, G., Rubin, I., & Bilenker, R. (Eds.). (1983). *Comprehensive management of cerebral palsy.* New York: Grune & Stratton.

Tripp, A. (1988). Comparison of attitudes of regular and adapted physical educators toward disabled individuals. *Perceptual and Motor Skills, 66,* 425–426.

Winnick, J. P., & Short, F. X. (1991). A comparison of the physical fitness of nonretarded and mildly mentally retarded adolescents with cerebral palsy. *Adapted Physical Activity Quarterly, 8,* 43–56.

Ylvisaker, M. (Ed.). (1985). *Head injury rehabilitation: Children and adolescents.* San Diego: College Hill.

CHAPTER

26

Deaf and Hard-of-Hearing Conditions

FIGURE 26.1

The Rome School for the Deaf has its own way of sideline conversation.

After you have studied this chapter, you should be able to:

1. Describe Gallaudet University, deaf sport, and the deaf community. Identify organizations for the deaf and outstanding deaf persons and discuss relevance to teaching physical education-recreation.

2. Differentiate between deafness and hard-of-hearing conditions. Discuss language and communication in relation to each, with an emphasis on the age that hearing loss was sustained and other factors that affect decision making.

3. Identify three approaches to teaching communication skills, discuss controversy, and state your own beliefs.

4. Explain hearing loss in terms of the three attributes of sound. Relate your explanation to understanding test results and adapting physical education instruction for different hearing loss classifications.

5. Develop three make-believe case studies in which you demonstrate understanding of (a) classification of hearing loss in decibels, (b) causes of hearing loss, (c) congenital and acquired conditions, (d) role of parents in development, and (e) probable physical education performance level.

6. Create two games for teaching persons the parts of the ear, how hearing loss occurs, and/or other concepts in this chapter.

7. Using your case studies or those assigned, write physical education IEPs. State and justify placement, goals, and objectives.

8. Develop an instructional unit or lesson plans to guide improvement of vestibular dysfunction and balance.

9. Explain speechreading, cued speech, different kinds of sign language, personal hearing aids, assistive listening devices and systems, and telecommunication devices for the deaf.

10. Discuss existing and needed research. Show evidence of reading research published in the last 3 years.

Deaf and hard-of-hearing (HH) students often excel in physical education. At Gallaudet University in Washington, DC, the only liberal arts college in the world for persons who are deaf, student interest in athletics is so high that men and women engage in several intercollegiate sports. This university, founded in 1864, is recognized worldwide for its leadership in sports, education, and sign language. The football huddle was invented at Gallaudet so opponents could not see the game strategies being communicated through sign. Here, too, was the famous revolt of March 1988, when students refused to attend classes until the Board of Regents appointed a deaf president who could use sign and would advocate for rights (Sacks, 1989). I. King Jordan, the new president, simultaneously signed and spoke his acceptance speech:

The world has watched the deaf community come of age. We will no longer accept limits on what we can achieve. . . . We know that deaf people can do anything hearing people can except hear.

The Gallaudet Modern Dance Group has performed in Europe and throughout the United States. Says Peter Wisher, founder of the group, "The majority of audiences are composed of hearing people, but they soon forget the dancers are deaf. They become tremendously involved with the kids, especially during the numbers using abstracted sign language" (Carney, 1971, p. 21).

Some deaf persons, like Denver Broncos football player Kenny Walker (previously University of Nebraska) and baseball player William "Dummy" Hoy (1862–1961) have gained recognition as outstanding members of hearing teams. Hoy played with both American and National leagues and instigated the development of umpire hand signals. More and more people who are deaf or HH are in mainstream physical education and sports. Some, however, opt to participate in deaf sport only, where most athletes sign (see Figure 26.1).

Deaf Sport and Deaf Community

Deaf sport, a term created by individuals who are deaf, is explained by David Stewart (1991) in his excellent book *Deaf Sport: The Impact of Sports Within the Deaf Community:*

Deaf sport is a social institution within which Deaf people exercise their right to self-determination, competition, and socialization surrounding Deaf sport activities. The magnitude and the complexity of Deaf sport reflects many of the dimensions of being deaf in a hearing society. In this sense, Deaf sport is a microcosm of the Deaf community (p. 2). . . . Deaf sport emphasizes the honor of being Deaf, whereas society tends to focus on the adversity of deafness. (p. 1)

Stewart, by birth a Canadian, is a professor at Michigan State University. See Chapter 2 for more information on Stewart.

Deaf sport refers to all of the sport opportunities provided by the *deaf community,* a term coined by people who are deaf to describe their cultural and linguistic separateness from the hearing, speaking world. Over the centuries, deaf persons have tended to cluster together and to take care of one another's needs. Their language is sign, and until recently, few hearing persons knew much about them. Deaf persons do not advocate person-first terminology. That is why this chapter refers to deaf people rather than people with deafness.

The rules, strategies, and skills of deaf sport are not adapted except for communication modes. Modifications are made only in starting and stopping signals and in the ways officials communicate with players. Deaf sport internationally is governed by the Comite International des Sports des Sourds (CISS), founded in France in 1924. The English translation of this is International Committee on Silent Sports, but the commonly used abbreviation (CISS) is derived from the French name. Summer World Games for the Deaf began in 1924, almost a quarter of a century before international competition was initiated for other special populations. The American Athletic Association for the Deaf (AAAD) was founded at the end of World War II (1945), long before organizations for athletes with disabilities were conceived. Every nation has a deaf community and deaf sport (e.g., the Canadian Deaf Sports Association, 1987).

Until 1991, the CISS did not associate itself with the worldwide sport for disabled athlete movement. Its resistance was based on the philosophy that deaf sport is unique and does not in any way relate to disability. Affiliation in 1991 did not represent a change in philosophy but was a political move in support of other special populations. The World Games for the Deaf will continue to be held at a different site from the Paralympics.

World Games for the Deaf, like the Olympics, are held every 2 years. Summer Games are held on a schedule that runs 1993, 1997, and so on, and Winter Games are held on a schedule that runs 1991, 1995, and so on. In 1985, the Summer Games were conducted in the United States for the second time; over 2,500 athletes from 30 nations competed in 13 different sports.

To be eligible for participation in deaf sport, athletes must have a hearing loss of 55 decibels (dB) or greater in the better ear. Deaf athletes are not classified according to severity of hearing loss. Hearing aids are not permitted during competition.

Table 26.1 presents the eight individual and five team summer sports in which deaf athletes can compete internationally. Competition in the Winter World Games includes alpine and nordic skiing, speed skating, and ice hockey. Additionally, deaf athletes have regional and national competitions. News about deaf sports is regularly published in magazines called *The Deaf American* and *Deaf Sports Review*. There is also a growing body of research (Stewart, McCarthy, & Robinson, 1988; Stewart, Robinson, & McCarthy, 1991).

In addition to AAAD, there are many other sport organizations for persons who are deaf. The oldest of these are the National Deaf Bowling Association and the U.S. Deaf Skiers Association, established in 1963 and 1968, respectively. Illustrative other organizations are the World Recreation Association of the Deaf (WRAD), American Deaf Volleyball Association, American Hearing Impaired Hockey Association, Deaf Athletic Federation of the United States, and National Racquetball Association of the Deaf. In Canada, there are several ice hockey organizations, and winter sports like curling are emphasized. Addresses of these organizations change frequently. For information, contact the

Table 26.1
Summer sports in which deaf persons compete internationally.

Individual	Team
Cycling (men)	Soccer (men)
Wrestling, Greco Roman and freestyle (men)	Water polo (men)
Swimming (men and women)	Handball (men)
Track and field (men and women)	Volleyball (men and women)
Tennis (men and women)	Basketball (men and women)
Table tennis (men and women)	
Badminton (men and women)	
Shooting (men and women)	

Athletic Department at Gallaudet University or the National Association of the Deaf, 814 Thayer Avenue, Silver Spring, MD 20910.

Definitions and Concepts

What do we call persons with a hearing loss? Many such individuals do not consider themselves disabled and prefer to be thought of as a cultural and linguistic minority (Butterfield, 1991; Stewart, 1991). They are often proficient in both sign and English and wonder why so much of the world can communicate only in one way. In particular, most world-class athletes who are deaf take this stance. In contrast, adults adjusting to a hearing impairment may mourn their loss in ways similar to persons with physical disabilities. Obviously, there are many individual differences.

Hearing loss is correctly termed *deaf* or *hard of hearing*, mainly depending on the degree of loss but sometimes on the communication ability of an individual. These are categories specified by both federal legislation and policy-making organizations. The term *deaf* may be used to encompass all conditions in which the loss is significant, as in the name of the American Athletic Association for the Deaf (AAAD) and the Canadian Deaf Sports Association (CDSA). Or a sharp distinction can be made, usually for funding or school purposes. *Deaf* describes a person who is unable to understand speech through use of the ears alone, with or without hearing aids. *Hard of hearing* (HH) is a condition that makes difficult, but does not prevent, the understanding of speech through use of the ears alone, with or without hearing aids. The generic term *hearing impairment* is losing favor.

The practice of linking auditory and visual deficits and discussing them in the same chapter or context as sensory impairments is now outdated. The conditions are much more different than alike. Blindness is primarily a disability of mobility, whereas deafness, if it is considered a disability, is a matter of communication and social acceptance.

Deafness is associated more closely with speech impairment and specific learning disability than other special education categories. About 6 to 8% of deaf and HH children

FIGURE 26.2

Dr. Stephen Butterfield, well-known researcher at the University of Maine, signs test instructions to a child.

have diagnosed learning disabilities (Cherow, 1985; Martin, 1991). In general, deaf persons have normal intelligence and perform as well on tasks that measure thinking as their hearing peers. Academic achievement depends largely on educational opportunity. Many deaf and HH people have problems with reading and writing beyond the fifth-grade level.

Language and Communication

The terms *language* and *communication* should not be used interchangeably. Language can be (a) inner, (b) receptive, or (c) expressive (see Chapter 18). Communication is typically described as verbal or nonverbal. Verbal methods are (a) oral, (b) written, and (c) sign (i.e., any modality that uses words). Nonverbal methods are facial expressions, postures, body language, or gestures. Nonverbal also refers to silent demonstrations.

Persons who are deaf or HH communicate in many ways, depending on (a) the age that the loss was sustained, (b) training, (c) ability, and (d) cultural affiliation. They may read lips, a skill called *speechreading,* or rely on *sign language,* a manual communication system in which fingers, hands, facial expressions, and body movements are used to convey meaning (see Figure 26.2). There are many forms of signing: American Sign Language (ASL), also called Ameslan; Pidgin Sign English (PSE), also called Siglish; and Manually Coded English (MCE). Of these, ASL is the recognized language of deaf and HH people who communicate manually. ASL has its own grammar and syntax, so sentences are not constructed in the same way that words are ordered in English.

Fingerspelling is a system in which a particular hand position is used for each letter of the alphabet. Each word is spelled letter by letter; because it is slower than signing, it is rarely used by itself. Fingerspelling may be the communication system of choice with hearing persons who do not know sign or with deaf-blind persons who cannot see sign. With the latter, the hand positions are made in the palm of the recipient's hand.

When hearing loss occurs before age 3, learning to speak English is slow and laborious. In older children, who lose the ability to hear their own speech and monitor pronunciation of new words, speaking may gradually become less easy. Problems occur because many listeners will not take the time to become familiar with a different speech pattern. This is the same kind of discrimination experienced by foreigners who speak English with an accent (or poorly).

Approaches to Communication

Three approaches to teaching communication skills are (a) manual, which includes fingerspelling and signing; (b) oral or speech only; and (c) total communication, which combines the best of manual and oral methods. Most school systems today use total communication. In the past, however, deaf education was characterized by bitter controversy over the better method, oral or manual. This intensified in the late 1800s, with Alexander Graham Bell (the inventor of the telephone) championing the oral method and Edward Gallaudet (founder and director of Gallaudet University) advocating the manual method. Both of these men had deaf mothers, but different attitudes prevailed in their households. Eventually, the oral method won, and sign was not taught in most classrooms until the 1970s, when total communication became the accepted philosophical approach.

Although sign was not allowed in the classroom, it continued to be used in everyday life. Many deaf people have always regarded sign as their major language, and today sign is widely accepted as a language. Many movies and videotapes depict communication and other issues. Among these, *Children of a Lesser God* (originally a play) is perhaps best known because Marlee Matlin, who is deaf, won an Oscar in 1987 as best actress for her role. Matlin signed her acceptance speech but later used her voice in various public appearances, thereby drawing criticism from some deaf persons. Since 1991 Matlin has starred in a television series called *Reasonable Doubt.* In contrast, Kitty O'Neal, who holds the world speed records for women in water skiing and various car racing events, defends the oral method in the video presenting her life story.

Sound and Vibration

Sound waves are really vibrations. They start at a particular point and spread, much like a rock tossed into a pond makes circles of waves. Most people both hear and feel vibrations. Total deafness means vibrations can only be felt. Consider a rock concert, especially the bass tones. Sounds are conducted to the inner ear through both air and bone conduction. Vibrations, however, are felt by the whole body and convey a basic beat or rhythm.

Central to the understanding of hearing loss are the three attributes of sound: intensity, frequency, and timbre or tone. Figure 26.3 depicts an audiogram that shows how intensity (the vertical axis) and frequency (the horizontal axis) are used to describe hearing loss. Perfect hearing would be noted by shading the 0 line across all frequencies. The loss depicted is a mild conductive one that can be simulated by placing your fingers in both ears. Figure 26.3 shows that the

FIGURE   26.3

Audiogram findings for mild conductive loss superimposed on illustration of various environmental and speech sounds at different frequencies and intensities.

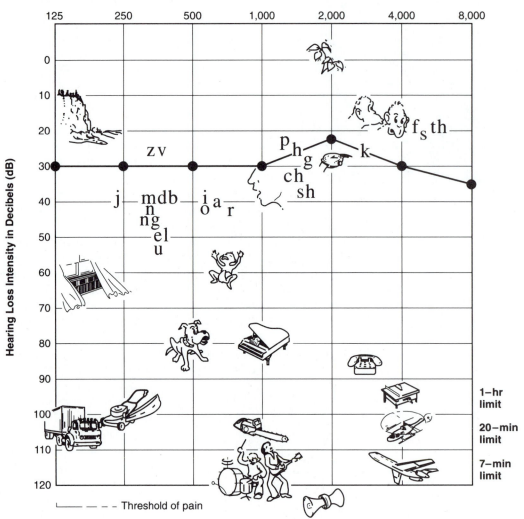

Frequency in Cycles per Second (Hz)

speech sounds *f, s,* and *th* at high frequencies (pitches) are the first to be lost, along with *p, h, z,* and *v* at lower frequencies. To better understand audiograms and hearing classifications, let's consider the attributes of sound.

Intensity

Intensity refers to the perception of loudness and softness. The unit of measurement that expresses the intensity of a sound is the *decibel* (dB). This term is named for Alexander Graham Bell and literally means one tenth of a bell. A sound at 0 level is barely audible. Speech can be heard from a distance of 10 to 20 ft when the loudness is 35 to 65 dB, depending on the pitch. When the intensity of sound ranges above 100 dB the sound may become painful.

Frequency

Frequency refers to the perception of high and low pitch. It is measured in terms of hertz (Hz). Most human beings can perceive frequencies from about 20 to 20,000 Hz. The au-

diogram includes only the frequencies between 125 and 8,000, since these are the most important in daily communication.

Three of these frequencies—500, 1,000, and 2,000 Hz—are emphasized in hearing tests. For instance, persons who do not hear frequencies above 2,000 Hz have difficulty in recognizing such high-frequency sounds as the letters *s, z, sh, zh, th* as in think, *th* as in that, *ch* as in chair, *j* as in Joe, *p, b, t, d, f, v,* and *h*.

Check your understanding of pitch on a piano. The lowest note on the keyboard (*A*) is 30 Hz. Middle *C* is 256 Hz. The highest *C* on the keyboard is 4,000 Hz.

Timbre or Tone

Timbre refers to all of the qualities besides intensity and frequency that enable us to distinguish between sounds, voices, and musical instruments. It is sometimes conceptualized as the resonance quality of a sound because it depends on the number and character of the vibrating body's overtones. Hearing persons deficient in this area are called *tone deaf.*

Table 26.2
Classification of hearing loss.

Degree of Loss	Loss in Decibels	Difficulty with
Slight	25–40	Whispered speech
Mild	41–54	Normal speech at distance greater than 3 to 5 ft
Marked or moderate	55–69	Understanding loud or shouted speech at close range; group discussions
Severe	70–89	Understanding speech at close range, even when amplified
Profound	90+	Hearing most sounds, including telephone rings and musical instruments (see Figure 26.3)

Note. 55 dB or worse in one ear is the criterion for sport eligibility in AAAD.

They can distinguish between some tones but not others. Vowel and vowel combinations (diphthongs) have more easily distinguished tones than consonants.

Testing and Classifying Hearing Loss

Formal hearing tests are conducted by an audiologist or speech and hearing therapist using an instrument called an audiometer. Table 26.2 presents the most widely used system for classifying hearing loss. In general, the first three classes (slight, mild, moderate) are considered HH, and the last two (severe, profound) are considered deaf.

Hearing loss is so complex that there are many individual differences in how persons with each classification function. Table 26.2 offers generalizations about hearing and speaking limitations. There are, of course, exceptions to the rule. Many persons with a 25- to 40-dB loss can benefit from hearing aids (Roeser & Downs, 1988), but 40 dB is the more traditional criterion.

A 3- to 5-ft criterion is useful in making classroom adaptations for slight and mild losses. Students farther away than this may miss as much as 50% of class instruction if they cannot see lips. Consider how this affects learning in various physical education settings.

The moderate classification (55 to 69 dB) is of particular interest because 55 dB is the minimum criterion for eligibility to participate in AAAD activities. The 55-dB and greater loss is associated with difficulty in following and contributing to small-group conversations and class discussions. Loud or shouted speech at close range may be heard but not totally understood because of distortions and background noise. Speech training becomes imperative at this level for correct pronunciation.

The 70-dB level is the accepted criterion for distinguishing between HH and deafness. Persons partially hear speech sounds within 1 ft, but they cannot understand most of them, even with amplification. Individuals at both the severe and profound levels may need intensive training in total communication. Interpreters and/or buddy systems are helpful in communicating with hearing people, especially in group settings.

Congenital and Acquired Conditions

Ability to communicate in conventional spoken English is largely dependent upon age that hearing loss occurs. Therefore, time of onset (congenital or acquired) must be considered in both education and research. A synonym for *acquired* is *adventitiously deaf.* The terms *prelingual* and *postlingual* further specify whether loss was sustained before or after the development of language.

With congenital hearing losses, knowing whether parents are hearing or deaf and what language (sign or spoken English) dominates in the home is critical. This affects all aspects of development, especially self-esteem. Deaf children born to deaf parents typically have significantly higher self-esteem than those born to hearing parents because they are immediately accepted and begin learning language (sign) at a very young age.

Only about 10% of deaf children have deaf parents. Illustrative of such persons among the leaders in deaf sport is Donalda Ammons (1986, 1990), who has served for many years as chairperson of the U.S. World Games for the Deaf Team Committee. Ammons is Director of Foreign Study Programs at Gallaudet. Her best sports are basketball and swimming.

Hearing children are often born of deaf parents. The excellent novel *In This Sign* by Greenberg (1970) is one of several that explore relationships in families and describe growing up deaf. In it, Abel and Janice Ryder (both born deaf) marry and have hearing children and grandchildren. The television presentation of this book—*Love Is Never Silent*—is well worth renting.

Acquired hearing losses vary in severity, depending on the degree of loss and age of onset. Among the many persons with acquired hearing losses are Ludwig van Beethoven, Bernard Baruch, and Thomas Alva Edison. The last 25 years of Beethoven's life were spent in almost total deafness. His famous Ninth Symphony, the *Missa Solemnis,* and many of his piano sonatas and string quartets were composed after he became totally deaf. At his last appearance at a public concert, in 1824, Beethoven was completely oblivious to the applause of the audience acclaiming his ninth and final symphony.

Deaf-Blind Conditions

Discussion of combined deaf-blind losses, covered in this chapter in earlier editions of this book, has been moved to Chapter 27 on blindness. This is because persons who are deaf-blind typically engage in sports under the auspices of the U.S. Association for Blind Athletes (USABA) rather than AAAD. Sight and hearing are seldom both totally lost. With regard to educational placement, knowing which loss is the greater and when each occurred is important. If the condition is prelingual, training in speech and language (i.e., deaf education) will probably be given more emphasis than mobility.

FIGURE 26.4

Three parts of the ear shown in relation to locations of disorder.
Descriptors for air conduction and sensorineural losses are summarized.

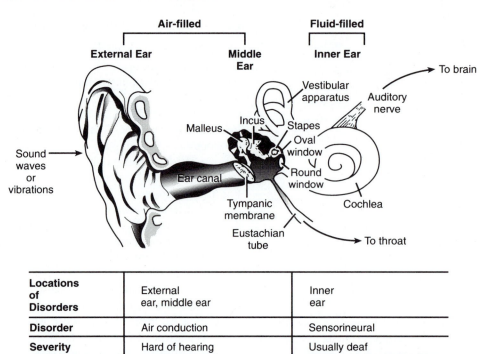

Locations of Disorders	External ear, middle ear	Inner ear
Disorder	Air conduction	Sensorineural
Severity	Hard of hearing	Usually deaf
Main Concern	Amplification	Distortion and amplification
Frequencies Affected	All, called a flat loss	Greatest for high frequencies and consonants
Speech Tendency	Too soft, otherwise OK	Too loud, words often mispronounced
Hearing Aid	Prognosis good	Some, but of limited help

Types and Causes of Hearing Loss

There are three types of hearing loss: (a) conductive, (b) sensorineural, and (c) mixed. Visualizing the three parts of the ear and the causes of disorders in each part is helpful (see Figure 26.4). The Greek word for ear is *otos*, so inflammation of the ear is *otitis*. The instrument used in an ear examination is an *otoscope*.

Conductive Loss

Conductive loss is diminished sound traveling through the air passages of the external and middle ear. Putting your finger in your ear canal creates about a 25-dB conductive loss. You can still hear, but not as well. A conductive loss results in an HH condition, not deafness.

Disorders of the external ear center around the size and shape of the ear canal. Occasionally, infants are born without a canal (atresia) or with one that is abnormally narrow. Usually, however, problems are caused by obstruction (impacted earwax), injury, or infection (external otitis) and respond well to treatment.

Disorders of the middle ear are more serious, often resulting in permanent damage. The middle ear is the small space between the eardrum (tympanic membrane) and the bony capsule of the inner ear. It includes the ossicles (malleus, incus, stapes), the small bones shaped, respectively, like a hammer, anvil, and stirrup that transmit sound waves to the inner ear much like a blacksmith once worked on horseshoes with a hammer. The middle ear also contains the Eustachian tube, which connects the nasopharynx passageway with the throat, and is much affected by colds, sinus infections, and allergies.

Inflammation of the middle ear, called *otitis media*, accounts for more conductive disorders than any other condition. Young children are especially at risk, because 76 to 95% have at least one ear infection before age 2. There are several kinds of otitis media. Some are *acute*, characterized by severe pain and swelling. Others are *chronic*, with persons adjusting to the discomfort and hardly aware of the fluid accumulation behind the eardrum. Many adults with a childhood history of colds, asthma, and respiratory infections do not realize the danger of this fluid until too late.

Otitis media (or any condition that causes the tubes to swell or clog) prevents the Eustachian tubes from performing their functions: (a) ventilating and keeping dry the middle air cavity and (b) equalizing air pressure on the two sides of the eardrum. If corrective measures are not taken, damage occurs. Antibiotics and other medications sometimes require several days to take effect.

When Eustachian tubes are clogged, flying and activities that involve changes in altitude (e.g., mountain climbing, biking) and pressure (swimming, diving, snorkeling) should be avoided. Obviously, colds and infections should be treated promptly to avoid or minimize Eustachian tube clogging.

Middle ear ventilation tubes are used when the Eustachian tubes are chronically blocked or infected, a condition more prevalent in younger than older children. These tubes are surgically inserted, under local or general anesthesia, with one end in the middle ear and the other just outside the eardrum. During the months that a tube is in place, swimming is contraindicated.

Sensorineural Loss

Sensorineural loss occurs in the inner ear, where sensory receptors convert sound waves into neural impulses that travel to the brain for translation. The hearing apparatus within the inner ear is the cochlea, so named because it resembles a snail shell in appearance. The oval and round windows are the passages through which sound waves enter the inner ear and disrupt the fluid and hair cells in the cochlea, the mechanism central to sensory reception. Also housed in the inner ear is the vestibular apparatus (semicircular canals) that governs balance. This explains why sensorineural hearing loss and balance deficits sometimes occur together (see Figure 26.5).

Sensorineural loss not only reduces sound but also causes distortions in residual hearing. In young children, this makes learning to speak a real challenge and delays development of language concepts. If loss is total, there is no need for a hearing aid because no amount of amplification will help. If loss is partial, hearing aids will help but not as much as in a conductive loss. Often, hearing aids are used only for auditory and speech training in a structured setting.

Most persons who are born deaf have sensorineural loss. Over 60 types of hereditary hearing loss have been identified, with autosomal recessive genes accounting for about 40% of childhood deafness (Kottke & Lehmann, 1990). Often, persons do not know they are carrying these genes. Only about 10% of deaf infants are born to parents who are deaf. Of these, about half have one parent who is hearing.

About 50% of all hearing losses in children have an unknown (idiopathic) etiology (Batshaw & Perret, 1986; Schildroth & Karchmer, 1986). This is largely because hearing losses are often not discovered until language delays are noted. Many of these losses may be genetic.

Among young children, *meningitis* (usually a bacterial infection) and various viral infections (e.g., mumps, scarlet fever, encephalitis, measles) often dramatically wipe out both hearing and balance. Meningitis carries a 1 in 5 risk of hearing loss. An infection of the meninges (coverings) surrounding the spinal cord and brain, meningitis is characterized by high fever, vomiting, and stiff neck. From 30 to 50% of its survivors have multiple disabilities.

Maternal illnesses during pregnancy often result in deafness. Many of these, like measles, are controlled by vaccines so widespread epidemics no longer occur. Herpes vi-

FIGURE 26.5

Sensorineural loss is linked to balance deficits.

ruses and toxoplasmosis (infection caused by protozoa found in animals and birds) continue to produce serious hearing defects.

Among adolescents and adults, noise is the main cause of new cases of hearing loss (Kottke & Lehmann, 1990). Several million Americans work in occupations with potentially hazardous noise levels (i.e., above 85 db). Federal laws govern the number of hours that persons can work at high decibel levels and require the wearing of hearing-protection devices, but these laws are not always followed. Additionally, life in big cities is increasingly noisy, especially time spent in travel. Some sports create noise levels that persons mask by wearing hearing-protection devices (e.g., shooting, snowmobiling, motorcycles). Rock concerts and personal earphones attached to stereo devices are also sources of hearing damage.

Lastly, parts of the sensorineural hearing mechanism deteriorate with age, just like other body parts. Reasons for the high prevalence of hearing loss with aging are not clear, but noise is believed to be a major factor. Parts of the conductive system may deteriorate also, but it is sensorineural loss that causes the problems widely associated with biological aging.

Mixed Loss and Tinnitus

Many persons have mixed (combined) conductive and sensorineural losses. This is particularly true of senior citizens.

Tinnitus is a sound sensation in one or both ears that affects about 6% of the population. Associated with both conductive and sensorineural losses, it is experienced as a whistling, hissing, buzzing, roaring, throbbing, or whining sound.

It can be sporadic but is continuous for many people. Medical management is sometimes effective, but most persons simply learn to block out their tinnitus.

Prevalence and Incidence of Hearing Loss

Most sources indicate that 7 to 15% of the population have significant hearing losses. Over 17 million Americans have hearing losses, of whom 2 million (about 1 person in 8) are profoundly deaf (Kottke & Lehmann, 1990). At all ages, hearing loss predominates in males.

Prevalence varies sharply, however, by age group, with senior citizens affected the most. Profound hearing loss is present in about 1 in 1,000 newborns (Roeser & Downs, 1988). Approximately 3 in every 1,000 children below age 6 have a moderate or greater sensorineural loss in both ears (Blackman, 1983). The rate is increased 15 to 30 times when mild sensorineural loss is included. Conductive losses are more difficult to track because mild conditions often remain undetected; all children who have had middle ear infections are at risk. Those with Down syndrome, cleft palate, and face/head malformations are at particular risk because of abnormally narrow ear canals. Numbers increase as disease, injury, and environmental noise take their toll. Among school-age children, about 5 to 7% could benefit from special education services for hearing losses.

The prevalence of hearing loss for the 45- to 64-year-old age group is about 11%, whereas that for the 65- to 74-year-old age group is 30%. By age 75, approximately 50% of the population has a significant loss. This is usually for the higher frequencies (i.e., consonants and high-pitched voices and sounds). Background noise (including music) intensifies problems. Speech discrimination is typically more of a problem than loudness; this means that hearing aids are of limited value.

Presbycusis is the term for degeneration of hearing with age. Although all parts of the auditory apparatus are subject to breakdown, presbycusic changes are primarily sensorineural rather than conductive (see Figure 26.6).

In summary, hearing loss is a high-prevalence condition when older age groups are included. It affects more persons than heart conditions, arthritis, blindness, and any chronic physical disability (Kottke & Lehmann, 1990).

Educational Placement

Of the special education conditions recognized by legislation, deafness was the first, historically, to receive attention. The first residential schools in the United States, founded in 1817 and 1818, respectively, were for deaf students (see Appendix G). Thomas Gallaudet, father of Edward (who founded Gallaudet University), started the first residential school. By the late 1800s, almost every state had a school for deaf students. Most of these had excellent physical education programs and encouraged sport competition. Historically, deaf sport has drawn most of its athletes from these schools (Stewart, 1991). This is partly because sport-inclined deaf students in public schools are typically coached by persons who know little or nothing about deaf sport.

FIGURE 26.6

Presbycusis is degeneration of hearing with age. It mostly causes sensorineural losses. (© Thomas Braise/The Stock Market)

Patterns of educating deaf children have varied, of course, from family to family. Some children have always lived at home while attending public or private schools. With the enactment of federal legislation in 1975 has come a definite trend away from residential school placement. Local communities are required to provide the services that deaf children need in regular public schools. Interpretation of need and compliance with law vary widely, however. Particularly underserved are over 4,000 students in small schools where they are the only persons who are deaf or HH (Butterfield, 1991).

Much debate currently centers on the question of what is the least restrictive educational environment for students who are deaf or HH. Where and how can they best learn total communication—in a special school, a special class within a regular school, a resource room pull-out arrangement, or the regular class with a tutor or interpreter? Who will be the leaders in resolving issues?

When a student who is deaf or HH attends a regular school, regardless of academic placement, he or she is likely to be assigned to regular physical education. This is because many persons on individualized education program (IEP) teams believe that physical education is a good place to work on socialization skills. In addition, conventional wisdom suggests that motor performance and fitness are not limited by hearing loss. The exception is the student with inner ear damage that has affected balance.

Some deaf students, like hearing ones, can benefit from adapted physical education services. Whenever assessment indicates that a student is functioning at a lower level than classmates and/or needs special assistance to succeed, adapted physical education services should be written into the IEP. These services do not necessarily mean separate or pull-out settings. Services are often consultant in nature, with a specialist supplying information to the regular educator and

FIGURE 26.7

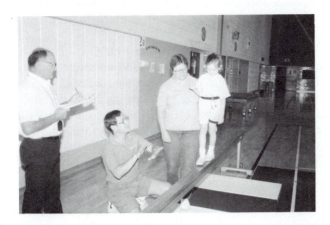

Three leading researchers from Michigan State University work together in data collection. From left to right, John Haubenstricker, David Stewart, and Gail Dummer.

facilitating attitude change. Many adapted physical activity personnel take sign classes so that they can use total communication and help others to learn basic sign.

Assessment of Performance

Federal law states that assessment, for purposes of placement, must be in the student's native language. For many deaf students, this is American Sign Language (ASL). Others, who rely mainly on speechreading, should have optimal lighting and a speaker they can understand. In some instances, an interpreter may be needed. Deaf students may demonstrate delays or perform below average simply because they do not understand test instructions. Dunn and Ponticelli (1988) statistically examined the effect of two communication modes (ASL and Signing Exact English) on the motor performance of prelingually deaf students and reported that ASL produced higher scores. Dummer, Haubenstricker, and Stewart (1989) indicated that communication difficulties (both instructional and motivational) affected scores of their 210 subjects. Stewart, Dummer, and Haubenstricker (1990) critically reviewed physical education research on deaf and HH persons and pointed out test administration weaknesses (see Figure 26.7).

Deaf and HH persons rely on a variety of communication modes. In both teaching and research, individual preferences should be honored. Rapport with the tester should be established before formal evaluation, with interpreters used as needed. Motivational cues (e.g., "good," "run faster," "throw harder") should be carefully planned, as should preliminary instructions. In reporting findings, a thorough description of communication methodology permits replication as well as valid comparisons of performance from year to year. It is not enough to say *total communication* because this term refers to a wide range of communication behaviors.

Physical Education Instruction

Instruction, regardless of setting, should be based on assessed needs in the nine physical education goal areas. The following presents research and pedagogy related to each goal for deaf and HH individuals.

Self-Concept

Feeling good about self in a particular domain determines amount of effort expended and, ultimately, success. Underachievement may occur in mainstream physical education (Garrison & Tesch, 1978; Hopper, 1988), where deaf and HH students experience communication difficulties and related problems of social acceptance. Perceived athletic competence varies, therefore, with the setting, with many persons preferring deaf sports. If assessment indicates low athletic self-concept in mainstream physical education, possible reasons should be carefully studied. The quality and frequency of communication should be examined and plans for improvement developed cooperatively. In particular, teacher and peers should make sure that praise and encouragement are heard, speechread, and seen (signed) to the same extent as other students.

Other reasons for low athletic self-concept are a school, community, or family that does not value abilities and/or a perception that significant others hold low expectations. Some parents are so concerned with language, speech, and hearing training that they feel there is not time for afterschool sports. Other parents may be overprotective. Some schools may stress academics so much that students feel nothing else is really important. In such cases, little energy is put into sports.

Little research has been conducted on athletic selfconcept of deaf and HH persons. Hopper (1988) studied children ages 10 to 14 at Washington State School for the Deaf and reported a relatively low athletic self-concept. Scores were highest in the scholastic domain and lowest in the social acceptance domain. The pattern of self-concepts in different domains may relate specifically to the school attended. Much research is needed in this area.

Socialization and Social Acceptance

An important goal of physical education is to help students make friends who will carry over into after-school leisure activities. Research shows that socialization occurs only when there is planned intervention that requires communication and cooperation. The noise level in most sport settings requires careful planning in this regard. Ideally, when a deaf student is being integrated for the first time, teacher and classmates should learn basic signs. A partner or buddy assures that class instructions are understood.

The IEP team that specifies socialization as a goal should ensure that the integrated setting has a class size and a curriculum that enables communication and cooperation. Obviously, the smaller the class, the less noise and the more opportunity for getting to know each other. Maximum class size (about 20) should be written into the IEP. The curriculum most conducive to communication and cooperation includes individual and dual sports, dance, movement education, aquatics, and cooperative games. These are activities that demand partners. The deaf student must be equal to or better than his or her hearing partner in motor skill and fitness to make the relationship one of mutual respect.

Deaf persons with good sport skills can also make lasting friends in team sport settings if the teacher monitors communication and ascertains inclusion. Research shows that members of winning teams like each other better than those on losing teams. The teacher should therefore see that deaf students are assigned to teams that are likely to win.

Some deaf students are shy about talking and may not take the initiative in making friends. They may tend to withdraw and not want to take their turn in leading class exercises. Such individuals need support and incentive systems. A friend who regularly asks, "What do you think?" is helpful. Socialization requires considerable empathy on the part of both hearing and deaf persons.

Fun/Tension Release

A goal of fun/tension release in physical education is especially important because speechreading and sign require tremendous concentration. Background noise creates tension in persons wearing hearing aids as well as in those who speechread without aids. Poor lighting conditions and other environmental barriers also raise frustrations.

Appropriate goals of physical education and sport on some days are (a) to relax and have fun and/or (b) to channel frustrations, tensions, and hostilities into the healthy outlet of physical activity. The former may be accomplished best by cooperative activities, whereas the latter may be best served by competitive sports. Fun is defined in many ways, and teachers should ascertain what is fun for each individual.

Motor Skills and Patterns

Performance in motor skills and patterns is the same as for hearing persons except when inner ear balance deficits exist. Experts widely agree that much of the published research on motor development and performance of deaf and HH groups is inaccurate. Reasons include (a) etiology was not considered, (b) communication of test instructions was not optimal, and (c) learning opportunities were not examined. Reviews of research literature (Goodman & Hopper, 1992; Savelsbergh & Netelenbos, 1992; Schmidt, 1985) thus indicate contradictory findings, with most experts concluding that nonvestibular impaired deaf and hearing persons perform similarly when opportunities are equal.

That opportunities are not equal is shown in recent studies that report motor delays. Stephen Butterfield, University of Maine, and David Stewart, Michigan State University, are researchers with many years of experience in deaf and HH sport. Studies spearheaded by them show delayed motor development in catching, kicking, jumping, and hopping (Butterfield, 1986) when assessed by the Ohio State University Scale of Intra Gross Motor Development (OSU-SIGMA) and in the hop, horizontal jump, leap, skip, and all object control skills (Dummer et al., 1989) when assessed by Ulrich's Test of Gross Motor Development (TGMD). Both SIGMA and TGMD (see Chapter 7) are qualitative tests that assess maturity of form, rather than distance, speed, and accuracy. This suggests communication difficulty in comprehending good form and emulating it. Communication is a two-way street, so the problem may be the expressive language of the teacher, the receptive language of the child, or both.

Butterfield, after examining the influence of age, sex, hearing loss, and balance on mature form, concluded that most skills are affected primarily by age and balance. Static balance and dynamic balance were examined separately (the correct procedure) and contributed in different amounts to skill (Butterfield, 1987, 1989, 1990; Butterfield & Ersing, 1988).

Static and dynamic balances of deaf and HH students should be thoroughly tested. When problems are identified, balance should become the targeted area of supplementary instruction. Gymnastics, trampoline, tumbling, dance, and movement exploration are particularly helpful (Butterfield, 1988). Physical education programming, however, should be balanced between using strengths and remediating weaknesses.

Leisure-Time Skills

Persons in the deaf community seem to participate more in deaf sports than those in integrated settings. This is closely linked to ease of communication and social acceptance.

Many deaf/HH persons watch lots of television, despite their hearing loss, and receive little encouragement from parents to develop active leisure lifestyles (Hattin, Fraser, Ward, & Shephard, 1986). An important role of physical activity personnel is to acquaint deaf/HH persons with the many available options and to help them get to know role models. This may entail going with them to various sport events, making introductions, and creating buddy and support systems (Stewart, 1984, 1991).

Physical Fitness

The most comprehensive study of the fitness of deaf ($N = 892$) and HH ($N = 153$) students, ages 10 to 17, showed that deaf/HH and hearing peers are similar in body composition, grip strength, sit-and-reach flexibility, 50-yd dash times, and 9- or 12-min endurance runs (Winnick & Short, 1986). Only on abdominal strength (sit-ups) are hearing students superior. This finding has not been explained and needs further research.

Studies with smaller sample sizes present conflicting evidence. Some report that deaf students are less fit than hearing peers (Campbell, 1983; Shephard, Ward, & Lee, 1987). In general, research on fitness of deaf/HH individuals has the same weaknesses as that on motor performance. Etiology and balance function require more attention because these factors affect running efficiency in endurance items, sit-ups, and other exercises.

Play and Game Behaviors

Young deaf children particularly need instruction in play and game behaviors because this area is closely associated with language concepts. Hearing peers pick up game rules, strategies, and behaviors in incidental ways and spontaneous neighborhood play. Opportunities for deaf children are limited, not only because of communication and social acceptance, but because speech, hearing, and language training may cut into the hours that others play.

FIGURE 26.8

Language concepts are reinforced through movement education
challenges given by sign.

Perceptual-Motor Function and Sensory Integration

Balance is probably the most important component in the area
of perceptual-motor function and sensory integration. Research shows a tendency for postural and body awareness activities to improve balance function in deaf and HH
individuals (Effgen, 1981; Lewis, Higham, & Cherry, 1985).
The damaged vestibular system cannot be cured, but compensatory measures are learned.

Body image training is essential for young children
who can learn signs for body parts and actions through movement. *Tap dance* teaches sounds the feet can make. The
teacher may tap the rhythm lightly on the child's head so
that he or she can perceive it via bone conduction while
moving the feet. Another possibility is positioning the child
so that his or her hand is on the record player, piano, or drum.
A system of flashing lights can also be devised to convey
rhythmic patterns.

Perceptual-motor activities also can be used to teach
language and academics (see Figures 26.8 and 26.9). Training
in prepositions (*up, down, toward, away from, in, out*) and
other speech forms is made fun by movement. Charades in
which partners move like different animals while class members try to guess which animal are fun when signs and words
are learned simultaneously.

Creative Expression

Much of deaf education is extremely structured. In particular, young children are repeatedly reinforced on the right
and wrong ways to form sounds with the mouth and signs
with the hands. The end results must be identical to the adult
they are imitating. There is little time for movement explo-

FIGURE 26.9

Games should be invented to reinforce classroom learnings in such
subjects as geography and social studies. "How fast and how accurately
can you trace the boundaries of the states I call out (sign)?" is the
challenge issued by the teacher.

ration and dance unless these are woven into physical education instruction. Several researchers show that creativity,
movement skill, and language can be improved when total
communication is used in movement exploration on climbing
apparatus (Lubin & Sherrill, 1980) and in dance instruction
(Reber & Sherrill, 1981).

Vestibular Dysfunction and Balance Training

The inner ear governs both hearing and balance. If the vestibular apparatus is damaged, static and/or dynamic balances are impaired. Balance is not a general ability that can
be measured by one or two tests. Balance is specific to task
requirements and body positions. It is particularly affected
by head movements and body righting reactions. *Thus, static
and dynamic balances should be assessed in many ways and
trained under variable conditions.*

Vestibular dysfunction is almost always present in
persons who have recovered from meningitis. Minor damage,
undiagnosed, may affect many persons whose inner ear deafness is not hereditary. With increasing age, when there are
lots of movement opportunities, people learn to compensate
for balance deficits. Balance normally improves from childhood through adolescence, when performance plateaus. Then,

FIGURE 26.10

Sack races help improve dynamic balance. Note that the starting signal must be visual.

in old age, when the inner ear mechanisms begin to degenerate, balance again becomes a problem. This explains why research that combines many ages seldom yields useful information about balance deficits.

Balance is also dependent upon good vision. Persons with vestibular deficits particularly need training in using the eyes. Balance beam walking, for example, is made easier by keeping the eyes focused on a wall spot. Activities performed with eyes closed or blindfolded obviously complicate balance problems and typically are contraindicated for deaf persons who need vision to enable communication.

Individuals, deaf or otherwise, who have balance problems should be given special instruction on the principles of equilibrium. Movement exploration sessions may be developed around the following themes:

1. **Center of Gravity.** "What is it? How do your movements affect it? In what movements can you keep the center of gravity centered over its supporting base? Can your hands be used as a supporting base? What happens when your center of gravity moves in front of the supporting base? In back of it? To the side of it? What activities lower your center of gravity? Raise it?"

2. **Broad base.** "How can you adapt different exercises so that the supporting base is larger than normal? In what directions can you enlarge your base—that is, how many stances can you assume? In which direction should you enlarge your base when throwing? Batting? Serving a volleyball? Shooting baskets?"

Persons learn quickly to compensate for poor balance by maintaining the body in a mechanically favorable position. Games and relays on skates, stilts, or using novel apparatus (sack races) teach compensation (see Figure 26.10). Activities should be planned to enhance vision and kinesthesis. All forms of dance and gymnastics increase body awareness. The increasingly popular Oriental exercise systems and martial arts—karate, kung fu, and Tai Chi—also contribute to this objective.

Speechreading and Cued Speech

Speechreading, formerly called lipreading, is a difficult skill because many sounds look identical. For example, *b, p,* and *m* are produced by bringing the lips together. *L, t,* and *d* are formed with the tongue on the roof of the mouth behind the front teeth. Words like *mama, papa, man, mat, mad, bat, bad, ban, pan, pad,* and *pat* look the same and can be understood only if the general idea or context of the speech is followed.

Several trap sentences illustrate the problem of speechreading: "What's that big loud noise?" looks the same as "What's that pig outdoors?" the title of an excellent autobiography by deaf journalist Henry Kisor (1990). Try saying "It rate ferry aren't hadn't for that reason high knit donned co" to someone with earplugs. Chances are that he or she will think you said, "It rained very hard and for that reason I didn't go." According to Kisor (1990), much of speechreading is guesswork. About 30 to 40% is understanding words, and the rest is *context guessing* to fill in the gaps.

Cued speech is a system whereby spoken words are supplemented with hand signs near the face to help persons interpret words that look the same, like *son/sun* and *bat/pat.* Eight specific hand shapes presented in four positions near the face provide a multitude of cues. This system was created by Cornett (1967).

Naturally, it is easier to speechread familiar acquaintances than strangers. During initial meetings, 50% or sometimes less is understood. With continued contact, comprehension increases. However, occasionally, there are persons (about 10%) who are impossible to speechread. These are typically people who move their lips very little, speak fast, show little expression and emotion, chew gum, or have a mustache.

Speechreading is particularly difficult in group conversations or discussions in which the speaker is frequently changing. Obviously, the deaf or HH individual must be able to see the lips of everyone talking but also fast in determining which new person is talking. Discussions seldom elicit much talk from speechreaders because they tend to be uncertain about when pauses occur for them to jump in and about the exact time a topic or focus changes. To facilitate involvement, restating the topic and asking the speechreader what he or she thinks is helpful.

Speechreading is much more fatiguing than ordinary auditory processing of words. Most persons speak over 120 words a minute. A cough, sneeze, or other distraction disrupts understanding. Success in speechreading demands high concentration. Young children, of course, focus for shorter periods than older ones. Instruction should be adapted to individual differences.

Proper lighting conditions facilitate speechreading. Care should be taken that deaf persons are not facing into the sun. This is also important in sign language. What other environmental adaptations should be made?

American Sign Language and Other Forms of Sign

American Sign Language (ASL) is a bona fide language like Spanish and French, with its own grammar and syntax. Much practice is necessary before communication level reaches the sophistication expected of adults. ASL can express abstract as well as concrete thoughts. It is the dominant language of the deaf community in the United States and Canada and has regional variations and dialects. Other countries have sign languages comparable to ASL (e.g., British and French sign). ASL is the fourth most commonly used language in the United States (Flodin, 1991). Only English, Spanish, and Italian rank ahead of it.

ASL sentence structure is different from that of English. For example, in English, we might say, "Have you been to Texas?" In ASL, this would be TOUCH FINISH TEXAS YOU QUESTION, with *you* and *question* signed simultaneously.

Most hearing people do not take the time to learn ASL syntax and grammar. Instead, they link signs together in the same order they speak words in English. The result is a form of signed English or English signing. In contrast, Pidgin sign refers to a mixture of English and ASL. When enrolling in sign language classes, it is wise to ask which kind of sign will be taught.

ASL generally is not the language used in total communication classes in public schools. Signed English permits signs to be presented in the same order that English is spoken and thus enhances the improvement of speechreading skills. Signed English has educational appeal because it may help deaf persons learn to speak, read, and write English. Some deaf persons are therefore bilingual in sign. They use ASL in the deaf community and signed English at school. Additionally, they learn to speak, read, and write English and other languages.

In becoming multilingual, deaf persons experience the frustrations common to learning foreign languages. Proficiency in English may not be as strong as that of persons who are unilingual. This affects academic achievement in a mainstream setting.

Learning Some Signs

Signs are useful substitutes for whistles and shouts in noisy physical education environments. An increasing number of teachers are weaving sign into sport and dance instruction. Many students cannot hear over the background noise, and so sign is a viable instructional supplement.

Signs are easily worked into early childhood games, creative dramatics, and action songs. They enrich the perspective of hearing children who, in the next decade, will be learning sign in elementary school, just as they do Spanish and French.

Learning sign often begins with fingerspelling (see Figure 26.11). Persons generally master their name first and then add signs for "Hi, my name is _____ ." See Figures 26.12, 26.13, and 26.14. Note that the explanation of *name* in Figure 26.12 refers to the *H* finger. The better we know the manual alphabet, the easier sign is. When instructions say to move clockwise or counterclockwise, this is from the viewpoint of the signer, not the watcher. Note that signs in instructional manuals are shown as they are seen by the watcher. The type of sign used by most beginners is manually coded English (MCE). Much formal instruction is needed to use systems like ASL and pidgin sign language (PSE).

FIGURE 26.11

Standard fingerspelling and number signs.

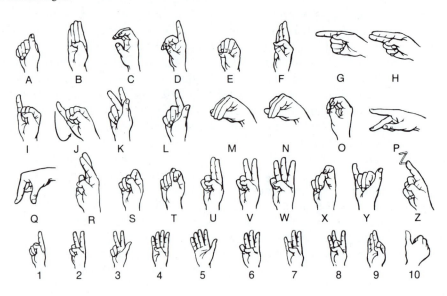

FIGURE 26.12

Signs to play the *Name Game*. Note eight signs: Four to say, "Hi, my name is _____ ;" two to say, "What is your name?;" and two to say, "I'm happy to meet you."

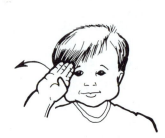

HI
Move the right *B* hand to the right from a position close to the right temple.

MY, MINE
Place the palm of the right flat hand on the chest.

Use sign for your name.

NAME
Cross the middle-finger edge of the right *H* fingers over the index-finger edge of the left *H* fingers.

PERSONAL NAME SIGN
Use a sign of your choice or fingerspell the letters of your name.

FIGURE 26.12 (continued)

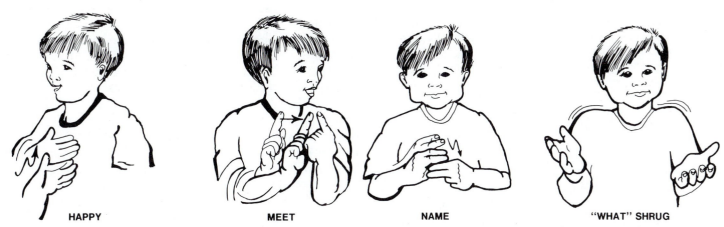

HAPPY — **MEET** — **NAME** — **"WHAT" SHRUG**

"I'm happy to meet you," in American Sign Language — "What is your name?" in American Sign Language

---

FIGURE 26.13

Signs to play start-stop games like *Red Light, Green Light*. Note that many games are played with only two signs. These signs are also important for classroom discipline.

Play Start, Stop Games Like Red Light, Green Light

START, BEGIN
Hold the left flat hand forward with the palm facing right. Place the tip of the right index finger between the left index and middle finger; then twist the right index in a *clockwise direction* once or twice.

STOP
Bring the little-finger side of the right flat hand down sharply at right angles on the left palm.

FIGURE 26.14

Signs to reinforce students. These signs should be used frequently in teaching and coaching.

Learn Reinforcers!

THANKS, THANK YOU, YOU'RE WELCOME
Touch the lips with the fingertips of one or both flat hands; then move the hands forward until the palms are facing up. It is natural to smile and nod the head while making this sign.

GOOD
Place the fingers of the right flat hand at the lips; then move the right hand down into the palm of the left, with both palms facing up.

Among the many books and articles that teach sign are the following:

Butterworth, R. R., & Flodin, M. (1989). *Signing made easy.* New York: Putnam.

Costello, E. (1983). *Signing: How to speak with your hands.* New York: Bantam.

Fant, L. (1983). *The American Sign Language phrase book.* Chicago: Contemporary Books.

Flodin, M. (1991). *Signing for kids.* New York: Putnam.

Riekehof, L. (1987). *The joy of signing* (2nd ed.). Springfield, MO: Gospel Publishing House.

Robinson, J., & Stewart, D. (1987). *Coaching deaf athletes.* Ontario: Canadian Deaf Sports Association.

Books and videotapes that teach and/or use ASL in exercise can be ordered from Gallaudet University Press, 800 Florida Avenue NE, Washington, DC 20002-3695 (Phone 800–451–1073). Particularly appropriate for physical education is an aerobic workout tape called "Sign 'n Sweat." This tape features a deaf instructor, Gina Oliva (1989), using total communication.

Signing can be viewed on television when church services for deaf persons are broadcast. It is also used by the National Theatre of the Deaf, which has toured both Europe and the United States since its establishment in 1967. Most of the company's professional actors are alumni of Gallaudet University. The National Theatre of the Deaf is housed in Waterford, Connecticut.

Interpreters and Transliteration

Transliteration is the process of transmitting information from English to ASL and vice versa. Persons trained to do this are called interpreters and can be located through speech and hearing personnel in schools and universities. Interpreters expect to be paid, just like other professionals. Transliteration is an exhausting activity, so several interpreters take turns when sessions are long.

Personal Hearing Aids

Who can benefit from a hearing aid? The 40-dB loss is the traditional criterion, but there is a trend toward prescribing them for 25- to 40-dB losses, especially in young children who need help in learning speech and language. Hearing aids amplify sound but do not ameliorate distortions. They are therefore used more in conductive than in sensorineural conditions. Losses over 90 dB typically leave too little residual hearing for amplification to be of help in communication. Hearing aids are not allowed in deaf sport competition.

Hearing aids work best when the listening environment is quiet and structured and the speaker is relatively close (not more than 4 or 5 ft away) or wearing a special device to transmit sound waves. Hearing aids have the same components as public address systems and amplify in the same way. Their five main parts are (a) input microphone, (b) amplifier, (c) earphone or output receiver, (d) battery, and (e) on-off switch.

Hearing aids are available in four styles, named according to their location: (a) chest or body-worn, (b) behind the ear, (c) eyeglass, and (d) in the ear. The chest style is worn primarily by young children or by persons with multiple disabilities. The behind-the-ear style is used mostly by school-age individuals, whereas adults may opt for any of the latter three.

Regardless of style, proper maintenance is a daily concern because parts are prone to breakdown. Most malfunctions are caused by dead or weak batteries, corrosion on battery contacts, or improper battery placement. Other problems include clogged earmolds, frayed cords, cracked tubing, excessive distortion, and poor frequency response. Teachers should not automatically assume that hearing aids are working correctly. Research shows that 30 to 50% of hearing aids of school-age children are not performing adequately on any given day (Roeser & Downs, 1988).

Moisture is a particular problem, especially for persons who perspire heavily during activity. Hearing aids can be dried with hair blowers. Swimming settings usually contraindicate use of aids. Contact sports, where there is danger to the aid or to the wearer, may also be contraindicated.

Deaf and HH persons have personal preferences about wearing aids in physical activity settings. These should be honored. A hearing aid amplifies *all* noise, not just word sounds. As a result, persons wearing aids may react negatively to prolonged noise and have frequent tension headaches. What implications does this have for integrated physical education and sport?

Assistive Listening Devices and Systems

Assistive listening devices and systems (ALDS) include all electronic and electromechanical devices except the personal hearing aid. Over 200 devices are available to amplify sounds, convert them to light or vibration systems, or in some way transmit meaning (e.g., closed-captioned television). Among the sounds relayed are the ring of the telephone, the buzz of an alarm clock, the chime of a doorbell, the warning of a fire alarm or smoke detector, and the cry of an infant.

Think about adaptations that might make housing safer, entertainment (television, theatre, sports) more enjoyable, and learning in a large lecture hall or gymnasium more effective! For the latter, AM and FM radio frequencies can transmit voice sounds when the speaker wears a special device. Decoders are now being built into all television sets so that they have the capacity for closed-captioning. New devices are available every day.

Telecommunication Device for the Deaf

A telecommunication device for the deaf permits telephone communication between two deaf persons or a deaf and hearing person. The TDD has three parts: (a) a portable typewriter, (b) a screen that displays one line of text at a time, and (c) two rubber cups into which a telephone handset can fit. The TDD is wired to a regular telephone that makes distinctive beeps when a TDD caller is on the line.

To send a TDD message, simply place the telephone handset on the rubber cups and type your first sentence. The message is converted into tones that are conveyed over the phone line to another TDD, which transforms the tones into words on the screen. The receiver then types back a message.

TDDs can be powered by either batteries or household current. In many ways, they resemble computers, but TDDs use the Baudot code to transmit information, whereas most computers use the ASCII code.

TTY, an abbreviation for teletypewriter, correctly refers to the early models of TDDs, first created in the late 1950s by a deaf Bell Telephone engineer. Some persons, however, continue to use TDD and TTY interchangeably. The important thing is that government, public, and private offices have available a device that permits communication with deaf persons. Letterhead stationary, advertisements, and public announcements should include TDD numbers. Where on your campus and in your community can you make TDD calls?

General Guidelines for Deaf and HH Conditions

1. When first meeting a deaf/HH person, ask if he or she can understand your speech. If not, find someone to help or use paper/pencil communication.

2. Remember that short sentences are easier to speechread than long ones.

3. Speak normally and remember that only 3 to 4 of every 10 words are distinguishable on the lips. Use facial expressions and body language to help convey meaning.

4. When a sentence is not understood, repeat it. If one repetition does not help, then rephrase, using different words. Remember that some words are harder to speechread than others. Many words look the same. Find alternatives.

5. If you do not understand the other person's speech, do not pretend. Ask for as many repetitions as you need. Suggest, "Tell me again in a different way."

6. Empty your mouth before speaking. This applies to chewing gum, food, tobacco, cigarettes, straws, and anything else that distorts sights and sounds.

7. Keep your lips fully visible. Avoid mustaches, hands in front of face, and Halloween masks. Do not talk while writing on the chalkboard unless your face is visible.

8. Keep lighting conditions optimal.

9. Avoid standing in front of a window or bright light that forces a deaf/HH person to cope with a glare.

10. When outdoors, position yourself so that you, rather than the deaf/HH person, face the sun.

11. Minimize background noise and distractions.

12. Do not raise your voice when speaking to a person with a hearing aid.

13. When teaching, use lots of visual aids and demonstrations. Have order of events and class rules posted.

14. When behavior problems occur, consider whether students are seeing and hearing adequately. Note that restlessness often signals fatigue.

15. Encourage students with hearing losses to move freely around the gymnasium in order to be within seeing and hearing ranges.

16. Learn basic signs and weave them into the class structure. Give attention to signs that praise performance and motivate personal bests. Use these signs concurrently with speech with all students, not just those with hearing losses.

17. Be aware that head and neck positions that enable persons to see starting signals may affect speed. Read the excellent article by Bressler (1990) on the deaf sprinter. Communication needs may also affect the way persons want to swim (face out of water) and other activities.

References

Ammons, D. A. (1986). World games for the deaf. In C. Sherrill (Ed.), *Sport and disabled athletes* (pp. 65–72). Champaign, IL: Human Kinetics.

Ammons, D. A. (1990). Unique identity of the world games for the deaf. *Palaestra, 6* (2), 40–43.

Batshaw, M. L., & Perret, Y. (1986). *Children with handicaps: A medical primer* (2nd ed.). Baltimore: Paul H. Brooks.

Blackman, J. A. (1983). *Medical aspects of developmental disabilities in children birth to three.* Iowa City, IA: University of Iowa.

Bressler, H. (1990). The deaf sprinter: An analysis of starting techniques. *Palaestra, 6* (4), 32–37.

Butterfield, S. A. (1986). Gross motor profiles of deaf children. *Perceptual and Motor Skills, 62,* 68–70.

Butterfield, S. A. (1987). The influence of age, sex, hearing loss, etiology, and balance ability on the fundamental motor skills of deaf children. In M. E. Berridge & G. R. Ward (Eds.), *International perspectives on adapted physical activity* (pp. 43–51). Champaign, IL: Human Kinetics.

Butterfield, S. A. (1988). Deaf children in physical education. *Palaestra, 4* (3), 28–30, 52.

Butterfield, S. A. (1989). Influence of age, sex, hearing loss, and balance on development of throwing by deaf children. *Perceptual and Motor Skills, 69,* 448–450.

Butterfield, S. A. (1990). Influence of age, sex, hearing loss, and balance on development of sidearm striking by deaf children. *Perceptual and Motor Skills, 70,* 361–362.

Butterfield, S. A. (1991). Physical education and sport for the deaf: Rethinking the least restrictive environment. *Adapted Physical Activity Quarterly, 8* (2), 95–102.

Butterfield, S. A., & Ersing, W. F. (1988). Influence of age, sex, hearing loss, and balance on development of catching by deaf children. *Perceptual and Motor Skills, 66,* 997–998.

Campbell, M. E. (1983). *Motor fitness characteristics of hearing impaired and normal hearing children.* Unpublished master's thesis, Northeastern University, Boston.

Canadian Deaf Sports Association. (1987). *Coaching deaf athletes.* Ontario: Author.

Carney, E. (Ed.). (Spring, 1971). Beat of a different drum. *Gallaudet Today,* p. 21.

Cherow, E. (Ed.). (1985). *Hearing-impaired children and youth with developmental disabilities.* Washington, DC: Gallaudet University Press.

Cornett, R. O. (1967). Cued speech. *American Annals of the Deaf, 112,* 3–13.

Dummer, G., Haubenstricker, J., & Stewart, D. A. (1989). *Performances of deaf children and youth on the Test of Gross Motor Development.* Paper presented at the First National Deaf Sports Conference, Canadian Deaf Sports Association, Ottawa, Ontario.

Dunn, J., & Ponticelli, J. (1988). The effect of two different communication modes on motor performance test scores of hearing impaired children. In *Abstracts: Research Papers, 1988 AAHPERD Convention.* Reston, VA: American Alliance for Health, Physical Education, Recreation, and Dance.

Effgen, S. K. (1981). Effect of an exercise program on the static balance of deaf children. *Physical Therapy, 61,* 873–877.

Flodin, M. (1991). *Signing for kids.* New York: Putnam.

Garrison, W. M., & Tesch, S. C. (1978). Self-concept and deafness: A review of research literature. *Volta Review, 80,* 457–466.

Goodman, J., & Hopper, C. (1992). Hearing impaired children and youth: A review of psychomotor behavior. *Adapted Physical Activity Quarterly, 9* (3), 214–236.

Greenberg, J. (1970). *In this sign.* New York: Holt, Rinehart, & Winston.

Hattin, H., Fraser, M., Ward, G. R., & Shephard, R.J. (1986). Are deaf children unusually fit? A comparison of fitness between deaf and blind children. *Adapted Physical Activity Quarterly, 3* (3), 268–275.

Hopper, C. (1988). Self-concept and motor performance of hearing impaired boys and girls. *Adapted Physical Activity Quarterly, 5* (4), 293–304.

Kisor, H. (1990). *What's that pig outdoors? A memoir of deafness.* New York: Penguin Books.

Kottke, F., & Lehmann, J. (1990). *Krusen's handbook of physical medicine and rehabilitation* (4th ed.). Philadelphia: W. B. Saunders.

Lewis, S., Higham, L., & Cherry, D. (1985). Development of an exercise program to improve the static and dynamic balance of profoundly hearing-impaired children. *American Annals of the Deaf, 130* (4), 278–284.

Lubin, E., & Sherrill, C. (1980). Motor creativity of preschool deaf children. *American Annals of the Deaf, 125,* 460–466.

Martin, D. S. (Ed.). (1991). *Advances in cognition, education, and deafness.* Washington, DC: Gallaudet University Press.

Oliva, G. A. (1989). Advocacy: Evolution or revolution? *Palaestra, 6* (1), 49–51, 59.

Reber, R., & Sherrill, C. (1981). Creative thinking and dance/movement skills of hearing impaired youth: An experimental study. *American Annals of the Deaf, 26* (9), 1004–1009.

Roeser, R., & Downs, M. (1988). *Auditory disorders in school children* (2nd ed.). New York: Thieme Medical Publishers.

Sacks, O. (1989). *Seeing voices: A journey into the world of the deaf.* Berkeley: University of California Press.

Savelsbergh, G., & Netelenbos, J. B. (1992). Can the developmental lag in motor abilities of deaf children be partly attributed to localization problems? *Adapted Physical Activity Quarterly, 9* (4), 343–352.

Schildroth, A. N., & Karchmer, M. (1986). *Deaf children in America.* Boston: Little, Brown.

Schmidt, S. (1985). Hearing impaired students in physical education. *Adapted Physical Activity Quarterly, 2* (4), 300–306.

Shephard, R., Ward, R., & Lee, M. (1987). Physical ability of deaf and blind children. In M. E. Berridge & G. R. Ward (Eds.), *International perspectives on adapted physical activity* (pp. 355–362). Champaign, IL: Human Kinetics.

Stewart, D. A. (1984). The hearing impaired student in physical education. *Palaestra, 1* (1), 35–37.

Stewart, D. A. (1991). *Deaf sport: The impact of sports within the deaf community.* Washington, DC: Gallaudet University Press.

Stewart, D. A., Dummer, G., & Haubenstricker, J. (1990). Review of administration procedures used to assess the motor skills of deaf children and youth. *Adapted Physical Activity Quarterly, 7,* 231–239.

Stewart, D. A., McCarthy, D., & Robinson, J. (1988). Participation in deaf sport: Characteristics of deaf sport directors. *Adapted Physical Activity Quarterly, 5* (3), 233–244.

Stewart, D. A., Robinson, J., & McCarthy, D. (1991). Participation in deaf sport: Characteristics of elite deaf athletes. *Adapted Physical Activity Quarterly, 8* (2), 136–145.

Winnick, J., & Short, F. (1986). Physical fitness of adolescents with auditory impairments. *Adapted Physical Activity Quarterly, 3* 58–66.

CHAPTER
27

Blindness and Visual Impairments

FIGURE 27.1

Charles Buell gives a blind child and his sighted opponent a first lesson in wrestling.

After you have studied this chapter you should be able to:

1. Differentiate between legal blindness, travel vision, motion perception, light perception, and total blindness. Explain deaf-blindness. Discuss physical education programming for each.

2. Identify some of the concerns, aspirations, and behaviors associated with blindness. Discuss implications for physical education.

3. Discuss the following in relation to assessment and instruction: (a) haptic perception, (b) spatial awareness, (c) trust and courage, (d) sound usage, (e) physical fitness, (f) orientation and mobility, and (g) adaptations of equipment and facilities.

4. Contrast public and residential facilities in the education of blind students.

5. Discuss the U.S. Association for Blind Athletes (USABA) and opportunities for competition.

6. Explain the three USABA classifications and discuss similarities and differences in the sport events recommended for each.

7. Describe the games of goal ball and beep baseball.

8. Discuss existing and needed research concerning vision loss and physical education. Review the contributions of such researchers as Charles Buell, Joseph Winnick, and James Mastro.

Never check the actions of the blind child; follow him, and watch him to prevent any serious accidents, but do not interfere unnecessarily; do not even remove obstacles which he would learn to avoid by tumbling over them a few times. Teach him to jump rope, to swing weights, to raise his body by his arms, and to mingle, as far as possible, in the rough sports of the older students. . . . Do not too much regard bumps upon the forehead, rough scratches, or bloody noses, even these may have their good influences. At the worst, they affect only the bark, and do not injure the system, like the rust of inaction.

Samuel Gridley Howe (1841)

T he previous statement was made by the first director of Perkins Institution in Boston, a residential school founded in the early 1800s for children who were blind. Perkins is known for its training of Anne Sullivan Macy, the teacher of Helen Keller, and for its outstanding physical education and sport program. Most states have a residential school for children who are blind, and a field trip to this facility is a good way to learn about physical education programming, which historically has been excellent (Buell, 1984). The trend today, however, is for children to live at home and to be educated in public schools, where resource room help is available.

Because blindness is a low-incidence condition in childhood, seldom is there more than one or two students with severe vision problems in the same school district. Regular physical educators have little experience in this area and tend to overprotect such children by excusing them from activity and excluding them from competitive sport. In general, motor skills and fitness of children with visual impairments (VI) in public schools are lower than those in residential schools.

Charles Buell, a versatile physical educator (1912–1992), emphasized that children with VI should be taught in mainstream settings and held to the same achievement standards as their sighted peers. Buell (1982, 1986) particularly recommended wrestling as a sport in which youth with VI can excel (see Figure 27.1). Buell, legally blind himself, held a doctorate from the University of California and was recognized worldwide as an athlete, physical educator, coach, and researcher.

Table 27.1
Sport classifications for USABA and IBSA.

Classification	Description
B1	No light perception in either eye up to light perception and inability to recognize the shape of a hand in any direction and at any distance
B2	Ability to recognize the shape of a hand up to a visual acuity of 2/60 and/or a limitation of field vision of 5°
B3	2/60 to 6/60 (20/200) vision and/or field of vision between 5 and 20°

Note. In 1982, this system was adopted in place of the system that used Classes A, B, C.

Definitions and Basic Concepts

Blindness and *visual impairment* are often used as synonyms, particularly in the sport world. The International Blind Sports Association (IBSA) and the U.S. Association for Blind Athletes (USABA) serve persons whose vision varies from 20/200 ft (6/18 m) to total blindness. Table 27.1 shows the three sport classifications. Persons in B1, B2, and B3 classes are significantly different from one another in sport ability. These terms are helpful therefore in writing physical education individualized education programs (IEPs).

Acuity (sharpness of vision) is typically measured by standing 20 ft from a Snellen chart and reading its lines of progressively smaller print. Educators often designate five categories as follows:

1. **Legal Blindness (20/200).** Ability to see at 20 ft what the normal eye sees at 200 ft (i.e., 1/10 or less of normal vision).

2. **Travel Vision (5/200 to 10/200).** Ability to see at 5 to 10 ft what the normal eye sees at 200 ft.

3. **Motion Perception (3/200 to 5/200).** Ability to see at 3 to 5 ft what the normal eye sees at 200 ft. This ability is limited almost entirely to motion.

4. **Light Perception (less than 3/200).** Ability to distinguish a strong light at a distance of 3 ft from the eye, but inability to detect movement of a hand at the same distance.

5. **Total Blindness (lack of visual perception).** Inability to recognize a strong light shown directly into the eye.

Since persons who are legally blind have considerable usable vision, these classifications often result in confusion. Buell (a Class B2) laughingly described the disbelief of his colleagues when he used a pocket magnifier to look up a telephone number in the city directory. "But you are blind," they said. He corrected them by stating that he was legally blind but he was nevertheless partially sighted.

At least 80% of people who are blind have some residual vision. These persons travel independently and rely on large-size print rather than braille. Given good light conditions to use residual vision, their sport performance is similar to that of sighted peers when instruction and practice are equal. They are most disadvantaged by weather (dark, rainy days) and scheduling of early or late practices when the sun is not overhead. Persons often profess to see more than they do, partly because of the desire for normalcy and partly because they have no experience upon which to judge normal vision. Some persons, although legally blind, are very sensitive about being called *blind*.

Prevalence of Blindness and Visual Impairment

Blindness and VI are largely problems of old age. Approximately a half-million persons in the United States are legally blind, and countless others have serious visual problems. At least two thirds of these persons are over 65 years of age.

The statistics concerning VI among school-age children vary with the definition used. Approximately 23,000 children with VI between the ages of 3 and 21 are receiving special education services. However, VI affects fewer children than any other disability, with the exception of the deaf-blind classification.

Causes of Blindness

Most blindness in school-age persons is attributed to birth defects (congenital cataracts, optic nerve disease, retinopathy) or retinopathy of prematurity (ROP), previously called retrolental fibroplasia. ROP occurs when oxygen is poorly regulated in incubators. Excessive oxygen damages the retina and sometimes causes mild brain damage and learning problems.

Infectious diseases, tumors, and injuries are minor causes of blindness. In older persons, cataracts and diabetes are leading causes. About 4% of visual disorders in children are caused by a genetic disorder called *albinism*. Because of congenital absence of pigment in the skin, hair, and eyes, these persons have very fair skin, platinum blond hair, and blue eyes. Related visual problems are myopia, photophobia (un-

usual intolerance of light), astigmatism, and nystagmus. Many persons with albinism compete as Class B3 athletes in USABA.

Deaf-Blindness

Deaf-blind means a combination of auditory and visual impairments that results in severe communication and other needs that require supplementary educational assistance beyond that provided in special education for one disability. The Individuals with Disabilities Education Act (IDEA), Part C (Section 1422) specifically addresses services for deaf-blindness, and over 1,600 children and youth ages 6 to 21 are classified as deaf-blind. About half of these receive instruction in state-operated schools, mainly residential facilities for the blind, and regional centers. The other half attend public schools. Because the widespread rubella epidemics of the early 1960s resulted in more deaf-blindness than any other factor, most persons with this condition are adults (an estimated 8,000).

A considerable body of literature on physical education and recreation for deaf-blindness was developed in the 1960s and 1970s, and the pedagogy therein remains relevant. A newer source is Kratz, Tutt, & Black (1987). Information can be accessed through the ERIC computer network or by contacting one of the 10 regional offices of the Helen Keller National Center for Deaf-Blind Youths and Adults (see list in April 1988 *American Annals of the Deaf*).

Causes

Deaf-blindness can be hereditary or acquired. Prenatal and perinatal conditions that affect the nervous system often damage both vision and hearing. Drug and alcohol abuse, sexually transmitted diseases, and maternal infections are associated with multiple disability. Childhood diseases linked with deaf-blindness are meningitis, rubella, and scarlet fever. In the hereditary category, *Usher's syndrome* is the leading cause. It is a genetic condition resulting in congenital deafness and a progressive blindness known as retinitis pigmentosa, which first appears in the early 30s. Usher's syndrome affects 3 of every 100,000 persons.

Deaf-blindness, of course, seldom results in total loss. Diagnosis aims at determining amount of residual vision and hearing and prescribing education, eyeglasses, hearing aids, and communication devices that will enable optimal function.

Deaf-Blind Role Models

The best known of deaf-blind persons was Helen Keller (1880–1968), who was disabled by an illness at 19 months of age. Helen Keller graduated *cum laude* from Radcliffe, mastered five languages, and wrote three books. Her autobiography (Keller, 1965) is among the classics that everyone should read. Her story has also been immortalized in a play and film called *The Miracle Worker*.

Still another deaf-blind person, Robert J. Smithdas, who suffered cerebral spinal meningitis at age 5, has gained recognition via an autobiography and his work as a public relations counselor and lecturer. At age 32, after completing a master of arts degree at New York University and working in a salaried position for several years, Smithdas wrote,

Loneliness was continually present in my life after I became deaf and blind. And even now, in adulthood, I find it with me despite all my adjustments to social living. Loneliness is a hunger for increasing human companionship, a need to be part of the activity that I know is constantly going on about me. . . . To share my moments of joy with someone else, to have others sympathize with my failures, appreciate my accomplishments, understand my moods, and value my intelligence—these are the essential conditions that are needed for happiness. (Smithdas, 1958, p. 259)

In 1988, one of the members of the USABA team to the Paralympics in Korea was deaf-blind. This 16-year-old had lost his vision as a toddler and then progressively lost all hearing by the age of 15. He was, however, an excellent competitive swimmer and practiced with a local swim team. He carried a small, portable TDD with him so that persons could type in communication, which he read via a braille tape output and then answered. He also could understand fingerspelling when hand positions for the various letters were made in the palm of his hand (see Figure 27.2). Unfortunately, few team and staff members had fingerspelling skills of sufficient speed to maintain his interest. His greatest problem thus was communication. Embedded in this was the need for sensory stimulation and companionship, especially for people to take the time to talk to him via the TDD or fingerspelling.

Coactive Movement Model

The coactive movement model is an instructional model that works well with toddlers and young children who are blind or deaf-blind and was popularized by Van Dijk of the Netherlands in the 1960s and incorporated into instructional programs throughout the world. The purpose of this model is to develop communication skills through movement instruction that progresses through several stages (Leuw, 1972; Van Dijk, 1966).

In the initial stage, the teacher sits with legs extended on the floor, places the child on his or her lap, and seat-scoots across the floor. Arms, legs, and trunks of the teacher and child touch so that body part movements are in unison. This coactive movement pattern is used also for creeping, with the teacher's chest touching the child's back and all eight limbs plastered against one another.

Surfaces of the two bodies are in as much contact as possible as new patterns (knee-walking, walking, rise-to-stand, stair climbing, and the like) are tried in a variety of environments: on mats, water beds, moon walks, trampolines, floors with carpets of various textures, grass, and wading pools. The teacher talks, sings, hums, or whistles the name of the activity throughout the coactive movement. If there is no residual hearing, fingerspelling or a tactual cue is used before, during, and after the movement.

In the second stage, the child and teacher cooperatively move together, but the distance between their bodies is gradually increased so that the action becomes mirroring or imitation. When the child links language with movement, then cues can be given to promote independent body action. Subsequent stages resemble perceptual-motor program-

FIGURE 27.2

Two ways to converse with a person who is deaf-blind. (*A*) Fingerspelling in palm of hand. (*B*) Use of a telecommunication device for the deaf (TDD) with braille output.

A

B

ming, with emphasis on imitation of total body movements, then limb actions, then hand gestures, and finally, fingerspelling and sign language. For children who have residual hearing, learning to follow verbal commands is stressed.

Concerns, Aspirations, and Models

The student who is totally blind has few, if any, restrictions in physical education. Nothing can worsen the vision. In contrast, students who are gradually losing visual acuity may fear falling, being hit in the eye by a ball, or other accidents that can rob them of remaining vision. These fears are generally unfounded.

Time of Onset

VI is typically designated as congenital (born with) or adventitious (diagnosed at age 2 or 3 or later). Congenital VI is often not recognized until motor or cognitive delays appear. Age of onset should always be indicated because it gives insight into amount of time the child had for developing space and form perception, visualization skills, and locomotor and object control patterns.

Delayed Motor Development

Motor development is delayed in blind infants, particularly in mobility- and locomotion-related behaviors (Adelson & Fraiberg, 1974; Fraiberg, 1977; Jong, 1990). The median age of walking is about 20 months. Mastery of motor milestones is in a different order from that of sighted infants, with milestones that require vision for motivation delayed most (e.g., raising the head from prone, reaching, crawling, creeping, and walking). Object control and manipulation tend to be delayed 3 to 6 months. This, in turn, prevents proper emergence of tactile perception abilities and related problem-solving skills.

Early intervention is beneficial but does not completely remediate delays (Levine, Carey, Crocker, & Gross, 1983; Norris, Spaulding, & Brodie, 1957). Of particular concern are delays in development of play and social skills. Children with VI cannot progress without help to parallel or cooperative play because of lack of awareness of others' presence.

Overemphasis on Academics

Reading and other academic skills require more time than average for individuals with VI. As a result, such children often spend time in study that others use for leisure and large muscle activity. This not only deprives them of skill and fitness but also interferes with making and keeping friends. With age, deficits in social competence become more and more obvious.

Unless helped with social development, the life experiences of persons with VI differ considerably from those of peers. This eventually may interfere with job success. Most jobs are lost, not because of inadequate vocational skills, but because of inability to get along with other workers.

Stereotyped Behaviors and Appearance

Stereotyped behaviors or *stereotypies* (previously called blindisms) are mannerisms like rocking backward and forward, putting fist or fingers into eyes (see Figure 27.3), waving fingers in front of face, whirling rapidly round and round, and bending the head forward. These same behaviors may be observed among sighted persons with emotional problems, autism, or limited opportunities to move. They can be prevented or at least minimized through the provision of vigorous daily exercise. Some persons like Ray Charles become quite successful in spite of stereotypies, but most need

FIGURE 27.3

Rubbing the eye is a stereotypy that should be called to the child's attention and extinguished.

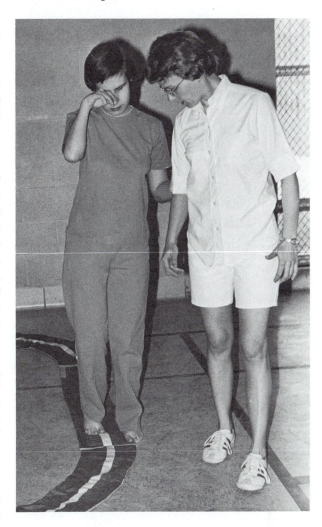

help in making appearance as normal as possible. Verbal correction often causes anxiousness and self-consciousness. A good approach is to agree on a tactile cue like a hand on the shoulder as a reminder to stop.

Persons with VI should be taught self-monitoring in relation to appearance, postures, and facial expressions. VI limits ability to imitate, thereby spontaneously learning appropriate behaviors and responses as do sighted persons. Verbal instructions are needed in many areas that individuals with normal vision take for granted.

Models

Models with VI are sources of inspiration, helping people with VI to realize what is possible. For sighted persons, models with VI help to change attitudes and dispel misconceptions. While live models are best, books and videotapes are also helpful.

The autobiographies of such persons as Harold Krents (1972) and Tomi Keitlen (1960) emphasize the importance of sport participation in making friends and gaining self-confidence. Krents recalls step-by-step how his brother

FIGURE 27.4

Dr. James Mastro (left), U.S. Association for Blind Athletes (USABA) gold medalist, conducts workshop on wrestling.

FIGURE 27.5

(*A*) Dr. Charles Buell (left) and Harry Cordellos (right), posing after a workshop. (*B*) Harry Cordellos performing on one ski.

A

B

taught him to catch a regulation football and to bat a 10-inch playground ball—skills he could have been taught by a physical educator but was not. In high school physical education, he was allowed to play touch football with his sighted classmates but was admonished to "Keep out of the way." The anecdotes leading to his acquisition of the nickname "Cannonball" make the book well worth reading. Tomi Keitlen describes in detail her first attempts at swimming, golf, horseback riding, fencing, and skiing after becoming totally blind at age 33. In addition to valuable accounts of how such sports can be learned and enjoyed without sight, Keitlen describes the problems of adjusting to blindness. The greatest battle, she stresses, is to avoid being segregated and labeled as different from sighted persons.

James Mastro, a B1 international athlete, has been active in USABA since its inception in 1976, repeatedly winning gold medals in wrestling, judo, shot put, and discus. Mastro was born with one eye sightless and injured the other while fencing with curtain rods in late childhood. In spite of countless surgeries, he lost all vision but light perception by age 18. This did not deter his becoming a member of the university wrestling team and eventually becoming an Olympic wrestler. A broken arm in the last qualifying bout kept him from winning and becoming a member of the U.S. Olympic Team, but he was named an alternate.

Since completing his doctorate in adapted physical education at Texas Woman's University, Dr. Mastro has provided leadership for the Braille Sports Foundation, been president of the National Beep Baseball Association, and conducted workshops throughout the world (see Figure 27.4). He is also a prolific researcher (see Sherrill, 1990, for review of his work). Dr. Mastro is the first totally blind person to earn a doctorate in physical education and is a strong model for others.

Harry Cordellos (1976, 1981) is another strong model whose autobiography *Breaking Through* is filled with sport stories (see Figure 27.5A). Cordellos, born with glaucoma and a heart murmur, was partially sighted throughout childhood but so overprotected by parents and teachers that he never engaged in vigorous play. In spite of 14 operations,

FIGURE 27.6

Standard English Braille alphabet.

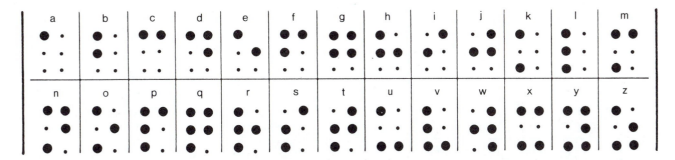

he was totally blind by age 20. Fortunately, he outgrew his heart problems. At age 20, he was introduced to sports via water skiing (see Figure 27.5B), and subsequently he dedicated his life to athletic training and educating the sighted world about the potential of persons with VI. Cordellos has run over 100 marathons; he does this with a sighted partner. His best time in the Boston Marathon is 2 hr, 57 min, 42 sec. Cordellos has run 50 mi in less than 8 hr and has competed in the Iron Man Triathlon in Hawaii (swimming 2.4 mi, biking 112 mi, and running 26.2 mi). He has demonstrated that there is no physiological reason why persons with VI cannot excel in sports.

Erling Stordahl, in Norway, is also an outstanding model. The creator of the world-famous sport center (Helsesportsenter) in Beitostølen, he has broadened horizons of persons with and without disabilities. He is particularly known for leadership in winter sports and innovations that permit persons with VI to ski.

Charles Buell, described in the opening section of this chapter, is another model. Until age 80, he continued to work out daily and to encourage mainstream acceptance of people with VI.

Find persons with VI, support their involvement in sports, and ask them to lecture in public schools and universities. Exposure to models is one of the best ways of ameliorating the problem of overprotection. University students can volunteer to serve as partners in long-distance runs, provide transportation, and the like.

Physical Assistance

Physical assistance should not be offered to persons with VI unless requested. *In tandem walking, for instance, persons with VI should hold onto the upper arm of the sighted partner, not vice versa.* Sighted persons, of course, bear the responsibility for making their presence known and should state their name when initiating a verbal exchange rather than assume that the other has an infallible auditory memory.

Implications of VI for Physical Education

Regular class physical education placement is recommended for students with VI (Nixon, 1988; 1989). Except for ball-handling activities, students with VI can participate with few adaptations. Their success depends in large part on the ability of the physical educator to give precise verbal instructions.

Like other students, they strive to fulfill their teacher's expectations. Falls, scratches, and bruises should be disregarded as much as possible to allow the dignity of recovering without oversolicitous help.

When activities are practiced in small groups, the teacher should ascertain that students with VI know the names of their classmates, the approximate space allocated to each, their place in the order of rotation if turns are being taken, and the direction of movement. Sight is not required for success on the trampoline, parallel bars, and other pieces of apparatus; for tumbling, free exercise, and dance; for weight lifting, fitness activities, swimming; or for many other sports.

Good lighting in the instructional environment is essential so that persons with VI can make use of residual vision. Availability of class handouts in large-size print and braille also increases success (see Figure 27.6). Last, noise must be minimized because persons with VI must be able to hear.

Especially recommended activities for persons with VI are wrestling, tumbling, gymnastics, bowling, swimming, weight training, judo, dart throwing, dance, roller skating, ice skating, shuffleboard, horseback riding, tandem cycling, hiking, camping, fishing, rowing, waterskiing, and surfing. These sports require little or no adaptation for students with VI to participate with the sighted (see Figure 27.7).

Athletes with VI can compete with the sighted on a comparatively equal basis in wrestling. Most residential schools have interscholastic wrestling teams, and many students excel over their sighted opponents in state and national events.

In the 1970s, special ball games for persons with VI, such as *beep baseball* and *goal ball,* became popular. Kickball with tandem running around the diamond gives children a chance to identify with big league baseball.

A study of the memories and opinions of adults with VI about physical education found that their favorite childhood outdoor sport was baseball/softball (Sherrill, Rainbolt, & Ervin, 1984). Respondents did not mention adaptations. Tying for second place were swimming, football, and horseback riding. Two thirds of the sample had been reared in residential schools. These persons expressed positive opinions about school-based physical education, but negative feelings about both past and present community, church, and family physical education and recreation—indicating that usually there were none.

FIGURE 27.7

Horseback riding is one of many lifetime sports that persons who are blind can enjoy with the sighted.

Haptic Perception Teaching Model

Haptic perception refers to the combined use of tactile sensations and kinesthesis. Persons with little or no residual vision must be taught through these modalities. The coactive movement model discussed earlier in the chapter in the section on deaf-blindness is one approach to haptic teaching. For children who can hear and understand language, however, haptic teaching is associated with auditory input to guide learning about space and form. The teacher must give concise, explicit directions that hold interest and result in desired behaviors. A good activity is to practice leading exercises and conducting obstacle course activities with blindfolded friends.

When planning movement exploration activities, the physical educator must realize that space is interpreted unconventionally by haptic-minded persons. Whereas the visually oriented child perceives distant objects as smaller than those nearby, the child with VI does not differentiate between foreground and background. The size of objects is not determined by nearness and farness, but rather by the objects' emotional significance and the child's imagination.

Children with VI experience difficulty in conceptualizing boundaries. Having no visual field to restrict them, their space is as large as their imagination. They tend, however, to think in parts rather than wholes since concepts are limited to the amount of surface they can touch at any given time. To familiarize themselves with the gymnasium, they may move from one piece of apparatus to another, feel the walls, discover windows and doors, and creep on the floor. They are, however, never completely certain how the unified whole feels or looks.

Three-dimensional models (similar to dollhouses) of the gymnasium, swimming pool, playground, campsite, and other areas are helpful. Miniature figures can be arranged on the simulated playground to acquaint students with playing positions, rules, and strategies. Dolls can also be used to teach spatial relationships among dancers in a group composition, cheerleaders in a pep squad demonstration, and swimmers in the assigned lanes of a meet. Unless dolls with movable joints are taken through such movements as forward rolls, cartwheels, and skin-the-snake on a parallel bar, the student with VI has no way of conceptualizing the whole prior to attempting a new activity.

FIGURE 27.8

Child with B1 classification brailles her medal.

Spatial Awareness Training

In spatial awareness training, objectives are manual identification of objects, orientation to stable and moving sounds, spatial orientation, improvement of movement efficiency, and mobility training. Children with VI need special training in recognizing the right-left dimensions of objects that are facing them (Cratty, 1971). Not capable of seeing, they have never received a mirror image; hence, the concept of someone facing them is especially difficult.

Children with VI must be provided with opportunities for learning about their own body parts as well as about those of animals and other human beings. This can be accomplished, at least partially, by tactual inspection. Three-dimensional figures must be available to teach similarities and differences between different body builds, male and female physical characteristics, and postural deviations. Movement exploration based on modifications of the dog walk, seal crawl, mule kick, and the like is meaningless unless the child can feel, smell, and hear the animal about to be imitated. Tactual inspection of persons, animals, and objects is called *brailling*. At meets, B1 persons often braille their medals (see Figure 27.8).

The following are other activities that help individuals with VI to organize and learn about space:

1. Practice walking a straight line. Without sight, persons tend to veer about 1.25 inches per step or walk a spiral-shaped pathway.
2. Practice facing sounds or following instructions to make quarter, half, three-quarter, and full turns.
3. Practice reproducing the exact distance and pathway just taken with a partner.
4. Take a short walk with a partner and practice finding the way back to the starting point alone.
5. Outside, where the rays of the sun can be felt, practice facing north, south, east, west. Relate these to goal cages and the direction of play in various games.
6. Practice determining whether the walking surface is uphill or downhill or tilted to the left or right; relate this to the principles of stability and efficient movement.
7. Practice walking different floor patterns. Originate novel patterns and then try to reproduce the same movement.

These and other space explorations offer fun and excitement for sighted youngsters who are blindfolded as well as for children with VI. Remember, however, that the blindfolded child is at a greater disadvantage than persons who have had several years to cope with spatial problems.

Guidewires and Sighted Partners

Students with VI and blindfolded friends should be provided with a *guidewire* stretched from one end of the playfield or gymnasium to the other to enable them to meet such challenges as "Run as fast as you can," "Roller skate as fast as you can," or "Ride a tricycle or bicycle as fast as you can." The students can hold onto a short rope looped around the guidewire. *Gliding fingers directly over the wire can cause burns.* Window-sash cord stretched at *hip height* is probably best for running practice. A knot at the far end of the rope warns the runner of the finish line. Residential schools erect permanent guidewires on their tracks. Students can improve their running efficiency or master a new locomotor skill *by grasping the upper arm of a sighted partner,* but the ultimate goal should always be self-confidence in independent travel.

Sound Usage in Locomotion and Sports

Students with VI can be grouped with individuals who have auditory perception deficits for special training in recognizing and following sounds. A continuous sound is better than intermittent ones. Whenever possible, the sound source should be placed in front of the student so that he or she is moving directly toward it. The next best position is behind the person so that he or she can proceed in a straight line away from it. Most difficult to perceive and follow are sounds to the side. A progression from simple to difficult should be developed. After success with a single sound source, students should be exposed to several simultaneous sounds, with instructions to pick out and follow only the relevant one.

Try the following activities, using a blindfold, to get an idea of competencies that must be developed for success in sport:

1. Discriminate between the bouncing of a small rubber ball for playing jacks, a tennis ball, a basketball, and a cageball.

2. Judge the height of the rebound of a basketball from its sound and thus be able to catch a ball bounced by you or by another.

3. Perceive the direction of a ground ball and thus be able to field or kick one being rolled toward your left, right, or center.

4. Discriminate, in bowling, the difference between sounds of a ball rolling down the gutter as opposed to the lane and also the difference between one bowling pin versus several falling.

5. Recognize, in archery, the sound of a balloon bursting when it is hit by an arrow or of an arrow penetrating a target made of a sound-producing material (see Figure 27.9).

6. Recognize the difference between the center of the trampoline and its outer areas by the sound of a ball attached to its undersurface.

7. Walk a nature trail or participate in a treasure hunt by following sounds from several tape cassettes located about the area.

8. Follow a voice or bell as you swim and dive in an open area.

9. Perceive the rhythm of a long rope alternately touching the ground and turning in the air so that you know when to run under and jump the rope.

Orientation and Mobility Training

Comprehensive physical education programs include units on orientation and mobility (O and M). Many children with VI are overprotected prior to entering school and hence need immediate help in adjusting to travel within the school environment. The physical educator must orient young children to the playground equipment as well as to space. Bells may be attached to the supporting chains of swings to warn of danger. Children who are blind often excel in climbing and hanging feats. Unable to see their distance from the ground, they seem fearless in the conquering of great heights and enjoy the wonder and praise of sighted classmates.

The following are illustrative objectives for a unit on the use of playground equipment for students with VI. Students should

1. Demonstrate how to play safely on all equipment.

2. Tell safety rules and reasons for each.

3. Display a cooperative attitude and express a willingness to learn.

FIGURE 27.9

Balloons attached to the target enable the child who is blind to hear a bull's-eye.

4. Walk a hand ladder (arm-swing from rung to rung).

5. Use the legs to pump while swinging (in a sitting position).

6. Climb to the top of both 8- and 14-ft slides alone and slide down feet first.

7. Perpetuate a tilted merry-go-round by swinging out on the downside and leaning in on the upside.

8. Play simple games on the jungle gym.

9. Use a seesaw safely with a companion.

Adaptations of Equipment and Facilities

Teachers and parents of children with VI should write to the American Foundation for the Blind for catalogs of special equipment. Each year, improvements are made in sound-source balls and audible goal locators that facilitate the

FIGURE   27.10

Electronic balls with beepers make basketball a possibility.

teaching of ball skills. Electronic balls with beepers are gradually replacing balls with bells (see Figure 27.10). *Balls should be painted orange or yellow for persons with partial sight.* In most primary school activities, beanbags with bells sewn inside are preferred over balls, which are harder to recover.

Outside softball diamonds should be of grass with mowed baselines or should have wide asphalt paths from base to base and from the pitcher's mound to the catcher. Inside, guidewires can be constructed from base to base. Boundaries for various games are marked by a change in floor or ground surfaces that can be perceived by the soles of the feet. Tumbling mats, for instance, can be placed around the outside periphery of the playing area to mark its dimensions.

Braille can be used on the swimming pool walls to designate the changing water depths. It can also be used on gymnasium floors and walls as aids in determining the colors, shapes, and sizes of targets.

Portable aluminum bowling rails 9 ft long and 3 ft high are available through the American Foundation for the Blind. These rails are easily assembled and broken down for transportation to different bowling alleys.

For the most part, however, equipment does not need to be adapted for individuals with VI. The play area should be quiet enough to facilitate use of sound and well lighted to enhance use of residual vision.

Physical and Motor Fitness

Most research shows that persons with VI have lower fitness than sighted peers (Shephard, 1990; Winnick, 1985). This is generally attributed to lack of instruction and practice, inactive lifestyles, and overprotection. Degree of VI, age, and sex affect fitness scores. The more severe the VI, the lower the fitness; this is probably because overprotection increases with severity. The performance gap between males and females with VI is greater than for sighted peers; presumably, this is because girls are more overprotected than boys. Boys improve steadily from ages 6 to 17, whereas girls plateau at about age 13 or 14.

Of the 14 items used in Project Unique (see Chapter 13), the greatest discrepancy between blind and sighted youth was in throwing, running, and jumping (Winnick, 1985). These findings partially support the work of Buell (1982), which showed greatest weakness in running and throwing events.

Most research also shows that persons with VI have greater skinfold thicknesses than sighted peers (Hopkins, Gaeta, Thomas, & Hill, 1987; Winnick, 1985). There is also a tendency toward shorter heights (Lee, Ward, & Shephard, 1985).

In general, youth with VI should take the same fitness tests as sighted peers. In health-related fitness, distance runs require a partner. Otherwise, few adaptations are needed except in motivation. Whereas sighted persons are challenged to personal bests by seeing others succeed, VI limits the motivational value of social comparison. Verbal input should be substituted.

VI also limits social comparisons of height and weight, the amount that others are eating, and exercise habits. Whereas we may see someone jogging on the other side of the street and be motivated to follow suit, persons with VI are more dependent on internal motivation. Whereas we can run, cycle, or drive to an exercise site at will, persons with VI must be assertive in finding companions.

Studies on cardiorespiratory fitness of persons with VI have shown fitness levels either equal to sighted persons or low fitness levels that significantly improve as a result of treadmill and bicycle ergometer training. Harry Cordellos, marathon runner who is blind and American Alliance for Health, Physical Education, Recreation, and Dance (AAHPERD) honor award recipient, has such outstanding fitness that he is the subject of an ongoing longitudinal study at the Cooper Aerobic Institute in Dallas. A film featuring Cordellos, entitled *Survival Run,* is available (Media Marketing, 1983).

When persons with VI are navigating unfamiliar areas, gaits become mechanically less efficient. This, in turn, contributes to early fatigue. Good fitness is needed to combat both fatigue and stress. Research shows that B1 and B2 sprinting patterns are less mechanically efficient than those of B3 (Gorton & Gavron, 1987; Pope, McGrain, & Arnhold, 1986). Long-distance runs that require a sighted partner heighten stress because of the required adjustment to new people.

USABA and Sport Competition

An understanding of national and international sport opportunities gives insight into programming for individuals with VI. While persons with VI can participate in many integrated activities, they should be given optimal training in areas where they are most likely to excel.

While sports have been well organized within the residential school network for years, the movement gained new impetus with the formation of USABA in 1976. In 1977, USABA sponsored its first national championships. These are now held every year, with international competition occurring every fourth year in conjunction with the Paralympics. Sanctioned sports for the national games include powerlifting, judo, swimming, track and field, wrestling, goal ball, women's gymnastics, winter sports (downhill and cross-country skiing), tandem cycling, and others as selected by the USABA board. Under consideration are crew rowing, sailing, archery, and competitive diving. The rules for these sports are based on those used by such organizations as the U.S. Gymnastics Federation (USGF), the National Collegiate Athletic Association (NCAA), the National Federation of State High School Associations (NFSHSA), and the International Blind Sports Association.

Track-and-Field Events

Track events include 100, 200, 400, 800, 1500, 3000 (women) 5000 (men) 10,000 meters 4 × 100 Relay, 4 × 400 Relay and the Marathon conducted separately for B1, B2, and B3 athletes. The 100 meter dash runners run independently on a 8-lane track using callers. In longer runs all B1 runners must use guide runners, B2 and B3 runners may or may not use guide runners, and the use of a tether is optional. A *contact tether* between partners is a nonelastic rope or cloth no more than 50 cm in length (see Figure 27.11). In such runs, the person with VI must always precede the sighted partner.

Field events include the long jump, triple jump, high jump, shot put, javelin, and discus. Regulation throwing implements are used. The pentathlon is an event also but for males only.

Gymnastics

Gymnastics events in which persons with VI compete are floor exercise, balance beam, uneven bars, vaulting, and all-round. Competitors are expected to have achieved a level of competence such that the aid of a coach or spotter is not necessary. Such persons may, however, be present for any move considered a risk. A 0.5 deduction is made for aid by a coach or spotter during competition. Added safety is provided by an extra layer of mats and padding covering all exposed metal parts of apparatus. Gymnastics competition, while presently for females only, will be sanctioned for males when sufficient numbers express interest. Currently, most men seem to prefer other sports.

FIGURE 27.11

(A) Harry Cordellos (left) with sighted partner, Randy Foederer. Note that both will take first step with inside foot. (B) Both hold onto a *contact tether* no more than 50 cm in length.

A

B

Goal Ball

A game created in Europe especially for veterans blinded in World War II, goal ball is played under the rules of the International Blind Sport Association (IBSA). The only required equipment is a bell ball. Each team consists of three players wearing knee and elbow pads and blindfolds. The playing area is the same for males and females (see Figure 27.12). Very important is the regulation that all field markings be 5 cm in width and made of a distinctive texture for easy player orientation.

Games are 14 min in duration, with 7-min halves. Each team tries to roll the ball across the opponent's goal while the other team tries to stop them (see Figure 27.13). A thrown ball may bounce, but it must be rolling before it reaches the opponent's throwing area or it becomes an infraction. The entire team helps with defense. The arriving ball can be warded off in a standing, kneeling, or lying position with any body part or the whole body (see Figure 27.14).

Because all team members are required to wear a blindfold, goal ball places persons with VI on equal terms with sighted peers and thus can be used in mainstream physical education. Rules are available through USABA or from physical educators at residential schools. Many adapted games and drills of this nature can be designed to give mainstream students a novel experience as well as excellent training in auditory perception. Goal ball is suitable for all age groups, beginning in about the third or fourth grade.

Beep Baseball

Although not a USABA regulation sport, beep baseball is played by many persons with VI (Montelione & Mastro, 1985). Its rules are governed by the National Beep Baseball Association, which was founded in 1976. These rules are different from the original game, invented by Charlie Fairbanks in 1964.

Current rules call for a regulation-size baseball diamond with grass mowed to an approximate height of 2 inches (see Figure 27.15). Grassy areas are used because they provide optimal safety and comfort for players who often dive onto the ground to field balls. The ball, which is available through the Telephone Pioneers (see the list of organizations in Appendix E), is a regulation softball 16 inches in circumference, with a battery-operated electronic sound device inside. A regulation bat is used. Bases are 48 inches tall, with the bottom part made of a 36-inch tall pliable plastic cone and the top part made of a long cylinder of foam rubber. An electronic buzzer is installed in each base.

A team is comprised of six blindfolded players and two sighted players who act as pitcher and catcher when their team is up to bat and act as spotters when their team is in the field. As spotters, their role is to call out the fielder's name to whom the hit ball is coming closest. Only one name is called, for obvious safety reasons.

Batters are allowed four strikes and one ball (1991 rule change). Except on the last strike, fouls are considered strikes. Batters must attempt to hit all pitched balls, with the option of letting one go by without penalty. When a fair ball is hit, the umpire designates which one of the two buzzing bases shall be activated. A run is scored if the batter gets to the designated base before the ball is fielded. Games are six innings, with three outs an inning. Teams are comprised of both males and females.

FIGURE 27.12

Playing area for goal ball.

		Note: Line width = 5 cm Line color = white		
Mat	Throwing/ landing area		Throwing/ landing area	Mat
		Neutral area (no players)		
2.5 m	3 m	7 m	3 m	2.5 m

Goal line

Goal line   8.5 m

FIGURE 27.13

Starting positions for the offensive team in goal ball.

For more information about beep baseball, write Dr. James Mastro, Braille Sports Foundation, 4601 Excelsior Boulevard, Minneapolis, MN 55416 or 612–574–9317.

Other addresses for information about sport for individuals with VI are

U.S. Association for Blind Athletes (USABA)
Roger Neppl, Executive Director
33 N. Institute Street
Brown Hall, Suite 015
Colorado Springs, CO 80903

American Foundation for the Blind (AFB)
15 West 16th Street
New York, NY 10011

References

Adelson, E., & Fraiberg, S. (1974). Gross motor development in infants blind from birth. *Child Development, 45,* 114–126.

Buell, C. (1982). *Physical education and recreation for the visually handicapped* (2nd ed.). Washington, DC: American Alliance for Health, Physical Education, Recreation, and Dance.

FIGURE   27.14

In goal ball, any part of the body or the whole body can be used to prevent the bell ball from rolling across the goal line.

FIGURE   27.15

Playing field for beep baseball. The circular foul line between 1st and 3rd bases is a constant distance of 40 ft from home plate. A batted ball must travel over this line to be considered *fair*. The pitcher stands 20 ft from home plate. The distance between home plate and each base location is 90 ft. The base is 5 ft outside the baseline.

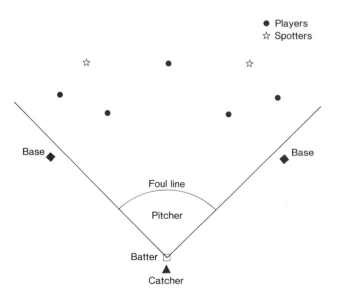

Buell, C. (1984). *Physical education for blind children* (2nd ed.). Springfield, IL: Charles C. Thomas.

Buell, C. (1986). Blind athletes successfully compete against able-bodied opponents. In C. Sherrill (Ed.), *Sport and disabled athletes* (pp. 217–223). Champaign, IL: Human Kinetics.

Cordellos, H. (1976). *Aquatic recreation for the blind.* Washington, DC: American Alliance for Health, Physical Education, and Recreation.

Cordellos, H. (1981). *Breaking through.* Mountain View, CA: Anderson World.

Cratty, B. (1971). *Movement and spatial awareness in blind children and youth.* Springfield, IL: Charles C. Thomas.

Fraiberg, S. (1977). *Insights from the blind: Comparative studies of blind and sighted infants.* New York: New American Library.

Gorton, B., & Gavron, S. (1987). A biomechanical analysis of the running pattern of blind athletes in the 100–m dash. *Adapted Physical Activity Quarterly, 4,* 192–203.

Hopkins, W. G., Gaeta, H., Thomas, A. C., & Hill, P. M. (1987). Physical fitness of blind and sighted children. *European Journal of Applied Physiology, 56,* 69–73.

Howe, S. G. (1841). *Perkins report.* Watertown, MA: Perkins Institute for the Blind.

Jong, C. G. A. (1990). The development of mobility in blind and multiply handicapped infants. In A. Vermeer (Ed.), *Motor development, adapted physical activity, and mental retardation* (pp. 56–66). Basel, Switzerland: Karger.

Keitlen, T. (1960). *Farewell to fear.* New York: Avon Book Division.

Keller, H. (1965). *The story of my life.* New York: Airmont Publishing.

Kratz, L. E., Tutt, L., & Black, D. A. (1987). *Movement and fundamental motor skills for sensory deprived children.* Springfield, IL: Charles C. Thomas.

Krents, H. (1972). *To race the wind.* New York: G. P. Putman's Sons.

Lee, M., Ward, G., & Shephard, R. J. (1985). Physical capacities of sightless adolescents. *Developmental Medicine and Child Neurology, 27,* 767–774.

Leuw, L. (1972). Co-active movement with deaf-blind children: The Van Dijk model. Videotape made at Michigan School for Blind. Available through many regional centers for deaf-blind.

Levine, M. D., Carey, W., Crocker, A., & Gross, R. (1983). *Developmental-behavioral pediatrics.* Philadelphia: W. B. Saunders.

Media Marketing. (1983). *Survival run.* (This 16-mm film can be ordered from Media Marketing, W-STAD, Brigham Young University, Provo, UT 84602.)

Montelione, T., & Mastro, J. (August, 1985). Beep baseball. *Journal of Physical Education, Recreation, and Dance,* pp. 60–61, 65.

Norris, M., Spaulding, P., & Brodie, F. (1957). *Blindness in children.* Chicago: University of Chicago Press.

Nixon, H. L. (1988). Getting over the worry hurdle: Parental encouragement and the sports involvement of visually impaired children and youths. *Adapted Physical Activity Quarterly, 5* (1), 29–43.

Nixon, H. L. (1989). Integration of disabled people in mainstream sports: Case study of a partially sighted child. *Adapted Physical Activity Quarterly, 6,* 17–31.

Pope, C., McGrain, P., & Arnhold, R. (1986). Running gait of the blind: A kinematic analysis. In C. Sherrill (Ed.), *Sport and disabled athletes* (pp. 173–180). Champaign, IL: Human Kinetics.

Shephard, R. J. (1990). *Fitness in special populations.* Champaign, IL: Human Kinetics.

Sherrill, C. (1990). Psychosocial status of disabled athletes. In G. Reid (Ed.), *Problems in movement control* (pp. 339–364). Amsterdam: North-Holland.

Sherrill, C., Rainbolt, W., & Ervin, S. (1984). Attitudes of blind persons toward physical education and recreation. *Adapted Physical Activity Quarterly, 1* (1), 3–11.

Smithdas, R. J. (1958). *Life at my fingertips.* New York: Doubleday.

Van Dijk, J. (1966). The first steps of the deaf-blind child towards language. *International Journal for the Education of the Blind, 15* (1), 112–115.

Winnick, J. (1985). The performance of visually impaired youngsters in physical education activities: Implications for mainstreaming. *Adapted Physical Activity Quarterly, 2* (4), 292–299.

A P P E N D I X

A

Prevalence and Incidence Statistics

Table A.1
Students, ages 6 to 21, receiving special education services, 1989–1990.

Type of Disability	IDEA, Part B		ESEA (SOP)		Total	
	Number	*Percent*	*Number*	*Percent*	*Number*	*Percent*
Specific learning disabilities	2,038,720	98.7	26,172	1.3	2,064,892	100.0
Speech or language impairments	964,829	98.8	11,357	1.2	976,186	100.0
Mental retardation	507,331	89.6	58,819	10.4	566,150	100.0
Serious emotional disturbance	340,059	88.9	42,511	11.1	382,570	100.0
Multiple disabilities	67,500	76.7	20,456	23.3	87,956	100.0
Hearing impairments	41,003	70.5	17,161	29.5	58,164	100.0
Orthopedic impairments	41,864	87.2	6,135	12.8	47,999	100.0
Other health impairments	49,233	92.6	3,932	7.4	53,165	100.0
Visual impairments	17,357	75.6	5,603	24.4	22,960	100.0
Deaf-blindness	813	49.8	821	50.2	1,634	100.0
All conditions	*4,068,709*	*95.5*	*192,967*	*4.5*	*4,261,676*	*100.0*

Source: U.S. Department of Education, Office of Special Education Programs, Washington, DC.

Note. Total U.S. population is 250,000,000 (1990 census).
Note. IDEA and ESEA (SOP—State Operated Programs,
Schools, or Institutions) indicate the laws that fund services.

Table A.2
Incidence of selected conditions for all age groups combined.

High-Incidence Conditions (Based on 1,000 Persons)		Moderate-Incidence Conditions (Based on 10,000 Persons)		Rare-Incidence Conditions (Based on 100,000 Persons)	
Anorexia nervosa	4[a]	Achondroplasia	1	Apert's syndrome	0.5
Arthritis	20	Arthrogryposis	3	Blindness	21.6
Asthma	3–6	Autism	5	Cri-du-chat	5
Cancer	250	Blindness	2	Friedreich's ataxia	1.8–2
Cerebral palsy	3.5	Cooley's anemia	9	Galactosemia	2.2
Cleft palate and/or lip	1	Cornelia de Lange syndrome	1	Barre-Guillain	1
Clubfoot (Talipes)	1.5	Cretinism	1.7	Huntington's disease	6.5
Congenital heart defects	6–10	Down syndrome	5	Hurler's syndrome	1
Congenital hip dislocation	1–3	Hemophilia	1	Marfan's syndrome	5
Convulsive disorders	5	Klinefelter's syndrome	2[b]	Multiple sclerosis	6
Cystic fibrosis	1	Neurofibromatosis	3	Muscular dystrophy	3
Deafness	9	Rubella syndrome	1	Osteogenesis imperfecta	3
Depression	120	Tourette's syndrome	1–5	Perthes disease	4–5
Diabetes	10	Trisomy 18	3	Phenylketonuria	7
Down syndrome	0.5	Turner's syndrome	1[a]	Prader-Willi	0.5
Fetal alcohol syndrome	1			Reye's syndrome	1
Fragile X syndrome	0.5–1			Spinal cord injury	5
Hard of hearing	32			Tuberous sclerosis	1
Learning disabilities	3–20				
Mental illness	166				
Mental retardation	30				
Noonan syndrome	1				
Obesity	150				
Schizophrenia	10				
Sickle-cell anemia	2[c]				
Spina bifida	1–3				

[a]Females only
[b]Males only
[c]Blacks only

APPENDIX

B

Medications (Family name first, then generic and trade names)

1. **Analgesics to relieve pain**
   aspirin, *a*cetyl*s*alicylic *a*cid (or ASA) (Anacin, Bufferin, Darvon, Excedrin)
   codeine
   ibuprofen (Advil, Motrin)
   methadone (Dolophine)

2. **Antiasthmatic drugs**
   bronchodilators that are nonsteroid, beta-adrenergic
   albuterol (Proventil, Ventolin)
   terbulatin (Bricanyl, Brethine)
   bronchodilators that are steroid
   beclomethazone (Vanceril)
   flunisolide (AeroBid)
   corticosteroids like prednisone (Deltazone)
   cromolyn sodium (Intal)
   xanthines like theophyllin (Bronkodyl, Slo-Phyllin, Theo-Dur)

3. **Anticancer drugs (chemotherapy)**
   chlorambucil (Leukeran)
   methotrexate (Folex, Mexate)
   tamoxifen (Nolvadex, Tamoxifen)

4. **Anticonvulsants for seizures (epilepsy)**
   ethosuximide (Zaronthin)
   phenobarbital (Luminal, Stental)
   phenytoin (Dilantin)
   primidone (Mysoline)

5. **Antidepressants (three types for management of depression)**
   Bicyclic, tricyclic, and tetracyclic drugs
   amitriptyline (Elavil, Endep)
   desipramine (Norpramin, Pertofrane)
   doxepin (Adapin, Sinequan)
   imipramine (Tofranil)
   nortriptyline (Aventyl)
   lithium (Carbolith, Eskalith, Lithobid)
   *mono*amine *o*xidase (MAO) inhibitors
   phenelzine (Nardil)

6. **Antihistamines for allergies and hayfever**
   astemizole (Hismanal)
   diphenhydramine (Benadryl)
   terfenadine (Seldane)

7. **Antihypertensives for high blood pressure**
   angiotensin-converting enzyme (ACE) inhibitors
   captopril (Capoten)
   enalapril (Vasotec)
   beta blockers
   acebutolol (Sectral)
   atenolol (Tenormin)
   betaxolol (Kerlone)
   carteolol (Cartrol)
   metoprolol (Lopressor)
   propranolol (Inderal)
   calcium channel blockers
   diltiazem (Cardizem)
   nicardipine (Cardene)
   nifedipine (Adalat, Procardia)
   verapamil (Calan, Isoptin)
   diuretics or thiazides
   chlorothiazide (Diuril)
   methyclothiazide (Duretic, Enduron)
   vasodilators (several families)
   arteriodilators, including hydralazine (Apresoline) and minoxidil (Loniten)
   venodilators, including nitroglycerin and other nitrates
   mixed, including ACE inhibitors

8. **Anti-infective drugs to fight infections (family names only)**
   antibiotics
   antimicrobials
   cephalosporins
   erythromycins
   penicillins
   sulfonamides
   tetracyclines

9. **Antipsychotic drugs for schizophrenia, bipolar disorders, and acute psychotic episodes**
   chlorpromazine (Thorazine)
   haloperidol (Haldol)
   lithium (Carbolith, Eskalith, Lithobid)
   thiothixene (Navine)

10. **Cardiovascular drugs**
    alpha blockers
    prazosin (Minipress)
    beta blockers (see antihypertensives)
    calcium channel blockers (see antihypertensives)
    digitalis preparations
    digoxin (Lanoxicaps, Lanoxin)
    diuretics (see antihypertensives)
    heart rhythm regulators
    digitalis, digoxin (Lanoxin)
    disopyramide (Norpace)
    propranolol (Inderal)
    quinidine (Quinidex, Quinaglute)
    nitrates
    nitroglycerin (Nitro-Bid, Nitroglyn)

11. **Cholesterol-reducing drugs (hyperlipidemic agents)**
cholestyramine (Questran)
colestipol (Colestid)
gembibrozil (Lopid)
lovastatin (Mevacor)
niacin (Antivert, Nicobid)

12. **Corticosteroids for severe inflammatory conditions**
beclomethasone (Vanceril)
cortisone
dexamethasone (Decadron, Deronil, Dexasone)
methylprednisolone (Medrol)
prednisone (Deltazone, Orasone)

13. **Hyperactivity management drugs**
dextroamphetamine (Dexedrine)
epinephrine (Adrenalin)
methylphenidate hydrochloride (Ritalin)
pemoline (Cylert)

14. **Insulin for diabetes, type I**

15. **Iron for anemia**

16. **Metal poisoning drugs**
edetate calcium disodium (Calcium Disodium Versenate)
penicillamine (Cuprimine, Depen)

17. **Muscle relaxants for spasticity and tightness**
baclofen (Lioresal)
chlorzoxazone (Paraflex)
cyclobenzaprine (Flexeril)
diazepam (Valium)

18. **Nonsteroidal anti-inflammatory drugs (NSAIDs), mainly used for arthritis**
aspirin or salicylates
fenamic acid derivatives like Meclofenamate (Meclodium, Meclomen)
fenoprofen (Nalfon)
piroxicam (Feldene)

19. **Sedatives and hypnotics, nonbarbiturates**
chloral hydrate (Noctec)
flurazepam (Dalmane)
temazepam (Restoril)
triazolam (Halcion)

20. **Sex hormones, mostly for menstrual and menopause problems**
female (Estrogens, Progestogens)
male (Androgens)

21. **Sulfonylureas for diabetes, type II**
chlorpropamide (Diabinese)
glipizide (Glucotrol)
glyburide (DiaBeta, Micronase)
tolazamide (Tolinase)
tolbutamide (Orinase)

22. **Tranquilizers or benzodiazepines (antianxiety drugs)**
alprazolam (Xanax)
buspirone (Buspar)
chlordiazepoxide (Librium)
clorazepate (Tranxene)
diazepam (Valium)
oxazepam (Serax)

23. **Vasodilators** (*see* **antihypertensives**)

24. **Xanthines**
theophylline and phylline drugs like aminophylline, oxtriphylline (Quibron, Slo-Phyllin, Theo-Dur)

APPENDIX C

Assessment Information

Table C.1
Guide to locating norms and standards in body of text.

The purpose of Table C.1 is to help you locate assessment information for writing IEPs and making placement decisions.

Figure		**Page**
5.7	Sherrill's Assessment and Programming Model	113
7.2	Denver II	156
10.29	Milani-Comparetti Evaluation	255
13.8	Triceps Skinfold Measures	347
Table		**Page**
5.5	Developmental Stages in Rules Conformity	117
5.6	Developmental Stages in Social Play	119
5.7	Developmental Levels in Cooperation-Competition Continuum	121
7.1	50-Yd Dash Norms for Ages 9–17+	158
7.2	AAHPERD Physical Best Criteria	159
10.1	Reflexes of Most Importance to Physical Educators	239
11.1	Walk and Run Skills	286
11.2	Stair Skills	288
11.3	Jump and Hop Skills	289
11.4	Object Control Skills	297
13.9	12-Min Walking/Running Test	361
18.4	Developmental Levels in Toy or Object Play	446
19.2	Adult Heights and Weights	456

Table C.2
Overarm throw softball distance scores (in feet) for grades 1 to 6.

	Boys						Girls					
Grade	1	2	3	4	5	6	1	2	3	4	5	6
Age	6	7	8	9	10	11	6	7	8	9	10	11
Mean	47	62	73	89	102	115	24	32	36	44	54	64
Standard Deviation	14	16	16	19	23	22	8	11	11	13	16	20
						Percentiles						
95	71	90	101	122	143	152	39	53	60	69	85	100
75	56	73	83	102	118	130	29	38	42	52	62	74
50	47	61	73	87	102	114	24	31	35	44	54	62
30	40	55	64	79	91	102	20	27	30	37	46	54
25	38	53	63	77	86	100	19	25	29	35	45	51
15	31	48	58	70	79	91	17	23	27	32	40	46
5	25	35	49	63	65	81	14	20	20	25	32	38

Note. From Margie Hanson, *Motor Performance Testing of Elementary School Age Children,* pp. 252, 265, 266, unpublished doctoral dissertation, University of Washington, Seattle.

Table C.3
Standing long jump scores (in inches) for grades 1 to 6.

	Boys						Girls					
Grade	1	2	3	4	5	6	1	2	3	4	5	6
Age	6	7	8	9	10	11	6	7	8	9	10	11
Mean	46	50	54	56	60	63	43	47	49	53	57	61
Standard Deviation	6	7	6	6	7	8	6	7	7	7	7	8
						Percentiles						
95	58	61	63	66	71	75	54	59	61	65	68	74
75	50	55	59	61	66	69	47	51	55	58	62	66
50	46	50	54	56	61	64	42	47	50	53	57	61
30	43	47	51	53	57	60	40	44	46	50	54	57
25	42	46	50	52	56	59	39	43	45	49	53	56
15	40	44	48	50	54	57	37	41	42	46	51	53
5	36	39	43	46	48	50	32	37	38	42	46	50

Note. From Margie Hanson, *Motor Performance Testing of Elementary School Age Children,* pp. 252, 265, 266, unpublished doctoral dissertation, University of Washington, Seattle.

Table C.4
50-yd dash times (in seconds) for grades 1 to 6.

	Boys							Girls					
Grade	1	2	3	4	5	6		1	2	3	4	5	6
Age	6	7	8	9	10	11		6	7	8	9	10	11
Mean	9.9	9.3	8.8	8.5	8.2	8.1		10.3	9.5	9.2	8.7	8.6	8.3
Standard Deviation	1.0	0.9	0.7	0.7	0.7	0.7		1.0	0.9	0.9	0.7	0.6	0.7
						Percentiles							
95	8.4	8.1	7.8	7.5	7.4	7.1		8.9	8.2	8.0	7.6	7.7	7.2
75	9.2	8.7	8.3	8.1	7.8	7.7		9.5	8.9	8.7	8.3	8.2	7.8
50	9.9	9.2	8.8	8.6	8.2	8.0		10.2	9.3	9.2	8.7	8.6	8.3
30	10.4	9.6	9.0	8.9	8.6	8.4		10.9	9.7	9.5	9.0	9.0	8.7
25	10.6	9.9	9.1	9.0	8.6	8.5		11.0	9.9	9.6	9.1	9.1	8.8
15	11.0	10.2	9.4	9.3	8.9	8.8		11.3	10.4	9.9	9.5	9.4	9.1
5	11.6	11.0	9.9	9.6	9.5	9.3		12.0	11.1	10.8	10.1	9.8	9.5

Note. From Margie Hanson, *Motor Performance Testing of Elementary School Age Children,* pp. 252, 265, 266, unpublished doctoral dissertation, University of Washington, Seattle.

Table C.5
Height-weight data for boys (in pounds).

Height (in inches)	5	6	7	8	9	10	11	12	13	14	15	16	17	18	19	Height (in inches)
38	34	34														38
39	35	35														39
40	36	36														40
41	38	38	38													41
42	39	39	39	39												42
43	41	41	41	41												43
44	44	44	44	44												44
45	46	46	46	46	46											45
46	47	48	48	48	48											46
47	49	50	50	50	50	50										47
48		52	53	53	53	53										48
49		55	55	55	55	55	55									49
50		57	58	58	58	58	58	58								50
51			61	61	61	61	61	61								51
52			63	64	64	64	64	64	64							52
53			66	67	67	67	67	68	68							53
54				70	70	70	70	71	71	72						54
55				72	72	73	73	74	74	74						55
56				75	76	77	77	77	78	78	80					56
57					79	80	81	81	82	83	83					57
58					83	84	84	85	85	86	87					58
59						87	88	89	89	90	90	90				59
60						91	92	92	93	94	95	96				60
61							95	96	97	99	100	103	106			61
62							100	101	102	103	104	107	111	116		62
63							105	106	107	108	110	113	118	123	127	63
64								109	111	113	115	117	121	126	130	64
65								114	117	118	120	122	127	131	134	65
66									119	122	125	128	132	136	139	66
67									124	128	130	134	136	139	142	67
68										134	134	137	141	143	147	68
69										137	139	143	146	149	152	69
70										143	144	145	148	151	155	70
71										148	150	151	152	154	159	71
72											153	155	156	158	163	72
73											157	160	162	164	167	73
74											160	164	168	170	171	74

Note. Data from Melvin H. Williams, *Nutrition for Fitness and Sports.* Copyright © 1983 Wm. C. Brown Publishers, Dubuque, IA. All Rights Reserved.

Table C.6
Height-weight data for girls (in pounds).

Height (in inches)	5	6	7	8	9	10	11	12	13	14	15	16	17	18	Height (in inches)
							Age								
38	33	33													38
39	34	34													39
40	36	36	36												40
41	37	37	37												41
42	39	39	39												42
43	41	41	41	41											43
44	42	42	42	42											44
45	45	45	45	45	45										45
46	47	47	47	48	48										46
47	49	50	50	50	50	50									47
48		52	52	52	52	53									48
49		54	54	55	55	56	56								49
50		56	56	57	58	59	61	62							50
51			59	60	61	61	63	65							51
52			63	64	64	64	65	67							52
53			66	67	67	68	68	69	71						53
54				69	70	70	71	71	73						54
55				72	74	74	74	75	77	78					55
56					76	78	78	79	81	83					56
57					80	82	82	82	84	88	92				57
58						84	86	86	88	93	96	101			58
59						87	90	90	92	96	100	103	104		59
60						91	95	95	97	101	105	108	109	111	60
61							99	100	101	105	108	112	113	116	61
62							104	105	106	109	113	115	117	118	62
63								110	110	112	116	117	119	120	63
64								114	115	117	119	120	122	123	64
65								118	120	121	122	123	125	126	65
66									124	124	125	128	129	130	66
67									128	130	131	133	133	135	67
68									131	133	135	136	138	138	68
69										135	137	138	140	142	69
70										136	138	140	142	144	70
71										138	140	142	144	145	71

Note. Data from Melvin H. Williams, *Nutrition for Fitness and Sports.* Copyright © 1983 Wm. C. Brown Publishers, Dubuque, IA. All Rights Reserved.

APPENDIX

D

Addresses of Sport Organizations

Table D.1
Disabled sport organizations (DSOs) under U.S. Olympic Committee.

Amputee
National Handicapped Sports
Kirk Bauer, Executive Director
451 Hungerford Dr., Suite 100
Rockville, MD 20850
(301) 217–0960

Program Services Division
Debra L. Feagans
Winter Competition
3595 E. Fountain Blvd.
Suite 1–1
Colorado Springs, CO 80910
(719) 574–4136

Blind
U.S. Association for Blind Athletes
Roger Neppl, Executive Director
33 N. Institute St.
Brown Hall, Suite 015
Colorado Springs, CO 80903
(719) 630–0422

Dr. Gay Clement, USABA Youth Sports
Benson Bldg., University of South Carolina
Columbia, SC 29208
(803) 777–4465

Cerebral Palsy and Traumatic Head Injury
U.S. Cerebral Palsy Athletic Association
National Office Moving
Western Regional Office
Jerry McCole
3810 W. NW Highway #205
Dallas, TX 75220
(214) 352–4100

Other Contacts for CP Sports
Jeffery A. Jones
VWW Sports Program
Rehabilitation Institute of Chicago
345 East Superior St.
Chicago, IL 60611
(312) 908–4292

Grant Peacock, USCPAA President
2593 Lake Erin Dr.
Tucker, GA 30084
(404) 996–2942

Deaf
American Athletic Association for the Deaf
Shirley Platt, Sec.-Treas.
1134 Davenport Dr.
Burton, MI 48529
(313) 239–3962

National Information Center on Deafness
Gallaudet University
800 Florida Ave. NE
Washington, DC 20002–3625

Dwarf
Dwarf Athletic Association of America
Dr. Len Sawisch, President
3725 W. Holmes Rd.
Lansing, MI 48911
(517) 393–3116

Janet Brown, Executive Director
418 Willow Way
Lewisville, TX 75067
(214) 317–8630

Les Autres

United States Les Autres Sports Association
Dave Stephenson, Executive Director
1101 Post Oak Blvd., Suite 9–486
Houston, TX 77056
(713) 521–3737

Mentally Retarded

Special Olympics International
Eunice Kennedy Shriver, Founder-Director
1350 New York Avenue NW
Suite 500
Washington, DC 20005
(202) 628–3630

Spinally Paralyzed

National Wheelchair Athletic Association
3595 East Fountain Blvd., Suite L-100
Colorado Springs, CO 80910
(719) 574–1150

Track & Field
Wheelchair Athletes of USA
Judy Einbinder
1475 W. Gray, #161
Houston, TX 77019
(713) 522–9769

Note. See *Sports' N Spokes* for single sport affiliated bodies.

Table D.2
Other disabled multisport organizations.

Canadian Wheelchair Sports Association
1600 James Naismith Dr.
Gloucester, Ontario K1B 5N4, Canada
(613) 748–5685/Fax (613) 748–5722

United States Organization for Disabled Athletes
143 California Ave.
Uniondale, NY 11553
(516) 485–3701

Braille Sports Foundation
Dr. James Mastro
38–66 Way
N.E. Fridley, MN 55432
(612) 574–9317

Canadian Deaf Sports Association
333 River Rd.
Ottawa, Ontario K1L 8H9

International Paralympic Committee
Dr. Robert Steadward
Rick Hansen Centre
W1–67 Van Vliet Centre
University of Alberta, Edmonton
Alberta, Canada T6G 2H9
(403) 492–3182

1996 Atlanta Paralympic Games
Mike Mushett
Andy Fleming
2020 Peachtree Rd, N.W.
Atlanta, GA 30309
(404) 588–1996

International Sports Organization for the Disabled (ISOD)
Stoke Mandeville Sports Stadium
Harvey Rd.
Aylesbury, Bucks
England

Table D.3
Sport organizations/resources for one sport.

Basketball
National Wheelchair Basketball Association
Dr. Stan Labanowich
110 Seaton Bldg.
University of Kentucky
Lexington, KY 40506

Boccia
Cathy Shea
3500 S.W. 10th
Topeka, KS 66604

Bowling
American Wheelchair Bowling Association
Daryl Pfister
N54 W15858 Larkspur Lane
Menominee Falls, WI 53051

American Blind Bowling Association
411 Sheriff
Mercer, PA 16137

Horseback Riding
National Center for Therapeutic Riding
P.O. Box 42501
Washington, DC 20015

North American Riding for the Handicapped
Association
P.O. Box 33150
Denver, CO 80233

Dressage for Disabled
U.S. Dressage Federation
Sandy Rafferty
Rt. 1, Box 369
Troy, MO 63379

Racquet Sports
International Foundation for Wheelchair
Tennis
Peter Burwash
2203 Timberloch Place, Suite 126
The Woodlands, TX 77380

National Foundation of Wheelchair Tennis
Brad Parks, Director
940 Calle Amanecer, Suite B
San Clemente, CA 92672

National Wheelchair Racquetball
Association
Joe Hagar
535 Kensington Rd., Apt. 4
Lancaster, PA 17603

Road Racing
International Wheelchair Road Racers Club, Inc.
Joseph M. Dowling, President
30 Myano Lane
Stamford, CT 06902
(203) 967–2231

Shooting
National Wheelchair Shooting Federation
Deanna Greene, President
P.O. Box 18251
San Antonio, TX 78218–0251

Skiing
National Handicapped Sports
Kirk Bauer, Executive Director
451 Hungerford Dr., Suite 100
Rockville, MD 20850

Ski for Light, Inc.
Jeff Pagels, Mobility-Impaired Coordinator
1400 Carole Lane
Green Bay, WI 54313
(414) 494–5572

Softball
National Wheelchair Softball Association
Jon Speake, Commissioner
1616 Todd Court
Hastings, MN 55033
(612) 437–1792

Water Sports/Recreation
American Red Cross
17th and D Street NW
Washington, DC 20006

Council for National Cooperation in Aquatics
Louise Priest
901 West New York St.
Indianapolis, IN 46223

United States Swimming, Inc.
1750 East Boulder St.
Colorado Springs, CO 80909

Quad Sports
United States Quad Rugby Association
Brad Mikkelsen
2418 West Fallcreek Court
Grand Forks, ND 58201
(701) 772–1961

Appendix

E

Addresses of Other Organizations and Agencies

Table E.1
Professional associations.

Adapted Physical Activity Academy
American Alliance for Health, Physical Education,
Recreation, and Dance-Arapces Substructure
1900 Association Dr.
Reston, VA 22091

American College of Sports Medicine
P.O. Box 1440
Indianapolis, IN 46206–1440

American Dance Therapy Association
2000 Century Plaza, Suite 108
Columbia, MD 21044

American Occupational Therapy Association
1383 Piccard Dr., Suite 301
Rockville, MD 20850-4375

American Physical Therapy Association
111 N. Fairfax St.
Alexandria, VA 22314

American Psychological Association
1200 17th St. NW
Washington, DC 20036

American Therapeutic Recreation Association
P.O. Box 15215
Hattiesburg, MS 39402–5212

Canadian Association for Health, Physical Education, and
Recreation (Suite 606)
1600 James Naismith Dr.
Gloucester, Ontario K1B 5N4

Canadian Association of Sport Sciences (Suite 311)
1600 James Naismith Dr.
Gloucester, Ontario K1B 5N4

Canadian Fitness and Lifestyle Research Institute (Suite 313)
1600 James Naismith Dr.
Gloucester, Ontario K1B 5N4

The Council for Exceptional Children
1920 Association Dr.
Reston, VA 22091

International Federation of Adapted Physical Activity
Contact Dr. Claudine Sherrill
89 Windjammer Dr.
Frisco, TX 75034

National Association of State Directors of Special Education
Suite 320, 1800 Diagonal Rd.
Alexandria, VA 22314

National Consortium for Physical Education and Recreation for
Individuals with Disabilities
(Address changes every 2 years with new president)
Contact Dr. Claudine Sherrill
89 Windjammer Dr.
Frisco, TX 75034

National Dance Association
1900 Association Dr.
Reston, VA 22091

National Rehabilitation Association
633 S. Washington St.
Alexandria, VA 22314

National Therapeutic Recreation Society
3101 Park Center Dr.
Alexandria, VA 22302

Rehabilitation International USA
25 East 21st St.
New York, NY 10010

Very Special Arts, John F. Kennedy Center for Performing Arts
Washington, DC 20566
Phone (202) 628–2800

Table E.2
Associations related to disabilities.

Autism
Autism Society of America
8601 Georgia Ave., Suite 503
Silver Springs, MD 20910
Phone (301) 565–0433

National Society for Autistic Children
1234 Massachusetts Ave. NW, Suite 1017
Washington, DC 20005

Blind
American Foundation for the Blind
15 West 16th St.
New York, NY 10011

Association for the Education and Rehabilitation of the Blind and Visually Impaired—Bulletin for Physical Educators
206 N. Washington St., Suite 320
Alexandria, VA 22314

The Seeing Eye, Incorporated
Morristown, NJ 07960

Ski for Light
Skiing for Visually Impaired and Physically Handicapped
1455 West Lake St.
Minneapolis, MN 55408

Telephone Pioneers of America
Beep Ball Information
22 Cortlandt St., Room 2588
New York, NY 10007

Cerebral Palsy and Traumatic Head Injury
American Academy for Cerebral Palsy and
Developmental Medicine
1910 Byrd Ave., No. 118
P.O. Box 11086
Richmond, VA 23230–1086

National Easter Seal Society
70 E. Lake St.
Chicago, IL 60601

National Head Injury Foundation
333 Turnpike Rd.
Southborough, MA 01772
Toll Free 1–800–444–6443

United Cerebral Palsy Associations
1522 K St. NW, Suite 1112
Washington, DC 20005

Dwarf
Little People of America
7238 Piedmont Dr.
Dallas, TX 75227–9324

Deaf
Alexander Graham Bell Association for the Deaf
3417 Volta Place NW
Washington, DC 20007

American Instructors of the Deaf
P.O. Box 2025
Austin, TX 78768–2025

Gallaudet College
National Information Center on Deafness
7th St. and Florida Ave. NE
Washington, DC 20002

Helen Keller National Center for Deaf-Blind Youths and Adults
111 Middle Neck Rd.
Sands Point, NY 11050

National Association of the Deaf
814 Thayer Ave.
Silver Spring, MD 20910

Learning Disabilities
Learning Disability Association of America (LDA)
(formerly ACLD)
4156 Library Rd.
Pittsburgh, PA 15234

Orton Dyslexia Society
724 York Rd.
Baltimore, MD 21204

Mental Retardation
American Association on Mental Retardation
1719 Kalorama Rd. NW
Washington, DC 20009

ARC (formerly Association for Retarded Citizens)
P.O. Box 6109
Arlington, TX 76005

National Down Syndrome Congress
1800 Dempster St.
Park Ridge, IL 60068–1146

National Down Syndrome Society
666 Broadway
New York, NY 10012

The Association for Persons with Severe Handicaps (TASH)
(formerly AAESPH)
11201 Greenwood Ave. N
Seattle, WA 98133

Physical Disabilities
National Spinal Cord Injury Association
600 W. Cummings Park, Suite 2000
Woburn, MA 01801

Paralyzed Veterans of America
801 18th St. NW
Washington, DC 20006

Spina Bifida Association of America
1700 Rockville Pike, Suite 250
Rockville, MD 20852

Table E.3
Voluntary health organizations.

American Cancer Society
1599 Clifton Rd. NE
Atlanta, GA 30329

American Diabetes Association
P.O. Box 25757
1660 Duke St.
Alexandria, VA 22314

American Heart Association
7272 Greenville Ave.
Dallas, TX 75231–4596
(214) 373–6300

American Lung Association
1740 Broadway
New York, NY 10019

American Red Cross
17th and D Streets NW
Washington, DC 20006

American Thoracic Society
1740 Broadway
New York, NY 10019–4374

The Arthritis Foundation
1314 Spring St. NW
Atlanta, GA 30309

Asthma and Allergy Foundation of America
1717 Massachusetts Ave., Suite 305
Washington, DC 20036
Toll Free 1–800–7–ASTHMA

Cystic Fibrosis Foundation
6931 Arlington Rd., No. 200
Bethesda, MD 20814

Epilepsy Foundation of America
4351 Garden City Dr.
Landover, MD 20785

Muscular Dystrophy Association
27th Floor
810 Seventh Ave.
New York, NY 10019

National Hemophilia Foundation
110 Green St., Room 406
New York, NY 10012

National Multiple Sclerosis Society
205 East 42nd St.
New York, NY 10017

Table E.4
Government offices/agencies.

National Center for Health Statistics
Public Health Service, HRA
Rockville, MD 20852

National Information Center for Children and Youth with
Disabilities (NICHCY)
P.O. Box 1492
Washington, DC 20013
Toll Free 1–800–999–5599

Office of Special Education and Rehabilitative Services (OSERS)
Mary E. Switzer Bldg., Room 3132
330 C Street SW
Washington, DC 20202–2524

Office of Special Education Programs (OSEP), one of three
offices comprising OSERS
400 Maryland Ave. SW
Donahoe Building
Washington, DC 20202

President's Council on Physical Fitness and Sports
Washington, DC 20001

State Agencies and Information on Disability—Contact
NICHCY (see previously listed address)

APPENDIX

F

Addresses for Purchasing Materials

Table F.1
Companies for books and journals.

Brown & Benchmark
2460 Kerper Blvd.
Dubuque, IA 52001
Toll Free 1–800–388–5578
Publishes several textbooks.

Challenge Publications
P.O. Box 508
Macomb, IL 61455
Phone (309) 833–1902
Publishes *Palaestra.*

Human Kinetics Publishers
Box 5076
Champaign, IL 61820
Toll Free 1–800–747–4457
Publishes *Adapted Physical Activity Quarterly* and several
textbooks.

Paralyzed Veterans of America, Inc.
5201 N. 19th Ave.
Suite 111
Phoenix, AZ 85015
Phone (602) 246–9426
Publishes *Sports 'N Spokes,* which is a major information source
for purchase of wheelchairs and products used by people in
wheelchairs.

Pro•Ed
8700 Shoal Creek Blvd.
Austin, TX 78758–6897
Phone (512) 451–3246
Publishes *Academic Therapy, Focus on Autistic Behavior,
Journal of Learning Disabilities, Topics in Early Childhood
Special Education,* and other journals.

SPORT Database
1600 James Naismith Dr.
Gloucester, Ontario, Canada KIB 5N4
Phone (613) 748–5658
Produces comprehensive reference lists and computerized data.

Table F.2
Companies for equipment.

Cosom/Mantua Industries, Inc.
Grandview Ave.
Woodbury Heights, NJ 08097
Phone (609) 853–0300.

Flaghouse, Inc.
150 N. MacQuesten Parkway
Mt. Vernon, NY 10550
Phone (914) 699–1900.

GSC/BSN Sports
P.O. Box 7726
Dallas, TX 75209
Toll Free 1–800–525–7510
Official supplier for U.S. Cerebral Palsy Athletic Association.
Good source for retractable handle bowling balls.

Jayfro Corporation
976 Hartford Turnpike
Waterford, CT 06385
Phone (203) 447–3001.

J. A. Preston Corporation
744 W. Michigan Ave.
Jackson, MI 49204
Toll Free 1–800–631–7277.

LS & S Products for Visually Impaired
P.O. Box 673
Northbrook, IL 60065
Toll Free 1–800–468–4789.

Rifton for People With Disabilities
Route 213
Rifton, NY 12471
Phone (914) 658–3141.

Sportime
One Sportime Way
Atlanta, GA 30340–1402
Toll Free 1–800–444–5700.

Wolverine Sports
745 State Circle
Ann Arbor, MI 48108
Toll Free 1–800–521–2832.

Table F.3
Companies for personal flotation devices.

Danmar Products, Inc.
2390 Winewood
Ann Arbor, MI 48102.

Excel Sports Science, Inc.
P.O. Box 5612
Eugene, OR 97405.

J & B Foam Fabricators, Inc.
P.O. Box 144
Ludington, MI 49431.

Table F.4
Companies for test and curriculum materials.

American Guidance Service (AGS)
P.O. Box 99
Circle Pines, MN 55014–1796
Toll Free 1–800–323–2560
Bruininks-Oseretsky Test and Body Skills, a motor development curriculum.

DLM,
One DLM Park
Allen, TX 75002
Toll Free 1–800–527–4747
Early childhood materials, Peabody developmental materials.

Pro·Ed
8700 Shoal Creek Blvd.
Austin, TX 78758–6897
Phone (512) 451–3246
I CAN physical education materials, Test of Gross Motor Development (TGMD), data-based gymnasium materials, behavior management and social skills curricula.

Western Psychological Services (WPS)
12031 Wilshire Blvd.
Los Angeles, CA 90025
Toll Free 1–800–222–2670
Self-concept and personality inventories, counseling materials.

A P P E N D I X

G

Important Events in Adapted Physical Activity

1817 The first residential schools established in the United States were for deaf students: the American School for the Deaf in Hartford, CT, and the New York School for the Deaf in White Plains, NY, founded in 1817 and 1818, respectively. Thomas Hopkins Gallaudet is credited with founding the school in Connecticut. In 1856, the institution now known as Gallaudet University, Washington, DC, evolved through the efforts of philanthropist Amos Kendall.

1830 The first residential schools for the blind were founded between 1830 and 1833 in Boston, New York, and Philadelphia. Only one of the early residential facilities, the Perkins Institution in Boston, provided physical education for its students.

1847 *The American Annals of the Deaf,* first published in 1847, is the oldest educational journal in the United States still in existence.

1848 The first residential institution for persons with mental retardation in the United States was organized in Massachusetts in 1848.

1863 The earliest residential facilities for persons with physical disabilities bore such names as Hospital of the New York Society for the Relief of the Ruptured and Crippled (1863) and the Children's House of the Home for Incurables in Philadelphia (1877).

1864 Edouard Seguin's classic book *Idiocy and Its Diagnoses and Treatment by the Physiological Method* was translated into English. This book provided the framework for the earliest attempts to train persons with mental retardation. Seguin was a student and protégé of Jean-Marc Itard, known for his work with Victor, the "Wild Boy of Aveyron," in the early 1800s.

1876 Establishment of the American Association on Mental Deficiency (AAMD). First president was Edouard Seguin. One of its original goals was to promote the development of residential facilities. During the first decade of AAMD's existence, 20 states created residential schools for persons with MR.

1885 Formation of the Association for the Advancement of Physical Education, the forerunner of AAHPERD. First president was Edward Hitchcock, MD. Almost all the early members were physicians.

1895 The National Education Association (NEA) organized a Department of Physical Education.

1899 Public schooling for persons with disabilities had begun, with the earliest documentation citing 100 large cities with special education classes. Among these were Boston, Chicago, Cleveland, Detroit, New York, and Milwaukee.

1902 The National Education Association organized a Department of Special Education. Alexander Graham Bell, pioneer in deaf education, spearheaded this recognition.

1906 Formation of the Playground Association of America, the forerunner of National Recreation and Park Association (NRPA), of which the National Therapeutic Recreation Society (NTRS) is a subdivision. First president was Dr. Luther Halsey Gulick.

1912 Establishment of Children's Bureau in Washington, DC, to promote the welfare of children and to prevent their exploitation in industry.

1917 Origin of the National Society for the Promotion of Occupational Therapy, the forerunner of the American Occupational Therapy Association (1921).

1919 National Easter Seals Society for Crippled Children and Adults founded.

1920 The National Civilian Vocational Rehabilitation Act, a forerunner of the Social Security Act, passed.

1921 Origin of forerunner of American Physical Therapy Association. First president was Mary McMillan, who strongly influenced early leaders in corrective physical education who were also physical therapists: George Stafford and Josephine Rathbone.

1922 Establishment of Council for Exceptional Children (CEC), the first organization to advocate for all groups with disabilities. First president was Elizabeth Farrell.

1928 First textbooks to use the term *corrective physical education* were published:
Stafford, G. T. (1928). *Preventive and corrective physical education.* New York: A. S. Barnes.
Lowman, C., Colestock, C., & Cooper, H. (1928). *Corrective physical education for groups.* New York: A. S. Barnes.

1930 Historic White House Conference on Child Health and Protection. The Committee on the Physically and Mentally Handicapped wrote the often-quoted Bill of Rights for Handicapped Children.

1935 Social Security Act passed.

1944, 1952, also **1915–17** Major epidemics of poliomyelitis, which left thousands of persons paralyzed. In 1952 alone, 57,628 cases of polio were reported.

1945 Formation of the American Athletic Association for the Deaf (AAAD). This was the first special population in the United States to form its own sport organization.

1946 Association for Physical and Mental Rehabilitation (APMR) established, the forerunner of American Kinesiotherapy Association (AKA). Name changed to American Corrective Therapy Association in 1967 and to AKA in 1983.

1949 Formation of the National Wheelchair Basketball Association (NWBA).

1950 The National Association for Music Therapy, Inc. (NAMT) formed.

1950 The National Association for Retarded Citizens (NARC) founded. Name changed in 1979 to Association for Retarded Citizens (ARC). In 1992, ARC became the name rather than the initials for words.

1952 First International Wheelchair Games held at Stoke Mandeville, England.

1955 Salk vaccine recognized as 80 to 90% effective against paralytic polio.

1956 Formation of National Wheelchair Athletic Association (NWAA).

1958 National Foundation for Infantile Paralysis became The National Foundation—March of Dimes and turned attention to birth defects and genetic counseling.

1958 PL 85–926 was passed, authorizing grants to universities and colleges and to state education agencies for training personnel in mental retardation. This legislation represents the beginning of the federal government's commitment to the rights of persons with disabilities.

1960 First Paralympic Games held in Rome. This was the first time that the International Stoke-Mandeville Games were held in conjunction with Olympic Games.

1961 Kennedy appointed the first President's Panel on Mental Retardation.

1963 PL 88–164 amended 1958 legislation to encompass all handicapped groups that required special education.

1964 Civil rights legislation (PL 88–352) passed.

1964 Association for Children with Learning Disabilities (ACLD) formed. Name changed in 1980 to ACLD, Inc. (An Association for Children and Adults with Learning Disabilities) and in 1990 to LDA (Learning Disability of America).

1965 PL 89–10, the Elementary and Secondary Education Act (ESEA), passed. Included Titles I to IV. Many innovative public school physical education programs, now nationally well known, were funded under Title III (now IVC). Among these programs were Vodola's Project ACTIVE in New Jersey and Long's Project PEOPEL in Arizona.

1965 The AAHPER Project on Recreation and Fitness for the Mentally Retarded was formed with a grant from the Joseph P. Kennedy, Jr. Foundation. This project was the forerunner of the Unit on Programs for the Handicapped, which served AAHPERD members from 1968 to 1981.

1966 American Dance Therapy Association, Inc. (ADTA) founded in New York City.

1966 Bureau of Education for the Handicapped (BEH) created by PL 89–750 within the Office of Education of HEW. BEH, which became the Office of Special Education Programs (OSEP) in 1980, has been the agency that funds university training programs in physical education and recreation for persons with disabilities.

1967 Formation of the National Handicapped Sports and Recreation Association (NHSRA), which governs winter and amputee sports. Name changed to National Handicapped Sports (NHS) in 1992.

1967 ESEA amended under PL 90–170, Title V, Section 502, to support training, research, and demonstration projects, specifically in physical education and recreation for individuals with disabilities. This was part of the Mental Retardation Amendments originally supported by Senator Edward Kennedy and signed by President Lyndon B. Johnson.

1967 National Therapeutic Recreation Society (NTRS) created as a branch of the National Recreation and Park Association.

1968 AAHPER Unit on Programs for the Handicapped approved. This replaced Project on Recreation and Fitness for the Mentally Retarded.

1968 PL 90–480, Elimination of Architectural Barriers to Physically Handicapped, passed. This was the first federal legislation pertaining to architectural barriers.

1968 First Special Olympics; AAHPER-Kennedy Foundation Special Fitness Awards established.

1970 Title VI, Public Law 91–230, Education of the Handicapped Act (EHA), passed. This was the first major legislation leading to the subsequent passage of PL 94–142 in 1975.

1970 Series of institutes sponsored by BEH held on the Development of AAHPER Guidelines for Professional Preparation Programs for Personnel Involved in Physical Education and Recreation for the Handicapped. Report published by AAHPER in 1973.

1972 Information and Research Utilization Center (IRUC) in Physical Education and Recreation for the Handicapped funded by BEH and established in conjunction with AAHPER Unit on Programs for the Handicapped.

1972 Title IX legislation (PL 92–318) passed.

1972 AC/FMR (Accreditation Council for Facilities for the Mentally Retarded) issued standards, including recreation services, which all residential and intermediate care facilities must implement in order to receive accreditation. New AC/FMR standards are issued periodically.

1973 Rehabilitation Amendments (PL 93–112) completely recodified the old Vocational Rehabilitation Act and placed emphasis on expanding services to clients with more severe disabilities. Section 504, the "nondiscrimination clause," which specified that no qualified persons with disabilities shall be excluded from federally assisted programs or activities, is the best-known part of the law. PL 93–112 was not implemented, however, until 1977, when its rules and regulations were agreed upon and published in the May 4, 1977, issue of the *Federal Register.*

1973 National Ad Hoc Committee on Physical Education and Recreation for the Handicapped formed by BEH project directors at Minneapolis (AAHPER) conference. This was the forerunner of the National Consortium (see 1975).

1973 International Federation of Adapted Physical Activity founded. First symposium held in Montreal in 1977.

1974 At the annual conference in Anaheim, California, AAHPER was reorganized as the American Alliance for Health, Physical Education, and Recreation with seven independent associations. Three of these included programs for people with disabilities: ARAPCS (Association for Research, Administration, Professional Councils and Societies), NASPE (National Association for Sport and Physical Education, and AALR (American Association for Leisure and Recreation).

1974 The National Diffusion Network (NDN) created by the United States Office of Education. This system facilitates optimal use of programs like Project ACTIVE through a network of state facilitators and developer/demonstrators. For additional information, contact Division of Educational Replication, USOE, ROB3 Room 3616, 400 Maryland Ave. SW, Washington, DC 20202.

1974 Formation of the American Association for the Education of the Severely/Profoundly Handicapped (AAESPH). In 1980, the name of this organization changed to The Association for the Severely Handicapped (TASH) and the title of its journal became *JASH, Journal of Association for Severely Handicapped.*

1975 National Consortium on Physical Education and Recreation for the Handicapped (NCPERH) evolved from National Ad Hoc Committee. First president was Leon Johnson, University of Missouri. Name changed in 1992 to National Consortium for Physical Education and Recreation for Individuals With Disabilities (NCPERIWD).

1975 PL 94–142 enacted. Called the "Education for All Handicapped Children Act," it stated specifically that *instruction in physical education* shall be provided for all children with disabilities.

1976 Formation of the U.S. Association for Blind Athletes (USABA).

1976 The Olympiad for the Physically Handicapped held in Canada in conjunction with the Olympic Games. This was the first time that blind athletes and amputees were recognized and allowed to participate.

1976 White House Conference on Handicapped Individuals (WHCHI) held, with delegates chosen from governors' conference in each state. The final report included 420 recommendations, several of which pertained to recreation and leisure.

1977 First National Championships, U.S. Association for Blind Athletes.

1977 Regulations to implement Section 504 of PL 93–112, the Rehabilitation Act of 1973, signed by the Secretary of HEW, Joseph Califano. This is the first civil rights law guaranteeing equal opportunities for Americans with disabilities.

1977 Regulations to implement PL 94–142 published in the August 23 issue of the *Federal Register.* (See Chapter 4.)

1977 First Annual National Wheelchair Marathon held in conjunction with the Boston Marathon (26.2 mi). This event is now sponsored annually by the National Spinal Cord Injury Foundation.

1978 Formation of the National Association of Sports for Cerebral Palsy (NASCP). Name changed in 1986 to U.S. Cerebral Palsy Athletic Association.

1978 PL 95–602, the Developmentally Disabled (DD) Assistance and Bill of Rights Act passed, updating DD legislation of 1970 and 1975.

1978 PL 95–606, the Amateur Sports Act, recognized the sport organizations of athletes with disabilities as part of the U.S. Olympic Committee structure.

1979 The American National Standards Institute (ANSI) published the revised ANSI standard A 117.1 (Specifications for Making Buildings and Facilities Accessible to and Usable by Physically Disabled People). This standard replaced the one established in 1961 and reaffirmed in 1971. ANSI is the governmental agency responsible for, among other things, setting standards for wheelchair accessibility. For more information, contact ANSI, 1430 Broadway, New York, NY 10018.

1979 AAHPER's name officially changed to AAHPERD (American Alliance for Health, Physical Education, Recreation, and Dance), thereby giving recognition to dance as a discipline separate from physical education.

1979 The U.S. Olympic Committee (USOC) organized a Committee for the Handicapped in Sports, with Kathryn Sallade Barclift elected as its first chairperson. This committee brought together for the first time representatives from the five major sport organizations for athletes with disabilities. Now named Committee on Sports for the Disabled (COSD).

1979 PL 96–88 changed the status of the old U.S. Office of Education within the Department of Health, Education, and Welfare (HEW) to a Department of Education. Shirley M. Hufstedler was appointed its first secretary. HEW was disbanded.

1980 Reorganization completed for the two new departments replacing HEW. These new structures are the Department of Education (ED) and the Department of Health and Human Services (HHS). Within ED's seven principal program offices, the Office of Special Education and Rehabilitative Services (OSERS) relates to people with disabilities. Principal components of OSERS are Office of Special Education Programs (OSEP), which replaces BEH; Rehabilitation Services Administration (RSA); and National Institute of Handicapped Research.

1981 New AAHPERD guidelines (competencies) on adapted physical education published.

1981 Declared the "International Year of the Disabled" by the United Nations.

1981 January 19 issue of *Federal Register* (Vol. 46, No. 12) devoted to IEPs, including clarifications for physical education.

1981 Formation of the U.S. Amputee Athletic Association (USAAA). Dissolved in 1990.

1982 First UNESCO-sponsored international symposium on physical education and sport programs for persons with physical and mental disabilities.

1984 International Games for the Disabled (blind, cerebral palsied, amputee, and les autres) held in Long Island, NY, with approximately 2,500 athletes competing. Seventh World Wheelchair Games (spinally paralyzed) held in England.

1984 *Adapted Physical Activity Quarterly* first published. This was first professional journal to be devoted specifically to adapted physical education.

1984 *Palaestra* first published. This was a specialized journal for adapted physical activity, sport, and recreation.

1986 *Sport and Disabled Athletes,* the proceedings of the Olympic Scientific Congress, published by Human Kinetics, Champaign, IL.

1986 Merger completed within AAHPERD of NASPE Adapted Physical Education Academy and ARAPCS Therapeutic Council. The new structure is called the Adapted Physical Activity Council and is housed within ARAPCS.

1988 Paralympics held in Korea. This was the first time that all athletes with physical disabilities competed at the same venue.

1990 Americans With Disabilities Act (PL 101–336) enacted.

1990 Individuals With Disabilities Education Act (PL 101–476) enacted.

1992 North American Federation of Adapted Physical Activity (NAFAPA) organized.

1992 Paralympics held in Barcelona. This was the first time that integrated classifications were used.

1993 First quadrennial International Special Olympics Meet held outside of USA. World Winter Games in Salzburg, Austria.

CREDITS

LINE ART, TABLES, TEXT

1

Figure 1.9. From M. Churton & J. R. Tompkins (1988) in C. Sherrill (Ed.). *Leadership training in adapted physical education,* p. 200, Champaign, IL: Human Kinetics.

2

Figure 2.11. From H. Yuker, J. Block, & J. Young (1966). *The measurement of attitudes toward disabled persons.* Albertson, NY: Human Resources Center.
Figure 2.12. From G. N. Siperstein (1980). *Instruments for measuring children's attitudes toward the handicapped.* University of Massachusetts Center for the Study of Social Acceptance, Boston.
Figure 2.13. From I. Ajzen & M. Fishbein (1980). *Understanding attitudes and predicting social behavior,* p. 220, Englewood Cliffs, NJ: Prentice Hall, Inc. With permission of Yale University Press. Based on Janis & Hovland, 1959.
Poem on p. 23 by La Ferne Ellis Price in *The Wonder of Motion: A sense of life for Woman* (p. 13). Copyright 1970 by American Alliance for Health, Physical Education, Recreation, and Dance.
Song on p. 27 by Nancy Anderson. From videotape *Look at Me.* By permission of Terry N. Terry, President, The Message Makers, 1217 Turner, Lansing, MI 48906.
Poem on p. 33 by Jean Caywood, Richardson, TX. No copyright.
Excerpt, pp. 30–31. Leo Buscaglia. *The Disabled and Their Parents: A Counseling Challenge.* (Thorofare, NJ: Charles B. Slack, Inc., 1975), pp. 19–20.
Excerpt, pp. 33–34. *Guidelines for Writing and Speaking About People With Disabilities,* Research and Training Center on Independent Living, University of Kansas, Lawrence.
Poem on p. 34. From Dave Compton, "OK Being Different" in *Proceedings of Special Populations Institute,* March 28–29, 1974. Ogleby Park, Wheeling, West Virginia: Northern Community College.

3

Figure 3.1. Adapted from unpublished work of Duncan Wyeth, Michigan Dept. of Education.

4

Figure 4.1. Adapted from table (p. 3) in *NICHCY News Digest, 1* (1), 1991. (Government publication, copyright permission not needed.)
Figure 4.9. Partly from Special education as developmental capital by E. Deno, *Exceptional Children, 37* (3), 1970, p. 235. Copyright 1970 by The Council for Exceptional Children. Reprinted with permission.

6

Figure 6.3. Developed from concepts on pp. 15–51, A. Maslow (1970). *Motivation and personality* (2nd ed.). New York: Harper & Row.
Table 6.1. Adapted from instrument supplied by C. Ennis, personal correspondence, 1988. Research using this instrument is in Ennis, C. (1985). Purpose concepts in an existing physical education curriculum. *Research Quarterly for Exercise and Sport, 56* (4), 323–333.
Figure 6.6. Based on concepts presented in A. Bandura (1977). Self-efficacy: Toward a unifying theory of behavioral change. *Psychological Review, 84* (7), 191–215.
Figures 6.9, 6.12, and 6.13. From S. Harter, *Manual for the Self-Perception Profile for Adolescents,* 1988. Reprinted with permission. Not copyrighted.
Figure 6.11. Reprinted with permission of Psychologists and Educators Inc., P.O. Box 513, Chesterfield, MO 63006.
Figure 6.15. Reprinted with permission of Dr. Dale Ulrich, Physical Education Dept., Indiana University, Bloomington, IN 47405.
Figure 6.16. From "The Self-Esteem Complex and Youth Fitness" by K. R. Fox, 1988, *Quest, 40,* pp. 233 and 237.
Figure 6.17. From K. R. Fox, 1990, *The Physical Self-Perception Profile Manual,* Office of Health Promotion, Northern Illinois University, DeKalb, IL 60115.
Figure 6.18. Based on content in M. R. Weiss, B. Bredemeier, & R. Shewchuk (1985). An intrinsic/extrinsic motivation scale for the youth sport setting. *Journal of Sport Psychology, 7,* 75–91.

Figure 6.19. From "Testing the Validity of the Griffin/Keogh Model for Movement Confidence by Analyzing Self-Report Playground Involvement Decisions of Elementary School Children," by M. E. Crawford & N. S. Griffin. This article is reprinted with permission from the *Research Quarterly for Exercise and Sport, vol. 57,* no. 1 (1986). The *Research Quarterly for Exercise and Sport* is a publication of the American Alliance for Health, Physical Education, Recreation and Dance, 1900 Association Drive, Reston, VA 22091.
Figure 6.20. From "Attributions of Athletes with Cerebral Palsy" by G. Dummer, M. Ewing, R. Habeck, & S. Overton, 1987, *Adapted Physical Activity Quarterly, 4* (4), p. 282. Reprinted with modification with permission.

7

Figure 7.2 Courtesy of William K. Frankenburg & Josiah B. Dodds, University of Colorado Medical Center, Boulder, CO.
Table 7.3 Content from Test of Gross Motor Development, 1985, by Dale A. Ulrich. PRO·ED, 8700 Shoal Creek Blvd., Austin, TX 78758.
Figures 7.3, 7.4, and 7.5. From G. S. D. Morris (1980). *How to Change the Games Children Play,* 2nd ed., Minneapolis: Burgess.
Figure 7.8. Reproduced with the permission of American Guidance Service, Inc. *Bruininks-Oseretsky Test of Motor Proficiency* by Robert N. Bruininks. Copyright 1978. All rights reserved.
Table 7.6. Based on content in Denver Developmental Screening Test Manual published by Denver Developmental Materials, Inc., P.O. Box 6919, Denver, CO 80206–0919.
Figure 7.17. From Special Olympics International. *Special Olympics Gymnastics Sports Skills Program,* pp. 28 and 64. Reprinted with permission.

8

Tables 8.4 and 8.5. Concepts from Janet Wessel's I CAN and ABC federally funded projects. Also included in J. Wessel and L. Kelly (1986). *Achievement-Based Curriculum Development in Physical Education.* Philadelphia: Lea & Febiger.

Figure 8.7. From *Cowstails and Cobras* (pp. 34, 36, 41, and 43) by Karl Rohnke, 1977, Hamilton, MA: Project Adventure. Copyright 1977 by Project Adventure. Reprinted by permission.
Checklist on pp. 200–204 adapted from unpublished dissertation of Nancy Megginson, 1982, Texas Woman's University, Denton.

9

Figure 9.4. From Muska Mosston, Teaching Physical Education—From Command to Discovery. Columbus, OH: Charles E. Merrill, 1966, 1981, p. 230.

10

Figure 10.6. Adapted from G. Sage (1977). *Introduction to Motor Behavior: A Neuropsychological Approach,* p. 106. Reading, MA: Addison-Wesley Publishing Co.
Figures 10.7, 10.35(a), 10.35(b), 10.36, and 10.38. From John W. Hole, Jr., *Human Anatomy and Physiology,* 2d ed. Copyright © 1981 Wm. C. Brown Communications, Inc., Dubuque, Iowa. All Rights Reserved. Reprinted by permission.
Figure 10.22. From *Fundamental Movement: A Developmental and Remedial Approach,* by Bruce A. McClenaghan and David L. Gallahue. Copyright © 1978 by W. B. Saunders Company.
Figure 10.29. Reprinted by permission of A. Milani-Comparetti and E. A. Gidoni, Italy. Reproduced by permission from Norris G. Haring, *Developing Effective Individualized Education Programs for Severely Handicapped Children and Youth* (Columbus, OH: Special Press, 1977, p. 79). Available for purchase from Crace Rossa Italiana, Comitato Provinciale De Firenze, Centro Di Educazione Motoria, "Anna Torrigiani," via Di Comerata 8, 50133 Firenze.
Figure 10.39. From Sylvia S. Mader, *Inquiry Into Life,* 4th ed. Copyright © 1985 Wm. C. Brown Communications, Inc., Dubuque, Iowa. All Rights Reserved. Reprinted by permission.
Figure 10.40. From "Rhythmical Stereotypes in Normal Infants" by E. Thelen, 1979, *Animal Behavior, 27* pp. 703, 706.

11

Figure 11.21. Adapted from *Fundamental Movement: A Developmental and Remedial Approach,* by Bruce A. McClenaghan and David L. Gallahue. Copyright © 1978 by W. B. Saunders Company.
Figure 11.23 (c) and (d) and 11.24 (d) and (e). Courtesy of Mr. Jeffery A. Jones, Rehabilitation Institute of Chicago.
Figure 11.25. Adapted from M. Wild, *Research Quarterly,* AAHPERD, 1938; redrawing from C. Corbin, *A Textbook of Motor Development,* 2d. ed. Copyright © 1980 Wm. C. Brown Publishers, Dubuque, Iowa. All Rights Reserved. Reprinted by permission.
Figure 11.27. Table portion from G. S. D. Morris (1980). *How to Change the Games Children Play,* 2nd ed., Minneapolis: Burgess. *Excerpts* from Test of Gross Motor Development, 1985, by Dale A. Ulrich. PRO·ED, 8700 Shoal Creek Blvd., Austin, TX 78758.

13

Figure 13.5. Adapted from R. Detrano & V. F. Froelicher (1988). Exercise testing: Uses and limitations considering recent studies. *Progress in Cardiovascular Diseases, 31* (3), 173–204. Figure on p. 178.
Table 13.4. Data based largely on a paper by Samuel M. Fox, M.D., Preventive Cardiology Program, Georgetown University Medical Center, and presented by W. L. Haskell at N.I.M.H. meeting, Washington, D.C., April 1984.
Figure 13.8(c). From Carl C. Seltzer and Jean Mayer, "A Simple Criterion of Obesity," *Postgraduate Medicine 38* (August, 1965): A101–107.
Figure 13.11(a). Courtesy of Mr. Jeffery A. Jones, Rehabilitation Institute of Chicago.
Figure 13.13. From Edward L. Fox, Richard W. Bowers, and Merle L. Foss, *The Physiological Basis of Physical Education and Athletics,* 4th ed. Copyright © 1989 Wm. C. Brown Communications, Inc., Dubuque, Iowa. All Rights Reserved. Reprinted by permission.

18

Figure 18.5. Redrawn from Shirley, M. M. "The First Two Years" in *Child Welfare Monograph* 7, 1933. © 1933, renewed 1960, University of Minnesota Press, Minneapolis.
Figure 18.6. From *The Cerebral Cortex of Man,* by Penfield and Rasmussen © 1985 by MacMillan Publishing Co.

19

Figure 19.6. From "Natural History of Human Atherosclerotic Lesions" by H. L. McGill, J. C. Geer, and J. P. Strong. In *Atherosclerosis and Its Origins* (p. 42) by M. Sandler and G. H. Bourne (Eds.), 1963, New York: Academic Press. Copyright 1963 by Academic Press. Reprinted by permission.
Figures 19.3 (center), 19.7, 19.8(b), 19.9 (a and b), 19.10, 19.14, 19.23, and 19.25. From John W. Hole, Jr.,

Human Anatomy and Physiology, 5th ed. Copyright © 1990 Wm. C. Brown Communications, Inc., Dubuque, Iowa. All Rights Reserved. Reprinted by permission.
Figure 19.3 (top left/bottom right). From Charles B. Corbin and Ruth Lindsey, *Concepts of Physical Fitness,* 7th ed. Copyright © 1990 Wm. C. Brown Communications, Inc., Dubuque, Iowa. All Rights Reserved. Reprinted by permission.
Figure 19.8(a). From Kent M. Van De Graaff and Stuart Ira Fox, *Concepts of Human Anatomy and Physiology,* 2d ed. Copyright © 1989 Wm. C. Brown Communications, Inc., Dubuque, Iowa. All Rights Reserved. Reprinted by permission.
Figure 19.12(a). From Stuart Ira Fox, *Laboratory Guide to Human Physiology,* 5th ed. Copyright © 1990 Wm. C. Brown Communications, Inc., Dubuque, Iowa. All Rights Reserved. Reprinted by permission.
Figure 19.13. From Herbert A. de Vries, *Physiology of Exercise for Physical Education and Athletics,* 4th ed. Copyright © 1986 Wm. C. Brown Communications, Inc., Dubuque, Iowa. All Rights Reserved. Reprinted by permission.
Figure 19.21(a). From Sylvia S. Mader, *Inquiry Into Life,* 4th ed. Copyright © 1985 Wm. C. Brown Communications, Inc., Dubuque, Iowa. All Rights Reserved. Reprinted by permission.

21

Figure 21.7. From John W. Hole, Jr., *Human Anatomy and Physiology,* 5th ed. Copyright © 1990 Wm. C. Brown Communications, Inc., Dubuque, Iowa. All Rights Reserved. Reprinted by permission.
Figure 21.8. From D. A. Sugden and J. F. Keogh (1990). *Problems in Movement Skill Development.* Columbia, South Carolina: University of South Carolina Press, p. 87. Redrawn from Dobbins, D. A., Garron, R., & Rarick, G. L. (1981). The motor performance of educable mentally retarded and intellectually normal boys after covariate control for differences in body size. *Research Quarterly for Exercise and Sport, 58,* 1–8.
Figure 21.10. From A. E. Wall, M. Bouffard, J. McClements, H. Findlay, & M. J. Taylor (1985). A knowledge-based approach to motor development: Implications for the physically awkward, p. 32, *Adapted Physical Activity Quarterly, 2* (1), 21–42.
Figure 21.11. From Special Olympics International. *Athletics Sports Skills Program.* Reprinted with permission.
Figure 21.12. From G. Reid, D. Montgomery, & C. Seidl, *Stepping Out for Fitness,* pp. 31–33. Copyright 1990 by Canadian Association for Health, Physical Education, and Recreation.
Figure 21.13. From E. J. Watkinson and A. E. Wall, *PREP: The Play Program: Play Skill Instruction for*

Mentally Handicapped Children, pp. 14 & 21. Copyright 1982 by Canadian Association for Health, Physical Education, and Recreation.
Figure 21.14. Adapted from Ruth C. Webb, "Sensory-Motor Training of the Profoundly Retarded," *American Journal of Mental Deficiency, 74* (September, 1969): 287.
Figures 21.16 and 21.17. From Special Olympics International (1989). *Special Olympics Motor Activities Training Guide.* Reprinted with permission.

23

Figure 23.4(a). From John W. Hole, Jr., *Human Anatomy and Physiology,* 5th ed. Copyright © 1990 Wm. C. Brown Communications, Inc., Dubuque, Iowa. All Rights Reserved. Reprinted by permission.
Figure 23.5. From G. G. Williamson (1987). *Children with Spina Bifida: Early Intervention and Preschool Programs* (p. 2). Baltimore, MD: Paul H. Brookes Publishing Co.; reprinted with permission.
Figure 23.9. From M. L. Barr & J. A. Kiernan (1988). *The Human Nervous System: A Medical Viewpoint* (5th ed.). Hagerstown, MD: Harper & Row. By permission of J. P. Lippincott, Philadelphia.

25

Figure 25.11. Redrawn from *Handling the Young Cerebral Palsied Child at Home,* 2nd edition, by Nancy R. Finnie. Copyright © 1974 by Nancy R. Finnie, F.C.S.P., additions for U.S. edition, copyright © by E.P. Dutton and Company, Inc.

26

Figure 26.3. From J. L. Northern & M. P. Downs (1991). *Hearing in Children* (4th ed.). Baltimore: Williams & Wilkins Co., p. 17. © Williams & Wilkins Co.

PHOTOGRAPHS

1

Figure 1.3. Comsom Games and Athletic Goods Company, Minneapolis, MN
Figure 1.6. B. Cadden, Valdez Public Schools in Alaska

2

Figure 2.6. Barron Ludlum, *Denton Record Chronicle*

5

Figure 5.3 (top left). Adapted Sports Program for Blind Students, Texas Woman's University
Figure 5.3 (bottom left). Dr. Ernest Bundschuh, University of Georgia
Figure 5.13. Cosom Games and Athletic Goods Company, Minneapolis, MN

9

Figure 9.1. Rae Allen
Figure 9.3. Dr. Garth Tymeson, Northern Illinois University

Figure 9.7. DeKalb Public Schools, Georgia
Figure 9.12. Dr. Lane Goodwin, University of Wisconsin at LaCrosse, Special Populations Programs

12

Figure 12.1. Creative Playground by Sharon Schmidt
Figure 12.11. Contributed by Dr. Ernest Bundschuh, University of Georgia

13

Figure 13.8. From Don R. Kirkendall, et al. *Measurement and Evaluation for Physical Educators,* Wm. C. Brown Company, Dubuque, IA

14

Figure 14.4. Reprinted by permission of Reedco Incorporated
Figure 14.7. Denton State School

15

Figure 15.3. Barron Ludlum, *Denton Record Chronicle*

17

Figure 17.1. Judy Newman
Figure 17.10. Longview, WA YMCA

19

Figure 19.1. Rae Allen
Figure 19.2. Fonda Johnstone

22

Figure 22.2. Ross Photos
Figure 22.3. Jim Estes

23

Figures 23.12–23.15. Dr. Horst Strohkendl, Universidat Koln, W. Germany
Figure 23.16. Paralyzed Veterans of America /*Sports 'n Spokes*
Figure 23.17 (both). *Sports 'n Spokes*
Figure 23.24(a). Beneficial Designs, Inc., Santa Cruz, CA

24

Figure 24.5 (both). Marilyn Butt, adapted physical education consultant from Ontario, Canada
Figures 24.6–24.8. University of Texas SWMS-Dallas, Department of Medical Art
Figure 24.15. Dr. Jo Cowden, University of New Orleans
Figure 24.33. National Academy of Sciences, National Research Council, Washington, DC

27

Figure 27.1. Steve Edmonds
Figures 27.7–27.9. Christian Record Braille Foundation. Photo by Robert L. Sheldon
Figure 27.10 Steve Edmonds
Figures 27.13 and 27.14. Provided by Rosanna Copeland, Parkview School for the Blind in Oklahoma

NAME INDEX

SUBJECT INDEX

Gallop age, 294
Gallop-skip-slide order of learning, 294
Games
  analysis, 192
  components, 192
  design model, 192–93, 510
  formations, 322, 326–27, 507
  rules understanding, 117
  severely disabled, 535
  skills, 211
  structured, 273
Gangrene, 466, 612
GAPES, 102, 104–5
Generalization, in attitude theory, 35, 39
Generalization in cognition, 116, 213, 220, 282, 284, 309–10, 517, 528, 537, 540, 553
Generic model, 9
Genu recurvatum, 387
Genu valga, varum, 387
Gestalt psychology, 42
Gibbosity, 496
Glasgow Coma Scale, 621
Glaucoma, 353, 666
Glucometer, 463
Glucose concentration, 461–63
Gluteus maximus lurch, 279
Gluteus medius lurch, 562
Goal ball, 667, 673–75
Goal setting, 130, 174–75, 355
Goals and objectives
  adapted physical activity, 13, 100, 102, 104–5
  areas, aspects, 101–2
  definitions, 13, 100, 106–7, 447
  IEP, relationship to, 87, 107, 275
  illustrative, 106–7, 530
  planning, relationship to, 100
  prioritizing, 102, 104–5, 127
  purposes, 100
  selection and assessment, 101, 107
  shortcuts, 276
  time required for achievement, 107
  writing, 107, 276, 322
Goals of Adapted Physical Education Scale, 102, 104–5
Goniometer, 353–54, 600
Good behavior game, 219, 551
Good form, 275
Good teaching, indicators, 72–73
Government Agencies/Offices
  Committee on Sports for Disabled, 82
  National Information Center for Children and Youth with Disabilities (NICHCY), 692
  Office of Civil Rights, 80
  Office of Special Education and Rehabilitative Services (OSERS), 692
  Office of Special Education Programs (OSEP), 56, 692
  President's Council on Physical Education and Sport, 173, 336, 692
  U.S. Department of Education, 93, 698–99
  U.S. Department of Health and Human Services, 86, 698–99
  U.S. Olympic Committee, 52, 81
Gower's sign, 592
Graded reversal of deterioration principle, 549, 553
Grading, 173
Graphing, 216–17
Group conversations and speechreading, 655
Growth retardation, 601
Guidelines for interacting, 30–32
Guidelines for speaking and writing, 33–34
Guidewires, 669, 672

H
Halliwick model, 414
Hallucinations, 546
Hallus valgus, 391–92
Hammock activities, 214, 236, 407–10, 417
Hand grasp, 109
  age, 295, 297
  development, 440, 446
  problems, 295–97, 444, 574, 596, 599
  reflex, 242, 256
Handicap, definition, 32
Handling technique principles, 634
Haptic perception, 322, 668
Hard-of-hearing, 642–59
Harrington surgery, 381–82
HDL-C, 460
Head control, 236, 248, 254, 276, 659
Health definition, 333
Health examination, 429–30
Health/safety concerns, swimming, 431
Hearing aids, 647, 649, 658
Hearings, 83–84, 93, 97
Heart conditions, 24, 353, 431, 465–77, 592, 621
Height/weight assessment, 346–48
Helbing's sign, 390–91
Hemiparesis, 522, 621
Hemiplegia, 277, 621, 624–26, 629–30, 635
Hemispheres, brain, 260–61, 263
Hemophilia, 431, 489, 497
Hemorrhage, 620
Hernias, 353, 377, 524
Herpes viruses, 649
Hertz, 646
Hierarchial brain function, 266–67
Hierarchial learning, 231
High blood pressure, 353, 477, 621
Hip problems, 381–82, 385–86, 599, 608–9, 635
History, adapted physical activity, 17–20, 696–99
HKAFOs, 636
Holism, 128, 220, 265, 336
Hollow chest, 384–85
Home/school/community programming, 5, 17, 506, 510
Homemade equipment, 303, 356, 363
Homeostasis, 60, 263, 455, 481
Homosexuality, 545
Hop age, 293
Hop rhythmic sequence, 293
Hopscotch, 293
Horseback riding, 253, 617, 634, 636, 666–68
Household ambulators, 558, 562
Human immunodeficiency virus, 496–99
Human rights movement, 78–82
Humanistic philosophy, 23, 127–35
Humanistic Theory
  ecological or field, 130–31
  fully functioning self, 130
  normalization, 130–31
  personal meaning, 132–33
  self-actualization, 129–30
  self-determination, 134–35
  self-efficacy, 133–34
  social-cognitive, 133
Hydrocephalus, 431, 521, 562–63
Hydrotherapy, 413, 594, 596
Hyperactivity, 123, 263, 394–99, 510–13
Hyperextended knees, 383, 387
Hyperhydration, 495
Hyperkinesis vs. hyperactivity, 510
Hyperopia, 237
Hypertension, blood pressure, 353, 477–78, 491, 568, 621
Hypertension, muscular/stress, 394–99
Hyperthermia, 355, 495
Hypertonus, 275

Hypertrophic scarring, 597
Hypertrophy, muscular dystrophy, 592
Hyperventilating, 424, 495
Hypoactivity, 123
Hypoglycemia, 463, 495
Hypokalemia (potassium loss), 455
Hypokinetic conditions, 333
Hypotension, 455
Hypothalamus, 263
Hypothermia, 355, 470
Hypotonia, 275, 523–24, 627
Hypovolemia (fluid loss), 455

I
I CAN, Wessel, 7, 188, 534
Identity disorders, 547
Idiot-savant, 310
Ileostomy, 567
Imagery, 43, 395–96, 406–7
Imitation, 441, 528
Imitation problems, 318–19, 321
Impulsivity, 310, 509
Inattention, 511
Inclusion, 38, 44–46, 184–88, 192–93, 651–52
Incomplete lesions, 558, 563, 565
Independence, productivity, integration, 85–86
Independence levels, 539
Independent variables related to persuasion, 40
Individual differences
  perspective, 109
  theory, 14–15, 49
  unifying theme, 9
Individual sports, 193, 595, 615
Individualization, 67–68, 209, 218
Individualized Education Program (IEP), 11, 188, 194, 197, 200, 275, 504
  dates, 92
  definition, 87
  length, 89
  meeting, 92, 171
  PAST-DE acronym, 88
  principles, 92
  procedural safeguards, 93
  process, 91–92
  purpose, 88
  sample PE-IEP, 90
  young children, 449–50
Individualized family service plan (IFSP), 92, 434, 448–49
Individuals With Disabilities Education Act (IDEA)
  age range covered, 86
  definitions, 86–89
  direct vs. related services, 80–81, 435
  evaluation procedures, 95
  funding, 83
  number of students served, 677
  parts A-H, 87
  part B, 80–81, 83, 86, 93
  part H, 83, 86
  physical education mentions, 89
  reauthorization, 82
  transitional services, 86, 91
Infantile spasms, 494
Infants and toddlers
  assessment/programming, 109, 229–69, 434–52
  HIV, 498–99
  postures, 265–66, 371–72, 376, 384, 387, 390
  services, 75, 92–93
  stereotypies, 268
Infarction, 466
Infections, 431, 519, 524, 591, 648–49
Information processing, 216, 509–10
Inhibition, 238, 245, 257, 264, 267, 633
Injuries, 559, 563, 585, 605, 607
Inner language, 447
Innervation, sensation, 565
In-service training, 56

Instruction and programming criteria, 201
Instructional stimulus enhancement principle, 503, 507, 513
Instructional units, 188–89, 202
Instructional/informational variables, 62–64
Instruments
  AAHPERD fitness tests, 158, 336
  AAHPERD Physical Best, 159, 166, 175, 332, 334, 336, 527
  ACTIVE basic motor ability test, 166
  Aerobic fitness walk/run test, 360–61
  Attitude inventories, list, 37
  Ayres Southern California perceptual-motor tests, 323
  Balance beam assessment checklist, 176
  Behavior evaluation scale-2, 166
  Bender-Gestalt test, 321
  Brigance diagnostic inventory, 159
  Bruininks-Oseretsky Test of Motor Proficiency, 157, 163–65, 172, 323, 506
  Canadian Standardized Test of Fitness, 346, 532
  Checklist for Evaluating Objectives, 107
  Checklist for evaluating school district APE, 200
  Checklist for evaluation of long jump, 292
  Checklist for evaluation of walking, 284
  Clipboard testing/teaching sheet, 274
  Cratty Self-Concept Scale, 140
  Cratty six-category gross motor test, 166, 321
  Data-based gymnasium assessment, 159
  Denver Developmental Screening Test, 155, 173
  Denver II, 155–56, 162–63, 448
  Floor exercise assessment checklist, 176
  Goals of Adapted Physical Education Scale, 102, 104–5
  Gymnastics assessment checklist with difficulty ratings, 175
  Harter Self-Perception Instruments, 138, 141–43
  Hughes gross motor assessment, 166
  I CAN assessment, 159
  Intelligence tests, list, 518
  Jump and hop skills TTP checklist, 289
  Locus of control instruments, list, 150
  Martinek-Zaichkowsky Self-Concept Scale, 138, 140–41
  Milani-Comparetti assessment, 254–55
  Morris motor skill profile sheets, 161–62
  Motor skill test product battery, 166
  Movement Purposes Inventory, 133
  Muscle strength/function tests, 339
  Neurological soft signs, tests for, 505
  New York posture test, 369
  Object control skills TTP checklist, 297
  Observation of Whole Child Form, 113
  OSU-SIGMA, 166–67
  Pain and dyspnea rating scales, 346
  Physical Self-Perception Profile, 144–45
  Pictorial checklist
    catching skills, 301
    long jump, 291
    overarm throw, 300
    running, 285